Handbook of Learning from Multiple Representations and Perspectives

In and out of formal schooling, online and off, today's learners must consume and integrate a level of information that is exponentially larger and delivered through a wider range of formats and viewpoints than ever before. The *Handbook of Learning from Multiple Representations and Perspectives* provides a path for understanding the cognitive, motivational, and socioemotional processes and skills necessary for learners across educational contexts to make sense of and use information sourced from varying inputs. Uniting research and theory from education, psychology, literacy, library sciences, media and technology, and more, this forward-thinking volume explores the common concerns, shared challenges, and thematic patterns in our capacity to make meaning in an information-rich society.

Peggy Van Meter is Associate Professor of Education and Director of Undergraduate and Graduate Studies in the Department of Educational Psychology, Counseling, and Special Education at the Pennsylvania State University, USA.

Alexandra List is Assistant Professor of Education in the Department of Educational Psychology, Counseling, and Special Education at the Pennsylvania State University, USA.

Doug Lombardi is Associate Professor in the Department of Human Development and Quantitative Methodology at the University of Maryland, USA.

Panayiota Kendeou is Professor in the Department of Educational Psychology, Guy Bond Endowed Chair in Reading, and Director of Graduate Studies at the University of Minnesota, USA.

Educational Psychology Handbook Series
Series Editor: Patricia A. Alexander

International Handbook of Research on Teachers' Beliefs
Edited by Helenrose Fives and Michelle Gregoire Gill

Handbook of Test Development, 2nd Edition
Edited by Suzanne Lane, Mark R. Raymond, and Thomas M. Haladyna

Handbook of Social Influences in School Contexts: Social-Emotional, Motivation, and Cognitive Outcomes
Edited by Kathryn R. Wentzel and Geetha B. Ramani

Handbook of Epistemic Cognition
Edited by Jeffrey A. Greene, William A. Sandoval, and Ivar Bråten

Handbook of Motivation at School, 2nd Edition
Edited by Kathryn R. Wentzel and David B. Miele

Handbook of Human and Social Conditions in Assessment
Edited by Gavin T.L. Brown and Lois R. Harris

Handbook of Quantitative Methods for Detecting Cheating on Tests
Edited by Gregory J. Cizek and James A. Wollack

Handbook of Research on Learning and Instruction, 2nd Edition
Edited by Patricia A. Alexander and Richard E. Mayer

Handbook of Self-Regulation of Learning and Performance, 2nd Edition
Edited by Dale H. Schunk and Jeffrey A. Greene

Handbook of Multiple Source Use
Edited by Jason L. G. Braasch, Ivar Bråten, Matthew T. McCrudden

Handbook of Strategies and Strategic Processing
Edited by Daniel L. Dinsmore, Luke K. Fryer, and Meghan M. Parkinson

Handbook of Learning from Multiple Representations and Perspectives
Edited by Peggy Van Meter, Alexandra List, Doug Lombardi and Panayiota Kendeou

Handbook of Learning from Multiple Representations and Perspectives

Edited by
Peggy Van Meter
Alexandra List
Doug Lombardi
Panayiota Kendeou

NEW YORK AND LONDON

First published 2020
by Routledge
52 Vanderbilt Avenue, New York, NY 10017

and by Routledge
2 Park Square, Milton Park, Abingdon, Oxon, OX14 4RN

Routledge is an imprint of the Taylor & Francis Group, an informa business

© 2020 selection and editorial matter, Peggy Van Meter, Alexandra List, Doug Lombardi and Panayiota Kendeou; individual chapters, the contributors

The right of Peggy Van Meter, Alexandra List, Doug Lombardi and Panayiota Kendeou to be identified as the authors of the editorial material, and of the authors for their individual chapters, has been asserted in accordance with sections 77 and 78 of the Copyright, Designs and Patents Act 1988.

All rights reserved. No part of this book may be reprinted or reproduced or utilized in any form or by any electronic, mechanical, or other means, now known or hereafter invented, including photocopying and recording, or in any information storage or retrieval system, without permission in writing from the publishers.

Trademark notice: Product or corporate names may be trademarks or registered trademarks, and are used only for identification and explanation without intent to infringe.

Library of Congress Cataloging-in-Publication Data
Names: Van Meter, Peggy, 1964- editor. | List, Alexandra, 1988- editor. | Lombardi, Doug, 1965- editor. | Kendeou, Panayiota (Pani), editor.
Title: Handbook of learning from multiple representations and perspectives/ edited by Peggy N. Van Meter, Alexandra List, Doug Lombardi, Panayiota (Pani) Kendeou.
Description: New York, NY : Routledge, 2020. | Includes bibliographical references and index.
Identifiers: LCCN 2019046148 (print) | LCCN 2019046149 (ebook) | ISBN 9780367001162 (hardback) | ISBN 9780367001179 (paperback) | ISBN 9780429443961 (ebook)
Subjects: LCSH: Cognitive learning. | Knowledge representation (Information theory) | Perspective (Linguistics) | Human information processing.
Classification: LCC LB1062 .H249 2020 (print) | LCC LB1062 (ebook) | DDC 370.15/23—dc23
LC record available at https://lccn.loc.gov/2019046148
LC ebook record available at https://lccn.loc.gov/2019046149

ISBN: 978-0-367-00116-2 (hbk)
ISBN: 978-0-367-00117-9 (pbk)
ISBN: 978-0-429-44396-1 (ebk)

Typeset in Minion Pro
by Swales & Willis, Exeter, Devon, UK

CONTENTS

List of contributors		ix
Chapter 1	Loggers and Conservationists: Navigating the Multiple Resource Forest through the Trees ALEXANDRA LIST; PEGGY VAN METER; DOUG LOMBARDI; PANAYIOTA KENDEOU	1
Section 1	**LEARNING FROM MULTIPLE REPRESENTATIONS**	**15**
Chapter 2	Cognitive and Socio-Cultural Theories on Competencies and Practices involved in Learning with Multiple External Representations MARTINA A. RAU	17
Chapter 3	Use of Multiple Representations by Experts and Novices ROBERT B. KOZMA	33
Chapter 4	Cognitive Processes Underlying Learning From Multiple Representations ANNE SCHÜLER	48
Chapter 5	Learning from Multiple Representations: Roles of Task Interventions and Individual Differences JENNIFER G. CROMLEY	62
Chapter 6	Interventions to Support Learning from Multiple External Representations PEGGY VAN METER; NICHOLAS STEPANIK	76
Chapter 7	Learning by Construction of Multiple Representations SHAARON AINSWORTH; RUSSELL TYTLER; VAUGHAN PRAIN	92

vi • Contents

| Chapter 8 | Problem Solving in Mathematics with Multiple Representations
DESPINA A. STYLIANOU | 107 |

Section 2 LEARNING FROM MULTIPLE PERSPECTIVES 121

Chapter 9	Beyond Trustworthiness: Comprehending Multiple Source Perspectives SARIT BARZILAI; MICHAEL WEINSTOCK	123
Chapter 10	On the Roles of Dispositions and Beliefs in Learning from Multiple Perspectives IVAR BRÅTEN; HELGE I. STRØMSØ	141
Chapter 11	Knowledge as Perspective: From Domain Perspective Learning to Interdisciplinary Understanding ALEXANDRA LIST	164
Chapter 12	Processes and Products of Encountering Belief-Related Information MATTHEW T. MCCRUDDEN	191
Chapter 13	The Role of Cognitive Conflict in Understanding and Learning from Multiple Perspectives JASON L.G. BRAASCH; LISA SCHARRER	205
Chapter 14	Learning from Multiple Complementary Perspectives: A Systematic Review CARLA M. FIRETTO	223
Chapter 15	Learning from Multiple Perspectives: Processes and Strategies Associated with Reading Dual-Position Texts CATHERINE M. BOHN-GETTLER	245
Chapter 16	The Role of Validation in Integrating Multiple Perspectives TOBIAS RICHTER; HANNES MÜNCHOW; JOHANNA ABENDROTH	259
Chapter 17	Students' Perspective Learning in a Disciplinary Multisource Task Environment BYEONG-YOUNG CHO; LINDA KUCAN; EMILY C. RAINEY	276

Section 3 THEORETICAL VIEWPOINTS ON THE INTEGRATION OF MULTIPLE REPRESENTATIONS AND MULTIPLE PERSPECTIVES 295

| Chapter 18 | The Roles of Executive Functions in Learning from Multiple Representations and Perspectives
D. JAKE FOLLMER; RAYNE A. SPERLING | 297 |

Chapter 19	Putting Self-Regulated Learning and Metacognition into Multiple Representations and Perspectives COURTNEY A. DENTON; KRISTA R. MUIS; BRENDAN MUNZAR; NESMA ETOUBASHI	314
Chapter 20	Values, Attitudes, and Beliefs: Cognitive Filters Shaping Integration of Multiple Representations and Multiple Perspectives DOUG LOMBARDI; BENJAMIN C. HEDDY; ANANYA M. MATEWOS	329
Chapter 21	Motivation and the Processing of Multiple Inputs DAVID B. MIELE; TIMOTHY J. NOKES-MALACH; SIDNEY MAY	346
Chapter 22	Emotions and Learning from Multiple Representations and Perspectives REINHARD PEKRUN; KRISTINA LODERER	373
Chapter 23	Relational Reasoning: The Bedrock of Integration within and across Multiple Representations, Documents, and Perspectives PATRICIA A. ALEXANDER; DISCIPLINED READING AND LEARNING RESEARCH LABORATORY	401
Chapter 24	Using Critical Thinking Frameworks to Understand Integration of Multiple Inputs BRIAN M. CARTIFF; JEFFREY A. GREENE	425
Section 4	**CHALLENGES AND SOLUTIONS**	**441**
Chapter 25	Assessing and Modifying Knowledge: Facts vs. Constellations DAVID N. RAPP; AMALIA M. DONOVAN; NIKITA A. SALOVICH	443
Chapter 26	The Challenge of Misinformation and Ways to Reduce its Impact JASMYNE A. SANDERSON; ULLRICH K. H. ECKER	461
Chapter 27	The Challenge of Fake News: Intellectual Survival in the Context of Multiple Representations and Perspectives PANAYIOTA KENDEOU; RINA HARSCH; REESE BUTTERFUSS; JOSEPH AUBELE; JASMINE KIM	477
Chapter 28	The Need for Personalized Learning and the Potential of Intelligent Tutoring Systems BRENT MORGAN; A. MARIE HOGAN; ANDREW J. HAMPTON; ANNE M. LIPPERT; ARTHUR C. GRAESSER	495
Chapter 29	Representational Affordances for Collaborative Learning in Technology-Enhanced Environments BODONG CHEN; FENG LIN	513

Chapter 30 The Challenge of Measuring Processes and Outcomes while Learning from Multiple Representations with Advanced Learning Technologies 532
ROGER AZEVEDO; MICHELLE TAUB

Conclusion 555

Chapter 31 The Multiple Resources Learning Framework: Learning from Multiple Representations and Multiple Perspectives 557
PEGGY VAN METER; ALEXANDRA LIST; PANAYIOTA KENDEOU; DOUG LOMBARDI

Index 589

CONTRIBUTORS

Shaaron Ainsworth is Professor and Director of the Learning Sciences Research Institute in the School of Education at the University of Nottingham. Her background includes psychology, artificial intelligence, and cognitive science and her research revolves around representational learning and how technology can support it. She has published over 100 papers and books on this topic as well as supervising 20 doctorates in this area.

Johanna Abendroth (formerly Maier) is a Postdoctoral Researcher in the Department of Psychology at the University of Würzburg. Johanna does research in educational psychology, cognitive science, and cognitive psychology. Her work has particularly focused on information evaluation and validation on the Internet.

Patricia A. Alexander is a University Distinguished Professor, Jean Mullen Professor of Literacy, and Distinguished Scholar-Teacher in the Department of Human Development, University of Maryland. She directs the Disciplined Reading and Learning Research Laboratory and is the author of over 300 publications. Her research interests include comprehension, relational reasoning, text-based learning, academic development, and models of multiple source use.

Joseph Aubele is the Lab Manager in the Reading and Learning Lab at the University of Minnesota – Twin Cities. His research interests are in early childhood reading and finding effective ways to assist struggling readers.

Roger Azevedo is a Professor in the Department of Learning Sciences and Educational Research at the University of Central Florida. He is also an affiliated faculty in the Departments of Computer Science and Internal Medicine at the University of Central Florida and the lead scientist for the Learning Sciences Faculty Cluster Initiative. His main research area includes examining the role of cognitive, metacognitive, affective, and motivational self-regulatory processes during learning with intelligent tutoring systems, serious games, and immersive virtual learning environments. He has published over 250 peer-reviewed papers, chapters, and refereed conference proceedings in the areas of educational, learning, cognitive, and computational sciences.

Sarit Barzilai is a Senior Lecturer in the Department of Learning, Instruction and Teacher Education and the Chair of the Educational Technologies Graduate Program. She is also the Primary Investigator in the Israel Center for Research Excellence (I-CORE) on Learning in a Networked Society (LINKS). Her research interests focus on learners' epistemic thinking (i.e. thinking about knowledge and knowing) and digital literacy. She is particularly interested in studying learners' epistemic thinking in digital media contexts such as learning from multiple online information sources and from digital games.

Catherine M. Bohn-Gettler is a Professor of Educational Psychology at the College of Saint Benedict – St. John's University, where she also serves as the Co-Director for Undergraduate Research. She completed her MA and PhD in Educational Psychology at the University of Minnesota – Twin Cities. Her research focuses on improving comprehension by understanding how a variety of factors interact to influence processing and memory. This work makes interdisciplinary connections across several fields, including discourse processing, cognition, emotion, and education.

Jason L.G. Braasch is an Assistant Professor in the Department of Psychology at the University of Memphis and an affiliate of the Institute for Intelligent Systems. His work focuses on students' reasoning about conflicting information and the role of sourcing in such reasoning. He is the recipient of the 2018 Early Career Impact Award from the Federation of Associations in Behavioral & Brain Sciences (FABBS).

Ivar Bråten is a Professor of Educational Psychology in the Department of Education at the University of Oslo, Norway. His main research interests are epistemic cognition, self-regulated learning, reading comprehension, and multiple document literacy.

Reese Butterfuss is a graduate student in the Department of Educational Psychology at the University of Minnesota. His research explores the conditions and processes that support knowledge revision and learning from texts.

Brian M. Cartiff is a doctoral student in the Learning and Psychological Studies Program in the School of Education at the University of North Carolina at Chapel Hill. He has degrees in chemistry and education and was a high school science teacher for over 20 years. His research interests include epistemic cognition, critical thinking, and the nature of science understanding as well as how these factors influence public understanding of science.

Bodong Chen is Associate Professor and Bonnie Westby Huebner Chair in Education and Technology at the University of Minnesota – Twin Cities. His work is focused on the design of digital environments for collaborative learning experiences that are conducive to essential competencies for knowledge societies. In particular, he devises pedagogical practices and technologies for collaborative learning, investigates complex learning processes in authentic settings, and applies nascent computational methods to both empirical research and software engineering. His scholarship is featured in journals such as *Educational Psychologist, International Journal of Computer-Supported Collaborative Learning, Computers & Education*, and *Journal of Learning Analytics*.

Byeong-Young Cho is an Associate Professor of Language, Literacy, and Culture in the School of Education, University of Pittsburgh, and a research scientist at Pitt's Learning Research and Development Center. Cho's research focuses on the cognitive, metacognitive, and epistemic processes of student reading in multisource textual environments. His recent work examines classroom practices that support student learning and engagement as they read, write, and think with multiple texts in disciplinary literacy instruction.

Jennifer Cromley is Professor of Educational Psychology at the University of Illinois at Urbana-Champaign. Her research concerns comprehension of illustrated scientific text and cognitive and motivational predictors of retention in science, technology, engineering, and mathematics majors. She has conducted basic and applied classroom intervention research in both areas, including fostering student comprehension of diagrams at the middle school and high school level, as well as research on the strategy of drawing-to-learn.

Courtney A. Denton is a third-year PhD student in the Learning Sciences program at McGill University. She is interested in how individuals integrate conflicting perspectives during online learning. Courtney's doctoral research explores digital literacy skills and their development.

Amalia M. Donovan is a graduate student in the Department of Learning Sciences in the School of Education and Social Policy at Northwestern University. Her research examines methods by which people's reliance on inaccurate information might be attenuated, with particular interest in the use of online resources in the service of validation.

Ullrich K.H. Ecker is an Associate Professor and Director of Community and Engagement at the University of Western Australia's School of Psychological Science. He is a cognitive psychologist studying human memory and in particular misinformation processing and debunking. He has published more than 60 articles and book chapters on these topics, including papers in *Psychological Science in the Public Interest*, the *Journal of Experimental Psychology: General*, and *Political Psychology*. His research is funded mainly by the Australian Research Council. He teaches Cognitive Psychology and Research Communication Skills, and has received multiple awards for both his teaching and research.

Nesma Etoubashi is a first-year PhD student in the School/Applied Child Psychology program at McGill University. She is passionate about education, equality, children, science, and all things psychology related. Her doctoral research will examine the effectiveness of an intervention aimed at fostering critical thinking skills and heuristic awareness in secondary students to prevent the formation of socio-scientific misconceptions.

Carla M. Firetto is an Assistant Professor of Educational Psychology at Arizona State University in the Mary Lou Fulton Teachers College. The overarching focus of her research aims to facilitate students' high-level comprehension of complex texts and content. Toward this end, she examines ways to help learners comprehend and integrate across multiple texts and think more critically and analytically as they learn. Firetto's research focuses on identifying the individual differences that account for variations in students' ability to read from multiple, complex texts as well as the mechanisms (e.g., small-group discussions) that promote students' comprehension and integration processes.

D. Jake Follmer is an Assistant Professor in the College of Education and Human Services at West Virginia University. His research focuses on the roles of cognitive and metacognitive skills in learning and strategy use. He is particularly interested in interdisciplinary research that examines the roles of cognitive and metacognitive skills and supports in learners' comprehension of expository text.

Arthur C. Graesser is a Professor in the Department of Psychology and the Institute of Intelligent Systems at the University of Memphis and a Senior Research Fellow in the Department of Education at the University of Oxford. His primary research interests are in cognitive science, discourse processing, and the learning sciences. He has served as editor of several academic journals and published over 500 articles in journals, books, and conference proceedings. Dr. Graesser and his colleagues have designed, developed, and tested software that integrates psychological sciences with learning, language, and discourse technologies, including the family of AutoTutor products and Coh-Metrix.

Jeffrey A. Greene is a Professor and Associate Dean for Academic Affairs in the School of Education at the University of North Carolina at Chapel Hill. He has a PhD in Educational Psychology and an MA in Educational Measurement, Statistics, and Evaluation. He was awarded the 2016 Richard E. Snow Award for Distinguished Early Contributions in Educational Psychology from Division 15 of the American Psychological Association. Greene's research focuses upon digital literacy, including student cognition, self-regulation, and epistemic cognition in science and history domains.

Andrew J. Hampton is a Research Scientist Assistant Professor at the Institute for Intelligent Systems and Department of Psychology, within the University of Memphis. His current duties include serving as project manager on the pioneering hybrid tutor ElectronixTutor and development leader on a conversational AI meant to aid in career planning through education and qualification tracking, intelligent recommendation, and mitigation of personal issues. His research interests include technologically mediated communication, psycholinguistics, semiotics, adaptive educational technology, artificial intelligence, political psychology, and the ethical implications of AI from a psychological perspective.

Rina Harsch is a graduate student in the Department of Educational Psychology at the University of Minnesota. Her research interests include reasoning and knowledge revision.

Benjamin Heddy is an Assistant Professor at the University of Oklahoma in the Department of Educational Psychology. Benjamin received his PhD in Urban Education from the University of Southern California. Currently, he teaches undergraduate and graduate courses on the topics of motivation, cognition, learning theory, human development, and research methods. His research program focuses on cognitive and motivational aspects of learning; including engagement, academic emotions, interest development, and further specializing in the investigation of learning activities that occur in everyday experience. As a second related line of research he studies the mechanisms of conceptual, emotion, and attitude change.

Marie Hogan is a corporate Project Manager specializing in Application Development, Mergers and Acquisitions, and Data Integrations. Marie is studying International Relations and Neuro-Behavioral Psychology at the University of Memphis. Her research interests are cognition, emotion, judgment and decision-making, and heuristics.

Panayiota Kendeou is a Professor and Guy Bond Chair in Reading in the Department of Educational Psychology at the University of Minnesota. Her research program focuses on examining the cognitive processes that support learning and memory in the context of reading comprehension. Dr. Kendeou won the Early Career Impact Award from the FABBS Foundation in 2015, the Tom Trabasso Young Investigator Award from the Society for Text & Discourse in 2012, and the Research in Literacy Award from the UK Literacy Association in 2009. Dr. Kendeou also serves as the incoming Editor for the *Journal of Educational Psychology* and on several other editorial boards (e.g., *Contemporary Educational Psychology, Scientific Studies of Reading, Learning and Instruction*).

Jasmine Kim is a graduate student in the Department of Educational Psychology at the University of Minnesota – Twin Cities. Her research explores text and reader characteristics that facilitate knowledge revision.

Robert B. Kozma is now retired and living in San Francisco. Robert Kozma was Professor of Education and Research Scientist at the University of Michigan before moving to Silicon Valley to direct the Center for Technology and Learning at SRI International. His research focused on media theory, instructional design, and the use of technology to support learning. Subsequently, he was an independent consultant working with ministries of education, multinational organizations, and high-tech companies to develop policies that used technology to support education reform that prepared students for the 21st century knowledge economy. He began his career as a primary school teacher in inner-city Detroit.

Linda Kucan is an Associate Pofessor in the University of Pittsburgh's School of Education. Her primary research focus is on comprehension and learning from text – particularly informational text. She also investigates discussion as a context for comprehension instruction and the role of tasks in mediating student learning from text. These research interests converge in her work in disciplinary literacy in history with an emphasis on student learning about the thinking practices of historians as they engage with multiple sources.

Feng Lin is a Lecturer at Singapore University of Social Sciences. Her main research interest focuses on the design of computer-supported collaborative learning environments for epistemic and conceptual growth. She is also interested in understanding collaborative learning process, teacher scaffolding, the nature of epistemic cognition, and pedagogy design for deeper science learning.

Anne Lippert is a Postdoctoral Research Fellow at the University of Memphis's Institute for Intelligent Systems. She received her PhD in cognitive psychology from the University of New Mexico. Dr. Lippert's primary research interests are cognitive science, knowledge representation, group decision-making, and the learning sciences. At the Institute for Intelligent Systems, Dr. Lippert is part of an interdisciplinary team of researchers who design, develop, and test intelligent tutoring software that integrates psychological sciences with learning, language, and discourse technologies. She is currently the project manager for the development of an Intelligent Tutoring System that teaches reading comprehension skills.

Alexandra List is an Assistant Professor in the Department of Educational Psychology, Counseling, and Special Education at the Pennsylvania State University. Her work examines how students learn from multiple texts, for instance, when learning about complex topics on the Internet. She is particularly interested in the cognitive processes involved when students evaluate information, integrate information across sources, and write based on multiple texts. She received her MA in Educational Measurement, Statistics, and Evaluation and her PhD in Educational Psychology from the University of Maryland, College Park.

Kristina Loderer is a Professor in the Department of Psychology at the University of Augsburg. Her research interests include achievement emotions and motivation, with a particular focus on the effects of emotions on learning, academic performance, and psychological health. Her current work also concentrates on functional and dysfunctional approaches to regulating achievement emotions, as well as the development of interventions targeting emotional competencies in students. Methodologically, her work has drawn on experimental study designs, field-based treatment evaluations, and advanced meta-analytic techniques for evidence synthesis.

Doug Lombardi is an Associate Professor in the Department of Human Development and Quantitative Methodology at the University of Maryland, College Park, USA. As the head of the Science Learning Research Group, he conducts research focusing on developing tools and strategies to facilitate students' reasoning about socio-scientific topics (i.e., those that pose local, regional, and global challenges, such as causes of climate change). Doug has received early career research awards from the American Educational Research Association's Division C, American Psychological Association's Division 15, the Society for Text & Discourse, and NARST: A Worldwide Organization for Improving Science Teaching and Learning Through Research.

Ananya M. Matewos is a Postdoctoral Research Fellow at Temple University in teaching and learning. Ananya received her PhD in Urban Education from the University of Southern California. Currently, she investigates science learning and motivation, with a focus on studying the critical evaluation of science topics through classroom interactions and discourse.

Sidney May is a doctoral student in the Applied Developmental and Educational Psychology Program at Boston College. Broadly, her research interests include motivation regulation, sense of belonging, and educational equity. She hopes to build research-practice partnerships around closing the opportunity gap in education.

Matthew T. McCrudden is an Associate Professor of Educational Psychology at the Pennsylvania State University. He has a PhD in learning and technology and an MA in cognition, learning, and development. He has also taught at the University of North Florida (2005–2008) and Victoria University of Wellington, New Zealand (2008–2018). He teaches courses in educational psychology and research methods. He has published numerous articles and books on human learning. His most recent co-edited volume is the *Handbook of Multiple Source Use*. His research interests include how learner characteristics and instructional tasks and materials relate to cognition and learning.

David B. Miele is an Associate Professor in the Department of Counseling, Developmental, and Educational Psychology at Boston College. He is also principal investigator of the Motivation, Metacognition, and Learning (MML) Laboratory at Boston College (https://www.bc.edu/mmllab). His research examines students' beliefs about their ability, learning, and motivation, and examines how these beliefs influence their engagement in academic tasks. At the broadest level, he is interested in what it takes for students to become effective, independent learners. He is also interested in how teachers' and parents' beliefs influence the ways in which they support students' learning.

Brent Morgan is the President and co-founder of MagicStat.co and a Visiting Assistant Professor at Rhodes College. His primary research interest is in bi-directional adaptability in human–computer interaction. He has also investigated how emotions influence cognition across a variety of tasks. He has led or contributed to numerous research projects in artificial intelligence in education, most notably ElectronixTutor, the first hybrid intelligent tutoring system (ITS), and the Personal Assistant for Life-Long Learning (PAL3). He is currently developing a hybrid ITS to complement an undergraduate statistics course in psychology.

Krista R. Muis is Professor and Canada Research Chair in Epistemic Cognition and Self-Regulated Learning at McGill University, Department of Educational and Counselling Psychology. Her research interests are in the areas of epistemic cognition, emotion, and self-regulated learning in the context of mathematics and science learning. She is interested in how students' epistemic cognition and emotions influence learning and academic performance. She also explores how individuals process complex, contradictory content on socio-scientific issues such as climate change. She examines what role misconceptions play when learning about these topics, and how beliefs and emotions facilitate or constrain learning.

Hannes Münchow is a Postdoctoral Researcher in the field of educational psychology at Julius-Maximilians-University Würzburg (Germany). In his research, he investigates cognitive, affective, and motivational processes in comprehending and evaluating scientific texts. He is also interested in learning from text and multiple media as well as emotional designing and digital game-based learning.

Brendan Munzar is a second-year PhD student. He is interested in the interplay between emotions and self-regulated learning during elementary students' mathematics problem solving. He is also interested in how emotions, attitudes, and epistemic cognition affect university students' learning about controversial socio-scientific topics like genetically modified organisms and vaccines.

Timothy J. Nokes-Malach is an Associate Professor of Psychology and a Research Scientist at the Learning Research and Development Center at the University of Pittsburgh. His research focuses on human learning, problem solving, and knowledge transfer, and most recently on the interactive effects of motivation and social interaction on those processes. His work has been supported with grants from the Pittsburgh Science of Learning Center, the National Science Foundation, the Department of Education's Institute for Education Sciences, and the James S. McDonnell Foundation.

Reinhard Pekrun is a Professor of Psychology at the University of Essex and Professorial Fellow at the Australian Catholic University. His research areas are achievement motivation and emotion, personality development, and educational assessment and evaluation. Pekrun is a highly cited scientist who pioneered research on emotions in education and originated the Control-Value Theory of Achievement Emotions. He has published 23 books and more than 250 articles and chapters. Pekrun is recipient of the Diefenbaker Award 2015, the Sylvia Scribner Award 2017, the EARLI Oeuvre Award 2017, and the Lifetime Achievement Award 2018 from the German Psychological Society.

Vaughan Prain is a Professor in Science Interdisciplinary Education Research at Deakin University, Australia. He has published widely on innovative teaching and learning approaches in primary and secondary science, focusing in recent years on students learning through engaging with representational affordances within and across visual, spatial, linguistic, and embodied modes. This has led to an increased interest in the conditions, tasks, and learning sequences that support student multimodal and creative reasoning.

Emily Rainey is an Assistant Professor of Literacy Education in the University of Pittsburgh's School of Education. She studies disciplinary literacy and adolescent literacy teaching and learning, with a focus on how young people may be supported to use disciplinary literacy practices as tools for reasoning and critique. To date, much of her work has focused on the academic domains of secondary English and history.

Martina A. Rau received her undergraduate/master's degree in Psychology from the University of Freiburg, Germany and a PhD in Human–Computer Interactions from Carnegie Mellon University. She is currently an Associate Professor in Educational

Psychology with an affiliate appointment in Computer Sciences. Her research focuses on learning with visual representations in STEM. Her empirical work has investigated the use of physical and virtual representations in math, chemistry, and engineering with students at the elementary, high-school, and college levels. She uses a multi-methods approach to integrate learning outcome measures with process-level measures of learning.

David N. Rapp is Professor in the Department of Psychology and in the School of Education and Social Policy, and a Charles Deering McCormick Professor of Teaching Excellence, at Northwestern University. His research examines the consequences of exposure to inaccurate information, with work funded by the National Science Foundation and the Institute for Education Sciences. His recent books include the co-edited volumes *Processing Inaccurate Information: Theoretical and Applied Perspectives from Cognitive Science and the Educational Sciences*, and *The Handbook of Discourse Processes, second edition*. He currently serves as Editor of the journal *Discourse Processes*.

Tobias Richter is Professor of Educational Psychology at Julius-Maximilians-University Würzburg (Germany). Formerly, he was Professor of Cognitive Psychology at the University of Kassel (Germany). He currently serves as speaker of the Educational Psychology Division of the German Psychological Society (Deutsche Gesellschaft für Psychologie, DGPs). In his research, he is interested in cognitive foundations of learning, language and text comprehension, learning from text and digital media, learning disorders, and assessment and intervention in education.

Nikita A. Salovich is a graduate student in Cognitive Psychology at Northwestern University. Her research investigates why people rely on inaccurate information even when they should know better, including factors that help predict the likelihood that individuals will engage in effective information evaluation.

Jasmyne A. Sanderson is a postgraduate researcher and a student in the combined Masters of Clinical Neuropsychology and PhD program at the School of Psychological Science at the University of Western Australia. Her research investigates the role of information integration and updating in the continued influence of misinformation.

Lisa Scharrer is a Researcher in the Department of Educational Sciences at the Ruhr-University Bochum in Germany. Her work focuses on learning with multiple documents and the evaluation of information and sources of information on the Internet. She is also interested in public scientific understanding and improving scientific communication.

Anne Schüler studied psychology at the University of Tübingen (Germany) and received her PhD there in 2010. Since 2009, she has been a Research Associate at the Leibniz-Institut für Wissensmedien (Tübingen, Germany). Currently, she is working as a postdoc in the Multiple Representation Lab, where she studies the cognitive foundations of multimedia learning (e.g., mental text-picture integration) and the support of self-regulated processes when learning with multimedia (e.g., Eye Movement Modeling Examples). Furthermore, she studies the processing and impact of conflicting information in videos and social media. She often uses the eye tracking techniques in her research.

Rayne A. Sperling is an educational psychologist. Her research examines the measurement and promotion of learners' self-regulation including their motivation, metacognition, and strategic processing. Her work also addresses effective instructional manipulations, in both traditional and technology-rich environments, that are designed to promote learners' self-regulation, comprehension, decision-making, and problem solving. Much of her work addresses issues of objective-based student assessment, construct measurement, and evaluation.

Nicholas Stepanik earned his Master of Science degree in Mathematics from the University of Connecticut and is currently a doctoral candidate in Educational Psychology at the Pennsylvania State University, University Park. His research interests include both mathematics and physics education, with a focus on how students use and understand multiple representations. His current research involves examining the effects of fluency and sense-making interventions with multiple representations in introductory-level calculus courses.

Helge I. Strømsø is a Professor of Higher Education in the Department of Education at the University of Oslo, Norway. His main research interests are teaching and learning in higher education, digital literacy, and thinking and reasoning about socioscientific issues.

Despina A. Stylianou is a Professor of Mathematics Education at the City College of New York and the Director of Mathematics in the City, a center for K-8 professional development for mathematics teachers. Her research interests lie in the area of mathematical cognition; her work explores the mathematical skills, sensibilities, and habits of mind and action that are critical to doing, learning, and using mathematics proficiently, particularly argumentation and representation.

Michelle Taub is an Assistant Professor in the Department of Learning Sciences and Educational Research, and core faculty of the learning sciences cluster at the University of Central Florida. Her research focuses on using multimodal multichannel data to examine how emotional and motivational states impact the use of cognitive and metacognitive self-regulatory processes during learning with advanced learning technologies. Specifically, she focuses on investigating how eye tracking, facial expressions, and log files can be used as measures of learning processes, and how they impact overall learning and performance with these technologies across different populations of learners and different learning contexts.

Russell Tytler is Alfred Deakin Professor and Chair in Science Education at Deakin University, Melbourne. He has researched and written extensively on student learning and reasoning in science. His interest in the role of representation as a multimodal language for reasoning and learning in science extends to pedagogy and teacher and school change. He researches and writes on interdisciplinary science and mathematics learning, school–community partnerships, and STEM curriculum policy and practice. He is widely published, and has been chief investigator on a range of Australian Research Council and other research projects.

Peggy Van Meter is an Associate Professor and the Director of Undergraduate and Graduate Education in the Department of Educational Psychology, Counseling, and Special Education at Pennsylvania State University. Her research addresses college student learning with multiple representations that include both verbal and visual representations. She has conducted a number of studies across different science and engineering courses testing interventions to support student learning from these representations.

Michael Weinstock is a Senior Lecturer in the Department of Education at Ben-Gurion University of the Negev. He received his PhD in Developmental Psychology from Teachers College, Columbia University. His work examines epistemology, argumentative reasoning, and critical thinking from a developmental lens.

1

LOGGERS AND CONSERVATIONISTS
Navigating the Multiple Resource Forest through the Trees

Alexandra List
PENNSYLVANIA STATE UNIVERSITY

Peggy Van Meter
PENNSYLVANIA STATE UNIVERSITY

Doug Lombardi
UNIVERSITY OF MARYLAND, COLLEGE PARK

Panayiota Kendeou
UNIVERSITY OF MINNESOTA

ABSTRACT

In this introduction to the *Handbook of Learning from Multiple Representations and Perspectives* we use the metaphor of "seeing the forest through the trees" to conceptualize the nature of multiple resource learning. First, in comparing resources to trees, we identify these as originating from sources (i.e., roots), including specific content (i.e., trunk), and taking on various representational formats (i.e., leaves). Second, we identify the cognitive processes involved when learners conceptualize individual resources (i.e., trees) and identifying the connections among them for holistic understanding (i.e., see the forest). Finally, we suggest that learners may be viewed as loggers and conservationists seeking to take advantage of the resources available within a multi-resource forest and to understand the complex ecosystems within it.

Key words: multiple representations, multiple perspectives, multiple resource learning

At the dawn of the Internet Age, Elm and Woods (1985) described a phenomenon of *getting lost*, wherein a learner "does not have a clear conception of relationships within the system, does not know his present location in the system ... and finds it difficult to decide where to look next within the system" (p. 927). Elm and Woods' lost learner may be described as having trouble navigating the dense forest of information through the trees, a problem that has, if anything, become more pronounced with the growing predominance of the Internet (Amadieu, Tricot, & Mariné, 2009; DeStefano & LeFevre, 2007). The ubiquity of the Internet and other technological developments mean not only that learners are inundated with an ever-expanding torrent of information, but that this information is both diverse and complex. Learners now encounter information mediums beyond text, including images and videos, with new formats introduced every day (e.g., infographics, gifs, emojis). Beyond these formatting differences, the information available on the Internet today is heterogenous. Gone is the age of editorial discretion and information gatekeeping (Coiro, 2003; Marchi, 2012; Metzger & Flanagin, 2013). Instead, today's learner encounters not only information that was created to inform and persuade but also to misdirect, mislead, and deceive (Lazer et al., 2018; List & Rubenstein, 2019; Tandoc, Lim, & Ling, 2018). Learners today need help making sense of the wealth and diversity of information on and offline. We conceived of this *Handbook* as an effort to do just that. We aim to help learners traverse the dense forest of information by integrating two independently unfolding lines of research – those of learning from multiple representations and from multiple perspectives. Learning from multiple representations occurs when individuals try to make sense of information presented across multiple, separable representations that differ in symbol systems, formats, or modalities (e.g., texts, diagrams, formulas), with separate representations typically providing content that is consistent and overlapping but not entirely redundant. Learning from multiple perspectives occurs when learners try to understand complex or controversial issues; such issues are often defined by there being a variety of viewpoints, requiring the juxtaposition and integration of these perspectives for learning. We believe that, although developing separately, these lines of research jointly capture the challenges inherent in learning in the 21st-century knowledge society – challenges associated with not only the volume of information available, but also its mixed modality, its potentially indeterminate or inexplicit origin and positionality, and its implicit inter-relatedness to a wealth of other multimodal, ambiguously sourced content.

We introduce the factors and mechanisms associated with learning from multiple representations (Section 1) and from multiple perspectives (Section 2) as well as the characteristics and skills that learners need to be successful at each pursuit (Section 3) and the challenges and opportunities that they may encounter (Section 4). We close this *Handbook* by introducing a framework, the Multiple Resource Learning Framework that, for the first time, explicitly links the learner characteristics and processes jointly involved in learning from both multiple representations and multiple perspectives, the contexts, tasks, and resources that shape such learning, and the constructions that are developed as a result. To foreground this ambitious pursuit, we use the expression of *seeing the forest through the trees* to conceptualize the fundamental goal that learners must accomplish when learning from information resources featuring multiple representations and multiple perspectives. Using this metaphor, we describe how (a) any multimodal and/or multi-positional information resource may be thought of as a tree, (b) how such trees may figure into a broader sylvan landscape of information, and (c) how learners may be conceptualized as loggers and conservationists trying to exploit and cultivate thorny thickets of information on their own and with various degrees of instructional support. We close this introduction with an overview of each *Handbook* section.

INFORMATION RESOURCES ARE LIKE A TREE

Trees have three main parts – the roots, the trunk, and the leaves. So too can information resources be described as having three main features: source, content, and representational format (List & Alexander, 2018). *Source* refers to accessible information about a resource's origin or purpose for being created, including information about author and publisher (Bråten, Strømsø, & Britt, 2009). In addition to serving as a basis for determining trustworthiness, the source contributes to the *perspective* of a resource. In this *Handbook* we define perspective as the collection of attitudes, values, beliefs, knowledge propositions, and goals that guide the presentation of information, including decisions about what content to focus on and which to exclude and which representational format(s) to use in what ways. These attitudes, values, beliefs, knowledge propositions, and goals may be expected to proceed from the author of a given resource, as well as the author's social, cultural, and epistemic (i.e., domain) communities. Nevertheless, while the bulk of prior work, particularly in the field of learning from multiple texts, has focused on understanding learners' determinations of source benevolence and expertise (Bråten et al., 2009; Stadtler & Bromme, 2014), we chose, in this *Handbook*, to focus on a source's perspective(s). Perspective, in addition to linking individual authors to broader sociocultural and epistemic communities (e.g., domains), also links author's positionality with their decisions around what content to include and what representational formats to feature in presenting information to an audience. For instance, similarly benevolent and expert authors may choose to include quotes or narrative descriptions as evidence vis-à-vis data tables and statistical analyses, depending on their epistemic and methodical perspective(s). Similarly, whether authors support or oppose a given proposal may be more a question of perspective than of expertise.

We view the different perspective(s) that authors hold and reproduce in the resources that they create as roots of a tree. Like roots, these perspectives are mostly hidden, rather than manifest, and uncovering these roots is oftentimes an effortful and deliberate process, as demonstrated by the literature on sourcing within the context of learning from multiple texts (Brante & Strømsø, 2018; Britt & Aglinskas, 2002; Strømsø & Bråten, 2014). Nevertheless, their covert nature makes roots or author's perspective no less foundational to the content and representational format of particular resources or trees of information.

We liken a resource's informational *content* to the trunk of a tree, constituting its substantive essence or core. Leaves, then, are the *representational format(s)* that particular resources take on. We use the term representational format to indicate the modalities or symbol system(s) encoding information within particular resources as well as the particular formatting of these systems. While the two primary modalities examined in prior work have been the visual and the linguistic (Mayer, 2001; Mayer & Anderson, 1992), symbol systems as varied as graphic representations, algebraic expressions, and musical notation all constitute different types of representational formats (Loughlin, Grossnickle, Dinsmore, & Alexander, 2015). In this *Handbook* and in the literature on learning from multiple representations, more broadly, our concern is primarily with informational materials that include within them more than one representational format (i.e., multimedia). Such materials characterize the vast majority of information that learners may be expected to encounter, across a range of educational contexts, including when learning using textbooks or the Internet. We do not consider a resource's representational format(s) to be a superficial matter of style, rather, we view these as a deliberate, perspective-driven choices on the part of authors (Schnotz & Baadte, 2015; Schnotz & Bannert, 2003). We further acknowledge that it is oftentimes the representational format that may suggest to learners the starkest contrasts among resources. That is, learners may much more readily perceive differences among texts, diagrams, and animations, even if these are representing the same content, than they would more subtle contrasts between authors holding different perspectives on a common issue. This is similar to how we perceive the differences among pines, oaks, and palms most starkly because of their leaves, despite these also varying in qualities of their roots and trunk.

To extend this metaphor further, source perspectives, content, and representational formats are inextricably linked as are roots, trunk, and leaves. Likewise, just as the nature of trees' roots, trunk, and leaves represent an environmental adaptation, so too can information resources be viewed as derived from and existing within their sociocultural and epistemic contexts. As an illustration, consider that the content and representational format characteristics of journal articles within any scholarly domain are a result not only of author perspective but also of the historical legacies and conventions of academic publishing. Likewise, the content of Tweets and any hashtags assigned are both a matter of author perspective and of Twitter communities' communicative practices.

As a final note, the term informational resource, or input, is used with intention both in this introduction and throughout this *Handbook*. Resources and inputs are broad terms that encapsulate the multitude of sources, texts, perspectives, and representations that learners may be expected to encounter during complex learning tasks, as reflected in the literatures on learning from multiple representations and from multiple perspectives. Moreover, resources hold a dual meaning as scaffolds provided to aid learners and as materials needed to be effortfully extracted and manufactured before they can be used. We consider these dual meanings to be particularly apt for capturing how resources are viewed in the fields of learning from multiple representations and from multiple perspectives. On the one hand, particularly in the literature on learning from multiple representations, resources are deliberately designed by teachers and researchers to aid learners in the process of learning. Indeed, color codes, in-text deictic references, labels, and other signaling devices (Lorch, Lemarié, & Grant, 2011; Scheiter & Eitel, 2015) have all been used as means of modifying multimodal instructional materials to be more accessible and effective resources for learners (Richter, Scheiter, & Eitel, 2016). On the other hand, both the literatures on learning from multiple perspectives and multiple representations recognize that learning from even the most optimally designed instructional resources is not an automatic or passive process for learners. Rather, these literatures approach learning as an active, deliberate, effortful, and strategic process. In the section that follows, we highlight some of the strategic processes that may be expected to be involved in individuals' learning from multimodal and multi-perspective resources. We frame these processes as those required to conceptualize the information forest through the various multimodal and multi-perspective trees.

MULTIPLE, MULTIMODAL, MULTI-PERSPECTIVE RESOURCES ARE LIKE TREES IN A FOREST

In the previous section, we established that trees constitute a potent metaphor to capture the source perspective, content, and representational format(s) that define any informational resource. In this section, we move from considering informational resources or trees in isolation to viewing these as part of a dense informational forest. Indeed, making sense of trees or informational sources in relation to one another may be the fundamental task inherent in learning from multiple representations and multiple perspective, or in seeing the forest through the trees. We consider such relational sense making to be guided by three features of multi-resource learning tasks.

First, multi-resource learning tasks require that each resource included be understood individually, as itself. That is, in order to form relations across information resources, each resource must be understood both holistically and analytically. This requires both understanding a given tree as a whole and decomposing the subcomponents within it and identifying the relations among these parts. We see such holistic and analytic comprehension processes manifest in both the literatures on learning from multiple representations and from multiple perspectives. In the literature on learning from multiple representations, it is common to analyze learners' distribution of attentional resources (e.g., gaze patterns) across individual representational components within a multimedia resource (e.g., a text and a diagram) and as shifting between these (Mason, Pluchino, Tornatora, & Ariasi, 2013; Ozcelik, Arslan-Ari, & Cagiltay, 2010). Likewise, the emergent literature on learning from multiple perspectives, stemming largely from the literature on learning from multiple texts, has focused on learners' mastery of outcomes associated with both comprehension and integration; while the former has been concerned with learners' understanding of individual texts and the perspectives provided within them, the latter has been concerned with learners' cross-perspective and cross-text relation formation across the resources available (Florit, Cain, & Mason, 2019; Gil, Bråten, Vidal-Abarca, & Strømsø, 2010; List, Lee, & Du, under review).

Second, as suggested by the examples above, multiple resource learning is foundationally an exercise in relation formation within and across multimedia resources. We see this relation formation evidenced both when learners link multimedia features within a single resource and when learners identify complementary, corroborative, causal, and conflicting relations across a set of resources provided (Ainsworth, 2006; Braasch, Bråten, Britt, Steffens, & Strømsø, 2014; Cromley, Snyder-Hogan, & Luciw-Dubas, 2010; List, Du, Wang, & Lee, 2019; Wiley et al., 2009). Here the metaphor of seeing the forest through the trees becomes even more potent. For there to be a forest, trees of various types need to be presented alongside one another. But it is not the physical positioning of trees side by side that makes up a forest; rather, the forest is an ecosystem with trees inter-related to one another in a variety of sophisticated ways. Symbiosis, mutualism, commensalism, parasitism, competition, and predation all describe relationships in the forest ecosystem. Yet these relationships are not readily apparent nor easily seen and thus uncovering these delicate interconnections requires deliberate analysis. Similarly, the relationships among multiple, multimedia resources are often complex and opaque so that learners must engage in careful analysis and construction in order to identify the relationships among these. These challenges may, in part, be a consequence of the nature of the relationships between resources, such as when perspectives disagree with, dispute, or discredit one another or when two representations serve different functional roles.

Finally, it is critical to recognize that seeing the forest through the trees is fundamentally a matter of perspective. Wandering through the forest allows for comparing trees to one another, but it is only by standing at its edge or flying above it that a forest could possibly be conceptualized in its entirety. This reminds us, first, that learners are not neutral observers; rather, it is their positionality within the forest that dictates what trees they see, how they perceive these, and their ability to discern the connections among these. This conclusion is well supported by literature indicating that how learners engage with multiple representations and multiple perspectives is influenced by a host of unique individual differences, including learners' own attitudes, perspectives, prior knowledge, and cognitive abilities (Kardash & Scholes, 1996; Lord, Ross, & Lepper, 1979; Rau, 2018; Taber & Lodge, 2006; Van Meter, Cameron, & Waters, 2017). At the same time, pragmatically, an entire forest, in its totality, can rarely, if ever, be seen, especially as its boundaries and constituencies are constantly in flux. Instead, learners are much more likely to study an area or a patch of land, as a proxy for the broader forest beyond. Such study requires the simultaneous recognition that the forest is a boundless information landscape and that we have limited capabilities to process or understand it all. This tension between information volume and individuals' limited processing capacities may be at the heart of the difficulties associated with learning from multiple resources and the driving force behind Elm and Woods' (1985) conceptualization of being lost.

The vastness of the information available and our correspondingly limited processing capacities are only some of the challenges associated with learning from multiple representations and from multiple perspectives. A forest represents a foreboding landscape not only because of the volume of trees within it or their varied nature but also because a forest represents a profound unknown, equally likely to contain trails that guide the way through and those that meander in circles. So too, in understanding learning from multiple representations and from multiple perspectives it is necessary to recognize that at least some of the challenges associated with learning from such resources come from learners approaching these with, definitionally, little knowledge of the information within them. Learners do not know the possible connections that could exist across representations or the range of perspectives that there may be on a given topic. To address this gap requires explicitly signaling connections across multimedia representations and using graphic organizers and other scaffolds to systematize and connect the perspectives that learners are likely to encounter. Although the former has extensively been done in the field of learning from multiple representations (Mayer, 2001; Richter et al., 2016), the latter is only now being introduced within the literature on learning from multiple perspectives (Barzilai & Eshet-Alkalai, 2015; Kiili & Leu, 2019; Luo & Kiewra, 2019).

The limited knowledge that learners may bring to bear on learning from multiple representations and multiple perspectives may be mitigated by effectively designing instructional resources, like clearly marked hiking trails through a forest. Nevertheless, a final aspect of viewing today's informational milieu as a forest landscape is recognizing that most of the journeys that learners are likely to take will not follow such well-worn trails. Learners instead are likely to wander along winding paths, some of which may leave them more lost than when they started. This describes the nature of learners' information use in the era of virality, truth decay, and deep fakes, all occurring alongside the decline of traditional notions of reliability and expertise (Kendeou, McCrudden, & Robinson, in press; Mills, 2012; Shao et al., 2018). It is for this type of wandering that we aim to equip learners through this *Handbook*. It is our hope that teaching learners to traverse the information forest more strategically will help them to better take advantage of the abundances within it.

LEARNERS AS LOGGERS AND CONSERVATIONISTS IN AN INFORMATION FOREST

While recognizing the challenges facing learners seeking to traverse the multi-resources forest, it is also the case that learners can, indeed, overcome such challenges. Extending our metaphor of the information forest, we suggest that learners may do so by adopting the roles of loggers or conservationists.

Loggers adopt a utility-focused approach to multiple resource use. While intimately familiar with the characteristics of different types of trees, they are ultimately focused on converting trees into logs of a fairly uniform and standard size. This parallels the focus on problem solving and application and transfer widely emphasized in the literature on learning from multiple representations (Brenner et al., 1997; Lesh, Post, & Behr, 1987; Schönborn & Bögeholz, 2009). Information users who are loggers deal with the complexity offered by the multitude of multimodal and multi-perspective resources available in the information forest by focusing on homogenization. That is, just as loggers seek to mitigate the complexity inherent in working with trees of many different shapes and sizes by stripping away the leaves and bark to create logs of uniform width and height, so too learners working with multiple resources select key information across resources and identify points of commonality across them in an effort to reduce information variety and volume. This process of reduction and coordination may be considered to be central to the logger approach to information use, as is the adoption of utility-focused goals.

Conservationists utilize a somewhat different approach. Although no less active in their engagement with information, conservationists are much more reflective in their resource use. Conservationists are concerned with understanding trees, the relationships among them, and the broader ecosystem. While deeply engaged in understanding and analyzing the information forest, in contrast to loggers, conservationists are less inclined to make bold use of the resources available. This parallels work on learning from multiple perspectives, which has thus far emphasized learners' comprehension and integration of multiple perspectives, but less so their use of multiple perspectives to solve problems or to develop perspectives of their own. Crucially, a key feature of the conservationist approach is its concern with sustainability and tree health, paralleling evaluative and epistemic considerations much emphasized in the literature on learning from multiple perspectives (Kohnen & Mertens, 2019; Stahl, Hynd, Britton, & McNish, 1996; Strømsø, Bråten, & Samuelstuen, 2003).

While loggers were described as managing information volume and resource complexity by engaging in selection and harmonization, conservationists are more inclined to appreciate, analyze, and seek to find patterns in, but not necessarily strive to reduce, information complexity. These learners may deal with the variability of resources populating an information forest by seeking to understand and systematize this variability, but not necessarily to eliminate or reduce it. Moreover, conservationists may be said to be less utility-focused in their multiple resource use, as compared to their logger counterparts. Rather, conservationist learners may be expected to be more academically oriented, viewing information resources and perspectives more intellectually as objects of inquiry, rather than only as resources to be used to accomplish some goal.

Of course, not all learners may be loggers or conservationists, both metaphors defined by the adoption of an active approach to resource use. Some learners may simply be survivalist. These learners, even when thrust into an information forest, may seek to limit their engagement within it and hope only to emerge on the other side, unscathed. Such survivalist orientations are demonstrated in the literature on learning from multiple representations in learners' tendencies to rely on text-driven processing even in the presence of additional visual representations (Bartholomé & Bromme, 2009; Mason, Pluchino, & Tornatora, 2015) and in the literature on learning from multiple perspectives in some learners' reluctant or deliberately limited information use (Lawless & Kulikowich, 1996; List & Alexander, 2017). In contrast to loggers and conservationists, these learners are unlikely to view the information forest as one of resource abundance. Rather, such learners may be profoundly aware of the perils of the information forest and to acutely fear "getting lost" within it. It is, in part, these learners that we seek to aid with this *Handbook*; learners wandering lost in the information forest or reluctant to proceed within it. That is, by integrating the literatures on learning from multiple representations and from multiple perspectives we hope to map the challenges presented by the multiple resource forest and to identify the trails and tools necessary to traverse these.

Sfard (1998), in presenting acquisition and participation as two different metaphors for learning, explicitly cautions about the dangers of relying on a single one. She writes:

> the relative advantages of each of the two metaphors make it difficult to give up either of them: Each has something to offer that the other cannot provide. Moreover, relinquishing either ... may have grave consequences, whereas metaphorical pluralism embraces a promise of a better research and a more satisfactory practice.
>
> (p. 10)

Within this *Handbook* we wholeheartedly embrace Sfard's (1998) proposition. Learners need to be taught to be both loggers and conservationists; to understand, evaluate, make use of, and integrate the resources that are abundant in the information forest, but are oftentimes quite difficult to grasp. That is, like loggers, learners must be taught to make efficient use of the resources available to solve problems; and, like conservationists, learners ought to be taught to engage with resources in an analytic and evaluative fashion – construing resources relationally and on an author's terms. As is the case for both loggers and conservationists, learners' development in these regards can only come from deliberate experiences engaging with diverse information resources in a variety of ways. These types of experiences are what future classrooms in the information age should afford.

The metaphors we offer throughout this chapter are obviously simplistic and woefully incomplete. Nevertheless, we use these to introduce the reader to subsequent discussions throughout this *Handbook* on learning from multiple representations and from multiple perspectives in an increasingly complex world. In the section that follows we introduce each section of the *Handbook* as cairns to guide the reader through.

HANDBOOK SECTIONS

Section 1 is focused on learning from multiple representations. Rau (Chapter 2) reviews theoretical frameworks for conceptualizing multiple representation learning. This chapter provides a broad view that encompasses both individuals' cognitive operations and disciplinary practices. Kozma (Chapter 2) examines expert–novice differences in the use of representations. This chapter considers multiple representations in the context of disciplinary practices and illuminates learners' developing abilities. Chapters in the middle half of this section focus on learning from multiple representations. The chapter by Schüler (Chapter 4) presents three different methodological approaches to uncovering the cognitive processes of multiple representations learning and reviews the findings from each. Cromley (Chapter 5) examines individual differences that are associated with multiple representations learning and examines the influence of these individual differences across tasks (e.g., fact recall, transfer) used in multiple representations research. Van Meter and Stepanik's chapter (Chapter 6) examines interventions designed to support multiple representations learning. Dividing these according to how the intervention supports the cognitive operations of multiple representations learning, this chapter reviews materials-, prompts-, and learner-driven interventions. The final two chapters of this section expand the notion of learning from multiple representations by considering representation construction. Ainsworth, Tytler, and Prain's (Chapter 7) focus is on learners' construction of their own science representations and the role of these construction processes in learning. Stylianou (Chapter 8) writes about how learners use representations to aid mathematics problem solving. Together, these final two chapters paint a picture of active learners engaged with representations in generative ways.

Section 2 is focused on learning from multiple perspectives. The section begins with a chapter by Barzilai and Weinstock defining what constitutes a *perspective*, particularly in light of prior work on the role of author or source in individuals' learning from multiple texts. Then, three chapters in this section focus on the individual difference factors involved in learning from multiple perspectives. These include a chapter by Bråten and Strømsø (Chapter 10) focusing on learners' epistemic and ontic beliefs; a chapter by List (Chapter 11) focusing on the role of learners' emergent domain understanding in multiple perspective learning; and a chapter by McCrudden (Chapter 12) examining how learners' attitudes and beliefs may be reflected in the perspectives that they themselves adopt when processing perspective-consistent and -inconsistent information. The next set of chapters focuses on the processes involved in individuals' learning from multiple perspectives. These include examinations of learning from both complementary (Firetto, Chapter 14) and conflicting (Braasch & Scharrer, Chapter 13) perspectives and validation and evaluation processes that are common to learning from multiple perspectives, related to one another in a variety of ways (Richter, Maier, & Münchow, Chapter 16). Finally, the last chapters in this section address how instructional materials and classroom tasks may be used to facilitate learning from multiple perspectives. These chapters include Bohn-Gettler (Chapter 15) discussing how different types of texts may be modified to foster learners' multiple perspective learning and Cho, Kucan, and Rainey (Chapter 17) demonstrating how multiple perspective learning may be fostered through historical inquiry tasks in the social studies classroom.

Section 3 draws on the major constructs and theories populating the educational psychology landscape to explore how such theories conceptualize the integration of multiple perspectives and multiple representations for learning. Follmer and Sperling (Chapter 18) discuss and delineate how executive functions can serve a key role and shape learning during the integration of multiple representations and multiple perspectives. Denton, Muis, Munzar, and Etoubashi (Chapter 19) examine how learners can use self-regulated learning and metacognitive strategies to make sense of multiple representations and multiple perspectives. Lombardi, Heddy, and Matewos (Chapter 20) propose a model suggesting that multiple representations and multiple perspectives mediate the relations between values, attitudes, and beliefs in learning situations. Similarly, Miele, Nokes-Malach, & May (Chapter 21) provide a motivational model of integrative processing, which identifies factors that may influence learners' motivation when integrating various types of representations and perspectives. Pekrun and Loderer (Chapter 22) review theories that inform our understanding of emotions present in learning situations and break down how multiple representations can guide learners' emotion-prompting appraisals and contrary perspectives can foster emotions that influence the processes and outcomes of learning. Alexander and the Disciplined Reading and Learning Research Laboratory (Chapter 23) make the argument that relational reasoning is a critical cognitive capability to facilitate learning from multiple representations and multiple perspectives. Cartiff and Greene (Chapter 24) conclude the section by providing a discussion of how theoretical and empirical work reveals ways that multiple representations and multiple perspectives can facilitate learning, particularly when learners are adept critical thinkers.

Section 4 is focused on the challenges and opportunities that learners encounter in the context of learning from multiple representations and multiple perspectives. The first three chapters in this section discuss the challenges posed by the ever increasing and unregulated information ecosystem that includes multiple representations and multiple perspectives, while also making distinctions between knowledge, misinformation, and fake news. Rapp, Donovan, and Salovich (Chapter 25) revisit an old problem, that of the nature of knowledge, and discuss the challenges that emerge as a result of different conceptualizations of knowledge representations: facts and constellations. Sanderson and Ecker (Chapter 26) focus on the challenge of misinformation, our susceptibility to it, and ways to reduce it. Kendeou, Harsch, Butterfuss, Aubele, and Kim (Chapter 27) discuss the challenges that fake news pose to our intellectual survival, and how human- and technology-level solutions can be applied in the context of the information ecosystem. The next two chapters look at how multiple representations and perspectives can be leveraged to optimize learning. Morgan, Hogan, Hampton, Lippert, and Graesser (Chapter 28) discuss how multiple representations can be integrated into intelligent tutoring systems in an effort to personalize and optimize individuals' learning experiences. Chen and Lin (Chapter 29) examine how multiple learners learn together and illustrate the ways in which multiple representations mitigate challenges and harness multiple perspectives of learners to surpass their individual understanding. In the final chapter, Azevedo and Taub (Chapter 30) discuss how measuring learners' processes and outcomes while using multiple representations can be accomplished using multimodal multichannel data.

REFERENCES

Ainsworth, S. (2006). DeFT: A conceptual framework for considering learning with multiple representations. *Learning and Instruction, 16*(3), 183–198.

Amadieu, F., Tricot, A., & Mariné, C. (2009). Prior knowledge in learning from a non-linear electronic document: Disorientation and coherence of the reading sequences. *Computers in Human Behavior, 25*(2), 381–388.

Bartholomé, T., & Bromme, R. (2009). Coherence formation when learning from text and pictures: What kind of support for whom? *Journal of Educational Psychology, 101*(2), 282. doi:10.1037/a0014312

Barzilai, S., & Eshet-Alkalai, Y. (2015). The role of epistemic perspectives in comprehension of multiple author viewpoints. *Learning and Instruction, 36*, 86–103.

Braasch, J. L. G., Bråten, I., Britt, M. A., Steffens, B., & Strømsø, H. I. (2014). Sensitivity to inaccurate argumentation in health news articles: Potential contributions of readers' topic and epistemic beliefs. In D. N. Rapp & J. L. G. Braasch (Eds.), *Processing inaccurate information: Theoretical and applied perspectives from cognitive science and the educational sciences* (pp. 117–137). Cambridge, MA: MIT Press.

Brante, E. W., & Strømsø, H. I. (2018). Sourcing in text comprehension: A review of interventions targeting sourcing skills. *Educational Psychology Review, 30*(3), 773–799.

Bråten, I., Strømsø, H. I., & Britt, M. A. (2009). Trust matters: Examining the role of source evaluation in students' construction of meaning within and across multiple texts. *Reading Research Quarterly, 44*(1), 6–28.

Brenner, M. E., Mayer, R. E., Moseley, B., Brar, T., Durán, R., Reed, B. S., & Webb, D. (1997). Learning by understanding: The role of multiple representations in learning algebra. *American Educational Research Journal, 34*(4), 663–689.

Britt, M. A., & Aglinskas, C. (2002). Improving students' ability to identify and use source information. *Cognition and Instruction, 20*(4), 485–522.

Coiro, J. (2003). Exploring literacy on the internet. *The Reading Teacher, 56*(5), 458–464.

Cromley, J. G., Snyder-Hogan, L. E., & Luciw-Dubas, U. A. (2010). Cognitive activities in complex science text and diagrams. *Contemporary Educational Psychology, 35*(1), 59–74.

DeStefano, D., & LeFevre, J. A. (2007). Cognitive load in hypertext reading: A review. *Computers in Human Behavior, 23*(3), 1616–1641.

Elm, W. C., & Woods, D. D. (1985, October). Getting lost: A case study in interface design. In; *Proceedings of the Human Factors Society Annual Meeting* (pp. 927–929). Los Angeles, CA: SAGE Publications.

Florit, E., Cain, K., & Mason, L. (2019). Going beyond children's single-text comprehension: The role of fundamental and higher-level skills in 4th graders' multiple-document comprehension. *British Journal of Educational Psychology*. https://doi.org/10.1111/bjep.12288

Gil, L., Bråten, I., Vidal-Abarca, E., & Strømsø, H. I. (2010). Summary versus argument tasks when working with multiple documents: Which is better for whom? *Contemporary Educational Psychology, 35*(3), 157–173.

Kardash, C. M., & Scholes, R. J. (1996). Effects of preexisiting beliefs, epistemological beliefs, and need for cognition on interpretation of controversial issues. *Journal of Educational Psychology, 88*(2), 260–271.

Kendeou, P., McCrudden, M., & Robinson, D. H. (in press). *Misinformation and Fake News in Education*. Charlotte, NC: Information Age Publishing, Inc.

Kiili, C., & Leu, D. J. (2019). Exploring the collaborative synthesis of information during online reading. *Computers in Human Behavior, 95*, 146–157.

Kohnen, A. M., & Mertens, G. E. (2019). "I'm always kind of double-checking": Exploring the information-seeking identities of expert generalists. *Reading Research Quarterly, 54*(3), 279–297.

Lawless, K. A., & Kulikowich, J. M. (1996). Understanding hypertext navigation through cluster analysis. *Journal of Educational Computing Research, 14*(4), 385–399.

Lazer, D. M., Baum, M. A., Benkler, Y., Berinsky, A. J., Greenhill, K. M., Menczer, F., ... Schudson, M. (2018). The science of fake news. *Science, 359*(6380), 1094–1096.

Lesh, R., Post, T., & Behr, M. (1987). Representations and translations among representations in mathematics learning and problem solving. In C. Janvier (Ed.), *Problems of representation in the teaching and learning of mathematics* (pp. 33–40). Hillsdale, NJ: Lawrence Erlbaum Associates.

List, A., & Alexander, P. A. (2017). Text navigation in multiple source use. *Computers in Human Behavior, 75*, 364–375.

List, A., & Alexander, P. A. (2018). Postscript: In pursuit of integration. *Learning and Instruction, 57*, 82–85.

List, A., & Rubenstein, L. D. (2019). Understanding susceptibility to educational inaccuracies: Examining the Likelihood of Adoption Model. In P. Kendeou, D. H. Robinson, & M. McCrudden (Eds.), *Misinformation, quackery, and fake news in education*. Charlotte, NC: Information Age Publishing.

List, A., Du, H., Wang, Y., & Lee, H. Y. (2019). Toward a typology of integration: Examining the documents model framework. *Contemporary Educational Psychology, 58*, 228–242.

List, A., Lee, H. Y., & Du, H. (under review). How do students integrate multiple texts? An investigation of top-down processing.

Lorch, R. F., Jr., Lemarié, J., & Grant, R. A. (2011). Three information functions of headings: A test of the SARA theory of signaling. *Discourse Processes, 48*(3), 139–160.

Lord, C. G., Ross, L., & Lepper, M. R. (1979). Biased assimilation and attitude polarization: The effects of prior theories on subsequently considered evidence. *Journal of Personality and Social Psychology, 37*(11), 2098–2109.

Loughlin, S., Grossnickle, E., Dinsmore, D., & Alexander, P. (2015). "Reading" paintings: Evidence for trans-symbolic and symbol-specific comprehension processes. *Cognition and Instruction, 33*(3), 257–293.

Luo, L., & Kiewra, K. A. (2019). Soaring to successful synthesis writing: An investigation of SOAR strategies for college students writing from multiple sources. *Journal of Writing Research., 11*(1), 163–209.

Marchi, R. (2012). With Facebook, blogs, and fake news, teens reject journalistic "objectivity". *Journal of Communication Inquiry, 36*(3), 246–262.

Mason, L., Pluchino, P., & Tornatora, M. C. (2015). Eye-movement modeling of integrative reading of an illustrated text: Effects on processing and learning. *Contemporary Educational Psychology, 41*, 172–187. doi:10.1016/j.cedpsych.2015.01.004

Mason, L., Pluchino, P., Tornatora, M. C., & Ariasi, N. (2013). An eye-tracking study of learning from science text with concrete and abstract illustrations. *Journal of Experimental Education, 81*(3), 356–384.

Mayer, R. E. (2001). *Multimedia learning*. London: Cambridge University Press.

Mayer, R. E., & Anderson, R. B. (1992). The instructive animation: Helping students build connections between words and pictures in multimedia learning. *Journal of Educational Psychology, 84*(4), 444–452.

Metzger, M. J., & Flanagin, A. J. (2013). Credibility and trust of information in online environments: The use of cognitive heuristics. *Journal of Pragmatics, 59*, 210–220.

Mills, A. J. (2012). Virality in social media: The SPIN framework. *Journal of Public Affairs, 12*(2), 162–169.

Ozcelik, E., Arslan-Ari, I., & Cagiltay, K. (2010). Why does signaling enhance multimedia learning? Evidence from eye movements. *Computers in Human Behavior, 26*(1), 110–117.

Rau, M. A. (2018). Making connections among multiple visual representations: How do sense-making skills and perceptual fluency relate to learning of chemistry knowledge?. *Instructional Science, 46*(2), 209–243. doi:10.1007/s11251-017-9431-3

Richter, J., Scheiter, K., & Eitel, A. (2016). Signaling text-picture relations in multimedia learning: A comprehensive meta-analysis. *Educational Research Review, 17*, 19–36.

Scheiter, K., & Eitel, A. (2015). Signals foster multimedia learning by supporting integration of highlighted text and diagram elements. *Learning and Instruction, 36*, 11–26.

Schnotz, W., & Baadte, C. (2015). Surface and deep structures in graphics comprehension. *Memory & Cognition, 43*(4), 605–618. doi:10.3758/s13421-014-0490-2

Schnotz, W., & Bannert, M. (2003). Construction and interference in learning from multiple representation. *Learning and Instruction, 13*(2), 141–156.

Schönborn, K. J., & Bögeholz, S. (2009). Knowledge transfer in biology and translation across external representations: Experts' views and challenges for learning. *International Journal of Science and Mathematics Education, 7*(5), 931–955.

Sfard, A. (1998). On two metaphors for learning and the dangers of choosing just one. *Educational Researcher, 27*(2), 4–13.

Shao, C., Ciampaglia, G. L., Varol, O., Yang, K. C., Flammini, A., & Menczer, F. (2018). The spread of low-credibility content by social bots. *Nature Communications, 9*(1), 4787.

Stadtler, M., & Bromme, R. (2014). The content–Source integration model: A taxonomic description of how readers comprehend conflicting scientific information. In D. N. Rapp & J. Braasch (Eds.), *Processing inaccurate information: Theoretical and applied perspectives from cognitive science and the educational sciences* (pp. 379–402). Cambridge, MA: MIT Press.

Stahl, S. A., Hynd, C. R., Britton, B. K., McNish, M. M., & Bosquet, D. (1996). What happens when students read multiple source documents in history?. *Reading Research Quarterly, 31*(4), 430–456.

Strømsø, H. I., & Bråten, I. (2014). Students' sourcing while reading and writing from multiple web documents. *Nordic Journal of Digital Literacy, 9*((02)), 92–111.

Strømsø, H. I., Bråten, I., & Samuelstuen, M. S. (2003). Students' strategic use of multiple sources during expository text reading: A longitudinal think-aloud study. *Cognition and Instruction, 21*(2), 113–147.

Taber, C. S., & Lodge, M. (2006). Motivated skepticism in the evaluation of political beliefs. *American Journal of Political Science, 50*(3), 755–769.

Tandoc, E. C., Jr, Lim, Z. W., & Ling, R. (2018). Defining "fake news" A typology of scholarly definitions. *Digital Journalism, 6*(2), 137–153.

Van Meter, P. N., Cameron, C., & Waters, J. R. (2017). Effects of response prompts and diagram comprehension ability on text and diagram learning in a college biology course. *Learning and Instruction, 49*, 188–198. doi:10.1016/j.learninstruc.2017.01.003

Wiley, J., Goldman, S. R., Graesser, A. C., Sanchez, C. A., Ash, I. K., & Hemmerich, J. A. (2009). Source evaluation, comprehension, and learning in internet science inquiry tasks. *American Educational Research Journal, 46*(4), 1060–1106.

Section 1
Learning from Multiple Representations

2

COGNITIVE AND SOCIO-CULTURAL THEORIES ON COMPETENCIES AND PRACTICES INVOLVED IN LEARNING WITH MULTIPLE EXTERNAL REPRESENTATIONS

Martina A. Rau

UNIVERSITY OF WISCONSIN – MADISON

ABSTRACT

Instruction often involves multiple external representations that use different symbol systems such as text and visuals. While multiple representations can help students learn by providing complementary information about complex concepts, they can hinder students' learning if students fail to understand how each representation shows information or how multiple representations relate to one another. Cognitive research has investigated which competencies help students learn with multiple representations. This line of research suggests that students need to acquire verbal sense-making competencies and nonverbal perceptual fluency with multiple representations, as well as meta-representational competencies. Socio-cultural research has investigated how students acquire representation practices while interacting with members of scientific, professional, or learning communities. This research suggests that enculturation in such communities involves both verbal and nonverbal communication processes that allow students to use representations to participate in disciplinary discourse. The goal of this chapter is to describe how these theoretical perspectives have influenced research on the processes through which students learn representational competencies and practices in learning with multiple representations. In doing so, I highlight overlap and differences between the cognitive and socio-cultural perspectives. As practical interventions are the focus of later chapters, I only briefly discuss how these perspectives can inform instruction.

Key words: multiple external representations, cognitive theories, socio-cultural theories, sense-making competencies, perceptual fluency

INTRODUCTION

STEM instruction heavily relies on a variety of external representations to illustrate complex concepts (Ainsworth, 2006; NRC, 2006). For example, students learning about chemical bonding typically read texts that describe foundational concepts of bonding (Fig. 2.1a), use equations to predict reactions (Fig. 2.1b), and visualize molecules with a variety of visual representations (Fig. 2.1c–e). The educational research literature defines multiple external representations as a combination of different presentations that illustrate the same content but use different symbol systems (e.g., symbolic versus visual).

The use of multiple external representations serves two goals, which have been examined by research from different theoretical perspectives (Rau, 2017). First, cognitive research focuses on the *pedagogical* goal of using representations to help students understand abstract concepts (e.g., Ainsworth, 2006; Schnotz, 2014). Second, socio-cultural research focuses on the *professional* goal of how representations can help students learn verbal and nonverbal communication practices of professional communities (e.g., Greeno & Hall, 1997; Latour, 1990). While these perspectives focus on different goals, both perspectives examine which *representational competencies* students need in order to successfully learn with multiple representations, which describe the knowledge and skills students need in order to depict information and use such depictions to solve problems (Rau, 2017). In this chapter, I focus on cognitive research that has investigated which representational competencies students need to successfully learn with multiple representations. Then, I briefly review socio-cultural research on how students acquire representation practices while highlighting overlap and differences between the two theoretical perspectives. While practical interventions are the focus of later chapters in this volume, I briefly discuss how the theoretical perspectives can be translated into instructional supports for learning with multiple representations.

LITERATURE REVIEW

Why are multiple representations so prevalent in instructional materials? Indeed, it is hard to find instructional materials that do not use visuals in addition to words and symbols. Multiple external representations can help students learn about complex concepts because they can provide complementary information, constrain the

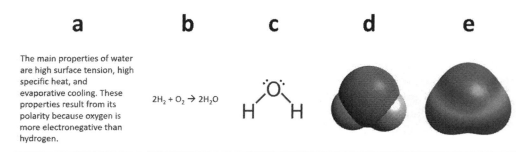

Figure 2.1 Multiple external representations about chemical bonding; (a) and (b) show symbolic representations (i.e., text and equation), whereas (c), (d), and (e) show visual representations (i.e., Lewis structure, space-filling model, and electrostatic potential map (EPM)).

interpretation of the information they depict, and encourage construction of deeper meaning (Ainsworth, 2006). Representations complement each other if they engage students in different processes and because they provide different information. For example, while texts can describe properties of water molecules (Fig. 2.1a), visual representations can complement the descriptions by showing bonded and unbonded electrons (Fig. 2.1c), bond angles (Fig. 2.1d), and electron distributions (Fig. 2.1e). Representations constrain one another if one representation provides information that helps students interpret the other representation. For example, the text (Fig. 2.1a) states that oxygen is more electronegative than hydrogen, which may help students interpret the color red in the EPM (Fig. 2.1e) as indicating regions of high electron density. Multiple representations can encourage students to construct deeper meaning because making connections between the representations as illustrated in the previous examples requires students to achieve insights that go beyond what can be shown in one single representation.

To understand why multiple external representations can help students learn, it is useful to first revisit how educational research defines representations.

What are Multiple External Representations and Why are They Helpful?

Representations are objects that stand for something else – a referent (Peirce, Hartshorne, Weiss, & Burks, 1935). For example, the referent of the visual representations in Fig. 2.1c–e is a water molecule. While representations provided in instructional materials are *external* representations because they are outside of the student, imagined representations are *internal* (Rau, 2017). For example, if the student mentally visualizes a water molecule when hearing the word "water," he/she draws on an internal representation of a water molecule. Internal representations are building blocks of mental models, which describe students' knowledge about a given topic. For example, a student's mental model may contain numerous internal representations of molecules that exemplify covalent, polar, and ionic types of bonds.

The distinction between internal and external representations is key to understanding how educational research defines the term *multiple* external representations. This term typically refers to a combination of external representations that use different symbol systems. A common distinction is between symbolic and visual symbol systems. For example, Schnotz (2014) defines symbolic representations as those that use features that are descriptive in that they have an arbitrary, convention-based mapping to the referent. For example, text or equations (Fig. 2.1a–b) contain letters, numbers, and symbols that carry no meaning in and by themselves, but that have an agreed-upon mapping to constructs such as that O stands for oxygen. By contrast, visual representations use features that are depictive in the sense that they have a similarity-based mapping to the referent. For example, the space-filling model in Fig. 2.1d uses concrete features such as the size of spheres that correlate with the actual size of atoms. Further, visual representations can be distinguished based on the degree to which they are abstract (i.e., they use features with low similarity to the referent) or concrete (i.e., they use features with high similarity to the referent). For example, the Lewis structure in Fig. 2.1c contains some symbolic features and some features with low similarity to the referent (e.g., dots for electrons), whereas the space-filling model in Fig. 2.1d uses features with higher similarity to the referent (e.g., sphere size).

The distinction between symbolic and visual representations is important because many educational theories assume that they are processed in different parts of working memory. This notion draws on the dual coding assumption, which suggests that working memory has a verbal part and a visual part (Baddeley, 2012; Chandler & Sweller, 1991; Paivio, 1986). As detailed below, one reason why multiple external representations are considered to be more effective than a single representation is that they are making more effective use of students' working memory capacity by drawing on both the verbal and visual parts (Mayer, 2005, 2009).

However, multiple external representations do not always live up to their potential to enhance students' learning. While we typically assume that multiple representations help students learn because they make abstract concepts accessible, abundant research shows that they can impede students' learning if students fail to understand how each representation depicts information or if they fail to integrate information across the different representations (Rau, Aleven, & Rummel, 2015). Because students often use representations they are unfamiliar with to learn concepts they are equally unfamiliar with, they face a *representation dilemma* (Dreher & Kuntze, 2015; Rau, 2017). That is, students do not know how the representations illustrate concepts, or what the concepts are but are expected to use the representations to learn the concepts. Consequently, when learning with external representations, students simultaneously learn about the representations and about the concepts (Rau, 2017).

Educational research describes knowledge about how representations show information in terms of *representational competencies* (diSessa, 2004; Kozma & Russell, 2005; NRC, 2006). This research can be distinguished by whether it takes a cognitive or a socio-cultural theoretical perspective (Nathan & Sawyer, 2014; Rau, 2017). Cognitive research seeks to resolve the representation dilemma by examining which types of representational competencies students need in order to benefit from multi-representational instructional materials (Ainsworth, 2006; NRC, 2006). Sociocultural theories consider the representation dilemma as a defining feature of scientific discourse where professional scientists continuously refine their understanding of representations through multiple iterations of creating representations of phenomena that allow reflecting on the phenomena (Justi & Gilbert, 2002; NRC, 2006). Hence, representational competencies are an ever-evolving cultural phenomenon that students acquire as they participate in discourse with members of the scientific community.

Cognitive Research on Representational Competencies

Cognitive research attempts to resolve the representation dilemma by investigating which representational competencies enable students to learn new content with multiple representations. Cognitive theories assume that competencies are the sum of many component skills and pieces of knowledge that constitute expertise in a given domain (Koedinger, Corbett, & Perfetti, 2012) – referred to as the "factoring assumption" (Nathan & Sawyer, 2014).

The factoring assumption can be illustrated with the example of two prominent theories about learning with multiple representations: Mayer's (2005, 2009) Cognitive Theory of Multimedia Learning (CTML) and Schnotz's (2005, 2014) Integrated Model of Text and Picture Comprehension (ITPC). The CTML assumes human capacity for information processing is limited. If processing of information exceeds a student's cognitive capacity, this results in cognitive overload, which can impede learning. Further, building on the dual channel assumption (Chandler & Sweller, 1991) the CTML posits that when verbal information is loaded into the verbal channel of working memory, students form a verbal mental model. Similarly, visual information results in a pictorial mental model in the visual channel. Learning happens when students actively integrate information from the mental models of the verbal and visual channels with prior knowledge that is retrieved from long-term memory. Multiple representations (e.g., text and visual) are more effective than a single representation (e.g., text only) because the verbal and visual channels each have their own working memory capacity. Hence, overall working memory capacity is increased when instructional materials present both verbal and visual information, compared to presenting only verbal or only visual information. Increased cognitive capacity reduces the risk of cognitive overload and thereby enhances learning. The CTML illustrates the factoring assumption because it considers information as being processed pieces (or "chunks") that can take up working memory capacity.

The ITPC (Schnotz, 2005, 2014) further specifies the nature of verbal and visual processing in the respective working memory channels. Verbal information (e.g., written or spoken text) is internally represented as symbolic propositions. To make meaning of these propositions, students draw on orthographic knowledge from long-term memory. This yields a descriptive mental model of the content of the text. By contrast, visual representations have direct correspondences to the referent. Therefore, visual information (e.g., an image) can be mapped directly to a pictorial mental model. Then, students can integrate both types of mental models with their prior domain knowledge, which constitutes learning. Because analog internal representations carry more concrete information, Schnotz (2014) proposes that they are more directly available for mental model formation than propositional internal representations, which are more abstract and flexible and therefore have to be interpreted in relation to the students' prior knowledge about the given topic before they can be integrated into the mental model. In sum, it is *because* of these complementary functions of analog and propositional internal representations for mental model formation that multiple external representations have the potential to enhance students' learning. Thus, similar to the CTML, the ITPC assumes that chunks of information can be extracted from different types of external representations and integrated with other chunks of information that are retrieved from long-term memory.

Overall, cognitive research distinguishes between three broader types of representational competencies based on qualitative differences between the processes they involve; namely, sense-making competencies, perceptual fluency, and meta-representational competencies (Rau, 2017). *Sense-making competencies* describe explicit, analytical knowledge that allows students to engage in verbal, explanation-based processes to map visual features of representations to domain-relevant concepts (Ainsworth, 2006; Rau, 2017). By contrast, *perceptual fluency* describes implicit, automatic knowledge that allows students to engage effortlessly and efficiently in recognition-based processes to quickly see information in visual representations (Goldstone, 1997; Kellman & Massey, 2013). Further, this research distinguishes multiple types of sense-making competencies and perceptual fluency, depending on how many visual representations are involved (Rau, 2017). Finally, *meta-representational competencies* describe students' knowledge about their knowledge about visual representations and hence subsumes their knowledge about their own sense-making competencies and perceptual fluency.

Sense-Making Competencies

With respect to sense-making competencies, research distinguishes *representational* sense-making and *connectional* sense-making competencies (Rau, 2017). *Representational sense-making competencies* describe students' ability to explain how an individual visual representation shows information about domain-relevant concepts (Ainsworth, 2006; Mayer, 2009; Schnotz, 2014). Based on the previously mentioned dual coding theory, Schnotz (2014) and Mayer (2009) describe these processes in terms of mapping visual features to prior knowledge about the referent that students internally represent in their mental model of the domain. For example, to make sense of the Lewis structure in Fig. 2.1c, students have to map the dots to unbonded valence electron pairs in a molecule. That is, they have to map the visual feature (i.e., the dots) to their conceptual knowledge about bonding (i.e., not all valence electrons participate in bonds).

According to structure mapping theory (Gentner & Markman, 1997), students establish these mappings based on similarities between the external representation and the referent. On the one hand, similarities in concrete visual representations can help students make mappings (e.g., the dots in the Lewis structure in Figure 2.1c are a more concrete depiction of electrons than the color coding in the EPM in Figure 2.1e). On the other hand, similarities between visual features and the referent may not be conceptually relevant. In this case, students also need to distinguish between relevant and irrelevant shared features; or else they might acquire misconceptions that can hinder future learning. For example, the dots in the Lewis structure in Fig. 2.1c could suggest the misconception that electrons are stationary and belong to one atom, rather than being shared across the entire molecule while having a certain likelihood of residing in a given area, as depicted by the EPM in Fig. 2.1e. In sum, representational sense-making competencies involve students' ability to distinguish relevant and irrelevant visual features of an individual representation and to explain how the relevant visual features map to their mental model of domain-relevant concepts.

Connectional sense-making competencies describe students' ability to make sense of connections among various representations (Ainsworth, 2006; Rau, 2017). Because analog internal representations of visual representations maintain similarity-based mappings between the visual representation's features and the referent, students have to distinguish between incidental and conceptually meaningful similarities among the representations. For example, both the space-filling model in Fig. 2.1d and the EPM in Fig. 2.1e use the color red, but the space-filling model uses red as a code for oxygen, whereas the EPM uses red for regions of high electron density. In the case of a water molecule, oxygen has high electron density, but this is a coincidence. Hence, mappings based on color could be confusing and potentially misleading to students. By contrast, all visual representations in Fig. 2.1c–e show that the water molecule is bent, which is an accurate representation of the geometry of water molecules. Hence, mappings based on the spatial features of the visual representations are conceptually meaningful. These examples illustrate that, when students distinguish between incidental and meaningful mappings, they build on their mental models of the domain content. Further, these examples illustrate that representational sense-making competencies about how each individual representation depicts information (e.g., EPMs use red to indicate regions of high electron density) can help students make sense of connections among multiple representations.

In addition, students need to make sense of differences between the representations (Ainsworth, 2006; Rau, Michaelis, & Fay, 2015); that is, they need to compare the representations with respect to what concepts one shows but the other one does not. For example, the Lewis structure in Fig. 2.1c shows two lone electron pairs, whereas the space-filling model and the EPM in Fig. 2.1d–e do not. Making sense of such differences allows students to use one representation to constrain their interpretation of another representation (Ainsworth, 2006). For example, the lone electron pairs by the oxygen molecule explain why the water molecule has a bent geometry, which is shown most reliably in the space-filling model. This example also illustrates that sense-making competencies involve the ability to combine information across multiple representations that provide complementary information about domain-relevant concepts (e.g., about lone electrons and molecular geometry). Finally, by making sense of these connections students construct deeper understanding of the content than would be possible with only one of these representations. In sum, connectional sense-making competencies involve the ability to explain comparisons among multiple representations based on conceptually relevant similarities and differences.

Perceptual Fluency

With respect to perceptual fluency, research distinguishes *representational* fluency and *connectional* fluency (Rau, 2017). *Representational fluency* describes students' ability to "see at a glance" what an individual representation shows quickly, automatically, and without perceived mental effort (Chi, Bassok, Lewis, Reimann, & Glaser, 1989; Kellman & Massey, 2013). With respect to Schnotz's (2014) ITPC, representational fluency indicates that students have achieved a high level of expertise that allows them to efficiently form accurate internal representations of external representations. Hence, representational fluency involves students' ability to quickly retrieve conceptual information shown by the representation from their mental model of the domain content (Chase & Simon, 1973; Kellman & Massey, 2013). For example, when students are presented with the Lewis structure in Fig. 2.1c, they should immediately see that it shows a water molecule.

The mechanisms through which students acquire representational fluency differ fundamentally from those through which students acquire sense-making competencies. According to perceptual learning research, students become representationally fluent via inductive processes involved in perceptual pattern learning (Gibson, 1969; Kellman & Massey, 2013; Richman, Gobet, Staszewski, & Simon, 1996). In terms of Schnotz's (2014) ITPC, representational fluency describes efficiency in retrieving conceptual information from mental models based on internal representations. This efficiency results from perceptual chunking; that is, rather than relying on feature-by-feature mappings between external representations and concepts, they can treat the entire external representation and its associated internal representation as a perceptual chunk to retrieve conceptual information (Richman et al., 1996). For example, when presented with the EPM in Fig. 2.1e, students immediately "see" a polar molecule that likely is water, which implies that the substance has high surface tension, high specific heat, etc.

Perceptual pattern-learning processes are not necessarily willful or planned; instead, they are experience-based, and often implicit to the degree that students may not even be aware of them (Kellman & Massey, 2013; Schooler, Fiore, & Brandimonte, 1997). For example, students' ability to quickly recognize various molecules based on their EPMs likely results from their exposure to numerous examples of such representations throughout their chemistry learning experiences. As a consequence, perceptual pattern recognition is not necessarily verbally accessible; in fact, some research suggests that trying to verbalize how or why one perceives information in perceptual stimuli can even interfere with the accuracy of perceptual pattern recognition (Schooler et al., 1997; Schooler, Ohlsson, & Brooks, 1993). For example, it is likely that students are able to explain why they infer which molecule an EPM shows, but doing so may decrease their accuracy in recognizing molecules based on EPMs. In sum, representational fluency describes students' ability to quickly recognize conceptual information based on individual visual representations.

Connectional fluency describes students' ability to quickly and effortlessly translate among multiple representations. Specifically, in addition to becoming perceptually fluent with each of the representations, students also need to learn to automatically "just see" whether two representations show the same information, to quickly combine information across different representations, and to translate among them without mental effort (Chase & Simon, 1973; Kellman & Massey, 2013). For example, when students see the Lewis structure and the EPM in Fig. 2.1c and 1e, they have to immediately see that they both show water and use the information about how many electrons (Fig. 2.1c) likely reside in which region of the molecule (Fig. 2.1e) to predict how the polarity of the molecule explains properties of water. This example illustrates that connectional fluency describes a student's ability to translate among multiple representations with high accuracy and efficiency.

In terms of Schnotz's (2014) ITPC, connectional fluency describes students' ability to map multiple internal representations of the multiple external representations to one another. Analogous to representational fluency, this competency results from perceptual chunking (Goldstone, Schyns, & Medin, 1997; Kellman & Massey, 2013). Instead of mapping particular features to one another, students learn to process the entire external representation as one perceptual chunk, which allows for efficient mappings among perceptual chunks. In sum, connectional fluency describes students' ability to quickly integrate conceptual information across multiple representations.

Meta-representational Competencies

Much research on meta-cognition has investigated how students acquire knowledge about their own knowledge (e.g., Hartman, 2002). Analogously, in addition to acquiring knowledge about the representations themselves, students also acquire knowledge about their knowledge about representations; typically referred to as meta-representational competencies (NRC, 2006; Rau, 2017). Meta-representational competencies allow students to select appropriate representations for a given problem, as well as to critique and modify representations (diSessa & Sherin, 2000).

Selecting appropriate representations involves two aspects: knowledge about which representation fits the demands of a given problem and knowledge about the student's own ability to successfully use the representation (Acevedo Nistal, Van Dooren, & Verschaffel, 2013; Ainsworth, 2006). Both aspects require sense-making competencies as well as perceptual fluency. First, connectional sense-making competencies are involved in comparing how different representations show relevant content, so as to make an informed decision about which information is needed to solve the problem. Similarly, connectional fluency is involved when the student compares representations in terms of how easily and efficiently it makes conceptual information about the problem available. Second, representational sense-making competencies are involved when the student assesses his/her own points of confusion about interpreting a given representation. This allows the student to make an informed decision about whether the representation will allow him/her to successfully solve the problem. Similarly, representational fluency is involved when the student assesses the ease and efficiency of solving the problem with the representation. For example, when solving a problem about predicting whether water dissolves acetone, a student may compare the representations in Fig. 2.1c–e with respect to how well they show polarity based on the distribution of electrons across the molecule (i.e., connectional sense-making). Based on this comparison, the student may select the EPM in Fig. 2.1e because it most accurately shows the distribution of electrons across the water molecule. However, the student may be aware that he/she is not fluent with this representation. The student knows that the location of electrons in Lewis structures does not always correspond to the most electron dense region in the EPM (i.e., connectional sense-making). By comparing the EPM to the Lewis structure in Fig. 2.1c, the student realizes that the location of the electrons in the Lewis structure corresponds to the more electron dense region in the EPM, so that the two representations provide similar information in the case of water. Hence, the student can trust the Lewis structure of water to provide easily accessible information about the location of electrons in the case of water (i.e., connectional fluency).

Critiquing and modifying representations also involves both sense-making competencies and perceptual fluency. Sense-making competencies are involved when students become aware of the limitations of each visual representation (Ainsworth, 2006; diSessa & Sherin, 2000). Representational sense-making competencies are involved when students critique a representation by comparing the information shown in the representation to their mental model of what other information is conceptually relevant. Connectional sense-making competencies are involved when students critique and modify a representation by comparing the information it shows to information that a different representation would show. Perceptual fluency is involved when students critique and modify representations based on the ease with which they show information compared to their mental model of relevant conceptual information (i.e., representational fluency) or compared to a different representation (i.e., connectional fluency). Further, perceptual fluency frees cognitive capacity for complex thinking (Kellman & Massey, 2013; Rau, 2017), which has been associated with increased creativity that may enhance students' ability to modify existing representations or to invent new ones (NRC, 2006). In sum, meta-representational competencies describe the ability to reflect on one's knowledge about representations, which involves both sense-making competencies and perceptual fluency.

Taken together, cognitive theories conceptualize representational competencies as a set of skills that allow students to understand and fluently interact with representations that complement and constrain one another because of the information they provide and because they are processed via different working memory channels.

Socio-Cultural Research on Learning with Multiple External Representations

In contrast to cognitive research, socio-cultural research does not consider the representation dilemma a problem but rather views it as a defining feature of scientific practices that involve modeling (Justi & Gilbert, 2002; NRC, 2006). Scientists tend to represent phenomena they find interesting, so that they can use the representations to reflect on the nature of the phenomenon, which may lead them to revise their representations, and so forth. Indeed, observational studies of expert scientists in chemistry and other STEM domains show that their problem-solving and communication practices critically rely on representation-reflection iterations (Kozma & Russell, 2005; Schwarz et al., 2009). Consequently, socio-cultural research focuses on group-level processes; specifically, on how students learn to participate in disciplinary practices with multiple representations (Wertsch, 1997; Wertsch & Kazak, 2011; see Kozma, Chapter 3 for additional discussion of expert use).

In line with this focus, socio-cultural research does not consider representational competencies as a learning outcome that can be separated from problem-solving and communication practices (Latour, 1986; Wertsch, 1997). Indeed, socio-cultural theories of learning reject the "factoring assumption" that is characteristic of cognitive theories, but instead assume that knowledge is invariably intertwined with and situated in the context of its use (Greeno & Engeström, 2014; Nathan & Sawyer, 2014). That is, socio-cultural theories focus on students' ability to use representations in the context of meaningful activities to a larger degree than cognitive theories do (Greeno & Hall, 1997). These activities are embedded in practices of scientific, professional, or learning communities – for example when students receive scaffolding from more knowledgeable peers or experts to interact with the representations (Johri & Lohani, 2011; Rogoff, 1995). Hence, students' learning with representations is inherently mediated by social interactions that involve both *verbal* and *nonverbal* communication.

Verbal Communication Mediates Learning with External Representations

Disciplinary practices involve the use of external representations to verbally discuss ideas and phenomena (Airey & Linder, 2009; Kozma & Russell, 2005; Wertsch & Kazak, 2011). Socio-cultural theories consider representations as cultural communication tools that have been shaped by the history of a given scientific, professional, or learning community (Vygotsky, 1978). Hence, as students participate in such communities, they learn conventions that describe, for instance, which representations are commonly used to support which kinds of arguments (Cobb & McClain, 2006) and how to use representations in collaborative problem-solving activities (Roschelle, 1992; Wertsch & Kazak, 2011).

These findings build on socio-cultural studies describing how experts combine multiple representations to solve disciplinary problems and to communicate with one another (Airey & Linder, 2009; Kozma, Chin, Russell, & Marx, 2000; Kozma & Russell,

2005). These social practices involve discussing how different representations show information more or less accurately so as to select suitable representations for a given activity (Kozma & Russell, 2005; Latour, 1990).

In sum, social practices of using representations for verbal communication involve explaining how individual representations show information and how multiple representations compare to one another. These practices engage students in processes similar to the cognitive processes that result in the sense-making competencies described above. However, rather than describing an individual student's sense-making competencies, they describe group-level sense-making processes involved in social communication practices.

Nonverbal Communication Mediates Learning with External Representations

In addition, representations play an important role in supporting nonverbal communication as part of disciplinary practices (Singer, 2017; Wertsch & Kazak, 2011). When collaborating, community members use nonverbal communication such as gesture to direct each other's attention to relevant features of artifacts and tools, including representations (Singer, 2017). Indeed, socio-cultural theories emphasize the importance of becoming fluent with a "multimodal language" students learn as part of disciplinary discourse, which involves thinking, learning, and expressing oneself in terms of multiple representations (Braden & Hortin, 1982).

As part of this multimodal language, community members automatically infer community-specific ways of interpreting individual representations beyond what is explicitly shown in a given representation (Airey & Linder, 2009). For example, even though the Lewis structure in Fig. 2.1c does not show polarity, chemists can "see" how the polarity of the water molecule implies properties of water such as surface tension. Further, the multimodal language involves fluently translating among multiple representations and switching flexibly between representations in ways that follow community-specific practices. Acquiring fluency in this multimodal language enculturates students into thinking and communicating about discipline-specific phenomena in ways that are characteristic of the given scientific, professional, or learning community (Schönborn & Anderson, 2006).

Socio-cultural research suggests that nonverbal communication plays an important role in students' acquisition of fluency in a community-specific visual language. For example, Airey and Linder (2009) describe how repeated collaborative interactions allow students to translate flexibly among representations to the extent that doing so becomes "almost second nature" (p. 10). When students see how other community members communicate with representations, they start imitating their communication practices (Wertsch & Kazak, 2011). In this process, gestures such as pointing at visual features help students attend to meaningful visual features (Rau & Patel, 2018; Singer, 2017). Such gestures can help students induce which parts of the representations provide information relevant to the tasks the community solves.

In sum, social practices of using representations for nonverbal communication involve becoming fluent in a multimodal language that allows students to seamlessly infer what information individual representations show about community-specific phenomena and to flexibly translate among multiple representations. The practices through which students acquire fluency in this multimodal language are similar to the cognitive learning processes that yield perceptual fluency as described above; but rather than describing an individual student's perceptual fluency, they describe group-level perceptual fluency in communication.

Reflection on Community Practices

By engaging in verbal and nonverbal communication practices with multiple representations, students also learn about how cultural conventions for using representations have developed historically (Kozma & Russell, 2005; Latour, 1986). For example, chemistry students may learn about how Lewis structures (Fig. 2.1c) were developed as tools to reason about new discoveries about bonding, which prior representations could not accurately depict (Kozma et al., 2000; Rocke, 2010). Through such reflections, students learn that representations are not static; rather, representations are flexible tools that support the community's reasoning about established concepts and new ideas (Donald, 1991; Latour, 1986). Hence, students experience that representations can change over time, and that communities often invent new representations as more sophisticated tools to reason about known phenomena and new discoveries (Donald, 1991; Lehrer & Schauble, 2004).

Such reflection practices that lead to modifications or inventions of representations involve both verbal and nonverbal forms of communication. Verbal communication is involved when community members discuss shortcomings of existing representations and reason about which aspects of phenomena are not adequately represented (Lehrer & Schauble, 2004, 2017). Nonverbal communication is involved when community members jointly modify existing representations (e.g., by sketching on top of an existing drawing) or create new representations (e.g., by drawing; Cooper, Stieff, & DeSutter, 2017; Prain & Tytler, 2012) or gesture to convey visuo-spatial information they cannot easily express verbally (Atit, Weisberg, Newcombe, & Shipley, 2016; Tversky, 2011).

In sum, socio-cultural research describes reflecting on, modifying, and inventing representations as an important aspect of the enculturation processes that allow students to participate in scientific, professional, and learning communities. These processes involve both verbal and nonverbal communication. From a cognitive perspective, these processes involve meta-representational competencies at the individual level, but the socio-cultural perspective focuses on reflection on representation practices at the community level.

IMPLICATIONS FOR INSTRUCTIONAL INTERVENTIONS

Even though cognitive and socio-cultural perspectives rely on qualitatively different theoretical assumptions, both perspectives emphasize the importance of verbally mediated sense-making and non-verbal inductive processes. Further, both perspectives describe learning processes focusing on individual representations as well as processes that involve the integration of multiple representations. Consequently, both theoretical perspectives imply that instructional interventions should help students (1) verbally explain how individual representations show information, (2) verbally explain how multiple representations show similar and different information, (3) nonverbally induce perceptual information from individual representations, (4) nonverbally integrate perceptual information across multiple representations, and (5) verbally reflect on and regulate the use of representations in problem solving.

The two theoretical perspectives differ in terms of their unit of analysis: while cognitive research focuses on learning and the level of individual students, socio-cultural research focuses on learning of students situated in physical (e.g., tools) and social (e.g., community members) contexts. Consequently, the two perspectives make different recommendations for supporting students' learning with multiple representations. Cognitive research suggests that engaging in the verbal and nonverbal processes described above yield representational competencies that can be learned independently of participating in community practices. Hence, this research has developed trainings for individual students that support representational competencies so as to prepare them for more complex activities. For example, cognitive research on learning with multiple representations has yielded training modules that support students' acquisition of sense-making competencies and perceptual fluency, which has been shown to enhance their learning of content knowledge (Rau, Aleven, & Rummel, 2017; Rau & Wu, 2018). Further, distinguishing different types of representational competencies allows cognitive research to investigate how trainings should sequence support for different competencies. For example, this research suggests that instruction should support sense-making competencies before perceptual fluency (Rau, 2018).

By contrast, socio-cultural research does not strictly distinguish learning processes from learning outcomes and consequently views the processes through which students acquire representational competencies as invariably intertwined with community representation practices. Hence, this research has examined ways of scaffolding students in using representations while they participate in community practices. For example, pairing students with more knowledgeable community members while working on meaningful, complex problems in the real world has been shown to help students acquire representation practices (Azevedo & Mann, 2018; Johri & Lohani, 2011). Rather than analyzing constituent competencies separately, socio-cultural research investigates how multiple ways of scaffolding can be combined to help students engage in verbal and nonverbal communication with multiple representations (Puntambekar & Kolodner, 2005; Wilkerson-Jerde, Gravel, & Macrander, 2015).

CONCLUSION

Because multiple representations are ubiquitous in instructional materials, students are inevitably confronted with them. Yet, they pose significant challenges for students that have been described as the *representation dilemma*: students use representations they do not know to learn concepts they do not know. Hence, students have to concurrently and iteratively learn about the representations as well as the concepts. Cognitive research focuses on these processes at the level of individual students who use representations to learn about domain-relevant concepts. Socio-cultural research focuses on these processes at the level of students participating in broader community practices. While these perspectives differ in fundamental theoretical assumptions about learning, research from both perspectives shows that successful learning with multiple representations hinges on students' engagement in verbal sense-making processes as well as nonverbal perceptual induction processes.

ACKNOWLEDGMENTS

This research was funded by NSF IIS CAREER 1651781 and NSF DUE-IUSE 1611782.

REFERENCES

Acevedo Nistal, A., Van Dooren, W., & Verschaffel, L. (2013). Students' reported justifications for their representational choices in linear function problems: An interview study. *Educational Studies, 39*(1), 104–117.

Ainsworth, S. (2006). DeFT: A conceptual framework for considering learning with multiple representations. *Learning and Instruction, 16*(3), 183–198.

Airey, J., & Linder, C. (2009). A disciplinary discourse perspective on university science learning: Achieving fluency in a critical constellation of modes. *Journal of Research in Science Teaching, 46*(1), 27–49.

Atit, K., Weisberg, S. M., Newcombe, N. S., & Shipley, T. F. (2016). Learning to interpret topographic maps: Understanding layered spatial information. *Cognitive Research: Principles and Implications, 1*, 2. https://cognitiveresearchjournal.springeropen.com/articles/10.1186/s41235-016-0002-y#citeas

Azevedo, F. S., & Mann, M. J. (2018). Seeing in the dark: Embodied cognition in amateur astronomy practice. *Journal of the Learning Sciences, 27*(1), 89–136.

Baddeley, A. (2012). Working memory: Theories, models, and controversies. *Annual Review of Psychology, 63*, 1–29.

Braden, R. A., & Hortin, J. A. (1982). Identifying the theoretical foundations of visual literacy. Paper presented at the 13th Annual Conference on Visual Literacy (Lexington, KY, October 31–November 3, 1981).

Chandler, P., & Sweller, J. (1991). Cognitive load theory and the format of instruction. *Cognition and Instruction, 8*(4), 293–332.

Chase, W. G., & Simon, H. A. (1973). Perception in chess. *Cognitive Psychology, 4*(1), 55–81.

Chi, M. T., Bassok, M., Lewis, M. W., Reimann, P., & Glaser, R. (1989). Self-explanations: How students study and use examples in learning to solve problems. *Cognitive Science, 13*(2), 145–182.

Cobb, P., & McClain, K. (2006). Guiding inquiry-based math learning. In R. K. Sawyer (Ed.), *The Cambridge handbook of the learning sciences* (1st ed., pp. 171–186). New York: Cambridge University Press.

Cooper, M. M., Stieff, M., & DeSutter, D. (2017). Sketching the invisible to predict the visible: From drawing to modeling in chemistry. *Topics in Cognitive Science, 9*(4), 902–920.

diSessa, A. A. (2004). Metarepresentation: Native competence and targets for instruction. *Cognition and Instruction, 22*(3), 293–331.

diSessa, A. A., & Sherin, B. L. (2000). Meta-representation: An introduction. *Journal of Mathematical Behavior, 19*(4), 385–398.

Donald, M. (1991). *Origins of the Modern Mind*. Cambridge, MA: Harvard University Press.

Dreher, A., & Kuntze, S. (2015). Teachers facing the dilemma of multiple representations being aid and obstacle for learning: Evaluations of tasks and theme-specific noticing. *Journal für Mathematik-Didaktik, 36*(1), 23–44.

Gentner, D., & Markman, A. B. (1997). Structure mapping in analogy and similarity. *American Psychologist, 52*(1), 45–56.

Gibson, E. J. (1969). *Principles of perceptual learning and development*. New York: Prentice Hall.

Goldstone, R. (1997). *Perceptual Learning*. San Diego, CA: Academic Press.

Goldstone, R. L., Schyns, P. G., & Medin, D. L. (1997). Learning to bridge between perception and cognition. *Psychology of Learning and Motivation, 36*, 1–14.

Greeno, J. G., & Engeström, Y. (2014). Learning in activity. In R. K. Sawyer (Ed.), *The Cambridge handbook of the learning sciences*. (pp. 128–50). Cambridge: Cambridge University Press.

Greeno, J. G., & Hall, R. P. (1997). Practicing representation. *Phi Delta Kappan, 78*(5), 361–367.

Hartman, H. J. (2002). *Metacognition in learning and instruction*. (2nd ed., H. J. Hartman, Ed.). Dordrecht: Kluwer Academic Publisher.

Johri, A., & Lohani, V. K. (2011). Framework for improving engineering representational literacy by using pen-based computing. *International Journal of Engineering Education, 27*(5), 958–967.

Justi, R., & Gilbert, J. K. (2002). Models and modelling in chemical education. In O. de Jong, R. Justi, D. F. Treagust, & J. H. van Driel (Eds.), *Chemical education: Towards research-based practice* (pp. 47–68). Dordrecht: Kluwer Academic Publishers.

Kellman, P. J., & Massey, C. M. (2013). Perceptual learning, cognition, and expertise. In B. H. Ross (Ed.), *The psychology of learning and motivation* (vol. 558, pp. 117–165). New York: Elsevier Academic Press.

Koedinger, K. R., Corbett, A. T., & Perfetti, C. (2012). The knowledge-learning-instruction framework: Bridging the science-practice chasm to enhance robust student learning. *Cognitive Science, 36*(5), 757–798.

Kozma, R., Chin, E., Russell, J., & Marx, N. (2000). The roles of representations and tools in the chemistry laboratory and their implications for chemistry learning. *Journal of the Learning Sciences, 9*(2), 105–143.

Kozma, R., & Russell, J. (2005). Students becoming chemists: Developing representational competence. In J. Gilbert (Ed.), *Visualization in science education* (pp. 121–145). Dordrecht: Springer.

Latour, B. (1986). Visualization and cognition: Thinking with eyes and hands. *Knowledge and Society: Studies in the Sociology of Culture Past and Present, 6*, 1–40.

Latour, B. (1990). Drawing things together. In M. Lynch & S. Woolgar (Eds.), *Representations in scientific practice* (pp. 19–68). Cambridge, MA: MIT Press.

Lehrer, R., & Schauble, L. (2004). Modeling natural variation through distribution. *American Educational Research Journal, 41*(3), 635–679.

Lehrer, R., & Schauble, L. (2017). The dynamic material and representational practices of modeling. In Tamer G. Amin & Olivia Levrini (Eds.), *Converging perspectives on conceptual change: Mapping an emerging paradigm in the learning sciences* (pp. 163–170).

Mayer, R. E. (2005). Cognitive theory of multimedia learning. In R. E. Mayer (Ed.), *The Cambridge handbook of multimedia learning* (pp. 31–48). New York: Cambridge University Press.

Mayer, R. E. (2009). Cognitive theory of multimedia learning. In R. E. Mayer (Ed.), *The Cambridge handbook of multimedia learning* (2nd ed., pp. 31–48). New York: Cambridge University Press.

Nathan, M. J., & Sawyer, R. K. (2014). Foundations of the learning sciences. In R. K. Sawyer (Ed.), *The Cambridge handbook of the learning sciences* (2nd ed., pp. 21–43). New York: Cambridge University Press.

NRC. (2006). *Learning to think spatially*. Washington, DC: National Academies Press.

Paivio, A. (1986). *Mental representations: A dual coding approach*. Oxford: Oxford University Press.

Peirce, C. S., Hartshorne, C., Weiss, P., & Burks, A. (1935). *Collected papers of Charles Sanders Peirce* (vols. 1–6). Cambridge, MA: Harvard University Press.

Prain, V., & Tytler, R. (2012). Learning through constructing representations in science: A framework of representational construction affordances. *International Journal of Science Education, 34*(17), 2751–2773.

Puntambekar, S., & Kolodner, J. L. (2005). Toward implementing distributed scaffolding: Helping students learn science from design. *Journal of Research in Science Teaching, 42*(2), 185–217.

Rau, M. A. (2017). Conditions for the effectiveness of multiple visual representations in enhancing stem learning. *Educational Psychology Review, 29*(4), 717–761.

Rau, M. A. (2018). Sequencing support for sense making and perceptual induction of connections among multiple visual representations. *Journal of Educational Psychology, 110*(6), 811–833.

Rau, M. A., Aleven, V., & Rummel, N. (2015). Successful learning with multiple graphical representations and self-explanation prompts. *Journal of Educational Psychology, 107*(1), 30–46.

Rau, M. A., Aleven, V., & Rummel, N. (2017). Supporting students in making sense of connections and in becoming perceptually fluent in making connections among multiple graphical representations. *Journal of Educational Psychology, 109*(3), 355–373.

Rau, M. A., Michaelis, J. E., & Fay, N. (2015). Connection making between multiple graphical representations: A multi-methods approach for domain-specific grounding of an intelligent tutoring system for chemistry. *Computers and Education, 82*, 460–485.

Rau, M. A., & Patel, P. (2018). A collaboration script for nonverbal communication enhances perceptual fluency with visual representations. In J. Kay & R. Luckin (Eds.), *Rethinking learning in the digital age: Making the learning sciences count (ICLS) 2018* (pp. 272–279). London: International Society of the Learning Sciences.

Rau, M. A., & Wu, S. P. W. (2018). Support for sense-making processes and inductive processes in connection-making among multiple visual representations. *Cognition and Instruction, 36*(4), 361–395.

Richman, H. B., Gobet, F., Staszewski, J. J., & Simon, H. A. (1996). Perceptual and memory processes in the acquisition of expert performance: The EPAM model. In K. A. Ericsson (Ed.), *The road to excellence? The acquisition of expert performance in the arts and sciences, sports and games* (pp. 167–187). Mahwah, NJ: Erlbaum Associates.

Rocke, A. J. (2010). *Image and reality: Kekulé, kopp, and the scientific imagination*. Chicago, IL: University of Chicago Press.

Rogoff, B. (1995). Observing socio-cultural activity on three planes. In J. V. Wertsch, P. D. Rio, & A. Alvarez (Eds.), *Pedagogy and practice: Culture and identities* (pp. 139–163). New York: Cambridge University Press.

Roschelle, J. (1992). Learning by collaborating: Convergent conceptual change. *Journal of the Learning Sciences, 2*(3), 235–276.

Schnotz, W. (2005). An integrated model of text and picture comprehension. In R. E. Mayer (Ed.), *The Cambridge handbook of multimedia learning* (pp. 49–69). New York: Cambridge University Press.

Schnotz, W. (2014). An integrated model of text and picture comprehension. In R. E. Mayer (Ed.), *The Cambridge handbook of multimedia learning* (2nd ed., pp. 72–103). New York: Cambridge University Press.

Schönborn, K. J., & Anderson, T. R. (2006). The importance of visual literacy in the education of biochemists. *Biochemistry and Molecular Biology Education, 34*(2), 94–102. doi:10.1002/bmb.2006.49403402094

Schooler, J. W., Fiore, S., & Brandimonte, M. A. (1997). At a loss from words: Verbal overshadowing of perceptual memories. *Psychology of Learning and Motivation: Advances in Research and Theory, 37*, 291–340.

Schooler, J. W., Ohlsson, S., & Brooks, K. (1993). Thoughts beyond words: When language overshadows insight. *Journal of Experimental Psychology: General, 122*(2), 166–183.

Schwarz, C. V., Reiser, B. J., Davis, E. A., Kenyon, L., Achér, A., Fortus, D., … Krajcik, J. (2009). Developing a learning progression for scientific modeling: Making scientific modeling accessible and meaningful for learners. *Journal of Research in Science Teaching, 46*(6), 632–654.

Singer, M. (2017). The function of gesture in mathematical and scientific discourse in the classroom. In B. Church & M. W. S. A. Kelly (Eds.), *Why gesture? How the hands function in speaking, thinking and communicating* (pp. 317–329). Amsterdam/Philadelphia: John Benjamins Publishing Company.

Tversky, B. (2011). Visualizing thought. *Topics in Cognitive Science, 3*(3), 499–535.

Vygotsky, L. S. (1978). Interaction between learning and development. In M. W. Cole, V. John-Steiner, S. Scribner, & E. Souberman (Eds.), *Mind in Society* (pp. 79–91). Cambridge, MA: Harvard University Press.

Wertsch, J. V. (1997). Properties of mediated action. In J. V. Wertsch (Ed.), *Mind as action* (pp. 23–72). New York: Oxford University Press.

Wertsch, J. V., & Kazak, S. (2011). Saying more than you know in instructional settings. In T. Koschmann (Ed.), *Theories of learning and studies of instructional practice* (pp. 153–166). New York: Springer.

Wilkerson-Jerde, M. H., Gravel, B. E., & Macrander, C. A. (2015). Exploring shifts in middle school learners' modeling activity while generating drawings, animations, and computational simulations of molecular diffusion. *Journal of Science Education and Technology, 24*(2/3), 396–415.

3

USE OF MULTIPLE REPRESENTATIONS BY EXPERTS AND NOVICES

Robert B. Kozma

SAN FRANCISCO

ABSTRACT

This chapter examines comparative studies of experts and novices as a research paradigm that contributed to and benefitted from advances in psychology and the design of educational environments. Specifically, it examines the use of multiple representations and their features by experts and novices in science, technology, engineering, and mathematic (STEM) domains. The chapter looks at ways that multiple representations and representational competence contribute to the understanding and practice of scientists, as well as the ways they present challenges to students of these disciplines. Finally, the chapter draws implications from these studies for the design of educational environments, psychological theory, and future research on the features, function, and use of multiple representations to support understanding and practice.

Key words: expert, novice, multiple representations, representational competence, STEM domains

OVERVIEW OF THE EXPERT-NOVICE PARADIGM

As psychology moved from a behaviorist, "black box" perspective of the 1950s and 1960s (Skinner, 1953), which focused on physical contexts ("stimuli") and observable behavior ("responses") and ascribed no role in research or theory for mentation, to a perspective which focused on the cognitive structures and processes behind behavior (Neisser, 1967; Newell & Simon, 1972; Simon, 1969), studies of expertise came to be the research topic of choice (Chi, Glaser, & Farr, 1988). Cognitive psychologists and computer scientists working in the nascent domain of artificial intelligence tried to construct models of how humans worked through problems. Researchers examined expert performance in complex domains, such as chess (De Groot, 1946/1978), computer programming (Soloway, Adelson, & Ehrlich, 1988), and X-ray diagnosis (Lesgold et al., 1988). A variety of research techniques, such as think-aloud protocols, latency response studies, and eye tracking, were used to make inferences about the otherwise-inaccessible mental structures and cognitive processes involved in human problem solving. These inferences included the information that experts held in memory, how it was organized, and how experts used this information to solve problems.

A complementary area of research emerged that focused on the performance of novices—students or those new to a domain. This research resulted in a description of their naïve knowledge, often erroneous relative to established knowledge in the domain, which was sometimes characterized as "pre-conceptions" or "misconceptions" (e.g., McCloskey, 1983; Zoller, 1990). This approach was sympathetic to constructivist learning theories (Bruner, 1966; Piaget, 1950; Vygotsky, 1978) that emphasized students' current knowledge that created "zones of proximal development" and had practical applications that allowed teachers or instructional programs to customize or personalize lessons to address students' patterned errors or developmental state. In some studies, novice knowledge was studied in parallel with a group of experts responding to the same task (e.g., Larkin, McDermott, Simon, & Simon, 1980; Schoenfeld & Herrmann, 1982). The purpose of these studies was to create dynamic computer models that characterized both a "beginning state" (novice) and an "end state" (expert), the challenge being to move the computer model from the former state to the latter or in its instructional application to move novices to experts. In its instructional application, the goal was not just to have students acquire a body of knowledge but to use that knowledge to solve problems in expert-like ways.

This cognitive approach to psychology, that focused on mentation and mental states, subsequently evolved to a more socio-cultural approach (Brown, Collins, & Duguid, 1989; Lave & Wenger, 1991), sometimes referred to as situated practice or cognitive apprenticeship, that emphasized human cognition and behavior in the context of social interactions and physical environments. While this, in some sense, was a return to the emphasis on context, so important in the behavioral frame, the physical environment from this perspective is treated as a set of resources with affordances that enable or constrain cognition, rather than a set of stimuli to which a person responds, and it implies a more interactive or transactional relationship between person and context. In this paradigm, the "stimulus" is extended to also include others—colleagues, customers, mentors, experts—who sometimes serve as the problem context but sometimes serve to scaffold or augment cognition and sometimes to provide a cultural arena within which certain behaviors and practices are valued and others not. The environment also includes other contextual elements, such as physical spaces and tools, that sometimes augment performance and sometimes represent challenges to performance. From this perspective, experts are distinguished from novices not just by their use of knowledge to solve problems but also by how they use it in a community of practice. And its implication for education is to create authentic problem situations and contexts in which students work to collaboratively build a body of knowledge and practice.

This chapter looks at a narrow slice of the research on both experts and novices: how they use a particular kind of physical resource—representations—either singly or together (i.e., multiple representations) to understand domains, to solve problems and to interact with others. The review also narrows the range of knowledge domains within which representations are used to those of science, technology, engineering, and mathematics, or STEM.

When cognitive psychologists use the term "representation" they typically refer to internal knowledge contents and structures in human memory and how those can be "represented" in a theory or computer model (Bobrow, 1975). However, this review examines the use of symbol systems or "external representations". That is, an artifact that "stands for" either a physical object or phenomena in the world or an internal idea or concept (Greeno, 1989). Representations can take a variety of forms that include words (spoken or written), pictures, diagrams, instrument read-outs, equations, formulae, etc. The relationship between the characteristics of a representation and that for which it stands (its referent) can be veridical in some ways (e.g. the relationship between a picture of a coin and a coin) or totally arbitrary (e.g., the relationship between the word "coin" and a coin) (Goodman, 1968). But characteristics of a good external representation, from a cognitive perspective, correspond to the important aspects of a phenomenon while ignoring the irrelevant aspects. A representation that gets this balance right, what Norman (1993) calls a "cognitive artifact", enhances one's ability to think and reason about the phenomenon, relative to operating on the phenomenon directly.

In the studies reviewed in this chapter, representations are sometimes embedded in the problem space to which subjects are responding and are sometimes resources, or tools, which the subjects draw on to respond to the problem. The goal of the chapter is to look at differences in the way experts and novices use various representations, both singly and together. Also included are studies in which solo subjects use representations and those in which two or more subjects together use representations. The review is not meant to be comprehensive but to organize the literature into certain trends and demonstrate these trends with specific studies. Finally, the chapter includes implications of this research for educational applications, theory development, and research methodology.

REVIEW OF THE LITERATURE

Experts' Use of Representations

Representations are ubiquitous in scientific fields and play a vital role in the development and expression of STEM knowledge. For example, historian Wilda Anderson (1984) documents that chemistry became a modern science as new language co-evolved with new chemical symbol systems that were uniquely suited to this new knowledge and its implementation in the laboratory. Lemke (1998) analyzed the use of various representations in academic journal articles in STEM fields and found extensive use of verbal text and a wide variety of representations, including figures, tables, charts, equations, maps, and photographs. And more recently, data visualization provides scientists with new representational tools to do their work (Owens, 2018).

Clearly STEM experts use representations but what role do representations play in STEM expertise? In their overview of research on expertise, Chi, Glaser, and Farr (1988) summarize the findings that characterize experts and expert performance. The most pronounced characteristic is that experts not only have a significant amount of knowledge about their domain, they organize this knowledge in large, principled patterns. In problem-solving situations, they spend a significant amount of time analyzing the problem, using underlying principles to do so, and then proceed to the solution with speed.

This principled pattern recognition is played out in experts' use of external representations. For example, in a study by Chi, Feltovich, and Glaser (1981), experts were asked to group a variety of stated physics problems, accompanied by diagrams, and explain their groupings. Experts formed groups around principles such as "conservation of energy" or "angular motion". Within these principled groupings, there were diagrams that looked quite different across groupings—inclined plane diagrams, pulley diagrams, and spring diagrams may have been sorted together as "conservation of energy". In effect, experts could "see" underlying principles across diverse representations. Similarly, Kozma and Russell (1997) gave expert chemists sets of chemistry representations in various static and dynamic forms: chemical equations, graphs, molecular animations, and videos of lab bench experiments. The experts were asked to sort representations and give explanations for their sorts. The experts based their sorts on chemical concepts such as "equilibrium" or "gas law". Significantly, the groupings of experts cut across representational forms. Experts were also able to transform one representation to another, selecting a graph that corresponded to a chemical equation, for example. And in mathematics, Stylianou and Silver (2004) studied problem solving by professors, giving them a set of challenging problems and found they used diagrams, along with equations, to represent problem situations and used diagrams as reasoning tools to help them solve the problems.

Kozma, Chin, Russell, and Marx (2000) examined professional chemists and chemistry professors as they conducted their research in the laboratory, alone and with colleagues. They observed that chemists used a variety of representations and employed different representations for different purposes. For example, they used structural diagrams to represent the composition and structural arrangement of elements of a compound they were trying to synthesize on the lab bench, as well as represent the reagents that they started with. They used equations to represent the process of molecular rearrangement they were trying to achieve with their lab bench procedures. And they used instrument read-outs to confirm that indeed they had produced their desired results. Yet another representational system—language—was used as a way to assign meaning to the other representations and to map one representation onto another and this mapping process was crucial to the experimental enterprise. So, for example, a chemist might use language and gestures to refer to specific features of a read-out (such as pointing to a cluster of peaks on a graph), claim they corresponded to specific structural features of the generated compound, as represented by diagrams, and argue thus that they had synthesized the intended product. This behavior is so typical of chemists that Nobel chemist Raold Hoffmann claimed, "In an important sense, chemistry is the skillful study of symbolic transformations applied to graphic objects" (Hoffmann & Laszlo, 1991, p. 11).

The ability to generate, read, and coordinate multiple representations to stand for aperceptual entities and processes and their associated concepts and principles is sometimes referred to as "representational competence" (Daniel, Bucklin, Leone, & Idema, 2018; Kozma & Russell, 2005, 1997). While the particulars of these skills vary with scientific discipline (Daniel et al., 2018), general principles can cut across disciplines. Kozma and Russell (1997) specify a set of competencies that include the ability to:

- Identify and analyze features of representations and use them as evidence to support claims, draw inferences, and make predictions.
- Transform one representation into another and explain their relationship.
- Create or select appropriate representation(s) to support claims.
- Select appropriate representations to use for a particular purpose and justify these selections
- Explain how distinct representations might convey the same information in different ways
- Explain how one representation might communicate unique information, that cannot be communicated via another representation.

In summary, STEM experts—individually and collectively—coordinate multiple representations to solve problems, express understanding, negotiate meaning, and warrant claims. There is a special role for language, often accompanied by gestures, as a mediating representation that coordinates all others. These multiple representations are not just alternative ways of saying the "same thing" but each representation often says something unique as well. Experts' ability to use various representations together is the foundation for the underlying abstract concepts and principles that they hold.

Novice's Use of Representations and Expert-Novice Comparisons

While the knowledge and practices of experts are organized around underlying principles within a domain, the knowledge and behavior of novices are very different. Many studies have found that student understanding of scientific phenomena is based on personal experience or the surface features of the phenomena rather than disciplined study. For example, Clement (1983) and McCloskey (1983) found that college students who had not had physics often demonstrated an understanding of motion, which is based on their experience with friction, that is contrary to established laws of physics, such as: An object remains in motion only as long as it is in contact with a mover, or an object should always move in the direction in which it is kicked. Kozma, Russell, Johnston, and Dershimer (1990) found that undergraduate students first taking chemistry often believed that although a system at equilibrium becomes dynamic when it is perturbed (e.g., a reagent was added), the reaction comes to a stop when the system reaches equilibrium, influenced by the observation that the color, for example, stops changing.

This focus on physical properties and surface features also effects novice use of representations. In their study of experts mentioned above, Kozma and Russell (1997) gave the same task of sorting various chemistry representation to first-term chemistry students, as well. While experts sorted representations based on chemistry concepts and their sorts cut across different representational forms, students often grouped all representations of the same type together, graphs, for example, even though they represented different chemical systems. Novices were also less able to transform one representational form to another. Similarly, in a study of representational use in physics by Kohl and Finkelstein (2008), first-term physics students were less skilled at using multiple representations than physics graduate students. The graduate students moved fluently among various representations, while first-term physics students were not only less likely to solve problems correctly, they were more likely to meander across different representations during problem solving, with no clear purpose for their use. Stylianou and Silver (2004) found that mathematics professors drew on mathematical principles in their use of diagrams to solve problems while mathematics underclass students could neither provide a set of visual representations nor use given ones to solve problems. These novices knew that they were supposed to draw a diagram but they did not know how to make diagrams a helpful tool.

In summary, novices lack both the central concepts and principles in a domain and representational skills; they do not have the principled knowledge to understand representational expressions nor do they have the representational competence that allows them to use representations to understand underlying concepts and principles. Instead, their understanding is based on their personal experiences with domain phenomena and they are influenced by the surface features of representations.

NEW INSIGHTS AND FUTURE DIRECTIONS

Educational Implications

Given the importance of representations in STEM domains, a logical question is: Can the instructional use of multiple representations help move novices to more expert-like understanding or performance? Since novices lack both principled knowledge and representational skills in a domain, it is not surprising that the research findings on the instructional use of multiple representations are mixed. For example, while experimental studies by Wu, Krajcik, and Soloway (2001), Moreno and Duran (2004), Berthold, Eysink, and Renki (2009), Eilam et al. (2008), Hand and Choi (2010), Taramopoulos and Psillos (2017) and Ott, Brunken, Vogel, and Malone (2018) found that multiple representations were more effective in STEM learning than single representations, Ainsworth, Bibby, and Wood (2002) and Coleman et al. (2018) found that multiple representations did not facilitate learning.

These mixed results require a more nuanced understanding of how students process multiple representations during learning and how multiple representations can be structured within learning environments to be more effective. Ainsworth et al. (2002) contrasted children learning estimation with two representations, either mathematical, pictorial, or a mixed system of one pictorial and mathematical representation. Pictures and mathematical representations each helped children learn but children who studied with the combination knew no more at the end of the study than they had at the beginning. In the study by Coleman et al. (2018), groups of 4th grade students were given several versions of science readings; one group received text-only while three other groups received text with pictures arranged in several different ways to examine design principles. None of the groups with pictures performed better than the group with text alone. Indeed, the group with text integrated with the pictures in a web-like way performed least well. These researchers concluded that the use of multiple representations may have resulted in cognitive overload that inhibited learning.

However, providing students with guidance during representational use helps them develop representational skills and, in turn, deepens their understanding of the subject. For example, in a study by Moreno and Duran (2004), two groups of grade school students in mathematics engaged in a computer-based environment to learn about addition and subtraction of signed numbers. Both groups were given two representational forms: equations and a pictorial number line for which students could use a joystick to move an animated character back and forth along the line. Students were asked to manipulate the character in a way that corresponded to the equation. In the Non-Guided group, students were merely given feedback on the correctness of their moves. In the Guided group, students were provided a verbal mapping of the elements and processes of the animated number line onto the symbolic elements of equation. As a result, the Guided group performed better than the Non-Guided group.

This guidance can be direct or indirect. The results from a study by van der Meij and de Jong (2011) engaged two groups of secondary students with a computer-based exploratory, multiple representation environment in physics. The difference between the two treatments was that in addition to their solution to the problems, one group was asked to explain their answer while the second group was also asked to explain the relationships between various representations. The group that gave their own explanation of the relationship between representations performed better on post-tests.

Rau and Wu (2017) examined how students could be supported in helping each other make sense of multiple representations. They conducted a quasi-experiment with undergraduate chemistry students to test the effectiveness of prompts to help students discuss visual representations. In a control condition, students collaboratively solved worksheet problems without a collaboration script. In an experimental condition, students solved the same problems with a collaboration script that prompted students to discuss visual representations. The experimental condition showed significantly higher learning gains on a transfer post-test and on a midterm exam three weeks later.

The relationship between talk and representational use can work the other way around: Not only can guided discussion help students make sense of representations, features of representations can shape discussions. In a study by Kozma (2000) which examined discourse among student partners and between students and instructor during wet lab experiments in a university organic laboratory course, the physical features of the wet lab (i.e., characteristics of the reagents, experimental equipment, and procedures) limited the discussion to physical procedures and the physical attributes of the reagents used and produced. There was essentially no discussion of the chemical composition or structure or of the compounds or reactions. On the other hand, students subsequently used a professional molecular modeling environment to construct and examine the molecular structure of the compound they produced in the wet lab. The features of this representation in the modeling environment shaped discussions among students and between them and the instructor such that they were filled with "chemical talk" of the sort witnessed in discussions among professional chemists (Kozma et al., 2000).

Finally, a growing research literature shows that student generation of representations, when accompanied by guidance, can also facilitate learning (Van Meter & Firetto, 2013; Ainsworth, Tyler, & Prain, Chapter 7). For example, in a study by Van Meter (2001), grade school students read to learn about the central nervous system.

Students in one group were instructed to make drawings to represent what they read, subsequently inspected provided illustrations, then answered prompting questions that directed comparison of drawings and illustrations, and, finally, modified their drawings accordingly. These students performed better on post-tests than did a group who drew, inspected provided illustrations, and modified drawings, but were not provided with comparison prompting questions. They also performed better than a drawing group with no provided illustrations and a non-drawing control group with provided illustrations only.

These findings from expert-novice studies can guide designers in their creation of representational environments and instructional practices that support learning. For example, an important finding from this research is that while experts "see" underlying principles when viewing representations, novices are focused on their surface features. Designers can create representations with surface features that serve as "training wheels" that bridge novice and expert representation use and domain understanding. For example, while physicists use static force vector diagrams to represent the cumulate effect of several forces on an object, students might benefit from software in which they can directly manipulate animated force vectors or values of the vector equation to see the impact of different forces on the resultant vector and the direction and speed of the object. Another finding is that novices are influenced by physical features of their personal experiences with scientific phenomena. New technologies, such as augmented reality (Cheng & Tsai, 2013, Gopalan, Abu Bakar & Zulkifli, 2017), could allow designers to overlay representations onto the physical phenomena that leaners observe (e.g., a dynamic graph or a molecular animation viewed over a chemical reaction in the wet lab) that might help them understand these phenomena in a more principled way. Research and development in this area would contribute to both practice and cognitive theory.

In summary, the use of multiple representations is both essential and problematic to STEM learning. STEM disciplines are filled with multiple representations and, thus, learning to use them is essential to the understanding and practice of science. Yet, because novices lack both understanding and representational skill, merely using multiple representations in instruction often results in cognitive overload and is not effective. However, their careful use in instruction can shape student thought and talk that benefits from verbal guidance, particularly that which supports student mapping of representations onto each other and particularly in the context of collaborative exploration and investigations.

Theoretical Implications

As mentioned at the beginning of the chapter, there are two theoretical foundations for the study of expertise and the educational use of multiple representations: information processing or cognitive theory and socio-cultural or situative theory (see Rau, Chapter 2, for a more detailed treatment of theory). These two approaches can and should be complementary (Greeno, 2011).

The leading cognitive proponents in this area are Richard Mayer (2009), Wolfgang Schnotz (2014), and others that build on their work (Ainsworth, 2006). Sometimes referred to as "multimedia theory", the work is based on several cognitive principles, such as dual-channel input, limited memory capacity, and active processing. Mayer draws on this foundation to present a set of instructional design principles, such as the multimedia principle, the contiguity principle, the modality principle, and so on (see Van Meter and Stepanik, Chapter 6). The application of these principles is meant to guide appropriate cognitive processing during learning without overloading the learner's cognitive system. For example, the multimedia principle, along with other principles, would suggest the careful design of text or verbal representations along with pictorial representations arranged in a way to reduce cognitive load and support the learner's active selection, organization, and integration of information. Other researchers (e.g., Rau & Matthews, 2017) have added cognitive-based principles related to the design of multimedia or multi-representational environments that guide designers in their construction and use of the various features, arrangements, and contexts of multiple representations so as to improve their effectiveness in contributing to the learning of STEM subjects.

From an expert-novice perspective, however, it is important to make a theoretical distinction between two types of representations in STEM as they contribute to or make demands on the cognitive constraints and resources of experts and learners. There is significant difference between the manipulatable number line in the Moreno and Duran (2004) study, for example, and the signed numbers that they used. The first is a "contrived" representation designed to help students understand a mathematic principle or procedure; the latter is an "authentic" representation used by mathematicians. Instructional designers have all kinds of control over the contrived representations and the instructional activities in which they are used. But designers have to accept as a given the authentic representations of mathematicians, chemists, physicists, etc. as part of the knowledge base of these domains. The understanding and use of these authentic representations, such as chemical equations in chemistry and force vectors in physics, and their use to solve problems is a curricular goal of STEM courses, not instructional devices. Cognitive theories of expertise should expand to include the analysis of specific features of authentic representations, how they differ between STEM disciplines, and the ways that calculus representations, for example, help mathematicians and molecular equations help chemists understand their domain. Clearly, authentic STEM representations present significant demands on the cognitive resources of novices. Cognitive multimedia theories must incorporate the distinction between authentic and contrived representations and elaborate on both the specific cognitive challenges authentic representations make on novices and the ways in which contrived representations and instructional activities can be designed to address these.

The second theoretical orientation for considering expertise and the use of multiple representations is socio-cultural. From this orientation, a STEM domain is not just seen as a body of knowledge but a set of epistemic practices by which scientists, mathematicians, and engineers engage in and come to understand their domains (Lynch, 1985; Lynch & Woolgar, 1990). In addition, representations are viewed not just as a part of the body of scientific knowledge but as epistemic resources by which scientists propose, communicate, evaluate, and legitimize knowledge claims (Amman & Knorr Cetina, 1990). From this perspective, these authentic epistemic practices become a curricular goal within the context of an inquiry approach to science education (Kelly & Licona, 2017). And situative theories of learning (Brown et al., 1989; Lave & Wenger, 1991) suggest that students be engaged in these activities within a community of practice, in its educational application.

Socio-cultural theory would benefit by explicitly addressing the authentic ways that STEM apprentices are coached in the use of representations as they are inducted into the field by experts. And by extension, situated learning theory should include the ways that multiple representations can support learning and collaborative practices, as suggested by Pea (1994) and others (e.g., Kozma, 2003; Roth & McGinn, 1998).

The construct of representational competence provides a bridge between cognitive and situative orientations and, although it does not cross the threshold of a theory itself, it can contribute to both theory development and educational practice (Pande & Chandrasekharan, 2017; Scheid, Müller, Hettmannsperger, & Schnotz, 2018). Representational competencies consist of both cognitive skills (e.g., transform one representation to another) and situated practices (e.g., use representations as evidence to support claims) (Kozma & Russell 1997). Elaboration on the cognitive and social demands and affordances of these skills and practices can contribute to both theoretical orientations and link them together (Rau, Chapter 2).

Research Implications

Future research on expert-novice use of multiple representations can inform both educational practice and theory development. From a cognitive perspective, more detail is needed on the ways that experts use representations to reason about their domain and the transactional relationship between current knowledge, use of representation, and the generation of new knowledge. An example of this practice is described in the study by Kozma et al. (2000), cited above, where a pharmaceutical chemist reasons with the specific features of an NMR graph to determine if the compound that she produced in the lab has the structure of the compound she intended to produce.

Also needed is an examination of the specific features of representations that support reasoning and discourse within disciplines. Alchemy, the discipline that preceded chemistry, was rich with symbolic forms, the use of which defined the domain and membership in it. However, the features of these representations did not afford insight into the chemical structures and processes. In the 18th century, a new language and representational system was invented that was the foundation of modern chemistry and the features of which afforded major discoveries in the field (Anderson, 1984). The features of these representations and others were studied by Kozma et al. (2000) and this kind of research is needed in other disciplines.

Of further interest would be how different features of domain-specific representations scaffold reasoning in one domain that is different than that in another domain or, conversely, how the use of representations in one domain might foster new knowledge or approaches when used in another domain. The near-universal use of mathematics representations across science domains comes to mind. What is it about mathematical representations and operations on them that makes them so universally useful in STEM domains?

Another important focus of research should be the special role and unique features of language, spoken or written, as a representational form. Words most often have only an arbitrary, rather than veridical, symbolic relationship with their referents (Goodman, 1968). Yet research reviewed above shows that both experts and novices use language, via explanations, questions, and argumentation, to understand other representations, individually and together. Does the arbitrary nature of language somehow serve as a "representational glue" that binds representations together and draws on their diverse features to abstract a common, underlying meaning?

Similarly, from a socio-cultural perspective, more detail is needed on the specific ways that experts coach STEM apprentices, as they induct these novices into the field by using representations to propose, communicate, evaluate, and legitimize knowledge claims, much as in the study by Kozma et al. (2000), where the professor models and coaches representational use and the graduate student engages in legitimate peripheral participation (Lave & Wenger, 1991) as he appropriates these practices. The educational application of findings on experts from both socio-cultural and cognitive studies would be rather limited, given their extensive domain knowledge, but they would inform theory and might provide general principles that could be transferred to education.

As for novices, more cognitive research is needed on the ways students struggle with the specific features of authentic representations and how the features of contrived representations and guidance in their use can support their understanding of these authentic representations as well as domain understanding, more generally (Forman, Ramirez-Del Toro, Brown, & Passmore, 2017). Situated research is needed, as well, on effective classroom practices of teachers and of student communities as students are guided in representational use and their discourse in learning communities is supported. Findings from such studies would inform both cognitive and situative theories of novice understanding, as well as the practices of instructional designers, a goal of design-based implementation research (Penuel et al., 2011).

Finally, continued research is needed in the area of representational competence (see Rau, Chapter 2), specify and validate these skills, for experts and novices, within and across domains (Kohl, 2005; Rau, 2017a; Rau, 2017b; Schank & Kozma, 2002; Steiff, 2011).

There is a growing number of educational contexts within which such research and theory development can happen (Michalchik, Rosenquist, Kozma, Kreikemeier, & Schank, 2008; Rau, 2017a). As more and more practice occurs online—both among experts and novices—it creates opportunities for researchers to access large amounts of data on authentic representation practices in the classroom and the laboratory that can be used to address issues in research and theory.

All of these lines of research will benefit from multi-disciplined collaboration. Only through the collective contributions of cognitive and learning scientists, cultural anthropologists, linguists, instructional designers, and domain experts will we thoroughly understand the representational use and practices of experts and the ways in which representations can support learning.

CONCLUDING THOUGHTS

In this final section, I would like to return, in a more personal way, to the starting educational assumption upon which expert-novice research is based and leave the reader with some general considerations. The assumption that underpins this chapter is that expertise—the knowledge, practices, and representational use of experts—is a model for curricular goals and instructional practices of education; expertise is the end-point to the novice starting point. That is, students should come to think and act in some important ways like experts think and act, including in their use of representations, and teachers and instructional designers should in some way incorporate these expert practices into their educational practices. This has certainly been a foundational assumption of much of my own research in this area.

But one might ask, is expertise and expert use of representations the, or the only, model we should use for building a STEM curriculum and instructional practices? It may make sense if novices are science majors and the goal of STEM education is to fill the science pipeline. The understanding and use of specialized, domain-specific representations is an important qualification for membership in the exclusive scientific community, as well as important to understanding its fundamental principles. But these representations and practices may not make sense if the goal is the widespread support for the scientific endeavor and value of scientific findings among the general population.

In an international survey of attitudes toward science conducted by 3M (2018), 86% of respondents said they knew "little" or "nothing" about science, 38% agreed that their everyday life would not be very different without science, 32% are skeptical about science, and 20% expressed distrust of scientists. More specific to the United States and to the topic of climate change, a survey by the Pew Research Center (Rainie, 2017) found that while 87% of the responding scientists believed that climate change was due primarily to human activity, only 50% of the general public believed so.

Perhaps rather than looking at the way scientists understand and practice science and using that as a curricular model for science classrooms, we should look at ways that representations can be used to convince non-science students and the general public of veracity of scientific findings, to create an emotional impact of these findings, and to compel the public to action, where appropriate. This curricular goal would have very different educational, theoretical, and research implications than the study of expert-novice differences.

From this perspective, representational competence might best be seen as a generative, general skill; a liberal art, rather than or in addition to a specialized scientific skill. And, much like critical thinking or creativity, representational competence could be applied across fields to not only help people understand science (and other domains) but to create new, more accessible and impactful ways to communicate about science to a skeptical general public.

REFERENCES

3M (2018). *3M state of science index.* https://multimedia.3m.com/mws/media/1515295O/presentation-3m-state-of-science-index-2018-global-report-pdf.pdf

Ainsworth, S. (2006). DeFT: A conceptual framework for considering learning with multiple representations. *Learning and Instruction, 16*, 183–198.

Ainsworth, S., Bibby, P., & Wood, D. (2002). Examining the effects of different multiple representational systems in learning primary mathematics. *Journal of the Learning Sciences, 11*(1), 25–61.

Amman, K., & Knorr Cetina, K. (1990). The fixation of (visual) evidence. In M. Lynch & S. Woolgar (Eds.), *Representation in scientific practice* (pp. 85–122). Cambridge, MA: MIT Press.

Anderson, W. (1984). *Between the library and the laboratory: The language of chemistry in eighteenth-century France.* Baltimore, MD: Johns Hopkins Press.

Berthold, K., Eysink, T., & Renki, A. (2009). Assisting self-explanation prompts are more effective than open prompts when learning with multiple representations. *Instructional Science, 37*(4), 345–363.

Bobrow, D. (1975). Dimensions of representations. In D. Bobrow & A. Collins (Eds.), *Representation and understanding: Studies in cognitive science* (pp. 1–34). New York: Academic Press.

Brown, J. S., Collins, A., & Duguid, P. (1989). Situated cognition and the culture of learning. *Educational Researcher, 18*, 32–42.
Bruner, J. (1966). *Toward a theory of instruction*. Cambridge, MA: Harvard University Press.
Cheng, K.-H., & Tsai, -C.-C. (2013). Affordance of augmented reality in science learning: Suggestions for future research. *Journal of Science Education and Technology, 22*(4), 449–462.
Chi, M., Feltovich, P., & Glaser, R. (1981). Categorization and representation by experts and novices. *Cognitive Science, 5*, 121–152.
Chi, M., Glaser, R., & Farr, M. (1988). *The nature of expertise*. Hillsdale, NJ: Erlbaum.
Clement, J. (1983). A conceptual model discussed by Galileo and used intuitively by physics students. In D. Genter & A. Stevens (Eds.), *Mental models* (pp. 325–340). Hillsdale, NJ: Erlbaum.
Daniel, K., Bucklin, C., Leone, E. A., & Idema, J. (2018). Toward a definition of representational competence. In K. Daniel (Ed.), *Toward a framework for representational competence in science education* (pp. 3–11). Heidelberg: Springer-Verlag.
De Groot, A. D. (1978). *Thought and choice in chess* (2nd ed.). The Hague Mouton; originally publ. 1946.
der Meij, V., & Jong, D. (2011). The effects of directive self-explanation prompts to support active processing of multiple representations in a simulation-based learning environment. *Journal of Computer Assisted Learning, 27*(5), 411–423.
Eilam, B., & Poyass, Y. (2008). Learning with multiple representations: Extending multimedia learning beyond the lab. *Learning and Instruction, 18*(4), 368–378.
Forman, E., Ramirez-Del Toro, V., Brown, L., & Passmore, C. (2017). Discursive strategies that foster an epistemic community for argument in a biology classroom. *Learning and Instruction, 48*, 32–39.
Goodman, N. (1968). *Languages of art: An approach to a theory of symbols*. New York: Bobbs-Merrill.
Gopalan, V., Abu Bakar, J., & Zulkifli, A. (2017). A brief review of augment reality science learning. American Institute of Physics Conference Proceedings, https://doi.org/10.1063/1.5005377
Greeno, J. G. (1989). Situations, mental models and generative knowledge. In D. Klahr & K. Kotofsky (Eds.), *Complex information processing: The impact of Herbert A. Simon* (pp. 109–144). Hillsdale, NJ: Erlbaum.
Greeno, J. G. (2011). A situative perspective on cognition and learning in interaction. In T. Koschmann (Ed.), *Theories of learning and studies of instructional practice* (vol. 1, pp. 41–71). Berlin: Springer.
Hand, B., & Choi, A. (2010). Examining the impact of student use of multiple representations in constructing arguments in organic chemistry. *Research in Science Education, 40*(1), 29–44.
Hoffmann, R., & Laszlo, R. (1991). Representation in chemistry. *Angewandte Chemi, 30*, 1–16.
Kelly, G., & Licona, P. (2017). Epistemic practices and science education. In M. Matthews (Ed.), *History, philosophy and science teaching* (pp. 139–165). New York: Springer.
Kohl, P., & Finkelstein, N. (2005). Student representational competence and self-assessment when solving physics problems. *Physical Review: Physics Education Research,* 010104-1/010104-11.
Kohl, P., & Finkelstein, N. (2008). Patterns of multiple representation use by experts and novices during physics problem solving. *Physical Review Physics Education Research,* 4.010111-1-12.
Kozma, R. (2000). Students collaborating with computer models and physical experiments. In C. Hoadley (Ed.), *Computer support for collaborative learning* (pp. 314–322). Mahwah, NJ: Erlbaum.
Kozma, R. (2003). The material features of multiple representations and their cognitive and social affordances for science understanding. *Learning and Instruction, 13*(2), 205–226.
Kozma, R., Chin, E., Russell, J., & Marx, N. (2000). The role of representations and tools in the chemistry laboratory and their implications for learning chemistry. *Journal of the Learning Sciences, 9*(2), 105–143.
Kozma, R., & Russell, J. (1997). Multimedia and understanding: Expert and novice responses to different representations of chemical phenomena. *Journal of Research in Science Teaching, 34*(9), 949–968.
Kozma, R., Russell, J., Johnston, J., & Dershimer, C. (1990). College students' understanding of chemical equilibrium. Paper presented at the annual meeting of the American Educational Research Association, Boston, MA.
Larkin, J., McDermott, J., Simon, D., & Simon, H. (1980). Expert and novice in solving physics problems. *Science, 208*, 1335–1342.
Lave, J., & Wenger, E. (1991). *Situated learning: Legitimate peripheral participation*. Cambridge: Cambridge University Press.
Lemke, J. (1998). Multiplying meaning: Visual and verbal semiotics in scientific text. In J. R. Martin & R. Veel (Eds.), *Reading science: Critical and functional aspects on discourse of science* (pp. 87–113). London: Routledge.

Lesgold, A., Rubinsin, H., Feltovich, P., Glaser, R., Klopfer, D., & Wang, Y. (1988). Expertise in a complex skill: Diagnosing X-ray pictures. In M. Chi, R. Glaser, & M. Farr (Eds.), *The nature of expertise* (pp. 311–342). Hillsdale, NJ: Erlbaum.

Lynch, M. (1985). *Art and artifact in laboratory science: A study of shop work and shop talk in a research laboratory*. London: Routledge.

Lynch, M., & Woolgar, S. (1990). Introduction: Sociological orientations to representational practice in science. In M. Lynch & S. Woolgar (Eds.), *Representation in scientific practice* (pp. 1–18). Cambridge, MA: MIT Press.

Mayer, R. E. (2009). Cognitive theory of multimedia learning. In R. E. Mayer (Ed.), *The Cambridge handbook of multimedia learning* (2nd ed., pp. 31–48). New York: Cambridge University Press.

McCloskey, M. (1983). Naive theories of motion. In D. Genter & A. Stevens (Eds.), *Mental models* (pp. 299–324). Hillsdale, NJ: Erlbaum.

Michalchik, V. K., Rosenquist, A., Kozma, R., Kreikemeier, P., & Schank, P. (2008). Representational resources for constructing shared understandings in the high school chemistry classroom. In J. Gilbert, M. Reiner, & M. Nakhleh (Eds.), *Visualization: Theory and practice in science education* (pp. 233–282). Berlin: Springer.

Moreno, R., & Duran, R. (2004). Do multiple representations need explanations? The role of verbal guidance and individual differences in multimedia mathematics learning. *Journal of Educational Psychology, 96*(3), 492–503.

Neisser, U. (1967). *Cognitive psychology*. New York: Appleton-Century-Crofts.

Newell, A., & Simon, H. A. (1972). *Human problem solving*. Englewood Cliffs, NJ: Prentice Hall.

Norman, D. (1993). *Things that make us smart: Defining human attributes in the age of the machine*. New York: Diversion Books.

Ott, N., Brunken, R., Vogel, M., & Malone., S. (2018). Multiple symbolic representations: The combination of formula and text supports problem solving in the mathematical field of propositional logic. *Learning and Instruction, 58*, 88–105.

Owens, J. (2018). Data visualization innovations in the life sciences and drug discovery. *Infomatics from Technology Networks*. www.technologynetworks.com/informatics/articles/data-visualization-innovations-in-life-sciences-and-drug-discovery-296360

Pande, P., & Chandrasekharan, S. (2017). Representational competence: Toward a distributed and embodied cognition account. *Studies in Science Education, 53*(1), 1–43.

Pea, R. (1994). Seeing what we build together: Distributed multimedia learning environments for transformative communications. *Journal of the Learning Sciences, 3*(3), 285–299.

Penuel, W., Fishman, B., Cheng, B., & Sabelli, N. (2011). Organizing research and development at the intersection of learning, implementation and design. *Educational Researcher, 40*(7), 331–337.

Piaget, J. (1950). *The psychology of intelligence*. New York: Routledge.

Rainie, L. (2017). *U.S. public trust in science and scientists*. Washington, DC: Pew Research Center.

Rau, M. (2017a). A framework for educational technologies that support representational competencies. *Transactions on Learning Technologies, 3*(10), 290–305.

Rau, M. (2017b). Conditions for the effectiveness of multiple visual representations in enhancing STEM learning. *Educational Psychological Review, 29*(4), 717–761.

Rau, M., & Matthews, P. (2017). How to make 'more' better? Principles for effective use of multiple representations to enhance students' learning about fractions. *ZDM: The International Journal on Mathematics Education, 49*(4), 531–544.

Rau, M., & Wu, S. (2017). Educational technology support for collaborative learning with multiple visual representations in chemistry. In B. K. Smith, M. Borge, E. Mercier, & K. Y. Lim (Eds.). *Making a difference: Prioritizing equity and access in CSCL, 12th International Conference on Computer Supported Collaborative Learning (CSCL) 2017* (vol. 1, pp. 79–86). Philadelphia, PA: International Society of the Learning Sciences.

Roth, W.-M., & McGinn, M. (1998). Inscriptions: Toward a theory of representing as social practice. *Review of Educational Research, 68*(1), 35–59.

Schank, P., & Kozma, R. (2002). Learning chemistry through the use of a representation-based knowledge building environment. *Journal of Computers in Mathematics and Science Teaching, 21*(3), 253–279.

Scheid, J., Müller, A., Hettmannsperger, R., & Schnotz, W. (2018). Representational competence in science education: From theory to assessment. In K. Daniel (Ed.), *Toward a framework for representational competence in science education* (pp. 263–277). Heidelberg: Springer-Verlag.

Schnotz, W. (2014). An integrated model of text and picture comprehension. In R. E. Mayer (Ed.), *The Cambridge handbook of multimedia learning* (2nd ed., pp. 72–103). New York: Cambridge University Press.

Schoenfeld, D., & Herrmann, D. (1982). Problem perception and knowledge structure in expert and novice mathematical problem solvers, *Journal of Experimental Psychology: Learning, Memory and Cognition, 8*(5), 484–494.

Simon, H. A. (1969). *Sciences of the artificial.* Cambridge, MA: MIT Press.

Skinner, B. F. (1953). *Science and human behavior.* New York: Free Press.

Soloway, E., Adelson, B., & Ehrlich, K. (1988). Knowledge and processes in the comprehension of computer programming. In M. Chi, R. Glaser, & M. Farr (Eds.), *The nature of expertise* (pp. 129–152). Hillsdale, NJ: Erlbaum.

Steiff, M. (2011). Improving representational competence using molecular simulations embedded in inquiry activities. *Journal of Research in Science Teaching, 48*(10), 1137–1158.

Stylianou, D., & Silver, E. (2004). The role of visual representations in advanced mathematical problem solving: An examination of expert-novice similarities and differences. *Mathematical Thinking and Learning, 6*(4), 353–387.

Taramopoulos, A., & Psillos, D. (2017). Complex phenomena understanding in electricity through dynamically linked concrete and abstract representations. *Journal of Computer Assisted Learning, 33*(2), 151–163.

Van Meter, P. (2001). Drawing construction as a strategy for learning from text. *Journal of Educational Psychology, 69,* 129–140.

Van Meter, P., & Firetto, C. (2013). Cognitive model of drawing construction: Learning through the construction of drawings. In G. Schraw, M. McCrudden, & D. Robinson (Eds.), *Learning through visual displays* (pp. 247–280). Charlotte, NC: Information Age Publishing.

Vygotsky, L. (1978). *Mind in society: The development of higher psychological processes.* Cambridge, MA: Harvard University Press.

Wu, H.-K., Krajcik, J., & Soloway, E. (2001). Promoting understanding of chemical representations: Students' use of a visualization tool in the classroom. *Journal of Research in Science Teaching, 38,* 821–842.

Zoller, U. (1990). Students' misunderstandings and misconceptions in college freshman chemistry (general and organic). *Journal of Research in Science Teaching, 27*(10), 1053–1065.

4

COGNITIVE PROCESSES UNDERLYING LEARNING FROM MULTIPLE REPRESENTATIONS

Anne Schüler

LEIBNIZ-INSTITUT FÜR WISSENSMEDIEN

ABSTRACT

This chapter focuses on the cognitive processes underlying learning from multiple representations (e.g., text-picture combinations). Knowing about the cognitive processes involved is important for two reasons: First, it allows evaluating the assumptions of multimedia theories. Second, it allows us to support those learners who do not benefit from multiple representations by helping them to better execute the cognitive processes necessary to take advantage of information presented across multiple representations. After a short review of the assumptions made by theories of multimedia learning, empirical studies providing evidence regarding the underlying cognitive processes are reported. In these studies, cognitive paradigms (i.e., often established experimental setups), eye tracking, or verbal protocols were used to shed light on the cognitive processes underlying learning with multiple representations. Additionally, a short overview of how individuals can differ regarding the use of cognitive processes is provided. Afterwards, an example is shown of how we can support individuals in performing adequate cognitive processes when learning from multiple representations. The chapter ends with an outlook on future research.

Key words: cognitive processes, multiple representations, multimedia learning, eye tracking, text-picture processing

Multiple representations can be defined as the combination of different representational formats like written or spoken texts, static illustrations, or animated pictures. Multiple representations are common in textbooks, where combinations of text, photos, schematic illustrations, and charts may be used to relay information. Learning from multiple representations is also common in digital learning environments, which may consist of spoken narratives, simulations, and videos. Even websites on the internet, like Wikipedia, Facebook, or Amazon, normally consist of multiple representation formats. Hence, multiple representations are a part of our daily lives.

A possible categorization of different multiple representation formats refers to the differentiation of verbal information (like written or spoken text) versus pictorial information (like static pictures as photos, illustrations, charts; or like dynamic pictures, animations or simulations). The combination of verbal and pictorial representations has also been called "multimedia" (e.g., Mayer, 2009). Therefore, in this chapter, I will use the terms multimedia and multiple representations interchangeably. There has been a lot of research in the area of learning with multimedia, and from this research we know that most learners benefit from the presentation of information using multimedia (for overviews, see Butcher, 2014; Mayer, 2009).

In this chapter I would like to answer the question of which cognitive processes play a central role in learning with multimedia. This is an important question for two reasons: First, the knowledge of the underlying cognitive processes supporting learning with multimedia allows for theory building. In particular, an understanding of cognitive processes can contribute both to the Cognitive Theory of Multimedia Learning (CTML; Mayer, 2009) and the Integrated Model of Text and Picture Comprehension (ITPC; Schnotz & Bannert, 2003). A key feature of these theories are assumptions about the cognitive processes involved in learning from multimedia presentations, assumptions that are investigated in this chapter. The second reason to consider the underlying cognitive processes is that understanding the cognitive processes necessary for learning from multimedia representations allows us to better support those learners who do not engage these cognitive processes and therefore do not benefit from affordances of multimedia learning.

Before I summarize the empirical findings regarding the underlying cognitive processes, I will briefly outline the assumptions behind leading theories of multimedia learning. I focus on the CTML (Mayer, 2009), which postulates three central cognitive processes when learning with multimedia: selection, organization, and integration. The theory assumes that learners engage actively in these three cognitive processes, that is, learners seek to make sense of multiple representations. Let's take a more detailed look at these processes: In a first step, learners select information from the learning materials. For example, a learner can decide to select a certain word or phrase from the written text and a certain pictorial element from the image. In the next step, learners must mentally organize the selected information, that is, they build internal connections (e.g., a cause and effect chain) among the selected words as well as among the selected pictorial elements to construct a mental representation of the selected verbal information and a mental representation of the selected pictorial information in their working memory. After this step, the learners have two mental representations in their working memory, namely a verbal mental representation of the text in verbal working memory and a pictorial mental representation of the image in pictorial working memory (cf. Schüler, Scheiter, & van Genuchten, 2011 for the involvement of working memory in multimedia learning). As a final step, the learners integrate the two mental representations, the verbal and the pictorial, with each other and with their prior knowledge, to form a coherent mental model. This step is often seen as the most important step, as the resulting integrated mental representation corresponds to deep learning and allows learners to transfer learned content to new situations.

According to Mayer (1997), the integration of the verbal and the pictorial mental model takes place through the production of one-to-one correspondences between both representations, that is, between their elements, actions, and causal relations. For example, to map the verbal description of a tornado's functioning to an image representing this process, learners must first identify the corresponding elements in text and illustration (e.g., they must recognize that the word "air" refers to the arrows depicted in the picture). Then they must map the actions described in the text to the actions depicted in the picture (e.g., they must recognize that the expression "warm air rises to the higher, cooler air masses" refers to red arrows pointing up into the sky). Thirdly, they must map causal relationships between the actions described in the text and the actions depicted in the picture (e.g., they must recognize that the causal relationship described in the text between "The warm air flows continuously upwards" and "The cumulus cloud becomes a storm cloud" is the same as the causal relationship depicted in the picture).

In summary, it can be said that, according to CTML (Mayer, 2009), learning with multiple representations involves three cognitive processes, which are actively executed by the learners: selection, organization, and integration, with integration seen as the most important cognitive process. This is also mirrored in the empirical studies summarized in the next sections, as these studies focused mainly on integration, and less on selection and organization processes.

EVIDENCE FROM EMPIRICAL STUDIES REGARDING COGNITIVE PROCESSES UNDERLYING LEARNING FROM MULTIPLE REPRESENTATIONS

In this chapter I will review empirical studies which aimed to investigate the cognitive processes underlying learning from multiple representations. I will differentiate between three categories of studies based on the method they used: first, studies using cognitive paradigms; second, studies using eye tracking; third, studies using verbal protocols.

Studies Using Cognitive Paradigms

One way to measure the cognitive processes underlying learning from multiple representations is to use cognitive paradigms; that is, certain, often established experimental setups, which allow making conclusions about the underlying mechanisms of a psychological phenomenon. One advantage of such paradigms is that they often allow the underlying processes to be measured more explicitly than is the case with learning setups, where conclusions about the underlying processes are drawn based on performance in a recall or transfer task (e.g., better performance in a transfer task is ascribed to the process of integration). Within a cognitive paradigm, for example, the distribution of information between text and picture can often be better controlled. This allows for later analyses to trace specific knowledge that is gained back to its representational source and to examine the degree to which integration occurred. In the following section, some studies are presented that have worked with such paradigms and from which conclusions can be drawn about the cognitive processes underlying learning from multimedia, especially the integration process.

In an early study by Glenberg and Langston (1992), participants were presented with texts describing several four-step procedures (e.g., how to write a paper: write a first draft/consider the structure/consider the audience/proof the paper), with the two middle steps of these procedures always described as occurring simultaneously. Although it was explicitly pointed out in the texts that both middle steps had to take place simultaneously (e.g., "The next two steps should be taken at the same time"), the texts described them sequentially, that is, step 2 was described before step 3. Half of the subjects received additional images showing the two middle steps as simultaneous (i.e., side by side; Experiment 1). Interestingly, subjects who only received texts represented the relationships between the four steps sequentially (i.e., they did not relate the middle steps equally strongly to the first and last steps of the procedure, despite their simultaneous occurrence). On the other hand, participants who received images related the middle steps equally strongly to the first and last step of the process, suggesting that they not only represented the sequential text structure, but that they integrated the temporal structure of the picture with the facts of the text.

Work by McNamara, Halpin, and Hardy (1992) provides additional evidence for the integration of text and pictures. The authors conducted a series of experiments in which they investigated whether subjects integrated spatial information about locations with non-spatial facts about these locations. The subjects first had to memorize a map with different locations (e.g., a roadmap which contained the location of 20 cities). After studying the map, subjects were asked to learn non-spatial facts about the cities shown on the map (e.g., that a city is famous for its large amusement park). In the next step, subjects performed a task in which they had to decide whether a particular city was in a particular region of the learned map or in another region. The integration of picture (i.e., the map) and text (i.e., the facts) in this task was investigated by comparing performance under two different conditions: In the "near" condition the city was primed (i.e. pre-activated) with a non-spatial fact of a nearby city on the road map, while in the "far" condition the city was primed with a non-spatial fact of a distant city on the road map. The authors showed a distance effect, such that the responses to the cities were more accurate if they were primed with a non-spatial fact about a nearby city, rather than if they were primed with a non-spatial fact about a distant city (Experiments 1 and 3). Overall, these results support the assumption that verbal information on non-spatial facts was integrated with pictorial information on locations, leading to the observed priming effects of facts as a function of distance.

In our own research (e.g., Schüler, Arndt, & Scheiter, 2015) we have used Gentner and Loftus's (1979) paradigm to investigate the integration of text and picture. Participants were instructed to memorize several combinations of sentences and pictures that differed in their degree of specificity (general vs. specific). Specific sentences and pictures provided additional information that the general sentences and pictures did not contain. For example, a general picture showed a teacher in front of an empty blackboard, while a specific picture showed a mathematics teacher in front of a formula-filled blackboard. The corresponding general sentence was "The teacher stands in front of the blackboard", while the corresponding specific sentence was "The mathematics teacher stands in front of the blackboard". Every participant saw one of the four possible sentence-picture combinations (i.e. general picture/general sentence; specific picture/specific sentence; general picture/specific sentence; specific picture/

general sentence). After memorizing all presented sentence-picture combinations, participants were presented with the general and the specific version of each sentence next to each other on one slide and had to decide which of both versions they had read in the learning phase. In addition, they completed a similar test regarding the pictures in which they decided whether they had seen the general or the specific version of each picture in the learning phase. The dependent variable was the frequency of selecting the specific version of sentences and pictures in the two tests. In cases where the generality or specificity of the picture and the sentence matched, sentences and pictures provided the same information (e.g., about a teacher or a mathematics teacher), and so it was expected that participants should have no problems correctly rejecting or accepting the respective version. However, in cases where sentences and pictures provided information at different levels of specificity (i.e. general pictures/specific sentences or specific pictures/general sentences), the integration of text and picture was expected to become evident. For example, if students had seen the general picture of the teacher in combination with the specific sentence about the mathematics teacher, the integrated representation should contain the information that the teacher is a mathematics teacher. Therefore, students should more often mistakenly choose the specific picture with the mathematics teacher instead of the general picture with the teacher. Similarly, students should more often wrongly choose the specific version of a sentence after seeing a specific picture/general sentence combination. In two studies we were able to show that text-picture integration took place, at least regarding the sentence test. This finding provides further evidence that learners indeed construct an integrated mental model of the information presented across texts and pictures.

In another set of studies, I used a paradigm from text comprehension research (inconsistency paradigm; cf. Albrecht & O'Brien, 1993) to investigate whether integration of multiple representations occurs during learning. The main idea of the inconsistency paradigm is that – if integration occurs – learners should become aware of inconsistent information presented across texts and images during reading. Imagine, for example, a sentence-picture combination, where the sentence states that "once the handle is released, the two disks start to drop again and do *not* separate from each other", whereas in the picture two disks are depicted as separated from one another. When learners are confronted with such inconsistent text-picture information, they should have difficulty cognitively integrating text and images. This, in turn, should be reflected in their eye-gaze behavior, such that they have longer fixation times on texts and images and more frequently switch between the two representations. It is precisely this pattern of findings that I have observed in two experiments (Schüler, 2017): Learners receiving inconsistent text-picture information showed more intensive gaze behavior when inconsistent information was presented, as compared to a control group not receiving inconsistent information. This finding indicates that learners try to map and integrate text and pictures mentally with each other. If this process is hampered by inconsistent information, learners show more intensive gaze behavior.

In sum, studies using cognitive paradigms to investigate the cognitive processes underlying learning from multiple representations underline the integration assumption made by theories of multimedia learning (e.g., Mayer, 2009). Hence, they speak in favor of the assumption that pictorial and verbal information are integrated with each other into one coherent mental model, as corresponding pictorial and verbal information seems to be highly connected leading to the effects reported by Glenberg and Langston (1992), McNamara et al. (1992), and Schüler et al. (2015). Moreover, the finding that learners are sensitive to inconsistencies between text and picture (Schüler, 2017) also underlines the assumption that learners try to connect the text to the image during learning.

Studies Using Eye Tracking

Probably the most common approach to measuring the cognitive processes underlying learning from multiple representations is eye tracking (for reviews, see Alemdag & Cagiltay, 2018; Scheiter & Eitel, 2016). Eye tracking records learners' eye movements when processing multiple representations, such as their attendance to text-image combinations. Eye tracking metrics such as looking at a representation (i.e., fixations) or switching between multiple representations (i.e., transitions) are not only seen as indicators of the distribution of students' visual attention. They are also used to draw conclusions about the cognitive processes (e.g., selection, organization, and integration) underlying learning (see eye-mind-assumption, Just & Carpenter, 1980; Van Gog & Scheiter, 2010). For example, the time to the first fixation on a word or image element is seen as an indicator for the selection of information; the total fixation time on a text or an image is seen as an indicator for organization of information (cf. Alemdag & Cagiltay, 2018); and the frequency with which learners switch their gaze between text and picture (e.g., Hannus & Hyönä, 1999; Hegarty & Just, 1993; Johnson & Mayer, 2012; Mason, Tornatora, & Pluchino, 2013) is seen as an indicator of learners' attempts to integrate information from text and image.

One of the first studies in multimedia learning using eye tracking was conducted by Hegarty and Just (1993, Experiment 2). A text on the functioning of a pulley system and an image of the pulley system were presented to learners. It turned out that learners alternately looked at the text and the picture, and that the learners switched to the picture at the end of a sentence. This can be an indication that learners build their mental model step by step; that is, they first construct a verbal mental representation based on text segments; then they switch to the corresponding part in the image to construct the pictorial mental representation; lastly they integrate both representations with each other. Furthermore, in reference to the image, two types of processing strategies were identified: local inspections, which refer to a few image elements, and global inspections, which refer to large parts of an image and may be used to construct a mental representation of the whole image. Local and global inspections may be seen as part of the pictorial organization process proposed by the CTML (Mayer, 2009).

In a more recent study by Mason et al. (2013), participants read a text combined with a picture on the subject of air. Cluster analyses of learners' gaze behavior identified three different groups of learners: First, high integrators were characterized by a high number of switches between text and image and long image fixation times. Second, low integrators were characterized by a low number of switches between text and image and low image fixation times. Third, medium integrators demonstrated some switches between text and pictures and rather short fixation times of the images. Interestingly, the three groups not only showed different viewing behavior, but also differed in learning performance: High integrators showed better learning performance than low integrators on most dependent measures. This shows that integration processes – indicated by students switching between text and image – and picture processing – reflected in fixation times on an image – are both important cognitive processes that support learning (for similar results, see also Hannus & Hyönä, 1999; Jian, 2017; Mason, Pluchino, & Tornatora, 2015; Mason, Pluchino, Tornatora, & Ariasi, 2013; O'Keefe, Letourneau, Homer, Schwartz, & Plass, 2014).

Another very interesting finding from eye-tracking research is that learning from multimedia materials is often heavily text driven. Thus, Hannus and Hyönä (1999) found that learning was heavily guided by text (about 80% of the learning time was spent on looking at text) and that participants (10-year-old children) inspected images only superficially (only about 6% of the learning time was spent on looking at images). This pattern has been replicated in several multimedia studies using eye tracking with adult participants (e.g., Jian & Wu, 2015; Johnson & Mayer, 2012; Schmidt-Weigand, Kohnert, & Glowalla, 2010). This finding is interesting insofar as this disequilibrium between text and picture processing is not explicitly considered in theories of multimedia learning.

One possible explanation for the neglect of pictures is that the information presented by images can be captured "at a glance". In contrast, reading requires the fixation on individual words, lexical access, as well as syntactic and semantic processing (cf. Schmidt-Weigand, 2009). Eitel, Scheiter, and Schüler (2012) were able to show that for images of causal systems, which are commonly used in multimedia learning scenarios, a viewing time of 50 milliseconds is sufficient to identify the rough theme of the image, or the so-called "gist". This gist mainly contains information about the spatial arrangement of essential elements of the image (Oliva & Torralba, 2006), which in turn is crucial for the formation of a mental model (Johnson-Laird, 1980). While the gist is extracted with the first fixation(s), the following fixations are used to add details to the image. Eitel, Scheiter, and Schüler (2013) and Eitel, Scheiter, Schüler, Nyström, and Holmqvist (2013, Experiment 3) showed that the gist extracted from an image can facilitate subsequent text processing. For example, people provided with a short image presentation prior to text presentation had shorter reading times of text passages describing the spatial configurations visualized in the image than people not presented with an image prior to reading. These differences in reading times indicate that even a brief examination of an image supports the construction of a spatial mental model from text, to such an extent that the corresponding parts of a text can be understood more quickly. Therefore, it is argued that images support learning from multimedia, because learners may use illustrations as a scaffold to construct a mental model when processing text (cf. Eitel et al., 2013, 2013; Glenberg & Langston, 1992; Gyselinck, Cornoldi, Dubois, De Beni, & Ehrlich, 2002; Gyselinck & Meneghetti, 2011; Gyselinck & Tardieu, 1999; Tardieu & Gyselinck, 2003). Future research is needed to examine this assumption more closely.

Another explanation for why learners spent less time looking at the images is that the importance of images for learning is underestimated by students, hence, leading them to ignore or superficially process images. If this is true, more intensive picture processing should lead to better learning performance, which has been confirmed by several empirical studies (e.g., Mason et al., 2013; Scheiter & Eitel, 2015).

In sum, studies using eye tracking show that especially processing of picture information (i.e., picture organization) and switches between text and pictures (i.e., integration) are associated with better performance. Furthermore, there is evidence that processing of multiple representations is heavily text-driven and that learners seem to neglect the images. One explanation for this finding could be that learners can extract the gist of the picture within a very short time frame, hence, a short glance at the picture is sufficient for its processing. It could also be, however, that learners do underestimate the importance of images for learning.

One drawback of eye tracking lays in the fact that it is sometimes difficult to interpret the cognitive processes which underlie a certain gaze behaviour. For example, do prolonged picture fixation times indicate that the organization process was successful? Or does it mean that the learner has difficulties in accomplishing the pictorial organization process? Here, verbal protocols, which are described in the next section, can give more insight.

Studies Using Verbal Protocols

Another possible way to measure online cognitive processes during learning are verbal protocols. In verbal protocols, learners are required to express aloud the thoughts coming to their mind during processing multiple representations (cf. Ericsson & Simon, 1993).

In a study by Butcher (2006, Experiment 2) participants were instructed to self-explain their thought process aloud during learning. Three groups were compared: a group presented with a text alone, a group presented with a text combined with a schematic, simplified picture, and a group presented with a text combined with a detailed picture. She found that presenting students with pictures generated a high number of correct self-explanation inferences during learning, whereas the amount of other statements (e.g., paraphrases, elaborations, monitoring statements) was not influenced by picture presentation. Additionally, it was observed that schematic, simplified pictures supported integrative inferences, that is, inferences that integrated previously stated information with the currently processed information. As learners receiving schematic pictures outperformed the other two groups on almost all outcome measures, Butcher concluded that integration inferences, in particular, are necessary to construct a mental representation of the content to be learned.

Kühl, Scheiter, Gerjets, and Gemballa (2011) also instructed learners to think-aloud during learning. Participants learned either with a text alone, with a text combined with static pictures, or with a text combined with dynamic pictures (i.e., animations). Similar to the results from Butcher (2006), learners receiving pictures reported that they did not understand the content (i.e., negative monitoring) less often and generated more inferences than learners receiving only texts. These processes were also related to performance: Negative monitoring was negatively related with factual knowledge, pictorial recall, and transfer knowledge, whereas generative inferences were positively related to the three dependent variables. Thus, differences in both types of strategy reports may explain the better performance of learners receiving pictures. Another interesting finding was that learners receiving dynamic pictures evaluated their learning process more positively, indicating that they were more confident that they had understood the learning content. However, the dynamic visualization group did not outperform the static visualization group, and, moreover, their positive evaluations of learning were not related to the learning outcome. This indicates that learners presented with dynamic visualization developed more illusions of understanding than the other two groups (for similar results, see also Eitel, 2016).

To summarize, the empirical findings from studies interested in the cognitive processes underlying learning from multimedia indicate the following: First, the postulated process of text-picture integration seems to take place as indicated by studies using cognitive paradigms and eye tracking. Second, eye-tracking studies showed that integration (e.g., switches between text and image) and picture organization (e.g., fixation time on picture) seem to be important strategies, as these gaze parameters were related with better performance. Third, learning from multimedia seems to be heavily text-driven (e.g., long fixation times on text and very short fixation times on images). And lastly, pictures seem to induce qualitatively different cognitive processes, like inferences, going beyond the presented content.

INDIVIDUAL DIFFERENCES REGARDING COGNITIVE PROCESSES WHEN LEARNING FROM MULTIMEDIA

The cognitive processes described above (i.e., selection, organization, and especially integration) are important prerequisites for learning successfully with multimedia. Not surprisingly, it has been shown that the quality of strategic processing differs between individuals learning from multiple representations. So, in the present section I want to give some examples regarding individual characteristics that can influence cognitive processing when learning from multimedia. (See Cromley, Chapter 5 for a more detailed description of individual differences and their influence on learning from multiple representations.)

An individual characteristic which seems to play a crucial role in the execution of cognitive processes is prior knowledge. For example, in the study by Mason et al. (2013) described above, another interesting finding was that learners with higher prior knowledge made more integrative transitions between the text and picture and fixated on the picture longer during rereading. The authors concluded that higher prior knowledge was associated with strategic behavior, which is crucial for successful learning from multimedia. Morrow et al. (2012) also used the eye-tracking technique and showed that participants (older adults over 60 years) with high and low prior knowledge differed in their processing behaviors: Learners with high prior knowledge initially looked longer at the text than low prior knowledge learners. Moreover, after reading the text once, they looked longer at the relevant pictures than learners with low prior knowledge. Low prior knowledge learners, as a contrast, looked at the pictures in a distributed fashion throughout the whole trial.

Similar results were observed by Hannus and Hyönä (1999), who differentiated their 10-year-old participants into high intellectual ability and low intellectual ability learners. The two groups differed in two ways regarding their processing behaviors: First, high-ability learners reread the text more often than low-ability students. Second, high-ability learners studied pertinent text and picture segments more intensively than low-ability learners, making more transitions between related text and picture components. Again, the behavior shown by the high-ability learners seems to be more appropriate for learning from multiple representations. In line with this observation, high-ability learners also showed better performance.

Another factor influencing the way multimedia materials are processed is whether a learner can be classified as a verbalizer or a visualizer. Verbalizers use verbal modes of thinking, whereas visualizers use visual, pictorial ways of thinking (Massa & Mayer,

2003). In a study by Koc-Januchta, Höffler, Thoma, Prechtl, and Leutner (2017) it was shown that verbalizers showed a heavily text-driven processing behavior. On the other side, visualizers showed a strong picture-oriented way of processing. Compared to verbalizers, they spent more time on the pictures. Moreover, verbalizers looked at picture elements irrelevant for learning sooner than visualizers. Notably, visualizers also showed higher learning performance.

To sum up, individual characteristics can influence what kind of cognitive processes are conducted. In the studies reviewed, higher prior knowledge, higher intellectual abilities, and a visual mode of thinking were associated with better cognitive strategies and better learning outcomes.

SUPPORTING LEARNERS' COGNITIVE PROCESSES DURING LEARNING FROM MULTIMEDIA

It should be obvious that engaging the appropriate cognitive processes during learning from multiple representations is a prerequisite for benefitting from multimedia instruction. At the same time, not all learners are able to engage the cognitive processes necessary or deploy these to a sufficient extent to learn from multimedia. Hence, an important question is how we can support learners who have difficulties in using the strategies required to learn from multiple representations. Two possibilities exist to support learners (cf. Renkl & Scheiter, 2017): a material-based approach and a learner-based approach. According to the material-based approach, we can design learning materials in such a way that they "prompt" the required cognitive processes. For example, one can present text and images in spatial proximity instead of presenting them separately to aid integration processes (cf., Johnson & Mayer, 2012). Or one can highlight corresponding elements in text and pictures to aid students in connecting these elements to one another (cf., Richter, Scheiter, & Eitel, 2016; Schneider, Beege, Nebel, & Rey, 2018).

Due to space limitations, I will not go further in detail regarding the material-based approach (see Van Meter and Stepanik, Chapter 6, for more discussion on this point). It is necessary, however, to note a particular disadvantage of the material-based approach as it relates to learner processes; namely that it is not always possible to adapt learning materials as needed (e.g., in the classroom context or in textbooks). A possible alternative is to teach learners facilitative processing strategies that they can apply independently to the processing of multimedia material, even if the material is poorly designed or does not elicit strategy engagement. This approach is called the learner-based approach (cf. Renkl & Scheiter, 2017; Van Meter and Stepanik, Chapter 6). For example, processing strategies can be taught through strategy trainings before the learning phase that provide learners with knowledge on how to effectively process multimedia learning materials (e.g., Scheiter, Schubert, Gerjets, & Stalbovs, 2015; Schlag & Ploetzner, 2011). Eye Movement Modeling Examples (EMMEs) are a special form of strategy training. Here, adequate processing strategies are modelled with the help of eye movements on concrete learning materials, that is, learners are given examples of how the strategies can be implemented. Processing strategies, which are normally not visible, are externalized with the help of the eye movements of a model (usually an experienced learner). Before the actual learning phase, learners are presented with short videos in which facilitative processing strategies are applied to the learning material with the help of the model's eye movements. For example, the intense viewing of the picture is visualized (i.e., picture organization processes) or the gaze changes between text and picture (i.e., integration processes) are shown. Research shows that EMMEs can both increase learning outcomes and lead to changes in learners' gaze behavior, suggesting the adoption of new processing strategies by learners (e.g., Mason et al., 2015; Mason, Scheiter, & Tornatora, 2017). Thus, for example, in the study by Mason et al. (2015) the EMME group (receiving EMME before the learning phase) was compared to a control group (receiving no strategy information before the learning phase). The EMME contained a text and an image on the water cycle. The video showed that the model initially read the entire text. Then, the model's gaze shifted from text segments to the corresponding image elements. During the subsequent learning phase, where all participants learnt about the food chain, participants' gaze behavior was measured. Results revealed that learners in the EMME group showed more integrative processing strategies than learners in the control group. Thus, for example, the EMME group spent more time in refixating relevant parts of the image while rereading the text, which is interpreted as an integrative processing behavior (see also Mason et al., 2017). Additionally, in the EMME group this gaze behavior was related to better transfer performance, confirming the assumption that integration is important for learning success.

In sum, learners can be taught facilitative processing strategies, for example, by using EMME. It has been shown that learners receiving EMME showed more adequate processing of multimedia materials and also showed better performance than learners without strategy trainings.

FUTURE DIRECTIONS

In the last section I want to address future directions concerning the cognitive processes underlying learning from multiple representations. First, in most of the research described above two external representations were combined with each other, most often written text and static image. In our daily lives, however, we are most often faced with materials consisting of more than two external representations. Hence, future research should investigate the cognitive processes underlying learning from more than two external representations.

Second, multimedia research should take into consideration the assumptions made in text comprehension research. For example, within the framework of memory-based theories it is assumed that the reactivation of information is a pivotal prerequisite for integration: as soon as information is reactivated it can be integrated with current information in working memory (Cook & O'Brien, 2014). Furthermore, it is widely accepted that reactivation and integration of information is initially a rather automatic, passive process (cf. Richter, 2015). This is inconsistent with assumptions in current multimedia theories where it is assumed that cognitive processes (e.g., selection, organization, and integration) are engaged actively and consciously by the learner. Further, text comprehension theories assume that, after connections are made, a more active process of validation takes place (Richter, 2015; Richter, Münchow, & Abendroth, Chapter 16), enabling subjects to evaluate whether there are inconsistencies within the materials or whether the integrated information is inconsistent with their background knowledge. Thus, future research may investigate whether the integration of text and picture information also occurs rather automatically, if there is a great deal of consistency or redundancy among them, or whether the integration process is more conscious when learning from multiple representations.

SUMMARY AND CONCLUSIONS

The cognitive theory of multimedia learning (Mayer, 2009) postulates three cognitive processes which are essential for learning from multimedia materials: selection, organization, and integration. Empirical research supports the assumption that integration occurs (e.g., studies using cognitive paradigms; eye-tracking studies) and that integration is pivotal for successful learning from multiple representations (e.g., Mason et al., 2013). Furthermore, picture processing seems to also be important for successful learning with multiple representations as spending more time on the pictures is related to better performance. As picture fixation times are interpreted as an indicator for pictorial organization processes, this emphasizes the assumption that organizing pictorial elements is necessary to benefit from multiple representations (e.g., Mason et al., 2013; Scheiter & Eitel, 2015). At the same time, learners often seem to underestimate the benefits of pictures and concentrate heavily on text (e.g., Hannus & Hyönä, 1999). It might be, however, that a short glance at a picture is sufficient to get the gist of the picture, which in turn seems to support mental model construction (e.g., Eitel et al., 2013), even absent further processing. Here, more research is needed to investigate possible boundary conditions of this finding (e.g., picture complexity; domain). Empirical research using verbal protocols showed that pictures stimulate learners to draw inferences which go beyond the content of the learning materials (Butcher, 2006). This can also explain why pictures are often beneficial for learning. As not all learners are able to engage the cognitive processes necessary to benefit from learning from multiple representations (e.g., learners with low prior knowledge), material- or learner-based measures can be used to help learners in performing the necessary cognitive processes.

In sum, knowledge about the cognitive processes underlying learning from multiple representations is important for theory building and allows us to support those learners who are unable to benefit from multiple representations on their own.

REFERENCES

Albrecht, J. E., & O'Brien, E. J. (1993). Updating a mental model: Maintaining both local and global coherence. *Journal of Experimental Psychology: Learning, Memory, and Cognition, 19*, 1061–1070. doi:10.1037/0278-7393.19.5.1061

Alemdag, E., & Cagiltay, K. (2018). A systematic review of eye tracking research on multimedia learning. *Computers and Education, 125*, 413–428. doi:10.1016/j.compedu.2018.06.023

Butcher, K. R. (2006). Learning from text with diagrams: Promoting mental model development and inference generation. *Journal of Educational Psychology, 98*, 182–197.

Butcher, K. R. (2014). The multimedia principle. In R. E. Mayer (Ed.), *The Cambridge handbook of multimedia learning* (2nd ed., pp. 174–205). New York: Cambridge University Press.

Cook, A. E., & O'Brien, E. J. (2014). Knowledge activation, integration, and validation during narrative text comprehension. *Discourse Processes, 51*, 26–49. doi:10.1080/0163853x.2013.855107

Eitel, A. (2016). How repeated studying and testing affects multimedia learning: Evidence for adaptation to task demands. *Learning and Instruction, 41*, 70–84. doi:10.1016/j.learninstruc.2015.10.003

Eitel, A., Scheiter, K., & Schüler, A. (2012). The time course of information extraction from instructional diagrams. *Perceptual and Motor Skills, 115*, 677–701. doi:10.2466/22.23.PMS.115.6.677-701

Eitel, A., Scheiter, K., & Schüler, A. (2013). How inspecting a picture affects processing of text in multimedia learning. *Applied Cognitive Psychology, 27,* 451–461. doi:10.1002/acp.2922

Eitel, A., Scheiter, K., Schüler, A., Nyström, M., & Holmqvist, K. (2013). How a picture facilitates the process of learning from text: Evidence for scaffolding. *Learning and Instruction, 28,* 48–63. doi:10.1016/j.learninstruc.2013.05.002

Ericsson, K. A., & Simon, H. A. (1993). *Protocol analysis: Verbal reports as data* (Rev. ed.). Cambridge, MA: MIT Press.

Gentner, D., & Loftus, E. F. (1979). Integration of verbal and visual information as evidenced by distortions in picture memory. *American Journal of Psychology, 92*(2), 363–375. doi:10.2307/1421930

Glenberg, A. M., & Langston, W. E. (1992). Comprehension of illustrated text: Pictures help to build mental models. *Journal of Memory and Language, 31,* 129–151. doi:10.1016/0749-596X(92)90008-L

Gyselinck, V., Cornoldi, C., Dubois, V., De Beni, R., & Ehrlich, M. F. (2002). Visuospatial memory and phonological loop in learning from multimedia. *Applied Cognitive Psychology, 16,* 665–685. doi:10.1002/acp.823

Gyselinck, V., & Meneghetti, C. (2011). The role of spatial working memory in understanding verbal descriptions. A window into the interaction between verbal and spatial processing. In A. Vandienrendonck & A. Szmalec (Eds.), *Spatial working memory* (pp. 159–180). New York: Psychology Press.

Gyselinck, V., & Tardieu, H. (1999). The role of illustrations in text comprehension: What, when, for whom, and why? In H. van Oostendorp & S. R. Goldman (Eds.), *The construction of mental representations during reading* (pp. 195–218). Mahwah, NJ: Erlbaum.

Hannus, M., & Hyönä, J. (1999). Utilization of illustrations during learning of science textbook passages among low- and high-ability children. *Contemporary Educational Psychology, 24,* 95–123. doi:10.1006/ceps.1998.0987

Hegarty, M., & Just, M. A. (1993). Constructing mental models of machines from text and diagrams. *Journal of Memory and Language, 32,* 717–742. doi:10.1006/jmla.1993.1036

Jian, Y. C. (2017). Eye-movement patterns and reader characteristics of students with good and poor performance when reading scientific text with diagrams. *Reading and Writing, 30,* 1447–1472. doi:10.1007/s11145-017-9732-6

Jian, Y. C., & Wu, C. J. (2015). Using eye tracking to investigate semantic and spatial representations of scientific diagrams during text-diagram integration. *Journal of Science Education and Technology, 24,* 43–55. doi:10.1007/s10956-014-9519-3

Johnson, C. I., & Mayer, R. E. (2012). An eye movement analysis of the spatial contiguity effect in multimedia learning. *Journal of Experimental Psychology: Applied, 18,* 178–191. doi:10.1037/a0026923

Johnson-Laird, P. N. (1980). Mental models in cognitive science. *Cognitive Science, 4,* 71–115. doi:10.1207/s15516709cog0401_4

Just, M. A., & Carpenter, P. A. (1980). A theory of reading: From eye fixations to comprehension. *Psychological Review, 87,* 329–354. doi:10.1037/0033-295X.87.4.329

Koc-Januchta, M. M., Höffler, T., Thoma, G.-B., Prechtl, H., & Leutner, D. (2017). Visualizers versus verbalizers: Effects of cognitive style on learning with texts and pictures – An eye-tracking study. *Computers in Human Behavior, 68,* 170–179. doi:10.1016/j.chb.2016.11.028

Kühl, T., Scheiter, K., Gerjets, P., & Gemballa, S. (2011). Can differences in learning strategies explain the benefits of learning from static and dynamic visualizations? *Computers and Education, 56,* 176–187. doi:10-1016/j.compedu.2010.08.008

Mason, L., Pluchino, P., & Tornatora, M. C. (2015). Eye-movement modelling of integrative reading of an illustrated text: Effects on processing and learning. *Contemporary Educational Psychology, 41,* 172–187. doi:10.1016/j.cedpsych.2015.01.004

Mason, L., Pluchino, P., Tornatora, M. C., & Ariasi, N. (2013). An eye-tracking study of learning from science text with concrete and abstract illustrations. *Journal of Experimental Education, 81*(3), 356–384. doi:10.1080/00220973.2012.727885

Mason, L., Scheiter, K., & Tornatora, C. (2017). Using eye movements to model the sequences of text-picture processing for multimedia comprehension. *Journal of Computer Assisted Learning, 33,* 443–460. doi:10.1111/jcal.12191

Mason, L., Tornatora, M. C., & Pluchino, P. (2013). Do fourth graders integrate text and picture in processing and learning from an illustrated science text? Evidence from eye-movement patterns. *Computers and Education, 60,* 95–109. doi:10.1016/j.compedu.2012.07.011

Massa, L. J., & Mayer, R. E. (2003). Three facets of visual and verbal learners: Cognitive ability, cognitive style, and learning preference. *Journal of Educational Psychology, 95,* 833–846. doi:10.1037/0022-0663.95.4.833

Mayer, R. E. (1997). Multimedia learning: Are we asking the right questions? *Educational Psychologist*, *32*, 1–19.
Mayer, R. E. (2009). *Multimedia learning* (2nd ed.). Cambridge: University Press.
McNamara, T. P., Halpin, J. A., & Hardy, J. K. (1992). The representation and integration in memory of spatial and nonspatial information. *Memory and Cognition*, *20*, 519–532.
Morrow, D., D'Andrea, L., Stine-Morrow, E. A. L., Shake, M., Bertel, S., Chin, J., … Murray, M. (2012). Comprehension of multimedia health information among older adults with chronic illness. *Visual Communication*, *11*, 347–362. doi:10.1177/1470357212446413
O'Keefe, P. A., Letourneau, S. M., Homer, B. D., Schwartz, R. N., & Plass, J. L. (2014). Learning from multiple representations: An examination of fixation patterns in a science simulation. *Computers in Human Behavior*, *35*, 234–242. doi:10.1016/j.chb.2014.02.040
Oliva, A., & Torralba, A. (2006). Building the gist of a scene: The role of global image features in recognition. *Progress in Brain Research*, *155*, 23–36. doi:10.1016/S0079-6123(06)55002-2
Renkl, A., & Scheiter, K. (2017). Studying visual displays: How to instructionally support learning. *Educational Psychology Review*, *29*, 599–621. doi:10.1007/s10648-015-9340-4
Richter, J., Scheiter, K., & Eitel, A. (2016). Signaling text-picture relations in multimedia learning: A comprehensive meta-analysis. *Educational Research Review*, *17*, 19–36. doi:10.1016/j.edurev.2015.12.003
Richter, T. (2015). Validation and comprehension of text information: Two sides of the same coin. *Discourse Processes*, *52*, 337–355. doi:10.1080/0163853X.2015.1025665
Scheiter, K., & Eitel, A. (2015). Signals foster multimedia learning by supporting integration of highlighted text and diagram elements. *Learning and Instruction*, *36*, 11–26. doi:10.1016/j.learninstruc.2014.11.002
Scheiter, K., & Eitel, A. (2016). The use of eye tracking as a research and instructional tool in multimedia learning. In C. Was, F. Sansosti, & B. Morris (Eds.), *Eye-tracking technology applications in educational research* (pp. 143–164). Hershey, PA: IGI Global.
Scheiter, K., Schubert, C., Gerjets, P., & Stalbovs, K. (2015). Does a strategy training foster students' ability to learn from multimedia? *Journal of Experimental Education*, *83*, 266–289. doi:10.1080/00220973.2013.876603
Schlag, S., & Ploetzner, R. (2011). Supporting learning from illustrated texts: Conceptualizing and evaluating a learning strategy. *Instructional Science*, *39*, 921–937. doi:10.1007/s11251-010-9160-3
Schmidt-Weigand, F. (2009). The influence of visual and temporal dynamics on split attention: Evidences from eye tracking. In R. Zheng (Ed.), *Cognitive effects of multimedia learning* (pp. 89–107). Hershey, PA: IGI.
Schmidt-Weigand, F., Kohnert, A., & Glowalla, U. (2010). A closer look at split visual attention in system- and self-paced instruction in multimedia learning. *Learning and Instruction*, *20*, 100–110. doi:10.1016/j.learninstruc.2009.02.011
Schneider, S., Beege, M., Nebel, S., & Rey, G. D. (2018). A meta-analysis of how signaling affects learning with media. *Educational Research Review*, *23*, 1–24. doi:10.1016/j.edurev.2017.11.001
Schnotz, W., & Bannert, M. (2003). Construction and interference in learning from multiple representations. *Learning and Instruction*, *13*, 141–156. doi:10.1016/S0959-4752(02)00017-8
Schüler, A. (2017). Investigating gaze behaviour during processing of inconsistent text-picture information: Evidence for text-picture integration. *Learning and Instruction*, *49*, 218–231. doi:10.1016/j.learninstruc.2017.03.001
Schüler, A., Arndt, J., & Scheiter, K. (2015). Processing multimedia material: Does integration of text and pictures result in a single or two interconnected mental representations? *Learning and Instruction*, *35*, 62–72. doi:10.1016/j.learninstruc.2014.09.005
Schüler, A., Scheiter, K., & van Genuchten, E. (2011). The role of working memory in multimedia instruction: Is working memory working during learning from text and pictures?. *Educational Psychology Review*, *23*, 389–411. doi:10.1007/s10648-011-9168-5
Tardieu, H., & Gyselinck, V. (2003). Working memory constraints in the integration and comprehension of information in multimedia context. In H. V. Oostendorp (Ed.), *Cognition in a digital world* (pp. 3–24). Mahwah, NJ: Erlbaum.
Van Gog, T., & Scheiter, K. (2010). Eye tracking as a tool to study and enhance multimedia learning. *Learning and Instruction*, *20*, 95–99. doi:10.1016/learninstruc.2009.02.09

5

LEARNING FROM MULTIPLE REPRESENTATIONS
Roles of Task Interventions and Individual Differences

Jennifer G. Cromley
UNIVERSITY OF ILLINOIS AT URBANA-CHAMPAIGN

ABSTRACT

Learning from multiple representations (MRs) is not an easy task for most people, despite how easy it is for experts. Different combinations of representations (e.g., text + photograph, graph + formula, map + diagram) pose different challenges for learners, but across the literature researchers find these to be challenging learning tasks. Each representation typically includes some unique information, as well as some information shared with the other representation(s). Finding one piece of information is only somewhat challenging, but linking information across representations and especially making inferences are very challenging and important parts of using multiple representations for learning. Coordination of multiple representations skills are rarely taught in classrooms, despite the fact that learners are frequently tested on them. Learning from MRs depends on the specific learning tasks posed, learner characteristics, the specifics of which representation(s) are used, and the design of each representation. These various factors act separately and in combination (which can be compensatory, additive, or interactive). Learning tasks can be differentially effective depending on learner characteristics, especially prior knowledge, self-regulation, and age/grade. Learning tasks should be designed keeping this differential effectiveness in mind, and researchers should test for such interactions.

Key words: individual differences, learning task × individual difference interactions

INTRODUCTION

Learning from multiple representations (MRs) – combinations of text, diagrams, tables, animations, graphs, formulas, maps, and other representations of information – is not an easy task for most people, despite how easy it is for experts. Different combinations of representations (e.g., text + photograph, graph + formula, map + diagram) pose different challenges for learners, but across the literature researchers find these to be challenging learning tasks. Each representation typically includes some unique information, as well as some information shared with the other representation(s). For example, in Figure 5.1 showing the anatomy of bones in the inner ear, the text explains that the eardrum would be found to the left of the malleus (hammer) bone shown in the diagram. The diagram shows that there are two joints among these three bones, and names the joints. Both text and diagram refer to all three bones, and also refer to the incus (anvil) as coming between the malleus (hammer) and stapes (anvil) bones.

In these types of multi-representational information sources, finding one piece of information is only somewhat challenging, but linking information across representations is a very challenging and important part of using multiple representations for learning. For example, linking information across text and diagram (often called coordinating multiple representations or CMR), such as finding only one of the bones in the diagram, is a relatively simple task (White, Chen, & Forsyth, 2010). A more challenging CMR task is using the information from the representations to draw conclusions or inferences; for example, a disease called otosclerosis involves extra bone growing at the base of the stapes. Understanding why this would cause hearing loss requires drawing a number of conclusions – the bones transmit sound between the eardrum and the inner ear, and the base of the stapes touches the inner ear, so extra bone could interfere with transmitting sound, which could cause hearing loss. The information in this case is provided in the MRs, but the reader needs to actively make

Anatomy

The ossicles are, in order from the eardrum to the inner ear (from superficial to deep), the malleus, incus, and stapes. The terms mean hammer, anvil, and stirrup.

The malleus (hammer) connects with the incus and is attached to the tympanic membrane (eardrum), from which vibrational sound pressure motion is passed.

The incus (anvil) is connected to both the other bones.

The stapes (stirrup) connects with the incus and is attached to the membrane of the fenestra ovalis, the elliptical or oval window or opening between the middle ear and the inner ear.

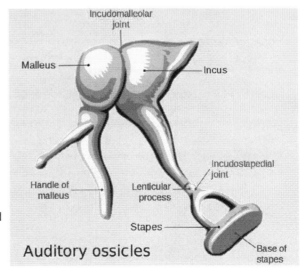

Figure 5.1 Example of Multiple Representations.

inferences (draw conclusions) from the information provided. Even the straightforward fact that the three bones are linked into a chain, and that the chain transmits sound, is not stated explicitly in this multi-representational text, and is an inference that the reader needs to make. The distinction between learning facts and making inferences from MRs is important, as supporting learners to engage in CMR sometimes requires different supportive or instructional methods for various types of learning outcomes.

Learning from multiple representations does not only depend on the learner actively searching or making inferences. Learning from multiple representations depends on a number of different factors, all of which are in play simultaneously:

- Learner characteristics – the focus of this chapter: Does the learner already have some knowledge of the topic, vocabulary knowledge (word meanings), or well-developed reading comprehension? Higher or lower spatial skills (such as mentally rotating a 3D shape in space), working memory (holding information in memory while solving a problem), or a learning disability? Motivation to learn about the topic (such as a person just diagnosed with otosclerosis)? Knowledge of specific symbols or conventions (e.g., color keys used in maps)? Other individual differences?
- Which representations are used: Maps and graphs use very specific conventions (e.g., compass rose, contour lines, X and Y axes), whereas photographs can be extremely varied. Static diagrams can be investigated at length, but animation or video goes by very quickly. Some diagrams are extremely formalized (e.g., free body diagrams in physics), whereas others are not.
- Design features of each representation: Both text and visuals can be made more comprehensible by changing the design. Headings can be bolded, words and visuals can be linked with lettering, numbering, color, highlighting, or animated cues/signals. Less-important parts of visuals can be made less prominent (e.g., not brightly colored). Distracting – albeit interesting – features can be removed. Speed controls can be provided for videos or other learning environments.
- What learning tasks are assigned:[1] The same set of multiple representations can be perceived as easy for certain learning tasks assigned to learners, but could be perceived as quite challenging for other tasks, as suggested by the find-a-bone vs. infer-a-cause tasks in the example above. Does the assignment require using a particular learning strategy, such as copying or making a diagram or using a hands-on model? Are students instructed in how to coordinate MRs? Do the tasks require finding an answer (receptive) or creating something new (productive)? We use the term *task intervention* to refer to a change in the tasks that learners carry out when learning from multi-modal materials. These range from full-scale strategy instruction programs to prompting of a single learning strategy, during-learning tasks such as interspersed fill-in-the blank activities, or directing learners to replay video or conduct multiple simulation trials.

In summary, learning from multiple representations depends on the specific learning tasks posed, learner characteristics, the specifics of which representation(s) are used, and the design of each representation. To make matters more complicated, these various factors can act separately and in combination, so that in some cases only learner spatial skills are in play, but sometimes required strategies (such as making a drawing to learn from the multiple representations) work better for high spatial learners and worse for low spatial learners, or vice versa.

When different learner, learning material, and/or learning task factors act in combination, we can think of them as being compensatory, additive, or interactive. *Compensatory* processes would be ones where a strength in one factor can compensate for a weakness on another factor. For example, Höffler and Leutner (2011) wrote about high spatial skills (strong on a learner characteristic) as compensating for poor multimedia design (weak on a design factor). *Additive* processes would be ones where a strength in one factor and a strength in another factor would yield better learning, exactly and only to the extent that one would expect by adding the effects of each. For example, Olympiou and Zacharia (2012) compared learning from a computer-simulated learner-controlled optics laboratory session versus a hands-on laboratory session versus a combination of computer-simulated and hands-on sessions. Learners' prior knowledge about optics was also collected. On a conceptual light and color test, the combined condition resulted in higher scores, and students who began the study with more topic knowledge had higher scores: participants' scores were the result of adding the benefits that one would expect from their experimental condition and the benefits that one would expect from their level of prior knowledge. *Interactive* processes would be ones where a strength in one factor and a strength on another factor yield results greater than what would be expected by simply adding the effects of each (interaction is sometimes called moderation, in the sense that how strong the effect of A on B depends on one's score on C, and C is called the moderator variable).

For example, in a computer-based simulation for learning about electrical circuits (Johnson, Ozogul, & Reisslein, 2015), students who were in a condition where relevant parts of a graph were pointed out with a signal (sometimes called a cue) scored higher on circuit problems than those in a condition without signals; students who had higher prior knowledge also scored higher on circuit problems. Combinations of signaling and prior knowledge had even stronger effects; students who were in the signals condition but started the study with low prior knowledge had much higher scores on circuit problems than those in the no-signals condition, thus closing the achievement gap between low and high prior knowledge learners. There was an interaction between condition and prior knowledge, in that effect of condition depended on level of prior knowledge (condition actually did not make a difference for the high prior knowledge participants), and effect of prior knowledge depended on condition (low prior knowledge students benefitted from the signaling condition, but high prior knowledge students scored the same regardless of condition). Interactions can be thought of as multiplying – not just adding – the effect of each factor, such as the prior knowledge × design interaction above.

The experiments above are samples from a wide range of methods that have been developed and tested to teach CMR skills. These methods of CMR instruction can be quite effective, depending on which representations are used (a task × representation interaction). Ironically, these CMR skills are rarely taught in actual classrooms, even though CMR skills are frequently tested in end-of-course tests, national and international assessments, and standardized achievement tests (LaDue, Libarkin, & Thomas, 2015).

REVIEW OF THE LITERATURE

I focus in this chapter on how individual differences play a role in learning from multiple representations, from a systematic search for peer-reviewed articles on learning in science, math, and engineering published 2005–16. In order to understand how individual differences and learning task × individual difference interactions might vary depending on the learning outcome measured, we[2] categorized dependent variables in the studies as

- Factual: tests that require recall or recognition of a single piece of information,
- Inferential: tests that require combining provided pieces of information, sometimes called comprehension by authors of the studies we reviewed,
- Procedural: tests that require remembering the order of problem-solving steps, or
- Transfer: tests that require applying learned skills and information to a new context.

We focused our review on comparisons of different conditions using the same multimedia (e.g., hypermedia with tutoring vs. hypermedia without tutoring). Despite the importance of comparing multimedia to regular instruction, it is difficult to determine in those studies whether differences are due to the medium or to the specific characteristics of the multimedia (e.g., is it the tutoring or the hypermedia that makes the difference?).

Individual Differences

As a basis for design principles, theories of multimedia learning most strongly emphasize background knowledge and working memory as individual differences that may affect learning. As with reading comprehension, background knowledge should aid in comprehending MRs, and knowledge is known to affect perceptual processes – learners who know more actually perceive differently (Shah & Freedman, 2011). The limited capacity of working memory is posited to be an important obstacle to learning in both Cognitive Load Theory (Paas & Sweller, 2014) and the Cognitive Theory of Multimedia Learning (Mayer, 2014), in the sense that learners can easily feel overwhelmed by the amount of information in MRs. In addition, developmental and cognitive psychologists who study spatial skills have emphasized the role of such skills in using visual representations (Kastens, Pistolesi, & Passow, 2014).

Many other individual differences have been studied in the multiple representations literature, including intelligence; logic skills; general academic ability; science, reading or math scores; self-regulated learning (SRL); effort; sex; affect/mood; and various motivational variables (e.g., interest, need for cognition).

Direct effects of individual differences on learning suggest that a particular individual characteristic matters for factual learning, for drawing inferences from what was learned, or for transfer of learning to new situations or domains. If working memory is important for inferential learning, then there should be a significant correlation between scores on a working memory measure and scores on an inference measure given after learning from text + diagrams (e.g., Isberner et al., 2013; $r = .34$).

In our literature review, we categorized correlations between individual differences and learning into ones that involve prior knowledge measures, motivational variables, reading comprehension, reasoning, spatial skills, working memory, and other. The number of studies reporting correlations, together with the number of effects, for each type of learning outcome is shown in Table 5.1.

Prior Knowledge

Prior knowledge has a mean correlation of $r = .42$ with factual outcomes from learning with multimedia and a mean correlation of $r = .37$ with transfer outcomes from learning with multimedia. These results were positive for learning about chemistry, biology, ecosystems, and machinery (pulley systems and flushing cistern). They held for middle school, high school, and undergraduate students. As with learning from text alone, a student's prior knowledge contributes to learning from animations, simulations, and text + diagrams. For factual learning, this is consistent with many different learning theories, as the learner with more existing topic-relevant information in memory can more easily connect the newly presented information to information in memory (an encoding advantage). For transfer of learning, this is consistent with models of analogical transfer, as the existing knowledge becomes a scaffold for an integrated mental model that is then mapped onto the novel (transfer) situation. It should be noted that a very large number of other studies measured prior knowledge, but did not report a correlation with learning outcomes (most often, groups were compared on pre-test prior knowledge).

Motivational Variables

Across a range of different motivational variables, motivation has a mean correlation of $r = .11$ with factual outcomes from learning with multimedia, a mean correlation of $r = .36$ with inferential outcomes, and a mean correlation of $r = .25$ for transfer. Although it is odd to combine results using different motivational variables, there are not enough studies using any one variable to analyze the main motivational constructs

Table 5.1 Number of Studies and Effects for Each Individual Difference Type and Learning Outcome.

Individual difference	Factual Outcome (no. of studies/ no. of effects)	Inferential Outcome (no. of studies/ no. of effects)	Transfer Outcome (no. of studies/ no. of effects)
Prior knowledge	5/11	0/0	4/4
Motivational variables	4/8	1/2	2/2
Reading comprehension	2/5	0/0	2/2
Deductive reasoning	2/5	2/8	0/0
Spatial skills	4/12	2/2	2/5
Working memory	2/6	1/1	0/0
Other	3/5	4/11	1/6

separately. The results for factual outcomes come from hypermedia, text + diagrams, and games; are predominantly with middle school students; and range from interest to mastery goals, self-concept, and entity self-beliefs about learning. The small effect is not surprising, as factual learning requires relatively low effort, so motivation would not be expected to have a large effect. By contrast, the more effortful inferential outcomes show a larger effect, though both come from the same study (Merchant et al., 2012) using virtual reality. The two transfer effects both come from text + diagram research. Perhaps the lower effect on transfer is due to the cognitive demands of transfer, which cannot be overcome simply with increased motivation.

Reading Comprehension

Comprehension of text would be expected to assist multimedia learning for at least two reasons: (1) it reflects general linguistic comprehension (whether print or spoken) and (2) it should boost comprehension of print text in multimedia that use print. Consistent with this expectation, reading comprehension has a mean correlation of $r = .44$ with factual outcomes from learning with multimedia and a mean correlation of $r = .49$ with transfer outcomes from learning with multimedia. It should be noted that all of these effects come from the same research team, and all are from middle school students learning from text + diagrams.

Deductive Reasoning

As with reading comprehension, there may be different reasons why deductive reasoning relates to learning from multimedia: (1) it may reflect a general intelligence factor (g) which would be expected to correlate with all types of learning outcomes, and (2) it uses the same skill tested in inferential learning measures from multimedia. As with all texts, the authors of multimedia do not make every relation explicit in the learning materials, and learners who can accurately draw their own conclusions are benefitted by having such deductive reasoning skills. Consistent with this expectation, deductive reasoning has a mean correlation of $r = .42$ with factual outcomes from learning with multimedia and a mean correlation of $r = .41$ with inferential outcomes from learning with multimedia. Even if specific during-learning inferences are not remembered at post-test, the declarative knowledge that went into those inferences might be remembered better, explaining the effects on factual learning from multimedia. These findings about deductive reasoning come from two studies, one on a simulation of machine operation and one on an animation of the cardiovascular system.

Spatial Skills

From a theoretical perspective, multimedia may be advantageous over text because visuals preserve the spatial relations among parts, and these spatial relations are hard to capture in words. This implies that learners' spatial skills may affect their learning from multimedia. However, competing hypotheses have been put forward – some have argued that low spatial students need the visuals because they explicitly show spatial relations, whereas others have argued that visuals are better understood by high spatial students. Published correlations strongly support the latter position – spatial skills correlate positively with learning from multimedia. The mean correlations are $r = .25$ with factual outcomes from learning with multimedia, a mean correlation of $r = .40$ with inferential outcomes, and a mean correlation of $r = .20$ for transfer. The research uses high school and undergraduate samples, mostly learning biology topics.

Factual measures often ask for information about one specific part or element named in the multimedia presentation, such as a definition. Inferences, by contrast, may require using spatial information such as blood entering the left atrium, being squeezed down through the mitral valve, and entering the left ventricle below. This could explain the larger relation of spatial skills to multimedia learning for inferential outcomes. As with motivation, perhaps the lower effect on transfer is due to the cognitive demands of transfer, which cannot be overcome simply with better spatial skills. It should be noted that thousands of spatial skills tests exist, which map onto dozens of spatial skills typologies. The most commonly used spatial tests in the multimedia literature are the Mental Rotations Test and various hidden figures/embedded figures tests. Different multimedia learning tasks might tap these skills differently – understanding steoreoisomers in organic chemistry draws strongly on rotation, whereas understanding a weather map requires distinguishing specific information within a complex 2D map.

Working Memory

Theories of multimedia rely strongly on the limited capacity assumption from models of memory. Despite the theoretical centrality of working memory (WM), studies have rarely measured learners' WM. Two studies of undergraduates, one on learning plant biology with hypermedia and one on learning about tectonic plates with animation, show a mean correlation of $r = .28$ with factual outcomes. Low WM capacity does indeed seem to interfere with factual learning from hypermedia and animation.

Other Individual Differences

Five correlations of other individual differences (SRL, paraphrasing, monitoring, satisfaction with learning materials, and game usability) were found for factual outcomes, 11 correlations (paraphrasing, monitoring, verbal ability, perceived ease of use, knowledge of visualization conventions) with inferential outcomes, and six correlations (reaction time on a dual task, lesson difficult rating, and self-reported mental effort) for transfer outcomes. The correlations for monitoring and paraphrasing are negative (i.e., monitoring indicates lapses in comprehension), and of the 22 correlations, 14 are small ($r < .20$).

In summary, direct effects of individual differences on learning are most often significant for prior knowledge (more knowledgeable learners gain more from MRs), reading comprehension (those better at reading comprehension gain more from MRs), and reasoning. Direct effects of these variables on learning are mixed for spatial skills, and small for motivation and 'other' individual differences. There are large literatures on pre-teaching to build knowledge, reading comprehension instruction, and methods for teaching reasoning; all of these individual differences can be strengthened with the aim of later improving learning from multimedia.

Task Intervention × Individual Differences Interactions

Putting together what we know about task interventions and individual differences, some task modifications might be more beneficial for students with certain individual characteristics. A strong prediction of Cognitive Load Theory (CLT) is that design features meant to help low knowledge learners might not help – or might even harm – high knowledge learners (called the expertise reversal effect). For example, could cues or signaling help low knowledge learners but not make a difference to high knowledge learners? We can generalize this beyond just the multimedia design features and knowledge that are the focus of CLT, to ask about task interventions and any individual differences, such as drawing helping high spatial learners but harming low spatial learners.

Across 27 task × individual difference interactions tested in articles in this literature review, we found that prior knowledge, self-regulated learning, mastery-approach goal orientation (motivation), and age/grade in school reliably interacted with task manipulations (see detailed descriptions of ten significant interactions below). Reading skills sometimes did, and rarely were there interactions with learner sex, interest, need for cognition, mental effort, or reasoning. One way of thinking about these interactions is in terms of closing known achievement gaps (e.g., between males and females or high-achieving and low-achieving students; expertise reversal) vs. worsening these known achievement gaps (i.e., benefitting those who are already at an advantage). That is, in some of the interactions we found, the intervention was more helpful to a traditionally lower performing group such as females in math; thus, the intervention helped to close the male–female achievement gap. In other interactions we found, the intervention was actually more helpful to the group that was already performing better such as high prior achievement students; thus, the intervention helped to make the achievement gap worse than it had been before the study.

Knowledge Interactions

Bodemer and Faust (2006) tested different computer-based text-and-diagram conditions for fostering CMR on a science topic (operation of a heat pump) with undergraduates. They found that drag-and-drop conditions benefitted high knowledge learners more than low knowledge learners. Bokosmaty, Sweller, & Kalyuga, 2015) compared different amounts of guidance for solving geometry problems using a computer-based text-and-diagram learning environment for 8th and 9th grade students. They found that less-elaborate instructional conditions (modeling solution steps *or* explaining which theorems supported the appropriate step, but not both) benefitted high knowledge learners more.

Skill-Level Interactions

Pachman, Sweller, and Kalyuga (2013) compared customized geometry problem assignments vs. free choice of geometry problem assignments using paper and pencil text-and-diagram learning for 8th grade students. They found that allowing students free choice of which problems to practice – rather than focusing on weak areas – benefitted lower skilled students more, but made little difference for high skilled students. Pachman, Sweller, and Kalyuga (2014) similarly tested customized and free choice geometry work for 8th grade students. They similarly found that focusing practice mostly on weak areas – rather than practicing all skills from a chapter – benefitted higher skilled students more, but made little difference for low skilled students.

Age Interaction

Mason and Tornatora (2016) tested instruction to compare-and-contrast, versus no instructions to compare, or sequential text-and-diagrams with 5th and 7th grade students learning about heat flow and states of matter. They found that 7th grade students benefitted more from comparing-and-contrasting instructions than did younger students.

Sex Interaction

DeLeeuw & Mayer (2011) found that fostering competitive play in an educational game about electrical flow through circuits helped level the playing field for female undergraduate players; when there were no messages fostering competition, females under-performed males.

Motivational Interactions

Yaman, Nerdel, and Bayrhuber (2008) found that worked examples showed extra benefits for high school students learning about cellular respiration from a simulation for high interest students. Duffy and Azevedo (2015) found that a hypermedia-based intelligent tutoring intervention on the circulatory system was more beneficial for undergraduate students focused on getting a higher grade than others, and led to lower scores for those focused on learning for understanding.

Reading Comprehension Interaction

Mason, Pluchino, and Tornatora (2015) tested effects of eye movement modeling (EMME) for seventh-grade students learning about aquatic food chains from text and diagrams. They found that students with lower reading comprehension were benefitted by eye movement guidance (showing them where and in what sequence to look at the page), whereas high comprehenders were not affected by EMME.

Self-Regulated Learning Interaction

Wang (2011) compared learning from animations about evolution using a peer recommendation system (fellow students recommend a learning resource vs. no peer recommendation system) for 7th grade students. Wang found that peer-recommended argumentation leveled the playing field for low SRL students, compared to the control condition which was significantly better for high SRL students.

Of these ten significant interactions, five made achievement gaps worse by benefitting already-advantaged students more (higher knowledge, skill, interest, or age), four closed achievement gaps by benefitting disadvantaged students more (lower skill, reading comprehension, SRL, or females), and one was neutral. Thus, testing task × individual difference interactions per se does not lead overwhelmingly to closing achievement gaps.

We can think about these task × individual difference interactions in a few ways:

(1) Some task interventions perhaps should only be used with a specific subset of learners: For example, if drawing-to-learn disadvantages low spatial learners, it should only be targeted to high spatial students. Alternatively, (2) some task modifications are inequitable, and perhaps should not be used if an equitable task modification exists: If verbally completing a partial diagram works as well on average but does not disadvantage a subgroup of students, then verbal completion should be chosen over visual completion. (3) In cases where a task intervention appears to not help learning, this could be because it was effective for a subgroup of learners (on an individual difference that was not tested) and ineffective for another subgroup of learners. In other words, when interactions are not tested, a non-significant main effect can hide a significant interaction. What to do about these three interpretations might depend on a number of factors, including whether the individual difference is easy enough to measure, whether data on the individual differences are readily available (prior reading achievement probably is, spatial skills probably are not), the makeup of a class (if all high spatial, there is no issue), and the availability of other task modifications (with these MRs on students at this age).

NEW INSIGHTS AND FUTURE DIRECTIONS

The nuanced pattern of results above, and the range of task intervention types, strongly suggests that coordinating MRs is not one "thing," it varies by representations and representation combinations, each of which are somewhat domain-specific (see Kozma, Chapter 3 and Stylianou, Chapter 8 of this volume for detailed discussions). Even a straightforward principle such as self-explanation is not consistently effective when implemented with MRs – learners may need to learn the discipline-specific representations and their unique conventions (e.g., Cartesian coordinate system, arrows in physics free body diagrams), and task interventions – i.e., instruction – needs to be customized to these. Furthermore, the most obvious task interventions, such as telling students to slow down animations, do not always have large effects. Other types of modifications such as animated cueing or using static diagrams to convey dynamic phenomena actually have larger effects. In addition, some task instruction appears to have effects on specific types of learning outcomes; self-explanation instruction – which includes fostering inferences – has effects more on inferential outcomes than on memory for facts.

A second insight from these task intervention studies is that effects vary across both dependent (i.e., learning outcome) variables and MR types. Whether to choose a task intervention or try to foster learning by designing the display differently might depend, for example, on whether the learner is using animation vs. a simulation. For inferential outcomes, learning from animation appears to be better fostered by design, whereas for games, self-explanation (especially pull-down self-explanation) appears to be a better way to achieve those ends.

A third insight concerns the paradox of testing for intervention × learner individual difference interactions: on the one hand, a seemingly ineffective intervention can be shown to be effective for subgroup(s) of learners. On the other hand, once researchers have found these interactions, the task intervention needs to be cautiously recommended only for the subgroup that benefitted (e.g., drag and drop is better for high-knowledge learners). Adaptive learning systems with MRs have been developed and tested, but results are mostly reported in conference proceedings, which were not reviewed here.

CONCLUSIONS/IMPLICATIONS

Implications for Design Teams

Helping learners become better able to learn from MRs is not a simple, straightforward task that can be accomplished with a few common principles. Design of learning tasks and task interventions (i.e., task supports) needs to simultaneously take into account the learner characteristics – especially knowledge, reading comprehension, and deductive reasoning – the multimedia type, the specific representations and their conventions and other design features, and the desired learning outcome (factual, inferential, procedural, transfer). Supports for the steps in the learning process appear to have larger effects than other types of instruction such as cueing specific parts of a representation. More 'active' strategies (e.g., drawing vs. filling in blanks) are not consistently better; their effectiveness depends on the fit to the task, person, and content in the learning environment. Designing collaborative MR activities seems to lead to less learning, despite the potential for other beneficial outcomes such as creativity or teamwork skills. Preliminary studies that reveal where learners face obstacles in certain tasks can help pinpoint exactly what task interventions should support. A formal, logical analysis of the task – called a task analysis – can also help identify what task interventions should support.

Research suggests many effective vehicles for delivering these interventions – through direct instruction by teachers, strategy cue cards, tutors, or embedded in the learning environment (e.g., via segmented worked examples with interspersed problems). In general, very complex multi-part strategy instruction is not recommended – it is less effective and less well taken up by learners (Bokosmaty et al., 2015) – whereas shorter, simpler suites of strategy instruction are recommended. In this sense, in this research we have overestimated learners and how quickly they can acquire new skills.

Implications for Researchers

In many studies we reviewed, researchers collected individual difference data but never tested for interactions with task interventions. If these data are collected, it is wise to always test for interactions; this would then result in some possible cautions to teachers and other end users (e.g., best suited for undergraduate students, etc.). Patterns in the literature above might help researchers avoid unproductive studies (e.g., self-explanation in text and diagrams). Focused literature review in the multimedia type and dependent variable(s) of interest should also point in productive directions.

Implications for Teachers

Implementing MR learning packages that try to change what learners do is a bigger challenge than just counting on design to lead to learning. After all, most representations are specific to a discipline, and no matter how well designed, students will need some instruction in how to use them, how to understand relations among different representations, and how to draw conclusions using them. On the other hand, these investments of time and effort can help learners become more independent and may be applicable to new learning situations (i.e., transfer). Learners benefit more when they get feedback on their use of new learning strategies, whether informally by observing learning, in feedback on their answers to questions posed during learning, or by other means. As noted above, simpler suites of strategy instruction appear to be more effective and more often actually practiced by learners, compared to extended, multi-part strategies. Solo work appears to lead to better learning than various types of collaboration. In addition, different strategies might be best for learning facts than for drawing conclusions, learning step-by-step procedures, or transferring skills to new contexts. Choosing instructional packages should take into account the desired outcome(s) and also the type of multimedia employed.

Our results point to a much more complex picture than perhaps has been conveyed previously about supporting learning from MRs. That complexity, though, reflects the realities of science, mathematics, and engineering content, as well as the complexities of human beings learning in social and material environments. Learning is not simple and straightforward, learning from MRs is not simple and straightforward, and supporting people in learning how to learn from MRs is not simple and straightforward.

ACKNOWLEDGEMENT

Produced with funding from the US National Science Foundation award #1661231. Opinions are the author's own and do not reflect the policies of the National Science Foundation or the US Government.

NOTE

1. We mean *task* in the same broad sense that it was used by Snow et al. (2000) in the Report of the National Reading Panel – all of the instructions and activities that surround a particular instance of reading, separate from the characteristics of the text and reader characteristics.
2. I am indebted to LuEttaMae Lawrence for her work locating, coding, and entering data from articles on this project.

REFERENCES

Bodemer, D., & Faust, U. (2006). External and mental referencing of multiple representations. *Computers in Human Behavior, 22*(1), 27–42.

Bokosmaty, S., Sweller, J., & Kalyuga, S. (2015). Learning geometry problem solving by studying worked examples: Effects of learner guidance and expertise. *American Educational Research Journal, 52*(2), 307–333.

DeLeeuw, K. E., & Mayer, R. E. (2011). Cognitive consequences of making computer-based learning activities more game-like. *Computers in Human Behavior, 27*(5), 2011–2016. doi:10.1016/j.chb.2011.05.008

Duffy, M. C., & Azevedo, R. (2015). Motivation matters: Interactions between achievement goals and agent scaffolding for self-regulated learning within intelligent tutoring system. *Computers in Human Behavior, 52*, 338–348.

Höffler, T. N., & Leutner, D. (2011). The role of spatial ability in learning from instructional animations: Evidence for an ability-as-compensator hypothesis. *Computers in Human Behavior, 27*(1), 209–216.

Isberner, M., Richter, T., Maier, J., Knuth-Herzig, K., Horz, H., & Schnotz, W. (2013). Comprehending conflicting science-related texts: Graphs as plausibility cues. *Instructional Science, 41*(5), 849–872. doi:10.1007/s11251-012-9261-2

Johnson, A. M., Ozogul, G., & Reisslein, M. (2015). Supporting multimedia learning with visual signalling and animated pedagogical agent: Moderating effects of prior knowledge. *Journal of Computer Assisted Learning, 31*(2), 97–115.

Kastens, K. A., Pistolesi, L., & Passow, M. J. (2014). Analysis of spatial concepts, spatial skills and spatial representations in New York State regents Earth science examinations. *Journal of Geoscience Education, 62*(2), 278–289.

LaDue, N. D., Libarkin, J. C., & Thomas, S. R. (2015). Visual representations on high school biology, chemistry, earth science, and physics assessments. *Journal of Science Education and Technology, 24*(6), 818–834.

Mason, L., Pluchino, P., & Tornatora, M. C. (2015). Eye-movement modeling of integrative reading of an illustrated text: Effects on processing and learning. *Contemporary Educational Psychology, 41*, 172–187.

Mason, L., & Tornatora, M. C. (2016). Analogical encoding with and without instructions for comparison of scientific phenomena. *Educational Psychology, 36*(2), 391–412.

Mayer, R. E. (2014). Cognitive theory of multimedia learning. In R. E. Mayer (Ed.), *The Cambridge handbook of multimedia learning* (pp. 43–71). NewYork: Cambridge University Press.

Merchant, Z., Goetz, E. T., Keeney-Kennicutt, W., Kwok, O. M., Cifuentes, L., & Davis, T. J. (2012). The learner characteristics, features of desktop 3D virtual reality environments, and college chemistry instruction: A structural equation modeling analysis. *Computers and Education, 59*(2), 551–568. doi:10.1016/j.compedu.2012.02.004

Olympiou, G., & Zacharia, Z. C. (2012). Blending physical and virtual manipulatives: An effort to improve students' conceptual understanding through science laboratory experimentation. *Science Education, 96*(1), 21–47.

Paas, F., & Sweller, J. (2014). Implications of cognitive load theory for multimedia learning. In R. E. Mayer (Ed.), *The Cambridge handbook of multimedia learning* (pp. 27–42). NewYork: Cambridge University Press.

Pachman, M., Sweller, J., & Kalyuga, S. (2013). Levels of knowledge and deliberate practice. *Journal of Experimental Psychology: Applied, 19*(2), 108–119.

Pachman, M., Sweller, J., & Kalyuga, S. (2014). Effectiveness of combining worked examples and deliberate practice for high school geometry. *Applied Cognitive Psychology, 28*(5), 685–692.

Shah, P., & Freedman, E. G. (2011). Bar and line graph comprehension: An interaction of top-down and bottom-up processes. *Topics in Cognitive Science, 3*(3), 560–578.

Wang, T. H. (2011). Developing web-based assessment strategies for facilitating junior high school students to perform self-regulated learning in an e-learning environment. *Computers & Education, 57*(2), 1801–1812.

White, S., Chen, J., & Forsyth, B. (2010). Reading-related literacy activities of American adults: Time spent, task types, and cognitive skills used. *Journal of Literacy Research, 42*(3), 276–307.

Yaman, M., Nerdel, C., & Bayrhuber, H. (2008). The effects of instructional support and learner interests when learning using computer simulations. *Computers and Education, 51*(4), 1784–1794.

6

INTERVENTIONS TO SUPPORT LEARNING FROM MULTIPLE EXTERNAL REPRESENTATIONS

Peggy Van Meter and Nicholas Stepanik

PENNSYLVANIA STATE UNIVERSITY

ABSTRACT

Students are often expected to learn from multiple external representations (MERs) that include both verbal and visual representations. This learning requires students to execute the cognitive operations of selecting key elements from all representations, organizing these into locally coherent representations, and integrating across representations and with prior knowledge to achieve global coherence. Despite the prevalence of MERs in instructional materials, many students are unable to fully exploit their learning potential. In this chapter, we review interventions that have been designed to improve this learning. The framework that organizes this review draws attention to the source that stimulates and supports the cognitive operations of MERs learning; i.e., the materials, the learner, or a response prompt. Regardless of the source, interventions that support the cognitive operations of MERs processing have positive effects on learning. Patterns within the current research and directions for future research are discussed.

Key words: multimedia, multiple representations, diagrams, science, learning interventions, learning

INTRODUCTION

MERs refer to material that uses more than one representation to convey information and typically include both verbal and nonverbal representations. Figure 6.1 shows an example of MERs that use a text and two graphs to explain the normal curve. MERs such as this are common in instructional material, with other examples including combinations of graphs and formulae to teach mathematical functions, physics text and diagrams explaining how forces work, and animation with audio narration explaining a biological system. As varied as these examples are, they share a defining feature of MERs which is that each representation conveys both unique and shared information. Because of this information distribution across representations, maximizing the learning potential of MERs requires the student to comprehend each representation and generate cross-representation connections to construct an integrated internal knowledge representation (Ainsworth, 1999; Mayer, 2014a). Students who engage in this ideal processing acquire higher quality knowledge than their peers with less ideal processing, and these advantages have been shown on measures of conceptual knowledge (Johnson & Mayer, 2012; Mason, Pluchino, Tornatora, & Ariasi, 2013), mental model revision (Butcher, 2006; Cromley, Snyder-Hogan, & Luciw-Dubas, 2010), and verbal-visual inferencing (Scheiter & Eitel, 2015; Van Meter, Cameron, & Waters, 2017). Despite the potential learning advantage of MERs, however, many students fail to achieve this ideal.

The Normal Curve

The normal curve is a graph of the normal distribution. This curve is also called a bell-curve because it is shaped like a bell. All normal curves are unimodal. They have only one (uni) mode, or peak. A set of values that is perfectly normally distributed, the mean, median, and mode will all be the same.

The specific shape of any normal curve is determined by both the mean and the standard deviation of the distribution. Figure 1 illustrates how the height and spread of normal curves are affected by differences in means and standard deviations. In all normal distributions, 68% of all values of the variable will be found within 1 standard deviation of the mean. 95% of the values will be found within 1.96 standard deviations from the mean. This pattern is symmetrical so that 34% of scores will fall between the mean and 1 standard deviation above the mean; 34% will fall between the mean and 1 standard deviation below the mean.

Figure A. Four normal curves with different means and standard deviations.

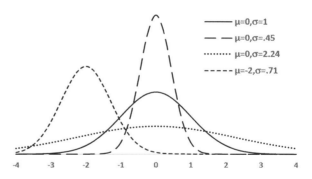

Figure B. Normal curves with standard deviations.

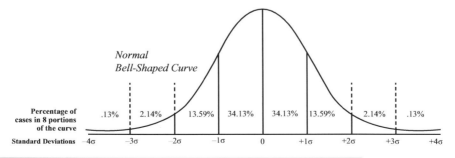

Figure 6.1 Example of Instructional Material Containing Multiple External Representations.

The discrepancy between the potential of MERs and students' ability to realize this potential has sparked research on interventions to improve this learning. This chapter reviews this literature. The assumption underlying the organization of this review is that the quality of learning is affected by the cognitive operations underlying MERs processing. To learn from MERs, that is, a student must execute essential operations such as attending to all representations and determining how they are related. One way of understanding the effects of MERs learning interventions is to consider how the intervention intends to affect these cognitive operations. More specifically, in this chapter, we organize these interventions according to the source of this support or the mechanism that has primary responsibility for initiating and supporting MERs learning operations. We have identified three primary sources; namely, the learning materials, the learner, or an embedded prompt. Before proceeding further with an explanation of these three categories, the following section identifies the cognitive operations that are targeted by these efforts.

Cognitive Operations and Learning from Multiple External Representations

Cognitive operations are mental activities that are applied to information (Van Meter et al., 2016). These activities operate on information that is externally presented or internally held and lead to the construction of mental representations. The Cognitive Theory of Multimedia Learning (CTML; Mayer, 2014a) provides the most comprehensive view of cognitive operations involved in MERs learning. This model describes MERs learning as involving the *selection* of key elements from each representation, the *organization* of these elements, and the *integration* of representations by drawing referential connections (Paivio, 1991) across organized representations and with prior knowledge. Organization entails constructing coherent internal representations of each external representation to achieve local (within representation) coherence formation (Seufert & Brunken, 2006). Integration involves using referential connections (Paivio, 1991) to generate inferences and achieve global (between representation) coherence formation (Seufert & Brünken, 2006). Students who successfully execute these operations achieve higher scores on measures such as conceptual reasoning or transfer (Schlag & Ploetzner, 2011; Van Meter et al., 2016) and verbal-visual inferencing (Scheiter & Eitel, 2015; Van Meter et al., 2017).

The CTML holds that selection, organization, and integration are executed within an information processing system whose architecture both permits and constrains their benefits. CTML, for instance, posits that optimal MERs learning requires generative processing (Wittrock, 1989), such as explaining, summarizing, and monitoring. These generative processes are necessary for MERs learning because these processes stimulate construction of meaningful relations across parts of the new material and between this material and prior knowledge (Fiorella & Mayer, 2016). At the same time, however, CTML also adopts the assumptions of Cognitive Load Theory (CLT; Paas & Sweller, 2014) and recognizes that these generative processes take place within a limited capacity system. These limitations constrain the amount of content a student can attend to at any one time including the attention directed at identifying cross-representation connections.

The picture of MERs learning that emerges is one in which a student must execute resource demanding cognitive operations, within a limited capacity system, and often in the context of challenging to-be-learned content. From this perspective, it is not surprising that many students do not maximize the potential of MERs. Educational scholars from across disciplinary perspectives have acknowledged that, although MERs play a critical role in communicating knowledge, many students struggle with these representations (e.g., Kohl & Finkelstein, 2006; Schönborn & Anderson, 2006). This is known as the representation dilemma in which students must learn concepts they do not know from representations they do not understand (see Rau, Chapter 2). The gap between learning demands and student abilities opens a promising avenue for intervention efforts: If the ability to learn from MERs is critical for learning, and a student is likely to struggle with MERs, then learning can be improved by supporting MERs processing.

LEARNING INTERVENTIONS

A variety of MERs learning interventions have been tested and these interventions can be organized in a number of ways. Interventions, for example, could be categorized according to the type of MERs tested, the nature of the to-be-learned content (e.g., conceptual or procedural), or even the age of the learner. For this chapter, we use a framework that categorizes interventions according to the source that is responsible for the initial stimulation of cognitive MERs learning operations. Source refers to the element that is manipulated in an intervention, with this manipulation intended to drive how MERs are studied. We have identified three such sources resulting in three different types of MERs learning interventions. The first of these are materials-driven interventions. In these interventions, some surface feature of the instructional material is manipulated so that the mapping between representations is more apparent; e.g. corresponding verbal and visual information are shown together, animations using spoken rather than written text. We classifiy these interventions as materials-driven because the materials manipulation is intended to be the source that causes the materials to be processed differently than they would be absent this manipulation.

Another category of interventions is learner-driven interventions. In these, the learner receives some explicit instruction on how best to study MERs such as how to comprehend diagrams (e.g. Cromley et al., 2013) or a text-diagram integration strategy (Schlag & Ploetzner, 2011). Following instruction, learners receive some new MERs set and are expected to apply the newly taught process to novel materials. The learner then is the stimulating source for the MERs learning operations because the learner must independently select and apply these operations to new materials.

Our materials- and learner-driven categories are similar to how Renkl and Scheiter (2017) organized this literature in their recent review of MERs interventions. We differ from their organization, however, by adding a distinct, third category of interventions: prompt-driven interventions. These interventions do involve materials manipulations, but the manipulation involves embedding some prompt that requires an overt response from the learner. A learner, for example, is required to respond to a prompt asking for an explanation of how two representations are related (e.g. van der Meij & de Jong, 2011). Although these interventions do involve materials manipulations, we distinguish these from materials-driven interventions because of the required overt response. It is the effort to generate this response that alters MERs learning processes. The following sections review the research and discuss future directions for each of these three types of MERs learning interventions.

Materials-Driven Interventions

As just discussed, materials-driven interventions are those that involve some manipulation to the surface features of representations, such as integrating verbal text within a diagram (Johnson & Mayer, 2012), altering diagram complexity (Butcher, 2006), and pairing animations with spoken, rather than written, text (Schmidt-Weigland, Kohnert, & Glowalla, 2010). These manipulations are considered to be surface-level because the content itself is not manipulated; only the manner in which the content is presented is changed. A typical test of a materials-driven intervention involves comparing learning outcomes for participants who receive materials containing the same content, but differ regarding the instructional design of the MERs.

The most widely known materials-driven interventions are those inspired by instructional design principles derived from the CTML. As discussed previously, the CTML posits that MERs learning involves the essential operations of selection, organization, and integration. CTML also assimilates CLT principles to draw attention to the cognitive load demands of MERs learning (Paas & Sweller, 2014). As an illustration, consider a student given the materials in Figure 6.1. Upon inspecting the text and graphs, the student must identify and derive the meaning of concepts such as distribution and mean (i.e., selection). Local coherence formation is achieved when the student determines how these concepts relate within representations (i.e., organization). The student must also connect the text and graphs to achieve global coherence formation (i.e., integration). The student may, for example, construct a mental model showing how changing the value of the mean shifts the location of the curve.

Each of these steps requires cognitive resources to hold elements and their relations in working memory while simultaneously carrying out essential cognitive operations. CLT has identified three specific sources for the cognitive demands of MERs learning (Paas & Sweller, 2014). *Intrinsic* cognitive load stems from the inherent qualities of the to-be-learned content and is tied to the number of elements and their interactivity. In Figure 6.1, for example, one can see that inter-related elements, such as standard deviation, mean, and distribution, create intrinsic cognitive load. *Germane* cognitive load comes from efforts to understand the content including the essential operations of MERs learning. For a learner studying the materials in Figure 6.1, germane cognitive load is created by, for example, working to understand how the concept of symmetry in the text relates to the percentages in the bottom graph. *Extraneous* cognitive load, the third type, is created by poorly designed materials that require directing resources toward non-essential activities (Sweller, van Merriënboer, & Paas, 2019). This is illustrated in Figure 6.1 where the text uses words for key concepts (e.g., mean) but the graph uses symbols (e.g., μ). This inconsistent labeling requires the student to dedicate resources toward determining the correspondence between different indicators of the same concept.

Recognition that MERs learning carries high cognitive load has led to development of instructional design principles to minimize extraneous load and support essential operations (Mayer & Fiorella, 2014). As one example, the temporal contiguity principle argues that content from external representations is brought into the cognitive system through different channels; auditory or visual. In MERs, representations may compete for the same input channel; e.g., the representations in Figure 6.1 all compete for the visual channel. According to temporal contiguity, materials that use different input channels support learning because the two representations can be processed simultaneously. This principle is demonstrated in research showing that learning improves when animations are paired with audio narration rather than written text (Berney & Bétrancourt, 2016). Temporal contiguity explains this finding by claiming that the verbal and visual representations can be simultaneously processed when they enter through separate processing channels, with this simultaneous processing easing the burden of determining cross-representation connections.

Temporal contiguity is just one of many principles that have been tested in materials-driven interventions. Other principles include (a) spatial contiguity: corresponding parts of verbal and visual representations are placed next to each other, (b) coherence: unnecessary, extraneous verbal, and nonverbal elements are removed, and (c) multimedia: people learn better from verbal and visual representations than from either alone. Because our space here is limited and these principles have been extensively reviewed elsewhere (e.g. Mayer, 2014b, 2017; Mayer & Fiorella, 2014), we will not focus on these specific principles further. Instead, the remainder of this section addresses two main conclusions that can be drawn from the research on materials-driven interventions.

Our first conclusion is that effective learning improves with materials-driven interventions that ease the demands of making accurate cross-representation connections. To illustrate this point, consider again the student studying the materials in Figure 6.1. The student selects standard deviation and mean from the text and, while working to understand their relationship, begins to inspect the top graph. As previously described, however, the student has to divert resources to translate between the words and symbols in the two representations. By the time "mean" is mapped to "μ", the student may not even recall the reason for initiating the search. Materials that lessen the demands of this search and support generation of accurate connections support learning compared to materials that require a more extensive or less certain search (e.g., Richter, Scheiter, & Eitel, 2016).

Scheiter and Eitel (2015) demonstrated this point in a study testing the effects of the signaling principle. Signaling entails manipulating surface features to make the correspondence between representations more obvious; i.e. to signal the points of connections across representations (Schneider, Beege, Nebel, & Rey, 2018). In Figure 6.1, for instance, the correspondence between *mean* and μ could be signaled by writing both in the same color (Ozcelik, Karakus, Kursun, & Cagiltay, 2009) or inserting hyperlinks (Seufert, Jänen, & Brünken, 2007). Scheiter and Eitel (2015) tested signals with college students learning from biology text and diagrams. In Experiment 1, signaling condition participants studied materials that included matching signals. Compared to participants in an unsignaled materials condition, matched-signaling condition participants had higher scores on a measure of text-diagram integration. While Experiment 1 demonstrates the value of signaling text-diagram connections, Experiment 2 demonstrates the importance of ensuring that these connections are accurate. In addition to the same control and matched-signaling conditions of Experiment 1, the second experiment added a mismatched-signals condition; i.e., a signal in the text did not match the signaled elements of the diagram. Post-test scores showed no differences between participants in the control and mismatched-signals condition while those in the matched-signals condition again had higher text-diagram integration scores.

As Scheiter and Eitel (2015) show, the benefits of signaling do not come from some general attentional focus between representations or by calling out key elements.

Instead, the benefits stem from supporting students' generation of accurate connections between corresponding elements. This pattern extends beyond the effects of signaling. Positive effects have also been found for other materials manipulations that ease cross-representation integration; e.g., embedding hyperlinks (Seufert et al., 2007), reducing the complexity of diagrams (Butcher, 2006), and allowing students to control the pace of animations (Schmidt-Weigand et al., 2010).

Our second conclusion is an extension of the first but draws on studies that have collected online process data such as eye tracking or think-alouds (see Schüler, Chapter 4). These data support the conclusion that the effects of materials-driven interventions can be traced to how these manipulations influence underlying cognitive operations. Specifically, these studies use process data to draw a direct link between surface feature manipulations and learning operations. One such study is Johnson and Mayer's (2012) test of the spatial contiguity principle, which states that integration is supported by placing corresponding content from different representations in close proximity. Johnson and Mayer tested this with college students who learned about a brake system by studying either integrated or separated text and diagrams. Integrated materials embedded text into the corresponding location of diagrams while separated materials displayed the text below the diagrams. In Experiments 1 and 2, participants in the integrated conditions had higher post-test scores than those who studied separated representations. Johnson and Mayer also collected participants' eye movements and found that this manipulation supports the cognitive operation of integration: participants who studied spatially integrated representations made more integrative transitions between text and diagrams than those studying separated materials. Similar effects have been shown with other materials-driven interventions such as signaling (e.g., Koning, Tabers, Rikes, & Paas, 2010) and the use of abstract versus concrete illustrations (Mason et al., 2013). Moreover, visual attention and transitions are not the only learning processes affected by materials-driven interventions. Materials design can also influence cognitive load (Schneider et al., 2018), affect (Plass, Heidig, Hayward, Homer, & Um, 2014) and self-explanations (Butcher, 2006).

Altogether, materials-driven interventions that stimulate essential MERs operations do improve MERs learning (see Mayer, 2014b; Renkl & Scheiter, 2017). The most significant weakness within this body of research, the area most in need of empirical attention, concerns the nature of the materials and the experimental settings in which these interventions are tested. The majority of this intervention work uses very brief, contrived materials with populations who have no particular investment in the presented concepts. It is unclear how findings generalize from these controlled settings and materials to students who are learning from MERs that are included in the instructional material of a course. The call for more tests of these interventions in applied settings is, in part, motivated by evidence that the most ideal, long-term benefits of MERs learning are not necessarily found with the most ideal materials design. For example, Schweppe and Rummer (2016) found that, although the expected advantage of studying animations with spoken, rather than written, text may be present on immediate posttests, participants who receive the two visual modalities (i.e., written text with animation) have the advantage on delayed transfer post-tests. Presumably, the greater effort at the time of learning paid off in greater long-term retention. In addition to potential long-term learning effects, there is also reason to question how these materials-driven interventions might fare with populations of students from applied settings. The population most commonly studied in this research are college students and typically, these study participants are drawn from courses unassociated with the content in the experimental materials. There is reason to question the generalizability of these findings to students who might be studying the materials as part of a course, however, because these course-embedded students are quite likely to differ along individual difference characteristics known to influence MERs learning. One would expect, that is, that course-embedded students would have higher levels of prior knowledge, more facilitative motivational states, and/or stronger knowledge of domain-specific MERs conventions than college students randomly selected from an unassociated course. Because these individual differences influence MERs learning (see Cromley, Chapter 5), tests of interventions in applied contexts are necessary. It is worth noting that this trend is not confined to materials-driven interventions. Indeed, this point also applies to many of the prompt- and learner-driven interventions covered in the next sections of this review.

Prompt-Driven Interventions

Prompt-driven interventions are ones in which prompts that require some explicit response from the learner are embedded in the instructional materials. Students' efforts to respond stimulate corresponding cognitive operations (Nokes, Hausmann, VanLehn, & Gershman, 2011) and prompts can be designed to stimulate the cognitive operations of MERs learning (Van Meter et al., 2017). Consider, for example, a student studying the materials in Figure 6.1 who encounters the prompt, "Explain what determines the shape of the normal curve." Responding to this prompt requires the selection of main concepts from the graphs, such as mean and standard deviation, and locating these in the text. Further, within-representation inferences may be generated to form coherent understandings of each main concept and cross-representation inferences may be required to construct a complete response. A student who successfully executes these operations will be able to explain how the mean and standard deviation affect the shape of the curve. We classify interventions of this type as prompt-driven because the embedded prompts, and efforts to respond to them, stimulate the cognitive operations that are applied to MERs.

In these interventions, self-explanation prompts are the most widely studied. Self-explanation is a strategic operation in which students generate inferences and activate prior knowledge to explain the "why" of some phenomenon (McNamara, 2017; Wylie & Chi, 2014). These strategic operations are well-matched to the demands of MERs learning because self-explanation stimulates selection of key concepts and generation of inferences necessary for local and global coherence formation (Wylie & Chi, 2014). And, in fact, this claim that self-explanation supports MERs learning is consistent with the empirical evidence. A typical manipulation in these studies involves presenting students with MERs that can be divided into separate sections (e.g., different pages, different problems) that each contain multiple representations. Each section includes an embedded prompt so that the student is prompted to explain the contents of each section. Prompt-driven interventions following this general structure have demonstrated that self-explanation prompts improve MERs learning with a variety of materials including worked examples (Berthold, Eysink, & Renkl, 2009), science text (Van Meter et al., 2017), animations (Yeh, Chen, Hung, Hwang, 2010), and educational games (Johnson & Mayer, 2010).

Although self-explanation prompts can be effective alone, they are typically most effective when some additional support is provided to assist students while explaining. This support effect is demonstrated in a study by Berthold et al. (2009) in which learning outcomes were compared for participants who received either unsupported, open explanation prompts or supported, assisting explanation prompts. Assisting prompts used a fill-in-the-blank form to structure explanations. Open prompts simply asked for an explanation. After studying worked examples covering concepts of probability theory, participants in the assisting prompt condition had higher scores on a measure of conceptual knowledge than no-prompt control and open-prompt condition participants. These findings are consistent with research testing other forms of support. Johnson and Mayer (2010), for example, found that participants learned more when self-explanations required selecting an appropriate principle from a drop-down menu rather than generating the principle independently. In a study by van der Meij and de Jong (2011), participants whose self-explanation prompts directed attention to a specific between-representation relationship had a learning advantage over those who received open-explanation prompts. Altogether then, prompting students to self-explain is a generally effective MERs learning intervention, but prompting effects are enhanced when explanation efforts are supported. The benefits of self-explanation can be traced to the alignment between the cognitive operations stimulated by this strategy and the additive effects of supporting self-explanation are likely due to improvements in the accuracy of explanation inferences (e.g., Fiorella & Mayer, 2016).

Self-explanation prompts are not the only type of prompt that have been tested in these interventions. Benefits have also been demonstrated for prompts that, for example, require metacognitive reflection on principle applications (Fiorella & Mayer, 2012), stimulate associative processing of cross-representational relations (Van Meter et al., 2016), and direct the construction and revision of students' self-generated drawings (Wu & Rau, 2018). That these prompts support MERs learning is not surprising because, similar to self-explanation, these prompts also stimulate deeper conceptual processing and inference generation. There is, however, evidence that prompts targeting other aspects of MERs learning are also effective. Rau (2018), for example, tested fluency prompts aimed at building the capacity for rapid, perceptual translations between representations. These prompts are grounded in the hypothesis that learning from multiple visual representations requires perceptual fluency or, the ability to rapidly and easily translate between representations (see Rau, Chapter 2; Rau, 2017). Rau (2018) tested the efficacy of these fluency-building prompts with college students learning basic chemical concepts. In the fluency-building condition, participants received prompts in which they saw a molecule represented in one form (e.g., Lewis structure) followed by two alternative representations (e.g., space-filling model) and had to rapidly select which alternative is the same as the initial representation. The effects of fluency-building prompts were evaluated against a sense-making prompt condition and a no-prompt control. Although the sense-making prompts were similar to self-explanation prompts that have been used in other research, Rau (2018) did not find positive effects for these prompts. There was, however, a significant interaction between prior knowledge and fluency prompts. Although fluency prompts improved learning for high prior knowledge participants, low prior knowledge participants in this condition scored significantly lower than control condition participants. This interaction suggests that some requisite level of conceptual knowledge may be necessary before students can take advantage of improved cross-representational fluency (Rau, Aleven, & Rummel, 2015). Nonetheless, these findings support Rau's (2017) assertion that the ability to rapidly translate between representations is a valuable skill underlying MERs learning.

Van Meter et al. (2017) also found support for prompts designed to influence how visual representations are studied within MERs sets. In this study, college students studied biology text and diagrams. Participants in the diagram-awareness condition received prompts that directed identification of important concepts in the diagrams on each page. Participants in another experimental condition received open self-explanation prompts while participants in a control condition were told to take notes. Both self-explanation and diagram-awareness condition participants had significantly higher post-test scores than control condition participants. Diagram-awareness condition participants, however, also had significantly higher scores than self-explanation condition participants on a subtest of items assessing diagram knowledge. Consistent with Rau's (2018) findings, Van Meter et al. (2017) concluded that prompting students' processing of visual representations improves MERs learning.

The literature reviewed in this section demonstrates that prompt-driven interventions positively impact MERs learning. Whether stimulating some form of self-explanation and conceptual reasoning or more specifically addressing processing of visual representations, learning is improved by inserting response prompts that stimulate cognitive operations aligned with MERs (Rau, 2018). Although this claim is supported by the evidence, the area we find that most needs attention in this body of research is the system, or rather the lack of a system, to categorize the response prompts tested across studies. Specifically, there are inconsistencies in how these prompts are labeled and operationalized across studies, and these inconsistencies affect how this evidence can be synthesized and interpreted. To illustrate this point, consider two of the studies discussed above that both claim to test open self-explanation prompts; one by Berthold et al. (2009) and one by Van Meter et al. (2017). Berthold et al. (2009) compared assisting and open-explanation prompts. Open prompts were in the form of a content-specific question that required an explanation (e.g., Why is a number calculated in a particular way?). Van Meter et al.'s (2017) study also included an open self-explanation prompting condition but, in this study, these prompts simply directed participants to "explain the important concepts". Van Meter et al. did test a condition in which participants responded to content specific questions similar to Berthold et al.'s (2009) open-explanation prompts (e.g., How does calcium change the thin filament?). Van Meter et al. (2017), however, labeled these questions as directed response prompts and treated the condition as a comparison control group. In short, what Berthold et al. (2009) considered to be open self-explanation prompts, Van Meter et al. (2017) treated as a meaningful control group in which prompts were "similar to adjunct questions" (p. 190).

Inconsistent operational definitions such as those illustrated above can be found throughout the literature on prompt-driven interventions (see e.g., Johnson & Mayer, 2010; van der Meij & de Jong, 2011). On the one hand, these inconsistencies bolster confidence in our causal claim regarding the effectiveness of prompt-driven interventions. Specifically, our claim that the probability of some response prompt improving MERs learning is tied to the probability that the prompt stimulates the essential cognitive operations of this learning. Moreover, this probability increases when support is provided to assist the construction of accurate inferences. Increased confidence in this conclusion comes from the fact that a variety of response prompts, rather than some one specific type, can effectively improve MERs learning. While stimulating the cognitive operations of selection, organization, and integration appears to be essential for MERs learning, it is not the case that there is only one way to achieve this. On the other hand, however, these inconsistencies are a significant limitation of the research. Because studies have used so many different types of prompts, we are unable to identify some specific form or structure to guide the composition of response prompts in prompt-driven interventions. Without such a guide, our ability to translate research to pedagogical recommendations is limited.

Learner-Driven Interventions

Learner-driven interventions are motivated by the belief that students do not maximize the potential of MERs because they do not know how to study them effectively. A student faced with the representations in Figure 6.1, for example, may not understand the conventions used to convey meaning in the two graphs, and thus, is unable to successfully select and organize elements from these representations. A student may also lack a strategic process for generating the cross-representation connections necessary for integration. Learner-driven interventions address these weaknesses by teaching students a technique for studying MERs. These interventions are classified as learner-driven because the effectiveness of the instruction is evaluated by how well the student is able to independently apply the taught techniques to a new set of materials.

One type of learner-driven intervention is the Conventions of Diagrams (COD) instruction developed by Cromley (e.g. Cromley et al., 2013; Miller, Cromley, & Newcombe, 2016). This instruction supports diagram comprehension by teaching students how to interpret conventions in science diagrams (e.g. arrows, color). Students in COD-intervention classrooms receive convention-comprehension tips that teach the meaning of conventions and how they can be used and answer questions that address convention uses. Tests of this intervention show that COD instruction improves diagram comprehension ability, with some evidence that this ability also supports knowledge acquisition (Cromley et al., 2013; Miller et al., 2016). While COD instruction alone targets diagram comprehension, Bergey, Cromley, and Newcombe (2015) extended this instruction to also support the integration of representations. This new instruction on Coordinating Multiple Representations (CMR) was embedded with COD so that students in COD + CMR instruction not only receive tips and questions about diagram conventions but also about how to connect verbal and visual representations. In this respect, these tips and questions extend to support MERs integration. Bergey et al. compared the effects of COD + CMR to COD-only instruction in two schools. Students in both conditions had improved diagram comprehension ability following the intervention, but there was a slight advantage for students in the COD + CMR on a measure of content knowledge. Specifically, students in the COD + CMR condition in both schools had significant knowledge increases while only one COD condition school showed significant gains.

Other learner-driven interventions have tested the effects of teaching MERs learning strategies. Learning strategies are self-directed operations that are executed to achieve a goal (e.g., Schlag & Ploetzner, 2011). In the context of MERs learning, these strategies could facilitate both within-representation comprehension and between-representation integration. Although there is substantial evidence that verbal text processing improves with strategy instruction (e.g., McNamara, 2017), few studies have tested MERs learning strategies. Those that have, however, indicate significant potential for this approach. This promise is illustrated in a study by Stalbovs, Scheiter, and Gerjets (2015) who taught college students implementation intentions (i.e., strategies) corresponding to text, diagram, and integration processes. A text-processing strategy, for example, directed participants to read the title first, while a diagram-processing strategy directed the selection of central diagram elements. An integration strategy directed participants to search the picture for corresponding information after reading a paragraph. Experimental conditions in this study compared learning outcomes for participants who learned different numbers and combinations of strategies (i.e., one vs. three strategies, one type vs. combined). Participants in all strategy conditions had higher post-test scores than no-strategy control condition participants, but those who were taught one strategy from each of the three categories (i.e., combined) had the greatest advantage.

A study by Schlag and Ploetzner (2011) also found positive effects of strategy instruction. Participants in this study learned a six-step strategy designed to support the selection, organization, and integration of representations. Steps 2–4 of this strategy, for example, directed participants to underline key terms in the text, locate those concepts in the diagram, and label them. Consistent with Stalbovs et al.'s (2015) results, strategy-instructed participants learned more than no-strategy control condition participants; i.e., participants who were taught the strategy had higher scores than control condition participants on measures of factual, conceptual, and transfer knowledge.

The results of strategy instruction studies are in line with findings from Eye Movement Modeling Example (EMME) research. EMME is a technique in which participants view a video showing the eye movement patterns of another individual completing the task in a successful way (Krebs, Schüler, Scheiter, 2018). This approach does not teach a specific strategy but rather models a holistic way to execute the task. The model, for example, spends time inspecting the diagram and transitions between the text and corresponding parts of the diagram during study. In a typical EMME study, experimental participants view this model and then study new material without any additional support. EMME studies show that this technique improves learning from science MERs for both middle school (Mason, Pluchino, & Tornatora, 2015) and college (Jarodzka, Van Gog, Dorr, Scheiter, & Gerjets, 2013; Skuballa, Fortunski, & Renkl, 2015) students.

Learner-driven interventions provide consistent evidence that teaching students how to work with MERs improves learning. In short, students can learn processes that support the selection and organization of elements from representations and the integration of these elements across representations. The main shortcoming we find in this area of research is that there are simply too few tests of these learner-driven interventions, particularly in comparison to the number of studies testing materials-driven interventions. We find this disheartening because "in everyday life, learners do not always encounter materials whose design is based upon [ideal design] principles" (Schlag & Ploetzner, 2011, p. 925). In this context, students would benefit from knowing and being able to apply effective MERs learning processes. The identification of these processes, along with the development of techniques for teaching them, should be a primary goal of MERs learning research.

CONCLUSIONS

The use of MERs, including both verbal and visual representations, is common in instructional material. Although students are often expected to learn from these materials, an unfortunate truth is that many struggle to successfully execute the operations of MERs learning. This representation dilemma (see Rau, Chapter 2; Rau, 2017) has stimulated development of interventions to support these operations. The specific operations of MERs learning are the *selection* and *organization* of elements from each representation and *integration* across representations and with prior knowledge (Mayer, 2014a). This review organized the research on MERs-learning interventions into three categories according to the source that stimulates and supports these operations; i.e., the materials, the learner, or a response prompt.

A major conclusion from our review is that all three types of interventions can improve MERs learning. Looking across our intervention categories, however, leads to three additional conclusions. First, the cognitive operations of selection, organization, and integration provide the mechanisms that can be leveraged to support MERs learning. The benefits of many of the interventions described in this chapter can be traced to how specific interventions influence those operations (see Schüler, Chapter 4). Second, the interventions developed to date can be implemented with relative ease. We found only one intervention, Cromley's (e.g., Miller et al., 2016) COD/COD + CMR instruction, that involved more than a single experimental session. Students, it seems, profit from only brief encounters with MERs-learning interventions. Finally, these interventions are particularly valuable because they tend to support the acquisition of higher-order knowledge. A consistent finding within this body of research is that improved MERs learning leads to improved performance on measures such as mental model revision (Butcher, 2006; Cromley et al., 2010), conceptual transfer and/or reasoning (Johnson & Mayer, 2012; Van Meter et al., 2016), and text-diagram integration (Scheiter & Eitel, 2015; Van Meter et al., 2017).

Even with all that has been done, still more work is needed. We recommend two main directions for future research. First, as previously noted, we encourage more research on learner-directed interventions. This approach is particularly promising because of the potential for learners to independently apply taught processes to materials encountered in their everyday lives (Schlag & Ploetzner, 2011). Although the existing evidence gives reason to be optimistic about this possibility, additional research is needed to better understand both the best strategies for MERs learning and how to support students' ability to transfer and apply taught methods over time. A second line of research concerns development of interventions that sit at the intersection of the three categories that organized this review. Though some studies do fit this mold (e.g., Bodemer & Faust, 2006; Schwonke et al., 2013), the majority of research can be classified into these categories, which means that few studies have tested interventions at their intersection. This is surprising because it is reasonable to expect that such intersectional efforts would reveal additive benefits. Imagine, for example, a student who is applying a newly learned intergration strategy while studying materials with embedded signals to support integration. Alternatively, a student might receive instruction on how to generate quality self-explanations before receiving materials with embedded explanation prompts.

Despite these additional research needs, the empirical evidence related to MERs learning interventions provides reason to be optimistic that students can be helped to maximize the learning potential of multiple external representations. Whether driving processing through materials manipulations, embedded prompts, or processing instruction, these interventions have demonstrated benefits for student learning. At the same time, it is equally clear that these interventions are needed. Although MERs are ubiquitous in instructional materials, many students are unable to capitalize on their potential. Without effective interventions, these students will continue to fall short of learning goals.

REFERENCES

Ainsworth, S. (1999). The functions of multiple representations. *Computers and Education, 33*(2), 131–152. doi:10.1016/S0360-1315(99)00029-9

Bergey, B. W., Cromley, J. G., & Newcombe, N. S. (2015). Teaching high school biology students to coordinate text and diagrams: Relations with transfer, effort, and spatial skill. *International Journal of Science Education, 37*(15), 2476–2502. doi:10.1080/09500693.2015.1082672

Berney, S., & Bétrancourt, M. (2016). Does animation enhance learning? A meta-analysis. *Computers and Education, 101*, 150–167. doi:10.1016/j.compedu.2016.06.005

Berthold, K., Eysink, T. H., & Renkl, A. (2009). Assisting self-explanation prompts are more effective than open prompts when learning with multiple representations. *Instructional Science, 37*(4), 345–363. doi:10.1007/s11251-008-9051-z

Bodemer, D., & Faust, U. (2006). External and mental referencing of multiple representations. *Computers in Human Behavior, 22*(1), 27–42. doi:10.1016/j.chb.2005.01.005

Butcher, K. R. (2006). Learning from text with diagrams: Promoting mental model development and inference generation. *Journal of Educational Psychology, 98*, 182–197. doi:10.1037/0022-0663.98.1.182

Cromley, J. G., Perez, T. C., Fitzhugh, S. L., Newcombe, N. S., Wills, T. W., & Tanaka, J. C. (2013). Improving students' diagram comprehension with classroom instruction. *Journal of Experimental Education, 81*(4), 511–537. doi:10.1080/00220973.2012.745465

Cromley, J. G., Snyder-Hogan, L. E., & Luciw-Dubas, U. A. (2010). Cognitive activities in complex science text and diagrams. *Contemporary Educational Psychology, 35*(1), 59–74. doi:10.1016/j.cedpsych.2009.10.002

De Koning, B. B., Tabbers, H. K., Rikers, R. M., & Paas, F. (2010). Attention guidance in learning from a complex animation: Seeing is understanding? *Learning and Instruction, 20*(2), 111–122. doi:10.1016/j.learninstruc.2009.02.010

Fiorella, L., & Mayer, R. E. (2012). Paper-based aids for learning with a computer-based game. *Journal of Educational Psychology, 104*(4), 1074. doi:10.1037/a0028088

Fiorella, L., & Mayer, R. E. (2016). Eight ways to promote generative learning. *Educational Psychology Review, 28*(4), 717–741. doi:10.1007/s10648-015-9348-9

Jarodzka, H., Van Gog, T., Dorr, M., Scheiter, K., & Gerjets, P. (2013). Learning to see: Guiding students' attention via a model's eye movements fosters learning. *Learning and Instruction, 25*, 62–70. doi:10.1016/j.learninstruc.2012.11.004

Johnson, C. I., & Mayer, R. E. (2010). Applying the self-explanation principle to multimedia learning in a computer-based game-like environment. *Computers in Human Behavior, 26*(6), 1246–1252. doi:10.1016/j.chb.2010.03.025

Johnson, C. I., & Mayer, R. E. (2012). An eye movement analysis of the spatial contiguity effect in multimedia learning. *Journal of Experimental Psychology: Applied, 18*(2), 178–191. doi:10.1037/a0026923

Kohl, P. B., & Finkelstein, N. D. (2006). Effects of representation on students solving physics problems: A fine-grained characterization. *Physical Review Special Topics – Physics Education Research, 2*(1), 010106. doi:10.1103/PhysRevSTPER.2.010106

Krebs, M. C., Schüler, A., & Scheiter, K. (2018). Just follow my eyes: The influence of model-observer similarity on eye movement modeling examples. *Learning and Instruction.* doi:10.1016/j.learninstruc.2018.10.005

Mason, L., Pluchino, P., & Tornatora, M. C. (2015). Eye-movement modeling of integrative reading of an illustrated text: Effects on processing and learning. *Contemporary Educational Psychology, 41*, 172–187. doi:10.1016/j.cedpsych.2015.01.004

Mason, L., Pluchino, P., Tornatora, M. C., & Ariasi, N. (2013). An eye-tracking study of learning from science text with concrete and abstract illustrations. *Journal of Experimental Education, 81*(3), 356–384. doi:10.1080/00220973.2012.727885

Mayer, R. E. (2014a). Cognitive theory of multimedia learning. In R. E. Mayer (Ed.), *The Cambridge handbook of multimedia learning* (2nd ed., pp. 43–71). New York: Cambridge University Press.

Mayer, R. E. (2014b). *The Cambridge handbook of multimedia learning* (2nd ed.). New York: Cambridge University Press.

Mayer, R. E. (2017). Using multimedia for e-learning. *Journal of Computer Assisted Learning, 33*(5), 403–423.

Mayer, R. E., & Fiorella, L. (2014). Principles for reducing extraneous processing in multimedia learning: Coherence, signaling, redundancy, spatial contiguity, and temporal contiguity principles (pp. 279–315). *The Cambridge handbook of multimedia learning.* New York: Cambridge University Press.

McNamara, D. S. (2017). Self-Explanation and Reading Strategy Training (SERT) Improves low-knowledge students' science course performance. *Discourse Processes, 54*(7), 479–492. doi:10.1080/0163853X.2015.1101328

Miller, B. W., Cromley, J. G., & Newcombe, N. S. (2016). Improving diagrammatic reasoning in middle school science using conventions of diagrams instruction. *Journal of Computer Assisted Learning, 32*(4), 374–390. doi:10.1111/jcal.12143

Nokes, T. J., Hausmann, R. G., VanLehn, K., & Gershman, S. (2011). Testing the instructional fit hypothesis: The case of self-explanation prompts. *Instructional Science, 39*(5), 645–666. doi:10.1007/s11251-010-9151-4

Ozcelik, E., Karakus, T., Kursun, E., & Cagiltay, K. (2009). An eye-tracking study of how color coding affects multimedia learning. *Computers and Education, 53*(2), 445–453. doi:10.1016/j.compedu.2009.03.002

Paas, F., & Sweller, J. (2014). Implications of cognitive load theory for multimedia learning. In R. E. Mayer (Ed.), *The Cambridge handbook of multimedia learning* (2nd ed., pp. 27–42). New York: Cambridge University Press.

Paivio, A. (1991). Dual coding theory: Retrospect and current status. *Canadian Journal of Psychology/Revue Canadienne de Psychologie, 45*(3), 255–287. doi:10.1037/h0084295

Plass, J. L., Heidig, S., Hayward, E. O., Homer, B. D., & Um, E. (2014). Emotional design in multimedia learning: Effects of shape and color on affect and learning. *Learning and Instruction, 29*, 128–140. doi:10.1016/j.learninstruc.2013.02.006

Rau, M. A. (2017). Conditions for the effectiveness of multiple visual representations in enhancing STEM learning. *Educational Psychology Review, 29*(4), 717–761. doi:10.1007/s10648-016-9365-3

Rau, M. A., Aleven, V., & Rummel, N. (2015). Successful learning with multiple graphical representations and self-explanation prompts. *Journal of Educational Psychology, 107*(1), 30–46. doi:10.1037/a0037211

Renkl, A., & Scheiter, K. (2017). Studying visual displays: How to instructionally support learning. *Educational Psychology Review, 29*(3), 599–621. doi:10.1007/s10648-015-9340-4

Richter, J., Scheiter, K., & Eitel, A. (2016). Signaling text-picture relations in multimedia learning: A comprehensive meta-analysis. *Educational Research Review, 17*, 19–36. doi:10.1016/j.edurev.2015.12.003

Scheiter, K., & Eitel, A. (2015). Signals foster multimedia learning by supporting integration of highlighted text and diagram elements. *Learning and Instruction, 36*, 11–26. doi:10.1016/j.learninstruc.2014.11.002

Schlag, S., & Ploetzner, R. (2011). Supporting learning from illustrated texts: Conceptualizing and evaluating a learning strategy. *Instructional Science, 39*(6), 921–937. doi:10.1007/s11251-010-9160-3

Schmidt-Weigand, F., Kohnert, A., & Glowalla, U. (2010). A closer look at split visual attention in system- and self-paced instruction in multimedia learning. *Learning and Instruction, 20*(2), 100–110. doi:10.1016/j.learninstruc.2009.02.011

Schneider, S., Beege, M., Nebel, S., & Rey, G. D. (2018). A meta-analysis of how signaling affects learning with media. *Educational Research Review, 23*, 1–24. https://doi.org/10.1016/j.edurev.2017.11.001

Schönborn, K. J., & Anderson, T. R. (2006). The importance of visual literacy in the education of biochemists. *Biochemistry and Molecular Biology Education, 34*(2), 94–102. doi:10.1002/bmb.2006.49403402094

Schweppe, J., & Rummer, R. (2016). Integrating written text and graphics as a desirable difficulty in long-term multimedia learning. *Computers in Human Behavior, 60*, 131–137. doi:10.1016/j.chb.2016.02.035

Schwonke, R., Ertelt, A., Otieno, C., Renkl, A., Aleven, V., & Salden, R. J. (2013). Metacognitive support promotes an effective use of instructional resources in intelligent tutoring. *Learning and Instruction, 23,* 136–150. doi:10.1016/j.learninstruc.2012.08.003

Seufert, T., & Brünken, R. (2006). Cognitive load and the format of instructional aids for coherence formation. *Applied Cognitive Psychology: The Official Journal of the Society for Applied Research in Memory and Cognition, 20*(3), 321–331. doi:10.1002/acp.1248

Seufert, T., Jänen, I., & Brünken, R. (2007). The impact of intrinsic cognitive load on the effectiveness of graphical help for coherence formation. *Computers in Human Behavior, 23*(3), 1055–1071. doi:10.1016/j.chb.2006.10.002

Skuballa, I. T., Fortunski, C., & Renkl, A. (2015). An eye movement pre-training fosters the comprehension of processes and functions in technical systems. *Frontiers in Psychology, 6,* 598. doi:10.3389/fpsyg.2015.00598

Stalbovs, K., Scheiter, K., & Gerjets, P. (2015). Implementation intentions during multimedia learning: Using if-then plans to facilitate cognitive processing. *Learning and Instruction, 35,* 1–15. doi:10.1016/j.learninstruc.2014.09.002

Sweller, J., van Merriënboer, J. J., & Paas, F. (2019). Cognitive architecture and instructional design: 20 years later. *Educational Psychology Review,* 1–32. doi:10.1007/s10648-019-09465-5

van der Meij, J., & de Jong, T. (2011). The effects of directive self-explanation prompts to support active processing of multiple representations in a simulation-based learning environment. *Journal of Computer Assisted Learning, 27*(5), 411–423. doi:10.1111/j.1365-2729.2011.00411.x

Van Meter, P. N., Cameron, C., & Waters, J. R. (2017). Effects of response prompts and diagram comprehension ability on text and diagram learning in a college biology course. *Learning and Instruction, 49,* 188–198. doi:10.1016/j.learninstruc.2017.01.003

Van Meter, P. N., Firetto, C. M., Turns, S. R., Litzinger, T. A., Cameron, C. E., & Shaw, C. W. (2016). Improving students' conceptual reasoning by prompting cognitive operations. *Journal of Engineering Education, 105*(2), 245–277. doi:10.1002/jee.20120

Wittrock, M. C. (1989). Generative processes of comprehension. *Educational Psychologist, 24*(4), 345–376. doi:10.1207/s15326985ep2404_2

Wu, S. P., & Rau, M. A. (2018). Effectiveness and efficiency of adding drawing prompts to an interactive educational technology when learning with visual representations. *Learning and Instruction, 55,* 93–104. doi:10.1016/j.learninstruc.2017.09.010

Wylie, R., & Chi, M. T. H. (2014). The self-explanation principle in multimedia learning. In R. E. Mayer (Ed.), *The Cambridge handbook of multimedia learning* (2nd ed., pp. 413–432). New York: Cambridge University Press.

Yeh, Y. F., Chen, M. C., Hung, P. H., & Hwang, G. J. (2010). Optimal self-explanation prompt design in dynamic multi-representational learning environments. *Computers and Education, 54*(4), 1089–1100. doi:10.1016/j.compedu.2009.10.013

7

LEARNING BY CONSTRUCTION OF MULTIPLE REPRESENTATIONS

Shaaron Ainsworth
UNIVERSITY OF NOTTINGHAM

Russell Tytler
DEAKIN UNIVERSITY, MELBOURNE

Vaughan Prain
DEAKIN UNIVERSITY, MELBOURNE

ABSTRACT

While research on students learning through interpreting expert representations in many fields has a long and valued history, what and how students learn when they construct, share and review their own multiple, multimodal representations remains a relatively emergent research area. In this chapter, we critically analyze: (a) the claims made for student multiple representation construction (MRC), both in terms of how it works and potential benefits; (b) the evidence for these claims; and (c) their theoretical underpinnings in cognitivist and socio-semiotic perspectives. We end by articulating some future challenges and directions for MRC as both technology and theory-informed pedagogy embrace new learning opportunities.

Key words: multiple representations, construction, science, cognition, communication

INTRODUCTION

Although the benefits (and costs) for learning by interpreting multiple representations have been actively researched for many decades, learning by constructing multiple representations has only recently begun to receive significant attention. Yet, consider how students enact the movement of the Moon around the Earth using their bodies before writing and drawing an explanation of tides in their workbooks. Or the liveliness of group reasoning around the creation of an animation or the translation of a text into two-dimensional or three-dimensional models. The benefit of focusing on and constructing such multimodal representations has been convincingly demonstrated by research on professional practice in domains as diverse as science, fashion design, mathematics, and archeology, all of which are rich with the construction, interpretation, and discussion of multiple modes of knowing. Consequently, in this chapter we will consider learning by the construction of multiple, primarily non-verbal, representations such as drawing, creating animations, building models, generating gestures, and enactments. In so doing, we build from both cognitive and socio-cultural/semiotic explanations of the importance of multi-representational construction (hereafter MRC), as well as consider the generative conditions and challenges associated with ensuring the success of such learning.

There is no universally agreed structural taxonomy of symbol systems. For some researchers, there are binaries such as modality (e.g., visual or textual) or dynamism (static or animated) whereas for others they are finer grained approaches (graphs, tables, graphical tables, time charts, networks, structure diagrams, process diagrams, maps, cartogram, icons, and pictures; e.g. Lohse, Biolsi, Walker, & Rueler, 1994) and of course graphs need not simply be graphs but could be, *inter alia*, bar charts, histograms, line graphs, or scatter plots. Given this complexity, we will be generous in our inclusion of what counts as multiple and include anything that *any* of these approaches would count as different representations. In defining MRC, we do not insist on the generation of multiple representations, only that taken as a whole the representational system includes multiple representations (so may include initial presented materials as well as new constructed forms).

We critically analyze: (a) the claims made for MRC, both in terms of how it works and the potential benefits; (b) the evidence for these claims; and (c) their theoretical underpinnings. We end by articulating some future directions for MRC as both technology and theory informed pedagogy embrace new opportunities for such learning.

REVIEW OF THE LITERATURE

To organize this review, we consider three main rationales for asking learners to engage in multi-representational construction activities:

1. Successful multi-representational construction involves cognitive processes that are central to deep learning.
2. It is a core disciplinary practice in many areas, especially, although not limited to, the science, technology, engineering, and mathematical (STEM) domains and consequently one that students need to learn how to engage in.
3. MRC supports communication between peers as they both construct and reason around artifacts. Teachers can use such activities as the basis for formative feedback and summative assessment.

We consider these roles of MRC as interdependent. For example, professionals construct multiple representations, not only because of their centrality to disciplinary epistemic processes but because of the cognitive and communicative benefits that this activity provides. Accordingly, we point out this synergy where most useful, whilst noting that the theoretical and methodological bases of such claims are often distinct.

MRC as a Constructive Cognitive Process

The first rationale for encouraging MRC rests on the argument that learning is more successful when learners are active in the construction of their own understanding. Clearly, this is a commonly articulated perspective in educational theory but we will rest our definition on that of Chi (2009). She defines two fundamental characteristics of constructive learning activities: they require learners to produce an overt output and this output is not simply a restatement of the learning material but goes beyond it in some way. Thus, typical constructive activities cited by Chi include explaining, elaborating, making predictions, and reflecting. This approach underpins our definition, but we require an addition to count as MRC – the overt constructive activity must be in a different representational form to any studied material. Thus, for us reading a text and then generating a reflective summary in note form of what you have read and understood, whilst constructive, is not MRC. But reading a text, and then drawing a picture of some of that read material would be MRC, as would watching a video and then writing an explanation of what you think it means. In Chi's definition, constructive activities need not be externalized, although they often are and may be particularly beneficial when they are. In our definition of MRC, outputs must be externalized, even if they are ephemeral: if a student read an account of planetary motion and then created a role play of how the Moon rotates around the Earth this would for us be a good example of MRC. Chi's account is general but there are specific theoretical frameworks and empirical studies that are focused on particular forms of MRC. Space limitations do not permit an account of them all but we will consider two examples: drawing as a lasting form of MRC and gesturing as an ephemeral one.

Van Meter & Firetto (2013) proposed a cognitive model of drawing construction where the focus is on explaining the generative learning that occurs when students draw from written text. Based upon a number of prior theories, they suggest that learners must first form a surface representation of the linguistic features of the text prior to semantic processes. This results in the construction of a propositional network that describes structural elements and relations in the to-be-drawn text. A drawing is then created by translating this information into a perceptual image, which will be strongly influenced by the drawer's prior knowledge, the goals they have in mind and their developing understanding. Thus, learning by drawing is not a simple linear process, nor is it effortless. To be successful, drawing as MRC is a metacognitive strategy requiring deep engagement with the original text as well as the emerging drawing and the learner's understanding. Drawing does not simply externalize what learners have in mind; it changes their mind.

This model is drawn from and has informed a large (and increasing) number of empirical studies. Typically, studies that have used drawing as a learning strategy (see Ainsworth, Prain, & Tytler, 2011), ask students to read text and then transform some of that text into a drawing, which also incorporates their prior understanding of the concepts (e.g., Gobert & Clement, 1999; Van Meter, Aleksic, Schwartz, & Garner,

2006). A recent meta-analysis by Fiorella and Zhang (2018) found a mean effect size of .41 for comprehension tests and .37 for transfer performance when drawing was used in this way. Consequently, research has now turned to consider the factors that enhance drawing as a strategy and two key insights can be seen to emerge from these studies. The first is that what students draw matters. A number of studies (e.g., Scheiter, Schleinschok, & Ainsworth, 2017; Schwamborn, Mayer, Thillmann, Leopold, & Leutner, 2010) have found that students who transform more of the key ideas in text into the resulting drawing learn more than those who draw fewer of them. This is true even when students' prior knowledge is taken into account. A second key insight is that drawing in this way can be supported either through prompting and scaffolding whilst students draw or through training before they begin. For example, Van Meter et al. (2006) found that providing 9–12-year-old children with model drawings to compare their own drawings led to enhanced learning. Scheiter et al. (2017) trained students in the features of good drawings first (focusing on selecting and externalizing key ideas) and again found that higher quality drawings were associated with better outcomes.

There is less research looking at drawing as MRC when learning from non-textual material, however, there are some studies looking at drawing to support learning from visualization. For example, Zhang and Linn (2011) asked high school students to draw their interpretation of molecular movement during chemical reactions that they had earlier explored with a visualization tool and compared them to students who only interacted with the visualization (though for extra time). They found the drawing group did learn more about chemical reactions. Similarly, Wu and Rau (2018) compared the benefits of being prompted to draw before, during, and after interacting with Chem Tutor, which provides different visual representations of atoms. They found that drawing throughout, especially when students revised what they drew, was particularly beneficial for learning. Mason, Lowe, and Tornatora (2013) found that drawing whilst watching an animation of Newton's Cradle helped children to understand the physical processes depicted, compared to those who traced drawings or did not draw at all. But, in contrast to these studies that focused on easy-to-draw visualizations, Ploetzner and Fillisch (2017) found that asking participants to draw rather than reflect on what they had observed in an animation of a four-stroke engine resulted in poor learning. They argued that drawing biased the learners to attend to structures rather than to important dynamic changes in the animation. In this and in all the studies reported above, the quality of what a student drew predicted their learning. Thus, this research suggests that drawing as MRC need not be limited to drawing from text. Constructing drawings when supported by visual materials can also be beneficial, but only to the extent that the drawing activity supports learners (with appropriate prior knowledge) to externalize the relevant aspects of the visualization. The key point seems to be that the drawing challenges students to actively select and abstract from a more complex visualization.

A second example of MRC is seen when considering how gesturing supports learning. It is now well accepted that gesturing is an important component of teaching and learning (even if the underlying generation mechanism for gestures is not fully understood). Gestures do, of course, support communication. When students observe the gestures of teachers as they explain a complex idea, especially when that gesture is simultaneously produced with speech, they learn better (e.g. Congdon et al., 2017).

However, the benefits of gesturing are not limited to observing the gestures of others; if people themselves gesture as they solve problems and reason, their understanding is enhanced (e.g. Goldin-Meadow & Wagner, 2005; Stieff, Lira, & Scopelitis, 2016). Gesturing is said to help learning as it reduces demands on working memory and engages the motor system. However, gesturing as MRC occurs when the learners themselves (not their teachers) use gestures in a representational way: i.e., the gestures are abstracted representational actions that depict "action, motion, or shape, or that indicate location or trajectory" (Kita, Alibali, & Chu, 2017, p 245). Novack and Goldin-Meadow (2017) argue that the way that representational gestures must abstract away from the specifics of the situation to highlight its key properties is fundamental to their value for supporting generalization and memory. Similarly, Kita et al. (2017) suggest that it is the schematic nature of representational gestures that supports the selection, activation, and manipulation of spatio-motoric information. Studies report the benefits of gesturing as MRC on a number of measures. For example, Chu and Kita (2011) found that people who solved spatial rotation tasks when encouraged to gesture solved them more accurately than people who were not permitted to gesture. Notably, this benefit was maintained even when the participants were prohibited from gesturing in a subsequent problem-solving phase. Cook, Mitchell, and Goldin-Meadow (2008) found that requiring children to gesture whilst they solved mathematics problems requiring grouping was equally effective as requiring them to verbally explain it. However, gesturing was associated with better retention of this grouping strategy four weeks afterward. Further, supporting the idea that it is abstraction that is important in representational gesturing, Novack et al. (2014) found that children taught a more abstract gesture to support grouping in addition tasks (a v-shaped gesture to group objects) were more successful than those who were taught a concrete holding gesture or those who held and manipulated physical objects.

The research on factors that predict the success of drawing as MRC is echoed in the research on gesturing as MRC. For example, the content of gestures matters. Goldin-Meadow, Cook, and Mitchell (2009) found that children who were taught a specific gesture to represent grouping in mathematical problem solving later solved similar problems more accurately than children who had been taught to gesture in general towards the problem or not encouraged to gesture at all. Similarly, gesturing as a learning strategy can be trained. Stieff et al. (2016) taught college students gestures that represented the spatial relationships depicted in diagrams of molecular representations. Compared to students who studied alone, or with an instructor who talked with gesture about the relationship between the representations, the gesturing students were more able to translate between representations. Moreover, Stieff et al. (2016) found that although using concrete models to solve these problems was an equally effective strategy to gesturing in this way, when students were subsequently tested under exam conditions without concrete models, the gesture condition students performed better.

It is not our intention to suggest that drawing or gesturing are equivalent. Clearly, each has different parts to play depending on the task. Rather, we propose that it is likely that similar but not identical constructive processes are involved when learning successfully through gesture and drawing as MRC. Moreover, we suggest that specific situations may call for one form rather than the other and research will help identify what those situations are. For example, it is likely that tasks that cannot easily be learned through static 2D representations such as the four-stroke engine of Ploetzner and Fillisch (2017) are unlikely to be best learned through drawing and these might best be supported through gesturing or the other types of MRC that the word limit has not allowed us to cover, such as animation construction (Chang, Quintana, & Krajcik, 2010) or writing (Keys, Hand, Prain, & Collins, 1999). Moreover, as we will discuss later, the forms that gesturing, drawing, and other forms of MRC take will change as the tools we are using to learn are changing.

MRC as Representing Core Disciplinary Practices

Alongside cognitive perspectives on the benefits of MRC sits a recent upsurge of research activity grounded in socio-cultural and semiotic perspectives on learning. From these perspectives, drawing on Vygotskian theory (Vygotsky, 1978), multiple representations are seen as mediating tools through which meanings and understandings are achieved in any subject, elevating their role to fundamental resources for thinking and reasoning. They are seen as the means through which learning occurs and is shared. The act of constructing representations enables new meanings to be created and noticed. Researchers such as Magnani (2015) have tried to integrate cognitive and socio-cultural perspectives. For Magnani, drawing on Peirce (1931–58) and Hutchins (1995), abductive, speculative reasoning in science is understood within an "eco-cognitive model of abduction" (Magnani, 2015, p. 290), where meaning-making through MRC is achieved through the use of informed interaction with the environment, including the manipulation of physical and cognitive resources.

From socio-cultural perspectives, MRC is researched with different emphases: (a) investigating the construction and transaction of meanings in classrooms that lead to understanding, so that context and social processes achieve greater prominence; (b) exploring MRC as fundamental to the literacies of different subjects – as multimodal language tools that students need to master; and (c) as allied to the material/semiotic practices through which knowledge is built in the discipline (Rau, Chapter 2). There are in this literature different perspectives on the extent to which students need to be actively involved in MRC as part of their induction into disciplinary ways of thinking. We will review research perspectives and findings concerning MRC for each of these particular emphases. Many of these studies are in the ethnographic and design-based research tradition, and some have pursued mixed method and quasi-experimental designs. We will look particularly at research in science and to some extent mathematics, as representative of these approaches.

Studies of teacher and student learning interactions in science have shown the fundamentally multimodal nature of classroom teaching and learning processes. Kress and van Leeuwen's (2006) research has taken a socio-semiotic perspective on the ways in which teachers shape students' learning through the orchestration of representations across different modes, involving the management of student production of text and visual representations to engage with meaningful interpretation of science. From their perspective, student meaning-making involves drawing on the multimodal resources of science (linguistic, visual, and mathematical) which constitute a new literacy which must be learned. Similarly, Lemke (2004) identified the complex orchestration of multimodal representations students face in any science classroom, and linked this to the development of scientific discursive practices interpreted as the development of the multimodal literacies of science. Lemke described the way a student in a chemistry classroom needs to not only have command of multiple literacies; verbal discourse formations, crystal diagrams, gestures indicating spatial directionality, algebraic and symbolic representations, and stoichiometric calculations, but needs also to be able to translate and integrate these in order to infer canonical meanings. From a broadly socio-cultural perspective, learning in any discipline is viewed as the purposeful induction into such practices.

These science education research programs have closely followed on from a new tradition in science studies that draw on how scientists build knowledge. There is now considerable evidence of the central role in scientific discovery practices of representational invention and manipulation, and modeling, in generating, interpreting, and justifying ideas (Nersessian, 2008). Latour (1990, 1999) showed how data are transformed into theory by a series of representational "passes" to end with the formalized linguistic, visual, and mathematical forms that constitute the scientific knowledge reported in journals. Similarly, Gooding (2004), in a study of Michael Faraday's diaries, and analysis of visualizations across a variety of scientific fields, showed how the creative invention and manipulation of new visual representational forms underpin new ideas in science. Klein (2001) argued that symbolic representational manipulation and refinement actively shaped the developments in chemical formulae in the early 1800s.

Drawing on this growing research tradition into the multimodal constructive processes underpinning scientific discovery, classroom researchers argue that if we are to induct students into these disciplinary practices, they must be actively involved in the construction, evaluation, and refinement of multiple representations (Duschl, 2008; Lehrer & Schauble, 2006; Prain & Tytler, 2012). Students benefit from having firsthand experience and understanding of how these multimodal representational tools are used to imagine, build, and validate knowledge (Ford & Forman, 2006).

Lehrer and Schauble (2006) have engaged in a long-term program of design-based research investigating the role of modeling and model-based reasoning in science and mathematics classrooms, showing impressive levels of student conceptual invention and performance through systematically immersing students in the epistemic practices of the discipline. This involves the invention, evaluation, and refinement of multimodal representational systems (Kobiela & Lehrer, 2019; Lehrer & Schauble, 2012). For instance, Lehrer, Kim, and Jones (2011) found that a program of invention, discussion, and refinement of statistical measures led to students attending to, and making explicit, characteristics of distributions not normally noticed. Similarly, Mulligan (2015) found that young children's invention and repeated critical reflection on and refinement of graphical representations enhanced a range of meta-representational competencies (the ability to optimize representational use for a task and to use novel representations productively, diSessa, 2004) and enhanced the early development of statistical concepts. Manz (2012) showed how 3rd graders' model construction practice codeveloped with their ecological knowledge over a long-term gardening design-based investigation.

Tytler, Prain, Hubber, and Waldrip (2013) have developed a guided inquiry approach to teaching and learning science (Representation Construction Approach – RCA) whereby students construct, evaluate, coordinate, and refine representations (often drawings, or 3D models, or role plays), being led towards canonical scientific representational practices such as the exploration of ideas through speculative drawing, gesture, and talk, or the coordination of measurement practices, sketches, tables, diagrams, and text in investigative processes. Underpinning the approach is a pragmatist semiotic perspective on knowledge and learning (Peirce, 1931–58). This approach to meaning-making in science draws on Peirce's semiotic theory where meaning-making and meaning-changing are understood as sign-dependent processes, where signs stand in for their referents and enable reflective analyses of intended and realized meanings by the sign-maker. From this perspective, learning in science entails students investing signs in science discourse with appropriate disciplinary meaning and usage. Creating, interpreting, and justifying MRCs in science is therefore understood as fundamental to reasoning and learning in this subject. The approach is linked to recent framings of MRC research around visualization (Gilbert, Reiner, & Nakleigh, 2008), conceived of as a crucial aspect of conceptual work across disciplines. This framing is particularly productive in fields such as chemistry where students must learn to coordinate visual representations of sub-micro phenomena with macro and symbolic representations.

The RCA program of design-based research has shown significant gains in learning outcomes, evidenced by the sophistication and complexity of student productions (Hubber & Tytler, 2017), by teacher attestation to deepened learning and discussion (Hubber, Tytler & Haslam, 2010; Waldrip, Prain, & Carolan, 2010), and in some cases by informal comparison of pre- and post-test results with non-intervention classes (Tytler, Prain, & Hubber, 2018). Interviews and pre-/post-tests of students engaged in the RCA program demonstrated gains in students' epistemological sophistication concerning the relation between representations and understanding (Hubber et al., 2010). These gains align with diSessa's (2004) construct of meta-representational competence, referring to students' capacity to interpret, critique, invent, compare, and relate representations. This research has also been informed by the increased recognition of the role of material practices in inquiry, including the manipulation of objects as resources for science learning. In theorizing how students learn from engaging with, and integrating, linguistic, visuospatial, mathematical, and embodied modes of thinking in science, Prain and Tytler (2012) proposed that different affordances in each of these modes contributed to meaning-making and meaning-sharing.

Research on non-linguistic MRCs has also led to new research on the affordances of talk and writing to clarify and explain other modes. Although historically viewed as the dominant mode for creating and assessing learning, writing is now understood as but one (albeit crucial) contributor to this multimodal claim-making in science (Prain & Hand, 2016). Hand and colleagues have extensively researched how writing enables science learning within an inquiry-based approach incorporating other modes (Keys et al., 1999). In this approach, students are immersed in guided claim-making as they follow a modified report framework called the Science Writing Heuristic that encourages them to make, share, justify, refine, and explain multimodal claims about topics. This immersive process has led to strong learning gains (Akkus, Gunel, & Hand, 2007). Drawing variously on cognitivist, pedagogical, and argumentation theorists (Ford & Forman, 2006; Halliday & Martin, 1993; Klein, 2006), this research program has focused more recently on how students coordinate linguistic modes with other modes of meaning-making, to construct multimodal claims in science (Hand & Choi, 2010). Chen, Park, and Hand (2016) found that talk and writing enabled students to clarify and explain how other modes served claim-making. Knain, Fredlund, Furberg,

Mathiasssen, Remmen, & Odegaard (2017) identified the key role of teacher-guided evaluation if students are to build on their everyday student-centered language to construct the multimodal representations (languages) of science. This process entails multiple forms of "transduction" (Volkwyn, Airey, Gregorčič, & Heijkenskjöld, 2016) in science learning, where learners are expected to remake the meaning of a sign in one mode into a sign in a different mode and to integrate these meanings across multiple modes. While there are emerging claims about the character of (and what enables) particular modal transductions, there is a need for more systematic research on how this process plays out in student MRC on particular topics and more generally.

Thus, it can be seen that in these socio-cultural traditions, MRC entails fundamental disciplinary processes of claim-making and sharing, and is characterized in classrooms as a core discursive practice that students need to be inducted into. As such, MRC is recognized as complex, encompassing multiple reasoning processes that draw on the affordances of different modes and their cross-modal coordination.

MRC Supports Communication and Collaboration

The final rationale we consider for MRC in learning is its role in supporting and shaping communication and collaboration. Multiple representations are constructed, shared, negotiated, developed, and redeveloped across a community of learners (and practitioners) often across extended periods of time. This occurs in the classroom as children collaborate to create representations of scientific phenomena they are investigating, between teachers and their students as students create representations to show their developing understanding for either formative or summative assessment, and in the workplace where co-workers develop shared understanding of problems. Research that explains how MRC works to support such communicative practices, therefore, draws on theoretical perspectives that highlight the cognitive benefits of representation construction in dialogue, argumentation, and reasoning, typically employing an account of cognition that emerged from situated (e.g., Hall, 1996) and distributed (e.g., Hutchins, 1995) traditions. As such, this work aligns well with the theoretical perspective drawn from socio-cultural accounts that identify creation, negotiation, and refinement of representational systems as a key disciplinary practice. Given this broad theoretical basis, it is unsurprising that research exploring MRC in communication and collaboration draws upon studies which have adopted a wide range of methods including experimental studies, case studies, and ethnographies.

One key benefit of MRC is that students can come to understand one another's perspectives as they develop shared knowledge via the construction of common ground (Clark & Wilkes-Gibbs, 1986). While this process is neither effortless nor automatic, representations can disambiguate communication between collaborators when they can be gestured towards or moved around (Roschelle & Teasley, 1995). Moreover, collaborative MRC requires learners to negotiate shared understanding, externalizing their own knowledge whilst eliciting the views of peers (Fischer & Mandl, 2005). Thus, Suthers (2014) suggests they act as "Negotiation Potentials" as collaborators become more aware of the need to discuss and agree on changes to the representation. This can, in turn, lead to them acting as a "referential resource" enabling collaborators to elaborate new shared understandings that have been made both memorable (Dillenbourg & Traum, 2006) and salient by their expression as external representations. Thus, a genuinely joint representation that emerges from such collaborative construction must be capable of coordinating the collaborators' different perspectives on the problem. This, Schwartz (1995) argues, is the reason that collaborating pairs constructed representations that were more abstract than the representations that were created during lone problem solving.

Another kind of communication supported by MRC can be that between a teacher and their students. MRC can allow teachers to gain insight into what their students understand, something that a single mode of representation may sometimes make less explicit. In this respect, MRC can also be powerful for diagnostic, formative, and summative assessment purposes (Tytler et al., 2013). For example, Cooper, Williams, and Underwood (2015) asked college students to draw and explain the inter-molecular forces in ethanol. By having both modes of representation, it was clearer that many students had an incorrect understanding of these inter-molecular forces. Another example of MRC for assessing student understanding can be seen when students gesture their understanding to others. For example, Breckinridge Church & Goldin-Meadow (1986) studied children solving Piagetian conservation tasks and found that some children had an inconsistency between their spoken response and the gestures that accompany it. What is striking is that, for children who produced these discordant responses, typically the gesture was correct and speech incorrect. Moreover, it was these students who made the greatest gains in their understanding when subsequently provided with instruction. Waldrip et al. (2010) found that tests developed with blank spaces for students to combine text and image provided greater insight into student understanding, but also developed the capacity to coordinate across different modes indicative of higher levels of achievement. This echoes the findings of Chen et al. (2016) concerning the value of writing for clarifying the meanings embedded in other modes.

NEW INSIGHTS AND FUTURE DIRECTIONS

The acts of MRC (talking, writing, gesturing and drawing) we have focused on in this review are those that have been used by humans to support learning for thousands of years. This section will briefly try to forecast how these traditional modes of MRC may evolve as we involve digital tools in MRC. Digitally supported MRC is increasingly commonplace across all levels of education as well as in informal settings. It can be seen when children use visual programming languages such as Scratch to write stories or make games (e.g. Maloney, Resnick, Rusk, Silverman, & Eastmond, 2010), or when they program a model of predator-prey evolution by drawing using SimSketch in a museum (Heijnes, van Joolingen, & Leenaars, 2018). Such constructive representational activities need not only be two-dimensional as tools such as three-dimensional printers allow students to make their engineering ideas concrete (e.g. Brown, 2015). There is also increasing interest in how gesture can be directly incorporated into digital learning tools (Sheu & Chen, 2014), with technologies ranging from off the shelf solutions such as the Nintendo Wii to experimental prototypes including data gloves and tangibles being used to support learning in fields as diverse as motor skills, storytelling, and physics. Participatory simulations do not simply include the learners' gestures but their whole bodies, as children act as viruses spreading "infection" as they touch others (Colella, 2000) or investigate virtual earthquakes in their classrooms by physically enacting trilateration with real string and digital measures (Moher et al., 2015). Finally, approaches such as e-textiles (e.g. Kafai, Fields, & Searle, 2014) show how very traditional materials can be integrated with digital tools to support learning by MRC. Thus, MRC can be seen as a fundamental component of the Maker Movement (e.g. Halverson & Sheridan, 2014).

When considering tools that support collaboration and communication between people as they engage in MRC again there are many exciting possibilities to enrich the activity. For example, a multi-touch table project (Higgins, Mercier, Burd, & Joyce-Gibbons, 2012) allowed children to conduct a historical investigation using representational resources. This facilitated the grounding processes described above as representations more easily became the subject of joint attention and shared viewing as they were "left" on the table where they could be resized, moved, and reorganized, and additionally came to represent the history of joint decision making and ultimate consensus. Learners need not only be co-present physically or even temporally to engage in joint MRC – for example, there are many examples of argumentation tools where students can jointly construct diagrams that make salient key points whilst managing the task demands in chat (see Kirschner, Buckingham-Shum, & Carr, 2012). Moreover, even though the potential of MRC to be utilized for digital assessment had not received much attention, this is beginning to change. For example, BeSocratic (Bryfczynski et al., 2015) has been used to mark assignments and give formative feedback to college students studying chemistry and CogSketch has been used to grade geology assessments (Garnier et al., 2017). This is important as not only does MRC reveal insights that are otherwise difficult to accomplish, it also offers an approach to assessment that embodies key epistemic activities in the disciplinary area, providing instructors with important insight as well as modeling for students the intended outcomes of all their studies.

Nonetheless, the future of MRC is not only about new technological possibilities, it should also be about new theoretical insights into our understanding of these possibilities, about how pedagogical practices in schools and universities should adapt to this changing world and also exploring new sites for MRC such as those found in informal education and the home.

CONCLUSIONS

This review points to emerging complementary insights arising from research based on cognitivist and socio-semiotic perspectives on what and how students learn when they are guided in multi-representational construction. The first perspective highlights cognitive processing challenges students face and overcome in constructing and clarifying meanings across modes, whereas socio-semiotic researchers focus more on the affordances of different modes and the challenges (and opportunities) for students when they integrate modes to clarify emerging meanings and create new ones. Both perspectives have generated persuasive claims about learning gains when students engage in MRC, but raise many questions. In terms of formal education and curricular design, which tasks, production resources, and teacher guidance are most conducive to students' learning gains, and for which students? How do new technologies enable and constrain these learning gains and how (when relevant) can teacher support be incorporated? What background conceptual and representational understandings do students need to acquire (and how do they acquire these) to participate productively?

Given that constructing multiple and multimodal representations entails students engaging in creative, unscripted remaking and creation of new meanings through shifts in modes and modal integration, what frameworks should guide practice and assessment? To what extent can tacit and informal imaginative meaning-making processes within and across multiple mode construction be researched and programmed? While current research perspectives and methodologies provide leads on these questions, there is scope for more intensive investigation of what students do, why, and what they notice, find illuminating, or learn when they create, share, judge, and refine their representational constructions. Given that MRC entails creative and critical reasoning processes before, during, and after the act of construction, and often exceeds straightforward meaning replication, there is a need to research in more depth, the interactive activities that support students' reasoning and their creation, manipulation, and argumentation concerning disciplinary sign-making. We suggest that only by integrating the insights gained from ongoing research in the different research traditions noted in this chapter can we truly make progress in understanding and facilitating further the role of MRC as a key learning process.

ACKNOWLEDGMENT

Russell Tytler and Vaughan Prain's research was funded by the Australian Research Council.

REFERENCES

Ainsworth, S., Prain, V., & Tytler, R. (2011). Drawing to learn in science. *Science*, *333*(6046), 1096–1097.

Akkus, R., Gunel, M., & Hand, B. (2007). Comparing an inquiry-based approach known as the science writing heuristic to traditional science teaching practices: Are there differences? *International Journal of Science Education*, *29*(14), 1745–1765.

Breckinridge Church, R., & Goldin-Meadow, S. (1986). The mismatch between gesture and speech as an index of transitional knowledge. *Cognition*, *23*(1), 43–71.

Brown, A. (2015). 3D printing in instructional settings: Identifying a curricular hierarchy of activities. *TechTrends*, *59*(5), 16–24.

Bryfczynski, S., Pargas, R. P., Cooper, M. M., Klymkowsky, M., Hester, J., & Grove, N. P. (2015). Classroom uses for BeSocratic. In T. Hammond, S. Valentine, A. Adler, & M. Payton (Eds.), *The impact of pen and touch technology on education* (pp. 127–136). Cham: Springer International Publishing.

Chang, H. Y., Quintana, C., & Krajcik, J. S. (2010). The impact of designing and evaluating molecular animations on how well middle school students understand the particulate nature of matter. *Science Education*, *94*(1), 73–94.

Chen, Y. C., Park, S., & Hand, B. (2016). Examining the use of talk and writing for students' development of scientific conceptual knowledge through constructing and critiquing arguments. *Cognition and Instruction*, *34*(2), 100–147.

Chi, M. T. H. (2009). Active-constructive-interactive: A conceptual framework for differentiating learning activities. *Topics in Cognitive Science*, *1*(1), 73–105.

Chu, M., & Kita, S. (2011). The nature of gestures' beneficial role in spatial problem solving. *Journal of Experimental Psychology-General*, *140*(1), 102–116.

Clark, H. H., & Wilkes-Gibbs, D. (1986). Referring as a collaborative process. *Cognition*, *22*(1), 1–39.

Colella, V. (2000). Participatory simulations: Building collaborative understanding through immersive dynamic modeling. *Journal of the Learning Sciences*, *9*(4), 471–500.

Congdon, E. L., Novack, M. A., Brooks, N., Hemani-Lopez, N., O'Keefe, L., & Goldin-Meadow, S. (2017). Better together: Simultaneous presentation of speech and gesture in math instruction supports generalization and retention. *Learning and Instruction*, *50*, 65–74.

Cook, S. W., Mitchell, Z., & Goldin-Meadow, S. (2008). Gesturing makes learning last. *Cognition*, *106*(2), 1047–1058.

Cooper, M. M., Williams, L. C., & Underwood, S. M. (2015). Student understanding of intermolecular forces: A multimodal study. *Journal of Chemical Education*, *92*(8), 1288–1298.

Dillenbourg, P., & Traum, D. (2006). Sharing solutions: Persistence and grounding in multimodal collaborative problem solving. *Journal of the Learning Sciences*, *15*(1), 121–151.

diSessa, A. (2004). Metarepresentation: Native competence and targets for instruction. *Cognition and Instruction*, *22*(3), 293–331.

Duschl, R. (2008). Science education in three-part harmony: Balancing conceptual, epistemic, and social learning goals. *Review of Research in Education*, *32*(1), 268–291.

Elkins, J. (2011). Visual practices across the University: A report. In O. Grau (Ed.), *Imagery in the 21st century*. Cambridge, MA: MIT Press.

Fiorella, L., & Zhang, Q. (2018). Drawing boundary conditions for learning by drawing. *Educational Psychology Review*, *30*(3), 1115–1137.

Fischer, F., & Mandl, H. (2005). Knowledge convergence in computer-supported collaborative learning: The role of external representation tools. *Journal of the Learning Sciences*, *14*(3), 405–441.

Ford, M. J., & Forman, E. A. (2006). Redefining disciplinary learning in classroom contexts. In J. Green & A. Luke (Eds.), *Review of educational research* (vol. 30, pp. 1–32). Washington, DC: American Education Research Association.

Garnier, B., Chang, M., Ormand, C., Matlen, B., Tikoff, B., & Shipley, T. F. (2017). Promoting sketching in introductory geoscience courses: Cogsketch geoscience worksheets. *Topics in Cognitive Science*, *9*(4), 943–969.

Gilbert, J., Reiner, M., & Nakhleh, M. (Eds.). (2008). *Visualization: Theory and practice in science education*. Dordrecht: Springer.

Gobert, J. D., & Clement, J. J. (1999). Effects of student-generated diagrams versus student-generated summaries on conceptual understanding of causal and dynamic knowledge in plate tectonics. *Journal of Research in Science Teaching*, *36*(1), 39–53.

Goldin-Meadow, S., Cook, S. W., & Mitchell, Z. A. (2009). Gesturing gives children new ideas about math. *Psychological Science*, *20*(3), 267–272.

Goldin-Meadow, S., & Wagner, S. M. (2005). How our hands help us learn. *Trends in Cognitive Sciences*, *9*(5), 234–241.

Gooding, D. C. (2004). Cognition, construction and culture: Visual theories in the sciences. *Journal of Cognition and Culture*, *3*(4), 551–593.

Hall, R. (1996). Representation as shared activity: Situated cognition and Dewey's cartography of experience. *Journal of the Learning Sciences*, *5*(3), 209–238.

Halliday, M., & Martin, J. (1993). *Writing science: Literacy and discursive power*. London: Falmer Press.

Halverson, E. R., & Sheridan, K. (2014). The maker movement in education. *Harvard Educational Review*, *84*(4), 495–504.

Hand, B., & Choi, A. (2010). Examining the impact of student use of multiple modal representations in constructing arguments in organic chemistry laboratory classes. *Research in Science Education*, *40*(1), 29–44.

Heijnes, D., van Joolingen, W., & Leenaars, F. (2018). Stimulating scientific reasoning with drawing-based modeling. *Journal of Science Education and Technology*, *27*(1), 45–56.

Higgins, S., Mercier, E., Burd, L., & Joyce-Gibbons, A. (2012). Multi-touch tables and collaborative learning. *British Journal of Educational Technology*, *43*(6), 1041–1054.

Hubber, P., & Tytler, R. (2017). Enacting a representation construction approach to teaching and learning astronomy. In D. Treagust, R. Duit, & H. Fischer (Eds.), *Multiple representations in physics education* (pp. 139–161). London: Springer.

Hubber, P., Tytler, R., & Haslam, F. (2010). Teaching and learning about force with a representational focus: Pedagogy and teacher change. *Research in Science Education*, *40*(1), 5–28.

Hutchins, E. (1995). *Cognition in the wild*. Cambridge, MA: MIT Press.

Kafai, Y. B., Fields, D. A., & Searle, K. A. (2014). Electronic textiles as disruptive designs: Supporting and challenging maker activities in schools. *Harvard Educational Review*, *84*(4), 532–556.

Keys, C. W., Hand, B., Prain, V., & Collins, S. (1999). Using the scientific writing heuristic as a tool for learning from laboratory investigations in secondary science. *Journal of Research in Science Teaching*, *36*, 1065–1084.

Kirschner, P. A., Buckingham-Shum, S. J., & Carr, C. S. (2012). *Visualizing argumentation: Software tools for collaborative and educational sense-making*. Berlin: Springer.

Kita, S., Alibali, M. W., & Chu, M. (2017). How do gestures influence thinking and speaking? The gesture-for-conceptualization hypothesis. *Psychological Review, 124*(3), 245–266.

Klein, P. (2006). The challenges of scientific literacy: From the viewpoint of second-generation cognitive science. *International Journal of Science Education, 28*(2-3), 143–178.

Klein, U. (2001). *Tools and modes of representation in the laboratory sciences*. Dordrecht and Boston, MA: Kluwer Academic Publishers.

Knain, E., Fredlund, T., Furberg, A., Mathiassen, K., Remmen, K. B., & Ødegaard, M. (2017). Representing to learn in science education: Theoretical framework and analytical approaches. *Acta Didactica Norge, 11*(3), 1–22.

Kobiela, M., & Lehrer, R. (2019). Supporting dynamic conceptions of area and its measure. *Mathematical Thinking and Learning, 21*(3), 178–206.

Kress, G., & van Leeuwen, T. (2006). *Reading images: The grammar of visual design* (2nd ed.). London and New York: Routledge.

Latour, B. (1999). *Pandora's hope: Essays on the reality of science studies*. Cambridge, MA: Harvard University Press.

Latour, B. (1990). Visualisation and cognition: Drawing things together. In M. Lynch & S. Woolgar (Eds.), *Representation in scientific practice* (pp. 19–68). Cambridge, MA: MIT Press.

Lehrer, R., Kim, M. J., & Jones, R. S. (2011). Developing conceptions of statistics by designing measures of distribution. *ZDM, 43*(5), 723–736.

Lehrer, R., & Schauble, L. (2006). *Cultivating model-based reasoning in science education*. Cambridge: Cambridge University Press.

Lehrer, R., & Schauble, L. (2012). Seeding evolutionary thinking by engaging children in modeling its foundations. *Science Education, 96*(4), 701–724.

Lemke, J. (2004). The literacies of science. In E. W. Saul (Ed.), *Crossing borders in literacy and science instruction: Perspectives on theory and practice* (pp. 33–47). Newark, DE: International Reading Association/National Science Teachers Association.

Lohse, G. L., Biolsi, K., Walker, N., & Rueler, H. (1994). A classification of visual representations. *Communications of the A.C.M., 37*(12), 36–49.

Magnani, L. (2015). The eco-cognitive model of abduction: Naturalizing the logic of abduction. *Journal of Applied Logic, 13*(3), 285–315.

Maloney, J., Resnick, M., Rusk, N., Silverman, B., & Eastmond, E. (2010). The Scratch programming language and environment. *ACM Transactions on Computing Education (TOCE), 10*(4), 16:1–16:16.

Manz, E. (2012). Understanding the codevelopment of modeling practice and ecological knowledge. *Science Education, 96*(6), 1071–1105.

Mason, L., Lowe, R., & Tornatora, M. C. (2013). Self-generated drawings for supporting comprehension of a complex animation. *Contemporary Educational Psychology, 38*(3), 211–224.

Moher, T. (2015). Knowledge construction in the instrumented classroom: Supporting student investigations of their physical learning environment. In O. Lindwall, P. Hakkinen, K. T. Tchounikine, S. Ludvigsen, et al. (Eds.), *Exploring the material conditions of learning: The CSCL Conference* (vol. 2, pp. 548–551). Gothenburg, Sweden: ISLS.

Mulligan, J. (2015). Moving beyond basic numeracy: Data modeling in the early years of schooling. *ZDM, 47*(4), 653–663.

Nersessian, N. (2008). Model-based reasoning in scientific practice. In R. Duschl & R. Grandy (Eds.), *Teaching scientific inquiry: Recommendations for research and implementation* (pp. 57–79). Rotterdam: Sense Publishers.

Novack, M. A., Congdon, E. L., Hemani-Lopez, N., & Goldin-Meadow, S. (2014). From action to abstraction: Using the hands to learn math. *Psychological Science, 25*(4), 903–910.

Novack, M. A., & Goldin-Meadow, S. (2017). Gesture as representational action: A paper about function. *Psychonomic Bulletin and Review, 24*(3), 652–665.

Peirce, C. S. (1931-58). *Collected papers of Charles Sanders Peirce* (vols. 1–6, Ed. C. Hartshorne, P. Weiss, and A. W. Burks, vols. 7–8, Ed. Arthur W. Burks). Cambridge, MA: Harvard University Press.

Ploetzner, R., & Fillisch, B. (2017). Not the silver bullet: Learner-generated drawings make it difficult to understand broader spatiotemporal structures in complex animations. *Learning and Instruction, 47*, 13–24.

Prain, V., & Hand, B. (2016). Coming to know more through and from writing. *Educational Researcher, 45*(7), 430–434.

Prain, V., & Tytler, R. (2012). Learning through constructing representations in science: A framework of representational construction affordances. *International Journal of Science Education, 34*(17), 2751–2773.

Roschelle, J., & Teasley, S. D. (1995). The construction of shared knowledge in collaborative problem solving. In C. O'Malley (Ed.), *Computer supported collaborative learning* (pp. 69–97). Berlin: Springer-Verlag.

Scheiter, K., Schleinschok, K., & Ainsworth, S. (2017). Why sketching may aid learning from science texts: Contrasting sketching with written explanations. *Topics in Cognitive Science, 9*(4), 866–882.

Schwamborn, A., Mayer, R. E., Thillmann, H., Leopold, C., & Leutner, D. (2010). Drawing as a generative activity and drawing as a prognostic activity. *Journal of Educational Psychology, 102*(4), 872–879.

Schwartz, D. L. (1995). The emergence of abstract representations in dyad problem solving. *Journal of the Learning Sciences, 4*(3), 321–354.

Sheu, F.-R., & Chen, N.-S. (2014). Taking a signal: A review of gesture-based computing research in education. *Computers and Education, 78*, 268–277.

Stieff, M., Lira, M. E., & Scopelitis, S. A. (2016). Gesture supports spatial thinking in STEM. *Cognition and Instruction, 34*(2), 80–99.

Suthers, D. D. (2014). *Empirical studies of the value of conceptually explicit notations in collaborative learning: Knowledge cartography* (pp. 1–22). London: Springer.

Tytler, R., Prain, V., & Hubber, P. 2018. Representation construction as a core science disciplinary literacy. In K.-S. Tang & K. Danielsson (Eds.), *Global developments in literacy research for science education* (pp. 301–317). Dordrecht: Springer.

Tytler, R., Prain, V., Hubber, P., & Waldrip, B. (2013). *Constructing representations to learn in science*. Rotterdam: Sense Publishers.

Van Meter, P., Aleksic, M., Schwartz, A., & Garner, J. (2006). Learner-generated drawing as a strategy for learning from content area text. *Contemporary Educational Psychology, 31*(2), 142–166.

Van Meter, P., & Firetto, C. (2013). Cognitive model of drawing construction: Learning through the construction of drawings. In G. Schraw, M. McCrudden, & D. Robinson (Eds.), *Learning through visual displays* (pp. 248–280). Scottsdale, AZ: Information Age Publishing.

Volkwyn, T., Airey, J., Gregorčič, B., & Heijkenskjöld, F. (2016). Multimodal transduction in secondary school physics. 8th International Conference on Multimodality, December 7–9, 2016. Cape Town, South Africa. http://urn.kb.se/resolve?urn=urn:nbn:se:uu:diva-316982.

Vygotsky, L. S. (1978). *Mind in society*. Cambridge, MA: Harvard University Press.

Waldrip, B., Prain, V., & Carolan, J. (2010). Using multi-modal representations to improve learning in junior secondary science. *Research in Science Education, 40*(1), 65–80.

Wu, S. P. W., & Rau, M. A. (2018). Effectiveness and efficiency of adding drawing prompts to an interactive educational technology when learning with visual representations. *Learning and Instruction, 55*, 93–104.

Zhang, Z. H., & Linn, M. C. (2011). Can generating representations enhance learning with dynamic visualizations?. *Journal of Research in Science Teaching, 48*(10), 1177–1198.

8

PROBLEM SOLVING IN MATHEMATICS WITH MULTIPLE REPRESENTATIONS

Despina A. Stylianou
CITY COLLEGE OF NEW YORK

ABSTRACT

Mathematics education has been a strong advocate of representation use. A multitude of studies have shown that representations can be a valuable tool during problem solving both in mathematics and in all the related sciences that use mathematics tools and theory. In this chapter we explore the various ways in which representations are used during problem solving as well as the various challenges associated with representation use and we make recommendations for further work in this area.

Key words: mathematics education, problem solving, representation, modeling, mathematical processes

Over the past two decades the mathematics education community has been increasingly viewing representations as "useful tools for communicating both information and understanding" (National Council of Teachers of Mathematics, 2000, p. 64). This awareness that representation is central to mathematics is clearly reflected in recent reform efforts, especially in the United States. It is particularly obvious in the position of the National Council of Teachers of Mathematics (NCTM) who in their national standards document elevated the status of representation to one of five process standards, that is, one of five broad goals of what mathematics instruction should enable students to do. It is now recommended that students at all levels "create and use representations to organize, record, and communicate mathematical ideas; select, apply, and translate among mathematical representations to solve problems; and use representations to model and interpret physical, social, and mathematical phenomena" (NCTM, 2000, p. 64). In other words, it is advocated that students should be fluent users of representations and classroom instruction should support students in learning how to navigate mathematical concepts and problem solving through the use of these multiple representations. More recently, NCTM reaffirmed its position on representation by designating representation as one of the eight effective teaching practices in Principles to Actions (National Council of Teachers of Mathematics, 2014). The "Use and Connect Mathematical Representations" practice describes teachers' and students' use of representations as a tool that enables the exploration and justification of mathematical ideas (Goldin & Shteingold, 2001). It is noted that "effective teaching of mathematics engages students in making connections among mathematical representations to deepen understanding of mathematics concepts and procedures and as tools for problem solving" (National Council of Teachers of Mathematics, 2014, p. 24). In other words, as students engage with representation, and they express, and justify their thinking through connections between representations, they demonstrate deeper conceptual understandings (Fuson, Kalchman, & Bransford, 2005).

As mathematics underlies reasoning across science and applied science disciplines (e.g., physics, engineering, and even biological sciences), one can argue that representation is a useful tool in most science as well. For example, in most sciences one works with data, various forms of data visualization such as graphs, as well as diagrams, tables, and symbols. Hence, by extension, we argue that questions of how representations are used and understood in mathematics are foundational to understanding how these are used in other sciences, technological, and applied disciplines.

In mathematics, the notion of multiple representations is quite specific. Hence, before we continue any further, we pause to consider what are these specific types of representations used in mathematics. A shared set of categories of representations has gradually emerged from the work in mathematics education, including five types of representations: visual, symbolic, verbal, contextual, and physical (Lesh, Post, & Behr, 1987b). Lesh and Doerr (2012) added two more types of representations, graphical and tabular, to this list. It is expected that one of the goals of mathematics instruction is to build capacity for students to move fluidly and with ease between representations as they engage in problem solving, as is shown in Figure 8.1 adapted from Lesh et al.

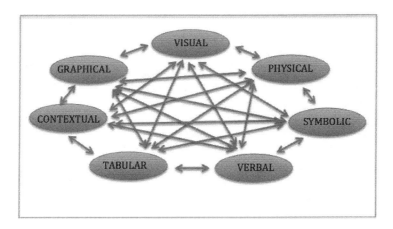

Figure 8.1 Five Types of Representations in Mathematics Problem Solving.

(1987b). Tripathi (2008) noted that using these "different representations is like examining [a mathematical] concept through a variety of lenses, with each lens providing a different perspective that makes the concept richer and deeper" (p. 439).

The figure depicts representations as connected nodes. It is argued that the depth of students' understanding is related to the strength of those connections among the various mathematical representations (Pape & Tchoshanov, 2001) as well as students' ability to move flexibly among representations (Stylianou & Silver, 2004). Students should be able to approach a problem from several points of view and be encouraged to switch among different representations until they are able to understand the situation and choose a path that will lead them to a successful solution.

In the sections that follow, first, we provide a theoretical background on representation in mathematics, and we describe the varied representations that teachers and students may use in the course of mathematics teaching and learning. Second, we describe the relationship between students' use of and connections between varied representations alongside their deepening mathematical understanding. In particular, we illustrate how students begin to see representational systems as tools for solving and communicating their thinking across a variety of problem types and we highlight challenges and questions with respect to representation that remain open for us to explore.

BACKGROUND ON REPRESENTATION

Note that researchers in mathematics education do not always agree on what representation means[1] (English, 1997; Goldin, 1998; Presmeg, 1997) and, thus, have adopted various theoretical perspectives to study the role of representation in problem solving (e.g., Cifarelli, 1998; Goldin, 1998; Kaput, 1998). Representations are broadly viewed as configurations that "stand for" or represent particular concepts, mental images, or processes. They are the choices we make for expressing mathematical ideas and the ways in which we use them. But despite the difficulty in articulating a tight definition for representation, mathematics educators have been able to identify the types of multiple representations that are used in mathematics: they can be drawings, diagrams, physical models, and also mathematical symbols – in short, the range of symbolic tools that can be used for representing aspects of the world.

As such, "'the term representation refers both to process and product – to the act of capturing a mathematical concept or relationship in some form and to the form itself'" (National Council of Teachers of Mathematics, 2000, p. 67). Hence, representation is an essential part of the mathematical activity and a vehicle for capturing mathematical concepts (e.g., Ball, 1993; Cai, 2005; Cobb, 2003; Cobb, Stephen, McClain, & Gravemeijer, 2002; Dufour-Janvier, Bednarz, & Belanger, 1987; Gravemeijer, Lehrer, Van Oers, & Verschaffel, 2002; Kaput, Noss, & Hoyles, 2008; Meira, 2003; Nunokawa, 1994).

With respect to "representation as process," research in mathematics education at a theoretical level has suggested a number of processes for working with representations. For example, Janvier (1987) described translation – the cognitive process of moving among different representations of the same mathematical concept as a way to better navigate one's way through problem solving. Kaput (1991) discussed the need to understand the cognitive processes for constructing and interpreting representations. It has been argued that the evolution of representational ability and the evolution of mathematical conceptions are mutually supportive (Lehrer & Schauble, 2002). Hence, the development of students' ability to represent ideas in different ways is fundamental to mathematical work.

With respect to "representation as product," empirical work has examined students' difficulties in understanding and using representations, particularly graphical and visual representations. For example, students are known to interpret graphs literally, including reading motion graphs as "walking paths" (Leinhardt, Zaslavsky, & Stein, 1990). These difficulties students face are contrasted with evidence that individuals who are skilled in problem solving in fact rely on multiple representations including visual representations as tools that add information in this process (e.g., Ochs, Jacoby, & Gonzales, 1994; Stylianou, 2002). One of the reasons underlying students' difficulties may be the fact that representations have often been taught and learned as if they were ends in themselves (Eisenberg & Dreyfus, 1994; Greeno & Hall, 1997; National Council of Teachers of Mathematics, 2000) – an approach that limits the power and utility of representations as tools for learning and doing mathematics.

REPRESENTATION IN INDIVIDUAL PROBLEM SOLVING

Representation is central to a person's understanding of a mathematical concept and a person's problem-solving activity. In particular, it has been argued that the use of a variety of representations, or multiple representations in a flexible manner, has the potential to making the learning of mathematics more meaningful and effective. Each representation has specific strengths, but it also has disadvantages, hence, their combined use can be a more effective tool by showing different facets of one mathematical idea (Cuoco, 2001; Kaput, 1992; National Council of Teachers of Mathematics, 2000).

The ability to choose an appropriate representation in mathematics and to "capitalize on the strengths of a given representation is an important component of understanding mathematical ideas" (Lesh, Behr, & Post, 1987a, p. 56). Similarly, different representations may need to be constructed for specific purposes during the problem-solving process and each one of these representations may serve a different purpose. A review of the literature on mathematical problem solving using the lens of representation suggests that representations can be used as tools to facilitate different subtasks of the process of problem solving (see Pimm, 1987; Stylianou, 2008).

(a) As a means to understand the information provided in the problem situation and set goals – one uses representation as a tool that helps one combine different aspects of the problem so as to see all the constraints and affordances of the problem and how these interact with one another. This is an important function of representation, as, often, not all aspects of a problem situation are immediately obvious to the reader (e.g., Schoenfeld, 1985).
(b) As recording tools – one uses a representation as a tool that combines all the information provided in the problem statement instead of trying to keep it "all in the mind." A representation may provide a compact and efficient means to record these thoughts (e.g., Newell & Simon, 1972).
(c) As tools that facilitate exploration of the concepts or problems at hand – one uses the representation as a flexible device that allows one to manipulate the

concepts at hand and reveal further information and implications of the given situation (e.g., Stylianou & Silver, 2004).

(d) As monitoring and evaluating devices to assess progress in problem solving (e.g., Gibson, 1998; Izsák & Gamoran Sherin, 2003). In this case, one may use a representation as a way to monitor her/his progress in problem solving and to make informed decisions when selecting subsequent goals and maintaining or revising current plans.

In an earlier study (Stylianou & Silver, 2004), I highlighted each of these four roles, particularly in the work of expert mathematicians. In that study, as each mathematician was given a problem to solve, they started using different representations (graphs, diagrams, symbolic notation) as they read the task, as a means of gathering and understanding the problem (first tool). They then often started annotating their representations as they began to explore the problem instead of keeping these exploratory thoughts in their heads, hence using their representations as recording tools (second tool). They subsequently changed their representation as they progressed in their thinking, looking for new information that could be missing or went unnoticed initially (third tool). Finally, as they made progress towards their solutions, they kept going back to their initial representations, checking that they were on track (fourth tool).

This discussion not only illustrates the different roles representation may play, but it also suggests that the meaning and utility of a representation can shift as problem-solving purposes and difficulties change, as is often the case in the work of expert mathematicians or by experienced users of mathematics (Hall, 1989; Stylianou & Silver, 2004). For research purposes, a representation generated by a student is a record of the process used during problem solving. Hence, as Cai (2005) suggests, a representation can be viewed in a similar manner to the solution strategies used in the solution process and can reveal similar information about the solver's reasoning.

Within this domain of individual representation use, some researchers have also explored affective factors such as the representational preferences of students. Most notably, DeBellis and Goldin (2006) performed a series of studies that suggested that feelings of success or frustration that students may experience in problem solving while engaging with a particular representation may impact (positively or negatively respectively) their subsequent interest in using that representation. Hence, these personal affective factors can impact students' interactions with representations.

REPRESENTATION AS A SOCIAL ACTIVITY IN MATHEMATICS

The complexities of representation use extend beyond its use as an individual or cognitive practice, to its use as a social process, closely related to students' understanding of the concepts and situations being represented (Monk, 2003). From this perspective, recent studies are beginning to address the complexities involved in negotiating individually constructed representations in the shared space of a group or a classroom as well as the teacher's role in facilitating these interactions (e.g., Gravemeijer et al., 2002; Silver, Ghousseini, Gosen, Charalambous, & Font Strawhun, 2005; Stein, Engle,

Smith, & Hughes, 2008). This work has emphasized the role of discourse and mechanisms, such as negotiation of meaning, by which taken-as-shared interpretations and uses of representation are established in classrooms (e.g., Cobb, Yackel, & McClain, 2000; Hall & Rubin, 1998; Sfard, 2000).

Hence from a social perspective, representations are used as tools to understand the mathematical concepts at hand and solve problems, but also as modes of communicating about these concepts and problem solving (e.g., Roth & McGinn, 1997). This use of representation fits relatively well with those found among mathematicians as well as the applied mathematics community (e.g., physicists and engineers). For example, Hall and Stevens (1995) studied the activity of civil engineers working on design projects and highlighted the various roles different representations (sketches, graphs, and sets of measurements) took on while the members of the design team communicated to each other different ideas and concerns they might have, and the central role these representations had during the negotiation of the final specifications of the proposed projects. In the realm of science, Ochs et al. (1994) analyzed the work of a group of physicists to show how professionals use representations to create a shared world of understanding. They described, for example, the visual representation used during a particular conversation as a "'stage on which scientists dramatize understanding of their own and others' works'" and argued that physicists are using this stage in such a way that "'when narrators are speaking, gesturing, and drawing, they are thus asking co-participants not only to look through the graph to some represented world but also at the graph as a referential object in and of itself'" (Ochs et al., 1994, p. 10).

REPRESENTATION IN INSTRUCTION

Teachers use representations as an integral part of their daily instruction. A representation is a vital part of explanations teachers provide of new concepts, illustrations of problem-solving processes, and to create connections among concepts. In the process of introducing a new concept, teachers often use more than one representation as "any representation will express some but not all of the information, stress some aspects and hide others" (Dreyfus & Eisenberg, 1996, pp. 267–268). Some representations may be more appropriate in illustrating a particular concept or process (Cobb, Yackel, & Wood, 1992; Leinhardt, 2001). However, as teachers may experience difficulties with mathematical content, they may also have gaps in their ability to use representations when doing and teaching mathematics (e.g., see Izsák & Gamoran Sherin, 2003). While the recommendations for increased and fluid use of representations in mathematics classrooms place significant demands on teachers, there is little evidence that teachers have received the necessary support to implement them; there is little evidence that either professional development programs or teacher preparation programs have been preparing teachers and prospective teachers to meet these demands and integrate them in instruction successfully (Ball, 1997; Ball & Cohen, 1999; Lampert & Ball, 1998; Putnam & Borko, 1997; Stein et al., 2008). Consequently, research is needed to study the teachers' conceptions of representation in the context of school mathematics, aiming to form a basis for suggestions to improve teacher education programs in that area.

Greeno (1987) examined the use of representation during mathematics instruction and suggests that, similar to the case of individual problem solving, different representations of the same mathematical concept or task can facilitate different subtasks of instruction. For example, a teacher may use a particular representation to facilitate an instructional explanation; that is, a representation can be an explanation tool (see, e.g., Leinhardt, 2001). The choice of a representation shared in class can impact the classroom discussion and help the teacher focus students' attention on particular mathematical connections and concepts; that is, representations can be tools that facilitate classroom discussion (e.g., Stein et al., 2008).

Finally, student-generated representations during problem solving can be used by the teacher as assessment tools to gain better insight into student reasoning (e.g., Stylianou, Kenney, Silver, & Alacaci, 2000; see also Ainsworth, Tytler, & Prain, Chapter 7). Cai (2005), who examined US and Chinese teachers' construction of representations to teach mathematics, found that the two groups of teachers use different types of representations. His analysis of these representations used in instruction by the two groups of teachers showed a different conceptual emphasis, differences in ways teachers evaluated student representations and solutions. This suggests that differences in teachers' values of representation can have an impact on teaching.

I mentioned earlier that students are having difficulty negotiating the various forms and functions of representations (see Heinze, Star, & Verschaffel, 2009; Nistal, Van Dooren, Clarebout, Elen, & Veschaffel, 2009). Similarly, for teachers, the use of multiple, conceptually based representations is a new dimension to the teaching of mathematics and many may have few instructional tools at their disposal to facilitate their students' development of this practice (see, e.g., Izsák & Gamoran Sherin, 2003; Stylianou, 2010).

SYMBOLIZATION AND MODELING IN REPRESENTATION ACTIVITY

We have observed a growing interest within the mathematics education community in the role of symbolization and modeling as part of representation. Indeed, the Common Core State Standards document (National Governors Association Center for Best Practices & Council of Chief State School Officers, 2010) no longer mentions representation as a core mathematical practice, but, instead, has elevated "model with mathematics" as one of eight core "processes and proficiencies" that "mathematics educators at all levels should seek to develop in their students" (p. 1).

The shift in the direction of "models and modeling" rather than "representations and representing" grew, partly, due to critique from both constructivist scholars and those who work within the framework of socio-cultural theory[2] – the two theories that dominate mathematics education currently. The former criticized a tendency to use external representations, particularly manipulatives, as bearers of meaning, while the latter also noted that representations or material objects only acquire meaning in social practices (Gravemeijer et al., 2002). Hence, instead of viewing representation as a mirror to reality, scholars start from the assumption of "models as structured forms of symbolization that can be taken as tools for organizing reality and communicating about it" (van Oers, 2002, p. 25).

The ultimate goal remains that students use representations to learn about concepts and procedures and as tools to solve future problems. Van Den HeuvelzPanhuizen (2003) refers to these student uses of representation as *model of* and *model for* – signifying the distinction between models that are developed as a representation of a problem situation and those that have become generalized tools *for* solving problems. In fact, Gravemeijer (1999) described four levels of mathematical activity that closely relate to models and modeling – problem-solving activity within the task, activity that refers back to work in the task, general activity, and formal activity. Students are expected to move gradually from the activity within the task to formal activity, that is, activity that allows them to generalize from the specific situation at hand to other, broader situations. As is often the case with development, this move is rarely linear; as students work with representations, they often move back and forth from the concrete representation to the abstraction.

This is a dynamic process of gaining and losing information in their representations; losing contextual detail and gaining abstracted information. Note that, particularly for students, representation is *dynamic*. Not only do students create and manipulate their own representations of problem situations, but students' representations co-evolve along with their reasoning as their reasoning becomes more abstract.

This dynamic, iterative cycle of representing and gradually altering one's representation to gain new meanings has also been described in the research literature as a "chain of signification" (e.g., Gravemeijer et al., 2002; Meira, 2002; Presmeg, 1997). A sign – a signifier of another object – gradually takes on a meaning in itself and can be acted on.

Representations, in this sense, are tools for understanding, exploration, and communication (Stylianou, 2011) and, as such, they are never invented in their final form. Their evolution sheds light on the evolution of student thinking, hence, allowing the teacher to provide appropriate support and scaffolding. When the students are grounded in the context, the teacher can see that the students are grappling with understanding the constraints of the task. It has been shown that highly contextual and specific representations – what Bieda and Nathan (2009) call grounding – might have negative impact on students' performance. Bieda and Nathan (2009) and Kaminski, Sloutsky, and Heckler (2008) conducted studies that showed that strong contextualizing and specific representations might direct learners towards superficial properties and distract them from the underlying mathematical structure, resulting in limited learning and difficulty in transferring learning.

Throughout my past work, students used representations as presentation tools for their work, both informally to their peers in their groups, and more formally to present their solutions to their class. Students also used their representations as tools to negotiate and co-construct meaning and strategy with their peers. In a particular task (Stylianou, 2011), students were asked to consider how many people can be seated when several tables are connected. While the reader is referred to the full article for more detail (Stylianou, 2011), observations of students' work in the study showed that their representations evolved gradually from the specific to the abstract and as that shift happened, so the students' thinking evolved from specific arithmetic to general and symbolic.

Abstracted representations appeared also to facilitate the creation of connections or relations among tasks or situations. Students established these connections when they noticed a similarity in representing situations, or a similarity in actions they performed on the representation during their explorations. When a few days later, students were asked to work on a growth pattern involving triangles, they soon noticed the connection with the square table task and their representations moved to the more general type more easily.

In order for students to see representations as generalized tools for solving problems (i.e., moving from "model of" to "model for"), they must consider a particular representation as appropriate in the given problem situation and judge it against other possible representations (Lesh & Doerr, 2012; Lesh & Zawojewski, 2007). Furthermore, students must interpret the underlying mathematical structures and relationships highlighted through the representation and then identify other mathematical situations that maintain the corresponding structure. Doing so requires mathematical representations to be viewed as part of a wider system within which meanings and conventions have been established (Goldin & Shteingold, 2001, p. 1), rather than an isolated *model of* any particular problem situation. Correspondingly, students' abilities to see representations as *models for* require flexibility in moving between representations modes (Lesh et al., 1987b; Superfine, Canty, & Marshall, 2009).

DIRECTIONS FOR FUTURE WORK

In this chapter we have looked closely at the research on representations in the teaching and learning of mathematics. We have seen the notion rise to significance in national standards documents and become one of the core aspects in calls for reform. But where does research stand and what are the questions that remain open for moving forward?

Cai and his colleagues (2014) when discussing mathematical modeling and its progress identified five areas for discussion: mathematics, cognition, curriculum, instruction, and teacher education. I will follow their lead in this chapter when discussing representations in mathematics education.

There is no question that representations are a part of mathematics, both applied and theoretical. And while we have begun to understand differences in how expert mathematicians and younger students use representations, more needs to be done to understand these differences and similarities and to create a roadmap for those expert uses of representations to be developed by students. Similarly, there has been a substantial body of work on the cognitive aspects of representation in mathematics, particularly in mathematics learning. Initially, this work focused on challenges that students face when attempting to use representations when engaging with problem solving, but over the past decade more nuanced work has shown that students are capable of using representations during problem solving in a way that is fruitful in their development. Indeed, students' use of representation allows them to engage with abstraction and generalization in encouraging ways. While this work is far from completed, more work needs to be done to capitalize on our understandings of students' use (and difficulties) in using representations in curriculum and instruction, particularly how teachers might encourage and scaffold the use of representations in mathematical problem solving in broader and more flexible ways. It is not clear how teachers engage their students in representation, and how they do so. Our current understanding of what happens in classrooms with respect to representation, including both instruction and assessment, is lacking. Questions remain as to how we can build representationally rich classrooms, and how to further infuse the use of representations in curriculum and instruction, particularly as a process rather than just a product.

In fact, just as our understanding of what happens in classrooms with respect to representation is lacking, we know even less about the role of representation in teachers' own training and education that might guide their work in the classroom. Despite our progress on understanding students' thinking about representation and engagement with the various representation, I am not sure that this work has found its way in teacher preparation programs around the world. In fact, we have good reason to believe that discrepancies between students' eagerness to use representation and teacher preparation is common.

In the opening paragraph of this chapter, I highlighted the education community's interest in representations, and the prominent role that representation has been gaining in reform efforts. Given these strong interests in representation in mathematics and its central role in current policy statements on the teaching and learning of mathematics, it is important that work on representation continues particularly in the context of classrooms.

NOTES

1. As Presmeg (2006) noted, the term representation "became imbued with various meanings and connotations in the changing paradigms of the last two decades" (p. 206). She further notes that the mathematics education community has had difficulty articulating an accurate definition of this term. Presmeg continues to quote Kaput (1987) that "an indication of this difficulty is that definitions for the term 'representation' often include the word 'represent'". Hence several researchers prefer to use the term "inscriptions" rather than representations. Here, I maintain the use of representation to stay closer to the majority of the literature; however, I use it as synonymous to "inscription."
2. Modeling is, of course, broader than simply a critique to representation as a bearer for meaning. Modeling has its roots in the 19th century, as a part of an effort to contextualize mathematics and make mathematics more application-oriented. Please see Kaiser (2017) for a historical view of modeling.

REFERENCES

Ball, D. L. (1993). Halves, pieces and twoths: Constructing and using representational contexts in teaching fractions. In T. Carpenter, E. Fennema, & T. Romberg (Eds.), *Rational numbers: An integration of research* (pp. 328–375). Hillsdale, NJ: Lawrence Erlbaum Associates, Inc.

Ball, D. L. (1997). What do students know? Facing challenges of distance, context, and desire in trying to hear children. In B. Biddle, T. Good, & I. Goodson (Eds.), *International handbook on teachers and teaching* (pp. 769–817). Dordrecht: Kluwer Academic Press.

Ball, D. L., & Cohen, D. (1999). Developing practice, developing practitioners: Toward a practice-based theory of professional education. In G. Sykes & L. Darling-Hammond (Eds.), *Teaching as the learning profession: Handbook of policy and practice* (pp. 3–32). San Francisco, CA: Jossey-Bass.

Bieda, K., & Nathan, M. (2009). Representational disfluency in algebra: Evidence from student gestures and speech. *ZDM-The International Journal on Mathematics Education, 41*, 637–650.

Cai, J. (2005). US and Chinese teachers' constructing, knowing and evaluating representations to teach mathematics. *Mathematical Thinking and Learning, 7*, 135–169.

Cai, J., Cirillo, M., Pelesko, J. A., Borromeo Ferri, R., Borba, M., Geiger, V., ... Kwon, O. N. (2014). Mathematical modeling in school education: Mathematical, cognitive, curricular, instructional and teacher education perspectives. In P. Liljedahl, C. Nicol, S. Oesterle, & D. Allan (Eds.), *Proceedings of the joint meeting of PME 38 and PME-NA 36* (vol. 1, pp. 145–172). Vancouver: PME.

Cifarelli, V. (1998). The development of mental representations as a problem solving activity. *Journal of Mathematical Behavior, 17*, 239–264.

Cobb, P. (2003). Modeling, symbolizing, and tool use in statistical data analysis. In K. Gravemeijer, R. Lehrer, B. van Oers, & L. Verschaffel (Eds.), *Symbolizing, modeling and tool use in mathematics education* (pp. 171–198). Dordrecht: Kluwer Academic Press.

Cobb, P., & Bauersfeld, H. (1995). *The emergence of mathematical meaning: Interaction in classroom cultures.* Hillsdale, NJ: Lawrence Erlbaum.

Cobb, P., Stephen, M., McClain, K., & Gravemeijer, K. (2002). Participating in classroom mathematical practices. *Journal of the Learning Sciences, 10*(1/2), 113–163.

Cobb, P., & Yackel, E. (1995). Constructivist, emergent, and sociocultural perspectives in the context of developmental research. In *Proceedings of PME-NA XXVII.* Roanoke, VA.

Cobb, P., & Yackel, E. (1996). Constructivist, emergent, and sociocultural perspectives in the context of developmental research. *Educational Psychologist, 31*, 175–190.

Cobb, P., Yackel, E., & McClain, K. (2000). *Symbolizing and communicating in mathematics classrooms: Perspectives on discourse, tools, and instructional design.* Mahwah, NJ: Lawrence Erlbaum.

Cobb, P., Yackel, E., & Wood, T. (1992). A constructivist alternative to the representational view of mind in mathematics education. *Journal for Research in Mathematics Education, 29*, 306–333.

Cuoco, A. (2001). *The roles of representation in school mathematics* (2001 Yearbook). Reston, VA: NCTM.

de Jong, T., Ainsworth, S., Dobson, M., van der Hulst, A., Levonen, J., & Reimann, P. (1998). Acquiring knowledge in science and math: The use of multiple representations in technology-based learning environments. In M. W. van Someren, P. Reimann, H. P. A. Boshuizen, & T. de Jong (Eds.), *Learning with multiple representations* (pp. 9–40). Amsterdam: Pergamon.

DeBellis, V., & Goldin, G. (2006). Affect and meta-affect in mathematical problem solving. A representational perspective. *Educational Studies in Mathematics, 63*(2), 131–147.

Dreyfus, T., & Eisenberg, T. (1996). On different facets of mathematical thinking. In R. J. Sternberg & T. Ben-Zeev (Eds.), *The nature of mathematical thinking* (pp. 253–284). Hillsdale, NJ: Lawrence Erlbaum Associates.

Dufour-Janvier, B., Bednarz, N., & Belanger, M. (1987). Pedagogical considerations concerning the problem of representation. In C. Janvier (Ed.), *Problems of representation in the teaching and learning of mathematical problem solving* (pp. 109–122). Hillsdale, NJ: Lawrence Erlbaum Associates.

Eisenberg, T., & Dreyfus, T. (1994). On understanding how students learn to visualize function transformations. *Research in Collegiate Mathematics Education, 1*, 45–68.

English, L. D. (1997). *Mathematical reasoning: Analogies, metaphors and images.* Mahwah, NJ: Lawrence Erlbaum Associates.

Fuson, K., Kalchman, M., & Bransford, J. D. (2005). Mathematical understanding: An introduction. In M. S. Donovan & J. D. Bransford (Eds.), *How students learn: History, mathematics, and science in the classroom* (pp. 217–256). Washington, DC: National Academies Press.

Goldin, G., & Shteingold, N. (2001). Systems of representations and the development of mathematical concepts. In A. Cuoco & F. Curcio (Eds.), *The roles of representation in school mathematics: 63rd yearbook of the National Council of Teachers of Mathematics* (pp. 1–23). Reston, VA: NCTM.

Goldin, G. A. (1998). Representational systems, learning, and problem solving in mathematics. *Journal of Mathematical Behavior, 17*, 137–165.

Gravemeijer, K. (1999). How emergent models may foster the constitution of formal mathematics. *Mathematical Thinking and Learning, 1*, 155–177.

Gravemeijer, K., Lehrer, R., Van Oers, B., & Verschaffel, L. (2002). *Symbolizing, modeling and tool use in mathematics education.* Dordrecht: Kluwer Academic Press.

Greeno, J. (1987). Instructional representations based on research about understanding. In A. Schoenfeld (Ed.), *Cognitive science and mathematics education* (pp. 61–88). New York: Academic Press.

Greeno, J., & Hall, R. (1997). Practicing representation. *Phi Delta Kappan, 78*(5), 361–368.

Hall, R. (1989). Exploring the episodic structure of algebra story problem solving. *Cognition and Instruction, 6*, 223–283.

Hall, R., & Rubin, A. (1998). There's five little notches in here: Dilemmas in teaching and learning the conventional structure of rate. In J. Greeno & S. Goldman (Eds.), *Thinking practices in mathematics and science learning* (pp. 189–235). Mahwah, NJ: Lawrence Erlbaum Associates, Inc.

Hall, R., & Stevens, R. (1995). Making space. In S. Star (Ed.), *The cultures of computing* (pp. 118–145). London: Basil Blackwell.

Heinze, A., Star, J., & Verschaffel, L. (2009). Flexible and adaptive use of strategies and representations in mathematics education. *ZDM-the International Journal on Mathematics Education, 41*, 535–540.

Izsák, A., & Gamoran Sherin, M. (2003). Exploring the use of new representations as a resource for teacher learning. *School Science and Mathematics, 103*, 18–27.

Janvier, C. (1987). Translation processes in mathematics education. In C. Janvier (Ed.), *Problems of representation in the teaching and learning of mathematics* (pp. 27–32). Hillsdale, NJ: Lawrence Erlbaum Associates.

Kaiser, G. (2017). The teaching and learning of mathematical modeling. In J. Cai (Ed.), *Compendium for research in mathematics education* (pp. 267–290). Reston, VA: NCTM.

Kaminski, J., Sloutsky, V., & Heckler, A. (2008). The advantage of abstract examples in learning math. *Science, 320*, 454–455.

Kaput, J. (1987). Representational systems and mathematics. In C. Janvier (Ed.), *Problems of representation in the teaching and learning of mathematics* (pp. 19–26). Hillsdale, NJ: Lawrence Erlbaum.

Kaput, J. J. (1991). Notations and representations as mediators of constructive process. In E. von Glasersfeld (Ed.), *Radical constructivism in mathematics education* (pp. 53–74). Dordrecht: Kluwer.

Kaput, J. J. (1992). Technology and mathematics education. In D. Grouws (Ed.), *Handbook of research on mathematics teaching and learning*. New York: Macmillan.

Kaput, J. J. (1998). Representations, inscriptions, descriptions and learning: A kaleidoscope of windows. *Journal of Mathematical Behavior, 17*(2), 265–281.

Kaput, J. J., Noss, R., & Hoyles, C. (2008). Developing new notations for a learnable mathematics in the computational era. In L. English (Ed.), *Handbook of international research in mathematics education* (2nd ed., pp. 693–715). New York: Routledge, Taylor & Francis.

Lampert, M., & Ball, D. (1998). *Teaching, multimedia and mathematics: Investigations of real practice*. New York: Teachers College Press.

Lehrer, R., & Schauble, L. (2002). Symbolic communication in mathematics and science: Co-constructing inscription and thought. In E. Amsel (Ed.), *The development of symbolic communication* (pp. 167–192). Mahwah, NJ: Erlbaum.

Leinhardt, G. (2001). Instructional explanations: A commonplace for teaching and location for contrast. In V. Richardson (Ed.), *Handbook for research on teaching* (pp. 333–357). Washington, DC: American Education Research Association.

Leinhardt, G., Zaslavsky, O., & Stein, M. K. (1990). Functions, graphs and graphing: Tasks, learning and teaching. *Review of Educational Research, 60*(1), 1–64.

Lesh, R., Behr, M., & Post, T. (1987a). Rational number relations and proportions. In C. Janvier (Ed.), *Problems of representation in the teaching and learning of mathematics* (pp. 41–58). Hillsdale, NJ: Lawrence Erlbaum Associates.

Lesh, R., & Doerr, H. (2012). Foundations of a model and modeling perspective on mathematics teaching, learning and problem solving. In R. Lesh & H. Doerr (Eds.), *Beyond constructivism: Models and modeling perspectives on mathematics problems solving, learning, and teaching* (pp. 3–33). Mahwah, NJ: Lawrence Erlbaum Associates.

Lesh, R., Post, T., & Behr, M. (1987b). Representations and translations among representations in mathematics learning and problem solving. In C. Janvier (Ed.), *Problems of Representations in the Teaching and Learning of Mathematics* (pp. 33–40). Hillsdale, NJ: Lawrence Erlbaum, 1987.

Lesh, R., & Zawojewski, J. (2007). Problem solving and modeling. In F. Lester (Ed.), *Second handbook of research on mathematics teaching and learning* (pp. 763–804). Charlotte, NC: Information Age Publishing; Reston, VA: NCTM.

Meira, L. (2003). Mathematical representations as systems of notations-in-use. In K. Gravemeijer, R. Lehrer, B. van Oers, & L. Verschaffel (Eds.), *Symbolizing, modeling and tool use in mathematics education* (pp. 87–104). Dordrecht: Kluwer.

Meira, L. (2002). Mathematical representations as systems of notations-in-use. In K. Gravenmeijer, R. Lehrer, B. van Oers, & L. Verschaffel (Eds.), *Symbolizing, modeling and tool use in mathematics education* (pp. 87–104). Dordrecht: Kluwer.

Monk, S. (2003). Representation in school mathematics: Learning to graph and graphing to learn. In J. Kilpatrick (Ed.), *A research companion to PSSM* (pp. 250–262). Reston, VA: NCTM.

National Council of Teachers of Mathematics. (2000). *Principles and standards for school mathematics*. Reston, VA: NCTM.

National Council of Teachers of Mathematics. (2014). *Principles to actions*. Reston, VA: NCTM.

National Governors Association Center for Best Practices & Council of Chief State School Officers. (2010). *Common core state standards for mathematics*. Washington, DC: Author. Retrieved from www.corestandards.org/assets/CCSSI_Math%20Standards.pdf.

Newell, A., & Simon, H. (1972). *Human problem solving*. Englewood Cliffs, NJ: Prentice Hall.

Nistal, A., Van Dooren, W., Clarebout, G., Elen, J., & Veschaffel, L. (2009). Conceptualizing, investigating and simulating representational flexibility in mathematical problem solving and learning: A critical review. *ZDM-the International Journal on Mathematics Education, 41*, 627–636.

Nunokawa, K. (1994). Solver's structures of a problem situation and their global restructuring. *Journal of Mathematical Behavior, 13*, 275–297.

Ochs, E., Jacoby, S., & Gonzales, P. (1994). Interpretive journeys: How physicists talk and travel through graphic space. *Configurations, 2*(1), 151–171.

Pape, S., & Tchoshanov, M. (2001). The role of representation(s) in developing mathematical understanding. *Theory into Practice, 40*(2), 118–127.

Pimm, D. (1987). *Speaking mathematically: Communication in mathematics classrooms*. London: Routledge.

Presmeg, N. (1997). Reasoning with metaphors and metonymies in mathematics learning. In L. English (Ed.), *Mathematical reasoning: Analogies, metaphors, and images* (pp. 267–279). Mahwah, NJ: LEA.

Presmeg, N. (2006). Research on visualization in learning and teaching mathematics. In A. Gutierrez & P. Boero (Eds.), *Handbook of research on the psychology of mathematics education* (pp. 205–235). Rotterdam: Sense Publishers.

Putnam, R., & Borko, H. (1997). Teacher learning: Implications of new views of cognition. In B. Biddle, T. Good, & I. Goodson (Eds.), *International handbook of teachers and teaching* (pp. 1223–1296). Dordrecht: Kluwer.

Roth, W. M., & McGinn, M. K. (1997). Graphing: Cognitive ability or practice? *Science and Education, 81*, 91–106.

Schoenfeld, A. H. (1985). *Mathematical problem solving*. New York: Academic Press.

Sfard, A. (2000). Steering (dis)course between metaphors and rigor. *Journal for Research in Mathematics Education, 31*(3), 296–327.

Silver, E., Ghousseini, H., Gosen, D., Charalambous, C., & Font Strawhun, B. (2005). Moving from rhetoric to praxis: Issues faced by teachers in having students consider multiple solutions for problems in the mathematics classroom. *Journal of Mathematical Behavior, 24*, 287–301.

Stein, M. K., Engle, R., Smith, M., & Hughes, E. (2008). Orchestrating productive mathematical discussions: Five practices for helping teachers move beyond show and tell. *Mathematical Thinking and Learning, 10*, 313–340.

Stylianou, D. (2002). Interaction of visualization and analysis: The negotiation of a visual representation in problem solving. *Journal of Mathematical Behavior, 21*, 303–307.

Stylianou, D. (2010). Teachers' conceptions of representation in the context of middle school mathematics. *Journal of Mathematics Teacher Education, 13*(4), 325–343.

Stylianou, D. A. (2008). Representation as a cognitive and social practice. In O. Figueras (Ed.), *Proceedings of the joint meeting of the 32nd Annual Meeting for the Psychology of Mathematics Education and Psychology of Mathematics Education – North America* (vol. 4, pp. 289–296). Morelia, Mexico: Centro de Investigacio´n y de Estudios Avanzados del IPN and Universidad Michoacana de San Nicolas de Hidalgo.

Stylianou, D. A. (2011). An examination of middle school students' representation practices in mathematical problem solving through the lens of expert work: Towards an organizing scheme. *Educational Studies in Mathematics, 76*, 265–280.

Stylianou, D. A., Kenney, P. A., Silver, E. A., & Alacaci, C. (2000). Gaining insight into students' thinking through assessment tasks. *Mathematics Teaching in the Middle Grades, 6*, 136–144.

Stylianou, D. A., & Silver, E. A. (2004). The role of visual representations in advanced mathematical problem solving: An examination of expert-novice similarities and differences. *Journal of Mathematical Thinking and Learning, 6*(4), 353–387.

Superfine, A., Canty, R., & Marshall, A. (2009). Translation between external representation systems in mathematics: All-or-none or skill conglomerate? *Journal of Mathematical Behavior, 28*(4), 217–236.

Tripathi, P. (2008). Developing mathematical understanding through multiple representations. *Mathematics Teaching in the Middle School, 13*(8), 438–445.

Van Den HeuvelzPanhuizen, M. (2003). The didactical use of models in realistic mathematics education: An example from a longitudinal trajectory on percentage. *Educational Studies in Mathematics, 54*, 9–35.

van Oers, B. (2002). Informal representations and their improvements. In K. Gravemeijer, R. Lehrer, B. van Oers, & L. Verschaffel (Eds.), *Symbolizing, modeling and tool use in mathematics education* (pp. 25–29). Dordrecht: Kluwer Academic Press.

Section 2
Learning from Multiple Perspectives

9

BEYOND TRUSTWORTHINESS
Comprehending Multiple Source Perspectives

Sarit Barzilai
UNIVERSITY OF HAIFA

Michael Weinstock
BEN-GURION UNIVERSITY OF THE NEGEV

ABSTRACT

To make sense of informational texts it is often necessary to grasp their authors' perspectives and how these underlie the presentation of information. Comprehending source perspectives can help readers make better judgments and develop deeper understanding through consideration of alternative approaches and viewpoints. The capabilities of engaging with multiple perspectives are increasingly important in 21st-century societies in which it has become all too easy for people to sequester themselves in "echo chambers" that resonate their own viewpoints. The aims of this chapter are to explicate what comprehension of multiple source perspectives involves, how this complex epistemic performance develops, and how it might be promoted in educational settings. We first define source perspectives and describe what representation of source perspectives of informational texts entails. Subsequently, we discuss how perspective comprehension is conceived according to three theoretical approaches: theory of mind research, theories of epistemic development, and the more recent AIR model of epistemic cognition. We show that these theoretical lenses shed light on different facets of this construct. In the last section, we suggest how growth in source perspective comprehension might be fostered by drawing on a new theory of epistemic growth, the Apt-AIR framework.

Key words: perspective comprehension, sourcing, multiple document comprehension, epistemic thinking, epistemic development

WHY PERSPECTIVES MATTER

To make sense of informational texts it is often necessary to grasp their authors' perspectives and how these underlie the presentation of information. For instance, do an author's arguments regarding a carbon tax stem from an economic or environmental outlook? Are the reasons provided for or against vaccination based on social, moral, or scientific norms and values? Is a proposed model of writing shaped by a cognitive or socio-cognitive theoretical approach? Comprehending the perspectives that underlie the production and communication of information can help readers interpret and evaluate information as well as relate it to other pieces of information that may reflect similar or different perspectives. Ultimately, it might help them develop better judgments or deeper understanding through consideration of alternative approaches and viewpoints.

The aims of this chapter are to explicate what comprehension of multiple source perspectives involves, how this complex epistemic performance develops, and how it might be promoted in educational settings. We use the term *source perspective comprehension* to refer to readers' understanding of authors' particular ways of thinking and knowing and how these inform authors' interpretation and representation of the issue at hand. This definition will be unpacked in the following section. Our particular interest is in the comprehension of perspectives represented in *multiple informational texts* rather than in oral discourse or fictional narratives. This area of perspective comprehension has so far received relatively little empirical and theoretical attention. Research on comprehension of multiple texts has extensively addressed how readers evaluate source trustworthiness and various dimensions of trustworthiness, such as expertise and benevolence (Bråten, Stadtler, & Salmerón, 2017). Surely, standards of trustworthiness are critical for the acceptance of information. However, even highly trustworthy documents typically represent only a single perspective or a limited range of perspectives regarding the issue at hand. Also, similarly trustworthy sources may reflect contrasting or competing perspectives. Comprehension of multiple perspectives goes beyond trustworthiness evaluation to address the fundamental diversity and complexity of knowledge.

Perspective comprehension is important for understanding texts that reflect diverse viewpoints, and developing well-informed arguments or explanations that consider ideas, claims, or evidence that stem from different viewpoints (Barzilai & Eshet-Alkalai, 2015; Britt & Rouet, 2012). Consideration of alternative perspectives can increase the accountability of knowledge building because different voices and approaches are acknowledged and weighed. This may sometimes result in a more refined commitment to one's own perspective, and at other times lead to an informed expansion or shift of perspective. The capabilities of engaging with multiple perspectives may be increasingly important in 21st-century societies in which social media and search algorithms can make it all too easy for people to sequester themselves into "echo chambers" that resonate their own viewpoints (Bakshy, Messing, & Adamic, 2015).

In the next section, we define perspectives and describe what representation of source perspectives involves. Subsequently, we discuss how perspective comprehension is conceived according to three theoretical approaches: theory of mind research, theories of epistemic development, and the more recent AIR model of epistemic cognition. We aim to demonstrate that interrogating the construct of perspective comprehension from different theoretical lenses helps shed light on important facets of this construct. In the last section, we suggest how growth in source perspective comprehension might be promoted by drawing on a new theory of epistemic growth, the Apt-AIR framework (Barzilai & Chinn, 2018).

PERSPECTIVES AND SOURCE PERSPECTIVES

Perspectives are often generally described as the distinct ways in which knowers "see" or "perceive" things (Miller & Boix Mansilla, 2004). Camp (2017, 2020) defined perspectives as *overarching interpretive principles* which organize one's thinking about the target subject. According to Camp, perspectives determine what information people notice and remember about the subject, guide how they organize, assimilate, and explain new information, and thus how they evaluate and respond to that information. Thus, perspectives are not propositions or claims but rather principles that guide interpretation of new information and experiences. They are tools for thinking rather than thoughts themselves (Camp, 2017).

Following Camp, we view perspectives as ways of thinking and knowing that inform interpretations and judgments. Perspectives are diverse and can include personal, professional, social, cultural, ideological, theoretical, methodological, etc. approaches, commitments, or frameworks (Britt & Rouet, 2012; Miller & Boix Mansilla, 2004). Differences in perspectives may result from differences in people's roles, social positions, experiences, education, and more.

In this chapter, our specific focus is on how readers comprehend source perspectives of informational texts. *Texts* or *documents* are artifacts that convey information to readers (Britt & Rouet, 2012). The term *source* refers to the origin of the text and the circumstances surrounding its production, such as its authorship, publication venue, time of publication, etc. (Bromme, Stadtler, & Scharrer, 2018). *Source perspectives* are the perspectives of the authors or organizations who create and communicate information using texts.[1] Authors' perspectives can shape how they interpret and represent events and phenomena, influence the information that they choose to include or exclude, determine which aspects they emphasize, and which conclusions they draw. For example, a journalist's ideological perspective might impact her reporting about the consequences of a new bill that is being passed through parliament.

According to the Documents Model Framework (DMF, Britt & Rouet, 2012; Perfetti, Rouet, & Britt, 1999), comprehension of multiple documents ideally involves forming an integrated mental representation of the situations or phenomena described in the documents, a representation of the sources of the document (e.g., their authorship, time, and venue of publication, etc.), a representation of the relations between sources and content (e.g., who said what), and a representation of the relations among sources (e.g., agreement or opposition).

The DMF helps explain how readers might make sense of multiple documents. Yet, to comprehend source perspectives, readers need to do more than represent sources and track "who said what", they also need to develop a metarepresentation (Perner, 1991) of each text as a representation that was constructed within a particular perspective, and to recognize that the phenomenon described in the text is the phenomenon *as seen* from that perspective. Building on Perner's (1991) analysis of metarepresentation, we suggest that developing such a metarepresentation requires decoupling the representation of the content of the document from the representation of the phenomenon it refers to, developing a representation of the representational relation between the content and the phenomenon, and grasping that this representational relation is likely influenced by the way the writer perceives the phenomenon.

To illustrate, Figure 9.1 depicts the various types of representations that readers have to construct in order to comprehend the perspective of a journalist who is reporting on a new bill: Readers need to represent (a) the hypothetical consequences of the bill as distinct from (b) the reporter's description of these consequences, and also to represent (c) the representational relation between the consequences of the bill and the representation of these consequences by the journalist. Readers also need to represent (d) the reporter's ideological perspective and (e) how this perspective could have shaped her analysis of the bill and (f) her description of its consequences. Readers might infer the journalist's perspective from various textual cues or from information available elsewhere about the journalist and the venue of publication.

Decoupling the representation of the phenomenon from its description may be difficult for readers, especially when they have low prior knowledge about the phenomenon. However, awareness that perspectives inform the production of knowledge can lead readers to *anticipate* that the document might reflect its author's perspective and that alternative representations of the phenomenon could exist. Such an awareness could lead readers to be more epistemically vigilant (Sperber et al., 2010) regarding the potential existence and influence of source perspectives.

Nonetheless, when readers read single texts, they might not necessarily pay attention to source perspectives. Furthermore, readers might not be able to successfully infer source perspectives if they only have the content of a single document and limited prior knowledge to build on. In contrast, if readers encounter multiple texts that reflect different viewpoints – for example, if they happen to read an alternative analysis of the new bill, published by an independent think-tank – they may notice differences in the ways that the bill is represented in the texts. These differences could alert them to differences in sources perspectives and inform their understanding of

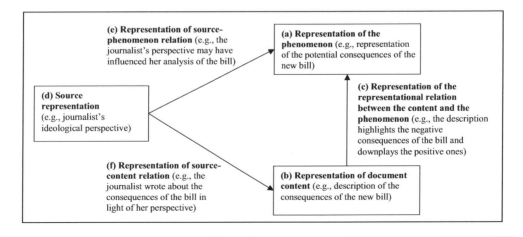

Figure 9.1 Metarepresentation of the source-content relation.

how these perspectives shape the descriptions of the bill. Indeed, conflicts between author viewpoints have been found to enhance viewpoint comprehension (Barzilai & Eshet-Alkalai, 2015). Thus, engaging with multiple texts can potentially make source perspectives more salient.

However, although multiple texts have the potential to bring multiple perspectives to the fore, identifying perspectives in informational texts is more difficult than identifying perspectives in everyday social interactions or in literary texts (Jucks & Bromme, 2011; Kim et al., 2018). Conversational cues that can help infer perspectives in social interactions, such as facial expressions and tone of voice, are missing. Moreover, the authors of expository texts are often rendered "invisible" by their impersonal, omniscient, and authoritative writing style (Paxton, 1997), and their perspectives are usually not explicitly described. Hence, readers need to actively infer authors' perspectives from the information provided about their backgrounds, affiliations, and credentials and from their explanations and arguments. Readers might also use lexical cues, such as use of technical terms, to infer writers' disciplines and areas of expertise (Jucks, Becker, & Bromme, 2008).

THREE LENSES ON SOURCE PERSPECTIVE COMPREHENSION

In the following sections, we explore source perspective comprehension from three complementary theoretical lenses (theory of mind research, theories of epistemic development, and the AIR model of epistemic cognition). Each of these approaches illuminates different aspects of how understanding of source perspectives develops and what this understanding entails.

Theory of Mind Lens: The Emergence of the Understanding of Multiple Perspectives

A likely precursor of source perspective comprehension is the psychological development of the understanding of multiple perspectives, which has been studied extensively in theory of mind research (Flavell, 2000). From before the age of 2, children understand that they might not see what someone else sees, or vice versa (Sodian, Thoermer, & Metz, 2007). However, it is not until the age of about 4 or 5, with the attainment of theory of mind (ToM), that children not only understand that all perspectives need not be the same but indicate that they can represent the mental states of others. In classic *first-order ToM* tasks, a child is presented with information that someone else does not have (e.g., that a crayon box actually has candles inside). When asked about what the other person thinks (e.g., what is inside the crayon box), the child with ToM will recognize that the other has a different knowledge representation than does the child and will have a different report about the state of things. This early understanding of perspectives involves the ability to represent others' mental states (including thoughts, emotions, desires, and intentions) and how these are related to their positioning in particular contexts (Flavell, 2000). It also involves the metarepresentational awareness that representations differ from reality and the recognition of the possibility of misrepresentation (Perner, 1991).

However, first-order ToM is hardly the last development in understanding multiple perspectives. At age 6, children can infer another's interpretation of an ambiguous picture and refer to a specific aspect of another's perspective in explaining why the other might misinterpret the content of such a picture (Pillow & Mash, 1998). With *second-order ToM* children can represent how someone else might represent the thinking of yet another person (Miller, 2009). With *interpretive ToM* (iToM), at age 7 to 8, one is not just able to compare one's own representations with another's, but can understand how other people might have different representations than each other, even if they have the same information (Carpendale & Chandler, 1996; Lalonde & Chandler, 2002). Unlike first-order ToM, with iToM one recognizes that the reason there may be more than one claim is not just because people have different objective knowledge, but because people have different subjective perspectives – which could include different interpretive processes, preferences, or ways of knowing. In an iToM task, children first see and describe a full picture, then they see the picture framed in such a way that only an ambiguous portion remains. They are then asked what each of two other people would say the occluded picture is of. A child who recognizes that the two other people might say different things about the picture is considered to have iToM; the child understands that even though the two people have seen the same ambiguous picture they each might interpret the information differently from one another. Children with iTOM understand that different perspectives arise not just from having different external information but from internal processes of knowing such as interpretation.

ToM development has been found to be related to comprehension of fiction and non-fiction texts, presumably due to increased representation of characters' thoughts and emotions (Dore, Amendum, Golinkoff, & Hirsh-Pasek, 2018). Additionally, better understanding of the representational nature of mental states can extend to an understanding that texts are also representations that can be interpreted in various ways (Lecce, Zocchi, Pagnin, Palladino, & Taumoepeau, 2010). Some evidence suggests that ToM development might also be related to the representation of multiple source perspectives. Weinstock and Israel (2017) found that 2nd graders who had exhibited iToM were much more likely to attribute differences in the claims made by two science experts to the fact that they were different people with different minds. By 4th grade, these early achievers of iToM were able to express how different ways of knowing were central to perspectives. For example, they described how experts had different ways of observing the phenomenon or different areas of expertise that led to their conclusions. Furthermore, Florit, Carli, Giunti, and Mason (2020) found that 4th and 5th grade students' second-order ToM uniquely predicted multiple-text comprehension even when considering prior topic knowledge, reading abilities, and topic and task differences. Students with more advanced second-order ToM were better able to represent and justify the different perspectives that were reflected in the texts. These studies suggest that developments in ToM might be a precursor of source perspective comprehension. As children develop understanding of how different claims might arise from different perspectives, they may later come to understand that single or multiple documents also represent claims from different author perspectives.

Epistemic Development Lens: Coming to Terms with the Legitimacy of Multiple Perspectives

The understanding that individual minds reflect perspectives and that there are multiple representing minds seems to be the basis for a generalized theory of knowledge

(Lalonde & Chandler, 2002; Osterhaus, Koerber, & Sodian, 2017; Weinstock & Madjar, 2018). That is, the awareness that people's perspectives shape how they interpret information can lead to a more generalized understanding that knowledge is produced within particular perspectives. Perry (1970/1999) described how college students' repeated interactions with competing perspectives about knowledge and values led to a new understanding of the multiplicity of knowledge and later of the possibility of forming a commitment within this multiplicity. From Perry's description, developmental researchers formed schemes of adolescent and adult epistemic development (e.g., King & Kitchener, 1994; Kuhn, 1991).

These descriptions of epistemic development go beyond ToM research to address not only awareness of multiple perspectives but also appreciation of their epistemic legitimacy and their value in constituting knowledge (Thomm, Barzilai, & Bromme, 2017). Following Perry (1970/1999), Kuhn (1991) proposed three basic epistemic positions; absolutism, multiplism, and evaluativism. Elsewhere, we have called these positions "epistemic perspectives" because they are best understood as epistemic preferences and modes of interpretation that inform epistemic reasoning (Barzilai & Weinstock, 2015). With *absolutism*, people understand knowledge to be objective and allowing of only one correct, objective, and legitimate viewpoint. Disagreements between claims arise because some people are mistaken or biased, and their view is not legitimate. Subjective perspectives are perceived as obstacles to knowing that should be overcome. With *multiplism*, people emphasize the subjective aspects of knowing. From idiosyncratic perspectives, people produce claims that essentially represent opinions. As everyone stands at their unique position in the world, there are inevitably multiple perspectives with no possibility of stepping outside of these perspectives and weighing them. The legitimacy of multiple perspectives is acknowledged, yet there is no common ground from which they can be evaluated or resolved. With *evaluativism*, people understand that information becomes knowledge through interpretation and that this interpretation takes place from particular perspectives and understandings of how we can know (Pepper, 1942). Perspectives in this sense are not idiosyncratic, but are grounded in shared theories, methodological approaches, or worldviews, so there are disciplinary, social, cultural, etc. perspectives. Multiple perspectives are not only legitimate; they also play a productive role in sound knowledge construction. Engaging with different perspectives can make people more aware of their own perspectives and lead them to examine their assumptions, approaches, and interpretations. This could contribute to wider and deeper understanding of the issue at hand as well as greater awareness of the limits of knowledge.

These epistemological developments have been found to be related to the coordination of multiple perspectives in knowledge construction and evaluation tasks. For example, among adults on a juror reasoning task, evaluativists were more likely than absolutists to anticipate how someone who might argue for a verdict choice different from theirs, to recognize and coordinate different perspectives on the evidence, and to produce arguments for their own verdict and against other verdicts (Weinstock, 2016; Weinstock & Cronin, 2003). This research shows how taking multiple perspectives into account improves knowledge construction. The theoretical basis for this is that knowing involves weighing one's claims within a framework of alternatives. Thus, skills in justifying a claim should reflect a consideration of alternative perspectives and an explanation of one's own perspective.

Epistemic perspectives have been found to be associated with understanding of source viewpoints. Barzilai and Zohar (2012) found that 6th grade students who expressed evaluativist views were more likely to evaluate the trustworthiness of websites based on author perspective or bias as compared to students who expressed absolutist views. When integrating information from multiple websites, those with evaluativist views were more likely to identify the viewpoints expressed by different websites, to compare these viewpoints, and ultimately to develop arguments based on more websites. Barzilai and Eshet-Alkalai (2015) subsequently documented that evaluativism is a unique positive predictor of author viewpoint comprehension. They proposed that because evaluativism acknowledges the role of subjectivity in knowledge construction, as well as the need to weigh alternative accounts, it may lead to greater attention to author viewpoints as readers attempt to understand and evaluate different accounts.

Epistemic perspectives have also been found to be related to how university students explain expert disagreement (Thomm et al., 2017). Specifically, multiplism was found to be positively associated with motivation-related explanations for why experts disagree, suggesting that subjective views of knowing may lead to the attribution of claims to personal causes. Evaluativism, in contrast, was associated with topic complexity explanations, complexity being defined as the existence of multiple interacting aspects or factors and the inconclusiveness of research into the topic (Thomm et al., 2017). Thus, evaluativism might sensitize readers to challenges that experts face in the interpretation of knowledge. Collectively, these studies suggest that readers' views of the legitimacy and value of multiple accounts and perspectives can play into their comprehension of source perspectives.

AIR Model Lens: Unpacking the Elements of Source Perspective Comprehension

The AIR model (Chinn, Rinehart, & Buckland, 2014) offers an alternative approach to the analysis of epistemic thinking. Holding that epistemic thinking is situated in specific situations and contexts, this approach is less concerned with defining overarching epistemic perspectives and more concerned with identifying specific epistemic components. According to the AIR model, epistemic thinking has three main components: (a) *Epistemic aims and value* refer to goals that have a representational nature, such as acquiring knowledge or developing explanations, and the importance of these goals; (b) *Epistemic ideals* are criteria or norms for evaluating whether epistemic aims have been achieved. Epistemic ideals are also used for evaluating epistemic products and justifying their acceptance; (c) *Reliable epistemic processes* include strategies or procedures that are likely to result in the achievement of epistemic aims. The AIR model is commensurate with an evaluativist approach to knowing because it foregrounds the central role of evaluation in the construction of knowledge. However, it goes beyond the notion that competing accounts should be critically weighed to expand upon the specific normative ideals and reliable processes that enable the evaluation and construction of knowledge. The AIR model also addresses a wider range of epistemic aims and their situated nature (Chinn et al., 2014).

To demonstrate how the AIR model might contribute to the analysis of source perspective comprehension, Table 9.1 exemplifies key ideals and reliable processes that might serve the achievement of two epistemic aims: developing knowledge *about* source perspectives and developing knowledge *through the consideration* of multiple source perspectives. The first aim, developing knowledge *about* source perspectives, relates to situations in which readers aim to know what is the perspective of the source and to determine if this perspective is worth taking into account. To do so, readers can engage in epistemic processes such as *attending to* the perspective of the author, accurately *identifying* this perspective, and critically *evaluating* it. Some of the ideals that can be used to evaluate source perspectives are their *relevance* to the reader's purpose, their *power* for generating novel ideas, explanations, or evidence, and their *justification* in light of available data, evidence, or norms. Such ideals can help readers judge if particular perspectives merit inclusion in their knowledge building efforts or if they can be reasonably ignored.

If readers identify multiple relevant and valuable perspectives, they may then engage with the aim of developing knowledge *through the consideration of* multiple source perspective. To do so, they can use epistemic processes such as *interpreting* the phenomenon in light of various perspectives and *resolving* these perspectives to develop knowledge about the topic (e.g., to develop an analysis of how carbon emissions from meat production can be reduced by coordinating biological, environmental, health, and socio-cultural perspectives regarding the problem). The resulting product can then be evaluated in light of epistemic ideals such as the *accuracy* of claims, *justification* based on reasons and evidence that arise from diverse perspectives, *comprehensiveness* of the aspects and perspectives that were considered, and the *coherence* of the connections formed between perspectives.

Although we are not aware of studies that have specifically examined readers' perspective-related ideals, making this an interesting topic for future research,

Table 9.1 AIR Analysis of Source Perspective Comprehension: Examples of Aims, Ideals, and Processes.

Epistemic aims	Developing knowledge *about* source perspectives	Developing knowledge *through the consideration of* multiple source perspectives
Epistemic ideals	Ideals for evaluating perspectives: • *Relevance* of perspective to one's aim • *Power* of perspective for generating novel ideas, explanations, or evidence • *Justification* of perspective in light of data sources, evidence, or norms	Ideals for evaluating knowledge that is based on multiple perspectives: • *Accuracy* of knowledge claims • *Justification* in light of reasons and evidence from multiple perspectives • *Comprehensiveness* of aspects and perspectives considered • *Coherence* of the connections formed between perspectives
Reliable epistemic processes	• *Attending to* perspectives (i.e., anticipating and seeking perspectives) • *Identifying* perspectives (i.e., correctly inferring writers' perspectives) • *Evaluating* the unique contribution of the perspective (i.e., using ideals to judge the legitimacy and value of the perspective)	• *Interpreting* in light of perspectives (i.e., understanding how perspectives underlie the presentation of information and that alternative interpretations may exist) • *Resolving* perspectives (i.e., prioritizing, coordinating, or integrating perspectives)

prior research indicates that readers can and do engage in the epistemic processes described in Table 9.1. In the following paragraphs we describe research findings related to the nature of student performance in each of these epistemic processes. The processes are loosely ordered: Attending to and identifying source perspectives are likely prerequisites for evaluating and interpreting these perspectives. However, evaluation and interpretation might not always follow attention and identification. Resolving source perspectives will often require some evaluation of these perspectives. However, these processes do not necessarily unfold linearly. For example, readers' attempts to resolve conflicts between perspectives might spur them to evaluate these perspectives.

Attending to source perspectives

Because authors' perspectives are usually not explicitly stated, readers need to actively anticipate and seek out these perspectives. Very few studies have examined whether readers spontaneously attend to author perspectives. Barzilai, Tzadok, and Eshet-Alkalai (2015) asked university students to think aloud while reading blog-posts that represented diverse viewpoints regarding seawater desalination. They found that only 39% of the students spontaneously mentioned the position of the authors (pro or con) and only 33% mentioned their disciplinary perspectives (e.g., ecological or economic). In a more recent think-aloud study, Tzadok, Barzilai, and Eshet-Alkalai (in preparation) found highly similar frequencies of attention to author positions (36%) and disciplinary perspectives (34%) while reading blog-posts about desalination and genetically modified food. In this study, Tzadok et al. added a condition in which students were prompted to evaluate sources. In this condition, mentions of author positions increased to 56% and mentions of author disciplinary perspectives increased to 71%. These results suggest that most university students are capable of attending to authors' viewpoints, but that they might not do so spontaneously, perhaps because of insufficient awareness of the value and importance of attending to these viewpoints.

Identifying source perspectives

Attending to source perspectives does not necessarily mean that readers are correctly and accurately inferring the nature of these perspectives. Empirical evidence suggests that many readers struggle to correctly infer author viewpoints. In their study with 6th grade students, Barzilai and Zohar (2012) found that on average 49% of participants were able to correctly identify the viewpoints of the majority of the websites they were reading. Similarly, Coiro, Coscarelli, Maykel, and Forzani (2015) found that 43% of their 7th grade participants were able to correctly identify the viewpoint of website authors. Hobbs and Frost (2003) found that when 11th grade students were asked to identify the viewpoints represented in media messages, they tended to repeat claims instead of describing viewpoints or to describe viewpoints in an unelaborated manner. Finally, Barzilai and Eshet-Alkalai (2015) found that university students correctly described authors' positions and disciplinary perspectives in only about half of cases. Thus, readers of all ages appear to find it difficult to correctly identify author viewpoints, even when prompted to do so.

Interpreting in light of source perspectives

Readers also need to interpret how authors' perspectives might underlie their arguments and explanations and anticipate alternative interpretations. Coiro et al. (2015) asked 7th grade students to consider how website authors' viewpoints might affect their words and images. They found that only 20% of responses included a clear description of how authors' viewpoints affected the words and/or images they used. Similar results are reported by Forzani (2018). Bromme, Thomm, and Wolf (2015) found that when university students are asked to explain the causes for disagreements between scientists' claims, some students attribute these conflicts to differences in experts' backgrounds, including their areas of specialization and knowledge, opinions, education, etc. Thomm et al. (2017) found that acknowledgment of the impact of researchers' backgrounds on their claims, including differences in areas of specialization, perspectives, or opinions, was lower in a biology controversy (30% of the participants) than in a history controversy (90%). Thus, awareness of how perspectives underlie interpretation might depend on discipline-specific assumptions regarding the production of knowledge. In some disciplines, the role of subjectivity in the construction of knowledge is acknowledged more readily (see List, Chapter 11, for a discussion of the role of domain in perspective taking).

Evaluating source perspectives

We are not aware of studies that have examined how readers evaluate source perspectives themselves. However, source perspectives have been found to come into play when readers evaluate documents. For example, in a qualitative study with high-school students, Stenseth and Strømsø (2019) found that 46% of the participants considered the representation of multiple perspectives in their justifications for selection of documents about climate change and nuclear energy. Students seemed to prefer reading documents that contributed alternative perspectives. In Barzilai and Eshet-Alkalai's (2015) study, 45% of the participants mentioned author viewpoints in their justifications of blog-post credibility judgments. In this study, evaluations tended to focus on critiquing the one-sidedness of source perspectives (e.g., "It does not consider the other side of the coin, which is the damages caused by seawater desalination (on the ecological side and not the economic side)," p. 93). Both of these studies suggest that readers may value the contribution of alternative perspectives to knowledge building, and that this can inform their document preferences and evaluations. However, in other studies, alternative perspectives have not emerged as an evaluation criterion (e.g., Kiili, Leu, Marttunen, Hautala, & Leppänen, 2018; List, Grossnickle, & Alexander, 2016). It is possible that evaluation of source perspectives is contingent on their relevance to task goals and on their salience in the texts. More research is needed to examine this issue.

Resolving source perspectives

Evaluation of source perspectives may lead to a conclusion that only one of these perspectives is relevant, valuable, and well-justified. However, if multiple pertinent and well-grounded perspectives have been identified, the challenge remains how to resolve the differences between these perspectives. One possibility is to prioritize a single perspective and to use it to guide one's reasoning. This might be reasonable if this perspective is better justified or has greater explanatory power than other perspectives. Yet, even in such a case, consideration of alternative perspectives can contribute to a better understanding of one's own perspective and a more informed commitment to this perspective. However, sometimes developing an explanation or solution can benefit from the consideration of multiple perspectives. For example, finding the best solution to a socio-scientific problem may require coordinating multiple stakeholder viewpoints and multiple disciplinary perspectives. Coordinating perspectives involves identifying the relationships among them, and then appropriately organizing or combining claims, while acknowledging their origins, to form an integrative understanding of the issue.

Do readers engage in such complex processes? In a think-aloud study, Cho, Woodward, and Li (2018) examined how high-school students processed online information sources about mountaintop removal coal mining. They found that more successful readers engaged more frequently in reconciling multiple viewpoints by comparing, contrasting, connecting, and juxtaposing these viewpoints to identify and resolve conflicts in the information, compared to less successful readers. In Barzilai and Eshet-Alkalai's (2015) study, participants were ultimately tasked with writing an argument regarding seawater desalination based on four blog-posts which represented distinct viewpoints. Participants based their arguments only on 1.7 blog-posts on average, indicating that they only partially took into account the range of available viewpoints. More research is needed to develop a more detailed account of the ways in which readers resolve multiple perspectives.

All in all, the studies described in this section indicate that comprehension of source perspectives can be a highly challenging task. In the next section, we suggest how source perspective comprehension might be supported in educational settings.

FOSTERING COMPREHENSION OF MULTIPLE SOURCE PERSPECTIVES

The research that we have surveyed indicates that source perspective comprehension is a complex epistemic performance that involves both epistemic understanding of the nature, legitimacy, and value of multiple perspectives, as well as capabilities to engage with epistemic processes and ideals for reasoning with multiple source perspectives, across diverse tasks and contexts. How might growth in such complex epistemic performance be fostered?

To address this question, we draw on a recent theoretical framework–the Apt-AIR framework (Barzilai & Chinn, 2018). This framework expands the AIR model (Chinn et al., 2014) in order to unpack the goals of promoting students' epistemic growth, in light of philosophical, educational, and psychological research on how people know. Drawing on the virtue epistemology of Ernest Sosa (2015), the Apt-AIR framework argues that education should promote growth in students' capabilities and dispositions to engage in *apt epistemic performance*, defined as performance that enables achievement of epistemic aims through epistemic competence.[2] According to the Apt-AIR framework, epistemic growth proceeds through increases in people's capabilities and dispositions to competently perform epistemic processes and apply epistemic ideals so that they successfully achieve epistemic aims.

The Apt-AIR framework further describes five interweaving aspects of apt epistemic performance that education should foster in order to advance epistemic growth: (1) engaging in reliable cognitive processes that lead to the achievement of epistemic aims; (2) adapting epistemic performance to diverse situations; (3) metacognitively regulating and understanding epistemic performance; (4) caring about and enjoying epistemic performance; and (5) participating in epistemic performance together with others (Barzilai & Chinn, 2018). In what follows, we discuss how these aspects might apply to promoting the comprehension of multiple source perspectives. Our analysis of these aspects integrates understandings from the literatures that we have reviewed earlier.

Engaging in Source Perspective Comprehension

This aspect emphasizes that epistemic growth is promoted when students have opportunities to develop their abilities to actively employ reliable epistemic processes and apply appropriate epistemic ideals to achieve epistemic aims. Activities that can provide students with such opportunities can be, for example, asking students to develop explanations or arguments by integrating texts that present multiple perspectives on an issue. However, simply providing texts that reflect diverse viewpoints might be insufficient for promoting the comprehension of their viewpoints. One reason for this is that, as the aforementioned evidence suggests, students might not spontaneously attend to these viewpoints and might find it difficult to appropriately identify, interpret, evaluate, and resolve them. A second reason is that multiple perspectives might be meaningfully processed only by students who have already developed an evaluativist understanding of the constructed nature of knowledge and of the value of taking into account multiple points of view. Hence, it may be productive to scaffold identification, interpretation, evaluation, and resolution of source perspectives as students work with the texts. For example, teachers can prompt students to identify authors' viewpoints and engage with them in the analysis of how these viewpoints influence authors' messages (Hobbs & Frost, 2003). Students might also be provided with scaffolds that encourage them to juxtapose viewpoints and to evaluate their relevance to the task at hand, their power for contributing valuable information and ideas, and their justification based on evidence. Teachers may also support students in integrating multiple perspectives by prompting them to attend to their relations.

Adapting Source Perspective Comprehension

Apt epistemic performance involves the ability to achieve epistemic aims in an adaptive manner that is responsive to task and context conditions. For example, the perspectives that need to be considered in order to solve a socio-scientific problem are different from the perspectives that need to be considered when explaining a historical event. Thus, students should ideally have opportunities to engage with various types of sources perspectives in multiple tasks from different disciplines, so that they develop a grasp of the value of multiple perspectives for different types of tasks, how to identify perspectives in different types of texts, how perspectives might be evaluated in different disciplines, and so forth. Students can also be invited to think about when it is important to consider multiple perspectives and when it might make more sense to adopt a single guiding perspective.

Metacognitively Understanding and Regulating Source Perspective Comprehension

According to the Apt-AIR framework, apt epistemic performance requires metacognitive understanding and regulation of epistemic performance. The studies that we have reviewed suggest that metacognitive understanding of the nature and legitimacy of multiple perspectives underlies comprehension of source perspectives. That is, development of the understanding that people can perceive and interpret phenomena in different ways and that different viewpoints can valuably contribute to knowledge construction appears to be a precursor to competent perspective comprehension. This understanding has a metacognitive nature because it involves knowing about how people know (Barzilai & Zohar, 2014). Hence, learners might benefit from activities that foster understanding of what perspectives are, how they emerge, how they can shape interpretations and judgements, and how texts reflect their authors' perspectives. They may also need to grasp when and why the consideration of multiple perspectives can advance epistemic aims and how to critically evaluate competing perspectives, including understanding the meaning and importance of ideals for evaluating perspectives. Students might also need to develop regulatory skills to manage the construction of knowledge from multiple perspectives. For example, when planning how to investigate a complex topic (e.g., immigration policy), students might be prompted to think in advance about which perspectives might be relevant and important for learning about this topic.

Multiple texts could potentially support development of the metacognitive understanding of how authors' perspectives shape the ways in which they construct and communicate knowledge. Olson (1994) has argued that because texts do not convey attitude or intent in the same direct way that speech does, readers must learn to actively recover the writers' intent and attitude using textual clues. According to Olson, the development of this ability is related to an increased understanding of subjectivity, which, in turn, can allow readers to reflect on their own and others' subjectivity. Thus, learning to interpret how perspectives shape authors' explanations and arguments might promote a grasp of how knowledge is constructed within perspectives and how language and texts can be used to represent intents and viewpoints. Furthermore, contrasts and tensions between texts can motivate readers to examine who wrote them in order to resolve conflicts and restore coherence (Braasch & Bråten, 2017). This might draw readers' attention to the role of authors' perspectives in the construction of knowledge (Barzilai & Eshet-Alkalai, 2015). However, we expect that engaging students in critical reflection or discussion regarding the perspectives they are reading might be needed in order to promote growth in metacognitive understanding. For example, students might be encouraged to consider how differences in historians' theoretical and methodological approaches might lead them to different conclusions (Barzilai, Thomm, & Shlomi-Elooz, 2019).

Caring about and Enjoying Source Perspective Comprehension

Critically engaging with multiple perspectives can be both time-consuming and effortful. Hence, learners may be unlikely to engage in this performance if they do not develop a deep appreciation of the importance of multiple perspectives and a commitment to engaging with multiple perspectives. We would like learners to *want to* understand others' perspectives, and to experience this not as an intimidating activity but rather as an interesting and intellectually satisfying one. To achieve this goal, it might be helpful to engage students in activities which highlight the value of figuring out authors' perspectives. For example, Monte-Sano, De La Paz, and Felton (2014) kicked off their historical literacy cognitive apprenticeship curriculum by juxtaposing documents that presented conflicting British and American colonist accounts of the dramatic events of the battle that started the American Revolutionary War. This example vividly demonstrates the critical importance of attending to source perspectives in the investigation of historical events. Students might also need to be supported when encountering source perspectives that conflict with their own deeply felt perspectives. Making it clear that multiple, different perspectives are legitimate and valued might help students develop resources for dealing with conflicting perspectives (Barton & McCully, 2012).

Participating in Source Perspective Comprehension

This aspect of the Apt-AIR framework addresses the importance of being able to achieve epistemic aims together with others. Comprehension of multiple perspectives is a fundamentally social epistemic performance, which lies at the core of learning from and with others. Engaging in this performance can develop an appreciation of the benefits and challenges of acquiring knowledge based on other people's testimony (i.e., telling) rather than through one's independent efforts. Relying on testimony requires grasping how testimony is shaped by people's situated perspectives. This grasp also involves an awareness that some perspectives can be better represented than others and of the epistemic injustice that can occur when perspectives of particular people and groups are systematically excluded from knowledge building. Thus, students can be invited to consider not only which viewpoints are represented in texts, but also which viewpoints are left out.

It is important to emphasize that the five aspects of apt epistemic performance that we have just described are not independent from each other, but are rather complementary and interacting (Barzilai & Chinn, 2018). Promoting the comprehension of multiple source perspectives in educational contexts is likely to require jointly addressing all of these aspects so that learners develop both skills and dispositions to engage in source perspective comprehension in and out of school. More research is needed to explore educationally productive ways of interacting with multiple texts and their diverse perspectives.

CONCLUSION

By analyzing the construct of source perspective comprehension, through multiple theoretical lenses, we have attempted to show that this performance is rooted in the development of people's ability to understand others' perspectives and in the ensuing epistemic understanding of the constructed nature of knowledge. Nevertheless, making sense of the perspectives of the authors of informational texts poses particular challenges and involves multiple specific epistemic processes and criteria that students can struggle to successfully employ. Finally, we have suggested several ways in which apt source perspective comprehension may be fostered in educational settings. Ultimately, developing learners' understanding of multiple source perspectives may not only promote deeper reading comprehension, but can also provide a valuable opportunity for promoting learners' epistemic growth.

NOTES

1. We acknowledge that texts can sometimes represent multiple perspectives or include embedded perspectives. However, for the sake of clarity and brevity, we focus at present on the simpler case in which each text reflects a single predominant perspective.
2. According to Sosa (2015), competence is a disposition to succeed when one tries, across a range of relevant conditions. Epistemic competence is a disposition to succeed in achieving epistemic aims, such as acquiring true beliefs.

REFERENCES

Bakshy, E., Messing, S., & Adamic, L. A. (2015). Exposure to ideologically diverse news and opinion on Facebook. *Science, 348*(6239), 1130–1132.

Barton, K. C., & McCully, A. W. (2012). Trying to "see things differently": Northern Ireland students' struggle to understand alternative historical perspectives. *Theory and Research in Social Education, 40*(4), 371–408.

Barzilai, S., & Chinn, C. A. (2018). On the goals of epistemic education: Promoting apt epistemic performance. *Journal of the Learning Sciences, 27*(3), 353–389.

Barzilai, S., & Eshet-Alkalai, Y. (2015). The role of epistemic perspectives in comprehension of multiple author viewpoints. *Learning and Instruction, 36*, 86–103.

Barzilai, S., Thomm, E., & Shlomi-Elooz, T. (2019). The impact of topic familiarity and disagreement explanation on source evaluation. Paper presented at the Biennial Conference of the European Association for Research on Learning and Instruction, Aachen, Germany.

Barzilai, S., Tzadok, E., & Eshet-Alkalai, Y. (2015). Sourcing while reading divergent expert accounts: Pathways from views of knowing to written argumentation. *Instructional Science, 43*(6), 737–766.

Barzilai, S., & Weinstock, M. (2015). Measuring epistemic thinking within and across topics: A scenario-based approach. *Contemporary Educational Psychology, 42*, 141–158.

Barzilai, S., & Zohar, A. (2012). Epistemic thinking in action: Evaluating and integrating online sources. *Cognition and Instruction, 30*(1), 39–85.

Barzilai, S., & Zohar, A. (2014). Reconsidering personal epistemology as metacognition: A multifaceted approach to the analysis of epistemic thinking. *Educational Psychologist, 49*(1), 13–35.

Braasch, J. L. G., & Bråten, I. (2017). The discrepancy-induced source comprehension (D-ISC) model: Basic assumptions and preliminary evidence. *Educational Psychologist, 52*(3), 167–181.

Bråten, I., Stadtler, M., & Salmerón, L. (2017). The role of sourcing in discourse comprehension. In M. F. Schober, D. N. Rapp, & M. A. Britt (Eds.), *Handbook of discourse processes* (2nd ed., pp. 141–166). New York: Routledge.

Britt, M. A., & Rouet, J.-F. (2012). Learning with multiple documents: Component skills and their acquisition. In J. R. Kirby & M. J. Lawson (Eds.), *Enhancing the quality of learning: Dispositions, instruction, and learning processes* (pp. 276–314). New York: Cambridge University Press.

Bromme, R., Stadtler, M., & Scharrer, L. (2018). The provenance of certainty: Multiple source use and the public engagement with science. In J. L. G. Braasch, I. Bråten, & M. T. McCrudden (Eds.), *Handbook of multiple source use* (pp. 269–284). New York: Routledge.

Bromme, R., Thomm, E., & Wolf, V. (2015). From understanding to deference: Laypersons' and medical students' views on conflicts within medicine. *International Journal of Science Education, Part B, 5*(1), 68–91.

Camp, E. (2017). Perspectives in imaginative engagement with fiction. *Philosophical Perspectives*, *31*(1), 73–102.

Camp, E. (2020). Imaginative frames for scientific inquiry: Metaphors, telling facts, and just-so stories. In P. Godfrey-Smith & A. Levy (Eds.), *The scientific imagination: Philosophical and psychological perspectives*. Oxford: Oxford University Press.

Carpendale, J. I., & Chandler, M. J. (1996). On the distinction between false belief understanding and subscribing to an interpretive theory of mind. *Child Development*, *67*(4), 1686–1706.

Chinn, C. A., Rinehart, R. W., & Buckland, L. A. (2014). Epistemic cognition and evaluating information: Applying the AIR model of epistemic cognition. In D. Rapp & J. Braasch (Eds.), *Processing inaccurate information* (pp. 425–454). Cambridge, MA: MIT Press.

Cho, B.-Y., Woodward, L., & Li, D. (2018). Epistemic processing when adolescents read online: A verbal protocol analysis of more and less successful online readers. *Reading Research Quarterly*, *53*(2), 197–221.

Coiro, J., Coscarelli, C., Maykel, C., & Forzani, E. (2015). Investigating criteria that seventh graders use to evaluate the quality of online information. *Journal of Adolescent and Adult Literacy*, *59*(3), 287–297.

Dore, R. A., Amendum, S. J., Golinkoff, R. M., & Hirsh-Pasek, K. (2018). Theory of mind: A hidden factor in reading comprehension? *Educational Psychology Review*, *30*(3), 1067–1089.

Florit, E., De Carli, P., Giunti, G., & Mason, L. (2020). Advanced theory of mind uniquely contributes to children's multiple-text comprehension. *Journal of experimental child psychology*, *189*, 104708.

Flavell, J. H. (2000). Development of children's knowledge about the mental world. *International Journal of Behavioral Development*, *24*(1), 15–23.

Forzani, E. (2018). How well can students evaluate online science information? Contributions of prior knowledge, gender, socioeconomic status, and offline reading ability. *Reading Research Quarterly*, *53*(4), 385–390.

Hobbs, R., & Frost, R. (2003). Measuring the acquisition of media-literacy skills. *Reading Research Quarterly*, *38*(3), 330–355.

Jucks, R., Becker, B.-M., & Bromme, R. (2008). Lexical entrainment in written discourse: Is experts' word use adapted to the addressee?. *Discourse Processes*, *45*(6), 497–518.

Jucks, R., & Bromme, R. (2011). Perspective taking in computer-mediated instructional communication. *Journal of Media Psychology: Theories, Methods, and Applications*, *23*(4), 192–199.

Kiili, C., Leu, D. J., Marttunen, M., Hautala, J., & Leppänen, P. H. T. (2018). Exploring early adolescents' evaluation of academic and commercial online resources related to health. *Reading and Writing*, *31*(3), 533–557.

Kim, H. Y., LaRusso, M. D., Hsin, L. B., Harbaugh, A. G., Selman, R. L., & Snow, C. E. (2018). Social perspective-taking performance: Construct, measurement, and relations with academic performance and engagement. *Journal of Applied Developmental Psychology*, *57*, 24–41.

King, P. M., & Kitchener, K. S. (1994). *Developing reflective judgment: Understanding and promoting intellectual growth and critical thinking in adolescents and adults*. San Francisco, CA: Jossey-Bass Publishers.

Kuhn, D. (1991). *The skills of argument*. New York: Cambridge University Press.

Lalonde, C. E., & Chandler, M. J. (2002). Children's understanding of interpretation. *New Ideas in Psychology*, *20*(2), 163–198.

List, A., Grossnickle, E. M., & Alexander, P. A. (2016). Undergraduate students' justifications for source selection in a digital academic context. *Journal of Educational Computing Research*, *54*(1), 22–61.

Lecce, S., Zocchi, S., Pagnin, A., Palladino, P., & Taumoepeau, M. (2010). Reading minds: The relation between children's mental state knowledge and their metaknowledge about reading. *Child Development*, *81*, 1876–1893.

Miller, M., & Boix Mansilla, V. (2004). *Thinking across perspectives and disciplines*. Cambridge, MA: Harvard Graduate School of Education.

Miller, S. A. (2009). Children's understanding of second-order mental states. *Psychological Bulletin*, *135*(5), 749–773.

Monte-Sano, C., De La Paz, S., & Felton, M. (2014). *Reading, thinking, and writing about history: Teaching argument writing to diverse learners in the common core classroom, grades 6-12*. New York: Teachers College Press.

Olson, D. R. (1994). *The world on paper: The conceptual and cognitive implications of writing and reading*. New York: Cambridge University Press.

Osterhaus, C., Koerber, S., & Sodian, B. (2017). Scientific thinking in elementary school: Children's social cognition and their epistemological understanding promote experimentation skills. *Developmental Psychology*, *53*(3), 450–462.

Paxton, R. J. (1997). "Someone with like a life wrote it": The effects of a visible author on high school history students. *Journal of Educational Psychology*, *89*(2), 235–250.

Pepper, S. C. (1942). *World hypotheses: A study in evidence.* Berkeley-Los Angeles, and London: University of California Press.

Perfetti, C. A., Rouet, J.-F., & Britt, M. A. (1999). Toward a theory of documents representation. In H. van Oostendorp & S. R. Goldman (Eds.), *The construction of mental representations during reading* (pp. 99–122). Mahwah, NJ: Lawrence Erlbaum Associates.

Perner, J. (1991). *Understanding the representational mind.* Cambridge, MA: MIT Press.

Perry, W. G. (1970/1999). *Forms of intellectual and ethical development in the college years.* San Francisco, CA: Jossey-Bass Publishers. (Original work published 1968).

Pillow, B. H., & Mash, C. (1998). Children's understanding of misinterpretation: Source identification and perspective-taking. *Merrill-Palmer Quarterly, 44*(2), 129–140.

Sodian, B., Thoermer, C., & Metz, U. (2007). Now I see it but you don't: 14-month-olds can represent another person's visual perspective. *Developmental Science, 10*(2), 199–204.

Sosa, E. (2015). *Judgment and agency.* Oxford: Oxford University Press.

Sperber, D., Clément, F., Heintz, C., Mascaro, O., Mercier, H., Origgi, G., & Wilson, D. (2010). Epistemic vigilance. *Mind & Language, 25*(4), 359–393.

Stenseth, T., & Strømsø, H. I. (2019). To read or not to read: A qualitative study of students' justifications for document selection in task-oriented reading. *Scandinavian Journal of Educational Research,63*(5), 771–788.

Thomm, E., Barzilai, S., & Bromme, R. (2017). Why do experts disagree? The role of conflict topics and epistemic perspectives in conflict explanations. *Learning and Instruction, 52,* 15–26.

Weinstock, M. (2016). Epistemic cognition in legal reasoning. In J. A. Greene, W. A. Sandoval, & I. Bråten (Eds.), *Handbook of epistemic cognition* (pp. 215–229). New York: Routledge.

Weinstock, M., & Cronin, M. A. (2003). The everyday production of knowledge: Individual differences in epistemological understanding and juror-reasoning skill. *Applied Cognitive Psychology, 17*(2), 161–181.

Weinstock, M., & Israel, V. (2017). Children's developing understanding of interpretation as a source of disagreement. Paper presented at the Biennial Conference of the European Association for Research on Learning and Instruction, Tampere, Finland.

Weinstock, M., & Madjar, N. (2018). From theory of mind to epistemology: Children's epistemic development. Paper presented at the Annual Meeting of the Jean Piaget Society, Amsterdam.

10

ON THE ROLES OF DISPOSITIONS AND BELIEFS IN LEARNING FROM MULTIPLE PERSPECTIVES

Ivar Bråten and Helge I. Strømsø

UNIVERSITY OF OSLO

ABSTRACT

This chapter reviews theory and research on the roles of dispositions and beliefs in learning from multiple perspectives and discusses implications for future research in the area. Learning from multiple perspectives is defined as the integration of different views on a particular topic, issue, or phenomenon. With regard to dispositions, more enduring and general individual difference factors related to personality are focused on, and with regard to beliefs, it is distinguished between beliefs about reality (i.e., ontic beliefs) and beliefs about knowledge and knowing about reality (i.e., epistemic beliefs). Different frameworks relevant for understanding how dispositions and beliefs may come into play when learning from multiple perspectives are discussed, and empirical work regarding the roles of dispositions, epistemic beliefs, and ontic beliefs in such learning is reviewed. In addition, the chapter launches and discusses the idea that beliefs may be more or less influenced by dispositions and, consequently, function differently in terms of learning from multiple perspectives. Based on this theoretical and empirical work, several theoretical and empirical issues that need further clarification and testing are highlighted.

Key words: dispositions, beliefs, ontic beliefs, epistemic beliefs, learning from multiple perspectives

INTRODUCTION

The purpose of this chapter is to review theory and research on the roles of students' dispositions and beliefs in learning from multiple perspectives, discuss implications for educational research and practice, and suggest future directions. We define learning from multiple perspectives as the integration of different views on a particular topic, issue, or phenomenon. Such views may be complementary or conflicting, with integration involving combining complementary views to achieve a more complete understanding or drawing bridging inferences across conflicting views to achieve conflict resolution or reconciliation (Latini, Bråten, Anmarkrud, & Salmerón, 2019; List & Alexander, 2019). Moreover, as recently noted by Bråten and Braasch (2018), such forms of integration are required not only when learners encounter different views in external sources, but also when they encounter views in external sources that differ from their own views or preconceptions about the issue in question.

A range of cognitive, metacognitive, and motivational factors have been discussed in relation to learning from multiple perspectives, such as when learners encounter different views on the same issue in multiple textual resources or documents (for reviews, see Barzilai & Strømsø, 2018; Bråten, Braasch, & Salmerón, in press). More enduring and general individual difference factors related to personality have been underfocused in this area of research, however. In this chapter, we therefore focus on the role of dispositions in learning from multiple perspectives. In the terminology of Allport's (1961) classic theory of personality, a disposition is a "neuropsychic structure having the capacity to render many stimuli functionally equivalent, and to initiate and guide equivalent (meaningfully consistent) forms of adaptive and expressive behavior" (p. 347). In other words, dispositions denote characteristics of a learner that exert their influence across situations and give consistency to his or her approach to different learning tasks (see also, VandenBos, 2007).

An additional focus in this chapter is on learners' beliefs (in this volume, beliefs are also discussed by Lombardi, Heddy, & Matewos, Chapter 20). While beliefs have been described in terms of what individuals accept as or want to be true regardless of external verification (e.g., Murphy & Mason, 2006), we, following Wolfe and Griffin (2018), define beliefs as positions or stances that individuals take about the truth value of propositions or statements. Some of these statements concern what is (i.e., reality). We term the positions people take about the truth value of such statements "ontic beliefs." For example, positions individuals take about the truth value of statements regarding climate change or evolution (e.g., "climate change is caused by human activity") represent their ontic beliefs. The positions that individuals take about such statements, for example as reflected in their agreement with items on a questionnaire, may be consistent or inconsistent with what is externally verified and confirmed by others (i.e., factual). That is, some people may believe that human-induced climate change is not happening or that the principles of evolution are false although the scientific evidence in both cases is overwhelming. Regarding other aspects of reality, however, these people may hold beliefs that are factual and consistent with scientific evidence, for example considering the truth value of the statement "smoking causes cancer" to be high. Of course, many people also hold beliefs about climate change and evolution that are consistent with scientific evidence, that is, they consider statements about these aspects of reality that are consistent with scientific evidence to be true.

Another class of statements do not directly concern what is (i.e., reality) but, rather, knowledge and knowing about what is. We term the positions individuals take about the truth value of such statements "epistemic beliefs." For example, in addition to taking positions about the truth value of statements regarding climate change or evolution, individuals may take positions about the truth value of statements regarding knowledge and knowing about climate change or evolution (e.g., "knowledge about climate change is complex"). Such beliefs may vary along several dimensions and be more or less adaptive in learning contexts, as thoroughly documented in the last decades (Greene, Sandoval, & Bråten, 2016). Typically, researchers try to measure individuals' epistemic beliefs independent of their ontic beliefs by asking them to express their agreement with statements concerning knowledge and knowing about aspects of reality (e.g., domains or topics) rather than aspects of reality themselves.[1]

Of note is that we use "ontic" instead of "ontological" beliefs in this chapter because the latter term may suggest that people hold beliefs about the philosophical study of being (i.e., ontology) rather than about what is real (i.e., ontic). For a similar reason, "epistemic beliefs" has replaced "epistemological beliefs" within personal epistemology research. Thus, non-philosophers seldom hold beliefs about the philosophical study of knowledge and knowing (i.e., epistemology), although they may hold beliefs about knowledge and the process of knowing (i.e., the epistemic; Kitchener, 2002). Presumably, both ontic and epistemic beliefs may vary in regard to level of specificity. Thus, just as beliefs concerning knowledge and knowing may range from domain-general to topic-specific beliefs (Sandoval, Greene, & Bråten, 2016), ontic beliefs may range from beliefs about the world in general to beliefs about specific topics, such as climate change or evolution (Boden, Berenbaum, & Gross, 2016), with the latter type often termed topic beliefs in the literature (e.g., Kardash & Howell, 2000; McCrudden & Sparks, 2014). Also, beliefs are typically regarded as dynamic rather than static, with their content as well as their level of conviction (i.e., strength) potentially changing as a function of different experiences (Boden et al., 2016). Presumably, both ontic and epistemic beliefs play important roles in learning from multiple perspectives. This is because beliefs about both reality and knowledge are likely to frame and filter learners' processing of information and, thus, influence the extent to which they create balanced mental representations from multiple perspectives.

Given these conceptual clarifications, we addressed the roles of dispositions and beliefs in learning from multiple perspectives in the following three main sections, with dispositions regarded as more stable and general and with beliefs regarded as more dynamic and varying with respect to level of specificity. In the first main section, we provide a theoretical background by discussing four models that, taken together, speak to the importance and functioning of dispositions and beliefs in learning from multiple perspectives. In the second, we review empirical work examining linkages between dispositions and beliefs on the one hand, and learning from multiple perspectives on the other. In this section, we will also take a look at some research that has included both dispositions and beliefs in one and the same study. Moreover, we will launch the idea that beliefs may be more or less influenced by dispositions and, consequently, function differently in terms of learning from multiple perspectives. In essence, we discuss the possibility that the more strongly beliefs are rooted in underlying dispositions (i.e., personality), the more widespread and robust the effects of those beliefs on learning from multiple perspectives might be. Finally, in the third main section, we summarize the results of our theoretical and empirical analysis and discuss some implications and future directions that may be derived from it.

THEORETICAL BACKGROUND

In this section, we briefly present and discuss four models or frameworks focusing on learning complex information from multiple sources. These models were developed within educational psychology during the last decade and extend our understandings of how dispositions and beliefs may come into play when individuals try to integrate different perspectives in the service of meaning-making. They are the Integrated Model of Epistemic Beliefs and Multiple-Text Comprehension, the Two-Step Model of Validation in Multiple-Text Comprehension, the Plausibility Judgments of Conceptual Change Model, and the Integrated Framework of Multiple Texts.

The Integrated Model of Epistemic Beliefs and Multiple-Text Comprehension

Theorists have highlighted the need to construct a coherent mental representation when learning from a single textual source (Graesser, Singer, & Trabasso, 1994; Kintsch, 1998; van den Broek, 2010). The documents model framework of Britt and colleagues (Britt, Perfetti, Sandak, & Rouet, 1999; Britt & Rouet, 2012; Perfetti, Rouet, & Britt, 1999; Rouet, 2006) describes additional representational structures that must be constructed when individuals learn from multiple sources dealing with the same topic, issue, or phenomenon from different perspectives. In such instances, learners must create a coherent interpretation that bridges or reconciles different perspectives, that is, an integrated mental model (Britt & Rouet, 2012). Moreover, it is essential to note the sources (e.g., the authors) of the different perspectives as well as the relationships between these sources (e.g., whether authors agree or disagree), with the representation of such source-content and source-source links termed the intertext model within the documents model framework (Perfetti et al., 1999; Rouet, 2006).

The Integrated Model of Epistemic Beliefs and Multiple Text Comprehension (Bråten, Britt, Strømsø, & Rouet, 2011) represents an attempt to describe how and explain why learners' beliefs about knowledge and knowing, that is, their epistemic beliefs, are related to the construction of the two subcomponents of the documents model. Thus, building on the multidimensional epistemic belief framework of Hofer and Pintrich (1997), including beliefs about the certainty of knowledge, the simplicity of knowledge, the source of knowledge, and the justification for knowing, Bråten et al. (2011) proposed that beliefs falling along these four dimensions would differentially affect the construction of the integrated mental model and the intertext model. Specifically, based on available empirical evidence linking epistemic beliefs to aspects of multiple text comprehension, they posited that beliefs concerning the simplicity of knowledge and the justification for knowing would mainly influence the construction of the integrated mental model, whereas beliefs concerning the certainty of knowledge and the source of knowledge would mainly influence the construction of the intertext model.

With respect to the integration of different perspectives (i.e., mental model construction), in particular, Bråten et al. (2011) argued that believing knowledge to consist of a body of interrelated concepts rather than an accumulation of isolated facts would make it more likely that learners define the task as requiring integration across different perspectives, aim to construct a coherent mental representation from these perspectives, and engage in elaborative processing across sources to achieve this aim. Moreover, believing that knowledge claims need to be justified through reason, rules of inquiry, and the evaluation and integration of multiple information sources rather than through personal opinion, first-hand experience, and common sense was assumed to promote the integration of different perspectives because it makes it more likely that learners engage in metacognitive thinking and corroboration when encountering multiple perspectives located in different sources.

While much of Bråten et al.'s (2011) discussion centered on the impact of topic-specific epistemic beliefs, these authors also acknowledged that epistemic beliefs at different levels of specificity may affect learning from multiple perspectives.

The Two-Step Model of Validation in Multiple Text Comprehension

Rather than focusing on beliefs about knowledge and knowing, the Two-Step Model of Validation in Multiple Text Comprehension (Richter & Maier, 2017, 2018) mainly concerns the effects of beliefs about the topics, issues, or phenomena discussed across multiple sources (see also Richter, Münchow, & Abendroth, Chapter 16). More specifically, this model describes what happens when there is consistency or inconsistency between such ontic beliefs and the perspectives encountered in external sources, such as in one or more texts.

In the first step of the model, learners routinely and automatically validate different perspectives encountered in external sources in light of their consistency or inconsistency with learners' prior beliefs about the topic or issue in question. When inconsistencies between beliefs and perspectives located in external sources are detected, for example, when a person believes that there are no negative health effects of using a cell phone but reads in a newspaper that cell phone radiation actually may cause cancer, learners tend to perceive these belief-inconsistent views as implausible and reject them, instead concentrating on other information that is consistent with their prior beliefs. According to Richter and Maier (2017), this will lead to a consistency effect, such that external perspectives that are perceived as plausible because they are consistent with learners' prior beliefs will receive more cognitive resources. Also, these will be better remembered and understood as compared to belief-inconsistent views on the topic or issue. Consequently, this automatic, first step of Richter and Maier's (2017, 2018)) model of validation will result in a belief-biased or unbalanced rather than an integrated mental model of multiple perspectives.

In the second step of the two-step model of validation, however, learners may engage in strategic, elaborative processing of belief-inconsistent information to resolve the discrepancy and create a balanced mental representation that incorporates different perspectives on the issue. Among the task- and learner-related variables that determine whether learners engage in this deliberate second step of validation are their epistemic beliefs, with a "well developed epistemological position" (Richter & Maier, 2017, p. 152) making it more likely that learners strategically elaborate information to create an integrated model of multiple perspectives. In this way, the two-step model of validation also acknowledges the potential importance of adaptive beliefs about knowledge and the process of knowing in learning from multiple perspectives.

Although Richter and Maier (2017, 2018)) primarily discussed the effects of beliefs about specific socio-scientific topics or issues, beliefs about reality at different levels of specificity and stability may exert an influence on learning from multiple perspectives within their model of validation. One precondition to this is that beliefs, regardless of their specificity, and the perspectives to which they are compared become coactivated in working memory.

The Plausibility Judgments in Conceptual Change Model

The main focus of the model of Plausibility Judgments in Conceptual Change (PJCC) is to describe how learners' judgment of the potential truthfulness (i.e., plausibility) of a scientific explanation may lead them to change their existing knowledge structures to become more consistent with the scientific understanding of the phenomenon (Lombardi, Nussbaum, & Sinatra, 2016). Thus, when learners encounter a scientific explanation of a phenomenon (e.g., climate change) that is inconsistent with their current understanding, the PJCC posits that they judge the plausibility of the scientific explanation to be greater when it is aligned with their background knowledge and comprehensible, perceived to have a solid foundation and come from a trustworthy source, and not countered by heuristics and biases activated in the context.

With respect to the plausibility judgment itself, Lombardi et al. (2016) considered this to range from implicit to explicit on a continuum, with degree of explicitness reflecting degrees of awareness and cognitive effort during information processing. Moreover, the extent to which learners will engage in a conscious, effortful form of plausibility judgment is assumed to depend on "individuals' dispositions to think deeply and be inclined to impartly consider alternative explanations" (Lombardi et al., 2016, p. 46). In the psychological literature, such dispositions are termed need for cognition and open-mindedness, respectively, with need for cognition defined as "a stable individual difference in the tendency to engage in and enjoy cognitively effortful activities across a wide range of domains" (Petty, Briñol, Loersch, & McCaslin, 2009, p. 319), and with open-mindedness defined as an enduring and general inclination to seriously consider alternative views and contradictory evidence rather than dogmatically sticking to one's own ideas or perspectives (Riggs, 2010; Stanovich & West, 1997; Svedholm-Häkkinen & Lindeman, 2018). Among the motivational factors that may influence the degree of explicitness of learners' plausibility judgments is personal interest, which refers to a relatively stable individual disposition to be attracted by and engaged in specific topics or domains (Schiefele, 1999; Schunk, Meece, & Pintrich, 2014). As such, personal interest is distinguished from situational interest, which refers to a transient affective engagement elicited by particular tasks or contexts (Hidi, 2001; Schunk et al., 2014). Sometimes, learners also have to be prompted or involved in particular instructional activities to critically evaluate alternative explanations in a more explicit way.

However, even when learners reflect upon alternative explanations with an open mind, they will not reconstruct their conceptual understanding if they judge the plausibility of the scientific explanation to be less plausible than their current understanding. According to Lombardi et al. (2016), other factors, such as learners' commitments, may also override increased plausibility for the scientific explanation in some instances. For example, learners may have adopted certain values that make conceptual change unlikely despite the perceived plausibility of the scientific explanation.² The PJCC is relevant to understanding learning from multiple perspectives because it describes how learners' explicit judgments of the plausibility of perspectives (i.e., scientific explanations) that conflict with their own perspectives may lead them to change their existing perspectives and construct new understandings of the phenomena in question.

The Integrated Framework of Multiple Texts

List and Alexander (2019) proposed the Integrated Framework of Multiple Texts (IF-MT) to describe a series of three stages through which multiple text use typically unfolds. First, in the preparation stage, learners establish a stance toward the completion of the reading task. Then, in the execution stage, they strategically process the texts. Finally, in the production stage, they construct a task product, for example, a written synthesis of the texts' content. In this conceptualization, the stances formed in the preparation stage are crucial because they also determine the strategic processing occurring in the execution stage and, consequently, what learners understand from the texts and their task products.

According to the IF-MT, several types of beliefs and dispositions influence learners' adoption of a particular stance or orientation to task completion in the preparation stage. Among them are learners' epistemic beliefs, especially beliefs about appropriate sources of knowledge and methods for justifying knowledge claims. Moreover, learners' motivational disposition in the form of personal or individual interest is assumed to play an important role, as are their attitudes toward the topic or domain discussed across texts. Of note is that evaluation is a defining attribute of any attitude, which can be conceived of as an enduring and global evaluation (i.e., positive or negative) of an object, issue, or domain (Bizer, Barden, & Petty, 2003).

Specifically, building on their Cognitive Affective Engagement Model (List & Alexander, 2017, 2018), List and Alexander (2019) proposed that learners' personal interests and attitudes combine with their multiple text proficiency (i.e., their pre-established habits in dealing with multiple texts in terms of source evaluation and content integration) to form a particular default stance or orientation toward task completion. Thus, when personal interest is low, attitudes weak, and multiple text proficiency low, learners are likely to adopt a disengaged stance. Conversely, when personal interest is high, attitudes strong, and multiple text proficiency high, learners are likely to adopt a critical analytic stance. With respect to the two stances falling in between, List and Alexander (2019) assumed that learners who are characterized by high personal interest and strong attitudes but lack multiple text proficiency will adopt an affectively engaged stance, and that learners who are characterized by low personal interest and weak attitudes in combination with high multiple text proficiency will adopt an evaluative stance. Of note is also that some epistemic beliefs about justification for knowing, such as beliefs in justification by multiple sources (Ferguson, Bråten, & Strømsø, 2012), are assumed to increase the likelihood that learners adopt an evaluative or critical analytic stance toward task completion. However, in terms of strategic processing in the execution stage, only learners adopting a critical analytic stance can be expected to engage in deep-level cross-text elaborative linking and monitoring in the service of bridging or reconciling different perspectives across trustworthy sources when working with multiple texts (List & Alexander, 2019).

Summary

To summarize, the four models we reviewed provide foundational, theoretical understanding of the roles of dispositions and beliefs in learning from multiple perspectives. Thus, these models highlight how various dispositions and beliefs may come into play when learners are required to integrate different perspectives to achieve a more complete understanding of an issue or reconcile conflicting views, which is the rule rather than the exception in the information saturated learning context of the 21st century (Bråten & Braasch, 2017). The models differ, however, with respect to whether their main focus is on the relationship between different perspectives located in external sources (e.g., texts) or the relationship between the learner's prior mental representation (beliefs or conceptual understanding) and differing views located in external sources. Thus, it seems fair to say that both Richter and Maier's (2017) Two-Step Model of Validation and Lombardi et al.'s (2016) Model of Plausibility Judgments in Conceptual Change mainly concern how learners come to terms with discrepancies between their own view and perspectives encountered in external sources, whereas Bråten et al.'s (2011) Integrated Model of Epistemic Beliefs and Multiple Text Comprehension and List and Alexander's (2019) Integrated Framework of Multiple Text Use mainly concern integration of different perspectives from external sources.

With respect to the dispositions and beliefs that are featured in these models, the models of Bråten et al. (2011) and Richter and Maier (2017, 2018) center on prior beliefs; the former on beliefs concerning knowledge about what is to be learned (e.g., knowledge about the causes of climate change) and the latter on beliefs about what is to be learned (e.g., the causes of climate change), termed epistemic and ontic beliefs, respectively, in the present chapter. In comparison, the models of Lombardi et al. (2016) and List and Alexander (2019) are more concerned with the effects of dispositions or personality traits such as need for cognition and open-mindedness (Lombardi et al., 2016), as well as with enduring trait-like characteristics such as personal interest, attitudes, and values (List & Alexander, 2019; Lombardi et al., 2016). Taken together, the four models highlight the need to integrate perspectives that, at the outset, are internal and external to the learner, as well as different external perspectives, and that learners' pre-existing dispositions and beliefs may play important roles in both scenarios.

EMPIRICAL WORK

In this section, we review empirical evidence on the roles of dispositions and beliefs in learning from multiple perspectives, focusing on text-based learning. In addition, we review some studies that speak to the relationship between dispositions and beliefs, including the possibility that dispositions may underlie beliefs and represent reasons why people believe what they do.

Dispositions and Learning from Multiple Perspectives

A number of studies have focused on how need for cognition and open-mindedness are related to processing and learning when readers are presented with different perspectives on a topic or issue. Regarding need for cognition, Kardash and Scholes

(1996), for example, had undergraduates read one text presenting two conflicting views on the HIV–AIDS relationship and asked them to write a concluding paragraph for that text. Results showed that need for cognition positively predicted the quality of students' conclusions, with students high in need for cognition more likely to represent the uncertainty and tentative nature of the evidence that was presented in the text. Thus, the stronger their disposition to engage in and enjoy complex and cognitively demanding tasks, the better participants represented the different perspectives in their written conclusions. Somewhat later, Kardash and Noel (2000) obtained similar results when undergraduates read one text discussing different energy resources: need for cognition contributed positively to students' memory and understanding of textual information.

Given that need for cognition by definition is linked to effortful cognitive processing (Cacioppo, Petty, Feinstein, & Jarvis, 1996; Petty et al., 2009), it seems likely that a positive relationship between need for cognition and learning from multiple perspectives is mediated by processing variables. This was tested in a study where upper-secondary school students read multiple texts presenting conflicting perspectives on sun exposure and health (Bråten, Anmarkrud, Brandmo, & Strømsø, 2014). Path analysis showed that need for cognition had a direct positive effect on participants' cross-text elaboration strategies and an indirect effect on the integration of multiple perspectives mediated by cross-text elaboration.

Likewise, Levin, Huneke, and Jasper (2000) demonstrated that need for cognition may facilitate the investment of cognitive effort in appropriate processing strategies when learning from multiple perspectives. These authors asked undergraduates to select one computer out of 16 as a gift to a friend, with information about a number of features presented by means of a "computer shop program." Results showed that participants with high need for cognition invested more effort, used more productive search strategies, and made higher quality decisions as compared to participants with low need for cognition.

Winter and Krämer (2012) invited parents to search a science blog for articles about the effects of media depictions of violence on children. Half of the articles contained two-sided materials, whereas the other half contained arguments for one position only. Results showed that need for cognition predicted participants' preference for selecting two-sided over one-sided articles (for further research on the presentation of multiple perspectives via single dual-positional texts, see Bohn-Gettler, Chapter 15). As another example, Mason, Boldrin, and Ariasi (2010) found that when university students were asked to research different information sources about a controversial topic, participants high in need for cognition evaluated both sources and content more thoroughly than did participants low in need for cognition. Although most studies examining the role of need for cognition in text-based learning have used expository texts, it has also been demonstrated that need for cognition may predict how readers cope with narrative texts presenting multiple perspectives (Dai & Wang, 2007).

Regarding open-mindedness, Stanovich and West (1997), inspired by previous work on thinking dispositions (e.g., Baron, 1993), developed a questionnaire intended to capture actively open-minded thinking, with subscales focusing on the consideration of information that disconfirms one's view and willingness to change when faced with contradictory evidence.[3] Stanovich and West (1997) had undergraduates read a number of propositions concerned with social and political issues, with each proposition followed by a counterargument and a rebuttal. Participants were asked to evaluate the quality of the rebuttal, and an argument quality score, corrected for prior beliefs, was calculated. Results showed a positive relationship between actively open-minded thinking and the evaluation of argument quality when cognitive ability was also controlled for.

Griffin, Wiley, Britt, and Salas (2012) studied the relationship between 7th graders' actively open-minded thinking and their learning from a multiple text inquiry task, using a subset of items from the measure constructed by Stanovich and colleagues (see also, Sá, West, & Stanovich, 1999). In addition, reports of reading skills, prior knowledge, and interest were included. Learning was measured by the inclusion of key concepts in students' essays and scores on an inference verification task. Results showed that actively open-minded thinking, together with reports of reading skills, positively predicted performance on both outcome measures. Thus, students' disposition to reason about evidence and openness to change their own views seemed to positively affect their identification of key concepts and their integration of information across different perspectives.

As a final example, Haran, Ritov, and Mellers (2013) studied the relationship between actively open-minded thinking and adults' persistence in information acquisition and ability to make informed predictions. To predict the outcome of football games, participants could look up different kinds of information about a team's record. Results showed that open-minded thinking predicted both information acquisition and the number of correct predictions made after controlling for expertise and need for cognition. Thus, participants' disposition to consider different kinds of information was positively related to their actual persistence in doing so, as well as to the quality of their predictions based on different information sources. Need for cognition was not related to the outcome measures in this particular study.

In summary, dispositions in terms of need for cognition and open-minded thinking have been shown to contribute to text-based learning from multiple perspectives. Moreover, there is some evidence to suggest that the relationship between such dispositions and learning outcomes is mediated by strategic processing with respect to search, evaluation, and integration.

Regarding the other trait-like individual characteristics discussed in the previous main section, evidence for the role of personal interest in learning from multiple perspectives seems to be quite meager. Thus, in research on the reading of multiple texts dealing with controversial issues from multiple perspectives, self-reports of personal interest have been only weakly associated with the integration of different perspectives, if at all (Bråten et al., 2014; Bråten, Brante, & Strømsø, 2018; List, Stephens, & Alexander, 2019; Salmerón, Gil, & Bråten, 2018; Stang Lund, Bråten, Brandmo, Brante, & Strømsø, 2019; Stang Lund, Bråten, Brante, & Strømsø, 2017; Strømsø & Bråten, 2009; Strømsø, Bråten, & Britt, 2010), and in only one study was personal interest a unique positive predictor of integration performance when other relevant variables were controlled for (Strømsø & Bråten, 2009).

With respect to attitudes, some studies have found that individuals may spend longer time processing and evaluating arguments that contradict their attitudes compared to arguments supporting their attitudes (Edwards & Smith, 1996; Taber, Cann, & Kucsova, 2009; Taber & Lodge, 2006), with such indications of more effortful processing of contradictory arguments suggesting that individuals strive to protect their attitudes and counterargue opposing views (Wolfe & Griffin, 2018). A study by van Strien, Kammerer, Brand-Gruwel, and Boshuizen (2016), however, did not find that students with strong attitudes processed websites that contradicted their attitudes more thoroughly than websites supporting their attitudes. Instead, van Strien and colleagues (van Strien, Brand-Gruwel, & Boshuizen, 2014; van Strien et al., 2016) found that students with strong attitudes judge the credibility of websites contradicting their attitudes to be lower and use less information from such websites in their written products. Recently, Schweiger and Cress (2019) found that strong prior attitudes led participants to prioritize information supporting their attitudes when reading as well as evaluating the content of blog-posts on a mental health issue.

Finally, regarding values, Gottlieb and Wineburg (2012) demonstrated that readers' values in the form of commitments to religious faith communities affected how they dealt with multiple perspectives presented across texts. In this study, religious (Jewish and Christian) and non-religious individuals read multiple texts presenting conflicting views on the biblical Exodus. Results showed that the religiously committed individuals judged the plausibility and evidentiary weight of texts respectively supporting and casting doubt on the historical authenticity of this event very differently than did non-religious individuals. In the same vein, Kahan et al. (2012) demonstrated the importance of cultural values in dealing with conflicting views on socio-scientific issues. Thus, the results of this study indicated that values shared in a group with which individuals identify may influence their judgments of the risks associated with climate change and nuclear power more than their science literacy skills. For further discussion of the roles of attitudes and values in learning from multiple perspectives, see Lombardi et al. (Chapter 20).

Beliefs and Learning from Multiple Perspectives

Epistemic beliefs

Beliefs about knowledge and knowing may exist at different levels of specificity (Muis, Bendixen, & Haerle, 2006). Accordingly, in this section, we distinguish between studies measuring domain-general, domain-specific, and topic-specific epistemic beliefs. When *domain-general* epistemic beliefs have been studied in the context of undergraduate and high-school students' reading of multiple perspectives, results indicate that learning is facilitated by beliefs about knowledge as tentative and complex rather than certain and simple (Kardash & Scholes, 1996; Qian & Alvermann, 1995; Rukavina & Daneman, 1996). For example, when high-school students read a refutation text about Newton's theory of motion (Qian & Alvermann, 1995), their tendency to view knowledge as tentative, evolving, and complex seemed to facilitate their comprehension of the phenomenon. In the same vein, research by Mason and colleagues (Mason & Boscolo, 2004; Mason & Scirica, 2006) has suggested that secondary school students' "general level of epistemological understanding" is adaptive when interpreting and evaluating two-sided texts on controversial topics.

Research on the relationship between *domain-specific* epistemic beliefs and learning from texts presenting multiple perspectives also suggests that beliefs about knowledge might affect learning positively. Epistemic beliefs at this level of specificity can be conceived of as developed in formal educational contexts, in tensions between the normative epistemologies of specific domains or disciplines and instructional practices experienced in school (including learning materials and evaluative practices; Muis et al., 2006; Sandoval et al., 2016). For example, believing knowledge in the domain of science to be tentative and complex has been found to contribute to learning from refutation texts, among both 5th graders (Mason, Gava, & Boldrin, 2008) and undergraduates (Kendeou, Muis, & Fulton, 2011). Other studies have focused on beliefs about the process of knowing in specific domains. Inspired by the work of Greene, Azevedo, and Torney-Purta (2008), Bråten, Ferguson, and colleagues conceptualized beliefs about justification for knowing as varying along three different dimensions, which they termed personal justification, justification by authority, and justification by multiple sources (Ferguson et al., 2012). When 10th graders read a set of partly conflicting texts on the issue of sun exposure and health, results showed a positive relationship between students' beliefs in justification of knowledge claims in science through corroboration across multiple sources and their integrated understanding of the issue. Reliance on personal justification, on the other hand, negatively predicted integration across texts (Bråten, Ferguson, Strømsø, & Anmarkrud, 2013; Ferguson & Bråten, 2013). Moreover, in a study with high-school students, the relationship between beliefs in justification by multiple sources in science and integrated understanding was found to be mediated by students' investment of effort and their use of cross-text elaboration strategies (Bråten et al., 2014). Beliefs concerning justification by multiple sources also seem to be particularly facilitative when students learn about scientific issues from single refutation texts (Kendeou, Braasch, & Bråten, 2016; Trevors, Kendeou, Bråten, & Braasch, 2017).

Regarding *topic-specific* epistemic beliefs, Bråten, Strømsø, and colleagues initiated research on beliefs at this level of specificity in relation to students' integrated understanding of multiple perspectives on particular topics that were discussed in a set of conflicting texts. Results showed that for undergraduates, but not for high-school students, believing that knowledge about a socio-scientific issue was tentative and evolving positively predicted their integrated understanding of the issue (Bråten & Strømsø, 2010a; Strømsø & Bråten, 2009; Strømsø, Bråten, & Samuelstuen, 2008). Also, believing knowledge about the topic to be complex rather than simple was found to contribute to the building of integrated understanding across texts (Bråten & Strømsø, 2010a, 2010b; Strømsø et al., 2008). Regarding beliefs about the source of knowledge about a topic, two studies indicated that when students encounter different perspectives on a relatively unfamiliar topic, they may be better off relying on external expertise than relying on themselves as the source of knowledge (Bråten, Strømsø, & Samuelstuen, 2008; Strømsø et al., 2008). Finally, with respect to topic-specific beliefs about justification for knowing, believing that knowledge claims need to be justified through reason, rules of inquiry, and the evaluation and integration of multiple sources was found to uniquely predict the construction of an integrated understanding of different perspectives on the topic (Bråten & Strømsø, 2010b; Strømsø & Bråten, 2009). Attention to this level of specificity is important because learners' beliefs about knowledge and knowing may vary among topics within a domain. For example, learners' beliefs about the certainty of knowledge may vary among different historical topics (e.g., depending on the distance in time) and reliance on justification by multiple sources may differ across medical topics (e.g., depending on the controversy surrounding the topic).

More recent studies suggest that the relationship between topic-specific epistemic beliefs and learning from multiple perspectives is mediated by other individual differences variables. In particular, emotions have been found to play a role in mediating relations between topic-specific beliefs about justification for knowing and learning from multiple perspectives, with curiosity seemingly being of special importance (Muis et al., 2015; Trevors, Muis, Pekrun, Sinatra, & Muijselaar, 2017). Further, Barzilai and Eshet-Alkalai (2015) found that students' topic-specific epistemic beliefs in terms of absolutist, multiplist, and evaluativist views on knowledge and knowing (Kuhn, 1991) indirectly affected their integrated understanding via their interpretation of the authors' viewpoints.

In summary, there is currently substantial evidence that epistemic beliefs at different levels of specificity may be related to learning from multiple perspectives (for reviews, see also Bråten, Strømsø, & Ferguson, 2016; Strømsø & Kammerer, 2016). Potential mediators of such relationships are still wide open for further research, however.

Ontic beliefs

When individuals encounter information in external sources that is inconsistent with their own beliefs about some aspect of reality, those beliefs have been found to influence their reasoning, learning, and comprehension in a range of studies (e.g., Bråten, Salmerón, & Strømsø, 2016; Kardash & Scholes, 1996; Lord, Ross, & Lepper, 1979; Maier & Richter, 2013; McCrudden & Barnes, 2016; McCrudden, Barnes, McTigue, Welch, & MacDonald, 2017; McCrudden & Sparks, 2014; Murphy & Alexander, 2004). Please remember that an ontic belief is considered to represent a position on the truth value of a proposition concerning some aspect of reality (Wolfe & Griffin, 2018). As such, ontic beliefs are distinguished from attitudes because attitudes represent general preferences (i.e., likes and dislikes) for something that cannot be proven incorrect (i.e., nonfactual), whereas ontic beliefs represent positions about the truth value of propositions that can be objectively refuted or substantiated by arguments or evidence. Examples of such propositions are "capital punishment reduces criminality," "human activities cause global warming," "HIV causes AIDS," and "cell phone use is perfectly safe."

In a classic study by Lord et al. (1979), people read and evaluated conflicting research evidence on capital punishment. These authors found that those who had strong initial beliefs on the topic evaluated more positively the evidence that supported their beliefs than evidence that opposed their beliefs. Moreover, reading conflicting evidence strengthened their initial beliefs on the topic. Building on Lord et al. (1979), Kardash and Scholes (1996) investigated the degree to which people's preexisting beliefs about the HIV–AIDS relationship were associated with the written conclusions that they produced after reading a text presenting arguments for two different positions on the topic (HIV is the sole cause of AIDS vs. HIV does not cause AIDS). Results showed that the stronger preexisting beliefs students held about this topic, the more certain conclusions they wrote from the inconclusive text favoring their own initial beliefs about the HIV–AIDS relationship. In the same vein, Murphy and Alexander (2004) found that students who read three single texts on different controversial topics – each presenting arguments as well as counterarguments for a particular position regarding the topic – strengthened their own pre-reading beliefs about the topic discussed in the text.

Several other authors have also found that people seem to be biased toward their own prior beliefs about aspects of reality when they evaluate arguments and conclusions about controversial issues or phenomena (McCrudden & Barnes, 2016; McCrudden et al., 2017; Strømsø & Bråten, 2017), as well as when they interpret the contents of belief-consistent and belief-inconsistent texts (Maier & Richter, 2013, 2014; Maier, Richter, Nauroth, & Gollwitzer, 2018b). Recent research has also confirmed that arguments consistent with students' prior beliefs are prioritized in their written products (Maier, Richter, & Britt, 2018a).

Although learners' understanding of different perspectives may be biased by prior beliefs, such beliefs do not necessarily impair their memory for the perspectives they oppose. This was demonstrated by Maier and Richter (2013, 2014), who found that students' understanding of a controversy was biased toward belief-consistent texts but that their memory actually was better for belief-inconsistent texts. Other studies have found no relationship between undergraduates' prior beliefs and their memory for textual content, however (Kardash & Howell, 2000; Strømsø, Bråten, & Stenseth, 2017; Wiley, 2005). For example, Strømsø et al. (2017) did not observe any belief-biased recall of conclusions when students read texts on controversial socio-scientific issues, although participants were found to trust belief-consistent conclusions more than belief-inconsistent conclusions. In that study, participants' ontic beliefs concerned their positions on the truth value of (i.e., agreement with) statements regarding the health effects of cell phone use and intake of artificial sweeteners. In brief, belief-inconsistent perspectives may well be attended to and remembered without being integrated into a coherent mental representation of the issue or phenomenon.

Regarding processing, there is evidence to suggest that students sometimes may spend more time processing belief-inconsistent than belief-consistent information (e.g., Maier & Richter, 2014; Maier et al., 2018a). This accords with the idea that people may strategically engage in effortful processing of belief-inconsistent information to arrive at a coherent mental representation of controversial issues (Richter & Maier, 2017, 2018). However, people may also process belief-inconsistent information more deeply in order to counterargue and refute that information (Klaczynski, Gordon, & Faulth, 1997), which is supported by results showing that students may produce more evaluative judgments when reading information that opposes their prior beliefs, compared to information with which they already agree (Kardash & Howell, 2000).

Finally, a study by Maier et al. (2018b) suggested that students' prior beliefs about a particular topic may influence their comprehension more strongly than their identification with relevant social groups. In the terminology of ontic beliefs, the beliefs that were targeted in that study were participants' positions on the truth value of (i.e., agreement with) statements regarding the effectiveness of different psychological treatments. Still, as noted previously, commitment to social or cultural groups also may affect how individuals deal with different perspectives on controversial issue (Kahan & Corbin, 2016; Kahan et al., 2012).

In summary, learners' ontic beliefs typically affect their interpretation of perspectives on controversial issues encountered in external sources. Such beliefs may affect their comprehension of those issues but not necessarily their memory for perspectives that oppose their prior beliefs. Effortful processing of belief-inconsistent information may sometimes strengthen a one-sided rather than an integrated representation of the issue in question.

Relationships between Dispositions and Beliefs

In this chapter, we have considered the dispositions of need for cognition and open-mindedness, in particular. Given the definitional characteristics of these dispositions, as described earlier, they could be expected to be positively related. This has also been confirmed in several studies (e.g., Sinatra & Kardash, 2004; Sinatra, Southerland, McConaughy, & Demastes, 2003; Svedholm-Häkkinen & Lindeman, 2018; Toplak, West, & Stanovich, 2014). In this section, however, we will focus on how these dispositions might relate to people's beliefs about knowledge and reality, respectively.

Regarding epistemic beliefs, Sinatra and Kardash (2004) found that students high in need for cognition were also more likely to believe that knowledge is evolving via the processes of integration and reorganization (i.e., knowledge-building) rather than through simple accumulating of factual information. Accordingly, Kardash and Scholes (1996) found that students high in need for cognition were less likely to believe that knowledge is simply handed down by authorities rather than constructed by learners through effortful processing. Of note is that both Sinatra and Kardash (2004) and Kardash and Scholes (1996) measured epistemic beliefs at a domain-general level, that is, as pertaining to knowledge in general. With respect to domain-specific epistemic beliefs, Bråten and colleagues have demonstrated that need for cognition is positively related to lower- and upper-secondary school students' beliefs in justification for knowing in science by means of corroboration across multiple sources (Bråten et al., 2014; Bråten & Ferguson, 2014). Moreover, need for cognition was found to be positively related to beliefs in justification by reliance on scientific expertise and negatively related to beliefs in justification for knowing in science by referring to personal opinion and experience (Bråten & Ferguson, 2014). Mason et al. (2010), who studied need for cognition in relation to epistemic beliefs that were activated during a web-based inquiry about a specific socio-scientific topic, found that university students high in need for cognition were also more likely to judge the credibility of websites on the basis of expertise and to justify knowledge claims by appealing to scientific evidence. Finally, some studies have demonstrated that actively open-minded thinking correlates positively with domain-general epistemic beliefs, especially with beliefs in knowledge as tentative and complex rather than certain and simple (Sinatra & Kardash, 2004; Sinatra et al., 2003).

Regarding ontic beliefs, Kardash and Scholes (1996) found that the higher participating undergraduates scored on need for cognition, the stronger their beliefs that HIV causes AIDS (although this relationship did not reach a conventional level of statistical significance with a two-tailed test). Moreover, when Haugtvedt and Petty (1992) had undergraduates read two conflicting messages about the safety of a particular food additive, students high in need for cognition were found to hold more elaborated beliefs about the issue than did students low in need for cognition, with such beliefs also less likely to change through persuasion. There is also some evidence to suggest that open-mindedness may be related to beliefs about aspects of reality (i.e., ontic beliefs). Thus, Kahan and Corbin (2016) demonstrated that people's actively open-minded thinking was positively related to their beliefs in scientifically supported human-induced climate change. However, when participants' commitments to political ideologies were also taken into account, the positive relation between open-mindedness and such beliefs were found to hold up only for those who endorsed liberal values. In contrast, for those who endorsed conservative values, there was a negative relation between actively open-minded thinking and beliefs consistent with a scientific explanation of climate change. This suggests that shared values within social or cultural groups may be important contributors to what people believe about the world, with such values also moderating the relationship between dispositions and beliefs about controversial issues.

Why do people believe what they do?

Moving beyond the correlational data discussed above, a perennial question concerns the basis of people's beliefs, that is, why they believe what they do (Boden et al., 2016). In the context of learning from multiple perspectives, this question is important because the basis of beliefs might impact the processing of different perspectives as well as learning outcomes (Wolfe & Griffin, 2018). In particular, the extent to which people's beliefs are influenced by stable and general dispositions or traits versus specific experiences in specific contexts seems important in this regard. One basic idea is that the more learners' beliefs are anchored in dispositions or traits, such as need for cognition or open-mindedness, the more stable and general those beliefs might be and the more pervasive their effects, with stable and general beliefs more likely to override a contextualization of beliefs according to specific topics and tasks.

Support for this idea comes from theoretical assumptions and empirical findings regarding the functions of beliefs, with some beliefs, for example, serving the purpose of gaining coherent, evidence-based representations of the world in all its complexity, and others primarily serving the purpose of providing a sense of belonging to a social or cultural group (Boden et al., 2016; Griffin, 2008; Wolfe & Griffin, 2018). In terms of dispositions, the former may be anchored in dispositions such as need for cognition and open-mindedness and the latter in individuals' commitments to a shared value system. Empirically, research has suggested that beliefs may be more or less dispositional in nature and that the dispositions underlying beliefs may influence processing and mental representation of different perspectives (Griffin, 2008; Wolfe & Griffin, 2018; Wolfe, Tanner, & Taylor, 2013). For example, learners' self-reported belief-basis (i.e., the reasons they claim to hold particular beliefs) has been shown to affect the processing and comprehension of controversial issues. Thus, individuals basing their beliefs on a need for or openness to considering available complex evidence seem more likely to process both sides of an issue thoroughly and construct mental representations that integrate different perspectives (Wolfe & Griffin, 2018; Wolfe et al., 2013). In contrast, individuals who base their beliefs on a need to achieve or maintain a sense of belonging or community may be more likely to bias their processing to reach a valued conclusion, such as by avoiding uncertainty and ambiguity introduced by taking diverse perspectives into consideration.

Although somewhat speculative at this point, beliefs might thus be more or less influenced by dispositional individual differences across domains and by features of specific topics or tasks, with beliefs sometimes reflecting underlying dispositions to the extent that they function as worldviews more generally filtering individuals' experiences and outcomes when learning from multiple perspectives. This idea about an interplay between dispositional and contextualized beliefs in learning from multiple perspectives is related to the notion of top-down and bottom-up processing within human cognition. When beliefs are firmly rooted in more enduring and general dispositions, they may contribute to a form of top-down processing of information that sometimes facilitates and sometimes constrain learning from multiple perspectives, depending on the kind of disposition that underlies the beliefs. On the other hand, when beliefs are formed and changed primarily in response to specific contextual influences, they may contribute to a form of bottom-up processing of information where the context and the nature of the information play a dominant role. Presumably, most beliefs that are activated during learning from multiple perspectives are not either dispositional or contexualized but rely on both types of sources.

CONCLUSIONS, IMPLICATIONS, AND FUTURE DIRECTIONS

The theoretical and empirical work discussed in this chapter highlights the roles of dispositions and beliefs in learning from multiple perspectives. We reviewed four theoretical accounts of how learners deal with the challenges of constructing a coherent mental representation when encountering different views on the same topic, issue, or phenomenon. This review clarified that enduring and general individual difference factors related to personality, as well as learners' beliefs about both knowledge and reality, are taken into consideration by contemporary theorists in this area. As our subsequent review of relevant empirical work showed, these theoretical considerations also have some empirical grounding. At the same time, however, further theoretical clarification and testing of hypotheses derived from theory are needed to improve our understanding of the nature and functioning of these constructs in the context of learning from multiple perspectives.

Thus, the relationship between different dispositions and their exact roles in learning from multiple perspectives need further clarification and testing. For example, although dispositions such as need for cognition and open-mindedness may be conceptually distinct, with the motivational aspect of need for cognition being more pronounced, the extent to which they independently or interactively may influence learning from multiple perspectives is currently not known, Moreover, such testing should involve theoretically derived hypotheses about which aspects of learning from multiple perspectives most likely are influenced by such dispositions, individually and in concert, which means that theoretical refinement and empirical work have to develop in tandem. Also, it is currently not known whether there are optimal levels of need for cognition and open-mindedness that are adaptive when learning from multiple perspectives, with too high levels possibly hindering rather than helping learners in making decisions and constructing balanced representations. Finally, an interesting and important question regarding these dispositions concerns whether they are malleable at all, or whether individuals displaying low levels of need for cognition and lack of open-mindedness on available tests are more or less doomed to constructing one-sided, biased representations from multiple perspectives.

Further information is also needed regarding the two types of beliefs discussed in this chapter, that is, epistemic and ontic beliefs, in relation to learning from multiple perspectives. In particular, knowledge about how these two types of beliefs may influence each other and interact in such a learning context is essentially lacking. Empirical studies addressing this issue should build on conceptualizations of how beliefs about knowledge and reality are related, which is currently not clearly specified in existing frameworks, which tend to focus on one type of beliefs at the expense of the other (see, however, Schraw & Olafson, 2008). At the psychological (if not conceptual) level, it is even an open question to what extent beliefs about knowledge and reality are clearly distinguishable. For example, when asking participants to consider the truth value of a statement concerning knowledge about the causes of climate change, to what extent are they actually distinguishing this statement from a statement concerning the causes of climate change? In brief, the possibility that learners' epistemic and ontic beliefs at different levels of specificity are psychologically intertwined deserves much more attention, theoretically as well as empirically, in future work. One reason this issue is important is that it is currently not known to what extent it is possible to change one type of beliefs in a sustainable way without addressing the other, for example, whether more adaptive (i.e., scientifically supported) beliefs about the causes of climate change may be promoted without simultaneously addressing learners' beliefs about knowledge and knowing concerning the causes of climate change (cf., Sinatra & Chinn, 2011).

Finally, we ventured well beyond safe empirical territory and launched the idea that learners' beliefs may be more or less anchored in enduring and general dispositions such as need for cognition and open-mindedness, which may make them less influenced by contextual factors in terms of specific topics and tasks. For example, learners with a strong disposition toward open-mindedness might hold identifiable epistemic beliefs (e.g., that knowledge is tentative and complex and that knowledge claims need to be justified by considering evidence from multiple sources), as well as ontic beliefs (e.g., considering a wider range of alternative, hypothetical models of reality; Stanovich & Toplak, 2019), across topics and tasks. As such, these learners' beliefs may reflect their personality more than contextual variations. It goes without saying that this idea needs further theoretical clarification and empirical backing. Thus, none of the models we reviewed conceptualized potential relationships between dispositions and beliefs. Based on such conceptualizations, future research should investigate how different types of beliefs are influenced by and possibly mediate the effects of dispositions on learning from multiple perspectives.

Of note is that the issues discussed in this chapter may have practical as well as theoretical significance. Learning by integrating multiple perspectives on the same topic, issue, or phenomenon may allow for deeper understanding and more applicable knowledge (Spiro, Klautke, & Johnson, 2015). Presumably, a better understanding of dispositions and beliefs that may facilitate (or constrain) such learning may make educators better equipped to adapt their instruction to and cultivate students' potentials for dealing with multiple perspectives.

NOTES

1 We return to this issue in the final section.
2 We define values as "internalized cognitive structures" that over time and across contexts "guide choices by evoking a sense of basic principles of right and wrong, a sense of priorities, and a willingness to make meaning and see patterns" (Oyserman, 2015, p. 36).
3 For a recent, critical discussion of the measurement of actively open-minded thinking, see Stanovich and Toplak (2019).

REFERENCES

Allport, G. W. (1961). *Pattern and growth in personality*. New York: Holt, Rinehart, & Winston.
Baron, J. (1993). Why teach thinking? An essay. *Applied Psychology: An International Review, 42*, 191–214.
Barzilai, S., & Eshet-Alkalai, Y. (2015). The role of epistemic perspectives in comprehension of multiple author viewpoints. *Learning and Instruction, 36*, 86–103.
Barzilai, S., & Strømsø, H. I. (2018). Individual differences in multiple document comprehension. In J. L. G. Braasch, I. Bråten, & M. T. McCrudden (Eds.), *Handbook of multiple source use* (pp. 99–116). New York: Routledge.
Bizer, G., Barden, J., & Petty, R. E. (2003). Attitudes. In L. Nadel (Ed.), *Encyclopedia of cognitive science* (vol. 1, pp. 247–253). Basingstoke, UK: Macmillan.
Boden, M. T., Berenbaum, H., & Gross, J. J. (2016). Why do people believe what they do? A functionalist perspective. *Journal of General Psychology, 20*, 399–411.
Bråten, I., Anmarkrud, Ø., Brandmo, C., & Strømsø, H. I. (2014). Developing and testing a model of direct and indirect relationships between individual differences, processing, and multiple-text comprehension. *Learning and Instruction, 30*, 9–24.
Bråten, I., & Braasch, J. L. G. (2017). Key issues in research on students' critical reading and learning in the 21st century information society. In C. Ng & B. Bartlett (Eds.), *Improving reading and reading engagement in the 21st century: International research and innovations* (pp. 77–98). Singapore: Springer.
Bråten, I., & Braasch, J. L. G. (2018). The role of conflict in multiple source use. In J. L. G. Braasch, I. Bråten, & M. T. McCrudden (Eds.), *Handbook of multiple source use* (pp. 184–201). New York: Routledge.
Bråten, I., Braasch, J. L. G., & Salmerón, L. (in press). Reading multiple and non-traditional texts: New opportunities and new challenges. In E. B. Moje, P. Afflerbach, P. Enciso, & N. K. Lesaux (Eds.), *Handbook of Reading Research* (vol. 5). New York: Routledge.
Bråten, I., Brante, E. W., & Strømsø, H. I. (2018). What really matters: The role of behavioural engagement in multiple document literacy tasks. *Journal of Research in Reading, 41*, 680–699.
Bråten, I., Britt, M. A., Strømsø, H. I., & Rouet, J. F. (2011). The role of epistemic beliefs in the comprehension of multiple expository texts: Toward an integrated model. *Educational Psychologist, 46*, 48–70.
Bråten, I., & Ferguson, L. E. (2014). Investigating cognitive capacity, personality, and epistemic beliefs in relation to science achievement. *Learning and Individual Differences, 36*, 124–130.
Bråten, I., Ferguson, L. E., Strømsø, H. I., & Anmarkrud, Ø. (2013). Justification beliefs and multiple-documents comprehension. *European Journal of Psychology of Education, 28*, 879–902.
Bråten, I., Salmerón, L., & Strømsø, H. I. (2016). Who said that? Investigating the plausibility-induced source focusing assumption with Norwegian undergraduate readers. *Contemporary Educational Psychology, 46*, 253–262.
Bråten, I., & Strømsø, H. I. (2010a). Effects of task instruction and personal epistemology on the understanding of multiple texts about climate change. *Discourse Processes, 47*, 1–31.
Bråten, I., & Strømsø, H. I. (2010b). When law students read multiple documents about global warming: Examining the role of topic-specific beliefs about the nature of knowledge and knowing. *Instructional Science, 38*, 635–657.
Bråten, I., Strømsø, H. I., & Ferguson, L. E. (2016). The role of epistemic beliefs in the comprehension of single and multiple texts. In P. Afflerbach (Ed.), *Handbook of individual differences in reading* (pp. 67–79). New York: Routledge.
Bråten, I., Strømsø, H. I., & Samuelstuen, M. S. (2008). Are sophisticated students always better? The role of topic-specific personal epistemology in the understanding of multiple expository texts. *Contemporary Educational Psychology, 33*, 814–840.

Britt, M. A., Perfetti, C. A., Sandak, R., & Rouet, J. F. (1999). Content integration and source separation in learning from multiple texts. In S. R. Goldman, A. C. Graesser, & P. van den Broek (Eds.), *Narrative, comprehension, causality, and coherence: Essays in honor of Tom Trabasso* (pp. 209–233). Mahwah, NJ: Erlbaum.

Britt, M. A., & Rouet, J. F. (2012). Learning with multiple documents: Component skills and their acquisition. In J. R. Kirby & M. J. Lawson (Eds.), *Enhancing the quality of learning: Dispositions, instruction, and learning processes* (pp. 276–314). New York: Cambridge University Press.

Cacioppo, J. T., Petty, R. E., Feinstein, J. A., & Jarvis, B. C. (1996). Dispositional differences in cognitive motivation: The life and times of individuals varying in need for cognition. *Psychological Bulletin, 119*, 197–253.

Dai, D. Y., & Wang, X. (2007). The role of need for cognition and reader beliefs in text comprehension and interest development. *Contemporary Educational Psychology, 32*, 332–347.

Edwards, K., & Smith, E. E. (1996). A disconfirmation bias in the evaluation of arguments. *Journal of Personality and Social Psychology, 71*, 5–24.

Ferguson, L. E., & Bråten, I. (2013). Student profiles of knowledge and epistemic beliefs: Changes and relations to multiple-text comprehension. *Learning and Instruction, 25*, 49–61.

Ferguson, L. E., Bråten, I., & Strømsø, H. I. (2012). Epistemic cognition when students read multiple documents containing conflicting scientific evidence: A think-aloud study. *Learning and Instruction, 22*, 103–120.

Gottlieb, E., & Wineburg, S. (2012). Between veritas and communitas: Epistemic switching in the reading of academic and sacred history. *Journal of the Learning Sciences, 21*, 84–129.

Graesser, A. C., Singer, M., & Trabasso, T. (1994). Constructing inferences during narrative text comprehension. *Psychological Review, 101*, 371–395.

Greene, J. A., Azevedo, R., & Torney-Purta, J. (2008). Modeling epistemic and ontological cognition: Philosophical perspectives and methodological directions. *Educational Psychologist, 43*, 142–160.

Greene, J. A., Sandoval, W. A., & Bråten, I. (Eds.). (2016). *Handbook of epistemic cognition*. New York: Routledge.

Griffin, T. D. (2008). Faith: Serving emotional epistemic goals rather than evidence coherence. In V. Sloutsky, B. Love, & K. McRae (Eds.), *Proceedings of the 30th Annual Conference of the Cognitive Science Society* (pp. 2059–2064). Austin, TX: Cognitive Science Society.

Griffin, T. D., Wiley, J., Britt, M. A., & Salas, C. R. (2012). The role of CLEAR thinking in learning science from multiple-document inquiry tasks. *International Electronic Journal of Elementary Education, 5*, 63–78.

Haran, U., Ritov, I., & Mellers, B. A. (2013). The role of actively open-minded thinking in information acquisition, accuracy, and calibration. *Judgment and Decision Making, 8*, 188–201.

Haugtvedt, C. P., & Petty, R. E. (1992). Personality and persuasion: Need for cognition moderates the persistence and resistance of attitude changes. *Journal of Personality and Social Psychology, 63*, 308–319.

Hidi, S. (2001). Interest, reading, and learning: Theoretical and practical considerations. *Educational Psychology Review, 13*, 191–209.

Hofer, B. K., & Pintrich, P. R. (1997). The development of epistemological theories: Beliefs about knowledge and knowing and their relation to learning. *Review of Educational Research, 67*, 88–140.

Kahan, D. M., & Corbin, J. C. (2016). A note on the perverse effects of actively open-minded thinking on climate-change polarization. *Research and Politics, 3*, 1–5.

Kahan, D. M., Peters, E., Wittlin, M., Slovic, P., Ouellette, L. L., Braman, D., & Mandel, G. (2012). The polarizing impact of science literacy and numeracy on perceived climate change risks. *Nature Climate Change, 2*, 732–735.

Kardash, C. A., & Howell, K. L. (2000). Effects of epistemological beliefs and topic-specific beliefs on undergraduates' cognitive and strategic processing of dual positional text. *Journal of Educational Psychology, 92*, 524–535.

Kardash, C. A., & Noel, L. K. (2000). How organizational signals, need for cognition, and verbal ability affect text recall and recognition. *Contemporary Educational Psychology, 25*, 317–331.

Kardash, C. A., & Scholes, R. J. (1996). Effects of preexisting beliefs, epistemological beliefs, and need for cognition on interpretation of controversial issues. *Journal of Educational Psychology, 88*, 260–271.

Kendeou, P., Braasch, J. L. G., & Bråten, I. (2016). Optimizing conditions for learning: Situating refutations in epistemic cognition. *Journal of Experimental Education, 84*, 245–263.

Kendeou, P., Muis, K. R., & Fulton, S. (2011). Reader and text factors in reading comprehension processes. *Journal of Research in Reading, 34*, 365–383.

Kintsch, W. (1998). *Comprehension: A paradigm for cognition*. Cambridge University Press.

Kitchener, R. F. (2002). Folk epistemology: An introduction. *New Ideas in Psychology, 20*, 89–105.

Klaczynski, P. A., Gordon, D. H., & Faulth, J. (1997). Goal-oriented critical reasoning and individual differences in critical reasoning biases. *Journal of Educational Psychology, 89*, 470–485.

Kuhn, D. (1991). *The skills of argument*. Cambridge: Cambridge University Press.

Latini, N., Bråten, I., Anmarkrud, Ø., & Salmerón, L. (2019). Investigating effects of reading medium and reading purpose on behavioral engagement and textual integration in a multiple text context. *Contemporary Educational Psychology, 59*, 101797.

Levin, I. P., Huneke, M. E., & Jasper, J. D. (2000). Information processing at successive stages of decision making: Need for cognition and inclusion-exclusion effects. *Organizational Behavior and Human Decision Processes, 82*, 171–193.

List, A., & Alexander, P. A. (2017). Cognitive Affective Engagement Model of multiple source use. *Educational Psychologist, 52*, 182–199.

List, A., & Alexander, P. A. (2018). Cold and warm perspectives on the cognitive affective engagement model of multiple source use. In J. L. G. Braasch, I. Bråten, & M. T. McCrudden (Eds.), *Handbook of multiple source use* (pp. 34–54). New York: Routledge.

List, A., & Alexander, P. A. (2019). Toward an integrated framework of multiple text use. *Educational Psychologist, 54*, 20–39.

List, A., Stephens, L. A., & Alexander, P. A. (2019). Examining interest throughout multiple text use. *Reading and Writing, 32*, 307–333.

Lombardi, D., Nussbaum, E. M., & Sinatra, G. M. (2016). Plausibility judgment in conceptual change and epistemic cognition. *Educational Psychologist, 51*, 35–56.

Lord, C. G., Ross, L., & Lepper, M. R. (1979). Biased assimilation and attitude polarization: The effects of prior theories on subsequently considered evidence. *Journal of Personality and Social Psychology, 37*, 2098–2109.

Maier, J., & Richter, T. (2013). Text-belief consistency effects in the comprehension of multiple texts with conflicting information. *Cognition and Instruction, 31*, 151–175.

Maier, J., & Richter, T. (2014). Fostering multiple text comprehension: How metacognitive strategies and motivation moderate the text-belief consistency effect. *Metacognition and Learning, 9*, 45–71.

Maier, J., Richter, T., & Britt, M. A. (2018a). Cognitive processes underlying the text-belief consistency effect: An eye-movement study. *Applied Cognitive Psychology, 32*, 171–185.

Maier, J., Richter, T., Nauroth, P., & Gollwitzer, M. (2018b). For me or for them: How in-group identification and beliefs influence the comprehension of controversial texts. *Journal of Research in Reading, 41*, S48–S65.

Mason, L., Boldrin, A., & Ariasi, N. (2010). Searching the web to learn about a controversial topic: Are students epistemically active?. *Instructional Science, 38*, 607–633.

Mason, L., & Boscolo, P. (2004). Role of epistemological understanding and interest in interpreting a controversy and in topic-specific belief change. *Contemporary Educational Psychology, 29*, 103–128.

Mason, L., Gava, M., & Boldrin, A. (2008). On warm conceptual change: The interplay of text, epistemological beliefs, and topic interest. *Journal of Educational Psychology, 100*, 291–309.

Mason, L., & Scirica, F. (2006). Prediction of students' argumentation skills about controversial topics by epistemological understanding. *Learning and Instruction, 16*, 492–509.

McCrudden, M. T., & Barnes, A. (2016). Differences in student reasoning about belief-relevant arguments: A mixed methods study. *Metacognition and Learning, 11*, 275–303.

McCrudden, M. T., Barnes, A., McTigue, E., Welch, C., & MacDonald, E. (2017). The effect of perspective-taking on reasoning about strong and weak belief-relevant arguments. *Thinking and Reasoning, 23*, 115–133.

McCrudden, M. T., & Sparks, P. C. (2014). Exploring the effect of task instructions on topic beliefs and topic belief justifications: A mixed methods study. *Contemporary Educational Psychology, 39*, 1–11.

Muis, K. R., Bendixen, L. D., & Haerle, F. C. (2006). Domain-generality and domain specificity in personal epistemology research: Philosophical and empirical reflections in the development of a theoretical framework. *Educational Psychology Review, 18*, 3–54.

Muis, K. R., Pekrun, R., Sinatra, G. M., Azevedo, R., Trevors, G., Meier, E., & Heddy, B. C. (2015). The curious case of climate change: Testing a theoretical model of epistemic beliefs, epistemic emotions, and complex learning. *Learning and Instruction, 39*, 168–183.

Murphy, P. K., & Alexander, P. A. (2004). Persuasion as a dynamic, multidimensional process: An investigation of individual and intraindividual differences. *American Educational Research Journal, 41*, 337–363.

Murphy, P. K., & Mason, L. (2006). Changing knowledge and beliefs. In P. A. Alexander & P. H. Winne (Eds.), *Handbook of educational psychology* (2nd ed., pp. 305–324). Mahwah, NJ: Erlbaum.

Oyserman, D. (2015). Psychology of values. In J. D. Wright (Ed.), *International encyclopedia of the social and behavioral sciences* (2nd ed., vol. 25, pp. 36–40). Oxford: Elsevier.

Perfetti, C. A., Rouet, J. F., & Britt, M. A. (1999). Towards a theory of documents representation. In H. van Oostendorp & S. R. Goldman (Eds.), *The construction of mental representations during reading* (pp. 99–122). Mahwah, NJ: Erlbaum.

Petty, R. E., Briñol, P., Loersch, C., & McCaslin, M. J. (2009). The need for cognition. In M. R. Leary & R. H. Hoyle (Eds.), *Handbook of individual differences in social behavior* (pp. 318–329). New York: Guilford.

Qian, G., & Alvermann, D. (1995). Role of epistemological beliefs and learned helplessness in secondary school students' learning science concepts from text. *Journal of Educational Psychology, 87*, 282–292.

Richter, T., & Maier, J. (2017). Comprehension of multiple documents with conflicting information: A two-step model of validation. *Educational Psychologist, 52*, 148–166.

Richter, T., & Maier, J. (2018). The role of validation in multiple-document comprehension. In J. L. G. Braasch, I. Bråten, & M. T. McCrudden (Eds.), *Handbook of multiple source use* (pp. 151–167). New York: Routledge.

Riggs, W. (2010). Open-mindedness. *Metaphilosophy, 41*, 172–188.

Rouet, J. F. (2006). *The skills of document use*. Mahwah, NJ: Erlbaum.

Rukavina, I., & Daneman, M. (1996). Integration and its effect on acquiring knowledge about competing scientific theories from text. *Journal of Educational Psychology, 88*, 272–287.

Sá, W. C., West, R. F., & Stanovich, K. E. (1999). The domain specificity and generality of belief bias: Searching for a generalizable critical thinking skill. *Journal of Educational Psychology, 91*, 497–510.

Salmerón, L., Gil, L., & Bråten, I. (2018). Effects of reading real versus print-out versions of multiple documents on students' sourcing and integrated understanding. *Contemporary Educational Psychology, 52*, 25–35.

Sandoval, W. A., Greene, J. A., & Bråten, I. (2016). Understanding and promoting thinking about knowledge: Origin, issues, and future directions of research on epistemic cognition. *Review of Research in Education, 40*, 457–496.

Schiefele, U. (1999). Interest and learning from text. *Scientific Studies of Reading, 3*, 257–279.

Schraw, G. J., & Olafson, L. J. (2008). Assessing teachers' epistemological and ontological worldviews. In M. S. Khine (Ed.), *Knowing, knowledge, and beliefs: Epistemological studies across diverse cultures* (pp. 25–44). Dordrecht: Springer.

Schunk, D. H., Meece, J. L., & Pintrich, P. R. (2014). *Motivation in education: Theory, research, and applications* (4th ed.). Columbus, OH: Pearson Merrill Prentice Hall.

Schweiger, S., & Cress, U. (2019). Attitude confidence and source credibility in information foraging with social tags. *PLoS ONE, 14*(1), e0210423.

Sinatra, G. M., & Chinn, C. (2011). Thinking and reasoning in science: Promoting epistemic conceptual change. In K. Harris, C. B. McCormick, G. M. Sinatra, & J. Sweller (Eds.), *Critical theories and models of learning and development relevant to learning and teaching* (vol. 1, pp. 257–282). Washington, DC: APA Publications.

Sinatra, G. M., & Kardash, C. A. (2004). Teacher candidates' epistemological beliefs, dispositions, and views on teaching as persuasion. *Contemporary Educational Psychology, 29*, 483–498.

Sinatra, G. M., Southerland, S. A., McConaughy, F., & Demastes, J. W. (2003). Intentions and beliefs in students' understanding and acceptance of biological evolution. *Journal of Research in Science Teaching, 40*, 510–528.

Spiro, R. J., Klautke, H., & Johnson, A. K. (2015). All bets are off: How certain kinds of reading to learn on the Web are totally different from what we learned from research on traditional text comprehension and learning from text. In R. J. Spiro, M. DeSchryver, M. S. Hagerman, P. M. Morsink, & P. Thompson (Eds.), *Reading at a crossroads? Disjunctures and continuities in current conceptions and practices* (pp. 45–50). New York: Routledge.

Stang Lund, E., Bråten, I., Brandmo, C., Brante, E. W., & Strømsø, H. I. (2019). Direct and indirect effects of textual and individual factors on source-content integration when reading about a socio-scientific issue. *Reading and Writing, 32*, 335–356.

Stang Lund, E., Bråten, I., Brante, E. W., & Strømsø, H. I. (2017). Memory for textual conflicts predicts sourcing when adolescents read multiple expository texts. *Reading Psychology, 38*, 417–437.

Stanovich, K. E., & Toplak, M. E. (2019). The need for intellectual diversity in psychological science: Our own studies of actively open-minded thinking as a case study. *Cognition, 187*, 156–166.

Stanovich, K. E., & West, R. F. (1997). Reasoning independently of prior belief and individual differences in actively open-minded thinking. *Journal of Educational Psychology, 89*, 342–357.

Strømsø, H. I., & Bråten, I. (2009). Beliefs about knowledge and knowing and multiple-text comprehension among upper secondary students. *Educational Psychology, 29*, 425–445.

Strømsø, H. I., & Bråten, I. (2017). Students' trust in research-based results about potential health risks presented in popular media. *Bulletin of Science, Technology, and Society, 37*, 3–14.

Strømsø, H. I., Bråten, I., & Britt, M. A. (2010). Reading multiple texts about climate change: The relationship between memory for sources and text comprehension. *Learning and Instruction, 18*, 513–527.

Strømsø, H. I., Bråten, I., & Samuelstuen, M. S. (2008). Dimensions of topic-specific epistemological beliefs as predictors of multiple text understanding. *Learning and Instruction, 18*, 513–527.

Strømsø, H. I., Bråten, I., & Stenseth, T. (2017). The role of students' prior topic beliefs in recall and evaluation of information from texts on socio-scientific issues. *Nordic Psychology, 69*, 127–142.

Strømsø, H. I., & Kammerer, Y. (2016). Epistemic cognition and reading for understanding in the Internet age. In J. A. Greene, W. A. Sandoval, & I. Bråten (Eds.), *Handbook of epistemic cognition* (pp. 230–246). New York: Routledge.

Svedholm-Häkkinen, A. M., & Lindeman, M. (2018). Actively open-minded thinking: Development of a shortened scale and disentangling attitudes towards knowledge and people. *Thinking and Reasoning, 24*, 21–40.

Taber, C. S., Cann, D., & Kucsova, S. (2009). The motivated processing of political arguments. *Political Behavior, 31*, 137–155.

Taber, C. S., & Lodge, M. (2006). Motivated skepticism in the evaluation of political beliefs. *American Journal of Political Science, 50*, 755–769.

Toplak, M. E., West, R. F., & Stanovich, K. E. (2014). Assessing misery information processing: An expansion of the Cognitive Reflection Test. *Thinking and Reasoning, 20*, 147–168.

Trevors, G. J., Kendeou, P., Bråten, I., & Braasch, J. L. G. (2017). Adolescents' epistemic profiles in the service of knowledge revision. *Contemporary Educational Psychology, 49*, 107–120.

Trevors, G. J., Muis, K. R., Pekrun, R., Sinatra, G. M., & Muijselaar, M. M. L. (2017). Exploring the relations between epistemic beliefs, emotions, and learning from texts. *Contemporary Educational Psychology, 48*, 116–132.

van den Broek, P. (2010). Using texts in science education: Cognitive processes and knowledge representation. *Science, 328*, 453–456.

van Strien, J. L. H., Brand-Gruwel, S., & Boshuizen, H. P. A. (2014). Dealing with conflicting information from multiple nonlinear texts: Effects of prior attitudes. *Computers in Human Behavior, 32*, 101–111.

van Strien, J. L. H., Kammerer, Y., Brand-Gruwel, S., & Boshuizen, H. P. A. (2016). How attitude strength biases information processing end evaluation on the web. *Computers in Human Behavior, 60*, 245–252.

VandenBos, G. R. (2007). *APA dictionary of psychology*. Washington, DC: American Psychological Association.

Wiley, J. (2005). A fair and balanced look at the news: What affects memory for controversial arguments? *Journal of Memory and Language, 53*, 95–109.

Winter, S., & Krämer, N. C. (2012). Selecting science information in web 2.0: How source cues, message sidedness, and need for cognition influence users' exposure to blog posts. *Journal of Computer-Mediated Communication, 18*, 80–96.

Wolfe, M. B., & Griffin, T. D. (2018). Beliefs and discourse processing. In M. F. Schober, D. N. Rapp, & M. A. Britt (Eds.), *The Routledge handbook of discourse processes* (pp. 295–314). New York: Routledge.

Wolfe, M. B., Tanner, S. M., & Taylor, A. R. (2013). Processing and representation of arguments in one-sided texts about disputed topics. *Discourse Processes, 50*, 457–497.

11

KNOWLEDGE AS PERSPECTIVE

From Domain Perspective Learning to Interdisciplinary Understanding

Alexandra List

PENNSYLVANIA STATE UNIVERSITY

ABSTRACT

This chapter introduces the construct of domain perspective learning as a mechanism for preparing students for later interdisciplinary learning and problem solving. Domain perspective learning involves (a) recognizing that the information presented by an author is, in part, a result of their domain perspective, or the objects of focus, methods of inquiry, and evaluative standards that characterize the domain that they are a part of; and (b) conceptualizing, comparing and evaluating, and integrating multiple domain perspectives for interdisciplinary learning and problem solving. In addition to introducing domain perspective learning and identifying the processes that this involves, this chapter concludes with a description of three strategies that may be used to enhance domain perspective learning in the classroom.

Key words: domain perspective learning, domain, knowledge, domain perspective, epistemic beliefs

Many complex problems facing society today, such as food insecurity, global migration, and automation, are multifaceted, complex, and *interdisciplinary* in nature; that is, addressing these issues requires knowledge and expertise from multiple fields. Correspondingly, among the trends in education reform, aiming to meet the demands of the 21st century, have been efforts to engage students in interdisciplinary learning and problem solving (Ivanitskaya, Clark, Montgomery, & Primeau, 2002; Jones, Rasmussen, & Moffitt, 1997). Interdisciplinary learning is defined as the integrative, rather than additive, process of contrasting and connecting different disciplines to achieve benefits for learning or *interdisciplinary understanding* (Spelt, Biemans, Tobi, Luning, & Mulder, 2009). At the same time, interdisciplinary learning has been identified as a process that is quite complex and demanding for learners, particularly those not yet in college and having little expertise in any domain, hampering their abilities to engage in interdisciplinary problem solving (Jones, 2010; Nariman & Chrispeels, 2016).

While engaging students in interdisciplinary learning and problem solving remains an important goal, such learning may be too demanding a process for novice learners who are only beginning to understand the characteristics of and differences between different academic domains. Instead, a distinct but related approach, that of domain perspective learning (DPL), is introduced in this chapter as a mechanism for supporting novice learners to develop an understanding of different domains and to draw on this understanding to think critically and to solve interdisciplinary problems. DPL is first defined in reference to the literature on perspective-based learning to describe how teaching students about domain perspectives may provide them with rich, coherent, and multidimensional lenses through which to understand and evaluate information. In addition to defining DPL, this chapter describes the processes that may be involved in domain perspective learning, including how domain perspectives may be conceptualized, compared and evaluated, and integrated. Finally, it closes with describing the functions or benefits of domain perspective learning and how these may be achieved in the classroom.

DEFINING PERSPECTIVE

Perspectives may be defined as "frames of reference" (McCrudden & Schraw, 2007, p. 116), orientations, or lenses on the world, generally; and lenses on information in texts, more specifically. In part, perspectives delineate what information is attended to or deemed to be important and what information is ignored, as well as how information is interpreted and evaluated, and what information is retained. Although a variety of factors, among them our attitudes (i.e., positive and negative judgments of objects) and epistemic beliefs (i.e., beliefs about knowledge and knowing, Buehl & Alexander, 2001), contribute to the perspectives on information that readers may hold (see McCrudden, Chapter 12), perspectives have commonly been operationalized as task goals assigned to students prior to reading (McCrudden & Schraw, 2007). For instance, a classic study by Pichert and Anderson (1977) asked students to read a text about a house from the perspective of either a burglar or a home-buyer. Assigned perspectives were found to result in differences in students' ratings of text-based statements importance and in differential text recall. Goetz, Schallert, Reynolds, and Radin (1983) asked students to read the same house passage from the perspective of a police officer, real estate agent, or education student. They found students to rate perspective-relevant, rather than perspective-irrelevant, sentences as more important, to spend more time reading these, and to better recall these after reading. Kaakinen, Hyönä, and Keenan (2002) confirmed these results using behavioral data from eye tracking. In particular, they found students' reading of relevant vis-à-vis irrelevant text passages to be marked by longer fixation times at both first-pass and second-pass reading. Thus, perspectives such as these, referred to as role-based, act as filters that students use to understand the world and sift through the information within it.

Rather than focusing on role-based perspectives (e.g., home buyer, police officer) assigned to students prior to reading, this chapter instead focuses on one specific type of perspective, *domain perspective*, that may be an especially powerful lens for students to use in information processing and during reading. Domain perspectives (DPs) are distinguishable from the role-based perspectives commonly examined in prior work (Goetz et al., 1983; Kaakinen & Hyönä, 2008; Pichert & Anderson, 1977) in the depth of knowledge, grounded in academic domains, that these demand of learners and ask them to apply to understanding information. While reading like a police officer asks that students have only a superficial conception of this role, reading like a criminologist or asking students to recognize a criminological perspective reflected in text, requires learners to have a considerably deeper understanding of criminology as a domain and the epistemic practices (i.e., how knowledge is developed, substantiated, and evaluated) within it. Moreover, while role-based perspectives have commonly been examined as externally assigned to students prior to reading, domain perspectives may be expected to be more personal in nature or more characteristic of individuals. As such, domain perspectives are reflected both when learners read from particular DPs as a function of their prior knowledge, interests, and beliefs (e.g., biology majors reading from a biological perspective) and when expert authors write texts from a DP (e.g., biologists writing from a biological perspective).

DEFINING DOMAINS

Although sometimes used interchangeably (e.g., Paulsen & Wells, 1998), in defining domains, it is first helpful to distinguish these from the broader disciplines from which they derive. Disciplines, characterized by their historical roots and generalizability (Foshay, 1962), are relatively few in number; identified by Alexander (1998) as including history, literature, science, and mathematics. Domains, then, constitute more specific and, typically, more applied areas of study (Biglan, 1973; Schommer-Aikins, Duell, & Barker, 2003). Rarick (1967) describes domains as originating from the scientific practice of "classify[ing] like things together for systematic and detailed study," which, over time has resulted in the domains or "segments of knowledge" that we have today (p. 49).

Schwab argues that disciplines, and therefore the domains that they perpetuate, can be thought of as having two components: "the body of imposed conceptions" and "its inquiry," thereby making reference to the declarative or conceptual knowledge that characterize a particular domain and to the processes and activities associated with its acquisition (i.e., procedural knowledge). Becher and Parry (2005) describe these latter processes as encompassing "techniques of inquiry," "established research methods," and a "set of required resources" (pp. 133–134). Drawing on these conceptualizations of disciplines and domains, in this chapter, domains are viewed as defined by and distinguished from one another in the (a) objects or subjects that they investigate, (b) the methods of inquiry that they use, and (c) the evaluative standards that they apply. Throughout this chapter, I refer to these objects and subjects of focus, methods of inquiry, and evaluative standards as *domain characteristics*, for the sake of conciseness. Objects and subjects of focus refer to the target(s) of investigation within domains or what may count as evidence, more specifically. Methods of inquiry refer to the domain-specific processes of how evidence is gathered, analyzed, and interpreted to formulate conclusions. Finally, standards for evaluation pertain to how determinations of evidence quality, appropriateness of processes, and the relative substantiation of conclusions and claims are made within domains. For instance, history may be defined, in part, by the study of documents and artifacts (i.e., objects), using techniques like corroboration and contextualization (i.e., Wineburg, 1991, methods), to achieve coherent interpretations that robustly account for the evidence available and conceptualize such evidence in a historically appropriate fashion (Lee & Ashby, 2001). Biology, as a contrast, maybe thought of as focused on the study of organisms (i.e., subjects), using techniques of observation and scientific experimentation (i.e., methods), to achieve discernible categorization or replicable results (i.e., evaluative standards, Hauslein, Good, & Cummins, 1992; Reindl, Strobach, Becker, Scholtz, & Schubert, 2015).

Beyond these domain-specific examples, Goldman et al. (2016) provide a comprehensive framework of the overarching concepts (i.e., similar to objects of inquiry), inquiry practices (i.e., similar to methods), (c) epistemologies (i.e., including evaluative standards), (d) forms of information representation (e.g., texts), and (e) discourse structures (i.e., language use) that define the disciplines of literature, history, and science. This chapter primarily focuses on domains, rather than disciplines, as more narrow and accessible fields of study. Nevertheless, to use Goldman et al.'s terminology (2016), in this chapter, overarching concepts, inquiry practices, and epistemologies are used to define domains. Later in this chapter, in the section on instructional implications to promote DPL, introducing domain-specific forms of information representation and discourse structures in the classroom are recommended as mechanisms for fostering DPL. Nevertheless, prior to identifying the processes involved in DPL and the instructional strategies that may be used to foster such learning, domain perspectives are first defined.

DEFINING DOMAIN PERSPECTIVES

Domain perspectives are lenses on the world, generally, and on information, more specifically. These perspectives are informed by an understanding of the objects of focus, methods of inquiry, and standards for evaluation that characterize a particular domain. Consistent with Goldman et al. (2016), domain perspectives can be further conceptualized as epistemic in nature. That is, such perspectives are distinct from role-based perspectives (e.g., reading like a home buyer) in that they specifically draw on domain-specific conceptions of what knowledge is and how knowledge may be developed and substantiated. For example, while reading from a role-based perspective may help students determine what information is relevant or not, reading from a domain perspective may further encourage students to ask critical questions and suggest to students the standards to apply in evaluating information. As such, simply directing students to read like an architect may draw students' attention to the design features of a home; however, teaching students about the domain of architecture and then encouraging them to read from an architectural perspective may prompt students to analyze and compare the features of a home to known architectural styles and question choices made in design. Domain perspective learning includes both students' adoption of a particular domain perspective during reading (e.g., read from the perspective of an economist) and their abilities to recognize and reason about domain-specific perspectives reflected in text (e.g., a text written from an economic perspective), with both of these approaches to DPL requiring students to have somewhat sophisticated conceptions of domain characteristics. That is, both reading from and recognizing and reasoning about domain perspectives require a deep and systematic knowledge base, as compared to the more limited and superficial knowledge required when students read from a role-based perspective.

Although both approaches to domain perspective learning (i.e., students reading from a domain perspective and recognizing and reasoning about domain perspectives in text) may require similar types of processing and information evaluation, this chapter focuses to a considerably greater extent on the latter of these two (i.e., learners recognizing domain perspectives in text). This is the case for at least two reasons. First, in a K-12 context, where students may be expected to be domain novices (Alexander, 2003a, 2003b; Kuhn, Cheney, & Weinstock, 2000), if they are aware of domains and domain characteristics at all (Brozo, Moorman, Meyer, & Stewart, 2013; Shanahan & Shanahan, 2008, 2014), it is unlikely that students may readily assume a domain perspective during reading. That is, elementary school students, in contrast to undergraduate biology majors or biology experts, are unlikely to automatically or deliberately read texts from a biological perspective. Moreover, assigning elementary or middle school students to "read like a biologist," with no deep-level understanding of what biology is as a domain or its domain characteristics, may result in students adopting the same superficial, role-based perspective, like asking students to "read like a homebuyer." Indeed, we may expect learners' assumption of domain perspectives during reading, as grounded in their understanding of domain characteristics, to only emerge at the undergraduate level, in the absence of specific instruction to the contrary (e.g., Alexander, 2003b; Goldman et al., 2016).

Second, while K-12 students may not readily adopt domain perspectives of their own during reading, they are certainly likely to encounter authors' domain perspectives, reflected in texts, when learning about complex or controversial topics. In part, such topics may be defined as requiring interdisciplinary understanding. Boix Mansilla and Duraising (2007) define interdisciplinary understanding as learners': "capacity to integrate knowledge and modes of thinking in two or more disciplines or established areas of expertise to produce a cognitive advancement ... in ways that would have been impossible or unlikely through single disciplinary means" (p. 219). This means that understanding complex, interdisciplinary problems, like resource scarcity or cultural globalization, requires that learners draw on information from diverse domains or areas of study, including texts written from economic, political science, historical, and geographic DPs. That is, students working to understand and potentially solve interdisciplinary problems need to recognize that experts from different domain perspectives are working to address these, understand how such problems are conceptualized and approached from different DPs, and compare, evaluate, and integrate DP-based information in determining possible solutions. As such, recognizing and reasoning about a variety of DPs is likely to be a much more necessary and fruitful endeavor for learners working to understand and solve interdisciplinary problems, more so than adopting a single domain perspective for reading. As such, students' abilities to recognize and reason about different domain perspectives represented in text constitute the focus of the remainder of this chapter. Nevertheless, understanding how students' own DPs, developed through their gradually increasing participation in domains as communities of practice (Goldman et al., 2016), shape the nature of their reading, problem solving, and information processing remains an important area for future work.

ORIGIN OF DOMAIN PERSPECTIVES IN TEXT

In addition to defining what is meant by a domain perspective, it is important to determine where domain perspectives come from. As discussed previously, students may develop the ability to adopt domain perspectives as a virtue of their knowledge building and advancement within particular domains or fields of study (e.g., majoring in biology). At the same time, at the K-12 level, such individual development of a robust domain perspective is unlikely to occur (Alexander, 2003b). But, students, even at the K-12 level, may be expected to much more commonly encounter domain perspectives through text, whether students are aware of these or not. These domain perspectives, represented through text, may be considered to be an attribute of source. Source refers to the features of text that pertain to text origin or reason(s) for being created. While a variety of features associated with source have been investigated in prior research (e.g., currency, publisher, Bråten, Strømsø, & Britt, 2009), author and author trustworthiness has received the greatest degree of attention in the literature (Bråten, Strømsø, & Salmerón, 2011; Reisman, 2012; Rouet, Favart, Britt, & Perfetti, 1997; Stahl, Hynd, Britton, McNish, & Bosquet, 1996). Author trustworthiness has been understood as based on author's benevolence and expertise (Stadtler & Bromme, 2014). *Author benevolence* refers to author intention to provide quality and accurate information and has often been conceptualized by students as an author's freedom from bias. Author expertise refers to an author's qualifications and knowledge and abilities to speak as an authority on a given topic. Investigated widely in prior work (Macedo-Rouet et al., 2019; Salmerón, Macedo-Rouet, & Rouet, 2016), such attributes may be viewed as reflective of the author as an individual. This chapter expands this view of author to further encompass the domain perspective(s) that the author holds and expresses in writing.

In particular, author may be defined by three interrelated dimensions (see Figure 11.1). The first of these dimensions refers to an author's topic stance. This dimension occurs at the intersection of an author's knowledge and beliefs and the topic that they are writing about and, generally, reflects whether an author stands in support of or in opposition to a particular issue or proposal. The second dimension captures an author's relevant individual characteristics, pertinent to their stance on a particular topic and the information that they provide about this topic. Chief among these characteristics are author's benevolence (i.e., motivation or intent for writing) and expertise (i.e., knowledge and authority). The third dimension, of particular interest in this chapter, reflects author's domain perspective or positioning within larger areas of study. While benevolence and expertise may be viewed as individual author characteristics, author's domain perspective necessarily connects them to a broader, domain community, holding shared epistemic orientations, practices, and values for knowledge-building. For instance, a report discussing the effects of deforestation in the Amazon may be said to reflect an author's particular position on this issue, the author's expertise and motivations for writing, as benevolent or not, and the author's domain perspective (e.g., in the domain of forestry). Jointly, author

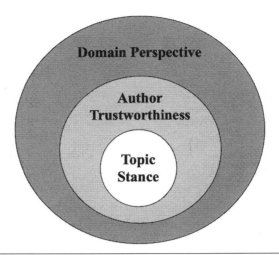

Figure 11.1 Representation of text's source.

benevolence, expertise, and domain perspective dictate the evidence that they draw on in formulating a topic stance and the information they elect to feature or exclude in their writing, as well as how this information is presented. More generally, the three author-related dimensions identified in Figure 11.1 and their inter-relations are important for students to consider when evaluating information in texts and the extent to which this information is credible, comprehensive, and convincing. As such, teaching students to recognize and reason about domain perspective is fundamentally asking them to attend to source. In this way, teaching students to engage in DPL aligns with broader intervention efforts aimed at teaching students to attend to source during reading and to use source in evaluating information (Brante & Strømsø, 2018; Pérez et al., 2018).

The depiction in Figure 11.1 is intended to convey at least three insights about author characteristics, as they are conceptualized in this chapter. First, Figure 11.1 represents an author's specific stance on a given topic as nested within the domain perspectives that they hold. In this way, Figure 11.1 makes the point that domain perspective does not necessarily dictate author's specific stance on a particular topic or issue. That is, authors within the same domain may be for or against particular proposals. As such, domain perspective only serves to determine the objects of analysis, methods of inquiry, and standards for evaluation that authors use in formulating a specific topic stance. Second, the representation in Figure 11.1 makes clear that the nature of authors' expertise comes from the domain communities of which they are a part. This specific aspect of Figure 11.1 may be said to reflect the "social" dimension of domains, identified by Becher and Parry (2005) as reflecting their organizational structure (e.g., within universities), their induction of new members, their social values, and their reciprocal recognition of experts by other experts. These, alongside the epistemic characteristics of domains (i.e., their objects of focus, methods of inquiry, and the evaluative standards that they apply for knowledge establishment), are encapsulated in the domain perspective that authors bring to various topics.

Finally, the third insight introduced in this representation reflects a distinction between author benevolence or potential bias, and author's domain perspective. Although research on how learners define bias and perceive author bias during reading is scant, the distinction between author bias and author's DP is essential to draw. Bias, when it is exhibited, may take the form of authors selectively or incompletely presenting information. This selective presentation of information for reasons of bias (i.e., personal motivations, reflecting a lack of benevolence) can be distinguished from the selective presentation of information for reasons of domain perspective. To underscore this point, an ecologist focused on the environmental, rather than on the economic, impacts of a particular proposal, should not be viewed as biased (i.e., not benevolent) or personally motivated to present information selectively (e.g., for financial gain). Rather, this ecologist should be viewed as epistemically motivated to describe an issue based on the characteristics of his or her domain. The information provided by such an author should be viewed as offering a domain-bound, rather than biased, perspective. As such, it should be distinguished from incomplete information provided by a property owner in the area, who may have a personal or financial motive (i.e., a lack of benevolence) for selective information presentation. With domain perspectives defined and positioned as stemming from characteristics of author or source, the section that follows describes the processes involved in DPL. These processes include conceptualizing individual domain perspectives as well as comparing and evaluating these and integrating them to solve problems.

PROCESSES INVOLVED IN DOMAIN PERSPECTIVE LEARNING

Conceptualizing a Single Domain Perspective

When students are presented with only one domain perspective (e.g., an economic argument for building a new shopping mall), the processes that are involved are those related to DP *recognition* and *construction*. Recognition and construction occur both when authors explicitly identify their DPs, allowing students to use this information in making inferences about the content provided in text, and when authors are not explicit in identifying their DPs, requiring students to instead deduce these based on the information provided (e.g., the type of evidence cited or the methods described).

Recognition

Recognition refers to students' attendance to explicit and implicit cues likely to signal a domain perspective. These cues may stem from features of the content included within a text (e.g., the type of evidence that is introduced), from author characteristics (e.g., credentials), or from features of text format (e.g., document types, like journal articles or policy briefs). These cues may further explicitly identify a domain perspective or may implicitly suggest it through the content that is introduced or how such content is presented.

Construction

Construction involves the definition and elaboration of a domain perspective according to its domain characteristics (i.e., the objects of focus, methods of inquiry, and evaluative standards that define that particular domain). Construction involves not only instantiating these various characteristics in association with a particular domain perspective but also applying these to understand what information may be presented by a specific, domain perspective-bound author and why. For instance, construction is involved in students recognizing that an economist predicting job growth in association with new shopping mall construction is introducing such predictions based on financial modeling (i.e., method of inquiry), aiming to maximize data fit (i.e., evaluative standard applied). As such, construction refers to students' cognitive representation of the domain perspective(s) reflected in a particular text and how these are associated with the information presented within it.

Inferential and Deductive Recognition and Construction

Conceptualizing a domain perspective, including both recognition and construction, may be viewed as either an inferential or a deductive process. It is sometimes the case that an author or source may explicitly identify themselves as offering a particular domain perspective on an issue. In such an instance, students may be expected to use this explicit positioning to make inferences about the domain characteristics that a particular author drew on to compose the information presented within a specific text.

Conversely, it is oftentimes the case that authors do not explicitly position themselves according to the domain perspective(s) that they are drawing on or represent. In such an instance, students are required, instead, to deduce an author's DP leanings, based on the objects of investigation that they discuss, the methods of inquiry that they use, and the evaluative standards that they apply. For instance, reading a text introducing projections and stress-tests of the traffic flow and congestion likely to result from shopping mall construction, should lead students to conclude that a particular text is written from an urban planning perspective, with this deduction allowing for further inferencing regarding the information that is included within a particular text. At the same time, this type of deduction may be expected to be considerably more challenging for learners to construct when they are unfamiliar with or unaware of different domains, as compared to when authors explicitly identify their domain perspective(s). In summary, students' conceptualization of a specific domain perspective requires both recognition and construction. Together, these processes result in students understanding the specific information included within a particular text as the result of author's domain perspective, defined by the characteristics of the domain(s) that they represent. The next section describes the processes involved in students' reasoning across multiple domain perspectives, as is required for interdisciplinary understanding.

REASONING ABOUT MULTIPLE DOMAIN PERSPECTIVES

At the outset of this chapter, engaging students in DPL was identified as a method for facilitating interdisciplinary understanding. For DPL to lead to such understanding requires students to do more than to conceptualize individual domain perspectives; rather students need to reason about multiple domain perspectives during learning and problem solving. Two key processes, namely (a) comparison and evaluation and (b) integration, are required for students to reason about multiple domain perspectives. These processes may be expected to take place after students have conceptualized a number of individual domain perspectives on a common topic. For instance, this may involve students individually considering the economic ramifications, social opportunities, and ecological costs of constructing a new shopping mall, as conceptualized across distinct domain perspectives. Once a number of domain perspectives on a common topic have been conceptualized, the processes of comparison and evaluation and of integration may ensue.

Comparison and Evaluation

Because domain perspectives are defined by distinct domain characteristics, it is difficult, if not impossible, to directly draw comparisons across these. That is, it is difficult to compare the economic effects of constructing a new shopping mall to its possible ecological harms. This is because economic vis-à-vis ecological domain perspectives are defined, in part, by differences in the objects and subjects of inquiry that they focus on. As such, because their objects of focus, alongside other domain characteristics, are distinct from one another, these DPs are impossible to directly compare. So, while we may expect an economic DP to analyze the effects of shopping mall construction on the local economy and an ecological DP to consider the constructions' environmental effects, direct comparing these DPs provides us with no mechanism for evaluating the relative importance of economic (e.g., more jobs) vis-à-vis environmental (e.g., increased pollution) impacts. As such, diverse domain perspectives on common topics, for the most part, can only be compared indirectly. Such indirect comparisons can occur through one of three means, through: (a) endogenous evaluation, (b) the comparison of conclusions drawn across domain perspectives according to universal values or ideals, or though (c) the personal weighing of DPs. All three of these approaches to the comparison of domain perspectives are intertwined with their evaluation. That is because the goal of comparing DPs, as described in this section, is to allow for competing conclusions, drawn across DPs, to be balanced and prioritized through learners' judgments of their relative merits and limitations.

Endogenous Evaluation

When presented with information from multiple DPs, one method for comparing these or selecting from among them is to compare the quality of the information included within them. This involves evaluating the arguments included in texts or judging the quality of the evidence introduced by specific authors, representing particular DPs, and the fidelity and robustness with which this evidence was analyzed, interpreted, and marshalled in support of claims. Such argument evaluation, however, is most likely to occur in accordance with evaluative standards that are endogenous to particular domains, or domain-specific, rather than domain-general, in nature. That is, evidence introduced in association with an economic analysis favoring shopping mall construction is likely to be evaluated according to economic-specific standards for evidence and methods quality (e.g., number of observations, identification strategy or estimation approach used), rather than according to the evaluative standards used in other domains (e.g., distinguishing primary and secondary sources in history). When evidence is analyzed and interpreted and resulting conclusions are evaluated in a domain-specific fashion, learners are able to determine the overall quality of

DP-specific arguments and position these along a continuum of strength and convincingness. Then, when arguments forwarded by different DPs diverge or conflict with one another, learners are able to use their endogenous or domain-specific evaluations of argument strength to compare and select from among these. That is, across arguments forwarded by different DPs, students may be expected to select the stronger argument over its weaker counterpart.

Nevertheless, there are three important caveats to such endogenous evaluation and its facilitation of DP comparison and selection. First, when comparing DP-based arguments according to their relative strength, this comparison is typically based on domain-specific standards of evaluation. Certainly, there are domain-general evaluative standards. For instance, sample size and representativeness are a concern common across domains. Nevertheless, even these domain general standards still tend to be applied in a domain-specific fashion (e.g., what constitutes an appropriate sample size differs across the domains of economics, sociology, and medicine). As such, even when introduced to domain-general standards for evaluation, students still need specific instruction in how these may be applied to understanding and evaluating domain-specific objects and methods. Second, in the case of endogenous evaluation, perspectives are still compared indirectly, according to their relative strength, rather than directly juxtaposed with one another. Third, while endogenous evaluation may be an effective comparison approach to use when the arguments forwarded by different DPs are of varying quality, this approach provides little guidance in helping students to compare and select from among DPs that are of comparable strength and convincingness. Indeed, this approach is reliant on students being able to accurately identify arguments, introduced across DPs, as comparable or discrepant in their relative strength.

Comparing Conclusions Drawn across Domain Perspectives

Endogenous evaluation is not possible when different domain perspectives introduce arguments that are of similar quality, as determined by domain-specific standards of evaluation. In these cases, arguments presented by competing DPs may need to be compared according to the conclusions that they draw. For example, comparing different DP-based arguments on shopping mall construction, that are comparable in strength, would involve determining whether authors representing different DPs are ultimately in favor of or in opposition to shopping mall construction. In this way, conclusions drawn across DPs act as a kind of common denominator or currency across arguments forwarded by different domain perspectives, allowing these to be compared. This is similar to how argument strength serves a common metric allowing DPs to be compared when an endogenous evaluation approach is adopted.

Once the conclusions that are arrived at via particular domain perspectives are identified, these can be juxtaposed with conclusions stemming from other, potentially conflicting, domain perspectives. At the most basic level, comparing conclusions across domain perspectives may involve determining how many DPs are in favor of a particular course of action, how many are opposed, and electing to decide with the majority. However, oftentimes a more nuanced or balanced approach is needed to evaluate the relative merits and limitations of conclusions forwarded across different domain perspectives.

Such a balanced or systematic approach to conclusion comparison involves evaluating conclusions from different DPs according to their alignment with *universal values* or ideals. The term universal values is used in this chapter to represent evaluative standards that are (a) domain-general in nature, or distinct from the domain-specific evaluative standards that are used to substantiate and evaluate the quality of knowledge claims within domains (e.g., replicability in science, corroboration in history); (b) relatively few in number, (c) exist on a cultural or societal level, rather than within specific domains, and are (d) broadly agreed upon within a particular society. For instance, in the United States, such values may include a respect for individual freedoms, a prioritizing of economic competition, and a commitment to law and order (Clarke & Aram, 1997; Perkins, 2002; Sen, 1999). Moreover, such universal values may be considered to be (e) abstract and (f) asymptotic in nature. This means that universal values, such as tradition or security (Schultz & Zelezny, 1999), can never be fully realized. Rather, such universal values are used as barometers of what specific domain perspective-based conclusions may be seeking to maximize or mitigate, at any given time.

Stated more simply, the benefits to job growth associated with building a new shopping mall can never be directly or meaningfully compared to the environmental harms of increased pollution, stemming from increased traffic to and from the retail core. However, the domain perspective-based conclusions regarding shopping mall construction can be evaluated according to the values they are seeking to maximize (e.g., opportunity) and any harms they may be looking to reduce (e.g., habitat destruction). Important to note is that such values are abstracted from the specific objects of focus that are examined within particular domains. That is, while the number of jobs created are not compared to the metric tons of emissions generated, the universal values that these effects correspond to can be questioned, balanced, and compared. Asking students to compare conclusions from diverse domain perspectives according to the values that they are seeking to maximize or diminish both helps students to apply DPs to real-world problems and better simulates the values-based judgments that often guide decision making in the real world. That is, deciding whether or not to move forward with shopping mall construction is oftentimes a values-based decision regarding what is prioritized and what is dismissed.

Personal Weighing

While comparing conclusions from competing DPs according to universal values may be considered to be the preferred approach to systematically weighing distinct DP-based arguments, it is also the case that such a systematic approach is often not the one adopted. Rather, the final way that students can determine which arguments, from different domain perspectives, they favor or oppose, is by aligning these arguments with a set of personally determined preferences or criteria. Such personal criteria are similar to endogenous evaluations of argument strength and universal values in that they serve as a common measuring stick that can be used to compare different DP-based arguments; but such personal criteria are distinct in that they may not be explicitly stated and, often, are not deliberately arrived at or interrogated. That is, students trying to make a decision on whether they support or oppose shopping mall construction and weighing economic benefits against ecological costs, may simply decide that they care much more about the environment than they do about any potential economy benefits that may result. While this type of personal weighing, like endogenous evaluation and the comparison of conclusions according to universal values, allows competing DP-based arguments to be compared, such comparison is based on individuals' preferences that may or may not be well-reasoned or systematically applied. Moreover, such individual preferences may or may not be more generally shared or easily communicable to others. As such, the comparison and selection of arguments from competing DPs based only on personally determined criteria, while common, may only constitute a starting point for engaging students in the comparison and evaluation of domain perspective-based arguments during learning.

In examining how DP-based arguments may be compared and evaluated, three possible approaches to such comparison have been identified. These include: (a) endogenous evaluation (i.e., evaluating the strength of arguments proposed by competing DPs using domain-specific standards), (b) the comparison of DP-based conclusion according to universal values, and (c) the weighing of competing DP-based arguments according to personally determined, rather than universal, criteria. Across these three approaches to DP-based argument comparison, the focus or goal of such comparison is to allow for the preferential selection of arguments or conclusions introduced by some DPs over others. At the same time, students' goals may not always be to preferentially select one DP-based argument over another; at times, students may be interested in DP integration or the linking of argument from across domain perspectives for interdisciplinary understanding or problem-solving. Such DP integration may likewise be thought of as involving the processes of comparison and evaluation, to varying extents; however, in the case of integration, such processes are focused on synthesis rather than on selection. The next section outlines the ways that disparate domain perspectives and the arguments that these introduce may be combined or integrated with one another to solve problems or to decide on courses of action.

Integration

Beyond comparison and evaluation for DP selection, students need to be able to connect or integrate different domain perspectives and the arguments that these introduce in order to solve problems. In fact, doing so is considered to be essential for interdisciplinary understanding and problem solving (Boix Mansilla & Duraising, 2007). Like comparison, DP integration is likely to unfold in one of three possible ways. These include selective, transformative, and structural approaches to DP integration. These approaches may be conceptualized as progressing in sophistication, with only the final approach reflecting the type of processing that is emblematic of true interdisciplinarity (Ivanitskaya et al., 2002; Van den Besselaar & Heimeriks, 2001). As a contrast, the first two approaches to DP integration discussed (i.e., selective, transformative), may best be characterized as multidisciplinary in nature, in that they draw on multiple domain perspective-based arguments without fully connecting these, in their entirety, as is required for interdisciplinarity (Van den Besselaar & Heimeriks, 2001). Nevertheless, in focusing on domain perspective learning, generally, rather than on interdisciplinary learning, more specifically, this chapter makes the case that all three of these approaches to DP integration are important and may serve specific learning and instructional aims in the classroom.

Selective

A selective approach to DP integration uses various domain perspectives to generate unique solutions to a common problem and then chooses from among these. As such, a selective approach is one that draws on diverse domain perspectives to create a "menu" of options that students can select from and additively combine to find a resolution to a common problem. For instance, the problem of a lack of accessible shopping options within a particular neighborhood may be solved by changing traffic patterns, increasing communication around existing store options, and offering subscription services, with these solutions potentially recommended by urban planning, communications, and marketing domain perspectives, respectively. Nevertheless, as suggested by the above example, a selective approach to DP integration is dependent on the variety of solutions suggested by different DPs being complementary in nature and amenable to combination. That is, a selective approach to DP integration becomes less effective when the advertisements that are distributed are for stores that are difficult to get to (i.e., when solutions introduced across DPs are incompatible). Moreover, a selective approach to DP integration is particularly unhelpful when the solutions that are offered across DPs are directly in conflict. For instance, while one DP may argue for increasing shopping options, another DP may argue for the same land being used for additional road construction or for a park, to increase foot traffic, more broadly. When solutions offered by different DPs are in conflict with one another these become quite difficult for students to reconcile, particularly when students have limited domain and cross-domain expertise. Indeed, in such instances of conflict students are likely to choose a solution offered by one DP over another for a variety of well-justified or arbitrary and ad-hoc reasons. These include DP selection based on endogenous evaluation or on the comparison of competing DP-based conclusions according to universal values or personal criteria, as is discussed in the previous section. While exercises in this type of comparison, evaluation, selection, and prioritization may be important for students to engage in, transformative and structural approaches to DP integration are further introduced as means of engaging students in more robust domain perspective integration.

Transformative

A transformative approach to DP integration is one that directs students' attention to the problems that they are seeking to address, rather than to DP-specific solutions, as is the case with a selective approach. A transformative approach to DP integration is one that is used to define, rather than solve, problems. As such, it emphasizes using domain perspectives as lenses on a common topic and looking across the insights originating from these various lenses to jointly specify and define problems in a way that is mutually negotiated and agreed upon, across domains. Thus, in a transformative approach to DP integration, problem definitions may be expected to be clarified, corroborated, and prioritized across DPs, until a joint problem scope is defined. Such comparison and prioritization may be expected to be more systematic or analytic, as compared to a selective DP integration approach, which may be expected to prioritize among DP-based solutions in a more ad hoc manner.

In a transformative approach to DP integration, the problems that students are asked to solve are not only addressed by different domain perspectives but rather are reconceptualized in light of these. For instance, the problem of deciding whether or not to construct a shopping mall may, rather, need to be broadened to consider how to make an area of a city more attractive to its residents and to define what may make an area of a city "attractive" and who may be defined as a "resident" across domains. This broader, analytic approach to question definition may provide a way for different DP approaches to be juxtaposed and put into conversation with one another. Indeed, the emphasis in transformative DP integration is not on the selective or ad hoc picking and choosing among maximally compatible DPs; rather it is on building consensus across domain perspectives by explicitly asking such perspectives to specify key priorities and concerns. In such a way, a transformative approach to DP integration further asks students to consider how different DPs may both define problems around a common topic and conceptualize such problems in terms of universal values or ideals. In contrast to a selective approach to DP integration, a transformative approach may be said to require students to develop a cross-domain understanding of problems, prior to engaging in cross-domain problem solving (e.g., solution generation) *per se*.

Yet, a transformative approach to DP integration is likely not to be considered to be truly interdisciplinary in nature (Van den Besselaar & Heimeriks, 2001). Such an approach nevertheless treats DPs as separate entities and only focuses on defining a shared or common language across these through problem definition. A final structural approach to DP integration is therefore proposed as an instance of true interdisciplinarity.

Structural

A structural approach to DP integration integrates multiple domain perspectives in and of themselves. That is to say that even absent any specific problems or efforts aimed at their resolution, a structural approach to DP integration seeks to connect domain perspectives in an effort to view the world in an enriched and multidimensionally informed way. As such, a structural approach to integrating domain perspectives requires redefining objects of focus, methods of inquiry, and evaluative standards across domains. In turn, this may result in whole novel objects of inquiry being considered, new and interdisciplinary methods being developed, and adaptive evaluative standards being established.

Within the context of structural integration, because it is domains themselves that are integrated, the selection of domains for integration must be especially purposeful or deliberate on the part of learners. Such deliberate selection should be guided by individuals' deep level knowledge of the to-be-integrated domains. At the expert level, such a structural approach to domain integration may be considered core to the development of interdisciplinary domains of public policy, behavioral economics, human–computer interaction, and gender studies. At the more novice level, such deliberate domain integration may be considered to be the focus of developing students' interdisciplinary understanding and problem solving only once a fairly advanced level of DPL has been achieved (e.g., once students have experience with selective and transformative DP integration).

Comparing Selective, Transformative, and Structural Approaches to DP Integration

Selective, transformative, and structural approaches to DP integration may be compared to one another along a number of dimensions. Principally, these differ in the extent to which multiple domain perspectives are truly integrated or simply consulted or combined. That is, selective DP integration adopts a functional view toward DPL, only drawing on multiple domain perspectives to generate a number of solutions without integrating solutions across domains, except in an additive manner. A transformative approach to DP integration is focused on building connections across domain perspectives in how they see the world and the problems they identify with in it. While a transformative approach is focused on analyzing and comparing insights introduced across domain perspectives and evaluating these according to shared standards or universal values, such an approach still does not integrate domains *per se*. Finally, a structural approach to DP integration systematically combines domains, in terms of their domain characteristics, to approach the world in an interdisciplinary, yet unitary fashion.

Further, approaches to DP integration may be considered to differ from one another in the stances toward interdisciplinary problems that they adopt. Selective approaches to DP integration are functional in nature and are focused on generating a number of domain perspective-based solutions to complex problems and choosing from among these. Transformative approaches shift the focus to defining problems in a broad and multiple domain perspective-informed fashion. Finally, a structural approach to DP integration first unifies multiple domain perspectives and then uses these as one common lens to define problems, propose solutions, and examine information in the world, more generally. As such, while selective and transformative approaches to DP integration may be said to view problems in a multidisciplinary (i.e., drawing on multiple domains) fashion, is it only transformative DP integration that is interdisciplinary in nature, or reflective of true cross-domain integration (Van den Besselaar & Heimeriks, 2001).

Finally, these different approaches to DP integration vary in how deliberate they are in the domains that they elect to consult and the criteria they use to select among and compare these. A selective approach to DP integration may be considered to be the most ad hoc. That is, such an approach may be expected to be focused on generating a large number of domain perspective-specific solutions to problems and combining these in ways that are convenient, most of all, rather than deliberately considered. A transformative approach to DP integration may be considered distinctive because, in analyzing and comparing problem conceptualizations across DPs, such an approach is purposeful in setting out the common criteria that may be used to judge or balance varied problem definitions, with these common criteria typically taking the form of universal values or ideals. Finally, a structural approach to DP integration is the most systematic in considering not only the criteria according to which insights from across DPs may be compared (i.e., as is done within a transformative approach to integration) but also in purposefully choosing the DPs that students ought to be asked to draw on. These various approaches to DP integration and the differences among them are summarized in Table 11.1.

Table 11.1 Comparing Approaches to Domain Perspective Integration.

	What is Integrated?	Method of Integration	Degree of Systemization
Selective	Multiple DP-specific solutions to problems	Additive	Limited
Transformative	Problem definitions across DPs	Corroboration and comparison	Problem definitions are systematically compared and held to common, universal standards
Structuralist	Features of domains (i.e., objects of focus, methods of inquiry, evaluative standards)	Synthetic and generative of new objects of focus, methods of inquiry, and evaluative standards	Highly purposeful in the domains that are chosen for integration

PURPOSE FOR DOMAIN PERSPECTIVE LEARNING

As is likely evident from the previous sections of this chapter, learning from multiple domain perspectives represents quite a challenging and demanding process for students. This begs the question of why learning from multiple domain perspectives should be an activity that students engage in at all, particularly when students, even at the undergraduate level, have difficulties reasoning even within the bounds of a single domain. In the section that follows, three distinct functions or purposes for teaching students to engage in domain perspective learning are identified. These are to build deeper understanding, enhance problem solving, and foster critical thinking.

Build Deeper Understanding

The fundamental purpose of learning from multiple domain perspectives rests in necessity. Much information in the world, particularly expert information and information written about complex topics, is necessarily written from a domain perspective, regardless of whether such a perspective is explicitly identified by the author or not. As such, meaningfully understanding and evaluating a great deal of complex information requires students to be able to conceptualize domain perspectives or to recognize how the domain characteristics associated with particular DPs inform the specific information included in DP-specific texts.

Engaging students in reasoning about the connection between domain perspectives and the information included in a text fosters their *epistemic cognition*. Maggioni and Parkinson (2008) define epistemic cognition as what individuals *do* when engaged in reflecting on what knowledge is and how it may be justified. For example, students engage in epistemic cognition when evaluating sources during reading to determine whether they are making credible knowledge claims or when corroborating information across texts to confirm its veracity (Barzilai & Zohar, 2012; Bråten et al., 2011). Despite the centrality of epistemic cognition in dictating how individuals view the world and process information, considerable empirical evidence suggests that students do not readily engage in epistemic cognition, rarely evaluating sources, detecting discrepancies, or corroborating information, unless explicitly instructed to do so (Kienhues, Stadtler, & Bromme, 2011; List, Alexander, & Stephens, 2017; Mason, Boldrin, & Ariasi, 2010; Stadtler & Bromme, 2007; Valanides & Angeli, 2005).

This chapter argues that beyond source evaluation, students' recognition of domain perspectives during reading reflects epistemic cognition or students' reasoning regarding what knowledge is and how it is established, in a domain-specific fashion (Chinn, Buckland, & Samarapungavan, 2011). Such DP-based epistemic cognition may involve inferring the methods of inquiry used to gather data (e.g., understanding that public opinion polls reflect survey data gathered via self-report) or applying domain-specific standards to evaluating information (e.g., questioning how replicable or reliable experimental findings may be). As such, asking students to recognize and conceptualize domain perspectives constitutes a form of epistemic cognition, with greater epistemic cognition associated with benefits for learning and academic achievement (Lodewyk, 2007; Muis, 2007).

Problem Solving

Problem solving is a secondary function served by helping students to conceptualize multiple domain perspectives and compare and integrate across these. Problem solving refers to the novel generation of solutions on the part of the learner (Mayer, 2006). Such solution generation may be achieved by selectively, transformatively, or structurally integrating domain perspectives to, at the most sophisticated level of DP integration, achieve interdisciplinary problem solving. As such, engaging students in domain perspective learning during problem solving results in their generating more domain-specific solutions (i.e., selective approach), reconceptualizing problems and problem spaces from multiple domain perspectives (i.e., transformative approach), and structurally integrating domain perspectives to develop novel methods and approaches to inquiry. This last, structural approach to problem solving and DP integration reflects the argument, introduced across a variety of domains, that some intractable problems that exist in the world today (e.g., inequality, climate change) can only be addressed interdisciplinarily. As reflected in a structural approach to DP integration, this would involve the deliberate and systematic application of novel modes of inquiry, developed based on practices from across disparate domains, to address these.

Critical Thinking

Finally, domain perspective learning may serve as a mechanism for fostering critical thinking. Here, one specific aspect of critical thinking is examined: the evaluation of statements or conclusions according to the information that they are based upon vis-à-vis the information that they ignore or exclude. Examples of this type of critical thinking include students' critiques of media for the stories and characters that it features or fails to portray and represent (Kellner, 1995) and critiques of medicine for its piecemeal focus on isolated ailments, rather than on a person as a whole and their environment, in an anthropologically informed manner (Baer, Singer, & Johnsen, 1986; Gee & Payne-Sturges, 2004). This type of critical thinking, focused on what is represented and what is excluded, may be considered to be an essential part of building interdisciplinary understanding. As explained by Feuerstein (1999): "The educational strategy for multi-dimensional thinking requires pupils to cope with multi-faceted tasks on a single issue. This demands defining the whole gamut of potential aspects which exist in a given situation" (p. 44). Here, Feuerstein defines multi-dimensional thinking in much the same way that this chapter defines critical thinking, as concerned with the myriad of "potential aspects" of a given situation. DPL may be viewed as a mechanism for helping students to identify and reason about such "potential aspects" or to engage in critical thinking.

Generally speaking, students have been found to struggle with critical thinking and analysis, even when evaluating arguments in only one domain (Marin & Halpern, 2011; Twardy, 2004). This struggle has been attributed, in part, to limitations in students' reasoning skills, with students lacking a framework to use in evaluating arguments against various standards (Ennis, 1991; Wu & Tsai, 2007). As suggested in this chapter, domain perspective learning may serve as a mechanism for helping students to engage in critical thinking and to apply evaluative standards from across domains to analyzing complex and multidimensional problems. For example, students may have difficulties thinking critically about a proposal to build a new shopping mall and may not question the economic benefits that it promises to deliver. Nevertheless, directing students to consider multiple domain perspectives on this issue may prompt them to both evaluate the promise of added jobs according to domain-specific evaluative standards in economics (e.g., how were job projections identified or estimated) and to further consider the sociological (e.g., who would benefit by having access to jobs and more consumer goods?), geographic (e.g., how would the mall fit into the urban landscape?), and political (e.g., who is involved in the decision making around building a new shopping mall?) ramifications of this plan.

Drawing on different perspectives as a mechanism for fostering critical thinking has been done in work by Kiili, Coiro, and Hämäläinen (2016). Specifically, to help students develop arguments and counterarguments during two-sided argumentation, Kiili et al. (2016) introduced students to a *perspective pallet*, listing educational, political, ideological, judicial, social, ethical, and global perspectives, among others. Once introduced, students were able to use this perspective pallet to generate a variety of arguments or to think critically about a common topic. Applied to DPL, such a perspective pallet may serve as the basis for introducing students to different domain perspectives and their associated domain characteristics. As students come to understand these different domains and their associated characteristics, they can use the DPs represented in a perspective pallet to think critically about complex topics.

Thus far, this chapter has suggested that the benefits of learning from multiple domain perspectives include building deeper level understanding of complex issues, improving problem solving, and fostering critical thinking. Nevertheless, despite these stated benefits, a cautionary note is needed regarding what may be expected of novices engaged in DPL vis-à-vis their expert counterparts.

CAUTIONARY NOTE ON NOVICES' DOMAIN PERSPECTIVE LEARNING

The goal of this chapter is to describe how domain novices may be engaged in domain perspective learning and, ultimately, in interdisciplinary problem solving. This novice focus is appropriate, first, because the majority of students in K-12 schools are just such domain novices, with no specific domain expertise. Second, this novice focus is appropriate since the domain-perspective reasoning of experts is quite different from that of novices (Grosslight, Unger, Jay, & Smith, 1991; Wineburg, 1991). In part, this is because an intrinsic aspect of expertise is that, once such expertise is achieved, processing information, including reading and writing, is inherently done from that expert's domain perspective. That is, an expert biologist does not need to be taught or directed to recognize the domain and sub-domain perspectives of their field represented in text or to judge these using domain-specific evaluate standards. A feature of their expertise is that such domain perspective-based reading and reasoning is almost second nature. Likewise, what is meant for an expert in one domain to reason across other domains is different than what may be expected of novices reasoning across domain perspectives. Although experts in one domain are not necessarily experts in another, their efforts to reason across domains may be much more likely to result in the structural integration of domains (i.e., in interdisciplinary understanding), rather than in more selective or transformative DP integration. This is because their expertise in one domain may bolster their understanding of the domain characteristics of another (Bruns, 2013; Schunn & Anderson, 1999). This may especially be the case when the domains that experts are integrating share certain characteristics, as reflected in interdisciplinary fields like biochemistry and political philosophy. Nevertheless, the degree of DP-based, interdisciplinary reasoning ascribed to experts can hardly be expected of novices.

Why, then, is it a worthwhile endeavor to engage domain novices in reasoning using various domain perspectives? As suggested previously, DPL allows novices to draw on and benefit from others' domain expertise (e.g., when reading texts written by experts), without yet having to have developed domain expertise of their own. These benefits extend to allowing novices to learn about the epistemic practices that define different domains and helping them to approach interdisciplinary problems more competently and strategically. At the same time, encouraging students to move fluidly across various domain perspectives, with little to no domain expertise of their own, runs the risk of fostering a kind of artificiality or epistemic ersatz. At worse, such learning may encourage students to treat domain perspectives in a superficial or heuristic fashion. For instance, an economic perspective may be viewed as synonymous with wanting to maximize profit while an ecological perspective may be conceptualized as unidimensionally opposed to development of any kind. Such epistemic ersatz may be especially likely to arise when curricula are not structured to support students' deep exploration of domain characteristics and domain-specific epistemic practices, alongside engaging in interdisciplinary problem solving. To guard against such epistemic ersatz, this chapter closes by identifying three instructional strategies that may be use to foster students' domain perspective learning in the classroom.

STRATEGIES TO FOSTER DOMAIN PERSPECTIVE LEARNING

There are three instructional strategies that can be used to promote domain perspective learning. These strategies are introduced with the recognition that not all tasks, and perhaps not even the majority of tasks, require interdisciplinary understanding. Teaching students to approach and investigate complex problems within, rather than across, domains should continue to be the central focus of instruction. Likewise, not all problems require interdisciplinary resolution. Nevertheless, when an interdisciplinary approach is required, three strategies can be used to promote students' domain perspective learning. These strategies are (a) making domains and domain characteristics explicit for learners, (b) asking students to read and write domain-specific texts, and (c) engaging students in identifying ill-structured and complex problems.

Making Domains and Domain Characteristics Explicit for Learners

The fundamental challenge associated with engaging learners in DPL and, ultimately, in interdisciplinary problem solving, is that students' DP-specific reasoning may be limited by their relative lack of domain knowledge or expertise. That is, novice learners may be expected to be both limited in their knowledge of domain content (e.g., events in history) and in their knowledge of domains, *per se* (e.g., the methods of inquiry and evaluative standards used in history). As such, a challenge for teachers rests in building these two aspects of domain knowledge simultaneously, when students need to understand domain characteristics to understand how content within domains has come to be determined and substantiated. For instance, teaching students about the causes of the Civil War also requires introducing them to the evidence sources (i.e., objects of focus) that historians examine to determine causality and to causal analysis as a method of historical reasoning.

While teaching domain content to novices can be said to characterize much of the instruction happening in today's schools, teaching students about domains, themselves, occurs to a much more limited extent (Goldman et al., 2016). This fact is underscored by the ease with which it is possible to essentialize domains only according to the content or concepts that they include, rather than considering domains' underlying characteristics. For instance, it is easy to view literature as only the reading of great texts or to view history as a collection of facts about wars and kings. Although domains are, of course, partially defined by the content that they include, the structure and epistemic characteristics of domains should be made more explicit to students. Indeed, DPL requires first and foremost that students come to understand domains and their essential characteristics. This would include helping students to conceptualize domains in terms of the objects and subjects that they study, the methods they use, and the evaluative standards that they apply. Such explicit identification can be done by introducing students to domain-specific, epistemic-related concepts (e.g., defining reliability or hypothesis testing) and by engaging students in the methods of inquiry and epistemic practices of different domains. This may include involving students in data collection in the classroom or helping students to use historical archives for research (Kanari & Millar, 2004; Roff, 2007; Tally & Goldenberg, 2005; Zhai, Jocz, & Tan, 2014). Moreover, such an understanding of domains and their essential characteristics may be fostered by modeling for students the kind of reasoning that characterizes methods in different domains and how to apply domain-specific standards to their evaluation. Collins, Brown, and Newman (1988) refer to this as *cognitive apprenticeship* and prescribe it as an antidote to the problem of "schools ... [being] relatively successful in organizing and conveying large bodies of conceptual and factual knowledge ... [but] render[ing] key aspects of expertise invisible to students" (p. 2).

Asking Students to Read and Write Domain-Specific Texts

An additional mechanism for fostering students' DPL and building their understanding of domains and domain characteristics, is engaging them in domain-specific reading and writing. Among the features distinguishing different domains or areas of study are their communicative practices, including the text formats and publication practices that may define each domain (Goldman et al., 2016). As such, when students read domain-specific texts this can develop their conceptions of domains, particularly if the communicative practices that are exhibited within each domain are identified and the evaluative standards used to make judgments within each domain are made explicit. For instance, this may include asking students to evaluate sample size and representativeness when reading studies in psychology or asking students to distinguish among primary and secondary sources in history. Likewise, helping students to build rich conceptualizations of domain perspectives may also be done by asking students to create domain-specific texts (e.g., policy briefs, lab reports). Doing so may not only serve as an academic exercise but also constitute a mechanism for engaging students in domain-specific practices. That is, while writing a laboratory report constitutes a common academic assignment, completing such a report can further develop students' understanding of how the structure of a laboratory report serves to meet the domain-specific evaluative standards of knowledge building in science (e.g., precision, replication). Doubtless, at present, this degree and depth of instruction about domain characteristics represents a relatively narrow sliver of US schooling (e.g., in Advanced Placement classes and apprenticeship courses, Bell, Blair, Crawford, & Lederman, 2003; Brophy & VanSledright, 1997). At the same time, sustained efforts aimed at building domain literacy suggest that many more students can be engaged in such learning even at very young ages (Driver, Newton, & Osborne, 2000; Goldman et al., 2016; Taylor, Barker, & Jones, 2003; VanSledright, 2002).

Engaging Students in Identifying Ill-Structured and Complex Problems

Beyond building students' understanding of domains and domain characteristics, engaging students in DPL is often an exercise in problem solving. Such problem solving requires that the focal problem topic or issue be sufficiently complex and multifaceted to warrant examination from multiple domain perspectives. As such, when determining what problems may be fruitful contexts for developing DPL and interdisciplinary problem solving, three standards may be used. First, such problems should be complex. Such complexity may come from problems being fairly abstract or general in nature (e.g., inequality) or consisting of many elements, related to one another in a variety of ways (e.g., shopping mall construction). These many elements may constitute different objects and subjects of inquiry that can be explored across domain perspectives.

Second, such problems should be open-ended or ill-structured in nature. As defined in classic typologies of problem solving (Simon, 1973), ill-structured problems may be characterized in a number of ways. To start, such problems are defined by having an ambiguous or incomplete problem space. This requires learners to define and make inferences about what, specifically, a problem entails and what the boundaries of a particular problem may be. Second, ill-structured problems, due to their ill-defined problem space, have no obvious or evident end-state and no optimal solution path for students to follow. This requires learners to self-determine how a particular problem ought to be solved and what the desired outcomes of a problem should be, with no objectively correct answers involved. This ambiguity in problem space, solution process, and problem outcomes provide room for each of these elements to be conceptualized differently according to the particular domain perspectives that students draw on. For instance, a selective approach to domain perspective integration may involve students generating a variety of possible solutions to an ill-structured problem, while a transformative approach to DP integration may, rather, involve learners defining problem spaces from a variety of domain perspectives. Although the ultimate goal may be for students to be able to structurally integrate DPs or to engage in interdisciplinary problem solving, such advanced problem solving is undergirded by students' selective and transformative DP integration.

Finally, in looking for problems for learners to address in an interdisciplinary fashion it is important that these be sufficiently important or high-stakes so as to be motivating for learners. Domain perspective learning is a challenging and demanding task. While participating in such a challenging and complex task may be inherently or intrinsically motivating for some learners, for others the value of task completion may need to be sufficiently high to warrant the necessary degree of cognitive engagement required. Such value may come from topic interest or from the importance that learners assign to the issues that they are asked to investigate or the problems that they are asked to solve.

In addition to selecting problems for learners that are complex, ill-structured, and motivating, a necessary approach to fostering DPL may be asking students to generate and define particular problems or topics of inquiry for themselves. As demonstrated in case studies of inter-disciplinary classrooms (Brown, 2002; Springer, 2006), such problem definition and topic generation often takes the form of question specification and serves an essential function for students in both helping them to conceptualize problems in a precise yet multifaceted manner and in motivating the problem solving process. Moreover, engaging students in question specification may result in the generation of problems rooted in students' local, school-based, and neighborhood concerns. Addressing such concerns, alongside more global issues affecting us all, is at the core of interdisciplinary understanding and problem solving.

CONCLUSION

This chapter introduces the construct of domain perspective learning as a precursor to students' development of interdisciplinary understanding and problem solving in the classroom. In particular, domain perspective learning is defined as students' recognition of information included in text as reflecting the objects of inquiry, methods, and evaluative standards that define particular domains. Moreover, DPL is defined as including students' use of domain perspectives to make inferences about and evaluate information in domain informed ways and their integration of domain perspectives to solve problems. In making the case for domain perspective learning, the benefits of DPL for building deeper understanding, improving problem solving, and fostering critical thinking are discussed. At the same time, DPL is fundamentally positioned not as an alternative to a-perspective or "objective" learning, as such learning does not exist. Rather, to the extent that students' processing of information in the world is always a matter of perspective, this chapter argues for developing students' understanding of domain perspectives as a way of enhancing and systematizing such processing.

REFERENCES

Alexander, P. A. (1998). The nature of disciplinary and domain learning: The knowledge, interest, and strategic dimensions of learning from subject-matter text. In C. Hynd (Ed.), *Learning from text across conceptual domains* (pp. 263–287). Mahwah, NJ: Erlbaum.

Alexander, P. A. (2003a). Profiling the developing reader: The interplay of knowledge, interest, and strategic processing. In C. M. Fairbanks, J. Worthy, B. Maloch, J. V. Hoffman, & D. L. Schallert (Eds.), *The fifty-first yearbook of the National Reading Conference* (pp. 47–65). Oak Creek, WI: National Reading Conference.

Alexander, P. A. (2003b). The development of expertise: The journey from acclimation to proficiency. *Educational Researcher, 32*(8), 10–14.

Baer, H. A., Singer, M., & Johnsen, J. H. (1986). Toward a critical medical anthropology. *Social Science & Medicine, 23*(2), 95–98.

Barzilai, S., & Zohar, A. (2012). Epistemic thinking in action: Evaluating and integrating online sources. *Cognition and Instruction, 30*(1), 39–85.

Becher, T., & Parry, S. (2005). The endurance of the disciplines. In I. Bleiklie & M. Henkel (Eds.), *Governing Knowledge* (pp. 133–144). Dordrecht: Springer.

Bell, R. L., Blair, L. M., Crawford, B. A., & Lederman, N. G. (2003). Just do it? Impact of a science apprenticeship program on high school students' understandings of the nature of science and scientific inquiry. *Journal of Research in Science Teaching: The Official Journal of the National Association for Research in Science Teaching, 40*(5), 487–509.

Biglan, A. (1973). The characteristics of subject matter. *Journal of Applied Psychology, 57*(3), 195–203.

Brante, E. W., & Strømsø, H. I. (2018). Sourcing in text comprehension: A review of interventions targeting sourcing skills. *Educational Psychology Review, 30*(3), 773–799.

Bråten, I., Britt, M. A., Strømsø, H. I., & Rouet, J. F. (2011). The role of epistemic beliefs in the comprehension of multiple expository texts: Toward an integrated model. *Educational Psychologist, 46*(1), 48–70.

Bråten, I., Strømsø, H. I., & Britt, M. A. (2009). Trust matters: Examining the role of source evaluation in students' construction of meaning within and across multiple texts. *Reading Research Quarterly, 44*(1), 6–28.

Bråten, I., Strømsø, H. I., & Salmerón, L. (2011). Trust and mistrust when students read multiple information sources about climate change. *Learning and Instruction, 21*(2), 180–192.

Brophy, J. E., & VanSledright, B. (1997). *Teaching and learning history in elementary schools*. New York: Teachers College Press.

Brown, D. F. (2002). Self-directed learning. *Educational Leadership, 60*(1), 54–58.

Brozo, W. G., Moorman, G., Meyer, C., & Stewart, T. (2013). Content area reading and disciplinary literacy: A case for the radical center. *Journal of Adolescent and Adult Literacy, 56*(5), 353–357.

Bruns, H. C. (2013). Working alone together: Coordination in collaboration across domains of expertise. *Academy of Management Journal, 56*(1), 62–83.

Buehl, M. M., & Alexander, P. A. (2001). Beliefs about academic knowledge. *Educational Psychology Review, 13*(4), 385–418.

Chinn, C. A., Buckland, L. A., & Samarapungavan, A. L. A. (2011). Expanding the dimensions of epistemic cognition: Arguments from philosophy and psychology. *Educational Psychologist, 46*(3), 141–167.

Clarke, R., & Aram, J. (1997). Universal values, behavioral ethics and entrepreneurship. *Journal of Business Ethics, 16*(5), 561–572.

Collins, A., Brown, J. S., & Newman, S. E. (1988). Cognitive apprenticeship: Teaching the craft of reading, writing and mathematics. *Thinking: The Journal of Philosophy for Children, 8*(1), 2–10.

Driver, R., Newton, P., & Osborne, J. (2000). Establishing the norms of scientific argumentation in classrooms. *Science Education, 84*(3), 287–312.

Ennis, R. (1991). Critical thinking: A streamlined conception. *Teaching Philosophy, 14*(1), 5–24.

Feuerstein, M. (1999). Media literacy in support of critical thinking. *Journal of Educational Media, 24*(1), 43–54.

Foshay, A. W. (1962). Education and the nature of a discipline. In A. Frazier (Ed.), *New dimensions in learning: A multidisciplinary approach* (pp. 1–8). Washington, DC: Association for Supervision and Curriculum Development, National Education Association.

Gee, G. C., & Payne-Sturges, D. C. (2004). Environmental health disparities: A framework integrating psychosocial and environmental concepts. *Environmental Health Perspectives, 112*(17), 1645–1653.

Goetz, E. T., Schallert, D. L., Reynolds, R. E., & Radin, D. I. (1983). Reading in perspective: What real cops and pretend burglars look for in a story. *Journal of Educational Psychology, 75*(4), 500–510.

Goldman, S. R., Britt, M. A., Brown, W., Cribb, G., George, M., Greenleaf, C., & Project, R. E. A. D. I. (2016). Disciplinary literacies and learning to read for understanding: A conceptual framework for disciplinary literacy. *Educational Psychologist*, 51(2), 219–246.

Grosslight, L., Unger, C., Jay, E., & Smith, C. L. (1991). Understanding models and their use in science: Conceptions of middle and high school students and experts. *Journal of Research in Science Teaching*, 28(9), 799–822.

Hauslein, P. L., Good, R. G., & Cummins, C. L. (1992). Biology content cognitive structure: From science student to science teacher. *Journal of Research in Science Teaching*, 29(9), 939–964.

Ivanitskaya, L., Clark, D., Montgomery, G., & Primeau, R. (2002). Interdisciplinary learning: Process and outcomes. *Innovative Higher Education*, 27(2), 95–111.

Jones, B. F., Rasmussen, C. M., & Moffitt, M. C. (1997). *Real-life problem solving: A collaborative approach to interdisciplinary learning*. Washington, DC: American Psychological Association.

Jones, C. (2010). Interdisciplinary approach-advantages, disadvantages, and the future benefits of interdisciplinary studies. *Essai*, 7(1), 26.

Kaakinen, J. K., & Hyönä, J. (2008). Perspective 2010 driven text comprehension. *Applied Cognitive Psychology*, 22(3), 319–334.

Kaakinen, J. K., Hyönä, J., & Keenan, J. M. (2002). Perspective effects on online text processing. *Discourse Processes*, 33(2), 159–173.

Kanari, Z., & Millar, R. (2004). Reasoning from data: How students collect and interpret data in science investigations. *Journal of Research in Science Teaching*, 41(7), 748–769.

Kellner, D. (1995). Cultural studies, multiculturalism and media culture. In G. Dines & J. Humez (Eds.), *Gender, race and class in media* (pp. 5–17). Thousand Oaks, CA: Sage.

Kienhues, D., Stadtler, M., & Bromme, R. (2011). Dealing with conflicting or consistent medical information on the web: When expert information breeds laypersons' doubts about experts. *Learning and Instruction*, 21(2), 193–204.

Kiili, C., Coiro, J., & Hämäläinen, J. (2016). An online inquiry tool to support the exploration of controversial issues on the internet. *Journal of Literacy and Technology*, 17(1/2), 31–52.

Kuhn, D., Cheney, R., & Weinstock, M. (2000). The development of epistemological understanding. *Cognitive Development*, 15(3), 309–328.

Lee, P. J., & Ashby, R. (2001). Empathy, perspective taking and rational understanding. In O. L. Davis, J.S. Foster, & E. Yaeger (Eds.), *Historical empathy and perspective taking in the social studies* (pp. 21–50). Boulder, CO: Rowman & Littlefield.

List, A., Alexander, P. A., & Stephens, L. A. (2017). Trust but verify: Examining the association between students' sourcing behaviors and ratings of text trustworthiness. *Discourse Processes*, 54(2), 83–104.

Lodewyk, K. R. (2007). Relations among epistemological beliefs, academic achievement, and task performance in secondary school students. *Educational Psychology*, 27(3), 307–327.

Macedo-Rouet, M., Potocki, A., Scharrer, L., Ros, C., Stadtler, M., Salmerón, L., & Rouet, J. F. (2019). How good is this page? Benefits and limits of prompting on adolescents' evaluation of web information quality. *Reading Research Quarterly*, 54(3), 299–321.

Maggioni, L., & Parkinson, M. M. (2008). The role of teacher epistemic cognition, epistemic beliefs, and calibration in instruction. *Educational Psychology Review*, 20(4), 445–461.

Mansilla, V. B., & Duraising, E. D. (2007). Targeted assessment of students' interdisciplinary work: An empirically grounded framework proposed. *Journal of Higher Education*, 78(2), 215–237.

Marin, L. M., & Halpern, D. F. (2011). Pedagogy for developing critical thinking in adolescents: Explicit instruction produces greatest gains. *Thinking Skills and Creativity*, 6(1), 1–13.

Mason, L., Boldrin, A., & Ariasi, N. (2010). Searching the web to learn about a controversial topic: Are students epistemically active? *Instructional Science*, 38(6), 607–633.

Mayer, R. E. (2006). Coping with complexity in multimedia learning. In J. Elen & R. E. Clark (Eds.), *Handling complexity in learning environments: Theory and research* (pp. 129–139). Oxford: Elsevier Press.

McCrudden, M. T., & Schraw, G. (2007). Relevance and goal-focusing in text processing. *Educational Psychology Review*, 19(2), 113–139.

Muis, K. R. (2007). The role of epistemic beliefs in self-regulated learning. *Educational Psychologist*, 42(3), 173–190.

Nariman, N., & Chrispeels, J. (2016). PBL in the era of reform standards: Challenges and benefits perceived by teachers in one elementary school. *Interdisciplinary Journal of Problem-Based Learning*, 10(1), 5. doi: https://doi.org/10.7771/1541-5015.1521

Paulsen, M. B., & Wells, C. T. (1998). Domain differences in the epistemological beliefs of college students. *Research in Higher Education, 39*(4), 365–384.

Pérez, A., Potocki, A., Stadtler, M., Macedo-Rouet, M., Paul, J., Salmerón, L., & Rouet, J. F. (2018). Fostering teenagers' assessment of information reliability: Effects of a classroom intervention focused on critical source dimensions. *Learning and Instruction, 58*, 53–64.

Perkins, M. (2002). International law and the search for universal principles in journalism ethics. *Journal of Mass Media Ethics, 17*(3), 193–208.

Pichert, J. W., & Anderson, R. C. (1977). Taking different perspectives on a story. *Journal of Educational Psychology, 69*(4), 309–315.

Rarick, G. L. (1967). The domain of physical education as a discipline. *Quest, 9*(1), 49–52.

Reindl, A., Strobach, T., Becker, C., Scholtz, G., & Schubert, T. (2015). Crab or lobster? Mental principles underlying the categorization of crustaceans by biology experts and non-experts. *Zoologischer Anzeiger: A Journal of Comparative Zoology, 256*, 28–35.

Reisman, A. (2012). Reading like a historian: A document-based history curriculum intervention in urban high schools. *Cognition and Instruction, 30*(1), 86–112.

Roff, S. (2007). Archives, documents, and hidden history: A course to teach undergraduates the thrill of historical discovery real and virtual. *The History Teacher, 40*(4), 551–558.

Rouet, J. F., Favart, M., Britt, M. A., & Perfetti, C. A. (1997). Studying and using multiple documents in history: Effects of discipline expertise. *Cognition and Instruction, 15*(1), 85–106.

Salmerón, L., Macedo-Rouet, M., & Rouet, J. F. (2016). Multiple viewpoints increase students' attention to source features in social question and answer forum messages. *Journal of the Association for Information Science and Technology, 67*(10), 2404–2419.

Schommer-Aikins, M., Duell, O. K., & Barker, S. (2003). Epistemological beliefs across domains using Biglan's classification of academic disciplines. *Research in Higher Education, 44*(3), 347–366.

Schultz, P. W., & Zelezny, L. (1999). Values as predictors of environmental attitudes: Evidence for consistency across 14 countries. *Journal of Environmental Psychology, 19*(3), 255–265.

Schunn, C. D., & Anderson, J. R. (1999). The generality/specificity of expertise in scientific reasoning. *Cognitive Science, 23*(3), 337–370.

Sen, A. K. (1999). Democracy as a universal value. *Journal of Democracy, 10*(3), 3–17.

Shanahan, C., & Shanahan, T. (2014). The implications of disciplinary literacy. *Journal of Adolescent and Adult Literacy, 57*(8), 628–631.

Shanahan, T., & Shanahan, C. (2008). Teaching disciplinary literacy to adolescents: Rethinking content-area literacy. *Harvard Educational Review, 78*(1), 40–59.

Simon, H. A. (1973). The structure of ill structured problems. *Artificial Intelligence, 4*(3-4), 181–201.

Spelt, E. J., Biemans, H. J., Tobi, H., Luning, P. A., & Mulder, M. (2009). Teaching and learning in interdisciplinary higher education: A systematic review. *Educational Psychology Review, 21*(4), 365–378.

Springer, M. (2006). *Soundings: A democratic, student-centered education*. Westerville, OH: National Middle School Association.

Stadtler, M., & Bromme, R. (2007). Dealing with multiple documents on the WWW: The role of metacognition in the formation of documents models. *International Journal of Computer-Supported Collaborative Learning, 2*(2/3), 191–210.

Stadtler, M., & Bromme, R. (2014). The content-source integration model: A taxonomic description of how readers comprehend conflicting scientific information. In D. N. Rapp & J. L. G. Braasch (Eds.), *Processing inaccurate information: Theoretical and applied perspectives from cognitive science and the educational sciences* (pp. 379–402). Cambridge, MA: MIT Press.

Stahl, S. A., Hynd, C. R., Britton, B. K., McNish, M. M., & Bosquet, D. (1996). What happens when students read multiple source documents in history? *Reading Research Quarterly, 31*(4), 430–456.

Tally, B., & Goldenberg, L. B. (2005). Fostering historical thinking with digitized primary sources. *Journal of Research on Technology in Education, 38*(1), 1–21.

Taylor, I., Barker, M., & Jones, A. (2003). Promoting mental model building in astronomy education. *International Journal of Science Education, 25*(10), 1205–1225.

Twardy, C. (2004). Argument maps improve critical thinking. *Teaching Philosophy, 27*(2), 95–116.

Valanides, N., & Angeli, C. (2005). Effects of instruction on changes in epistemological beliefs. *Contemporary Educational Psychology, 30*(3), 314–330.

Van den Besselaar, P., & Heimeriks, G. (2001), Disciplinary, multidisciplinary, interdisciplinary: Concepts and indicators. In M. Davis & C. S. Wilson (Eds.), *Proceedings 8th International Conference on Scientometrics and Informetrics* (pp. 705–716). Sydney: ISSI.

VanSledright, B. A. (2002). Fifth graders investigating history in the classroom: Results from a researcher-practitioner design experiment. *Elementary School Journal, 103*(2), 131–160.

Wineburg, S. S. (1991). Historical problem solving: A study of the cognitive processes used in the evaluation of documentary and pictorial evidence. *Journal of Educational Psychology, 83*(1), 73–87.

Wu, Y. T., & Tsai, C. C. (2007). High school students' informal reasoning on a socio-scientific issue: Qualitative and quantitative analyses. *International Journal of Science Education, 29*(9), 1163–1187.

Zhai, J., Jocz, J. A., & Tan, A. L. (2014). "Am I like a scientist?" Primary children's images of doing science in school. *International Journal of Science Education, 36*(4), 553–576.

12

PROCESSES AND PRODUCTS OF ENCOUNTERING BELIEF-RELATED INFORMATION

Matthew T. McCrudden

PENNSYLVANIA STATE UNIVERSITY

ABSTRACT

This chapter focuses on the role of beliefs and attitudes on the processes readers use to engage with information from multiple sources, often presenting multiple perspectives, and the products of those processes. The chapter provides an overview of the possible ways in which beliefs and attitudes influence the processes and products of reading information from multiple perspectives. Indeed, this chapter views students' beliefs and attitudes as types of perspectives in-and-of themselves. The chapter begins with an overview of memory-based and reader-directed processing, and how both can influence the ways in which we process belief-related information. A model is introduced to describe how memory-based and reader-directed processing unfolds when individuals read belief-related information. This model captures the interaction between the perspectives that learners may bring to a text and those that they encounter during reading. Directions for future research are provided.

Key words: beliefs, attitudes, memory-based processing, reader-directed processing

Beliefs and attitudes play influential roles in our everyday lives. A *belief* is an idea that an individual wants to be true that does not require verification (Murphy & Mason, 2006), or is the acceptance of an idea as being true (Moshman, 2015). An *attitude* is "an evaluation of an object of thought", although there are more nuanced definitions in the literature (Bohner & Dickel, 2011, p. 392). While watching an interview, a viewer may believe that an interviewee is credible and form an attitude based on the person's appearance and manner. Following a meal, a person may believe that a particular restaurant serves the best lasagna in town and may form a favorable attitude about the restaurant based on the ambience and service. While reading an online article about a politically contentious issue, readers' beliefs and attitudes may affect their perceptions of the author's ideas and conclusions. These examples illustrate how our beliefs and attitudes can play a role in our daily lives. This chapter discusses the role beliefs and attitudes play in processing and learning from multiple sources of information. A source can be defined as the person or entity to whom information is attributed (Macedo-Rouet, Braasch, Britt, & Rouet, 2013), such as the author of a text or an author referenced within a text. These sources can present a variety of perspectives on a topic and can communicate such perspectives through a variety of formats or representations (e.g., text, visual display).

Clearly, our beliefs and attitudes can affect how we evaluate information. Importantly, two people who read the same information may interpret and evaluate the information differently based on their beliefs and attitudes. As such, in this chapter, I look not only at the types of perspectives that may be represented by a source, but also examine reader beliefs and attitudes as providing them with a perspective or lens that is used to process information. A seminal study by Lord, Ross, and Lepper (1979) illustrates this point. Lord et al. asked undergraduates to report their beliefs about the deterrent efficacy of capital punishment and their attitudes towards capital punishment. Subsequently, they identified undergraduates who supported or opposed capital punishment and asked them to read two fictitious research studies. One study reported evidence that capital punishment deters homicide, whereas the other study provided evidence that capital punishment does not deter homicide. After reading each study, the participants rated its convincingness and how well or poorly the study had been conducted. Participants rated the perspective-consistent study as better conducted and more convincing than the perspective-inconsistent study. For instance, participants who were pro-deterrence (i.e., believed that capital punishment is a deterrent and were in favor of capital punishment) rated the pro-deterrence study as more convincing and better conducted than the anti-deterrence study.

What this study and other studies like it illustrate is that our beliefs and attitudes can serve as perspectives or as a lens through which we interpret and evaluate information (Kunda, 1990; Nickerson, 1998), which at times is defensible (Koslowski, 1996; Moshman, 2011). However, our beliefs and attitudes can also interfere with our ability to interpret information or otherwise prevent us from revising our beliefs and attitudes in the face of reasonable evidence. For instance, a person who believes that vaccination shots are unnecessary or that they have side effects that are not substantiated by sound evidence may ignore or refute evidence that challenges these beliefs (Nyhan, Reifler, Richey, & Freed, 2014). That is, beliefs and attitudes may undermine thinking and reasoning when possible revision of one's knowledge, beliefs, or attitudes may be warranted.

The focus of the current chapter is on the role of beliefs and attitudes in the processes and activities that occur as readers engage with information from multiple sources, in addition to the products of those enacted processes. What follows is a summary and integration of previous research that considers how readers might process information from multiple sources that include belief-related information, how goals might influence these processes, and the products that readers generate during and after their engagement with this information. Thus, this chapter is intended as an overview of the possible ways in which beliefs and attitudes function as perspectives, influencing the processes and products of reading information from multiple sources. The chapter begins with an overview of memory-based and reader-directed processing. Initially, these processes will be described in the context of how readers process belief-neutral information. Later, these processes will be described in the context of how readers process belief-related information or information that presents perspective-consistent or inconsistent information. A model is introduced to describe how memory-based and reader-directed processing unfolds when individuals read belief-related information. This model intends to capture how the processes and products of reading are the result of readers' own perspectives, in the form of attitudes and beliefs, and of the information that learners may encounter during reading. Directions for future research are provided.

MEMORY-BASED PROCESSING

When an individual is reading, ideas previously available in long-term memory are activated, which can influence comprehension. This happens automatically through a process known as *passive activation* (i.e., the autonomous access of information already available in memory). Memory-based views of text processing explain how basic memory processes lead to the activation of information already available in long-term memory (Kendeou & O'Brien, 2014; Kendeou, Smith, & O'Brien, 2013). Of particular relevance to the present chapter, memory-based views can explain how beliefs, attitudes, and knowledge in long-term memory, collectively making up a reader's perspective or lens on texts, can be activated when individuals encode newly encountered information. When newly encoded information enters into the focus of attention (i.e., the working memory system), information in long-term memory that overlaps with it gains activation. Some information shares more overlap than other information; information that shares more overlap becomes activated in working memory and can affect subsequent processing, independently of whether the recently activated ideas promote or impede comprehension.

This has important implications for the processing of belief-related information. When newly encoded information and recently activated ideas (e.g., beliefs) are consistent with each other, comprehension processes unfold in a routinized manner because there is little or no discrepancy between these two sources of information. However, when a discrepancy arises, this can lead to a slow-down in reading and prompt attempts to establish coherence (i.e., relations between ideas stated in the text and the reader's prior experience; Kendeou & O'Brien, 2014), monitor comprehension (Kendeou, Butterfuss, Kim, Van Boekel, 2019), or to validate the information (i.e., use knowledge and beliefs to monitor truth or plausibility; Richter & Maier, 2017; 2018; Richter, Münchow, & Abendroth, Chapter 16).

Evidence of how memory-based processing affects reading can be seen in research on refutation texts. Refutation texts are designed to promote conceptual change by stating misconceptions, refuting them, and providing explanations of the correct ideas (Bohn-Gettler, Chapter 15; Hynd, 2001). This research has shown changes in processing that result from discrepancies between co-activated ideas in working memory (e.g., newly encoded information and activation of long-term memory). For instance, in Kendeou and van den Broek (2007), undergraduates with and without misconceptions about physics read refutation or non-refutation texts. In the first experiment, participants verbalized their thoughts as they read (think-aloud methodology); in the second experiment, participants read the text one sentence at a time as reading time was recorded (reading time methodology). The results showed that when readers without misconceptions read the refutation statements, they were less likely to express conflict between their prior knowledge and the information in the text and they had faster reading times. By contrast, when readers with misconceptions read the refutation statements, they were more likely to express conflict between their prior knowledge and the information in the text and they had slower reading times. Thus, when there is no discrepancy between newly encoded information and recently activated ideas, comprehension unfolds relatively smoothly. Conversely, when such a discrepancy exists, readers use more effortful processes while attempting to address the discrepancy. Similarly, increases in attention allocation can be seen in research in which readers encounter information that challenges their beliefs, for instance by reading texts from conflicting perspectives (e.g., Maier, Richter, & Britt, 2018; Richter, Münchow, & Abendroth, Chapter 16). Attempts to address such discrepancies, when detected, are actively guided by readers. Importantly, such conflict or consistency between readers' long-term memory and information in texts may arise regardless of whether it is readers' knowledge, attitudes, beliefs, or some combination of these that are activated by a particular text. As such, I examine perspective here as a general filter that guides reader interactions with texts in either an automatic or deliberate fashion.

READER-GUIDED PROCESSING

A complement to memory-based views of processing is reader-guided views of processing (McNamara & Magliano, 2009; Rapp & van den Broek, 2005; van den Broek, Rapp, & Kendeou, 2005). Reader-guided processing refers to readers' intentional use of effortful processes in a deliberate attempt to create meaning (Cho, Afflerbach, & Han, 2018; Graesser, Singer, & Trabasso, 1994). Reading is a goal-directed activity, such as when individuals read to answer questions or to solve problems (McCrudden & Schraw, 2007).

According to reader-guided views of processing (e.g., Rouet, Britt, Durik, 2017), readers construct a task model that is based on their interpretations of the reading task, as they begin a reading experience, such as when a student reads to prepare for a class discussion or an assessment (e.g., essay, test). A task model includes the formation of goals for reading, plans for realizing one's goals for reading, and the establishment of criteria for determining the relevance of information in relation to their reading goals, which can be updated as the reading experience unfolds. Reader goals are important because they affect: (1) *why* individuals read, or their goals for reading (Alexander & Jetton, 1996; Jetton & Alexander, 1997; Ramsay & Sperling, 2011); (2) *what* they read, including what documents or sources they select (Bråten, McCrudden, Lund, Brante, & Strømsø, 2018; McCrudden, Stenseth, Bråten, & Strømsø, 2016); and (3) *how* they read, or strategies that could be useful for task completion (Cerdán & Vidal-Abarca, 2008; Gil, Bråten, Vidal-Abarca, & Strømsø, 2010; Linderholm, Kwon, & Wang, 2011; Lorch, Lorch, & Klusewitz, 1993; Magliano, Trabasso, & Graesser, 1999; van den Broek, Lorch, Linderholm, & Gustafson, 2001). For instance, students use different reading strategies when they read for different purposes (e.g., van den Broek et al., 2001). Thus, a task model is a mental representation of the specific goals for reading, ideas about how to realize those goals, and value placed on realizing those goals (Britt, Rouet, & Durik 2017). As such, task instructions can serve as an externally assigned perspective that students use as a lens or filter to determine relevance and guide the course of processing.

Individuals construct a mental model of text, which may include information or visual displays from different sources. A *coherent* mental model is a network of interrelated ideas that reflect the explicit information in text, and the inferences that establish how the explicit information is interconnected across texts and related to background knowledge (Kintsch, 1998; Magliano, McCrudden, Rouet, & Sabatini, 2018; Zwaan & Radvansky, 1998). A reader's mental model can include content information from the texts as well as information about the sources to whom it is attributed (Bråten & Braasch, 2018; Rouet et al., 2017).

Individuals update and evaluate their mental models before, during, and after reading which can be influenced by reader-guided processing (Rapp & McCrudden, 2018). Three main factors can contribute to readers' decisions to invoke reader-guided processing when reading text from a variety of sources or perspectives. The first factor is *content relevance*, which refers to the perceived instrumental value of content in relation to a goal for reading. Information that more effectively helps readers realize their goals is *more relevant*, whereas information that less effectively helps readers realize their goals is comparatively *less relevant*. When readers make determinations of relevance, they apply standards of relevance, which are the criteria readers use to determine the relevance of text information in relation to their goals (Lehman & Schraw, 2002; McCrudden, Magliano, & Schraw, 2011; McCrudden & Schraw, 2007). Readers can make determinations of relevance when they select documents to read/view and when they process the content and source information in a document.

The second factor is s*ource credibility*, which refers to a reader's perceptions of an author's expertise and trustworthiness (Pornpitakpan, 2004). *Author expertise* refers to the reader's perception of the author's ability to make correct assertions. *Author trustworthiness* refers to the reader's perception that the author believes the information that s/he communicates is true. In the context of learning from multiple perspectives, source credibility can affect the extent to which the reader uses the information. For instance, perceptions of source credibility may influence whether readers select, process, or use the information (Anmarkrud, Bråten, & Strømsø, 2014; Bråten et al., 2018). Further, a reader needs to judge the pertinence of author expertise (i.e., ability to accurately decide who is capable of providing a needed piece of knowledge; Bromme & Thomm, 2016).

The third factor is *comprehensibility*, which refers to a reader's ability to understand information in a text or visual display. A reader is more likely to use information that is comprehensible. Difficulty in comprehending text or a visual display will likely decrease the usefulness of the information to the reader (Danielson & Sinatra, 2017).

These three factors can work in concert. A reader is more likely to use text information that has content relevance, is from a credible source, and that is comprehensible. However, the salience of each of these factors may be amplified depending on the context. For instance, a reader may rely more heavily on the source when the information is more difficult to comprehend or the topic is less familiar (Bråten et al., 2018).

INTEGRATING AUTOMATIC AND EFFORTFUL PROCESSING

The Landscape model of text comprehension explains the dynamic and reciprocal interaction between memory-based and reader-directed processing that take place as readers construct a mental model during text comprehension (van den Broek, Risden, Fletcher, & Thurlow, 1996). As a reader progresses through a text, concepts fluctuate in activation; some concepts remain active, others decline in activation, and others are reactivated. If the information active in memory meets the reader's standards of coherence, then there is no need to engage in effortful processing. *Standards of coherence* "consist of a set of implicit or explicit criteria that a reader adopts for a particular reading situation, reflecting his/her desired level of understanding" (van den Broek, Bohn-Gettler, Kendeou, Carlson, & White, 2011, p. 125). However, if it does not meet the reader's standards of coherence, the reader may actively search his/her memory or the text to re-establish coherence (van den Broek et al., 2011). Importantly, the perspectives that readers bring to a given text can influence their standards of coherence. That is, readers' standards of coherence should be influenced by the perspectives that they bring to a text and the perspective(s) they encounter within a text. Moreover such standards may not only apply to how well information is understood but also how information is evaluated, for example.

Dual Processing Theories

Memory-based processing is considered to operate independently of reader beliefs, whereas reader beliefs can influence reader-directed processing. A complementary literature has identified the type of processing that readers may engage when encountering belief-consistent or belief-inconsistent information. Dual process theories identify two qualitatively distinct types of processing (Evans & Stanovich, 2013; Stanovich & Toplak, 2012). Type 1 processing is autonomous and involves the passive activation of heuristics (i.e., mental shortcuts people use to solve problems and make judgements quickly) that can affect how we interpret and use newly encoded information. Heuristics, such as those created by one's beliefs, are the default response unless Type 2 processing is enacted. Type 2 processing is deliberate and requires working memory resources. It is effortful and involves conscious thought, and thus can mitigate the effects of one's beliefs and attitudes, such as when an individual uses an analytic mode of thinking (e.g., Evans, Newstead, Allen, & Pollard, 1994; Stupple, Ball, Evans, & Kamal-Smith, 2011). That is, Type 2 processing can override Type 1 processing; however, Type 2 processing is still susceptible to biasing effects from belief and attitudes (McCrudden & Barnes, 2016). Memory-based and Type 1 processing both involve automatic processing, whereas reader-guided and Type 2 processing both involve effortful processing. However, the constructs are not interchangeable. For instance, Type 1 processing is not equivalent to memory-based processing although both involve automatic processing via activation. Type 1 processing deals with reasoning heuristics, whereas memory-based processing generally deals with semantic activation. One factor that can affect that nature of reader-guided and Type 2 processing is reader goals.

Accuracy and Directional Goals

Readers' goals can play an important role in why individuals read, what they read, and how they read (McCrudden, Magliano, & Schraw, 2010). Readers can adopt two general categories of goals for reading: accuracy and directional goals. Researchers generally assume that readers have the goal of understanding an author's intended meaning; that is, to accurately interpret the text and use the information to realize some goal or purpose. In many ways, the assumption that readers hold *accuracy goals* (i.e., goals focused on arriving at an accurate interpretation or conclusion) is a useful assumption. However, in the context of reading belief-related information, readers might also espouse a different kind of goal: a *directional goal* (i.e., goals focused on arriving at a desired interpretation or conclusion). As such, when readers more strongly espouse directional goals, their attitudes and beliefs may have a more biasing influence on processing.

When individuals espouse a directional goal, they may show a tendency to interpret information in a way that preserves or maintains their beliefs (e.g., confirmation bias). For instance, they may evaluate information differently based on whether it is compatible with their beliefs (Bohn-Gettler & McCrudden, 2018) and apply stricter standards of evaluation to belief-inconsistent information (McCrudden & Barnes, 2016). Klaczynski (2000) used a dual processing framework to propose two dispositions that influence how people process belief-related information: people who are belief-driven and people who are knowledge-driven. The foci of individuals who display these tendencies resemble directional goals (belief-driven) and accuracy goals (i.e., knowledge-driven).

People who espouse belief-driven goals process information in a way that enables them to assimilate ideas, which preserves or maintains their views; thus, they tend to display directional goals. They may use Type 1 processing for belief-consistent information; they may not seriously evaluate information that is compatible with their preexisting beliefs, and thus may overlook flaws or weaknesses. Similarly, when encountering belief-inconsistent information they may use Type 1 processing such that they may not seriously consider alternative ideas, immediately dismissing them because they are incongruent with their beliefs. Or, they may use Type 2 processing to critique belief-inconsistent information, but not apply the same standards to belief-consistent information. Thus, they maintain their beliefs by using heuristics to process belief-relevant information (Type 1 processing), or by applying comparatively more critical standards of evaluation to belief-inconsistent information (Type 2 processing). As such, these readers may be expected to be heavily biased by their perspectives.

Conversely, people who espouse a knowledge-driven goal use analytic thought in such a way that the goal to acquire knowledge overrides the goal to preserve their beliefs in their current form; thus, they tend to display accuracy goals. Individuals who espouse knowledge-driven goals can hold topic beliefs, but they are able to reason in a relatively unbiased way. When people encounter belief-related information, if accuracy goals exceed directional goals, they engage in Type 2 processing independently of whether the information is belief-consistent. They subject belief-consistent and belief-inconsistent information to similar levels of scrutiny. As a result, they may preserve their theories, or they may revise their theories to account for new ideas. Thus, in contrast to directional goals, accuracy goals are more likely to result in modifications to one's beliefs (although this may not change the overall direction of the beliefs; McCrudden & Sparks, 2014).

Research on argument evaluation provides evidence for how accuracy goals and directional goals can affect how individuals process belief-related arguments. For instance, a mixed methods study by McCrudden and Barnes (2016) illustrates how espoused goals can affect evaluation of belief-related arguments. In the quantitative strand, high-school students rated the strength of stronger and weaker arguments for and against climate change. A pre-test measure of beliefs was used to determine whether the arguments were consistent or inconsistent with their beliefs. The results indicated that participants rated belief-consistent arguments more favorably than belief-inconsistent arguments; however, they also rated strong arguments more favorably than weak arguments. This latter finding indicated that participants did not evaluate the arguments exclusively on whether they were belief-consistent. In the follow-up qualitative strand, interviews were conducted with two groups of participants. Both groups were similar in that they rated strong arguments more favorably than weak arguments, which indicated that they had used Type 2 processing to evaluate the arguments; however, they differed in how they rated belief-consistent and belief-inconsistent arguments. Some students appeared to espouse accuracy goals; they applied the same evaluation criteria to arguments independently of whether they were belief-consistent. However, students in the other group applied different evaluation criteria to equally compelling arguments, rating the belief-consistent arguments more favorably. Thus, directional goals can affect how individuals interpret and evaluate information, demonstrating that readers may hold accuracy goals, directional goals, or potentially both when they process belief-related information. Moreover, as illustrated in the above example, many reading situations may generally be viewed as an intersection between readers' own perspectives and the perspectives forwarded by sources and texts.

PROCESSES AND PRODUCTS IN READING BELIEF-RELATED INFORMATION

In this section I integrate memory-based and reader-directed views of processing and dual processing theories as they relate to the processes and products of reading belief-related information. Memory-based processing (e.g., automatic activation) involves the passive activation of information already in memory; that is, it operates independently of readers' beliefs. However, goals can affect reader-directed processing (i.e., intentional strategy use). The relations between memory-based and reader-directed processing, and the products that result from these processes, can be depicted in a visual display (see Figure 12.1), which provides testable hypotheses, some of which are compatible with empirical evidence from research in cognitive psychology, educational psychology, social psychology, and discourse processes. As such, the model in Figure 12.1 reflects the types of processing and products that may result when readers' perspectives (i.e., belief or attitudes on certain topics) encounter perspective-consistent or -inconsistent information in text(s).

When belief-related information is encoded and enters into the focus of attention, information in long-term memory that overlaps with it gains activation. Information that has greater overlap becomes activated in working memory, independently of whether the recently activated ideas are belief-consistent. Once the newly encoded information and recently activated ideas are both in the focus of attention (co-activated), the extent to which automatic, memory-based processes fulfill a reader's

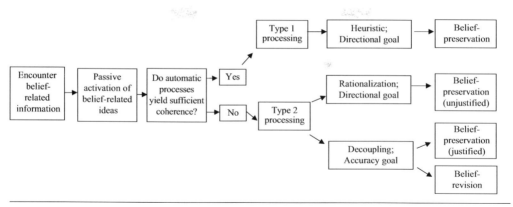

Figure 12.1 Processing and Products of Encountering Belief-Related Information.

desired level of understanding (i.e., coherence) will influence whether Type 1 or Type 2 processing is utilized.

If memory-based processes generally yield sufficient coherence, readers will rely predominantly on Type 1 processing and default to a directional goal. If newly encoded and recently activated information are compatible, readers will see no need to engage in effortful, strategic processing of the information, particularly if they detect little or no discrepancy between the newly encoded information and the recently activated ideas. If the newly encoded information and recently activated information are *not* compatible, readers may detect a discrepancy; however, they will summarily dismiss this information because it is incompatible with their existing beliefs. In either case, these readers might incorporate the newly encoded information into their existing knowledge structures, but their beliefs remain intact and unchanged in any meaningful way. The outcome is belief-preservation.

Conversely, if automatic processes do *not* yield sufficient coherence, readers will rely predominantly on Type 2 processing. There are two qualitatively different forms of Type 2 processing. One form is *rationalization* (Pennycook, Fugelsang, & Koeler, 2015), in which readers seek to reaffirm their beliefs and predominantly espouse a directional goal. They can articulate an explanation for why the newly encoded information should be supported (or opposed); however, this explanation does not involve serious consideration of critiques of their viewpoint. So, while an explanation is provided, it is unjustified because it involves case-building (i.e., justification of a pre-drawn conclusion; Nickerson, 1998) or myside bias (i.e., when individuals evaluate and generate ideas that are biased towards their existing beliefs and attitudes; Stanovich, West, & Toplak, 2013). The outcome is belief-preservation.

Importantly, when readers rationalize, they can process belief-related information in a number of ways (Bohn-Gettler & McCrudden, 2018). For instance, a reader might: (a) only apply a high standard of coherence to belief-consistent information with the aim of bolstering or strengthening his/her views (confirmation bias); (b) only apply a high standard of coherence to belief-inconsistent information with the aim of refuting and disconfirming the information (disconfirmation bias); or (c) aim to both strengthen existing views and refute alternative views. All of these instances describe how readers' perspectives may shape the course of processing.

A second form of Type 2 processing is *decoupling* (Pennycook et al, 2015), in which readers separate their beliefs from the reasoning process and predominantly espouse an accuracy goal. They can articulate an explanation for the why the newly encoded information should be supported (or refuted); this explanation involves serious consideration of the information independently of their viewpoint. The outcome can be belief-preservation or belief-revision. *Belief-preservation* occurs when the individual generates an explanation for why the newly encoded information should be supported (or refuted). This differs from belief-preservation that results from rationalization because the decoupling involves serious consideration of alternative viewpoints and criticisms of one's beliefs, whereas rationalization does not. *Belief-revision* occurs when the individual develops a more sophisticated understanding of the ideas related to one's beliefs. This can involve the acceptance of the information, although it may not necessarily result in an overall directional change in one's beliefs (i.e., gradations of belief acceptance; McCrudden & Sparks, 2014). When readers effectively use decoupling, they are able to hold their perspectives in greater abeyance during processing. As a result, their perspectives have a less (or no) biasing effect on both processing and its products.

DIRECTIONS FOR FUTURE RESEARCH

There are several areas that warrant further investigation. First, it is important to understand relations among beliefs, the strength of those beliefs, and knowledge in contributing to the perspectives that readers adopt toward texts. For instance, suppose a student is asked to read several sources that present varied perspectives about the use of drones to write an argument to address the following question: Should governments use drone strikes abroad as an instrument of policy? Beliefs pertain to one's position on a topic (e.g., Should governments use drone strikes abroad as an instrument of policy? Yes or no). This differs from the strength of one's beliefs, which pertain to how strongly or weakly those beliefs are held (which may be measured, for example, by asking participants to rate the strength of their beliefs on a seven-point Likert-type scale). That is, a student may believe that governments should use drone strikes abroad but the student's belief may be held with moderate strength (e.g., moderately agree). On the other hand, knowledge pertains to what a person knows about a topic. Two particularly relevant forms of knowledge are domain knowledge (i.e., general knowledge about the domain) and topic knowledge (i.e., specific knowledge about a topic in a domain; Alexander, Kulikowich, & Schulze, 1994). For instance, general knowledge about instruments of policy or foreign relations differs from topic knowledge about the accuracy of drone strikes and their impact on civilians. Although in this chapter, I have examined attitudes, beliefs, and knowledge as collectively reflected in the reader perspectives, future work should further consider the individual contributions of each of these. In the context of academic freedom, students have the right to believe whatever they want to believe, and schools cannot require students to change their beliefs (Moshman, 2009). However, students can be expected to understand evidence and arguments that form the basis of experts' positions on particular topics. As such, when investigating processes and products of learning from multiple perspectives, the educational focus should be on promoting comprehension and building knowledge, independently of the strength and direction of their beliefs.

Along these lines, a second area for future research involves the use of longitudinal research designs. Taking such an approach can provide insights into the developmental trajectory of beliefs, attitudes, and knowledge. When students have limited knowledge about a topic, longitudinal designs can provide insights into the ways in which people develop their perspectives about topics and what role knowledge can play in this development over time.

A third related area for future work pertains to the role of emotions when learning from multiple representations about belief-related ideas. Affective responses play an important role in our receptivity to information the conflicts with our beliefs, attitudes, and knowledge about ideas that we view as threatening (Trevors, Kendeou, & Butterfuss, 2017). There is a need for more empirical work on the impact of emotions on memory-based and reader-directed processing of information reflecting multiple perspectives (see Bohn-Gettler, 2019, for a framework of how emotions influence the processes involved in reading comprehension and Pekrun & Loderer, Chapter 22).

Lastly, an area that needs further attention is the role of group processes when learning from multiple perspectives. Multiple sources of information often provide readers access to multiple ideas and views about a topic. Interacting with other students or peers affords the opportunity to engage with others when attempting to make meaning from multiple perspectives. What skills are needed to negotiate meaning from documents and from interactions with others some of whom may have different experiences? How does group composition influence interactions among students? These and other important questions need further attention.

CONCLUSION

Beliefs and attitudes, as reflected in learners' perspectives, play an influential role in how we appraise information, reflect on an experience, and make decisions. Empirical evidence from research in cognitive psychology, educational psychology, social psychology, and discourse processes highlights the processes and activities that occur as readers engage with texts, in addition to the products of those enacted processes. Work in this area has the potential to inform theoretical accounts of how beliefs, attitudes, and knowledge, together encompassing learners' perspectives, influence what we believe and how we learn from multiple perspectives.

REFERENCES

Alexander, P. A., & Jetton, T. L. (1996). The role of importance and interest in the processing of text. *Educational Psychology Review, 8*(1), 89–122.

Alexander, P. A., Kulikowich, J. M., & Schulze, S. K. (1994). The influence of topic knowledge, domain knowledge, and interest on the comprehension of scientific exposition. *Learning and Individual Differences, 6*, 379–397.

Anmarkrud, Ø., Bråten, I., & Strømsø, H. I. (2014). Multiple-documents literacy: Strategic processing, source awareness, and argumentation when reading multiple conflicting documents. *Learning and Individual Differences, 30*, 64–76. doi:10.1016/j.lindif.2013.01.007

Bohner, G., & Dickel, N. (2011). Attitudes and attitude change. *Annual Review of Psychology, 62*, 391–417.

Bohn-Gettler, K. (2019). Getting a grip: The PET framework for studying how reader emotions influence comprehension. *Discourse Processes, 56*, 386–401. doi:org/10.1080/0163853X.2019.1611174

Bohn-Gettler, K., & McCrudden, M. T. (2018). The effects of task relevance instructions and topic beliefs on reading processes and memory. *Discourse Processes, 55*(4), 410–431. doi:10.1080/0163853X.2017.1292824

Bråten, I., & Braasch, J. L. G. (2018). Strategic processing in accessing, comprehending, and using multiple sources online. In J. L. G. Braasch, I. Bråten, & M. T. McCrudden (Eds.), *Handbook of multiple source use* (pp. 133–150). New York: Routledge.

Bråten, I., McCrudden, M. T., Lund, E. S., Brante, E. W., & Strømsø, H. I. (2018). Task-oriented learning with multiple documents: Effects of topic familiarity, author expertise, and content relevance on document selection, processing, and use. *Reading Research Quarterly, 53*(3), 345–365. doi:10.1002/rrq.197

Britt, M., Rouet, J., & Durik, A. M. (2017). *Literacy beyond text comprehension*. New York: Routledge.

Bromme, R., & Thomm, E. (2016). Knowing who knows: Laypersons' capabilities to judge experts' pertinence for science topics. *Cognitive Science, 40*(1), 241–252.

Cerdán, R., & Vidal-Abarca, E. (2008). The effects of tasks on integrating information from multiple documents. *Journal of Educational Psychology, 100*, 209–222.

Cho, B., Afflerbach, P., & Han, H. (2018). Strategic processing in accessing, comprehending, and using multiple sources online. In J. L. G. Braasch, I. Bråten, & M. T. McCrudden (Eds.), *Handbook of multiple source use* (pp. 133–150). New York: Routledge.

Danielson, R. W., & Sinatra, G. M. (2017). A relational reasoning approach to text-graphic processing. *Educational Psychology Review, 29*(1), 55–72. doi:10.1007/s10648-016-9374-2

Evans, J. S., Newstead, S. E., Allen, J., & Pollard, P. (1994). Debiasing by instruction: The case of belief bias. *European Journal of Cognitive Psychology, 6*, 263–285. doi:10.1080/09541449408520148

Evans, J. S., & Stanovich, K. E. (2013). Dual-process theories of higher cognition: Advancing the debate. *Perspectives on Psychological Science, 8*(3), 223–241. doi:10.1177/1745691612460685

Gil, L., Bråten, I., Vidal-Abarca, E., & Strømsø, H. I. (2010). Summary versus argument tasks when working with multiple documents: Which is better for whom?. *Contemporary Educational Psychology, 35*, 157–173.

Graesser, A. C., Singer, M., & Trabasso, T. (1994). Constructing inferences during narrative text comprehension. *Psychological Review, 101*, 371–395.

Hynd, C. E. (2001). Refutational texts and the change process. *International Journal of Educational Research, 35*, 699–714.

Jetton, T. L., & Alexander, P. A. (1997). Instructional importance: What teachers value and what students learn. *Reading Research Quarterly, 32*, 290–308.

Kendeou, P., Butterfuss, R., Kim, J., & Van Boekel, M. (2019). Knowledge revision through the lenses of the three-pronged approach. *Memory and Cognition, 47*, 33–46.

Kendeou, P., & O'Brien, E. J. (2014). The Knowledge Revision Components (KReC) framework: Processes and mechanisms. In D. N. Rapp & J. L. G. Braasch (Eds.), *Processing Inaccurate Information: Theoretical and Applied Perspectives from Cognitive Science and the Educational Sciences* (pp. 353–377). Cambridge, MA: MIT Press.

Kendeou, P., Smith, E. R., & O'Brien, E. J. (2013). Updating during reading comprehension: Why causality matters. *Journal of Experimental Psychology: Learning, Memory, and Cognition, 39*(3), 854–865.

Kendeou, P., & van den Broek, P. (2007). The effects of prior knowledge and text structure on comprehension processes during reading of scientific texts. *Memory and Cognition, 35*, 1567–1577.

Kintsch, W. (1998). *Comprehension: A paradigm for cognition*. New York: Cambridge University Press.

Klaczynski, P. A. (2000). Motivated scientific reasoning biases, epistemological beliefs, and theory polarization: A two-process approach to adolescent cognition. *Child Development, 71*, 1347–1366.

Koslowski, B. (1996). *Theory and evidence: The development of scientific reasoning*. Cambridge, MA: MIT Press.

Kunda, Z. (1990). The case for motivated reasoning. *Psychological Bulletin, 108*(3), 480–498. doi:10.1037/0033-2909.108.3.480

Lehman, S., & Schraw, G. (2002). Effects of coherence and relevance on shallow and deep text processing. *Journal of Educational Psychology, 94*, 738–750.

Linderholm, T., Kwon, H., & Wang, X. (2011). The effects of reading purpose on advanced readers. In M. T. McCrudden, J. P. Magliano, & G. Schraw (Eds.), *Text relevance and learning from text* (pp. 197–222). Greenwich, CT: Information Age Publishing.

Lorch, R. F., Jr., Lorch, E. P., & Klusewitz, M. A. (1993). College students' conditional knowledge about reading. *Journal of Educational Psychology, 85*(2), 239–252.

Lord, C., Ross, L., & Lepper, M. (1979). Biased assimilation and attitude polarization: The effects of prior theories on subsequently considered evidence. *Journal of Personality and Social Psychology, 37*, 2098–2109.

Macedo-Rouet, M., Braasch, J. L. G., Britt, A. M., & Rouet, J.-F. (2013). Teaching fourth and fifth graders to evaluate information sources during text comprehension. *Cognition and Instruction, 31*(2), 204–226.

Magliano, J., McCrudden, M. T., Rouet, J. F., & Sabatini, J. (2018). The modern reader: Should changes to how we read affect research and theory?. In M. F. Schober, D. N. Rapp, & M. A. Britt (Eds.), *Handbook of discourse processes* (2nd ed., pp. 343–361). Abingdon, UK: Taylor & Francis.

Magliano, J. P., Trabasso, T., & Graesser, A. C. (1999). Strategic processing during comprehension. *Journal of Educational Psychology*, *91*, 615–629.

Maier, J., Richter, T., & Britt, M. A. (2018). Cognitive processes underlying the text-belief consistency effect: An eye-movement study. *Applied Cognitive Psychology*, *32*, 171–185.

McCrudden, M. T., & Barnes, A. (2016). Differences in student reasoning about belief-relevant arguments: A mixed methods study. *Metacognition and Learning*, *11*(3), 275–303. doi:10.1007/s11409-015-9148-0

McCrudden, M. T., Magliano, J., & Schraw, G. (2010). Exploring how relevance instructions affect personal reading intentions, reading goals, and text processing: A mixed methods study. *Contemporary Educational Psychology*, *35*(4), 229–241.

McCrudden, M. T., Magliano, J., & Schraw, G. (Eds.). (2011). *Text relevance and learning from text*. Charlotte, NC: Information Age Publishing.

McCrudden, M. T., & Schraw, G. (2007). Relevance and goal-focusing in text processing. *Educational Psychology Review*, *19*(2), 113–139.

McCrudden, M. T., & Sparks, P. C. (2014). Exploring the effect of task instructions on topic beliefs and topic belief justifications: A mixed methods study. *Contemporary Educational Psychology*, *39*(1), 1–11.

McCrudden, M. T., Stenseth, T., Bråten, I., & Strømsø, H. I. (2016). The effects of topic familiarity, author expertise, and content relevance on Norwegian students' document selection: A mixed methods study. *Journal of Educational Psychology*, *108*(2), 147–162.

McNamara, D. S., & Magliano, J. P. (2009). Towards a comprehensive model of comprehension. In B. Ross (Ed.), *The psychology of learning and motivation* (pp. 297–384). New York: Elsevier.

Moshman, D. (2009). *Liberty and learning*. Portsmouth, NH: Heinemann.

Moshman, D. (2011). *Adolescent rationality and development: Cognition, morality, and identity (3rd ed.)*. New York: Taylor & Francis.

Moshman, D. (2015). *Epistemic cognition and development: The psychology of justification and truth*. New York: Taylor & Francis.

Murphy, P. K., & Mason, L. (2006). Changing knowledge and beliefs. In P. A. Alexander & P. H. Winne (Eds.), *Handbook of educational psychology* (pp. 305–324). Mahwah, NJ: Lawrence Erlbaum.

Nickerson, R. S. (1998). Confirmation bias: A ubiquitous phenomenon in many guises. *Review of General Psychology*, *2*(2), 175–220.

Nyhan, B., Reifler, J., Richey, S., & Freed, G. L. (2014). Effective messages in vaccine promotion: A randomized trial. *Pediatrics*, *133*, e835–842.

Pennycook, G., Fugelsang, J. A., & Koehler, D. J. (2015). What makes us think? A three stage dual-process model of analytic engagement. *Cognitive Psychology*, *80*, 34–72. doi:10.1016/j.cogpsych.2015.05.001

Pornpitakpan, C. (2004). The persuasiveness of source credibility: A critical review of five decades' evidence. *Journal of Applied Social Psychology*, *34*, 243–281.

Ramsay, C. M., & Sperling, R. A. (2011). The relevance of purpose: Why purpose situates relevance instructions. In M. T. McCrudden, J. P. Magliano, & G. Schraw (Eds.), *Text relevance and learning from text* (pp. 243–265). Greenwich, CT: Information Age Publishing.

Rapp, D. N., & McCrudden, M. T. (2018). Relevance before, during, and after discourse experiences. In J. Strassheim & H. Nasu (Eds.), *Relevance and irrelevance: Theories, factors, and challenges* (pp. 141–160). Berlin: De Gruyter.

Rapp, D. N., & van den Broek, P. (2005). Dynamic text comprehension: An integrative view of reading. *Current Directions in Psychological Science*, *14*, 276–279.

Richter, T., & Maier, J. (2017). Comprehension of multiple documents with conflicting information: A two-step model of validation. *Educational Psychologist*, *52*, 148–166.

Richter, T., & Maier, J. (2018). The role of validation in multiple document comprehension. In J. L. G. Braasch, I. Bråten, & M. T. McCrudden (Eds.), *Handbook of multiple source use* (pp. 151–167). New York: Routledge.

Rouet, J. F., Britt, M. A., & Durik, A. M. (2017). RESOLV: Readers' representation of reading contexts and tasks. *Educational Psychologist*, *52*(3), 200–215.

Stanovich, K. E., & Toplak, M. E. (2012). Defining features versus incidental correlates of type 1 and type 2 processing. *Mind and Society*, *11*, 3–13. doi:10.1007/s11299-01-0093-6

Stanovich, K. E., West, R. F., & Toplak, M. E. (2013). Myside bias, rational thinking, and intelligence. *Current Directions in Psychological Science, 22*(4), 259–264. doi:10.1177/0963721413480174

Stupple, E. J. N., Ball, L. J., Evans, J. S., & Kamal-Smith, E. N. (2011). When logic and belief collide: Individual differences in reasoning times support a selective processing model. *Journal of Cognitive Psychology, 23*, 931–941.

Trevors, G. J., Kendeou, P., & Butterfuss, R. (2017). Emotion processes in knowledge revision. *Discourse Processes, 54*, 406–426. doi:10.1080/0163853X.2017.1312201

van den Broek, P., Bohn-Gettler, C., Kendeou, P., Carlson, S., & White, M. J. (2011). When a reader meets a text: The role of standards of coherence in reading comprehension. In M. T. McCrudden, J. Magliano, & G. Schraw (Eds.), *Text relevance and learning from text* (pp. 123–140). Greenwich, CT: Information Age Publishing.

van den Broek, P., Lorch, R. F., Linderholm, T., & Gustafson, M. (2001). The effects of readers' goals on inference generation and memory for texts. *Memory and Cognition, 29*, 1081–1087.

van den Broek, P., Rapp, D. N., & Kendeou, P. (2005). Integrating memory-based and constructionist processes in accounts of reading comprehension. *Discourse Processes, 39*, 299–316.

van den Broek, P., Risden, K., Fletcher, C. R., & Thurlow, R. (1996). A "landscape" view of reading: Fluctuating patterns of activation and the construction of a stable memory representation. In B. K. Britton & A. C. Graesser (Eds.), *Models of understanding text* (pp. 165–187). Mahwah, NJ: Erlbaum.

Zwann, R. A., & Radvansky, G. A. (1998). Situation models in language comprehension and memory. *Psychological Bulletin, 123*, 162–185.

13

THE ROLE OF COGNITIVE CONFLICT IN UNDERSTANDING AND LEARNING FROM MULTIPLE PERSPECTIVES

Jason L. G. Braasch

UNIVERSITY OF MEMPHIS

Lisa Scharrer

RUHR-UNIVERSITÄT BOCHUM

ABSTRACT

This chapter focuses on readers' processing of discrepant information that might be encountered within a single text, between multiple texts, or when content conflicts with the reader's prior knowledge, beliefs, and attitudes. Based on theoretical models of single and multiple text comprehension, we describe the cognitive processes in which readers engage when they experience cognitive conflict, and when they engage in strategies that serve to re-establish cognitive equilibrium. We focus specifically on the role that sourcing strategies play at different stages of processing, including in attributing the origin of cognitive conflict, in explaining why a discrepancy has occurred, in resolving coherence breaks by evaluating each source's credibility, and in mentally representing conflicting perspectives. Based on our conceptual and empirical analysis, we discuss implications for adapting current theoretical models to consider readers' attention to, and evaluation and representation of source perspectives, and we consider how the mechanisms described could be tested empirically.

Key words: cognitive conflict, memory representation, multiple perspectives, source evaluation, text comprehension

INTRODUCTION

In the modern age, we rely heavily on digital resources retrieved from the Internet to understand a situation or issue. Since virtually anyone can publish situation- or issue-related content on the Internet regardless of how knowledgeable and credible they are, readers access an array of resources that may be consistent, complementary, or discrepant with one another (Goldman, 2004). In the current chapter, we focus on readers' interactions with discrepant content, whether that be within a single text, across multiple texts, or content as it is weighed against the individual's current knowledge, beliefs, and attitudes. Based on previous literature, we propose that experiences of cognitive conflict stemming from a perceived discrepancy guide readers towards a sequence of cognitive processes that serve to alleviate this mental discomfort. To do so, readers first attribute an origin to the cognitive conflict. Depending on these attributions, readers may invoke inappropriate or appropriate ways to re-establish cognitive equilibrium. We specifically focus on the importance of one way for achieving mental comfort, that is, in enacting "sourcing strategies." These are defined as attending to, evaluating, representing, and using available and accessible information about the sources of texts (e.g., author, publication venue) (Bråten, Stadtler, & Salmerón, 2018). The prominent role that sourcing can play in returning to mental equilibrium at the different phases of processing motivates our core assumption that conflict acts as a stimulating factor for readers' sourcing activities. Whereas a mounting body of research has focused on how conflict facilitates attention to and representation of source features, far less experimental work has focused on the reasons that people evaluate each source's perspective. We define evaluations of a source's perspective as a consideration of the perceived knowledge, intentions, motives, and biases that each source has. Thus, these kinds of evaluations reflect more critical reflections than just processing the semantic content to understand what a website is saying. Readers typically produce these kinds of evaluations based on inferences about any source features that are available, such as the author's credentials (or lack thereof), the type and date of publication, and the venue in which the text was published, to name but a few.

The remainder of this chapter is divided into four main sections. A first section provides a general overview of cognitive processes specified in many theoretical models that underlie text comprehension. A second section more specifically reviews the cognitive processes in which readers engage to support understanding and learning from multiple sources, especially when they contradict one another. Whereas a third section reviews research on individuals' propensities to evaluate multiple perspectives, it concludes by stressing that research is limited with respect to manipulations of whether a discrepancy was or was not present. Thus, no studies to date directly test the role that cognitive conflict may play in evaluating multiple perspectives during reading; nor have studies considered how these processes support representing and using source perspectives. In a fourth and final section, we summarize the outcome of our conceptual and empirical analysis, discuss implications for adapting current theoretical models to consider how readers evaluate and represent information about source perspectives, and prescribe future work that could inform the viability of these adaptations.

OVERVIEW OF COGNITIVE PROCESSES SPECIFIED IN MODELS OF TEXT COMPREHENSION

Theoretical models of single text comprehension have not specifically addressed the kinds of inferences readers make about source perspectives during reading and how these relate to their mental representation of information for later use. However, more general processes are first reviewed to provide a foundation for understanding how people encode and represent texts, in general. Text comprehension theories suggest that individuals incrementally construct a mental representation of a situation or issue described in a text. They do this by connecting incoming propositions (typically sentences) with information that is part of the current mental representation (Kintsch, 1998). As each independent text proposition is read, they enter working memory and, as such, serve as retrieval cues. Some theoretical models focus on the description and empirical validation of these passive, "bottom up" processes (Kendeou & O'Brien, 2014; McKoon & Ratcliff, 1998; O'Brien & Myers, 1999). In this sense, the more that retrieval cues share feature overlap with activated traces from long-term memory, the more likely the latter will be returned to working memory (O'Brien & Myers, 1999). For example, if someone read a text stating "climate change has nothing to do with human depletion of fossil fuels," the idea that "human consumption of fossil fuels has caused the Earth's temperatures to rise" may become activated from long-term memory due to a substantial degree of overlap between the two. In this sense, information retrieval is considered an unrestricted and "dumb" process (Kintsch, 1998), that is, any information can return to working memory irrespective of its accuracy or relevance to the current context (O'Brien, Cook, & Gueraud, 2010; O'Brien, Rizzella, Albrecht, & Halleran, 1998). With each new input of information, textual propositions passively connecting to other propositions are increasingly likely to become a part of the reader's final mental representation. As a contrast, inappropriate, irrelevant, and redundant propositions are gradually eliminated from the mental representations that readers form (Kintsch, 1998). These processes of integration and elimination result in an associative network of propositions (with contributions from text and knowledge) that constitutes an edited, integrated, and coherent mental representation. For example, if a person consistently reads about connections between fossil fuel use, production of carbon dioxide, and increasing temperatures, these ideas will become strengthened and integrated. To contrast, the idea "fossil fuels are formed from decayed plants and animals" would have little to no connections to the evolving representation. As such, the "decayed plants and animals" idea would, itself, decay and be eliminated from the mental representation.

In addition to passive memory-based retrieval processes, other theoretical models state that readers also engage in more active, strategic, and "top down" processes during text comprehension (Graesser, Singer, & Trabasso, 1994; Long, Seely, & Oppy, 1996; Magliano, Trabasso, & Graesser, 1999). Readers can selectively attend to information based on the particular reading goals they may have adopted (Graesser, 2007). Accordingly, reading goals may guide how actively someone will "search for meaning," that is strategically construct explanations for situations and issues described by texts. Such cognitive activities are thought to facilitate construction of a representation that gains local as well as global coherence. Important for the current work, when individuals experience coherence breaks during reading, they appear to increase cognitive efforts to strategically resolve them by way of inferences and reinterpretations of the information described in texts with contributions from relevant background knowledge (Long & Lea, 2005).

Taken together, these two overarching classes of text comprehension models illustrate that successful comprehension may require that readers rely on both "bottom-up" (i.e., passive, automatic) and "top-down" (i.e., effortful, resource-consuming, strategic) processes. In the following sections, we theorize that whereas passive mechanisms likely underlie experiences of cognitive conflict, attributions of the origins of cognitive conflict, attempts to re-establish coherence, and evaluation of source perspectives reflect more effortful, strategic attempts to "search after meaning."

Cognitive Processes that Support Understanding and Learning from Multiple Sources

The description of the cognitive processes involved in readers' understanding of conflicting information is inspired by the Content-Source Integration (CSI) model of Stadtler and Bromme (2014). Their model presents an ordered sequence of stages to deal with conflicting content, although they specifically focus on contradictions that occur across multiple texts. In their model, readers first detect a conflict that is present between multiple documents; after, they attempt to restore coherence by ignoring it, creating inferences to reconcile the conflict, or attributing it to conflicting sources. A final CSI stage states that if the methods used in the second stage cannot restore coherence, then readers will instead evaluate which proposition is true as a way to resolve conflict by applying at least one of two strategies: First, they may evaluate the validity of the propositions directly by assessing their epistemic strength, which would be based on their own prior knowledge and beliefs (first-hand evaluations). Second, they may determine the propositions' validity indirectly by evaluating the credibility of the respective sources, and thus the extent to which the source's proposition can be trusted (second-hand evaluations). We build on and update this work by providing a more comprehensive characterization of the ways that several processes might unfold during the sequence of these three stages (see Figure 13.1 for a visualization). Most notably, we focus on added theorization and empirical support for a *potential cause* of these processes. First, we explore several different kinds of situations that could stimulate cognitive conflict. These include discrepancies across multiple texts (CSI's primary focus), but also within texts and between text content and the reader's prior knowledge, beliefs, or attitudes (see Braasch & Bråten, 2017). Moreover, additional intermittent processes based on other phenomena explored within recent research are included. In particular, we offer an in-depth characterization of the role that sourcing strategies play at several different stages of processing, including in attributing the origin of cognitive conflict, in explaining why a discrepancy has occurred, in resolving coherence breaks by way of evaluating each source's credibility, and in mentally representing conflicting perspectives.

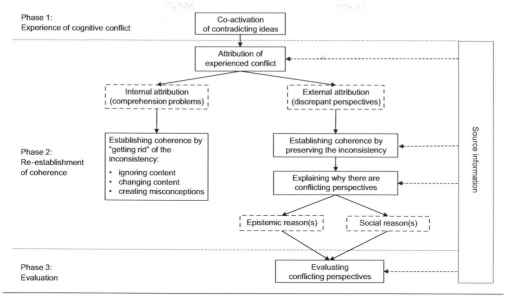

Figure 13.1 Cognitive Processes Unfolding during Readers' Understanding of Conflicting Content.

Experiences of Cognitive Conflict

Experiences of cognitive conflict can occur when discrepancies are present within a single text, between a text and reader factors (knowledge-, belief- or attitude-inconsistent statements), or across two or more texts. When a person specifically encounters one of these kinds of discrepancies during reading, there are several assumptions based on the processes specified above. In models of single text comprehension, the input sentence passively and automatically activates information from long-term memory and, as a result, a matching process ensues between the focal idea and memory traces that receive sufficient activation based on some degree of feature overlap (Kendeou & O'Brien, 2014; Kintsch, 1998; O'Brien & Myers, 1999). If during this process a discrepant proposition is returned, both would be co-activated in working memory (Kendeou & O'Brien, 2014; van Den Broe, & Kendeou, 2008). As such, the assumption is that this co-activation of concepts is the mechanism by which a person would experience cognitive conflict.

Empirical evidence to date has mainly focused on situations where discrepant sentences occur within the same text. They are typically, however, separated by several sentences. Thus, the paradigm allows for an examination of the process by which inactive information becomes activated again, returning from long-term back into working memory. Experiments frequently replicate that sentences introducing a discrepancy cause participants to slow down during reading as compared to sentences that are consistent with previously read information (Albrecht & O'Brien, 1993; Hakala & O'Brien, 1995; Rapp, Gerrig, & Prentice, 2001). Work by Beker, Jolles, Lorch, and van den Broek (2016) extended the inconsistency paradigm to a multiple text reading scenario, demonstrating that content encountered in a first text slows down participants' reading of sentences in a second text more if it is inconsistent with the first. Thus, good readers appear to notice when contradictions arise, resulting in experiences of cognitive conflict.

Conflict Attribution

Detection of an inconsistency may serve as an impetus for a second more active, stage of processing. These changes in moment-by-moment processing may reflect a "search for meaning" in efforts to restore coherence. As depicted in Figure 13.1, readers will attempt to reduce experiences of cognitive conflict by somehow attributing the origin of the perceived discrepancy. They may attempt to identify the reason for their conflict experience either *internally*, that is reflecting problems in their own understanding, or *externally*, that is to an objective conflict between sources with discrepant perspectives on the issue (Kienhues & Bromme, 2011; Otero, 2002; Stadtler, Scharrer, & Bromme, 2013). For example, if someone read a text stating: "climate change has nothing to do with human depletion of fossil fuels," they could either attribute an experience of cognitive conflict internally to their own misunderstanding of the sentence, or externally as an objective conflict between sources with discrepant perspectives concerning the role fossil fuel use might play in global warming.

Internal Attributions of an Experienced Conflict.

Readers may interpret their experience of cognitive conflict as a subjective problem, and conclude that the perceived inconsistency stems from their lack of competence to fully understand the provided information rather than from an actual textual conflict. Readers who attribute the experienced conflict internally believe that they are unable to integrate the provided content correctly or lack the prior topic knowledge required for making the inferences that would reconcile the seemingly inconsistent claims. In the literature on text comprehension and education, various researchers have used related terms to describe this phenomenon including "internal attribution" (Otero, 2002) "self-related explanation" (Stadtler et al., 2013), or "ability explanation" (Kienhues & Bromme, 2011).

Readers may be particularly inclined to attribute an experienced conflict internally if they believe the knowledge about the given subject matter to be certain and free of controversy, making it unlikely that there are actually conflicting perspectives on the issue (Stadtler & Bromme, 2014). Apart from epistemic beliefs, readers' tendency to ascribe a conflict to internal causes may be affected by information they have obtained about the text source(s). Internal attribution may be particularly likely if readers perceive a large discrepancy in topic knowledge between themselves and the text author(s), for example when a layperson reads a scientific text authored by an expert in the field. Readers may then be particularly inclined to perceive their own competence as insufficient to fully comprehend the subject matter (Stadtler et al., 2013). This was also shown in findings from Otero and Campanario (1990) who asked a group of secondary school students to read a scientific text containing several conflicting statements. The participants were instructed to highlight those sentences they perceived to be conflicting. Afterwards, they were interviewed about their reasons for highlighting or not highlighting any objective textual conflicts. This showed that students who reported that they had experienced some cognitive conflict but nonetheless had refrained from highlighting the corresponding sentences had frequently done so because they perceived that they did not have enough knowledge about the topic to confidently judge whether a conflict actually existed.

Attributing Cognitive Conflict Experiences to Discrepant Perspectives

Readers may also attribute their experience of cognitive conflict to *external* reasons, specifically to objectively existing textual conflict that results from multiple, contradictory perspectives disagreeing on the subject matter. Such contradictory perspectives can arise from the fact that knowledge about the topic at hand is still developing, inconsistent, or uncertain (Kienhues & Bromme, 2011), or from variations in the sources' ability or communicative intent (Stadtler et al., 2013). Readers' attribution of conflict to different perspectives has been referred to as "external attribution" (Otero, 2002), or as "epistemic and source explanations" (Kienhues & Bromme, 2011; Stadtler et al., 2013).

Unlike internal attributions, attributions of discrepant perspectives may be particularly likely if the reader considers themselves to have a high level of topic knowledge and ability, preventing them from attributing experienced inconsistencies to their own comprehension difficulties. In addition, readers may be more likely to attribute experienced conflict to different perspectives if they have low coherence expectations for the encountered text materials (see Stadtler & Bromme, 2014). For example, Stadtler et al. (2013) had a group of secondary school students read partly conflicting information about a medical topic, after they had been explicitly warned that the text materials might contain conflicting propositions. Not surprisingly, readers were more inclined to attribute encountered conflicts externally rather than to any personal comprehension difficulties when they were warned that conflict might occur. Apart from such explicit warnings, low coherence expectations may also emerge if the reader endorses epistemic beliefs on the topic reflecting knowledge about the topic being uncertain and inconsistent (cf. Kienhues & Bromme, 2011), or if the reader believes that sources vary in their ability and motivation to provide accurate information.

Inappropriate Strategies Readers Use to Re-establish Coherence

As visualized in Figure 13.1, different attributions of the origins of cognitive conflict experienced may guide further information processing as well. That is, they may constrain the kinds of strategies that a reader will engage to restore the coherence of their mental representation. As the following will detail, all strategies are not equally successful in preserving the discrepancies that readers encounter by including these inconsistencies in their mental representation.

When readers attribute cognitive conflict experiences internally, they may be more likely to enact strategies that afford opportunities to "get rid" of the inconsistency (ignoring or changing content; creating inaccurate semantic links that nullify the conflict). When readers attribute experiences of cognitive conflict externally to different perspectives, they may be more likely to enact strategies that afford opportunities for preserving inconsistency in their mental representation through sourcing. Theoretical assumptions in the CSI model (Stadtler & Bromme, 2014) and a long history of empirical research demonstrate that individuals do, in fact, employ a host of different strategies for restoring coherence once they have experienced cognitive conflict (Blanc, Kendeou, van den Broek, & Brouillet, 2008; Braasch & Bråten, 2017; Chinn & Brewer, 1998; Hakala & O'Brien, 1995; Otero & Kintsch, 1992).

Ignoring Semantic Content

One strategy reflects that readers restore coherence by ignoring the content of one of the discrepant texts they read altogether. For example, in Chinn and Brewer (1998), participants read a first text about an initial scientific theory; a second text presented data that were anomalous with the theory described in text 1. Participants responded in many different ways reflecting continued endorsement of the initial theory and disbelief in the anomalous data. In a related literature, researchers consistently replicate a "continued influence" effect such that people receiving a correction to misinformation about a news event remain influenced by the initial account when subsequently reasoning about the event (Seifert, 2014). Thus, one coherence-restoring strategy people adopt is to simply ignore content information from one discrepant text to preserve their mental representation of the other.

Changing Semantic Content

A second strategy reflects that readers may attempt to restore a break in coherence by distorting or "hedging" one or more aspects of the contradictory ideas. For example, in Otero and Kintsch (1992), participants read a single text about the science topic of superconductivity which presented two contradictory sentences. When recalling the texts, readers generated unwarranted inferences (e.g., people obtained superconductivity in the past through cooling, but now there is another method – using extremely high temperatures). In recent work by Rouet and colleagues (2016), participants read brief news stories that did or did not contain contradictions and were instructed to summarize what they read. The results suggest that people attempted to restore coherence through various forms of hedging, such as tagging one of the discrepant propositions as uncertain (e.g., maybe, possibly) or using terms of scope (e.g., many, some). Thus, empirical examples demonstrate another strategy people adopt to restore coherence: downplaying a discrepancy in terms of time and/or degree.

Creating Misconceptions about Semantic Content

Third, readers may attempt to restore a coherence break by creating and representing unwarranted, incorrect relationships between discrepant propositions presented across texts. For example, in Blanc et al. (2008), participants read a series of news reports, providing think-aloud comments after every other sentence. An initial cause of the focal event was presented early in the story; a second cause was presented later. Towards the end, a sentence was manipulated to support the first or second cause or to be neutral to the causes. Think-aloud comments confirmed that readers created novel causal connections between the two discrepant sentences in an attempt to establish coherence. Thus, in this case, the strategy appears to result in mentally representing misconceptions about the news events.

Using Sourcing Strategies to Re-establish Coherence

The previous three strategies allowed readers to create somewhat coherent models of a discrepancy. However, they resulted in either incomplete (strategy 1) or inaccurate accounts (strategies 2 and 3) of the situation or issue. Instead, people sought to negate the discrepancy's existence. Strategies that require the consideration of any available source feature information can, however, allow for processing that preserves the inconsistency in terms of conflicting perspectives. Thus, when readers attribute experiences of cognitive conflict externally to different perspectives, they may enact a fourth strategy: attempting to restore a break in coherence by creating links between information sources and their respective discrepant propositions, and links between the sources themselves (Stadtler & Bromme, 2014).

Two theoretical models focus on the ways that people process and represent multiple sources from texts and are, thus, relevant for review in the current chapter. The Documents Model Framework (DMF) describes how good readers mentally represent multiple texts in terms of the information sources conveyed within them (Britt, Perfetti, Sandak, & Rouet, 1999; Perfetti, Rouet, & Britt, 1999). In the DMF, people mentally represent information from multiple texts in terms of an integrated mental model and an intertext model. The integrated mental model includes connections made across propositions upon which multiple texts agree, complement, or contradict one another (Britt & Rouet, 2012). An intertext model, however, involves a representation of the source features of texts (e.g., authors, publication venues) by way of relationships between sources and their respective content information (e.g., "Author A says ... "; "Author B says ... ") and relationships between the sources themselves ("Author A agrees with Author B" and "Author A contradicts Author B").

Whereas the DMF primarily describes the end result of a good reader building a coherent mental representation of a situation or issue described in texts, the Discrepancy-Induced Source Comprehension (D-ISC) theoretical model characterizes how sourcing processes unfold *during reading* as individuals actively attempt to remediate experiences of cognitive conflict that stem from detected discrepancies (Braasch & Bråten, 2017; Braasch, Rouet, Vibert, & Britt, 2012; Rouet et al., 2016). In particular, D-ISC states that, upon detecting a discrepancy, readers will strategically shift their attentional resources toward constructing a mental representation of the described situation or issue that also includes source features (e.g., the authors of the messages, the venues publishing that article) as organizational components in the manner of an intertext model (Britt & Rouet, 2012). Hence, unlike the three problematic strategies that readers employ to "get rid" of a discrepancy, and thus fail to include it in their mental representation, sourcing strategies are, in fact, the only method that authentically preserves a conflict in readers' representation as a function of differences between two or more sources. This is especially an important approach when there is no clear indication of who is right or wrong, as can be the case in many authentic reading contexts.

When an individual reads a sentence that is discrepant with the same text, a different text, or their prior knowledge, beliefs, and attitudes, it is assumed that the proposition would return to working memory based on passive, automatic, and memory-based processes outlined previously (Kintsch, 1998; Myers & O'Brien, 1998). Co-activation of the discrepancy in working memory should result in readers' experiences of cognitive conflict (Kendeou & O'Brien, 2014). The D-ISC assumes that this break in coherence promotes adoption of sourcing strategies, including increased attention to and evaluation of any available source information present during reading. Studies incorporating online measures of text processing (e.g., eye movements, verbal protocols) have verified this assumption. For example, in Braasch et al. (2012), readers spent more time looking at segments of texts featuring source when reading news stories presenting discrepant, relative to consistent, propositions. In Kammerer, Kalbfell, and Gerjets (2016), readers of discrepancies produced more evaluative judgments when thinking aloud about the "about us" information on conflicting websites relative to students reading consistent websites.

Moreover, the D-ISC model predicts an increased presence of source-content links in readers' mental representations of controversial content measured *after reading has concluded*. For example, in Braasch et al. (2012) and Rouet et al. (2016), when participants were given a cued recall task after reading, they displayed better identification of the sources making assertions within discrepant relative to consistent news stories. In another example by Kammerer and Gerjets (2012), participants read four discrepant or consistent websites to write an essay from memory making a recommendation on a focal health topic. People referred to more sources (the types or names of web pages) in their recommendations if the previously read websites contradicted one another, rather than if they had not. Thus, there is some support that cognitive conflict stimulates readers to strive towards re-establishing coherence by making connections between sources and their respective propositions.

One study examined whether experiences of cognitive conflict might also stimulate readers to re-establish coherence by forming source–source links, i.e. between the information sources themselves. Saux, Le Bigot, Burin, and Rouet (2017) provided news stories, again with sources making discrepant or consistent proposition, and measured participants' memory for one source given the other as a retrieval cue. Conflicts in news stories appeared to prompt readers to pay closer attention to relationships between sources, which resulted in their greater presence in students' mental representations of what was read. Taken together, these patterns suggest that sourcing strategies may provide a way for individuals to preserve a conflict by creating an intertext model of the overarching situation or issue described across text(s) (Britt & Rouet, 2012).

Depending on their goal, readers may not be satisfied with the level of coherence achieved by attending to and remembering different source features. Rather than simply representing that their cognitive conflict is attributable to discrepant sources, readers who aim to acquire a full understanding of the texts' content may also seek to find an explanation for *why* these discrepancies have occurred. In a series of studies, Thomm and colleagues have investigated how readers explain the occurrence of conflict between multiple scientific sources (Thomm, Barzilai, & Bromme, 2017; Thomm & Bromme, 2016). Their findings show that readers consider two types of explanations that give rise to conflicting perspectives: social reasons, i.e. differences in the sources' ability or motivation, and epistemic reasons, i.e. the complexity of knowledge and the process of scientific knowledge production. Consequently, readers appear to consider information about the sources in their search for conflict explanations, with their endorsement of social reasons varying depending on the sources' reported level of ability and motivation (Thomm & Bromme, 2016). As such, sourcing strategies not only support the restoration of coherence by affording opportunities to create an intertext model, but also by supporting inferences that can help explain why there are conflicting perspectives (Figure 13.1). The latter aspect does not appear to be of primary concern in the DMF.

EVALUATING MULTIPLE PERSPECTIVES

Depending on their reading goal, readers may not be satisfied with forming a coherent mental representation of conflicting perspectives. Instead, they may seek to form a personal opinion about the topic at hand, which implies that they resolve any discrepancy by determining which perspective is more believable or plausible (Lombardi, Nussbaum, & Sinatra, 2016; Stadtler & Bromme, 2014). As proposed in the CSI model, there are principally two ways by which readers can evaluate multiple perspectives. First, readers may attempt to evaluate the provided content directly in terms of its epistemic strength. They may accomplish such first-hand evaluations by checking the proposed arguments for their logical consistency or for coherence with their own prior knowledge, beliefs, and attitudes about the topic (Bromme & Goldman, 2014; Bromme, Kienhues, & Porsch, 2010). Research has shown that readers frequently engage in first-hand evaluations (Brem, Russell & Weems, 2001; Kiili, Laurinen, & Marttunen, 2008; van Strien, Brand-Gruwel, & Boshuizen, 2014). A number of descriptive studies have asked participants which evaluation strategies they would use in a reading situation. Readers frequently report that they would assess the quality of the content directly (Brem, Russell, & Weems, 2001; Rowley, Johnson, & Sbaffi, 2015). For example, Brem, Russell, and Weems (2001) provided students in grades 9 to 12 with websites on various scientific topics and interviewed them about the evaluation criteria they would apply to evaluate the arguments they contained. Overall, readers deemed content-related evaluation criteria to be most important, among them evaluating website content for coherence with prior knowledge and evaluating its precision and the level of detail.

In line with these studies using self-report to capture students' evaluation criteria, further descriptive studies have characterized readers' in situ evaluation behavior while completing an authentic reading task (Kiili et al., 2008; van Strien et al., 2014). As in the self-report studies, these studies also found that readers often base their evaluations at least in part on features of the text content. van Strien et al. (2014) asked 11th grade students to read multiple conflicting documents about a scientific issue. After reading, students wrote an essay about the topic. Analyses of the essays showed that the position that students adopted about the issue was biased toward their prior attitude, indicating that they based their evaluation of content credibility on consistency with their prior opinion.

Apart from evaluating the epistemic strength of the obtained content directly, readers may also judge information validity indirectly by determining whether the content is proposed by a credible source. Such "second-hand evaluations" help readers to ascertain whether the content proposed by the source can be trusted to be valid (Bromme & Goldman, 2014; Bromme et al., 2010; Stadtler & Bromme, 2014). That is, individuals could think about how much they trust the text content by referring to metadata information embedded within or provided outside the body of text, including its origin, context, and purpose for being written, to name but a few features (Barzilai & Strømsø, 2018). Theoretical models and frameworks of source evaluation have suggested two central conditions that need to be met for a source to be deemed credible. First, the reader needs to perceive that the source is sufficiently able to make competent and fully informed propositions about the topic at hand. Second, the reader needs to perceive that the source has her or his interests at heart, and thus is motivated to pass on only correct information (Bromme & Goldman, 2014; Bromme, Stadtler, Scharrer, & Thomm, 2015). Whereas the former reflects the source's *knowledge*, the latter point reflects its *biases* and *intentions*.

Studies have confirmed that readers can, at times, use information about a source's knowledge or competence to judge the validity of assertions that are being made (Bromme et al., 2015; Hendriks, Kienhues, & Bromme, 2015; Stadtler, Scharrer, Macedo-Rouet, Rouet, & Bromme, 2016). For example, Bromme et al. (2015, Study 1) asked undergraduate students to read conflicting pairs of documents about a health topic, while manipulating level of source expertise. After reading, participants rated perceived source credibility and indicated their acceptance of the proposed claims. Results showed that a source was perceived to be more credible when presented as an expert rather than as a layperson. In addition, claim acceptance was higher when it was reported by a source with a high level of expertise.

Further studies have also demonstrated that readers can, at times, use information about a source's biases or intentions to support inferences about credibility (Bromme et al., 2015; Kammerer et al., 2016; Scharrer, Stadtler, & Bromme, 2019). For example, Kammerer et al. (2016) asked undergraduate students to judge the trustworthiness of two sources providing information about a nutritional topic. Participants rated the source reflecting a possible vested commercial interest to be less trustworthy than the source with no commercial interests. In a recent study by Scharrer et al. (n.d.), a group of non-experts read information about a socio-scientific issue, which presented a scientific claim with ethical implications (the claim referred to the effectiveness of a drug used in lethal injections and thus had implications for the ethical debate about capital punishment). Readers agreed more with the claim if its source was unlikely to be influenced by an ethical bias, although such a bias was only considered as detrimental for the source's persuasiveness if their ethical position was incongruent with the reader's own stance.

The extant research does indicate that indirect evaluation through the assessment of source credibility is particularly important when readers possess only limited prior topic knowledge (Bromme & Goldman, 2014; Bromme et al., 2010). Due to a division of cognitive labor in modern societies (Bromme et al., 2010; Keil, Stein, Webb, Billings, & Rozenblit, 2008), most people are non-experts regarding the majority of domains and topics. Because adequate content evaluation often requires extensive knowledge and experience within the content domain that can usually only be obtained through specialized training, direct evaluations of assertions are often beyond a non-expert's epistemic capabilities. Rather than relying on their own judgment of the content, low knowledge readers are usually better advised to base their judgment on second-hand evaluations (Bromme et al., 2010).

To summarize, first- and second-hand evaluations, alone or in combination, can lead to accurate evaluations of content validity, potentially providing readers some ways to adequately resolve a discrepancy between multiple perspectives. Depending on reading goals, an individual's mental comfort may be conditional on resolving any encountered discrepancies. It is conceivable that conflict stimulates readers' evaluative strategies, including their consideration of source information. However, there is a paucity of studies that actually manipulate whether there was or was not a discrepancy (that is, discrepancy is typically held constant). Thus, it appears to be the case that research is limited with respect to causal connections between discrepancy (assuming cognitive conflict as a result) and considerations of sources' knowledge, biases, or intentions.

CONCLUSIONS, IMPLICATIONS, AND FUTURE DIRECTIONS

In the modern age, we often encounter discrepant information, whether that be within a single text, across multiple texts, or when weighed against our current knowledge, beliefs, and attitudes. These types of discrepancies often result in experiences of cognitive conflict, that is, mental discomfort that the reader wants to alleviate. One way to do so is to make attributions about the origins of the perceived discrepancy, these can be due to internal or external factors. Although the relationships are untested as of yet, attributions may also guide the kinds of strategies readers engage as they attempt to restore coherence. These include inappropriate ways to "resolve" a discrepancy by nullifying its existence. Others may use sources to organize their representation of text(s), apply a more appropriate coherence-restoration strategy. Importantly, this strategy allows a reader to accurately preserve the controversy in terms of the respective sources making conflicting claims.

This chapter also presented theoretical models derived by cognitive and educational psychologists to describe the mechanisms that allow readers to mentally represent controversies vis-à-vis sources (Braasch & Bråten, 2017; Britt & Rouet, 2012; Stadtler & Bromme, 2014). Empirical support suggests that discrepancies within and across texts, and between a text and prior beliefs, do in fact produce experiences of cognitive conflict, which result in greater source *attention* and *memory* (Braasch et al., 2012; Bråten, Salmerón, & Strømsø, 2016; Kammerer et al., 2016). However, theorization and research are limited with respect to characterizing whether experiences of cognitive conflict stimulate *evaluations of source perspectives* including making inferences about their *knowledge, intentions*, and *biases*.

Prominent theoretical models of comprehension could be adapted to better characterize the ways that cognitive conflict may stimulate readers to evaluate each source's perspective, including their knowledge, intentions, and biases. The Documents Model Framework (DMF) describes an intertext model, in which a person represents source features of texts (e.g., authors, publication venues) in terms of relationships between sources and their respective content assertions, and relationships between the sources themselves (Britt & Rouet, 2012). Those relationships, referred to as "intertext predicates," could include inferences about each source's competency, and any comparisons between them to evaluate which source seems to be more knowledgeable. Other intertext predicates could reflect inferences about whether a source is or is not well-intentioned in making their claims. Similarly, intertext predicates could reflect inferences about each source's potential biases, and any comparisons between them to evaluate which seems to be the least biased. Thus, the DMF could be easily adapted to specify a broader range of relationships that readers might ultimately represent. Whereas the DMF primarily focuses on the outcomes of reading, the D-ISC model characterizes the ways that sourcing processes unfold during reading. As such, adaptations of the model could characterize how evaluations of sources' perspectives including knowledge, intentions, and biases unfold during reading, over and above the more often researched attention to sources. To review D-ISC's main mechanisms, it is assumed that co-activation of discrepant claims in working memory promote cognitive conflict. In hopes of alleviating this mental discomfort, individuals may more actively evaluate each source's perspective as a means by which a more coherent understanding of the situation or issue can be achieved.

Clearly, in adapting theoretical models to accommodate assumptions about source evaluation, empirical validation is required. We suggest three initial directions for future research. First, to examine the sequence and time course of how these processes unfold during reading, studies should incorporate measures of "online" processing including verbal protocols, either separately or in conjunction with measuring readers' eye movements. Analyses incorporating microgenetic methods (Siegler, 2006) could provide key insights into the ways that readers transition between experiences of cognitive conflict, attributions of their origins, and the strategies in which people engage to restore coherence. For example, a future experiment could collect verbal protocols while individuals read texts that are manipulated to contradict or to be consistent with one another. Instructions could specify that readers should, for every comprehension difficulty they experience, state out loud where they think the difficulty stems from, and how they will rectify it. Microgenetic analysis of reader comments could validate whether internal attributions lead to strategies that reduce cognitive conflict by ignoring or changing some content, or by creating new unwarranted connections. At the same time, examinations could identify whether external attributions guide considerations of a discrepancy as an objective issue between two or more sources coming from different perspectives. Of course, these studies should also involve measures that seek to move beyond memory. For example, studies could investigate how readers transfer inferences about a source's knowledge, intentions, and biases to novel contexts, e.g., when attempting to comprehend a new article on a website that has already been deemed untrustworthy based on prior experiences.

Second, expansions of processes outlined by the CSI model (Stadtler & Bromme, 2014) in this chapter may be moderated by individual and contextual factors, as well as their interaction. Studies could incorporate individual differences factors such as level of a reader's prior knowledge and beliefs, and the strength of their attitudes, to help characterize relationships with different strategies for resolving coherence breaks that arise from discrepancies. A focus on reader characteristics would align with ideas presented in Bråten and Strømsø's chapter in this volume (Chapter 10), which discusses contributions of dispositions and beliefs to reasoning from various perspectives.

To give an example, if readers with lower domain knowledge notice discrepancies, they may choose to restore coherence by ignoring any content information that is inconsistent with their current position (Wiley, 2005). This scenario would obviate a need to consider the information sources making their respective conflicting claims. Readers with higher domain knowledge, however, may be more likely to detect a discrepancy and as such experience cognitive conflict. They may choose to restore coherence by evaluating source information including potential intentions and biases, and by thinking about whether one source is more knowledgeable than the other. Similarly, studies could manipulate contextual factors. For example, research could examine the degree to which the processes outlined in Figure 13.1 depend on a person's reading goal, such as if they are reading for personal fulfillment versus to complete coursework (van den Broek, Lorch, Linderholm, & Gustafson, 2001).

Finally, experimental research could more firmly establish causal relations between different forms of text-based discrepancies and evaluations of sources' perspectives. Very few studies provide causal evidence that the two are related. In a recent study, Saux and colleagues (2018, Experiment 2) manipulated discrepancies in brief news stories and provided features for each story that indicated the source's knowledge and appearance (the journalist who interviewed several witnesses and had a black moustache). Although online processing measures were not captured, the results confirmed that discrepant content information enhanced recall of knowledge features, while having no impact on recall for appearance features. There is a clear need for more studies incorporating online measures of text processing (eye movements, verbal protocols). It is an open research question whether different kinds of discrepancies stimulate people to evaluate whether one text's source is more knowledgeable than another source during reading. Equally important are studies investigating whether discrepancies result in more evaluations about whether some sources have more beneficent intentions, or are less biased relative to other sources. In concert with online processing, such studies could document whether discrepancies result in a greater inclusion of evaluations about potential source knowledge, intentions, and biases within the mental representations that people construct about text(s). Based on the theoretical considerations described in this chapter, predictions are that discrepancies promote these processes and mental representations of these facets of sources, including their perspectives, but only when features afford opportunities to do so. Although major questions remain, further research in this vein could better specify conditions that support routine inferences about source knowledge, intentions, and biases. These kinds of evaluations surely lead to more efficient, effective inquiry, and thus are a worthy research endeavor to pursue.

ACKNOWLEDGEMENT

This chapter was funded, in part, by a Spencer Foundation grant to Jason L. G. Braasch (No. 201900066). Any opinions, findings, and conclusions or recommendations expressed in this material are those of the authors, and do not necessarily reflect the views of the Spencer Foundation.

REFERENCES

Albrecht, J. E., & O'Brien, E. J. (1993). Updating a mental model: Maintaining both local and global coherence. *Journal of Experimental Psychology: Learning, Memory, and Cognition, 19*, 1061–1070.

Barzilai, S., & Strømsø, H. I. (2018). Individual differences in multiple document comprehension. In J. L. G. Braasch, I. Bråten, & M. T. McCrudden (Eds.), *Handbook of multiple source use* (pp. 99–116). New York: Routledge.

Beker, K., Jolles, D., Lorch, R. F., & van Den Broek, P. (2016). Learning from texts: Activation of information from previous texts during reading. *Reading and Writing, 29*, 1161–1178.

Blanc, N., Kendeou, P., van Den Broek, P., & Brouillet, D. (2008). Updating situation models during reading of news reports: Evidence from empirical data and simulations. *Discourse Processes, 45*, 103–121.

Braasch, J. L. G., & Bråten, I. (2017). The Discrepancy-Induced Source Comprehension (D-ISC) model: Basic assumptions and preliminary evidence. *Educational Psychologist, 52*, 167–181.

Braasch, J. L. G., Rouet, J. F., Vibert, N., & Britt, M. A. (2012). Readers' use of source information in text comprehension. *Memory and Cognition, 40*, 450–465.

Bråten, I., Salmerón, L., & Strømsø, H. (2016). Who said that? Investigating the plausibility-induced source focusing assumption with Norwegian undergraduate readers. *Reading and Writing, 46*, 253–262.

Bråten, I., Stadtler, M., & Salmerón, L. (in press). The role of sourcing in discourse comprehension. In M. F. Schober, M. A. Britt, & D. N. Rapp (Eds.), *Handbook of discourse processes* (2nd ed.). New York: Routledge.

Brem, S. K., Russell, J., & Weems, L. (2001). Science on the web: Student evaluations of scientific arguments. *Discourse Processes, 32*, 191–213.

Britt, M. A., Perfetti, C. A., Sandak, R., & Rouet, J. F. (1999). Content integration and source separation in learning from multiple texts. In S. R. Goldman, A. C. Graesser, & P. van Den Broek (Eds.), *Narrative, comprehension, causality, and coherence: Essays in honor of Tom Trabasso* (pp. 209–233). Mahwah, NJ: Erlbaum.

Britt, M. A., & Rouet, J. F. (2012). Learning with multiple documents: Component skills and their acquisition. In J. R. Kirby & M. J. Lawson (Eds.), *Enhancing the quality of learning: Dispositions, instruction, and learning processes* (pp. 276–314). New York: Cambridge University Press.

Bromme, R., & Goldman, S. R. (2014). The public's bounded understanding of science. *Educational Psychologist, 49*, 59–69.

Bromme, R., Kienhues, D., & Porsch, T. (2010). Who knows what and who can we believe? Epistemological beliefs are beliefs about knowledge (mostly) attained from others. In L. D. Bendixen & F. C. Feucht (Eds.), *Personal epistemology in the classroom: Theory, research, and implications for practice* (pp. 163–193). Cambridge: Cambridge University Press.

Bromme, R., Stadtler, M., Scharrer, L., & Thomm, E. (2015). A scientist through and through? How the source's commitment to science affects readers' evaluation of source and content in the domain of medicine. Paper presented at the annual meeting of the Society for Text and Discourse, Minneapolis, MN.

Bromme, R., & Thomm, E. (2016). Knowing who knows: Laypersons' capabilities to judge experts' pertinence for science topics. *Cognitive Science, 40*, 241–252.

Chinn, C. A., & Brewer, W. F. (1998). An empirical test of a taxonomy of responses to anomalous data in science. *Journal of Research in Science Teaching, 35*, 623–654.

Graesser, A. C. (2007). An introduction to strategic reading comprehension. In D. S. McNamara (Ed.), *Reading comprehension strategies: Theories, interventions, and technologies* (pp. 137–172). Mahwah, NJ: Erlbaum.

Goldman, S.R. (2004). Cognitive aspects of constructing meaning through and across multiple texts. In N. Shuart-Faris & D. Bloome (Eds.), *Uses of intertextuality in classroom and educational research* (pp. 317–351). Greenwich, CT: Information Age.

Graesser, A. C., Singer, M., & Trabasso, T. (1994). Constructing inferences during narrative text comprehension. *Psychological Review, 101*, 371–395.

Hakala, C. M., & O'Brien, E. J. (1995). Strategies for resolving coherence breaks in reading. *Discourse Processes, 20*, 167–185.

Hendriks, F., Kienhues, D., & Bromme, R. (2015). Measuring laypeople's trust in experts in a digital age: The Muenster Epistemic Trustworthiness Inventory (METI). *PLoS ONE 10*, e0139309.

Kammerer, Y., & Gerjets, P. (2012). The impact of discrepancies across web pages on high-school students' trustworthiness evaluations. In E. de Vries & K. Scheiter (Eds.), *Proceedings EARLI Special Interest Group Text and Graphics: Staging knowledge and experience: How to take advantage of representational technologies in education and training?* (pp. 97–99). Grenoble, France: Université Pierre-Mendes-France.

Kammerer, Y., Kalbfell, E., & Gerjets, P. (2016). Is this information source commercially biased? How contradictions between web pages stimulate the consideration of source information. *Discourse Processes, 53*, 430–456.

Keil, F. C., Stein, C., Webb, L., Billings, V. D., & Rozenblit, L. (2008). Discerning the division of cognitive labor: An emerging understanding of how knowledge is clustered in other minds. *Cognitive Science, 32*, 259–300.

Kendeou, P., & O'Brien, E. J. (2014). The knowledge revision components (KReC) framework: Processes and mechanisms. In D. Rapp & J. Braasch (Eds.), *Processing inaccurate information: Theoretical and applied perspectives from cognitive science and the educational sciences* (pp. 353–377). Cambridge, MA: MIT Press.

Kienhues, D., & Bromme, R. (2011). Beliefs about abilities and epistemic beliefs: Aspects of cognitive flexibility in information rich environments. In J. Elen, E. Stahl, R. Bromme, & G. Clarebout (Eds.), *Links between beliefs and cognitive flexibility: Lessons learned* (pp. 105–124). New York: Springer.

Kiili, C., Laurinen, L., & Marttunen, M. (2008). Students evaluating internet sources: From versatile evaluators to uncritical readers. *Journal of Educational Computing Research, 39*, 75–95.

Kintsch, W. (1998). *Comprehension: A paradigm for cognition*. New York: Cambridge University Press.

Lombardi, D., Nussbaum, E. M., & Sinatra, G. M. (2016). Plausibility judgments in conceptual change and epistemic cognition. *Educational Psychologist, 51*, 35–56.

Long, D. L., & Lea, R. B. (2005). Have we been searching for meaning in all the wrong places: Defining the "search after meaning" principle in comprehension. *Discourse Processes, 39*, 279–298.

Long, D. L., Seely, M. R., & Oppy, B. J. (1996). The availability of causal information during reading. *Discourse Processes, 22*, 145–170.

Magliano, J. P., Trabasso, T., & Graesser, A. C. (1999). Strategic processing during comprehension. *Journal of Educational Psychology, 9*, 615–629.

McKoon, G., & Ratcliff, R. (1998). Memory based language processing: Psycholinguistic research in the 1990s. *Annual Review of Psychology, 49*, 25–42.

Myers, J. L., & O'Brien, E. J. (1998). Accessing the discourse representation during reading. *Discourse Processes, 26*, 131–157.

O'Brien, E. J., Cook, A. E., & Gueraud, S. (2010). Accessibility of outdated information. *Journal of Experimental Psychology: Learning, Memory, and Cognition, 36*, 979–991.

O'Brien, E. J., & Myers, J. L. (1999). Text comprehension: A view from the bottom up. In S. R. Goldman, A. C. Graesser, & P. van Den Broek (Eds.), *Narrative comprehension, causality, and coherence: Essays in honor of Tom Trabasso* (pp. 35–53). Mahwah, NJ: Erlbaum.

O'Brien, E. J., Rizzella, M. L., Albrecht, J. E., & Halleran, J. G. (1998). Updating a situation model: A memory-based text processing view. *Journal of Experimental Psychology: Learning, Memory, and Cognition, 24*, 1200–1210.

Otero, J. (2002). Noticing and fixing difficulties while understanding science texts. In J. Otero, J. A. Leon, & A. C. Graesser (Eds.), *The psychology of science text comprehension* (pp. 281–308). Mahwah, NJ: Erlbaum.

Otero, J., & Campanario, J. M. (1990). Comprehension evaluation and regulation in learning from science texts. *Journal of Research in Science Teaching, 27*, 447–460.

Otero, J. M., & Kintsch, W. (1992). Failures to detect contradictions in a text: What readers believe versus what they read. *Psychological Science, 3*, 229–235.

Perfetti, C. A., Rouet, J. F., & Britt, M. A. (1999). Towards a theory of documents representation. In H. van Oostendorp & S. R. Goldman (Eds.), *The construction of mental representations during reading* (pp. 99–122). Mahwah, NJ: Erlbaum.

Rapp, D. N., Gerrig, R. J., & Prentice, D. A. (2001). Readers' trait-based models of characters in narrative comprehension. *Journal of Memory and Language, 45*, 737–750.

Rouet, J. F., Le Bigot, L., de Pereyra, G., & Britt, M. A. (2016). Whose story is this? Discrepancy triggers readers' attention to source information in short narratives. *Reading and Writing, 29*, 1549–1570.

Rowley, J., Johnson, F., & Sbaffi, L. (2015). Students' trust judgements in online health information seeking. *Health Informatics Journal, 21*, 316–327.

Saux, G., Britt, A., Le Bigot, L., Vibert, N., Burin, D., & Rouet, J. F. (2017). Conflicting but close: Readers' integration of information sources as a function of their disagreement. *Memory and Cognition, 45*, 151–167.

Saux, G., Ros, C., Britt, M. A., Stadtler, M., Burin, D., & Rouet, J. F. (2018). Readers' selective recall of source features as a function of claim discrepancy and task demands. *Discourse Processes, 55*, 525–544.

Scharrer, L., Stadtler, M., & Bromme, R. (n.d.). When biased readers encounter biased sources: How ethical (dis-)agreement between reader and author affects evaluation of scientific information. *Manuscript submitted for publication*.

Seifert, C. M. (2014). The continued influence effect: The persistence of misinformation in memory and reasoning following correction. In D. N. Rapp & J. L. G. Braasch (Eds.), *Processing inaccurate information: Theoretical and applied perspectives from cognitive science and the educational sciences* (pp. 39–71). Cambridge, MA: MIT Press.

Siegler, R. S. (2006). Microgenetic analyses of learning. In W. Damon, R. Lerner, D. Kuhn, & R. S. Siegler (Eds.), *Handbook of child psychology, vol 2. Cognition, perception, and language* (6th ed., pp. 464–510). Hoboken, NJ: Wiley.

Stadtler, M., & Bromme, R. (2014). The content-source integration model: A taxonomic description of how readers comprehend conflicting scientific information. In D. N. Rapp & J. L. G. Braasch (Eds.), *Processing inaccurate information: Theoretical and applied perspectives from cognitive science and the educational sciences* (pp. 379–402). Cambridge, MA: MIT Press.

Stadtler, M., Scharrer, L., & Bromme, R. (2013). How do readers explain the occurrence of conflicts in science texts? Effects of presentation format and source expertise. In M. Knauff, N. Pauen, N. Sebanz, & I. Wachsmuth (Eds.), *Proceedings of the 35th annual conference of the Cognitive Science Society* (pp. 3448–3453). Austin, TX: Cognitive Science Society.

Stadtler, M., Scharrer, L., Macedo-Rouet, M., Rouet, J.-F., & Bromme, R. (2016). Improving vocational students' consideration of source information when deciding about science controversies. *Reading and Writing, 29*, 705–729.

Thomm, E., Barzilai, S., & Bromme, R. (2017). Why do experts disagree? The role of conflict contexts and epistemic perspectives in conflict explanations. *Learning and Instruction, 52*, 15–26.

Thomm, E., & Bromme, R. (2016). How source information shapes lay interpretations of science conflicts: Interplay between sourcing, conflict explanation, source evaluation, and claim evaluation. *Reading and Writing, 29*, 1629–1652.

van Den Broek, P., & Kendeou, P. (2008). Cognitive processes in comprehension of science texts: The role of co-activation in confronting misconceptions. *Applied Cognitive Psychology, 22*, 335–351.

van Den Broek, P., Lorch, R. F., Linderholm, T., & Gustafson, M. (2001). The effects of readers' goals on inference generation and memory for texts. *Memory and Cognition, 29*, 1081–1087.

van Strien, J. L. H., Brand-Gruwel, S., & Boshuizen, H. P. A. (2014). Dealing with conflicting information from multiple nonlinear texts: Effects of prior attitudes. *Computers in Human Behavior, 32*, 101–111.

14

LEARNING FROM MULTIPLE COMPLEMENTARY PERSPECTIVES
A Systematic Review

Carla M. Firetto

ARIZONA STATE UNIVERSITY

ABSTRACT

Individuals often face contexts in which they must learn from multiple perspectives, but relatively little research has specifically examined how learners integrate information when the perspectives are complementary in nature. This chapter presents a systematic review that explores the trends and findings across extant research conducted on learning from complementary perspectives. A comprehensive, multipronged search approach identified 20 unique articles examining learning from multiple complementary perspectives. Key information (e.g., focus, theoretical frame(s), sample, perspectives, measures, and findings) from the identified studies is presented along with trends and patterns across the body of work. Critical gaps that need further examination are also forwarded to propel future research in this emerging area.

Key words: complementary perspectives, multiple perspectives, integration, content area learning, systematic review

Individuals often face contexts in which they must learn from multiple perspectives. Consider Josephine, an undergraduate student, who took a series of general education courses during her first semester of college in world history, introductory biology, calculus, and general psychology. Each course had an unspoken expectation that Josephine would learn from multiple perspectives to build strong foundational knowledge of the course content. However, the different courses each employed substantively different learning materials, potentially having far-reaching impacts on her learning of the respective domains.

As part of her world history course, Josephine learned about the history of the French Revolution from various sources presenting multiple perspectives, including a historical film, a series of original sources (e.g., translated diaries and historical maps), and the course textbook. Notably, as is common in the domain of history, each perspective included information that conflicted with the other perspectives. Thus, to effectively develop a cohesive understanding of the French Revolution, Josephine had to identify and resolve the discrepancies between perspectives as well as assess the veracity of the different sources to establish a sound understanding of the content.

In contrast, she also encountered multiple perspectives in her introductory biology course as she learned about the various physiological systems (e.g., cardiovascular or respiratory) in the human body. For each system she read from the assigned course textbook chapter, attended course lectures, and completed an online module that visually depicted the system functions. Each of those perspectives presented complementary information about the function of a given system. Further, the course continued to present complementary information from additional perspectives as subsequent physiological systems were introduced throughout the semester. As she studied, she focused on connecting the complementary information presented both *within* and *across* the physiological systems to build a cohesive understanding of how the human body worked.

Consistent with Barzilai and Weinstock's (Chapter 9) notion of source perspective, Josephine learned from multiple perspectives (i.e., stand-alone informational texts or documents from various origins with different purposes or functions) through lectures, textbooks, and sundry other sources in both courses. Importantly, however, the relationship across the multiple perspectives was notably different in the two courses. In particular, the perspectives presented in her world history course were characterized by the inclusion of discrepant or conflicting information, while the perspectives in her introductory biology course only contained complementary information. The inclusion or exclusion of conflicting information exerts a strong influence on how individuals integrate and synthesize information from multiple perspectives (Braasch & Bråten, 2017; Bråten & Braasch, 2018) and, consequently, would have a profound impact on Josephine's learning in the two courses.

Substantive theoretical (Braasch & Bråten, 2017; Stadtler & Bromme, 2014) and empirical (see Bråten & Braasch, 2018 for a review) research has been conducted to examine how individuals learn from perspectives with discrepant or conflicting information. However, comparatively little research has examined how learners integrate information when faced with complementary perspectives. A recent review of research on multiple text integration by Barzilai, Zohar, and Mor-Hagani (2018) found that fewer than 5% of the identified intervention studies employed texts presenting complementary perspectives, while 44% employed texts presenting discrepant or conflicting perspectives. Given that much of the seminal research on multiple text integration falls within the domain of history (e.g., Wineburg, 1991; see Fox & Maggioni, 2018), it is not surprising that much of the extant research focuses on perspectives with discrepant or conflicting information; historians are often tasked with synthesizing across primary and secondary sources (e.g., newspaper articles, personal diaries, letters, or government documents) that inherently contain conflicting accounts or perspectives.

The body of research examining multiple conflicting perspectives is rapidly expanding (Anmarkrud, Bråten, & Strømsø, 2014; Braasch & Bråten, 2017; Brante & Strømsø, 2018; Bråten & Braasch, 2018). However, this research is unlikely to generalize to the context of complementary perspectives, given the central role of conflicting information for the comprehension of multiple perspectives (Braasch & Bråten, 2017; Bråten & Braasch, 2018; Stadtler & Bromme, 2014). In addition, a thorough literature search did not yield comparable systematic reviews focusing on multiple complementary perspectives. Consequently, this chapter aims to thoroughly explore the trends and findings across research conducted on multiple complementary perspectives, while also forwarding a set of directions to propel future research in this area.

A SYSTEMATIC REVIEW OF EXTANT RESEARCH ON MULTIPLE COMPLEMENTARY PERSPECTIVES: METHOD AND RESULTS

Search Procedures

A comprehensive, multi-pronged approach identified publications employing multiple complementary texts. First, publications examining research on multiple texts identified by two recent systematic literature reviews were considered (Barzilai et al., 2018; Primor & Katzir, 2018). Second, a limited search was conducted to independently and broadly identify additional related articles. The following inclusion criteria were used: (1) the article must examine learning from multiple complementary perspectives (i.e., more than two texts or sources, broadly defined), (2) the article must employ a specific set of perspectives (e.g., articles where participants learned from an infinite potential of perspectives through an Internet search were excluded), (3) the article must report an empirical study with at least one purported measure of integration or cross-perspective synthesis, (4) the article must be published in a peer-reviewed journal, and (5) the article must be published in English.

Based on a set of 61 articles employing multiple texts, Barzilai and colleagues (2018) conducted a systematic review of the tasks or instructional activities designed to support a learner's ability to integrate perspectives. As part of their review, they conducted an in-depth examination on a subset of studies that focused on the influence of activities designed to promote integration. The 21 studies from this subset were classified into three categories based on the employed perspectives: three explicitly indicated using complementary texts, seven explicitly indicated using contrasting or contradictory texts, and the remaining 11 did not explicitly indicate the text type. All three of the articles explicitly noting the use of complementary texts met the criteria for inclusion in this review (i.e., Cerdán & Vidal-Abarca, 2008; Martinez, Mateos, Martín, & Rijlaarsdam, 2015; Mateos & Solé, 2009). To broaden the search beyond the subset of intervention studies and to identify articles that employed complementary texts without explicitly indicating so, the remaining 51 articles (i.e., 40 non-intervention studies and 11 intervention studies that did not explicitly specify perspective type) were examined for inclusion. As a result, eight additional articles were identified for inclusion (Blaum, Griffin, Wiley, & Britt, 2017; Boscolo, Arfé, & Quarisa, 2007; Daher & Kiewra, 2016; Hilbert & Renkl, 2008; Le Bigot & Rouet, 2007; Linderholm, Kwon, & Therriault, 2014; Mateos, Martín, Villalón, & Luna, 2008; Wiley & Voss, 1999).

Primor and Katzir's (2018) systematic review examined the ways in which multiple text integration has been assessed in the literature. They identified 50 articles that examined multiple text integration and classified whether the studies employed contradictory or conflicting texts (i.e., A ≠ B), complementary texts (i.e., A + B), or both (i.e., A ≠ B and A + B). All articles with complementary texts were examined, and six articles were identified for inclusion (i.e., A + B, Cerdán & Vidal-Abarca, 2008; Griffin, Wiley, Britt, & Salas, 2012; Le Bigot & Rouet, 2007; Linderholm, Therriault, & Kwon, 2014; Wiley & Voss, 1999; both A ≠ B and A + B; Barzilai & Eshet-Alkalai, 2015).

Finally, an independent search was conducted using the PSYCHinfo database. Peer-reviewed articles were searched for using the following search query: ("Multiple Texts") OR ("Multiple Documents"). No limitation was made for year, but the search was conducted in January of 2019 in order to obtain all articles published prior to and including 2018. The search yielded a total of 129 results, seven which met the inclusion criterion (Braasch, McCabe, & Daniel, 2016; Cerdán & Vidal-Abarca, 2008; Firetto & Van Meter, 2018; Karimi, 2015; Karimi & Atai, 2014; Lehmann, Rott, & Schmidt-Borcherding, 2019; List, 2018).

Altogether, this comprehensive, multi-pronged approach identified 20 unique articles examining learning from complementary perspectives that met the preestablished inclusion criteria (i.e., several of the articles were identified in more than one of the search approaches). Over half (i.e., 12) were published within the last five years and all but one since 2007, indicating emerging interest in this area and further establishing the need for a comprehensive review. While the number of identified articles was somewhat limited in quantity, the search approach yielded a wide breadth of research. Key information from the 20 identified studies is presented in Table 14.1 including: study focus, theoretical framework(s), sample description, perspective features, integration measures, and key findings. Trends and patterns across these studies are reported in the sections below as they relate to this key information. In addition, based on these trends and patterns, critical gaps that need to be further examined are also noted with the hope that this review may serve to inspire future research in this emerging area. Finally, two broader themes emerged overall, and future directions are forwarded.

Theoretical framework(s)

Trends and patterns

In addition to Kintsch's Construction-Integration theory (Kintsch, 1988; Van Dijk & Kintsch, 1983), the Documents Model (Perfetti, Rouet, & Britt, 1999) and the Multiple Documents Task-Based Relevance and Content Extraction model (MD-TRACE; Rouet & Britt, 2011) were the predominant theoretical frameworks employed. With few exceptions, most studies (i.e., 16) explicitly indicated one or more of these respective frameworks as the undergirding theoretical frame(s) of their research. While the majority of studies were guided by the aforementioned multiple texts theoretical framing, several utilized theoretical framing based on the various forms of integration support. For example, Jairam and Kiewra (2009) developed an integration support based on Mayer's SOI model (1996), while Hilbert and Renkl (2008) were guided

Table 14.1 Key Information from Identified Studies Examining Multiple Complementary Perspectives.

Author(s) Year	Study Focus	Theoretical Frame(s)	Sample Description	Perspective Features	Integration Measures	Key Findings
Barzilai & Eshet-Alkalai 2015	*Individual differences*: epistemic perspectives *Perspective manipulations*: conflicting vs. converging	• Kintsch Documents Model • MD-TRACE	$N = 170$ Hebrew-speaking university students; various majors	Topic: Seawater desalination; Conflicting condition: 2 "For" & 2 "Against" blogs; Converging condition: 4 "For" blogs; ~214 words each	Written response scoring (argument writing): scored for argument structure & argument sources	Conflict had a significant positive effect on viewpoint comprehension for learners with high levels of multiplist or evaluist perspectives; evaluativism positively predicted viewpoint comprehension, which mediated the relationship between epistemic perspectives and integration
Blaum, Griffin, Wiley, & Britt 2017	*Integration support*: causal prompt vs. causal-plus-solution prompt *Perspective manipulations*: a core document set without vs. with a policy-related document	• Kintsch • MD-TRACE	$N = 46$ 7th grade students; science class	Topic: Global climate change; Core document set condition: 7 documents, ~300 words each; Core document set with policy condition: 7 documents + 1 policy text, 234 words	Written response scoring (explanatory essay): scored for coverage, causal structure, use of policy information, and presence of source references; 18-item Inference Verification Task (IVT)	Learners who read the core document set with the policy document included more policy statements in their essays with fewer causal connections and causal explanations, but no difference was found with regard to the use of references or on the inference verification task; there were no differences in the essays regarding the two prompts, but causal-plus-solution learners outperformed those receiving the causal prompt on the IVT
Boscolo, Arfé & Quarisa 2007	*Integration support*: writing synthesis workshop	• Kintsch • Spivey	$N = 52$ undergraduate psychology students in an Italian university	Topics: Motivation & Creativity; 3 texts, ~450 words each	Written response scoring (written synthesis): scored for units of integration via (a) information across texts connected through cohesion devices and (b) information across texts was connected into a new unit	Learners' scores increased from pre-test to post-test on four measures of text quality but did not improve regarding integration; the intervention only had a minimal impact on learners' beliefs about writing

(Continued)

Table 14.1 (Continued)

Author(s) Year	Study Focus	Theoretical Frame(s)	Sample Description	Perspective Features	Integration Measures	Key Findings
Braasch, McCabe, & Daniel 2016 Experiment 3	*Perspective manipulations*: congruent vs. distinct semantic information	• Kintsch • Documents Model • MD-TRACE	N = 82 undergraduate students from an introductory psychology course	Topic: Social media; 24 sentences (12 congruent and 12 distinct)	Written response scoring (comprehensive essay): scored for proportion of accurate distinct and congruent text claims, number of sources correctly attributed, number of essay details	Learners had an increased recall of congruent claims and evidence, including both repeated and unique evidence; there was a negative correlation between the recall of content and the recall of source information for learners reading the congruent sentences, but the correlation was not present for learners reading distinct sentences
Cerdán & Vidal-Abarca 2008	*Integration support*: intertext essay vs. intratext questioning *Processes*: mental processes	• Kintsch • Documents Model	N = 56 undergraduate psychology students in a university in Spain	Topic: Antibacterial resistance; 3 texts from trustworthy websites, ~500 words each	Transfer test: ability for learners to apply knowledge to a new situation; Process measures: frequency count of "nonconsecutive readings of relevant units of information" & single-unit pattern of processing	Learners who completed the intertext essay outperformed learners who answered intratext questions on the transfer test, even though no differences were found on measures of comprehension; task condition differences were also identified for both process measures of integration; task condition performance and transfer test scores were correlated with both integration process measures
Daher & Kiewra 2016	*Integration support*: SOAR study strategy vs. learners' preferred study strategy	• Mayer's SOI Model/Information Processing • Kintsch • TRACE/MD-TRACE	N = 134 undergraduate students from a learning strategies course	Topic: Apes; Study materials: 5 texts on different apes, ~280 words each	Achievement test: included open-ended relationship items which assessed "unstated similarities between or among apes" (p. 15) at either local or global levels	Learners who completed the SOAR strategy outperformed those who studied using their preferred study strategy for all three achievement test items (i.e., fact, concept, and relationship); the benefits of the SOAR strategy were evidenced for both local relations and global relations items

Author(s) Year	Study Focus	Theoretical Frame(s)	Sample Description	Perspective Features	Integration Measures	Key Findings
Firetto & Van Meter 2018	*Integration support*: integration vs. comprehension vs. control task *Processes*: strategy use *Perspective Manipulation*: multiple texts vs. single text	• Kintsch Documents Model • MD-TRACE	N = 617 undergraduate biology students	Topic: Human anatomy, edited from textbook chapters; Multiple texts condition: 2 texts, ~1750 words each; Single text condition: 1 text with information combined, ~3500 words	Written response scoring (open-ended free recall question): coded for whether or not participants spontaneously integrated	Learners who engaged in the integration prompt/task were more likely to integrate than learners in the other two conditions; learners who read one text were more likely to integrate than those who read two texts; self-reported integration strategy use mediated the effect of the integration task on learners' integrated response
Griffin, Wiley, Britt, & Salas 2012	*Individual differences*: CLEAR thinking	• Kintsch Documents Model • MD-TRACE	N = 59 7th grade students; science class	Topic: Global climate change; 7 texts from online sources adapted for grade level, ~350 words each	18-item IVT	There was a statistically significant positive correlation between inquiry task essay scores and IVT scores; CLEAR thinking (i.e., Commitment to Logic, Evidence, and Reasoning) and reading skill accounted for unique variance in learners' IVT scores
Hilbert & Renkl 2008	*Integration support*: concept maps *Individual differences*: verbal and spatial ability *Processes*: cognitive processes	• Ausubel's assimilation theory of cognitive learning	N = 38 German-speaking undergraduate students	Topic: Stem-cells; 6 newspaper articles, 2,116 words total, 80–1,029 words each	Integration test: 7 multiple-choice items requiring learners to integrate knowledge from at least two articles	Spatial ability scores and integration scores were positively correlated; integration scores were also correlated positively with the number of correctly labeled concept map links and negatively with the number of unlabeled links; in think alouds, learners who reflected more on the relationships as well as those who verbalized planning/controlling scored higher on the integration test

(Continued)

Table 14.1 (Continued)

Author(s) Year	Study Focus	Theoretical Frame(s)	Sample Description	Perspective Features	Integration Measures	Key Findings
Karimi 2015	*Integration support & Perspective manipulation:* strategy instruction with single or multiple text vs. no strategy instruction with single or multiple text *Processes:* strategy use	• Kintsch • Multiple documents-based literacy	N = 76 Farsi-speaking learners enrolled in a language center to learn English; subsample of n = 32 for process measures	Topics: Various (e.g., ADHD, cybercrime, heart attack, global warming, alternative medicine, dyslexia); multiple texts from various sources (e.g., Internet, textbooks), ~1,200 words each	Full sample: 20-item IVT Subsample: report of mental processes, qualitatively examined for strategic processes and intertextual awareness	Learners who read multiple texts in the intervention period scored statistically significantly higher on the integration measure than learners who read single texts; those who read multiple texts with strategy instruction outperformed those who read multiple texts without strategy instruction on the integration measure; learners who read multiple texts with strategy instruction reported the most use of integration strategies
Karimi & Atai 2014	*Individual differences:* epistemological beliefs	Epistemological beliefs: • Perry's unidimensional • Schommer's multidimensional	N = 64 midwifery students in their first semester in Iran (English for Specific/Academic Purposes)	Topic: Multi-fetal pregnancy; 4 texts from various sources (e.g., textbook chapter, popular science text), ~1,000 words each	20-item IVT	Learners with more sophisticated epistemological beliefs had higher scores on both intratextual and intertextual inferential learning; all dimensions of epistemological beliefs predicted integration (i.e., simple knowledge, certain knowledge, omniscient authority, innate ability, and quick learning)

Author(s) Year	Study Focus	Theoretical Frame(s)	Sample Description	Perspective Features	Integration Measures	Key Findings
Le Bigot & Rouet 2007	*Individual differences*: prior knowledge *Integration support*: summary vs. argument writing *Perspective manipulations*: organized by topic vs. by source	• Kintsch • Documents Model	N = 52 French-speaking undergraduate and graduate students	Topic: Social influence; 7 texts revised from psychology textbooks, ~145 words each	Comprehension questionnaire: 16-item multiple-choice test with microstructure (local details) and macrostructure (global details) questions at both the situation model and the text-based level	Learners with high prior knowledge scored higher on the post-test with particularly pronounced differences on macrostructure-text-based questions; there was no main effect of task or presentation format, but a three-way interaction revealed that students who completed the summary task and read texts organized by sources answered microstructure questions more accurately
Lehmann, Rott, & Borcherding 2019[a]	*Integration support*: unspecific vs. argument writing task *Integration support*: with vs. without integration focus questions	• Kintsch • MD-TRACE	N = 93 German-speaking pre-service elementary mathematics teachers	Topic: Shulman's types of teacher knowledge; 3 texts, ~2,000 words each; documents derived from published sources and slightly modified	Written response scoring (writing task): scored for integrative elaboration and frequency of switches between sources; 14-item IVT	Learners responding to the argument task had more integrative elaborations and switches than those responding to the unspecific writing task, as did learners who received integration focus questions compared to those who did not; neither task condition effect was replicated with the IVT measure, but when motivation was added as a covariate there was an effect of focus questions as well as an interaction

(Continued)

Table 14.1 (Continued)

Author(s) Year	Study Focus	Theoretical Frame(s)	Sample Description	Perspective Features	Integration Measures	Key Findings
Linderholm, Kwon, & Therriault 2014 Experiment 1 (E1) and Experiment 2 (E2)	*Integration support*: self-explanation definition-only strategy vs. self-explanation definition-plus-modeling strategy vs. control	• Documents Model • MD-TRACE	E1: $N = 132$ undergraduate students in an educational psychology course E2: $N = 64$ undergraduate students in an educational psychology course	Topic: Electricity; 3 texts, ~441 words each, modified for consistency in length and structure	E1/E2: 10 short-answer essay questions assessing common and unique information, four questions were classified as "integrated comprehension" items; E2: Written response scoring (writing task prompting the use of all three texts): composite score (8 points) based on integration	E1: Strategy had an effect on learners' reading comprehension, and participants in the definition-only condition outperformed the control; no statistically significant differences were detected for integrated comprehension items, even though differences were present for factual items; E2: Findings noted from E1 were replicated with regard to the reading comprehension measure; strategy had an effect on learners' composite writing scores
Linderholm, Therriault, & Kwon 2014 Study 1 (S1) and Study 2 (S2)	*Processes*: cognitive processes *Integration support*: self-explanation strategy vs. control	• Documents Model	S1: $N = 26$ undergraduate students in an introductory educational psychology course S2: $N = 118$ undergraduate students in an introductory educational psychology course	Topic: Electricity; 3 texts, ~441 words each, modified for consistency in length and structure	S1: Written response scoring (writing task prompting use of all three texts): sentences coded into categories, including one for "integrated information"; think alouds coded for "integrated explanations"; S2: 10 short-answer essay questions assessing common and unique information across the texts	S1: The majority of sentences in response to the writing task were paraphrased (77%) with few instances of integrated information from across at least two of the three texts (14%); integrated explanations in the think alouds were rare (1.55 on average, per individual); the only cognitive processes to positively correlate with integrated information in writing were those associated with learners' verbalized understanding; S2: Learners who participated in a self-explanation condition scored higher on the comprehension test than a control group

Author(s) Year	Study Focus	Theoretical Frame(s)	Sample Description	Perspective Features	Integration Measures	Key Findings
List 2018	*Processes*: strategic processes *Perspective manipulations*: video vs. text	• Kintsch • Documents Model	$N = 78$ undergraduate students	Topic: Species preservation; Video condition: 2 videos, created by TEDEd, selected for similarity in length and style; Text condition: 2 texts transcribed from the videos, ~700 words	Written response scoring (argument prompt): coded for degree of integration; Written response scoring (compare and contrast prompt): coded for points of similarity and difference	There were no differences between perspective type for integration scores of written responses, potentially due to limited integration overall; strategies of directing attention and connecting content with prior knowledge were predictive of both integration scores
Martinez, Mateos, Martín, & Rijlaarsdam 2015	*Integration support & Perspective manipulation*: Strategies for Writing Syntheses to Learn (SWSL) with two texts vs. a conventional task with a regular textbook	• Kintsch • Documents Model • Spivey	$N = 62$ 6th grade primary students in Spain; subsample of $n = 32$ for process measures	Topic: Contemporary history; Two texts: pairs of texts, ~250 words each; Regular textbook: used course textbook	Written response scoring (synthesis): scored for integration and averaged with other quality indicators; writing processes were coded for interactions (e.g., text switches)	There were statistically significant interactions between time and condition for both product quality and interactions (i.e., switches), such that the pre-to-post gains were markedly greater for the SWSL participants
Mateos, Martín, Villalón, & Luna 2008	*Integration support & Perspective manipulation*: summary task with single text vs. synthesis task with multiple texts *Processes*: cognitive and metacognitive processes	• Spivey	$N = 9$ 15-year old secondary students from a state-run school in Spain	Summary/single text condition: Topic: Medieval cities; 1 adapted text, 261 words; Synthesis/multiple text condition: Topic: Spanish immigration; 2 adapted texts, ~225 words each	Written response scoring (synthesis): categorized into (1) ideas from one text, (2) alternating ideas from both texts, and (3) connecting ideas	Only one student produced a high-quality written synthesis with type 3 integration; five produced type 2 integration; three produced type 1 integration; participants evidenced similar cognitive and metacognitive processes for both summary and synthesis tasks, with the exception of inter-integrating events which were only present when learners were engaged in the synthesis task by definition

(Continued)

Table 14.1 (Continued)

Author(s) Year	Study Focus	Theoretical Frame(s)	Sample Description	Perspective Features	Integration Measures	Key Findings
Mateos & Solé 2009	Integration support: various types of synthesis tasks Individual differences: educational level	• Spivey	N = 45 split across four class levels: 7th grade, 9th grade, 11th grade, and undergraduate psychology students[b] in Spain	Topic: Cartography, 7th grade, 2 texts; Topic: Immigration, 9th grade, 2 texts; Topic: Social change, 11th grade, 2 texts; all adapted from textbooks, etc.	Written response scoring (synthesis): scored 1 to 5 from non-synthesis to successful synthesis (later recategorized into 3 categories)	Despite high reading and writing abilities, learners did not generally produce strong written syntheses; only one learner reading complementary perspectives produced a "successful synthesis" (i.e., at the 16-17 y/o level); learners at lower educational levels produced poorer quality syntheses than those at higher educational levels; task complexity increased with educational level
Wiley & Voss 1999 Experiment 1	Integration support: argument vs. narrative vs. summary vs. explanation Perspective manipulation: separate source documents vs. textbook-like chapter	• Kintsch	N = 64 undergraduate introductory psychology students	Topic: Ireland from 1800–1850; Separate source documents condition: 8 documents (e.g., map, biographies), ~220 words each; Textbook-like chapter condition: 8 documents combined, 1,571 words	Written response scoring (essays): scored for transformation, integration, and causal connections	Learners who responded to argument tasks outperformed those responding to narrative, summary, or explanation tasks on transformation, integration, and causality, particularly when learners were reading from multiple sources

[a] published online and indexed in 2018
[b] results pertaining to the sample of university participants were excluded due to the exclusive focus on contrasting perspectives

by Ausubel's assimilation theory of cognitive learning (Ausubel, Novak, & Hanesian, 1978), and many of those focusing on writing as an intervention support (Boscolo et al., 2007; Martinez et al., 2015; Mateos et al., 2008; Mateos & Solé, 2009) cited Spivey (1997). Overall, however, there was remarkable consistency across the studies with regard to their theoretical framing.

Gaps and future directions

There is presently no theoretical framework specifically established to frame research on learning from complementary perspectives. Consequently, the Documents Model (Perfetti et al., 1999) and the MD-TRACE model (Rouet & Britt, 2011) have framed much of the research employing texts with either complementary or contrasting perspectives. Yet, the extent to which these models apply to complementary perspectives is unclear. For example, the Documents Model places a strong emphasis on the use of source tagging, which may be less crucial when individuals are learning from complementary texts written by the same author (Firetto & Van Meter, 2018). In contrast, there may be key components specific to complementary texts that are not addressed by existing models. Recently, List and Alexander (2018) have forwarded the Integrated Framework of Multiple Texts (IF-MT), which explicitly accounts for the nature of the relationship between multiple perspectives. Specifically, the IF-MT model includes a component whereby learners identify the relational designation (e.g., complementary or contrasting) between sets of texts which can consequently inform the processes they engage in (e.g., synthesis or reconciliation). Moving forward, researchers in this area should consider the IF-MT as a potential theoretical framework to guide future studies or develop new frameworks specific to multiple complementary perspectives.

Sample Description

Trends and Patterns

Participant descriptions were sufficiently elaborated in accordance with APA Guidelines. Among the 20 studies, 22 participant samples (i.e., both studies by Linderholm and colleagues [2014] presented findings of two experiments which both fit the inclusion criteria) employed a diverse range of sample sizes (i.e., $N = 9$ to $N = 617$). For participant age/academic level, undergraduate students were the predominant level studied (i.e., 15 out of 20 studies). Only five of the samples were composed of learners in K-12 schools (i.e., 6th grade, Martinez et al., 2015; 7th grade, Griffin et al., 2012; Blaum et al., 2017; 15-year-olds, Mateos et al., 2008; 7th grade, 9th grade, and 11th grade; Mateos & Solé, 2009).

Research on multiple perspectives is burgeoning worldwide. About half of the research (i.e., nine out of 20 studies) was conducted with American, English-speaking undergraduate students while the other half (i.e., 11 out of 20 studies) was conducted with learners outside of the United States, those speaking languages other than English, or those learning English as a second language. For example, Barzilai and Eshet-Alkalai (2015) recruited samples of Hebrew-speaking participants in Israel, Hilbert and Renkl (2008) and Lehman and colleagues (2019) both recruited German-speaking participants in Germany, and Le Bigot and Rouet (2007) recruited French-speaking participants in France. Further, Karimi recently studied two different populations of L2 English learners in Iran (Karimi, 2015; Karimi & Atai, 2014).

Gaps and Future Directions

At present, the body of literature is largely based on how undergraduate students read multiple complementary texts. Consequently, the generalizability of the published findings is limited for K-12 education. Researchers should consider conducting more studies in K-12 contexts to better understand how younger learners read and integrate multiple complementary perspectives. Likewise, while the body of research is being conducted across multiple languages, future researchers should consider expanding upon the findings of Karimi and colleagues (Karimi, 2015; Karimi & Atai, 2014) by recruiting learners in English language learning contexts or those acquiring a second language.

Perspective Features

Trends and Patterns

Perspectives ranged widely with regard to the number of perspectives (i.e., from two to eight), however, pairs of two or sets of three perspectives were employed in about half of the studies (i.e., nine out of 20 studies). All studies included at least one condition with a perspective presented in the form of a text. About half of the studies employed texts that were 200–500 words each (i.e., 11 out of 20 studies), but texts ranged from several sentences (Braasch et al., 2016) to about 2,000 words each (Lehmann et al., 2019). Perspectives were also presented in the form of maps (Wiley & Voss, 1999) and videos (List, 2018). Topics varied widely (e.g., electricity, climate change, antibacterial resistance) but were most commonly within the domain of science (i.e., 12 out of 20 studies). Some authors specifically mentioned that perspectives were adapted from original sources to fit the context of the study. For example, Griffin and colleagues (2012) adapted online texts to be more developmentally appropriate for their 7th grade participants, while Linderholm and colleagues (2014) modified the texts to ensure consistency in length and structure across the different perspectives.

Gaps and Future Directions

Overall, many of the perspectives that were employed were in the form of strikingly short texts. As such, it is unclear how learning from these abbreviated texts can be generalized to typical learning contexts with long, complex texts. To address this limitation, researchers should use longer text-segments, chapters, or books as well as experimentally assess the degree to which text length influences learners' integration. Additionally, much of the extant research focuses on traditional written texts in the domain of science. Two notable exceptions that provide unique and valuable contributions include List's (2018) comparison of videos to texts, as the only identified study that experimentally examined complementary *non-textual* perspectives, and Lehmann and colleagues' (2019) study which employed texts in the domain of education. Further examining the influence of medium for complementary perspectives as well as perspectives from domains other than science would prove fruitful for future research.

Integration Measures

Trends and Patterns

Many researchers utilized measures of integration that involved learners' written responses (i.e., 13 out of 20 studies). Yet, the written response measures varied widely both in how they were structured as well as how they were scored. For example, some writing measures involved learners' generation of written arguments (Barzilai & Eshet-Alkalai, 2015; List, 2018), whereas others involved written syntheses that explicitly prompted learners to integrate texts (Boscolo et al., 2007; Martinez et al., 2015; Mateos et al., 2008; Mateos & Solé, 2009). Written responses were scored in a number of different ways. For example, Boscolo and colleagues (2007) scored for units of integration, including instances where information from different texts were connected in the written response. Lehmann and colleagues (2019) scored written responses similarly and called the coding category "integrative elaborations." Another mechanism used to examine integration was the frequency with which participants referred to, or switched between, different sources (Lehman et al., 2019; Martinez et al., 2015). Alternatively, other researchers categorically classified responses based on the presence or absence of "spontaneous integration" (Firetto & Van Meter, 2018) or scored them based on the degree of integration (List, 2018; Mateos et al., 2008; Mateos & Solé, 2009). Mechanisms for measuring integration also included open-ended (Daher & Kiewra, 2016) or multiple-choice (Hilbert & Renkl, 2008; Le Bigot & Rouet, 2007) integration questions and Intertextual Inference Verification Tasks (IVT; Blaum et al., 2017; Griffin et al., 2012; Karimi, 2015; Karimi & Atai, 2014; Lehmann et al., 2019).

Gaps and Future Directions

Because there is no universal standard measure of integration, researchers employ a wide variety of outcome measures, each operationalizing integration differently. Further, even narrowing down to only the studies that employed open-ended writing measures, no two studies used the same prompts or the same scoring. As such, it is hard to draw comparisons across the different studies. New measures need to be developed with evidence of both reliability and validity that can be used across a variety of contexts where learners are faced with multiple complementary perspectives.

Focus and Key Findings

Trends and Patterns

Based on the aims and key findings of the identified studies, three clear foci emerged. The body of research primarily focused on: (a) developing mechanisms to support learners' integration of multiple complementary perspectives, (b) examining how learner characteristics and processes were associated with learners' integration of multiple complementary perspectives, and (c) investigating various features of complementary perspectives that influence learners' integration. Importantly, all 20 manuscripts could be classified as having one or more of these foci. The key findings are reviewed in the sections below as they relate to each of these three foci.

INTEGRATION SUPPORTS

The most predominant of the three foci (i.e., 15 of the 20 studies) was identifying mechanisms (e.g., prompts, tasks, interventions, strategies) to support learners' integration of multiple complementary perspectives. Within this focus, integration supports took the form of concept maps (Hilbert & Renkl, 2008; Karimi, 2015), graphic organizers or matrices (Daher & Kiewra, 2016; Firetto & Van Meter, 2018), self-elaborations (Linderholm et al., 2014, 2014), and writing tasks. Specific writing tasks included causal explanations (Blaum et al., 2017), written arguments (Le Bigot & Rouet, 2007; Lehmann et al., 2019; Wiley & Voss, 1999), and written intertext (Cerdán & Vidal-Abarca, 2008) or synthesis essays (Boscolo et al., 2007; Martinez et al., 2015; Mateos et al., 2008; Mateos & Solé, 2009). Importantly, irrespective of the form, the intervention supports were overwhelmingly effective at supporting learners' integration. With only two exceptions (Boscolo et al., 2007; Le Bigot & Rouet, 2007), the integration supports resulted in positive impacts on integration outcomes, either via increases from pre-test to post-test or in comparison to other conditions.

Despite surface-level differences, there were clear similarities in the deep structure of these intervention supports, related to the stimulation of learners' cognitive and strategic processes and the ways in which the supports were employed. The first similarity was that researchers often designed integration supports to bolster similar key strategic processes. In most instances, supports were designed to (a) guide learners in selecting key relevant and related information that could be integrated across perspectives, (b) help learners organize and build a coherent internal knowledge structure, and/or (c) elaborate and generate inferences or connections with prior knowledge (Boscolo et al., 2007; Cerdán & Vidal-Abarca, 2008; Daher & Kiewra, 2016; Firetto & Van Meter, 2018; Hilbert & Renkl, 2008; Karimi, 2015; Linderholm et al., 2014, 2014; Martinez et al., 2015; Mateos et al., 2008; Mateos & Solé, 2009; Wiley & Voss, 1999). In addition, several supports also focused on guiding learners' regulation and metacognition (Daher & Kiewra, 2016; Firetto & Van Meter, 2018; Hilbert & Renkl, 2008; Karimi, 2015; Martinez et al., 2015).

When describing how these supports were implemented, many researchers reported procedures aligning with various aspects of effective strategy instruction (see Graham & Harris, 2005). Researchers often provided learners with: (a) the goal of integrating or the purpose of engaging in the strategy (Boscolo et al., 2007; Firetto & Van Meter, 2018; Karimi, 2015; Lehmann et al., 2019), (b) explicit instruction in the intervention and/or its use (Boscolo et al., 2007; Daher & Kiewra, 2016; Hilbert & Renkl, 2008; Linderholm et al., 2014, 2014; Mateos & Solé, 2009), (c) modeling and/or examples (Boscolo et al., 2007; Daher & Kiewra, 2016; Firetto & Van Meter, 2018; Hilbert & Renkl, 2008; Karimi, 2015; Linderholm et al., 2014; Martinez et al.,

2015), (d) guided and/or independent practice (Boscolo et al., 2007; Daher & Kiewra, 2016; Karimi, 2015; Le Bigot & Rouet, 2007; Martinez et al., 2015), (e) collaboration (Martinez et al., 2015), and (f) feedback (Daher & Kiewra, 2016; Karimi, 2015). Notably, these aspects were present in intervention supports that emphasized writing as well as in those that did not. Given the well established theoretical and empirical literature of strategy instruction, the use and subsequent efficacy of these supports is not surprising.

INDIVIDUAL DIFFERENCES AND PROCESSES

Another major focus of the extant research centered around examining individual differences associated with learners' integration of multiple complementary perspectives as well as the cognitive processes learners engaged in while reading (i.e., nine of the 20 studies). The findings revealed that the learners who were more competent at integrating across the perspectives were those with: higher prior knowledge (Le Bigot & Rouet, 2007), more advanced spatial ability (Hilbert & Renkl, 2008), better reasoning capability (Griffin et al., 2012), and more sophisticated epistemological beliefs (Karimi & Atai, 2014). In addition, learners showed greater integration at higher education levels (Mateos & Solé, 2009). In contrast, neither learners' verbal ability (Hilbert & Renkl, 2008) nor their epistemological perspectives (Barzilai & Eshet-Alkalai, 2015) had a direct influence on integration. Certain cognitive and strategic processes were associated with integration when learners were engaged in reading from multiple complementary perspectives. For example, connecting to prior knowledge was associated with integration (List, 2018) as was reflecting on the relationship between concepts (Hilbert & Renkl, 2008). Regulation processes were also associated with integration, specifically as they related to positive (Linderholm, Therriault, & Kwon, 2014) and negative (Hilbert & Renkl, 2008; Linderholm et al., 2014) monitoring as well as planning and controlling (Hilbert & Renkl, 2008).

PERSPECTIVE MANIPULATIONS

The final focus revolved around experimental manipulations to the perspectives (i.e., 10 of the 20 studies). Both Braasch and colleagues (2016) as well as Barzilai and Eshet-Alkalai (2015) examined the role of conflict by including conditions with and without conflicting or discrepant information. Braasch and colleagues (2016) found that learners took longer to read and integrated more when reading congruent (i.e., complementary) perspectives than when reading perspectives containing discrepant information. In contrast, learners reading complementary perspectives had poorer scores on sourcing measures than those reading perspectives with discrepant information. Barzilai and Eshet-Alkalai (2015) found a similar trend, but they identified a key nuance as it related to learners' epistemic perspectives – conflict only improved learners' comprehension when they had high levels of multiplism or evaluatism. In addition, five studies employed conditions with both multiple and single perspectives. Three of them, however, were designed such that the single perspective condition was confounded with the integration support (Karimi, 2015; Martinez et al., 2015; Mateos et al., 2008). Further, the two studies that directly compared reading from single or multiple perspectives found opposing results. Wiley and Voss (1999) found that learners who read multiple perspectives wrote essays with more transformed sentences, had more connections and causal connections, and had a lesser proportion of borrowed sentences than learners who read the same information presented in the form of a single perspective. In contrast, Firetto and Van Meter (2018) found that fewer learners who read multiple perspectives integrated than learners who read the same information presented as a single perspective.

Gaps and Future Directions

Across all three of the foci, research has produced valuable contributions toward the understanding of how learners integrate multiple complementary perspectives. In the future, investigations of the relationship among these foci by examining integration supports in combination with various individual differences may create better understandings of what works and for whom. Additionally, researchers should conduct direct comparisons between single and multiple perspectives given the limited and conflicting findings.

DISCUSSION

Broader Themes

Based on the aforementioned trends, two broader cross-cutting themes pertaining to the feasibility and alignment of the research also emerged. First, there was a clear association between the examined sample and employed methodology. For example, the two studies with the smallest sample sizes (e.g., $N = 9$, Mateos et al., 2008; $N = 26$, Linderholm et al., 2014) both examined think-aloud protocols of participants as they engaged in the multiple complementary perspective reading task in addition to conducting a quantitative coding of participants' essays. In contrast, the two studies with the largest sample sizes (i.e., $N = 170$, Barzilai & Eshet-Alkalai, 2015; $N = 617$; Firetto & Van Meter, 2018) employed Likert-type scales to examine the relationship between learners' individual differences and integration, as evidenced in written responses. Given the intensive resources required to collect and analyze think-aloud data, it is likely that the studies utilized small sample sizes in order to maintain feasibility. In contrast, by employing outcome measures that were comparatively less resource intensive (i.e., Likert-type scales), researchers could leverage the statistical power afforded by larger samples.

Additionally, all five of the studies that recruited learners from K-12 schools employed texts relevant to their class. For example, both studies by Griffin et al. (2012, 2017) were conducted in 7th grade science classrooms, and students in these studies learned from multiple complementary perspectives about global climate change. Likewise, students in Martinez and colleagues' (2015) study read content that was part of their regular history curriculum that had not yet been taught. Thus, these students engaged in learning from multiple complementary perspectives from texts related to what they were learning. This alignment between the sample and the perspective content was also evident in four of the 15 undergraduate-level studies (Boscolo et al., 2007; Firetto & Van Meter, 2018; Karimi & Atai, 2014; Lehmann et al., 2019). For example, Karimi and Atai (2014) recruited midwifery students and examined their learning from multiple complementary texts about multi-fetal pregnancies and Firetto and Van Meter (2018) recruited students from an introductory biology course and used texts about content that would be taught later in that course, like Martinez and colleagues' (2015) study.

Overall Future Directions

Building on the broader themes, researchers should aim to increase the authenticity of their research. Authenticity can be increased by using perspectives more similar to those in traditional learning contexts (e.g., longer texts or topics that align with learners' typical learning contexts). Karimi and Atai's (2014) study serves as an illustrative example of authenticity, as the midwifery participants learned from long texts (i.e., about 1,000 words each) about multi-fetal pregnancies. In essence, they learned from texts that were likely similar to other texts in their course and that also held both utility value and intrinsic interest (Eccles et al., 1983). By increasing authenticity, the results may be more externally valid and generalizable. Thus, researchers should consider using naturally occurring texts consistent with those read by their sample of interest.

Another noteworthy point relates to the level of detail researchers offer in their publications, particularly in their descriptions of the perspectives. Researchers often did not explicitly note the relationship between perspectives in their publications. This was evident by the fact that Barzilai and colleagues (2018) classified less than half of the intervention studies in their review as either complementary or conflicting, as they only classified studies when the relationship was explicitly stated by the authors. While it is often possible for readers to obtain this information through a careful read of the manuscript or by reaching out to the author for clarification, ideally researchers should include these labels explicitly in their published research.

Finally, within the research reviewed herein, there appear to be nuanced differences between studies with regard to the nature of the complementary relationship. For example, there were varying degrees of overlap between the perspectives in the different studies. While all of the studies employed multiple perspectives, some complementary perspectives were comprised of independent texts (e.g., Daher & Kiewra, 2016) while others had substantial overlap (e.g., Karimi, 2015). Likewise, there may be other levels of distinction that characterize multiple complementary perspectives (e.g., within or across domain, whether or not the perspectives reference each other) and subsequently influence individuals' learning. Given that research in this area is in the nascent stages, it is unclear what key aspects or subtypes of complementary perspectives may emerge, but greater detail regarding descriptions of the employed texts and their characteristics will aid future investigations along these lines.

CONCLUSION

As the author aimed to synthesize this body of literature, the writing of this chapter actually served as an exercise in integrating across multiple perspectives. The set of

20 manuscripts derived from the multi-pronged literature search made up the multiple (primarily) complementary perspectives. Key information from each of these perspectives was organized using a table. Serving as a form of integration support, the table enabled the author to derive a set of trends and patterns across the body of research in order to identify gaps and forward recommendations that will ideally serve to propel future investigations in this area. It is this author's hope that such future research will enable leaners like Josephine to better integrate information from multiple complementary perspectives, such as that learned in her introductory biology course.

ACKNOWLEDGMENTS

I wish to extend my sincere thanks to both S. Barzilai and L. Primor for kindly providing the citation lists from their respective reviews.

REFERENCES

*indicates article included in the review.

Anmarkrud, Ø., Bråten, I., & Strømsø, H. I. (2014). Multiple-documents literacy: Strategic processing, source awareness, and argumentation when reading multiple conflicting documents. *Learning and Individual Differences, 30*, 64–76.

Ausubel, D. P., Novak, J. D., & Hanesian, H. (1978). *Educational psychology: A cognitive view*. New York: Holt: Rinehart, & Winston.

*Barzilai, S., & Eshet-Alkalai, Y. (2015). The role of epistemic perspectives in comprehension of multiple author viewpoints. *Learning and Instruction, 36*, 86–103.

Barzilai, S., Zohar, A. R., & Mor-Hagani, S. (2018). Promoting integration of multiple texts: A review of instructional approaches and practices. *Educational Psychology Review*, doi:http://dx.doi.org.ezproxy1.lib.asu.edu/10.1007/s10648-018-9436-8

*Blaum, D., Griffin, T. D., Wiley, J., & Britt, M. A. (2017). Thinking about global warming: Effect of policy-related documents and prompts on learning about causes of climate change. *Discourse Processes, 54*(4), 303–316.

*Boscolo, P., Arfé, B., & Quarisa, M. (2007). Improving the quality of students' academic writing: An intervention study. *Studies in Higher Education, 32*(4), 419–438.

Braasch, J. L. G., & Bråten, I. (2017). The Discrepancy-Induced Source Comprehension (D-ISC) Model: Basic assumptions and preliminary evidence. *Educational Psychologist, 52*, 167–181. doi:https://doi.org/10.1080/00461520.2017.1323219

*Braasch, J. L. G., McCabe, R. M., & Daniel, F. (2016). Content integration across multiple documents reduces memory for sources. *Reading and Writing, 29*(8), 1571–1598.

Brante, E. W., & Strømsø, H. I. (2018). Sourcing in text comprehension: A review of interventions targeting sourcing skills. *Educational Psychology Review, 30*(3), 773–799.

Bråten, I., & Braasch, J. L. G. (2018). The role of conflict in multiple source use. In J. L. G. Braasch, I. Bråten, & M. T. McCrudden (Eds.), *Handbook of multiple source use* (pp. 184–202). New York: Routledge.

*Cerdán, R., & Vidal-Abarca, E. (2008). The effects of tasks on integrating information from multiple documents. *Journal of Educational Psychology, 100*(1), 209–222. doi:http://dx.doi.org.ezproxy1.lib.asu.edu/10.1037/0022-0663.100.1.209

*Daher, T. A., & Kiewra, K. A. (2016). An investigation of SOAR study strategies for learning from multiple online resources. *Contemporary Educational Psychology, 46*, 10–21.

Eccles, J. S., Adler, T. F., Futterman, R., Goff, S. B., Kaczala, C. M., Meece, J. L., & Midgley, C. (1983). Expectancies, values, and academic behaviors. In J. T. Spence (Eds.), *Achievement and achievement motivation* (pp. 75–146). San Francisco, CA: W. H. Freeman.

*Firetto, C. M., & Van Meter, P. N. (2018). Inspiring integration in college biology students reading multiple texts. *Learning and Individual Differences, 65*, 123–134. doi:https://doi.org/10.1016/j.lindif.2018.05.011

Fox, E., & Maggioni, L. (2018). Multiple source use in history. In J. L. G. Braasch, I. Bråten, & M. T. McCrudden (Eds.), *Handbook of multiple source use* (pp. 205–220). New York: Routledge.

Graham, S., & Harris, K. R. (2005). *Writing better: Effective strategies for teaching students with learning difficulties*. Baltimore, MD: Brookes.

*Griffin, T. D., Wiley, J., Britt, M. A., & Salas, C. R. (2012). The role of CLEAR thinking in learning science from multiple-document inquiry tasks. *International Electronic Journal of Elementary Education*, 5(1), 63–78.

*Hilbert, T. S., & Renkl, A. (2008). Concept mapping as a follow-up strategy to learning from texts: What characterizes good and poor mappers?. *Instructional Science*, 36(1), 53–73.

Jairam, D., & Kiewra, K. (2009). An investigation of the SOAR study method. *Journal of Advanced Academics*, 20(4), 602–629.

*Karimi, M. N. (2015). EFL learners' multiple documents literacy: Effects of a strategy-directed intervention program. *Modern Language Journal*, 99(1), 40–56. doi:http://dx.doi.org.ezproxy1.lib.asu.edu/10.1111/modl.12192

*Karimi, M. N., & Atai, M. R. (2014). ESAP students' comprehension of multiple technical reading texts: Insights from personal epistemological beliefs. *Reading Psychology*, 35(8), 736–761. doi:http://dx.doi.org.ezproxy1.lib.asu.edu/10.1080/02702711.2013.802753

Kintsch, W. (1988). The role of knowledge in discourse comprehension: A construction-integration model. *Psychological Review*, 95(2), 163.

*Le Bigot, L., & Rouet, J.-F. (2007). The impact of presentation format, task assignment, and prior knowledge on students' comprehension of multiple online documents. *Journal of Literacy Research*, 39(4), 445–470.

*Lehmann, T., Rott, B., & Schmidt-Borcherding, F. (2019). Promoting pre-service teachers' integration of professional knowledge: Effects of writing tasks and prompts on learning from multiple documents. *Instructional Science*, 47(1), 99–126. doi:http://dx.doi.org.ezproxy1.lib.asu.edu/10.1007/s11251-018-9472-2

*Linderholm, T., Kwon, H., & Therriault, D. J. (2014). Instructions that enhance multiple-text comprehension for college readers. *Journal of College Reading and Learning*, 45(1), 3–19.

*Linderholm, T., Therriault, D. J., & Kwon, H. (2014). Multiple science text processing: Building comprehension skills for college student readers. *Reading Psychology*, 35(4), 332–356. doi:10.1080/02702711.2012.726696

*List, A. (2018). Strategies for comprehending and integrating texts and videos. *Learning and Instruction*, 57, 34–46. doi:https://doi.org/10.1016/j.learninstruc.2018.01.008

List, A., & Alexander, P. A. (2018). Toward an integrated framework of multiple text use. *Educational Psychologist*, doi:10.1080/00461520.2018.1505514

*Martinez, I., Mateos, M., Martín, E., & Rijlaarsdam, G. (2015). Learning history by composing synthesis texts: Effects of an instructional programme on learning, reading and writing processes, and text quality. *Journal of Writing Research*, 7(2), 275–302.

*Mateos, M., Martín, E., Villalón, R., & Luna, M. (2008). Reading and writing to learn in secondary education: Online processing activity and written products in summarizing and synthesizing tasks. *Reading and Writing*, 21(7), 675–697.

*Mateos, M., & Solé, I. (2009). Synthesising information from various texts: A study of procedures and products at different educational levels. *European Journal of Psychology of Education*, 24(4), 435–451.

Mayer, R. (1996). Learning strategies for making sense out of expository text: The SOI model for guiding three cognitive processes in knowledge construction. *Educational Psychology Review*, 8(4), 357–371.

Perfetti, C. A., Rouet, J.-F., & Britt, M. A. (1999). Towards a theory of documents representation. In H. van Oostendorp & S. R. Goldman (Eds.), *The construction of mental representations during reading* (pp. 99–122). Mahwah, NJ: Erlbaum.

Primor, L., & Katzir, T. (2018). Measuring multiple text integration: A review. *Frontiers in Psychology*, 9, 1–16. doi: 10.3389/fpsyg.2018.02294

Rouet, J.-F., & Britt, M. A. (2011). Relevance processes in multiple document comprehension. In M. T. McCrudden, J. P. Magliano, & G. Schraw (Eds.), *Text relevance and learning from text* (pp. 19–52). Greenwich, CT: Information Age.

Spivey, N. N. (1997) *The constructivist metaphor: Reading, writing and the making of meaning*. San Diego, CA: Academic Press.

Stadtler, M., & Bromme, R. (2014). The content-source integration model: A taxonomic description of how readers comprehend conflicting scientific information. In D. N. Rapp & J. L. G. Braasch (Eds.), *Processing inaccurate information: Theoretical and applied perspectives from cognitive science and the educational sciences* (pp. 379–402). Cambridge, MA: MIT Press.

Van Dijk, T. A., & Kintsch, W. (1983). *Strategies of discourse comprehension* (pp. 11–12). New York: Academic Press.

*Wiley, J., & Voss, J. (1999). Constructing arguments from multiple sources: Tasks that promote understanding and not just memory for text. *Journal of Educational Psychology, 91*(2), 301–311.

Wineburg, S. (1991). Historical problem solving: A study of the cognitive processes used in the evaluation of documentary and pictorial evidence. *Journal of Educational Psychology, 83*, 73–87. doi:http://dx.doi.org/10.1037/0022-0663.83.1.73

15

LEARNING FROM MULTIPLE PERSPECTIVES
Processes and Strategies Associated with Reading Dual-Position Texts

Catherine M. Bohn-Gettler
COLLEGE OF SAINT BENEDICT – ST. JOHN'S UNIVERSITY

ABSTRACT

Learning from multiple perspectives is influenced by both the textual material and the reader's strategies. One text structure, dual-position texts, can be a vehicle for fostering thinking about two opposing views on an issue, appropriate strategy use, and a developing of a balanced understanding of multiple perspectives on controversial issues. In the context of a classification system for expository texts addressing multiple perspectives, dual-position texts are considered neutral (i.e., with the intent to inform, not persuade), two-sided, nonrefutation texts. The strategies readers apply while learning from dual-position texts occur in the context of the automatic and strategic processes associated with reading comprehension, such as epistemic validation. These processes can influence how readers engage, comprehend, and are persuaded by dual-position texts. However, optimal learning of multiple perspectives from dual-position texts varies as a function of complex, interactive variables such as text features, knowledge, contexts, and beliefs. This chapter synthesizes work in this field to create a more coherent frame for research and practice.

Key words: dual-position text, expository, text structures, comprehension, processing

Our current society often requires that we process ambiguous and complex issues, making it vital for readers to engage with and understand multiple and competing perspectives. Making informed decisions about controversial issues requires effective reasoning and critical thinking in which readers compare and contrast multiple sides of an issue, evaluate the soundness and reasoning behind each argument, integrate competing ideas, and carefully consider evidence to inform justified conclusions

(Nussbaum, 2011; West, Toplak, & Stanovich, 2008). Although effortful, this type of processing prevents readers from drawing overly simplistic or absolutist conclusions about a topic for which the evidence may be inconclusive. In short, engaging in critical thinking and effective reasoning, based in an understanding of both sides of an issue, helps readers make informed and justified decisions.

It is therefore vital to understand what text structures might best support such critical thinking. For example, students may be asked to read a single text presenting arguments in favor of and opposed to teaching intelligent design in science classrooms (Bohn-Gettler & McCrudden, 2018), or whether genetically modified food should be marketed (Mason & Boscolo, 2004). Or students may be asked to consider multiple texts, in which each text conveys a different, conflicting perspective on topics such as global warming or vaccinations (Maier, Richter, & Britt, 2018). In this chapter, we consider one text type (i.e., dual-position text) as a means of engaging students in thinking critically and evaluatively about multiple perspectives. This chapter will situate dual-position texts in the context of other texts types, describe the processes underlying the comprehension of dual-positions texts, consider the ways in which dual-position texts may support learning from multiple perspectives, and reflect upon directions for future research.

Although dual-position texts are a common avenue through which readers encounter descriptions of multiple perspectives, most research focuses on one-sided texts or learning from multiple one-sided documents. The careful study of one-sided texts and multiple documents is important for learning from multiple perspectives, but it is likewise critical to understand dual-position texts given their prevalence and potential for supporting the development of an informed citizenry who can engage in critical thinking through the consideration of multiple alternative perspectives (Lombardi, Danielson, & Young, 2016; West et al., 2008). This chapter defines dual-position texts by situating them in the context of other expository text structures, explains how readers process dual-position texts, considers how dual-position texts interact with other factors to influence learning, and proposes implications and future directions for the field.

SITUATING DUAL-POSITION TEXTS: CLASSIFYING TEXT STRUCTURES FOR MULTIPLE PERSPECTIVES

The primary goal of dual-positions text is to convey opposing perspectives related to a controversial issue. Dual-position texts are sometimes called two-sided nonrefutational texts (Andiliou, Ramsay, Murphy, & Fast, 2012; Buehl, Alexander, Murphy, & Sperl, 2001) because their intention is not to persuade or refute a specific perspective, but instead to inform the reader of the rationale behind conflicting perspectives. As such, dual-position texts can be found in media, digital environments, and textbooks – any source in which the goal is to provide a neutral and balanced perspective on an issue (Wiley, 2005).

Dual-position texts represent a subtype of expository text. Expository texts provide factual information related to a particular topic (Wolfe, 2005). They often contain a hierarchical organization such that an overarching topic or argument is presented, which is then supported by other subtopics and arguments related to the overarching topic (Hyönä, Lorch, & Kaakinen, 2002). Prior work has examined the varying structures of expository texts, such as compare-contrast, problem-response, chronological, and descriptive. This work yields a variety of important findings, such as revealing how different text structures vary in cohesion and organization (Meyer & Freedle, 1984) and interact with other variables, such as working memory and reading goals, to influence moment-by-moment processing and comprehension (Bohn-Gettler & Kendeou, 2014; Hyönä et al., 2002).

Although prior research describes larger categories of expository text (e.g., Meyer & Freedle, 1984), a classification system for expository texts that specifically addresses one or more perspectives on a controversial issue is warranted. There are conflicting findings regarding how readers process and learn from texts addressing controversial issues. For example, some studies document that readers spend more time reading belief-inconsistent arguments to refute them (Edwards & Smith, 1996; Kardash & Howell, 2000), whereas other studies found that readers spend more time processing belief-consistent information (Taber & Lodge, 2006). Other studies found that processing time depended on text structure (Maier & Richter, 2013) or argument quality (Wolfe, Tanner, & Taylor, 2013), and textual memory depended on task relevance (Bohn-Gettler & McCrudden, 2018). It may be that differences in the text formats used in these studies could explain discrepancies in findings.

Texts addressing multiple perspectives can vary widely in terms of content, aims, and structure. For example, does the text describe one or multiple viewpoints? Is the intent of the text to persuade the reader, and if so, how? Therefore, before describing the processing invoked when reading dual-position texts and the implications for learning from multiple perspectives, I first propose a classification system for texts that address multiple perspectives. Please see Figure 15.1 for a schematic of the classification system. (Note that this classification system is not only important for single texts, but each format may also extend to multiple text situations.)

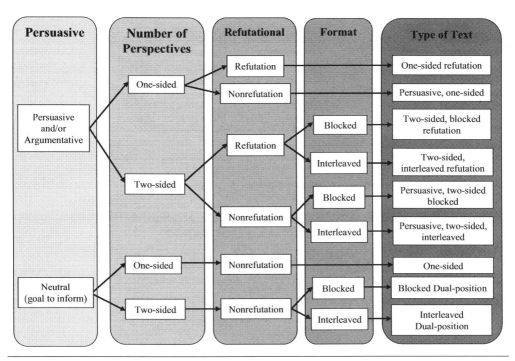

Figure 15.1 Classification of Expository Texts Describing Issues for which there are Multiple Perspectives.

This classification system applies to texts that address a topic for which there are opposing viewpoints, and may include topics about which readers have misconceptions. The type of text is then defined by the following questions: Is the intent of the text to persuade the reader? If the text is written to persuade the reader, is it refutational or nonrefutational? Regardless of whether it intends to persuade the reader, does the text address one or multiple opposing perspectives? And finally, if the text addresses multiple opposing perspectives, is the text presented in a blocked or interleaved manner? Please note that these categories may not always be mutually exclusive – for example, there can be gradations in the persuasiveness of a text. In addition, although many other factors are informative to the quality of the text (such as the quality and plausibility of the arguments, or whether the sources are credible), this classification system deals with the structure, not the content or source, of the text.

Is the Text Written to Persuade the Reader?

Texts addressing multiple perspectives can adopt one of two stances: to persuade readers (i.e., to advocate for a particular position), or to provide information to readers in a neutral manner (i.e., not advocating for a particular position). Although there can be gradations of persuasiveness, for the purposes of this chapter, persuasiveness is defined based on the intent of the author to persuade, and not defined based on the text's impact on the reader. Note that argumentative texts are a type of persuasive text, but not all persuasive texts are argumentative. Argumentative texts attempt to persuade readers by providing an overarching claim followed by supporting arguments that are justified by reasons, evidence, and/or data (Britt, Kurby, Dandotkar, & Wolfe, 2007). (Also note, however, that the quality of the arguments may vary; Diakidoy, Christodoulou, Floros, Iordanou, & Kargopoulos, 2015). Persuasive texts can be found in a variety of places, such as books, websites, blogs, essays, editorials in news media, and more.

A large body of work has examined persuasive and argumentative texts in various forms (Diakidoy et al., 2015; Iordanou, 2010; Murphy, Holleran, Long, & Zeruth, 2005). Argumentative texts have been found to be effective for modifying readers' beliefs (but only when readers positively evaluate the text; Diakidoy et al., 2015), and improve recall when readers approach argumentative texts with an evaluation goal. Although argumentative texts can be persuasive, they can be complex because they contain claims, qualifiers, questions, concessions, and more. Two-sided argumentative texts may further contain counterclaims and refutations (Diakidoy, Ioannou, & Christoudoulou, 2017). This complexity can cause readers to experience difficulty distinguishing between main claims and individual arguments (Diakidoy et al., 2015; Larson, Britt, & Larson, 2004).

In contrast, some texts are written to be neutral, meaning that they are written with the intent to inform the reader about a topic, and are not written with the intention to persuade or influence the reader's views or actions. For the purposes of this chapter, these will be labelled as "neutral" texts.[1] Neutral texts can be found in media articles attempting to present a balanced perspective, textbooks and learning resources when describing various sides of a debate, and more. Dual-position texts are considered neutral because they are informative without seeking to persuade: they seek to describe varying perspectives on an issue in a neutral manner for the purposes of learning. Although readers may be persuaded by dual-position texts, the goal of the text is to be neutral, that is, to inform but not sway the reader in one direction or another.

Does the Text Address One or Multiple Perspectives?

Regardless of whether the goal is to persuade or inform, texts can vary in terms of the number of opposing arguments presented. A one-sided text presents one point of view, whereas a two-sided text provides two opposing, or alternate, points of view. When reading one-sided texts, readers are likely to engage in strategies that confirm their pre-existing knowledge and beliefs and disconfirm any statements that oppose their beliefs. Hence, readers tend to engage with such texts to build a case for their current beliefs, often paying attention to content that supports their point of view. If a reader is engaging with a text that conflicts with their pre-existing beliefs, they may either avoid reading it, engage in refutational strategies, or ignore arguments conflicting with their perspective. In this way, readers' views tend to become more extreme. Therefore, one-sided texts are often less effective at persuasion in comparison to two-sided texts (Andiliou et al., 2012; Buehl et al., 2001).

Two-sided texts present both opposing sides, and can be persuasive or neutral. There is some evidence that two-sided texts are more effective at helping readers to develop a deeper understanding of both sides of the issue and in modifying readers' beliefs (Andiliou et al., 2012; Buehl et al., 2001). However, the effectiveness of two-sided texts depends on several key variables, such as text structure, prior beliefs, and more. Dual-position texts are considered two-sided, neutral texts. (Note that, in Figure 15.1, two-sided texts can be persuasive. Dual-position texts contain two opposing viewpoints but do not attempt to persuade, and hence are only listed in the non-persuasive category.)

If the Text is Persuasive, does it Utilize Refutation?

Refutation texts present a misconception or invalid argument, explain why it is incorrect, and then provide the correct information with supporting evidence (Hynd, 2001). Therefore, refutation texts always promote one perspective over another, and are consequently persuasive (Alexander, Buehl, & Sperl, 2001; Guzzetti, Snyder, Glass, & Gamas, 1993). Refutation texts are often one-sided (but can sometimes be two-sided) and can be presented in a blocked or interleaved manner (which will be described in the next section).

Refutation texts are one of the most persuasive text forms, because they provide explanations for why a misconception is incorrect (Braasch, Goldman, & Wiley, 2013; Kendeou & O'Brien, 2014). Because refutation texts force readers to consider alternative perspectives even when they hold initially strong beliefs, they are among the most powerful ways to bring about conceptual change and convince readers to alter their views (Buehl et al., 2001; Kendeou & O'Brien, 2014; Murphy, Long, Holleran, & Esterly, 2003).

Nonrefutation texts do not refute a particular idea or misconception. Instead, they simply present ideas and evidence, as is the case for dual-position texts. Although dual-position texts are not refutational, some characteristics of refutation texts may have implications for dual-position texts. When readers hold misconceptions, explicit refutation is considered required for knowledge revision to occur (implying that dual-position texts, because they do not contain refutation, would not be successful at promoting knowledge revision). Such refutation highlights conflicts between misconceptions and the correct ideas, making both conflicting pieces of information active in working memory simultaneously – a principle referred to as co-activation. Co-activation allows the new, conflicting information to be integrated with prior knowledge and beliefs, leading to increased critical evaluation, an increased likelihood of identifying challenges, and improved post-reading knowledge and learning (Kendeou & O'Brien, 2014). Although dual-position texts are not refutational, they can present conflicting information in a manner that could enable co-activation. This is more likely to occur when the text is interleaved than when blocked, a topic to which we now turn.

If the Text is Two-Sided, is it Structured in a Blocked or Interleaved Format?

Recall that two-sided texts present two opposing perspectives, side A and side B. In a blocked format, the entirety of side A is presented, followed by the entirety of side B. In an interleaved format, the text alternates back and forth between sides A and B, sometimes in a point-counterpoint fashion (Wiley, 2005). Dual-position (i.e., two-sided nonpersuasive) and two-sided persuasive texts can come in either format. However, because one-sided texts only present one perspective on an issue, they are not interleaved. The distinction between blocked and interleaved can matter in terms of processing, memory, persuasiveness, and more (Maier & Richter, 2013; Wiley, 2005). In particular, although dual-position texts do not refute, interleaved dual-position texts bear some similarities to refutation texts: Interleaved dual-position texts can enable coactivation of competing concepts, which is described later in this chapter.

DUAL-POSITION TEXTS

With this classification system, researchers can consider the varying structures of expository texts describing issues for which there are multiple perspectives. The classification system demonstrates how varying properties can combine in complex ways to influence the structure of the text and may provide a frame for understanding discrepant findings regarding why some texts result in belief change or conceptual change, whereas others do not influence learning or change.

In this classification system, because dual-position texts maintain a neutral perspective by seeking to inform, and present two opposing perspectives, they are considered neutral (i.e., not intended to persuade), two-sided, and nonrefutational (Guzzetti et al., 1993). When readers hold moderate initial positions on the topic, dual-position texts tend to be more persuasive than one-sided nonrefutational texts, but less persuasive than refutational texts (Buehl et al., 2001). In contrast, when readers hold a strong initial position on the topic, the effectiveness of dual-position texts in promoting understanding of both sides of the issue decreases as readers shift to belief-maintenance processing (Andiliou et al., 2012). However, dual-position texts with an interleaved structure tend to be more persuasive than texts with a blocked structure (although it is unknown how interleaved dual-position texts compare with refutation texts) for reasons that lie in the cognitive processes behind the processing of dual-position text (Maier et al., 2018; Wiley, 2005).

PROCESSES UNDERLYING THE COMPREHENSION OF DUAL-POSITION TEXTS

This chapter situates learning from dual-position texts in prominent models of text comprehension, including the construction-integration model (Kintsch & van Dijk, 1978), the RI-Val model (Cook & O'Brien, 2014), and the Landscape model (van den Broek, Risden, Fletcher, & Thurlow, 1996). The construction-integration model describes how readers can encode information from a text along three levels: the surface structure, representing the exact words from the text; the textbase, where readers encode gist meanings from the text; and the situation model, where readers make inferences to connect current text with prior knowledge and earlier text. The situation model level is assumed to be the deepest level of comprehension (Kintsch & van Dijk, 1978).

Comprehension models also assume that readers approach texts with limited cognitive resources: Working memory, or how much information readers can mentally manipulate at a single time, is limited (Kintsch & van Dijk, 1978; Miller, 1956). In addition, knowledge in memory is organized as a network of concepts called schemata. When one concept becomes activated, other related concepts are then activated. Readers attempt to integrate the new textual information with the activated knowledge. If an inconsistency between the new information and the activated concepts is detected, readers can resolve this conflict by either suppressing some concepts while strengthening other concepts (i.e., ignoring the inconsistent information), or work to integrate the conflicting information (Cook & O'Brien, 2014; Kintsch & van Dijk, 1978; van den Broek et al., 1996). To accomplish such integration, epistemic validation may be required.

Epistemic Validation

Recall that dual-position texts often highlight conflicting information by comparing and contrasting different perspectives, which increases the likelihood that it will be noticed by readers. Because such incongruities may occur, epistemic validation (Richter, 2011, 2015; Richter, Münchow, & Abendroth, Chapter 16) may be required, in which a reader validates the incoming text information against their prior knowledge and beliefs to make judgements regarding whether the information is true or plausible. To accomplish this, readers utilize prior knowledge and their own criteria for validity. Epistemic validation, or epistemic monitoring, can occur either automatically (i.e., without the reader's active control or awareness) or strategically (i.e., in which the reader is consciously applying a particular strategy; Richter, 2011).

Automatic epistemic monitoring occurs when readers automatically, or without being explicitly aware of it, monitor whether incoming information is consistent or inconsistent with prior text and prior knowledge. Automatic epistemic monitoring occurs through a nonconscious spread of activation, and the existing schemata do not change. Instead, consistent information is strengthened, and inconsistent information is suppressed or ignored. This type of processing does not place many demands on readers' limited cognitive resources. Readers' goals can influence whether they engage in such automatic processing. For example, if readers are motivated to strengthen their current beliefs or have little motivation to deeply process the text (a goal that does not require epistemic elaboration, which will be discussed next), the default will be this automatic mode of processing (Richter, 2011; McCrudden, Chapter 12).

However, what happens when inconsistent information cannot be ignored? Depending on its structure, dual-position texts make it difficult to ignore inconsistent information because these texts explicitly compare similar and conflicting arguments for opposite sides of a controversial issue. When inconsistent information cannot be ignored, or if readers have a goal to actively consider conflicting viewpoints, readers can engage in a more effortful process known as epistemic elaboration (Richter, 2011). Epistemic elaboration is a strategic, knowledge-based process that requires motivation, cognitive resources, and prior knowledge. Despite being effortful, it is crucial for readers to achieve the cognitive flexibility necessary to understand an issue from both perspectives (Richter, 2011).

Epistemic elaboration is often accompanied by other reading strategies, such as text-based and knowledge-based inferences, to build a rich and coherent situation model (Richter, 2011). Text-based inferences occur when readers connect the information in the sentence they are currently reading to information presented earlier in the text. Knowledge-based inferences occur when readers connect information they are currently reading to prior knowledge (van den Broek, Risden, & Husebye-Hartmann, 1995). The combination of epistemic elaboration with other coherence-building processes helps readers to build a rich situation model that is balanced. This can then support the building of an informed perspective based on knowledge of both positions.

THE CONDITIONS UNDER WHICH DUAL-POSITION TEXTS CAN SUPPORT LEARNING FROM MULTIPLE PERSPECTIVES

Readers routinely engage in automatic processing, but do not regularly engage in epistemic elaboration. It is possible that the structure of a text could be one route for encouraging epistemic elaboration to enhance comprehension of both sides of a controversial issue and could perhaps be a route to change readers' stances. Unfortunately, surprisingly little research compares dual-position texts with other structures to directly test these assertions.

One hypothesis might be that dual-position texts persuade readers to change their stances because they evenly and neutrally present both sides of an issue. However, there are mixed findings in terms of the persuasiveness of two-sided nonrefutational (i.e., dual-position) texts (Andiliou et al., 2012; Mason & Boscolo, 2004; Wiley, 2005). Dual-position texts might be less consistent in promoting change because they are nonrefutational and therefore do not explicitly force readers to consider if they have any misconceptions and why such misconceptions may be incorrect. Another potential reason for the mixed findings may be related to reader motivation and beliefs. For example, if readers are motivated to engage in assimilative processing, they could actively ignore information that competes with their perspective. Further, if readers hold strong initial beliefs, they are less likely to be swayed by a dual-position text. In fact, dual-position texts sometimes lead readers to strengthen their initial positions (Andiliou et al., 2012).

Unfortunately, the literature remains inconclusive because other research suggests that dual-position texts may facilitate improved processing by fostering deep (as opposed to surface) learning. Because the goal of dual-position text is to integrate different perspectives, dual-position texts highlight inconsistencies and directly require readers to make connections and integrate the different perspectives. However, other than a handful of studies, there is surprisingly little research directly testing this assertion. One study found that dual-position texts increase readers' perceived knowledge of the text in comparison to their perceived knowledge after reading separate texts containing the same information (Andiliou et al., 2012). Other studies found that dual-position texts can improve the balance of the situation model, but only when texts are interleaved and when certain conditions are in place (Bohn-Gettler & McCrudden, 2018; Wiley, 2005). Therefore, the extant literature suggests that the effects of dual-position texts are often moderated by other variables, such as text format, topic beliefs, goals, and more.

Blocked versus Interleaved Formats of Dual-Position Texts

One moderating variable for the conditions under which dual-position texts influence processing, memory, and persuasion is whether the text is blocked or interleaved. A few studies provide evidence that interleaved texts support the building of situation models that better integrate both opposing perspectives. First, Wiley (2005) found that an interleaved format (compared to a blocked format) decreased readers' use of belief-supporting strategies – especially for readers with low prior knowledge. When the text was presented in a blocked format, readers with low prior knowledge engaged in strategies to confirm their beliefs and disconfirm belief-inconsistent information. After reading, readers with higher prior knowledge demonstrated increased knowledge for both sides of the position. In contrast, readers with lower prior knowledge were only able to build a more balanced and complete situation model with the interleaved text. After reading the blocked text, readers with lower prior knowledge demonstrated improved memory for belief-consistent information. Second, Bohn-Gettler and McCrudden (2018) found that, after engaging with an interleaved dual-position text, readers' recall was not biased by their beliefs. Third, Maier and Richter (2013) presented readers with texts presenting opposing perspectives on an issue. The interleaved presentations led to stronger situation models for both sides of the argument and reductions in belief biases. (Although Maier and Richter utilized multiple one-sided texts instead of a dual-position text, the results nevertheless align with Wiley, 2005.)

There are several reasons why interleaved dual-position texts may help readers build stronger situation models containing both opposing perspectives. Recall that, when readers encounter new information in a text, related concepts in their mental schema are automatically activated (Cook & O'Brien, 2014; Kintsch & van Dijk, 1978; van den Broek et al., 1996). Further, recall that refutation texts are particularly beneficial for learning, conceptual change, and persuasion because of the co-activation principle: competing information is activated simultaneously, which highlights differences and may encourage elaborative coherence-building processing in readers (Kendeou, Butterfuss, Kim, & Van Boekel, 2019; Kendeou & O'Brien, 2014). These principles may inform why blocked versus interleaved dual-position texts differentially support processing and the building of a balanced situation model containing accurate details about both competing perspectives.

When arguments are alternated in dual-position texts, they are closer in proximity. This keeps the conflicting ideas active in readers' limited working memories, thereby increasing the likelihood that they will be integrated with one another and with prior knowledge on a continuous basis (Maier & Richter, 2013; Wiley, 2005). This is because the concepts are more likely be co-activated (Kendeou & O'Brien, 2014) when the conflicting arguments are in closer proximity, which then heightens readers' awareness of the inconsistencies. Because readers are then more able to detect inconsistencies, they are more likely to engage in elaborative processes that build coherence and understanding (Maier et al., 2018; Wiley, 2005). This can therefore lead to a more balanced situation model (Maier & Richter, 2013).

In contrast, blocked structures result in conflicting arguments being farther in proximity. This makes the co-activation of conflicting ideas less likely, which can lead to assimilative and belief-biased processing. In addition, readers' pre-existing schemata for belief-consistent information tends to be richer, with more concepts and connections between concepts. This enables readers to more easily integrate belief-consistent information into their mental models, leading to a stronger network and a richer representation for belief-consistent information relative to belief-inconsistent information. When confronted with arguments inconsistent with their beliefs, the schemata is not as rich, reducing the number of possible connections (Maier et al., 2018; Wiley, 2005). Therefore, in blocked texts where conflicting arguments are farther in proximity, the likelihood of coactivating competing concepts is further reduced.

Knowledge, Goals, and Beliefs

In addition to text structure, a reader's knowledge, goals, and epistemological beliefs may produce conditions under which dual-position texts can optimally support learning. In fact, understanding such factors may help to transform our understandings of how and when dual-positions texts can foster versus hinder processing and comprehension – especially for texts in which readers may hold strong topic beliefs. (See Bråten & Strømsø, Chapter 10, for more information on epistemic beliefs; List, Chapter 11, for considerations of domain knowledge; and McCrudden, Chapter 12, for additional content regarding the influence of topic beliefs on processing.)

For example, Wiley (2005) found that possessing higher prior knowledge about a topic may allow readers to better integrate new information, even belief-inconsistent information, into their mental schema to form a more coherent situation model. When prior knowledge is low, readers may revert to relying upon their topic beliefs when encoding information into memory and later retrieving it, because they do not have enough prior knowledge to fully integrate the new incoming information (Wiley, 2005). Given that prior knowledge may support overcoming belief-biased processing, it is interesting to consider that high-knowledge readers who are sufficiently motivated to engage in epistemic elaboration showed improved comprehension processing when texts contained implausible information or invalid arguments. In contrast, the comprehension of low-knowledge readers decreased when texts contained implausible information. This interaction represents a reverse validity effect (Richter, 2011).

Importantly, the reverse validity effect occurs when readers are *sufficiently motivated* to engage in epistemic elaboration, introducing the idea that reader goals and motivations are important to consider regarding dual-position texts. To examine this, Bohn-Gettler and McCrudden (2018) asked readers to think-aloud about an interleaved dual-position text with the goal of focusing on either side A or side B. When evaluating the text content during reading, readers engaged in confirmation strategies for belief-consistent information, and disconfirmation strategies for belief-inconsistent information – overriding their goals to focus on a particular side, and consistent with other research (Edwards & Smith, 1996; Maier et al., 2018). However, readers' post-reading recall was not influenced by topic beliefs. Instead, participants asked to focus on side A recalled more content relevant to side A, and participants asked to focus on side B recalled more content relevant to side B (Bohn-Gettler & McCrudden, 2018), aligning with prior work on relevance and reading goals (McCrudden, Magliano, & Schraw, 2010). Therefore, although beliefs can influence processing for dual-position texts, reader goals may, in some cases, reduce belief-biased processing (Bohn-Gettler & McCrudden, 2018).

Another factor that may influence readers' goals and motivation when approaching a dual-position text is their epistemological beliefs (Moshman, 2015). (See Bråten & Strømsø, Chapter 11, for more information on this topic.) Complex epistemological beliefs, such as the belief that knowledge is uncertain and changing, increase the likelihood that readers will use more effortful epistemic strategies to enhance learning, evaluate the quality of evidence, and be willing to change prior conceptions (Mason & Boscolo, 2004; Richter & Schmid, 2010). In contrast, naïve epistemological beliefs, such as beliefs that knowledge is certain, are associated with oversimplified conclusions (Schommer, 1990), the usage of fewer cognitive strategies, and ignoring and distorting information (Kardash & Howell, 2000).

If readers have strong pre-existing topic beliefs about a controversial issue and hold naïve beliefs about learning, it increases the likelihood of ignoring and distorting belief-inconsistent information. Kardash and Howell (2000) found that, when interacting with dual-position texts, beliefs about the speed of learning influence the overall number of cognitive processes that readers demonstrated. Schommer (1990) similarly found that readers with naïve beliefs provided oversimplified and absolute conclusions after reading a dual-position text. Mason and Boscolo (2004) elaborated on this work by presenting a blocked dual-position text. Although all participants became more neutral toward the controversial topic, possessing complex epistemological beliefs facilitated this change. Therefore, supporting the development of complex epistemological beliefs can foster readers' understandings of multiple perspectives from dual-position texts.

CONCLUSION

Given the complexity of the issues facing our current society, it is important to understand how varying text structures can facilitate readers' comprehension of multiple, conflicting perspectives. Understanding the structures that are most beneficial for learning and for encouraging thinking about different views on an issue is vital for helping citizens make educated, reasoned, and justified decisions. Dual-position texts may offer a format to introduce readers to multiple competing perspectives in a neutral way, such that the intent of the text is not to persuade the reader. This can be appealing to many readers seeking to learn and may present benefits for comprehension and processing (albeit under certain conditions). In particular, dual-position texts may help readers integrate opposing sides of an issue when the text is interleaved, can support readers with less knowledge about a topic, and are especially beneficial for readers with more complex epistemological beliefs.

However, understanding how dual-position texts may or may not differ from other expository text structures that address multiple perspectives is critical. This chapter proposed a classification system that may help guide future research in the building of a more coherent body of work on dual-position texts. Such work would examine whether differences in the varying text structures identified facilitate or debilitate learning from multiple perspectives regarding complex topics. Furthermore, the description of how dual-position texts are likely processed aligns with work examining texts of other structures (e.g., Richter, 2011), making it important for future work to examine how each processing component applies specifically to dual-position texts. This could lead to a better understanding of what processes extend across varying text structures, and how particular text structures and content may elicit variations in strategies and learning. Another fruitful area for future research might be to determine whether certain text structures, such as dual-position texts, can mitigate the effects of belief bias, or reduce the moderating effects of variables such as epistemological beliefs and prior knowledge. In addition, considering how emotions may interact with beliefs to influence the comprehension of dual-position texts would be an important consideration (Bohn-Gettler, 2019). Furthermore, this chapter did not consider the quality of the arguments presented in dual-position texts, but connections to such work would be beneficial to our understanding of how to promote learning from multiple perspectives (Lombardi et al., 2016). Finally, future work would benefit from studying the expansion of use of dual-position texts to capture more multifaceted and multi-positional issues.

Dual-position texts play an important role in learning, although this is somewhat dependent on their structure, the reader, and the context. When dual-position text is interleaved, it can especially support readers with lower prior knowledge, can facilitate integration, lead to the building of a more balanced situation model, and potentially increase strategic epistemic elaboration. Understanding how to support students as they engage with dual-position texts and learning how to respond when students have varying levels of prior knowledge, epistemological beliefs, and topic beliefs, can support learning. In addition, helping students develop in their critical thinking skills to deeply consider two sides of an issue and evaluate the plausibility of various arguments will foster critical thinking skills when engaging with dual-position texts.

NOTE

1   Some literature utilizes the term *expository* texts to refer to texts with a neutral stance (Andiliou et al., 2012). However, other literature defines *expository* as texts providing factual information about a topic (Wolfe, 2005), which can come in a variety of structures and adopt either a particular stance *or* a neutral stance. Hence, this chapter utilizes the term *neutral* to avoid confusing terminology.

REFERENCES

Alexander, P. A., Buehl, M. M., & Sperl, C. T. (2001). The persuasiveness of persuasive discourse. *International Journal of Educational Research, 35*, 651–674. doi:10.1016/S0883-0355(02)00008-3

Andiliou, A., Ramsay, C. M., Murphy, P. K., & Fast, J. (2012). Weighing opposing positions: Examining the effects of intratextual persuasive messages on students' knowledge and beliefs. *Contemporary Educational Psychology, 37*, 113–127. doi:10.1016/j.cedpsych.2011.10.001

Bohn-Gettler, C. M. (2019). Getting a grip: The PET framework for studying how reader emotions influence comprehension. *Discourse Processes*, doi:10.1080/0163853X.2019.1611174

Bohn-Gettler, C. M., & Kendeou, P. (2014). The interplay of reader goals, working memory, and text structure during reading. *Contemporary Educational Psychology, 39*(3), 206–219. doi:10.1016/j.cedpsych.2014.05.003

Bohn-Gettler, C. M., & McCrudden, M. T. (2018). Effects of task relevance instructions and topic beliefs on reading processes and memory. *Discourse Processes, 55*(4), 410–431. doi:10.1080/0163853X.2017.1292824

Braasch, J. L. G., Goldman, S. R., & Wiley, J. (2013). The influences of text and reader characteristics on learning from refutation in science texts. *Journal of Educational Psychology, 105*(3), 561–578. doi:10.1037/a0032627

Britt, M. A., Kurby, C. A., Dandotkar, S., & Wolfe, C. R. (2007). I agreed to what? Memory for simple argument claims. *Discourse Processes, 45*(1), 52–84. doi:10.1080/01638530701739207

Buehl, M. M., Alexander, P. A., Murphy, P. K., & Sperl, C. T. (2001). Profiling persuasion: The role of beliefs, knowledge, and interest in the processing of persuasive texts that vary by argument structure. *Journal of Literary Research, 33*(2), 269–301.

Cook, A. E., & O'Brien, E. J. (2014). Knowledge activation, integration, and validation during narrative comprehension. *Discourse Processes, 51*(1/2), 26–49. doi:10.1080/0163853X.2013.855107

Diakidoy, I.-A. N., Christodoulou, S. A., Floros, G., Iordanou, K., & Kargopoulos, P. V. (2015). Forming a belief: The contribution of comprehension to the evaluation and persuasive impact of argumentative text. *British Journal of Educational Psychology, 85*, 300–315.

Diakidoy, I.-A. N., Ioannou, M. C., & Christoudoulou, S. A. (2017). Reading argumentative texts: Comprehension and evaluation goals and outcomes. *Reading and Writing, 30*, 1869–1890. doi:10.1007/s11145-017-9757-x

Edwards, K., & Smith, E. E. (1996). A disconfirmation bias in the evaluation of arguments. *Journal of Personality and Social Psychology, 71*, 5–24.

Guzzetti, B. J., Snyder, T. E., Glass, G. V., & Gamas, W. S. (1993). Promoting conceptual change in science: A comparative meta-analysis of instructional interventions from reading education and science education. *Reading Research Quarterly, 28*(2), 116–159.

Hynd, C. (2001). Refutational texts and the change process. *International Journal of Educational Research, 35*(7/8), 699–714.

Hyönä, J., Lorch, R. F., & Kaakinen, J. K. (2002). Individual differences in reading to summarize expository text: Evidence from eye fixation patterns. *Journal of Educational Psychology, 94*(1), 44–55.

Iordanou, K. (2010). Developing argument skills across scientific and social domains. *Journal of Cognition and Development, 11*, 293–327. doi:10.1080/15248372.2010.485335

Kardash, C. M., & Howell, K. L. (2000). Effects of epistemological beliefs and topic-specific beliefs on undergraduates' cognitive and strategic processing of dual-positional text. *Journal of Educational Psychology, 92*(3), 524–535. doi:10.1037/0022-0663.92.3.524

Kendeou, P., Butterfuss, R., Kim, J., & Van Boekel, M. (2019). Knowledge revision through the lenses of the three-pronged approach. *Memory and Cognition, 47*(1), 33–46. doi:10.3758/s13421-018-0848-y

Kendeou, P., & O'Brien, E. J. (2014). The Knowledge Revision Components (KReC) framework: Processes and mechanisms. In D. N. Rapp & J. L. G. Braasch (Eds.), *Processing inaccurate information: Theoretical and applied perspectives from cognitive science and the educational sciences* (pp. 353–377). Cambridge, MA: MIT Press.

Kintsch, W., & van Dijk, T. A. (1978). Toward a model of text comprehension and production. *Psychological Review, 85*(5), 363–394. doi:10.1037/0033-295X.85.5.363

Larson, M., Britt, M. A., & Larson, A. A. (2004). Disfluencies in comprehending argumentative texts. *Reading Psychology, 25*, 205–224. doi:10.1080/02702710490489908

Lombardi, D., Danielson, R. W., & Young, N. (2016). A plausible connection: Models examining the relations between evaluation, plausibility, and the refutation text effect. *Learning and Instruction, 44*, 74–86. doi:10.1016/j.learninstruc.2016.03.003

Maier, J., & Richter, T. (2013). Text belief consistency effects in the comprehension of multiple texts with conflicting information. *Cognition and Instruction, 31*(2), 151–175. doi:10.1080/07370008.2013.769997

Maier, J., Richter, T., & Britt, M. A. (2018). Cognitive processes underlying the text-belief consistency effect: An eye-movement study. *Applied Cognitive Psychology, 32*, 171–185. doi:10.1002/acp.3391

Mason, L., & Boscolo, P. (2004). Role of epistemological understanding and interest in interpreting a controversy and in topic-specific belief change. *Contemporary Educational Psychology, 29*, 103–128.

McCrudden, M. T., Magliano, J. P., & Schraw, G. (2010). Exploring how relevance instructions affect personal reading intentions, reading goals, and text processing: A mixed methods study. *Contemporary Educational Psychology, 35*(4), 229–241. doi:10.1016/j.cedpsych.2009.12.001

Meyer, B. J. F., & Freedle, R. O. (1984). Effects of discourse type on recall. *American Educational Research Journal, 21*(1), 121–143. doi:10.2307/1162357

Miller, G. A. (1956). The magical number seven, plus or minus two: Some limits on our capacity for processing information. *Psychological Review, 63*(2), 81–97. doi:10.1037/0033-295X.101.2.343

Moshman, D. (2015). *Epistemic cognition and development: The psychology of justification and truth.* New York: Taylor & Francis.

Murphy, P. K., Holleran, A. T., Long, F. J., & Zeruth, A. J. (2005). Examining the complex roles of motivation and text medium in the persuasion process. *Contemporary Educational Psychology, 30*, 418–438. doi:10.1016/j.cedpsych.2005.05.001

Murphy, P. K., Long, J. F., Holleran, T. A., & Esterly, E. (2003). Persuasion online or on paper: A new take on an old issue. *Learning and Instruction, 13*, 511–532.

Nussbaum, E. M. (2011). Argumentation, dialogue theory, and probability modeling: Alternative frameworks for argumentation research in education. *Educational Psychologist, 46*, 84–106.

Richter, T. (2011). Cognitive flexibility and epistemic validation in learning from multiple texts. In J. Elen, E. Stahl, R. Bromme, & G. Clarebout (Eds.), *Links between beliefs and cognitive flexibility* (pp. 125–140). Berlin: Springer.

Richter, T. (2015). Validation and comprehension of text information: Two sides of the same coin. *Discourse Processes, 52*, 337–354.

Richter, T., & Schmid, S. (2010). Epistemological beliefs and epistemic strategies in self-regulated learning. *Metacognition and Learning, 5*, 47–65.

Schommer, M. (1990). Effects of beliefs about the nature of knowledge on comprehension. *Journal of Educational Psychology, 82*, 498–504.

Taber, C. S., & Lodge, M. (2006). Motivated skepticism in the evaluation of political beliefs. *American Journal of Poligical Science, 50*(3), 755–769. doi:10.1111/j.1540-5907.2006.00214.x

van den Broek, P., Risden, K., Fletcher, C. R., & Thurlow, R. (1996). A "landscape" view of reading: Fluctuating patterns of activation and the construction of a stable memory representation. In B. K. Britton & A. C. Graesser (Eds.), *Models of understanding text* (pp. 165–187). Mahwah, NJ: Erlbaum.

van den Broek, P., Risden, K., & Husebye-Hartmann, E. (1995). The role of readers' standards for coherence in the generation of inferences during reading. In R. F. Lorch & E. J. O'Brien (Eds.), *Sources of coherence in reading* (pp. 353–373). Hillsdale, NJ: Erlbaum.

West, R. F., Toplak, M. E., & Stanovich, K. E. (2008). Heuristics and biases as measures of critical thinking: Associations with cognitive ability and thinking dispositions. *Journal of Educational Psychology, 100*(4), 930–941.

Wiley, J. (2005). A fair and balanced look at the news: What affects memory for controversial arguments?. *Journal of Memory and Language, 53*, 95–109.

Wolfe, M. B. W. (2005). Memory for narrative and expository text: Independent influences of semantic associations and text organization. *Journal of Experimental Psychology: Learning, Memory, and Cognition, 31*, 359–364. doi:10.1037/0278-7393.31.2.359

Wolfe, M. B. W., Tanner, S. M., & Taylor, A. R. (2013). Processing and representation of arguments in one-sided texts about disputed topics. *Discourse Processes, 50*(7), 457–497. doi:10.1080/0163853X.2013.828480

16

THE ROLE OF VALIDATION IN INTEGRATING MULTIPLE PERSPECTIVES

Tobias Richter, Hannes Münchow, and Johanna Abendroth
UNIVERSITY OF WÜRZBURG

ABSTRACT

The Internet is the primary source of information about a broad range of topics, which may range from consumer and medical decisions to political and socio-scientific issues. The relevant information is often available in the form of written texts that convey divergent perspectives, such as different opinions, competing theoretical assumptions, arguments and counterarguments, and evidence and counterevidence. What are the challenges and potential problems associated with comprehending texts that convey multiple perspectives? How can students be supported to make the most of this obviously complicated reading situation? This chapter attempts to answer these questions from a particular theoretical perspective that revolves around the notion that readers routinely validate text information against pertinent and accessible knowledge and beliefs. We will discuss how validation acts in concert with the two other major component processes of text comprehension, activation and integration. This discussion will be followed by an outline of the Two-Step Model of Validation, a model that makes predictions about circumstances that enable or hinder readers in forming a coherent and consistent mental representation based on multiple perspectives.

Key words: beliefs, comprehension, integration, multiple texts, validation

In this digital age, information about almost everything is available for almost everyone at one's fingertips. The Internet is the primary source of information whenever we wish to know more about a topic, which may range from consumer (e.g., *Should I buy this new smartphone?*) and medical decisions (e.g., *Should my child have this vaccination?*) to political and socio-scientific issues (e.g., *Should nuclear power plants be shut down?*). In most cases, the relevant information is available in the form of written texts and these texts often convey divergent perspectives, such as different opinions, competing theoretical assumptions, arguments and counterarguments, and evidence and counterevidence. How readers make sense of multiple perspectives is a highly relevant theoretical question but also a pressing issue for educational practitioners. What are the challenges and potential problems associated with comprehending texts that convey multiple perspectives? How can students be supported to make the most of this obviously complicated reading situation?

This chapter attempts to answer these questions from a particular theoretical perspective that revolves around the notion that readers routinely monitor the plausibility of text information with pertinent and accessible knowledge and beliefs (*validation*, Richter, 2015; Singer, 2013). Proceeding from single to multiple text comprehension, we will discuss how validation acts in concert with the two other major component processes of text comprehension, activation and integration. This discussion will be followed by an outline of the Two-Step Model of Validation, a model that relies on the notion of validation to make predictions about circumstances that enable or hinder readers in forming a coherent and consistent mental representation based on multiple perspectives (Richter & Maier, 2017). The Two-Step Model of Validation assumes that, per default, this representation is bound to be biased towards readers' prior beliefs in the form of a better comprehension of belief-consistent texts compared to belief-inconsistent texts (text-belief consistency effect). However, the model also specifies conditions that support readers to construct a mental representation of multiple perspectives that includes belief-consistent and belief-inconsistent information to a similar extent. These conditions have certain educational implications, especially for the design of training interventions that might help readers to successfully comprehend multiple texts in terms of reducing the preferential processing and comprehension of belief-consistent and plausible information.

THREE MAJOR COMPONENT PROCESSES OF COMPREHENSION: ACTIVATION, INTEGRATION, AND VALIDATION

When readers comprehend a text, they use the information in the text and their prior knowledge to construct a more or less complete mental representation of what the text is about. This type of referential representation has been termed a situation model or mental model, which can be distinguished from (although it is based on) the representation of the text itself and its propositional content (van Dijk & Kintsch, 1983). Situation models are built, enriched, and updated continuously as a reader moves forward in a text. In this process, the words and larger segments of a text function as retrieval cues that passively activate information from long-term memory (through a resonance-like mechanism, O'Brien & Myers, 1999). The activated information can be based on previous portions of the text (contextual information) or on prior knowledge and beliefs. New information from a text is then integrated with the activated information to form a situation model of the text content. Integration is usually described as a passive, text-driven process that is based on semantic associations between information from the text and information in long-term memory. For example, the Construction-Integration model (Kintsch, 1988) assumes a spreading activation process that is iterated until the network of propositions from the text and from prior knowledge reaches a stable pattern. Propositions with many connections are strengthened and remain active in the reader's situation model, whereas propositions with few connections are weakened and are eventually deactivated. The integration mechanisms result in a network of interconnected propositions from the text and from prior knowledge, which together form the current situation model.

This now classical notion that comprehension is largely based on passive activation and integration processes has proven to be quite powerful for explaining experimental findings and designing useful applications (for an overview, see McNamara & Magliano, 2009). However, its limits become apparent when a reader encounters text information that conflicts with the contents of the current situation model. For example, O'Brien, Rizzella, Albrecht, and Halleran (1998) presented readers with short narratives that introduced a character (e.g., *Mary is a vegetarian*). When later on in the narrative that character performed actions that contradicted the initial description (e.g., *Mary ordered a cheeseburger*) and the initial information is still active (or reactivated), reading times were increased. This and many similar findings obtained with this inconsistency paradigm have traditionally been interpreted as integration difficulties but they seem to reflect more than that: Apparently, readers possess a mechanism that checks the consistency of text information with the contents of the current situation model and accessible background knowledge. Singer, Halldorson, Lear, and Andrusiak (1992) have coined the term *validation* to refer to this mechanism.

An increasing number of researchers have adopted the idea that the commonly known dyad of basic and passive comprehension processes is in fact a triad, consisting of activation, integration, and validation (Isberner & Richter, 2014a; Richter, 2015; Richter & Singer, 2017). For instance, O'Brien and Cook (2016) proposed the Resonance-Integration-Validation Model (RI-Val) that describes how activation, integration, and validation act in concert during reading. The model proposes that after a certain amount of knowledge has been activated in the course of reading, integrating the activated knowledge with the text information begins. After the integration process has achieved a sufficient conceptual overlap between activated knowledge and text information, the activated, integrated information is validated against activated relevant background knowledge. Once the validation process has established a certain coherence threshold, the reader moves on in the text.

The general assumption that readers routinely validate information against active parts of their prior knowledge and the discourse context is supported by a wealth of evidence from reading time and eye-tracking experiments, studies with event-related potentials, and experiments based on the epistemic Stroop paradigm (for an overview, see Isberner & Richter, 2014a). The latter is particularly informative because it shows that validation entails the rejection of false or implausible information and, hence, goes beyond mere integration problems. In the epistemic Stroop paradigm, participants read words presented one-by-one in rapid succession (e.g., 300 ms per word) on a computer screen (Richter, Schroeder, & Wöhrmann, 2009). The words successively form sentences that can be true (e.g., *Libraries have books*) or false (e.g., *Computers have emotions*). The presentation stops at the word in the sentence at which the truth value of the sentence can, in principle, be computed. At this point, participants are prompted to provide a binary response for a task that is unrelated to the content of the sentence or the semantics of the word. For example, they can be asked to judge whether the word is spelled correctly (Richter et al., 2009). When the experimental sentence is false (*Computers have emotions*), but the required response (prompted at the word *emotions*) is "yes" (because the word is spelled correctly), participants' responses are slowed down as compared to true sentences (e.g., *Libraries have books*). This epistemic Stroop effect seems to be very robust. It has been shown with different tasks, for example, spelling judgments (like in Richter et al., 2009), judgments about whether the word has changed color (Isberner & Richter, 2013, Experiment 2), or simple reactions to the probe words TRUE or FALSE with the appropriate key (Isberner & Richter, 2014b). It has also been shown with different types of materials, including true vs. false sentences (like in Richter et al., 2009), sentences that are plausible vs. implausible in the discourse context (e.g., *Frank has a broken leg. He calls the* doctor/plumber; Isberner & Richter, 2013), or deictic sentences (e.g., *This is a car*) presented auditorily together with a matching or mismatching picture (Piest, Isberner, & Richter, 2018). In sum, the epistemic Stroop effect obtained across these different tasks and materials strongly suggests that comprehenders routinely and involuntarily validate linguistic information. Moreover, it suggests that information that is inconsistent with readers' prior knowledge or their beliefs, evokes a negative response tendency, that is, a tendency to give a "no"-response in an unrelated task.

If validation is indeed a routine component of comprehension as suggested by the presented research, it is likely to serve comprehension in relevant ways. The negative response tendency allows for the conclusion that one of these functions is to assist readers to build and maintain coherent and internally consistent mental representations during comprehension by detecting and rejecting information that does not fit into the current mental model. In line with this reasoning, Schroeder, Richter, and Hoever (2008) have shown that, for the comprehension of expository texts, implausible information is less likely to be integrated into the situation model of the text content. On the other hand, information that is part of the situation model is more likely to be judged as plausible. Similarly, a strong link between the perceived plausibility of information and its integration into the situation model has been found for multiple text comprehension (Maier & Richter, 2013a). The strong relationship between plausibility and the situation model constructed during reading suggests that validation and integration work in concert during comprehension. How this collaboration can be described for the case of comprehending multiple perspectives will be discussed in more detail next.

INTEGRATION AND VALIDATION IN THE COMPREHENSION OF TEXTS CONVEYING MULTIPLE PERSPECTIVES

Integration is more demanding if texts convey multiple perspectives. For example, when readers read multiple texts dealing with the same topic but from different angles, they need not only to integrate text information with their prior knowledge and earlier parts of the text, but also with information from the other text(s).

Sometimes, single texts offer different perspectives, for example, when a text cites different sources, such as a textbook describing competing theoretical explanations of the same phenomenon. Regardless of whether multiple perspectives are presented in multiple texts or in single texts, they necessitate readers to update their situation model and shift to a new representational structure (Gernsbacher, 1990) because seamless integration into the existing situation model is not possible. Validation might serve an important function in this process as it signals to the reader the need for updating (Richter & Singer, 2017).

On a general level, two types of reading situations involving multiple perspectives may be distinguished, depending on whether the different parts of a text or, more often, multiple texts present componential or conflicting information (e.g., Bråten, Braasch, & Salmeron, in press). The role of validation and its interplay with integration differs between these types of situations, as described next.

Integration and Validation in Multiple Texts Presenting Componential Information

The *componential reading situation* may be illustrated by a reader gathering information about a specific topic or question and reading several texts that provide partly overlapping but also unique information. It resembles a puzzle that readers need to solve by finding matching pieces and putting them together in the right way. An experiment by Cerdán and Vidal-Abarca (2008) sheds light on the specifics of this situation. They provided undergraduate students of psychology three longer texts about antibiotics resistance (length 390–684 words), each covering different aspects of the topic. Cerdan and Vidal-Abarca found that comprehension depended on the task they gave to their participants: An intertextual task (writing an essay on a question that required participants to refer to all three texts) that promoted the integration of information across texts lead to superior performance, as compared to an intratextual task that directed readers to focus on single texts (answering intratextual questions). Moreover, participants given the intertextual task spent more time reading relevant parts of the text and went back and forth between texts more frequently than participants given the intratextual task. Hence, in this componential reading situation participants assigned to the intertextual task integrated different matching pieces of information across texts and were able to combine these more successfully into a complete picture of the issue, as compared to participants assigned to the intratextual task.

In a componential reading situation, the effects of validation often do not become explicitly apparent. However, that is not to say that validation does not play a role. Rather, the validation process works in the background and continuously evaluates the consistency of ideas from the text with activated information. In such a reading situation, validation might create the prerequisites for updating by signaling to the reader when a piece of information does not fit into the current situation model (Richter & Singer, 2017) and whether a new structure has to be initiated. For example, in the study by Cerdán and Vidal-Abarca (2008), readers might have used validation to determine whether information presented in a later text about the "Genetics of bacteria resistance" fits into the situation model constructed during reading the previous text on "New perspectives on bacteria resistance". If validation determines that the information presented in the second text does not fit into the current situation model based on the first text, the construction of a new situation model is initiated. Similar, validation might also signal to the reader to reread specific information, for example from a previously read text. Apparently, successful integration, at least across longer texts in an authentic reading situation, goes beyond the passive integration as described by the Construction-Integration model (Kintsch, 1988) or the RI-Val model (O'Brien & Cook, 2016). Rather, it seems to be strategic to some extent and to require cognitive effort and validation processes, as indicated by the longer reading times on task-relevant portions of the texts in the study from Cerdán and Vidal-Abarca (2008).

Integration and Validation in Multiple Texts Presenting Conflicting Information

In a *reading situation involving conflicting information*, validation plays a more conspicuous role because readers are more likely to encounter information that is inconsistent with previously read information or their prior beliefs. Many studies in the field of multiple text comprehension have focused on the comprehension of texts that convey (partly) conflicting information. For example, the seminal work by Rouet, Britt, Mason, and Perfetti (1996) and Britt, Perfetti, Sandak, and Rouet (1999) involved students reading multiple and partially conflicting historical documents and secondary texts about a historic event, the US occupation of the Panama Canal. These texts represented different perspectives of American politicians, historians, and Panamanians. Other studies followed their lead using multiple texts representing different and partially conflicting perspectives on (socio-)scientific issues such as climate change (e.g., Maier & Richter, 2013a; McCrudden & Barnes, 2016), vaccinations (Maier & Richter, 2013b), the link between violent computer games and aggression (van Strien, Brand-Gruwel, & Boishuizen, 2014) or health risks caused by the electromagnetic radiation caused by cell phone use (e.g., Anmarkrud, Bråten, & Strømsø, 2014; Maier & Richter, 2016). These topics are controversially debated in public and readers who search the Internet to learn more about any of them are likely to encounter texts that present arguments and counterarguments, contrary evidence, and conflicting information, which is often due to differences in perspective.

The first question to ask is whether readers notice multiple perspectives at all when they read a text. There is evidence that they do, at least if the conflicting information is presented closely enough so that the earlier information is reactivated, and that differences in perspective may play a role in resolving such conflicts. For example, Braasch, Rouet, Vibert, and Britt (2012) conducted an eye-tracking experiment with two-sentence news articles in which two people (e.g., an art critic vs. a lighting technician) made claims about various topics (e.g., an opera show). The claims were either consistent or inconsistent with one another. Braasch et al. found that discrepant news reports lead to more and longer fixations on source information, i.e. the person making the claim, and a better memory for that information. Hence, participants in this study did notice the multiple perspectives in the texts. The authors interpret these findings in light of the Discrepancy-Induced Source Comprehension assumption (D-ISC), according to which readers who encounter discrepant or inconsistent information in a text become more attentive to sources, possibly in an attempt to resolve the discrepancy. Similarly, experiments by Beker, Jolles, Lorch, and van den Broek (2016) show that readers monitor the consistency of information even across texts. Beker et al. used a multiple-text version of the inconsistency paradigm with pairs of short expository texts (average length of five to six sentences) on different topics. Using this paradigm, they showed that reading times were prolonged for target sentences in the second text when these were inconsistent (as opposed to consistent) with information in the sentence preceding the target sentence. Again, such a finding indicates readers' awareness of multiple perspectives. Importantly, however, the slowdown in inconsistent target sentences did not occur when an explanation resolving the inconsistency had been provided in the first text. This finding suggests that readers spontaneously activated information from previously read texts and validated the consistency of information across texts. However, it must be noted that the texts used in the experiments by Beker et al. were very short, implying that information from Text 1 and Text 2 were read shortly after one another, which provides quite favorable conditions for the activation of information from Text 1 while reading Text 2.

If readers are affected by inconsistencies even across texts, how is it possible for them to achieve a coherent and consistent mental representation from texts presenting multiple perspectives with conflicting information? When the information comes from multiple texts, the ideal reader would integrate conflicting information by forming a documents model (Perfetti, Rouet, & Britt, 1999), a complex mental representation that contains a more or less complete situation model for each individual text plus an intertext model that includes source information (e.g., information about the author(s), the publication date, publication type, and outlet) and the argumentative relationships between the texts. Moreover, the ideal reader would use the source information to judge the credibility of texts and weigh the information accordingly. Likewise, the ideal reader would judge the quality of the arguments presented in each of the texts to arrive at an informed and justified point of view. Although the documents model has been proposed as a representational framework for multiple text comprehension, a similar type of representation seems suitable also for building a representation of the context of a single text that describes multiple perspectives, for example, a scientific text describing multiple theoretical viewpoints, which are ascribed to different sources (i.e., scientists).

There is evidence, for example from the study by Braasch et al. (2012), that readers indeed use source information to resolve information conflicts when that information is readily available. And, of course, readers sometimes also evaluate the quality of arguments presented in a text to arrive at an informed and justified point of view. However, they do not seem to engage in these processes routinely. For example, research on multiple texts has shown that readers by no means regularly attend to source information (e.g., Britt & Aglinskas, 2002), often do not use this information properly for judging text credibility (e.g., von der Mühlen, Richter, Schmid, Schmidt, & Berthold, 2016a), and do not properly evaluate the quality of the presented arguments (von der Mühlen, Richter, Schmid, Schmidt, & Berthold, 2016b). Most important in the present context, readers frequently adopt certain positions in such controversies, holding strong beliefs about what is true or false (or what is right and wrong), and these beliefs can affect their comprehension of texts conveying multiple perspectives. For example, most people are either pro or contra nuclear power but they typically know very little about the potential risks and safeguards in effect for nuclear reactions, not to mention the underlying physical processes. These beliefs affect comprehension of multiple texts. In particular, readers' situation models are biased towards their prior beliefs, with stronger situation models for texts conveying belief-consistent as compared to belief-inconsistent information (Maier & Richter, 2013b). In the following section, we will sketch a model that can account for this text-belief consistency effect and place it in a broader context of the role of validation in the comprehension of multiple perspectives.

THE TWO-STEP MODEL OF VALIDATION: HOW READERS COMPREHEND CONFLICTING INFORMATION IN MULTIPLE TEXTS

Richter and Maier (2017, 2018) have proposed the Two-Step Model of Validation to describe the cognitive processes involved in the comprehension of multiple texts with conflicting information (for a preliminary version of the model, see also Richter, 2011). One aim of this model is to explain the text-belief consistency effect i.e., the better comprehension of belief-consistent as compared to belief-inconsistent information (Maier & Richter, 2013b), which is regarded as a consequence of routine validation processes during comprehension. The Two-Step Model of Validation has been formulated to explain belief-biases in the comprehension of multiple texts on controversially debated issues, but in principle, the model applies to single texts conveying multiple perspectives as well. We view the processes described in the Two-Step Model of Validation as fundamental to how readers make sense of text conveying multiple perspectives, whenever they possess strong and accessible prior beliefs towards an issue.

The basic idea of the Two-Step Model of Validation is that routine validation enables readers to maintain a coherent and consistent mental representation of controversial topics without the need to invest much cognitive resources. However, such processing comes at the costs of a one-sided mental representation, in which belief-inconsistent information is integrated to a lesser extent. A second aim of the model is to account for conditions that are known to moderate the occurrence of the text-belief consistency effect.

In particular, Richter & Maier (2017) propose that two steps may be involved in readers' comprehension of texts with multiple perspectives (Figure 16.1). Step 1 is obligatory and demands little cognitive resources because it relies solely on routine and passive comprehension processes, i.e. the triad of activation, integration, and validation of information during reading. When readers possess strong and accessible beliefs about a controversial issue, these beliefs will be used to validate text information, which may lead to a belief bias in the comprehension of multiple texts (see next section for details). Step 2 is optional, resource demanding and depends on the specific goals of the reader. When readers undertake this step, they engage more strongly in elaborative processing of information that might be able to reduce detected inconsistencies between texts conveying multiple perspectives. In most cases, this will include

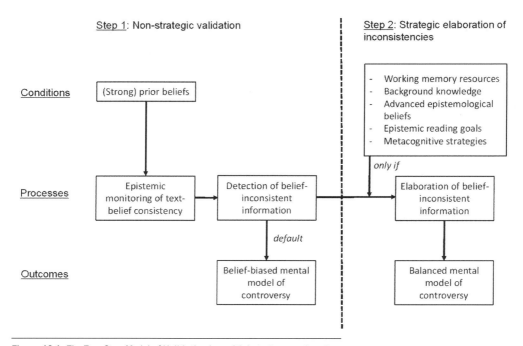

Figure 16.1 The Two-Step Model of Validation in multiple text comprehension.

better processing of belief-inconsistent information, as such information was processed to a lesser extent due to the monitoring process of Step 1 as outlined in the next section. Nevertheless, belief-consistent information might be additionally processed to resolve inconsistencies during Step 2. The elaborative processing of Step 2 requires certain conditions to occur, which will be outlined in the next sections. Arguably, elaborated processing increases the chances that belief-inconsistent information is integrated into the mental representation of a controversial issue.

Step 1: Routine Validation of Conflicting Information Based on Prior Knowledge and Beliefs

Being a passive process, validation occurs regardless of readers' goals; it is an integral component of comprehension (Isberner & Richter, 2014b; O'Brien & Cook, 2016). During this routine validation, text information is monitored for consistency with the current situation model and with the contents of long-term memory that are activated through concepts and propositions in the text. For the comprehension of single as well as multiple texts on controversial issues, it is important that validation can be based not only on prior knowledge but also on prior beliefs. Research on argument comprehension has shown that readers holding pertinent and accessible beliefs are as fast to evaluate aclaim as they are to comprehend it (Voss, Fincher-Kiefer, Wiley, & Silfies, 1993). Moreover, using the epistemic Stroop paradigm, Gilead, Sela, and Maril (2018) have shown that claims that are consistent or inconsistent with participants' beliefs (e.g., *The Internet has made people more* isolated/sociable) elicit the same negative response tendencies as false or implausible statements. This result suggests that readers' prior beliefs are also reactivated and used for validation, alongside knowledge, without readers' strategic attempts to do so. Moreover, these results suggest that validation continuously generates implicit plausibility judgments based on the consistency of new information with readers' prior beliefs as a by-product of comprehension.

The Two-Step Model of Validation assumes that in the comprehension of multiple perspectives, these implicit plausibility judgments serve as a kind of heuristic that helps readers to regulate their cognitive resources during reading and to maintain a coherent and consistent situation model. Per default, readers tend to process information perceived as plausible more deeply than information that they find less plausible. On a global level, this mechanism leads to a text-belief consistency bias in multiple documents comprehension (Maier & Richter, 2013a): Situation models for texts that are consistent with one's own beliefs in a controversy are stronger than those for belief-inconsistent texts. On a local level, it leads to a plausibility bias (Maier & Richter, 2013b): Belief-consistent information in a text is integrated more easily than belief-inconsistent information.

Both the (global) text-belief consistency effect and the (local) plausibility bias seem to be robust findings that occur in different groups of readers, from adolescents to university students, and with different topics and comprehension tasks (for a systematic review of the text-belief consistency effect, see Richter & Maier, 2017). For example, Maier and Richter (2013b) found a stronger situation model (measured with an inference recognition task) for belief-consistent compared to belief-inconsistent texts when university students read four multiple texts arguing for opposing positions with regard to global warming (man-made vs. natural causes) and vaccinations (more benefits vs. more risks) in a blocked fashion (first two texts on one position, then two texts on the opposing position). These results have been replicated in a sample of adolescents (Abendroth & Richter, 2019). Other studies have used essay-writing tasks. For example, Anmarkrud et al. (2014) presented undergraduates with six texts providing different views on whether the use of cell phones is associated with health risks. Most participants wrote essays that contained only reasons in support of their own position but did not provide any counterarguments or arguments for an alternative position. A third method that has been used in studies on text-belief consistency effects to measure comprehension outcomes is argument evaluation. An experiment by Kobayashi (2010, Experiment 1) is a case in point. Japanese undergraduates read texts that argued for or against the introduction of daylight savings time in Japan and rated the convincingness of the arguments presented. Belief-consistent arguments were rated as more convincing than belief-inconsistent arguments. Moreover, the argument's evaluation was correlated with the pro- and con-arguments in a subsequent essay task. The more participants were in favor of daylight savings time the fewer favorable statements they produced in response to the counterarguments provided in text. Thus, Kobayashi also found a link between the consistency of information with readers' prior beliefs and the perceived plausibility of such information, as well as with the (im)balance of the resulting mental representation of the controversy (similar to Maier & Richter, 2013b; Schroeder et al., 2008). In sum, these results are in line with the assumption of the Two-Step Model of Validation that readers per default process belief-inconsistent information in a shallower manner when reading multiple texts on conflicting information.

The first step of the Two-Step Model of Validation, with its assumption that readers use a plausibility (or belief-consistency) heuristic to regulate comprehension and the construction of situation models for multiple texts with conflicting information, is reminiscent of the well-known constructs of selective exposure (Festinger, 1957) and confirmation bias (Nickerson, 1998). However, the Two-Step Model differs from the latter constructs and the associated theories in that plausibility or text-belief consistency effects are assumed to take effect already during comprehension – to be more precise, as a by-product of regular comprehension processes. This proposal stands in sharp contrast to the classical view, which is also adopted by most work on confirmation biases, that the plausibility of information is evaluated in a separate step of information processing that occurs *after* comprehension has been completed (e.g., Connell & Keane, 2006; Gilbert, 1991).

Step 2: Elaborative Processing of Conflicting Information

Shallower processing of belief-inconsistent information seems to be the default way to process this type of information. Nevertheless, there can be no doubt that readers sometimes devote even more cognitive resources to belief-inconsistent information to actively resolve the inconsistency. There are cases when readers who encounter a belief-inconsistent claim do not reject or ignore this claim but search their long-term memory or additional sources for alternative reasons that support or refute the implausible information. Such *elaboration of information* is likely to improve the comprehension of conflicting information, especially belief-inconsistent information (for a review of available studies, see Richter & Maier, 2017).

The Two-Step Model further assumes that, unlike the routine validation processes in the first step, the elaboration of belief-inconsistent information is under the strategic control of the reader. Importantly, this assumption implies that strategic elaboration of inconsistent information occurs only in a specific motivational state characterized by students' assumption of an epistemic reading goal (Richter, 2003). Epistemic reading goals are those that include the acquisition of knowledge in a classical (philosophical) sense, that is, the acquisition of true and justified beliefs (e.g., Ichikawa & Steup, 2018). Such reading goals can be contrasted with, among others, receptive reading goals that involve memorizing information regardless of its truth value or justification (imagine, for example, a student memorizing information for a multiple-choice test). Epistemic reading goals can take many forms, such as reading a text out of epistemic curiosity (Richter & Schmid, 2010, Study 2), reading a text to scrutinize the position of an opponent (Edwards & Smith, 1996), or reading a text to gather information to make an important decision (e.g., about medical treatment). Adopting such a goal benefits the comprehension of multiple texts. For example, in a study by Wiley and Voss (1999) participants wrote more coherent essays with stronger causal links and scored better in comprehension tasks when they were instructed to write an argumentative essay (which is likely to induce an epistemic reading goal) as compared to being instructed to write a summary or a narrative text (which is likely to induce a receptive reading goal).

At the metacognitive level, epistemological beliefs may be relevant for whether readers adopt epistemic reading goals at all. For example, readers need to be aware that knowledge can change in light of new evidence. They also need to endorse the belief that although people can make different knowledge claims, knowledge is not arbitrary but needs to be justified in an appropriate way. Thus, a mature epistemological position such as commitment within relativism (Perry, 1970) or reflective judgment (King & Strohm Kitchener, 1994) is an important precondition for the elaborative processing of belief-inconsistent information.

Besides being motivated to do so, readers must also be able to engage in the strategic elaboration of belief-inconsistent information. Elaborative processing is costly in terms of cognitive resources and requires prior knowledge. Therefore, the Two-Step Model of Validation assumes that time pressure, low working memory capacity, or low prior knowledge make it unlikely that readers strategically elaborate on belief-inconsistent information (Richter & Maier, 2017).

EDUCATIONAL IMPLICATIONS OF THE TWO-STEP-MODEL: FOSTERING THE INTEGRATION OF CONFLICTING INFORMATION IN MULTIPLE TEXT COMPREHENSION

Using validation and the implicit plausibility judgments to regulate comprehension is to some extent beneficial for the comprehension of multiple texts as readers are able to preserve cognitive resources. Validation reflects a basic form of epistemic vigilance, i.e., the ability not to trust information blindly (Sperber et al., 2010). As such, it can protect the mental system from inaccurate information (although this protection is far from perfect). Moreover, it allows readers to construct and maintain coherent and consistent mental representations even if they are confronted with conflicting or even contradictory information (Isberner & Richter, 2014a). However, the crux of the matter is that validation can also be based on false and subjective beliefs, in which case it contributes to the persistence of such beliefs. On a more general level, whenever there is a rational dispute with arguments presented for different viewpoints (e.g., in scientific controversies, Britt, Richter, & Rouet, 2014), it is desirable that readers consider, comprehend, and scrutinize arguments that run against their beliefs to the same extent as arguments that are in line with their beliefs. In this sense, the ability to construct a balanced mental representation of conflicting information – or to integrate belief-inconsistent information in multiple text comprehension – is an important aspect of open-mindedness and cognitive flexibility (Richter, 2011). Fostering this ability may be considered as an important goal of education.

The Two-Step Model of Validation has clear implications for how this educational goal may be reached. Given that validation is a routine, non-strategic component of comprehension that further supports comprehension in important ways, it seems neither possible nor advisable to design interventions that suppress validation during reading multiple texts. In other words, for someone holding strong beliefs on a controversy, it does not make sense to try to adopt a neutral stance during reading multiple texts on that issue. In contrast, interventions that promote engagement in strategic elaboration of conflicting information, that is, engagement in Step 2 according to the Two-Step Model of Validation, seem promising. In line with this idea, a growing body of research indicates that the readers' skills related to strategic validation in multiple texts can be improved through suitable instruction and training interventions, as discussed next.

A number of studies have focused on sourcing, that is, being aware of source characteristics and using them for evaluating information, as a means of increasing the comprehension of multiple perspectives (e.g., Macedo-Rouet, Braasch, Britt, & Rouet, 2013; Stadtler & Bromme, 2008). Source characteristics of texts providing conflicting information can be useful to assess the general trustworthiness or credibility of these texts. For example, a text on nitrogen oxides is more trustworthy when written by an independent scientist than by an employee of a car manufacturer. Teaching sourcing strategies aims at improving the readers' evaluation of the credibility and usefulness of a document's source (Macedo-Rouet et al., 2013) and enhancing source awareness (Strømsø, Bråten, & Britt, 2010). Paul, Cerdán, Rouet, and Stadtler (2018) reported that, although children in elementary school were able recognize source information, they failed to use this information when they were asked to judge short controversial texts on health-related issues. Similarly, Paul, Stadtler, and Bromme (2017) could show that children in elementary school who received a sourcing prompt reported more source characteristics when judging controversial texts. However, there were no differences in the judgements of the texts between children who received the sourcing prompt and those who did not. Hence, the mere instruction to consider source information when processing conflicting information may not be sufficient to improve readers' sourcing skills (see Stadtler, Scharrer, Macedo-Rouet, Rouet, & Bromme, 2016, for a discussion). A more promising approach was examined by Stadtler and Bromme (2008) who improved laypersons' knowledge about sources and the use of source information with a computer-based tool that repeatedly prompted students to evaluate the source of incoming information. Wiley and colleagues (2009) successfully taught undergraduate university students to evaluate the reliability of information sources in order to enhance students' skills in searching for reliable information. Britt and Aglinskas (2002) developed a computer-based tutoring and practice environment to teach high-school students the strategies of sourcing and corroborating. Multiple documents with varying source characteristics (e.g., document type, document date) about the same historical controversies were presented to high school students, either by a lecturer, via textbook or embedded in the computer-based tutorial. Results showed that students who received the training more often attended to source information in an intertextual essay-writing task and answered more sourcing-related questions correctly as compared to the other conditions. In sum, empirical research has shown that sourcing skills can be improved by training interventions. However, what we do not know at this point is whether and to what extent sourcing interventions also improve integration of belief-inconsistent information and can help readers to achieve a more balanced mental representation. According to Braasch, McCabe, and Daniel (2016), there seems to be a trade-off between memory for sources and content integration. In three experiments, these authors varied the semantic congruence of multiple texts and found that integration was better but memory for sources was poorer for semantically more congruent texts.

Another way to foster strategic elaboration of conflicting information is to improve readers' abilities to decode the internal structure of arguments and to discriminate weak from strong arguments. Multiple texts contain arguments of varying quality. Thus, the comprehension and proper evaluation of arguments is a key competence for making sense of multiple texts with conflicting information. Despite the importance of these skills, high-school students and university students at the beginning of their studies have difficulties in the proper evaluation of arguments, in particular their internal consistency and plausibility (e.g., Larson, Britt, & Kurby, 2009; von der Mühlen et al., 2016b). Training interventions have focused on conveying knowledge about the functional structure of informal arguments (often on the basis of the argumentation model of Toulmin, 1958) and on practicing the skills to identify functional argument components (such as claim, reason, warrant, and rebuttal). Another approach is to provide information about argumentation fallacies combined with practice in identifying fallacies. For example, Larson et al. (2009) taught undergraduate university students about typical argumentation flaws and how to recognize the claim in informal arguments. Results of three studies showed that university and high school students in the training conditions outperformed those students that were not given the treatment.

Von der Mühlen, Richter, Schmid, and Berthold (2018) found similar results in an experimental study that evaluated the effectiveness of training university students to grasp the functional structure of informal arguments. The students' ability to recognize and allocate argument components was measured before and immediately after the training intervention in a four-week follow-up. Moreover, argument complexity was varied in order to distinguish between arguments with typical or less typical structure. Results showed that students who completed the training intervention performed better after the training compared to students in an active control condition (speed reading exercise) especially for the more complex arguments and when the students had demonstrated higher abilities prior to the training.

A study by Dwyer, Hogan, and Stewart (2012) used an argument mapping training intervention in which participants were taught to visualize functional components of text-based arguments and their inferential relationships. University students who worked with this technique showed higher skills in critical thinking and evaluating the quality of arguments as compared to students in a passive control condition. In sum, several experimental training studies show that a training about the structure of informal arguments and argumentation fallacies combined with practice tasks can enhance students' abilities to evaluate the structure of informal arguments and to judge their plausibility. Nevertheless, like for the sourcing training, evidence that a training in argument comprehension and evaluation can improve the comprehension of belief-inconsistent information in multiple text comprehension is still needed.

Finally, the Two-Step Model of Validation implies that improving readers' metacognitive knowledge about and strategies for the processing of conflicting information should be effective in achieving a better integration of belief-inconsistent information and overcoming text-belief consistency effects and plausibility biases. One simple approach is to create an awareness of potential biases resulting from routine validation processes, along with strategies that can be used to control the outcomes of these processes. Maier and Richter (2014) provided a short training of three metacognitive strategies, becoming aware of the effects of routine validation, actively using of prior knowledge to evaluate arguments, and scrutinizing intertextual argumentative relationships. When this training was combined with favorable motivational conditions (created with positive performance feedback), the text-belief consistency effect was eliminated.

CONCLUSION

In formal and informal learning, it is common for readers to deal with multiple perspectives, in our case, multiple texts that present conflicting information on controversial topics. The Two-Step Model of Validation uses the assumption that validation is a routine part of comprehension as the basis for explaining why readers often have difficulties comprehending information that is not in line with their beliefs. Specifically, it is suggested that readers often rely on a simple plausibility heuristic that leads to the preferential processing and comprehension of belief-consistent information and as a consequence to the text-belief consistency effect in the mental representation of multiple texts. Moreover, an epistemic reading goal as well as sufficient cognitive resources are postulated by the Two-Step Model of Validation as motivational and cognitive prerequisites for readers to resolve consciously noted inconsistencies through elaborative processing.

The Two-Step Model of Validation can be used to explain robust findings in multiple text comprehension such as the text-belief consistency effect and the plausibility effect. In addition, paying attention to the role of validation in multiple text comprehension also allows deriving interesting and promising approaches for trainings and interventions in the field. Nevertheless, the role of validation for multiple perspectives based on different types of representations, such as visualizations or auditory information, needs to be clarified in future research. Similarly, the relationship between validation and the other two component processes of comprehension – activation and integration – needs to be further narrowed and refined. Both avenues of future research will increase our knowledge about the role validation plays for readers' integration of multiple streams of information.

ACKNOWLEDGMENT

This research was supported by the German Federal Ministry of Education and Research (Grant no. 01PK15009B).

REFERENCES

Abendroth, J., & Richter, T. (2019). Text-belief consistency effect in adolescents' comprehension of multiple documents from the web. *Journal for the Study of Education and Development.*

Anmarkrud, Ø., Bråten, I., & Strømsø, H. I. (2014). Multiple-documents literacy: Strategic processing, source awareness, and argumentation when reading multiple conflicting documents. *Learning and Individual Differences, 30,* 64–76. doi:10.1016/j.lindif.2013.01.007

Beker, K., Jolles, D., Lorch, R. F., & van den Broek, P. (2016). Learning from texts: Activation of information from previous texts during reading. *Reading and Writing, 29,* 1161–1178. doi:10.1007/s11145-016-9630-3

Braasch, J. L., McCabe, R. M., & Daniel, F. (2016). Content integration across multiple documents reduces memory for sources. *Reading and Writing, 29,* 1571–1598.

Braasch, J. L., Rouet, J. F., Vibert, N., & Britt, M. A. (2012). Readers' use of source information in text comprehension. *Memory and Cognition, 40,* 450–465. doi:10.3758/s13421-011-0160-6

Bråten, I., Braasch, J. L. G., & Salmeron, L. (in press). Reading multiple and non-traditional texts. In E. B. Moje, P. Afflerbach, P. Enciso, & N. K. Lesaux (Eds.), *Handbook of reading research* (vol. 5). New York: Routledge.

Britt, M. A., & Aglinskas, C. (2002). Improving students' ability to identify and use source information. *Cognition and Instruction, 20,* 485–522. doi:10.1207/S1532690XCI2004_2

Britt, M. A., Perfetti, C. A., Sandak, R., & Rouet, J.-F. (1999). Content integration and source separation in learning from multiple texts. In S. R. Goldman, A. C. Graesser, & P. van den Broek (Eds.), *Narrative comprehension, causality, and coherence: Essays in honor of Tom Trabasso* (pp. 209–233). Mahwah, NJ: Erlbaum.

Britt, M. A., Richter, T., & Rouet, J.-F. (2014). Scientific literacy: The role of goal-directed reading and evaluation in understanding scientific information. *Educational Psychologist, 49,* 104–122. doi:10.1080/00461520.2014.916217

Cerdán, R., & Vidal-Abarca, E. (2008). The effects of tasks on integrating information from multiple documents. *Journal of Educational Psychology, 100,* 209–222. doi:10.1037/0022-0663.100.1.209

Connell, L., & Keane, M. T. (2006). A model of plausibility. *Cognitive Science, 30,* 95–120. doi:10.1207/s15516709cog0000_53

Dwyer, C. P., Hogan, M. J., & Stewart, I. (2012). An evaluation of argument mapping as a method of enhancing critical thinking performance in e-learning environments. *Metacognition and Learning, 7,* 219–244. doi:10.1007/s11409-012-9092-1

Edwards, K., & Smith, E. E. (1996). A disconfirmation bias in the evaluation of arguments. *Journal of Personality and Social Psychology, 71,* 5–24. doi:10.1037/0022-3514.71.1.5

Festinger, L. (1957). *A theory of cognitive dissonance.* Stanford, CA: Stanford University Press.

Gernsbacher, M. A. (1990). *Language comprehension as structure building.* Hillsdale, NJ: Erlbaum.

Gilbert, D. T. (1991). How mental systems believe. *American Psychologist, 46,* 107–119. doi:10.1037/0003-066X.46.2.107

Gilead, M., Sela, M., & Maril, A. (2018). That's my truth: Evidence for involuntary opinion confirmation. *Social Psychological and Personality Science, 10,* 393–401. doi:10.1177/1948550618762300

Ichikawa, J. J., & Steup, M. (2018). The analysis of knowledge. In E. N. Zalta (Ed.), *The Stanford encyclopedia of philosophy* [Online Document]. Retrieved from. https://plato.stanford.edu/archives/sum2018/entries/knowledge-analysis/

Isberner, M.-B., & Richter, T. (2013). Can readers ignore implausibility? Evidence for nonstrategic monitoring of event-based plausibility in language comprehension. *Acta Psychologica, 142,* 15–22. doi:10.1016/j.actpsy.2012.10.003

Isberner, M.-B., & Richter, T. (2014a). Comprehension and validation: Separable stages of information processing? A case for epistemic monitoring in language comprehension. In D. N. Rapp & J. Braasch (Eds.), *Processing inaccurate information: Theoretical and applied perspectives from cognitive science and the educational sciences* (pp. 245–276). Boston, MA: MIT Press.

Isberner, M.-B., & Richter, T. (2014b). Does validation during language comprehension depend on an evaluative mindset?. *Discourse Processes, 51,* 7–25. doi:10.1080/0163853X.2013.855867

King, P. M., & Strohm Kitchener, K. (1994). *Developing reflective judgment.* San Francisco, CA: Jossey-Bass.

Kintsch, W. (1988). The role of knowledge in discourse comprehension: A construction-integration model. *Psychological Review, 95,* 163–182. doi:10.1016/S0166-4115(08)61551-4

Kobayashi, K. (2010). Strategic use of multiple texts for the evaluation of arguments. *Reading Psychology, 31*, 121–149. doi:10.1080/02702710902754192

Larson, A. A., Britt, M. A., & Kurby, C. (2009). Improving students' evaluation of informal arguments. *Journal of Experimental Education, 77*, 339–365.

Macedo-Rouet, M., Braasch, J. L. G., Britt, M. A., & Rouet, J.-F. (2013). Teaching fourth and fifth graders to evaluate information sources during text comprehension. *Cognition and Instruction, 31*, 204–226. doi:10.1080/07370008.2013.769995

Maier, J., & Richter, T. (2013a). How nonexperts understand conflicting information on social science issues: The role of perceived plausibility and reading goals. *Journal of Media Psychology, 25*, 14–26. doi:10.1027/1864-1105/a000078

Maier, J., & Richter, T. (2013b). Text-belief consistency effects in the comprehension of multiple texts with conflicting information. *Cognition and Instruction, 31*, 151–175. doi:10.1080/07370008.2013.769997

Maier, J., & Richter, T. (2014). Fostering multiple text comprehension: How metacognitive strategies and motivation moderate the text-belief consistency effect. *Metacognition and Learning, 9*, 54–71. doi:10.1007/s11409-013-9111-x

Maier, J., & Richter, T. (2016). Effects of text-belief consistency and reading task on the strategic validation of multiple texts. *European Journal of the Psychology of Education, 31*, 479–497. doi:10.1007/s10212-015-0270-9

McCrudden, M. T., & Barnes, A. (2016). Differences in student reasoning about belief-relevant arguments: A mixed methods study. *Metacognition and Learning, 11*, 275–303. doi:10.1007/s11409-015-9148-0

McNamara, D. S., & Magliano, J. P. (2009). Towards a comprehensive model of comprehension. In B. Ross (Ed.), *The psychology of learning and motivation* (vol. 51, pp. 297–384). New York: Elsevier.

Nickerson, R. S. (1998). Confirmation bias: A ubiquitous phenomenon in many guises. *Review of General Psychology, 2*, 175–220. doi:10.1037/1089-2680.2.2.175

O'Brien, E. J., & Cook, A. E. (2016). Separating the activation, integration, and validation components of reading. In B. Ross (Ed.), *The psychology of learning and motivation* (vol. 65, pp. 249–276). New York: Academic Press.

O'Brien, E. J., & Myers, J. L. (1999). Text comprehension: A view from the bottom up. In S. R. Goldman, A. C. Graesser, & P. van den Broek (Eds.), *Narrative comprehension, causality, and coherence: Essays in honor of Tom Trabasso* (pp. 35–53). Mahwah: NJ: Erlbaum.

O'Brien, E. J., Rizzella, M. L., Albrecht, J. E., & Halleran, J. G. (1998). Updating a situation model: A memory-based text processing view. *Journal of Experimental Psychology: Learning, Memory, and Cognition, 24*, 1200–1210. doi:10.1037/0278-7393.24.5.1200

Paul, J., Stadtler, M., & Bromme, R. (2017). Effects of a sourcing prompt and conflicts in reading materials on elementary students' use of source information. *Discourse Processes, 56*, 155–169. doi:10.1080/0163853X.2017.1402165

Paul, J. M., Cerdán, R., Rouet, J.-F., & Stadtler, M. (2018). Exploring fourth graders' sourcing skills. *Journal for the Study of Education and Development, 41*, 536–580. doi:https://doi.org/10.1080/02103702.2018.1480458

Perfetti, C. A., Rouet, J. F., & Britt, M. A. (1999). Toward a theory of documents representation. In H. van Oostendorp & S. R. Goldman (Eds.), *The construction of mental representations during reading* (pp. 99–122). Mahwah, NJ: Erlbaum.

Perry, W. G. (1970). *Forms of intellectual and ethical development in the college years: A scheme*. New York: Holt, Rinehart, & Winston.

Piest, B. A., Isberner, M. B., & Richter, T. (2018). Don't believe everything you hear: Routine validation of audiovisual information in children and adults. *Memory and Cognition, 46*, 849–863. doi:10.3758/s13421-018-0807-7

Richter, T. (2003). *Epistemologische Einschätzungen beim Textverstehen [Epistemic validation in text comprehension]*. Lengerich, Germany: Pabst.

Richter, T. (2011). Cognitive flexibility and epistemic validation in learning from multiple texts. In J. Elen, E. Stahl, R. Bromme, & G. Clarebout (Eds.), *Links between beliefs and cognitive flexibility* (pp. 125–140). Berlin: Springer.

Richter, T. (2015). Validation and comprehension of text information: Two sides of the same coin. *Discourse Processes, 52*, 337–352. doi:10.1080/0163853X.2015.1025665

Richter, T., & Maier, J. (2017). Comprehension of multiple documents with conflicting information: A two-step model of validation. *Educational Psychologist, 52*, 148–166. doi:10.1080/00461520.2017.1322968

Richter, T., & Maier, J. (2018). The role of validation in multiple source use. In J. Braasch, I. Bråten, & M. McCrudden (Eds.), *Handbook of multiple source use* (pp. 151–167). New York: Routledge.

Richter, T., & Schmid, S. (2010). Epistemological beliefs and epistemic strategies in self-regulated learning. *Metacognition and Learning, 5,* 47–65. doi:10.1007/s11409-009-9038-4

Richter, T., Schroeder, S., & Wöhrmann, B. (2009). You don't have to believe everything you read: Background knowledge permits fast and efficient validation of information. *Journal of Personality and Social Psychology, 96,* 538–558. doi:10.1037/a0014038

Richter, T., & Singer, M. (2017). Discourse updating: Acquiring and revising knowledge through discourse. In M. F. Schober, D. N. Rapp, & M. A. Britt (Eds.), *The Routledge handbook of discourse processes* (2nd ed., pp. 167–190). New York: Routledge. doi:10.4324/9781315687384-11

Rouet, J.-F., Britt, M. A., Mason, R. A., & Perfetti, C. A. (1996). Using multiple sources of evidence to reason about history. *Journal of Educational Psychology, 88,* 478–493. doi:10.1037/0022-0663.88.3.478

Schroeder, S., Richter, T., & Hoever, I. (2008). Getting a picture that is both accurate and stable: Situation models and epistemic validation. *Journal of Memory and Language, 59,* 237–255. doi:10.1016/j.jml.2008.05.001

Singer, M. (2013). Validation in reading comprehension. *Current Directions in Psychological Science, 22,* 361–366. doi:10.1177/0963721413495236

Singer, M., Halldorson, M., Lear, J. C., & Andrusiak, P. (1992). Validation of causal bridging inferences in discourse understanding. *Journal of Memory and Language, 31,* 507–524. doi:10.1016/0749-596X(92)90026-T

Sperber, D., Clément, F., Heintz, C., Mascaro, O., Mercier, H., Origgi, G., & Wilson, D. (2010). Epistemic vigilance. *Mind and Language, 25,* 359–393. doi:10.1111/j.1468-0017.2010.01394.x

Stadtler, M., & Bromme, R. (2008). Effects of the metacognitive tool met.a.ware on the web search of laypersons. *Computers in Human Behavior, 24,* 716–737. doi:10.1016/j.chb.2007.01.023

Stadtler, M., Scharrer, L., Macedo-Rouet, M., Rouet, J.-F., & Bromme, R. (2016). Improving vocational students' consideration of source information when deciding about science controversies. *Reading and Writing, 29,* 705–729. doi:10.1007/s11145-016-9623-2

Strømsø, H. I., Bråten, I., & Britt, M. A. (2010). Reading multiple texts about climate change: The relationship between memory for sources and text comprehension. *Learning and Instruction, 20,* 192–204. doi:https://doi.org/10.1016/j.learninstruc.2009.02.001

Toulmin, S. E. (1958). *The uses of argument.* Cambridge, MA: Cambridge University Press.

van Dijk, T., & Kintsch, W. (1983). *Strategies of discourse comprehension.* New York: Academic Press.

van Strien, J. L. H., Brand-Gruwel, S., & Boishuizen, H. P. A. (2014). Dealing with conflicting information from multiple nonlinear texts: Effects of prior attitudes. *Computers in Human Behavior, 32,* 101–111. doi:10.1016/j.chb.2013.11.021

von der Mühlen, S., Richter, T., Schmid, S., & Berthold, K. (2018). How to improve argumentation comprehension in university students: Experimental test of a training approach. *Instructional Science, 47,* 215–237. doi:10.1007/s11251-018-9471-3

von der Mühlen, S., Richter, T., Schmid, S., Schmidt, L. M., & Berthold, K. (2016a). The use of source-related strategies in evaluating multiple psychology texts: A student-scientist comparison. *Reading and Writing, 8,* 1677–1698. doi:10.1007/s11145-015-9601-0

von der Mühlen, S., Richter, T., Schmid, S., Schmidt, L. M., & Berthold, K. (2016b). Judging the plausibility of argumentative statements in scientific texts: A student-scientist comparison. *Thinking and Reasoning, 22,* 221–249. doi:10.1080/13546783.2015.1127289

Voss, J. F., Fincher-Kiefer, R., Wiley, J., & Silfies, L. N. (1993). On the processing of arguments. *Argumentation, 7,* 165–181. doi:10.1007/BF00710663

Wiley, J., Goldman, S. R., Graesser, A. C., Sanchez, C. A., Ash, I. K., & Hemmerich, J. A. (2009). Source evaluation, comprehension, and learning in internet science inquiry tasks. *American Educational Research Journal, 46,* 1060–1106. doi:10.3102/0002831209333183

Wiley, J. F., & Voss, J. F. (1999). Constructing arguments from multiple sources: Tasks that promote understanding and not just memory for text. *Journal of Educational Psychology, 91,* 310–311. doi:10.1037//0022-0663.91.2.30

17

STUDENTS' PERSPECTIVE LEARNING IN A DISCIPLINARY MULTISOURCE TASK ENVIRONMENT

Byeong-Young Cho, Linda Kucan, and Emily C. Rainey

UNIVERSITY OF PITTSBURGH

ABSTRACT

This chapter focuses on how students learn about and develop perspectives when working with multiple sources in disciplinary classrooms. This chapter begins with a proposal for considering multiple facets of perspective learning, involving acknowledging, comparing, and co-constructing perspectives. It situates these perspective-learning processes in a historical literacy task environment that engages students in an examination of multiple historical sources. The chapter explores the nature of students' perspective learning within a series of classroom vignettes in which students used competing perspectives and consulted multiple sources in an investigation into their local area and its history. It draws on specific moments of classroom discourse from a research project conducted with 8th graders in an urban school, which examined student learning within a multisource task environment designed to promote disciplinary practices of historical reading, writing, and thinking. The chapter concludes with a discussion of observations of student engagement in this literacy task and suggestions about possible considerations for designing classroom environments that support perspective learning.

Key words: student perspectives, task environment, disciplinary literacy, historical inquiry, multiple sources

This chapter focuses on how students learn about and develop perspectives when working with multiple sources in disciplinary classrooms. We begin with a proposal for considering multiple facets of perspective learning, involving acknowledging, comparing, and co-constructing perspectives. We situate these perspective-learning processes in a historical literacy task environment that engages students in an examination of multiple historical sources. Next, we explore the nature of students' perspective learning within a series of classroom vignettes in which students used competing perspectives and consulted multiple sources in an investigation into their local area and its history. For this, we draw on specific moments of classroom discourse from a research project we conducted with 8th graders in an urban school, which examined student learning within a multisource task environment designed to promote disciplinary practices of historical reading, writing, and thinking. Finally, we discuss our observations of student engagement in this disciplinary literacy task and suggest possible considerations for designing classroom environments that support perspective learning.

A FRAMING OF PERSPECTIVE LEARNING IN DISCIPLINARY CLASSROOMS

We propose the idea of *perspective learning* to explore a way of supporting student engagement in the challenging work of assessing, negotiating, and developing multiple perspectives in subject area classrooms. Perspective learning is the process of knowing *with* and *about* the stances, viewpoints, and positioning involved in inquiries into specific problems and questions that are relevant and meaningful to learners and the communities of which they are a part. Through that learning, multiple perspectives are elaborated and enhanced over time by the students taking on the roles and responsibilities of active knowers. In classrooms that support perspective learning, students are scaffolded to activate and engage various perspectives coexisting in the classroom, including their own, as resources for classroom learning. In such environments, perspective learning can empower students to develop new ways of viewing and examining specific topics, problems, and questions.

Perspective learning is promoted with enriched opportunities for students to read, write, and think with diverse texts, particularly in the context of disciplinary literacy learning. The work of disciplinary literacy scholars (e.g., Goldman et al., 2016; Moje, 2007; Wineburg, 2001) suggests that disciplinary reading, writing, and reasoning support students in developing informed ways of acquiring and producing knowledge with texts that are represented in multiple formats, modes, and contexts. Disciplinary literacy instruction is therefore meant to guide student participation in epistemic practices for accessing, processing, and interrogating such texts (Lave & Wenger, 1991; Sandoval, Greene, & Bråten, 2016) through approximating the work of disciplinary experts (Moje, 2015; Van Drie & van Boxtel, 2008; Wineburg, 1991). Further, disciplinary literacy instruction can provide a context in which students are motivated to identify and develop legitimate perspectives and stances toward justifying the competing knowledge claims of others and of themselves.

Loosely structured disciplines especially rely on analysis and interpretation of documents and facts, and of the claims and perspectives of others. History, in particular, requires sophisticated work with varying perspectives (Carr, 1961). Historical arguments are a type of perspective that historians, and students of history, can generate, communicate, and compare. However, the process of historical reasoning also requires the consideration of multiple perspectives by first reading sources and discerning what the authors' perspectives were in relation to the particular contexts in which the documents were created and used (Wineburg, 1991). A wide range of historical sources (e.g., original documents, witness interviews, historical photos, contemporary accounts) may be examined, some with clearer sourcing, and therefore more perspective-related information, than others.

Historical inquiry, for example, involves considering how perspectives of contemporary figures relate to one another and what those perspectives collectively suggest about an event or issue of the past (Seixas, 1996). To this inquiry process, the historian or history student must bring a stance of historical empathy (Ashby & Lee, 1987; Foster, 2001); this means that it is crucial to prioritize understanding the beliefs, values, assumptions, and practices of people as they were without simply imposing judgment on them through a contemporary lens. In these ways, historical work involves negotiating multiple perspectives in order to construct evidence-based claims (e.g., Bain, 2006; Wineburg, 2001). This is deeply challenging work for young people to learn to do (Duhaylongsod, Snow, Selman, & Donovan, 2015; VanSledright, 2002).

Components of Perspective Learning

Perspective learning in history is complex and multifaceted. It encompasses a range of cognitive and social processes. We propose that perspective learning involves three major processes that students can coordinate at different moments of learning: (a) acknowledging perspectives, (b) comparing perspectives, and (c) co-constructing perspectives. In what follows, we describe how each of these processes may serve students' perspective learning in history classrooms.

Acknowledging Perspectives

An initial (and ongoing) process of perspective learning is detecting and recognizing what perspectives are available. Learners notice the perspectives of others including their peers, teachers, or authors of the texts used in classrooms. They are also able to retrieve their own perspectives as a reference point to recognize others' perspectives and react to any ambiguities in the perspectives. In history learning, for example, a class activity in which students must choose and defend a claim based on their interpretation of textual evidence makes such a process concrete. That is, engaging in this activity requires seeing that there are different perspectives and that these can be defended in more or less compelling ways.

Acknowledging perspectives is not easy. Looking deeply into one's own perspectives and articulating what they mean to others is not only difficult but rarely attempted, especially by inexperienced learners (Baker & Brown, 1984; Flavell, 1979; Kuhn, 2000; Pintrich, 2002). Productive self-reflection requires accurate awareness and appraisal of what is or is not known (e.g., What do I know about my topic of urban renewal in the 1950s? How can I make sense of it?), and the will to squarely face one's abilities (e.g., How capable am I of collecting texts relevant to my topic? How complete are the resources I am consulting?).

Further, perspectives on different aspects of historical inquiry may come into play as students analyze not only the specific historical problem being investigated (e.g., What were the adverse consequences of urban renewal practices for under-resourced minority communities in the city?) but also essential features of the tasks being conducted such as their objectives (e.g., What would I like to achieve through my investigation?), procedures (e.g., How well can I express my ideas?), or expected outcomes (e.g., What would I like to produce in the end?).

Comparing Perspectives

Perspective learning can engage students in constructive meaning making if students are guided to compare multiple perspectives by identifying the sources of various perspectives and then building multiple linkages across those perspectives. For example, in a classroom discussion about multiple accounts about an event, students may begin to see a focal historical problem from various perspectives by talking about what they learned from eyewitnesses' reports, photographs, and newspaper articles. They can identify different perspectives and evaluate the merits and limitations of each. In the process, students become more agentive in comparing and orchestrating various perspectives as resources for learning through these activities.

In such a classroom environment, perspectives that are developing in the minds of individual learners become a community product (Brown, Collins, & Duguid, 1989; Engeström, 1999; Lave & Wenger, 1991). A co-constructed perspective is the result of an environment in which students hold themselves accountable for their actions toward achieving a shared goal for historical understanding (e.g., to reconstruct an account of how black communities were demolished by the city's urban renewal projects) without losing their distinctive ways of viewing that history (e.g., Why had black people chosen to live in those communities? What were their reactions to racial practices?). As well, students may be encouraged to share their feedback with one another and help the classroom community direct attention and effort to assessing the specific merits and benefits of understanding the new opportunities and challenges brought about by their comparison of different perspectives.

Co-constructing Perspectives

Another aspect of perspective learning engages students in orchestrating the multiple perspectives that they have identified and reconciling them through collaborative effort. In history learning, for example, the process of co-constructing perspectives is driven by the emerging purpose of developing a salient and usable perspective (e.g., How does my inquiry suggest to me a viable perspective for understanding what has happened in our city in the past?), seeing the focal problem from the new perspective (e.g., What new aspects of the city's history are revealed from that perspective?), and justifying the perspective by considering alternative ways of perceiving and evaluating the problem space (e.g., How new are the newly revealed aspects? How do I weigh what I knew and what we have newly learned?). During such processes of perspective co-construction, students may have opportunities to challenge both others' and their own original perspectives with the newly framed perspective (e.g., Did I change how I respond to the practice of urban renewal in the 1950s? Do I see it differently now? If so, how?). Such learning can be supported when students are involved in completing a task by working with other students to impose coherence on information in order to present a unified claim.

We emphasize that these processes of perspective learning in history – acknowledging, comparing, and co-constructing perspectives – are scaffolded by engaging students in well-designed task environments. Several questions then arise: What is meant by a "task environment"? What role does it play in student learning? What essential features must be considered in designing a supportive task environment for perspective learning? We respond to these questions in the next section.

The Role of Multisource Task Environments in Perspective Learning

To begin, we consider the uses of the term "task" in order to describe what a task environment for perspective learning is like, drawing especially on education research on academic tasks (e.g. Doyle, 1983; Doyle & Carter, 1984; Marx & Walsh, 1988; Stein & Lane, 1996). Doyle identifies three aspects of academic tasks (1983, p. 161). First, academic tasks define the *products* that students generate and formulate, such as quiz responses, original essays, or oral presentations. They also include the *operations* students use to generate the product, such as cognitive strategies (e.g., memorization, comprehension, evaluation), sets of knowledge (e.g., content knowledge, domain knowledge, strategic knowledge), and pathways to understanding (e.g., conceptual learning, inquiry learning). Finally, academic tasks offer the *resources* that are to be used by students to create the task product, including material and human resources (e.g., a list of terms to remember, model essays, texts and charts, guidelines and rubrics, teachers and classmates).

This description of academic tasks helps determine how classroom tasks are created. At the same time, however, it reminds us that the specific classroom setting in which tasks are embedded must also be considered in the task design. In our account of task environments, therefore, we focus on the materialistic, conceptual, and contextual settings of a classroom where students carry out their intellectual work to generate the expected products with an array of learning strategies and resources that contribute to the production process. Likewise, task environments for perspective learning in history classrooms must be designed in ways that support students' generation of expected outcomes (e.g., formulating informed perspectives on a specific historical problem), engagement of learning processes (e.g., acknowledging, comparing, and co-constructing various perspectives on the problem), and coordination of resources (e.g., teacher modeling of historical thinking, relevant historical sources, class interactions, peer feedback for perspective development in history).

With this notion of classroom settings in mind, we characterize task environments that support students' perspective learning in history in the following manner. Such tasks are (a) intertextual and (b) dialogic, and they foreground (c) the epistemic stances of historians working on authentic questions and problems. When designed with these considerations, such classroom environments may provide "opportunities for students to regulate their own task activity" (Anderson, Stevens, Prawat, & Nickerson, 1988, p. 281) as they learn with and develop perspectives with texts and concepts from history.

Intertextual Commitment

Perspective learning is enabled by working within intertextual task environments. This means that a task environment should offer multiple sources of information, knowledge, and arguments that can support not only students' learning of content or information but also their literacy learning as they identify and use multiple texts to achieve the goal of developing evidence-based perspectives. Supporting and eliciting text-based interactions among students who have access to multiple sources are essential features of such task environments. Students can become more aware of intertextuality (with respect to how their thoughts and ideas are becoming mutually informed, influenced, and related through reading, writing, and conversing) through identifying various perspectives represented in texts and by other class participants and then building multiple linkages across these perspectives.

Dialogic Participation

Perspective learning is facilitated dialogically (Bakhtin & Holquist, 1981). In a dialogic classroom, students acknowledge the perspectives of others and take those perspectives into account in the process of completing a task that requires the participation of others. In such a setting, the perspectives of students, as well as those represented in the task environment in which they are working (i.e., by their peers, text authors, and teachers), are recognized, activated, and used as valuable resources for learning (Hammer & Elby, 2003). The task requires students to collaborate in order to develop a salient and usable perspective in relation to existing perspectives, to justify one's own perspective to others, and to reconcile competing or conflicting perspectives. Through such activity, perspectives are problematized and become grist for critical engagement (Greeno & van der Sande, 2007).

Epistemic Engagement

The kind of classroom setting designed for perspective learning facilitates students' literacy learning through epistemic engagement with multiple texts and sources. In this task environment, perspective learning can occur as students are supported in choosing and using a variety of different texts toward constructing their own standpoints and justifying them through their textual inquiry processes. An epistemically engaging task environment promotes sophisticated learning in which reading and writing activity is situated within particular contexts of use and conducted for specific purposes of knowledge work (Brown et al., 1989; Hammer & Elby, 2003). Therefore, the classroom as an epistemic community develops and flourishes through the active participation of its members in the epistemic practices of acknowledging, analyzing, and constructing perspectives.

In summary, our take on perspective learning offers implications for pedagogical practices that engage students in actively identifying and using the range of perspectives coexisting in the classroom as important resources to develop, test, and refine distinctive ways of viewing the world. It also implies that perspective learning can be promoted if students are working within a carefully designed task environment that elicits the sophisticated use of multiple resources to work with others engaged in the same effort. In what follows, we further explore students' perspective learning with classroom vignettes from our analysis of student discourse in a historical multisource task environment for middle school learners.

CLASSROOM VIGNETTES OF STUDENTS' PERSPECTIVE LEARNING

In this section, we describe how students at an urban middle school in Pittsburgh (Dunbar Academy, hereafter) worked during a history unit about Pittsburgh's Hill District (Kucan, Rainey, & Cho, 2019). We represent this unit as a task environment that supported students' engagement in historical perspective learning. We offer an analysis of students' perspective learning by focusing on selected vignettes of dialogic interactions (Miles, Huberman, & Saldana, 2014). Our goal is not to present examples of students' perspective taking, but rather to demonstrate the potential of historical multisource task environments for inviting students to engage in perspective learning. We note that these vignettes are not necessarily representative of the interactions students tended to have in our study; rather, we have selected them because of their clarity in illustrating students' work with perspectives, work that is often not observable because it happens internally. It is the clarity of these vignettes brought about through students' talk with one another that enables us to closely analyze the dimensions of these interactions and the conditions that seemed to support them.

A Brief History of the Pittsburgh Hill District

To begin, we provide some historical background about the Hill District in Pittsburgh as the focus of the unit. The history of the Hill District is essential for understanding race relations, economic patterns, and housing conditions in Pittsburgh today (Trotter & Day, 2010). Also known as "the Hill," the Hill District is a Pittsburgh neighborhood with a large black population that flourished during the 1930s–1940s. Segregated from commercial and entertainment venues in downtown Pittsburgh, residents of the Hill created their own businesses as well as churches and fraternal organizations. Urban renewal efforts in the 1950s effectively destroyed much of the Hill District. Specifically, the construction of the Civic Arena, a multi-use entertainment complex, resulted in the removal of hundreds of black families from their homes. A new highway also isolated the remaining neighborhood from downtown. Activism was centered in the Hill as black Pittsburghers protested their exclusion from construction jobs and displacement from their homes. Following the assassination of Martin Luther King Jr. in 1968, the Hill was the scene of violent demonstrations, and the mayor called in the National Guard.

A Multisource Task Environment for the Hill District Unit

We designed a unit to engage students in learning about the history of the Hill District. The motivation for that work was a then-recent news story about plans to reconnect the Lower Hill and downtown with a pedestrian bridge and park that would also feature displays to celebrate the unique history of the Hill. Specifically, we provided Dunbar students with contemporary sources that foregrounded the rich cultural history of the Hill as well as primary sources that focused on the low-level jobs and the blighted housing conditions of many Hill residents. For example, news articles about the construction of the Civic Arena depicted the Hill in bleak terms, while the Arena with its retractable dome was lauded as a wondrous edifice. Students viewed video clips about the vibrant entertainment scene in the Hill with its nightclubs and ball field. However, they also learned that most of the patrons of the clubs were white, and that the ball field was for black players in the Negro Leagues who were excluded from major league baseball teams. As these sources suggested, the history of the Hill District is complex, and investigating that history involves considering different perspectives.

We are committed to exploring ways of designing and testing text-rich task environments contextualized in social studies classrooms. This project's task environment therefore included the following features that served students' perspective learning:

- *Epistemic engagement.* Inquiry cycles scaffolded students to question, investigate, and communicate their own and others' perspectives and to make use of these epistemic resources for their learning about a historical event.
- *Intertextual commitment.* Disciplinary literacy tasks involved students in examining multiple historical sources in multiple formats. These sources included documentary video excerpts, photographs, newspaper articles, interviews, census data, and maps. Some of these sources were provided as paper documents, while others were available online in digital formats.
- *Dialogic participation.* Discursive activities and participation structures encouraged students to think together to activate, develop, and learn from different perspectives. These activities included working with a partner, small-group talk, and presenting reports to the entire class.

The culminating task for the unit was for students to design a multimedia presentation that provided responses to three questions: (1) What was the Hill District like in the past? (2) What happened to the Hill District? and (3) What should the city do with the Hill District now? The task required students to organize their responses to each question in a claim-evidence-reasoning framework. We made the framework available in an accessible sentence format to scaffold students to structure their responses easily. For example, a framework for responding to the first question includes:

- The Hill District was _____ in the past. [Claim]
- We examined historical documents, including _____, to investigate what the Hill was like. [Source of evidence]
- Together, these historical documents support our claim because _____. [Reasoning]

The task asked students to work with a partner to access historical sources in print as well as digitally in an online repository we created for them, so that they could include in their presentations video excerpts, maps, photographs, newspaper accounts, and interviews with Hill residents. Our purpose in designing this task was to support students in developing perspectives about the research and readings they had completed across the unit. Students were encouraged to present their perspectives about what happened in the Hill District and what could be envisioned for the present Hill community.

We provided pairs of students with video recorders, which they positioned on their tables as they worked together to complete the unit project. In the following section, we use selected transcripts from students' video-recorded discussions to present two vignettes that make visible students' use of and development of perspectives. We use each vignette to describe a notable moment at which Dunbar students were engaged in epistemic practices of acknowledging, comparing, and co-constructing perspectives related to their claims about the Hill District.

Perspective Learning of Denise and Isaiah

To begin, we offer a vignette that reveals two students negotiating the purpose of the task they were to complete. Denise and Isaiah, as a pair, were looking together at a rubric that detailed their task, which was to produce a clear argument with evidence and reasoning. As they represented what would be involved in completing the assigned task, they were *acknowledging* their own perspectives as well as the existence of their partner's perspectives.

Denise: Alright. Argumentative. This should be good because you like to make an argument.
Isaiah: Debating was my favorite part of history class last year.
Denise: I feel like, when we present, we can have that split down the middle and have the different arguments inside ... Make sense?
Isaiah: I'm not getting the entire picture.
Denise: Because, like, it's supposed to be like the argument for talking about the different points.
Isaiah: Yeah, like both sides.
Denise: Yeah, like the evidence.
Isaiah: Like the bad and the good.
Denise: And I'm saying you're probably going to have a different opinion on one thing, and I'll have a different opinion on another thing. We could talk about it in a different point of view on what we're talking about, when we explain and present. Okay?
Isaiah: Yeah.

At the outset, Denise seemed to represent the argumentative task as a debate or presentation of opposing perspectives. When Isaiah identified his lack of understanding of Denise's perspective on the historical task ("I'm not getting the entire picture"), Denise immediately responded by elaborating what she meant by "argumentative" ("talking about the different points"). In their back and forth, they *compared* their different perspectives as related to the task of building a historical argument together. In doing so, they clarified their common task goal or direction and potentially reinforced their mutual trust for working out the process of completing the task together, as suggested by Denise's comment that they would each probably have different points of view and that the final project could incorporate both opinions.

In this moment, the students had not yet engaged with the actual task, or connected "both sides" or "the bad and the good" to any specific event or situation related to the history of the Hill District. Later, however, Denise and Isaiah did just that when they were working together to create a claim to address the first question in the final task: What was the Hill District like in the past?

Denise: I was going to say that the Hill District is full of diversity, thriving, as an independent community ...

Isaiah: I'm trying to get onto History.com, and try to find something about the Hill District.

Denise: We can look that up in a minute. <Points to a box on Isaiah's screen.> We need to fill out the claim. The Hill District was full of diversity, and thriving as an independent community?

Isaiah: Yeah. That works.

Denise: So our claim was that the Hill District was full of diversity and thriving as an independent community, and then now we're looking for our sources to back up our claim.

Isaiah: ... I'm going through different sources to try to find our claim better.

Denise: I found one. <Reads> "In the Hill District in the same house where she grew up. She was one of nine children, two blocks up from Centre Avenue. Hers is the house with the bright red exterior, built in 1920. The home was the last in a row of 4 ... One of the homes was ... condemned." So, we could put this in our reasoning. We could put like a person came directly from ... you can trust this source because it ends in dot org. And it says, you can see pictures and stuff ...

Isaiah: This is a good site ... a quote from her said "her and her neighbors were able to find everything they needed right within the community. Clothing, shoes, food, and fun." So basically, now they're saying that the people took away and destroyed all their homes.

Isaiah: Yeah, it's like the one video we watched where it was a thriving community. They said you could walk into a barbershop, and then right across the street you had a barbeque shop, you had ...

Denise: Restaurants.

Isaiah: Yeah. Definitely. You had different types of restaurants, not just American, Italian, you had different types, and by black people, African Americans.

In this interaction, there are multiple indications of work with perspectives. Most visibly, this interaction depicts Denise and Isaiah *co-constructing* a claim by testing a drafted claim against specific evidence. Initially, Denise took the lead by making the explicit claim that the Hill District was "full of diversity, thriving, as an independent community." Responding to Denise, Isaiah kept his conclusion tentative. He agreed that the claim "works," but he continued to look for more sources of evidence that might assist the pair in revising the claim ("I'm going through different sources to try to find our claim better"). Denise stayed on task while acknowledging the effort of Isaiah and participating with him in the search for further sources to refine the current claim and reasoning ("now we're looking for our sources to back up our claim").

It was Denise who found a relevant source first in an online newspaper article published by a Pittsburgh non-profit journalism group. Isaiah and Denise immediately noticed the article's title, "The Hill District, a Community Holding On through Displacement and Development" and a vivid photo accompanying it, which was taken during an interview with an 80-year-old black woman who lived in the same Hill

District home where she grew up. They also noted a powerful quote from the woman in the photo and identified the article as a useful source to "back up" their claim, because they could use it to consider a perspective from a Hill resident as a historical participant.

Denise was confident in presenting her perspective, but Isaiah's tentativeness engaged them both in further investigation. That investigation involved the location of a new source and connecting that source to a previously accessed source (the video). By the end of the exchange, Isaiah seemed to be in agreement with Denise's initial claim, indicated by his use of the word "thriving," which she had introduced at the outset.

Although less explicit, there are also glimpses of the students *acknowledging* and *comparing* perspectives in this excerpt. When Denise suggested the initial claim to Isaiah, she did so with an upward intonation that signaled a question ("The Hill District was full of diversity, and thriving as an independent community?"). Isaiah, hearing this potential claim as a question, replied, "Yeah. That works." Denise's turn suggests an acknowledgment that Isaiah might have an alternate perspective, one that is different from her own. Similarly, when the students read the experience of the 80-year-old Hill District resident, they first examined it for additional information (potentially with the implicit understanding that the interviewee's perspective could challenge their own) and compared it to another source, a video that they had watched earlier in the unit.

In the vignette above, the students' work showcases an instance in which they were extending their initial perspective through compiling evidence. However, work with perspectives can also involve the revision of an existing perspective based on new ideas or information that challenges that perspective. After the aforementioned interaction, Isaiah and Denise and the rest of the class watched a PowerPoint presentation created by another pair, Dylan and Jeremiah. The first slide of the presentation read:

- *The Hill District in the past was a community that was discriminated at this time.*
- *According to our DocPack, it shows percentages of how many whites had job opportunities compared to African Americans.*
- *So what they did was make art to entertain their community.*
- *In 1948 Mary Dee became the first African American Female to become a radio DJ and radio pioneer.*

In response to his classmates' presentation, Isaiah raises his hand to offer a comment.

Uh, I am kind of agreeing with [Dylan and Jeremiah], but where I got my source from is the website that you had sent us. And it's, it is chapter, it is "A World of Their Own." So basically, it's racist because people, black people weren't allowed, really treated well outside the Hill. That's why it was thriving within it because there you were able to get a job by a black employer.

Here, Isaiah acknowledges the perspective of Dylan and Jeremiah as well as his own; he indicates some difference between the two perspectives; and he demonstrates perspective constructing by revising the claim that he and Denise had previously developed ("Yes, the Hill was a thriving community with its own restaurants and businesses, but that was because of racism."). As Isaiah says, "It's because ... black people weren't treated well outside the Hill. That's why it [the Hill neighborhood] was thriving within it [the Hill] because there you were able to get a job by a black employer." This episode briefly demonstrates the importance of finding out about the perspectives developed by other students for perspective learning.

Perspective Learning of Taye and Darius

Taye and Darius provide another example of acknowledging, comparing, and constructing perspectives. The episode involved them working together to respond to the third task question: What should the city do with the Hill District now?

Taye: The question is ... what should the city do with the Hill District now?
Darius: Are you asking what I think?
Taye: Ah, yeah.
Darius: What I think they should do is like, put in, like tear off all the ... what they made. Like you know how they made where the Civic Arena was into a parking area now? They shouldn't have done that. They should have rebuilt those houses because that's ... that's a lot of living space.
Taye: <simultaneous talk> Good idea, but since that's in the past, what are we going to do now?
Darius: Now just grow some grass.
Taye: Grow some grass in the ...
Darius: In that spot.
Taye: Yeah. I think they're planning to build an overlook, right? You know that.
Darius: We need grass!
Taye: Okay. So, build a park?
Darius: Yeah. Where people can just walk and kids can just play dodge ball.
Taye: Do it for stress relieving and just to forget about.
Darius: And recreational purposes.

At first, Darius argued that the city should never have paved a part of the land to make a parking lot. By *acknowledging* Darius's comment, Taye provided feedback and prompting ("Good idea, but since that's in the past, what are we going to do now?"). Then, together they considered what should happen now. Darius advocated for the city to grow grass in the spot where the parking lot is now, and the two of them built on one another's ideas (by *comparing* their perspectives) as important resources that they used to ultimately determine that a park should be created that would serve both "stress relieving" and "recreational" purposes. In this moment, Taye's comments worked to help Darius activate and present his perspective on a future plan for the redevelopment of the former Arena site (currently, a huge empty parking lot), and then both students engaged in the building of an emerging perspective by collaboratively justifying that historically informed perspective on the present and future of the Lower Hill (*co-constructing* a perspective).

Taye and Darius's discussion then provides an interesting example of perspective taking by attributing a perspective to an imagined audience. Taye offered his perspective on the planned deck that will reconnect the Hill District and downtown Pittsburgh. The plan includes a wall with historical information and an avatar to guide viewers through the display, and describes the avatar as a young black girl with braids, tentatively named Keisha.

Taye: And [the park] cannot include like you know Keisha. So Keisha, it's [the city redevelopers are] going to make this little mural I guess. With the black girl with braids and stuff. But I think they should just make a park without any kind of race anything, so everybody can go there and feel comfortable. Because if they don't, then it's not going to be a sense of calmness and comfortability. If that's a word.

Darius: Alright, in class I said this. That it's like racial profiling, it's like racial profiling for it to be, for it to assume to be a "black girl". <*acts out air quotes*> To assume that all black girls have braids, because <*looks around the room*> that's a bad example. <*points at one girl and laughs*> That's a good example. That's another good example, and that's also a good example. Not all black girls have braids …

Taye: It shouldn't have any racial connections or anything, so everyone can feel …

Darius: No racial profiling.

Taye: Because people think differently than each other, so one might think, Yay! They finally put …

Darius: Something.

Taye: A black woman on a wall, or something like that. Or made a mural about her. But some people might think, why does she have braids? You're only saying that because she's black or something. And then maybe some caucasian people might come and say, why don't you put any white people on the walls? And then maybe some other races come and say, why don't you put our people on the walls? And then it's just going to be, it's just going to get worse and worse. So, if you just keep off race and stuff, you'll be fine.

Taye takes exception to the planned design with the Keisha avatar because he thinks it will detract from the calmness of the park and overemphasize race. Darius agrees, referring to his comments in class about "racial profiling." He sees the choice of having Keisha wear braids as an example of such profiling, expressing that it is a singular and narrow representation of the actual complexity of black girls and women as a group. With Keisha as their focus, Darius and Taye anticipate the potential perspectives of "people [who] think differently." According to Taye, having a black girl as the guide could provoke negative responses from white people and people of other races. In this way, Taye tries to anticipate the perspective of people who might have different opinions and stances on the use of Keisha in the design of a mural that should, from his perspective, "keep off race."

Taken together, the moment-to-moment processes demonstrated in the classroom vignettes suggest that middle-school learners may be able to consider the rhetorical context of historical perspective taking in which multiple people and parties (e.g., classmates, teachers, others outside the classroom) may collaborate to generate a consensus and also compete to push perspectives of their own through manifold debates on a historical problem. That is, middle-school learners have the potential for thoughtful disciplinary learning given a context that supports their awareness of the meanings and values attached to diverse perspectives. As part of their learning, they may be supported to reevaluate such meanings and values by considering possible situations in which a given perspective is questioned and challenged.

WHAT THE HILL DISTRICT UNIT TELLS US ABOUT PERSPECTIVE LEARNING IN A HISTORICAL MULTISOURCE TASK ENVIRONMENT

Our work at Dunbar Academy has enabled us to observe the complexity of perspective learning in relation to social studies learning. We have offered instances in which middle-school students appeared to move among multiple dimensions of perspective learning. Students acknowledged their own perspectives and compared them to those of others, they co-constructed new perspectives by building on what their partners suggested, and they revised their perspectives by considering perspectives that challenged their own.

Our examination of these classroom interactions through the lens of perspective learning leads us to ask: if perspective learning is important work for students to undertake and accomplish in classrooms, in part because subject-area and literacy learning demand it, and if perspective learning is also a major source of challenge for students, then how are students best supported to understand what they can do and achieve through perspective learning? In what follows, we offer a few tentative pedagogical implications.

First of all, a rich task environment that encourages students to recognize and understand the contradictory or competing stances emanating from multiple sources may support students' perspective learning (Kucan et al., 2019). The task environment of our Hill District unit engaged students in a historical inquiry process that began with questions of local significance (i.e., What was the Hill like in the past? What happened to the Hill District? What should the city do with the Hill now?). These questions invited students into an ongoing local debate about how to best use city and state funds to repair damages to infrastructure and people that resulted from past policy decisions. In keeping with the literature on providing rich problem spaces for learning (Newell & Simon, 1972), our designed task environment sought to engage students in a rich multisource problem space that would enable opportunities for their perspective learning.

In addition, students' perspective learning may be supported by a dialogic environment in which the questions under consideration are open and students' interactions are focused on the creation of shared stances (Nystrand & Gamoran, 1991; Wertsch & Toma, 1995). Our Hill District unit was marked by routine reading and writing tasks and daily opportunities for co-constructing meaning within a range of participation structures. These opportunities provided the space for students to come to understand and compare one another's perspectives as well as those of the authors represented in the texts under study. In fact, processes of considering, connecting, synthesizing, and evaluating various perspectives underpin most academic discourses and practices (Moje, 2015). Naming and supporting these processes is likely to facilitate students' learning of how to use them.

It can be challenging work to learn about multiple perspectives and to reconcile them with one's own perspectives. Therefore, the emotional and psychological demands of perspective learning should not be overlooked. Questions of perspective (mine, yours, a focal community's) and the texts (and discourses) that represent it are, in some ways, questions of power, privilege, and identity (Gee, 2008; Luke, 1995). In other words, the process of monitoring, taking, and building perspectives is far from neutral or dispassionate. Students may experience invitations to interrogate their own perspectives and potentially change them as welcome; considering and interrogating perspectives is, in many ways, the most authentic type of work that people can do with texts. But students may also experience such requests as risky and complicated; to give up a closely held perspective, or even to be willing to consider such a proposition, may be seen as putting distance between oneself and one's friends, family, and/or culture. The emotional and relational aspects of perspective learning work in classrooms must be carefully considered, supported, and honored.

Our illustrations suggest some of the challenges that can arise for students when reconciling others' perspectives with their own, especially when their own heritage or cultural groups or practices are implicated. In our particular case, given the race-specific historical trauma centered in the Hill, and students' close proximity to the consequences of that racism, our unit may have created additional demands for students' perspective learning. Learning about a history of racism, employing historical empathy when reading a primary source written by a racist, or considering distant communities of people who might still misunderstand or disregard your own community – these are potentially painful moments, even if they also support students' developing understandings of the world. We join with others working to understand and do this work in emancipatory ways (Britzman, 2000; Farley, 2009; Garrett, 2011; Paris & Alim, 2014).

Further, given the ways in which schools have historically silenced, marginalized, and dismissed groups of children and their communities (e.g., Delpit, 1988; Ladson-Billings, 1995), educators and researchers must ask critical questions about how, when, and whether to weigh in about the quality of newly emerging or previously held perspectives. There is a risk that challenging the perspectives students bring to the classroom could serve not only as a locus of dissonance for individual students but as part of a longer tradition of enculturating non-dominant groups of children into dominant hegemonic ideologies. It is our stance that explicitly valuing processes of perspective learning could enable teachers to resist such unjust traditions. Further, as our model implies, by creating opportunities for students to be open to reading, listening to, and understanding others' views and voices, without losing the integrity of their current perspectives as legitimate resources for learning, we might invite students and teachers to question dominant ideologies and perspectives and to think about ways in which deliberately considering and holding perspectives can become acts of empowering the self.

CONCLUDING THOUGHTS

We often urge teachers to teach students how to analyze and develop perspectives. However, questions remain about what the term "perspective" means and what that meaning implies for pedagogical practice. The absence of common language or an easily accessible framework limits efforts to help students learn for, from, and with perspectives. In this chapter, we explored what "perspective learning" could mean in a social studies classroom setting. We hope this preliminary attempt inspires further work that will contribute to building a robust and detailed framework for perspective learning. We believe such a framework could assist students in developing into informed citizens who are able to acknowledge, consider, and construct their distinctive ways of viewing the world.

We note that perspective learning needs to be approached with care. Misguided instruction can reinforce the dangerous perception that learning about others' perspectives means replacing one's own with those of others such as teachers, textbook authors, or smarter classmates. Further, an overemphasis on discrete cognitive skills may decontextualize student engagement, alienating learners from their authentic goals and questions, which should drive their learning. Nonetheless, our observations suggest that creating a considerate task environment has promise for perspective learning that facilitates students' abilities to activate and make use of various perspectives by taking into account multiple sources and authorities to be acknowledged, challenged, and justified.

Notions of perspective learning also present challenges and questions for the field. For example, we need research that will inform pedagogical decision-making on which perspectives ought to be considered for potential incorporation into classrooms and what standards of argumentation and perspective building are privileged. We also need a knowledge base that will enable us to respond to questions about the cognitive and social processes involved in trajectories of perspective learning, as well as about the additional cognitive and social demands (for students and for teachers) brought about by task environments specifically designed to promote perspective learning. Last but not least, we need to understand how we may better support teachers to learn to facilitate students' perspective learning. We acknowledge that many questions remain open, and we believe the field will benefit from further thoughtful examinations of students' experiences in the learning of perspectives and the pedagogical practices that best support this kind of sophisticated learning.

ACKNOWLEDGMENT

The study described in this chapter was supported by a Spencer Small Research Grant (Reference #201900021).

REFERENCES

Anderson, L. M., Stevens, D. D., Prawat, R. S., & Nickerson, J. (1988). Classroom task environments and students' task-related beliefs. *The Elementary School Journal, 88*(3), 281–295.

Ashby, R., & Lee, P. J. (1987). Children's concepts of empathy and understanding in history. In G. Portal (Ed.), *The history curriculum for teachers* (pp. 62–88). Philadelphia, PA: Falmer Press.

Bain, R. B. (2006). Rounding up unusual suspects: Facing the authority hidden in the history classroom. *Teachers College Record, 108*(10), 2080–2114.

Baker, L., & Brown, A. L. (1984). Metacognitive skills and reading. In R. Barr, P. D. Pearson, M. L. Kamil, & P. B. Mosenthal (Eds.), *Handbook of reading research* (vol. 1, pp. 353–394). Mahwah, NJ: Lawrence Erlbaum.

Bakhtin, M. M., & Holquist, M. (1981). *The dialogic imagination: Four essays*. Austin, TX: University of Texas Press.

Britzman, D. P. (2000). Teacher education in the confusion of our times. *Journal of Teacher Education, 51*(3), 200–205.

Brown, J. S., Collins, A., & Duguid, P. (1989). Situated cognition and the culture of learning. *Educational Researcher, 18*(1), 32–42.

Carr, E. H. (1961). *What is history?*. Cambridge: Cambridge University Press.

Delpit, L. D. (1988). The silenced dialogue: Power and pedagogy in educating other people's children. *Harvard Educational Review, 58*(3), 280–298.

Doyle, W. (1983). Academic work. *Review of Educational Research, 53*, 159–199.

Doyle, W., & Carter, K. (1984). Academic tasks in classroom. *Curriculum Inquiry, 14*(2), 129–149.

Duhaylongsod, L., Snow, C. E., Selman, R. L., & Donovan, M. S. (2015). Toward disciplinary literacy: Dilemmas and challenges in designing history curriculum to support middle school students. *Harvard Educational Review, 85*(4), 587–608.

Engeström, Y. (1999). Activity theory and individual and social transformation. In Y. Engeström, R. Miettinen, & R.-L. Panamäki (Eds.), *Perspectives on activity theory* (pp. 19–38). Cambridge: Cambridge University Press.

Farley, L. (2009). Radical hope: Or, the problem of uncertainty in history education. *Curriculum Inquiry, 39*(4), 537–554.

Flavell, J. H. (1979). Metacognition and cognitive monitoring: A new area of cognitive-developmental inquiry. *American Psychologist, 34*(10), 906–911.

Foster, S. J. (2001). Historical empathy in theory and practice; Some final thoughts. In O. L. Davis, E. A. Yeager, & S. J. Foster (Eds.), *Historical empathy and perspective taking in the social studies* (pp. 167–189). Lanham, MD: Rowman & Littlefield.

Garrett, H. J. (2011). The routing and re-routing of difficult knowledge: Social studies teachers encounter when the levees broke. *Theory and Research in Social Education, 39*(3), 320–347.

Gee, J. P. (2008). *Social linguistics and literacies: Ideology in discourses* (3rd ed.). New York: Routledge.

Goldman, S. R., Britt, M. A., Brown, W., Cribb, G., George, M., Greenleaf, C., … Shanahan, C. Project READI. (2016). Disciplinary literacies and learning to read for understanding: A conceptual framework for disciplinary literacy. *Educational Psychologist, 51*(2), 219–246.

Greeno, J., & van der Sande, C. (2007). Perspectival understanding of conceptions and conceptual growth in interaction. *Educational Psychologist, 42*(1), 9–23.

Hammer, D., & Elby, A. (2003). Tapping epistemological resources for learning physics. *Journal of the Learning Sciences, 12*(1), 53–90.

Kucan, L., Rainey, E. C., & Cho, B.-Y. (2019). Engaging middle school students in disciplinary literacy through culturally relevant historical inquiry. *Journal of Adolescent and Adult Literacy, 63*(1), 15–27.

Kuhn, D. (2000). Metacognitive development. *Current Directions in Psychological Science, 9*(5), 178–181.

Ladson-Billings, G. (1995). Toward a theory of culturally relevant pedagogy. *American Educational Research Journal, 32*(3), 465–491.

Lave, J., & Wenger, E. (1991). *Situated learning: Legitimate peripheral participation*. Cambridge: Cambridge University Press.

Luke, A. (1995). When basic skills and information processing just aren't enough: Rethinking reading in new times. *Teachers College Record, 97*(1), 95–115.

Marx, R. W., & Walsh, J. (1988). Learning from academic tasks. *The Elementary School Journal, 88*(3), 207–219.

Miles, M. B., Huberman, A. M., & Saldana, J. (2014). *Qualitative data analysis: A methods sourcebook*. Thousand Oaks, CA: Sage.

Moje, E. B. (2007). Developing socially just subject-matter instruction: A review of the literature on disciplinary literacy teaching. *Review of Research in Education, 31*, 1–44.

Moje, E. B. (2015). Doing and teaching disciplinary literacy with adolescent learners: A social and cultural enterprise. *Harvard Educational Review, 85*(2), 254–301.

Nystrand, M., & Gamoran, A. (1991). Instructional discourse, student engagement, and literature achievement. *Research in the Teaching of English, 25*(3), 261–290.

Paris, D., & Alim, H. S. (2014). What are we seeking to sustain through culturally sustaining pedagogy? A loving critique forward. *Harvard Educational Review, 84*(1), 85–100.

Pintrich, P. R. (2002). The role of metacognitive knowledge in learning, teaching and assessing. *Theory into Practice, 41*(4), 219–225.

Sandoval, W. A., Greene, J. A., & Bråten, I. (2016). Understanding and promoting thinking about knowledge: Origins, issues, and future directions of research in epistemic cognition. *Review of Research in Education*, *40*(1), 457–496.

Seixas, P. (1996). Conceptualizing the growth of historical understanding. In D. R. Olson & N. Torrance (Eds.), *The handbook of education and human development* (pp. 765–783). Oxford: Blackwell Publishers.

Newell, A., & Simon, H. A. (1972). *Human problem solving*. Englewood Cliffs, NJ: Prentice-Hall.

Stein, M. J., & Lane, S. (1996). Instructional tasks and the development of student capacity to think and reason: An analysis of the relationship between teaching and learning in a reformed mathematics project. *Educational Research and Evaluation*, *2*(1), 50–80.

Trotter, J. W., & Day, J. N. (2010). *Race and renaissance: African Americas in Pittsburgh since World War II*. Pittsburgh, PA: University of Pittsburgh Press.

Van Drie, J., & van Boxtel, C. (2008). Historical reasoning: Towards a framework for analyzing students' reasoning about the past. *Educational Psychology Review*, *20*(2), 87–110.

VanSledright, B. (2002). *In search of America's past: Learning to read history in elementary school*. New York: Teachers College Press.

Wertsch, J. V., & Toma, C. (1995). Discourse and learning in the classroom: A sociocultural approach. In L. P. Steffe & J. Gale (Eds.), *Constructivism in education* (pp. 159–174). Hillsdale, NJ: Lawrence Erlbaum.

Wineburg, S. S. (1991). Historical problem solving: A study of the cognitive processes used in the evaluation of documentary and pictorial evidence. *Journal of Educational Psychology*, *83*(1), 73–87.

Wineburg, S. S. (2001). *Historical thinking and other unnatural acts: Charting the future of teaching the past*. Philadelphia. PA: Temple University Press.

Section 3
Theoretical Viewpoints on the Integration of Multiple Representations and Multiple Perspectives

18

THE ROLES OF EXECUTIVE FUNCTIONS IN LEARNING FROM MULTIPLE REPRESENTATIONS AND PERSPECTIVES

D. Jake Follmer
WEST VIRGINIA UNIVERSITY

Rayne A. Sperling
PENNSYLVANIA STATE UNIVERSITY

ABSTRACT

Executive functions serve an integral role in varied learning processes and outcomes. Yet, the study of the contributions of core executive functions to learners' effective integration and comprehension of multiple inputs reflects an underexplored area of inquiry. The primary aims of this chapter were to discuss and delineate the roles of executive functions in learners' integration of multiple representations and perspectives. After conceptualizing executive function, we propose key executive processes theoretically supported in the integration of multiple representations and texts. We then summarize critical task, text and source, and learner factors likely to impact learners' interactions with multiple inputs. We conclude the chapter by extending recommendations and considerations to augment the study of executive functions in the integration of multiple representations and perspectives.

Key words: executive function, multiple perspectives, multiple representations, integration, information literacy

The ability to integrate and derive meaning from multiple representations and perspectives is a complex and multifaceted skillset that informs learners' information literacy and facilitates understanding of and reasoning with complex information. Both established and developing models of learning with varied informational sources and representations (Ainsworth, 2006; Braasch & Bråten, 2017; Britt & Rouet, 2012;

Goldman, 2003; List & Alexander, 2017a; Rouet & Britt, 2011) posit critical context, task, text, and learner factors that influence learning of and comprehension with and through such complex information. This chapter examines the role of select learner factors in accounting for the integration of multiple inputs that come from representations, texts, and perspectives.

Specifically, the aims of this chapter are to discuss and delineate the roles of executive functions in learners' integration of multiple representations and perspectives. We begin by defining and explaining key terms of the chapter. In particular, we first conceptualize executive function and synthesize key features and components of executive skills (i.e., via the unity-diversity model of executive function; see, e.g., Miyake & Friedman, 2012; Miyake et al., 2000). Then, to situate the current chapter, we discuss the roles of specific executive functions in comprehension broadly (Butterfuss & Kendeou, 2017; Follmer, 2018). In this discussion, we highlight important individual difference characteristics that stand to influence the contributions of executive functions to comprehension processes (e.g., Best, Rowe, Ozuru, & McNamara, 2005; McNamara & Magliano, 2009).

Next, we present a review of research examining the contributions of cognitive factors to the integration of multiple inputs. Based in part on existing theoretical and empirical work, we then extend a summary of the mechanisms by which specific executive functions may influence learners' integration. Given the paucity of available work in this area, we identify key issues based on the relative lack of empirical attention explicitly linking executive processes to learners' integration across representations and perspectives. Within this approach, we articulate critical areas of need for future research and categorize these areas based on potential interactions among executive functions and key context and task (e.g., task complexity; task origin), source (e.g., representational features, complexity, and variability; text easability), and learner (e.g., prior knowledge; perceptions of relevance) factors. We then extend recommendations and considerations for future work to augment the study of executive functions in the integration of multiple representations and perspectives. We conclude by summarizing and presenting takeaways from the chapter.

REVIEW OF THE LITERATURE

Conceptualization of Executive Function

Executive function is commonly defined as a set of independent but related cognitive processes, engaged during novel or complex tasks, that facilitate the coordination and control of cognition, emotion, and behavior in service of a future goal (Follmer, 2018; Miyake & Friedman, 2012; Miyake et al., 2000; Welsh, Friedman, & Spieker, 2006). While models of executive function vary (e.g., Borkowski & Burke, 1996; Jacob & Parkinson, 2015), there is commonality across models in emphasis on core executive functions, namely inhibition, shifting, and updating. Inhibition (also referred to as response inhibition and inhibitory control) describes the ability to suppress or override a prepotent response in favor of a subdominant response. In the context of information literacy, inhibition is particularly involved in learners' ability to process information for importance, relevance, and consistency in support of meaning making.

Shifting (also referred to as flexibility and, less commonly, switching) refers to the ability to switch flexibly between mental sets, tasks, and goals. Shifting enables learners to process different types and sources of information effectively as well as deploy strategies flexibly during information processing. Updating refers to learners' ability to monitor and update information processed in working memory. It affords integration of incoming ideas and information – from varied sources – with prior knowledge. These core executive functions have been shown to play facilitative roles in complex cognitive and academic skills and processes (Borella, Carretti, & Pelegrina, 2010; Butterfuss & Kendeou, 2017; Eason, Goldberg, Young, Geist, & Cutting, 2012; Follmer & Sperling, 2018a; Fuhs, Nesbitt, Farran, & Dong, 2014) and are believed to directly support learners' referential processing and integration across informational sources.

A developing approach to synthesizing features and components of executive functions is the unity/diversity framework (Miyake & Friedman, 2012). This framework is undergirded by the premise that executive function demonstrates unity (based on the existence of a common underlying executive ability) as well as diversity (based on correlational evidence of separability among dissociable executive processes). In essence, this framework suggests that different executive functions correlate with one another, suggesting overlap with a common executive factor, but also demonstrate independence, suggesting that specific executive functions may relate differentially to specific outcomes and processes. Intersecting with this framework is additional work by Friedman and colleagues (2008) that suggests that individual differences in executive function rely considerably on genetic influence (i.e., are heritable). Further, as indicated by Miyake and Friedman (2012), individual differences in executive function also demonstrate stability across development. That is, longitudinal work has produced evidence of inter-individual stability in scores on tasks that recruit inhibition, shifting, and updating among both infants (14 to 36 months) and young adults (17 to 23 years), as examples (e.g., Friedman, Miyake, Robinson, & Hewitt, 2011; Mischel et al., 2010; Miyake & Friedman, 2012). Importantly, however, the framework also affords an important role of individual (i.e., intra-individual) growth and development, and developing work examining training and intervention effects on these executive functions shows some promise (see Diamond & Lee, 2011, for a review of effective mechanisms for improving executive functions; cf. Jacob & Parkinson, 2015).

The unity/diversity framework of executive function presents a number of advantages applicable to this work. First, it clearly signals the need to acknowledge and attempt to minimize measurement error commonly associated with the assessment of executive function (i.e., through a latent variable approach; see, e.g., Snyder, Miyake, & Hankin, 2015). That is, the framework advocates the modeling of exemplar tasks designed to alleviate the well-known task-impurity problem associated with assessing executive function, resulting in more accurate estimates of individuals' executive processing that can then be examined. In addition, the unity/diversity framework aligns well with existing developmental and behavioral genetic evidence supporting the genetic contributions to and developmental stability of executive function across learners' development. Finally, as suggested, the framework relies strongly on the established and empirically supported executive functions of inhibition, shifting, and updating as effective ways of examining the nature and organization of individual differences in executive functions.

Based in part on these advantages, we leverage the unity/diversity framework of executive function to examine the roles of inhibition, shifting, and updating in learners' integration of multiple representations and perspectives. For the purposes of this work, we extend a conceptualization of executive function to include and emphasize key cognitive processes (i.e., inhibition, shifting, and updating) that coordinate and control learners' cognition, emotion, and behavior toward goal-directed integration of multiple inputs. We use this conceptualization to ground our review of the roles of executive processes in learners' integration of multiple inputs.

Multiple Representations and Perspectives

Information literacy necessitates the effective integration of and learning from varied representations and perspectives (e.g., Ainsworth, 2008; Schnotz & Bannert, 2003). This subsection examines what is currently known about the roles of executive functions in learners' processing and comprehension of multiple representations and perspectives. We begin with an overview of the contributions of executive functions to comprehension processes broadly. Next, we use this overview to situate and organize a broader review of the role of cognitive processes in learning from multiple inputs. We orient this review around a central issue identified in this work: the paucity of research explicitly examining the roles of executive functions in learners' understanding of and learning from multiple representations and perspectives.

Executive Functions and Comprehension Processes

Comprehension is a multifaceted process relying on a host of critical learner (e.g., inferencing, knowledge-based and retrieval processes, goals, standards for coherence) and task (e.g., text type and complexity, source cohesion) characteristics (Afflerbach & Cho, 2009; McNamara & Magliano, 2009) that are embedded within contexts (Rouet, Britt, & Durik, 2017). Components and processes of prominent comprehension models (e.g., construction-integration models; Kintsch, 1988; Pearson & Cervetti, 2017) apply comparably to varied informational sources, including both text- and discourse-based sources (McNamara & Magliano, 2009). Among the characteristics that contribute to discourse comprehension, inferencing in particular serves as a hallmark of learners' ability to integrate information across texts and sources – a core ability that has been shown to depend critically on learners' working memory processes (e.g., Best et al., 2005). This integration has likewise been shown to support deep-level processing of and learning from text (Kintsch, 1998).

Existing work has suggested an important role of executive functions in comprehension processes as they support understanding of both texts and perspectives (e.g., Follmer, 2018; Georgiou & Das, 2016; Kendeou, Smith, & O'Brien, 2013). For example, numerous studies have implicated updating in readers' ability to develop and maintain an accurate mental representation of discourse, in part through facilitating the integration of incoming discourse information with readers' existing knowledge (e.g., Miller et al., 2014). Further, research has also demonstrated that dimensions of working memory are positively related to growth in comprehension skills (Stipek & Valentino, 2015) as well as problem-solving (Swanson & Fung, 2016; Yeh, Tsai, Hsu, & Lin, 2014).

Likewise, existing research (Kieffer, Vukovic, & Berry, 2013; Latzman, Elkovitch, Young, & Clark, 2010) has supported shifting as critical in allowing readers to deploy strategies that require flexibility in and regulation of attention, including, as examples, rereading and dynamically adjusting processing speed to facilitate comprehension. Shifting is believed to be particularly involved in the integration and understanding of multiple discourse elements and perspectives (e.g., context of narrative text, character perspectives/points of view, author/source perspectives, conflicting text and source information) such that readers are able to construct accurate and organized mental models of discourse information. In short, shifting is believed to foster readers' ability to process different components of discourse concurrently to form new concepts during reading as well as employ strategies flexibly to facilitate the development of an accurate mental representation of discourse during processing (Follmer, 2018).

In addition to updating and shifting, existing work has also supported inhibition as facilitative of readers' ability to suppress textual information that is situationally irrelevant during text processing (Kieffer et al., 2013). Additional work (e.g., Borella et al., 2010) has found that inhibitory processes may help readers to resist proactive interference during reading such that they are better able to control the current relevance of information processed during reading. Similar to the presumed effect of shifting, one overarching effect of inhibition is believed to be the construction of a more accurate mental representation during reading comprehension (e.g., Butterfuss & Kendeou, 2017).

These existing studies demonstrate the critical role executive functions can play while readers navigate a text source. It is likely, however, that the importance of executive functions would increase as the complexity of comprehension across multiple text sources also increases.

In the case of multiple representations that may not include solely text sources, evidence from existing studies demonstrates the important roles of executive functions in the processing of alternative forms of information. Executive functions are found to predict performance across academic domains (e.g., Latzman et al., 2010), lending additional support that executive functions likely play important roles in integration processes. Regarding the roles of spatial and visual representations and text, the relations between spatial ability and executive function are also established in preschool-aged children. For example, Verdine, Irwin, Golinkoff, & Hirsh-Pasek (2014) found significant relations among executive function, early reading indicators, as well as scores on manipulative spatial ability mathematics problem-solving tasks. The established relationship between spatial ability and executive function is therefore likely to influence the integration of text and other inputs. In fact, as Kellems, Gabrielsen, & Williams (2016) suggest, the role of visual supports, such as graphics and diagrams, may be a means to accommodate and compensate for dense text and discourse inputs.

More recent work examining reader–text interactions has obtained evidence of differential contributions of executive functions to comprehension processes based on varied text (expository, narrative) and question (inferential, literal) types, as well as on text both with and without representations (Eason et al., 2012; Follmer & Sperling, 2018b). Taken together, this and other work (Follmer, 2018) posits executive functions as critical domain-general processes that in part explain learners' dynamic interactions with text and discourse. Yet, much of this existing work examining the roles of executive functions as key cognitive processes influencing comprehension has evaluated comprehension on a text-by-text basis. For example, as noted by Sesma and colleagues (2009), after controlling for other individual difference variables, executive function contributed to reading comprehension as measured by a standardized achievement test. Few studies, however, have systematically examined the roles of core executive functions in learners' integration across multiple texts and representations (e.g., two texts with opposing views of the use of vaccinations; see Maier & Richter, 2014).

Cognitive Factors and Learning from Multiple Inputs

Recent work examining the roles of cognitive processes in learning from multiple inputs has thus far suggested important contributions of executive and working memory processes to learning from a variety of informational and multimedia sources. Begolli et al. (2018), for example, found that individual differences in executive functions played an important role in middle-level students' learning (e.g., via procedural and conceptual knowledge) from a task involving both misconceptions and correct solutions as well as successive mathematical representations. The authors leveraged their findings to suggest possible variations in the presentation (e.g., sequential vs. simultaneous) of representations as a mechanism for supporting learning through reductions in executive demand (see also Wu, Lin, & Hsu, 2013 for work examining the importance of representational sequencing).

In a well-known study, Cromley, Snyder-Hogan, & Luciw-Dubas (2010) examined the cognitive processes (e.g., inferencing, productive strategies, metacognitive strategies, low-level strategies) involved in the reading of expository science text and complex diagrams (i.e., multiple figures and a flow chart). They obtained evidence that college students' monitoring of strategy use – a cognitive process often attributed to executive functions (Latzman et al., 2010) – was implicated similarly in the reading of text compared with the processing of diagrams (see their table 3, p. 66). This and other work (Ainsworth & Loizou, 2003; Butcher, 2006; Jacob & Parkinson, 2015; Peng & Fuchs, 2016) suggests that monitoring and related executive skills may play both a domain- and an input-general role in processing of complex texts and representations. That is, preliminary evidence suggests that executive and metacognitive skills contribute similarly to information processing across domains (i.e., verbal, visuospatial) and inputs (i.e., texts, perspectives, and representations).

Other research (e.g., Gyselinck, Jamet, & Dubois, 2008) has strongly implicated working memory processing in the integration of information coming from multiple sources, including expository texts and diagrams. Bartholomé and Bromme (2009) found that college students' working memory capacity correlated significantly with their verbal retention, visual understanding, and global understanding when reading expository texts (presented in hypertext format) with hyperlinked illustrations. Working memory, however, did not moderate the role of instructional effects (i.e., mapping support and instructional guidance) on integration, perhaps suggesting a consistent contribution to learners' retention and understanding when comprehending complex textual and pictorial information. This and other work (e.g., Yeh et al., 2014) suggests an important role of working memory processing in both problem-solving and integration of information coming from varied representations. Further, the role of working memory and executive function in the integration of multiple representations, by extension, suggests involvement in the integration of multiple perspectives. In recent work, for example, Mason, Zaccoletti, Carretti, Scrimin, & Diakidoy (2019) illuminated the role of inhibition in the comprehension of refutational text in fourth and fifth graders learning about energy. As inhibitory control predicts comprehension within a single refutational text, the role of executive function in effective integration and comprehension is likely to increase when learners tackle multiple perspectives and sources.

NEW INSIGHTS AND FUTURE DIRECTIONS

The ability to effectively make sense of and integrate information from multiple inputs is essential in supporting deep-level processing. Yet, the presence and presentation of multiple representations and perspectives places important processing demands on learners (Bodemer, Ploetzner, Feuerlein, & Spada, 2004; Moreno & Durán, 2004). In light of this, learners need to be equipped to effectively manage such demands as they engage with varied multiples. As indicated, however, the study of the roles of executive functions in multiple representations and perspectives is nascent, and additional work is clearly needed to explicate the specific contributions of these executive processes to learners' integration of information in support of learning.

Executive Functions in Integration of Multiple Inputs

Given our review of existing work and the unity/diversity framework of executive function (Miyake & Friedman, 2012), we are now in a position to extend a summary of the possible roles of specific executive functions in learners' integration of multiple inputs (Laski & Dulaney, 2015; Lee, Ng, & Ng, 2009). We acknowledge at the outset that while these proposed processes are theoretically grounded, empirical work supporting them is in its infancy. In part for this reason, this summary is intended to ground future work and instigate specific avenues for future research. Accordingly, we present summaries of select executive processes influencing integration and comprehension of both multiple representations (see Table 18.1) and multiple texts and perspectives (see Table 18.2). In the latter summary, we integrate the specific contributions to multiple texts and perspectives into a combined input, as multi-text reading often entails the communication and processing of different perspectives coming from distinct sources and authors with distinct sets of assumptions, points of view, and emphases (e.g., Bråten, Britt, Strømsø, & Rouet, 2011).

In presenting these summaries, we elucidate abbreviated definitions of the core executive functions reviewed, specific executive processes that stand to influence the integration and comprehension of multiple inputs, and factors likely to impact learners' interactions with multiple representations and perspectives. In so doing, we categorize these factors impacting learners' interactions with multiple inputs based loosely on the framework proposed by List and Alexander (2017a), underscoring key

Table 18.1 Roles of Executive Functions in Integration and Comprehension of Multiple Representations.

Executive Function: Definition[a]	Possible Executive Processes Influencing Integration of Multiple Representations	Factors Impacting Learners' Interactions with Multiple Representations
Inhibition: Ability to suppress or override a prepotent or dominant response	– suppression of situationally irrelevant representational information – selection and use of relevant representations/representational information during processing – control of relevance of representational information during processing – resistance of distraction or interference from working memory	Context and Task Factors: – task origin (internally/externally prompted) – context and task demands – task instructions – task setting – task complexity – learning outcomes and goals – learning assessments
Shifting: Ability to switch flexibly between mental sets, tasks, and goals	– forging of connections between representations and between textual and representational information – construction of global inferences that support knowledge bridging between representation and domain – deployment of strategies to facilitate understanding and integration of representations	Representational Features: – representational setting[b] – representational complexity – perceptual variability[c] – representational complementarity[c] – dynamicity of representation(s)[d] – description of representation(s) – representational sequence[d]
Updating: Ability to monitor and update information stored in working memory	– integration of representational information with learners' domain knowledge – monitoring of comprehension of representational information – supporting of coherence formation and maintenance across representations and sources – allocation of attentional resources toward effective processing of representational information	Learner Factors: – prior domain knowledge – representational knowledge/competence[e] – domain and topic interest – perceptions of relevance – learner goals – standards for coherence[f]

Notes. This table presents possible executive processes underlying learners' integration of multiple representations, but these are not intended to be exhaustive. The list of factors impacting learners' interactions with multiple representations may serve as moderating variables, mediating variables, or covariates to be accounted for in the examination of the contributions of specific executive functions to comprehension of multiple representations.

[a] Definitions adapted from Follmer and Sperling (2018a) and based in part on Miyake et al., 2000.
[b] Setting may encompass placement of representation in source/text as well as degree of interaction between representation and source.
[c] See Ainsworth, 1999, 2006.
[d] See Wu et al., 2013.
[e] See Tippett, 2016.
[f] See McNamara & Magliano, 2009.

learner factors (emphasizing relevant individual differences variables), source and representational features (emphasizing material and design features of representations and texts), and context and task factors (emphasizing contextual, goal-related, and assessment-based factors).

Table 18.2 Roles of Executive Functions in Integration and Comprehension of Multiple Texts and Perspectives.

Executive Function: Definition[a]	Possible Executive Processes Influencing Integration of Multiple Texts and Perspectives	Factors Impacting Learners' Interactions with Multiple Texts and Perspectives
Inhibition: Ability to suppress or override a prepotent or dominant response	– suppression of situationally irrelevant information – control of relevance and processing of information during reading – resistance of distraction or interference from working memory	Context and Task Factors: – family and home literacies[b] – task origin (internally/externally prompted) – context and task demands – task instructions – task complexity – learning goals (internally/externally given) – learning assessments
Shifting: Ability to switch flexibly between mental sets, tasks, and goals	– forging of connections across texts and varied perspectives – identification and processing of complementary or refutational information across sources – construction of global inferences that support knowledge bridging across texts and perspectives – deployment of reading strategies to facilitate understanding and integration of source information	Text/Perspective Features: – text type and genre – text and perspective complexity/easability – text and perspective complementarity – text presentation/format
Updating: Ability to monitor and update information stored in working memory	– evaluation of information for relevance and importance to readers' integrated mental models – supporting of coherence formation and maintenance across texts and perspectives information – allocation of attentional resources toward effective source processing – monitoring of comprehension across sources – integration of textual information with learners' domain knowledge	Learner Factors: – requisite reading skills[c] – prior domain knowledge – cultural background[d] – native language considerations – domain and topic interest – perceptions of relevance – perceptions of source credibility – standards for coherence – reading motivation[e]

Notes. As in Table 18.1, the list of factors impacting learners' interactions with multiple texts and perspectives may serve as moderating variables, mediating variables, or covariates to be accounted for in the examination of the contributions of specific executive functions to comprehension.

[a] Definitions adapted from Follmer and Sperling (2018a) and based in part on Miyake et al., 2000.
[b] Emphasizes broader reading context(s) and home/familial factors (Edwards, Protacio, Peltier, & Hopkins, 2017).
[c] Those requisite reading skills most relevant to comprehension of multiple texts and perspectives will vary according to learners' developmental trajectories.
[d] Includes recent work on culturally sustaining pedagogies (see Fairbanks, Cooper, Webb, & Masterson, 2017).
[e] Reading motivation encompasses varied dimensions, including perceived control, involvement, self-efficacy, and social collaboration (see Taboada, Tonks, Wigfield, & Guthrie, 2013).

Executive Functions in Multiple Representations

As can be seen in Table 18.1, executive functions are believed to play key roles in learners' ability to interpret, comprehend, and effectively integrate multiple and varied representations. In particular, we invoke inhibition in learners' abilities to: suppress representational information that may be less relevant (or situationally irrelevant) during processing; select, use, and extract information from specific, relevant representational components or features; and control the current relevance of information being processed from multiple representations. In addition, based on previous discourse comprehension work (Borella et al., 2010; McNamara & Magliano, 2009), we propose an ancillary role of inhibition in supporting learners' resistance to distraction and interference during the processing of representations. One overarching function of inhibition is believed to be the co-construction of an accurate and integrated mental model of representational information during processing of multiple representations (e.g., such as when readers are tasked with forming a coherent model of representational information across diagrams that depict, in the context of biology, interactions among cells and unfolding cell processes; see, e.g., Cromley et al., 2010). This position is commensurate with recent findings by Mason and colleagues (2019).

Shifting is likely to support the development of connections and inferences across representational information. Paralleling existing evidence of shifting's role in text comprehension, shifting is believed to support learners' processing of disparate components of representations as well as learners' abilities to forge relationships among and across representational units and information. These relationships are proposed as requisite for effective integration across representations. Further, shifting is believed to also be involved in learners' deployment of strategies to foster – and augment – understanding from multiple representations. A primary function of shifting, then, is believed to be the maintenance of learners' overall cognitive flexibility in the processing of representations, enacted in part via inferencing from and strategic processing of representations.

Finally, updating is believed to serve a higher-level, monitoring function in learners' ability to evaluate dimensions of representations and current comprehension of them. Paralleling established work on readers' developed situation models (e.g., Zwaan & Singer, 2003), a learner's mental model of representational information is believed to be aided by executive function to the extent that higher-level relationships among this information are implicit and must be inferred. In this role, updating may facilitate integration of representational information with existing domain knowledge, in part through comprehension monitoring as learners process different representations. Key products of this integration may be both global coherence (i.e., an organized mental structure representing learners' connected models of relationships across representations) and knowledge revision (e.g., Suh & Trabasso, 1993). In a broader role, updating is also likely to promote the effective allocation and deployment of attentional resources toward processing (and re-processing) of representational information.

Executive Functions in Multiple Texts and Perspectives

Recent theoretical models of comprehension that accommodate multiple sources recognize that learners must consider and evaluate perspective in source documents. These models, such as the documents model framework (e.g., Britt & Rouet, 2012), posit important roles of relevance processing, source evaluation, information verification, and reconciliation of conflicting information, as examples, in the processing and integration of multiple perspectives (Braasch & Bråten, 2017; Bråten, Anmarkrud, Brandmo, & Strømsø, 2014; Britt & Rouet, 2011; Britt & Rouet, 2012; Broughton,

Sinatra, & Reynolds, 2010; List & Alexander, 2017b; Richter & Maier, 2017; Rouet et al., 2017). Richter and Maier (2017), in their two-step model of validation in multiple text comprehension, propose working memory resources and metacognitive strategies as critical in promoting strategic and elaborative processing of conflicting information in multiple documents (List & Alexander, 2017a). Based on this and other work (e.g., Strømsø, Bråten, & Britt, 2010; Swanson & Fung, 2016), we propose similar executive processes supporting learners' comprehension and integration of multiple texts, documents, and perspectives (see Table 18.2).

In the case of inhibition, a primary role appears to again be the suppression of situationally irrelevant textual information during processing of multiple texts and perspectives (Gernsbacher, 1990). Likewise, inhibitory processes seem particularly applicable to learners' ability to control the relevance of current textual information across sources. Each of these processes, combined with the more general process of resisting interference in working memory, supports the formation of accurate crosstextual inferences to ground understanding of relationships both within and across texts. Implicitly, inhibition may be particularly involved in readers' relevance processing and information verification when perspectives and points of view do not align (Richter & Maier, 2017; Rouet et al., 2017) or when alternative or conflicting perspectives are presented.

Shifting is directly involved in both relevance processing and the evaluation and processing of refutational and conflicting information across text. That is, shifting is likely to be implicated in learners' abilities to forge connections across texts and perspectives, process and make sense of conflicting or refutational information, and construct inferences across textual information to support integrated understanding of both related (i.e., complementary or aligning) and less related (i.e., disparate or conflicting) ideas and information. As a whole, shifting may support a reader's ability to "move" flexibly between texts and perspectives and to integrate incoming cross-textual inferences with existing knowledge. As with our analysis presented in Table 18.1, shifting also serves a more general purpose of facilitating the deployment of targeted reading strategies to repair breakdowns in comprehension of and inconsistencies in beliefs based on multiple texts (Richter & Maier, 2017), thus enriching understanding toward deep-level comprehension (e.g., Best et al., 2005; Maier & Richter, 2014).

Updating, as with the processing of multiple representations, is proposed to support evaluation of textual and perspective-based information for relevance and importance to comprehension, in part via readers' developed situation models (i.e., via organized, inferred connections between and among separate parts of text and discourse that are linked with readers' domain knowledge). Updating is also believed to support more general processes of comprehension monitoring and allocation of attentional resources to text and perspective processing (e.g., Broughton et al., 2010). Comprehension monitoring in multiple text comprehension in turn may impose increased burden on readers' coherence during processing – that is, on readers' ability to establish and maintain clear standards for coherence and fit an organized structure to the relationships among idea units across discourse constituents (e.g., McNamara & Magliano, 2009). Overall, updating may be leveraged to a greater degree in the processing of multiple texts and perspectives as a process facilitative of inference generation (i.e., elaborations) as well as information evaluation and integration.

Consideration of Other Factors

At this point, it seems fruitful to represent our conceptualization of executive functions in this chapter as including and emphasizing key cognitive processes (i.e., inhibition, shifting, and updating) that coordinate and control learners' cognition, emotion, and behavior toward goal-directed integration of multiple inputs. Overall and across our brief review of Tables 18.1 and 18.2, there is commonality (if not redundancy) in the roles that specific executive functions are believed to play in learners' integration of multiple inputs. That is, executive functions appear to serve as critical, domain-general processes that foster the development and maintenance of an accurate and coherent mental model of information across representations, texts, and perspectives (see Schüler, Arndt, & Scheiter, 2015 for evidence of learners forming a single integrated mental representation when integrating multiple representations in the processing of multimedia materials). Yet, in many ways, this summary presents a relatively simplistic account of the influence of these executive processes on effective integration of multiple inputs. In other words, this summary does not take into account critical context, task, source, and learner factors, mentioned earlier in this chapter, that stand to impact learners' interactions with these multiple inputs. As such, a consideration of the impact of these broad factors is necessary. While a comprehensive discussion of the influence of each of these factors is beyond the scope of this chapter, we find it important to cast a broad overview of these factors and to highlight the specific interactive roles of select factors in learners' effective integration.

Of particular importance to learners' effective (and strategic) integration of multiple inputs are learner factors such as prior knowledge. Early work examining interactions between readers' prior knowledge and features of text demonstrated that low-knowledge readers benefited from text with greater cohesion, in part because cohesion supported the development of knowledge-based inferences among those readers with lower background knowledge (McNamara, Kintsch, Songer, & Kintsch, 1996). Complementary effects may likely exist when examining interactions between learners' executive function and prior knowledge in the comprehension of multiple representations and perspectives. That is, learners' executive processing – of multiple representations, texts, or perspectives – may be leveraged to a greater or lesser degree based on the depth and quality of their domain knowledge. Simply put, what is strategic for one or more readers is likely to be influenced heavily by those readers' existing knowledge (i.e., of the text or representational content, concepts, etc.). A varyingly intensive or effortful processing approach via readers' executive processing may not be "needed" if learners also possess richer and more interconnected domain knowledge of the material discussed.

Similarly, material and source features of both texts (Best et al., 2005; Bråten et al., 2016; Follmer & Sperling, 2018b) and representations (Ainsworth, 2006; Kozma, 2003) are likely to interact with readers' executive processing to differentially support comprehension of multiple inputs. For example, text and representational complexity as well as the degree to which multiple texts, perspectives, and representations complement or contradict one another are likely to impose differential burden on executive processing such that a coherent understanding (i.e., integrated mental model) of information can be constructed. Indeed, the greater the degree of source complexity or refutation and differentiation across representations, the greater the need may be for readers to engage specific executive processes (e.g., shifting) to compensate for the difficulties imposed from such source and material features. Likewise, the greater the degree of inconsistency or conflicting information presented among perspectives in texts and sources (see existing work evaluating the role of refutation texts in supporting knowledge revision; e.g., Broughton et al., 2010; Danielson, Sinatra, & Kendeou, 2016), the greater the need may be for executive processes to facilitate integration and coherence across source information.

At a broader level, contextual and task-related factors are likely to be instrumental in eliciting learners' executive processing during interaction with multiple inputs. For example, learning tasks (e.g., reading and integration tasks) may be externally or instructionally prompted or may be pursued individually; task instructions may vary in complexity, organization, and cohesion; learners may adopt similar or different goals for the same or different learning tasks; and learning may be assessed in varied ways through myriad approaches. Based preliminarily on existing work demonstrating differential recruitment of executive function in task learning based on factors such as text cohesion (Follmer & Sperling, 2018b), level of comprehension assessed (Follmer & Sperling, 2018a), and question types used to assess comprehension of different text types (Eason et al., 2012), the possible effects of such contextual and task-related factors on readers' need for and use of executive processing are not trivial. Future research would benefit greatly from a holistic and nuanced examination of the roles of such contextual and task-based factors in shaping learners' need to leverage executive processing to foster effective integration of multiple inputs.

CONCLUSIONS

This chapter examined the roles of executive functions in the integration and comprehension of multiple representations, texts, and perspectives. Grounded in a broad review of existing work, we hypothesized and presented specific, theoretically grounded executive processes believed to influence the integration of multiple inputs. We leveraged this process summary to situate suggestions for future research and highlighted as a critical issue the paucity of research explicitly examining the roles of executive functions in learners' understanding of and learning from multiple representations and perspectives. We propose this as a necessary and fruitful area of future work in order to more clearly elucidate the dynamic and interactive factors that account for learners' integration of multiple inputs that come from representations, texts, and perspectives. We concluded the chapter by offering an overview of approaches to understanding the contribution of core executive processes to the integration of and learning from multiple inputs.

REFERENCES

Afflerbach, P., & Cho, B.-Y. (2009). Identifying and describing constructively responsive comprehension strategies in new and traditional forms of reading. In S. E. Israel & G. G. Duffy (Eds.), *Handbook of research on reading comprehension* (pp. 69–90). New York: Routledge.

Ainsworth, S. (2006). DeFT: A conceptual framework for considering learning with multiple representations. *Learning and Instruction*, *16*(3), 183–198.

Ainsworth, S. (2008). The educational value of multiple-representations when learning complex scientific concepts. In J. K. Gilbert, M. Reiner, & M. Nakhleh (Eds.), *Visualization: Theory and practice in science education* (pp. 191–208). Dordrecht: Springer.

Ainsworth, S., & Loizou, A. T. (2003). The effects of self-explaining when learning with text or diagrams. *Cognitive Science, 27*(4), 669–681.

Ainsworth, S. E. (1999). The functions of multiple representations. *Computers and Education, 33*(2/3), 131–152.

Bartholomé, T., & Bromme, R. (2009). Coherence formation when learning from text and pictures: What kind of support for whom? *Journal of Educational Psychology, 101*(2), 282.

Begolli, K. N., Richland, L. E., Jaeggi, S. M., Lyons, E. M., Klostermann, E. C., & Matlen, B. J. (2018). Executive function in learning mathematics by comparison: Incorporating everyday classrooms into the science of learning. *Thinking and Reasoning, 24*(2), 280–313.

Best, R. M., Rowe, M., Ozuru, Y., & McNamara, D. S. (2005). Deep-level comprehension of science texts: The role of the reader and the text. *Topics in Language Disorders, 25*(1), 65–83.

Bodemer, D., Ploetzner, R., Feuerlein, I., & Spada, H. (2004). The active integration of information during learning with dynamic and interactive visualisations. *Learning and Instruction, 14*(3), 325–341.

Borella, E., Carretti, B., & Pelegrina, S. (2010). The specific role of inhibition in reading comprehension in good and poor comprehenders. *Journal of Learning Disabilities, 43*(6), 541–552. doi:10.1177/0022219410371676

Borkowski, J. G., & Burke, J. E. (1996). Theories, models, and measurements of executive functioning: An information processing perspective. In G. R. Lyon & N. A. Krasnegor (Eds.), *Attention, memory, and executive function* (pp. 235–261). Baltimore, MD: Paul H. Brookes Publishing.

Braasch, J. L., & Bråten, I. (2017). The discrepancy-induced source comprehension (D-ISC) model: Basic assumptions and preliminary evidence. *Educational Psychologist, 52*(3), 167–181.

Bråten, I., Anmarkrud, Ø., Brandmo, C., & Strømsø, H. I. (2014). Developing and testing a model of direct and indirect relationships between individual differences, processing, and multiple-text comprehension. *Learning and Instruction, 30*, 9–24.

Bråten, I., Britt, M. A., Strømsø, H. I., & Rouet, J. F. (2011). The role of epistemic beliefs in the comprehension of multiple expository texts: Toward an integrated model. *Educational Psychologist, 46*(1), 48–70.

Britt, M. A., & Rouet, J. F. (2011). Research challenges in the use of multiple documents. *Information Design Journal, 19*(1), 62–68.

Britt, M. A., & Rouet, J. F. (2012). Learning with multiple documents: Component skills and their acquisition. In M. J. Lawson & J. R. Kirby (Eds.), *Enhancing the Quality of Learning: Dispositions, Instruction, and Learning Processes* (pp. 276–314). Cambridge: Cambridge University Press.

Broughton, S. H., Sinatra, G. M., & Reynolds, R. E. (2010). The nature of the refutation text effect: An investigation of attention allocation. *Journal of Educational Research, 103*(6), 407–423.

Butcher, K. R. (2006). Learning from text with diagrams: Promoting mental model development and inference generation. *Journal of Educational Psychology, 98*(1), 182.

Butterfuss, R., & Kendeou, P. (2017). The role of executive functions in reading comprehension. *Educational Psychology Review, 30*(3), 801–826.

Cromley, J. G., Snyder-Hogan, L. E., & Luciw-Dubas, U. A. (2010). Cognitive activities in complex science text and diagrams. *Contemporary Educational Psychology, 35*(1), 59–74.

Danielson, R. W., Sinatra, G. M., & Kendeou, P. (2016). Augmenting the refutation text effect with analogies and graphics. *Discourse Processes, 53*(5/6), 392–414.

Diamond, A., & Lee, K. (2011). Interventions shown to aid executive function development in children 4 to 12 years old. *Science, 333*(6045), 959–964.

Eason, S. H., Goldberg, L. F., Young, K. M., Geist, M. C., & Cutting, L. E. (2012). Reader–text interactions: How differential text and question types influence cognitive skills needed for reading comprehension. *Journal of Educational Psychology, 104*(3), 515–528. doi:10.1037/a0027182

Edwards, P. A., Protacio, M. S., Peltier, M., & Hopkins, L. (2017). Family literacy initiatives and reading comprehension. In S. E. Israel (Ed.), *Handbook of research on reading comprehension* (2nd ed., pp. 568–600). New York: Guilford Press.

Fairbanks, C. M., Cooper, J. E., Webb, S. M., & Masterson, L. A. (2017). Reading comprehension research and the shift toward culturally sustaining pedagogy. In S. E. Israel (Eds.), *Handbook of research on reading comprehension* (2nd ed., pp. 459–478). New York: Guilford Press.

Follmer, D. J. (2018). Executive function and reading comprehension: A meta-analytic review. *Educational Psychologist, 53*(1), 42–60. doi:10.1080/00461520.2017.1309295

Follmer, D. J., & Sperling, R. A. (2018a). A latent variable analysis of the contribution of executive function to adult readers' comprehension of science text: The roles of vocabulary ability and level of comprehension. *Reading and Writing*, 1–27. In press, doi:10.1007/s11145-018-9872-3.

Follmer, D. J., & Sperling, R. A. (2018b). Interactions between reader and text: Contributions of cognitive processes, strategy use, and text cohesion to comprehension of expository science text. *Learning and Individual Differences, 67*, 177–187.

Friedman, N. P., Miyake, A., Robinson, J. L., & Hewitt, J. K. (2011). Developmental trajectories in toddlers' self-restraint predict individual differences in executive functions 14 years later: A behavioral genetic analysis. *Developmental Psychology, 47*(5), 1410.

Friedman, N. P., Miyake, A., Young, S. E., DeFries, J. C., Corley, R. P., & Hewitt, J. K. (2008). Individual differences in executive functions are almost entirely genetic in origin. *Journal of Experimental Psychology: General, 137*(2), 201–225.

Fuhs, M., Nesbitt, K., Farran, D., & Dong, N. (2014). Longitudinal associations between executive functioning and academic skills across content areas. *Developmental Psychology, 50*, 1698–1709. doi:10.1037/a0036633

Georgiou, G. K., & Das, J. P. (2016). What component of executive functions contributes to normal and impaired reading comprehension in young adults? *Research in Developmental Disabilities, 49*, 118–128. doi:10.1016/j.ridd.2015.12.001

Gernsbacher, M. A. (1990). *Language comprehension as structure building*. Hillsdale, NJ: Erlbaum.

Goldman, S. R. (2003). Learning in complex domains: When and why do multiple representations help?. *Learning and Instruction, 13*(2), 239–244.

Gyselinck, V., Jamet, E., & Dubois, V. (2008). The role of working memory components in multimedia comprehension. *Applied Cognitive Psychology, 22*(3), 353–374.

Jacob, R., & Parkinson, J. (2015). The potential for school-based interventions that target executive function to improve academic achievement: A review. *Review of Educational Research, 85*, 512–552. doi:10.3102/0034654314561338

Kellems, R. O., Gabrielsen, T. P., & Williams, C. (2016). Using visual organizers and technology: Supporting executive function, abstract language comprehension, and social learning. In T. A. Cardon (Ed.), *Technology and the Treatment of Children with Autism Spectrum Disorder* (pp. 75–86). Cham: Springer.

Kendeou, P., Smith, E. R., & O'Brien, E. J. (2013). Updating during reading comprehension: Why causality matters. *Journal of Experimental Psychology: Learning, Memory, and Cognition, 39*(3), 854.

Kieffer, M. J., Vukovic, R. K., & Berry, D. (2013). Roles of attention shifting and inhibitory control in fourth-grade reading comprehension. *Reading Research Quarterly, 48*(4), 333–348.

Kintsch, W. (1988). The use of knowledge in discourse processing: A construction integration model. *Discourse Processes, 16*, 193–202.

Kintsch, W. (1998). *Comprehension: A paradigm for cognition*. New York: Cambridge University Press.

Kozma, R. (2003). The material features of multiple representations and their cognitive and social affordances for science understanding. *Learning and Instruction, 13*(2), 205–226.

Laski, E. V., & Dulaney, A. (2015). When prior knowledge interferes, inhibitory control matters for learning: The case of numerical magnitude representations. *Journal of Educational Psychology, 107*(4), 1035.

Latzman, R. D., Elkovitch, N., Young, J., & Clark, L. A. (2010). The contribution of executive functioning to academic achievement among male adolescents. *Journal of Clinical and Experimental Neuropsychology, 32*, 455–462. doi:10.1080/1380339090316 4363

Lee, K., Ng, E. L., & Ng, S. F. (2009). The contributions of working memory and executive functioning to problem representation and solution generation in algebraic word problems. *Journal of Educational Psychology, 101*(2), 373–387.

List, A., & Alexander, P. A. (2017a). Analyzing and integrating models of multiple text comprehension. *Educational Psychologist, 52*(3), 143–147.

List, A., & Alexander, P. A. (2017b). Cognitive affective engagement model of multiple source use. *Educational Psychologist, 52*(3), 182–199.

Maier, J., & Richter, T. (2014). Fostering multiple text comprehension: How metacognitive strategies and motivation moderate the text-belief consistency effect. *Metacognition and Learning, 9*(1), 51–74.

Mason, L., Zaccoletti, S., Carretti, B., Scrimin, S., & Diakidoy, I. A. N. (2019). The role of inhibition in conceptual learning from refutation and standard expository texts. *International Journal of Science and Mathematics Education, 17*(3), 483–501.

McNamara, D. S., Kintsch, E., Songer, N. B., & Kintsch, W. (1996). Are good texts always better? Interactions of text coherence, background knowledge, and levels of understanding in learning from text. *Cognition and Instruction, 14*, 1–43.

McNamara, D. S., & Magliano, J. P. (2009). Towards a comprehensive model of comprehension. In B. Ross (Eds.), *The psychology of learning and motivation* (vol. 51, pp. 297–384). New York: Elsevier Science.

Miller, A. C., Davis, N., Gilbert, J. K., Cho, S. J., Toste, J. R., Street, J., & Cutting, L. E. (2014). Novel approaches to examine passage, student, and question effects on reading comprehension. *Learning Disabilities Research and Practice, 29*(1), 25–35. doi:.doi.org/10.1111/ldrp.12027

Mischel, W., Ayduk, O., Berman, M. G., Casey, B. J., Gotlib, I. H., Jonides, J., … Shoda, Y. (2010). "Willpower" over the life span: Decomposing self-regulation. *Social Cognitive and Affective Neuroscience, 6*(2), 252–256.

Miyake, A., & Friedman, N. P. (2012). The nature and organization of individual differences in executive functions: Four general conclusions. *Current Directions in Psychological Science, 21*(1), 8–14.

Miyake, A., Friedman, N. P., Emerson, M. J., Witzki, A. H., Howerter, A., & Wager, T. D. (2000). The unity and diversity of executive functions and their contributions to complex "frontal lobe" tasks: A latent variable analysis. *Cognitive Psychology, 41*(1), 49–100.

Moreno, R., & Durán, R. (2004). Do multiple representations need explanations? The role of verbal guidance and individual differences in multimedia mathematics learning. *Journal of Educational Psychology, 96*(3), 492.

Pearson, P. D., & Cervetti, G. N. (2017). The roots of reading comprehension instruction. In S. E. Israel (Eds.), *Handbook of research on reading comprehension* (2nd ed., pp. 12–56). New York: Guilford Press.

Peng, P., & Fuchs, D. (2016). A meta-analysis of working memory deficits in children with learning difficulties: Is there a difference between verbal domain and numerical domain? *Journal of Learning Disabilities, 49*(1), 3–20.

Richter, T., & Maier, J. (2017). Comprehension of multiple documents with conflicting information: A two-step model of validation. *Educational Psychologist, 52*(3), 148–166.

Rouet, J. F., & Britt, M. A. (2011). Relevance processing in multiple document comprehension. In M. T. McCrudden, J. P. Magliano, & G. Schraw (Eds.), *Text relevance and learning from text* (pp. 19–52). Greenwich, CT: Information Age.

Rouet, J. F., Britt, M. A., & Durik, A. M. (2017). RESOLV: Readers' representation of reading contexts and tasks. *Educational Psychologist, 52*(3), 200–215.

Schnotz, W., & Bannert, M. (2003). Construction and interference in learning from multiple representation. *Learning and Instruction, 13*(2), 141–156.

Schüler, A., Arndt, J., & Scheiter, K. (2015). Processing multimedia material: Does integration of text and pictures result in a single or two interconnected mental representations?. *Learning and Instruction, 35*, 62–72.

Sesma, H. W., Mahone, E. M., Levine, T., Eason, S. H., & Cutting, L. E. (2009). The contribution of executive skills to reading comprehension. *Child Neuropsychology, 15*(3), 232–246.

Snyder, H. R., Miyake, A., & Hankin, B. L. (2015). Advancing understanding of executive function impairments and psychopathology: Bridging the gap between clinical and cognitive approaches. *Frontiers in Psychology, 6*, 328.

Stipek, D., & Valentino, R. A. (2015). Early childhood memory and attention as predictors of academic growth trajectories. *Journal of Educational Psychology, 107*(3), 771.

Strømsø, H. I., Bråten, I., & Britt, M. A. (2010). Reading multiple texts about climate change: The relationship between memory for sources and text comprehension. *Learning and Instruction, 20*, 192–204.

Suh, S., & Trabasso, T. (1993). Inferences during reading: Converging evidence from discourse analysis, talk-aloud protocols and recognition priming. *Journal of Memory and Language, 32*, 279–300.

Swanson, H. L., & Fung, W. (2016). Working memory components and problem-solving accuracy: Are there multiple pathways? *Journal of Educational Psychology, 108*(8), 1153–1177.

Taboada, A., Tonks, S. M., Wigfield, A., & Guthrie, J. T. (2013). Effects of motivational and cognitive variables on reading comprehension. In D. Alvermann, N. Unrau, & R. Ruddall (Eds.), *Theoretical models and processes of reading* (6th ed., pp. 589–610). Newark, DE: International Reading Association.

Tippett, C. D. (2016). What recent research on diagrams suggests about learning with rather than learning from visual representations in science. *International Journal of Science Education, 38*(5), 725–746.

Verdine, B. N., Irwin, C. M., Golinkoff, R. M., & Hirsh-Pasek, K. (2014). Contributions of executive function and spatial skills to preschool mathematics achievement. *Journal of Experimental Child Psychology, 126*, 37–51.

Welsh, M., Friedman, S., & Spieker, S. (2006). Executive functions in developing children: Current conceptualizations and questions for the future. In K. McCartney & D. Phillips (Eds.), *Blackwell handbook of early childhood development* (pp. 167–187). Malden, MA: Blackwell.

Wu, H. K., Lin, Y. F., & Hsu, Y. S. (2013). Effects of representation sequences and spatial ability on students' scientific understandings about the mechanism of breathing. *Instructional Science*, *41*(3), 555–573.

Yeh, Y. C., Tsai, J. L., Hsu, W. C., & Lin, C. F. (2014). A model of how working memory capacity influences insight problem solving in situations with multiple visual representations: An eye tracking analysis. *Thinking Skills and Creativity*, *13*, 153–167.

Zwaan, R. A., & Singer, M. (2003). Text comprehension. In A. Graesser, M. A. Gernsbacher, & S. Goldman (Eds.), *Handbook of Discourse Processes* (pp. 83–121). Mahwah, NJ: Lawrence Erlbaum.

19

PUTTING SELF-REGULATED LEARNING AND METACOGNITION INTO MULTIPLE REPRESENTATIONS AND PERSPECTIVES

Courtney A. Denton, Krista R. Muis, Brendan Munzar, and Nesma Etoubashi

MCGILL UNIVERSITY

ABSTRACT

There is an abundance of information in our digital society. Access to this information is beneficial to learning when an individual is able to employ effective strategies to make sense of incoming information, which may come from multiple inputs. Individuals must go far beyond comprehension – they are required to determine what is useful, extraneous, or misleading. Self-regulated learning and metacognitive strategy-use are promising means to sort facts from fiction. In this chapter, we present theoretical frameworks of self-regulated learning and metacognition to examine individuals' integration of multiple inputs. These frameworks, along with empirical research that support them, will assist in identifying future avenues for research and interventions to achieve better competence when integrating information on important issues.

Key words: self-regulated learning, metacognition, epistemic metacognition, integration, Internet-based learning

The proliferation of information and its sources brings many opportunities to access and create knowledge. In the age of NewsNow and Twitter, everyone can be a seeker as well as a source. Given the volume and diversity of available information, individuals are required to fluently engage with multiple inputs simultaneously in real-time. Specifically, individuals must search for, interpret, and coordinate sources and then link information across these texts, images, videos, and audio files. No easy feat.

Here, fluency entails a strong grasp of knowledge, in both its form and its function. To effectively sort fact from fiction, individuals may be required to split their attention and maintain cognitive flexibility when processing large amounts of information. Effective participation in our knowledge economy demands that individuals go far beyond comprehension – they must critically evaluate the 5Ws of incoming information to determine what is useful, extraneous, or misleading. Individuals must be aware of the information's source (i.e., *w*ho published the material, *w*here it was published, *w*hen it was published), *w*hat the material contains (e.g., content, multiple representation), and *w*hy this information was published (i.e., author's purpose or perspective).

Although access to multiple inputs poses its challenges, we argue that access is also beneficial to learning when an individual is able to employ effective strategies to make sense of incoming information. Chief among these strategies is information integration. In this chapter, we draw from theoretical frameworks of self-regulated learning (SRL) and metacognition to assess the vital role these skills play in promoting the utility of access to information with multiple inputs. Consistent with the conceptualization of this *Handbook*, we define multiple inputs as multiple symbolic forms and points of view. Within multiple inputs, multiple representations and multiple perspectives are included. Multiple representations are defined as content that may take multiple symbolic forms (e.g., alphabetic, graphic). For example, individuals may be required to monitor discrepancies between different representations (e.g., Scheiter & Eitel, 2015; Trevors, Feyzi-Behnagh, Azevedo, & Bouchet, 2016) or integrate textual and graphical information in illustrated texts (e.g., Mason, Pluchino, & Tornatora, 2015a). Multiple perspectives refer to varying points of view, where authors and sources may have distinct assumptions or purposes in communicating information. Here, individuals may be required to examine conflicting perspectives (e.g., Muis et al., 2015) or to develop a coherent mental model by integrating these perspectives (Rouet & Britt, 2011). To better understand how individuals engage with information that takes multiple forms, we first turn to theoretical frameworks and models of SRL.

SELF-REGULATED LEARNING (SRL)

In a sea of information, self-regulated learners provide exemplars for controlled learning. Rather than getting bogged down by the volume of available information, they are able to align their goals and products through constant comparison via monitoring. Zimmerman (1989) explained that an individual is self-regulated to the extent that they are metacognitively, motivationally, and behaviorally active in their own learning process. As such, when an error is detected, self-regulated learners may change their learning strategy to ensure that they make it back to shore.

Theorists have generally agreed that SRL encompasses (a) the preparatory phase, where an individual may plan how they will complete their task; (b) the performance phase, where an individual enacts their plans; and (c) the appraisal phase, where an individual may evaluate their products (Panadero, 2017). Within these general phases, theoretical models have also discussed cognitive (Winne & Hadwin, 1998; Zimmerman & Moylan, 2009), motivational (Pintrich, 2000), and affective (Boekaerts, 2011; Efklides, 2011) aspects of learning. Although many models have been proposed, we adopted Muis, Chevrier, & Singh's (2018) integrated model to describe SRL in greater depth given that it is the most inclusive SRL model to date. Similar to previous models (e.g., Winne & Hadwin, 1998, 2008), Muis et al.'s (2018) model includes four phases where individuals constantly monitor their progress against standards to achieve goals. These four phases include task definition, planning and goal setting, enactment, and evaluation. Muis et al. (2018) posited that regulation during these phases can occur across five areas: cognitive, motivational, affective, behavioral, and contextual.

To illustrate the phases of SRL and areas for regulation, imagine an individual is asked to learn as much as possible about climate change from a website that has text, images, and videos. In the first phase of SRL, the individual generates a perception of the task, context, and self in relation to the task (Muis, 2007). This perception is generated from information about the task's external contextual conditions (e.g., instructions about the task requirements) as well as internal conditions, which may include information from the five areas for regulation, such as prior knowledge (cognitive condition), self-efficacy for carrying out the task (motivational condition), curiosity (affective condition), or time available to complete the task (behavioral condition). The individual may recall what they already know about the causes and consequences of climate change and weigh the motivational, affective, and contextual conditions of the task. In phase two, the individual sets goals (e.g., time on task goals, achievement goals) and epistemic aims (i.e., goals for achieving knowledge or understanding) for the task and plans which strategies to use to complete the task. The individual may give themselves 30 minutes to learn as much as they can about climate change. To meet this time goal, the individual may prioritize reading the text over examining the images or videos. They may also plan to seek information from other websites, or perspectives, to corroborate what they find online.

In the third phase, the individual enacts the planned strategies. Lastly, in the fourth phase, the individual may evaluate their progress in relation to their goals and epistemic aims. The individual may keep track of time spent learning to respect time-related goals. They may also monitor their understanding of the causes and consequences of climate change. The individual may switch back-and-forth between the four phases of SRL to complete the task. In addition, metacognitive processing (e.g., monitoring and control) may occur in all phases. This processing may provide feedback to update the individual's task understanding, plans, and goals as they relate to the task. For example, if an evaluation of progress (i.e., Phase 4) generates a knowledge gap, the individual may revise their plan to complete the task (i.e., Phase 2) by inspecting images or videos related to the information needed.

Muis and colleagues (Muis, 2007; Muis et al., 2018) extended Winne and Hadwin's (1998) model of SRL by describing the role of emotions in learning. Although affective aspects of learning have been incorporated into previous models of SRL (Boekaerts, 2011; Efklides, 2011), Muis et al. (2018) specifically discussed knowledge-generating emotions, called epistemic emotions. Epistemic emotions, such as surprise, curiosity, and confusion, are often triggered by novel or discrepant information, such as differing viewpoints about climate change. These emotions can facilitate or constrain learning during all phases of SRL. For example, if information is novel to the individual, surprise is expected to occur, especially if the level of novelty is sufficiently high. To illustrate, an individual may be surprised to learn that global average temperatures are increasing about two or three degrees. When an individual reaches an impasse to learning goals, such as encountering differing perspectives about the impact of increasing global average temperatures, they will experience cognitive disequilibrium, which may also trigger surprise, followed by curiosity, should they perceive themselves capable of overcoming the complexity of the task and understanding the information. To navigate differing perspectives, the individual may seek more information about both perspectives to resolve the disequilibrium. Alternatively, the individual may experience surprise, followed by confusion, if the incongruity is perceived as difficult to resolve. If the individual cannot overcome the complexity or impasse, then the individual's confusion may lead to frustration, anxiety, and possibly boredom (see Pekrun & Loderer, Chapter 22, for further discussion of emotions and learning). According to Muis et al. (2018), epistemic emotions predict the quality of subsequent SRL processes and outcomes, including the degree to which a task can be completed. Thus, when presented with multiple inputs, individuals may experience both positive and negative epistemic emotions that may promote or hinder learning.

In summary, SRL describes the process by which individuals consciously manage their thoughts, behaviors, and emotions during learning activities. Theorists have identified four phases of SRL, where task definition, planning and goal setting, enactment, and evaluation play integral roles in learning outcomes. Moreover, SRL is closely tied to metacognitive processes, with the latter often being attributed to the evaluation phase. However, metacognitive processes can be employed at any stage of SRL. We turn to theoretical frameworks of metacognition to delineate these processes and examine their role in learning from multiple inputs.

METACOGNITION

Metacognition is a broad term that refers to one's understanding of their own cognition. As Kuhn (2000) explained, metacognition is the ability to reflect, monitor, and/or regulate first-order cognition. Metacognition theorists define its component parts in overlapping, yet distinct ways. These parts include metacognitive knowledge, skills, and experiences. Metacognitive knowledge, in particular, has been labeled in numerous ways. Flavell, Miller, and Miller (2002) conceptualized metacognitive knowledge as a means of understanding people as "cognitive creatures," where an individual has knowledge, beliefs, ideas, and theories about people, including how people interact with cognitive tasks and strategies. An individual's metacognitive knowledge informs their task definition and goal setting as they determine the criteria and extent to which information must be evaluated to complete the task.

Within metacognitive knowledge, there are three subcategories: knowledge of persons, knowledge of tasks, and knowledge of strategies. Knowledge of persons describes self-knowledge about the variables that influence one's own thinking, knowledge about others' cognitions, and understanding of commonalities between individuals' cognition. For example, when an individual possesses knowledge of others' thinking, they may use what they know about the expertise of an environmentalist to determine the reliability of information presented about climate change. By weighing the level of expertise across sources the individual can decide whether or not to integrate information during source coordination. Knowledge of tasks describes understanding how task conditions, goals, and demands influence one's own thinking. An individual's knowledge of the task may direct them to seek out different viewpoints. Knowledge of strategies describes an individuals' awareness of the thinking, learning, and problem-solving strategies that are at their disposal to accomplish their goals. When integrating information sources, an individual's knowledge of strategies will guide them as they decide when they need to validate or corroborate information across viewpoints.

For Kuhn (2000), the acquisition of new knowledge occurs through a controlled metacognitive process. Kuhn differentiated between metacognitive knowing and metastrategic knowing, such that metacognitive knowing refers to a meta-level knowing that something works (i.e., declarative knowledge, Schraw & Moshman, 1995), whereas metastrategic knowing refers to a meta-level understanding of how something works (i.e., procedural knowledge, Schraw & Moshman, 1995). This new term, metastrategic knowing, includes awareness of thinking strategies, their purpose, and how and when to use thinking strategies to reach learning objectives. Metastrategic knowing is further broken down into two subcategories: (a) metatask knowledge, or the knowledge of task goals, which is comparable to Flavell and colleagues' (2002) knowledge of tasks, and (b) metastrategic knowledge, or the knowledge of available strategies to achieve task goals, which is similar to Flavell and colleagues' (2002) knowledge of strategies and Schraw and Moshman's (1995) conditional knowledge.

The second component of metacognition is metacognitive skills, which refer to the techniques and processes used to regulate cognition and learning, where planning, monitoring, and evaluation play important roles in successful regulation. Whereas Schraw and Moshman (1995) included these three categories within metacognitive skills, Flavell and colleagues (2002) distinguished metacognitive monitoring from metacognitive self-regulation. Similar to the second phase of SRL, planning constitutes setting goals, selecting strategies, making predictions, strategy sequencing, and resource allocation. According to Schraw and Moshman (1995), this allows the individual to regulate their learning before beginning the task, which provides the individual with the opportunity to more efficiently use their resources and learning strategies. For example, an individual may plan to learn about the causes of climate changes separately from the consequences of climate change to organize their understanding. If they already know more about the causes, on the other hand, the individual may choose to spend more time researching the consequences of climate change. As they progress in their learning, the learner may monitor their performance, where monitoring involves the active awareness of comprehension and performance in relation to goals. For instance, the individual may monitor their progress toward answering the question about the causes and consequences of climate change or they may monitor information from one website to corroborate another website. Lastly, evaluation refers to assessing the products and efficiency of learning and thinking (e.g., self-reflection). If the individual is unsatisfied with the information or viewpoints that they have found, they may change their search strategy as a result of this evaluation.

According to Barzilai and Zohar (2012), evaluations can involve assessing thinking as well as assessing the object of that thinking. Referred to as epistemic metacognition, the object of thinking is knowledge for this form of metacognitive knowledge. Discussions about the nature of knowledge and knowing are particularly relevant to the examination of multiple perspectives. To illustrate, an individual who believes that knowledge is objective and certain may defer to authority figures when presented with contradictory information. By default, these individuals do not consider the multitude of perspectives on any given topic. On the other hand, an individual who believes that knowledge contains both objective and subjective components may weigh the evidence of two conflicting perspectives. During this process of integration, the learner must pay close attention to features such as the author's purpose and relevance to their goals to develop a coherent mental model (Rouet & Britt, 2011). As such, metacognitive skills play an important role during integration, as individuals assess whether to (a) seek information from another source to comprehend the topic, (b) continue processing information (i.e., reading), or (c) update their mental model of the topic. The knowledge of available strategies to achieve integration goals may anchor individuals, so that they use their metacognitive skills to look for and identify differences in perspectives based on evidence and reasoning.

The final component of metacognition is metacognitive experiences, which were outlined by Flavell and colleagues (2002) as the cognitive and affective moments that relate to more complex cognitive processing, such as confusion experienced when processing information. Efklides (2011) extended Flavell and colleagues' (2002) definition, explaining that an individual's interactions with the task will bring about different affective experiences. An individual's affect provides information that should be monitored before, during, and following completion of the task (Efklides, 2011). For instance, if a task feels difficult, this can signal that effort needs to be regulated, help needs to be sought, or different strategies should be used. Efklides (2011) linked metacognitive experiences with metacognitive knowledge, and posited that metacognitive experiences occur during the evaluation phase of SRL. Efklides' (2011) MASRL model includes two levels: The Person level and the Task × Person level. Metacognition resides within the Person level, where metacognitive knowledge, metacognitive skills, attitudes, emotions, motivation, self-concept, and cognitive ability are described. Similar to previous theorists, Efklides (2011) represented metacognitive knowledge as the declarative knowledge, beliefs, and theories concerning thinking, tasks, people, strategies, and goals. Metacognitive skills regulate the thinking process via use of procedural knowledge, self-monitoring, planning, and evaluation. Efklides (2011) included metacognitive knowledge in the forethought phase of SRL, explaining that it is either activated automatically or by metacognitive skills.

In summary, metacognition describes an individual's understanding of their thinking process, and is composed of metacognitive knowledge, skills, and experiences. Flavell and colleagues (2002) described metacognitive knowledge as an individual's knowledge, beliefs, ideas, and theories of other people; Kuhn (2000) viewed metacognitive knowing as the knowledge about a concept; Schraw and Moshman (1995) viewed metacognitive knowledge more broadly, as they included declarative, procedural, and conditional knowledge under this category; and, Efklides (2011) described metacognitive knowledge as the knowledge and beliefs about cognition, tasks, people, and goals. Schraw and Moshman (1995) and Efklides (2011) most resemble one another in their conceptualization of metacognitive knowledge. Metacognitive skills are similarly conceptualized across theorists as the skills or strategies used to regulate the learning process, such as planning, monitoring, and evaluation. Finally, Efklides (2011) also included metacognitive experience in the MASRL model, which describes the interaction between an individual's affect and the task and how this informs the learning process.

SRL AND METACOGNITIVE PROCESSES DURING INTEGRATION

Given this brief review of two theoretical constructs, we now discuss how SRL and metacognition impact integration of multiple inputs. To situate our discussion, we first reviewed empirical research on the integration of multiple inputs. Studies were selected if they examined SRL or metacognitive processes while individuals interacted with multiple inputs. SRL and metacognitive components included metastrategic knowing and strategy sequencing. Studies were chosen if these processes were the main focus of investigation, a secondary examination, or a minor focus. We first delineate the specific search procedures used to identify studies and then provide a critical summary and analysis of our findings with exemplary studies for illustrative purposes.

Search Procedures

Due to the specificity of our search, we did not restrict publications based on publication date. Three electronic databases (PsycINFO, ERIC, and Web of Science) were searched in September 2018 and May 2019 with the following keywords: "self-regul* OR metacog* AND representation* OR perspective* OR input", "self-regul* OR metacog* AND integration." This search resulted in a total of 1337 items. Eleven duplicate entries from the three databases and 40 dissertation abstracts were removed from the list. All abstracts of the remaining 1286 items were scanned to identify potentially relevant articles. Other articles that were removed included 1192 that focused on only one component of the search (e.g., measurement of an aspect of SRL but no multiple representation), 49 that were conference abstracts, 23 that were non-empirical, and another seven that fell into an "other" category. Items classified as "other" dealt with SRL or metacognition and other research areas, such as neuroscience and creativity work. Of the initial 1337 items identified from the database searches, a subtotal of 19 articles met the inclusion criteria and were selected for detailed review. Multiple representations were examined in 14 articles, and multiple perspectives were examined in five articles. Following initial review, an additional six articles were added to the detailed review that included multiple inputs and SRL or metacognition but did not explicitly state aspects of the theoretical frameworks. No articles examined both multiple representations and multiple perspectives with measures of SRL or metacognition.

Of the studies reviewed, learning contexts with multiple inputs were used to investigate the sequences of individual SRL or metacognitive processes and learning outcomes. Online integration processes were measured with eye-tracking technology or think-aloud protocols. In investigations of learning, integration was commonly inferred from outcome measures (e.g., post-test score, essay quality). We discuss findings from empirical work across four categories: integrating multiple representations, learning with multiple representations, integrating multiple perspectives, and learning from multiple perspectives. In the two sections on integration strategies, we describe process-focused and outcome-focused studies that measured integration. For the two sections on learning, we discuss empirical studies that measured the sequence of learning or learning gains, separating studies that focused on multiple perspectives from multiple representations. Intervention studies are included in all four sections.

Integrating Multiple Representations

Individuals may encounter multiple representations when learning, such that the content is represented in two or more symbolic forms (e.g., alphabetic, graphic, symbolic). If an individual is not adept at switching between these forms, they may have difficulty integrating information to build their mental representation of the topic or completing their task. Research has investigated visual transitions between text and graphics to identify individuals' integration strategies as they read illustrated texts. Mason, Tornatora, and Pluchino (2015b) utilized eye-tracking technology to identify 7th graders' integrative processing patterns as they read illustrated texts. Second-pass reading, or delayed processing where text or pictures were reinspected, was found to predict verbal and graphical recall as well as application of new knowledge in a transfer task. Students with stronger integrative processing demonstrated longer fixation times during second-pass reading as they transitioned from corresponding or non-corresponding text segments to corresponding or non-corresponding graphic segments. The distance between text and graphic has been found to affect these transitions, with less distance encouraging attempts to integrate (Johnson & Mayer, 2012). Scaffolds to support integrative processing have also been developed.

To improve recall and comprehension during integration of multiple representations, Seufert (2019) examined the effectiveness of training university students to use lower-level SRL strategies, such as prior knowledge activation and identifying important information, and metacognitive monitoring of the training checklist. Participants in the training group were introduced to reading and integration strategies, provided examples, and given opportunities to practice using the strategy for three weeks. Individuals assigned to the control group were involved in group discussions unrelated to the strategy training for the same length of time. At the end of three weeks, all participants were presented materials with both text and graphics where they were asked to relate text to the correct graphic. Their ability to recall and comprehend the materials was also assessed at post-test. Results revealed that training on lower-level SRL strategies, as opposed to higher-level strategies such as knowledge elaboration or critical thinking, did not improve participants' recall or comprehension of the materials. The emphasis on lower-level strategies in the training content and the intervention design may account for these null findings. Training using modelling, rather than declarative knowledge via checklist, has been successful in improving integration strategy-use and learning outcomes (Mason et al., 2015a). Theoretical frameworks of SRL and metacognition provide a strong foundation for research on strategy-use when training and measures are aligned.

In summary, access to multiple representations is beneficial to learning if students are able to employ appropriate SRL and metacognitive strategies to manage information in different formats (Cromley, Azevedo, & Olson, 2005). Eye-tracking technologies have provided behavioral evidence of deeper-level integrative processing, especially during second-pass reading of text and graphics. Additional research is required on the explicit role of SRL and metacognition in integrating multiple representations to inform interventions that employ deeper-level strategy instruction.

Learning with Multiple Representations.

Researchers have also examined how scaffolds and embedded feedback support the use of specific SRL and metacognitive processes during learning with multiple representations, such as planning and monitoring, especially for individuals with low prior knowledge (Lehmann, Hähnlein, & Ifenthaler, 2014; Schwonke et al., 2013; Taub, Azevedo, Bouchet, & Khosravifar, 2014). For example, Taub et al. (2014) examined how university students engaged in SRL while learning in a computer-based learning environment (CBLE) that featured multiple representations, including text and diagrams. SRL strategy scaffolds were embedded into the CBLE to support study of the material (e.g., creating summaries, judgments of learning, monitoring of progress toward goals, and note-taking). Participants in the "prompt and feedback" group also received scaffolding and feedback from the system's pedagogical agents. During analysis, participants were further separated into two groups: high and low prior knowledge about the learning content. Taub and colleagues found that individuals with low prior knowledge, no matter the group they were assigned, used more SRL strategies than high prior knowledge individuals. Cognitive strategy-use (e.g., note-taking, prior knowledge activation) did not differ between groups. In fact, both groups began their learning task by planning their approach and activating prior knowledge. However, these groups differed on their metacognitive strategy-use (e.g., monitoring progress toward goals), where high prior knowledge participants engaged in monitoring and evaluation (Phase 4) earlier than low prior knowledge participants. These results suggest that the sequence of strategy-use may influence learning efficiency as individuals who recognize their lack of understanding may be able to change learning strategies when they first detect (through monitoring) that they have not met their goal (Tuysuzoglu & Greene, 2015). To aid individuals in developing SRL competencies when learning with multiple representations, strategic scaffolds can be incorporated into learning activities.

Lehmann et al. (2014) investigated the role of one such strategic scaffold, SRL reflection prompts, as undergraduates constructed multiple representations of their knowledge (i.e., written knowledge and knowledge map). Pre-reflection and reflection prompts were used to support activation of key SRL processes before a learning activity, including planning, monitoring, and evaluating their learning. Metacognitive awareness was measured using self-report questionnaires (i.e., items related to metacognitive knowledge and metastrategic knowledge), which weakened the authors' ability to discuss the role of metacognition in knowledge construction. Participants were assigned to one of three groups: (1) directed pre-reflection, where prompts were intended to induce specific SRL processes; (2) general pre-reflection, where general prompts provided a suggestion before the SRL task; or, (3) general reflection, where prompts provided general instructions for planning and reflecting on the SRL task. Learning was measured via a post-test essay and concept map about the development of a black hole. The directed pre-reflection group had higher learning gains on their post-test essay than either group that received more general instruction. Essay quality was also associated with higher levels of self-reported metacognitive regulation. These findings suggest that direct instruction to activate SRL processes may lead to higher quality knowledge construction in multiple formats.

In summary, the order of strategy-use may influence learning efficiency and effectiveness as individuals who recognize their lack of understanding may be able to change their strategy to achieve their goal (Taub et al., 2014). Direct instruction and reflection prompts can be used to stimulate SRL and metacognitive processes during the enactment phase of a learning activity, such as planning, monitoring, and evaluation of products, which may lead to better learning gains (Lehmann et al., 2014). We now turn to empirical work that has examined learning when interacting with multiple perspectives.

Integrating Multiple Perspectives

Whereas research on integrating multiple representations has focused on coordinating information within the same source, research on integrating multiple perspectives has focused on combining and corroborating information from multiple sources. In addition to this layer of complexity, individuals must also take into account the source of information and justifications used to support knowledge claims when deciding how to integrate content into a coherent conceptual understanding (Barzilai & Zohar, 2012). As described in Barzilai and Weinstock (Chapter 9), individuals are required to identify relationships between perspectives and then integrate information while keeping source reliability in mind (e.g., author expertise). Individuals can also hold beliefs about the content of the task at hand that may influence learning. Barzilai and colleagues (Barzilai & Ka'adan, 2017; Barzilai & Zohar, 2012) examined the role of these beliefs and epistemic metacognition in integrating multiple perspectives from online sources.

In Barzilai and Zohar's (2012) study, 6th graders engaged in two online inquiry tasks at their home where they encountered conflicting perspectives. To capture epistemic metacognition, individuals were asked to reflect upon the websites they used during their inquiry task in retrospective interviews. Individuals' epistemic metastrategic knowledge about online learning strategies was found to relate to their beliefs about the nature of knowledge. That is, individuals' metastrategic knowledge was related to their beliefs about the subjective and objective dimensions of knowledge. Individuals who believed that knowledge has both objective and subjective dimensions had more awareness of multiple perspectives and discussed the concept of trustworthiness more in their retrospective interview responses. Although individuals demonstrated the same range of metastrategic knowledge about integrating perspectives, individuals who believed in both dimensions of knowledge focused on the integration component rather than corroboration or plausibility. Barzilai and Zohar explained that critical integration requires individuals to account for differences between distinct sources that may have varying purposes, biases, and levels of credibility. Individuals who acknowledge the subjective and objective dimensions of knowledge may be more attuned to look for and identify these differences and use their metastrategic knowledge to enact strategies for successful integration.

In a subsequent study, Barzilai and Ka'adan (2017) tested the efficacy of strategic and metastrategic scaffolds on 9th-grade students' ability to integrate multiple perspectives from divergent information sources. Students were assigned to one of three conditions: a control condition wherein students did not receive any scaffolds, a strategic condition wherein students received a strategic scaffold, or a metastrategic condition wherein students received both strategic and metastrategic scaffolds. The strategic scaffold supported source evaluation and text integration, whereas the metastrategic scaffold supported conditional knowledge, such as knowing how, when, and why to use a certain strategy. Source evaluation was viewed as an important precursor to source integration. Support tools for source evaluation took a matrix form, where participants were asked to reflect on source features such as author credentials, timeliness of the text, and purpose of the text. Source integration support took the form of a mind map, where arguments, sources, and connections between the two were made visible. For metastrategic strategy instruction, students identified and reflected on integration strategies. It is important to acknowledge that this study measured integration performance at three timepoints (pre, post, delayed), which provides better insight into the effectiveness of their instructional manipulation. Overall, Barzilai and Ka'adan (2017) found that individuals with strategic support had the greatest improvement in integration performance. This improvement was classified as gradual as opposed to the metastrategic support group, whose integration performance improved as well, but peaked at the immediate post timepoint. Integration improvement for individuals that received metastrategic support was found to occur by way of an increase in epistemic metacognitive knowledge about strategies and tasks.

In summary, individuals' beliefs about the subjective and objective nature of knowledge are related to their metastrategic knowledge when interacting with multiple perspectives online. For example, when tasked to integrate multiple perspectives, an individual's beliefs about knowledge may influence their knowledge of strategies that are available to achieve integration goals. Since this interaction would occur in the first phase of SRL (i.e., task definition), all subsequent phases might be affected. Barzilai and Ka'adan's (2017) study demonstrated that metastrategic knowledge can be developed with explicit instruction and, in turn, can support integration of multiple perspectives. However, direct strategic instruction was more effective in supporting integration, which suggests that instruction geared at the enactment phase of SRL (e.g., look for and identify differences in perspective) may play a more important role in successful integration. We next turn to empirical work which has utilized multiple perspectives to assess learning.

Learning from Multiple Perspectives

Research that requires individuals to process multiple perspectives has afforded a better understanding of how individuals engage in learning activities (Greene, Copeland, Deekens, & Seung, 2018; Muis et al., 2015). Muis and colleagues (2015) examined relationships between undergraduates' epistemic beliefs (i.e., beliefs about the nature of knowledge and knowing), epistemic emotions, SRL strategies, and learning gains. To capture epistemic emotions and the types of learning strategies used in real-time, individuals were asked to think out loud as they read conflicting perspectives about the causes and consequences of climate change from multiple perspectives of varying source quality. Think-out-loud data were coded based on the four macro phases of SRL described in Muis et al. (2018; i.e., task definition, planning and goal setting, enactment, and evaluation), where micro codes within each macro code included prior knowledge activation and task definitions (Phase 1), planning and goal setting (Phase 2), reproduction of information, rereading, knowledge elaboration, and critical thinking (Phase 3), and monitoring and evaluation of products (Phase 4).

Muis et al. (2015) found that individuals' beliefs about the nature of knowledge predicted the emotions experienced when reading conflicting perspectives, the types of learning strategies used, and the level of achievement, which coincide with Barzilai and Zohar's (2012) findings. Regarding the relationship between emotions and learning strategies, higher levels of surprise, curiosity, enjoyment, and confusion predicted higher levels of metacognitive self-regulation. Curiosity, enjoyment, and confusion predicted more critical thinking, and surprise, confusion, and anxiety predicted greater rehearsal. Lastly, curiosity and enjoyment were also related to knowledge elaboration. The emotions individuals experienced were likely a function of cognitive disequilibrium caused by conflicting information. This may have indicated to the individual that integration or resolution strategies were necessary to resolve conflicting perspectives. As such, individuals may have used more critical thinking and elaboration strategies to achieve this resolution, which resulted in better learning outcomes (Muis et al., 2018). As Muis et al. (2018) argued, these emotions can facilitate or constrain knowledge construction during all phases of SRL. See Pekrun and Loderer (Chapter 22) for further discussion of emotions and learning.

When constructing knowledge, researchers have augmented tasks to evaluate differences in individuals' SRL practices when interacting with multiple perspectives. For example, Greene et al. (2018) examined differences in undergraduates' SRL as they engaged with multiple perspectives during an online search. Participants were assigned to complete one learning task designed with different goals in mind: knowledge acquisition (i.e., knowledge test) or construction of understanding (i.e., writing an evidence-based argumentative essay). To capture SRL processes in real-time, participants were asked to think out loud. Learning was gauged using a pre-test/post-test design. Individuals in the essay task condition demonstrated more engagement in planning, monitoring, and epistemic cognition than their counterparts in the knowledge acquisition condition. By designing a task that requires deeper level strategy-use, individuals can be supported to develop these skills for future use.

Analysis of the cognitive and metacognitive strategies individuals adopt in real-time lays the groundwork to promote deeper level strategy-use and optimize the benefits of learning from multiple perspectives. What seems critical to develop is individuals' ability to integrate multiple perspectives via metacognitive processes that target comparison of incoming information with previously processed information to allow for a coherent integration of that information. Epistemic emotions may be key indications to individuals that perspectives are complementary or conflicting. Consider the example before about an individual researching climate change. This individual may experience surprise and then confusion when encountering articles outlining scientific evidence that contradicts previously held notions. If the individual cannot resolve the underlying contradictions, the confusion may lead to frustration and potentially result in disengagement from the learning task (D'Mello & Graesser, 2012). The confusion may also benefit the individual in that it highlights specifically where the individual should focus their attention and deploy strategies to resolve that confusion (D'Mello & Graesser, 2012). In this way, epistemic emotions inform individuals as to which strategies are needed to successfully integrate information and gain a deeper understanding of the content.

LIMITATIONS AND FUTURE DIRECTIONS

Empirical work examining SRL and metacognition as individuals integrate multiple inputs is limited but growing. Examination of these processes when encountering both multiple representations and perspectives has yet to be explored. A review of the literature revealed that individuals' beliefs about knowledge and knowing may predict their knowledge of strategies (Barzilai & Zohar, 2012) and the actual strategies they use (Muis et al., 2015) to achieve learning goals. Since this interaction between beliefs and knowledge of strategies occurs in the first phase of SRL (i.e., task definition), all subsequent phases may be affected. Further, the order of SRL strategy-use may predict learning effectiveness as individuals who recognize their lack of understanding may be able to change their strategies when goals are not being achieved (Taub et al., 2014). It also appears that direct instruction (Barzilai & Ka'adan, 2017) and SRL reflection prompts (Lehmann et al., 2014) can support integration and learning, respectively.

Above and beyond using contexts that feature multiple inputs, such as CBLEs and the Internet, research tasks must be created with deeper-level strategy-use in mind, as Greene et al.'s (2018) findings suggested. In and of itself, the task of integrating multiple inputs challenges the individual by requiring them to actively construct their understanding. As seen in the lasting effects for individuals in Barzilai and Ka'adan's (2017) strategic group, learning benefits from effortful cognitive and metacognitive processing. As individuals experience desirable difficulties, they require appropriate SRL and metacognitive strategies to manage information.

Research has demonstrated the value of think-aloud protocols in providing insight into individuals' SRL and metacognitive processes as they manage information in real-time (e.g., Barzilai & Zohar, 2012). When interacting with multiple representations, use of trace methodologies, such as eye-tracking or screen capture in combination with think-aloud protocols (e.g., summarizing) could be triangulated to better understand how integration of multiple inputs occurs. Based on this triangulation, strategic scaffolds could be designed to help students identify and use the appropriate strategies when interacting with an animation as opposed to text and diagrams. Future work may also explore the complex processes that occur as individuals construct knowledge using multiple representations.

Despite findings that have identified the importance of SRL and metacognition when dealing with multiple inputs, research has yet to explore which SRL or metacognitive strategies or supports are vital for individuals to effectively navigate, integrate, and manage information. This is one area of research that requires greater attention, especially as we live in a world where complex, contradictory information is readily accessible on the Internet. Drawing from digital literacy literature (e.g., Eshet-Alkalai & Chajut, 2009, 2010) may be useful to examine SRL strategies and behaviors on the Internet, such as deciphering multiple representations in design software, reorganizing and integrating multiple inputs during knowledge construction, navigating digital environments, and processing mass amounts of information in real-time. This body of research has situated the individual as an active creator of knowledge, where they seek and contribute. That is, the individual creates for themselves and for others. They actively create their own understanding during their search for information and they may create content to share with individuals that they know or that they don't know. Integration strategies play a central role in managing purposeful thinking in environments with multiple inputs – these strategies keep us afloat.

CONCLUSIONS

With access to information that may come in various formats and points of view, effective SRL and metacognitive processes are more important than ever. Research has examined how individuals integrate, learn from, and behave when interacting with multiple representations and perspectives. Highly self-regulated individuals tend to use resources more effectively and selectively, with learning gains highest when deep cognitive processing occurs. The order of strategy-use may influence learning efficiency and effectiveness as individuals who recognize their lack of understanding may be able to change their strategy to achieve their learning goals. Therefore, fostering SRL and metacognitive processes may help develop the skills necessary to allow individuals to successfully navigate the sea of complex and often contradictory information.

ACKNOWLEDGMENTS

Support for this research was provided by a grant to Krista R. Muis from the Social Sciences and Humanities Research Council of Canada (grant # 435-2014-0155) and the Canada Research Chairs program.

REFERENCES

Barzilai, S., & Ka'adan, I. (2017). Learning to integrate divergent information sources: The interplay of epistemic cognition and epistemic metacognition. *Metacognition and Learning, 12*(2), 193–232.

Barzilai, S., & Zohar, A. (2012). Epistemic thinking in action: Evaluating and integrating online sources. *Cognition and Instruction, 30*(1), 39–85.

Boekaerts, M. (2011). Emotions, emotion regulation, and self-regulation of learning. In D. H. Schunk & B. Zimmerman (Eds.), *Handbook of self-regulation of learning and performance* (pp. 408–425). New York: Taylor & Francis.

Cromley, J., Azevedo, R., & Olson, E. (2005). Self-regulation of learning with multiple representations in hypermedia. In C.-K. Looi (Ed.), *Artificial intelligence in education* (pp. 184–191). Amsterdam: IOS Press.

D'Mello, S., & Graesser, A. (2012). Dynamics of affective states during complex learning. *Learning and Instruction, 22*(2), 145–157.

Efklides, A. (2011). Interactions of metacognition with motivation and affect in self-regulated learning: The MASRL model. *Educational Psychologist, 46*(1), 6–25.

Eshet-Alkalai, Y., & Chajut, E. (2009). Changes over time in digital literacy. *CyberPsychology and Behavior, 12*(6), 713–715.

Eshet-Alkalai, Y., & Chajut, E. (2010). You can teach old dogs new tricks: The factors that affect changes over time in digital literacy. *Journal of Information Technology Education: Research, 9*(1), 173–181.

Flavell, J. H., Miller, P. H., & Miller, S. A. (2002). *Cognitive development* (vol. 338, 4th ed.). Englewood Cliffs, NJ: Prentice-Hall.

Greene, J. A., Copeland, D. Z., Deekens, V. M., & Seung, B. Y. (2018). Beyond knowledge: Examining digital literacy's role in the acquisition of understanding in science. *Computers and Education, 117*, 141–159.

Johnson, C. I., & Mayer, R. E. (2012). An eye movement analysis of the spatial contiguity effect in multimedia learning. *Journal of Experimental Psychology: Applied, 18*(2), 178.

Kuhn, D. (2000). Metacognitive development. *Current Directions in Psychological Science, 9*(5), 178–181.

Lehmann, T., Hähnlein, I., & Ifenthaler, D. (2014). Cognitive, metacognitive and motivational perspectives on preflection in self-regulated online learning. *Computers in Human Behavior, 32*, 313–323.

Mason, L., Pluchino, P., & Tornatora, M. C. (2015a). Eye-movement modeling of integrative reading of an illustrated text: Effects on processing and learning. *Contemporary Educational Psychology, 41*, 172–187.

Mason, L., Tornatora, M. C., & Pluchino, P. (2015b). Integrative processing of verbal and graphical information during re-reading predicts learning from illustrated text: An eye-movement study. *Reading and Writing, 28*(6), 851–872.

Muis, K. R. (2007). The role of epistemic beliefs in self-regulated learning. *Educational Psychologist, 42*(3), 173–190.

Muis, K. R., Chevrier, M., & Singh, C. A. (2018). The role of epistemic emotions in personal epistemology and self-regulated learning. *Educational Psychologist, 53*(3), 165–184.

Muis, K. R., Pekrun, R., Sinatra, G. M., Azevedo, R., Trevors, G., Meier, E., & Heddy, B. C. (2015). The curious case of climate change: Testing a theoretical model of epistemic beliefs, epistemic emotions, and complex learning. *Learning and Instruction, 39*, 168–183.

Panadero, E. (2017). A review of self-regulated learning: Six models and four directions for research. *Frontiers in Psychology, 8*, 422.

Pintrich, P. R. (2000). The role of goal orientation in self-regulated learning. In M. Boekaerts, P. R. Pintrich, & M. Zeidner *Handbook of self-regulation* (pp. 451–502). Amsterdam: Elsevier.

Rouet, J.-F., & Britt, M. A. (2011). Relevance processes in multiple document comprehension. In M. T. McCrudden (Ed.), *Text relevance and learning from text* (pp. 311–328). Charlotte, NC: Information Age Publishing Inc.

Scheiter, K., & Eitel, A. (2015). Signals foster multimedia learning by supporting integration of highlighted text and diagram elements. *Learning and Instruction, 36*, 11–26.

Schraw, G., & Moshman, D. (1995). Metacognitive theories. *Educational Psychology Review, 7*(4), 351–371.

Schwonke, R., Ertelt, A., Otieno, C., Renkl, A., Aleven, V., & Salden, R. J. (2013). Metacognitive support promotes an effective use of instructional resources in intelligent tutoring. *Learning and Instruction, 23*, 136–150.

Seufert, T. (2019). Training for coherence formation when learning from text and picture and the interplay with learners' prior knowledge. *Frontiers in Psychology, 10*, 1–11.

Taub, M., Azevedo, R., Bouchet, F., & Khosravifar, B. (2014). Can the use of cognitive and metacognitive self-regulated learning strategies be predicted by learners' levels of prior knowledge in hypermedia-learning environments? *Computers in Human Behavior, 39*, 356–367.

Trevors, G., Feyzi-Behnagh, R., Azevedo, R., & Bouchet, F. (2016). Self-regulated learning processes vary as a function of epistemic beliefs and contexts: Mixed method evidence from eye tracking and concurrent and retrospective reports. *Learning and Instruction, 42*, 31–46.

Tuysuzoglu, B. B., & Greene, J. A. (2015). An investigation of the role of contingent metacognitive behavior in self-regulated learning. *Metacognition and Learning, 10*(1), 77–98.

Winne, P. H., & Hadwin, A. F. (1998). Studying as self-regulated learning. *Metacognition in Educational Theory and Practice, 93*, 27–30.

Winne, P. H., & Hadwin, A. F. (2008). The weave of motivation and self-regulated learning. In D. H. Schunk & B. J. Zimmerman (Eds.), *Motivation and self-regulated learning: Theory, research and applications* (pp. 297–314). New York: Lawrence Erlbaum Associates.

Zimmerman, B. J. (1989). Models of self-regulated learning and academic achievement. In B. J. Zimmerman (Ed.), *Self-regulated learning and academic achievement* (pp. 1–25). Dordrecht: Springer.

Zimmerman, B. J., & Moylan, A. R. (2009). Self-regulation: Where metacognition and motivation intersect. In D. J. Hacker, J. Dunlosky, & A. C. Graesser (Eds.), *Handbook of metacognition in education* (pp. 311–328). New York: Routledge.

20

VALUES, ATTITUDES, AND BELIEFS
Cognitive Filters Shaping Integration of Multiple Representations and Multiple Perspectives

Doug Lombardi
UNIVERSITY OF MARYLAND

Benjamin C. Heddy
UNIVERSITY OF OKLAHOMA

Ananya M. Matewos
TEMPLE UNIVERSITY

ABSTRACT

Values, attitudes, and beliefs are integral to the learning process and influenced by both multiple representations and multiple perspectives. In this chapter, we propose a hypo-predictive model that posits a sequential relation between values, attitudes, and beliefs, where multiple inputs would mediate these relations. The chapter examines the literature serving as the foundation to the model's development and then presents a few exemplar learning and teaching situations to illustrate the application of this model in both educational research and practice.

Key words: beliefs, attitudes, values, multiple representations, multiple perspectives

INTRODUCTION

Students in their Earth Science class are working on group projects to create a poster demonstrating the science behind climate change and to propose a corresponding policy idea addressing how to reduce carbon emissions. In facilitating the groups, the teacher finds that students are experiencing conflict and confusion as some students remain uncertain about the role humans play in global warming. Other students are unconvinced policy changes related to carbon emissions can help and believe such actions may harm the economy. Some groups are at an impasse regarding policy solutions, while other groups were unable to finalize even the first part of the poster explaining the scientific phenomenon underlying climate science. Students appeared to be confused by an assortment of conflicting evidence and claims across the Internet and media sources, with one student even pulling up an online conspiracy theory video on the great climate hoax. It occurred to the teacher that the students already had values, attitudes, and beliefs around the issue of climate and each student's learning was influenced further by how they interpreted multiple representations and perspectives around climate related information sources.

The vignette above reveals that values, attitudes, and beliefs operate on people, including oneself, objects, issues, processes, and behaviors. Psychologists have been researching the intersections of values, attitudes, and beliefs for many decades. For the purpose of this article, we operationalize *values* as general and durable individually and socially derived standards, resulting from instrumental relations and outcomes of objects and behaviors (Rokeach, 1979). *Attitudes* are dichotomous (pro and con) evaluations of objects and behaviors that can vary in strength along a continuum (e.g., very pro or con, slightly pro or con, null, etc.; Ostrom, 1989). Finally for the purpose of connecting to this book's specific topic (learning in the context of multiple representations and multiple perspectives), we characterize *beliefs* as the salient information (i.e., the relatively small amount of information that can be cognitively processed at any one time) in which individuals use to determine their actions and inactions (Ajzen, 1991) and toward which they have a certain level of commitment (Lombardi, Nussbaum, & Sinatra, 2016). Beliefs enable people "to achieve desired outcomes and avoid untoward ones" as they exercise individual and collective agency (Bandura, 2001, p. 3).

The purpose of this chapter is to characterize the relations between values, attitudes, and beliefs in situations when learners experience multiple inputs, a common situation today and one that will likely remain common for the foreseeable future. Throughout this book, the authors and editors view multiple inputs as a general umbrella term that includes *multiple representations* – i.e., presentations of the same or complementary content via a variety of symbol systems (e.g., alphabetic, graphic, numeric) – and *multiple perspectives* – i.e., points of view on multifaceted or controversial topics, defined by coming from distinct sources and authors, each with a distinct set of assumptions, points of view, target audiences, and goals. In the 21st century, multiple representations include ephemeral text and images on electronic screens, as well as more stable text and images on relatively permanent media (e.g., paper). Also included in the multiple representation category are audio and tactile modes of presentation that may accompany text and other symbols. Multiple perspectives reflect viewpoints and positions from different institutions (e.g., government agencies), groups (e.g., political parties), and individuals (e.g., a celebrity on Twitter).

Our overall hypothesis is that multiple representations and multiple perspectives mediate the relations between values, attitudes, and beliefs in learning situations. Figure 20.1 is a schematic of our hypothesized model, which represents how we view

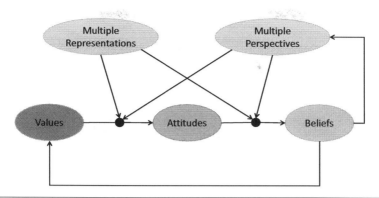

Figure 20.1 A Simple Feedback Model Representing the Interactions between Values, Attitudes, Beliefs with Multiple Representations and Multiple Perspectives.

the relations between these constructs as a double loop, simple feedback, between learners' beliefs, attitudes, and values, and how multiple representations and multiple perspectives interact with these relations as mediators. Our model of value, attitudes, and beliefs when learners interact with multiple representation and multiple perspectives is comprised of different relational paths. The model's core sequential path, i.e., values to attitudes to beliefs, is based on Fishbein's (1963) foundational expectancy-value (EV) framework relating attitudes and beliefs. Specifically, this early EV framework suggested that values, along with other factors (e.g., goals), can lead to pro or con evaluations (i.e., an attitude), which in turn is a mediator to a summative judgment that forms the basis of belief. In our model, we posit that beliefs feedback to values, with no direct feedback to attitudes. Although this may seem counter to Ajzen and Fishbein's (1980, 2008) seminal theories of reasoned action and planned behavior, where beliefs about the consequences of a certain action influence attitudes about the behavior, feedback to values only is in accordance with these theories because it is the subjective value of the consequence in combination with the belief that forms the attitude (Ajzen & Fishbein, 2008). The remainder of the chapter is divided into two sections. The first section reviews the literature that acts as a foundation to how we are conceptualizing the relations between values, attitudes, and beliefs. The second section presents suggestions for how educational researchers and practitioners could use our proposed hypo-predictive model.

REVIEW OF THE LITERATURE

Values

Values play an important role in people's everyday lives and may be both individually and socially based. Rokeach (1979) says that individual and superindividual (e.g., group, organizational, institutional, and/or societal) values relate to each other reciprocally and act as criteria for desirability for material objects and behaviors. As such, values differ from norms, which more closely relate to expected socio-cultural behaviors, rather than the desirable standard mode of behavior (Williams, 1979). For example, Miyake et al. (2010) found that female undergraduate physics students who affirmed their personal values about the importance of family, friends, etc. had greater gains in achievement than other female students who reflected on norms (i.e., other people's values that are not as personally important to these students). This difference in achievement underscores the personal relevance of values in learning situations, compared to norms, which may or may not have personal relevance.

Values may be a particularly important construct when individuals interact with multiple representations and multiple perspectives. In everyday learning situations that extend beyond classroom settings, learners often encounter multiple inputs in which they are intrinsically motivated and values are particularly salient (Brophy, 1999). For example, a community may be affected by a crisis when learning of high toxicity levels in their local drinking water supply. This news may be expressed in traditional print media (e.g., pamphlets) or visual electronic media (e.g., television news). How people value a mode of communication over another, such as print versus electronic broadcast, may impact the message expressed on these media, as well as the message perceived by the individual. Likewise, lower socio-economic groups that are typically disempowered and disproportionately affected by poor drinking water (i.e., because of a greater economic burden imposed by purchasing clean, bottled water) may have a completely different perspective on the problem than those from a higher socio-economic status. For leaders and members of the community to learn about and act on the crisis, they must value the types of information sources discussing the crisis, as well as value the perspectives of those adversely affected.

Values about Knowledge, Knowing, and Learning

Values have often been associated with motivation for learning. In their expectancy-value theory of motivation, Wigfield and Eccles (2000) see both values and expectations (i.e., beliefs about upcoming task outcomes) as critical components for students' achievement. These researchers suggested that four types of values are present when students engage in achievement tasks: (a) intrinsic values, associated with the level of enjoyment derived from the task or the depth of interest in the task; (b) attainment values, associated with the level of personal identification and self-belonging that the task supports; (c) utility values, associated with the worth and importance of the task toward a particular goal; and (d) cost values, associated with the negative aspects of a task. Brophy (1999) says that values are more important than expectancies when learners are "engaged in primarily intrinsically motivated activities," where goals are more implicit and less achievement oriented (p. 75). If an individual's goal is to construct and acquire knowledge either inside or outside a classroom context, that person must either already value the knowledge to be constructed or begin to value this knowledge through some sort of mediated process (e.g., a value reflected by a group's perspective). In such situations, a perspective (e.g., a conservative or liberal political position) may have more influence in shaping value about a topic of knowledge than that from a particular representation. Furthermore, identification with a group (e.g., identifying as a gender) may favor valuing types of knowledge (e.g., sports knowledge versus fashion knowledge). How one values the relevance of a group's perspective may have a similar effect in an individual's knowledge construction and acquisition. For example, a person relying on a watershed for drinking water may value the utility knowledge available from an environmental group that is dedicated to protecting and restoring the watershed (i.e., a utility value). In such a case, this person may learn about the watershed only from information obtained from this environmental group based solely on utility value alignment.

People have different values about knowledge and knowing that impact their motivation to learn and understand. Such values, often called epistemic values, specifically refer to the relative importance of some types of knowledge over others and indicate intentions to understand in a situation (Chinn, Rinehart, & Buckland, 2014; Torsney, Lombardi, & Ponnock, 2018). Such situational understanding is an epistemic achievement that is valued by the learner and broadens the notion of knowledge and knowing (Chinn, Buckland, & Samarapungavan, 2011). In the case of epistemic values, individuals may place varying degrees of value on both the nature of the knowledge and understanding (e.g., for someone concerned about their weight, understanding the connections between various dietary trends and health might have higher value than knowledge about gourmet recipes) and the nature of how relevant understanding is constructed (e.g., an adolescent may value knowledge construction processes through peer interactions over knowledge acquisition from a parent's "lecturing"). Many see epistemic value as related to achieving a learning goal (Torsney et al., 2018). Specifically, in some academic and professional settings, abstract, theoretical knowledge can be viewed as more valuable than applied, practical knowledge, whereas, in other situations, practical knowledge may have more value (Shulman, 1986). Epistemic values are tied to people's evaluation of the processes by which they construct certain knowledge and understandings. Thus, epistemic values are related to ideals and virtues of ways to effectively learn. Furthermore, such ideals and virtues may relate to how a learner views multiple representations (e.g., evaluations of expertise from scientific publications compared to articles in newspapers) and multiple perspectives (e.g., evaluations of trustworthiness of one political group over another).

Values about Conceptual Topics

Individuals also have various levels of value on specific learning topics, with many of these topics related to perceived relevance or connectivity. Pugh (2011) sees value as a critical component to learning through transformative experiences, which builds upon the Deweyan notion that the purpose of education is to "enrich and expand everyday experience" (p. 108). Transformative experience occurs in situations where students act on the classroom knowledge outside of the school context. For example, a student may have learned about local groundwater depletion in an Earth Science class and when reflecting on that lesson at home, may have sought information on how to mitigate local groundwater issues. Such research may have led to the student developing a rain garden in the backyard. In this case, transformative experience may have led the student to a particular representation of information (e.g., current information available on the Internet) and from a particular perspective (e.g., environment conservation groups). Experiential values are an important characteristic of transformative experiences and emerge from "the valuing of content for the experience it provides" (Pugh, 2011, p. 113).

Certain conceptual topics may elicit certain values. For example, Lundholm and colleagues (2013, 2018) suggest that value judgments are integral to understanding and conceptual development of certain social science topics, including economics and environmental studies (e.g., respect for nature and environmental protection to sustain a healthy and prosperous ecosystem may promote deeper understanding into wetlands as a resource rather than as a nuisance). Likewise, other researchers have seen topic-specific values related to controversial and/or abstract socio-scientific topics such as biological evolution (Heddy & Sinatra, 2013), genetically modified organisms (Mason, Junyent, & Tornatora, 2014), and cause of the common cold (Johnson & Sinatra, 2013; Jones, Johnson, & Campbell, 2015).

Attitudes

Attitudes toward things (e.g., material objects, processes, ideas, and events) are generally predictive of a set of behaviors that represent a general broad category. In a historical review of the relations between attitudes and behaviors, Ajzen, Fishbein, Lohmann, & Albarracín (2018) stressed that even though an attitude will not predict a specific behavior (e.g., attitudes about gender are not well correlated with a single vote for a particular candidate), attitudes do relate well to general patterns reflective of aggregate measures of associated behaviors (e.g., attitudes about God are well correlated with general trends in religiosity). Ajzen et al. (2018) call this "the principle of aggregation," where attitudes reliably predict broad patterns of behavior. For example, Ness (2011) found that elementary teachers' attitudes about text genre were associated with their instructional beliefs, specifically with a positive attitude about informational text relating to stronger beliefs about the instructional utility of informational text to increase students' literacy. Similarly, attitudes may influence beliefs about different perspectives. For example, Oxley et al. (2008) found that attitudes about the military, crime, and abortion, among other things, were associated strongly with political orientation beliefs.

Attitudes about Knowledge, Knowing, and Learning

Attitudes can operate on knowledge as an entity, whatever the form of knowledge may be (i.e., conceptual, procedural, and metacognitive). Specifically, attitudes about knowledge are valanced evaluations (pro or con, like or dislike), where individuals can have deep knowledge about a particular concept (e.g., stem cells), but have a pro or con evaluation about this knowledge (e.g., dislike the concept of stem cells because this type of research is opposed to a religious value; Sinatra & Seyranian, 2015).

Attitudes about knowledge are likely domain, and even topic, specific. Take for instance, the types of attitudes that may be activated when encountering information that is scientific in nature. One type is a *scientific attitude*, which may emerge from engaging in scientific practices (e.g., as a scientist, as a science student; Tytler & Osborne, 2012) and adopting scientific values (e.g., a positive attitude about empirical studies that are supported by credible and probative evidence; Chinn et al., 2014). Another type is associated with *attitudes toward science*, which researchers have investigated extensively. For non-scientists, attitudes toward science are somewhat distinct from a scientific attitude, and specifically relate to affective and motivational variables (e.g., enjoyment and interest in science and science activities) and the nature of the content (e.g., positive attitudes towards scientists and their findings; Osborne & Collins, 2001). Similar to science, people can have various attitudes toward mathematics, reading, writing, history, and other subjects, with these varying attitudes often related to cultural and gender differences (see, e.g., Gunderson, Ramirez, Levine, & Beilock, 2012; McKenna, Kear, & Ellsworth, 1995; Murphy & Beggs, 2003; Osborne, Simon, & Collins, 2003).

Attitudes toward a subject can spill over into learning about the subject because conceptual, procedural, and metacognitive understanding is tied closely to the content-to-be-learned (Neale, 1969). Therefore, in terms of multiple representations, people may have an attitude about a textbook, an image, a video recording, etc. because of its topic (e.g., disliking graphs because one dislikes mathematics). Similarly, attitudes about a perspective from a group may be related to a topic promoted by the group (e.g., in favor of perspectives taken by the American Association for the Advancement of Science because one favors science content).

Attitudes about Controversial Topics.

Clear attitude demarcation (e.g., strongly pro or strongly con) are often associated with controversial topics, such as vaccine safety and reading teaching methods. We generally consider a topic as controversial when that topic is characterized by conflicting sets of evidence and claims (Sinatra & Seyranian, 2015). Learning about controversial topics may therefore be strongly influenced by attitudes, where multiple perspectives could cause learners to be uncertain or construct knowledge inconsistent with expert understanding. In fact, learners may be particularly susceptible to adopting the attitudinal position of a group when placed in a learning situation that causes them to adopt that group's position (Lowry & Johnson, 1981). Such situations may exist in a relatively recent educational phenomenon, called "teaching the controversy," based on a campaign for promoting non-scientific viewpoints in science classrooms (Foran, 2014). For example, instructors may teach the causes of current climate change as a scientific controversy with alternative perspectives (e.g., sun-induced climate change, promoted by the fossil fuel industry) receiving equal attention to scientific perspectives (i.e., human-induced climate change). If both sides are taught as equal positions, a requirement in "teaching the controversy," some instructional techniques (e.g., pro and con debating) may lead to non-expert knowledge construction.

Learning about controversial topics may require purposeful and explicit thinking, especially when the learner conceptions conflict with the expert consensus conceptions about the topic to be learned (aka, the novel conception). Because strong attitudes are often associated with controversial topics, purposeful attitude change may also be necessary to facilitate learners' knowledge reconstruction (Heddy, Danielson, Sinatra, & Graham, 2017a). Thus, learners must be motivated and open to assess the central merits of the novel conceptions, as well as the background knowledge, which would deepen their thinking (i.e., through elaboration and critique). This process of purposeful and elaborative thinking is a central route to attitude change (Petty & Cacioppo, 1986), and as Dole and Sinatra (1998) have theorized, increases the likelihood of knowledge construction consistent with experts.

Beliefs

The term belief has many different meanings depending on the context of its use. For example, some philosophers view belief as a type of knowledge (e.g., belief as subjective knowledge; Kant, 1781/1998; or belief as incomplete knowledge, Mill, 1865/1979). Dewey (1910) suggests that beliefs are one dimension of knowing and learning, an idea which relates closely to Alexander, Schallert, & Hare's (1991) notion that knowledge consists of many components, such as information, skills, experiences, memories, with beliefs front and center as a necessary ingredient. Further, Lombardi et al. (2016) suggested that belief differs from other components involved in epistemic cognition because belief strength is based on individuals' level of commitment to some information (i.e., strong beliefs having a high level of commitment and weak beliefs having low or no level of commitment). Associating beliefs to various commitment levels reflects Ajzen's et al.'s (2018) notion that beliefs influence cognitive evaluations about behaviors, either implicitly (i.e., automatically with little or no conscious thought on the part of the learner), or explicitly (i.e. purposefully, with appreciable conscious thought on the part of the learner). Therefore, in the process of learning, learners may implicitly and explicitly employ their beliefs when integrating multiple representations and multiple perspectives.

The following examples reflect the dependency of an individual's belief on their level of commitment toward information. A simple visit to the grocery store can result in very different shopping behaviors depending on the shopper's beliefs around food production. For example, some people have very strong beliefs around the word "organic" and depending on how committed one is to understanding all the information surrounding that term, people can make very deliberate choices. For some, organic implies farm fresh, no pesticides, or artificial agents. Taking it a step further, some may believe that organic means that the food is not genetically modified (i.e., non-GMO). Based on these beliefs, people either justify the potential upcharge in prices and will only buy food labeled organic, or they avoid the word organic as it only signifies higher cost.

Beliefs about Knowledge, Knowing, and Learning

Philosophers situate their thinking about knowledge and knowing in an area of study called epistemology. However, thinking about knowledge and what it means to know is not limited to philosophers. In fact, almost all people engage in thinking processes about knowledge and knowing, and researchers often refer to these processes as epistemic cognition (Greene, Azevedo, & Torney-Purta, 2008). Historically, some researchers have referred to laypeople's cognition processes about knowledge as personal epistemologies (see, e.g., Bendixen & Rule, 2004); however, we view the idea of personal epistemologies as somewhat limited because most people's thoughts about knowledge and knowing often involve little reflection and explicit cognitive processing (King & Kitchener, 1994). Therefore, people's thoughts about knowledge and knowing probably do not constitute the full status of a personal theory or personal epistemology (i.e., most people do not purposefully study their own knowledge and knowing). Beliefs constitute an important and much studied aspect of epistemic cognition, which researchers sometimes refer to as epistemological beliefs (see, e.g., Hofer & Pintrich, 1997). However, for the purposes of precision, we use the term epistemic beliefs, rather than epistemological beliefs, because most people do not have well formed, or even implicit, beliefs about the philosophical study of knowledge (i.e., epistemology).

Developmental perspectives (see, e.g., King & Kitchener, 1994) view people's epistemic beliefs as transitioning from absolute and dualistic (e.g., knowledge is external with clear right and wrong positions) to subjective and relative (e.g., knowledge is internal with all opinions equally valid) to evaluative and reflective (e.g., knowledge is constructed and refined to greater validity through critical and creative criteria). Thus, when confronting multiple representations of information, absolutists may believe that "words in print are better than words on a digital device because print is the only way to really learn" (see, e.g., Baron, 2016). Relativists may say that digital and print are equally valid and based on personal preference because personally one likes reading on a tablet rather than reading from a traditional book; whereas their grandparents liked reading only from books (see, e.g., Harkaway, 2014). Evaluativists may be aware that perceptions may differ via different media and be able to gauge under which conditions digital media are effective for learning and deficient for learning (see, e.g., Gee & Hayes, 2011).

Similarly, people's epistemic beliefs may align with a stance that favors some perspectives over others (perspectives from a religious group or political party, where both may act as sources of information through which personal experiences may be filtered; Buehl & Alexander, 2001). For example, Klaczynski (2000) found that adolescents suspend analytical and critical thinking when their "theory preservation goals" align with a viewpoint (i.e., aligned with the goals of an adolescent's religious group; p. 1360). Thus, absolutists may heuristically align with groups favoring dualistic positions, multiplists may align with groups favoring subjectivity, and evaluativists may align with groups favoring critical and reflective positions. But, regardless of epistemic stance, purposeful and deliberate and analytical thinking may be heuristic when information emerges from a group aligned with one's perspective (Sinatra, Kienhues, & Hofer, 2014).

Instructional environments can bring epistemic beliefs to the forefront, and in some situations, help learners' to be more purposeful and reflective about evaluating their beliefs. In analyzing and critiquing research on the development of epistemic beliefs, Hofer and Pintrich (1997) say that learners "are likely to have ideas about knowledge and knowing that are activated in everyday educational settings and which affect their learning on a routine basis" (p. 103). Hofer and Pintrich (1997) also state that multiplist "beliefs take on the status of personal possessions, to which each individual is entitled;" whereas, evaluative beliefs compare viewpoints "to assess relative merit" and that "knowledge may be modified as a result" (p. 104).

Beliefs and Controversy

We take the position that one primary purpose of education is to transform people's beliefs (Dewey, 1916; Southerland, Sinatra, & Matthews, 2001). In many cases, academic knowledge (i.e., knowledge taught in school and other learning settings) may be fully consistent with individuals' beliefs. Research has established that in such cases, pre-existing beliefs aligned with academic knowledge benefit deeper learning

(McNamara, Kintsch, Songer, & Kintsch, 1996). But sometimes, academic knowledge can conflict with people's beliefs and may inhibit knowledge construction consistent with expert conceptions (Buehl & Alexander, 2001; Dole & Sinatra, 1998). Thus, in the face of controversy where there are conflicting sets of evidence and claims, people's pre-existing beliefs could inhibit deeper learning.

Beliefs about academic knowledge often vary by domain (Schommer & Walker, 1995). Therefore, different representations of knowledge associated with a domain, such as the way information is presented in a mathematics textbook, may interact with learners' beliefs about that domain, where some believe that mathematics is well-structured (Buehl & Alexander, 2001). In this example, if the learner encounters mathematical information that is represented in a less structured format, this representation may conflict with their beliefs about the highly structured domain of mathematics. Beliefs about domain structure (e.g., that mathematics is inherently well-structured) may also be a commonly held belief by those of various perspectives (e.g., non-experts in mathematics, such as students and some mathematics teachers). Such naïve beliefs could conflict with other perspectives (e.g., mathematical experts who may see the domain as somewhat ill-structured) preventing effective teaching and deep learning in a domain.

Multiple representations and multiple perspectives may be particularly relevant when individuals encounter sets of conflicting lines of evidence and claims that may also clash with beliefs. In their seminal work, Kardash and Scholes (1996) found that both epistemic beliefs – specifically, beliefs about certainty of knowledge – and personal beliefs – which they operationalized as degree of agreement about a controversial statement at the time of the study, e.g., "HIV (human immunodeficiency virus) causes AIDS" (p. 263) – affected readers' comprehension of a dual-position text that related different perspectives on the topic. A number of researchers have built upon the seminal findings of Kardash and Scholes (1996) by examining relations between beliefs and various evaluations and integrations of controversial information from both multiple representations (see, e.g., Bråten, Britt, Strømsø, & Jean-François Rouet, 2011) and multiple perspectives (see, e.g., Lombardi, Seyranian, & Sinatra, 2014). Many of these studies involved controversial science topics, such as the causes of current climate change or connections between cell phone use and brain cancer), with results showing that individuals' beliefs about various representations and perspectives related strongly to their deep learning. Specifically, naïve and alternative beliefs acted as a barrier to understanding scientifically accurate conceptions.

Summary of the Literature

The literature review strongly suggests that values, attitudes and beliefs are distinct but interacting constructs. Furthermore, this review supports our hypothesized model (Figure 20.1), wherein learners' values, attitudes, and beliefs are mediated by multiple representations and multiple perspectives. We now conclude the chapter by demonstrating some applications of the model. These examples are contextualized within practical situations for integrating of values, attitudes, and beliefs to promote deeper learning when interacting with multiple representations and multiple perspectives.

PRACTICAL LEARNING IMPLICATIONS FOR INTEGRATING VALUES, ATTITUDES, AND BELIEFS

As learners encounter new information, this information is filtered through the values, attitudes, and beliefs of that learner. Depending on how that information is represented, and what perspectives are available as sources, the outcomes of knowledge construction may be unreliable and unpredictable. This is particularly complex in a classroom where teachers are expecting learners (each with their own set of values, attitudes, and beliefs) to reach singular learning objectives as a class. In the following subsections, we look at various pathways suggested by the model and how multiple representations and multiple perspectives may interact with these pathways in applied instructional settings.

Scaffolded Instruction

Both cognitive and social resources shape a learner's interpretation and construction of knowledge. Cognitive resources include the values, attitudes, and beliefs, along with concepts and motivations from a person's experience that influence their behaviors in various activities. These cognitive resources are often culture and context-bound, and therefore interact with a person's social resources (Allchin, 1999). In science, epistemic values guide many scientific practices, such as reliable methods for measurement. These epistemic values that guide scientific research are also embedded within scientists' cultural setting. Therefore, cultural values also influence construction of scientific knowledge. Learning about science and other subjects (e.g., history, language arts, and even mathematics) in an authentic way might then be facilitated by engaging students in incorporating both epistemic values inherent in the knowledge building practice and cultural values to which the learner can connect.

For example, some learners who live in low-lying and coastal communities may place a high value on wetlands that buffer flooding. Other learners, however, may think of wetlands as swampy zones that only serve as breeding zones for pests. They may place a higher value on filling wetlands for commercial and residential development. In this case, teachers could position critique and evaluation inherent within the scientific enterprise to weigh lines of evidence with these two alternative value judgments – wetlands provide ecosystem services that contribute to human welfare versus wetlands are a nuisance to humans and provide little overall benefit – to arrive at greater understanding (Holzer, Lombardi, & Bailey, 2016). Learners' could productively use diverse cultural and cognitive resources to frame questions and compare alternative explanations and solutions based on available scientific evidence.

Instructional methods that directly teach value judgments within a particular context may facilitate such comparisons. In a classroom setting, teachers may relate values about a concept based on the personal utility, relevance, and aesthetic (Heddy, Sinatra, Seli, Taasoobshirazi, & Mukhopadhyay, 2017b). Learners maintain values, attitudes, and beliefs, which influences the ways that they perceive the world. Therefore, investigating methods for facilitating application of classroom content to learners' everyday experiences can be a useful way to explore the ways that values, attitudes, and beliefs shape a learner's interaction with multiple representations and perspectives.

Pugh (2004) designed a pedagogical approach meant to facilitate transformative experiences within the context of science learning, called the Teaching for Transformative Experience in Science (TTES) model. The TTES model is based on Dewey's (1934/1958) constructivist approach to education that emphasizes experiencing the content and teaching through cognitive apprenticeship. More specifically, the TTES model has three components including: (a) framing content as ideas, (b) scaffolding reseeing, and (c) modeling transformative experience (Pugh, Bergstrom, Heddy, & Krob, 2017). TTES is designed to use instructor modeling and scaffolding of transformative experiences to facilitate students' learning. Similarly, Heddy and colleagues (2017), implemented Use, Change, Value (or more simply, UCV) discussions to facilitate transformative experiences, where peers facilitate modeling and scaffolding. Students form small groups and discuss occasions where they used the concepts to resee phenomena in their everyday experience, how the content changed their perception, and why this experience was valuable. These discussions can take place in face-to-face or virtual discussion board formats and have deepened learning (Heddy et al., 2017a) and interest (Heddy & Sinatra, 2017).

Additionally, teachers could employ instructional scaffolds (e.g., Model-Evidence Link Diagrams; Chinn & Buckland, 2012; Lombardi, 2016) allowing students to engage in the scientific practice of evaluating the connection between lines of evidence and alternative models. According to our posited model, such scaffolded and explicit learning of values by comparing multiple representations (e.g., different forms of evidentiary data) and multiple perspectives (e.g., different viewpoints on the value of wetlands) could then influence learners' attitudes toward the position promoting the utility of science and potentially also a belief that critical evaluation associated with scientific thinking could productively solve problems. In line with our model, we speculate that explicitly judging values could influence both attitudes and beliefs about wetlands. This working hypothesis is supported by evidence suggesting that, when students engage in this activity, they explicitly reappraise plausibility of the alternatives and deepen their scientific knowledge on the topic, which is akin to the belief feedback loop in our model.

Teacher's Epistemic Reflexivity

Teachers' values, attitudes, and beliefs directly influence what and how they teach. For example, Lombardi and Sinatra (2013) interviewed teachers regarding how they teach about climate change. One teacher, who was skeptical of scientific claims that human activities were the cause of current climate change, said that she consulted primary sources (i.e., scientific journal articles) to design her climate change lessons. She placed a higher value on scientific source material rather than more popular interpretations of scientific findings (e.g., results shown in the documentary, *An Inconvenient Truth*). However, this same teacher clearly had a negative attitude toward the scientific explanation of human-induced climate change by questioning the motives of scientists (i.e., "who are they [scientists] being funded by … who's paying their salary;" Lombardi & Sinatra, 2013, p. 183). Finally, this teacher's negative attitude expressed a strong belief that scientists are lying about human-caused climate change and explicitly taught this belief to her students. This teacher example illustrates the complex relations between teachers' values, attitudes, and beliefs, as well as how teachers' thinking about knowledge within a domain (e.g., science, and in the case of the example above, climate specifically) impacts their teaching.

Because of the importance of teachers' epistemic cognition in guiding what and how they teach, many have called for teachers to explicitly consider how multiple representations and multiple perspectives influence their own values, attitudes, and beliefs (see, e.g., Brownlee, 2004; Kazempour & Sadler, 2015; Sadler, Amirshokoohi, Kazempour, & Allspaw, 2006). Such explicit reflection about the influence of multiple inputs is termed *epistemic reflexivity* (Lunn Brownlee, Ferguson, & Ryan, 2017). As teachers navigate and manage their multiple stakeholders, it is productive to employ epistemic reflexivity, which involves using internal dialogue to evaluate and understand multiple perspectives, to either maintain or change courses of action that are consistent with expert thinking (Archer, 2010).

Teachers' values, attitudes, and beliefs may involve predispositions and experiences that are firmly entrenched. However, explicit and informed reflexivity, or the intentional revising of teaching decisions based on evaluation of multiple representations and multiple perspectives, can become a learned teacher practice (Buehl & Fives, 2016). We would suggest that teachers explicitly consider sequential and dynamic relations between values, attitudes, and beliefs in a practice of epistemic reflexivity. We also suggest teachers consider how multiple representations and multiple perspectives mediate these relations, per our posited model, to help them craft instruction that promotes students' to be more critical thinkers and reflective of their own learning.

INSIGHTS, EMERGING QUESTIONS, AND FUTURE RESEARCH

Returning to our classroom vignette in which we started the chapter, the teacher could use scaffolding, epistemic reflexivity and TTES to help students evaluate their own values, attitudes, and beliefs and how it impacts their construction of new knowledge. This would involve comparison of alternative explanations about the phenomenon of current climate change, which represents multiple perspectives. In doing so, the teacher could expose students to different representations of data (e.g., graphical, numerical, narrative) that together present different facets of current climate change, and together, would constitute lines of evidence. Scaffolds could help facilitate coordination of both multiple representations and multiple perspectives when considering value judgements, attitudes, and beliefs about climate change. In using scaffolding, teachers could engage in modeling epistemic reflexivity to probe their own values, attitudes, and beliefs about climate change progressively to further their own scientific thinking as well as their students' learning about climate change. Finally, TTES could be fostered by actively thinking about how climate change may impact the school and surrounding community (e.g. creating geo-climate models across various time points). This could possibly prompt students to engage in epistemic agency, where they would become authors of their own contributions, accountable to the classroom learning community, and have the authority to think about and solve problems (Nussbaum & Asterhan, 2016; Pickering, 1995).

Our vignette, above, demonstrates how researchers and practitioners could use our hypothesized model (Figure 20.1) to predict productive changes in students' values, attitudes, and beliefs that are consistent with scientific consensus and would promote science learning. However, we realize this is a specific scenario that might not apply to all science topics, or to all learning domains (e.g., mathematics, language arts, and social studies). Although we speculate that our model would work with other science topics and other domains, we wonder specifically how mediation by multiple representations and multiple perspectives might influence values, attitudes, and beliefs more broadly. We also wonder about the usefulness of scaffolding, reflexivity, and transformative experiences for other domains beyond science learning. We do suggest that researchers could use this model to help determine researchable relationships, and potentially, curriculum designers to craft interventions that might shift values, attitudes, and beliefs toward those that are productive for society. We acknowledge that these relations are most likely dynamic and may be multidirectional, which is certainly an empirical question best answered by future research.

ACKNOWLEDGMENTS

Special thanks to Mr. Timothy G. Klavon for reviewing an earlier draft of this chapter. The National Science Foundation (NSF), under Grant No. DRL-1316057 and Grant No. DRL-1721041, supported some of the research presented in this chapter. Any opinions, findings, conclusions, or recommendations expressed are those of the authors and do not necessarily reflect the NSF's views.

REFERENCES

Ajzen, I. (1991). The theory of planned behavior. *Organizational Behavior and Human Decision Processes, 50*(2), 179–211. doi:https://doi.org/10.1016/0749-5978(91)90020-T

Ajzen, I., & Fishbein, M. (1980). *Understanding attitudes and predicting social behavior*. Englewood Cliffs, NJ: Prentice-Hall.

Ajzen, I., & Fishbein, M. (2008). Scaling and testing multiplicative combinations in the expectancy–Value model of attitudes. *Journal of Applied Social Psychology, 38*(9), 2222–2247.

Ajzen, I., Fishbein, M., Lohmann, S., & Albarracín, D. (2018). The influence of attitudes on behavior. In D. Albarracín & B. T. Johnson (Eds.), *The handbook of attitudes,* vol. 1. *Basic principles* (pp. 197–256). New York: Routledge.

Alexander, P. A., Schallert, D. L., & Hare, V. C. (1991). Coming to terms: How researchers in learning and literacy talk about knowledge. *Review of Educational Research, 61*, 315–343.

Allchin, D. (1999). Values in science: An educational perspective. *Science and Education, 8*(1), 1–12.

Archer, M. (2010). Introduction: The reflexive re-turn. In M. Archer (Ed.), *Conversations about reflexivity* (pp. 1–14). London: Routledge.

Bandura, A. (2001). Social cognitive theory: An agentic perspective. *Annual Review of Psychology, 52*(1), 1–26.

Baron, N. (2016). Why digital reading is no substitute for print. *The New Republic* (July). https://newrepublic.com/article/135326/digital-reading-no-substitute-print

Bendixen, L. D., & Rule, D. C. (2004). An integrative approach to personal epistemology: A guiding model. *Educational Psychologist, 39*(1), 69–80.

Bråten, I., Britt, M. A., Strømsø, H. I., & Rouet, J. F. (2011). The role of epistemic beliefs in the comprehension of multiple expository texts: Toward an integrated model. *Educational Psychologist, 46*(1), 48–70.

Brophy, J. (1999). Toward a model of the value aspects of motivation in education: Developing appreciation for particular learning domains and activities. *Educational Psychologist, 34*(2), 75–85.

Brownlee, J. (2004). Teacher education students' epistemological beliefs: Developing a relational model of teaching. *Research in Education, 72*(1), 1–17. doi:10.7227/RIE.72.1

Buehl, M. M., & Alexander, P. A. (2001). Beliefs about academic knowledge. *Educational Psychology Review, 13*(4), 385–418.

Buehl, M. M., & Fives, H. (2016). The role of epistemic cognition in teacher learning and praxis. In J. A. Greene, W. A. Sandoval, & I. Bråten (Eds.), *Handbook of epistemic cognition* (pp. 247–264). New York: Routledge.

Chinn, C. A., & Buckland, L. (2012). Model-based instruction: Fostering change in evolutionary conceptions and epistemic practices. In K. S. Rosengren, E. M. Evans, S. Brem, & G. M. Sinatra (Eds.), *Evolution challenges: Integrating research and practice in teaching and learning about evolution* (pp. 211–232). New York: Oxford University Press.

Chinn, C. A., Buckland, L. A., & Samarapungavan, A. L. A. (2011). Expanding the dimensions of epistemic cognition: Arguments from philosophy and psychology. *Educational Psychologist, 46*(3), 141–167.

Chinn, C. A., Rinehart, R. W., & Buckland, L. A. (2014). Epistemic cognition and evaluating information: Applying the AIR model of epistemic cognition. In D. N. Rapp & J. L. G. Braasch (Eds.), *Processing inaccurate information: Theoretical and applied perspectives from cognitive science and the educational sciences* (pp. 425–453). Cambridge, MA: MIT Press.

Dewey, J. (1910). Science as subject-matter and as method. *Science, 31*(787), 121–127.

Dewey, J. (1916). *Democracy and education*. New York: Free Press.

Dewey, J. (1934/1958). *Art as experience*. New York: Perigee Books.

Dole, J. A., & Sinatra, G. M. (1998). Reconceptualizing change in the cognitive construction of knowledge. *Educational Psychologist, 33*(2/3), 109–128.

Fishbein, M. (1963). An investigation of the relationships between beliefs about an object and the attitude toward that object. *Human Relations, 16*(3), 233–239.

Foran, C. (2014). The plan to get climate-change denial into schools. The Atlantic (Dec.). www.theatlantic.com/education/archive/2014/12/the-plan-to-get-climate-change-denial-into-schools/383540/

Gee, J. P., & Hayes, E. R. (2011). *Language and learning in the digital age*. London: Routledge.

Greene, J. A., Azevedo, R., & Torney-Purta, J. (2008). Modeling epistemic and ontological cognition: Philosophical perspectives and methodological directions. *Educational Psychologist, 43*(3), 142–160.

Gunderson, E. A., Ramirez, G., Levine, S. C., & Beilock, S. L. (2012). The role of parents and teachers in the development of gender-related math attitudes. *Sex Roles, 66*(3–4), 153–166.

Harkaway, N. (2014). Paper vs digital reading is an exhausted debate. www.theguardian.com/books/booksblog/2014/mar/31/paper-vs-digital-reading-debate-ebooks-tim-waterstone

Heddy, B. C., Danielson, R. W., Sinatra, G. M., & Graham, J. (2017a). Modifying knowledge, emotions, and attitudes regarding genetically modified foods. *Journal of Experimental Education, 85*(3), 513–533.

Heddy, B. C., & Sinatra, G. M. (2013). Transforming misconceptions: Using transformative experience to promote positive affect and conceptual change in students learning about biological evolution. *Science Education, 97*(5), 723–744.

Heddy, B. C., & Sinatra, G. M. (2017). Transformative parents: Facilitating transformative experiences and interest with a parent involvement intervention. *Science Education, 101*(5), 765–786.

Heddy, B. C., Sinatra, G. M., Seli, H., Taasoobshirazi, G., & Mukhopadhyay, A. (2017b). Making learning meaningful: Facilitating interest development and transfer in at-risk college students. *Educational Psychology, 37*(5), 565–581.

Hofer, B. K., & Pintrich, P. R. (1997). The development of epistemological theories: Beliefs about knowledge and knowing and their relation to learning. *Review of Educational Research, 67*(1), 88–140.

Holzer, M. A., Lombardi, D., & Bailey, J. M. (2016). Wetlands: Good or bad? Evaluating competing models. *Earth Scientist, 32*(2), 17–21.

Johnson, M. L., & Sinatra, G. M. (2013). Use of task-value instructional inductions for facilitating engagement and conceptual change. *Contemporary Educational Psychology, 38*(1), 51–63.

Jones, S. H., Johnson, M. L., & Campbell, B. D. (2015). Hot factors for a cold topic: Examining the role of task-value, attention allocation, and engagement on conceptual change. *Contemporary Educational Psychology, 42*, 62–70.

Kant, I. (1781/1998). *Critique of pure reason*. Cambridge: Cambridge University Press.

Kardash, C. M., & Scholes, R. J. (1996). Effects of preexisiting beliefs, epistemological beliefs, and need for cognition on interpretation of controversial issues. *Journal of Educational Psychology, 88*(2), 260.

Kazempour, M., & Sadler, T. D. (2015). Pre-service teachers' science beliefs, attitudes, and self-efficacy: A multi-case study. *Teaching Education, 26*(3), 247–271.

King, P. M., & Kitchener, K. S. (1994). *Developing reflective judgment: Understanding and promoting intellectual growth and critical thinking in adolescents and adults*. San Francisco, CA: Jossey-Bass.

Klaczynski, P. A. (2000). Motivated scientific reasoning biases, epistemological beliefs, and theory polarization: A two-process approach to adolescent cognition. *Child Development, 71*(5), 1347–1366.

Lombardi, D. (2016). Beyond the controversy: Instructional scaffolds to promote critical evaluation and understanding of earth science. *The Earth Scientist, 32*(2), 5–10.

Lombardi, D., Nussbaum, E. M., & Sinatra, G. M. (2016). Plausibility judgments in conceptual change and epistemic cognition. *Educational Psychologist, 51*(1), 35–56.

Lombardi, D., Seyranian, V., & Sinatra, G. M. (2014). Source effects and plausibility judgments when reading about climate change. *Discourse Processes, 51*(1/2), 75–92.

Lombardi, D., & Sinatra, G. M. (2013). Emotions about teaching about human-induced climate change. *International Journal of Science Education, 35*(1), 167–191.

Lowry, N., & Johnson, D. W. (1981). Effects of controversy on epistemic curiosity, achievement, and attitudes. *Journal of Social Psychology, 115*(1), 31–43.

Lundholm, C., & Davies, P. (2013). Conceptual change in the social sciences. In S. Vosniadou (Ed.), *International handbook of research in conceptual change* (2nd ed., pp. 288–304). London: Routledge.

Lunn Brownlee, J., Ferguson, L. E., & Ryan, M. (2017). Changing teachers' epistemic cognition: A new conceptual framework for epistemic reflexivity. *Educational Psychologist, 52*(4), 242–252.

Mason, L., Junyent, A. A., & Tornatora, M. C. (2014). Epistemic evaluation and comprehension of web-source information on controversial science-related topics: Effects of a short-term instructional intervention. *Computers and Education, 76*, 143–157.

McKenna, M. C., Kear, D. J., & Ellsworth, R. A. (1995). Children's attitudes toward reading: A national survey. *Reading Research Quarterly, 30*(4), 934–956.

McNamara, D. S., Kintsch, E., Songer, N. B., & Kintsch, W. (1996). Are good texts always better? Interactions of text coherence, background knowledge, and levels of understanding in learning from text. *Cognition and Instruction, 14*(1), 1–43.

Mill, J. S. (1865/1979). *An examination of Sir William Hamilton's philosophy* (vol. 9). Toronto: University of Toronto Press.

Miyake, A., Kost-Smith, L. E., Finkelstein, N. D., Pollock, S. J., Cohen, G. L., & Ito, T. A. (2010). Reducing the gender achievement gap in college science: A classroom study of values affirmation. *Science, 330*(6008), 1234–1237.

Murphy, C., & Beggs, J. (2003). Children's perceptions of school science. *School Science Review, 84*, 109–116.

Neale, D. C. (1969). The role of attitudes in learning mathematics. *Arithmetic Teacher, 16*(8), 631–640.

Ness, M. (2011). Teachers' use of and attitudes toward informational text in K-5 classrooms. *Reading Psychology, 32*(1), 28–53.

Nussbaum, E. M., & Asterhan, C. S. (2016). The psychology of far transfer from classroom argumentation. In F. Paglieri (Ed.), *The psychology of argument: Cognitive approaches to argumentation and persuasion* (pp. 407–423). London: College Publications.

Osborne, J., & Collins, S. (2001). Pupils' views of the role and value of the science curriculum: A focus-group study. *International Journal of Science Education, 23*(5), 441–467.

Osborne, J., Simon, S., & Collins, S. (2003). Attitudes towards science: A review of the literature and its implications. *International Journal of Science Education, 25*, 1049–1079.

Ostrom, T. M. (1989). Interdependence of attitude theory and measurement. In A. R. Pratkanis, S. J. Beckler, & A. G. Greenwald (Eds.), *Attitude structure and function* (pp. 11–36)). Hillsdale, NJ: Lawrence Erlbaum.

Oxley, D. R., Smith, K. B., Alford, J. R., Hibbing, M. V., Miller, M. S., Hatemi, P. K., et al. (2008). Political attitudes vary with physiological traits. *Science, 321*, 1667–1670.

Petty, R. E., & Cacioppo, J. T. (1986). The elaboration likelihood model of persuasion. In L. Berkowitz (Ed.), *Advances in experimental social psychology* (vol. 19, pp. 123–205). New York: Academic.

Pickering, A. (1995). *The mangle of practice: Time, agency, and science*. Chicago, IL: University of Chicago Press.

Pugh, K. J. (2004). Newton's laws beyond the classroom walls. *Science Education, 88*(2), 182–196.

Pugh, K. J. (2011). Transformative experience: An integrative construct in the spirit of Deweyan pragmatism. *Educational Psychologist, 46*(2), 107–121.

Pugh, K. J., Bergstrom, C. M., Heddy, B. C., & Krob, K. E. (2017). Supporting deep engagement: The teaching for transformative experiences in science (TTES) model. *Journal of Experimental Education, 85*(4), 629–657.

Rokeach, M. (1979). *Understanding human values*. New York: Free Press.

Sadler, T. D., Amirshokoohi, A., Kazempour, M., & Allspaw, K. M. (2006). Socioscience and ethics in science classrooms: Teacher perspectives and strategies. *Journal of Research in Science Teaching, 43*(4), 353–376.

Schommer, M., & Walker, K. (1995). Are epistemological beliefs similar across domains? *Journal of Educational Psychology, 87*(3), 424–432.

Shulman, L. S. (1986). Those who understand: Knowledge growth in teaching. *Educational Researcher, 15*(2), 4–14.

Sinatra, G. M., Kienhues, D., & Hofer, B. K. (2014). Addressing challenges to public understanding of science: Epistemic cognition, motivated reasoning, and conceptual change. *Educational Psychologist, 49*(2), 123–138.

Sinatra, G. M., & Seyranian, V. (2015). Warm change about hot topics: The role of motivation and emotion in attitude and conceptual change about controversial science topics. In L. Corno & E. Anderman (Eds.), *APA handbook of educational psychology* (pp. 245–256). Washington, DC: APA Publications.

Southerland, S. A., Sinatra, G. M., & Matthews, M. R. (2001). Belief, knowledge, and science education. *Educational Psychology Review, 13*(4), 325–351.

Torsney, B. M., Lombardi, D., & Ponnock, A. (2018). The role of values in pre-service teachers' intentions for professional engagement. *Educational Psychology*. Advance online publication. doi: 10.1080/01443410.2018.1504892.

Tytler, R., & Osborne, J. (2012). Student attitudes and aspirations towards science. In B. J. Fraser, K. Tobin, & C. J. McRobbie (Eds.), *Second international handbook of science education* (pp. 597–625). New York: Springer International.

Wigfield, A., & Eccles, J. S. (2000). Expectancy–Value theory of achievement motivation. *Contemporary Educational Psychology, 25*(1), 68–81.

Williams, R. M. (1979). Change and stability in values and values systems: A sociological perspective. In M. Rokeach (Ed.), *Understanding human values* (pp. 15–46). New York: Free Press.

21

MOTIVATION AND THE PROCESSING OF MULTIPLE INPUTS

David B. Miele
BOSTON COLLEGE

Timothy J. Nokes-Malach
UNIVERSITY OF PITTSBURGH

Sidney May
BOSTON COLLEGE

ABSTRACT

In the present chapter, we explore what motivates students to integrate multiple viewpoints and connect pieces of information from multiple representational formats (e.g., text and images) when working on academic tasks. We begin by introducing a motivational model of integrative processing that centers on students' adoption of an epistemic mastery goal (i.e., the goal of increasing one's knowledge about a particular topic or developing expertise in a particular domain). We then use the model to identify both proximal and distal determinants of students' motivation to pursue such goals. Proximal factors include students' expectancies, values, and perceived costs, whereas distal factors include individual difference variables (e.g., need for cognition, growth mindsets, individual interests), as well as features of the context/environment (e.g., time constraints, stimulating content, and classroom goal structures). But even when students are strongly motivated to pursue epistemic mastery goals, they may not attempt to integrate multiple inputs. We therefore focus on two additional factors: (a) the epistemic beliefs that students draw on in order to evaluate their progress toward their mastery goals, and (b) the modes of thinking associated with qualitatively distinct types of motivation, some of which may be particularly adaptive for the integrative processing of multiple inputs.

Key words: motivation, mastery goals, epistemic beliefs, expectancy-value, multiple perspectives, multiple representations

Consider a scenario in which two high school students in a United States history class have been tasked by their teacher with reading multiple texts about slavery written by Abraham Lincoln and then writing an essay that describes how his view of slavery and race changed from the beginning to the end of the American Civil War. Imagine that the ideas espoused by Lincoln in each of the texts appear at first glance to be inconsistent, even contradictory. Imagine also that the students are presented with a timeline that they can use to visualize precisely when each text was written in relation to other important events from the Civil War. Faced with a set of "discrete and seemingly contradictory pieces of text," the first student's approach is to do "the easiest thing a reader can do," which "is to leave each text as is: each an island unto itself" (Wineburg, 1998, p. 337). The essay this student ends up writing is simply a chronological account of the different things Lincoln said about slavery throughout his lifetime. In contrast, the second student attempts to form a coherent and nuanced understanding of Lincoln's view of slavery by shifting back and forth between the texts and the timeline and, in some cases, seeking out additional primary and secondary source materials. The essay that this student writes posits a single, multi-faceted view of slavery and explains how it evolved over time as Lincoln dealt with various challenges posed by the Civil War.

This scenario poses an important question: Why does the second student decide to engage in the integrative processing of multiple viewpoints and to draw on information presented in multiple representational formats (i.e., text vs. graphical timeline) whereas the first student does not? If we assume that the students are equally knowledgeable (or unknowledgeable) about the topic, have the same cognitive capacity, and possess similar sets of study strategies, the explanation is likely to be motivational in nature. For instance, one possibility is that (unlike the second student) the first student does not hold the epistemic mastery goal of forming a deep and coherent understanding of the topic and therefore sees no need to identify or reconcile any inconsistencies that might exist between the assigned texts or to refer to the timeline in order situate the texts within a broader historical context. Perhaps the student does not see the importance of learning about American history and would prefer to work on an assignment for a different class or to engage in some non-academic activity. Instead of adopting a mastery goal, the student might focus on putting in the minimum amount of effort needed to pass the assignment (i.e., adopt a work-avoidance goal; Harackiewicz, Durik, Barron, Linnenbrink-Garcia, & Tauer, 2008).

Such a scenario does not seem particularly far-fetched when you consider the amount of mental effort involved in learning from multiple inputs, especially when those inputs are somewhat contradictory or presented in different formats. For instance, in order to successfully process multiple conflicting texts, students must construct a coherent understanding of the topic by continually updating and reorganizing their mental representations to accommodate the novel information they encounter while reading each text (Bråten, Anmarkrud, Brandmo, & Strømsø, 2014). Likewise, in order to successfully integrate relevant information from an image with information from a text, students must build "connections between corresponding portions of the pictorial and verbal models [that they have constructed] as well as with relevant knowledge from long-term memory" (Mayer, 2014, p. 57). Both forms of integration are cognitively demanding and presumably require a greater amount of executive control (in the form of selective attention, working memory, and cognitive flexibility; Banich, 2009) than does processing a single text that includes relatively few inconsistencies or contradictions.

This suggests that in order to successfully integrate multiple inputs during learning, students must not only hold a mastery goal, they must be sufficiently motivated to expend the high levels of mental effort needed to achieve it. Therefore, one focus of the present chapter is on identifying factors that influence the strength or *quantity* of students' motivation to pursue mastery goals that involve integrative processing. As a framework for discussing such factors, we draw on Eccles and Wigfield's expectancy-value model of achievement motivation (see Wigfield, Tonks, & Klauda, 2016).

According to this model, the effort and discomfort associated with processing multiple inputs can be considered the perceived *costs* of attempting to form a deep and nuanced understanding of a topic. The factors that should most directly predict whether students will be sufficiently motivated to take on and overcome these costs are the extent to which they *value* the goal and *expect* to succeed at it. In the first part of the chapter, we outline the different types of values and expectancies that contribute to students' motivation and then go on to discuss a number of more distal factors that may indirectly influence students' motivation to engage in integrative processing via their values and expectancies (see also Lombardi, Heddy, & Matewos, Chapter 20). Some of these distal factors are individual difference variables, such as need for cognition (Cacioppo & Petty, 1982), need for cognitive closure (Kruglanski, 1990; Webster & Kruglanski, 1994), and implicit beliefs about intelligence (i.e., growth mindsets; Dweck, 2000), that may predict students' general tendencies to invest effort in their cognitive processing across a broad range of educational activities. Other factors, such as time pressure (Gigerenzer & Goldstein, 1996), personality traits (Roberts, Lejuez, Krueger, Richards, & Hill, 2014), and classroom goal structures (Ames, 1992) can be considered contextual variables that are more likely to predict students' levels of cognitive engagement within specific situations.

Returning to our example of the two students working on a history assignment, another reason why the first student might not be motivated to engage in integrative processing pertains to her beliefs about what it means to have a deep and nuanced understanding of a topic and how one goes about forming such an understanding. That is, the first student may in fact hold a strong epistemic mastery goal, but (unlike the second student) not realize that, in some cases, this goal can only be achieved by actively seeking and integrating multiple inputs that may vary in terms of their point of view and/or their representational format. As a result, this student may still end up working very hard on the task; but, as opposed to trying to identify and resolve inconsistencies between the texts, she may put a lot of time and effort into carefully processing each of the texts as isolated sources of information, without consulting the graphical timeline provided by the teacher. In line with this possibility, another focus of our chapter is on identifying the different kinds of *epistemic beliefs* (i.e., beliefs about the nature of knowledge and knowing) that are likely to influence students' motivation to engage in the integrative processing of multiple inputs. As a framework for discussing such beliefs, we draw on the model by Bråten, Britt, Strømsø, & Rouet

(2011), which distinguishes between beliefs about the simplicity, certainty, source, and justification of knowledge.

Finally, there is a third explanation for why one of the students in our example engaged in less integrative processing than the other student. As in the previous explanation, the two students may have been equally motivated to pursue the mastery goal of forming a deep and nuanced understanding of Lincoln's view of slavery. However, in this case, the difference in the students' processing of the materials may have been due in part to them experiencing qualitatively distinct forms of motivation, rather than holding distinct epistemic beliefs about what constitutes a deep understanding of the topic. That is, the second student may have experienced a type of motivation (e.g., a prevention orientation) that led her to automatically engage in a convergent *mode of thinking* that is conducive to the integration of multiple inputs, whereas the first student may have instead experienced a type of motivation (e.g., a promotion orientation) that led her to engage in a divergent mode of thinking that is less likely to facilitate integrative processing. Thus, a final focus of our chapter is to discuss the trade-offs between *qualitatively distinct* motivation states (e.g., intrinsic vs. extrinsic motivation, promotion vs. prevention orientation), with the aim of identifying specific states that may be more likely than others to predict the integrative processing of multiple inputs (especially when controlling for the overall strength or quantity of students' motivation). In pursuing this aim, we draw on the metamotivational framework posited by Miele, Scholer, and colleagues (Miele & Scholer, 2016; 2018; Miele, Scholer, & Fujita, in press; Scholer & Miele, 2016; Scholer, Miele, Murayama, & Fujita, 2018; see also Miele & Wigfield, 2014).

In the remainder of the chapter, we provide a preliminary outline of a motivational model of integrative processing and then use this model as a framework for reviewing the empirical literature. Note that there are relatively few studies that directly examine the association between motivational variables and integrative processing, thus many of the studies we discuss assess correlates of such processing (such as the use of deep strategies) and provide only tentative support for our arguments. Also note that our review of the literature is by no means comprehensive; the reader should assume that there are relevant studies (some of which may contradict our claims) that we were either unaware of at the time or unable to discuss due to page constraints. Ultimately, the purpose of this chapter is to provide a speculative framework that can be used by researchers to ask important questions about motivation and integrative processing and to guide future research on this topic.

A MOTIVATIONAL MODEL OF INTEGRATIVE PROCESSING

The Role of Achievement Goals

As depicted in Figure 21.1, our motivational model of integrative processing centers around students' identification and pursuit of what we refer to as an *epistemic mastery goal* – a specific type of mastery goal that involves wanting to increase one's knowledge about a topic or to develop expertise in a particular domain. This conception is similar to what some philosophers and psychologists mean by "epistemic aim" (Chen & Barger, 2016; Chinn, Buckland, & Samarapungavan, 2011); however, we prefer to retain the term "mastery goal" in order to make an explicit connection to the achievement goal

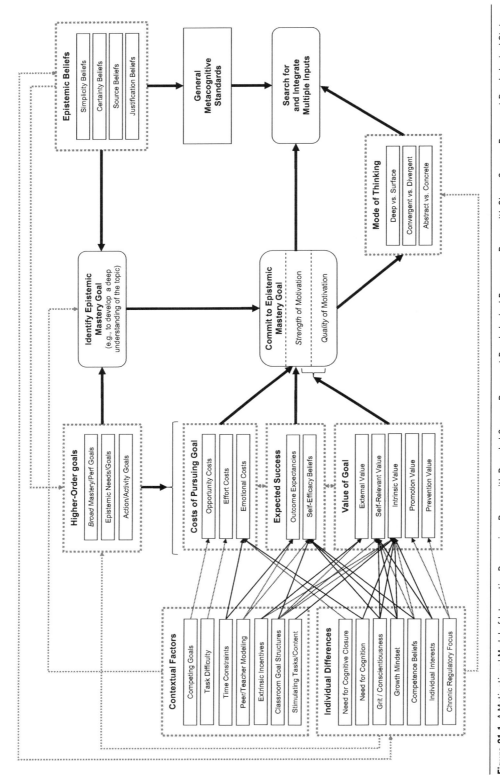

Figure 21.1 A Motivational Model of Integrative Processing. Boxes with Rounded Corners Represent Psychological Processes. Boxes with Sharp Corners Represent Psychological States (Including Perceived Features of the Task or Context). Solid Arrows Represent Paths of Influence that are Highlighted in this Chapter. Dotted Arrows Represent Paths that are Not Discussed.

literature. According to this literature, the standards one sets for oneself when adopting a mastery goal are typically personal (e.g., performing better than before or subjectively perceiving oneself to have learned a lot) or task-based (e.g., receiving an "A" on a paper or answering 95% of test questions correctly). Mastery goals are often contrasted with the performance goal of wanting to demonstrate one's ability by achieving some normative standard (e.g., wanting to outperform one's peers or wanting to match their success with less effort; Senko, 2016; Senko & Tropiano, 2016).

A primary assumption of our model is that, in most cases, students work to integrate multiple inputs because they hold an epistemic mastery goal of wanting to deeply understand the material. This is not to say that this is the only type of goal that motivates integrative processing. In some cases, students may choose to integrate multiple inputs because they want to know the material better than their peers (e.g., in order to earn one of the better grades in the class); however, we would argue that (in such cases) the students are likely to set a mastery subgoal (i.e., to try to understand the material deeply *in order* to achieve their higher-order performance goal). In fact, because we assume that goals are organized hierarchically (Carver & Scheier, 1998; Duckworth & Gross, 2014), our model posits that *all* epistemic mastery goals are subgoals (i.e., are subordinate to some higher-order goal). Other higher-order goals that may lead to the adoption of a mastery subgoal include a general need or desire to possess a coherent understanding of the world (i.e., *epistemic motivation*; De Dreu, Nijstad, & van Knippenberg, 2008), or a desire to engage in some behavior (i.e., an *action/activity goal*) that requires one to develop a sophisticated skill (e.g., learning how to program in order to build an app for one's phone).

As depicted in Figure 21.1, the motivational processes described in the present chapter begin with students considering (at an implicit or explicit level) what they can do to achieve their higher-order goal. In some cases, this leads them to *identify* an epistemic mastery subgoal as a potential means of satisfying the higher-order goal. As described in the next section, the specific representation of this subgoal is partly dependent on the students' epistemic beliefs. When considering whether to *commit* to the mastery subgoal or to instead pursue some other course of action, students weigh the costs associated with pursuing the goal against its perceived value, as well as the perceived likelihood of successfully accomplishing it. The magnitude of these costs, values, and expectancies are influenced by a broad set of contextual and individual difference factors, some of which are discussed in later sections.

Support for the central role played by mastery goals in our model comes from a number of studies that have found a positive association between students' endorsement of general or topic-specific mastery goals and their engagement in tasks that require the integration of multiple viewpoints. For instance, Darnon, Muller, Schrager, Panuzzo, and Butera (2006) asked college students in an introductory psychology class to imagine debating another student about the findings of a famous research study. The students were later asked to report the extent to which they would regulate sociocognitive conflict in an epistemic manner (e.g., "try to think of a solution that could integrate both points of view"), as well as in a self-affirming manner (e.g., "try to resist by maintaining your initial position"). The results indicated that participants' epistemic conflict regulation was significantly predicted by their mastery-approach goals (e.g., "I want to learn as much as possible from this class"), but not their performance-approach goals (e.g., "It is important for me to do better than other students"). In contrast, self-affirming (or "relational") conflict regulation was significantly predicted by both types of goals.

A subsequent study (Darnon & Butera, 2007) showed that for participants who were induced to hold a mastery goal, there was a significant association between how much they perceived themselves as having disagreed with an actual interaction partner and their self-reported level of epistemic conflict regulation; this was not the case for participants who were induced to hold a performance goal or who were in the control condition. In another follow-up study (Darnon, Butera, & Harackiewicz, 2007), participants who experienced disagreement with a supposed interaction partner learned more when they had initially been induced to hold a mastery goal compared to when they had been induced to hold a performance goal or were not exposed to a goal induction (see also Asterhan, 2018; Butera, Sommet, & Darnon, 2019).

Further support for the link between mastery goals and integrative processing comes from a study by Belenky and Nokes-Malach (2012). After reporting their mathematics achievement goals at the beginning of the study, participants engaged in an activity that involved learning a new statistical concept and then completed a post-test that assessed whether they could transfer what they had learned to a novel problem. The researchers manipulated the way in which the learning activity was introduced, such that only a subset of participants received the traditional "tell-and-practice" instructions. They also manipulated the availability of a learning resource during the post-test, such that only some participants were presented with a worked example. Importantly, solving the critical problem on the post-test required participants to integrate knowledge acquired from multiple inputs, including information from the earlier learning activity and the worked example. The results of the study showed that there was a large effect of the worked example on post-test problem-solving performance. Importantly, for the participants who were given the traditional instructions, the likelihood of successful transfer was only predicted by their mastery-approach goals and not any other achievement goal.

In addition to studies that have directly examined the association between mastery goals and measures of integrative processing, there are a number of studies showing a positive association between mastery goals and the use of deep learning strategies (e.g., elaborating the material and making connections between concepts; for a review, see Senko, Hulleman, & Harackiewicz, 2011). Such strategies are likely to be adaptive when students engage in tasks that require them to integrate multiple representations or viewpoints, so long as they attempt to use the strategies to make connections between the inputs. Support for this possibility comes from a study by Bråten and Strømsø (2011) in which college students were asked to read seven texts that presented conflicting viewpoints regarding global warming. The results showed that students' self-reported use of cross-text elaboration strategies (e.g., "I tried to compare different causal explanations of climate change") was marginally associated with their performance on a test of multiple-text comprehension, which assessed their ability to draw inferences *across* the texts (see also Bråten et al., 2014; Firetto & Van Meter, 2018).

The Role of Epistemic Beliefs

Another assumption of our model is that students are likely to assess progress toward their mastery goal or subgoal using personal standards that are metacognitive in nature (i.e., that involve reflecting on the depth and coherence of their own understanding). Some of these standards may be articulated prior to learning and are included as part of the goal representation itself, while others may exist as part of a more general set of metacognitive standards that only become salient *during* learning. Importantly, whether the students' standards actually require them to engage in the integrative processing of multiple inputs should depend in part on their *epistemic beliefs* about what constitutes "deep knowledge." This claim is consistent with Muis's (2007; Muis, Chevrier, & Singh, 2018) integrated model of epistemic cognition and self-regulated learning, which posits that "epistemic beliefs influence the types of standards students set when goals are produced" (Muis, 2007, p. 183; see also Denton, Muis, Munzar, & Etoubashi, Chapter 19). To illustrate this point, Muis references an example from Hofer (2004) in which a student explained that a book from 1908 would be adequate for learning about bees because "'in biology when they know it, it's not likely to change'" (p. 53). As Hofer goes on to explain, if students hold the epistemic belief that "knowledge is simple, there is little need to seek further evidence or to integrate information from multiple sources" (p. 53).

In addition to beliefs about the simplicity of knowledge, what other kinds of epistemic beliefs are likely to influence students' processing of multiple inputs? To answer this, we draw on Bråten et al.'s (2011) integrated model of epistemic beliefs and multiple-text comprehension (see also Bråten & Strømsø, Chapter 10). As alluded to in the previous section, multiple-text comprehension involves more than just piecing together a coherent set of arguments that happen to be distributed across multiple texts. Instead, "attempts to provide well-founded answers [based on multiple expository texts] require that individuals synthesize or integrate information from source materials expressing diverse and even contradictory viewpoints" (Bråten et al., 2011, p. 48). Thus, the model by Bråten and colleagues seems directly relevant for understanding how epistemic beliefs influence students' processing of multiple *perspectives* (though it is perhaps only indirectly relevant for understanding their processing of multiple representations).

Building on the work of Hofer and Pintrich (1997), the model posits that epistemic beliefs vary along several key dimensions. Two of these dimensions (simplicity and certainty) concern the nature of knowledge; with the *simplicity* dimension ranging from the belief that knowledge represents an accumulation of isolated facts to the belief that knowledge consists of a network of highly interrelated concepts, and the *certainty* dimension ranging from the belief that knowledge is an absolute and unchanging entity to the belief that knowledge is tentative and evolves over time. Two other dimensions of epistemic beliefs pertain to the nature of knowing. One of these is the *source* dimension, which ranges from the belief that knowledge originates from an external authority that resides outside of the self to the belief that knowledge is actively constructed through one's interactions with others; and the other is the *justification* dimension, which ranges from the belief that knowledge can be justified on the basis of observation and authority or what feels right to the belief that the justification of knowledge can be based on rules of inquiry and on the evaluation and integration of multiple sources.

A number of studies have demonstrated an association between the four dimensions of epistemic beliefs and students' successful integration of multiple perspectives (see Bråten et al., 2011); however, few seem to have examined the mediating role of motivation and engagement. One exception is a study by Bråten et al. (2014) that showed that secondary school students' beliefs about the importance of justifying claims with information from multiple sources (e.g., "Just one source is never enough to decide what is right in natural science") were indirectly associated with their integrated understanding of multiple texts via their effort (assessed in terms of reading time) and their use of cross-text elaboration strategies (e.g., "I tried to note disagreements between the texts").

In contrast to the various studies examining the associations between students' epistemic beliefs and their integration of multiple perspectives, there appears to be relatively little research directly examining the associations between these beliefs and students' processing of multiple representations. Furthermore, the few studies that we could find either did not highlight the role of effort, engagement, or motivation, or did not examine a large enough sample to make generalizable claims. For instance, Bendixen and Hartley (2003) showed that college students' beliefs about whether knowledge is derived from an "omniscient" authority or source uniquely predicted their learning of factual information from a hypermedia environment that contained text, links to relevant terms, and images; however, it was unclear whether the associations between students' beliefs and test performance were mediated by the effort that they put into integrating information from multiple representational formats (e.g., text and images). Another study of epistemic beliefs (Mishra & Yadav, 2006) did directly examine students' efforts at integrating multiple representations; but it employed a time-intensive mixed-method research design with a sample of only four students.

Levels of Expectancy, Value, and Cost as Determining the Strength of Motivation

Our model draws on Eccles and Wigfield's expectancy-value theory of achievement motivation (see Wigfield et al., 2016) in specifying expectancies, values, and costs as the most proximal determinants of how *strongly* motivated students are to pursue an achievement goal. However, in contrast to their theory, we do not consider cost to be a type of value; instead, we follow Barron and Hulleman (2015) in positing it as a distinct component.

Expectancies

Expectancies can be defined as students' estimates of how well they are likely to perform on an upcoming task. According to Bandura (1977), people base their expectancies on their beliefs about whether a given behavior or activity will lead to certain outcomes (i.e., their outcome expectations), as well as their beliefs about whether they are capable of successfully performing the behavior (i.e., their self-efficacy). It is important to distinguish between these types of expectancies because both are thought to be necessary in order for students to be motivated to engage in a task. If a student perceives a specific activity (e.g., developing a concept map) to be useful for synthesizing multiple inputs, but does not feel particularly capable of executing this activity, she may decide not to engage in it. Conversely, if the student perceives herself to be quite capable of carrying out the task, but views it as a waste of time, she may again decide not to engage in it. Although some studies have shown that outcome expectations do not capture much variance in motivation or behavior beyond what is predicted by self-efficacy (e.g., Manning & Wright, 1983), other studies suggest that this might be because the items used by researchers sometimes confound the two types of expectancies (Maddux, Norton, & Stoltenberg, 1986).

At a conceptual level, expectancy-value theory distinguishes between students' expectancies and their beliefs about their ability or competence in a particular domain (sometimes referred to as their academic self-concept; Marsh et al., 2019). Competence beliefs include students' assessments of their ability on an absolute scale (e.g., very little ability vs. a lot of ability), as well as how they think of themselves relative to their peers (e.g., a lot less ability vs. a lot more ability). However, at an empirical level, students' expectancies and competence beliefs are often indistinguishable. For instance, in studies of children and adolescents conducted by Eccles and Wigfield (see Wigfield & Eccles, 2000, for a review), items assessing domain-specific expectancies and competence beliefs have tended to load onto the same factor.

There is a good deal of empirical support for the role played by expectancy-related constructs in our model. For instance, a review by Locke, Latham, and Erez (1988) described a number of studies in which either expectancies or self-efficacy pertaining to a particular task or goal predicted commitment to that goal. At a broader level, numerous studies have shown an association between students' competence beliefs or self-efficacy in an academic domain or course and their domain- or course-specific achievement goals. For instance, in a study by Diseth (2011), students' self-efficacy in a college psychology course was positively associated with their endorsement of both performance approach goals and mastery goals, which in turn were associated with their self-reported use of deep learning strategies (though these strategies were more strongly predicted by mastery goals than by performance goals). A recent meta-analysis by Huang (2016) suggests that the associations between students' self-efficacy and their approach goals are fairly robust, with the correlation between self-efficacy and *mastery* approach goals being particularly strong ($r = .45$).

To the extent that mastery goals promote the use of deep learning strategies that are adaptive for integrating information from multiple inputs, our model predicts that self-efficacy should be indirectly associated with measures of integrative processing. Support for this prediction comes from a study by Bråten, Ferguson, Anmarkrud, and Strømsø (2013) in which high-school students' efficacy for understanding natural science texts was positively correlated with their comprehension of five texts that provided varying perspectives about the relation between sun exposure and health. Similar to the study by Bråten et al. (2014), comprehension was assessed based on students' responses to three questions assessing their integration of multiple perspectives (e.g., "Could more than one view on the relationship between sun exposure, health, and illness be correct? Yes or no? If no, why not? If yes, why?").

In contrast, a study by Song, Kalet, and Plass (2016) showed that medical students' self-efficacy for learning about a particular topic (i.e., carotid artery diseases) did *not* uniquely predict their learning performance within a multimedia environment that included animations and video. It is possible that the lack of an association is partly due to the manner in which self-efficacy was measured. When asked about their confidence in learning a particular topic, the students may have imagined a more conventional form of learning that involved only a single representational format. That is, they may have assessed their self-efficacy with respect to a task or goal that was somewhat different from the task in which they actually engaged. Perhaps if the students had been asked about their self-efficacy for learning about carotid artery diseases within a complex multimedia environment, these beliefs would have been more predictive of their learning performance (though, admittedly, the measure of self-efficacy in the previous study by Bråten et al., 2013, was not this specific). This possibility is consistent with Bandura's recommendation that self-efficacy be measured at the same level of specificity as the outcome variable (Pajares, 1996). It is also consistent with a meta-analysis by Stajkovic and Luthans (1998) which showed that the association between self-efficacy and task performance was weaker for high-complexity tasks than for low-complexity tasks.

Values

From the perspective of expectancy-value theory (Wigfield et al., 2016), values can be thought of as the subjective qualities of a task that lead an individual to experience it as desirable and worthwhile. Eccles and colleagues have proposed three distinct components of value (in addition to cost, which we consider to be a distinct construct) (Wigfield et al., 2016). These components include finding the task or topic to be interesting/enjoyable (i.e., intrinsic value), important (i.e., attainment value), and/or useful for achieving some broader goal (i.e., utility value). Following Miele and Scholer (2018), our model retains two of these components (attainment value, which were refer to as self-relevant value, and intrinsic value),[1] and adds a third component pertaining to the value derived from the incentives or demands imposed by some external force (i.e., *external value*). In accordance with self-determination theory (Deci & Ryan, 2000), our model posits that these three components fall along an autonomy-control continuum, such that intrinsic value and self-relevant value (compared to external value) lead students to experience a greater sense of autonomy and to engage in tasks in a more complex, creative, and flexible manner.

In addition to these types of value, our model includes two components originally proposed by regulatory focus theory (Higgins, 1997, 2012). The first of these stems from our fundamental need for growth, such that the outcomes of a task/goal are valued as ideals that one hopes to attain (i.e., promotion value). The second component stems from our fundamental need for safety/security, such that outcomes are instead valued as responsibilities that one feels obligated to attain (i.e., prevention value). As discussed in more detail later in the chapter, these two types of value lead people to engage in tasks in qualitatively distinct ways. Whereas promotion value is associated with eagerly seeking out opportunities for advancement (i.e., gain-oriented strategies), prevention value leads people to vigilantly guard against potential threats (i.e., loss-oriented strategies). It is important to note that promotion and prevention value are not mutually exclusive from the components that vary along the autonomy-control continuum. For example, a person can experience a personally important task as an ideal (self-relevant promotion value) or as a responsibility (self-relevant prevention value). For more on how these various components of value relate to each other at a theoretical level, see Miele and Scholer (2018).

In line with expectancy-value theory, our model stipulates that an increase in any of the value components associated with a particular task/goal will increase the strength of students' motivation and make it more likely that they will engage in the task. Support for this general claim comes from a study by Eccles and Harold (1991) in which the extent to which children perceived a domain (math, English, or sports) to be important, useful, or enjoyable was positively associated with the amount of time they spent engaging in activities in that domain outside of school. Other studies have found similar associations, but often while examining broader outcomes (such as course selection or career intentions; e.g., Durik, Vida, and Eccles, 2006).

One particularly relevant study (Plante, O'Keefe, & Théorêt, 2013) found that the association between domain-specific values (e.g., the perceived importance of math) and career intentions was mediated by participants' mastery goals – but note that for at least one of the mastery goal items, perceived value and goal endorsement were confounded (i.e., "It is important for me to master the knowledge and abilities that we are supposed to learn in math classes"). This study provides some support for our more specific claim that the magnitude of the value associated with an epistemic mastery goal positively predicts students' pursuit of this goal. However, values were assessed at the domain level, while our model posits task-specific values as more direct predictors of goal commitment. Though task-specific values are likely shaped by broader domain values, there are a number of other factors that can strengthen or weaken the values associated with a particular task or goal.[2] We discuss a number of these contextual and individual difference factors in subsequent sections.

To the extent that mastery goals promote the use of deep learning strategies that are adaptive for processing multiple inputs, our model also predicts that task values should be indirectly associated with measures of integrative processing (at least when mastery goals are salient). Several studies have investigated this association and provide mixed support for our prediction. The study by Bråten et al. (2013) described in the previous section found that, although multiple-text comprehension (which involved the integration of multiple perspectives) was predicted by students' self-efficacy, it was not predicted by a measure of task value that included items about the perceived importance, usefulness, and enjoyableness of reading natural science texts. Similarly, the previously described study by Song et al. (2016) found that medical students' learning performance within a multimedia environment (which presumably required the integration of multiple representations) was not uniquely predicted by a measure of perceived topic value. In contrast, other studies have shown that multiple-text comprehension (Bråten et al., 2014; Strømsø & Bråten, 2009; cf. Strømsø, Bråten, & Britt, 2010) and hypermedia learning (Akbulut, 2008)[3] are predicted by measures of task and/or topic interest, which are closely related to the concepts of intrinsic and self-relevant value.

Costs

In a general sense, perceived costs are what individuals think they need to sacrifice (e.g., the opportunity to socialize with friends), endure (e.g., anxiety), or put into a task (e.g., effort) in order to complete it successfully. Thus, unlike values (which specify what the individuals think they will get out of the task), costs tend to be negatively associated with task engagement and academic achievement.

Although this negative association can exist independently of values and expectancies (Jiang, Rosenzweig, & Gaspard, 2018; Perez et al., 2019), it can potentially take the form of an indirect path *through* values and/or expectancies. For example, believing that a task, topic, or course is very challenging and effortful may lead students to conclude that they are incapable of performing well (Feldon, Franco, Chao, Peugh, & Maahs-Fladung, 2018; Likourezos & Kalyuga, 2017), which may in turn make them less motivated to engage in it. Conversely, costs can also serve as mediators of the relation between values and task engagement or achievement, such that students who strongly value a task may perceive it as having limited downsides and, thus, as being worth engaging in (Perez et al., 2019). Finally, it is important to note that perceived costs (depending on how they are defined or operationalized) might actually have a positive or curvilinear association with motivation and task engagement under certain conditions. For example, as a task becomes more challenging, students may come to see it as more interesting or worthwhile, so long as the task does not grow so difficult that it becomes aversive (Abuhamdeh & Csikszentmihalyi, 2012).

Three types of perceived costs were initially proposed by Eccles and colleagues (Eccles-Parsons et al., 1983): *opportunity costs*, or the valued activities or events that individuals forgo by engaging in a particular task; *psychological/emotional costs*, or the emotional discomfort individuals experience (or expect to experience) while engaged in the task; and, *effort costs*, or the amount of effort that the task demands of the individuals. For the most part, this typology of costs has been validated by recent empirical studies (e.g., Perez, Cromley, & Kaplan, 2014), though at least one study found evidence for two distinct types of effort costs (e.g., Flake, Barron, Hulleman, McCoach, & Welsh, 2015).

With respect to the integration of multiple inputs, the type of cost that is perhaps most salient to students is the amount of effort that this integration requires (i.e., effort costs). To the extent that this effort is perceived to be aversive or not worthwhile (given the perceived value of the task), students may decide not to engage in integrative processing. Feldon, Callan, Juth, and Jeong (2019) recently suggested that it is worth considering this possibility in terms of cognitive load theory. In their review, they conceptualize load as "the total burden placed on working memory by the instructional materials in the context of the learner's prior knowledge" (p. 321). Because processing information in working memory is effortful, tasks that impose high levels of cognitive load require that learners expend high levels of mental effort in order to be successful. Building on cognitive load theory, Mayer (2014) has argued that tasks involving multimedia learning impose particularly high levels of load and require a large investment of mental effort by students (see also Anmarkrud, Andresen, & Bråten, 2019). This is in part because such tasks involve:

> a change from having two separate representations – a verbal model and a pictorial model – to having an integrated representation in which corresponding elements and relations from one model are mapped onto the other ... In addition, the integrated model includes connections with relevant knowledge.
>
> (Mayer, 2014, p. 57).

The question then is whether students are aware of these processing demands and whether this awareness sometimes functions as a cost that affects their motivation and task commitment.

The findings pertaining to this question are mixed. A highly cited study by Salomon (1984) showed that American 6th-grade students held reliable beliefs about how easy vs. difficult it would be to learn from different types of media (e.g., television vs. print). Though these beliefs were characterized by Salomon in terms of perceived self-efficacy, they seem to also reflect students' perceptions of the costs associated with each medium. Another important finding from the study was that beliefs about the ease of learning from television were negatively associated with the amount of effort students reported expending on a television task, whereas beliefs about learning from print were positively associated with their effort on a comparable text task (see also Salomon & Leigh, 1984). However, it is unclear to what extent students' effort ratings reflected differences in motivation; and, in addition, the associations between beliefs and effort ratings have been absent in other studies (e.g., Beentjes, 1989; Cennamo, Savenye, & Smith, 1991).

Interestingly, the study by Salomon (1984) found that the medium requiring students to process multiple representations (i.e., video) was actually perceived as easier to learn from than the medium requiring students to process a single type of representation (i.e., print). Salomon suggests that this was because "television, unlike print, is a source of information that is perceived by children as highly familiar, overlearned, and lifelike" (p. 650). Although this difference was not found by Beentjes (1989) in a sample of Dutch 6th-graders, it at least raises the possibility that younger students may sometimes fail to perceive the effort costs associated with tasks that require students to integrate information from multiple modalities.

Types of Values as Determining the Quality of Motivation

In addition to varying in strength, motivation also varies in kind. Drawing on prominent motivational theories from social and educational psychology (Deci & Ryan, 2000; Higgins, 1997), our model posits that students can experience qualitatively distinct types of motivation and that each type is elicited by a different value component. Specifically, a student who perceives a task to be interesting and enjoyable (high intrinsic value) or as pertaining to important aspects of her identity (high self-relevant value) is likely to experience an autonomous form of motivation (including intrinsic motivation). But a student who instead perceives the task as leading to some kind extrinsic reward or punishment (high external value) is more likely to experience a controlled form of motivation. Furthermore, a student who views her pursuit of a task as helping to achieve some ideal or aspiration (high promotion value) is likely to experience promotion motivation, whereas a student who view the task as a responsibility that she must uphold (high prevention value) is more likely to experience prevention motivation.

Importantly, our model draws on the metamotivational framework posited by Miele, Scholer, and colleagues (Miele & Scholer, 2016; 2018; Miele et al., in press; Scholer & Miele, 2016; Scholer et al., 2018; see also Miele & Wigfield, 2014) in positing that each *qualitatively distinct* type of motivation is associated with a different mode of thinking and that certain modes might be more adaptive for tasks that require integrative processing than others (we return to the concept of metamotivation at the end of the chapter). For example, in line with self-determination theory (Deci & Ryan, 2000), autonomous forms of motivation (including intrinsic motivation) tend to be associated with information processing that is relatively complex, creative, and flexible (see Cerasoli, Nicklin, & Ford, 2014); and this mode of processing might be particularly adaptive when trying to form connections between multiple perspectives or multiple representations. In contrast, controlled forms of motivation are associated with processing that is relatively simple and more repetitive, which is presumably less adaptive when it comes to forming connections between multiple inputs.

It is important to note that both autonomous *and* controlled forms of motivation can lead to integrative processing in so far as they strengthen students' commitment to an epistemic mastery goal. That is, a student who feels that she is being made to pursue an epistemic mastery goal (e.g., who feels controlled by her parents or teachers) is more likely to take the necessary steps to achieve that goal (e.g., to compare and contrast conflicting viewpoints) than a student who does not particularly care about the task (i.e., who is amotivated). However, our primary point in this section is that, when holding the strength of students' motivation constant, the *quality* of their motivation may partly determine how effective they are at identifying and implementing the steps needed to achieve an epistemic mastery goal. That is, when two students want to achieve an epistemic mastery goal to the same extent, the student who experiences this motivation in an autonomous manner might be more effective at integrating multiple inputs than the student who experiences this motivation in a controlled manner.

Tentative support for this possibility comes from a study by Sommet and Elliot (2017) in which college students reported the extent to which they (a) pursued mastery and performance goals in their classes (e.g., "My aim is to completely master the material presented in my classes" vs. "My goal is to perform better than the other students"), (b) generally pursued goals for autonomous and controlled reasons (e.g., "In my classes, I pursue goals because I find them personally valuable goals" vs. "In my classes, I pursue goals because I have to comply with the demands of others such as parents, friends, and teachers"), and (c) specifically pursued mastery and performance goals for autonomous and controlled reasons (i.e., their "goal complexes"; e.g., "My aim is to completely master the material presented in my classes because I find this a personally valuable goal" vs. "My aim is to completely master the material presented in my classes because I have to comply with the demands of others such as parents, friends, and teachers").

In addition to completing these motivational measures, the students also completed a number of outcomes measures, including a ten-item questionnaire assessing their use of deep learning strategies. The questionnaire was adapted from a subscale of Kirby, Knapper, Evans, Carty, and Gadula's (2003) Approaches to Learning at Work Questionnaire, which included items such as, "I find that studying for new tasks can often be really exciting and gripping," "I spend a good deal of my spare time learning about things related to my work," and "I find it helpful to 'map out' a new topic for myself by seeing how the ideas fit together." The results of the study showed that, when *controlling for the magnitude of students' mastery and performance goals*, the extent to which students generally or specifically engaged in goals for autonomous reasons (but not controlled reasons) significantly predicted their use of deep learning strategies. In so far as (a) the course-level mastery goals assessed in this study are likely to be correlated with task-specific epistemic mastery goals and (b) the deep learning strategies assessed in the study are likely to promote the integration of multiple inputs, these findings provide tentative support for the idea that integrative processing is determined by both the quantity and quality of students' motivation.

Autonomy and control are not the only types of motivation associated with distinct modes of information processing. In line with regulatory focus theory (Higgins, 1997), research suggests that promotion motivation tends to be associated with associative, divergent, and flexible processing and behavior, whereas prevention motivation is more closely associated with analytic, convergent, and careful processing (see Scholer, Cornwell, & Higgins, 2019). Although it is possible that one of these types of processing is generally more adaptive for the integration of multiple inputs than the other, it seems more likely that such integration involves both divergent and convergent thinking at different times. For instance, when working on a task that requires them to integrate multiple perspectives on a topic, students may perform best when they begin the task with a promotion focus and are to able form numerous associations between the different perspectives. However, at some point it may be helpful for the student to shift to a prevention focus so that they are better able to convergently synthesize these connections into a single, coherent understanding of the topic. Although this possibility is intriguing, it currently lacks empirical support. Thus, future studies should directly examine the influence of promotion and prevention motivations on the integrative processing of multiple inputs.

The Role of Individual Difference Factors

According to our model, individual differences can have an important influence on students' motivation to engage in the integrative processing of multiple perspectives or representations. Drawing on an expectancy-value framework we hypothesize that the expectancies, values, and costs that directly determine students' commitment to epistemic mastery goals are themselves shaped by individual differences in their thinking dispositions, mindsets, personality traits, and interests. Said another way, we posit that certain individual difference factors *indirectly* influence students' pursuit of epistemic mastery goals and their engagement in epistemic processing via their perceived expectancies, values, and costs.

Thinking Dispositions

Thinking dispositions can be thought of as broad preferences for regulating one's thinking in a particular manner. According to Toplak, West, and Stanovich (2014), "examples of some thinking dispositions that have been investigated by psychologists are: actively open-minded thinking, need for cognition, consideration of future consequences, need for closure, reflectivity, superstitious thinking, and dogmatism" (p. 1039). In this section, we focus specifically on need for cognition and need for closure, as they are both motivational in nature and likely to influence students' integrative processing via values and perceived costs.

Cacioppo, Petty, Feinstein, and Jarvis (1996) define the *need for cognition* as "a stable individual difference in people's tendency to engage in and enjoy effortful cognitive activity" (p. 198). We therefore expect students with high need for cognition to intrinsically value tasks that require deep levels of thinking, such as those involving the integration of multiple inputs. Support for this expectation comes from research showing that the need for cognition is positively associated with intrinsic interest and motivation and negatively associated with extrinsic motivation (for a review, see Cacioppo et al., 1996). For example, one study found that need for cognition was positively correlated with college students' intrinsic interest in science and predicted variation in this interest above and beyond the variance accounted for by big five personality factors (e.g., openness, conscientiousness, etc.; Feist, 2012).

Because people who are high in the need for cognition enjoy effortful cognitive processing, they should be willing to work hard on tasks that involve searching for and integrating discrepant information from multiple sources. In support of this possibility, Cacioppo et al. (1996) found that "individuals high in need for cognition are more likely to seek information about a wide range of tasks, issues, and current events than are individuals low in need for cognition" (p. 239). In addition, the previously described study by Bråten et al. (2014) showed a positive indirect association between secondary school students' need for cognition and their integrated understanding of multiple texts. Furthermore, this association was mediated by students' use of cross-text elaboration strategies (e.g., "I tried to note disagreements between the texts"), though it was not mediated by the measure of task effort (i.e., reading time).

The *need for cognitive closure* (Kruglanski, 1990; Webster & Kruglanski, 1994) is marked by a strong desire for a relevant answer (any answer) to a question and an aversion towards ambiguity (Kruglanski, 1990). Individuals with a high need for nonspecific closure are hypothesized to process *less* information during learning than individuals with a low need. This deficit in information processing can be at least partly attributed to the tendency of people high in need for closure to "seize" on the first piece of information relevant to the problem solution and then "freezing" on that information without seeking any additional information or integrating across information sources. This individual difference has been found to be negatively related to the need for cognition (Cacioppo et al., 1996).

Given these prior relations we expect that those in high need for closure will show less commitment to epistemic mastery goals. Mixed support for this claim comes from a series of studies by DeBacker, Crowson, and colleagues, including a study (Harlow, DeBacker, & Crowson, 2011) in which high-school students filled out surveys about their need for academic closure, achievement goals (mastery, performance-approach, and performance-avoidance), and their approaches to learning (shallow versus deep processing strategies). The results showed that students' preference for certainty (i.e., their "discomfort with ambiguity," which is one component of the need for closure; Webster & Kruglanski, 1994) *negatively* predicted their endorsement of a class mastery goal and, in turn, their self-reported use of deep cognitive processing strategies (e.g., "I create new examples of my own to check my understanding of theories and concepts learned in my classes"; see also DeBacker & Crowson, 2006). As previously mentioned, such strategies are likely to be adaptive when students engage in tasks that require them to integrate multiple representations or viewpoints. Interestingly, students' preference for structure (another component of need for closure) *positively* predicted their endorsement of a mastery goal and use of deep strategies. It is possible that these positive associations were driven by the academic framing of the closure scale used by the researchers (rather than by a general preference for structure), considering that a well-ordered academic environment is likely to be predictive of academic success. Of course, a similar argument could also be made to explain the negative association between preference for certainty and endorsement of mastery goals.

Mindsets

Much research has examined children's and adults' *beliefs about intelligence* (or mindsets; Dweck, 2000; Dweck & Leggett, 1988). Dweck and her colleagues have extensively examined two types of intelligence mindsets. Individuals with growth (or incremental) mindsets believe that intelligence can be changed (presumably via experience and practice), whereas individuals with a fixed (entity) mindset believe that intelligence cannot be substantially modified. Much research has shown that these beliefs can impact learning and performance outcomes, as well as the goals and strategies that students adopt in order to achieve these outcomes (see Burnette, O'Boyle, VanEpps, Pollack, & Finkel, 2013; Yeager & Dweck, 2012, for reviews). When students are faced with a setback or receive negative feedback, people with a growth mindset are particularly likely to adopt mastery goals and engage in mastery-oriented strategies, which involve responding to the setback with increased effort. In contrast, people with a fixed mindset are more likely to adopt performance goals and engage in helpless-oriented strategies, which involve withdrawing effort when faced with a setback (see Burnette et al., 2013, for a meta-analytic review).

This difference in behavior suggests that growth mindsets may lead people to interpret the costs associated with challenging tasks in a constructive manner and to form relatively positive task values and expectancies for success. Mixed support for the idea that growth mindsets may indirectly influence academic motivation and achievement through expectancies and values (which is in line with our model) comes from a recent study by Degol, Wang, Zhang, and Allerton (2018). In this study, math value was found to mediate the relation between high-school students' growth mindsets and their STEM-related career aspirations. In addition, math competence beliefs (which served as a measure of expectancies) mediated the interaction effect of gender and mindsets on students' end-of-year math grades, controlling for their previous math grades.

To the extent that students with growth mindsets maintain a positive sense of task value and efficacy in the face of challenge and are willing to invest more effort in the task, they should perform well on tasks that require them to integrate multiple perspectives or representations (as such tasks demand high levels of mental resources and effort). Tentative support for this possibility comes from a study by Braasch, Bråten, Strømsø, and Anmarkrud (2014) that assessed students' growth mindsets and multiple-text comprehension. However, the results of the study should be interpreted with care because the regression analyses included fixed mindsets as a separate variable, and there was a strong negative correlation between fixed and growth mindsets.

Personality Traits

Two additional individual difference constructs that we hypothesize will affect students' motivation to engage in the integrative processing of multiple inputs are grit and conscientiousness. *Grit* has been defined as trait-level perseverance and passion for long-term goals (Duckworth, Peterson, Matthews, & Kelly, 2007) and *conscientiousness* can be thought of as a tendency to follow rules and diligently complete tasks (Roberts et al., 2014). Although these variables are very highly correlated, and some have even questioned whether they represent distinct constructs (Credé, Tynan, &

Harms, 2017), researchers have typically investigated them as part of separate (but overlapping) literatures.

The prior work on grit has shown that individual differences in this construct are related to effort regulation, achievement goals, deliberate practice, self-efficacy, and value (Duckworth, Kirby, Tsukayama, Berstein, & Ericsson, 2011; Muenks, Yang, & Wigfield, 2018; Wolters & Hussain, 2015). Similarly, the research on conscientiousness has found it to be positively related to the motivational constructs of goal-setting, expectancies, and self-efficacy (see Judge & Ilies, 2002, for a meta-analytic review). Because, in our model, these constructs are considered to be proximal predictors of integrative processing, we expect that students who are high in grit or conscientiousness to perform well on tasks that require such processing. Preliminary support for this expectation comes from a study by Wolters and Hussain (2015) which showed a positive association between college students' "perseverance of effort" (a component of grit) and their self-reported use of cognitive and metacognitive strategies, such as rehearsal, elaboration, organization, monitoring, and planning – some of which may facilitate the integrative processing of multiple perspectives or representations (see Bråten & Strømsø, 2011). Importantly, grit's strength as a predictor of both cognitive and metacognitive strategies was reduced when academic value and self-efficacy were entered into the regression models. Thus, in line with our model, there may have been an indirect effect of grit on students' use of deep processing strategies through their expectancies and values.

Individual Interests

Yet another individual difference factor that should influence the integrative processing of multiple inputs is students' individual interest in a particular domain or task. Motivational theories of interest typically differentiate between *individual interest*, which is people's stable or long-lasting interest in a topic or domain, and *situational interest*, which refers to a more temporary state (similar to intrinsic value) that is driven by features of the stimulus or environment (Hidi & Renninger, 2006). Researchers have found individual interest to be positively associated with a number of constructs that are relevant to our model, such as task value, achievement goals (particularly mastery goals), effort, prolonged engagement, and deep strategy use (Harackiewicz et al., 2008; Hulleman, Durik, Schweigert, & Harackiewicz, 2008; Lipstein & Renninger, 2006; Renninger & Hidi, 2002; see Hidi & Renninger, 2006, for a review). It is therefore possible that individual interest indirectly influences students' integrative processing of multiple inputs via a set of more proximal variables.

Support for this possibility comes from the study by Bråten et al. (2014) described above. The authors found that a measure of students' individual interest in science reading (e.g., "I really like to understand the texts that I read in natural science") was indirectly associated with students' integrated understanding of multiple texts (which varied in perspective) via a measure of task effort (i.e., reading times). Individual interest also predicted a more situational measure of students' interest that was administered while they were reading the texts ("I am interested in understanding what I am reading in this text"), and both situational interest and effort were associated with students' use of cross-text elaboration strategies. Considering that these strategies were directly associated with the comprehension measure, it is possible that there was an indirect effect of individual interest on comprehension through situational interest and then strategy use (which would be in line with our model); however, a test of this sequential pathway was not reported by the authors (see also Strømsø & Bråten, 2009; cf. Strømsø et al., 2010).

The Role of Contextual Factors

Contextual factors that potentially influence students' motivation to engage in the integrative processing of multiple inputs include competing goals, time constraints, parent/teacher modeling, extrinsic incentives, classroom goal structures, and stimulating tasks and content. We will not review all of these factors and how they relate to the model due to space limitations, but instead will describe a few representative examples.

Time Constraints

Time constraints can indirectly influence integrative processing by shaping the perceived costs of a task. When given a relatively short amount of time to complete a complex task, even confident students may infer that they do not have enough time to deeply learn the material (i.e., form low expectancies) and, as a result, they may be unlikely to adopt an epistemic mastery goal or to engage in the integrative processing needed to achieve this goal. Support for this possibility comes from a study (Beck & Schmidt, 2013) in which students enrolled in an undergraduate statistics course reported their perceived time pressure (e.g., "I am constantly running out of time for this class") and their achievement goals during the week leading up to each of the four course exams. Both the within-subject and between-subject analyses showed that perceived time pressure was negatively correlated with students' endorsement of mastery goals (e.g., "In statistics class, I look for opportunities to develop new skills and knowledge"), but positively correlated with their endorsement of performance avoidance goals (e.g., "I prefer to avoid parts of statistics class where I might perform poorly"); the effects for performance approach goals were less consistent across analyses (see also De Dreu, 2003; Rieskamp & Hoffrage, 2008).

Another way in which time constraints may influence integrative processing is by increasing the *emotional* costs associated with completing the task. Consistent with the previous study (Beck & Schmidt, 2013), students' concerns about not being able to accurately or effectively complete the task in the allotted time may lead them to adopt performance avoidance goals. In turn, these goals may elicit feelings of anxiety (Elliot & McGregor, 1999; cf. Neff, Hsieh, & Dejitterat, 2005) and ruminative thoughts about competence (Dickhäuser, Buch, Dickhäuser, 2011) that consume students' attentional and memory resources (Ashcraft & Kirk, 2001; Eysenck & Calvo, 1992).

Ultimately, reductions in available executive function resources may leave students unable to engage in the kinds effortful processing strategies that would allow them to successfully coordinate multiple perspectives or connect information from different representational formats. In line with this possibility, González, Rodríguez, Faílde, & Carrera (2016) examined two samples of undergraduate students and found that class-related anxiety (e.g., "before statistics class, I worry whether I will be able to understand the subject") was strongly negatively correlated with students' self-reported use of self-regulatory strategies (e.g., "When I finish working a statistics problem, I check my answer to see if it is reasonable") and deep processing strategies (e.g., "When I work a statistics problem, I analyse it to see if there is more than one way to get the right answer"), as well as their persistence when faced with difficult tasks (e.g., "When I run into a difficult homework problem, I keep working at it until I've solved it").

Stimulating Content

Another feature of the task that might impact students' motivation to engage in integrative processing is the extent to which its content is tailored to students' individual interests or is designed to stimulate interest in a novel topic. For example, Bernacki and Walkington (2018) examined the effects of matching the content of algebra story problems to students' personal interests (e.g., sports or arts) and found that, when there was a match, students were more efficient in solving problems in a cognitive tutoring system and performed better on classroom exams. They also found evidence that students who were presented with personalized content exhibited more situational interest and value for the tasks. Similarly, researchers have found that including content that is perceived as novel, surprising, vivid, or intense can trigger students' situational interest (see Hidi & Harackiewicz, 2000); and, as previously discussed, situational interest was found to predict students' use of cross-text elaboration strategies, which involve integrating multiple perspectives (Bråten et al., 2014).

Classroom Goal Structures

Several features of the academic environment have been examined in terms of their contribution to classroom goal structures (Ames, 1992; Ames & Archer, 1988). Ames (1992) conducted a theoretical analysis of these goal structures that focused on six dimensions of the environment including: (1) Task, (2) Authority, (3) Recognition, (4) Grouping, (5) Evaluation, and (6) Timing (TARGET). Based on their location along these dimensions, instructional practices can be categorized as potentially fostering mastery goals (e.g., assigning meaningful and challenging tasks) or performance goals (e.g., assigning rote tasks). Several studies that have measured students' or teachers' perceptions of classroom or school goal structures have found that they are associated with a variety of motivational and academic outcomes, some of which are relevant for our model. For example, in studies by Kaplan and Maehr (1999) and Roeser, Midgley, and Urdan (1996), perceiving a school as mastery focused was positively associated with students' self-efficacy and their endorsement of mastery goals (though in these studies, personal goals were generally modeled as mediating the effects of goal structures on self-efficacy, which is contrast to our model).

FUTURE DIRECTIONS

In this chapter, we have outlined a motivational model of integrative processing and, in doing so, identified a number of factors that are likely to influence students' motivation to integrate multiple representations and viewpoints. In many cases, we were able to reference strong empirical support for the hypothesized relations between the constructs in our model. In other cases, the support was either mixed or missing altogether, often because no studies have yet been conducted that directly examine the relation in question. Ultimately, by helping to identify potential gaps in the literature, our model can be used by researchers to ask important questions about motivation and integrative processing and to guide future research on this topic.

Once the research community has developed a deeper understanding of how motivational factors influence the integrative processing of multiple inputs, a next step will be to be think through the implications of this understanding for educational practice. For example, how can motivational states that facilitate integrative processing be bolstered through classroom instruction or educational interventions? In addition to investigating how educators can foster adaptive motivational states in students, we encourage researchers to begin exploring the ways in which students can foster these states in themselves. Recent research on the topic of metamotivation by Miele, Scholer, Fujita, and colleagues has shown that students are surprisingly sensitive to the potential performance trade-offs associated with different kinds of motivation (see Miele et al., in press, for a review). For instance, in a study by Scholer and Miele (2016) college students believed that preparatory activities that have previously been shown to induce a prevention motivation would lead them to perform better on tasks that required convergent processing (compared to tasks that called for divergent processing). In contrast, the same students believed that activities that have been shown to induce a promotion motivation would lead them to perform better on tasks that required divergent processing. Researchers should investigate whether students can use this kind of metamotivational knowledge about self-regulation strategies and task demands to optimize their performance on tasks that call for the integrative processing of multiple perspectives or representations.

ACKNOWLEDGMENTS

This writing of this chapter was supported by funding from the Buehler Sesquicentennial Assistant Professorship, grant DUE-1534829 from the National Science Foundation, and Collaborative Grant No. 220020483 from the James S. McDonnell Foundation.

NOTES

1. Our model does not include a utility value component because, within a hierarchical system of goals, we consider perceive utility as the mean by which value is transmitted from a superordinate goal to a subordinate/task goal (see Miele & Scholer, 2018).
2. This point about the task- vs. domain-specificity of the constructs in our model should be kept in mind when interpreting the findings of a number of the studies reviewed in this chapter.
3. Note that in this and other hypermedia or multimedia studies, it is not always clear to what extent test/learning performance is dependent on the integrative processing of information from multiple representational formats.

REFERENCES

Abuhamdeh, S., & Csikszentmihalyi, M. (2012). The importance of challenge for the enjoyment of intrinsically motivated, goal-directed activities. *Personality and Social Psychology Bulletin, 38*(3), 317–330.

Akbulut, Y. (2008). Predictors of foreign language reading comprehension in a hypermedia reading environment. *Journal of Educational Computing Research, 39*(1), 37–50.

Ames, C. (1992). Classrooms: Goals, structures, and student motivation. *Journal of Educational Psychology, 84*(3), 261–271.

Ames, C., & Archer, J. (1988). Achievement goals in the classroom: Students' learning strategies and motivation processes. *Journal of Educational Psychology, 80*(3), 260–267.

Anmarkrud, Ø., Andresen, A., & Bråten, I. (2019). Cognitive load and working memory in multimedia learning: Conceptual and measurement issues. *Educational Psychologist, 54*(2), 61–83.

Ashcraft, M. H., & Kirk, E. P. (2001). The relationships among working memory, math anxiety, and performance. *Journal of Experimental Psychology: General, 130*, 224–237.

Asterhan, C. S. (2018). Exploring enablers and inhibitors of productive peer argumentation: The role of individual achievement goals and of gender. *Contemporary Educational Psychology, 54*, 66–78.

Bandura, A. (1977). Self-efficacy: Toward a unifying theory of behavioral change. *Psychological Review, 84*(2), 191–215.

Banich, M. T. (2009). Executive function: The search for an integrated account. *Current Directions in Psychological Science, 18*(2), 89–94.

Barron, K. E., & Hulleman, C. S. (2015). Expectancy-value-cost model of motivation. *Psychology, 84*, 261–271.

Beck, J. W., & Schmidt, A. M. (2013). State-level goal orientations as mediators of the relationship between time pressure and performance: A longitudinal study. *Journal of Applied Psychology, 98*(2), 354–363.

Beentjes, J. W. (1989). Learning from television and books: A Dutch replication study based on Salomon's model. *Educational Technology Research and Development, 37*(2), 47–58.

Belenky, D. M., & Nokes-Malach, T. J. (2012). Motivation and transfer: The role of mastery-approach goals in preparation for future learning. *Journal of the Learning Sciences, 21*(3), 399–432.

Bendixen, L. D., & Hartley, K. (2003). Successful learning with hypermedia: The role of epistemological beliefs and metacognitive awareness. *Journal of Educational Computing Research, 28*(1), 15–30.

Bernacki, M. L., & Walkington, C. (2018). The role of situational interest in personalized learning. *Journal of Educational Psychology, 110*(6), 862–881.

Braasch, J. L. G., Bråten, I., Strømsø, H. I., & Anmarkrud, Ø. (2014). Incremental theories of intelligence predict multiple document comprehension. *Learning and Individual Differences, 31*, 11–20.

Bråten, I., Anmarkrud, Ø., Brandmo, C., & Strømsø, H. I. (2014). Developing and testing a model of direct and indirect relationships between individual differences, processing, and multiple-text comprehension. *Learning and Instruction, 30*, 9–24.

Bråten, I., Britt, M. A., Strømsø, H. I., & Rouet, J. F. (2011). The role of epistemic beliefs in the comprehension of multiple expository texts: Toward an integrated model. *Educational Psychologist, 46*(1), 48–70.

Bråten, I., Ferguson, L. E., Anmarkrud, Ø., & Strømsø, H. I. (2013). Prediction of learning and comprehension when adolescents read multiple texts: The roles of word-level processing, strategic approach, and reading motivation. *Reading and Writing, 26*(3), 321–348.

Bråten, I., & Strømsø, H. I. (2011). Measuring strategic processing when students read multiple texts. *Metacognition and Learning, 6*(2), 111–130.

Burnette, J. L., O'Boyle, E. H., VanEpps, E. M., Pollack, J. M., & Finkel, E. J. (2013). Mind-sets matter: A meta-analytic review of implicit theories and self-regulation. *Psychological Bulletin, 139*(3), 655–701.

Butera, F., Sommet, N., & Darnon, C. (2019). Sociocognitive conflict regulation: How to make sense of diverging ideas. *Current Directions in Psychological Science, 28*(2), 145–151.

Cacioppo, J. T., & Petty, R. E. (1982). The need for cognition. *Journal of Personality and Social Psychology, 42*(1), 116–131.

Cacioppo, J. T., Petty, R. E., Feinstein, J. A., & Jarvis, W. B. G. (1996). Dispositional differences in cognitive motivation: The life and times of individuals varying in need for cognition. *Psychological Bulletin, 119*, 197–253.

Carver, C. S., & Scheier, M. F. (1998). *On the self-regulation of behavior*. New York: Cambridge University Press.

Cennamo, K. S., Savenye, W. C., & Smith, P. L. (1991). Mental effort and video-based learning: The relationship of preconceptions and the effects of interactive and covert practice. *Educational Technology Research and Development, 39*(1), 5–16.

Cerasoli, C. P., Nicklin, J. M., & Ford, M. T. (2014). Intrinsic motivation and extrinsic incentives jointly predict performance: A 40-year meta-analysis. *Psychological Bulletin, 140*(4), 980–1008.

Chen, J. A., & Barger, M. M. (2016). Epistemic cognition and motivation. In J. A. Greene, W. Sandoval, & I. Bråten (Eds.), *Handbook of epistemic cognition* (pp. 425–438). New York: Routledge.

Chinn, C. A., Buckland, L. A., & Samarapungavan, A. (2011). Expanding the dimensions of epistemic cognition: Arguments from philosophy and psychology. *Educational Psychologist, 46*, 141–167.

Credé, M., Tynan, M. C., & Harms, P. D. (2017). Much ado about grit: A meta-analytic synthesis of the grit literature. *Journal of Personality and Social Psychology, 113*(3), 492–511.

Darnon, C., & Butera, F. (2007). Learning or succeeding? Conflict regulation with mastery or performance goals. *Swiss Journal of Psychology, 66*(3), 145–152.

Darnon, C., Butera, F., & Harackiewicz, J. M. (2007). Achievement goals in social interactions: Learning with mastery vs. performance goals. *Motivation and Emotion, 31*(1), 61–70.

Darnon, C., Muller, D., Schrager, S. M., Pannuzzo, N., & Butera, F. (2006). Mastery and performance goals predict epistemic and relational conflict regulation. *Journal of Educational Psychology, 98*(4), 766–776.

De Dreu, C. K. (2003). Time pressure and closing of the mind in negotiation. *Organizational Behavior and Human Decision Processes, 91*(2), 280–295.

De Dreu, C. K., Nijstad, B. A., & van Knippenberg, D. (2008). Motivated information processing in group judgment and decision making. *Personality and Social Psychology Review, 12*(1), 22–49.

DeBacker, T. K., & Crowson, H. M. (2006). Influences on cognitive engagement: Epistemological beliefs and need for closure. *British Journal of Educational Psychology, 76*, 535–551.

Deci, E. L., & Ryan, R. M. (2000). The "what" and "why" of goal pursuits: Human needs and the self-determination of behavior. *Psychological Inquiry, 11*(4), 227–268.

Degol, J. L., Wang, M. T., Zhang, Y., & Allerton, J. (2018). Do growth mindsets in math benefit females? Identifying pathways between gender, mindset, and motivation. *Journal of Youth and Adolescence, 47*(5), 976–990.

Dickhäuser, C., Buch, S. R., & Dickhäuser, O. (2011). Achievement after failure: The role of achievement goals and negative self-related thoughts. *Learning and Instruction, 21*(1), 152–162.

Diseth, Å. (2011). Self-efficacy, goal orientations and learning strategies as mediators between preceding and subsequent academic achievement. *Learning and Individual Differences, 21*(2), 191–195.

Duckworth, A., & Gross, J. J. (2014). Self-control and grit: Related but separable determinants of success. *Current Directions in Psychological Science, 23*(5), 319–325.

Duckworth, A. L., Kirby, T. A., Tsukayama, E., Berstein, H., & Ericsson, K. A. (2011). Deliberate practice spells success. *Social Psychological and Personality Science, 2*(2), 174–181.

Duckworth, A. L., Peterson, C., Matthews, M. D., & Kelly, D. R. (2007). Grit: Perseverance and passion for long-term goals. *Journal of Personality and Social Psychology, 92*(6), 1087–1101.

Durik, A. M., Vida, M., & Eccles, J. S. (2006). Task values and ability beliefs as predictors of high school literacy choices: A developmental analysis. *Journal of Educational Psychology, 98*(2), 382–393.

Dweck, C. S. (2000). *Self-theories: Their role in motivation, personality, and development.* Philadelphia, PA: Taylor & Francis.

Dweck, C. S., & Leggett, E. L. (1988). A social-cognitive approach to motivation and personality. *Psychological Review, 95*(2), 256–273.

Eccles, J. S., & Harold, R. D. (1991). Gender differences in sport involvement: Applying the Eccles' expectancy-value model. *Journal of Applied Sport Psychology, 3*(1), 7–35.

Eccles-Parsons, J. S., Adler, T. F., Futterman, R., Goff, S. B., Kaczala, C. M., Meece, J. L., & Midgley, C. (1983). Expectancies, values, and academic behaviors. In J. T. Spence (Ed.), *Achievement and achievement motives: Psychological and sociological approaches* (pp. 75–146). San Francisco, CA: Freeman.

Elliot, A. J., & McGregor, H. A. (1999). Test anxiety and the hierarchical model of approach and avoidance achievement motivation. *Journal of Personality and Social Psychology, 76*(4), 628–644.

Eysenck, M. W., & Calvo, M. G. (1992). Anxiety and performance: The processing efficiency theory. *Cognition and Emotion, 6*, 409–434.

Feist, G. J. (2012). Predicting interest in and attitudes towards science from personality and need for cognition. *Personality and Individual Differences, 52*, 771–775.

Feldon, D. F., Callan, G., Juth, S., & Jeong, S. (2019). Cognitive load as motivational cost. *Educational Psychology Review, 31*, 319–337.

Feldon, D. F., Franco, J., Chao, J., Peugh, J., & Maahs-Fladung, C. (2018). Self-efficacy change associated with a cognitive load-based intervention in an undergraduate biology course. *Learning and Instruction, 56*, 64–72.

Firetto, C. M., & Van Meter, P. N. (2018). Inspiring integration in college students reading multiple biology texts. *Learning and Individual Differences, 65*, 123–134.

Flake, J. K., Barron, K. E., Hulleman, C., McCoach, B. D., & Welsh, M. E. (2015). Measuring cost: The forgotten component of expectancy-value theory. *Contemporary Educational Psychology, 41*, 232–244.

Gigerenzer, G., & Goldstein, D. G. (1996). Reasoning the fast and frugal way: Models of bounded rationality. *Psychological Review, 103*(4), 650–669.

González, A., Rodríguez, Y., Faílde, J. M., & Carrera, M. V. (2016). Anxiety in the statistics class: Structural relations with self-concept, intrinsic value, and engagement in two samples of undergraduates. *Learning and Individual Differences, 45*, 214–221.

Harackiewicz, J. M., Durik, A. M., Barron, K. E., Linnenbrink-Garcia, L., & Tauer, J. M. (2008). The role of achievement goals in the development of interest: Reciprocal relations between achievement goals, interest, and performance. *Journal of Educational Psychology, 100*(1), 105–122.

Harlow, L., DeBacker, T. K., & Crowson, H. M. (2011). Need for closure, achievement goals, and cognitive engagement in high school students. *The Journal of Educational Research, 104*, 110–119.

Hidi, S., & Harackiewicz, J. M. (2000). Motivating the academically unmotivated: A critical issue for the 21st century. *Review of Educational Research, 70*, 151–179.

Hidi, S., & Renninger, K. A. (2006). The four-phase model of interest development. *Educational Psychologist, 41*, 111–127.

Higgins, E. T. (1997). Beyond pleasure and pain. *American Psychologist, 52*(12), 1280–1300.

Higgins, E. T. (2012). Regulatory focus theory. In P. A. M. Van Lange, A. W. Kruglanski, & E. T. Higgins (Eds.), *Handbook of theories of social psychology* (vol. 1, pp. 483–504). Thousand Oaks, CA: Sage.

Hofer, B. K. (2004). Epistemological understanding as a metacognitive process: Thinking aloud during online searching. *Educational Psychologist, 39*(1), 43–55.

Hofer, B. K., & Pintrich, P. R. (1997). The development of epistemological theories: Beliefs about knowledge and knowing and their relation to learning. *Review of Educational Research, 67*(1), 88–140.

Huang, C. (2016). Achievement goals and self-efficacy: A meta-analysis. *Educational Research Review, 19*, 119–137.

Hulleman, C. S., Durik, A. M., Schweigert, S. B., & Harackiewicz, J. M. (2008). Task values, achievement goals, and interest: An integrative analysis. *Journal of Educational Psychology, 100*(2), 398–416.

Jiang, Y., Rosenzweig, E. Q., & Gaspard, H. (2018). An expectancy-value-cost approach in predicting adolescent students' academic motivation and achievement. *Contemporary Educational Psychology, 54*, 139–152.

Judge, T. A., & Ilies, R. (2002). Relationship of personality to performance motivation: A meta-analytic review. *Journal of Applied Psychology, 87*(4), 797–807.

Kaplan, A., & Maehr, M. L. (1999). Achievement goals and student well-being. *Contemporary Educational Psychology, 24*(4), 330–358.

Kirby, J. R., Knapper, C. K., Evans, C. J., Carty, A. E., & Gadula, C. (2003). Approaches to learning at work and workplace climate. *International Journal of Training and Development, 7*(1), 31–52.

Kruglanski, A. W. (1990). Lay epistemic theory in social-cognitive psychology. *Psychological Inquiry, 1*(3), 181–197.

Likourezos, V., & Kalyuga, S. (2017). Instruction-first and problem-solving-first approaches: Alternative pathways to learning complex tasks. *Instructional Science, 45*(2), 195–219.

Lipstein, R., & Renninger, K. A. (2006). "Putting things into words": 12–15-year-old students' interest for writing. In P. Boscolo & S. Hidi (Eds.), *Motivation and writing: Research and school practice*. New York: Kluwer Academic/Plenum.

Locke, E. A., Latham, G. P., & Erez, M. (1988). The determinants of goal commitment. *Academy of Management Review, 13*(1), 23–39.

Maddux, J. E., Norton, L. W., & Stoltenberg, C. D. (1986). Self-efficacy expectancy, outcome expectancy, and outcome value: Relative effects on behavioral intentions. *Journal of Personality and Social Psychology, 51*(4), 783–789.

Manning, M. M., & Wright, T. L. (1983). Self-efficacy expectancies, outcome expectancies, and the persistence of pain control in childbirth. *Journal of Personality and Social Psychology, 45*(2), 421–431.

Marsh, H. W., Pekrun, R., Parker, P. D., Murayama, K., Guo, J., Dicke, T., & Arens, A. K. (2019). The murky distinction between self-concept and self-efficacy: Beware of lurking jingle-jangle fallacies. *Journal of Educational Psychology, 111*(2), 331–353.

Mayer, R. E. (2014). Cognitive theory of multimedia learning. In R. E. Mayer (Ed.), *The Cambridge handbook of multimedia learning* (2nd ed., pp. 43–71). New York: Cambridge University Press.

Miele, D. B., & Scholer, A. A. (2016). Self-regulation of motivation. In K. R. Wentzel & D. B. Miele (Eds.), *Handbook of motivation at school* (2nd ed., pp. 363–384). New York: Routledge.

Miele, D. B., & Scholer, A. A. (2018). The role of metamotivational monitoring in motivation regulation. *Educational Psychologist, 53*(1), 1–21.

Miele, D. B., Scholer, A. A., & Fujita, K. (in press). Metamotivation: Emerging research on the regulation of motivational states. In A. Elliot (Ed.), *Advances in Motivation Science* (Vol. 7). Cambridge, MA: Academic Press.

Miele, D. B., & Wigfield, A. (2014). Quantitative and qualitative relations between motivation and critical-analytic thinking. *Educational Psychology Review, 26*(4), 519–541.

Mishra, P., & Yadav, A. (2006). Using hypermedia for learning complex concepts in chemistry: A qualitative study on the relationship between prior knowledge, beliefs, and motivation. *Education and Information Technologies, 11*(1), 33–69.

Muenks, K., Yang, J. S., & Wigfield, A. (2018). Associations between grit, motivation, and achievement in high school students. *Motivation Science, 4*(2), 158–176.

Muis, K. R. (2007). The role of epistemic beliefs in self-regulated learning. *Educational Psychologist, 42*(3), 173–190.

Muis, K. R., Chevrier, M., & Singh, C. A. (2018). The role of epistemic emotions in personal epistemology and self-regulated learning. *Educational Psychologist, 53*(3), 165–184.

Neff, K. D., Hsieh, Y. P., & Dejitterat, K. (2005). Self-compassion, achievement goals, and coping with academic failure. *Self and Identity, 4*(3), 263–287.

Pajares, F. (1996). Self-efficacy beliefs in academic settings. *Review of Educational Research, 66*(4), 543–578.

Perez, T., Cromley, J. G., & Kaplan, A. (2014). The role of identity development, values, and costs in college STEM retention. *Journal of Educational Psychology, 106*(1), 315–329.

Perez, T., Dai, T., Kaplan, A., Cromley, J. G., Brooks, W. D., White, A. C., … Balsai, M. J. (2019). Interrelations among expectancies, task values, and perceived costs in undergraduate biology achievement. *Learning and Individual Differences, 72*, 26–38.

Plante, I., O'Keefe, P. A., & Théorêt, M. (2013). The relation between achievement goal and expectancy-value theories in predicting achievement-related outcomes: A test of four theoretical conceptions. *Motivation and Emotion, 37*(1), 65–78.

Renninger, K. A., & Hidi, S. (2002). Student interest and achievement: Developmental issues raised by a case study. In A. Wigfield & J. S. Eccles (Eds.), *Development of achievement motivation* (pp. 173–195). New York: Academic.

Rieskamp, J., & Hoffrage, U. (2008). Inferences under time pressure: How opportunity costs affect strategy selection. *Acta Psychologica, 127*(2), 258–276.

Roberts, B. W., Lejuez, C., Krueger, R. F., Richards, J. M., & Hill, P. L. (2014). What is conscientiousness and how can it be assessed? *Developmental Psychology, 50*(5), 1315–1330.

Roeser, R. W., Midgley, C., & Urdan, T. C. (1996). Perceptions of the school psychological environment and early adolescents' psychological and behavioral functioning in school: The mediating role of goals and belonging. *Journal of Educational Psychology, 88*(3), 408–422.

Salomon, G. (1984). Television is" easy" and print is" tough": The differential investment of mental effort in learning as a function of perceptions and attributions. *Journal of Educational Psychology, 76*(4), 647–658.

Salomon, G., & Leigh, T. (1984). Predispositions about learning from print and television. *Journal of Communication, 20*, 119–135.

Scholer, A. A., Cornwell, J. F. M., & Higgins, E. T. (2019). Regulatory focus theory and research: Catching up and looking forward after 20 years. In R. Ryan (Ed.), *The Oxford handbook of human motivation* (2nd ed., pp. 75–95). New York, NY: Oxford University Press.

Scholer, A. A., & Miele, D. B. (2016). The role of metamotivation in creating task-motivation fit. *Motivation Science, 2*(3), 171–197.

Scholer, A. A., Miele, D. B., Murayama, K., & Fujita, K. (2018). New directions in self-regulation: The role of metamotivational beliefs. *Current Directions in Psychological Science, 27*(6), 437–442.

Senko, C. (2016). Achievement goal theory: A story of early promises, eventual discords, and future possibilities. In K. Wentzel & D. Miele (Eds.), *Handbook of motivation at school* (2nd ed., pp. 75–95). New York: Routledge.

Senko, C., Hulleman, C. S., & Harackiewicz, J. M. (2011). Achievement goal theory at the crossroads: Old controversies, current challenges, and new directions. *Educational Psychologist, 46*(1), 26–47.

Senko, C., & Tropiano, K. L. (2016). Comparing three models of achievement goals: Goal orientations, goal standards, and goal complexes. *Journal of Educational Psychology, 108*(8), 1178–1192.

Sommet, N., & Elliot, A. J. (2017). Achievement goals, reasons for goal pursuit, and achievement goal complexes as predictors of beneficial outcomes: Is the influence of goals reducible to reasons?. *Journal of Educational Psychology, 109*(8), 1141–1162.

Song, H. S., Kalet, A. L., & Plass, J. L. (2016). Interplay of prior knowledge, self-regulation and motivation in complex multimedia learning environments. *Journal of Computer Assisted Learning, 32*(1), 31–50.

Stajkovic, A. D., & Luthans, F. (1998). Self-efficacy and work-related performance: A meta-analysis. *Psychological Bulletin, 124*(2), 240–261.

Strømsø, H. I., & Bråten, I. (2009). Beliefs about knowledge and knowing and multiple-text comprehension among upper secondary students. *Educational Psychology, 29*(4), 425–445.

Strømsø, H. I., Bråten, I., & Britt, M. A. (2010). Reading multiple texts about climate change: The relationship between memory for sources and text comprehension. *Learning and Instruction, 20*(3), 192–204.

Toplak, M. E., West, R. F., & Stanovich, K. E. (2014). Rational thinking and cognitive sophistication: Development, cognitive abilities, and thinking dispositions. *Developmental Psychology, 50*(4), 1037–1048.

Webster, D. M., & Kruglanski, A. W. (1994). Individual differences in need for cognitive closure. *Journal of Personality and Social Psychology, 67*(6), 1049–1062.

Wigfield, A., & Eccles, J. S. (2000). Expectancy-Value theory of achievement motivation. *Contemporary Educational Psychology, 25*(1), 68–81.

Wigfield, A., Tonks, S. M., & Klauda, S. L. (2016). Expectancy-value theory. In K. R. Wentzel & D. B. Miele (Eds.), *Handbook of motivation at school* (2nd ed., pp. 55–74). New York: Routledge.

Wineburg, S. (1998). Reading Abraham Lincoln: An expert/expert study in the interpretation of historical texts. *Cognitive Science, 22*(3), 319–346.

Wolters, C. A., & Hussain, M. (2015). Investigating grit and its relations with college students' self-regulated learning and academic achievement. *Metacognition and Learning, 10*(3), 293–311.

Yeager, D. S., & Dweck, C. S. (2012). Mindsets that promote resilience: When students believe that personal characteristics can be developed. *Educational Psychologist, 47*(4), 302–314.

22

EMOTIONS AND LEARNING FROM MULTIPLE REPRESENTATIONS AND PERSPECTIVES

Reinhard Pekrun
UNIVERSITY OF ESSEX AND AUSTRALIAN CATHOLIC UNIVERSITY

Kristina Loderer
UNIVERSITY OF AUGSBURG

ABSTRACT

Using control-value theory as a conceptual framework, we review the literature on the role of emotions in learning from multiple inputs. We first provide a conceptual definition of emotion and an overview of the different types of emotions that play a role during learning, including achievement, epistemic, topic, and social emotions. Next, we discuss theoretical propositions about the origins and functions of these emotions. In the third section, we review empirical evidence on emotions during learning from multiple representations, both in terms of the sensory channels used and in terms of structures of multiple representations that guide learners' emotion-prompting appraisals. Most of this evidence has been gathered in studies on technology-enhanced multimedia learning, such as learning with intelligent tutoring systems, simulations, and games. Subsequently, we summarize recent findings on learning from multiple perspectives, such as contradictory perspectives provided in texts on controversial issues or refutation texts targeting conceptual change. In conclusion, we discuss directions for future research and implications for practice.

Key words: achievement emotion, epistemic emotion, appraisal, control-value theory, multimedia learning

Traditionally, research on emotions in education has focused on learners' anxiety, such as their test anxiety or math anxiety (Zeidner, 1998). However, learning can prompt a broad range of different emotions, including negative emotions other than anxiety, such as anger, frustration, confusion, shame, hopelessness, and boredom, as well as positive emotions like enjoyment of learning, hope for success, pride, and contentment. It seems likely that the occurrence and intensity of these various emotions can be even further enhanced when learning from multiple inputs. For example, the demands of such learning can prompt increased enjoyment in learners who enjoy the challenge, but trigger frustration and confusion in those who lack the competencies needed to deal with complex materials (see also D'Mello, 2013).

Over the past 20 years, researchers have started to investigate the multiple emotions occurring during learning (for overviews, see Pekrun & Linnenbrink-Garcia, 2014a). While the bulk of these studies pertained to learning from single representations (such as text) and single perspectives (such as current scientific knowledge in a given discipline), researchers who focus on multimedia learning or learning about controversial topics have started to also investigate the emotions accompanying learning from multiple inputs. In this chapter, we review theory and evidence on these emotions.

We first provide a conceptual definition of emotion and an overview of the different types of emotions that play a role during learning. Next, we use Pekrun's (2006, 2018, 2019a, Pekrun & Perry, 2014) control-value theory (CVT) as a conceptual framework to discuss propositions about the origins and functions of emotions during learning. In the third section, we review empirical evidence on emotions during learning from multiple representations. Much of this evidence has been gathered in studies on technology-enhanced multimedia learning, such as learning with intelligent tutoring systems, simulations, and games using different sensory channels and representational formats. Subsequently, we summarize recent findings on learning from multiple perspectives, such as contradictory perspectives presented in texts on controversial issues or refutation texts targeting conceptual change. In closing, we outline directions for future research and implications for practice.

CONCEPTS OF EMOTION

Emotion, Mood, and Affect

Emotions are multifaceted phenomena that consist of several interrelated component processes (Shuman & Scherer, 2014), including subjective feelings (affective component), cognitions (cognitive component), motivational tendencies (motivational component), physiological processes (physiological component), and expressive behavior (expressive component). For instance, a student experiencing anxiety when confronted with contradictory information may feel uneasy and nervous (affective), think about possible failure in resolving the contradictions (cognitive), want to avoid dealing with the material (motivational), have sweaty palms (physiological), and display an anxious facial expression (expressive component).

In comparison to emotions, *moods* are of lower intensity, have less specific reference objects, and are typically of longer duration. Some authors define emotion and mood as categorically distinct phenomena – whenever you experience enjoyment, anger, or anxiety, this state falls into either the category of emotion or the category of mood (Rosenberg, 1998). Alternatively, since moods show similar qualitative differences as emotions (as in cheerful, angry, or anxious mood), they can also be regarded as low-intensity emotions (Pekrun, 2006).

Different emotions and moods are often compiled in more general concepts of *affect.* Two variants of this term are used in the research literature. In the educational literature, affect is often employed to denote a broad variety of non-cognitive constructs including emotion, but also self-concept, beliefs, motivation, etc. (see, e.g., McLeod & Adams, 1989). In contrast, in emotion research, affect refers to emotions and moods more specifically. In this research, the term is often used to refer to more global variables of positive versus negative emotions or moods, with *positive affect* including various positive emotions (e.g., enjoyment, pride, satisfaction) and *negative affect* various negative emotions (e.g., anger, anxiety, frustration).

Two important dimensions describing emotions, moods, and affect are *valence* and *activation* (Barrett & Russell, 1998). Valence denotes the degree of pleasantness, making it possible to distinguish positive (i.e., pleasant) states, such as enjoyment and happiness, from negative (i.e., unpleasant) states, such as anger, anxiety, or boredom. In terms of activation, physiologically activating states can be distinguished from deactivating states, such as activating excitement versus deactivating relaxation. By classifying affective states using these two dimensions, four broad categories of emotions can be distinguished, including *positive activating* emotions such as enjoyment, excitement, hope, and pride; *positive deactivating* emotions such as relief, relaxation, and contentment; *negative activating* emotions like anger, anxiety, and shame; and *negative deactivating* emotions like hopelessness and boredom (see Table 22.1).

Table 22.1 Valence × Activation Taxonomy of Emotions

Activation	Valence	
	Positive (pleasant)	*Negative (unpleasant)*
Activating	Enjoyment	Anxiety
	Hope	Anger
	Pride	Frustration [c]
	Gratitude	Shame
	Surprise [a]	Envy
	Curiosity [b]	Surprise [a]
		Confusion
Deactivating	Relief	Disappointment
	Contentment	Frustration [c]
	Relaxation	Boredom
		Sadness
		Hopelessness

Note. This classification is based on established taxonomies of achievement emotions and epistemic emotions (Pekrun & Stephens, 2012; Pekrun & Perry, 2014).

[a] Frustration can comprise elements of (activating) anger and (deactivating) disappointment.
[b] Valence may vary based on emotion-eliciting event (positive, negative).
[c] Curiosity is considered as unpleasant in some conceptions (see Loewenstein, 1994; Pekrun, 2019b).

Emotions Related to Learning

Emotions differ according to the events and objects that trigger them. As such, emotions can also be grouped according to their *object focus* (Pekrun & Stephens, 2012). Regarding the influence of emotions on students' learning, object focus is critical because it determines if emotions pertain to the learning task at hand or not. In terms of object focus, the following broad groups of emotions and moods may be most important for learning from multiple inputs.

General and Specific Moods

By definition, moods may not be directly tied to a specific learning activity. Nevertheless, they have the potential to shape students' learning. For example, when you are in a joyful mood, you may be better disposed to creatively solve a complex task involving multiple perspectives than when you are in an anxious or angry mood.

Achievement Emotions

These are emotions that relate to achievement activities, such as studying and taking tests, and to the achievement outcomes of these activities (i.e., success and failure). Accordingly, two groups of achievement emotions are *activity emotions*, such as enjoyment, anger, frustration, or boredom during learning, and *outcome emotions*, such as hope and pride (related to success) or anxiety, hopelessness, and shame (related to failure). Many of the emotions experienced in academic settings can be classified as achievement emotions because they relate to activities and outcomes that are judged according to competence-based standards of quality.

Past research on achievement emotions predominantly focused on outcome emotions. Two important traditions of research on outcome emotions are test anxiety studies and studies on the links between perceived causes of success and failure and subsequent emotions, such as pride and shame (Weiner, 1985; Zeidner, 1998). Though outcome emotions are of critical importance for achievement strivings, emotions directly pertaining to the activities performed in achievement settings (i.e., activity emotions) are of equal relevance for learning.

Epistemic Emotions

The term "epistemic" is derived from ancient Greek and denotes thoughts and activities that aim to expand human knowledge. Thinking, however, is not just based on pure cognitive reasoning alone ("cold cognition"). Rather, it is closely tied to emotions such as surprise, curiosity, or confusion. Because they relate to the knowledge-generating qualities of cognitive tasks, these emotions have been called *epistemic emotions* (Brun, Doğuoğlu, & Kuenzle, 2008; Pekrun & Stephens, 2012). Epistemic emotions serve evolutionary-based purposes of acquiring knowledge about the world and the self. A prototypical situation for the arousal of epistemic emotions like surprise, curiosity, and confusion is contradictory information and cognitive incongruity, which imply that different pieces of information are not compatible and do not fit together.

A typical sequence of epistemic emotions induced by cognitive incongruity may involve (1) surprise; (2) curiosity and situational interest if the surprise is not dissolved; (3) anxiety in case of severe incongruity and information that deeply disturbs existing beliefs about the world, thus making clear that knowledge is not certain; (4) enjoyment and delight when recombining information such that the problem gets solved; or (5) frustration when this seems impossible (Pekrun & Stephens, 2012). For example, a student who believes that climate change is due to natural causes but who is confronted with convincing information that a major part of climate change is human-made may be surprised and become curious about this information. Alternatively, the discrepancy between prior beliefs and current information may trigger confusion, and, if the incongruity continues, then this may be quite frustrating for the student. However, if students are able to reconcile these different perspectives, they may be delighted by the solution they found. Importantly, epistemic confusion and frustration are not generated by the topic (such as climate change) itself; rather, they are driven by the cognitive conflict between existing beliefs and discrepant new information.

Topic Emotions

Emotions can be triggered by the contents covered by learning material. Examples are the empathetic emotions pertaining to a protagonist's fate when reading a novel, the emotions triggered by political events dealt with in political lessons, or the emotions related to topics in science class, such as the frustration experienced by American children when they were informed by their teachers that Pluto was reclassified as a dwarf planet (Broughton, Sinatra, & Nussbaum, 2013). In contrast to achievement and epistemic emotions, topic emotions do not directly pertain to learning and problem solving. However, they can influence students' engagement by affecting their interest and motivation in an academic domain (Ainley, 2007).

Social Emotions

Learning is situated in social contexts. Even when learning alone, students do not act in a social vacuum; rather, the goals, contents, and outcomes of learning are socially constructed. By implication, academic settings induce a multitude of emotions related to other persons. These emotions include both social achievement emotions (such as admiration, envy, contempt, or empathy related to the success and failure of others) and non-achievement emotions (such as love or hate in the relationships with classmates and teachers). Social emotions can directly influence students' engagement with academic tasks, especially when learning is situated in teacher–student or student–student interactions. They can also indirectly influence learning by motivating students to engage or disengage in task-related interactions with teachers and classmates.

ORIGINS AND FUNCTIONS OF EMOTIONS: CONTROL-VALUE THEORY

To discuss the origins and functions of emotions related to learning, we use Pekrun's (2006, 2018, 2019a, Pekrun & Perry, 2014) control-value theory of achievement emotions as a conceptual framework. Propositions of CVT explain learners' appraisals that function as proximal antecedents of their emotions, the role of learning tasks and environments, and the effects of emotions on processes and outcomes of learning. The theory pertains to learners' emotions across types of learning tasks. As such, it can also be used to explain emotions during learning from multiple inputs.

Appraisals as Proximal Antecedents

Perceived Control and Value

CVT posits that appraisals of control over, and the value of, achievement activities and their outcomes function as proximal antecedents of achievement emotions. Succinctly stated, the theory proposes that learners experience these emotions when feeling in control over, or out of control of, achievement activities and outcomes that are subjectively important. Perceived control comprises expectations to be able to successfully perform actions (i.e., self-efficacy expectations) and attain outcomes (outcome expectations) as well as attributions of success and failure to different causes. Perceived value pertains both to the intrinsic, interest-based value of achievement activities, and to their extrinsic value to attain success and avoid failure (achievement value) or to obtain further outcomes such as praise from parents or future career opportunities (utility value; see also Lombardi, Heddy, & Matewos, Chapter 20).

Prospective emotions related to future outcomes, such as hope for success and fear of failure, are thought to depend on expectations of these outcomes, combined with perceptions of their value. For example, a student who expects to succeed on an exam will experience hope and anticipatory enjoyment, provided that the exam is sufficiently important to be emotionally arousing. Conversely, a student who feels out of control will feel anxious. *Retrospective emotions* related to past achievement outcomes, such as pride and shame, are thought to depend on causal attributions of these outcomes, in line with Weiner's (1985) attributional theory of achievement emotions. Pride is thought to be triggered when success is attributed to internal causes such as ability or effort, and shame when failure is attributed to lack of ability or effort. *Activity emotions* such as enjoyment and boredom during learning are thought to be triggered by perceived competence to perform the activity and the perceived value of the activity. For example, students can enjoy learning if they feel competent to master the material and are interested in the contents. Boredom is experienced when learning lacks any incentive value, and when perceived competence is either too low relative to task demands (over-challenge) or too high (under-challenge). The extant empirical evidence supports these propositions (for reviews, see Pekrun & Perry, 2014; Putwain et al., 2018).

Cognitive Incongruity

For epistemic emotions such as surprise, curiosity, and confusion, appraisals of cognitive incongruity are relevant. Cognitive incongruity can be due to discrepancies between prior knowledge and current information, between current information and desired information, or between different pieces of current information (Pekrun & Stephens, 2012; see also Muis, Chevrier, & Singh, 2018). Discrepancies between prior expectancies and current information are thought to trigger surprise (Scherer, 2009). Gaps between current knowledge and desired knowledge give rise to curiosity (Loewenstein, 1994). Discrepancies between different pieces of currently available information prompt confusion, if not resolved quickly. As outlined below (section on emotions and learning from multiple perspectives), empirical findings support the importance of cognitive incongruity for the arousal of epistemic emotions during learning. For example, research by Muis, Pekrun et al. (2015) has shown that contradictory texts on the causes of climate change (natural vs. man-made) and its effects (positive vs. negative) can increase learners' surprise and confusion.

Non-Cognitive Induction of Emotion

Learners' emotions need not always be mediated by appraisals. There are two alternative, non-cognitive routes to emotion arousal. First, appraisal-based emotion induction can routinize during repeated occurrence of the same emotional situation. For example, repeatedly feeling out of control and fearful before math exams can lead to the formation of an emotion schema that directly triggers fear upon the math teacher's announcement of the next exam, further deliberation not being necessary. Second, other persons or features of the learning material can directly transmit emotions through entrainment and emotional contagion (see also Loderer, Pekrun, & Plass, in press).

Entrainment is a process through which physical or biological systems become synchronized over time by way of interacting with each other (Trost, Labbé, & Grandjean, 2017). Entrainment drives changes in emotions by influencing physiological and motor-expressive components. Similarly, emotions can be "caught" directly from external stimuli by means of emotional contagion. Emotional contagion is held to be driven by observation and automatic imitation of others' emotionally expressive behaviors (e.g., facial expression; Hatfield, Cacioppo, & Rapson, 1994). Such contagion may also occur in learning environments that allow for learning from multiple representations, such as multimedia learning games in which video- or voice chat-supported social interactions with fellow learners (Admiraal, Huizenga, Akkerman, & ten Dam, 2011) or digital agents (Gratch & Marsella, 2005; Krämer, Kopp, Becker-Asano, & Sommer, 2013) constitute one among multiple available channels for providing content.

Learning Environments as Antecedents

Given the role of appraisals as proximal antecedents, CVT proposes that learning tasks and environments influence learners' emotions through their appraisals (except for non-cognitive emotion induction as outline above). As such, features of tasks and environments that influence learners' perceptions of control, value, and incongruity will also influence their emotions. Relevant factors include task demands and the cognitive quality of learning materials; scaffolding by teachers or virtual agents; support of learners' autonomy; incentives and goal structures in the environment; and social interaction. As all of these factors are important features of tasks and environments providing multiple representations, they will be discussed in the section on emotions and learning from multiple representations.

Functions for Learning and Performance

The cognitive-motivational model of emotion effects that is part of CVT (Pekrun, 2006, 2018) proposes that emotions impact learning outcomes through various cognitive and motivational mechanisms (for a similar view, see Plass & Kaplan, 2016). This idea is grounded in research showing that affective states influence cognitive processes such as allocation of attention, memory storage and retrieval, and problem solving as well as motivational tendencies and behavior (Barrett, Lewis, & Haviland-Jones, 2016). We consider four mechanisms that are particularly important for learning from multiple inputs.

Cognitive Resources

Resource allocation models of emotion (Ellis & Ashbrook, 1988; Meinhardt & Pekrun, 2003) and cognitive load theory (Sweller, 1994) suggest that emotions impose extraneous cognitive load, that is, that they require working memory resources, which are then not available to perform complex learning tasks. CVT proposes a more differentiated view that considers the object focus of emotions. Emotions with task-external referents such as worries about problems in the relationship with a friend disrupt attentional focus. In contrast, enjoyment or curiosity targeted at the learning activity itself may focus attention on task completion.

Findings from multimedia learning studies support this view. These studies indicate that task-extraneous positive emotions induced via autobiographical recall of emotional events can distract attention and impede learning (e.g., Knörzer, Brünken, & Park, 2016). In contrast, positive states elicited by the visual design of multimedia environments can reduce cognitive load (Plass, Heidig, Hayward, Homer, & Um, 2014; Um, Plass, Hayward, & Homer, 2012) and sustain focus on the task (Park, Knörzer, Plass, & Brünken, 2015). One explanation for the latter finding may be that certain characteristics of visual design trigger low-intensity positive moods that increase learners' motivation to stay focused (Park, Flowerday, & Brünken, 2015).

Motivation to Learn

Positive activating emotions (Table 22.1) are thought to promote students' motivation to learn (see also Miele, Nokes-Malach, & May, Chapter 21). Specifically, enjoyment and curiosity can fuel investment of effort in learning tasks. In contrast, *negative deactivating emotions* like boredom and hopelessness undermine motivation. Boredom especially may increase tendencies to engage in off-task thought such as daydreaming and mind wandering. *Positive deactivating* and *negative activating emotions* can have more variable motivational effects. Positive deactivating emotions such as relief over unexpected success can undermine immediate motivation to invest effort, but may support reengagement with the learning task in the long term. Negative activating emotions such as anxiety and shame can undermine intrinsic motivation to learn, but can induce extrinsic motivation to increase effort and avoid failure, which has been observed both in the classroom (Turner & Schallert, 2001) and in multimedia learning environments (Loderer, Pekrun, & Lester, 2018). Anger or envy in response to others' achievements may also motivate students to learn more and outperform peers.

Memory Processes and Learning Strategies

Emotions facilitate different modes of processing information (see also Follmer & Sperling, Chapter 18). Experimental mood research indicates that positive states promote top-down, relational, and flexible processing, whereas negative states lead to bottom-up, analytical, and more rigid thinking (Fiedler & Beier, 2014). One implication is that emotions impact encoding and retrieval of learning material. While positive emotions can enhance the integration of information from multiple inputs in memory, negative emotions can increase accuracy in processing of single units of information (Spachtholz, Kuhbandner, & Pekrun, 2014) but possibly hinder flexible integration of information.

Accordingly, *positive activating emotions* should promote the use of flexible and deep learning strategies such as elaboration, organization of material, or critical thinking. As such, these emotions should facilitate the integration of information from multiple inputs. In contrast, *negative activating emotions* such as anxiety are thought to facilitate use of more rigid strategies such as simple rehearsal. Furthermore, confusion may instantiate critical thinking as a means to reduce cognitive incongruity. *Deactivating emotions* can undermine any strategic efforts, yielding superficial processing. This may be particularly true for boredom and hopelessness. Evidence from studies with multimedia learning environments supports these propositions (Artino & Jones, 2012; Loderer et al., 2018; Plass et al., 2014; Sabourin & Lester, 2014; Um et al., 2012).

Self-regulation of Learning

Self-regulation requires flexibility to adapt thought and action to task demands and individual goals (see Denton, Muis, Munzar, & Etoubashi, Chapter 19). This is particularly important in learning from multiple representations and perspectives that puts learners in charge of managing different inputs. Given that positive activating emotions promote flexible strategy use, they likely facilitate self-regulation of learning. In contrast, negative emotions like anxiety or shame should lead to increased reliance on external guidance, and negative deactivating emotions reduce overall engagement in learning. In line with these propositions, enjoyment and curiosity have been found to relate positively, and boredom to relate negatively, to learners' self-regulation in both traditional and multimedia learning environments (Artino & Jones, 2012; Muis, Psaradellis, Lajoie, Di Leo, & Chevrier, 2015; Pekrun, Goetz, Titz, & Perry, 2002).

Learning Outcomes

Due to the multifaceted influence of emotions on different learning mechanisms, their effects on overall learning outcomes are inevitably intricate. Net effects are a function of the interplay between tasks demands, interindividual learner attributes (e.g., working memory capacity; self-regulatory competencies), and the different cognitive and motivational processes set off by emotion. Positive activating emotions likely enhance learning under most conditions, including learning from multiple inputs. Supporting these assumptions, our meta-analysis revealed significant positive relations of enjoyment and curiosity with performance outcomes across diverse technology-based environments including multimedia environments (Loderer et al., 2018). In contrast, negative deactivating emotions like boredom impede learning (Tze, Daniels, & Klassen, 2016).

Achievement effects of positive deactivating and negative activating emotions are less straightforward. As noted, positive deactivating emotions may reduce task attention and strategic efforts but increase long-term motivation to learn. It remains unclear whether the interplay of these mechanisms facilitates or hinders overall achievement. Negative activating emotions generate task-irrelevant thinking and undermine intrinsic motivation to learn, but can increase extrinsic motivation and facilitate rehearsal of contents, which can be conducive to specific tasks that require rote memorization. However, the modal impact of these emotions on cognitive outcomes from learning with multiple inputs is likely to be negative (see also Goetz & Hall, 2013).

In sum, CVT proposes that emotions are key drivers of learning. However, simply equating pleasant emotions with positive effects and unpleasant emotions with negative effects does not account for the complex ways in which emotions can shape learning processes and outcomes.

Theoretical Corollaries: Reciprocal Causation

The propositions of CVT have a number of theoretical implications for the domain specificity of learning-related emotions, the role of individual antecedents, the regulation of these emotions, and their relative university across genders, contexts, and cultures (Pekrun, 2018). Of specific importance for the role of emotions in learning, CVT implies that emotions, their antecedents, and their outcomes are linked by reciprocal causation. Learning environments shape emotions through individual appraisals and emotional transmission, and these emotions, in turn, impact learning. However, learning activities and their outcomes reciprocally influence emotions and their antecedents (Pekrun, Lichtenfeld, Marsh, Murayama, & Goetz, 2017).

Specifically, success and failure at learning are important informants of learners' control beliefs and the emotions they trigger. Furthermore, in classroom contexts, learners' expressed emotions and achievements can shape the reactions of teachers or peers, including emotional responses (e.g., pity, anger) as well as instrumental behavior (e.g., design of appropriate learning tasks). Similarly, in collaborative multimedia environments, emotionally expressive virtual or human instructors may reciprocate learners' emotions. Affect-aware environments offer interventions designed to reduce maladaptive emotions and foster adaptive emotions based on continuous real-time analysis of learners' emotions (Calvo & D'Mello, 2012). Thus, learners' emotions may affect current representations provided in the environment which, in turn, shape their subsequent emotional trajectories.

EMOTIONS AND LEARNING FROM MULTIPLE REPRESENTATIONS

In this section, we summarize extant evidence on how features of multiple representations impact learners' emotions. We first review studies that focused on effects of combining multiple sensory features, which are often due to entrainment and emotional contagion as discussed earlier. Subsequently, we discuss structural features of learning environments that are likely to influence learners' appraisals and the emotions that are contingent on these appraisals. Finally, we highlight that research has not yet systematically examined how multiplicity and connectedness of representations influence learners' emotions, the study by Schneider, Dyrna, Meier, Beege, and Rey (2018) being an exception. Throughout this section, we use the term "multimedia learning" to denote learning from instruction that uses input from different sensory channels, or input from one channel using different symbolic representations, such as words versus pictures (Stark, Malkmus, Stark, Brünken, & Park, 2018).

Sensory Features of Multimedia Learning Tasks

Visual Design

The basic "look" is one of the first characteristics learners process when they encounter a learning task or environment. Egenfeldt-Nielsen, Smith, and Tosca (2008) argue that visuals "add to the atmosphere, provide a sense of realism, and generally make the world seem alive." In a meta-analysis of emotions in multimedia and computer-based learning environments, learners' curiosity differed across aesthetic designs of learning environments (Loderer et al., 2018). While visual design seems to be a superficial quality, learners may disengage from a learning task if its overall look is unappealing (McNamara, Jackson, & Graesser, 2010).

Basic emotion-relevant features of visual design include color and shape, both of which can affect mood. Um et al. (2012) found that infusing multimedia learning environments with bright and saturated warm colors (yellow, pink, and orange) increased learners' positive emotions and enhanced their comprehension as well as knowledge transfer, in comparison to an environment using grey coloring. This finding which has been replicated by Mayer and Estrella (2014). Children tend to associate bright colors with positive, and dark colors with negative emotions (Boyatzis & Varghese, 1994).

However, other findings suggest a more nuanced picture of the effects of bright colors. Specifically, the color red may signal danger or, in achievement contexts, failure (Elliot, Maier, Moller, Friedman, & Meinhardt, 2007), thus prompting negative emotions. In contrast, green colors can prompt positively connoted associations of hope, growth, and success (Lichtenfeld, Elliot, Maier, & Pekrun, 2012). In addition, there may be cultural and individual differences in color preference (Taylor, Clifford, & Franklin, 2013), such that it may be useful to allow for adapting color schemes of environments to personal tastes.

Elements of shape can also influence learners' emotions. Plass et al. (2014) showed that round face-like shapes in a multimedia learning environment induced positive emotions. This might be attributable to the fact that round shapes resemble human physical appearance and baby-like attributes signify innocence, safety, and honesty (baby-face bias; Plass & Kaplan, 2016). Shape and color may also aid in guiding attention to increase positive and reduce negative emotions by facilitating experiences of mastery and control over learning. This also applies to more complex visual effects such as learning from dynamic, multidimensional simulations of scientific phenomena (Plass, Homer, & Hayward, 2009).

In a similar vein, the visual appearance of virtual agents can impact learners' emotions. This can be done by adhering to general principles of aesthetics, but also by attending to the perceived similarity between learners and the agent (Domagk, 2010). Physical attractiveness as well as realistic, lifelike design and motion can foster positive emotional reactions to virtual characters (Shiban et al., 2015). Agents that resemble the learner in age, gender, and expertise (peer vs. expert agents) are rated as more likable and are evidently more effective in promoting positive emotions (Arroyo, Burleson, Tai, Muldner, & Woolf, 2013). Furthermore, enabling learners to design and personalize avatars (i.e., impersonations representing the learner in the computerized environment) can lead learners to identify more strongly with their virtual character (Turkay & Kinzer, 2014). Fidelity and realism in visual representation further impact the intensity of learners' emotional involvement (Yee & Bailenson, 2007).

Musical Score

Some multimedia learning environments, such as game-based environments, use sound and music to enliven their narrative. Auditory stimuli can amplify learners' enjoyment by enriching sensory experience. In addition, music directly influences emotions through rhythmic entrainment and by triggering associations to real-world events based on their emotional tone. Incorporating audible feedback into the environment may increase the perceived pleasantness of interacting with the learning tasks, irrespective of specific audio qualities (Nacke, Grimshaw, & Lindley, 2010). Husain, Thompson, and Schellenberg (2002) found that when confronting participants with different versions of a Mozart sonata, higher musical tempo increased perceived arousal, whereas mode (major vs. minor) impacted emotional valence. Moreover, self-reported enjoyment as well as achievement on a spatial abilities task were highest for the fast-major rendition, confirming that positive activating emotions are particularly beneficial for cognitive performance.

A closely related design feature is the vocal sound of characters in computerized learning tasks. As summarized by Baylor (2011), research indicates a human (as opposed to a computer-generated) voice can enhance social presence and lead to increased interest because it is perceived as more likable and engaging. Similarly, vocal sounds can be emotionally infectious. For example, an agent articulating excitement over a fun learning activity may lead learners to join in positive emotion.

Much like visual elements, acoustic qualities of learning environments can also influence their effectiveness in guiding attention to important content and emotional events within the environment (e.g., an approaching enemy; Collins, 2009). Explanations that need to be integrated with visual information (e.g., diagrams) enhance retention if presented in auditory instead of visual mode, especially when both sources of input contribute to understanding and thus are complementary (e.g., Fiorella, Vogel-Walcutt, & Schatz, 2012). Sound can further be used to provide performance feedback and to make learners aware of mistakes. Such sound feedback can either be used to downplay failure or to add a celebratory note to success to foster positive emotions.

Features of Multimedia Learning Tasks that Shape Learners' Appraisals

Beyond simple sensory features, learning tasks can be designed to influence learners' appraisals, such as their perceived control and value related to learning. Mediated by these appraisals, such design can also influence learners' emotions and resulting learning outcomes.

Task Demands and Clarity

Perceived control is enhanced when task demands match learner's competencies and when instruction is clearly structured and uses illustrative explanations. In addition, the match between task demands and competencies can influence learners' valuing of learning. Demands that are either too high or too low may reduce the intrinsic value of tasks to the extent that boredom is aroused (Pekrun, 2006). Clarity and comprehension can be promoted by considering known constraints (e.g., limited working memory capacity) and reducing extraneous cognitive load (Plass, Homer, & Hayward, 2009). As comprehension leads to higher perceived control, enhancing clarity should be emotionally adaptive. To promote clarity in learning, instructional designers can attend to principles such as representing key information through iconic information rather than symbolic information which requires more effortful processing (Plass, Homer, Milne, et al., 2009).

Scaffolding

Perceived control is also enhanced when others help learners through scaffolding. Cognitive scaffolding can entail modifying task difficulty, repeating content, providing additional explanations, using advance organizers to structure information and assist navigation in the learning environment, as well as the use of supportive and encouraging messages (Arroyo, Muldner, Burleson, & Woolf, 2014). Metacognitive scaffolding can be used to prompt effective problem-solving behaviors (e.g., providing hints), modify ineffective strategies (e.g., "Let's think again: What are the steps we have to carry out to solve this one?"; Arroyo et al., 2014, p. 82), and promote goal setting as well as self-monitoring. The meta-analysis by Loderer et al. (2018) found that cognitive and metacognitive scaffolding resulted in higher levels of enjoyment.

However, the dosage of scaffolding may determine its impact on learners' perceptions of mastery. Frequent reminders or hints to change one's learning approach may gradually lead learners to rely on external sources of guidance rather than promote self-regulation, which can diminish perceived autonomy and control. As such, intelligent environments that continuously track learners' knowledge levels to adjust and potentially fade degrees of scaffolding, account for individual differences in prior knowledge and learning pace, and intervene only where necessary may be most effective (Janning, Schatten, & Schmidt-Thieme, 2016). In intelligent systems, this can be achieved by implementing algorithms that allow for learner-based problem selection, including open learner models (e.g., visualizations of a systems' learning analytics that reveal learning progress; Long & Aleven, 2017) or sending personalized cues (e.g., "That was too easy for you. Next time, go for a more challenging problem – it's much more exciting and it will help you increase your learning!"; Arroyo et al., 2014, p. 81). Such scaffolds can be used to prevent loss of control when students are overwhelmed by too much autonomy (e.g., due to poor planning).

Autonomy Support

Providing learners with a sense of autonomy over their learning can also enhance their perceived control and any emotions shaped by control. In an experimental study with German 10th graders, Stark et al. (2018) tested propositions of Pekrun's (2006, 2018) CVT. They manipulated learners' control over, and perceived value of, a multimedia science learning task and examined effects on learning-related emotions and learning outcomes. The computer-based task consisted of 11 screens that contained information about the structure and function of the ATP synthase molecule. Each screen contained text and a static picture. Positive and negative learning-related emotions were measured using combinations of the learning-related positive and negative emotion scales of the Achievement Emotions Questionnaire (AEQ; Pekrun, Goetz, Frenzel, Barchfeld, & Perry, 2011). Learning outcomes were assessed with an achievement test.

Supporting CVT assumptions, the findings showed that control and value exerted synergistic, interactive effects on learners' positive learning-related emotions as well as their learning outcomes. As predicted, positive emotions and performance were highest when both control and value were high. Furthermore, positive emotions served as a mediator in the effects of control and value on performance, demonstrating the impact of learners' emotions on their achievement. These findings suggest that providing learners with autonomy by giving them the choice between tasks, or between different strategies to perform a task, can support their positive emotions and learning.

Incentives and Goal Structures

Learning environments can provide incentives (i.e., reward and punishment) that enhance learners' perceptions of the value of learning, thus influencing their emotions. For example, in multimedia learning games, incentive systems can take on the form of progress bars, point score systems, badges, opportunities to change the environment (e.g., appearance of one's avatar), or systematic unlocking of game levels or virtual goods. Because they are typically contingent on learners' performance, these incentives also comprise feedback about individuals' learning progress that influences their perceived control.

Incentives can vary in terms of their instrumental value. Rewards that entail access to additional fun activities or to new levels with new content can serve to build value through intrinsically valuable content. Such incentives may be particularly conducive to increasing enjoyment or curiosity (McNamara et al., 2010). Extrinsic incentives include rewards that enable learners, for instance, to exchange points for changing their avatar, or score tallying for comparisons with other learners through leaderboards. Such external compensation can enhance the value of learning. This can be a helpful tool for emotionally engaging learners who perceive the content as little intriguing, and to build interest value in the long run.

Incentives can also vary in their emphasis of certain goal orientations. Different standards for defining achievement can involve individualistic (mastery), cooperative, or competitive (normative) goal structures. These structures can be communicated through incentive structures (e.g., rewards for individual improvement vs. for outperforming others) and via feedback (e.g., referencing improvement in correct solutions vs. performance relative to others). Incentives and feedback reflecting mastery- or performance-approach goals can promote positive emotions (Pekrun, Cusack, Murayama, Elliot, & Thomas, 2014). Mastery standards and mastery-approach goals are held to be most emotionally adaptive, because they hone learners' focus in on the intrinsic values of learning activities. Nevertheless, normative standards and performance-approach orientations can provide enticing challenge and excite learners to engage with the learning task.

For example, Plass and colleagues (Biles & Plass, 2016) found that administering badges accentuating social comparison (e.g., "You figured out the straight angle rule faster than most players!") can yield better learning outcomes than mastery-related badges (e.g., "You have mastered the triangle rule!"). In the mastery condition, learners reporting high situational interest in the game contents outperformed those with low situational interest. Situational interest did not affect performance in the performance badge and no badge conditions. These findings point to interactions between goal-priming incentives and interest, but more research is needed to clarify these relations.

Mastery-oriented feedback can be combined with control-enhancing statements derived from attributional retraining (Perry, Chipperfield, Hladkyj, Pekrun, & Hamm, 2014). Arroyo et al. (2014) found that focusing feedback on the controllability of learning and the importance of effort (e.g., "Good job! See how taking your time to work through these questions can make you get the right answer?"; p. 81) can reduce frustration and anxiety. Such messages are designed to prompt adaptive control appraisals and thereby increase adaptive emotions. To reduce emotions like boredom, feedback can focus on appraisals of the utility value of learning contents (see Harackiewicz & Priniski, 2018).

Two additional emotionally relevant aspects pertain to learner choice and salience of rewards. Choice between different rewards can increase perceived autonomy and control over learning, but may result in learners becoming distracted by marginal elements of rewards such as modifying the visual layout of the multimedia environment (McNamara et al., 2010). With regard to salience, visually ornate or acoustically augmented extrinsic rewards can enhance their emotional pull, but may undermine intrinsic valuation of learning (Abramovich, Schunn, & Higashi, 2013). Specifically, frequently displaying badges during learning can overemphasize the value of achievement, which can be detrimental to learners who are struggling with the learning task and experience failure. For these students in particular, providing feedback and incentives based on individual learner progress rather than normative standards or raw achievement (see Arroyo et al., 2014, for examples) may be particularly helpful.

Social Interaction

Multimedia learning environments can comprise social interaction with fellow learners, teachers, or virtual agents. Social interaction can shape learner emotions in two ways. First, interaction partners may influence one another by way of emotional contagion and empathy. This makes it possible to regulate learners' emotions through modeling (e.g., enthusiastic expressions such as "This task looks cool!"), parallel empathy (i.e., replicating the learners' state), and reactive empathy (i.e., displaying emotions that differ from the learners' state in order to alter it). The features of agent design described earlier may be important moderators of the effectiveness of such interventions. For instance, realistic agents might provide more convincing role models and thus more powerful interventions.

Second, social exchange may cater to students' needs for relatedness and thereby make the learning task more exciting for learners (Sheldon & Filak, 2008). However, frequent social interaction *per se* may not be sufficient for triggering positive emotions: The perceived quality, rather than quantity, of interaction is key (Heidig & Clarebout, 2011). Supportive and empathic interaction is likely most beneficial. For instance, polite "face-saving" measures such as displaying hints employing collectives (e.g., "How about *we* solve for x?") rather than directives (e.g., "You need to solve for x"; Lane, 2016, p. 51) can elicit more positive learner affect.

In addition, the cooperative or competitive structure of interaction can influence students' emotions by impacting their goals during learning. While both structures may increase situational interest and enjoyment relative to individual learning settings, cooperation seems to be most beneficial from an emotional point of view (Ke & Grabowski, 2007). Competition can induce performance-avoidance goals (Murayama & Elliot, 2012), which shift learners' attention toward potential failure and lack of control, thus increasing the probability of experiencing negative emotions. Moreover, in competitive settings, some learners are bound to experience failure and, as a consequence, negative emotions. As such, cooperative formats, perhaps infused with carefully designed competitive activities, might be most beneficial to learners' emotions.

Multiplicity and Connectedness of Representations

The studies summarized in this section demonstrate how features of multimedia learning tasks can influence learners' emotions and performance. However, research has yet to address the emotional impact of the multiplicity of representations itself. To this end, it would be necessary to compare the effects of single versus multiple representations, or the effects of different combinations of representations. Related studies are largely lacking. An exception is the study by Schneider et al. (2018). In three experiments, learning material was presented that consisted of text and pictures that were either strongly or weakly connected. The first two experiments included instructional texts about South Korea, the third experiment included a text about the human body. The pictures were either affectively positively or negatively charged, and text and pictures were either strongly or weakly connected. As expected, positive pictures led to positive self-reported changes in affect (measured with an adapted version of the Positive Affect Negative Affect Schedule, PANAS; Watson, Clark, & Tellegen, 1988), whereas negative pictures led to negative changes. In contrast, the degree of connectedness did not influence affect. In addition, positively charged pictures led to better learning outcomes than negatively charged pictures. The analyses revealed that this effect was likely due to irrelevant thinking promoted by the negative pictures.

These findings confirm that the affective contents of learning materials can influence both learners' emotions and their learning outcomes. In contrast, the relations between different representations in terms of their connectedness may not exert a strong influence on emotions. Connectedness had positive effects on performance, similar to the effects of positive affective contents, but these effects were not mediated by emotion. It is an open question if such emotional irrelevance of cognitive relations between representations also holds for other types of representations, other types of relations, and other types of learning materials. It also remains open to question if the findings would generalize to discrete emotions that may be more susceptible to effects of connectedness, such as confusion that could be prompted if representations are not well connected.

EMOTIONS AND LEARNING FROM MULTIPLE PERSPECTIVES

Multiple perspectives on learning contents can be complementary or contradictory. The nascent research on emotions prompted by multiple perspectives has focused on the latter case: Contradictory information that prompts epistemic emotions such as surprise, curiosity, confusion, frustration, or delight when the contradiction can be resolved. Specifically, surprise, curiosity, and confusion have attracted researchers' attention. These three emotions are epistemic by definition, because they are specifically generated by cognitive incongruity as outlined earlier.

Epistemic Emotions: Surprise, Curiosity, and Confusion

Surprise is triggered by unexpected or schema-discrepant events (e.g., Berlyne, 1960; Noordewier, Topolinski, & Van Dijk, 2016; Reisenzein, Horstmann, & Schützwohl, 2019; Scherer, 2009). Surprise is likely to be the first emotional reaction to unexpected events. Surprise fixates individuals' gaze (i.e., visual attention) on the unexpected event (e.g., Horstmann & Herwig, 2015), elicits interest (Renninger & Hidi, 2016), facilitates curiosity and exploratory behavior (Berlyne, 1960; Litman, Hutchins, & Russon, 2005; Loewenstein, 1994), and promotes recall of the unexpected event (e.g., Parzuchowski & Szymkow-Sudziarska, 2008).

Curiosity has been labelled as a "drive to know" (Berlyne, 1954, p.187). Unexpected information or events that reveal gaps in one's knowledge arouse curiosity (Loewenstein, 1994). Curiosity is typically viewed as a gateway for meaningful learning in educational contexts (von Stumm, Hell, & Chamorro-Premuzic, 2011) and has been shown to promote exploration of new knowledge (Berlyne, 1954, 1960; Litman et al., 2005) and to enhance retention for new information (Gruber, Gelman, & Ranganath, 2014; Kang et al., 2009).

Confusion arises when learners are confronted with novel and complex information, or when new information is discrepant from previous knowledge and the resulting incongruity cannot be immediately resolved (Muis et al., 2018; Pekrun & Stephens, 2012). Confusion can stimulate task engagement (D'Mello & Graesser, 2012) because impasses (and the associated state of confusion) require active engagement and effortful cognitive processing in order to be overcome (Brown & VanLehn, 1980). For confusion to be productive, however, it is crucial that incongruity is ultimately resolved (D'Mello & Graesser, 2014). One way of achieving such resolution may be to explore or construct new knowledge (Berlyne, 1954, 1960).

Contradictory Perspectives and Epistemic Emotions during Learning

Learning from multiple, contradictory perspectives is a special case of processing contradictory information more generally. In contrast to effects of other types of contradictory information, such as unexpected events, the impact of contradictory learning materials on emotions has received scant attention. However, a few recent studies have focused on epistemic emotions prompted by contradictory learning contents.

Contradictory Perspectives in Social Interaction

Collaborative learning can involve having to deal with diverging opinions expressed by fellow learners or teachers. In two experiments, D'Mello, Lehman, Pekrun, and Graesser (2014) examined the effects of contradictory opinions on learners' confusion and performance. The learning material related to scientific reasoning knowledge, including topics such as construct validity, random assignment, or experimenter bias. In trialogues, learners interacted with a virtual tutor and a virtual peer who either agreed or disagreed with the learner, or among themselves, by providing correct or incorrect opinions. Confusion was measured via retrospective self-report or a more objective measure of learners' confusion visible in their responses to questions on the learning material. Specifically, frequency of incorrect answers after communication of contradictory perspectives was considered as an objective indicator of confusion.

The findings showed that contradictory opinions tended to increase learners' confusion, especially as assessed through the objective measure. The delayed retrospective self-report measure may not have been sufficiently sensitive to fully detect learners' momentary affective states. Confusion, in turn, influenced learners' performance as measured with immediate and delayed performance tests. Specifically, confusion had positive effects on performance when there were contradictory opinions, likely due to enhanced efforts to resolve the contradictions. As such, the findings suggest that confusion can be beneficial for learning from multiple perspectives.

Prior Beliefs and Learning from Contradictory Texts

Muis and her colleagues (Muis, Pekrun et al., 2015) introduced an experimental paradigm that connects research on epistemic emotions with inquiry on conceptual change and learning from refutation texts. In this paradigm, two levels of contradictory perspectives are considered, and the impact of these multiple perspectives on epistemic emotions and resulting learning outcomes is explored. The first level involves multiple *cognitive* perspectives represented by contradictory texts on controversial issues, such as climate change, genetically modified foods, or vaccination of children. For example, in our original study (Muis et al., 2018), participants were provided with two scientific texts arguing that climate change is either man-made (Text 1) or due to natural causes (Text 2), and two texts arguing that climate change has either negative (Text 3) or positive consequences (Text 4). The second level involves multiple *metacognitive* perspectives in terms of the congruity, or lack of congruity, between participants' epistemic beliefs and the task of reading contradictory texts. Epistemic emotions were assessed using the *Epistemic Emotion Scales* (EES; Pekrun, Vogl, Muis, & Sinatra, 2017).

We hypothesized that contradictory texts prompt epistemic emotions, including surprise, curiosity, and confusion, and that these emotions, in turn, would influence students' learning strategies when reading the texts as well as their learning outcomes. Furthermore, we expected lack of congruity between epistemic beliefs and learning from contradictory materials to also influence epistemic emotions. Specifically, we expected non-constructivist beliefs (i.e., beliefs that scientific knowledge is simple, certain, and defined by authority) to enhance emotions such as surprise and confusion when reading contradictory texts.

The findings provided support for some of these propositions. As expected, reading contradictory texts increased participants' surprise and confusion. Furthermore, some of the epistemic beliefs also were predictors of epistemic emotions. For example, belief in the simplicity of scientific knowledge positively predicted confusion, anxiety, and boredom, and belief in the certainty of knowledge positively predicted anxiety and frustration. Epistemic emotions, in turn, predicted use of learning strategies, such as curiosity predicting elaboration, critical thinking, and metacognitive self-regulation. Finally, elaboration and critical thinking were positive predictors of achievement. Metacognitive self-regulation was negatively related to achievement, likely due to difficulties in understanding the material prompting efforts to regulate one's learning.

Using the same experimental paradigm, Trevors, Muis, Pekrun, Sinatra, and Muijselaar (2017) replicated the Muis, Pekrun et al. (2015) study. Again, we found support for some of the proposed links. Reading the contradictory texts again increased surprise and confusion. The epistemic beliefs were predictors of emotions, such as a belief in justification of knowledge through inquiry positively predicting curiosity. Some of the emotions, in turn, predicted participants' increase in understanding. Specifically, curiosity tended to positively predict participants' understanding, whereas confusion was a negative predictor.

In related research on the role of self-beliefs for the effects of multiple perspectives on emotions and learning, Trevors, Muis, Pekrun, Sinatra, and Winne (2016) examined the "backfire effect" that can occur when attempting to change individuals' attitudes. This effect involves strengthening rather than changing attitudes through intervention, and can occur when individuals are emotionally invested in their attitudes. We asked participants to report about their diet self-concept and to read either an expository text on genetically modified foods that presented scientific information, or a refutation text that contained the same information but presented within a format that identified misconceptions and refuted them. Participants who read the refutation text and believed in the importance of keeping a healthy diet reported more negative epistemic emotions than participants who cared less about diet, likely because the refutation text made contradictions between these beliefs and scientific information more salient. Negative emotions, in turn, negatively predicted attitude change after reading, and negatively predicted knowledge change after reading the refutation text specifically. Positive emotions did not predict change of knowledge or attitude.

Finally, Trevors, Kendeou, and Butterfuss (2017) examined the role of emotions in learning from refutation texts. By directly addressing the misconception, refutation texts induce cognitive incongruity, thus presumably also prompting epistemic emotions. The texts addressed common misconceptions that were found to be frequent among undergraduate students, such as the belief that meteors that land on earth (meteorites) are hot; that chameleons change color to match their surroundings; or that reading in dim light ruins your eyes. Using a within-person experimental design, participants read both refutation texts and non-refutation texts dealing with these misconceptions. Emotions during reading the texts were assessed with a think-aloud protocol. As compared with non-refutation texts, reading refutation texts prompted surprise early during reading and enhanced learning. Furthermore, surprise positively predicted learning outcomes and mediated the effects of text condition on these outcomes.

Overall, the findings of these studies suggest that contradictory perspectives can prompt epistemic emotions. This seems to be true both for cognitive perspectives (contradictory texts, refutation texts) and metacognitive perspectives (prior beliefs vs. the nature of the current learning task). Surprise and curiosity were found to have positive effects on learning, whereas negative epistemic emotions can hinder learning from contradictory texts, especially so if these perspectives contradict individuals' prior self-beliefs.

Prior Beliefs and Learning After Unexpected Feedback

Most studies in this field, and in educational and psychological research more generally, have used between-person designs, with few exceptions like the study by Trevors et al. (2017) cited above. However, our theories typically pertain to within-person psychological functioning, such as theories of achievement and epistemic emotions as discussed earlier. Between-person approaches are not well suited to examine within-person functioning, because between- and within-person parameters (such as covariation between variables) can differ widely. By implication, it is imperative to supplement traditional between-person approaches with intra-individual analysis.

As such, and following calls to conduct within-person research (see Murayama et al., 2017), we used within-person analysis in a recent series of three experimental studies exploring the emotional effects of cognitive incongruity (Vogl, Pekrun, Murayama, & Loderer, 2019; for a replication, see Vogl, Pekrun, Murayama, Loderer, & Schubert, 2019). Specifically, we investigated the effects of incongruity prompted by high-confidence errors during a trivia task. The task consisted of 20 questions that relate to common misconceptions, similar to the material used by Trevors et al. (2017) as cited earlier (e.g., "Popes cannot have children legitimately" – true or false?). High-confidence errors are incorrect answers that individuals had believed to be correct, thus involving a lack of congruity between prior confidence and current negative feedback. We examined the effects of such feedback on three epistemic emotions (surprise, curiosity, and confusion), two achievement emotions (pride and shame), and participants' exploration of the correct answer. Multi-level analysis was used to explore the effects of feedback (Level 1: questions within persons, Level 2: persons).

Between-person analysis of the relations between these variables did not yield a clear pattern of findings. In contrast, within-person results were strong and consistent across studies. As expected, feedback on the trivia task induced both epistemic and achievement emotions but under different circumstances. Specifically, correct answers (i.e., success) predicted pride, and incorrect answers (i.e., failure) predicted shame. Incorrect answers also triggered the epistemic emotions surprise, curiosity, and confusion. However, for these emotions, the effects were specified by an interaction with prior confidence in the accuracy of the answer. Surprise, curiosity, and confusion were induced by high-confidence errors; their intensity depended on participants' confidence in the answers that turned out to be incorrect, thus generating cognitive incongruity. The results also shed light on the dynamic interplay of multiple epistemic emotions suggesting that surprise may precede curiosity (Loewenstein, 1994) and confusion (D'Mello & Graesser, 2012).

In addition, surprise and curiosity related positively to subsequent motivation to explore as well as actual exploratory behavior. The findings suggest that cognitive incongruity promotes exploration, and that surprise and curiosity are mediators in this relationship. Confusion also was a positive predictor of exploration. However, the effects for confusion were relatively weak, maybe due to variable effects on motivation. Negative activating emotions like confusion can strengthen motivation in individuals who expect to successfully solve the problem, but undermine motivation and knowledge exploration when a solution seems unlikely.

DIRECTIONS FOR FUTURE RESEARCH AND IMPLICATIONS FOR PRACTICE

Directions for Research

The findings summarized in this chapter provide clear evidence that features of multiple inputs can influence learners' emotions, and that these emotions, in turn, can impact on performance. Specifically, various sensory features of multimedia learning were found to influence affective state, likely due to processes of emotional entrainment and contagion. Furthermore, features of multimedia learning that are likely to influence learners' appraisals, such as task demands, scaffolding, autonomy support, incentives, and social interaction, were also found to influence emotions. However, one caveat is that the extant studies typically examined single features of multiple inputs but did not investigate how they interact in influencing appraisals and emotions. In addition, in a few recent studies on the impact of multiple perspectives on the same topic, it was found that contradictory perspectives can prompt epistemic emotions such as surprise, curiosity, and confusion.

The extant evidence from these three lines of research also suggests that the emotions during learning that were prompted in these ways can influence processes and outcomes of learning. However, so far the number of available studies is too small, and the evidence from these studies not sufficiently consistent to reach firm conclusions. As argued by D'Mello (2013, p. 1083), there is a lot of theory but "a dearth of data" in the field, "leaving many fundamental questions about how affective states arise, morph, decay, and impact learning outcomes largely unanswered ... Systematic research focused on answering basic questions ... is still in its infancy." As such, intensified efforts are needed to understand how emotions relate to learning from multiple inputs. As part of such efforts, research should be conducted along the following lines (see also Pekrun & Linnenbrink-Garcia, 2014b).

First, the theories that guide research on emotion and learning need to be further developed. The available theories need better integration, which may be feasible given that they are largely complementary rather than contradictory. For example, Scherer's (2009) component process model of emotion, models of effects of emotion on cognition (e.g., Fiedler & Beier, 2014), Moreno's (2006) and Plass and Kaplan's (2016) cognitive-affective models of multimedia learning, Muis et al.'s (2018) model of epistemic emotions, and Pekrun's CVT share basic assumptions about the mechanisms that mediate effects of antecedents on emotions, and effects of emotions on outcomes. Theory-building in the field also needs to attend to recent progress in basic research on emotions, such as cognitive and neuro-scientific evidence on the appraisal processes that guide emotion.

Second, many of the current findings need replication with sufficiently large and diversified samples before conclusions on generalizability can be reached. While some of the research cited in this chapter included series of studies involving conceptual replications (e.g., D'Mello et al., 2014; Muis, Pekrun et al., 2015, combined with Trevors et al., 2017), much of the research consisted of isolated, single studies with small, non-representative samples, thus leaving the field in a state of fragmentation overall. Use of small convenience samples and lack of statistical power is a general problem of studies especially in technology-based and multimedia learning, largely due to the costs for conducting this kind of research. Following the models developed in social psychology, organizing multi-lab studies may be a way to tackle this problem.

Third, most studies used between-person designs. Given that these designs are not well suited to investigate learning processes within individuals as argued earlier, future research should make increased use of within-person designs. This is complicated to achieve especially for controlled laboratory studies, given that sufficient a number of measurement occasions need to be available for each participant to render robust estimates for within-person effects. Using small tasks such as the trivia tasks in the research by Vogl, Pekrun, Murayama, and Loderer (2019) can solve this problem but comes at the cost of jeopardizing the authenticity of the learning tasks. Findings on trivia tasks may not be representative for learning with more complex materials.

Furthermore, with few exceptions, the available studies relied on self-report of emotions. Self-report is advantageous as it can represent a broad range of affective and cognitive facets of learners' emotions. For a nuanced picture of these emotions, self-report is indispensable. However, self-report is also known to have major disadvantages. Self-report is subject to response sets and memory biases, is limited to reports about consciously accessible emotion, and cannot capture dynamic processes of emotion in real-time (Pekrun & Bühner, 2014). As such, self-report needs to be complemented by other channels including physiological and behavioral measures.

On a related note, most of the available studies used one-shot assessments of emotion and did not assess the development of emotions over time during learning. Studies are needed that assess emotions in real-time throughout different phases of the learning process. In addition, studies are needed that examine the development of learning-related emotions over the lifespan. The extant studies focused on high-school and university students' emotions; studies should also investigate emotions during learning from multiple inputs in other age groups, using cohort-sequential and longitudinal designs. It would be especially important to analyze emotions and learning from multiple inputs in the pre-school and elementary school years. These years may be critically important for affective development, as competencies underlying cognitive appraisals (e.g., competencies to process causal expectancies and attributions) and an understanding of emotions develop at this age.

Finally, once the role of emotions in learning has been more firmly established, it will also be important to more fully explore the mechanisms that mediate effects. In this chapter, effects of multiple inputs have been theoretically explained by mechanisms of appraisals and emotional transmission, but these mediating mechanisms have rarely been directly investigated in research on learning from multiple inputs. In other words, studies have investigated effects of multiple inputs on emotions, but have failed to examine the processes that presumably cause these effects. Similarly, various motivational and cognitive mechanisms are held responsible for the effects of emotions on success in learning from multiple inputs, but these mechanisms typically have not been directly assessed either. For more fully explaining effects of emotions, it will be especially important to simultaneously consider different mechanisms that mediate learning, as it is necessary to understand the synergistic interplay of these mechanisms to more fully understand effects on learning outcomes.

Implications for Practice

Given the preliminary nature of the available evidence, caution should be exerted in deriving recommendations for instructional design and educational practice. Nevertheless, even if preliminary, it seems possible to infer a number of general guidelines. For example, in terms of *sensory features* of multimedia learning materials, it makes sense to design features in a way that facilitates positive affect through emotional entrainment and contagion, as argued earlier. A range of related design principles can be derived, for example, from the literature on multimedia design as summarized in the section on sensory features (see also Clark, Tanner-Smith, & Killingsworth, 2016; D'Mello, Blanchard, Baker, Ocumpaugh, & Brawner, 2014; Dickey, 2015; Graesser, D'Mello, & Strain, 2014; Ke, 2016; Loderer et al., 2018; Plass, Homer, & Kinzer, 2015).

In terms of the *representational structures*, it is advisable to construct learning tasks and environments such that learners' perceptions of control and value are promoted. The summary provided in the section on emotion and multiple representations suggests that this can be achieved by calibrating task demands based on learners' competencies, thus preventing under- or over-challenge; by scaffolding learner's activities to facilitate the development of competencies and a related sense of control; by providing incentive structures that promote emotional engagement; by avoiding excessive use of competitive goal structures, as these structures can exacerbate failure-related emotions such as anxiety and hopelessness in those who cannot win the competition; and by providing interaction with peers, teachers, or virtual agents to fulfill needs for social relatedness.

Finally, the nascent literature on emotions in learning from *multiple perspectives* suggests that it can be fruitful to provide learners with contradictory information that can stimulate surprise, curiosity, and confusion. However, for these emotions to be conducive to learning, it seems necessary to also provide learners with the opportunity to resolve contradictions. Learners who are competent to self-regulate their learning and integrate complex information may often be able to productively use confusing situations on their own. For others, guidance through scaffolding may be needed to let these emotions benefit learning.

REFERENCES

Abramovich, S., Schunn, C., & Higashi, R. M. (2013). Are badges useful in education? It depends upon the type of badge and expertise of learner. *Educational Technology Research and Development, 61,* 217–232.

Admiraal, W., Huizenga, J., Akkerman, S., & Dam, G. T. (2011). The concept of flow in collaborative game-based learning. *Computers in Human Behavior, 27,* 1185–1194.

Ainley, M. (2007). Being and feeling interested: Transient state, mood, and disposition. In P. A. Schutz & R. Pekrun (Eds.), *Emotion in education* (pp. 147–163). San Diego, CA: Academic Press.

Arroyo, I., Burleson, W., Tai, M., Muldner, K., & Woolf, B. P. (2013). Gender differences in the use and benefit of advanced learning technologies for mathematics. *Journal of Educational Psychology, 105,* 957–969.

Arroyo, I., Muldner, K., Burleson, W., & Woolf, B. P. (2014). Adaptive interventions to address students' negative activating and deactivating emotions during learning activities. In R. A. Sottilaire, A. C. Graesser, X. Hu, & B. Goldberg (Eds.), *Design recommendations for adaptive intelligent tutoring systems* (Vol. 2, Instructional management, pp. 79–91). Orlando, FL: US Army Research Laboratory.

Artino, A. R., & Jones, K. D. (2012). Exploring the complex relations between achievement emotions and self-regulated learning behaviors in online learning. *The Internet and Higher Education, 15,* 170–175.

Barrett, F. L., Lewis, M., & Haviland-Jones, J. M. (Eds.). (2016). *Handbook of emotions* (4th ed.). New York: Guilford.

Barrett, L. F., & Russell, J. A. (1998). Independence and bipolarity in the structure of current affect. *Journal of Personality and Social Psychology, 74,* 967–984.

Baylor, A. L. (2011). The design of motivational agents and avatars. *Educational Technology Research and Development, 59,* 291–300.

Berlyne, D. E. (1954). A theory of human curiosity. *British Journal of Psychology. General Section, 45,* 180–191.

Berlyne, D. E. (1960). *Conflict, arousal, and curiosity.* New York: McGraw-Hill.

Biles, M. L., & Plass, J. L. (2016). Good badges, evil badges: The impact of badge design on cognitive and motivational outcomes. In L. Y. Muilenburg & Z. L. Berge (Eds.), *Digital badges in education: Trends, issues, and cases* (pp. 39–52). New York: Taylor & Francis.

Boyatzis, C. J., & Varghese, R. (1994). Children's emotional associations with colors. *Journal of Genetic Psychology, 155,* 77–85.

Broughton, S. H., Sinatra, G. M., & Nussbaum, E. M. (2013). "Pluto has been a planet my whole life!" Emotions, attitudes, and conceptual change in elementary students' learning about Pluto's reclassification. *Research in Science Education, 43,* 529–550.

Brown, J. S., & VanLehn, K. (1980). Repair theory: A generative theory of bugs in procedural skills. *Cognitive Science, 4,* 379–426.

Brun, G., Doğuoğlu, U., & Kuenzle, D. (Eds.). (2008). *Epistemology and emotions.* Aldershot, UK: Ashgate.

Calvo, R. A., & D'Mello, S. (2012). Frontiers of affect-aware learning technologies. *IEEE Intelligent Systems, 27,* 86–89.

Clark, D. B., Tanner-Smith, E. E., & Killingsworth, S. S. (2016). Digital games, design, and learning: A systematic review and meta-analysis. *Review of Educational Research, 86,* 79–122.

Collins, K. (2009). An introduction to procedural music in video games. *Contemporary Music Review, 28,* 5–15.

D'Mello, S. K., Blanchard, N., Baker, R., Ocumpaugh, J., & Brawner, K. (2014). I feel your pain: A selective review of affect-sensitive instructional strategies. In R. A. Sottilaire, A. C. Graesser, X. Hu, & B. Goldberg (Eds.), *Design recommendations for adaptive intelligent tutoring systems* (Vol. 2, Instructional management, pp. 35–48). Orlando, FL: US Army Research Laboratory.

D'Mello, S., & Graesser, A. (2012). Dynamics of affective states during complex learning. *Learning and Instruction, 22,* 145–157.

D'Mello, S., & Graesser, A. (2014). Confusion and its dynamics during device comprehension with breakdown scenarios. *Acta Psychologica, 151,* 106–116.

D'Mello, S., Lehman, B., Pekrun, R., & Graesser, A. (2014). Confusion can be beneficial for learning. *Learning and Instruction, 29,* 153–170.

Dickey, M. D. (2015). *Aesthetics and design for game-based learning.* New York: Routledge.

Domagk, S. (2010). Do pedagogical agents facilitate learner motivation and learning outcomes?. *Journal of Media Psychology, 22,* 84–97.

Egenfeldt-Nielsen, S., Smith, J. H., & Tosca, S. P. (2008). *Understanding video games: The essential introduction.* New York: Routledge.

Elliot, A. J., Maier, M. A., Moller, A. C., Friedman, R., & Meinhardt, J. (2007). Color and psychological functioning: The effect of red on performance attainment. *Journal of Experimental Psychology: General, 136*, 154–168.

Ellis, H. C., & Ashbrook, P. W. (1988). Resource allocation model of the effects of depressed mood states on memory. In K. Fielder & J. Forgas (Eds.), *Affect, cognition and social behaviour* (pp. 25–43). Toronto, Canada: Hogrefe.

Fiedler, K., & Beier, S. (2014). Affect and cognitive processes in educational contexts. In R. Pekrun & L. Linnenbrink-Garcia (Eds.), *International handbook of emotions in education* (pp. 36–55). New York: Taylor & Francis.

Fiorella, L., Vogel-Walcutt, J. J., & Schatz, S. (2012). Applying the modality principle to real-time feedback and the acquisition of higher-order cognitive skills. *Educational Technology Research and Development, 60*, 223–238.

Goetz, T., & Hall, N. C. (2013). Emotion and achievement in the classroom. In J. Hattie & E. M. Anderman (Eds.), *International guide to student achievement* (pp. 192–195). New York: Routledge.

Graesser, A. C., D'Mello, S. K., & Strain, A. C. (2014). Emotions in advanced learning technologies. In R. Pekrun & L. Linnenbrink-Garcia (Eds.), *International handbook of emotions in education* (pp. 473–493). New York: Taylor & Francis.

Gratch, J., & Marsella, S. (2005). Lessons from emotion psychology for the design of lifelike characters. *Applied Artificial Intelligence, 19*, 215–233.

Gruber, M. J., Gelman, B. D., & Ranganath, C. (2014). States of curiosity modulate hippocampus-dependent learning via the dopaminergic circuit. *Neuron, 84*, 486–496.

Harackiewicz, J. M., & Priniski, S. J. (2018). Improving student outcomes in higher education: The science of targeted intervention. *Annual Review of Psychology, 69*, 409–435.

Hatfield, E., Cacioppo, J., & Rapson, R. L. (1994). *Emotional contagion*. New York: Cambridge University Press.

Heidig, S., & Clarebout, G. (2011). Do pedagogical agents make a difference to student motivation and learning? *Educational Research Review, 6*, 27–54.

Horstmann, G., & Herwig, A. (2015). Surprise attracts the eyes and binds the gaze. *Psychonomic Bulletin and Review, 22*, 743–749.

Husain, G., Thompson, W. F., & Schellenberg, E. G. (2002). Effects of musical tempo and mode on arousal, mood, and spatial abilities. *Music Perception, 20*, 151–171.

Janning, R., Schatten, C., & Schmidt-Thieme, L. (2016). Perceived task-difficulty recognition from log-file information for the use in adaptive intelligent tutoring systems. *International Journal of Artificial Intelligence in Education, 26*, 855–876.

Kang, M. J., Hsu, M., Kajbich, I. M., Loewenstein, G., McClure, S. M., Wang, J. T., & Camerer, C. F. (2009). The wick in the candle of learning: Epistemic curiosity activates reward circuitry and enhances memory. *Psychological Science, 20*, 963–973.

Ke, F. (2016). Designing and integrating purposeful learning in game play: A systematic review. *Educational Technology Research and Development, 64*, 219–244.

Ke, F., & Grabowski, B. (2007). Gameplaying for maths learning: Cooperative or not?. *British Journal of Educational Technology, 38*, 249–259.

Knörzer, L., Brünken, R., & Park, B. (2016). Facilitators or suppressors: Effects of experimentally induced emotions on multimedia learning. *Learning and Instruction, 44*, 97–107.

Krämer, N., Kopp, S., Becker-Asano, C., & Sommer, N. (2013). Smile and the world will smile with you: The effects of a virtual agents' smile on users' evaluation and behavior. *International Journal of Human-Computer Studies, 71*, 335–349.

Lane, H. C. (2016). Pedagogical agents and affect: Molding positive learning interactions. In S. Y. Tettegah & M. Gartmeier (Eds.), *Emotions, technology, design, and learning* (pp. 47–62). London, UK: Elsevier.

Lichtenfeld, S., Elliot, A. J., Maier, M. A., & Pekrun, R. (2012). Fertile green: Green facilitates creative performance. *Personality and Social Psychology Bulletin, 38*, 784–797.

Litman, J., Hutchins, T., & Russon, R. (2005). Epistemic curiosity, feeling-of-knowing, and exploratory behaviour. *Cognition and Emotion, 19*, 559–582.

Loderer, K., Pekrun, R., & Lester, J. C. (2018). Beyond cold technology: A systematic review and meta-analysis on emotions in technology-based learning environments. *Learning and Instruction*, Advance online publication doi:10.1016/j.learninstruc.2018.08.002.

Loderer, K., Pekrun, R., & Plass, J. L. (in press). Emotional foundations of game-based learning. In J. L. Plass, B. D. Homer, & R. E. Mayer (Eds.), *Handbook of game-based learning*. Cambridge, MA: MIT Press.

Loewenstein, G. (1994). The psychology of curiosity: A review and reinterpretation. *Psychological Bulletin, 116*, 75–98.

Long, Y., & Aleven, V. (2017). Enhancing learning outcomes through self-regulated learning support with an open learner model. *User Modeling and User-Adapted Interaction, 27*, 55–88.

Mayer, R. E., & Estrella, G. (2014). Benefits of emotional design in multimedia instruction. *Learning and Instruction, 33*, 12–18.

McLeod, D. B., & Adams, V. M. (Eds.). (1989). *Affect and mathematical problem solving: A new perspective*. New York: Springer.

McNamara, D. S., Jackson, G. T., & Graesser, A. C. (2010). Intelligent tutoring and games (ITaG). In Y. K. Baek (Ed.), *Gaming for classroom-based learning: Digital role-playing as a motivator of study* (pp. 44–65). Hershey, PA: IGI Global.

Meinhardt, J., & Pekrun, R. (2003). Attentional resource allocation to emotional events: An ERP study. *Cognition and Emotion, 17*, 477–500.

Moreno, R. (2006). Does the modality principle hold for different media? A test of the methods-affect-learning hypothesis. *Journal of Computer Assisted Learning, 23*, 149–158.

Muis, K. R., Chevrier, M., & Singh, C. A. (2018). The role of epistemic emotions in personal epistemology and self-regulated learning. *Educational Psychologist, 53*, 165–184.

Muis, K. R., Pekrun, R., Sinatra, G. M., Azevedo, R., Trevors, G., Meier, E., & Heddy, B. C. (2015). The curious case of climate change: Testing a theoretical model of epistemic beliefs, epistemic emotions, and complex learning. *Learning and Instruction, 39*, 168–183.

Muis, K. R., Psaradellis, C., Lajoie, S. P., Di Leo, I., & Chevrier, M. (2015). The role of epistemic emotions in mathematics problem solving. *Contemporary Educational Psychology, 42*, 172–185.

Murayama, K., & Elliot, A. J. (2012). The competition-performance relation: A meta-analytic review and test of the opposing processes model of competition and performance. *Psychological Bulletin, 138*, 1035–1070.

Murayama, K., Goetz, T., Malmberg, L.-E., Pekrun, R., Tanaka, A., & Martin, A. J. (2017). Within-person analysis in educational psychology: Importance and illustrations. In D. W. Putwain & K. Smart (Eds.), *British Journal of Educational Psychology Monograph Series II: Psychological Aspects of Education – Current Trends: The Role of Competence Beliefs in Teaching and Learning* (pp. 71–87). Oxford, UK: Wiley.

Nacke, L. E., Grimshaw, M. N., & Lindley, C. A. (2010). More than a feeling: Measurement of sonic user experience and psychophysiology in a first-person shooter game. *Interacting with Computers, 22*, 336–343.

Noordewier, M. K., Topolinski, S., & Van Dijk, E. (2016). The temporal dynamics of surprise. *Social and Personality Psychology Compass, 10*, 136–149.

Park, B., Flowerday, T., & Brünken, R. (2015). Cognitive and affective effects of seductive details in multimedia learning. *Computers in Human Behavior, 44*, 267–278.

Park, B., Knörzer, L., Plass, J. L., & Brünken, R. (2015). Emotional design and positive emotions in multimedia learning: An eyetracking study on the use of anthropomorphisms. *Computers and Education, 86*, 30–42.

Parzuchowski, M., & Szymkow-Sudziarska, A. (2008). Well, slap my thigh: Expression of surprise facilitates memory of surprising material. *Emotion, 8*, 430–434.

Pekrun, R. (2006). The control-value theory of achievement emotions: Assumptions, corollaries, and implications for educational research and practice. *Educational Psychology Review, 18*, 315–341.

Pekrun, R. (2018). Control-value theory: A social-cognitive approach to achievement emotions. In G. A. D. Liem & D. M. McInerney (Eds.), *Big theories revisited 2: A volume of research on sociocultural influences on motivation and learning* (pp. 162–190). Charlotte, NC: Information Age Publishing.

Pekrun, R. (2019a). Self-appraisals and emotions: A control-value approach. Chapter prepared for T. Dicke, F. Guay, H. W. Marsh, R. G. Craven, & D. M. McInerney (Eds) (forthcoming). *Self – a multidisciplinary concept*. Charlotte, NC: Information Age Publishing.

Pekrun, R. (2019b). The murky distinction between curiosity and interest: State of the art and future directions. *Educational Psychology Review, 31*, 905–914.

Pekrun, R., & Bühner, M. (2014). Self-report measures of academic emotions. In R. Pekrun & L. Linnenbrink-Garcia (Eds.), *International handbook of emotions in education* (pp. 561–579). New York: Taylor & Francis.

Pekrun, R., Cusack, A., Murayama, K., Elliot, A. J., & Thomas, K. (2014). The power of anticipated feedback: Effects on students' achievement goals and achievement emotions. *Learning and Instruction, 29*, 115–124.

Pekrun, R., Goetz, T., Frenzel, A. C., Barchfeld, P., & Perry, R. P. (2011). Measuring emotions in students' learning and performance: The Achievement Emotions Questionnaire (AEQ). *Contemporary Educational Psychology, 36*, 36–48.

Pekrun, R., Goetz, T., Titz, W., & Perry, R. P. (2002). Academic emotions in students' self-regulated learning and achievement: A program of qualitative and quantitative research. *Educational Psychologist, 37*, 91–105.

Pekrun, R., Lichtenfeld, S., Marsh, H. W., Murayama, K., & Goetz, T. (2017). Achievement emotions and academic performance: Longitudinal models of reciprocal effects. *Child Development, 88*, 1653–1670.

Pekrun, R., & Linnenbrink-Garcia, L. (Eds.). (2014a). *International handbook of emotions in education.* New York: Taylor & Francis.

Pekrun, R., & Linnenbrink-Garcia, L. (2014b). Conclusions and future directions. In R. Pekrun & L. Linnenbrink-Garcia (Eds.), *International handbook of emotions in education* (pp. 659–675). New York: Taylor & Francis.

Pekrun, R., & Perry, R. P. (2014). Control-value theory of achievement emotions. In R. Pekrun & L. Linnenbrink-Garcia (Eds.), *International handbook of emotions in education* (pp. 120–141). New York: Taylor & Francis.

Pekrun, R., & Stephens, E. J. (2012). Academic emotions. In K. R. Harris, S. Graham, T. Urdan, J. M. Royer, & M. Zeidner (Eds.), *APA educational psychology handbook* (vol. 2, pp. 3–31). Washington, DC: American Psychological Association.

Pekrun, R., Vogl, E., Muis, K. R., & Sinatra, G. M. (2017). Measuring emotions during epistemic activities: The Epistemically-Related Emotion Scales. *Cognition and Emotion, 31*, 1268–1276.

Perry, R. R., Chipperfield, J. G., Hladkyj, S., Pekrun, R., & Hamm, J. M. (2014). Attribution-based treatment interventions in some achievement settings. In S. A. Karabenick & T. C. Urdan (Eds.), *Advances in motivation and achievement* (vol. 18, pp. 1–35). Bingley, UK: Emerald.

Plass, J. L., Heidig, S., Hayward, E. O., Homer, B. D., & Um, E. (2014). Emotional design in multimedia learning: Effects of shape and color on affect and learning. *Learning and Instruction, 29*, 128–140.

Plass, J. L., Homer, B. D., & Hayward, E. O. (2009). Design factors for educationally effective animations and simulations. *Journal of Computing in Higher Education, 21*, 31–61.

Plass, J. L., Homer, B. D., & Kinzer, C. K. (2015). Foundations of game-based learning. *Educational Psychologist, 50*, 258–283.

Plass, J. L., Homer, B. D., Milne, C., Jordan, T., Kalyuga, S., Kim, M., & Lee, H. (2009). Design factors for effective science simulations: Representation of information. *International Journal of Gaming and Computer-Mediated Simulations, 1*, 16–35.

Plass, J. L., & Kaplan, U. (2016). Emotional design in digital media for learning. In S. Y. Tettegah & M. Gartmeier (Eds.), *Emotions, technology, design, and learning* (pp. 131–161). Amsterdam, The Netherlands: Elsevier.

Putwain, D. W., Pekrun, R., Nicholson, L. J., Symes, W., Becker, S., & Marsh, H. W. (2018). Control-value appraisals, enjoyment, and boredom in mathematics: A longitudinal latent interaction analysis. *American Educational Research Journal, 55*, 1339–1368.

Reisenzein, R., Horstmann, G., & Schützwohl, A. (2019). The cognitive-evolutionary model of surprise: A review of the evidence. *Topics in Cognitive Science, 11*, 50–74.

Renninger, K. A., & Hidi, S. (2016). *The power of interest for motivation and learning.* New York: Taylor & Francis/Routledge.

Rosenberg, E. L. (1998). Levels of analysis and the organization of affect. *Review of General Psychology, 2*, 247–270.

Sabourin, J. L., & Lester, J. C. (2014). Affect and engagement in game-based learning environments. *IEEE Transactions on Affective Computing, 5*, 45–56.

Scherer, K. R. (2009). The dynamic architecture of emotion: Evidence for the component process model. *Cognition and Emotion, 23*, 1307–1351.

Schneider, S., Dyrna, J., Meier, L., Beege, M., & Rey, G. D. (2018). How affective charge and text-picture connectedness moderate the impact of decorative pictures on multimedia learning. *Journal of Educational Psychology, 110*, 233–249.

Sheldon, K. M., & Filak, V. (2008). Manipulating autonomy, competence, and relatedness support in a game-learning context: New evidence that all three needs matter. *British Journal of Social Psychology, 47*, 267–283.

Shiban, Y., Schelhorn, I., Jobst, V., Hörnlein, A., Puppe, F., Pauli, P., & Mühlberger, A. (2015). The appearance effect: Influences of virtual agent features on performance and motivation. *Computers in Human Behavior, 49*, 5–11.

Shuman, V., & Scherer, K. R. (2014). Concepts and structures of emotions. In R. Pekrun & L. Linnenbrink-Garcia (Eds.), *International handbook of emotions in education* (pp. 13–35). New York: Taylor & Francis.

Spachtholz, P., Kuhbandner, C., & Pekrun, R. (2014). Negative affect improves the quality of memories: Trading capacity for precision in sensory and working memory. *Journal of Experimental Psychology: General, 143*, 1450–1456.

Stark, L., Malkmus, E., Stark, R., Brünken, R., & Park, B. (2018). Learning-related emotions in multimedia learning: An application of control-value theory. *Learning and Instruction, 58*, 42–52.

Sweller, J. (1994). Cognitive load theory, learning difficulty, and instructional design. *Learning and Instruction, 4*, 295–312.

Taylor, C., Clifford, A., & Franklin, A. (2013). Color preferences are not universal. *Journal of Experimental Psychology: General, 142*, 1015–1027.

Trevors, G. J., Kendeou, P., & Butterfuss, R. (2017). Emotion processes in knowledge revision. *Discourse Processes, 54*, 406–426.

Trevors, G., Muis, K. R., Pekrun, R., Sinatra, G. M., & Muijselaar, M. M. (2017). Exploring the relations between epistemic beliefs, emotions, and learning from texts. *Contemporary Educational Psychology, 48*, 116–132.

Trevors, G. J., Muis, K. R., Pekrun, R., Sinatra, G. M., & Winne, P. H. (2016). Identity and epistemic emotions during knowledge revision: A potential account for the backfire effect. *Discourse Processes, 53*, 339–370.

Trost, J. W., Labbé, C., & Grandjean, D. (2017). Rhythmic entrainment as a musical affect induction mechanism. *Neuropsychologia, 96*, 96–110.

Turkay, S., & Kinzer, C. K. (2014). The effects of avatar-based customization on player identification. *International Journal of Gaming and Computer-Mediated Simulations (IJGCMS), 6*(1), 1–25.

Turner, J. E., & Schallert, D. L. (2001). Expectancy-value relationships of shame reactions and shame resiliency. *Journal of Educational Psychology, 93*, 320–329.

Tze, V. M. C., Daniels, L. M., & Klassen, R. M. (2016). Evaluating the relationship between boredom and academic outcomes: A meta-analysis. *Educational Psychology Review, 28*, 119–144.

Um, E. R., Plass, J. L., Hayward, E. O., & Homer, B. D. (2012). Emotional design in multimedia learning. *Journal of Educational Psychology, 104*, 485–498.

Vogl, E., Pekrun, R., Murayama, K., & Loderer, K. (2019). Surprised – curious – confused: Epistemic emotions and knowledge exploration. *Emotion*, Advance online publication doi:10.1037/emo0000578.

Vogl, E., Pekrun, R., Murayama, K., Loderer, K., & Schubert, S. (2019). Surprise, curiosity, and confusion promote knowledge exploration: Evidence for robust effects of epistemic emotions. *Frontiers in Psychology (Section Emotion Science), 10*:2474.

von Stumm, S., Hell, B., & Chamorro-Premuzic, T. (2011). The hungry mind: Intellectual curiosity is the third pillar of academic performance. *Perspectives on Psychological Science, 6*, 574–588.

Watson, D., Clark, L. A., & Tellegen, A. (1988). Development and validation of brief measures of positive and negative affect: The PANAS scales. *Journal of Personality and Social Psychology, 54*, 1063–1070.

Weiner, B. (1985). An attributional theory of achievement motivation and emotion. *Psychological Review, 92*, 548–573.

Yee, N., & Bailenson, J. (2007). The proteus effect: The effect of transformed self-representation on behavior. *Human Communication Research, 33*, 271–290.

Zeidner, M. (1998). *Test anxiety: The state of the art*. New York: Plenum.

23

RELATIONAL REASONING

The Bedrock of Integration within and across Multiple Representations, Documents, and Perspectives

Patricia A. Alexander
and
Disciplined Reading and Learning Research Laboratory
UNIVERSITY OF MARYLAND, COLLEGE PARK

ABSTRACT

The purpose of this chapter is to establish the foundational role of relational reasoning in the quality integration of multiple representations, documents, and perspectives. To achieve that purpose, we first explicate the nature and forms of relational reasoning (i.e., the discernment of meaningful patterns in any stream of information). Then we consider what integration means, what it entails, and how it is assessed. Next, we explore the interplay of relational reasoning and integration within the three phases of the Integrated Framework of Multiple Texts (IF-MT; List & Alexander, 2018)—preparation, execution, and production. This exploration was informed by a classroom-based, multiple-source, multimodal activity focused on the controversial topic of the detrimental effects of students' overdependence on social media. The final product of this activity was an argumentative essay evaluated on the quality of integration manifested. Overall, the results of this examination provided support for the claim that relational reasoning is, in fact, the bedrock of quality integration when multiple documents incorporating multiple representations and multiple perspectives are processed.

Key words: relational reasoning, multiple source use, text integration

It is obvious that all advance in knowledge must consist of both [discrimination and association]; for in the course of our education, objects appearing separately are brought together and appear as new compound wholes to the mind. Analysis and synthesis are thus the incessantly alternating mental activities, a stroke of the one preparing the way for a stroke of the other.

(James, 1893, p. 253)

In this chapter, it is our mission to provide convincing and compelling evidence that *relational reasoning*, the ability to derive meaningful patterns from seemingly disparate objects, ideas, or experiences, is foundational to achieving the laudable outcomes described throughout this volume. Whether learners are deriving meaning from multiple representations or multiple documents, reconciling contrasting views, discerning "truth" from fallacious information, or generating a new insight from distinct sources, it is our bold contention that they must ultimately be engaged in relational reasoning.

PHILOSOPHICAL AND PSYCHOLOGICAL ROOTS

While the label we put to the orchestration of mental processes that comprise relational reasoning may differ, other "credible sources" have voiced similar arguments over the centuries. We observe it in Aristotle's *Categories* (Barnes, 2014), as he forwards a scheme for categorizing all that exists, and in Douglas Hofstadter's (1979) Pulitzer Prize-winning book, *Gödel, Escher, and Bach*, as he eloquently establishes the similarities between the mathematical formulae of Gödel, the mindboggling drawings of Escher, and the intricate fugues by Bach. Further support for relational reasoning's foundational nature can be found in the writings of William James (1893), as the opening quote demonstrates. Indeed, it is one of James's principles of psychology that comparison – discerning both similarities and differences – is mandatory for learning.

It was James's assertion that if attention were drawn only to the similarities between objects, ideas, or experiences, then critical differences were overlooked. Conversely, if attention were focused only on what separates or distinguishes one thing from another, a failure to notice what objects, ideas, and experiences have in common would result. Only when attention is directed to both similarities and differences can individuals truly understand how objects, ideas, and experiences, however distant in form or function they may appear, are integrated. Moreover, to James, "the faculty by which we perceive the resemblance upon which the genus is based is just as ultimate and inexplicable a mental endowment as that by which we perceive the differences upon which the species depend" (1890, p. 529). To James's psychological precept, we would only add that the faculty by which individuals *integrate* such similarities and differences into some new representation is likewise an endowment to be nurtured. In our theoretical and empirical work, we regard these "faculties" of noticing and attending to similarities and differences within an informational stream, and then integrating them into a meaningful pattern, as the essence of relational reasoning (e.g., Alexander & The Disciplined Reading and Learning Research Laboratory [DRLRL], 2012a; Dumas, Alexander, & Grossnickle, 2013).

CONTEMPORARY RESEARCH

One need not rely on classic works of philosophy or psychology or writings of a literary genius to establish the significance of relational reasoning to human learning. Contemporarily, the importance of relational reasoning is well addressed in the field of cognitive neuroscience (Baggetta & Alexander, 2016; Holyoak, 2012; Krawczyk, 2012). Consistent with the definition we have articulated in our research, cognitive neuroscientists characterize relational reasoning as "the integration of multiple relations between mental representations," and as a requisite to higher-order thinking and problem solving (Waltz et al., 1999, p. 119). Predictably linked to the prefrontal cortex, relational reasoning is, thus, recognized as an executive function (Chapter 18, this volume; Wendelken, Nakhabenko, Donohue, Carter, & Bunge, 2008). Simply described, an *executive function* is a cognitive process associated with the control and monitoring of behavior; that is, processes needed to achieve desired ends (Baggetta & Alexander, 2016). Basic executive functions that underlie all manner of cognitive performance (Crone et al., 2009) include attentional control, cognitive inhibition, inhibitory control, working memory, and cognitive flexibility.

Within the cognitive neuroscience literature, there are also higher-order executive functions that engage the aforementioned basic processes, but in performance of more complex cognitive acts such as planning, reasoning, and decision-making (Diamond, 2013; Krawczyk, 2012). While the prefrontal cortex remains the focal point of these acts, other brain regions can be implicated depending on the precise nature of the task (Goel, Navarrete, Noveck, & Prado, 2017). Relational reasoning is one of these higher-order executive functions (Krawczyk, 2012; Waltz et al., 1999). It encompasses the analysis and synthesis needed to discern similarities and differences between and among objects, ideas, and experiences. It also involves the integration of individual elements and components into a consolidated and meaningful outcome (Grossnickle, Dumas, Alexander, & Baggetta, 2016), what cognitive neuroscientists describe as *relational integration* or the re-assemblage of components required for problem solution or resolution (Parkin, Hellyer, Leech, & Hampshire, 2015). Certainly, such a higher-order ability as relational reasoning would be indispensable to students comparing written texts with visual displays, weighing claims and evidence in multiple documents, or deciding which position on a contentious issue they support.

DISCUSSION FRAMEWORK

In the ensuing discussion, we systematically craft our case for the foundational role of relational reasoning in learning from multiple representations, documents, and perspectives by first delving deeper into its theoretical and empirical underpinnings. Drawing on our research and that of others, we explore its very nature. This exploration encompasses one of our principal contributions to this domain of inquiry, the various forms of relational reasoning that may emerge when its component processes are fully engaged and ultimately integrated. We also examine how relational reasoning has been measured and how its varied forms can manifest differently in accordance with individuals' level of development, the domain in question, or the task at hand.

The next step we take in constructing our case is to investigate *integration*, which we describe as a meaningful consolidation of elements derived through analysis and synthesis. We view this step as necessary given the emphasis placed on integration in our conception of relational reasoning (hereafter referred to as RR), and the pivotal role such assemblages play in learning from multiple representations, documents, or perspectives. Our theoretical guide for this analysis is the Integrated Framework of Multiple Texts (IF-MT; List & Alexander, 2018). Mirroring the processes of RR, List and Alexander created this consolidation through the analysis and synthesis of various models of multiple source use (MSU) that populate the literature. Our interest here is not the authors' process of model building, which relies on RR, but the specific manner in which integration is positioned within the IF-MT.

Finally, drawing on the preceding analyses, we focus on the interplay between RR and integration required as learners attempt to generate a coherent representation from information dispersed over multiple representations, documents, and perspectives, which we collectively label as information sources. To concretize this discussion, we describe a recent study that occurred in one of our courses that made the bedrock nature of RR and the process of integration it entails all that more apparent to us. We also use this experience to illustrate how and why learning can be precarious even for mature and capable students who must be planful, self-regulatory, and goal-oriented as they navigate a task consisting of various information sources.

CONCEPTUALIZATION AND OPERATIONALIZATION OF RELATIONAL REASONING

Theoretical and Empirical Foundations

Although we offered a brief definition of RR in the opening paragraphs, a more formal definition seems warranted. Specifically, *relational reasoning is an orchestration of component processes purposefully evoked to derive meaningful associations within disparate information conveyed in any modality (e.g., visually, auditorily, or linguistically) or representational system (e.g., symbolic, numeric, or linguistic)* (Alexander & the DRLRL, 2012a; Jablansky, Alexander, Dumas, & Compton, 2016). That is, RR demands both attentional and perceptual abilities to infer relations among lower-order elements and map those relations to higher-order relations (Sternberg, 1977a).

Importantly, it is not only the discernment of relations, but also the capacity to synthesize relations into coherent representations that epitomizes RR (Alexander, Jablansky, Singer, & Dumas, 2016b). This is precisely why the definition of RR under which we operate speaks to "meaningful," consolidated patterns as the expected outcome of the reasoning process (Dumas et al., 2013). Moreover, by encouraging deeper processing among disparate elements, RR is indicative of learning and fosters transfer of knowledge across domains, texts, and perspectives by building connections between prior knowledge and new information (Alexander, Singer, Jablansky, & Hattan, 2016c; Dinsmore, Baggetta, Doyle, & Loughlin, 2014; Murphy, Firetto, & Greene, 2017). For example, in their analysis of the high-school students' discussions in their chemistry and physics classes, Murphy et al. (2017) offered evidence that RR was linked to students' integration of textual and graphic content in readings, their richer conceptualizations of magnitude and scale, and their revision of prior knowledge, including pre-existing misconceptions.

As noted, RR has enjoyed a long history in the domains of philosophy and psychology. Medieval philosophers, including Thomas Aquinas, William of Ockham, and Immanuel Kant, stressed the metaphysical nature of relations, such that relations do not represent entities in themselves, but rather a bridge between entities. This is precisely what is meant when we say that RR demands the identification of patterns "inherently composed of relations among relations" (Dumas, Alexander, Baker, Jablansky, & Dunbar, 2014, p. 1021). The importance of RR was later instantiated in Gestalt psychology (Koffka, 1922; Köhler, 1925) and information-processing theory (Duncker, 1945; Newell, Shaw, & Simon, 1958) that emphasized the role of patterning in perception and problem-solving, respectively. Importantly, both theories positioned the ability to detect and reason about relations as critical for organizing cognitive processes (Newell, 1980). The particular form of reasoning that has garnered the greatest attention in the literature is analogical – the search for relational similarities (Gick & Holyoak, 1980; Sternberg, 1977b). However, this rather singular emphasis on similarities overlooks the essential role that *dissimilarities* play in the recognition of meaningful patterns.

Manifestations of Relational Reasoning

The importance of considering both similarities *and* dissimilarities is evident in foundational studies related to perception (Köhler, 1925; Wertheimer, 1938), assessment (Cattell, 1940; Spearman, 1927), and mathematical set theory (Russell, 1903). Therefore, in the conceptualization of RR, Alexander and the DRLRL (2012a) acknowledged three forms based on the identification of differences (i.e., anomaly, antinomy, and antithesis). An *anomaly* represents an aberration, abnormality, or marked irregularity from an established pattern. Consequently, anomalous reasoning requires the recognition that some idea, object, or experience deviates from other related counterparts. For example, researchers who inspect their dataset for outliers are engaging in anomalous reasoning.

An *antithesis* denotes a relation of relative distinction or opposition, where ideas, objects, or experiences are set in relative contrast on the basis of certain characteristics. We describe these contrasts as *relative*, because even though individuals may verbally treat the ideas, objects, or experiences as dichotomous (i.e., as polar opposites), there are in reality innumerable graduations or variations that exist between them. For example, within the multiple source literature, there are frequent references to credible or non-credible sources or to controversial or non-controversial topics (e.g., Bråten, Ferguson, Strømsø, & Anmarkrud, 2014). In reality, while there are guidelines that can be articulated regarding credibility, there is no definitive way to separate credible from non-credible sources or controversial from non-controversial topics. Thus, when conflicting views or perspectives must be weighed, or when readers must decide whether a particular document seems more or less credible, antithetical reasoning is implicated.

Although *antinomy*, like antithesis, focuses on contrast, those contrasts represent a true categorical or dichotomous distinction (i.e., paradox). In effect, with antinomies, the choices are mutually exclusive with no degrees or variations possible, as there are with antitheses. Moreover, while antinomies are rare in the social sciences, they are often found in the sciences and in mathematics. In biology, for example, something can be either alive *or* dead, a plant *or* animal, a vegetable *or* fruit, but never both. Similarly, in mathematics, a number can either be even *or* odd, rational *or* irrational. Unlike antitheses, there are also no degrees of evenness or oddness, rationalness or irrationalness when it comes to numbers. In each of the aforementioned examples, the antinomous reasoning is evidenced when an individual compares ideas, objects, or experiences and determines their relation to be one of paradox or mutual exclusivity.

Assessment of Relational Reasoning

As with all latent constructs, RR occurs in the "black box" of the mind. Thus, the challenge for those studying this executive function is how to gain access to those processes and document their effects. In a recent review, Dumas (2017) categorized the studies of RR according to their investigative approach. Two of those classifications are especially relevant to this discussion: *in vivo* and *in vitro* studies. *In vivo* studies are investigations where data are gathered in real-time within naturalistic contexts free of researcher manipulation. For instance, studies have shown how engineers or engineering students reason relationally when exploring potential responses to specific design problems by discussing what in the past has worked (analogical reasoning) or has proven unworkable (antinomous reasoning) for comparable problems (Chan & Schunn, 2015; Jablansky, Alexander, & Schmidt, 2018). Similarly, data from residents and attending physicians making diagnostic and therapeutic decisions showed how the process often initiates with a resident detailing the anomalous symptoms exhibited by a patient. The diagnosis continues until an analogous case is forwarded and either accepted or rejected based on antinomous conditions (Dumas et al., 2014). There are also investigations of the reasoning patterns of expert or non-expert meteorologists as they attempt to interpret seemingly anomalous weather data (Trickett, Trafton, & Schunn, 2009), along with an observational study showing students demonstrating antinomous reasoning as they categorize substances as either metals or non-metals following their teacher's lesson on the nature of metals (Sun, Alexander, & Zhao, 2018). In such studies, the primary means of documenting RR was through the systematic analysis of verbal discourse that was recorded.

In vitro research, by comparison, involves some level of experimental control over the context or the content of the study, such as the inclusion of dedicated measures or particular manipulations. One *in vitro* study focused on the role of RR in students' abilities to determine the purpose for and evaluate the aesthetics of familiar and unfamiliar technologies at given time points (Jablansky et al., 2016) and over a two-year time span (Jablansky, Alexander, Dumas, & Compton, 2019). Jablansky and colleagues found that students in kindergarten through 12th grade used all four forms of RR when explaining the "fitness for purpose" (i.e., whether a product does what it was built to do) and "good design" (i.e., whether the product accommodates its user and demonstrates good aesthetics) for both familiar and unfamiliar technological objects. Other *in vitro* studies have used experimental or quasi-experimental paradigms to demonstrate the association between RR and creativity with divergent thinking tasks (Dumas & Schmidt, 2015), working memory via think-aloud protocols (Grossnickle et al., 2016), and mathematical abilities as demonstrated on visuospatial reasoning measures (Zhao, Alexander, & Sun, 2019).

With the exception of the Raven's Progressive Matrices (Raven, 1941), the gold standard among fluid intelligence measures and the principal tool for cognitive neuroscientists studying RR (Prabhakaran, Smith, Desmond, Glover, & Gabrieli, 1997), there were no dedicated measures of RR of which we were aware. Moreover, the Raven's tests matrix analogies only. For that reason, Alexander and colleagues developed and validated three measures of RR to more explicitly assess its four manifestations. Those measures are *The Test of Relational Reasoning* (TORR; Alexander & the DRLRL, 2012b) and the *Verbal Test of Relational Reasoning* (vTORR; Alexander & the DRLRL,

2014; Alexander et al., 2016c), for both older adolescents and adults; and the *Test of Relational Reasoning-Junior* (TORRjr; Alexander & the DRLRL, 2018) suitable for children and young adolescents. All measures consist of 32 items organized into four eight-item scales assessing analogical, anomalous, antinomous, and antithetical reasoning. As with the Raven's, the TORR and TORRjr are fluid ability measures consisting of visuospatial problems. The TORR has been "meaningfully calibrated, normed, and scored in adolescent and adult populations like those enrolled in higher education" and is invariant for gender, ethnicity, and race (Dumas & Alexander, 2018, p. 9). Similar calibration studies are underway for the TORRjr.

Relational Reasoning Summations

To establish RR as a bedrock to integration across multiple sources and multiple representations, we offer the several summations about this process that will serve to guide later discussion of its foundation role in integration. What these summations are intended to capture is how RR manifests in different forms that collectively and interactively underlie the process through which individuals attempt to extract meaningful patterns from the flood of disparate information they continuously encounter. Although that disparate information exists in many forms, we are particularly focused in this chapter on the textual and visual information with which students interact as part of MSU tasks that not only entail multiple documents and multiple modes of representation but also convey different and even conflicting perspectives.

The process of identifying points of similarity and difference within and across information sources is essentially the enactment of RR. When encountering various information sources, students attempting to forge a coherent representation of the information through analysis and synthesis must inevitably identify similarities and differences within and across those sources. In effect, the foundation of comprehending and learning from varied information sources is RR. Of course, it remains to be determined whether students effectively and efficiently use RR in their analyses and syntheses.

The forms of RR frequently work in concert during learning and problem-solving. There is ample evidence that these RR forms rarely function in isolation when complex problem solving is implicated (Dunbar, 1995). Rather, these forms work together in some orchestrated manner to resolve a problem (Jablansky et al., 2016; Sun et al., 2018). This was most evident in the study by Dumas et al. (2014) that examined the collaborative reasoning of resident doctors and their attending physician engaged in patient diagnosis. The researchers described the systematic unfolding of the forms during diagnosis moving logically from anomalies to analogies to antinomies and so forth.

Moreover, the manner in which tasks are communicated can influence students' RR approach. For instance, in their observation study of science and mathematics teachers, Sun et al. (2018) found that the lesson topic was influential to the forms of RR that dominated classroom discourse. For example, when the focus of the lesson was distinguishing between metals and non-metals, antinomous reasoning was frequently recorded. For this lesson, the teacher first demonstrated that heating non-metals produced acid oxide, which turned the pH indicator red (acid). Heating metals did not result in the same chemical reaction, leaving the pH indicator blue (alkaline).

After this demonstration, the students were tasked with testing other materials for the purpose of categorizing them as metals or non-metals. Both in the teacher's demonstration and in the students' task performance, verbalizations revolved around making categorical determinations.

There is evidence of a developmental trajectory in students' reliance on or proficiency in the use of various reasoning forms. In a longitudinal research study, Jablansky et al. (2019) found that even kindergarteners were able to use all four forms of RR when asked to judge the "fit for purpose" and "good design" of particular technologies (e.g., spoon holder). Nonetheless, there was evidence that younger students (K, 2nd, and 4th grades) relied mainly on analogical reasoning, followed by antinomous reasoning, whereas the older students (10th and 11th) showed more facility with anomalous and antithetical reasoning. Other researchers employing alternative methodologies and tasks have similarly suggested that certain forms of reasoning (e.g., analogical) may be less cognitively demanding than others (e.g., antithetical) that require more nuanced judgments of similarities and differences (Alexander, Dumas, Grossnickle, List, & Firetto, 2016a; Gentner & Rattermann, 1991).

INTEGRATION: WHAT IT MEANS, WHAT IT ENTAILS, AND HOW IT IS ASSESSED

Integration Defined

In order to understand the crucial role that relational reasoning plays in the processing of multiple representations, documents, and perspectives, it is essential to delve into the concept of integration. *Integration* is the meaningful consolidation of elements found within and across information sources that results from the analysis and synthesis of their contents. So defined, integration can occur throughout the processing of sources of any form (e.g., textbooks or photographs) and any symbolic representations (e.g., linguistic, numeric, figural, or pictorial). Further, this processing can result in outcomes that are more tacit (e.g., comprehension or confusion; Anmarkrud, Bråten, & Strømsø, 2014) or more explicit (e.g., summary statement or argumentative essay; Perfetti, Rouet, & Britt, 1999).

Yet, regardless of the form, symbolic system, or outcome, there are foundational processes that must be initiated if integration is to occur (Britt & Rouet, 2012). For example, integration requires a level of perception and attention to both surface features (e.g., domain or task objectives), and deeper, less evident components (e.g., authors' message or viewpoint). Attention to these surface and deeper elements are certainly predicated on the knowledge, affect, beliefs, interests, and intentions individuals bring to these sources (Bråten, Britt, Strømsø, & Rouet, 2011; Chapters 20, 21, 22, this volume).

Of course, integration can be facilitated or hampered by the characteristics of the sources, the context in which those sources are accessed, or the task guiding the engagement (Anmarkrud et al., 2014). Specifically, the clarity, novelty, or complexity of the representations, documents, or perspectives can significantly influence efforts to integrate within and across them (Wolfe & Goldman, 2005). As a rule, the clearer, more familiar, and simpler the sources, the more likely individuals are to consolidate information successfully (Braasch & Bråten, 2017). Conversely, when topics or source types are unfamiliar, or if the expected outcomes are novel, the process of integration is likely to be more demanding and the results more precarious (Gil, Bråten, Vidal-Abarca, & Strømsø, 2010). Moreover, if the environment is non-supportive or non-facilitative, then even the processing of clear, familiar, and relatively simple sources can prove challenging (Vidal-Abarca, Mañá, & Gil, 2010).

The Process of Integration

Beyond the necessity of attending to and perceiving features of information sources, there are three core cognitive processes foundational to integration: analysis, synthesis, and cohesion. Drawing on the IF-MT (List & Alexander, 2019), we explore these core processes operating at each stage of the framework: preparation, execution, and production. Although this integrated framework is designed with multiple documents in mind, the components, processes, and stages can be readily extrapolated to multiple representations and perspectives. For example, let's assume that students in a science class are asked to write an explanatory paper on what volcanoes are and why they erupt, using a library of documents that include both visuals and text. In the preparation stage, these students might thumb through the resources to see which might prove useful in completing their assignment – including visuals that might show the parts of volcanoes and even depict the process of eruption. In the execution stage, students might begin to construct their response to the task mentally by analyzing and synthesizing relevant information found in the different resources and in both the visuals and texts. They could determine what complementary or conflicting information in the visual and text pairings should be integrated into the final explanatory paper, during the production stage.

Preparation

The *preparation* stage of the IF-MT is the time when effective learners orient themselves to the task at hand. They may use this time to consider task demands and parameters, as well as assess how their performance will be evaluated (Rouet & Britt, 2012). Learners may also inspect the available instructional resources vis-à-vis their personal goals, knowledge, beliefs, and motivations (List & Alexander, 2017). As this suggests, there is evidence of analysis even within this initial stage. By *analysis*, we refer to the scrutiny or examination of some object, idea, or process that allows for greater understanding of its nature or constituent parts (Meyer & Ray, 2011).

According to List and Alexander (2017), this preliminary analysis of the task, instructional materials, and personal goals and characteristics can lead individuals to assume a certain stance toward task engagement from the outset. Specifically, some may be *disengaged*, aiming just to get the task done with minimal effort or personal investment. Others may find themselves *affectively engaged*, interested or motivated by the task or topic but not cognitively well equipped to accomplish it skillfully or effectively. Other individuals have habituated an approach to processing varied information sources that generally works for them. Yet, those exhibiting this *evaluative* stance fail to implement more cognitively demanding or epistemically competent processes that would be particularly well suited to some specific task. Finally, there are learners who come to a task involving information sources with not only the adequate knowledge of topic and source types and an understanding of the task objectives, but also the interest and personal investment in the topic and task to engage critically and analytically with the content conveyed in those sources. Those assuming this *critical-analytic* stance can be expected to purposefully, elaboratively, and reflectively process content within and across the information sources (Murphy, Rowe, Ramani, & Silverman, 2014). Of course, the products that result from tasks involving information sources should also reflect the extent and depth of learners' engagement during task execution.

Execution

The second stage in the IF-MT is *execution*, where students develop inter- and intratextual links to content conveyed in the various information sources. The execution stage is facilitated by individuals' ability to enact a variety of cognitive and metacognitive or self-regulatory strategies (Rouet, 2006). For instance, execution requires learners to be aware of the content dispersed across sources that may be complementary or conflicting. When complementary, synthesis entails the consolidation or summarization of the information spread across representations, documents, or perspectives (List & Alexander, 2019). However, when there are disagreements or discrepancies found within or across sources, synthesis may not only involve identifying such conflicts but also potentially reconciling them (Barzilai, Zohar, & Mor-Hagani, 2018).

During execution, individuals are expected to undertake four steps that require analysis and synthesis and that lead to integration: (a) identification, (b) separate representations, (c) simultaneous relation, and (d) relational elaboration (List & Alexander, 2019). *Identification* encompasses recognizing specific points of similarity or difference within and across information sources. The integration manifested here is between learners' existing knowledge base and the source content (Beker, Jolles, Lorch, & van den Broek, 2016). Learners also create a mental representation (synthesis) of each contributing source. These individual mental representations are then compared, and relevant relations between and among them are formulated (i.e., *simultaneous relations*). This mode of relational processing is essential for the production stage that follows since it creates a consolidated or integrated view of the various information sources and the specific issues, features, or aspects for which those sources converge or diverge (Wolfe & Goldman, 2005). Achieving this integrated, consolidated view and expanding and describing its nature is what is referred to as *relational elaboration* (Anmarkrud, McCrudden, Bråten, & Strømsø, 2013).

Production

The *production* stage entails learners using the understandings and viewpoints formed in the execution stage as the bases for generating internal and external outcomes (Rouet & Britt, 2012). The internal outcomes that might be realized include increased knowledge of the topics or issues analyzed and synthesized, a clearer understanding of the complexity or diversity of ideas or perspectives that exist, changed or deepened beliefs, heightened emotions, and stronger articulation of arguments posed on various sides of controversial or contentious issues (Perfetti et al., 1999). These internal outcomes can also manifest externally in the form of various products that are often created in response to a specific task. Such products can take the form of oral (e.g., debate or discussion), written (e.g., explanatory piece, argumentative essay, or position paper), or audiovisual (e.g., video or graphic) products that can be shared and evaluated (Segev-Miller, 2004).

Even if learners form viable mental representations of the sources they encounter and produce a relevant relational comparison of those sources, there is no assurance that the product they construct will be cohesive. *Cohesion* refers to the manner in which ideas expressed as thoughts or linguistic units, such as phrases, sentences, or paragraphs, flow from one to the next in a manner that creates a meaningful message (Witte & Faigley, 1981). In effect, cohesion requires not only the synthesis of content across information sources, but also the analytical ability to produce inferences that bridge the informational gaps that will inevitably exist (Stadtler & Bromme, 2014). Where the content in those sources is complementary, cohesion requires consolidating similar information (Britt & Aglinskas, 2002). When the content is diverse or conflicting, cohesion requires making inferences to achieve resolution, reconciliation, or the determination that one source or viewpoint offers stronger evidence (Braasch & Bråten, 2017).

Although the number of information sources examined during execution may be unrelated to the cohesiveness of any production, it could be assumed that the use of more information sources increases demands for analysis, synthesis, and integration, which may indirectly impact efforts to generate either an internally or externally coherent product (McCrudden & Schraw, 2007). If the number or types of information sources do not directly influence cohesion, such elements along with other task requirements may well come into play when products are evaluated. Factors such as task goals and requirements and the intended audience can indirectly affect the level of cohesion manifested in the final product (Coiro, 2003). Nonetheless, how well such tasks are performed will depend on learners' relevant knowledge, goals, and motivations to achieve, as well as how they interpret the task.

We will now briefly overview this process with an example of how learners would follow the IF-MT with multiple representations. For example, if students were presented with a science text that included both a visual and written text on how volcanoes erupt, we would expect them to begin in the preparation stage by considering their task demands and parameters. If the assigned task was to create an essay describing the eruption process, students might be expected to analyze the text and visual to decide how to incorporate the information from both sources into their final product. Now entering the execution stage, we would expect them to look across the sources in order to synthesize the information describing the eruption process via the text and visual. By synthesizing the information from multiple representations, the learner would determine what information is complementary or conflicting within the visual and text pairing. Finally, taking their understanding of the text and visual pairing, the students are able to consolidate the information from both sources to produce both internal (i.e., personal understanding of the eruption process) and external outcomes (i.e., a written essay describing how a volcano erupts) in the production stage.

Measuring Integration

Having explicated the process of integration, we next address how integration in each IF-MT stage has often been measured. Our goal is to underline how different measurement approaches afford different insights into integration during the preparation, execution, and production stages of multiple representation, document, and perspective inquiry. Depending on the stage in which measurement takes place, methods can differ along various parameters, such as overall form (e.g., *in vitro* versus *in vivo*), level of objectivity, or grain size of data. Of course, it is also vital to keep in mind that measurement approaches and what they can reveal will ultimately be shaped by a variety of factors including researchers' questions, the specific textual resources, characteristics of the participants, and the study setting.

Preparation

Although it is certainly possible to assess integration at any point in the process, its measurement is most often discussed in relation to the last two stages of the IF-MT, execution and production (Braasch, Bråten, Strømsø, & Anmarkrud, 2014). This is understandable, given the presence of external behaviors or products that can be inspected and analyzed. Nonetheless, what transpires during the preparation stage merits consideration, as it sets the stage for the execution and production stages and can provide critical baseline assessment data (Bråten, Anmarkrud, Brandmo, & Strømsø, 2014).

For example, during preparation there is opportunity for learners to direct attention to the conditions for integration, such as task parameters, source features, or desired outcomes. Although the results of this enhanced attention could remain tacit, it is also possible to create some external traces of these evaluations, as has been done in the research on task analysis (Cerdán & Vidal-Abarca, 2008), source evaluations (Bråten, Strømsø, & Britt, 2009), and goal setting (Schunk, 2003). Moreover, preparation is the point where learners engage in self-assessment relative to the tasks and resources at hand. This self-assessment is likely to include judgments of cognitive abilities (e.g., topic knowledge), beliefs about self (e.g., intellectual capacity) or about the topic (e.g., pro, con, or indifferent), their specific goals for the task (e.g., task orientation), and their motivations for engagement (e.g., interest).

Again, such self-evaluations may remain internal or they can be captured by means of specific measures or activities (e.g., self-efficacy; Schunk, 2003). In fact, within the literature dealing with information sources, it is quite common for researchers to gather cognitive and motivational data that they presume will have a significant effect on the learners' task execution and the products they ultimately generate (Bråten, Gil, & Strømsø, 2011). Later, performance on these pre-task measures could be used to construct profiles of learner engagement that correspond to the stances that List and Alexander (2017, 2019), describe or those data could be used in analyses of the final products that learners generate.

In fact, many studies have gathered data on individual characteristics, such as prior or topic knowledge (Hagen, Braasch, & Bråten, 2014), achievement motivations (Taboada, Tonks, Wigfield, & Guthrie, 2009), interest (Schiefele, Schaffner, Möller, & Wigfield, 2012), issue-specific beliefs (Bråten & Strømsø, 2010), and epistemic beliefs

(Bråten et al., 2011). Further, these characteristics have been found to influence the processes that learners undergo during the execution stage (Bråten et al., 2011) and to be related to the outcomes generated as part of the production stage (Taboada et al., 2009). In both these areas, integration remains a key to what transpires and what results. The more that researchers can ascertain about participants' individual differences, personal goals and motivations, understanding of task parameters and evaluation criteria, and their initial judgments of source features, the better equipped those researchers will be to interpret what happened during the execution and production stages and why.

Execution

A primary goal of measuring integration in the execution stage of the IF-MT is to identify what is transpiring in real-time while students are engaged in processing multiple representations, documents, or perspectives. Such real-time assessment has been undertaken through a variety of techniques, including think-alouds and eye tracking. Think-alouds capture the integration process by requiring participants to express what they are thinking as they process information sources (Wolfe & Goldman, 2005). Evidence of integration would be found through the analysis of learners' verbalizations as they describe how aspects of multiple sources relate to each other or are in conflict.

Because the process of verbalization of otherwise unvoiced thought processes might detract from the primary integration task, List (2019) constructed a think-aloud variation by having students draw a diagram to visually represent all relations between the given texts as they were reading, rather than requiring verbalization. Another frequently employed method to circumvent the shortcomings of think-alouds is to require verbalization of thought processes only at certain moments, using embedded prompts, rather than continuously (Van den Boom, Paas, Van Merriënboer, & Van Gog, 2004). In addition, eye-tracking methods have been employed to capture the integration of multiple representations (Schüler, 2017), documents (Braasch, Rouet, Vibert, & Britt, 2012), and perspectives (Tippett, 2010). Eye tracking is a relatively non-intrusive measure of visual behavior during execution.

Although there is controversy surrounding whether eye tracking reflects attention, the paradigm assumes that there is an important correspondence between where the eyes look and what the mind contemplates (Just & Carpenter, 1980). However, it is argued that this assumption only holds if the visual stimuli available to participants are pertinent to the task researchers are investigating (Hyönä, 2010). As a counterpoint to this argument, certain *in vivo* researchers using eye-tracking methods have worked to control the process sufficiently to overcome this issue. For example, Mason, Tornatora, and Pluchino (2013) identified three visual behavior patterns during the processing of inconsistent text-picture information that were found to be predictive of recall. These researchers also found that higher learning performances could be predicted by greater integrative processing of the illustrative text, as measured by rapid eye-movements (saccades) between text and illustrations. Also, eye-tracking has been used by researchers measuring integration during the processing of single texts that convey diverse viewpoints on controversial topics with the intention to instigate conceptual change (Broughton, Sinatra, & Nussbaum, 2011).

Prior literature has also shown that different strategies are employed depending on the reader's level of misconception (Tippett, 2010). For instance, increased conceptual change has been linked to time spent rereading sections that were in conflict with readers' misconceptions (Mikkilä-Erdmann, Penttinen, Anto, & Olkinuora, 2008). In effect, changes in conceptual understanding, resulting from processing one text or multiple documents, stand as evidence that integration has occurred during task engagement.

Production

In general, integration has most often been assessed through the analysis of the external products that are generated during the production stage. Such external products can include test performance (e.g., Braasch et al., 2014); written or oral summaries, explanations, or arguments (e.g., Barzilai & Ka'adan, 2017); or conceptual and attitudinal change (e.g., Mikkilä-Erdmann et al., 2008). The nature of that external product is frequently aligned with the assigned task and reflective of reader and source characteristics. For instance, when processing information sources covering similar or complementary content, the assigned task is to consolidate and summarize that content (List, 2019).

Conversely, when the task pertains to a controversial issue or when information sources present contrasting or conflicting content, then integration likely involves multiple steps that can be captured in a variety of products (List, 2019). For one, it is essential for learners to recognize the points of conflict that arise across the information sources and the contrasting orientations that represent these alternative views (Barzilai & Ka'adan, 2017). Whether required by the task or not, learners will likely position themselves with regard to the various views being conveyed and weigh the arguments and evidence in the information sources through that filter. Frequently, integration tasks require an argumentative essay, particularly when refutational text or multiple texts offering different views on a controversial issue must be integrated (Anmarkrud et al., 2013). These essays often require students to state their position on the central topic and to support their position with evidence from the sources. It is also common to require some acknowledgment of opposing or alternative arguments and to critique the nature of the evidence referenced in the sources, and to identify alternative scopes that might emerge around the key points.

A FOUNDATION OF RELATIONAL REASONING WITHIN INTEGRATION

To wed RR more concretely to integration of multiple information sources, we situate the prior discussion in the context of an MSU study conducted in the first author's undergraduate class. This study is particularly relevant to our discussion because there were not only multiple documents involved, but also multiple representations and perspectives on a controversial issue (Singh, Sun, & Zhao, 2019). Further, in this study, it was evident that multiple forms of RR worked in concert to enable students to identify similarities and differences within and across multiple information sources, representations, and perspectives, as well as between their existing knowledge and beliefs and the new and sometimes conflicting information they encountered. Here, we draw on the findings of this naturally occurring investigation to illustrate how RR underlies analysis, synthesis, and cohesion at each stage of the IF-MT framework (List & Alexander, 2019).

In this study, 114 undergraduates enrolled in an educational psychology course completed an MSU task addressing the controversial claim that: *Students today are overly dependent on technology to the detriment of their social, physical, emotional, and academic well-being.* Prior to the study, students' RR capacities were measured using the TORR (Alexander, 2012b; Alexander et al., 2016a). At the outset of the task, students indicated their initial position on this controversial topic on a 100mm line from strongly agree to strongly disagree, and briefly justified that position. Next, they were presented with a library of sources that resembled a Google search page. The library included ten documents that varied in terms of perspectives (pro, con, and neutral), source credibility (e.g., scientific reports, personal blogs), and information representations (e.g., text, graphics). They were directed to (a) select at least four documents to process in depth; (b) highlight information they deemed trustworthy and untrustworthy; and (c) judge the credibility and usefulness of each source they used. At the conclusion of this phase, students indicated their final position on the claim and composed an argumentative essay. As we will illustrate, the task features (e.g., claim and sources) and directives (e.g., number of sources and final product) shaped how RR was enacted and entwined with integration at each stage.

Preparation

In the preparation stage, RR manifested as students analyzed the task features and requirements. Their prior knowledge and beliefs were reflected in the frequency and forms of RR enacted. For instance, although students were not explicitly told to look for opposing views, their prior experiences with argumentation may have signaled the importance of justifying claims with evidence from the readings and acknowledging counterarguments. Thus, students' search and processing behaviors (e.g., time spent on each document, access to documents with similar or different perspectives to their own, access to documents of high or low source credibility) suggested that they initially scanned multiple documents to locate several that presented opposing views and seemed credible before they decided which sources merited further reading. Such a comparison among sources is certainly indicative of RR.

Moreover, we found evidence of the initial stances that List and Alexander (2017, 2019), described. For instance, certain "disengaged" students chose the minimum or fewer documents without even a cursory survey of their contents or credibility; more "evaluative" students started out with strong initial beliefs on the topic and chose documents and content that supported that position while disputing any counterarguments. It was students exhibiting a more critical-analytic stance that took time to peruse more documents than required and selected those higher in credibility. They were also as likely to counter as to support their initial views. Interestingly, students who showed higher degrees of position change after reading also scored higher on the TORR, which supports this critical-analytic stance.

Execution

The role of RR was more evident in the execution stage. For students, this stage involved the continuous process of (a) sculpting and resculpting mental representations from the stream of information within the multimodal documents; (b) recognizing conflicting views and evidence; and (c) judging content against their prior knowledge and beliefs – all of which require thinking relationally. In the notes students took while reading, we saw evidence of the comparisons and contrasts they made across documents, and between the ideas in those documents and their own beliefs, illustrating analogical and antithetical reasoning. Further, students' ratings of the sources read in terms of credibility and usefulness were signs of antithetical reasoning. For instance, one student, Justin[1] rated an article from a shoddy source with alarmist claims and dubious evidence as low on overall credibility and usefulness (37 and 61 points, respectively, on the 0–100 scale) and gauged another from a well-known press agency, describing the results of a recent research study, as high for credibility and usefulness (70 and 85 points, respectively). By doing so, he was essentially enacting antithetical reasoning to position these articles on opposite ends of the continua of credibility and usefulness.

As students read the documents, they could highlight specific content (e.g., source information, sentences, graphics) they deemed particularly trustworthy in green or untrustworthy in red. Their employment of antinomous reasoning manifests as they make dichotomous judgments about the trustworthiness of specific information. We noticed that some students tended to judge concrete data (e.g., statistics from national surveys) and specific research results as trustworthy, whereas unsubstantiated opinions and anecdotal quotes were more likely marked as untrustworthy. Additionally, in some cases, claims incorrectly substantiated by credible pieces of evidence were called out as such, as students employed antinomous reasoning to discern logical fallacies in argumentation. This was evident, for instance, when Justin highlighted a statistic ("the majority of Americans had a cell phone by the end of 2012, according to the Pew Center") as trustworthy but marked the claim directly following from it which tried to attribute increasing loneliness to increased cell phone use as untrustworthy ("… the pattern of loneliness begins to increase around 2012").

We also observed that some students were highly attuned to the logical structure of the articles, symbolically representing the flow of claims, counterarguments, and evidence in their written notes. Occasionally these students noted inconsistent or incompatible statements made within and across the documents, exhibiting anomalous and antinomous reasoning in the process. These patterns of analysis were also seen in comments pertaining to the visual and textual content within the multimodal documents. For example, some students processed information from a graph about a decrease in teenage drinking over the years and evaluated the data in relation to the text that claimed technology is positively impacting teenagers by reducing hedonistic tendencies. They used antinomous reasoning to conclude that correlation is not causation. One student, Katie, for example, made a note in her journal after taking down a claim from an article that linked social media use to loneliness, that "can't absolutely prove causation."

As we came to recognize in this study, analysis and synthesis go hand-in-hand. Specifically, even as the students were reading and comprehending the individual sources or portions of those sources (analysis), they were integrating within and across sources and identifying similarities and differences in the ideas and perspectives conveyed (synthesis). This interplay of analysis and synthesis is predicated on RR, since the students must discern patterns, categorize, and agglomerate information in a strategic and purposeful manner (Grossnickle et al., 2016). We found evidence to support this contention in students' written notes. For example, some students indicated in their notes whether the overall stance of particular documents was more pro or con technology. Some even organized the sources they read into pro or con groups in their journals. There were also those students who made judgments about stance at the level of content and not at the document level. Specifically, these students noted whether a particular statement that they copied or paraphrased in their notes could be used to support or refute the claim statement.

RR also manifested in students' monitoring behaviors during reading. Some students reported that the articles they initially chose lacked credibility or inadequately addressed the topic, so they went back and selected more credible or informative ones. Such reassessment and reselection would seem contingent on the students' comparative analysis of the sources and their content (i.e., their RR).

Production

The foundational nature of RR to integration was most clearly evident in the production stage. It is here that students externalized the mental representations built in the execution stage in the form of argumentative essays. To evaluate their essays, we created a rubric that included both global components core to integration (i.e., critical analysis, synthesis, and cohesion) and task-specific parameters (i.e., stating a claim, providing justifications, considering counterarguments, and writing well). Each global component and task-specific parameter was evaluated for its manifest quality on a 0 to 2 scale. A score of 0 represented omission or very poor response quality (e.g., no consideration of counterarguments; disconnected paragraphs; or poor flow across paragraphs). A score of 1 indicated that the component was addressed but in a marginally clear or unelaborated way (e.g., justification attempted but not fully elaborated or clearly explanatory; limited critical analysis manifested as superficial treatment or limited critical evaluation of sources or information from sources). Finally, a score of 2 indicated that the specific component or parameters had been well-addressed (e.g., a well-articulated claim statement; clear evidence of synthesis of information from sources within and across paragraphs). In light of the elements within the rubric and the different levels of quality represented, we used the summed score for the components and parameters as our measure of integration.

It was our determination that RR was integral to the aforementioned global components and the task-specific parameters, and was, thus, the bedrock for a well-executed argumentative essay involving sources that were multimodal and that varied in perspective. As evidence of this claim, we present an exemplary argumentative essay from the MSU project. In our exemplary case, the student, Marisa, drew from five sources (more than the four required) representing differing perspectives to support her claim that today's students are overly dependent on technology to the detriment of their well-being. At the document level, her essay was highly cohesive. She wove evidence extracted from the various sources into her essay that she organized around social, physical, emotional, and academic impacts of technology, respectively. She moved seamlessly between the pros and cons of technology within each of these areas, while ensuring that her claim of detrimental effects was more strongly supported. The smooth transition of ideas within and across paragraphs and the coordination of pro and con evidence would not be possible if Marisa had not reasoned relationally. Moreover, the quality of Marisa's production rested upon analysis and synthesis of the sources and content, which also required RR.

For instance, identifying areas that supported one position or another across the documents required recognizing patterns of similarities (i.e., analogical reasoning). In one case, Marisa reported findings from a PISA survey stating that "the percentage of 15-year-olds that say it is easy to make friends has decreased" and connected it to a psychologist's opinion that students are losing opportunities to make emotional bonds due to increasing use of social media. Also, Marisa's attention to opposing views on the topic was evidence of antithetical reasoning. In one such case, having made the point in one paragraph that "technology [negatively] impacts how a person is physically," she quickly moved to discuss the oppositional view in the subsequent paragraph: "However, articles have shown that not all the physical impacts of technology are negative." Similarly, after citing research supporting the enhancement of companionship between friends due to 24/7 online contact, Marisa immediately turned to other data in the same article that countered this claim: "However, in the same article it is discussed how technology can have harmful impacts on friendships in that rumors ... can be spread much more quickly."

Further, Marisa refuted authors' counterarguments by noting the untrustworthiness of their data or their lack of sound logic. Such processes demonstrate her antinomous reasoning. In several places, she rebutted the authors' opposing views by highlighting their error of drawing causal conclusions from correlational data. This discernment of ontological boundaries between correlation and causation was a display of antinomous reasoning. For example, one author claimed that the rise of technology has led to decreases in the rate of teenagers' risky behaviors. She countered this claim by saying that "While this does seem to be positive in that students are not spending their free time drinking heavily, smoking, ... these are correlations and thus it cannot be determined that because of technology these risky behaviors have gone down." Additionally, the relegation of evidence from the various sources into the categories of social, emotional, and physical impacts of technology that formed her essay's overall organizational structure also required antinomous reasoning.

Marisa's ability to spot opinions in the documents that were aberrant when examined against her relevant knowledge was indicative of anomalous reasoning. In one instance, she provided an alternate explanation for a trend in the data than the one offered by the author: "the percentage of 25- to 34-year-olds with tertiary degrees has risen from 26% to 43%. This phenomenon could be [due to the] high demand of employers looking for employees to have ... higher education rather than the increase in technology." The authors' explanation was unsatisfactory in her judgment precisely because it did not fit with her knowledge on the topic. She recognized the author's position on this matter as anomalous.

Further support for the foundational role of RR to integration came from our quantitative analyses. We examined how students' TORR performance was related to the quality of integration they manifested on the argumentative essay, and to their execution of the concomitant processes of critical analysis, synthesis, and cohesion. What we determined was that critical analysis was positively correlated with overall RR ability, and specifically to students' performance on the analogy and antithesis scales. Further, we used Bayesian Network analysis to model the process entailed in creating of a well-integrated essay. Based on theory, we created a network that represented the interrelations among the various task parameters and integration components and their conditional dependence on each other. We found that the probability of achieving higher levels of synthesis and overall cohesion on the essays increased when critical analysis was strong.

Based on the aforementioned analyses, we concluded that critical analysis was crucial to constructing a well-integrated argumentative essay. We also determined that the connection between RR and critical analysis was particularly salient to producing a quality argumentative essay. We also found that students with higher antithetical reasoning ability cited more documents that disagreed with their initial positions on the issue. Moreover, the overall level of detail that accompanied citations to particular sources (e.g., citing specific data versus a cursory mention of a document) was positively associated with students' RR capacity, particularly their level of analogical and antinomous reasoning. Additionally, students who were more detail-oriented in their citations also produced better-integrated essays. It may be that higher RR capability allowed students to grasp critical similarities and differences conveyed in the multiple sources. The mental patterns they thus formed of pro/con and credible/non-credible sources and evidence could then serve as the basis for a well-integrated argumentative essay that sought to support or refute the central claim for this MSU task (i.e., the detrimental effects of students' over-dependency on technology). In our judgment, these findings from this MSU task support our contention that RR in its various manifestations is foundational to students' engagement with multiple and multimodal documents that represent contrasting views or that convey conflicting evidence on a topic.

CONCLUDING THOUGHTS

In this chapter, it was our goal to forward and substantiate the claim that relational reasoning is an essential cognitive capability that allows individuals to derive meaning from information dispersed across multiple sources and conveyed by diverse modalities. It was also our contention that relational reasoning is implicated whenever conflicting or opposing viewpoints are encountered and solution or resolution is sought. Specifically, through "incessantly alternating mental activities" of analysis and synthesis (James, 1893, p. 253) – attending to similarities and dissimilarities – those engaged with multiple representations, documents, and perspectives achieve deeper understanding. That deeper understanding is then brought to bear when a meaningful consolidation or integration takes form, either internally as a mental representation or externally as a demonstrable product. Given the historical and contemporary theories proffered, findings from empirical research summarized, and the outcomes from a particular ecologically-valid study conducted, we feel that our goal has been achieved and our claim upheld. Further, we hope that readers, considering the arguments and evidence we have presented, will agree.

AUTHOR NOTES

Direct correspondence to Patricia A. Alexander, Department of Human Development and Quantitative Methodology, University of Maryland, College Park MD 20742-1131, 301-405-2821, palexand@umd.edu, ORCID: 0000-0001-7060-2582.

Contributors to this chapter include Jannah Fusenig, Sophie Jablansky, Eric Schoute, Anisha Singh, Yuting Sun, Lauren Singer Trakhman, Julianne van Meerten, and Hongyang Zhao.

NOTES

1. Pseudonyms are used for specific students in the study.

REFERENCES

Alexander, P. A. & the Disciplined Reading and Learning Research Laboratory. (2012a). Reading into the future: Competence for the 21st century. *Educational Psychologist, 47*, 259–280. doi:10.1080/00461520.2012.722511

Alexander, P. A. & the Disciplined Reading and Learning Research Laboratory (2012b). Test of Relational Reasoning. College Park, MD: University of Maryland.

Alexander, P. A. & the Disciplined Reading and Learning Research Laboratory (2014). *Verbal* Test of Relational Reasoning. College Park, MD: University of Maryland.

Alexander, P. A. & the Disciplined Reading and Learning Research Laboratory (2018). Test of Relational Reasoning-Junior. College Park, MD: University of Maryland.

Alexander, P. A., Dumas, D., Grossnickle, E. M., List, A., & Firetto, C. M. (2016a). Measuring relational reasoning. *Journal of Experimental Education, 84*, 119–151. doi:10.1080/00220973.2014.963216

Alexander, P. A., Jablansky, S., Singer, L. M., & Dumas, D. (2016b). Relational reasoning: What we know and why it matters. *Policy Insights from the Behavioral and Brain Sciences, 3*(1), 36–44. doi:10.1177/2372732215622029

Alexander, P. A., Singer, L. M., Jablansky, S., & Hattan, C. (2016c). Relational reasoning in word and in figure. *Journal of Educational Psychology, 108*, 1140–1152. doi:10.1037/edu0000110

Anmarkrud, Ø., Bråten, I., & Strømsø, H. I. (2014). Multiple-documents literacy: Strategic processing, source awareness, and argumentation when reading multiple conflicting documents. *Learning and Individual Differences, 30*, 64–76. doi:10.1016/j.lindif.2013.01.007

Anmarkrud, Ø., McCrudden, M. T., Bråten, I., & Strømsø, H. I. (2013). Task-oriented reading of multiple documents: Online comprehension processes and offline products. *Instructional Science, 41*(5), 873–894. doi:10.1007/s11251-013-9263-8

Baggetta, P., & Alexander, P. A. (2016). Conceptualization and operationalization of executive function. *Mind, Brain and Education, 10*, 10–33. doi:10.1111/mbe.12100

Barnes, J. (Ed.). (2014). *Complete works of Aristotle: The revised Oxford translation* (vol. 1). Princeton, NJ: Princeton University Press.

Barzilai, S., & Ka'adan, I. (2017). Learning to integrate divergent information sources: The interplay of epistemic cognition and epistemic metacognition. *Metacognition and Learning, 12*(2), 193–232. doi:10.1007/s11409-016-9165-7

Barzilai, S., Zohar, A. R., & Mor-Hagani, S. (2018). Promoting integration of multiple texts: A review of instructional approaches and practices. *Educational Psychology Review, 30*(3), 973–999. doi:10.1007/s10648-018-9436-8

Beker, K., Jolles, D., Lorch, R. F., & van den Broek, P. (2016). Learning from texts: Activation of information from previous texts during reading. *Reading and Writing, 29*(6), 1161–1178. doi:10.1007/s11145-016-9630-3

Braasch, J. L. G., & Bråten, I. (2017). The Discrepancy-Induced Source Comprehension (D-ISC) model: Basic assumptions and preliminary evidence. *Educational Psychologist, 52*, 167–181. doi:10.1080/00461520.2017.1323219

Braasch, J. L. G., Bråten, I., Strømsø, H. I., & Anmarkrud, Ø. (2014). Incremental theories of intelligence predict multiple-documents comprehension. *Learning and Individual Differences, 31*, 11–20. doi:10.1016/j.lindif.2013.12.012

Braasch, J. L. G., Rouet, J. F., Vibert, N., & Britt, M. A. (2012). Readers' use of source information in text comprehension. *Memory and Cognition, 40*(3), 450–465. doi:10.2758/s13421-011-0160-6

Bråten, I., Anmarkrud, Ø., Brandmo, C., & Strømsø, H. I. (2014). Developing and testing a model of direct and indirect relationships between individual differences, processing, and multiple-text comprehension. *Learning and Instruction, 30*, 9–24. doi:10.1016/j.learninstruc.2013.11.002

Bråten, I., Britt, M. A., Strømsø, H. I., & Rouet, J. F. (2011). The role of epistemic beliefs in the comprehension of multiple expository texts: Toward an integrated model. *Educational Psychologist, 46*(1), 48–70. doi:10.1080/00461520.2011.538647

Bråten, I., Ferguson, L. E., Strømsø, H. I., & Anmarkrud, Ø. (2014). Students working with multiple conflicting documents on a scientific issue: Relations between epistemic cognition while reading and sourcing and argumentation in essays. *British Journal of Educational Psychology, 84*, 58–85. doi:10.1111/bjep.12005

Bråten, I., Gil, L., & Strømsø, H. I. (2011). The role of different task instruction and reader characteristics when learning from multiple expository texts. In G. Schraw, M. T. McCrudden, & J. P. Magliano (Eds.), *Text relevance and learning from text* (pp. 95–122). Charlotte, NC: Information Age Pub.

Bråten, I., & Strømsø, H. I. (2010). When law students read multiple documents about global warming: Examining the role of topic-specific beliefs about the nature of knowledge and knowing. *Instructional Science, 38*(6), 635–657. doi:10.1007/s11251-008-9091-4

Bråten, I., Strømsø, H. I., & Britt, M. A. (2009). Trust matters: Examining the role of source evaluation in students' construction of meaning within and across multiple texts. *Reading Research Quarterly, 44*(1), 6–28. doi:10.1598/RRQ.44.1.1

Britt, M. A., & Aglinskas, C. (2002). Improving students' ability to identify and use source information. *Cognition and Instruction, 20*(4), 485–522. doi:10.1207/S1532690XCI2004_2

Britt, M. A., & Rouet, J.-F. (2012). Learning with multiple documents: Component skills and their acquisition. In M. J. Lawson & J. R. Kirby (Eds.), *Enhancing the quality of learning: Dispositions, instruction, and learning processes* (pp. 276–314). New York: Cambridge University Press.

Broughton, S. H., Sinatra, G. M., & Nussbaum, E. M. (2011). "Pluto has been a planet my whole life!" emotions, attitudes, and conceptual change in elementary students' learning about pluto's reclassification. *Research in Science Education, 43*(2), 529–550. doi:10.1007/s11165-011-9274-x

Cattell, R. B. (1940). A culture-free intelligence test. I. *Journal of Educational Psychology, 31*, 161–179. doi:10.1037/h0059043

Cerdán, R., & Vidal-Abarca, E. (2008). The effects of tasks on integrating information from multiple documents. *Journal of Educational Psychology, 100*(1), 209–222. doi:10.1037/0022-0663.100.1.209

Chan, J., & Schunn, C. (2015). The impact of analogies on creative concept generation: Lessons from an in vivo study in engineering design. *Cognitive Science, 39*, 126–155. doi:10.1111/cogs.12127

Coiro, J. (2003). Exploring literacy on the internet: Reading comprehension on the internet: Expanding our understanding of reading comprehension to encompass new literacies. *The Reading Teacher, 56*(5), 458–565. doi:10.2307/20205224

Crone, E. A., Wendelken, C., Van Leijenhorst, L., Honomichl, R. D., Christoff, K., & Bunge, S. A. (2009). Neurocognitive development of relational reasoning. *Developmental Science, 12*, 55–66. doi:10.1111/j.1467-7687.2008.00743.x

Diamond, A. (2013). Executive functions. *Annual Review of Psychology, 64*, 135–168. doi:10.1146/annurev-psych-113011-143750

Dinsmore, D. L., Baggetta, P., Doyle, S., & Loughlin, S. M. (2014). The role of initial learning, problem features, prior knowledge, and pattern recognition on transfer success. *Journal of Experimental Education, 82*(1), 121–141. doi:10.1080/00220973.2013.835299

Dumas, D. (2017). Relational reasoning in science, medicine, and engineering. *Educational Psychology Review, 29*, 73–95. doi:10.1007/s10648-016-9370-6

Dumas, D., & Alexander, P. (2018). Assessing differential item functioning on the test of relational reasoning. *Frontiers in Education, 3*, 1–11. doi:10.3389/feduc.2018.00014

Dumas, D., Alexander, P. A., Baker, L. M., Jablansky, S., & Dunbar, K. N. (2014). Relational reasoning in medical education: Patterns in discourse and diagnosis. *Journal of Educational Psychology, 106*, 1021–1035. doi:10.1037/a0036777

Dumas, D., Alexander, P. A., & Grossnickle, E. M. (2013). Relational reasoning and its manifestations in the educational context: A systematic review of the literature. *Educational Psychology Review, 25*, 391–427. doi:10.1007/s10648-013-9224-4

Dumas, D., & Schmidt, L. (2015). Relational reasoning as predictor for engineering ideation success using TRIZ. *Journal of Engineering Design, 26*, 74–88. doi:10.1080/09544828.2015.1020287

Dunbar, K. (1995). How scientists really reason: Scientific reasoning in real-world laboratories. In R. J. Sternberg & J. Davidson (Eds.), *The nature of insight* (pp. 365–396). Cambridge, MA: MIT Press.

Duncker, K. (1945). On problem-solving (L. S. Lees, Trans.). *Psychological Monographs, 58*, 5 (Whole #270). Washington, DC: American Psychological Association.

Gentner, D., & Rattermann, M. J. (1991). Language and the career of similarity. In S. A. Gelman & J. P. Byrnes (Eds.), *Perspectives on language and thought: Interrelations in development* (pp. 225–277). New York: Cambridge University Press.

Gick, M. L., & Holyoak, K. J. (1980). Analogical problem solving. *Cognitive Psychology, 12*(3), 306–355. doi:10.1016/0010-0285(80)90013-4

Gil, L., Bråten, I., Vidal-Abarca, E., & Strømsø, H. I. (2010). Understanding and integrating multiple science texts: Summary tasks are sometimes better than argument tasks. *Reading Psychology, 31*(1), 30–68. doi:10.1080/02702710902733600

Goel, V., Navarrete, G., Noveck, I. A., & Prado, J. (2017). The reasoning brain: The interplay between cognitive neuroscience and theories of reasoning. *Frontiers in Human Neuroscience, 10*, 673. doi:10.3389/fnhum.2016.00673

Grossnickle, E. M., Dumas, D., Alexander, P. A., & Baggetta, P. (2016). Individual differences in the process of relational reasoning. *Learning and Instruction, 42*, 141–159. doi:10.1016/j.learninstruc.2016.01.013

Hagen, Å. M., Braasch, J. L. G., & Bråten, I. (2014). Relationships between spontaneous note-taking, self-reported strategies and comprehension when reading multiple texts in different task conditions. *Journal of Research in Reading, 37*, 141–157. doi:10.1111/j.1467-9817.2012.01536.x

Hofstadter, D. R. (1979). *Gödel, escher, bach: An eternal golden braid*. New York: Basic Books.

Holyoak, K. J. (2012). Analogy and relational reasoning. In K. J. Holyoak & R. G. Morrison (Eds.), *The Oxford handbook of thinking and reasoning* (pp. 234–259). New York: Oxford University Press.

Hyönä, J. (2010). The use of eye movements in the study of multimedia learning. *Learning and Instruction, 20*(2), 172–176. doi:org/10.1016/j.learninstruc.2009.02.013

Jablansky, S., Alexander, P. A., Dumas, D., & Compton, V. (2016). Developmental differences in relational reasoning among primary and secondary school students. *Journal of Educational Psychology, 108*, 592–608. doi:10.1037/edu0000070

Jablansky, S., Alexander, P. A., Dumas, D., & Compton, V. (2019). The development of relational reasoning in primary and secondary school students: A longitudinal investigation in technology education. *International Journal of Technology and Design Education*.

Jablansky, S., Alexander, P. A., & Schmidt, L. S. (2018). Relational reasoning in engineering design teams. In Teaching critical thinking: Assessing and improving students' and teachers' reasoning skills. Symposium presented at the annual meeting of the American Educational Research Association, chaired by T. van Gog, New York, April.

James, W. (1890). *Principles of psychology*. New York: Henry Holt & Co.

James, W. (1893). *Psychology: A briefer course*. New York: Henry Holt & Co.

Just, M. A., & Carpenter, P. (1980). A theory of reading: From eye fixations to comprehension. *Psychological Review, 87*, 329–354. doi:10.1037/0033-295X.87.4.329

Koffka, K. (1922). Perception: An introduction to the Gestalt-Theories. *Psychological Bulletin, 19*(10), 531–585. doi:10.1037/h0072422

Köhler, W. (1925). An aspect of gestalt psychology. *The Pedagogical Seminary and Journal of Genetic Psychology, 32*, 691–723. doi:10.1080/08856559.1925.9944846

Krawczyk, D. C. (2012). The cognition and neuroscience of relational reasoning. *Brain Research, 1428*, 13–23. doi:10.1016/j.brainres.2010.11.080

List, A. (2019). *How do students integrate multiple texts?: An investigation of top-down processing*. [Manuscript submitted for publication]. Department of Educational Psychology, Counseling, and Special Education, The Pennsylvania State University.

List, A., & Alexander, P. A. (2017). Cognitive affective engagement model of multiple source use. *Educational Psychologist, 52*, 182–199. doi:doi.org/10.1080/00461520.2017.1329014

List, A., & Alexander, P. A. (2018). Toward an integrated framework of multiple text use. *Educational Psychologist*. Advance online publication. doi: 10.1080/00461520.2018.1505514.

Mason, L., Tornatora, M. C., & Pluchino, P. (2013). Do fourth graders integrate text and picture in processing and learning from an illustrated science text? Evidence from eye-movement patterns. *Computers and Education, 60*, 95–109. doi:10.1016/j.compedu.2012.07.011

McCrudden, M. T., & Schraw, G. (2007). Relevance and goal-focusing in text processing. *Educational Psychology Review, 19*(2), 113–139. doi:10.1007.s10647-006-9010-7

Meyer, B. J., & Ray, M. N. (2011). Structure strategy interventions: Increasing reading comprehension of expository text. *International Electronic Journal of Elementary Education, 4*(1), 127–152. doi:10.1515.1.1982

Mikkilä-Erdmann, M., Penttinen, M., Anto, E., & Olkinuora, E. (2008). Constructing mental models during learning from science text: Eye tracking methodology meets conceptual change. In D. Ifenthaler, P. Pirnay-Dummer, & J. M. Spector (Eds.), *Understanding models for learning and instruction* (pp. 63–79). New York: Springer.

Murphy, P. K., Firetto, C. M., & Greene, J. A. (2017). Enriching students' scientific thinking through relational reasoning: Seeking evidence in texts, tasks, and talk. *Educational Psychology Review, 29*(1), 105–117. doi:10.1007/s10648-016-9387-x

Murphy, P. K., Rowe, M. L., Ramani, G., & Silverman, R. (2014). Promoting critical-analytic thinking in children and adolescents at home and in school. *Educational Psychology Review, 26*(4), 561–578. doi:10.1007/s10648-014-9281-3

Newell, A. (1980). Physical symbol systems. *Cognitive Science, 4*(2), 135–183. doi:10.1207/s15516709cog0402_2

Newell, A., Shaw, J. C., & Simon, H. A. (1958). Elements of a theory of human problem solving. *Psychological Review, 65*(3), 151–166. doi:10.1037/h0048495

Parkin, B. L., Hellyer, P. J., Leech, R., & Hampshire, A. (2015). Dynamic network mechanisms of relational integration. *Journal of Neuroscience, 35*, 7660–7673. doi:10.1523/JNEUROSCI.4956-14.2015

Perfetti, C. A., Rouet, J.-F., & Britt, M. A. (1999). Toward a theory of documents representation. In H. van Oostendorp & S. R. Goldman (Eds.), *The construction of mental representations during reading* (pp. 99–122). Mahwah, NJ: Lawrence Erlbaum.

Prabhakaran, V., Smith, J. A., Desmond, J. E., Glover, G. H., & Gabrieli, J. D. (1997). Neural substrates of fluid reasoning: An fMRI study of neocortical activation during performance of the raven's progressive matrices test. *Cognitive Psychology, 33*, 43–63. doi:10.1006/cogp.1997.0659

Raven, J. C. (1941). Standardisation of progressive matrices, 1938. *British Journal of Medical Psychology, X19*(1), 137–150.

Rouet, J.-F. (2006). *The skills of document use: From text comprehension to web-based learning.* Mahwah, NJ,: Lawrence Erlbaum.

Rouet, J.-F., & Britt, M. A. (2012). Relevance processes in multiple document comprehension. In M. T. McCrudden, J. P. Magliano, & G. Schraw (Eds.), *Text relevance and learning from text* (pp. 19–52). Charlotte, NC: Information Age.

Russell, B. (1903). *Principles of mathematics.* New York: W. W. Norton & Co.

Schiefele, U., Schaffner, E., Möller, J., & Wigfield, A. (2012). Dimensions of reading motivation and their relation to reading behavior and competence. *Reading Research Quarterly, 47*(4), 427–463. doi:10.1002/RRQ.030

Schüler, A. (2017). Investigating gaze behavior during processing of inconsistent text-picture information: Evidence for text-picture integration. *Learning and Instruction, 49*, 218–231. doi:10.1016/j.learninstruc.2017.03.001

Schunk, D. H. (2003). Self-efficacy for reading and writing: Influence of modeling, goal setting, and self-evaluation. *Reading and Writing Quarterly, 19*(2), 159–172. doi:10.1080/10573560308219

Segev-Miller, R. (2004). Writing from sources: The effect of explicit instruction on students' processes and products. *L1-Educational Studies in Language and Literature, 4*(1), 5–33. doi:10.1023/B:ESLL.0000033847.00732.af

Singh, A., Sun, Y., & Zhao, H. (2019). Defining and assessing integration in the context of argumentative essays based on multiple sources. In *Integration: A critical competency for the digital age.* Symposium presented at the annual meeting of the American Educational Research Association, chaired by P. A. Alexander, Toronto. April.

Spearman, C. (1927). *The abilities of man: Their nature and measurement.* New York: Macmillan.

Stadtler, M., & Bromme, R. (2014). The content-source integration model: A taxonomic description of how readers comprehend conflicting scientific information. In D. N. Rapp & J. L. G. Braasch (Eds.), *Processing inaccurate information: Theoretical and applied perspectives from cognitive science and the educational sciences* (pp. 379–402). Cambridge, MA: MIT Press. Retrieved from www.jstor.org/stable/j.ctt9qf9b7

Sternberg, R. J. (1977a). Component processes in analogical reasoning. *Psychological Review, 84,* 353–378. doi:10.1037/0033-295X.84.4.353

Sternberg, R. J. (1977b). *Intelligence, information processing, and analogical reasoning: The componential analysis of human abilities.* Mahwah, NJ: Lawrence Erlbaum.

Sun, Y., Alexander, P. A., & Zhao, H. (2018). Influence of teacher discursive moves on students' relational reasoning in science classrooms. Poster presented at the annual meeting of the American Educational Research Association, New York, April.

Taboada, A., Tonks, S. M., Wigfield, A., & Guthrie, J. T. (2009). Effects of motivational and cognitive variables on reading comprehension. *Reading and Writing, 22*(1), 85–106. doi:10.1007/s11145-008-9133-y

Tippett, C. (2010). Refutation text in science education: A review of two decades of research. *International Journal of Science and Mathematics Education, 8*(6), 951–970. doi:10.1007/s10763-010-9203-x

Trickett, S. B., Trafton, J. G., & Schunn, C. D. (2009). How do scientists respond to anomalies? Different strategies used in basic and applied science. *Topics in Cognitive Science, 1,* 711–729. doi:10.1111/j.1756-8765.2009.01036.x

Van den Boom, G., Paas, F., Van Merriënboer, J. J., & Van Gog, T. (2004). Reflection prompts and tutor feedback in a web-based learning environment: Effects on students' self-regulated learning competence. *Computers in Human Behavior, 20*(4), 551–567. doi:10.1016/j.chb.2003.10.001

Vidal-Abarca, E., Mañá, A., & Gil, L. (2010). Individual differences for self-regulating task-oriented reading activities. *Journal of Educational Psychology, 102*(4), 817–826. doi:10.1037/a0020062

Waltz, J. A., Knowlton, B. J., Holyoak, K. J., Boone, K. B., Mishkin, F. S., de Menezes Santos, M., ... Miller, B. L. (1999). A system for relational reasoning in human prefrontal cortex. *Psychological Science, 10,* 119–125. doi:10.1111/1467-9280.00118

Wendelken, C., Nakhabenko, D., Donohue, S. E., Carter, C. S., & Bunge, S. A. (2008). "Brain is to thought as stomach is to?" Investigating the role of rostrolateral prefrontal cortex in relational reasoning. *Journal of Cognitive Neuroscience, 20,* 682–693. doi:10.1162/jocn.2008.20055

Wertheimer, M. (1938). Laws of organization in perceptual forms. In W. D. Ellis (Ed.), *A source book of gestalt psychology* (pp. 71–88). London: Kegan Paul, Trench, Trubner & Co.

Witte, S. P., & Faigley, L. (1981). Coherence, cohesion, and writing quality. *College Composition and Communication, 32,* 189–204. doi:10.2307/356693

Wolfe, M. B. W., & Goldman, S. R. (2005). Relations between adolescents' text processing and reasoning. *Cognition and Instruction, 23*(4), 267–502. doi:10.1207/s1532690xci2304_2

Zhao, H., Alexander, P., & Sun, Y. (2019). *Relational reasoning's contributions to mathematical performance in Chinese elementary and middle-school students.* [Manuscript submitted for publication]. Department of Human Development and Quantitative Methodology, University of Maryland.

24

USING CRITICAL THINKING FRAMEWORKS TO UNDERSTAND INTEGRATION OF MULTIPLE INPUTS

Brian M. Cartiff and Jeffrey A. Greene
UNIVERSITY OF NORTH CAROLINA AT CHAPEL HILL

ABSTRACT

The digital age has provided both opportunities and challenges to learning. Concepts that were once represented in text or static pictures now also can be shown in dynamic visuals or interactive animations. The advent of new technologies, such as social media as well as virtual and augmented realities, has allowed people to discover a myriad of perspectives on issues and ideas. Theoretical and empirical work has shown that use of these multiple representations and perspectives should and can benefit learning. However, there is also ample evidence that these benefits are infrequently achieved. Scholars have identified reasons why people might struggle to learn with multiple inputs, but there still are gaps in the literature. In this chapter, we suggest that critical thinking frameworks can enrich an understanding of learning from multiple inputs and identify some of the difficulties that learners face. We specifically address how critical thinking models might contribute to an understanding of how learners identify key features and credible evidence, which critical thinking dispositions might contribute to better use of multiple inputs, and how cognitive biases interfere with learning.

Key words: critical thinking, multiple representations, multiple perspectives, cognitive biases, epistemic cognition

Today's technologically advanced world is becoming more complex, in part due to the unprecedented proliferation of multiple information representations, perspectives, and sources (OECD, 2016). For example, a recent poll of nearly 20,000 adults in the US indicated that people are increasingly relying on Internet sources and social media for information (Gallup, 2018). This abundance of information and its easy accessibility have many positive aspects, but there are causes for concern as well, as scholars have noted that much of this information is unregulated (Britt & Aglinskas, 2002), unsubstantiated (Wopereis & van Merriënboer, 2011) and lacks credibility (Kienhues, Stadtler, & Bromme, 2011). These concerns may be why people around the world reported that it is increasingly difficult to feel truly informed when confronted with the sheer number of sources available to them (Gallup, 2018; Pew Research Center, 2018).

The mere existence of a plethora of inputs and information does not ensure that people will be able to select, interpret, and evaluate them in a meaningful way (Halpern, 1998). Many readers fail to successfully weigh and integrate alternative perspectives when considering positions on an issue (Britt, Perfetti, Sandak, & Rouet, 1999) and instead simply try to accumulate as much information as they can (Barzilai & Zohar, 2012). People also have difficulties in understanding, organizing, and integrating multiple representations of novel concepts (Ainsworth, 2006). Such challenges are concerning given learning from multiple representations is a crucial 21st-century skill that is necessary to understand complex topics in the modern world (NCTM, 2006; NRC, 2006; Rau & Matthews, 2017).

There is still much to be learned about how people integrate multiple inputs, or fail to do so, especially in authentic learning contexts inside and outside of school (Bråten & Strømsø, 2011; Mason, Tornatora, & Pluchino, 2013; Stadtler & Bromme, 2013; Stieff, Hegarty, & Deslongchamps, 2011). In particular, more research is needed regarding how higher order thinking processes, like critical thinking, can help people better understand, synthesize, and critique information when it is presented in multiple ways and from multiple perspectives (Greene & Yu, 2016). Though experts and novices alike differ on a formal definition of critical thinking, it can be viewed as the "ability to engage in purposeful, self-regulatory judgment" (Abrami et al., 2008, p. 1102) necessary for problem-solving and conceptual understanding. Employers, policymakers, and educators alike consider critical thinking to be a vital outcome of education, given the complexity of the multiple forms and sources of information found in the modern world (Tsui, 2002). In this chapter, we show how critical thinking frameworks might provide new ways of examining the difficulties that learners encounter when attempting to integrate these multiple inputs. In line with the other chapters in this *Handbook*, we consider *multiple inputs* to include both *multiple representations* and *multiple perspectives*.

MULTIPLE INPUTS

Multiple Representations

It is not always clear what is meant by multiple representations. This challenge is in part because there are various taxonomies that have been proposed that do not clearly map onto each other (Ainsworth, 2018), and also because emerging technologies continue to open up new possibilities for representations (e.g., augmented and virtual realities). In this chapter, we employ a broad and general definition of multiple representations as any two or more external representations (e.g., textual, pictorial, graphical, symbolic, animation, etc. outside of the human mind) used to illustrate a particular concept or its facets.

Each type of representation has its strengths and weaknesses for conveying information (Carney & Levin, 2002). Textual information is flexible and ubiquitous. Pictorial or visual representations may help people envision entities too small to see, such as atoms, or too large to see, such as galaxies, thus making these abstract concepts more comprehensible (Schnotz, 2014; Uttal & O'Doherty, 2008). Graphical representations can enhance the perception of patterns in numerical data that symbolic, alphanumeric representations may not reveal (van der Meij & de Jong, 2006). Animations can promote understanding of processes that static representations do not illustrate. Given representation types have different strengths, they can be used together to serve different purposes (Larkin & Simon, 1987) and promote deeper understanding (Ainsworth, 1999). Multiple representations can complement each other by spreading information out, which keeps any one of the representations from being overwhelming (Seufert, 2003). They can also facilitate interpretation, as more familiar representations can be used to interpret less familiar ones (Ainsworth, 1999). However, the affordances of multiple representations come to fruition only when those representations are accurate and useful. When confronted with multiple representations of dubious quality, people must engage in critical thinking to determine which representations to select, organize, and integrate (Halpern, 2003; Mayer, 2014). Many studies, though, demonstrate that learners often do not use multiple representations fruitfully (e.g., Hannus & Hyönä, 1999; Kozma & Russell, 1997; Schwonke, Berthold, & Renkl, 2009), in some cases because they do not even attempt to integrate the information from the different representations (Tabachneck, Leonardo, & Simon, 1994).

Multiple Perspectives

In accordance with other authors in this textbook, we define multiple perspectives as multiple viewpoints about an idea, issue, or occurrence. For example, in the domain of history, multiple perspectives can include different narratives about an event, from one or more sources (Wansink, Akkerman, Zuiker, & Wubbels, 2018). These narratives may be dependent on the source's cultural, ethical, or regional background, or on the primary sources chosen to produce a secondary account. There are different ways that these perspectives can be interpreted and integrated, and people successfully navigating this process can learn more than those who use only a perspective from a single source. However, critical thinking is necessary to determine how to integrate multiple perspectives most effectively (VanSledright & Maggioni, 2016).

On the other hand, with regard to socio-scientific issues, multiple perspectives might involve stances on controversial topics based on divergent interpretations of scientific evidence or due to differences in funding agencies, religious beliefs, or political stances. Negotiating and making decisions regarding multiple perspectives requires critical thinking and is an important component of scientific literacy (Fowler, Zeidler, & Sadler, 2009). Research has shown that, as with multiple representations, people of all ages struggle to synthesize information from multiple perspectives in meaningful and appropriate ways (e.g., Brand-Gruwel & Stadtler, 2011; Wiley et al., 2009).

In this chapter, we argue that research on critical thinking can afford new insights on why people struggle to integrate and use multiple inputs, as well as new directions for research. To provide grounding for our claims about the role of critical thinking in the integration of multiple inputs, we present a guiding example of a complex issue. The multiple inputs necessary to understand this issue provide a fertile base from which to discuss the role of critical thinking in integration.

Guiding Example: The Great Pacific Garbage Patch

USAToday.com has published several op-eds (e.g., Rice, 2018) on the Great Pacific Garbage Patch (GPGP), which is a large floating accumulation of trash in the ocean moving about the subtropical waters between California and Hawaii, primarily due to the movements of the Kuroshio, North Pacific, California, and North Equatorial currents (Lebreton et al., 2018). These op-eds contain multiple perspectives, including differing arguments about the main source of the plastics and other detritus making up the GPGP, how large the area and volume of the GPGP actually is, and contrary opinions on the best way to clean it up. The op-eds also include multiple representations, including photographs of the floating plastic in the GPGP, graphs showing global plastic production and use over time, aerial images of the GPGP used to identify the amount and location of debris and to determine plastic concentrations, and pictures and animations of the Pacific Ocean currents. A person wishing to understand the GPGP, and what if anything to do about it, must select, organize, and integrate these multiple inputs, and we argue that doing so successfully requires critical thinking.

CRITICAL THINKING

Concerns about people's ability to engage in critical thinking stretch at least back to the times when Socrates would challenge people and their assumptions in the ancient Athenian markets (Durant, 1933). Dewey (1933) is generally credited with identifying critical thinking as a major educational issue, and he defined it as the ability to engage in reflective judgments about beliefs and actions (see Lombardi, Matewos, & Heddy, Chapter 20, for more on Dewey's thoughts about education and his positions on beliefs). Given these foundations, it is perhaps not surprising that most critical thinking frameworks can be differentiated into those based in philosophy or psychology (Lewis & Smith, 1993). Philosophical models have been proposed by many scholars (e.g., Ennis, 1996; Paul, 1992) and have focused primarily on formal logical systems (Sternberg, 1986). On the other hand, psychological frameworks (e.g., Bransford & Stein, 1984; Halpern, 2003) describe how critical thinking is performed by specific people in particular contexts (Sternberg, 1986) and focus on how people can gain and employ particular critical thinking skills and dispositions (Abrami et al., 2008).

These different foundations result in some distinctions between critical thinking models, such as which criteria should be used for judging successful critical thinking and different views regarding whether and how critical thinking transfers from one subject area to another (Lai, 2011), but there are also important similarities across frameworks. These overlaps were revealed in two attempts to find consensus on the definition of critical thinking. Peter Facione (1990) conducted a Delphi study on critical thinking under the auspices of the American Philosophical Association. The panelists, including experts in philosophy, education, social sciences, and physical sciences, were not in total agreement on all aspects, but did manage to produce a consensus definition of critical thinking as a "purposeful, self-regulatory judgment which results in interpretation, analysis, evaluation, and inference, as well as explanation of the evidential, conceptual, methodological, criteriological, or contextual considerations upon which the judgment is based" (Facione, 1990, p. 3; see Denton, Muis, Munzar, & Etoubashi, Chapter 19, for more on the role of self-regulated learning in learning from multiple inputs). These experts also largely agreed about the affective dispositions and cognitive skills (e.g., being open-minded, reasoning) that need to be in place and employed in order for a person to be an ideal critical thinker.

The second major attempt at gaining consensus on critical thinking, organized by the American Educational Research Association, started in 2013. Participating scholars from a variety of disciplines recognized that major changes in US national curricula (e.g., Common Core State Standards; National Governors Association Center for Best Practices and Council of Chief State School Officers, 2010) called for new attempts to define the construct they referred to as "critical-analytic thinking" (Alexander, 2014; Byrnes & Dunbar, 2014). Despite not coming to a definitive definition, these scholars were able to gain consensus on a number of points, including the ideas that critical thinking needs to be based on credible evidence, it involves effortful evaluation of arguments and claims (Byrnes & Dunbar, 2014), and that there are both costs and benefits to critical thinking (Alexander, 2014).

In addition to these two collective attempts at gaining consensus among scholars, most critical thinking models (e.g., Facione, 1990; Halpern, 1998, 2003; Paul & Elder, 2006) have areas of commonality. These include a recognition of the crucial role of prior knowledge in both creating new knowledge (Bransford & Johnson, 1972) and in identifying and focusing on the most pertinent information (Halpern, 2003), the existence of multiple specific critical thinking skills and dispositions, the role of intellectual standards (e.g., accuracy, relevance, and significance of information; Paul & Elder, 2006), and the importance of metacognition. In Table 24.1, we identify some of the dispositions and skills listed in prominent models of critical thinking, showing both their similarities and differences.

Some of the differences in critical thinking models result from disagreements among scholars as to whether critical thinking is primarily domain-general or domain-specific. Those who support the domain-general stance (e.g., van Gelder, 2005) believe it can be taught and learned in a general way and then applied across different domains (Lai, 2011). Halpern (1993) asserted that empirical evidence across numerous studies, including gains in IQ scores, student self-reports, and student mental representations after completion of a critical thinking class all support a domain-general view. Likewise, both Lipman (1988) and Siegel (1992) recognized that specific criteria for judging apt critical thinking may be subject-specific but maintained that the fundamental nature of critical thinking is generalizable. For example, a fundamental aspect of critical thinking is evaluating the reliability of a source, but the criteria for making that judgment can vary by domain or discipline. Therefore, people should vet a newspaper article using different criteria than they would for a peer-reviewed journal article.

Table 24.1 Critical Thinking Dispositions and Skills across Different Models

	Alexander (2014), Byrnes and Dunbar (2014)	Facione (1990)	Paul (1992); Paul and Elder (2006); Foundation for Critical Thinking (2014)	Halpern (1998, 2003)
Dispositions	Effortful	Persistent in seeking results which are as precise as possible	Intellectual perseverance	Persistence in problem-solving and at complex tasks
	Open-minded	Open-minded	Intellectual courage (recognizing the need to face and fairly address ideas, beliefs or viewpoints toward which we have strong negative emotions and to which we have not given a serious hearing)	Open-mindedness
	Unbiased	Honest in facing personal biases	Intellectual humility (realizing the limits of one's knowledge and being sensitive to self-deception and bias)	
		Flexible	Intellectual empathy (recognizing the need to imaginatively put oneself in the place of others in order to genuinely understand them)	Flexibility
		Fair-minded in evaluation	Fairmindedness	Fairmindedness
		Trustful of reason	Confidence in reason	
		Reasonable in the selection of criteria	Intellectual integrity (recognizing that one needs to follow consistent, rigorous standards in thinking)	
	Skeptical and moderately distrusting			
		Well-informed		
		Diligent in seeking relevant information		
		Willing to reconsider		
		Habitually inquisitive		

	Alexander (2014), Byrnes and Dunbar (2014)	Facione (1990)	Paul (1992); Paul and Elder (2006); Foundation for Critical Thinking (2014)	Halpern (1998, 2003)
			Intellectual autonomy *(having rational control of one's beliefs, values, and inferences)*	Awareness of the social realities that need to be overcome (e.g., gaining consensus) so that thoughts can become actions
Skills	Reflective	Self-regulation	Self-directed, self-monitored	
	Analytic	Analysis		Argument analysis
	Evaluative	Evaluation		
		Interpretation	Interpretation	
		Inference	Inference	
		Explanation		
	Weighing costs and benefits			Problem-solving
				Verbal reasoning
				Hypothesis testing
				Livelihood and uncertainty
				Decision-making

Similar concepts appear in the same row.

Scholars advocating a domain-general view would say that effective critical thinkers could appropriately weigh the different arguments and pieces of evidence presented in the USAToday.com op-eds and decide which ones are better and more meaningful. These effective critical thinkers would be skeptical of accepting the arguments of an op-ed author who works in the plastics industry. Also, they would be able to employ appropriate reasoning to choose the best method of cleaning up the GPGP by analyzing the costs and benefits of each approach and evaluating the likely consequences of the proposed actions.

Scholars endorsing a domain-specific view of critical thinking would argue that the average person would likely struggle to understand and vet the multiple inputs presented in the USAToday.com op-eds. McPeck (1990), one of the proponents of a domain-specific view of critical thinking, maintained that there are "almost as many different kinds of critical thinking as there are different kinds of things to think about" (p. 10). He admitted that there are a small number of general thinking skills (e.g., not contradicting oneself), but also argued that the more general the skill, the less useful it is because most complex problems require discipline or domain-specific skills. Willingham (2007) agreed, asserting that educational programs aimed at improving critical thinking have been largely ineffectual because of their focus on teaching generalized skills, an opinion that seems to have empirical support (Abrami et al., 2008). Bailin (2002) pointed out that domain-specificity is a key facet of critical thinking because the epistemic practices, such as judging what kinds of evidence are valid and what types of standards to use, depend largely on the domain or discipline involved.

Advocates of the domain-specific view of critical thinking would point out that the reasoning strategies and ability to think critically are "tightly bound to domain knowledge" (Chinn & Duncan, 2018, p. 79). People possessing historical knowledge would use that specific domain knowledge to guide their thinking about the GPGP, for example by recognizing the historical causes for increased plastic production (e.g., World War II; Nicholson & Leighton, 1942), and would also employ disciplinary practices such as checking the alignment of the information presented in the op-eds with agreed-upon knowledge in history (Chinn & Duncan, 2018). Those with greater science knowledge, on the other hand, would diagnose that there is important information missing from the GPGP op-eds, such as the rates at which different plastics degrade, and would recognize that drawing inferences about the GPGP and how to clean it up without such pertinent information is an unreliable epistemic process (Chinn, Buckland, & Samarapungavan, 2011). There is insufficient empirical evidence to be definitive regarding whether critical thinking is domain-general, domain-specific, or both. Therefore, more research investigating this issue is needed.

CRITICAL THINKING FRAMEWORKS AND MULTIPLE INPUT INTEGRATION

There are many reasons why people might struggle to integrate information from different representations or perspectives (cf. Schnotz, 2014), but a few specific to critical thinking are: (1) failure to identify key features or ideas and instead focusing on easily noticeable, but superficial, ones, (2) failure to judge whether presented evidence is credible, (3) a lack of the necessary dispositions to effectively integrate information, and (4) falling victim to cognitive biases that interfere with successful integration.

Key Features

Whereas scholars believe that in most circumstances learners can benefit from multiple inputs, there is also evidence that complex representations may distract learners (Stern, Aprea, & Ebner, 2003), or lead them to focus on perceptually engaging, but relatively unimportant features (Lowe, 2003). As Facione (1990) pointed out, an ideal critical thinker will be diligent in seeking *relevant* information, but many people seem to struggle to identify and extract these particular components of multiple representations (Goldman, 2003). Knowing what the key features are, as opposed to superficial ones, likely involves domain-specific knowledge. In the GPGP example, readers might look at the text and graph describing how the production of various types of plastic has increased over time but focus primarily on the different colors used to identify the types of plastics as opposed to the more important y-axis information showing the magnitude of the increase. As another example, they may watch the animations of the currents in the Pacific Ocean and find them interesting as dynamic representations, but fail to make connections to the text that describes how difficult it is to find and examine the GPGP because it is moving and unstable. When reading the different op-eds, they may focus on how well-written the arguments are at the expense of appropriately analyzing the evidence presented in them. These failures to distinguish relevant and key features from less important ones are breakdowns in critical thinking that could keep people from learning efficiently from multiple inputs.

Credible Evidence

A related issue that is not addressed much in the multiple representation literature is how learners assess the credibility of the information and evidence in various depictions. This is likely, from our review of the literature, because researchers in the field have concentrated mostly on learning environments in school and expect that the representations presented there are accurate. On the other hand, there has been significant research into how people judge evidence to be credible in the multiple perspectives literature (e.g., multiple document comprehension; Kendeou & O'Brien, 2018). Nonetheless, in the digital age, people encounter both kinds of multiple inputs in a variety of contexts, many of them unregulated and uncurated. Even in curated informational sources, like our USAToday.com example, there is the possibility for misinformation, including misleading or inaccurate representations. Therefore, critical thinkers must actively evaluate inputs and sources for credibility, which is one of many aspects of epistemic cognition (i.e., the ways that people gain, justify, use, and produce knowledge; Greene, Sandoval, & Bråten, 2016; Greene & Yu, 2016).

For example, GPGP stories online and in print (e.g., Newitz, 2012), are frequently accompanied by photographs of large pieces of plastic essentially composing an island of floating trash. These pictures are alarming and eye-catching, fitting most people's expectations (National Geographic Society, 2012). However, they are also inaccurate, as they depict a single, relatively stable and easily visible mound of trash, instead of the two (Eastern and Western) general areas of unstable (i.e., moving and changing), partially submerged, microplastic accumulation they actually are (Evon, 2015; Goldstein, 2012). Rather than integrating these representations into their understanding of the GPGP, successful learners could employ one facet of critical thinking, epistemic cognition, to determine that these pictures are misleading. People with adaptive domain-specific epistemic cognition are better able to recognize what evidence is credible (Barzilai & Eshet-Alkalai, 2015), and these people would recognize that a picture of the GPGP as a mound of trash in the water around a person in a small canoe, a frequently employed image, is inconsistent with other pieces of information that indicate that GPGP is remote and difficult to access (i.e., unlikely that a person in a canoe would paddle into it).

Dispositions

Dispositions (i.e., the consistent, internal motivation to act a particular way; Facione, Facione, & Giancarlo, 2000) are another aspect of critical thinking models that might help researchers understand people's struggles to integrate multiple inputs. Some examples of relevant dispositions, which are domain-general to a large extent, are intellectual humility, concern for precision, and fair-mindedness, all of which can be crucial for critical thinking. As Halpern (1998) pointed out, even if people have the ability to engage in acts of critical thinking, such as inhibiting impulsive behaviors (i.e., they have strategies to accomplish this), they must also have the disposition to do so (i.e., they must want to be less impulsive). People who lack this disposition may become frustrated and overwhelmed (e.g., cognitive load; Rouet, 2009; Segers & Verhoeven, 2009) by a large number of multiple representations and be unable to inhibit this response, causing them to use only the simplest or most superficial representations (Schnotz, 2014). In our GPGP example, they may hastily discount pictures and graphs as unnecessary or extraneous and assume that they can learn all they need to from the text alone or vice versa.

Alternatively, if these learners feel they already have accurate ideas about the GPGP, they may ignore certain representations due to a lack of intellectual humility (Paul & Elder, 2006). In actuality, the satellite photos of the GPGP, graphs about plastic production and use, animations about the currents in the Pacific, and textual commentaries are complementary to each other and are all needed to create a more complete understanding of the phenomenon. Nonetheless, if learners lack the disposition to seek as much precision as the situation requires (Facione, 1990), then they are likely to focus on isolated representations or simply choose the one they find easiest to understand.

Certain dispositions are even more important when coordinating multiple perspectives. If learners lack fair-mindedness (Paul & Elder, 2006), then they might not see the need to integrate multiple perspectives. The various op-eds about the GPGP have some similarities, but also have different pieces of information and different interpretations of evidence. Learners who are fair-minded will weigh these each in turn. Along the same lines, if people lack the disposition to understand the opinions of others (Paul & Elder, 2006), are not flexible "in considering alternatives and opinions" (Facione, 1990, p. 25), or are not willing to revise their views when new information and personal reflection suggest that this is warranted (Ennis, 1991), then it is unlikely they will engage with or interpret across multiple perspectives.

Another critical thinking disposition, honesty in facing one's own biases (Ennis, 1991; Facione, 1990), may be another important avenue for future multiple input research. People with this critical thinking disposition are more likely to evoke strategies for addressing possible cognitive biases (Facione & Facione, 2001; West, Toplak, & Stanovich, 2008). This is important because cognitive biases are another reason why people struggle to integrate information from multiple inputs (Dwyer, Hogan, & Stewart, 2014).

Cognitive Biases

Cognitive biases are often the result of heuristics, which are cognitive shortcuts or simplifying strategies that people employ to deal with complex issues (Newell & Simon, 1972). These shortcuts produce proper judgments in many cases, but can also lead to systematic errors (i.e., cognitive biases; Tversky & Kahneman, 1974). In many cases, these biases appear domain-general, as they are produced by heuristics that people employ across multiple domains. The literature on these biases is extensive (see Kahneman, 2011) and beyond the scope of this chapter, but a few of these biases that might affect multiple input integration are overconfidence bias, focalism, confirmation bias, disconfirmation bias, and the backfire effect.

If learners already have some familiarity with a topic, they may not seek to integrate the information in multiple inputs because they are overconfident in their existing understanding, a well-founded bias (Trivers, 1991). The tendency to use only one or a few of the available representations may also be a result of a version of focalism, which is a cognitive bias resulting from people's tendency to put too much weight on one particular piece of information or event (Hanko, 2007). People who are not employing proper critical thinking may fall victim to one or both of these biases during their examination of the GPGP op-eds and miss vital information in creating an accurate mental representation of the phenomenon.

Confirmation bias, which refers to people's tendency to look only for information that supports their currently held beliefs (Tsipursky & Morford, 2018), or to perceive only information that aligns with their beliefs as valuable and credible (Lord, Ross, & Lepper, 1979), is also a major impediment to effective multiple input integration. People who believe that environmentalists have exaggerated claims about the GPGP likely will discount any perspectives that make similar claims. Alternatively, but leading to similar issues with regard to integration, people may exhibit disconfirmation bias, which occurs when they spend larger amounts of time and energy scrutinizing ideas that contradict their current beliefs or hold these discrepant ideas to higher standards than their current beliefs (Edwards & Smith, 1996). In fact, they may become even more intransigent in their beliefs about the GPGP and less likely to even consider differing perspectives if they experience the backfire effect, which occurs as beliefs become more entrenched as people are faced with contradictory evidence (Nyhan & Reifler, 2010, 2015). Clearly, cognitive biases, which are antithetical to critical thinking, can impede effective multiple input integration.

CONCLUSION AND FUTURE DIRECTIONS

Multiple representations and perspectives are essential for a complete understanding of certain concepts and ideas (Shanahan & Shanahan, 2008). The importance of multiple input integration is easily recognized, but it is not easily accomplished. Recognizing this, educators and policymakers have emphasized the ability to "integrate and evaluate multiple sources of information ... in order to address a question or solve a problem" (National Governors Association Center for Best Practices, 2010, p. 61). We have argued here that one way educators and scholars should go about investigating how to promote effective multiple input integration is by incorporating work on critical thinking. Such work may reveal that people who struggle with multiple input integration do not have particular critical thinking dispositions that would serve them favorably in vital stages of this integration. Alternatively, these struggles might be the product of cognitive biases, which result from mental shortcuts that people are apt to take when learning or trying to solve a problem.

One possible avenue for research is to investigate how critical thinking interventions affect learners' ability to integrate multiple inputs. There are many critical thinking interventions that vary widely in their implementations and outcomes (Abrami et al., 2008). Domain-general interventions that target critical thinking dispositions might be one possible avenue to follow, as there is some evidence that better critical thinking is associated with a willingness to change misconceptions, a key aspect of effective multiple input use (Kowalski & Taylor, 2004). Also, scholars have proposed various explanations for the origins and circumstances of cognitive biases (Battersby & Bailin, 2013), and there are specific interventions that have been found to help learners become more aware of them (e.g., Kray & Galinsky, 2003; Royce, Hayes, & Schwartzstein, 2019). Scholars in the field of multiple inputs might examine whether these mostly domain-general interventions have any impact on integration of various representations and perspectives.

Finally, we believe that more focus should be centered on learners' epistemic cognition. Epistemic cognition appears to be related to many different areas of academic achievement (Greene, Cartiff, & Duke, 2018), but it is still not prominently featured in critical thinking frameworks (Greene & Yu, 2016; Sinatra, Kienhues, & Hofer, 2014). It is likely that both domain-general aspects of epistemic cognition (i.e., views about the nature of knowledge and knowing in general) and domain-specific aspects (i.e., understanding what convincing evidence is and how knowledge is justified in specific fields) have some impact on multiple input integration. Research has shown that availing epistemic cognition can have a positive effect on people's ability to integrate multiple perspectives (e.g., Barzilai & Zohar, 2012), but more research is needed. Capturing and coordinating the ways epistemic cognition and critical thinking occur during multiple input integration should reveal promising new directions for helping people engage in that integration more successfully, thus helping them succeed in the modern world.

ACKNOWLEDGMENTS

The authors of this chapter would like to acknowledge their colleague, Rebekah F. Duke, for suggesting the Great Pacific Garbage Patch example used in this chapter.

REFERENCES

Abrami, P. C., Bernard, R. M., Borokhovski, E., Wade, A., Surkes, M. A., Tamim, R., & Zhang, D. (2008). Instructional interventions affecting critical thinking skills and dispositions: A stage 1 meta-analysis. *Review of Educational Research, 78*(4), 1102–1134.

Ainsworth, S. (1999). The functions of multiple representations. *Computers and Education, 33*(2/3), 131–152.

Ainsworth, S. (2006). DeFT: A conceptual framework for considering learning with multiple representations. *Learning and Instruction, 16*(3), 183–198.

Ainsworth, S. E. (2018). Multi-modal, multi-source reading: A multi-representational reader's perspective. *Learning and Instruction, 57,* 71–75.

Alexander, P. A. (2014). Thinking critically and analytically about critical-analytic thinking: An introduction. *Educational Psychology Review, 26*(4), 469–476.

Bailin, S. (2002). Critical thinking and science education. *Science and Education, 11*(4), 361–375.

Barzilai, S., & Eshet-Alkalai, Y. (2015). The role of epistemic perspectives in comprehension of multiple author viewpoints. *Learning and Instruction, 36,* 86–103.

Barzilai, S., & Zohar, A. (2012). Epistemic thinking in action: Evaluating and integrating online sources. *Cognition and Instruction, 30*(1), 39–85.

Battersby, M., & Bailin, S. (2013). Critical thinking and cognitive biases. In D. Mohammed & M. Lewiński (Eds.), *Virtues of argumentation: Proceedings of the 10th international conference of the Ontario Society for the Study of Argumentation (OSSA)* (pp. 1–9). Windsor, ON: OSSA.

Brand-Gruwel, S., & Stadtler, M. (2011). Solving information-based problems: Evaluating sources and information. *Learning and Instruction, 21,* 175–179.

Bransford, J. D., & Johnson, M. K. (1972). Contextual prerequisites for understanding: Some investigations of comprehension and recall. *Journal of Verbal Learning and Verbal Behavior, 11*(6), 717–726.

Bransford, J. D., & Stein, B. S. (1984). *The ideal problem solver: A guide for improving thinking, learning and creativity.* San Francisco, CA: Freeman.

Bråten, I., & Strømsø, H. I. (2011). Measuring strategic processing when students read multiple texts. *Metacognition and Learning, 6*(2), 111–130.

Britt, M. A., & Aglinskas, C. (2002). Improving students' ability to identify and use source information. *Cognition and Instruction, 20*(4), 485–522.

Britt, M. A., Perfetti, C. A., Sandak, R., & Rouet, J. (1999). Content integration and source separation in learning from multiple texts. In S. R. Goldman, A. C. Graesser, P. van den Broek, S. R. Goldman, A. C. Graesser, & P. van den Broek (Eds.), *Narrative comprehension, causality, and coherence: Essays in honor of Tom Trabasso* (pp. 209–233). Mahwah, NJ: Lawrence Erlbaum.

Byrnes, J. P., & Dunbar, K. N. (2014). The nature and development of critical-analytic thinking. *Educational Psychology Review, 26*(4), 477–493.

Carney, R. N., & Levin, J. R. (2002). Pictorial illustrations still improve students' learning from text. *Educational Psychology Review, 14*(1), 5–26.

Chinn, C. A., Buckland, L. A., & Samarapungavan, A. (2011). Expanding the dimensions of epistemic cognition: Arguments from philosophy and psychology. *Educational Psychologist, 46*(3), 141–167.

Chinn, C. A., & Duncan, R. G. (2018). What is the value of general knowledge in scientific reasoning? In F. Fischer, C. A. Chinn, K. Engelmann, & J. Osborne (Eds.), *Scientific reasoning and argumentation: The roles of domain-specific and domain-general knowledge* (pp. 77–101). New York: Routledge.

Dewey, J. (1933). *How we think, a restatement of the relation of reflective thinking to the educative process.* Washington, DC: Heath & Co.

Durant, W. (1933). *The story of philosophy: The lives and opinions of the world's greatest philosophers.* New York: Simon & Schuster.

Dwyer, C. P., Hogan, M. J., & Stewart, I. (2014). An integrated critical thinking framework for the 21st century. *Thinking Skills and Creativity, 12,* 43–52.

Edwards, K., & Smith, E. E. (1996). A disconfirmation bias in the evaluation of arguments. *Journal of Personality and Social Psychology, 71*(1), 5–24.

Ennis, R. H. (1991). Critical thinking: A streamlined conception. *Teaching Philosophy, 14*(1), 5–24.

Ennis, R. H. (1996). *Critical thinking.* Upper Saddle River, NJ: Prentice-Hall.

Evon, D. (2015). Fact check: The Great Pacific Garbage Patch. July 30. www.snopes.com/fact-check/great-pacific-garbage-patch/

Facione, P. A. (1990). *The Delphi report: Committee on pre-college philosophy.* Millbrae, CA: California Academic Press.

Facione, P. A., & Facione, N. C. (2001). Analyzing explanations for seemingly irrational choices: Linking argument analysis and cognitive science. *International Journal of Applied Philosophy, 15*(2), 267–286.

Facione, P. A., Facione, N. C., & Giancarlo, C. A. (2000). The disposition toward critical thinking: Its character, measurement, and relationship to critical thinking skill. *Informal Logic, 20*(1), 61–84.

Foundation for Critical Thinking (2014). Valuable intellectual virtues. Retrieved from www.criticalthinking.org/pages/valuable-intellectual-traits/528

Fowler, S. R., Zeidler, D. L., & Sadler, T. D. (2009). Moral sensitivity in the context of socioscientific issues in high school science students. *International Journal of Science Education, 31*(2), 279–296.

Gallup. (2018). *American views: Trust, media and democracy.* Washington, DC: Author.

Goldman, S. R. (2003). Learning in complex domains: When and why do multiple representations help? *Learning and Instruction, 13*(2), 239–244.

Goldstein, M. (2012). Three ways of looking at the Great Pacific Garbage Patch. Aug. 20. Retrieved from www.deepseanews.com/2012/08/three-ways-of-looking-at-the-great-pacific-garbage-patch/

Greene, J. A., Cartiff, B. M., & Duke, R. F. (2018). A meta-analytic review of the relationship between epistemic cognition and academic achievement. *Journal of Educational Psychology, 110*(8), 1084–1111.

Greene, J. A., Sandoval, W. A., & Bråten, I. (2016). *Handbook of epistemic cognition.* New York: Routledge.

Greene, J. A., & Yu, S. B. (2016). Educating critical thinkers: The role of epistemic cognition. *Policy Insights from the Behavioral and Brain Sciences, 3*(1), 45–53.

Halpern, D. F. (1993). Assessing the effectiveness of critical-thinking instruction. *Journal of General Education, 42*(4), 238–254.

Halpern, D. F. (1998). Teaching critical thinking for transfer across domains. *American Psychologist, 53*(4), 449–455.

Halpern, D. F. (2003). *Thought and knowledge: An introduction to critical thinking* (4th ed.). Mahwah, NJ: Lawrence Erlbaum.

Hanko, K. (2007). Focalism. In R. F. Baumeister & K. D. Vohs (Eds.), *Encyclopedia of social psychology* (vol. 1, pp. 352–353). Thousand Oaks, CA: SAGE.

Hannus, M., & Hyönä, J. (1999). Utilization of illustrations during learning of science textbook passages among low- and high-ability children. *Contemporary Educational Psychology, 24*(2), 95–123.

Kahneman, D. (2011). *Thinking fast and slow.* New York: Farrar: Straus & Giroux.

Kendeou, P., & O'Brien, E. J. (2018). Reading comprehension theories: A view from the top down. In M. F. Schober, D. N. Rapp, & M. A. Britt (Eds.), *The Routledge handbook of discourse processes* (pp. 7–21). New York: Routledge.

Kienhues, D., Stadtler, M., & Bromme, R. (2011). Dealing with conflicting or consistent medical information on the web: When expert information breeds laypersons' doubts about experts. *Learning and Instruction, 21*(2), 193–204.

Kowalski, P., & Taylor, A. K. (2004). Ability and critical thinking as predictors of change in students' psychological misconception. *Journal of Instructional Psychology, 31*(4), 297–303.

Kozma, R. B., & Russell, J. (1997). Multimedia and understanding: Expert and novice responses to different representations of chemical phenomena. *Journal of Research in Science Teaching, 34*(9), 949–968.

Kray, L. J., & Galinsky, A. D. (2003). The debiasing effect of counterfactual mind-sets: Increasing the search for disconfirmatory information in group decisions. *Organizational Behavior and Human Decision Processes, 91*(1), 69–81.

Lai, E. R. (2011). *Critical thinking: A literature review.* Pearson research report. Iowa City, IA: Pearson.

Larkin, J. H., & Simon, H. A. (1987). Why a diagram is (sometimes) worth ten thousand words. *Cognitive Science, 11*, 65–99.

Lebreton, L., Slat, B., Ferrari, F., Sainte-Rose, B., Aitken, J., Marthouse, R., … Reisser, J. (2018). Evidence that the Great Pacific Garbage Patch is rapidly accumulating plastic. *Scientific Reports, 8*, 1.

Lewis, A., & Smith, D. (1993). Defining higher order thinking. *Theory into Practice, 32*(3), 131–137.

Lipman, M. (1988). Critical thinking: What can it be?. *Educational Leadership, 46*(1), 38–43.

Lord, C. G., Ross, L., & Lepper, M. R. (1979). Biased assimilation and attitude polarization: The effects of prior theories on subsequently considered evidence. *Journal of Personality and Social Psychology, 37*(11), 2098–2109.

Lowe, R. K. (2003). Animation and learning: Selective processing of information in dynamic graphics. *Learning and Instruction, 13*(2), 157–176.

Mason, L., Tornatora, M. C., & Pluchino, P. (2013). Do fourth graders integrate text and picture in processing and learning from an illustrated science text? Evidence from eye-movement patterns. *Computers and Education, 60*(1), 95–109.

Mayer, R. E. (2014). Cognitive theory of multimedia learning. In R. Mayer (Ed.), *The Cambridge handbook of multimedia learning* (2nd ed., pp. 43–71). Cambridge: Cambridge University Press.

McPeck, J. E. (1990). Critical thinking and subject specificity: A reply to Ennis. *Educational Researcher, 19*(4), 10–12.

National Geographic Society. (2012). Great Pacific Garbage Patch. Oct. 9. www.nationalgeographic.org/encyclopedia/great-pacific-garbage-patch/

National Governors Association Center for Best Practices, Council of Chief State School Officers. (2010). Common core standards Washington, DC: Author. Retrieved from www.corestandards.org/the-standards

NCTM. (2006). *Curriculum focal points for prekindergarten through grade 8 mathematics: A quest for coherence.* Reston, VA: NCTM.

Newell, A., & Simon, H. A. (1972). *Human problem solving.* Englewood Cliffs, NJ: Prentice Hall.

Newitz, A. (2012). Lies you've been told about the pacific Garbage Patch. May 21. https://io9.gizmodo.com/5911969/lies-youve-been-told-about-the-pacific-garbage-patch

Nicholson, J. L., & Leighton, G. R. (1942). Plastics come of age. *Harper's Magazine, 185* (Aug.), 300–307.

NRC. (2006). *Learning to think spatially.* Washington, DC: National Academies Press.

Nyhan, B., & Reifler, J. (2010). When corrections fail: The persistence of political misperceptions. *Political Behavior, 32*(2), 303–330.

Nyhan, B., & Reifler, J. (2015). Does correcting myths about the flu vaccine work? An experimental evaluation of the effects of corrective information. *Vaccine, 33*(3), 459–464.

OECD. (2016). *Trends shaping education 2016.* Paris: OECD.

Paul, R. (1992). *Critical thinking: What every person needs to survive in a rapidly changing world* (2nd ed.). Rohnert Park, CA: Foundation for Critical Thinking.

Paul, R. W., & Elder, L. (2006). *The miniature guide to critical thinking: Concepts and tools* (4th ed.). Dillon Beach, CA: Foundation for Critical Thinking.

Pew Research Center (2018). Western Europeans under 30 view news media less positively, rely more on digital platforms than older adults. Oct. www.journalism.org/2018/10/30/western-europeans-under-30-view-news-media-less-positively-rely-more-on-digital-platforms-than-older-adults/

Rau, M. A., & Matthews, P. G. (2017). How to make "more" better? Principles for effective use of multiple representations to enhance students' learning about fractions. *ZDM, 49*(4), 531–544.

Rice, D. (2018). World's largest collection of ocean garbage is twice the size of Texas. Dec. 28. www.usatoday.com/story/tech/science/2018/03/22/great-pacific-garbage-patch-grows/446405002/

Rouet, J.-F. (2009). Managing cognitive load during document-based learning. *Learning and Instruction, 19*(5), 445–450.

Royce, C. S., Hayes, M. M., & Schwartzstein, R. M. (2019). Teaching critical thinking: A case for instruction in cognitive biases to reduce diagnostic errors and improve patient safety. *Academic Medicine, 94*(2), 187–194.

Schnotz, W. (2014). Integrated model of text and picture comprehension. In R. Mayer (Ed.), *The Cambridge handbook of multimedia learning* (2nd ed., pp. 72–103). Cambridge: Cambridge University Press.

Schwonke, R., Berthold, K., & Renkl, A. (2009). How multiple external representations are used and how they can be made more useful. *Applied Cognitive Psychology, 23*(9), 1227–1243.

Segers, E., & Verhoeven, L. (2009). Learning in a sheltered internet environment: The use of Webquests. *Learning and Instruction, 19*(5), 423–432.

Seufert, T. (2003). Supporting coherence formation in learning from multiple representations. *Learning and Instruction, 13*(2), 227–237.

Shanahan, T., & Shanahan, C. (2008). Teaching disciplinary literacy to adolescents: Rethinking content-area literacy. *Harvard Educational Review, 78*(1), 40–59.

Siegel, H. (1992). The generalizability of critical thinking skills, disposition, and epistemology. In S. P. Norris (Ed.), *The generalizability of critical thinking: Multiple perspectives on an educational ideal* (pp. 97–108). New York: Teachers College Press.

Sinatra, G. M., Kienhues, D., & Hofer, B. K. (2014). Addressing challenges to public understanding of science: Epistemic cognition, motivated reasoning, and conceptual change. *Educational Psychologist, 49*(2), 123–138.

Stadtler, M., & Bromme, R. (2013). Multiple document comprehension: An approach to public understanding of science. *Cognition and Instruction, 31*(2), 122–129.

Stern, E., Aprea, C., & Ebner, H. G. (2003). Improving cross-content transfer in text processing by means of active graphical representation. *Learning and Instruction, 13*(2), 191–203.

Sternberg, R. J. (1986). *Critical thinking: Its nature, measurement, and improvement.* Washington, DC: National Institute of Education.

Stieff, M., Hegarty, M., & Deslongchamps, G. (2011). Identifying representational competence with multi-representational displays. *Cognition and Instruction*, *29*(1), 123–145.

Tabachneck, H. J. M., Leonardo, A. M., & Simon, H. A. (1994). How does an expert use a graph? A model of visual and verbal inferencing in economics. In A. Ram & K. Eiselt (Eds.), *16th annual conference of the Cognitive Science Society* (pp. 842–847). Hillsdale, NJ: Erlbaum.

Trivers, R. (1991). Deceit and self-deception: The relationship between communication and consciousness. In M. Robinson & L. Tiger (Eds.), *Man and beast revisited* (pp. 175–191). Washington, DC: Smithsonian.

Tsipursky, G., & Morford, Z. (2018). Addressing behaviors that lead to sharing fake news. *Behavior and Social Issues*, *27*, AA6-AA10.

Tsui, L. (2002). Fostering critical thinking through effective pedagogy: Evidence from four institutional case studies. *Journal of Higher Education*, *73*(6), 740–763.

Tversky, A., & Kahneman, D. (1974). Judgment under uncertainty: Heuristics and biases. *Science*, *185*(4157), 1124–1131.

Uttal, D. H., & O'Doherty, K. (2008). Comprehending and learning from 'visualizations': A developmental perspective. In J. K. Gilbert, M. Reiner, & M. Nakhleh (Eds.), *Visualization: Theory and practice in science education* (pp. 53–72). OECD: Springer.

van der Meij, J., & de Jong, T. (2006). Supporting students' learning with multiple representations in a dynamic simulation-based learning environment. *Learning and Instruction*, *16*(3), 199–212.

van Gelder, T. (2005). Teaching critical thinking: Some lessons from cognitive science. *College Teaching*, *53*(1), 41–48.

VanSledright, B., & Maggioni, L. (2016). Epistemic cognition in history. In J. A. Greene, W. A. Sandoval, & I. Bråten (Eds.), *Handbook of epistemic cognition* (pp. 128–146). New York: Routledge.

Wansink, B., Akkerman, S., Zuiker, I., & Wubbels, T. (2018). Where does teaching multiperspectivity in history education begin and end? An analysis of the uses of temporality. *Theory and Research in Social Education*, *46*(4), 495–527.

West, R. F., Toplak, M. E., & Stanovich, K. E. (2008). Heuristics and biases as measures of critical thinking: Associations with cognitive ability and thinking dispositions. *Journal of Educational Psychology*, *100*(4), 930–941.

Wiley, J., Goldman, S. R., Graesser, A. C., Sanchez, C. A., Ash, I. K., & Hemmerich, J. A. (2009). Source evaluation, comprehension, and learning in Internet science inquiry tasks. *American Educational Research Journal*, *46*(4), 1060–1106.

Willingham, D. T. (2007). Critical thinking: Why is it so hard to teach? *Arts Education Policy Review*, *109*(4), 21–32.

Wopereis, I. G. J. H., & van Merriënboer, J. J. G. (2011). Evaluating text-based information on the World Wide Web. *Learning and Instruction*, *21*(2), 232–237.

Section 4
Challenges and Solutions

25

ASSESSING AND MODIFYING KNOWLEDGE

Facts vs. Constellations

David N. Rapp, Amalia M. Donovan, and Nikita A. Salovich

NORTHWESTERN UNIVERSITY, EVANSTON

ABSTRACT

There is a rich philosophical and empirical history associated with examinations of the nature of knowledge. Epistemological queries have focused on determining how to characterize knowledge, and on developing methods of supporting people's accurate understandings. The resulting work has led to contentious debates about whether, when, and how knowledge is amenable to change. These are timely disputes given contemporary concerns about the consequences of exposure to inaccurate information from multiple perspectives (including but not limited to social media, fake news, and unsubstantiated reports), and how information from competing sources influences people's understandings of the world. Emerging investigations have focused on when and in what ways people might modify what they know. In the current chapter, we highlight two distinct ways that "what people know" has been characterized – as declarative ideas and as constellations of ideas. Different concepts and topics might reflect either of these representational possibilities, which has crucial implications for epistemological investigations and claims about how to modify knowledge. We highlight the challenges and problems that can emerge when researchers confabulate distinct conceptualizations of knowledge representation. These are important considerations for selecting methodological approaches, deriving theoretical models, and arguing for (or against) the generalizability of findings. Suggestions for wrestling with these issues are offered.

Key words: knowledge, epistemology, updating, learning, mental representation

Classic and contemporary accounts of learning and comprehension are informed by philosophical and empirical examinations of knowledge, including ontological origins, development, and epistemology. This has also guided the design and implementation of instructional interventions in formal and informal learning settings. Fields including cognitive science, computer science, learning science, educational psychology, STEM content domains, literacy initiatives, history and civics education, curriculum design, special education, and philosophy have offered data, models, criticisms, and hypotheses about the way knowledge is constructed and how knowledge acquisition can be supported. In addition to many points of commonality, there are clear disciplinary differences across these fields with respect to how knowledge is studied, influencing the accounts proffered as speaking to the structure and contents of what people know (Hofer & Pintrich, 1997; Koedinger, Corbett, & Perfetti, 2012).

With respect to the nature of knowledge, two critical issues are regularly foregrounded by both academic and lay audiences given contemporary concerns about news reporting, media or authorial bias, information dissemination, and the spread of inaccurate information. The first involves determining how to characterize people's misunderstandings. The second involves identifying best practices for helping people reflect on and correct inaccurate understandings. These issues are the focus of this chapter, and are central to intellectual investigations of the nature and scope of knowledge. They reflect core topics within the theoretical philosophy of epistemology, namely, understanding what knowledge is and how it is constructed (e.g., Bonjour, 2002). Answering these fundamental questions proves relevant to concerns about people's exposure to, propagation of, and reliance on inaccurate information. They are also crucial considerations for discussing how people deal with information provided by multiple sources, as perspectives and presentations from both unreliable and reliable informants can include discrepancies, inconsistencies, and falsehoods (see Sanderson & Ecker, Chapter 26, for a discussion of "misinformation," and Kendeou et al., Chapter 27, for a discussion of "fake news"). Understanding when and why people notice and act on such issues requires clear explications of what knowledge is, including the processes and products involved in acquiring understandings and modifying what we know.

Addressing these issues involves identifying what is meant by terms including "misunderstandings" and "inaccurate understandings." A preliminary definition might identify an inaccurate understanding as running counter to what experts, evidence, and logic have determined to be valid. For example, someone who claims that the Earth is flat has failed to take into account an accumulated body of evidence to the contrary, and misunderstands the shape of the planet (and, as a result, other related issues). Not all misunderstandings, though, fit this easy definition. Many misunderstandings are associated with ideas and concepts for which there is substantial debate, including evidence for both sides of an argument, which makes assessments of accuracy less than trivial. For example, physics and metaphysical investigations of the nature of matter are sometimes presented as divided with respect to whether matter is composed of particles or strings. The two accounts involve sets of assumptions, sometimes overlapping and sometimes diverging, that make them difficult to reconcile. And yet specific elements of each account may be more or less viable under different circumstances depending on the evidence marshalled, the logical arguments provided, and the context of the particular physics problem being investigated.

This highlights a general consideration for discussions of epistemology in a variety of content areas and knowledge domains, in no way restricted just to this physics example, and directly pertinent to inaccurate understandings. Namely, aspects of what people seem to understand might be correct or incorrect depending on the time, context, and method by which knowledge is invoked. Misunderstandings therefore are a function of agreed upon principles and evidence, at times dependent upon situational considerations (Halldén, Scheja, & Haglund, 2008; Vosniadou & Brewer, 1992). While some misunderstandings are circumscribed, such as being wrong about particular facts (e.g., that the Atlantic is the biggest ocean in the world when in fact the Pacific is the largest), other misunderstandings can involve a variety of components that are difficult to disentangle, and that can motivate additional inferences and ideas that speak to other conceptual topics and issues (e.g., misconstrued accounts of complex phenomena such as the causes of economic crises or the repercussions of legislation on society).

But what precisely constitutes the knowledge inherent in people's misunderstandings? This question necessitates identifying the fundamental architecture of knowledge, which means the form and structure of what people know. If knowledge is, for example, rigidly held, with ideas encoded as fully fleshed out accounts and theories, our expectations about the best methods for addressing potential misunderstandings, and how easy they will be to address, will be quite different than if knowledge is more malleable, with concepts variably invoked as a function of experience, credibility, available evidence, context, and so on. These possibilities are actually the skeletal versions of two sides of rigorous debate between researchers in the cognitive and learning sciences (diSessa, 2008; Özdemir & Clark, 2007; Smith, diSessa, & Roschelle, 1993).

Specifying the nature of knowledge and misunderstandings is therefore a more challenging issue than might be addressed in a single chapter or volume. Nevertheless, we begin (some might say revisit) this issue with a discussion of two general ways that knowledge has been characterized to help outline what "inaccurate understandings" are or might be. This discussion is necessary for addressing the earlier identified issues – determining how to characterize people's knowledge, and using that information to help people build and maintain more accurate understandings. These concerns necessarily move beyond purely philosophical questions about the nature of knowledge, motivating applied considerations relevant for developing effective assessments, curricula, and instructional supports.

CONTEMPORARY ACCOUNTS OF KNOWLEDGE

Theorists and researchers have characterized knowledge in a variety of ways, which has led to vociferous theoretical debates. Differing opinions about those characterizations, as informed by empirical examinations, has resulted in opposing orientations and frameworks not just with respect to emerging epistemological accounts, but also for derived recommendations about the design of instructional materials and environments. It is beyond the scope of this chapter to describe all of the various accounts and empirical projects supporting these views. Rather, in defining accounts and implications related to the nature of knowledge, we will draw heavily on literature from domains dedicated to studying the modification of knowledge, as this is the primary focus of this chapter. In doing so, we will separate prevailing accounts into two groupings, fully realizing that such a dichotomous organization eliminates nuances associated with the accounts. However, this organization captures critical elements of the character of such accounts, and allows for highlighting critical considerations and limitations of their underlying arguments. (More generally, these disparate views connect with the theme of this volume, highlighting the differing perspectives that routinely emerge in people's investigations and arguments concerning the nature of knowledge.)

One set of views focuses on knowledge as complete, organized contents stored in memory. These "packets" of knowledge are well-formed, being encoded, stored, and retrieved wholesale from memory. Accounts endorsing this perspective are often termed *theory* or *holistic* views (e.g., Caramazza, McCloskey, & Green, 1981; Carey, 1985; Chi, 2005; McCloskey, 1983; Vosniadou, 1994). A crucial component of these accounts is that knowledge is stored in coherent, organized groupings involving relatively stable components. Thus, knowledge may be consistent over time, particularly in the absence of any substantial intervention aimed at encouraging the encoding or construction of new understandings. In practice, such views of knowledge often highlight declarative facts and schematic understandings as being applied during comprehension. Because these representations are holistic, any attempt at modifying them requires adopting a new schema or idea that is more viable or accurate than a previous one. Rather than attempting to shift or mold singular ideas in a direction more in line with expert understandings, for example, holistic views of knowledge may suggest that learners need to rely upon entirely *new* understandings instead of their pre-existing knowledge structures (McCloskey, 1983; Posner, Strike, Hewson, & Gertzog, 1982). As a result, inaccurate understandings obstruct the development of more rigorous understandings.

Another set of views has been positioned in opposition to these holistic accounts contending that when people encode, store, or retrieve information from memory, no set or organized system or even predictable structure is involved. Rather, disparate pieces of knowledge may be recruited, depending on individual and situational variables associated with an encoding or retrieval context (Clark, 2006; Saglam, Karaaslan, & Ayas, 2010; Smith et al., 1993). This view contends that during comprehension, people draw upon a range of different "bits" of knowledge and attempt to establish coherence among them, with the particular bits a learner utilizes varying across time and setting. Accounts endorsing this perspective have been termed *knowledge-in-pieces* or *fragmented* views (e.g., diSessa, 1993; diSessa, Gillespie, & Esterly, 2004; Smith et al., 1993). By these accounts, when individuals acquire information, newly constructed representations are of course potentially stored in long-term memory, but those representations are not guaranteed to be accessed routinely or consistently later on. This creates distinct challenges for learning, requiring more than simply updating or replacing coherent, consistently retrieved knowledge structures. Because the ideas underlying knowledge are less than systematic, coherent, or holistic, and are instead informed by many different experiences and contexts, attempts to completely modify what someone may understand can be difficult and unlikely to succeed. Even if modification is successful, as demonstrated with the acquisition of a more valid understanding, it need not guarantee the same valid understanding will routinely emerge in the future because of the interaction of factors described above. Conceptualizing knowledge as fragmented can allow for fine-grained examinations of the knowledge that learners possess, as it requires attending to and characterizing individual aspects of knowledge on its own terms. One argument is that such attention affords more precisely targeted interventions for fostering the development of rigorous understandings by leveraging elements of inaccurate understandings that may be useful in different circumstances.

Again, our characterizations here simplify the varied conceptualizations of knowledge that have been offered by theorists and researchers across fields. Nevertheless, this dichotomization helps elucidate two well-established perspectives that more nuanced accounts often endorse to a greater or lesser extent. Some views have even attempted to integrate holistic and knowledge-in-pieces views in efforts to describe human epistemology and explain how knowledge develops over time (e.g., Alexander & Baggetta, 2014; Hammer & Elby, 2002). To illustrate, consider an important contrast between expert and novice representations of knowledge: Experts, as compared to novices, often hold not just a greater quantity of knowledge, but also demonstrate more effective use of that knowledge to solve problems. Experts can flexibly draw upon a range of different concepts and relational connections during problem solving in their domain of expertise (Chi, Glaser, & Rees, 1982). Novices, who have considerably less experience to draw upon, may not process incoming information as effectively, or readily recognize meaningful patterns (Chase & Simon, 1973). For example, while experts place problems into groups based on the underlying semantic similarities core to the problems, novices organize problems based on potentially irrelevant surface features and descriptors (Chi, Feltovich, & Glaser, 1981; Novick, 1988). Novice knowledge may therefore reflect more disparate, piecemeal organizations that include varied features related or unrelated to underlying core concepts in a domain. With continued experience and practice, their representations may become more theory-based, allowing for easier identification and classification of the crucial elements and relational connections that characterize problems. We have described this integrated possibility not necessarily as an endorsement of its validity, but to illustrate how accounts have been leveraged in theoretically intriguing (and not uncontroversial) ways that attempt to bridge holistic and piecemeal views.

MODIFYING FACTS VS. CONSTELLATIONS OF KNOWLEDGE

The perspectives articulated above have, as critical to their accounts, provided explicit notions of how easy or challenging it might be to modify knowledge. We have opted to use the relatively generic term *modify* when referring to any attempt to alter what people know as it could involve a variety of processes and activities, including but not limited to assimilation (i.e., adding to what is already known), accommodation or revision (i.e., changing what is known), compartmentalization (i.e., tagging some portion of knowledge as relevant under some circumstances or situations but not others), conceptual change (i.e., impacting networks of interconnected ideas that are part of larger conceptual structures), and restructuration (i.e., building new representations and ways of thinking). (We will later focus on some of these cases to highlight specific kinds of investigations with respect to modifying knowledge.) The term updating is also popular, although it might be taken to mean that previous information is no longer available, despite a considerable body of evidence indicating that not to be the case even with projects that explicitly use the term (e.g., O'Brien, Rizzella, Albrecht, & Halleran, 1998; Taylor & Rapp, 2006).

Our decision to rely on the term modify relates not just to the range of effects that may or may not occur during learning experiences, but also aligns with the line of argument we will attempt to put forward: The ways in which researchers and theorists conceptualize knowledge, and whether and how modification might occur, is linked to their methodological decisions and any derived empirical claims being offered. These issues could be discussed in a variety of ways. We focus on how prevailing accounts conceptualize people's inaccurate understandings, as these constitute situations in which it would be preferable for people to modify what they know. This necessitates explicating what is constrained by the nature of knowledge articulated in the accounts, and also what might be expected or likely to obtain following attempts to modify knowledge, as based on empirical findings.

We begin by considering how *holistic* accounts of knowledge tend to conceptualize inaccurate understandings. Recall that these accounts hypothesize that knowledge is typically stored in coherent structures, which may be correct or incorrect. The goal is to attempt to modify incorrect accounts with valid and accurate understandings. As an example, consider someone possessing an incorrect declarative idea, such as where a country is located (e.g., Mexico being part of South America rather than North America), or the timeframe of a particular historical event (e.g., that the French and Indian War occurred in the 1800s rather than 1700s). If a factual misunderstanding can be modified to reflect accurate understandings, the resulting changes in learner knowledge could be classified as *knowledge revision*, with the previous inaccuracies replaced by new knowledge. To clarify this point, imagine a learner who has a factual misunderstanding that the capital of Illinois is Chicago. The goal of instruction would be to revise that incorrect understanding with the correct fact. Negating the idea that Chicago is the capital and offering the correct idea that Springfield is the capital can thus be helpful. Additional activities can strengthen and maintain this new understanding in memory, such as including repeated exposures to the accurate idea, asking learners to generate the idea rather than simply reading it (Jacoby, 1978; Roediger & Karpicke, 2006), and offering supplemental explanations (e.g., that state capitals are not necessarily, or even all that often, located in the most populous cities within a state). These activities help learners correct misunderstandings and maintain more coherent, valid knowledge (e.g., Rapp & Kendeou, 2007).

Of course, not all knowledge can be appropriately categorized as involving declarative facts, and may thus be less likely to enjoy benefits from these modestly designed instructional activities. But many kinds of misunderstandings *do* involve unitary, stable ideas that have been encoded based on evidence or claims. These declarative misunderstandings should not be characterized as unimportant to people's everyday considerations as they often underlie and inform deeper and more elaborate understandings. For example, identifying the locations of US state capitals could support inferences about historical events, economic developments, and other socio-historical conjectures and hypotheses. A focus on declarative misunderstandings allows for envisioning some knowledge structures as amenable to relatively simple and direct prompts for modification.

The requisite processes underlying such modification have been articulated in a variety of models, such as the Knowledge Revision Components (KReC) Framework (Kendeou & O'Brien, 2014). There are several stipulations associated with the framework, but we focus on three critical to the discussion here. When learners are presented with information running counter to what they know, they first engage in *co-activation*. This requires simultaneously considering newly presented information and relevant prior knowledge. The new information must then be *integrated* with prior knowledge to allow for modifying existing understandings and to connect new and old information in memory. The remaining challenge is that learners need to *activate* their new understandings, perhaps as prompted by instructions or other external motivators, to a greater degree than their prior incorrect knowledge. If multiple sets of competing, co-activated ideas are equally available, people may be confused and/or default to what they had learned previously (Rapp & Salovich, 2018). Revision, in this framework, necessitates the encoding of new ideas in mental structures, with learners privileging those new ideas over previous structures if sufficient attention, evidence, and practice are applied to those newly encoded memories. A critical assumption of this model, and others including the Landscape model (van Den Broek, Rapp, & Kendeou, 2005), the Discrepancy-Induced Sources Comprehension Model (Braasch & Bråten, 2017), and the RI-Val model (O'Brien & Cook, 2016), is that revision does not result in prior understandings being completely overwritten or eliminated. Rather, new structures receive more support and activation that afford their use. Any resulting understandings might therefore be classified as successful knowledge revision. The term *reliance* rather than revision is sometime invoked to refer to people's use of a particular set of ideas or understandings over others (Donovan, Theodosis, & Rapp, 2018; Rapp, Hinze, Kohlhepp, & Ryskin, 2014; Rapp & Salovich, 2018).

A variety of methods for encouraging reliance on more appropriate and valid ideas have been proposed. Empirically validated methods often involve the use of materials that confront people' misunderstandings by highlighting discrepancies between what they know or believe and what they *should* know or believe (Braasch & Bråten, 2017; Braasch, Rouet, Vibert, & Britt, 2012). An example involves refutation texts, which are written materials that point out prominent misunderstandings, discount their utility and validity, and provide accurate accounts intended to counter the misunderstandings (Hynd & Alvermann, 1986; Sinatra & Broughton, 2011; Tippett, 2010). Refutation texts support updating by facilitating the processes that underlie knowledge revision as articulated above. They present information such that inaccurate and accurate structures are potentially co-activated, present the accounts in close proximity with explicit descriptions intended to integrate them, and include explanations highlighting one co-activated idea as more reasonable or more accurate than the other, increasing the likelihood that the highlighted idea will be available and activated during subsequent opportunities to apply knowledge (Kendeou & O'Brien, 2014).

A large body of literature has consistently shown that refutation texts support the development of accurate understandings, with readers more likely to remember, endorse, and use accurate as compared to inaccurate information after reading refutation texts relative to texts that simply present ideas (e.g., Guzzetti, Snyder, Glass, & Gamas, 1993; Hynd & Alvermann, 1986; Sinatra & Broughton, 2011; Tippett, 2010). Readers exhibit more frequent efforts to integrate text content with prior knowledge after reading refutation texts as compared to after reading non-refutation texts, as measured with verbal productions during reading (Kendeou & van Den Broek, 2007). Readers also remember more content generally, and more accurate content specifically, after reading refutation compared to non-refutation texts as measured with free recall tasks (Donovan, Zhan, & Rapp, 2018). They also show enhanced performance on a variety of comprehension measures (e.g., recall and recognition tests for text content) after reading refutations relative to non-refutation texts, with the resulting memory benefits retained over time (Frède, 2008; Nussbaum, Cordova, & Rehmat, 2017).

Much of what we know, however, exhibits greater complexity than should be associated with separable, declarative facts. As examples, understandings of the role of vaccinations in maintaining public health, the antecedents and consequences of military conflicts, or even the causes of climate change (see Lombardi, Danielson, & Young, 2016 for a discussion of climate-related considerations), cannot be easily broken down into disparate facts amenable to simple correction. Instead, they interact with contextual factors as well as with people's existing knowledge, beliefs, and identities. This is not meant to diminish the importance of factual accuracy, but rather to indicate that many ideas and concepts are complicated, necessitating different considerations for theoretical accounts and remediations. If these understandings involve many interacting elements, holistic approaches are unlikely to encourage modification. When the representations underlying someone's perceptions and understandings of the world invoke multiple moving parts that are differentially active and appropriate under different circumstances, and that lack a clear and easily constructed set of explanations, these complex knowledge structures are more likely associated with a knowledge-in-pieces rather than a holistic view. When understandings involve a network of related ideas, each of which might fall along a continuum of accuracy, with the connections between them also conveying more or less accuracy, it is less likely that a targeted intervention designed to dispute a particular element from a holistic perspective would be particularly effective.

This is worth deep consideration given the range of perspectives that are often associated with various complicated topics, and for which we might hope to encourage modifications to support evaluative and accurate understandings. Consider claims about vaccinations as an example. Different forms of knowledge could be drawn upon in attempts to explain the impact that vaccinations have on public health (Zingg & Siegrist, 2012). People's understandings of scientific findings regarding the efficacy of vaccinations for reducing or eradicating diseases, their conceptualizations of the hallmarks of rigorous scientific inquiry, and their exposure to pertinent concepts like "herd immunity," could all be critically implicated. Social constructions about the roles of doctors, schools, pharmaceutical companies, and other actors in proposals for and against vaccinations may likewise come into play. Further, direct interactions with disease outbreaks, health sciences, and healthcare service providers, among numerous other possibilities, however idiosyncratic, also influence people's understandings of vaccines. A plethora of personal experiences and information obtained through primary and secondary sources of differing credibility and with differing presentation goals can make understanding complex concepts and models (such as inoculation) difficult (see Moran, Lucas, Everhart, Morgan, & Prickett, 2016). Even experts who regularly convey accurate ideas can hold pieces of incorrect understandings, although they are better than non-experts at suppressing reliance on those inaccuracies (Kelemen, Rottman, & Seston, 2013; Masson, Potvin, Riopel, & Brault-Foisy, 2014). Thus, the sets of experiences and information people activate, defer to, or discount as they debate and make decisions about vaccinations is influenced by the situations and contingencies in which they are having those debates and making those decisions.

Delineating an exhaustive list of the kinds of knowledge of potential importance to the topic of vaccinations, or to any other topic or account, would be impossible. Examples such as this one are therefore intended to illustrate that different kinds of interventions may be necessary for different misunderstandings, given the potential diversity in their constituent components. Interventions intended to encourage reliance on a particular correct piece of information may have limited utility when the underlying misunderstandings incorporate many and variable pieces of knowledge. When knowledge involves constellations of different ideas coalescing into moment-by-moment understandings that need not remain consistent or coherent over time, *conceptual change* may be necessary rather than the previously discussed revision approaches. We discuss this next as it requires (and exemplifies) a specifically knowledge-in-pieces approach to modifying knowledge.

Conceptual change involves modifications to central or core aspects of particular understandings in a network of knowledge (made up of encoded facts, percepts, interpretations, and so on), and is considered an especially challenging and time-consuming form of learning (diSessa & Sherin, 1998; Gentner et al., 1997). Unfortunately, the term conceptual change has at times been applied to *any* attempt to modify knowledge, whether involving a single fact or a complicated network of ideas. Distinguishing conceptual change from the modification of singular ideas is integral for developing precise accounts of knowledge change and suitable interventions to induce it (Kendeou, Butterfuss, Van Boekel, & O'Brien, 2017). We endorse the view that, in contrast to knowledge revision, conceptual change necessitates modification of elements of knowledge networks and constellations (which again are no more or less important than other types or forms of knowledge), and is a gradual, effortful process (diSessa & Sherin, 1998; Smith et al., 1993).

To differentiate the ways conceptual change gets liberally used and the specific instances to which it should refer, consider some concrete examples. When a student encodes a new idea into their existing body of factual knowledge about vaccines (e.g., that Edward Jenner pioneered the development of the smallpox vaccine), conceptual change would not be the most appropriate explanation for such learning. This example involves encoding a single idea or fact that does not necessitate reorganizing or restructuring knowledge networks. Similarly, some kinds of inaccurate ideas (e.g., misunderstanding vaccines to be a contemporary invention rather than dating back to the 18th century) can be discounted and revised by providing a single case or example of why that idea is incorrect. In stark contrast, if someone held the conviction that the choice of whether to vaccinate is an independent, free decision with no ramifications for society, a brief refutation would be insufficient for addressing this idea, given it is likely informed by many other related understandings (or misunderstandings) about public health, disease spread and prevalence, the development and implementation of vaccinations, and so on. Any effort to modify this misunderstanding would require addressing the multiple, interrelated ideas and concepts associated with it. Conceptual change, as exemplified here, requires more than a single contradictory example or even extended refutation, given that changing one element of a constellation has no guarantee of enacting cascading effects on related knowledge components. Activities associated with conceptual change require multiple experiences and approaches to redress constellations of knowledge (diSessa & Sherin, 1998). When our understandings are buffeted and informed by diverse perspectives involving different values, beliefs, forms of evidence (or views on what counts as evidence), logical claims, flawed arguments, perceptual experiences, and so on, repeated exposures to accurate information offered through potentially different modalities proves crucial for supporting conceptual change.

By this view, whether misunderstandings are constrained and bounded or made up of many interacting representations, traditional teaching methods involving direct instruction and attempts to correct inaccuracies are often insufficient for promoting accurate understandings (Chi, 2008; Simpson & Marek, 1988). They can fail to identify or address ideas in students' knowledge, or the ways those ideas are organized and related in memory, that are implicated in the misunderstanding. Communicating accurate ideas without careful assessment of learners' pre-existing knowledge about a topic may not lead to substantive changes in the quality of learners' complex misunderstandings. And if only some aspects of a complex misunderstanding are addressed, or if the accurate explanations offered map poorly onto a learner's prior knowledge, misunderstandings are likely to remain (Chi, 2005; Fisher, 2004).

Conceptual change therefore repositions the design of instructional experiences from the direct teaching of accurate ideas to the deep consideration of a student's existing knowledge on a given topic, and the value that knowledge may hold for the development of more rigorous understandings (diSessa & Minstrell, 1998; Swanson & Collins, 2018). Rather than simply presenting correct ideas about vaccinations in a public health class, an instructor might instead frame the learning experience as a discussion about vaccinations to which students would contribute their current understandings of the topic. This activity can then provide the foundation for more nuanced understandings to be developed through scaffolded tasks and discourse (Lombardi, Bailey, Bickel, & Burrell, 2018). What makes this approach valuable is that it emphasizes the utility of a learner's existing knowledge. By drawing on and highlighting pieces of knowledge that learners possess about a topic, rather than focusing on the flaws or inaccuracies in those understandings, instructors can "take stock" of learners' knowledge, both formatively and summatively, during remediation. Such an approach is not easy, not without potential drawbacks, and not appropriate for all learning environments or topics. But a focus on sharing and building upon existing knowledge may be useful in attempts to develop more sophisticated understandings of topics involving constellations of knowledge. Some approaches that explicitly endorse this perspective, albeit with variability in the particular learning goals of interest, have included constructivist and constructionist learning environments (e.g., Wilensky & Reisman, 2006; Wilensky & Resnick, 1999), problem-based learning tasks (e.g., Hmelo-Silver, 2004), and analogical reasoning activities (e.g., Brown & Clement, 1989; Chi, Roscoe, Slotta, Roy, & Chase, 2012). It is worth noting that these approaches highlight the need for addressing misunderstandings by exposing learners to ideas from multiple perspectives and using multiple representations, with careful design to ensure the accompanying presentations provide consistent evidence for valid ideas and inferences.

CHALLENGES FOR ADDRESSING INACCURATE UNDERSTANDINGS

Following from the discussion above, knowledge revision should be specific to modifying people's use of particular declarative facts and ideas, while conceptual change should reference attempts to address multiple critical elements of ideas in a shifting knowledge space. When considered this way, many contemporary empirical investigations and theoretical discussions seem to confound processes of knowledge revision and conceptual change. This happens in at least two ways. First, it occurs when researchers hypothesize about or argue that their attempts at addressing inaccurate declarative ideas demonstrate broader modifications to knowledge. For example, people's misidentification of Chicago as the capital of Illinois likely involves a declarative misunderstanding rather than some larger set of ideas coalescing into the inaccurate notion. Categorizing this example as an instance of conceptual change overstates the degree of modification that is required, and the modification that results after an accurate version of the fact has been provided to correct the misunderstanding.

Second, projects can inappropriately describe complicated, piecemeal knowledge organizations as having been successfully modified following some modest attempt at remediation. In these cases, the problematic account might focus on how a rich understanding of some STEM topic has been instantiated by addressing a specific fact or idea. For example, an attempt to address people's misunderstandings about vaccinations might apply a specific game-like activity to indicate how a lack of vaccinations can lead to disease outbreaks. This tack, while useful, only addresses one element worth considering with respect to understanding vaccinations. As previously discussed, people's understandings of vaccinations, and many other topics, are likely to implicate a wide and idiosyncratic range of understandings. Focusing specifically on one element of the topic, such as disease propagation for vaccinations, addresses only a subset of the knowledge required to elicit a desired change.

In some cases, addressing a particularly important component of knowledge can have crucial utility, perhaps leading to cascading modifications of related knowledge structures as foundational elements are reconsidered and knowledge undergoes restructuration (Chi, 2008). But the effectiveness of such a targeted attempt to modify knowledge is dependent upon the sophistication and rigor with which researchers have ascertained the particular knowledge structures in question (including but not limited to how central the issues to be redressed are, and whether they are malleable on their own or not). In lieu of such an analysis, it is possible that individuals involved in the intended modification activity might reconsider one element of the situation or issue, but nevertheless endorse alternative explanations that still allow for understanding vaccinations as problematic even in the face of, or perhaps despite, the dangers of disease propagation.

To summarize: Given that inaccurate understandings can exhibit notably different characteristics, it is crucial to utilize appropriate terms and their underlying propositions in projects attempting to address them. If an approach designed to promote revision of factual misunderstandings is implemented to address constellations of inaccurate ideas, some components underlying the inaccurate understandings may receive insufficient attention or be overlooked. The desired conceptual change may therefore not be attained. Similarly, conceptual change activities might not be necessary to effectively revise specific declarative understandings, and might even encourage new, incorrect understandings if applied inappropriately.

An important, related concern is that researchers often utilize different methods to describe and address people's misunderstandings. Diverse approaches and perspectives, in principle, are fine and probably preferred, as different methods can offer useful epistemological insights or inform practical guidelines for instruction. But a challenge is that the particular method used to measure or address people's understandings might bias expectations for the kinds of knowledge issues attended to, as well as influence the approach selected to address any misunderstandings. Consider, for example, if a researcher uses intensive prompt-driven, semi-clinical interviews to elicit discussions of issues related to a concept, such as understandings of vaccinations. Such clinical interview methods are common in assessing knowledge modification (Posner & Gertzog, 1982), and can promote responses that appear to reflect piecemeal knowledge as a function of the methodology. This is because the conversational and open-ended nature of interviews affords speakers the chance to contribute more moment-by-moment productions, which can result in understandings often appearing more disjointed and varied than those elicited by other methodologies (Sherin, Krakowski, & Lee, 2012; VanSledright & Brophy, 1992; Vosniadou & Brewer, 1992). As a contrasting example, when people are asked to judge the validity of single sentences, the obtained results do not provide nuanced insight into the nature of the underlying knowledge structures being retrieved (or not) to make those decisions. Characterizing knowledge as declarative in this latter case is unsurprising, as the methodological tool here constitutes declarative statements, limiting or disallowing consideration of more spontaneous and elaborative productions (Posner & Gertzog, 1982). In a more extreme case, the method chosen to assess knowledge can even fail to detect existing misunderstandings. Consider that when children are asked to report the shape of the Earth, many correctly identify it as round. However, when instructed to provide a visual representation of their understandings, some draw erroneous shapes (such as flat pancakes) and, when asked to describe their understandings via interviews, may admit to thinking that people could fall off the surface of the Earth (Vosniadou & Brewer, 1992). Focusing on one method can only provide partial insight, or even prove invalid, for identifying what people know.

As an additional challenge, the particular method selected, and how it might be applied, can be informed by *a priori* expectations about the ways in which knowledge is structured or organized. This establishes obvious concerns about researchers finding evidence for claims or accounts they hope to find evidence for, rather than allowing for a grounded approach to observing trends and patterns in data. It also incites worries that a method might be utilized because it is associated with a particular methodological expertise or theoretical investment at the exclusion, intended or not, of other valuable approaches. This is not to devalue any particular methodology in promoting or assessing the learning or modification of knowledge. Both holistic retrieval and open-ended discourse can promote learning (or relearning) of information (Murphy, Wilkinson, Soter, Hennessey, & Alexander, 2009; Roediger & Karpicke, 2006). Rather, the upshot is that the methods researchers use to assess inaccurate understandings are necessarily motivated by, and consequently motivate how, knowledge will be examined and described (Bryce & Blown, 2016). Projects that collect open-ended responses from large bodies of conversational data, and/or that afford moment-by-moment insights into productions often offer more elaborative, nuanced, and piecemeal indicators of understanding than do projects that allow premeditated responses and/or that restrict the range of responses or decisions an individual can provide on a task (Posner & Gertzog, 1982; Sherin et al., 2012). These differences should be both acknowledged and appreciated by researchers and theorists collecting and reviewing the data.

Again, this is not meant to suggest that projects involving interviews or statement judgments are always problematic, or that one is always preferred over the other. Rather, our assertion is that researchers should be aware of and up front about how their selected dependent measures and research tasks embody potential predispositions as to how knowledge will be conceptualized and characterized. (See Rapp & Mensink, 2011, for a similar discussion more generally related to methodological decisions.)

NEW INSIGHTS AND FUTURE DIRECTIONS

Different characterizations of knowledge inform the ways in which scholars attempt to measure and discuss misunderstandings, and the accompanying interventions highlighted as most fruitful for addressing them. This necessitates careful consideration of whether the specific misunderstandings of interest involve singular declarative ideas or constellations of ideas. Empirical examinations could usefully document the consequences of an inappropriate match between the nature of a misunderstanding and the method used for its correction, as well as when context, credibility, prior learning, and other interacting factors are promoted or neglected in attempts at intervention. Consider that incomplete or mismatched attempts could relate to so-called backfire effects, in which projects that intend to target specific interventions, rather than having hypothesized beneficial effects, actually result in greater investment in inaccurate ideas as well as rejection of correct propositions (Nyhan & Reifler, 2010).

Fruitful examinations must also recognize and attend to the challenges associated with assessing knowledge. Any misunderstandings being assessed (e.g., the risks of vaccines, how governments operate, the impact of immigration on the economy) may or may not reflect actual or emerging constellations of ideas, and researcher intuitions about whether misunderstandings are declarative or not are insufficient for cataloging the nature of people's knowledge. Moreover, in efforts to categorize misunderstandings, we must acknowledge that the methods underlying assessments influence the emerging characterizations of knowledge, and associated expectations as to the appropriateness of particular intervention approaches. We call for careful consideration of the constraints and limits of methods used to address epistemological questions, and deep contemplation as to where, when, how, and from whom any expected norms of understandings are derived.

The question, then, is how to be more mindful in the assessment and modification of people's understandings. Projects that attempt to apply multiple methods, assessing both moment-by-moment thinking and the resulting products of such activity, should prove useful for informing epistemological accounts and instructional designs. Other approaches and strategies can effectively supplement multi-method projects. For example, the development and application of effective assessments would benefit from collaborations with experts in various content domains (e.g., STEM content areas). Expert insight into how knowledge is constructed and organized in a given topic area can inform decisions as to what would constitute evidence of accurate understandings and modified knowledge. This relates to a more general concern that studies purporting to examine such issues often fail to apply appropriate pre-test or pre-intervention assessments, calling into question whether learning is actually being tested as part of the project. Whether projects attempt to describe the preconceptions people possess using microgenetic analyses of interview responses, or develop experimental investigations to highlight the utility of refutation texts, some account of what people knew prior to participating in those procedures proves crucial for characterizing the contents of knowledge and the consequences of modification activities.

Although modifying inaccurate understandings may be difficult, attempts to do so are not fruitless. Many of the intuitive ideas that people have about the world are modified through formal and informal educational experiences, and maintained over time (e.g., Chi, 2008). Contemporary accounts should benefit from attending to methods that have successfully yielded substantial, durable change in people's understandings in content domains. This should also involve consideration as to whether and how these beneficial experiences might be applied to a broader range of topics. Efforts to surface the root(s) of a misunderstanding through deliberate assessment, including consideration of the complex individual and contextual factors that play a role in people's understandings, proves crucial for developing theoretical accounts and applied interventions that support people's thinking.

Future work also needs to consider the varied inputs that feed into people's experiences with the world, which can inform accurate and inaccurate understandings. Some accounts have highlighted the perceptual experiences that underlie understandings of STEM topics (e.g., Andre & Ding, 1991; diSessa, 1993), while others have explicated how carefully designed textual presentations can address STEM misunderstandings (Hynd, Alvermann, & Qian, 1997; Kendeou & van Den Broek, 2007; Sungur, Tekkaya, & Geban, 2001). These accounts focus on particular subsets of presentations as provided through grounded systems or through symbol systems. And yet our understandings about the world are informed by a diverse array of presentations, ranging from direct interactions with physical objects, to indirect information claimed and conjectured by others, to abstracted accountings derived across multiple experiences. Wrestling with the challenge of both how to account for these diverse experiences, as well as how to effectively examine them using qualitative and quantitative methodologies, is important for the field going forward. Identifying which sources people rely on and why proves necessary for establishing accounts of when and how people acquire and modify knowledge. In addition, contemporary concerns about the validity of what we routinely encounter from news outlets, social media sites, word-of-mouth, and so forth, call into question how we reconcile information presented from sources that may or may not be invested in presenting the truth. Future work should interrogate how people experience complex information environments, and the consequences of those experiences for knowledge acquisition and application during everyday problem solving and decision making. This requires establishing rich theoretical accounts that inform applied considerations with respect to describing and supporting people's learning from and about the world.

CONCLUSIONS

Researchers often laud different instructional approaches for helping people develop sophisticated understandings, including but not limited to refutation-based experiences, direct challenges to pertinent claims, hands-on construction activities, and traditional lectures. The approaches that might be most successful for promoting useful understandings crucially depend upon what people already know as well as the nature of the knowledge that underlies their comprehension. Greater care and clarity must be applied in articulating these features at the outset of instructional design, such that an intended approach aligns with the characteristics of the knowledge in question. We reiterate that research and application is necessary for effectively modifying both people's declarative understandings as well as their integrated knowledge structures. In many cases, our conceptual understandings are derived from declarative facts, in addition to many of our declarative claims being based on complicated accumulations of disparate ideas and experiences. Instructional approaches are required to help people develop correct understandings of the capital of Illinois *and* what roles vaccinations play in maintaining public health, although the methods most suitable for targeting misunderstandings across these kinds of topics may and most likely need to differ.

REFERENCES

Alexander, P. A., & Baggetta, P. (2014). Percept-concept coupling and human error. In D. N. Rapp & J. L. G. Braasch (Eds.), *Processing inaccurate information: Theoretical and applied perspectives from cognitive science and the educational sciences* (pp. 297–328). Cambridge, MA: MIT Press.

Andre, T., & Ding, P. (1991). Student misconceptions, declarative knowledge, stimulus conditions, and problem solving in basic electricity. *Contemporary Educational Psychology, 16*, 3030–3313.

Bonjour, L. (2002). *Epistemology: Classic problems and contemporary responses*. Lanham, MD: Rowman & Littlefield.

Braasch, J. L. G., & Bråten, I. (2017). The discrepancy-induced source comprehension (D-ISC) model: Basic assumptions and preliminary evidence. *Educational Psychologist, 52*, 167–181.

Braasch, J. L. G., Rouet, J.-F., Vibert, N., & Britt, M. A. (2012). Readers' use of source information in text comprehension. *Memory & Cognition, 40*, 450–465.

Brown, D. E., & Clement, J. (1989). Overcoming misconceptions via analogical reasoning: Factors influencing understanding in a teaching experiment. *Instructional Science, 18*, 237–262.

Bryce, T. G. K., & Blown, E. J. (2016). Manipulating models and grasping the ideas they represent. *Science & Education, 25*, 47–93.

Caramazza, A., McCloskey, M., & Green, B. (1981). Naïve beliefs in "sophisticated" subjects: Misconceptions about trajectories of objects. *Cognition, 9*, 117–123.

Carey, S. (1985). *Conceptual change in childhood*. Cambridge, MA: Bradford Books, MIT Press.

Chase, W. G., & Simon, H. A. (1973). Perception in chess. *Cognitive Psychology, 4*, 55–81.

Chi, M. T., Roscoe, R. D., Slotta, J. D., Roy, M., & Chase, C. C. (2012). Misconceived causal explanations for emergent processes. *Cognitive Science, 36*, 1–61.

Chi, M. T. H. (2005). Commonsense conceptions of emergent processes: Why some misconceptions are robust. *Journal of the Learning Sciences, 14*, 161–199.

Chi, M. T. H. (2008). Three types of conceptual change: Belief revision, mental model transformation, and categorical shift. In S. Vosniadou (Eds.), *Handbook of research on conceptual change* (pp. 61–82). Hillsdale, NJ: Erlbaum.

Chi, M. T. H., Feltovich, P. J., & Glaser, R. (1981). Categorization and representation of physics problems by experts and novices. *Cognitive Science, 5*, 121–152.

Chi, M. T. H., Glaser, R., & Rees, E. (1982). Expertise in problem solving. In R. J. Sternberg (Eds.), *Advances in psychology of human intelligence* (vol. 1, pp. 7–75). Hillsdale, NJ: Erlbaum.

Clark, D. B. (2006). Longitudinal conceptual change in students' understanding of thermal equilibrium: An examination of the process of conceptual restructuring. *Cognition and Instruction, 24*, 467–563.

diSessa, A., & Minstrell, J. (1998). Cultivating conceptual change with benchmark lessons. In J. Greeno & S. Goldman (Eds.), *Thinking practices in mathematics and science learning* (pp. 155–188). Mahwah, NJ: Lawrence Erlbaum.

diSessa, A. A. (1993). Toward an epistemology of physics. *Cognition and Instruction, 10*, 105–225.

diSessa, A. A. (2008). A bird's-eye view of the "pieces" vs. "coherence" controversy (from the "pieces" side of the fence). In S. Vosniadou (Eds.), *International handbook of research on conceptual change* (pp. 35–60). New York: Routledge.

diSessa, A. A., Gillespie, N. M., & Esterly, J. B. (2004). Coherence versus fragmentation in the development of the concept of force. *Cognitive Science, 28*, 843–900.

diSessa, A. A. A., & Sherin, B. (1998). What changes in conceptual change?. *International Journal of Science Education, 20*, 1155–1191.

Donovan, A. M., Theodosis, E., & Rapp, D. N. (2018). Reader, interrupted: Do disruptions during encoding attenuate misinformation effects?. *Applied Cognitive Psychology, 32*, 775–786.

Donovan, A. M., Zhan, J., & Rapp, D. N. (2018). Supporting historical understandings with refutation texts. *Contemporary Educational Psychology, 54*, 1–11.

Fisher, K. M. (2004). The importance of prior knowledge in college science instruction. In D. W. Sunal, E. L. Wright, & J. Bland Day (Eds.), *Reform in undergraduate science teaching for the 21st century* (pp. 69–84). Greenwich, CT: Information Age Publishing.

Frède, V. (2008). Teaching astronomy for pre-service elementary teachers: A comparison of methods. *Advances in Space Research, 42*, 1819–1830.

Gentner, D., Brem, S., Ferguson, R. W., Markman, A. B., Levidow, B. B., Wolff, P., & Forbus, K. D. (1997). Analogical reasoning and conceptual change: A case study of Johannes Kepler. *Journal of the Learning Sciences, 6*, 3–40.

Guzzetti, B., Snyder, T., Glass, G., & Gamas, W. (1993). Promoting conceptual change in science: A comparative meta-analysis of instructional interventions from reading education and science education. *Reading Research Quarterly, 28*, 117–155.

Halldén, O., Scheja, M., & Haglund, L. (2008). The contextuality of knowledge: An intentional approach to meaning making and conceptual change. In S. Vosniadou (Eds.), *International handbook of research on conceptual change* (pp. 509–532). New York: Routledge.

Hammer, D., & Elby, A. (2002). On the form of a personal epistemology. In B. K. Hofer & P. R. Pintrich (Eds.), *Personal epistemology: The psychology of beliefs about knowledge and knowing* (pp. 169–190). Mahwah, NJ: Lawrence Erlbaum.

Hmelo-Silver, C. E. (2004). Problem-based learning: What and how do students learn?. *Educational Psychology Review, 16*, 235–266.

Hofer, B. K., & Pintrich, P. R. (1997). The development of epistemological theories: Beliefs about knowledge and knowing and their relation to learning. *Review of Educational Research, 67*, 88–140.

Hynd, C., Alvermann, D., & Qian, G. (1997). Pre-service elementary school teachers' conceptual change about projectile motion. *Science Education, 81*, 1–27.

Hynd, C., & Alvermann, D. E. (1986). The role of refutation text in overcoming difficulty with science concepts. *Journal of Reading, 29*, 440–446.

Jacoby, L. L. (1978). On interpreting the effects of repetition: Solving a problem versus remembering a solution. *Journal of Verbal Learning and Verbal Behavior, 17*, 649–667.

Kelemen, D., Rottman, J., & Seston, R. (2013). Professional physical scientists display tenacious teleological tendencies: Purpose-based reasoning as a cognitive default. *Journal of Experimental Psychology General, 142*, 1074–1083.

Kendeou, P., Butterfuss, R., Van Boekel, M., & O'Brien, E. J. (2017). Integrating relational reasoning and knowledge revision during reading. *Educational Psychology Review, 29*, 27–39.

Kendeou, P., & O'Brien, E. J. (2014). The knowledge revision components (KReC) framework: Processes and mechanisms. In D. N. Rapp & J. L. G. Braasch (Eds.), *Processing inaccurate information: Theoretical and applied perspectives from cognitive science and the educational sciences* (pp. 353–377). Cambridge, MA: MIT Press.

Kendeou, P., & van Den Broek, P. (2007). The effects of prior knowledge and text structure on comprehension processes during reading of scientific texts. *Memory & Cognition, 35*, 1567–1577.

Koedinger, K. R., Corbett, A. T., & Perfetti, C. (2012). The knowledge-learning-instruction framework: Bridging the science-practice chasm to enhance robust student learning. *Cognitive Science, 36,* 757–798.

Lombardi, D., Bailey, J. M., Bickel, E. S., & Burrell, S. (2018). Scaffolding scientific thinking: Students' evaluations and judgments during earth science knowledge construction. *Contemporary Educational Psychology, 54,* 184–198.

Lombardi, D., Danielson, R. W., & Young, N. (2016). A plausible connection: Models examining the relations between evaluation, plausibility, and the refutation text effect. *Learning and Instruction, 44,* 74–86.

Masson, S., Potvin, P., Riopel, M., & Brault-Foisy, L.-M. (2014). Differences in brain activation between novices and experts in science during a task involving a common misconception in electricity. *Mind, Brain and Education, 8,* 44–55.

McCloskey, M. (1983). Naive theories of motion. In D. Gentner & A. L. Stevens (Eds.), *Mental models* (pp. 299–323). Hillsdale, NJ: Erlbaum.

Moran, M. B., Lucas, M., Everhart, K., Morgan, A., & Prickett, E. (2016). What makes anti-vaccine websites persuasive? A content analysis of techniques used by anti-vaccine websites to engender anti-vaccine sentiment. *Journal of Communication in Healthcare, 9,* 151–163.

Murphy, P. K., Wilkinson, I. A. G., Soter, A. O., Hennessey, M. N., & Alexander, J. F. (2009). Examining the effects of classroom discussion on students' high-level comprehension of text: A meta-analysis. *Journal of Educational Psychology, 101,* 740–764.

Novick, L. R. (1988). Analogical transfer, problem similarity, and expertise. *Journal of Experimental Psychology: Learning, Memory, and Cognition, 14,* 510–520.

Nussbaum, E. M., Cordova, J. R., & Rehmat, A. P. (2017). Refutation texts for effective climate change education. *Journal of Geoscience Education, 65,* 23–34.

Nyhan, B., & Reifler, J. (2010). When corrections fail: The persistence of political misperceptions. *Political Behavior, 32,* 303–330.

O'Brien, E. J., & Cook, A. E. (2016). Coherence threshold and the continuity of processing: The RI-Val model of comprehension. *Discourse Processes, 53,* 326–338.

O'Brien, E. J., Rizzella, M. L., Albrecht, J. E., & Halleran, J. G. (1998). Updating a situation model: A memory-based text processing view. *Journal of Experimental Psychology: Learning, Memory, and Cognition, 24,* 1200–1210.

Özdemir, G., & Clark, D. B. (2007). An overview of conceptual change theories. *Eurasia Journal of Mathematics, Science and Technology Education, 3,* 351–361.

Posner, G. J., & Gertzog, W. A. (1982). The clinical interview and the measurement of conceptual change. *Science Education, 66,* 195–209.

Posner, G. J., Strike, K. A., Hewson, P. W., & Gertzog, W. A. (1982). Accommodation of a scientific conception: Toward a theory of conceptual change. *Science Education, 66,* 211–227.

Rapp, D. N., Hinze, S. R., Kohlhepp, K., & Ryskin, R. A. (2014). Reducing reliance on inaccurate information. *Memory & Cognition, 42,* 11–26.

Rapp, D. N., & Kendeou, P. (2007). Revising what readers know: Updating text representations during narrative comprehension. *Memory & Cognition, 35,* 2019–2032.

Rapp, D. N., & Mensink, M. C. (2011). Focusing effects from online and offline reading tasks. In M. T. McCrudden, J. P. Magliano, & G. Schraw (Eds.), *Text relevance and learning from text* (pp. 141–164). Greenwich, CT: Information Age Publishing.

Rapp, D. N., & Salovich, N. A. (2018). Can't we just disregard fake news? The consequences of exposure to inaccurate information. *Policy Insights from the Behavioral and Brain Sciences, 5,* 232–239.

Roediger, H. L., III, & Karpicke, J. D. (2006). Test-enhanced learning: Taking memory tests improves long-term retention. *Psychological Science, 17,* 249–255.

Saglam, Y., Karaaslan, E. H., & Ayas, A. (2010). The impact of contextual factors on the use of students' conceptions. *International Journal of Science and Mathematics Education, 9,* 1391–1413.

Sherin, B., Krakowski, L. M., & Lee, V. R. (2012). Some assembly required: How scientific explanations are constructed during clinical interviews. *Journal of Research in Science Teaching 49,* 166–198.

Simpson, W. D., & Marek, E. A. (1988). Understandings and misconceptions of biology concepts held by students attending small high schools and students attending large high schools. *Journal of Research in Science Teaching, 25,* 361–374.

Sinatra, G. M., & Broughton, S. H. (2011). Bridging reading comprehension and conceptual change in science education: The promise of refutation text. *Reading Research Quarterly, 46,* 374–393.

Smith, J. P., III, diSessa, A. A., & Roschelle, J. (1993). Misconceptions reconceived: A constructivist analysis of knowledge in transition. *Journal of the Learning Sciences, 3*, 115–163.

Sungur, S., Tekkaya, C., & Geban, O. (2001). The contribution of conceptual change texts accompanied by concept mapping to students' understanding of the human circulatory system. *School Science and Mathematics, 101*, 91–101.

Swanson, H., & Collins, A. (2018). How failure is productive in the creative process: Refining student explanations through theory-building discussion. *Thinking Skills and Creativity, 30*, 54–63.

Taylor, H. A., & Rapp, D. N. (2006). Updating human spatial memory. *Animal Spatial Cognition*. www.pigeon.psy.tufts.edu/asc/Taylor.

Tippett, C. D. (2010). Refutation text in science education: A review of two decades of research. *International Journal of Science and Mathematics Education, 8*, 951–970.

van Den Broek, P., Rapp, D. N., & Kendeou, P. (2005). Integrating memory-based and constructionist processes in accounts of reading comprehension. *Discourse Processes, 39*, 299–316.

VanSledright, B., & Brophy, J. (1992). Storytelling, imagination, and fanciful elaboration in children's historical reconstructions. *American Educational Research Journal, 29*, 837–859.

Vosniadou, S. (1994). Capturing and modeling the process of conceptual change. *Learning and Instruction, 4*, 45–69.

Vosniadou, S., & Brewer, W. F. (1992). Mental models of the Earth: A study of conceptual change in childhood. *Cognitive Psychology, 24*, 535–585.

Wilensky, U., & Reisman, K. (2006). Thinking like a wolf, a sheep or a firefly: Learning biology through constructing and testing computational theories – An embodied modeling approach. *Cognition and Instruction, 24*, 171–209.

Wilensky, U., & Resnick, M. (1999). Thinking in levels: A dynamic systems approach to making sense of the world. *Journal of Science Education and Technology, 8*, 3–19.

Zingg, A., & Siegrist, M. (2012). Measuring people's knowledge about vaccination: Developing a one-dimensional scale. *Vaccine, 30*, 3771–3777.

26

THE CHALLENGE OF MISINFORMATION AND WAYS TO REDUCE ITS IMPACT

Jasmyne A. Sanderson and Ullrich K. H. Ecker

UNIVERSITY OF WESTERN AUSTRALIA

ABSTRACT

Misinformation can influence people's memory, reasoning, and decision making even after they have received a correction – this is known as the continued influence effect of misinformation (CIE). There are a number of factors that contribute to misinformation's influence, both cognitive – including failures in the integration/updating of information and its later retrieval – and motivational – including the impact of pre-existing attitudes and worldviews. With the rise of the internet and social media, exposure to misleading and/or inaccurate information has arguably become more common, and there is a lack of gatekeepers to ensure information's quality and veracity; further challenges lie in the formation of echo chambers and filter bubbles. In this information environment, it is difficult for individuals to evaluate information and identify misinformation. This chapter briefly reviews theoretical accounts of the CIE and the challenges associated with the impact of misinformation in the current information landscape. It also discusses how some people may be more susceptible to misinformation effects, and suggests some recommendations on how to reduce the impact of misinformation, touching on both the specifics of how corrections should be presented and broader systemic factors.

Key words: misinformation, continued influence effect, memory updating, debunking, post-truth

People are exposed to large amounts of information on a daily basis, with constant and immediate access to information through both traditional news sources (i.e., radio, television) and social media and the Internet. Unfortunately, a significant share of this information will be incomplete, contradictory, or even inaccurate and misleading –

even if euphemisms such as "alternative facts" are being applied (Lewandowsky, Ecker, & Cook, 2017b). This leaves individuals with the difficult task of appraising the quality and credibility of the information they receive. Given the sheer volume of information available to people at their fingertips, individuals' ability to assess veracity is hindered: People have limited resources (either cognitive, motivational, or temporal) and therefore need to rely on heuristics – mental shortcuts such as the superficial visual aspects of a website (Fogg et al., 2003; Metzger & Flanagin, 2013) – to evaluate credibility. Such reliance on heuristics can lead to bias (Metzger & Flanagin, 2013). Moreover, the task is further complicated by the rise of fake accounts and deepfakes (i.e., artificial intelligence-based technology used to produce or alter video content; Fogg et al., 2003). It is estimated that 48 million Twitter accounts and 66 million Facebook profiles may be fake accounts or bots (i.e., an account impersonating a human) designed to boost the prevalence and distribution of false information, as seen in the use of Russian bots during the 2016 US Presidential Election (Chang, 2018; Lazer et al., 2018; Varol, Ferrara, Davis, Menczer, & Flammini, 2017). Therefore, people are faced with growing amounts of misinformation but they are not necessarily well-equipped to deal with it.

Misinformation is defined here as objectively false information that is presented as valid (and plausible enough to be initially believed by some) but is subsequently found to be incorrect (Johnson & Seifert, 1994; Wilkes & Leatherbarrow, 1988). While we assume the objective falsity of misinformation can be established at least in principle (e.g., by subject matter experts or independent fact-checkers), the increasing prevalence of misinformation means that information consumers must increasingly make veracity judgments of their own. Misinformation has many forms, ranging from rumors to fully elaborated fake news stories (see Kendeou et al., Chapter 27, for a discussion of fake news), but it is currently unclear how these forms differ in terms of impact. Moreover, while some misinformation may be benign (e.g., the false belief that the Great Wall of China is visible from space; see Rapp et al., Chapter 25, for related discussion), other misinformation can have serious and lasting negative implications. One of the most prevalent examples of impactful misinformation involves childhood vaccinations, specifically the claim in a now retracted paper published in the *Lancet* that there was a causal link between the MMR (mumps, measles, rubella) vaccine and autism (Murch et al., 2004; Wakefield et al., 1998). This demonstrably caused significant and long-lasting drops in vaccination rates in both the US and UK (e.g., Smith, Ellenberg, Bell, & Rubin, 2008; Thompson, 2009), despite widespread, clear and credible retractions, and abundant evidence discrediting the false claim (Demicheli, Jefferson, Rivetti, & Price, 2005).

There have been a number of proposed ways of classifying different types of misinformation. Recently, McCright and Dunlap (2017) proposed a taxonomy of four main types of misinformation: (1) truthiness, (2) bullshit, (3) systemic lies, and (4) shock and chaos. Truthiness refers to misinformation that is considered valid based simply on a feeling that it might be true rather than evidence. Bullshit is purposely deceptive and self-serving misinformation spread solely to persuade without any concern for reason or veracity. Systemic lies are carefully crafted misinformation campaigns specifically designed as a means to further ideological interests. Finally, a shock and chaos approach is used to confuse and fatigue publics in order to derail societal institutions to gain power. These different types of misinformation vary with respect to the amount of effort required to produce and sustain the misinformation. For example, campaigns of systemic lies (e.g., the climate change denial movement) require greater effort compared to bullshit, which is easily manufactured by individuals (e.g., conspiracy theories). For information consumers, it is important to be aware of these nuances in order to recognize misinformation when it is encountered. However, it is currently unclear how best to counteract the various types of misinformation; thus, presenting specific solutions to deal with the different types of misinformation is beyond the scope of this chapter, although we will provide general suggestions in the recommendations section.

This chapter will discuss the impact misinformation can have on a person's memory, reasoning, and decision making. It will outline the cognitive mechanisms that contribute to misinformation's persistence as well as briefly touching on the role of motivational factors. We will then discuss some of the challenges posed by misinformation, before making recommendations on ways to reduce the impact of misinformation.

THE CONTINUED INFLUENCE EFFECT

In light of the increasing prevalence of misinformation, there is a need to be able to successfully correct it. Unfortunately, this is a challenging task as once a person has been exposed to misinformation, it cannot simply be removed from memory, and it is therefore difficult to completely eliminate its influence. This means that misinformation can have a measurable impact on individuals' inferential reasoning, decision making, and judgments, even after a clear correction is provided that explicitly refutes the misinformation. This is known as the *continued influence effect* of misinformation (CIE; Johnson & Seifert, 1994; Wilkes & Leatherbarrow, 1988; for review, see Lewandowsky, Ecker, Seifert, Schwarz, & Cook, 2012).

Psychological research has demonstrated the CIE in a wide variety of settings, both in the lab and online, and using common myths (e.g., playing Mozart to your baby will make it smarter [it will not]), real-world misinformation (e.g., climate change is a hoax [it is not]), or fictional event reports. Using fictional event reports not only allows tight experimental control, but can also help demonstrate that the effect is not purely motivational, but essentially a cognitive phenomenon. In these studies, participants typically read a fictitious news report that contains a target piece of critical information – for example, that a warehouse fire was caused by negligent storage of volatile materials (Johnson & Seifert, 1994; Wilkes & Leatherbarrow, 1988). This information is either retracted (i.e., it is explained that there were no volatile materials) or not. Participants then answer a series of inferential reasoning questions that probe details of the report (e.g., "what may have caused the explosion?"). Such studies have found that *retractions* – merely stating that the critical information is incorrect – are relatively ineffective; that is, they reduce but do not eliminate the influence of the critical information on people's reasoning. Typically, a retraction is found to approximately halve the number of references to the critical information relative to a no-retraction control condition. Notably, this occurs even when people can remember and report the retraction (Ecker, Hogan, & Lewandowsky, 2017; Ecker, Lewandowsky, Fenton, & Martin, 2014; Ecker, Lewandowsky, & Tang, 2010; Johnson & Seifert, 1994; Wilkes & Leatherbarrow, 1988). This result is highly reliable and has been found even with subtle or implied misinformation (Chan, Jones, Hall Jamieson, & Albarracín, 2017; Ecker, Lewandowsky, Chang, & Pillai, 2014; Rich & Zaragoza, 2016; Walter & Murphy, 2018). For example, pairing a news article with a misleading (vs. accurate) headline can affect people's memory for the article and their inferential reasoning about the article's implications (Ecker et al., 2014). A more effective method, which will be discussed in the recommendations section, is to include an explanation with the retraction statement as to why the misinformation is incorrect.

It is important to note that a large proportion of CIE research has only examined the effect of corrections on individuals' reasoning, and there is less clear evidence of the *behavioral* effects. Some research has examined how corrections influence voting behaviors (Aird, Ecker, Swire, Berinsky, & Lewandowsky, 2018; Swire, Berinsky, Lewandowsky, & Ecker, 2017a), as well as health behaviors such as vaccinations (Nyhan, Reifler, Richey, & Freed, 2014) and the purchase of multivitamin supplements (MacFarlane, Hurlstone, & Ecker, 2018). These studies demonstrate that corrections do not necessarily translate to behavioral change – that is, corrections may have a larger effect on reasoning measures than behavioral measures. For example, it has been found that fact-checks of politicians' statements can change people's beliefs about those statements without, however, changing voting intentions (unless the number of false statements from a particular politician far outweighed the number of factual statements; Aird et al., 2018; Swire et al., 2017a).

COGNITIVE EXPLANATIONS FOR THE CIE

There are two dominant cognitive explanations for the CIE. One position suggests that the CIE occurs due to a failure at *retrieval* (Ayers & Reder, 1998; Ecker et al., 2010; Swire, Ecker, & Lewandowsky, 2017b). According to this view, misinformation and valid information (e.g., a retraction) are stored separately in different memory representations and compete for activation during retrieval; misinformation thus influences reasoning when it is selectively retrieved while the correction is not (Ayers & Reder, 1998; Ecker et al., 2010; Swire et al., 2017b). One particular version of this account assumes dual processes: automatic retrieval processes on the one hand and strategic retrieval and monitoring processes on the other. If misinformation is activated by cues and automatically retrieved, strategic processes are required to assess the validity of the information retrieved, and/or recollect any relevant correction. As these strategic processes are cognitively demanding, they often fail, resulting in the CIE (Ecker et al., 2010).

The retrieval failure account is supported by the finding that specific warnings reduce the influence of misinformation, presumably because warnings promote the use of strategic monitoring processes (Ecker et al., 2010). Additional evidence comes from work on familiarity effects: Swire et al. (2017b) found that longer retention intervals were associated with increased misinformation reliance. They argued that as the retention interval increased, recollection of the retraction became more difficult, while familiarity-driven automatic retrieval of the misinformation remained relatively intact.

Alternatively, the mental-model account suggests that failures of *information integration and updating* drive the CIE. This account assumes that people create mental models of events or causalities that are used to reason and draw inferences (Bower & Morrow, 1990; Wilkes & Leatherbarrow, 1988). When relevant new information – such as a retraction or correction – is encountered, the mental model requires updating and revision (Bower & Morrow, 1990). However, retractions by nature disrupt the mental model by invalidating a piece of critical information; this disruption threatens model coherence and may thus lead to the retraction being discounted and poorly integrated into the model (Gordon, Brooks, Quadflieg, Ecker, & Lewandowsky, 2017). This lack of integration between retraction and misinformation may be due to people's preference for complete over incomplete mental models, even when the complete model may contain dubious elements (Johnson & Seifert, 1994; Lewandowsky et al., 2012). A failure to integrate a retraction and subsequently update the mental model will lead to misinformation reliance (Gordon et al., 2017; Kendeou, Walsh, Smith, & O'Brien, 2014).

Behavioral and neuropsychological evidence has supported the mental-model account. At a basic level, this includes the finding that provision of a causal alternative explanation boosts the efficacy of a retraction (e.g., in the fictitious warehouse fire example, a statement that "there were no volatile materials present, but arson materials have been found"; see Chan et al., 2017; Ecker, O'Reilly, Reid, & Chang, 2019; Swire et al., 2017b; Walter & Murphy, 2018). This is easily explained by the mental-model account: if an alternative is provided that can replace the retracted element of the mental model, then there is no reason to discount the retraction because there is no threat to model coherence. Behaviorally, the finding that working memory capacity predicts people's susceptibility to the CIE (Brydges, Gignac, & Ecker, 2018) supports the mental-model account because information integration and model updating require working memory resources. Furthermore, a neuroimaging study using functional magnetic resonance imaging found neural activity differed for the encoding of retractions compared to non-retractions in regions associated with information integration, suggesting that a failure of memory integration/updating may contribute to the CIE (Gordon et al., 2017). Research has suggested that integration is more likely to fail if individuals do not use full cognitive resources (e.g., when under cognitive load during retraction encoding; Ecker, Lewandowsky, Swire, & Chang, 2011), or if the initial mental model is highly plausible, based on stereotypical information, and/or in line with individuals' expectations and worldview, which we will discuss below (Ecker et al., 2014).

To summarize, the retrieval-failure account suggests that the CIE arises when there is a failure in information selection and suppression occurring at the retrieval stage, whereas the mental-model account suggests a failure at the earlier integration/updating stage. It is important to note that these two views are not mutually exclusive; it is likely that failures with both integration/updating and retrieval contribute to the continued influence of misinformation.

THE ROLE OF MOTIVATIONAL FACTORS

Cognitive factors alone cannot explain reliance on misinformation entirely; motivational factors such as pre-existing attitudes, differing perspectives, and worldviews – fundamental beliefs about how society should operate (e.g., political worldviews; Cook, Lewandowsky, & Ecker, 2017) – also need to be considered. Individuals are motivated to maintain their view of the world and often attend to and interpret information in light of this view through attitude-driven processing (Kunda, 1990). For example, one study had left- and right-wing participants read fictitious articles about political misconduct (Ecker & Ang, 2019). Both participant groups mentioned worldview-consistent information more (i.e., mentioned misconduct by a politician of the opposing party more than their own party). This means correcting misinformation can be particularly challenging when the misinformation is congruent with people's attitudes and worldview. Worldview-incongruent corrections can be ineffective (Ecker & Ang, 2019), and under certain conditions, may even "backfire", that is, ironically increase belief in the misinformation being corrected (Lewandowsky et al., 2012; Nyhan & Reifler, 2010). Such backfire effects have been reported in the domains of climate change, vaccinations, and the presence of weapons of mass destruction in Iraq (Hart & Nisbet, 2012; Nyhan & Reifler, 2010; Nyhan et al., 2014). However, other research has failed to produce these effects despite using similarly contentious topics (Ecker et al., 2014; Wood & Porter, 2019). More fully explaining the impact of motivational factors thus remains a target for future research. Suggestions to counter motivational factors include framing the correction in line with individuals' worldview (Feinberg & Willer, 2013), having an in-group member present the correction (Benegal & Scruggs, 2018; Berinsky, 2017), or bolstering people's feelings of self-worth (e.g., through self-affirmations) before presenting the correction (Nyhan & Reifler, 2018).

CHALLENGES OF MISINFORMATION

Apart from the fact that misinformation is generally difficult to correct, there are particular challenges. One challenge is that some people are particularly susceptible to misinformation and its effects (Bensley, Lilienfeld, & Powell, 2014; Lewandowsky et al., 2013; Pennycook & Rand, 2018, 2019a). Generally, older adults are more likely to share misinformation online due to unfamiliarity with the internet and limited knowledge of how to evaluate online information (Grimes, Hough, Mazur, & Singnorella, 2010; Guess, Nagler, & Tucker, 2019). Older adults are also more vulnerable to the CIE, being more likely to incorrectly remember a corrected false claim as being true, particularly over longer intervals (Skurnik, Yoon, Park, & Schwarz, 2005; Swire et al., 2017b). These age-related differences are thought to arise from the general decline in cognitive functions, and more specifically less efficient strategic memory processes (Swire, et al., 2017b). Additionally, cognitive abilities including working memory capacity and verbal intelligence have been found to predict susceptibility to misinformation effects (Brydges et al., 2018; De keersmaecker & Roets, 2017). That is, even with no difference in initial misinformation belief, individuals with lower cognitive ability (i.e., WMC and verbal intelligence) tend to display less belief adjustment following the correction of false information compared to those with higher ability. Efforts to reduce the impact of misinformation should therefore be particularly geared towards groups that are most vulnerable to it.

Other challenges arise from the shape of the contemporary media landscape. This can be seen in the formation of echo chambers and filter bubbles – personalized information environments (e.g., social media feeds) where specific information is circulated based on user preferences and behavior (Lewandowsky et al., 2017b; Pariser, 2011; Sunstein, 2002; Zollo et al., 2017). This personalization – driven by both active personal decisions and preference-based algorithms – permits selective exposure to information that is consistent with one's attitudes and worldview, consequently limiting exposure to and learning from divergent views (Kahne & Bowyer, 2017; Lewandowsky, Cook, & Ecker, 2017a). Selective exposure can foster attitude polarization and research has found that the degree of homogeneity and polarization within social networks is associated with increased acceptance of misinformation (Dylko et al., 2017; Garrett, Weeks, & Neo, 2016). Attempts to address this personalization include adapting algorithms to "burst" filter bubbles (Resnick, Garrett, Kriplean, Munson, & Stroud, 2013), or simply informing people of how filter bubble algorithms work, as many are unaware that algorithms use data on online consumer behaviors and preferences to shape people's information diet (Eslami et al., 2015). Moreover, in contrast to traditional news media – at least some of which have ethics and integrity guidelines and responsible editors who act as gatekeepers – there are few such regulatory mechanisms on the Internet, and algorithms largely determine how news is distributed and to whom, thus fostering the creation and distribution of misinformation. There are obvious issues with the practicality of internet regulation that does not encroach on people's democratic rights; however, given the issues arising from misinformation, some argue that regulation may be an important tool to reduce the spread of misinformation (e.g., Nechushtai & Lewis, 2019).

Finally, societal factors such as the decline of social capital, social inequality and the associated broad discontent and political polarization, as well as either press monopolies or an information environment that allows anyone to publish information without gatekeeping mechanisms present more fundamental challenges relating to misinformation. For example, discontent arising from social inequality fosters vulnerability to targeted misinformation campaigns (e.g., ideological political polarization between parties tends to increase during periods of high income inequality; Garand, 2010; McCarty, Poole, & Rosenthal, 2006). Furthermore, combating misinformation is difficult when either one agency or platform has near exclusive control over media content or it is completely unregulated (see Lewandowsky et al., 2017a, 2017b; also Garand, 2010; Iyengar & Westwood, 2015; Wilkinson & Pickett, 2009). These are important factors to consider in the fight against misinformation, even though they are largely beyond the scope of this chapter.

RECOMMENDATIONS

We will now discuss some recommendations to combat misinformation and the CIE. These recommendations are broken down into suggestions for (1) presenting the correction, (2) helping individuals to detect misinformation and, (3) broader systemic changes.

Correction Design

Recommendation 1: Refutations

One of the most effective methods for reducing reliance on misinformation is a refutation. In comparison to a retraction, which simply states that a piece of information is incorrect, a *refutation* explains *why* the information is incorrect (and/or why people assumed it to be correct) and provides some factual information (Tippett, 2010).

Multiple studies including several meta-analyses have supported the effectiveness of refutations for both constructed and real-world misinformation (Chan et al., 2017; Ecker et al., 2019; Paynter et al., 2019; Swire et al., 2017b; Walter & Murphy, 2018). Refutations have been found particularly useful in situations characterized by mutual trust and availability of sufficient motivational and temporal resources, such as correcting scientific misconceptions in educational settings (Guzzetti, Snyder, Glass, & Gamas, 1993; Kowalski & Taylor, 2009; Tippett, 2010).

There are three reasons for a refutation's effectiveness. First, refutations promote the co-activation of misinformation and retraction. Models of conceptual change argue that in order for knowledge revision to occur both the misconception and correction need to be co-activated and a discrepancy noticed (Kendeou et al., 2014). Accordingly, refutations that make the discrepancy between the valid and invalid information salient have been found to facilitate integration/updating and reduce the CIE (Ecker et al., 2017).

Secondly, as briefly mentioned before, to the extent that a refutation includes factual information, it can serve to fill the gap created in a person's mental model by a retraction (Johnson & Seifert, 1994). For example, in the warehouse fire scenario people rely on misinformation less when they are given the alternative arson explanation (Johnson & Seifert, 1994). Naturally, utilizing this mechanism is not possible if no clear factual alternative is readily available. One explanation for the difficulty dispelling the vaccine-autism myth is that the causes of (the various types of) autism are not yet fully understood (Leonard et al., 2010).

Thirdly, refutations provide additional recollectable detail. In terms of the retrieval failure account sketched earlier, strategic recollection processes will easily fail if only scarce corrective information (e.g., "X is not true") is available in memory. A richer, more elaborate representation of corrective information will be better able to compete with the misinformation at retrieval (Ecker, Lewandowsky, Jayawardana, & Mladenovic, 2018; Kendeou et al., 2014).

Although refutations are demonstrably effective, there has been debate within the literature as to whether the misconception should be repeated in the correction. It is argued that repetition of the misinformation may inadvertently increase its familiarity and subsequent acceptance (Lewandowsky et al., 2012; Schwarz, Newman, & Leach, 2016; Schwarz, Sanna, Skurnik, & Yoon, 2007). However, research has not found much evidence for the existence of this so-called familiarity backfire effect (Ecker et al., 2017; Ecker et al., 2019; Pashler, Kang, & Mozer, 2013; Swire et al., 2017b). Pashler et al. (2013) found that reviewing previous incorrect information actually improved memory for new correct information. In line with this, the reconsolidation literature argues that retrieving information puts it in a labile and malleable state; this allows the memory representation to be updated and revised before again being stabilized by a reconsolidation process (Elsey & Kindt, 2017). Therefore, repeating the misinformation in a correction may induce the labilization process and better allow the correction to be incorporated into the original memory representation.

Recommendation 2: Warnings

Where possible, before people are exposed to misinformation the publisher or content platform should provide explicit warnings stating that the information people are going to receive may not be true. Warnings put people cognitively on guard, therefore reducing the depth of information encoding and increasing strategic monitoring processes at retrieval (Cook et al., 2017; Ecker et al., 2010). Social media platforms have trialed the use of warnings, although its effectiveness is unclear (Blair et al., 2017; Pennycook & Rand, 2019b). Blair et al. (2017) found that a "disputed" flag warning about false news stories – as per Facebook's original strategy against misinformation (Lyons, 2017) – modestly reduced the perceived accuracy of flagged stories; however, another study found that warnings also increased the perceived accuracy of non-flagged stories regardless of their veracity (Pennycook & Rand, 2019b). Additionally, researchers are developing fake news detection systems which may predict misinformation surges by identifying polarizing topics on social media, which may be used to optimize warnings about misinformation (Del Vicario, Quattrociocchi, Scala, & Zollo, 2018).

Recommendation 3: Graphical Displays

Information is often encountered across multiple representations including texts, graphs, or visual images. Corrections should be presented in a simple format that facilitates comprehension and retention. Graphical representations are choice formats because they achieve this goal, while quantifying and specifying the corrective information, which can prevent motivational counter-arguing (e.g., a graph showing data from several independent sources that quantify the exact amount of temperature rise over time is more difficult to counter-argue than a verbal statement that temperatures have increased; Nyhan & Reifler, 2018; also see Ecker et al., 2019; Paynter et al., 2019; van der Linden, Leiserowitz, Feinberg, & Maibach, 2014; but see Pluviano, Watt, & Della Sala, 2017). While visual representations are effective, it is important to note that they can easily be distorted and become misleading. For example, deceptive data visualizations (i.e., truncated or inverted axes) can lead to misinterpretation of data even if they are accompanied by accurate text explanations (O'Brien & Lauer, 2018; Vargas-Restrepo, Yang, Stanley, & Marsh, n.d.). Furthermore, the credibility of misinformation itself may be bolstered by visual representations, as people perceive graphs as "scientific" and visuals as a direct index of reality that are less easily manipulated than text, which is particularly concerning given the advent of deepfakes (Hameleers, Powell, Van der Meer, & Bos, n.d.; Messaris & Abraham, 2001; Smith, Best, Stubbs, Archibald, & Roberson-Nay, 2002). Thus, while corrections are likely to benefit from the use of multiple representations, individuals must also be aware of potentially deceitful use.

Educational Approaches

Recommendation 4: Information and media literacy training

General training in information and media literacy is a preemptive step to provide individuals with the skills and resources necessary to evaluate and recognize misinformation (Bensley et al., 2014; Lewandowsky et al., 2013; Lewandowsky et al., 2017b; Pennycook & Rand, 2019a). This involves fostering healthy skepticism and teaching individuals critical thinking skills, which are important for the recognition and rejection of misinformation (Bensley et al., 2014; Lewandowsky et al., 2013; Pennycook & Rand, 2019a). An important aspect of information literacy is source evaluation. People use trustworthiness over expertise as a heuristic for evaluating information (in the misinformation context, see Guillory & Geraci, 2013); however, people are not good at determining whether a source is trustworthy and therefore interventions must teach individuals source evaluation skills (McGrew, Breakstone, Ortega, Smith, & Wineburg, 2018). Interventions must also utilize available technologies (e.g., debunking sites, fake-news detection) to be able to rival the progression of misinformation on the Internet. There is preliminary evidence supporting the effectiveness of literacy interventions with improvements in students' abilities to identify inaccurate political information (Craft, Ashley, & Maksl, 2017; Kahne & Bowyer, 2017; Walton & Hepworth, 2011). These effects are found even when the information aligned with partisan ideology, suggesting such training has the potential to overcome personal motivational biases (Kahne & Bowyer, 2017). Some have argued, however, that these interventions could backfire by making people hyper-skeptical of information sources and well-established facts (Mihailidis, 2009). It is important to note that critical thinking should not be thought of as an abstract skill entirely independent of factual knowledge, as one often needs subject-relevant knowledge in order to appraise new information critically. Obtaining subject-relevant knowledge is a challenge given the inherent difficulty in reading scientific texts and individuals' low levels of understanding of scientific processes (Britt, Richter, & Rouet, 2014; Ozuru, Dempsey, & McNamara, 2009).

Recommendation 5: Inoculation

Inoculation is a pre-bunking strategy aimed to stop the spread and aid the detection of misinformation (Cook et al., 2017; Lewandowsky et al., 2017b; van der Linden, Leiserowitz, Rosenthal, & Maibach, 2017). Inoculation involves a warning about potential false information that attempts to challenge beliefs, followed by a specific, weakened example of such an attempt that highlights the techniques used and the logical flaw in the argument made. It thus acts like a "psychological vaccination" that helps to develop resistance against stronger, more persuasive attempts in the future (Cook et al., 2017). For example, such strategies have been found effective in the domain of climate change (Cook et al., 2017; van der Linden et al., 2017). Inoculation strategies may be incorporated as part of broader interventions against misinformation including literacy training programs and technology-based interventions. For example, Roozenbeek and van der Linden (2019) have had preliminary success with a "fake news game", which teaches players about misleading techniques by having them take on the role of a news editor whose only objective is to build a media empire using false news articles.

Broader Systemic Changes

Recommendation 6: Technocognition approach

Technology is progressing at a rapid rate and technological techniques to identify misinformation are developing just as quickly; for example, fact-checking is becoming automated and machine-learning algorithms are being built to automatically detect misinformation online (Del Vicario et al., 2018; Pérez-Rosas, Kleinberg, Lefevre, & Mihalcea, 2017). However, technological approaches alone will not be able to tackle the problem of misinformation. Instead, Lewandowsky et al. (2017b) proposed a "technocognition" approach which combines psychological principles including insights from behavioral economics with technological innovation in an attempt to reduce the impact of misinformation. An example of this is broadening of filter bubbles and diversification of information sources. Psychological research has shown that exposure to alternative perspectives can increase understanding and acceptance of those perspectives, or reduce polarization of one's own attitudes (Grönlund, Herne, & Setälä, 2015; Lord, Lepper, & Preston, 1984). For example, deliberation between people who were either restrictive or permissive in their attitudes towards immigration has been found to result in lowered anti-immigration attitudes for those who were initially restrictive (Grönlund et al., 2015). Websites can incorporate this idea by changing their algorithms to promote content that is different to individuals' views and may reduce the acceptance of misinformation in line with them. However, some have questioned the utility of this approach (Bail et al., 2018; Haim, Graefe, & Brosius, 2018).

Recommendation 7: Social change

As mentioned briefly before, societal factors can play an important role in misinformation susceptibility and thus in efforts to reduce misinformation's impact. Interventions may include the passing of anti-misinformation laws, with many countries having already introduced legislation governing the distribution of misinformation on social media; however, with government regulation a balance must be maintained between freedom of speech and distribution of misinformation (Goldzweig, Wachinger, Stockmann, & Römmele, 2018). Additionally, vulnerability to misinformation effects will be lowered by efforts to reduce social inequality and political polarization: the former leads to marginalization and discontent, which are breeding grounds for misinformation that serves to ostensibly explain the unjust state of affairs; the latter creates social division and can thus increase belief in misinformation about outgroups (see Deb, Donohue, & Glaisyer, 2017; Garand, 2010; Lewandowsky et al., 2017a; Tucker et al., 2018). Finally, interventions could involve improved communication and reinforcement of existing social norms – socially accepted rules that govern worldviews and behaviors – in order to build a culture that values and promotes truth, particularly regarding the creation and sharing of information online (Lazer et al., 2018; Pankoke-Babatz & Jeffrey, 2002).

FUTURE DIRECTIONS

Misinformation is a growing problem in current society and research continues to grow with it. Currently, research is beginning to go beyond survey approaches, assessing the impact of misinformation and corrections on actual behaviors, and using neuroimaging techniques to gain a better understanding of the neural basis of the CIE. Further research is needed to investigate and create specific strategies to target the different types of misinformation. It is also becoming apparent with misinformation in the "post-truth" era that this is an interdisciplinary problem that will require interdisciplinary solutions (Lewandowsky et al., 2017b). As such, research from different disciplines must join forces to find effective ways forward.

ACKNOWLEDGMENTS

Preparation of this chapter was supported by a Bruce and Betty Green Postgraduate Research Scholarship and an Australian Government Research Training Program Scholarship to Jasmyne Sanderson.

REFERENCES

Aird, M., Ecker, U. K. H., Swire, B., Berinsky, A., & Lewandowsky, S. (2018). Does truth matter to voters? The effects of correcting political misinformation in an Australian sample. *Royal Society Open Science, 5,* 180593.

Ayers, M. S., & Reder, L. M. (1998). A theoretical review of the misinformation effect: Predictions from an activation-based memory model. *Psychonomic Bulletin & Review, 5,* 1–21.

Bail, C. A., Argyle, L. P., Brown, T. W., Bumpus, J. P., Chen, H., Hunzaker, M. F., ... & Volfovsky, A. (2018). Exposure to opposing views on social media can increase political polarization. *Proceedings of the National Academy of Sciences, 115,* 9216–9221.

Benegal, S. D., & Scruggs, L. A. (2018). Correcting misinformation about climate change: The impact of partisanship in an experimental setting. *Climatic Change, 148,* 61–80.

Bensley, D. A., Lilienfeld, S. O., & Powell, L. A. (2014). A new measure of psychological misconceptions: Relations with academic background, critical thinking, and acceptance of paranormal and pseudoscientific claims. *Learning and Individual Differences, 36,* 9–18.

Berinsky, A. J. (2017). Rumors and health care reform: Experiments in political misinformation. *British Journal of Political Science, 47,* 241–262.

Blair, S., Busam, J. A., Clayton, K., Forstner, S., Glance, J., Green, G., ... & Zhou, A. (2017) Real solutions for fake news? Measuring the effectiveness of general warnings and fact-check tags in reducing belief in false stories on social media. https://dartmouth.edu/223Cnyhan/fake-news-solutions.pdf.

Bower, G. H., & Morrow, D. G. (1990). Mental models in narrative comprehension. *Science, 247,* 44–48.

Britt, M. A., Richter, T., & Rouet, J. F. (2014). Scientific literacy: The role of goal-directed reading and evaluation in understanding scientific information. *Educational Psychologist, 49,* 104–122.

Brydges, C. R., Gignac, G. E., & Ecker, U. K. H. (2018). Working memory capacity, short-term memory capacity, and the continued influence effect: A latent-variable analysis. *Intelligence, 69,* 117–122.

Chan, M. P. S., Jones, C. R., Hall Jamieson, K., & Albarracín, D. (2017). Debunking: A meta-analysis of the psychological efficacy of messages countering misinformation. *Psychological Science, 28,* 1531–1546.

Chang, L. (2018). Facebook removed 583 million fake accounts in the first quarter of 2018. https://www.digitaltrends.com/social-media/facebook-fake-accounts/.

Cook, J., Lewandowsky, S., & Ecker, U. K. H. (2017). Neutralizing misinformation through inoculation: Exposing misleading argumentation techniques reduces their influence. *Plos One, 12,* e0175799.

Craft, S., Ashley, S., & Maksl, A. (2017). News media literacy and conspiracy theory endorsement. *Communication and the Public, 2,* 388–401.

Deb, A., Donohue, S., & Glaisyer, T. (2017). Is social media a threat to democracy? *Omidyar Group.* www.omidyargroup.com/pov/2017/10/09/social_media_and_democracy.

De Keersmaecker, J., & Roets, A. (2017). 'Fake news': Incorrect, but hard to correct. The role of cognitive ability on the impact of false information on social impressions. *Intelligence, 65,* 107–110.

Del Vicario, M., Quattrociocchi, W., Scala, A., & Zollo, F. (2018). Polarization and fake news: Early warning of potential misinformation targets. https://arxiv.org/pdf/1802.01400

Demicheli, V., Jefferson, T., Rivetti, A., & Price, D. (2005). Vaccines for measles, mumps and rubella in children. *Cochrane Database of Systematic Reviews, 2,* 1–161.

Dylko, I., Dolgov, I., Hoffman, W., Eckhart, N., Molina, M., & Aaziz, O. (2017). The dark side of technology: An experimental investigation of the influence of customizability technology on online political selective exposure. *Computers in Human Behavior, 73,* 181–190.

Ecker, U. K. H., & Ang, L. C. (2019). Political attitudes and the processing of misinformation corrections. *Political Psychology, 40,* 241–260.

Ecker, U. K. H., Hogan, J. L., & Lewandowsky, S. (2017). Reminders and repetition of misinformation: Helping or hindering its retraction? *Journal of Applied Research in Memory and Cognition, 6,* 185–192.

Ecker, U. K. H., Lewandowsky, S., Chang, E. P., & Pillai, R. (2014). The effects of subtle misinformation in news headlines. *Journal of Experimental Psychology: Applied, 20*, 323–335.

Ecker, U. K. H., Lewandowsky, S., Fenton, O., & Martin, K. (2014). Do people keep believing because they want to? Preexisting attitudes and the continued influence of misinformation. *Memory & Cognition, 42*, 292–304.

Ecker, U. K. H., Lewandowsky, S., Jayawardana, K., & Mladenovic, A. (2018). Refutations of equivocal claims: No evidence for an ironic effect of counterargument number. *Journal of Applied Research in Memory and Cognition, 8*, 98–107.

Ecker, U. K. H., Lewandowsky, S., Swire, B., & Chang, D. (2011). Correcting false information in memory: Manipulating the strength of misinformation encoding and its retraction. *Psychonomic Bulletin & Review, 18*, 570–578.

Ecker, U. K. H., Lewandowsky, S., & Tang, D. T. W. (2010). Explicit warnings reduce but do not eliminate the continued influence of misinformation. *Memory & Cognition, 38*, 1087–1100.

Ecker, U. K. H., O'Reilly, Z., Reid, J. S., & Chang, E. P. (2019). The effectiveness of short-format refutational fact-checks. *British Journal of Psychology.* Advance online publication. doi:10.1111/bjop.12383

Elsey, J. W., & Kindt, M. (2017). Breaking boundaries: Optimizing reconsolidation-based interventions for strong and old memories. *Learning & Memory, 24*, 472–479.

Eslami, M., Rickman, A., Vaccaro, K., Aleyasen, A., Vuong, A., Karahalios, K., … & Sandvig, C. (2015). I always assumed that I wasn't really that close to [her]: Reasoning about invisible algorithms in news feeds. In *Proceedings of the 33rd annual ACM conference on human factors in computing systems* (pp. 153–162). Seoul: ACM.

Feinberg, M., & Willer, R. (2013). The moral roots of environmental attitudes. *Psychological Science, 24*, 56–62.

Fogg, B. J., Soohoo, C., Danielson, D. R., Marable, L., Stanford, J., & Tauber, E. R. (2003). How do users evaluate the credibility of web sites? A study with over 2,500 participants. In *Proceedings of the 2003 Conference on Designing for User Experiences* (pp. 1–15). San Francisco, CA: ACM.

Garand, J. C. (2010). Income inequality, party polarization, and roll-call voting in the U.S. Senate. *Journal of Politics, 72*, 1109–1128.

Garrett, R. K., Weeks, B. E., & Neo, R. L. (2016). Driving a wedge between evidence and beliefs: How online ideological news exposure promotes political misperceptions. *Journal of Computer-Mediated Communication, 21*, 331–348.

Goldzweig, R., Wachinger, M., Stockmann, D., & Römmele, A. (2018). *Beyond Regulation: Approaching the Challenges of the New Media Environment* (Working Paper No. 6, Dec.). Retrieved from www.dahrendorf-forum.eu/wp-content/uploads/2018/12/Beyond-Regulation_Final.pdf

Gordon, A., Brooks, J. C. W., Quadflieg, S., Ecker, U. K. H., & Lewandowsky, S. (2017). Exploring the neural substrates of misinformation processing. *Neuropsychologia, 106*, 216–224.

Grimes, G. A., Hough, M. G., Mazur, E., & Signorella, M. L. (2010). Older adults' knowledge of internet hazards. *Educational Gerontology, 36*, 173–192.

Grönlund, K., Herne, K., & Setälä, M. (2015). Does enclave deliberation polarize opinions? *Political Behavior, 37*, 995–1020.

Guess, A., Nagler, J., & Tucker, J. (2019). Less than you think: Prevalence and predictors of fake news dissemination on Facebook. *Science Advances, 5*, eaau4586.

Guillory, J. J., & Geraci, L. (2013). Correcting erroneous inferences in memory: The role of source credibility. *Journal of Applied Research in Memory and Cognition, 2*, 201–209.

Guzzetti, B. J., Snyder, T. E., Glass, G. V., & Gamas, W. S. (1993). Promoting conceptual change in science: A comparative meta-analysis of instructional interventions from reading education and science education. *Reading Research Quarterly, 28*, 117–159.

Haim, M., Graefe, A., & Brosius, H. B. (2018). Burst of the filter bubble? Effects of personalization on the diversity of Google News. *Digital Journalism, 6*, 330–343.

Hameleers, M., Powell, T. E., Van der Meer, G. L. A., & Bos, L. (n.d.). A picture paints a thousand lies? The effects and mechanisms of multimodal disinformation and rebuttals via social media. Manuscript submitted for publication.

Hart, P. S., & Nisbet, E. C. (2012). Boomerang effects in science communication: How motivated reasoning and identity cues amplify opinion polarization about climate mitigation policies. *Communication Research, 39*, 701–723.

Iyengar, S., & Westwood, S. J. (2015). Fear and loathing across party lines: New evidence on group polarization. *American Journal of Political Science, 59*, 690–707.

Johnson, H. M., & Seifert, C. M. (1994). Sources of the continued influence effect: When misinformation in memory affects later inferences. *Journal of Experimental Psychology: Learning, Memory, and Cognition, 20*, 1420–1436.

Kahne, J., & Bowyer, B. (2017). Educating for democracy in a partisan age: Confronting the challenges of motivated reasoning and misinformation. *American Educational Research Journal, 54*, 3–34.

Kendeou, P., Walsh, E. K., Smith, E. R., & O'Brien, E. J. (2014). Knowledge revision processes in refutation texts. *Discourse Processes, 51*, 374–397.

Kowalski, P., & Taylor, A. K. (2009). The effect of refuting misconceptions in the introductory psychology class. *Teaching of Psychology, 36*, 153–159.

Kunda, Z. (1990). The case for motivated reasoning. *Psychological Bulletin, 108*, 480–498.

Lazer, D. M., Baum, M. A., Benkler, Y., Berinsky, A. J., Greenhill, K. M., Menczer, F., … & Zittrain, J. L. (2018). The science of fake news. *Science, 359*, 1094–1096.

Leonard, H., Dixon, G., Whitehouse, A. J., Bourke, J., Aiberti, K., Nassar, N., … & Glasson, E. J. (2010). Unpacking the complex nature of the autism epidemic. *Research in Autism Spectrum Disorders, 4*, 548–554.

Lewandowsky, S., Cook, J., & Ecker, U. K. H. (2017a). Letting the gorilla emerge from the mist: Getting past post-truth. *Journal of Applied Research in Memory and Cognition, 6*, 418–424.

Lewandowsky, S., Ecker, U. K. H., & Cook, J. (2017b). Beyond misinformation: Understanding and coping with the "post-truth" era. *Journal of Applied Research in Memory and Cognition, 6*, 353–369.

Lewandowsky, S., Ecker, U. K. H., Seifert, C. M., Schwarz, N., & Cook, J. (2012). Misinformation and its correction: Continued influence and successful debiasing. *Psychological Science in the Public Interest, 13*, 106–131.

Lewandowsky, S., Stritzke, W. G., Freund, A. M., Oberauer, K., & Krueger, J. I. (2013). Misinformation, disinformation, and violent conflict: From Iraq and the "War on Terror" to future threats to peace. *American Psychologist, 68*, 487–501.

Lord, C. G., Lepper, M. R., & Preston, E. (1984). Considering the opposite: A corrective strategy for social judgment. *Journal of Personality and Social Psychology, 47*, 1231–1243.

Lyons, T. (2017). News feed FYI: Replacing disputed flags with related articles. https://newsroom.fb.com/news/2017/12/news-feed-fyi-updates-in-our-fight-against-misinformation/

MacFarlane, D., Hurlstone, M. J., & Ecker, U. K. H. (2018) Reducing demand for ineffective health remedies: Overcoming the illusion of causality. *Psychology & Health, 33*, 1472–1489.

McCarty, N., Poole, K. T., & Rosenthal, H. (2006). *Polarized America: The dance of ideology and unequal riches*. Cambridge, MA: MIT Press.

McCright, A. M., & Dunlap, R. E. (2017). Combatting misinformation requires recognizing its types and the factors that facilitate its spread and resonance. *Journal of Applied Research in Memory and Cognition, 6*, 389–396.

McGrew, S., Breakstone, J., Ortega, T., Smith, M., & Wineburg, S. (2018). Can students evaluate online sources? Learning from assessments of civic online reasoning. *Theory & Research in Social Education, 46*, 165–193.

Messaris, P., & Abraham, L. (2001). The role of images in framing news stories. In S. D. Reese, O. H. Gandy, & A. E. Grant (Eds.), *Framing public life* (pp. 215–226). Mahwah, NJ: Erlbaum.

Metzger, M. J., & Flanagin, A. J. (2013). Credibility and trust of information in online environments: The use of cognitive heuristics. *Journal of Pragmatics, 59*, 210–220.

Mihailidis, P. (2009). Beyond cynicism: How media literacy can make students more engaged citizens (doctoral dissertation). http://drum.lib.umd.edu/handle/1903/8301

Murch, S. H., Anthony, A., Casson, D. H., Malik, M., Berelowitz, M., Dhillon, A. P., … & Walker-Smith, J. A. (2004). Retraction of an interpretation. *The Lancet, 363*, 750.

Nechushtai, E., & Lewis, S. C. (2019). What kind of news gatekeepers do we want machines to be? Filter bubbles, fragmentation, and the normative dimensions of algorithmic recommendations. *Computers in Human Behavior, 90*, 298–307.

Nyhan, B., & Reifler, J. (2010). When corrections fail: The persistence of political misperceptions. *Political Behavior, 32*, 303–330.

Nyhan, B., & Reifler, J. (2018). The roles of information deficits and identity threat in the prevalence of misperceptions. *Journal of Elections, Public Opinion and Parties, 29*, 222–244.

Nyhan, B., Reifler, J., Richey, S., & Freed, G. L. (2014). Effective messages in vaccine promotion: A randomized trial. *Pediatrics, 133*, e835.

O'Brien, S., & Lauer, C. (2018). Testing the susceptibility of users to deceptive data visualizations when paired with explanatory text. In *Proceedings of the 36th ACM International Conference on the Design of Communication* (p. 7). Milwaukee, WI: ACM.

Ozuru, Y., Dempsey, K., & McNamara, D. S. (2009). Prior knowledge, reading skill, and text cohesion in the comprehension of science texts. *Learning and Instruction, 19*, 228–242.

Pankoke-Babatz, U., & Jeffrey, P. (2002). Documented norms and conventions on the Internet. *International Journal of Human-Computer Interaction, 14*, 219–235.

Pariser, E. (2011). *The filter bubble: What the internet is hiding from you*. London: Penguin UK.

Pashler, H., Kang, S. H., & Mozer, M. C. (2013). Reviewing erroneous information facilitates memory updating. *Cognition, 128*, 424–430.

Paynter, J., Luskin-Saxby, S., Keen, D., Fordyce, K., Frost, G., Imms, C., … & Ecker, U. K. H. (2019). Evaluation of a template for countering misinformation: Real-world autism treatment myth debunking. *Plos One, 14*, e0210746.

Pennycook, G., & Rand, D. G. (2018). Lazy, not biased: Susceptibility to partisan fake news is better explained by lack of reasoning than by motivated reasoning. *Cognition, 188*, 39–50.

Pennycook, G., & Rand, D. G. (2019a). Who falls for fake news? The roles of analytic thinking, motivated reasoning, political ideology, and bullshit receptivity. https://papers.ssrn.com/sol3/papers.cfm?abstract_id=3023545.

Pennycook, G., & Rand, D. G. (2019b). The implied truth effect: Attaching warnings to a subset of fake news stories increases perceived accuracy of stories without warnings. https://papers.ssrn.com/sol3/papers.cfm?abstract_id=3035384.

Pérez-Rosas, V., Kleinberg, B., Lefevre, A., & Mihalcea, R. (2017). Automatic detection of fake news. https://arxiv.org/pdf/1708.07104.pdf

Pluviano, S., Watt, C., & Della Sala, S. (2017). Misinformation lingers in memory: Failure of three pro-vaccination strategies. *Plos One, 12*, e0181640.

Resnick, P., Garrett, R. K., Kriplean, T., Munson, S. A., & Stroud, N. J. (2013). Bursting your (filter) bubble: Strategies for promoting diverse exposure. In *Proceedings of the 2013 conference on computer supported cooperative work companion* (pp. 95–100). San Antonio, TX: ACM.

Rich, P. R., & Zaragoza, M. S. (2016). The continued influence of implied and explicitly stated misinformation in news reports. *Journal of Experimental Psychology: Learning, Memory, and Cognition, 42*, 1–13.

Roozenbeek, J., & van der Linden, S. (2019). The fake news game: Actively inoculating against the risk of misinformation. *Journal of Risk Research, 22*, 570–580.

Schwarz, N., Newman, E., & Leach, W. (2016). Making the truth stick and the myths fade: Lessons from cognitive psychology. *Behavioral Science & Policy, 2*, 85–95.

Schwarz, N., Sanna, L. J., Skurnik, I., & Yoon, C. (2007). Metacognitive experiences and the intricacies of setting people straight: Implications for debiasing and public information campaigns. *Advances in Experimental Social Psychology, 39*, 127–161.

Skurnik, I., Yoon, C., Park, D. C., & Schwarz, N. (2005). How warnings about false claims become recommendations. *Journal of Consumer Research, 31*, 713–724.

Smith, L. D., Best, L. A., Stubbs, D. A., Archibald, A. B., & Roberson-Nay, R. (2002). Constructing knowledge: The role of graphs and tables in hard and soft psychology. *American Psychologist, 57*, 749–761.

Smith, M. J., Ellenberg, S. S., Bell, L. M., & Rubin, D. M. (2008). Media coverage of the measles-mumps-rubella vaccine and autism controversy and its relationship to MMR immunization rates in the United States. *Pediatrics, 121*, 836–843.

Sunstein, C. R. (2002). *Republic.com*. Princeton, NJ: Princeton University Press.

Swire, B., Berinsky, A. J., Lewandowsky, S., & Ecker, U. K. H. (2017a). Processing political misinformation: Comprehending the Trump phenomenon. *Royal Society Open Science, 4*, 160802.

Swire, B., Ecker, U. K. H., & Lewandowsky, S. (2017b). The role of familiarity in correcting inaccurate information. *Journal of Experimental Psychology: Learning, Memory, and Cognition, 43*, 1948–1961.

Tippett, C. D. (2010). Refutation text in science education: A review of two decades of research. *International Journal of Science and Mathematics Education, 8*, 951–970.

Tucker, J., Guess, A., Barberá, P., Vaccari, C., Siegel, A., Sanovich, S., … & Nyhan, B. (2018). *Social media, political polarization, and political disinformation: A review of the scientific literature*. https://core.ac.uk/download/pdf/154423139.pdf

Thompson, G. (2009). *Measles and MMR statistics*. London: House of Commons. http://researchbriefings.files.parliament.uk/documents/SN02581/SN02581.pdf

van der Linden, S. L., Leiserowitz, A. A., Feinberg, G. D., & Maibach, E. W. (2014). How to communicate the scientific consensus on climate change: Plain facts, pie charts or metaphors? *Climatic Change, 126*, 255–262.

van der Linden, S., Leiserowitz, A., Rosenthal, S., & Maibach, E. (2017). Inoculating the public against misinformation about climate change. *Global Challenges, 1,* 1600008.

Vargas-Restrepo, C., Yang, B. W., Stanley, M. L., & Marsh, E. J. (n.d.). Judgments of deceptive visualizations: The truncated effect for bar graphs. Manuscript submitted for publication.

Varol, O., Ferrara, E., Davis, C. A., Menczer, F., & Flammini, A. (2017). Online human-bot interactions: Detection, estimation, and characterization. International AAAI conference on web and social media.

Wakefield, A. J., Murch, S. H., Anthony, A., Linnell, J., Casson, D. M., Malik, M., ... & Walker-Smith, J. A. (1998). RETRACTED: Ileal-lymphoid-nodular hyperplasia, non-specific colitis, and pervasive developmental disorder in children. *Lancet, 351,* 637–641.

Walter, N., & Murphy, S. T. (2018). How to unring the bell: A meta-analytic approach to correction of misinformation. *Communication Monographs, 85,* 423–441.

Walton, G., & Hepworth, M. (2011). A longitudinal study of changes in learners' cognitive states during and following an information literacy teaching intervention. *Journal of Documentation, 67,* 449–479.

Wilkes, A. L., & Leatherbarrow, M. (1988). Editing episodic memory following the identification of error. *Quarterly Journal of Experimental Psychology, 40,* 361–387.

Wilkinson, R., & Pickett, K. (2009). *The spirit level: Why more equal societies almost always do better.* London: Allen Lane.

Wood, T., & Porter, E. (2019). The elusive backfire effect: Mass attitudes' steadfast factual adherence. *Political Behavior, 41,* 135–163.

Zollo, F., Bessi, A., Del Vicario, M., Scala, A., Caldarelli, G., Shekhtman, L., ... & Quattrociocchi, W. (2017). Debunking in a world of tribes. *Plos One, 12,* e0181821.

27

THE CHALLENGE OF FAKE NEWS

Intellectual Survival in the Context of Multiple Representations and Perspectives

Panayiota Kendeou, Rina Harsch, Reese Butterfuss, Joseph Aubele, and Jasmine Kim

UNIVERSITY OF MINNESOTA

ABSTRACT

In this chapter, we identify challenges that fake news poses to our intellectual survival. We view fake news as a contaminant to our information ecosystem and propose the *Fake News Pyramid* by incorporating parallels to models of disease spread. Our discussion of challenges and solutions is situated in the "information disorder" framework, with a distinction between the human and technology level at each phase of the news cycle. We conclude that to comprehensively combat the creation, exposure, and distribution of fake news, we must propose actionable solutions drawing on multiple perspectives and representations.

Key words: fake news pyramid, intellectual survival, information disorder, humans, technology

THE NOTION OF INTELLECTUAL SURVIVAL

In 2013, the World Economic Forum warned of the increasing danger of misinformation being spread in the web, the difficulty of correcting misinformation, and the danger corrective efforts may pose to freedom of speech. At the time, the spreading of misinformation was termed a "digital wildfire" and was elevated at the same threat level as economic failures, environmental dangers, and diseases. Notably, this was well before the 2016 US presidential elections during which the terms "fake news" and "post-truth" were introduced.

The current information ecosystem is incredibly complex and includes *multiple representations* (i.e., presentations via a variety of symbol systems) and *multiple perspectives* (i.e., points of view). Navigating effectively this system is no longer just a job for journalists or academics; it is an integral skill to our individual and collective intellectual survival in a post-truth era. We view human resistance to fake news as a necessary part of our *intellectual survival*. In this chapter, we identify challenges that fake news poses to our intellectual survival at the human and technology level and propose solutions at each phase of the news cycle: creation, exposure, detection, and distribution.

WHAT IS FAKE NEWS?

Fake news has been defined as "false stories" (Allcott & Gentzkow, 2017) or as "fabricated information that mimics news media content in form but not in organizational process or intent" (Lazer et al., 2018, p. 1094). At the same time, the term has also been used to encompass a wide range of phenomena, including news satire, news parody, fabrication, and manipulation (Tandoc, Lim, & Ling, 2018). Fake news has seen a spike in recent years thanks, in part, to ongoing political campaigns and widespread information-seeking on social media platforms. Unfortunately, many individuals who are exposed to fake news stories believe them to be true (Ecker, Hogan, & Lewandowsky, 2017). This is problematic given the pervasiveness of fake news (Ciampaglia et al., 2015; Lazer et al., 2018). In fact, the most popular mainstream news stories are shared *less* widely than the most popular fake news stories (Menczer, 2016).

We situate our discussion of fake news in the context of the *Information Disorder* conceptual framework (Wardle & Derakhshan, 2017), which distinguishes information in terms of falseness and potential to cause harm. Within this framework, *misinformation* captures information that is false (see Rapp et al., Chapter 25) or manipulated, but was not created with the intent of causing harm to a person, group, organization, or country (see Sanderson & Ecker, Chapter 26), whereas *disinformation* captures information that is false and was created with the intent of causing harm. Finally, *malinformation* captures information that is *not* false but is used to cause harm (e.g., leaks of privileged information). Given these definitional distinctions, fake news may be aptly operationalized as *misinformation* or *disinformation*, depending on whether the creators of the content intended to cause harm or were merely misinformed themselves.

KEY FACTORS AND PHASES OF THE NEWS CYCLE

In order to disentangle specific challenges presented by the problem of fake news, we conceptualize the spread of news as a cycle with key factors and multiple phases. With respect to key factors, we draw on the *Disease Pyramid* in the plant pathology literature (Browning, Simons, & Torres, 1978). In plant pathology, the pyramid describes how different factors contribute differentially to the spread of plant disease. Four disease components are mapped onto a triangular based pyramid; the *pathogen*, *host*, and *environment* make up the edges of the triangular base, and

The Challenge of Fake News • 479

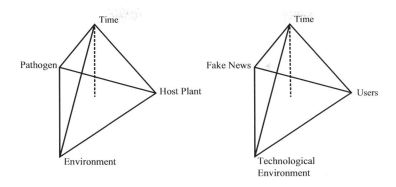

Figure 27.1 The Disease Pyramid and the Corresponding Fake News Pyramid.

time is a vector orthogonal to the base, giving the pyramid its third dimension (Figure 27.1, left). The nature of the pathogen, the hosts that carry the pathogen, and the characteristics of the environment that make it conducive to the proliferation of the pathogen interact over some period of time. If these four factors could be quantified, the volume of the pyramid would give the amount of disease in the plant population.

We propose the *Fake News Pyramid* (Figure 27.1, right), in which the spread of fake news is analogous to the spread of pathogens; the role of online users who are exposed, fail to detect, and then disseminate the fake news to virtual neighbors is analogous to the role of infected carriers that spread the pathogen to neighboring plants. Similarly, the technological environment is characterized by multiple perspectives and representations that inadvertently facilitate the dissemination of fake news, much like the natural environment has properties, such as temperature, which may be conducive to the propagation of a disease. As such, we have adopted this framework to conceptualize the interactions between key factors in the spread of fake news. We focus specifically on humans or users (with various perspectives) and the technological environment (with multiple representations) as factors in the spread of fake news in the information ecosystem over time.

With respect to time or the phases of the news cycle, we draw on the recently proposed framework for the spread of fake news by the Council of Europe, which includes three phases: *creation, production*, and *distribution* (Wardle & Derakhshan, 2017). Creation refers to the ideation of the false content or fake news; production refers to the conversion of that idea to a product that is accessible to information consumers; finally, distribution refers to the sharing or spread of fake news. To better understand distribution, we also need to consider *exposure* (contact with or consuming fake news) and *detection* (identification of fake news). For this reason, we expanded this framework by adding these two phases.

Thus, we focus our discussion on the role of human and technology factors as sources of challenges and solutions in each of the four[1] essential phases of the fake news ecosystem – creation, exposure, detection, and dissemination. An overview is presented in Table 27.1.

Table 27.1 Overview of Human and Technology Challenges and Solutions across the Fake News Cycle

		Creation	Exposure	Detection	Dissemination
Human	Challenges	- Ideology - Money	- Echo Chambers - Illusory-truth effect	- Gatekeeping - Motivated reasoning	- Sensational and emotional headlines
	Solutions	- Educational interventions - Social pressure	- Broadening searching practices - Accountability system	- Warning and retractions - Educational interventions	- Holding users accountable
Technology	Challenges		- "Personalized" exposure - Filter bubbles	- Social media as news sources - Trolls	- Social bots
	Solutions		- Ban certain publishers from profiting - Algorithms to promote higher quality content - Expose low-quality info consumers to high quality alternatives and elaborations	- Diffusion patterns - Network-based features - Machine learning	- Bot detection technologies - Disseminate counter/anti-misinformation

THE CREATION PHASE

Challenges at the Human Level

Those who create fake news do so for a variety of reasons, including the desire to spread their ideology, profit, or to disrupt the media cycle. Different techniques and strategies are used to accomplish these goals, and each technique poses a different threat to our intellectual survival. We identify prominent methods of creating fake news and major drivers for their creation.

Argumentum Ad Populum

Argumentum ad populum, or the appeal to "common knowledge," refers to the notion that information is true because many people believe it. People can be convinced by such arguments that common knowledge claims are validated by virtue of being shared by their peers (Godden, 2008). Consequently, they see no reason to empirically test them or argue for their veracity. Following this approach, creators of fake news frame information as common knowledge. This creates an ecosystem very susceptible to misinformation.

Ad hominem strategy

Ad hominem strategy refers to undermining someone's point of view by bringing up negative aspects of that person (Hansen, 2017). One type of ad hominem strategy is *abusive* ad hominem or the assertion that an argument shouldn't be accepted because of someone's past. For example, if an arguer committed a crime, then their argument cannot be trusted. The second type is *circumstantial* ad hominem or the assertion that an arguer is taking a position because that position serves their personal interest, not because the position is accurate. For example, arguers from "big business" or "corporate America" hold positions that have no basis because their position only serves themselves. The final type is *tu quoque*. Tuquoque arguments suggest that if an arguer does not follow their own advice, then the advice should be rejected. For example, negative ads are common during political campaigns, and many politicians denounce them. However, those same politicians still use negative ad campaigns. Some voters may use this as a basis to label those politicians as untrustworthy (Walton, 2006).

Political Polarization

Currently, the two ends of the political spectrum in the US are further apart now than they have been in recent memory. This has led to the creation of fake news to support each side's own beliefs and perspectives. In fact, when liberals and conservatives seek news about politics and government, the sources in which they place their trust do not overlap (Mitchell, Gotfried, Kiley, & Matsa, 2014). Moreover, the growing mutual hostility towards individuals on opposing ends of the political spectrum poses a civic threat because individuals with partisan views are more likely to read and share news articles that are exclusively aligned with their pre-existing beliefs (Bakshy, Messing, & Adamic, 2015). Compounding the problem, partisan viewers perceive more bias in news programs that do not align with their political perspective (Coe et al., 2008).

Money

Creating fake news presents many opportunities for monetary gain. Importantly, many fake news stories do not originate in the United States (Tandoc et al., 2018). This suggests that the generators of large amounts of fake news may not be politically motivated, but are simply pursuing economic incentives (Bakir & McStay, 2018).

Solutions at the Human Level

Educational Interventions

Educational interventions and news literacy programs appear to be the best recourse against incidental creation of fake news (i.e., misinformation) as they can teach people to assess the credibility of the information they encounter, investigate multiple perspectives on a given issue, and be aware of the various biases that may influence their understanding of information (McGrew, Breakstone, Ortega, Smith, & Wineburg, 2018; Wineburg & Reisman, 2015). There is also recent evidence that teaching individuals how fake news is being created in a game-based environment significantly improves their ability to detect and resist such fake news, building their "cognitive immunity" (Roozenbeek & van der Linden, 2019). In addition to teaching people how to detect fake news, interventions and games also educate people on their vulnerability to fake news (Rajaram & Marsh, 2019). This is important, as people tend to think that they are less vulnerable to fake news than others (Jang & Kim, 2018).

Social Pressure

Combatting the creation of fake news appears to be a greater challenge when it is intentional or involves financial incentives (Allcott & Gentzkow, 2017). Even if users are aware of the consequences of their actions, monetary incentives may motivate them to still create fake news. The social pressure that results from user-centered efforts to mitigate fake news (e.g., crowdsourcing) may encourage online platforms to take down such sources. However, despite our best attempts, fake news will be created and disseminated online (Vosoughi, Roy, & Aral, 2018). Thus, it is also important to address the different human- and technological-level challenges that occur during the exposure phase of the fake news cycle.

THE EXPOSURE PHASE

Challenges at the Human Level

Echo Chambers

Echo chambers refer to the amplified communication and repetition of ideas inside a closed system. In echo chambers, people are mostly exposed to information that confirms their own beliefs. Seeking news sources that align with one's ideology and beliefs is not a new problem, but it is considerably exacerbated by social media (Flaxman, Goel, & Rao, 2016). The lack of contradictory or different information or points of view in echo chambers can lead people to insulate themselves in distinct and polarized online environments that are unlikely to interact with one another (Del Vicario et al., 2016a, 2016b; Zollo et al., 2017). Even when information that contradicts or corrects misinformation breaches echo chambers, a "backfire effect" (Nyhan & Reifler, 2010) may occur and people may strengthen their misconceived beliefs.

Illusory-Truth Effect

The illusory-truth effect refers to our tendency to believe information to be correct after repeated exposure (Hasher, Goldstein, & Toppino, 1977). This effect has been amplified by social media and the belief that people no longer have to seek out the news, but the news finds them (Toff & Nielsen, 2018). The belief that news is everywhere and ambient (Hermida, 2010) is particularly prevalent now that we are constantly connected to the news world via various platforms (e.g., Facebook, Twitter) and devices (e.g., smartphones, tablets). This ambient exposure has serious consequences. To illustrate, as long as a news headline is believable, even a single exposure is enough to increase its perceived accuracy (Rapp & Salovich, 2018). This is the case even when there is a disclaimer indicating that a third-party fact-checking service has disputed the claims made (Pennycook, Cannon, & Rand, 2018) and when people possess knowledge that they could have used to evaluate it (Fazio, Brashier, Payne, & Marsh, 2015).

Solutions at the Human Level

Because people can become susceptible to believing fake news simply by being exposed to it, it is important to identify ways in which the presence of fake news in digital environments can be reduced. Importantly, people must be educated on how algorithms, filter bubbles, and echo chambers influence the content they are exposed to. Specifically, the content people view online is determined by complex algorithms that take into account an individual's online behavior, social networks, and information being shared by friends within those networks (Bode & Vraga, 2015; Gillespie, 2014). It follows that people may be able to reduce their exposure to fake news by changing the way they behave in digital environments. For example, people can reduce their exposure to misinformation by broadening search practices when seeking new information. Although some online platforms allow people to actively explore different types of information, people tend to focus on *popularity* as an indicator of quality. However, popularity is not always an accurate indicator of quality. In fact, a popularity search bias may actually hinder the quality of the content or information users seek, especially if users focus unduly on highly ranked items at the expense of exploring other options (Ciampaglia, Nematzadeh, Menczer, & Flammini, 2017).

Unlike online platforms that allow users to flexibly explore content (e.g., Google search), social media platforms allow much less flexibility. Still, as members of various social networks, people can monitor their own online behavior and hold each other accountable for the information they share. This could manifest as an *accountability system* where users are given the opportunity to flag specific content as fake news (Kim, Tabibian, Oh, Schölkopf, & Gomez-Rodriguez, 2018). After receiving enough flags, the disputed content can be evaluated by experts or an independent third-party fact-checker. Individual users can also choose to unfollow or block content from friends or acquaintances who regularly share fake news on social media platforms. Users could also work together to pressure social media platforms to remove specific profiles that are known for disseminating fake news.

Challenges at the Technological Level

"Personalized" Exposure

As noted earlier in this chapter, social media amplify the problem of fake news due to the presence of digital echo chambers in which users exclusively see content and posts that agree with their pre-existing beliefs (Pariser, 2011). Indeed, information on social media and the Internet is increasingly becoming more *personalized* (Borgesius et al., 2016). Before the "information age," news outlets typically offered the exact same content to all users. Now, those same news outlets can provide each user personalized content.

To capture the idea of content personalization, Pariser (2011) coined the term "filter bubble," meaning a *unique universe of information for each user*. One predominant concern regarding filter bubbles is that individuals may lock themselves within information cocoons (i.e., echo chambers). For example, an individual may seek only liberal-leaning blogs and websites, may listen to only liberal radio, and watch only liberal television. When forming political ideas or engaging in political discourse and decision making, such users may encounter relatively few opinions and arguments on the conservative spectrum, and thus have only limited understanding about opposing viewpoints (Borgesius et al., 2016).

Borgesius et al. (2016) distinguished between two different types of personalization within the context of filter bubbles. The first is *self-selected personalization,* in which users choose to encounter exclusively opinions that concur with their own. An example is a Twitter user only following other users whose opinions agree with their own. The second is *pre-selected personalization,* in which content may be chosen by the user, but may also be chosen by the information outlet. An example is when Facebook preselects a collection of news about "Friends," and makes that newsfeed available to the user. Borgesius et al. (2016) highlighted several concerns about filter bubbles, including effects on democracy and gatekeeping and influencing public opinion. Most important, because filter bubbles are a relatively recent idea, it is unknown what the long-term effects these concerns may have in terms of decision making, information exposure, and information use.

Solutions at the Technological Level

What can online platforms do to prevent consumer exposure to misinformation or to reduce this exposure relative to exposure to credible and accurate information? Research has highlighted three strategies that can be employed to this end. The first strategy is to prevent producers and distributors of disinformation from profiting financially from the traffic to their pages. For example, in 2016 Google took steps to remove over 200 publishers of misleading information and scams from its Adsense advertising network (Spencer, 2017). In 2017, Facebook announced that it would not allow advertisers that consistently link to stories that have been flagged as false by third-party fact-checkers to run ads on their site. By removing the financial incentive for certain publishers to distribute fake news, platforms can curb the amount of disinformation distributed in their networks, and in turn reduce the exposure of consumers to fake news.

The second strategy is to adjust algorithms to promote high-quality content. Many websites operate under the "wisdom of the crowd" assumption (Surowiecki, 2005), which is the notion that high-quality options will be chosen and gain early popularity, and in turn, this early popularity will make them more visible to others and thus more likely chosen. Another assumption that is implicit in this approach is that popularity is a reliable indicator of quality; however, this is not always the case, as popularity metrics can be skewed due to lack of independence of crowd members or manipulated by social bots, fake reviews, or astroturf (i.e., political campaigns run by organizations or individuals disguised as grassroots campaigns) (Ciampaglia et al., 2017). Thus, by promoting higher quality content or changing the popularity bias in algorithms to alter the rank of items, websites can sculpt information ecosystems that guide consumers towards high quality information.

The third strategy is to expose consumers of low-quality information to relevant high-quality information to help mitigate the negative effects of initial exposure. There is evidence that presenting users who have encoded misinformation and / or misconceptions with correct information reduces their misconceptions to some extent (Bode & Vraga, 2015; Butterfuss & Kendeou, in press; Kendeou, Butterfuss,

Kim, & Van Boekel, 2019; Kendeou, Walsh, Smith, & O'Brien, 2014; McCrudden & Kendeou, 2014). For example, Facebook has started presenting users viewing a post with a link to an article that has been flagged by a third-party fact-checker as false with a "Related Articles" section, which features fact-checking articles on the same issue (Lyons, 2017). Further information about the source can help users to assess credibility (Hughes, Smith, & Leavitt, 2018), which can influence processing of accurate information (Van Boekel, Lassonde, O'Brien, & Kendeou, 2017). For example, Facebook has rolled out a context button next to each article, which gives information about the publisher, articles about the same topic, and sharing statistics (Hughes et al., 2018).

Thus, online platforms can take measures to change the structure of their networks such that users are exposed to less low-quality information and more high-quality information. Financially disincentivizing problematic generators of misleading information, changing ranking algorithms so that they rank based on quality or maximize choice of higher quality information, and giving additional high-quality information and relevant contextual information to users who have been exposed to low-quality content are all strategies toward this end. Some websites such as Google and Facebook have started to implement policies that are consistent with these findings. Further research is necessary to verify the effectiveness of these policies and to find ways to further develop them.

THE DETECTION PHASE

Challenges at the Human Level

Gatekeeping

Gatekeeping refers to a multi-level verification process traditionally used by journalists, newspapers, and other forms of print media to control the kind of information that would be reported to the masses. Even though gatekeeping continues to take place, information shared in social media is not only from news organizations or organizations that employ some sort of quality control – for example, libraries (Williams & Delli Carpini, 2000). Thus, gatekeeping has shifted to a large extent to the individual. Now, gatekeepers include friends, family, or anyone else with whom we may interact with on social media (Bro & Wallberg, 2014). Successful gatekeeping requires the individual user to detect which news stories are real or fake (Williamset al., 2000). Unfortunately, even younger populations who have grown up in the digital age struggle with discerning real from fake news (McGrew et al., 2018). In part, this is because younger populations ("digital natives") not only consume more news on social media, but also tend to believe most of this news is true (Marchi, 2012). In other words, more news exposure does not translate into better detection skills. This phenomenon raises questions about the efficacy of the current gatekeeping model (Vos, 2015) as well as the need for education of "digital natives."

Motivated Reasoning

Motivated reasoning is a form of reasoning in which individuals evaluate arguments in a biased fashion to arrive at a preferred conclusion. Motivated reasoning has been implicated as a source of individuals' failures to accurately discern fact from fiction.

For example, Schaffner and Roche (2017) found that individuals may interpret a fact differently depending on how that fact aligns with their political ideologies. This shows that hard facts can become subjective to individuals who seek to use them to match their own motivations (for a review, see Kahan, 2013). However, a recent study by Pennycook and Rand (2019) found that susceptibility to fake news is not driven by motivated reasoning, but by lazy thinking instead. Thus, more research is needed to understand these contradicting findings.

Solutions at the Human Level

Warnings and Retractions

If people are unable to effectively distinguish between fake and real news, tagging fake news with warnings should help facilitate detection and reduce reliance on misinformation. To some extent, these approaches help; however, warnings or even retractions fail to completely eliminate the negative consequences of being exposed to misinformation (Butterfuss & Kendeou, in press; Chan, Jones, Hall Jamieson, & Albarracín, 2017; Ecker, Lewandowsky, & Tang, 2010). Warnings and corrections that include the misinformation may even make fake news familiar and easy to process during later encounters, increasing its perceived accuracy (Pennycook et al., 2018). However, warnings and corrections provided by friends and family members may encourage people to recognize the falsehood of information they read and endorse accurate information (Hannak, Margolin, Keegan, & Weber, 2014), particularly if the correction provides a causal explanation that supports the accurate information (Kendeou, Smith, & O'Brien, 2013; Kendeou et al., 2014).

Educational Interventions

Detection of fake news should start in the classroom, where students can be taught about the continued influence of misinformation and the cognitive biases that make them susceptible to misinformation (Breakstone, McGrew, Smith, Ortega, & Wineburg, 2018). Educational interventions should encourage scepticism in students so that they pay greater attention to the quality and source of information and feel compelled to search for more sources of information that provide diverse and conflicting perspectives on the same topic, especially when they read about controversial issues. Also, as noted earlier, educational games that require students to create fake news articles may help reduce their susceptibility to actual fake news articles (Roozenbeek & van der Linden, 2018, 2019). Students should also be taught specific strategies that will help them examine the validity and plausibility of arguments (Cook, Ellerton, & Kinkead, 2018; Lombardi, Bailey, Bickel, & Burrell, 2018). Making plausibility judgments is an important skill to foster because identifying fake news as implausible can effectively inoculate against the illusory-truth effect (Pennycook et al., 2018). Finally, students should be taught to monitor their emotions when they are conducting research online. Negative emotions may reduce people's ability to critically evaluate information about controversial topics such as climate change and may also impair their ability to identify fake news (Lombardi & Sinatra, 2013).

Challenges at the Technological Level

Social Media as News Sources

The internet, and social media more specifically, have become a primary information source for both journalists and ordinary news readers (Schifferes & Newman, 2013; Su, Akin, Brossard, Scheufele, & Xenos, 2015). In fact, news organizations may expect journalists to be fluent in social media as a means to disseminate news. Likewise, mainstream news media outlets are integrating more and more social media content into their output. This complicates the relation between professional news organizations and social media. For example, in the US, 62% of adults reported that they get news from social media networks (Gottfried & Shearer, 2016). In the UK, 40% of adults use social media as a regular news source, yet less than 10% trust information on social media networks like Twitter and Facebook (Newman, Fletcher, Kalogeropoulos, & Nielsen 2019).

Trolls

The Pew Research Center (Rainie, Anderson, & Albright, 2017) recently reported that internet "trolls" who spread fake news will persist, and the steadily expanding scale and complexity of Internet discourse will make it difficult to deal with problematic content and contributors. Trolls often impersonate a real organization or person and include messages designed to provoke predictable responses (Griffiths, 2014). Trolls participating in the propagation of fake news may persist because overseeing and moderating online content comes at a steep cost. In addition, increased surveillance may also result in censoring public debate and free speech, making it risky for big tech companies.

Solutions at the Technological Level

The challenges from technology-enhanced spreading of fake news online necessitates solutions that are also technology-enhanced. In this section, we highlight the ways in which technology can be wielded to detect misinformation, rumors, and fake campaigns online. Researchers have investigated some characteristic features that distinguish fake news from real news. This research has primarily focused on revealing traits of misinformation itself as well as its spreaders (Wu, Morstatter, Hu, & Liu, 2016). Using these characteristic features as input, learning algorithms can be trained to identify fake news.

Diffusion Patterns

One distinctive feature of fake news is the pattern of diffusion. Fake news spread from one agent to another in a network. In contrast to the agents organically spreading news they find interesting, disseminators of fake news often share information prolifically with the intention of making the news viral. Once information gains traction and reaches a certain spread threshold, the information cascades across a network, establishing a sense of credibility (Ratkiewicz et al., 2011). In order to promote distribution of fake news across the network, spreaders will share and retweet fake news prolifically by using multiple accounts and bots. Identifying dyads of multiple accounts in a network or consistently interacting, especially through retweets, can be instrumental in identifying which pieces of information could be fake news (Ratkiewicz et al., 2011). One solution to the challenge of detecting fake news is therefore to utilize an algorithm to analyze diffusion patterns.

Network-Based Features

Platform-based features can also be used to identify fake news. Platform features such as hashtags and URLs can be used by users to find useful information about themes of interest or users with similar interests and worldviews. However, misinformation distributors can also capitalize on the wide network reach made available by these features. Researchers have found that certain Twitter hashtags or URLs are associated with rumors or astroturfing (Qazvinian, Rosengren, Radev, & Mei, 2011; Ratkiewicz et al., 2011). Researchers also found that hashtags could be used to evaluate whether a user finds a piece of information to be consistent with their views, credible with regards to its source, and having consensus more generally (Kumar & Geethakumari, 2014; Lewandowsky, Cook, Fay, & Gignac, in press). However, because users sometimes spread rumors without using hashtags or URLs, reliance only on platform features will not generate a comprehensive set of misinformation (Qazvinian et al., 2011). Manually setting algorithms to look for fake news associated hashtags and URLs gathers reliably numerous information that can be helpful in fake news detection.

Machine Learning

Researchers found that certain features are better indicators of misinformation than others at different phases in the life cycle of the misinformation. For example, user-based metadata was the strongest feature for identifying fake news in the early stages before the information went viral; network-based feature analysis was strongest after a rumor has gone viral and passed its trending threshold (Varol, Ferrara, Menczer, & Flammini, 2017); and content-based features were reliable regardless of time (Qazvinian et al., 2011; Varol et al., 2017). While using algorithms that take multiple features of misinformation into account can yield precise and thorough collections of misinformation, several of these procedures rely on manually annotated datasets of online tweet information and other time-consuming, laborious methods (Grinberg, Joseph, Friedland, Swire-Thompson, & Laser, 2019). Several of them also rely on manually decided features or rules, which limits the extent to which they can uncover more latent features and correlates of misinformation. A proposed alternative is to use machine learning models, specifically recursive neural networks (Ma et al., 2016).

THE DISTRIBUTION PHASE

Challenges at the Human Level

Fake news spreads because humans spread it. Indeed, humans spread fake news more quickly and widely than they spread real news (Vosoughi et al., 2018). This finding is particularly true for fake political news, which is spread three times faster than other fake news.

Sensational and Emotional Headlines

Gabielkov, Ramachandran, Chaintreau, and Legout (2016) gathered a database of 75 billion potential views and 2.8 million shares of tweets. Of the total number of URLs looked at, only 2% were of Primary URLs, or URLs from five selected major news sources; 98% were of Secondary URLs, or URLs from sources that shared news, even news from a Primary URL. Of that 98% Secondary URLs, 60% of the stories were never clicked; users only read the headline. This means that people are sharing news stories without actually reading them. Furthermore, the sensationalized nature of fake news headlines and the emotions they incite, such as surprise and disgust, lead users to share the stories more rapidly than real news, which typically incites sadness, anticipation, and trust (Vosoughi et al., 2018). This is particularly problematic given evidence in the extant literature that emotional content in textual information can influence learning (Trevors, Kendeou, & Butterfuss, 2017).

Solutions at the Human Level

Holding Users Accountable

Interviews with people who shared misinformation on social media platforms suggest that people understand their potential role in spreading misinformation, especially when they use social media information to cope with a crisis (e.g., after the Boston Marathon bombings) or help friends in need (Huang, Starbird, Orand, Stanek, & Pedersen, 2015). When people realize that they have spread misinformation, they may be able to reflect on their online sharing behavior. This self-reflection may serve to facilitate change in such behavior in the future. Finally, these interviews highlight a greater need to understand the spread of misinformation in social media platforms during times of crisis so that users can be educated to anticipate and respond appropriately to information spread on social media.

Challenges at the Technological Level

Social Bots

A core challenge is the spread of misinformation by bots, or software-controlled social media profiles or accounts (Varol et al., 2017). Bots can interact with legitimate users and post content just as real users can. To this end, bots capitalize on our psychological tendencies to attend to what is popular, trust information shared in a social setting (Jun, Meng, & Johar, 2017), and trust those in our social circle (Jagatic, Johnson, Jakobsson, & Menczer, 2007).

Shao et al. (2018b, 2018a) attempted to provide a quantitative account of the impact of social bots on Twitter following the 2016 US presidential campaign. Overall, results indicated that social bots amplified the spread of misinformation and fake news by exposing individuals to low-credibility content from low-credibility sources and induced them to share that content. Specifically, low-credibility sources published approximately 100 articles per week, each of which garnered approximately 30 tweets per week. In fact, the distribution of popularity for low-credibility articles was nearly indistinguishable from that of fact-checked articles, which suggests that low-credibility articles are as likely to spread and go "viral" as are credible articles.

Shao et al. (2018b, 2018a) identified key strategies social bots use to spread low-credibility articles. First, bots get involved in the first few seconds after an article is published on Twitter, which results in many users being exposed to low-credibility articles early, increasing the chances of them going viral. Second, bots may mention influential users (i.e., users with a high number of followers) in tweets that link to low-credibility articles to give the appearance that the content they are sharing is widely shared, which increases the likelihood that others will reshare content to their followers, which in turn increases the perceived credibility of the low-credibility articles.

Solutions at the Technological Level

Whereas information overload and the difficulty of discriminating fake from true information can overwhelm users, technological solutions can be used to slow the spread of misinformation. For example, technology can be harnessed to detect bots that spread misinformation or to start a campaign that spreads real information to counter the misinformation.

Bot Detection Technologies

Most bot detection technologies are based on algorithms that classify users as bots or legitimate users, based on various features, including the content they share, user metadata, and network activity. User metadata and content feature analysis have been said to be most effective in detecting bots (Varol et al., 2017). Simple bots tend to interact with more sophisticated bots that behave like legitimate, human accounts (Varol et al., 2017). Thus, abnormalities in inter-bot connectivity and bot linkage structure within the node network have also been utilized as a feature for detection (Zhao et al., 2009). While these methods detect bots after the accounts have already spread misinformation, another method to detect a bot as soon as the account has been created is an algorithm based on username as a bot feature (Lee & Kim, 2014). Because bot controllers rely on an enormous number of bots to share misinformation, usernames are often created automatically using the same algorithm.

Algorithms can err; they do not have absolute precision and are not always comprehensive. If platforms automatically suspend all accounts that are detected as bots, some legitimate accounts will inevitably become suspended by accident, which would lead to concerns about censorship. As such, automatic suspension may not be a viable option for some platforms. Platforms can also detect bots by requiring a CAPTCHA before a user can disseminate information on the platform as an additional measure. While this would obstruct completely benign accounts such as emergency response accounts or mainstream news accounts that use automated systems, CAPTCHA deployment makes it easier to prevent the automatic spread of misinformation (Shao et al., 2018b).

Another method for curbing the dissemination of misinformation is the spread of correct information. A counter campaign that disseminates correct information can minimize the cascading spread of misinformation (Budak, Agrawal, & Abbadi, 2011). The question that follows is: what is the minimal number of users that need to be convinced to spread the correct information in order to curb misinformation spread?

Researchers have found that these users are often highly influential nodes in a network and can be identified through network analysis (Nguyen, Yan, Thai, & Eidenbenz, 2012). While highly effective, this method is also computationally costly.

CONCLUDING REMARKS

As a "post-truth" world becomes a more concrete reality, fake news, in its many forms, will persist as a prevalent contaminant to our information ecosystem. In the present chapter we identified challenges that fake news poses to our *intellectual survival* at the human and technology level and proposed solutions at each phase of the news cycle: creation, exposure, detection, and distribution. In doing so, we synthesized literature from multiple disciplines, including education, psychology, information sciences, journalism, and communication science. Our discussion of challenges and solutions was situated in the "information disorder" framework (Wardle & Derakhshan, 2017). We proposed the *Fake News Pyramid* by incorporating parallels to models of disease spread, given our view that fake news is a contaminant to our information ecosystem. Our proposed expanded framework incorporates interdisciplinary views that reflect the complex and dynamic nature of the threats to our intellectual survival. More work is necessary to further refine our current understanding of the problems and to identify and test targeted solutions in order to intellectually survive within an ever-changing information ecosystem.

ACKNOWLEDGMENTS

Writing of this paper was supported by the Guy Bond Chair from the College of Education and Human Development at the University of Minnesota to P. Kendeou.

NOTES

1   We discuss production in the creation phase.

   Correspondence concerning this paper should be addressed to Panayiota Kendeou, Department of Educational Psychology, University of Minnesota, 56 East River Road, Minneapolis, MN 55455; E-mail: kend0040@umn.edu.

REFERENCES

Allcott, H., & Gentzkow, M. (2017). Social media and fake news in the 2016 election. *Journal of Economic Perspectives*, *31*(2), 211–236.

Bakir, V., & McStay, A. (2018). Fake news and the economy of emotions: Problems, causes, solutions. *Digital Journalism*, *6*(2), 154–175.

Bakshy, E., Messing, S., & Adamic, L. (2015). Exposure to ideologically diverse news and opinion on Facebook. *Science*, *348*, 1130–1132.

Bode, L., & Vraga, E. K. (2015). In related news, that was wrong: The correction of misinformation through related stories functionality in social media. *Journal of Communication*, *65*(4), 619–638.

Borgesius, F. J., Trilling, D., Möller, J., Bodó, B., de Vreese, C. H., & Helberger, N. (2016). Should we worry about filter bubbles?. *Internet Policy Review*, *5*(1), 1–16.

Breakstone, J., McGrew, S., Smith, M., Ortega, T., & Wineburg, S. (2018). Why we need a new approach to teaching digital literacy. *Phi Delta Kappan*, *99*(6), 27–32.

Bro, P., & Wallberg, F. (2014). Digital gatekeeping: News media versus social media. *Digital Journalism*, *2*(3), 446–454.

Browning, J., Simons, M., & Torres, E. (1978). Managing host genes: Epidemiologic and genetic concepts. In J. Horsfall & E. Cowling (Eds.), *Plant disease: An advanced treatise* (pp. 191–212). Cambridge, MA: Academic Press.

Budak, C., Agrawal, D., & Abbadi, A. E. (2011). Limiting the spread of misinformation in social networks. In *Proceedings of the twentieth international conference on world wide web* (pp. 665–674). New York: ACM.

Butterfuss, R., & Kendeou, P. (in press). Reducing interference from misconceptions: The role of inhibition in knowledge revision. *Journal of Educational Psychology*.

Chan, M. P. S., Jones, C. R., Hall Jamieson, K., & Albarracín, D. (2017). Debunking: A meta-analysis of the psychological efficacy of messages countering misinformation. *Psychological Science, 28*(11), 1531–1546.

Ciampaglia, G. L., Nematzadeh, A., Menczer, F., & Flammini, A. (2017). How algorithmic popularity bias hinders or promotes quality. *Scientific Reports, 8*(1), 1–10.

Ciampaglia, G. L., Shiralkar, P., Rocha, L. M., Bollen, J., Menczer, F., & Flammini, A. (2015). Computational fact checking from knowledge networks. *PLoS ONE, 10*, 1–13.

Coe, K., Tewksbury, D., Bond, B. J., Drogos, K. L., Porter, R. W., Yahn, A., & Zhang, Y. (2008). Hostile news: Partisan use and perceptions of cable news programming. *Journal of Communication, 58*(2), 201–219.

Cook, J., Ellerton, P., & Kinkead, D. (2018). Deconstructing climate misinformation to identify reasoning errors. *Environmental Research Letters, 13*(2), 1–7.

Del Vicario, M., Bessi, A., Zollo, F., Petroni, F., Scala, A., Caldarelli, G., ... Quattrociocchi, W. (2016a). The spreading of misinformation online. *Proceedings of the National Academy of Sciences, 113*(3), 554–559.

Del Vicario, M., Vivaldo, G., Bessi, A., Zollo, F., Scala, A., Caldarelli, G., & Quattrociocchi, W. (2016b). Echo chambers: Emotional contagion and group polarization on Facebook. *Scientific Reports, 6*, 37825.

Ecker, U. K., Hogan, J. L., & Lewandowsky, S. (2017). Reminders and repetition of misinformation: Helping or hindering its retraction? *Journal of Applied Research in Memory and Cognition, 6*(2), 185–192.

Ecker, U. K., Lewandowsky, S., & Tang, D. T. (2010). Explicit warnings reduce but do not eliminate the continued influence of misinformation. *Memory and Cognition, 38*(8), 1087–1100.

Fazio, L. K., Brashier, N., Payne, K., & Marsh, E. (2015). Knowledge does not protect against illusory truth. *Journal of Experimental Psychology: General, 144*(5), 993–1002.

Flaxman, S., Goel, S., & Rao, J. (2016). Filter bubbles, echo chambers, and online news consumption. *Public Opinion Quarterly, 80*(1), 298–320.

Gabielkov, M., Ramachandran, A., Chaintreau, A., & Legout, A. (2016). Social clicks: What and who gets read on twitter?. *ACM SIGMETRICS Performance Evaluation Review, 44*(1), 179–192.

Gillespie, T. (2014). The relevance of algorithms. In T. Gillespie, P. Boczkowski, & K. Foot (Eds.), *Media technologies* (pp. 167–194). Cambridge, MA: MIT Press.

Godden, D. (2008). On common knowledge and ad populum: Acceptance as grounds for acceptability. *Philosophy and Rhetoric, 41*(2), 101–129.

Gottfried, J., & Shearer, E. (2016). News use across social media platforms 2016. www.journalism.org/2016/05 26/news-use-across-social-media-platforms-2016

Griffiths, M. D. (2014). Adolescent trolling in online environments: A brief overview. *Education and Health, 32*(3), 85–87.

Grinberg, N., Joseph, K., Friedland, L., Swire-Thompson, B., & Lazer, D. (2019). Fake news on twitter during the 2016 US Presidential election. *Science, 363*(6425), 374–378.

Hannak, A., Margolin, D., Keegan, B., & Weber, I. (2014). Get back! You don't know me like that: The social mediation of fact checking interventions in twitter conversations. Paper presented at the 8th international aaai conference on weblogs and social media, Ann Arbor, June.

Hansen, H. (2017). Fallacies. In E. Zalta (Ed.), *Stanford Encyclopedia of Philosophy* (Fall 2017 Ed.). https://plato.stanford.edu/archives/fall2017/entries/fallacies/#toc

Hasher, L., Goldstein, D., & Toppino, T. (1977). Frequency and the conference of referential validity. *Journal of Verbal Learning and Verbal Behavior, 16*(1), 107–112.

Hermida, A. (2010). Twittering the news. *Journalism Practice, 4*(3), 297–308.

Huang, Y. L., Starbird, K., Orand, M., Stanek, S. A., & Pedersen, H. T. (2015). Connected through crisis: Emotional proximity and the spread of misinformation online. In *Proceedings of the 18th ACM conference on computer supported cooperative work* and *social computing* (pp. 969–980). New York: ACM.

Hughes, T., Smith, J., & Leavitt, A. (2018). Helping people better assess the stories they see in news feed with the context button. https://newsroom.fb.com/news/2018/04/news-feed-fyi-more-context/

Jagatic, T. N., Johnson, N. A., Jakobsson, M., & Menczer, F. (2007). Social phishing. *Communications of the ACM, 50*(10), 94–100.

Jang, S. M., & Kim, J. K. (2018). Third person effects of fake news: Fake news regulation and media literacy interventions. *Computers in Human Behavior, 80*, 295–302.

Jun, Y., Meng, R., & Johar, G. V. (2017). Perceived social presence reduces fact-checking. In S. T. Fiske (Ed.), *Proceedings of the National Academy of Sciences* (pp. 5976–5981). Washington, DC: National Academy of Sciences.

Kahan, D. (2013). A risky science communication environment for vaccines. *Science, 342*(6154), 53–54.

Kendeou, P., Butterfuss, R., Kim, J., & Van Boekel, M. (2019). Knowledge revision through the lenses of the three-pronged approach. *Memory and Cognition, 47*(1), 33–46.

Kendeou, P., Smith, E. R., & O'Brien, E. J. (2013). Updating during reading comprehension: Why causality matters. *Journal of Experimental Psychology: Learning, Memory, and Cognition, 39*, 854–865.

Kendeou, P., Walsh, E. K., Smith, E. R., & O'Brien, E. J. (2014). Knowledge revision processes in refutation texts. *Discourse Processes, 51*(5/6), 374–397.

Kim, J., Tabibian, B., Oh, A., Schölkopf, B., & Gomez-Rodriguez, M. (2018). Leveraging the crowd to detect and reduce the spread of fake news and misinformation. In *Proceedings of the eleventh ACM international conference on web search and data mining* (pp. 324–332). New York: ACM.

Kumar, K. P., & Geethakumari, G. (2014). Detecting misinformation in online social networks using cognitive psychology. *Human-centric Computing and Information Sciences, 4*(14), 1–22.

Lazer, D. M., Baum, M. A., Benkler, Y., Berinsky, A. J., Greenhill, K. M., Menczer, F., ... Schudson, M. (2018). The science of fake news. *Science, 359*(6380), 1094–1096.

Lee, S., & Kim, J. (2014). Early filtering of ephemeral malicious accounts on Twitter. *Computer Communications, 54*, 48–57.

Lewandowsky, S., Cook, J., Fay, N., & Gignac, G. E. (in press). Science by social media: Attitudes towards climate change are mediated by perceived social consensus. *Memory and Cognition*.

Lombardi, D., Bailey, J. M., Bickel, E. S., & Burrell, S. (2018). Scaffolding scientific thinking: Students' evaluations and judgments during earth science knowledge construction. *Contemporary Educational Psychology, 54*, 184–198.

Lombardi, D., & Sinatra, G. M. (2013). Emotions about teaching about human-induced climate change. *International Journal of Science Education, 35*(1), 167–191.

Lyons, T. (2017). Replacing disputed flags with related articles. https://newsroom.fb.com/news/2017/12/news-feed-fyi-updates-in-our-fight-against-misinformation/

Ma, J., Gao, W., Mitra, P., Kwon, S., Jansen, B. J., Wong, K. F., & Cha, M. (2016). Detecting rumors from microblogs with recurring neural networks. *International joint conference on article intelligence, 2016-January*, (pp. 3818–3824). New York: Association for Computing Machinery.

Marchi, R. (2012). With Facebook, blogs and fake news, teens reject journalistic "objectivity". *Journal of Communication Inquiry, 36*(3), 246–262.

McCrudden, M. T., & Kendeou, P. (2014). Exploring the link between cognitive processes and learning from refutational text. *Journal of Research in Reading, 37*, 116–140.

McGrew, S., Breakstone, J., Ortega, T., Smith, M., & Wineburg, S. (2018). Can students evaluate online sources? Learning from assessments of civic online reasoning. *Theory and Research in Social Education, 46*(2), 165–193.

Menczer, F. (2016). The spread of misinformation in social media. In J. Bourdeau, J. Hendler, R. Nkambou, I. Horrocks, & B. Y. Zhao (Eds.), *Proceedings of the 25th international conference on world wide web* (p. 717). Montreal: International World Wide Web Conferences Steering Committee.

Mitchell, A., Gotfried, J., Kiley, J., & Matsa, K. E. (2014). *Political polarization and media habits. Report for the Pew Research Internet Project*. www.journalism.org/2014/10/21/political-polarization-media-habits

Newman, N., Fletcher, R., Kalogeropoulos, A., & Nielsen, R. (2019). *Reuters institute digital news report 2019*. Oxford: Reuters Institute for the Study of Journalism.

Nguyen, N. P., Yan, G., Thai, M. T., & Eidenbenz, S. (2012). Containment of misinformation spread in online social networks. In *Proceedings of the Fourth Annual ACM Web Science Conference* (pp. 213–222). New York: ACM.

Nyhan, B., & Reifler, J. (2010). When corrections fail: The persistence of political misperceptions. *Political Behavior, 32*(2), 303–330.

Pariser, E. (2011). *The filter bubble: What the Internet is hiding from you*. London: Penguin UK.

Pennycook, G., Cannon, T., & Rand, G. (2018). Prior exposure increases perceived accuracy of fake news. *Journal of Experimental Psychology: General, 147*(12), 1865–1880.

Pennycook, G., & Rand, D. (2019). Lazy, not biased: Susceptibility to partisan fake news is better explained by lack of reasoning than by motivated reasoning. *Cognition, 188*, 39–50.

Qazvinian, V., Rosengren, E., Radev, D. R., & Mei, Q. (2011). Rumor has it: Identifying misinformation in microblogs. In *Proceedings of the conference on empirical methods in natural language processing* (pp. 1589–1599). Stroudsburg, PA: Association for Computational Linguistics.

Rainie, H., Anderson, J. Q., & Albright, J. (2017). *The future of free speech, trolls, anonymity and fake news online*. Washington, DC: Pew Research Center.

Rajaram, S., & Marsh, E. J. (2019). Cognition in the internet age: What are the important questions? *Journal of Applied Research in Memory and Cognition, 8*(1), 46–49.

Rapp, D. N., & Salovich, N. A. (2018). Can't we just disregard fake news? The consequences of exposure to inaccurate information. *Policy Insights from the Behavioral and Brain Sciences, 5*(2), 232–239.

Ratkiewicz, J., Conover, M., Meiss, M., Goncalves, B., Flammini, A., & Menczer, F. (2011). Detecting and Tracking Political Abuse in Social Media. In *Proceedings of the fifth international AAAI conference on weblogs and social media* (pp. 297–304). Menlo Park, CA: Association for the Advancement of Artificial Intelligence.

Roozenbeek, J., & van der Linden, S. (2018). The fake news game: Actively inoculating against the risk of misinformation. *Journal of Risk Research, 22*, 570–580.

Roozenbeek, J., & van der Linden, S. (2019). Fake news game confers psychological resistance against online misinformation. *Palgrave Communications, 5*, 1–12.

Schaffner, B., & Roche, C. (2017). Misinformation and motivated reasoning. *Public Opinion Quarterly, 81*(1), 86–110.

Schifferes, S., & Newman, N. (2013). Verifying news on the social web: Challenges and prospects. In *Proceedings of the 22nd international conference on world wide web* (pp. 875–878). New York: ACM.

Shao, C., Ciampaglia, G. L., Varol, O., Yang, K., Flammini, A., & Menczer, F. (2018b). The spread of low-credibility content by social bots. *Nature Communications, 9*(1), 1–9.

Shao, C., Hui, P., Wang, L., Jiang, X., Flammini, A., Menczer, F., & Ciampaglia, G. L. (2018a). Anatomy of an online misinformation network. *PLos ONE, 13*(4), 1–23.

Spencer, S. (2017). How we fought bad ads, sites and scammers in 2016. www.blog.google/technology/ads/how-we-fought-bad-ads-sites-and-scammers-2016

Su, L. Y. F., Akin, H., Brossard, D., Scheufele, D. A., & Xenos, M. A. (2015). Science news consumption patterns and their implications for public understanding of science. *Journalism and Mass Communication Quarterly, 92*(3), 597–616.

Surowiecki, J. (2005). *The Wisdom of Crowds*. New York: Anchor.

Tandoc, E., Lim, Z. W., & Ling, R. (2018). Defining "fake news": A typology of scholarly definitions. *Digital Journalism, 6*(2), 137–153.

Toff, B., & Nielsen, R. K. (2018). "I just google it": Folk theories of distributed discovery. *Journal of Communication, 68*(3), 636–657.

Trevors, G. J., Kendeou, P., & Butterfuss, R. (2017). Emotion processes in knowledge revision. *Discourse Processes, 54*(5/6), 406–426.

Van Boekel, M., Lassonde, K. A., O'Brien, E. J., & Kendeou, P. (2017). Source credibility and the processing of refutation texts. *Memory and Cognition, 45*(1), 168–181.

Varol, O., Ferrara, E., Menczer, F., & Flammini, A. (2017). Early detection of promoted campaigns on social media. *EPJ Data Science, 6*, 1–19.

Vos, T. (2015). Revisiting gatekeeping theory during a time of transition. In T. Vos & F. Heinderyckx (Eds.), *Gatekeeping in Transition* (pp. 17–38). New York: Routledge.

Vosoughi, S., Roy, D., & Aral, S. (2018). The spread of true and false news online. *Science, 359*(6380), 1146–1151.

Walton, D. N. (2006). Poisoning the well. *Argumentation, 20*(3), 273–307.

Wardle, C., & Derakhshan, H. (2017). *Information disorder: Toward an interdisciplinary framework for research and policy making* (Council of Europe Report DGI(2017)09). https://firstdraftnews.org/wp-content/uploads/2017/11/PREMS-162317-GBR-2018-Report-de%CC%81sinformation-1.pdf

Williams, B., & Delli Carpini, M. (2000). Unchained reaction: The collapse of media gatekeeping and the Clinton-Lewinsky scandal. *Journalism, 1*(1), 61–85.

Wineburg, S., & Reisman, A. (2015). Disciplinary literacy in history: A toolkit for digital citizenship. *Journal of Adolescent and Adult Literacy, 58*(8), 636–639.

Wu, L., Morstatter, F., Hu, X., & Liu, H. (2016). Mining misinformation in social media. In M. Thai, W. Wu, & H. Xiong (Eds.), *Big data in complex and social networks* (pp. 1–34). Boca Raton, FL: Taylor & Francis Group.

Zhao, Y., Xie, Y., Yu, F., Ke, Q., Yu, Y., Chen, Y., & Gillum, E. (2009). BotGraph: Large scale spamming botnet detection. In *Proceedings of the sixth USENIX symposium on networked systems design and implementation* (pp. 321–334). Berkeley, CA: USENIX Association.

Zollo, F., Bessi, A., Del, V., Scala, A., Caldarelli, G., Shekhtman, L., & Quattrociocchi, W. (2017). Debunking in a world of tribes. *PLoS One, 12*(7), 1–27.

28

THE NEED FOR PERSONALIZED LEARNING AND THE POTENTIAL OF INTELLIGENT TUTORING SYSTEMS

Brent Morgan, A. Marie Hogan, Andrew J. Hampton, Anne Lippert, and Arthur C. Graesser

UNIVERSITY OF MEMPHIS

ABSTRACT

Intelligent Tutoring Systems (ITS) are computer learning environments that offer personalized instruction to help learners master knowledge and skills. ITSs are superior to typical computer-based training because their intelligent algorithms can adapt to the needs of the individual learner at a fine-grained level. However, most ITSs do not take advantage of the inherent benefit of incorporating multiple representations of the knowledge they teach. This chapter discusses how multiple representations can be integrated into a single system using knowledge components, and how this is incorporated into an expanded student model. As an example, we describe ElectronixTutor, which integrates five ITSs as well as a number of other learning resources to teach electronics.

Key words: intelligent tutoring systems, hybrid intelligent tutoring systems, multiple representations, system integration, educational technology

This chapter begins with a discussion of the role of multiple representations in the context of learning. For our purposes here, "representation" refers to the modality in which a piece of information is presented (e.g., verbal, diagrammatic, text, etc.). Next, we introduce intelligent tutoring systems (ITS), adaptive computer learning environments that offer personalized instruction, the state-of-the-art in education technology. We then identify a number of successful ITSs that use multiple representations to enhance learning. Among these is a new kind of ITS, a *hybrid* tutor, that integrates multiple other ITSs (and therefore multiple representations); we introduce the first hybrid tutor, *ElectronixTutor*. Finally, we conclude with some thoughts on the future, including stealth assessment (wherein the learner is unaware of the assessment), computer-supported collaborative learning, and optimal selection of representations (i.e., how should a hybrid ITS select the ideal representation(s) to present to the learner?).

MULTIPLE REPRESENTATIONS IN DIGITAL LEARNING TECHNOLOGIES

Multimedia learning environments employ multiple representations to improve understanding of conceptual and procedural information. According to Ainsworth (1999, 2018), multiple representations assist conceptual understanding by emphasizing differences or similarities as a learner is building a mental model, an internal representation of interconnecting information about a topic or concept (Johnson-Laird, 2010). With multiple representations, the inherent weaknesses of one representation can be mitigated by providing additional representations (see also Chapter 7). A single representation may not contain all the relevant information a learner may need; squeezing all of the information into a single representation may cause it to become cluttered and overcomplicated. A primary benefit of multiple representations is the adaptive selection of representation (e.g., depictive versus descriptive) for maximum efficacy. Conceptual understanding improves when multiple representations reflect varied interpretations of the concept, such as when fractions can be displayed as pie graphs, as parts of a group of items, or as shaded areas of a single item (Rau, Aleven, Rummel, & Pardos, 2014). Increased understanding of the concept being taught occurs when the learner (1) analyzes the representations to identify differences and commonalities between them, and (2) begins to contrast and integrate that new information with prior knowledge (Ainsworth, 1999). Multiple representations can be used to gradually familiarize a learner with more complex, abstract, or ambiguous representations by highlighting similarities (or contrasting differences) in a more familiar representation to extend or revise understanding (Ainsworth, 1999, 2018).

Design choices heavily influence the efficacy of multiple representations as a tool to improve learning outcomes. In addition to the content within multiple representations, learning outcomes are also influenced by the number of representations, the way the information is distributed, the sequence of representations, the form of the representational system, and support for translation between representations. These considerations are outlined in the DeFT framework (**De**sign parameters, pedagogical **F**unction, cognitive **T**asks), which is based on research in cognitive psychology, science, education, artificial intelligence, and curriculum studies (Ainsworth, 2006).

An example of how design choices can affect learning is an experiment wherein an ITS taught fractions (Rau et al., 2014; see also Chapter 2). The sequence and frequency of representations (shaded circles (A), rectangles (B), and number lines (C)) were evaluated for over 108 questions. One condition ("blocked") presented each representation for 36 questions in a row (e.g., 36 As followed by 36 Bs followed by 36 Cs). A second "moderately interleaved" condition transitioned after every sixth question from a blocked presentation to partially interleaved (e.g., AAAAAA-BBBBBB-CCCCCC) presentation. In a third "fully interleaved" condition, students were presented with a different representation after each question (e.g., A-B-C-A-B-C). Finally, in a fourth "increasingly interleaved" condition, students were presented with interleaved representations that gradually decreased in frequency of repetition from 12 problems at the beginning (e.g., 12 As followed by 12 Bs followed by 12 Cs) to every six problems (e.g., AAAAAA-BBBBBB-CCCCCC) to a fully interleaved single problem in the end (e.g., A-B-C-A-B-C). The fully interleaved condition demonstrated more consistent learning gains for low prior knowledge students, thereby illustrating the importance of supporting connection-making between representations for novice learners.

Learning outcomes are expected to improve when the learner has the opportunity to manipulate and engage with multiple representations, where an interaction with one representation results in a dynamic update of the second representation. Hence, multiple representations are more effective when they promote increased levels of cognitive engagement. The ICAP framework (Chi & Wylie, 2014) presents a hierarchy linked to promoting different levels of learning relative to the level of cognitive engagement with the content, specifically **I**nteractive > **C**onstructive > **A**ctive > **P**assive. When in the passive mode of engagement, the learner attends to received information without any other mental or physical activity (e.g., listening to a lecture without taking notes). In the active mode of engagement, learners manipulate the material in some way (e.g., highlighting a text). The constructive mode of engagement requires the learner to generate new material in some way (e.g., making concept maps; paraphrasing). Lastly, the interactive mode of engagement is when two or more learners interact with each other and each member of the group contributes constructively (e.g., debating). When using multiple representations, the learner's ability to actively manipulate, control, or interact with representations affords more opportunity to create more defined mental models of conceptual information and promote deeper learning.

Although multiple representations can improve performance, they are not universally beneficial. For example, one study suggested that multiple representations may be more effective when learning conceptual topics rather than procedural ones (Rau et al., 2014). Efficacy undoubtedly depends on the types of representations used, the way they are presented, the content cohesion, and the way a learner interacts with representations. These factors must all work in concert to result in meaningful learning. The misuse of multiple representations can interfere with the process of selecting relevant images, making connections, and integrating that information with prior knowledge. When a learner is presented with a representation that does not contain conceptually relevant information, it can result in a detrimental *coherence effect* (Mayer, Heiser, & Lonn, 2001). Presenting redundant representations (e.g., simultaneously presenting a complete transcript of narration along with a video) has also been shown to sometimes reduce recall and application of knowledge (*redundancy effect*; Mayer et al., 2001).

A very important threat to learning when using multiple representations is *cognitive overload* (Sweller, 1988). Meaningful learning consists of a process of selecting relevant words and images, organizing those words and images into a mental model that incorporates the verbal and visual media, and integrating them with prior knowledge (Mayer & Moreno, 2003). Unfortunately, for a novice, prior knowledge typically consists of disorganized fragments so the learner ends up focusing on surface features and missing the deeper connection between representations or how to apply them (Cook, 2006). Cognitive overload is manifest when task demands exceed the learner's working memory capacity. The overload can result from attending to too many extraneous irrelevant representations or from difficulty in making sense of how the representations are related. Unsurprisingly, cognitive overload results in reduced learning outcomes for recall and knowledge transfer tasks (Mayer & Moreno, 2003). Therefore, another important factor necessary for learning with multiple representations is *representational fluency*. Representational fluency is achieved when a learner understands the properties and format of a representation and how to connect and apply it to what they are learning (Rau, Aleven, Rummel, & Rohrbach, 2012). When a learner is presented with an unfamiliar representation (e.g., a complex diagram), part of their working memory is devoted to deciphering the nature of the representation itself, leaving a reduced amount for understanding the content within the representation or how to apply it.

The benefits of multiple representations are included in the list of key affordances of digital learning technologies in the second volume of *How People Learn* in a consensus report of the National Academy of Sciences, Engineering, and Medicine (National Academies of Sciences, Engineering, and Medicine, 2018). The complete list and description of the affordances are listed in Table 28.1. Twenty years ago, many of these affordances were beyond the capability of most computer learning environments. Linked representations were static if they were present at all. In today's computer-based adaptive instructional systems, learners can manipulate representations within the learning environment and the system responds adaptively and sometimes intelligently. In this chapter, we focus on intelligent tutoring systems, the current state-of-the-art in learning technologies.

Table 28.1 Key Affordances of Learning Technologies from *How People Learn II* (NAESEM)

Interactivity	The technology systematically responds to actions of the learner. For example, some serious games immerse learners in virtual worlds through role-playing and interaction with a gaming community. Reading a book, listening to an audiotape, and viewing a film are not interactive technologies because these do not present new information in response to the actions of the learner.
Adaptivity	The technology presents information that is contingent on the behavior, knowledge, and characteristics of the learner. A technology can be interactive but not adaptive, as in a game that offers the users choices but does not alter the options in response to the users' choices or actions. Conversely, intelligent adaptive learning programs are designed to be adaptive and interactive, so that when learners use the software, it assesses and may respond selectively to every task-related action on the part of the learner, including giving right and wrong answers, length of time taken in making decisions, and the learner's individual decision-making strategies.
Feedback	The technology gives feedback to the learner on the quality of the learner's performance, sometimes including how the quality could be improved. The feedback can range from a short message that a learner's input or response was correct or incorrect to an explanation of why the input was correct or incorrect. Task-relevant feedback can range from responses to short-term events that last a few seconds to long-term performance extending over (for instance) a school semester.
Choice	The technology gives students options for what to learn and how to learn so they can regulate their own learning. For example, choice is low for an instruction-oriented technology that pushes an agenda with few options for learner exploration. Choice is high, for instance, when students explore the Internet to find answers to their personal questions.

Nonlinear access	The technology allows the learner to select or receive learning activities in an order that deviates from a set order. Many commercial learning technologies offer a linear presentation in which material and major concepts are experienced in the same order by all learners. However, other technologies provide nonlinear access to information: the order of presentation depends on the learners' choices or varies by virtue of intelligent adaptivity.
Linked representations	The technology provides quick connections between representations for a topic that emphasize different conceptual viewpoints, pedagogical strategies, and media, such as between spoken messages, texts, diagrams, videos, and interactive simulations. Such connections support cognitive flexibility and encoding variability to support learning.
Open-ended learner input	The technology allows learners to express themselves through natural language, drawing pictures, and other forms of open-ended communication that encourage active learning.
Communication with other people	The learner communicates with one or more other "persons," who may range from peers to subject-matter experts. The communication may include text-based computer-mediated communication (email, chat, discussion rooms), multimedia computer-mediated communication, computer-supported collaborative learning, conversational agents, tutors on demand, and crowdsourcing.

INTELLIGENT TUTORING SYSTEMS

ITSs are computer learning environments that teach students by implementing intelligent algorithms that can adapt to the needs of the individual student with respect to the mastery of subject matter knowledge, cognitive skills, motivation, and sometimes emotions (Graesser, Hu, & Sottilare, 2018; Graesser, Rus, & Hu, 2017). Traditional computer-based training, in contrast, offers minimal adaptivity. In traditional computer-based training, learners typically study a given topic, are assessed with a multiple-choice test, are presented rudimentary feedback, and repeat the topic if performance does not exceed some threshold. The instructional events within a topic are predetermined and selected either rigidly or randomly rather than dynamically selected according to fine-grained intelligent algorithms. An ITS provides the intelligent adaptivity that is sensitive to the student's prior performance, student model of the subject matter, and other psychological characteristics.

The standard ITS architecture includes four primary components: the *domain model*, the *student model*, the *tutor model*, and the *user interface* (Sottilare, Graesser, Hu, & Holden, 2013; Woolf, 2009). The domain model is the conceptual representation of the domain to be learned, including common learner misconceptions. The ITS uses this expert knowledge to evaluate learner performance. The learner model is the ITS's representation of the learner's cognition, including knowledge, affect, motivation, and other psychological characteristics. The learner model is often compared to the domain model to track student progress. The domain model and learner model provide information to the tutor model, which then determines what action(s) the tutor does next. ITSs typically have two loops, an outer loop and an inner loop (VanLehn, 2006). The outer loop selects the optimal task or problem for the learner, whereas the inner loop governs actions for each step within that task (feedback, hints, etc.). Finally, the user interface is how the learner communicates with the tutor, including text, speech, sketches, and clicks. This can even include emotions that are derived from the verbal interactions, speech, facial expressions, and body posture (D'Mello & Graesser, 2010).

Reviews and meta-analyses have confirmed that ITSs frequently outperform classroom instruction, reading texts, and other traditional learning methods. These meta-analyses typically report effect sizes (signified by d), which refer to the difference between the ITS condition and a control condition, calibrated in standard deviation units. The reported meta-analyses show positive effect sizes varying from $d = 0.05$ (Dynarsky et al., 2007; Steenbergen-Hu & Cooper, 2014) to $d = 1.08$ (Dodds & Fletcher, 2004), with most between $d = 0.40$ and $d = 0.80$ (Kulik & Fletcher, 2015; Ma, Nesbit, J. C., & Liu, 2014; Steenbergen-Hu & Cooper, 2013; VanLehn, 2011). Our current best meta-meta estimate from all of these meta-analyses is 0.60. This performance is comparable to human tutoring which varies between 0.20 and 0.80 (Cohen, Kulik, & Kulik, 1982; VanLehn, 2011), depending on the expertise of the tutor. Human tutors have not varied greatly from ITSs in direct comparisons between ITSs and trained human tutors (Graesser, 2016; VanLehn, 2011).

These meta-analyses are based upon a number of successful ITSs. A curated list of ITSs is shown in Table 28.2. In addition to their primary domains, Table 28.2 lists their primary and secondary representations, the modality of learner input, and learner autonomy. The final autonomy column refers to the relative level of self-regulation available to the learners, especially in reference to their choice of the type representation. Some interesting conclusions can be drawn from this analysis. The two middle columns show that most ITSs incorporate multiple representations. This is perhaps unsurprising, given that ITSs are often designed by teams of learning scientists. Many ITSs also offer multiple modalities for learner input, with some even allowing open-ended verbal input. The final column, however, shows that although multiple representations and modalities are present, the learner has minimal ability to choose between them. ITSs typically specialize in their distinctive pedagogical approaches to the learning domain, but the systems have rarely considered learners making these decisions themselves. A hybrid system that integrates multiple resources would presumably increase *cognitive flexibility* (the ability think about and/or switch between multiple concepts simultaneously; Spiro, Coulson, Feltovich, & Anderson, 1988; Spiro, Klautke, Cheng, & Gaunt, 2017). This would allow researchers to orchestrate learning pedagogy theoretically, or alternatively, to have learners make decisions.

Integrating multiple learning resources would presumably further improve the efficacy of ITSs; however, this has remained relatively unexplored for a variety of reasons. First, ITSs are difficult and costly to develop, so there are relatively few ITSs in comparison to traditional computer-based training. Second, ITS developers must choose between quantity and quality, with an acknowledgment that any system with narrow scope is less useful for real-world applications. Additional representations might require a costly redesign of the system. Third, some ITS developers may have low interest in incorporating additional representations because they are more interested in specific research questions related to their primary research agenda and targeted domain knowledge. Fourth, there is a tendency in research and development to "do one thing and do it well." Multiple representations may not be high in priority.

Table 28.2 List of ITSs, Domains, Representations, and Learner Interaction

System Name	Domain	Primary Representation	Secondary Representation	Input	Learner Autonomy
AutoTutor Graesser et al., 2005	Various	Conversational	Diagrammatic	Text (open-ended)	Low
Dragoon VanLehn et al., 2017	Electronics	Diagrammatic	Mathematical	Click & Drag	Low
LearnForm Kumar et al., 2015	Electronics	Diagrammatic	Mathematical	Click	Low
BEETLE-II Dzikovska et al., 2014	Electronics	Verbal	Graphical	Text (open-ended)	Low
Fractions Tutor Aleven et al., 2016	Mathematics	Graphical	Verbal	Click	Low
Digital Tutors Fletcher, 2011	Various	Conversational	-	Text (open-ended)	Low
Ellie DeVault et al., 2014	Counseling	Conversational	-	Speech (open-ended)	Low
Sherlock Lesgold et al., 1992	Electronics	Scenario	Voice-over	Click	Low
COMET Suebnukarn & Haddawy, 2007	Medical	Scenario	Virtual classroom	Click	Low
TECH8 Dolenc & Aberšek, 2015	Technology	Diagrammatic	Mathematical	Click & Fill-in	Low
ELM-ART Brusilovsky et al., 1996	Programming	Interactive text	Hypermedia	Click	Low
SQL-Tutor Mitrovic & Martin, 2000	SQL	Textual	Verbal instruction	Click or Fill-in	Low
ZOSMAT Keleş et al. 2009,	Various	Diagrammatic	Mathematical	Click or Fill-in	Low
SEATS Davidovic et al., 2003	Programming	Mathematical	Spatial relationship	Code or click	Low
Cognitive Tutor Aleven & Koedinger, 2002	Math	Textual	Graphical	Click or Graph	Low
Betty's Brain Biswas et al., 2010	Science	Diagrammatic	Verbal	Click	Low
Andes VanLehn, 1996	Physics	Diagrammatic	Verbal	Fill-in	Low
Why2-Atlas Jordan et al., 2003	Physics	Conversational	-	Text (open-ended)	Low
SASO-ST Traum et al., 2008	Reasoning	Conversational	Paralinguistic	Speech	Low
iStart McNamara et al., 2004	Reading	Verbal	Graphical	Text & Click	Low
ARIES/ARA Millis et al., 2011	Critical Thinking	Scenario	Graphical	Text or Click	Low
KERMIT Mitrovic et al., 2007	Databases modeling	Diagrammatic	Scenario	Click & Drag	Low
AETS Zachary et al., 1998	Team Training	Graphical	Conversational	Keystroke, Eye-tracking, Speech	Medium
ALEKS Canfield, 2001	Mathematics	Mathematical	Graphical	Click & Fill-in	Medium
Coach Mike Lane et al., 2011	Programming	Conversational	Diagrammatic	Click, physical action	Medium
DeepTutor Rus et al., 2013	Physics	Conversational	Simulation	Text (open-ended)	Medium
Crystal Island Rowe et al., 2011	Critical Thinking	Virtual reality	Diagrammatic	Mouse & Arrow keys	Medium
Wayang Outpost Arroyo et al., 2004	SAT Math	Visuospatial	Scenario	Click	High

One important point is that multiple representations can also include multiple perspectives (i.e., contrasting or nuanced points of view). However, multiple perspectives are not often incorporated into ITSs. ITSs typically teach core concepts in well-defined domains (such as introductory STEM courses) which limits the potential for contrasting or nuanced points of view: most questions only have a single right answer. Furthermore, ITSs often have only one agent (if any at all), and thus typically present a single perspective. However, two (or more) agents afford a number of possible conversational designs (Graesser, Cai, Morgan, & Wang, 2017), including agents contradicting each other to induce confusion (Lehman et al., 2013), which has been shown to be beneficial to learning (D'Mello, Lehman, Pekrun, & Graesser, 2014).

A HYBRID ITS: ELECTRONIXTUTOR

The Office of Naval Research commissioned a new type of ITS through its STEM Grand Challenge (Craig, Graesser, & Perez, 2018). This new *hybrid* ITS, called *ElectronixTutor*, integrates a number of existing learning resources into a single application. ElectronixTutor was designed to teach the material covered in Apprentice Technician Training courses conducted by the Navy Educational Training Command. This content ranges from basic circuitry concepts (such as Ohm's law) to complex multistage amplifiers. ElectronixTutor is used to augment traditional classroom instruction with homework or laboratory work, with the opportunity of learners to self-regulate and learn by themselves. For classroom use, ElectronixTutor offers a calendar that can be aligned to a course syllabus.

ElectronixTutor features numerous learning resources integrated into one system. Most of the learning resources are ITSs, but others are non-adaptive, conventional resources, which can be utilized by ElectronixTutor for a more adaptive experience. We now turn to the learning resources of ElectronixTutor. Each system's affordances are displayed in Table 28.3.

AutoTutor

AutoTutor presents learners with two conversational agents who encourage reasoning and conceptual understanding through natural language interaction (Graesser, 2016; Nye, Graesser, & Hu, 2014). A tutor agent asks difficult questions that facilitate conceptual reasoning, followed by a multi-turn conversation that adaptively probes aspects of a complete answer that learners may have omitted. For example, if an ideal answer has five components but a learner initially only articulates three of them, the tutor agent uses hints and prompts to encourage the learner to express what they know about the other two, and corrects as necessary. A peer student agent provides flexibility in conversational roles and facilitates more natural exchanges. As an example, one question on Zener diodes is: "How does current flow through a Zener diode differently in the two bias conditions?" The expected answer from the student would be: "It conducts in forward bias. It also conducts in reverse bias beyond the breakdown voltage."

Dragoon

Dragoon focuses on mental model construction and simulation (VanLehn, Wetzel, Grover, & Van De Sande; Wetzel et al., 2016). In this ITS, learners must manipulate aspects of a complex circuit diagram in order to understand how variations in one parameter will change the behavior as a whole. These provide difficult problems, incorporating both conceptual relationships and mathematical reasoning in a holistic model of complex circuits.

LearnForm

LearnForm challenges the learner with complex problem-solving tasks. A learning task consists of an overarching problem statement, contributory multiple-choice questions, feedback on performance, and a summary of a complete correct answer. When a learner solves a complex problem incorrectly, LearnForm responds by breaking the problem down into its individual components to identify where the error occurred.

ASSISTments

This facilitates the online development of learning content, assessments, and other related technologies by instructors and other non-programmers (Heffernan & Heffernan, 2014). This platform provided the original learning management system for ElectronixTutor before it was migrated to the open-source Moodle platform. ASSISTments provides "skill builders" that give the learner drill and practice on the mathematics of basic electronics laws (Ohm's, Kirchhoff's).

BEETLE-II

BEETLE-II is a conversation-based ITS which explores basic electricity and electronics (Dzikovska, Steinhauser, Farrow, Moore, & Campbell, 2014). The problems are on open and closed circuits and using voltage to find a circuit fault. This is a beginner-level interactive resource that was supplied by the Naval Air Warfare Center Training Systems Division. The circuit problems and pedagogical structures were incorporated in ElectronixTutor in the form of multiple choice questions because those components best explained learning gains in the empirical evaluation of BEETLE-II (Dzikovska et al., 2014). In contrast, the fine-grained natural language interaction components did not predict learning gains in that study so they were not incorporated in ElectronixTutor.

Static Reading Materials

Conventional, non-adaptive learning resources provide additional pedagogical content at relatively low cost. These static resources allow learners total control over their study, potentially helping those who prefer free selection, unguided exploration, and self-regulated learning. Static resources include the Navy Electronics and Electricity Training Series (US Navy, 1998), which includes over 5,000 pages of content which form the basis for Navy electronics technician training. Each major topic also includes a summary for trainees to read and study in ElectronixTutor. The summary was constructed by domain experts at ASU and UM. Each summary contains a few pages (two to five) of essential information, including diagrams and hyperlinks to related web-based references (e.g., Wikipedia).

Point & Query

Although asking questions is associated with learning gains, learners often struggle to ask appropriate questions. A *Point & Query* utility (Graesser et al., 2018b) addresses this issue. In Point & Query, learners can hover their mouse over a hot-spot on an image (e.g., a resistor or capacitor), causing questions to pop up (e.g., "What is this part?"; "What is the function of this part?"). Mousing over one of the provided questions reveals the answer. Learners can then leverage common questions and answers, indexed to the relevant portion of the circuit in question. Point & Query induces a dramatic increase in the number of questions asked to about 120 per hour, or approximately 700 times the classroom rate (Graesser & Person, 1994) (Table 28.3).

The resources listed above were designed to engage learners at myriad levels of analysis and methods of interaction. The resources differ substantially in content, detail, media, and instructional approaches. Although each individual resource does not typically cover all of the available topics, each topic includes at least two resources that learners can leverage to explore the avenue of understanding that suits them best. Further, the beginning topics typically have more resources available (specifically, the easier, more fundamental problems provided by LearnForm and ASSISTments), as learners orient themselves to a new field. Integrating these resources into a single platform provides unprecedented breadth, depth, and flexibility.

The diversity of the learning resources also necessitated a tool to integrate them through subject matter content at an intermediate grain size. To that end, *knowledge components* (Koedinger, Corbett, & Perfetti, 2012) were adopted to form the basis of an interlingua that compares learner behavior across the constellation of learning

Table 28.3 Key Affordances of Learning Technologies from How People Learn II (NASEM)

Affordance	AutoTutor	Dragoon	Learnform	ASSISTments	BEETLE-II	ElectronixTutor
Interactivity	X	X	X	X	X	X
Adaptivity	X	X	X		X	X
Feedback	X	X	X	X	X	X
Choice	X					X
Nonlinear access	X	X	X	X	X	X
Linked representations	X	X	X	X	X	X
Open-ended learner input	X	X			X	X
Communication with other people	X				X	X

resources. A knowledge component is defined by Koedinger et al. (2012) as "an acquired unit of cognitive function or structure that can be inferred from performance on a set of related tasks." For example, a knowledge component in geometry might be finding the area of a triangle by multiplying ½ times the base times the height. Knowledge components are inherently hierarchical because multiplication, fractions, area, and parts of a triangle are themselves knowledge components; however, this is not a strict hierarchy because a single knowledge component (e.g., Diode Behavior Forward) can be associated with multiple topics (e.g., Zener Diodes & Regulators, Filters, P-N Junctions, Diode Limiters & Clampers). Each knowledge component in ElectronixTutor is specified as a topic-frame pair, where each topic is a concrete component in the curriculum (e.g., transistors, filters, PN junction), and each frame is the epistemic frame or schema (e.g., structure, function, behavior, parameter) specified by a domain expert. Hence, an example topic-frame pair would be "Diode Behavior Forward – Filters": understanding the forward behavior of a diode is critical to understanding why a filter is necessary. In ElectronixTutor, knowledge components are used for multiple purposes, including checking completeness of the curriculum, linking various learning resources, identifying difficulty level of learning items, and tracking learners' progress.

The most complete version of the ElectronixTutor interface resides on Moodle (see Figure 28.1 for a screenshot). The left banner of the ElectronixTutor interface includes the Topic of the Day, three recommendations, and the list of 15 topics. The Topic of the Day is the primary topic to focus on for the trainee on a given day as deemed by the instructor (or a default calendar). The Recommender System offers three recommendations based on an intelligent algorithm which incorporates the domain model, student model, and tutor model. The list of 15 topics offers freedom for the self-regulated students; they can select what they want to do by clicking on a topic, followed by clicking on an option in a hierarchically embedded second level of Learning Resources. Within the two system-guided options (Topic of the Day, Recommender System), ElectronixTutor has *three* loops. The outer loop still selects the topic, and the inner loop still determines actions for each tutoring step within the current system, but a *middle loop* selects the representation.

To the right of the left banner is the activity space in which the student interacts with the learning resource. In Figure 28.1 there is an AutoTutor trialogue with the teacher and student agents, a circuit diagram, an input area for the learner to type responses, and a chat history (not shown, but near the learner input area. Point & Query is also activated in the circuit diagram.

We have begun collecting preliminary data on ElectronixTutor with undergraduate electrical engineering students in beginner, intermediate, and advanced circuitry and electronics courses. In general, users did quite well on the attempted problems, with an average knowledge component score of 0.78 (i.e., they have expressed mastery of 78% of the concepts contained across all learning items they have attempted that contain that knowledge component). Participation was voluntary, and some students used the system far more than anticipated, indicating they found the system valuable. However, our recommendation would be for ElectronixTutor to be directly incorporated into the curriculum (i.e., mandatory) for maximum impact.

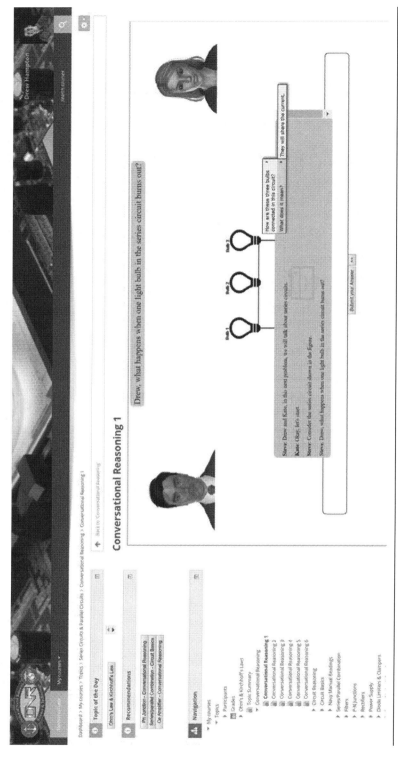

Figure 28.1 Screenshot of ElectronixTutor.

NEW INSIGHTS AND FUTURE DIRECTIONS

As stated above, we are currently collecting early data on ElectronixTutor, so we have no knowledge of its efficacy yet. However, each of the ITSs included in ElectronixTutor has been independently empirically validated, so we have some confidence that learning gains for each ITS will persist (if not improve) when integrated with other ITSs. However, this is not assured. There are four distinct outcome possibilities, described in Table 28.4. Here, "1 + 1" refers the integration of two systems, and the right of the equals sign roughly corresponds to student learning.

In the first outcome, a lack of representational fluency could confuse learners. In this case, additional resources actually hinder learning. In the second outcome, representations are not sufficiently different to increase or build upon understanding, or are not different enough to cater to individual preferences. This results in learning gains that fall within the previously defined range of the individual resources. In the third outcome, each resource is independently effective, and we see learning gains beyond those from a single resource. Although the resources complement each other (i.e., they approach the content from different perspectives without redundancy), there is no synergy among resources. Finally, in the fourth outcome, each resource enhances understanding of the others, resulting in cross-representational fluency and increased learning beyond what each resource could achieve independently.

Assessments of learner progress once revolved around the standard pre-post experimental design. Assessing a learner's progress is difficult and steals time from furthering learning. Hence, another area where ITSs offer advancements is *stealth assessments*, where the system gathers data while the learner engages with content. This type of seamless assessment evaluates the learner's progress and delivers tailored content without interrupting flow (Shute, 2011). Although all ITSs employ stealth assessment to some degree (which drives the adaptive component), the amount of stealth assessment can be increased, including cognitive, metacognitive, personality, social, etc. measures such as working memory, fluency, grit, impetuousness, self-regulated learning, and collaborative learning. This can lead to increased adaptability across all three loops of a hybrid ITS. In the inner loop, the system might note that the user always immediately asks for hints and explains the value of attempting to solve the problem on his/her own first. In middle loop, the system can use information about the learner to better recommend resources. For example, if the learner is high in grit, the system might more readily change resources, knowing that the learner is likely to persevere. For the outer loop, the system could provide more information about the learner's progress towards topic mastery. These can lead to a truly customized learning experience.

Table 28.4 Possible Outcomes of Integrating Learning Resources.

Outcome	Explanation
1 + 1 = 0	Additional resources cause confusion; no learning
1 + 1 = 1	Additional resources are redundant; learning is constant.
1 + 1 = 2	Additional resources have an additive effect on learning
1 + 1 = 3	Additional resources have an interactive effect on learning

Another critical activity where ITSs can help facilitate flow is *collaborative problem-solving* (CPS), one of the most frequently mentioned 21st-century skills (Fiore, Graesser, & Greiff, 2018; Graesser et al., 2018; National Research Council, 2012; OECD, 2017). However, teaching CPS skills is a nontrivial issue: in classroom settings, students may not be able to collaborate for a number of reasons, including insufficient knowledge in the content area, lack of access to appropriate resources, lack of knowledge on how to use resources, skill and social deficits, language and cultural differences, and problems with course materials (Costaguta, García, & Amandi, 2011; Onrubia & Engel, 2012; Varvel, 2007). One solution is to use ITSs to teach collaboration skills (Gilbert et al., 2018; Sottilare, Graesser, Hu, & Sinatra, 2018). Because communication with other people is an affordance of learning technologies (see Table 28.1), ITSs can not only assess task skills (how learners interact with the system), but also team skills (how learners interact with team members). ITSs are uniquely capable of providing a wide range of critical feedback (both immediate and delayed) to both the individual and the team (Gilbert et al., 2018).

One important research question for hybrid ITSs going forward is what representation is optimal to recommend at a given moment. For example, is it best to recommend resources that a trainee performs well on, where they are destined to receive gratifying positive feedback? Or is it best to expand their horizons, push the envelope, and promote cognitive flexibility? Initially, one strategy would be to simply recommend the resource the learner prefers to increase learner adoption: a sub-optimal representation is better than none at all. Eventually, however, the system would increasingly recommend alternative representations to promote cognitive flexibility. Another open research question is the relative contribution of each individual representation within an ITS. This can be answered with ablation studies which systematically remove one representation at a time to measure its efficacy. Thus, we can identify which representations are helpful, which are redundant (or cause overload), and which are synergistic.

As we have discussed, design choices such as the content of representations, sequence of representations, and types of representations heavily influence learning outcomes. Learners often have difficulty making sense of representations without additional integration and connection-making support to aid in development of the representational fluency necessary to benefit from multiple representations (Rau, Aleven & Rummel, 2012).

When presented with multiple representations, learners are tasked with identifying relevant information and determining how it relates within each individual representation (intra-representational coherence) and then how the representations relate to each other (inter-representational coherence) to formulate a coherent knowledge structure (Seufert, 2003). Rigidly designed learning environments with reductive representations risk oversimplifying the knowledge domain and can lead to an inability to transfer knowledge outside of the exact constraints presented in the learning environment. Thus, employing different conceptual representations should increase cognitive flexibility and lead to improved outcomes on transfer tasks within the environment and outside of the environment when the skills learned must be applied to real-time problem solving (Spiro, 1988; Spiro et al., 2017).

As user interfaces in consumer technology advance, educational technology must strive to keep up. Users are accustomed to more and more interactive environments in phones, games, TVs, and so on, which has raised the threshold for sustaining the user's attention. Hence, multiple representations continue to play a central role in educational technology, as evidenced by the number of ITSs which already include them. Integrating these ITSs into a hybrid tutor, then, gives learners unparalleled autonomy to learn via a diverse combination of representations.

REFERENCES

Ainsworth, S. (1999). The functions of multiple representations. *Computers and Education*, 33(2-3), 131–152.

Ainsworth, S. (2006). DeFT: A conceptual framework for considering learning with multiple representations. *Learning and Instruction*, 16(3), 183–198.

Ainsworth, S. (2018). Multiple representations and multimedia learning. In F. Fischer, C. E. Hmelo-Silver, S. R. Goldman, & P. Reimann (Eds.), *International handbook of the learning sciences* (pp. 96–105). New York: Routledge.

Aleven, V. A., & Koedinger, K. R. (2002). An effective metacognitive strategy: Learning by doing and explaining with a computer-based cognitive tutor. *Cognitive Science*, 26(2), 147–179. [Cognitive Tutor].

Aleven, V., McLaren, B. M., Sewall, J., Van Velsen, M., Popescu, O., Demi, S., & Koedinger, K. R. (2016). Example-Tracing tutors: Intelligent tutor development for non-programmers. *International Journal of Artificial Intelligence in Education*, 26(1), 224–269. [Fractions Tutor].

Arroyo, I., Beal, C., Murray, T., Walles, R., & Woolf, B. (2004). Wayang outpost: Intelligent tutoring for high stakes achievement tests. In James C. Lester, Rosa Maria Vicari, & Fábio Paraguaçu (Eds.), *Proceedings of the 7th international conference on intelligent tutoring systems* (pp. 468–477). Berlin/Heidelberg: Springer. [Wayang Outpost].

Biswas, G., Jeong, H., Kinnebrew, J., Sulcer, B., & Roscoe, R. (2010). Measuring self-regulated learning skills through social interactions in a teachable agent environment. *Research and Practice in Technology-Enhanced Learning*, 5, 123–152. [Betty's Brain].

Brusilovsky, P., Schwarz, E., & Weber, G. (1996). ELM-ART: An intelligent tutoring system on World Wide Web. In *International conference on intelligent tutoring systems* (pp. 261–269). Berlin, Heidelberg: Springer. [ELM-ART].

Canfield, W. (2001). ALEKS: A web-based intelligent tutoring system. *Mathematics and Computer Education*, 35(2), 152–158. [ALEKS].

Chi, M. T., & Wylie, R. (2014). The ICAP framework: Linking cognitive engagement to active learning outcomes. *Educational Psychologist*, 49(4), 219–243.

Cohen, P. A., Kulik, J. A., & Kulik, C. C. (1982). Educational outcomes of tutoring: A meta-analysis of findings. *American Educational Research Journal*, 19, 237–248.

Cook, M. P. (2006). Visual representations in science education: The influence of prior knowledge and cognitive load theory on instructional design principles. *Science Education*, 90(6), 1073–1091.

Costaguta, R., Garcia, P., & Amandi, A. (2011). Using agents for training students collaborative skills. *IEEE Latin America Transactions*, 9(7), 1118–1124.

Craig, S. D., Graesser, A. C., & Perez, R. S. (2018). Advances from Office of Naval Research STEM grand challenge: Expanding the boundaries of intelligent tutoring systems. *International Journal of STEM Education*, 5(15), 1–4.

D'Mello, S., & Graesser, A. C. (2010). Multimodal semi-automated affect detection from conversational cues, gross body language, and facial features. *User Modeling and User-Adapted Interaction*, 20, 147–187.

D'Mello, S., Lehman, B., Pekrun, R., & Graesser, A. C. (2014). Confusion can be beneficial for learning. *Learning and Instruction*, 29(3), 153–170.

Davidovic, A., Warren, J., & Trichina, E. (2003). Learning benefits of structural example-based adaptive tutoring systems. *IEEE Transactions on Education*, 46(2), 241–251. [SEATS].

DeVault, D., Artstein, R., Benn, G., Dey, T., Fast, E., Gainer, A., & Lucas, G. (2014). SimSensei Kiosk: A virtual human interviewer for healthcare decision support. In A. Lomuscio, P. Scerri, A. Bazzan, & M. Huhns (Eds.), *Proceedings of the 2014 international conference on Autonomous agents and multi-agent systems* (pp. 1061–1068). Paris: International Foundation for Autonomous Agents and Multiagent Systems. [Ellie].

Dodds, P. V. W., & Fletcher, J. D. (2004). Opportunities for new "smart" learning environments enabled by next generation web capabilities. *Journal of Education Multimedia and Hypermedia*, 13, 391–404.

Dolenc, K., & Aberšek, B. (2015). TECH8 intelligent and adaptive e-learning system: Integration into technology and science classrooms in lower secondary schools. *Computers and Education, 82,* 354–365. [TECH8].

Dynarsky, M., Agodina, R., Heaviside, S., Novak, T., Carey, N., Campuzano, L., & Sussex, W. (2007). *Effectiveness of reading and mathematics software products: Findings from the first student cohort.* Washington, DC: US Department of Education, Institute of Education Sciences.

Dzikovska, M., Steinhauser, N., Farrow, E., Moore, J., & Campbell, G. (2014). BEETLE II: Deep natural language understanding and automatic feedback generation for intelligent tutoring in basic electricity and electronics. *International Journal of Artificial Intelligence in Education, 24,* 284–332. [BEETLE-II].

Fiore, S. M., Graesser, A. C., & Greiff, S. (2018). Collaborative problem-solving education for the twenty-first-century workforce. *Nature Human Behaviour, 2*(6), 367–369.

Fletcher, J. D. (2011). *DARPA education dominance program: April 2010 and November 2010 digital tutor assessments* (No. IDA-NS-D-4260). Alexandria, VA: Institute for Defense Analyses. [Digital Tutors].

Gilbert, S. B., Slavina, A., Dorneich, M. C., Sinatra, A. M., Bonner, D., Johnston, J., ... Winer, E. (2018). Creating a team tutor using GIFT. *International Journal of Artificial Intelligence in Education, 28*(2), 286–313.

Graesser, A. C. (2016). Conversations with AutoTutor help students learn. *International Journal of Artificial Intelligence in Education, 26,* 124–132.

Graesser, A. C., Cai, Z., Morgan, B., & Wang, L. (2017). Assessment with computer agents that engage in conversational dialogues and trialogues with learners. *Computers in Human Behavior, 76,* 607–616.

Graesser, A. C., Chipman, P., Haynes, B. C., & Olney, A. (2005). AutoTutor: An intelligent tutoring system with mixed-initiative dialogue. *IEEE Transactions on Education, 48*(4), 612–618. [AutoTutor].

Graesser, A. C., Fiore, S. M., Greiff, S., Andrews-Todd, J., Foltz, P. W., & Hesse, F. W. (2018). Advancing the science of collaborative problem solving. *Psychological Science in the Public Interest, 19,* 59–92.

Graesser, A. C., Hu, X., Nye, B. D., VanLehn, K., Kumar, R., Heffernan, C., & Baer, W. (2018). ElectronixTutor: An intelligent tutoring system with multiple learning resources for electronics. *International Journal of STEM Education, 5*(15), 1–21.

Graesser, A. C., Hu, X., & Sottilare, R. (2018). Intelligent tutoring systems. In F. Fischer, C. E. Hmelo-Silver, S. R. Goldman, & P. Reimann (Eds.), *International handbook of the learning sciences* (pp. 246–255). New York: Routledge.

Graesser, A. C., & Person, N. K. (1994). Question asking during tutoring. *American Educational Research Journal, 31,* 104–137.

Graesser, A. C., Rus, V., & Hu, X. (2017). Instruction based on tutoring. In R. E. Mayer & P. A. Alexander (Eds.), *Handbook of research on learning and instruction* (pp. 460–482). New York: Routledge Press.

Heffernan, N., & Heffernan, C. (2014). The ASSISTments ecosystem: Building a platform that brings scientists and teachers together for minimally invasive research on human learning and teaching. *International Journal of Artificial Intelligence in Education, 24,* 470–497.

Johnson-Laird, P. N. (2010). Mental models and human reasoning. *Proceedings of the National Academy of Sciences, 107*(43), 18243–18250.

Jordan, P., Makatchev, M., & VanLehn, K. (2003). Abductive theorem proving for analyzing student explanations. In U. Hoppe, F. Verdejo, & J. Kay (Eds.), *Proceedings of artificial intelligence in education* (pp. 47–54). Amsterdam: IOS Press. [Why2-Atlas].

Keleş, A., Ocak, R., Keleş, A., & Gülcü, A. (2009). ZOSMAT: Web-based intelligent tutoring system for teaching–Learning process. *Expert Systems with Applications, 36*(2), 1229–1239. [ZOSMAT].

Koedinger, K. R., Corbett, A. C., & Perfetti, C. (2012). The Knowledge-Learning-Instruction (KLI) framework: Bridging the science-practice chasm to enhance robust student learning. *Cognitive Science, 36*(5), 757–798.

Kulik, J. A., & Fletcher, J. D. (2015). Effectiveness of intelligent tutoring systems: A meta-analytic review. *Review of Educational Research, 85,* 171–204.

Kumar, R., Chung, G. K., Madni, A., & Roberts, B. (2015). First evaluation of the physics instantiation of a problem-solving-based online learning platform. In C. Conati, N. Heffernan, A. Mitrovic, & M. F. Verdejo (Eds.), *Proceedings of the 17th international conference on artificial intelligence in education* (pp. 570–573). Cham: Springer. [LearnForm].

Lane, H. C., Noren, D., Auerbach, D., Birch, M., & Swartout, W. (2011). Intelligent tutoring goes to the museum in the big city: A pedagogical agent for informal science education. In G. Biswas, S. Bull, J. Kay, & A. Mitrovic (Eds.), *International journal of artificial intelligence in education,* (pp. 155–162). Heidelberg: Springer. [Coach Mike].

Lehman, B., D'Mello, S. K., Strain, A., Mills, C., Gross, M., Dobbins, A., ... Graesser, A. C. (2013). Inducing and tracking confusion with contradictions during complex learning. *International Journal of Artificial Intelligence, special issue: Best of AIED 2011, 22*(2), 71–93.

Lesgold, A., Lajoie, S. P., Bunzo, M., & Eggan, G. (1992). SHERLOCK: A coached practice environment for an electronics trouble-shooting job. In J. H. Larkin & R. W. Chabay (Eds.), *Computer assisted instruction and intelligent tutoring systems: Shared goals and complementary approaches* (pp. 201–238). Hillsdale, NJ: Erlbaum. [Sherlock].

Ma, W. A., Nesbit, J. C., O. O., & Liu, Q. (2014). Intelligent tutoring systems and learning outcomes: A meta-analytic survey. *Journal of Educational Psychology, 106*, 901–918.

Mayer, R. E., Heiser, J., & Lonn, S. (2001). Cognitive constraints on multimedia learning: When presenting more material results in less understanding. *Journal of Educational Psychology, 93*(1), 187–198.

Mayer, R. E., & Moreno, R. (2003). Nine ways to reduce cognitive load in multimedia learning. *Educational Psychologist, 38*(1), 43–52.

McNamara, D. S., Levinstein, I. B., & Boonthum, C. (2004). iSTART: Interactive strategy trainer for active reading and thinking. *Behavioral Research Methods, Instruments, and Computers, 36*, 222–233. [iStart].

Millis, K., Forsyth, C., Butler, H., Wallace, P., Graesser, A. C., & Halpern, D. (2011). Operation ARIES! A serious game for teaching scientific inquiry. In M. Ma, A. Oikonomou, & J. Lakhmi (Eds.), *Serious games and edutainment applications* (pp. 169–196). London: Springer-Verlag. [OPERATION ARIES!/ARA].

Mitrovic, A., & Martin, B. (2000). Evaluating the effectiveness of feedback in SQL-Tutor. In Kinshuk, C. Jesshope, & T. Okamoto (Eds.), *Proceedings international workshop on advanced learning technologies. IWALT 2000. Advanced learning technology: Design and development issues* (pp. 143–144). Palmerston North, New Zealand: IEEE. [SQL-Tutor].

Mitrovic, A., Martin, B., & Suraweera, P. (2007). Intelligent tutors for all: The constraint-based approach. *IEEE Intelligent Systems, 22*, 38–45. [KERMIT].

National Academies of Sciences, Engineering, and Medicine. (2018). *How people learn II: Learners, contexts, and cultures.* Washington, DC: National Academies Press.

National Research Council. (2012b). *Improving measurement of productivity in higher education.* Washington, DC: National Academies Press.

Nye, B. D., Graesser, A. C., & Hu, X. (2014). AutoTutor and family: A review of 17 years of natural language tutoring. *International Journal of Artificial Intelligence in Education, 24*(4), 427–469.

OECD (2017). *PISA 2015 Results (vol. 5): Collaborative Problem Solving.* Paris: OECD.

Onrubia, J., & Engel, A. (2012). The role of teacher assistance on the effects of a macro-script in collaborative writing tasks. *International Journal of Computer-Supported Collaborative Learning, 7*(1), 161–186.

Rau, M., Aleven, V., Rummel, N., & Rohrbach, S. (2012). Sense making alone doesn't do it: Fluency matters too! ITS support for robust learning with multiple representations. In S. Cerri, W. Clancey, G. Papadourakis, & K. Panourgia (Eds.), *Intelligent Tutoring Systems* (vol. 7315, pp. 174–184). Berlin/Heidelberg: Springer.

Rau, M. A., Aleven, V., Rummel, N., & Pardos, Z. (2014). How should intelligent tutoring systems sequence multiple graphical representations of fractions? A multi-methods study. *International Journal of Artificial Intelligence in Education, 24*(2), 125–161.

Rowe, J. P., Shores, L. R., Mott, B. W., & Lester, J. C. (2011). Integrating learning, problem solving, and engagement in narrative-centered learning environments. *International Journal of Artificial Intelligence in Education, 21* (1/2), 115–133. [Crystal Island].

Rus, V., D'Mello, S. K., Hu, X., & Graesser, A. C. (2013). Recent advances in intelligent systems with conversational dialogue. *AI Magazine, 34*, 42–54. [DeepTutor].

Seufert, T. (2003). Supporting coherence formation in learning from multiple representations. *Learning and Instruction, 13*(2), 227–237.

Shute, V. J. (2011). Stealth assessment in computer-based games to support learning. *Computer Games and Instruction, 55*(2), 503–524.

Sottilare, R., Graesser, A., Hu, X., & Holden, H. (Eds.) (2013). *Design Recommendations for Intelligent Tutoring Systems: Learner Modeling* (vol. 1). Orlando, FL: Army Research Laboratory.

Sottilare, R., Graesser, A. C., Hu, X., & Sinatra, A. (Eds.) (2018). *Design Recommendations for Intelligent Tutoring Systems: Team Tutoring* (vol. 6). Orlando, FL: US Army Research Laboratory.

Spiro, R. J.,Coulson, R. L.,Feltovich, P. J., &Anderson, D. K. (1988). Cognitive flexibility theory: Advanced knowledge acquisition in ill-structured domains. In V. Patel (Ed.), *Tenth annual conference of the cognitive science society* (pp. 375–383). Hillsdale, NJ: Erlbaum.

Spiro, R. J., Klautke, H. A., Cheng, C., & Gaunt, A. (2017). Cognitive flexibility theory and the assessment of 21st-century skills. In C. Secolsky & D. B. Denison (Eds.), *Handbook on measurement, assessment, and evaluation in higher education* (pp. 631–637). New York: Routledge.

Steenbergen-Hu, S., & Cooper, H. (2013). A meta-analysis of the effectiveness of intelligent tutoring systems on college students' academic learning. *Journal of Educational Psychology, 106*, 331–347.

Steenbergen-Hu, S., & Cooper, H. (2014). A meta-analysis of the effectiveness of intelligent tutoring systems on K-12 students' mathematical learning. *Journal of Educational Psychology, 105*, 971–987.

Suebnukarn, S., & Haddawy, P. (2007). COMET: A collaborative tutoring system for medical problem-based learning. *IEEE Intelligent Systems, 22*(4), 70–77. [COMET].

Sweller, J. (1988). Cognitive load during problem solving: Effects on learning. *Cognitive Science, 12*(2), 257–285.

Traum, D., Swartout, W., Gratch, J., & Marsella, S. (2008). A virtual human dialogue model for non-team interaction. In L. Dybkjær and W. Minker (Eds.), *Recent trends in discourse and dialogue* (pp. 45–67). Dordrecht: Springer . [SASO-ST].

US Navy. (1998). *Navy electricity and electronics training series* (vols. 1–24). Pensacola, FL: Naval Education and Training Professional Development and Technology Center.

VanLehn, K. (1996). Conceptual and meta learning during coached problem solving. In *International Conference on Intelligent Tutoring Systems* (pp. 29–47). Berlin, Heidelberg: Springer. [Andes].

VanLehn, K. (2006). The behavior of tutoring systems. *International Journal of Artificial Intelligence in Education, 16*, 227–265.

VanLehn, K. (2011). The relative effectiveness of human tutoring, intelligent tutoring systems and other tutoring systems. *Educational Psychologist, 46*, 197–221.

VanLehn, K., Wetzel, J., Grover, S., & Van De, S. B. (2017). Learning how to construct models of dynamic systems: An initial evaluation of the dragoon intelligent tutoring system. *IEEE Transactions on Learning Technologies, 10*(2), 154–167. [Dragoon].

Varvel, V. E. (2007). Master online teacher competencies. *Online Journal of Distance Learning Administration, 10*(1), 1–41.

Wetzel, J., VanLehn, K., Chaudhari, P., Desai, A., Feng, J., Grover, S., & van de Sande, B. (2016). The design and development of the Dragoon intelligent tutoring system for model construction: Lessons learned. *Interactive Learning Environments*. doi:10.1080/10494820.2015.1131167.

Woolf, B. P. (2009). *Building intelligent interactive tutors*. Burlington, VT: Morgan Kaufmann Publishers.

Zachary, W., Cannon-Bowers, J., Burns, J., Bilazarian, P., & Krecker, D. (1998). An advanced embedded training system (AETS) for tactical team training. In B. P. Goettl, H. M. Halff, C. L. Redfield,& V. J. Shute (Eds.), *International conference on intelligent tutoring systems* (pp. 544–553). Berlin, Heidelberg: Springer. [AETS].

29

REPRESENTATIONAL AFFORDANCES FOR COLLABORATIVE LEARNING IN TECHNOLOGY-ENHANCED ENVIRONMENTS

Bodong Chen

UNIVERSITY OF MINNESOTA

Feng Lin

SINGAPORE UNIVERSITY OF SOCIAL SCIENCES

ABSTRACT

Human learning is increasingly multi-representational. Despite substantial efforts to design multiple external representations for individual learning, little has been systematically synthesized about how external representations can be mobilized to help multiple learners learn together. In this chapter we first outline five key challenges facing collaborative learning including: (a) Establishing and maintaining a joint problem space, (b) Communicating with one another, (c) Creating a shared knowledge base, (d) Supporting epistemic practices; and (e) Coordinating, monitoring, and regulating collaborative processes. We then illustrate the ways in which multiple representations are provided to mitigate these challenges and to harness multiple perspectives of learners to surpass their individual understanding.

Keywords: external representations, computer tools, collaborative learning, computer-mediated communication

INTRODUCTION

Humans are predisposed by biology to live in the barbarism of the deep past. Only by an effort of will and through use of our invented representations can we bring ourselves into the present and peek into the future. Our educational systems must find ways to help children meet that challenge.

(Kay, 1991, p. 140)

Representation[1] is the use of signs and symbols to depict something else. Throughout human history, to portray our understanding of the world we have invented representations of all kinds, which in turn dictate how we come to understand reality and how we communicate with each other. Human languages – both spoken and written – are invented representations of human thoughts that have transformed how we think and communicate. Modern mathematical notation, which comprises representations symbolizing mathematical objects and ideas, has transformed the way we think and communicate mathematically. More recently, through multimedia stimuli, immersive virtual reality can engender senses of perception, presence, interaction, and compassion that are detached from the physical world. At a fundamental level, our invented representations dictate what we behold as human beings. Through inventing new representations – as well as new media to convey these representations – we expand what is collectively thinkable for humanity and hereby reinvent who we are.

It is therefore understandable that human learning is increasingly multi-representational (Ainsworth, 2018; see also Chapter 7 of this volume). Drawing perspectives from cognition, situated cognition, socio-cultural learning, and technology design, learning scientists are interested in investigating and designing multiple representations for learning in various contexts. In mathematics, a function can be represented in multiple ways – as a formula, a table, a graph, words – to facilitate mathematical reasoning. New digital technologies enable novel representations such as dynamic mathematical representations that facilitate student understanding of mathematical ideas and procedures (Moreno-Armella, Hegedus, & Kaput, 2008). In science, multiple representations can facilitate various scientific processes such as asking questions, constructing explanations, and conducting investigations (Wu & Puntambekar, 2012). In these cases, learners are presented with carefully crafted multiple representations to learn domain-specific content and/or important skills. In the meantime, given the appreciated benefits of multiple representations, besides using representations, learners are increasingly charged with creating, modifying, combining, and evaluating representations by themselves (Roque, Rusk, & Resnick, 2016). What has become crucial for contemporary learning is to develop metarepresentational competence that goes beyond learning basic representations to encompass higher levels of representational competence including critiquing, comparing, and explaining representations in use, as well as inventing and designing new representations (diSessa, 2004).

Despite these efforts to use multiple representations to facilitate individual learning (e.g., Ainsworth, 2008; Ainsworth, 2018), little has been synthesized about how representations can be mobilized to help multiple learners learn collaboratively together, a scenario that has its unique prospects and challenges. While collaborative learning exposes learners to multiple perspectives, it also necessitates mutual awareness (being aware of peers and their ideas), intersubjectivity (having a shared set of meanings), and effective coordination of group interactions (Suthers, 2003). Computer-Supported Collaborative Learning (CSCL) as a research field is particularly interested in mitigating these challenges through technology tools and multimedia artifacts. However, representational support for collaborative learning is seldom explicitly addressed in multiple representations or CSCL literature. In general, supporting collaborative learning remains an after-thought in studies of multiple representations, while CSCL research rarely discusses technological affordances of multiple representations for facilitating multiple perspectives. To bridge this gap, in this chapter we discuss key challenges facing CSCL and the affordances provided by multiple representations for addressing these challenges.

COLLABORATIVE LEARNING AND ITS CHALLENGES

Collaboration is heralded as an essential competency in modern societies and professions, leading to its widespread presence in educational standards and policy documents (e.g., Binkley et al., 2012; National Research Council, 2012). To learn collaboratively, multiple learners need to work together toward a shared learning goal. During the process, they may need to externalize their own perspectives, consider and integrate multiple perspectives, and come up with newer, bigger ideas to address problems of understanding. Supporting such learning experiences that are truly collaborative is challenging, with the success depending on multiple factors working synergistically.

While collaboration as a term is often used loosely in public discourse, many researchers have specific ideas about what can be considered collaboration. For decades, research fields such as Computer-Supported Collaborative Learning (CSCL) and Computer Supported Cooperative Work (CSCW) have been invested in supporting collaboration. As an interdisciplinary field, CSCL is concerned with "the practices of meaning making in the context of joint activity, and the ways in which these practices are mediated through designed artifacts" (Koschmann, 2002, p. 18). In research on collaborative problem-solving, collaboration is defined as "a coordinated, synchronous activity that is the result of a continued attempt to construct and maintain a shared conception of a problem" (Roschelle & Teasley, 1995, p. 70). In this case, to attain and maintain a joint problem place within a student group is a hallmark of collaboration. Such an emphasis on joint problems and shared goals is used to distinguish collaborative learning from cooperative learning (Johnson & Johnson, 2009). In cooperative learning, students "split the work, solve sub-tasks individually and then assemble the partial results into the final output" (Dillenbourg, 1999, p. 8), whereas collaborative groups engage in crucial processes of negotiation, shared meaning making, goal coordination, and knowledge co-construction (Jeong & Hmelo-Silver, 2016). Because meanings are created intersubjectively among learners within a shared context and are no longer attributable to individual learners, collaborative learning is fundamentally a group phenomenon that cannot be explained by the sum of individual learners (Stahl, 2006). In other words, meaning making in collaborative learning is an interactional achievement shared by learners rather than a solely internal process within individual minds (Stahl, Koschmann, & Suthers, 2014).

To support learning that is truly collaborative is not an easy task. Support for collaborative learning needs to go far beyond idea sharing to facilitate intersubjective meaning making among learners. Based on a thematic analysis of the literature, we identify the following challenges of collaborative learning that researchers attempt to address.

1. Establishing and maintaining a joint problem space. Collaboration necessitates a shared goal toward which learners work together. Establishing a shared goal requires learners to create a joint problem space through externally mediated negotiation and discussion (Roschelle & Teasley, 1995; Stahl, 2006). Having

a joint problem space highlights the importance of tagging into multiple perspectives of learners. This process of establishing such a space varies across pedagogical frameworks. For example, the Knowledge Building pedagogy involves learners to bring in authentic problems from everyday experiences into their class community, setting the stage for them to produce and continually improve ideas as a collective (Scardamalia & Bereiter, 2014). In other pedagogical scenarios, the problem space can be introduced by externally designed simulations (Hmelo-Silver, Jordan, Eberbach, & Sinha, 2016; Moher, 2006), and students are supported to introduce problems and articulate a joint problem they would pursue collaboratively. Without a shared perception of the joint problem space, group work becomes muddled and collaboration nonexistent.
2. Communicating with one another. Regardless of the context, to collaborate learners need to communicate with each other. Among themselves, learners ask questions, put forward ideas, identify gaps, and coordinate efforts. Some CSCL settings are face-to-face. The physical proximity in the face-to-face situation usually allows learners to communicate with fewer barriers. But face-to-face collaboration has its unique challenges. For example, one multi-touch table can only accommodate a handful of learners working together; they may communicate with each other effortlessly in the moment, thanks to the table's mediation, but they would face significant challenges if their collaboration needs to extend across multiple weeks and if they need to keep track of their dialogues during these weeks. In CSCL settings that are virtual, peer communication is completely mediated by digital media designed to facilitate particular expressive actions. In this situation, technological supports are intended to overcome the physical distance and the lack of social cues. Regardless of settings, supporting communication among learners is key for the negotiation of goals and exchange of perspectives in collaborative learning processes.
3. Creating a shared knowledge base. In CSCL activities, communication is turned into substance (Dillenbourg, 2005), producing artifacts representing knowledge and knowledge structures that would further facilitate collaborative progress. A significant challenge in various stages of collaborative learning is to build a shared knowledge base to maintain resources and ideas contributed by learners. A shared knowledge space allows multiple perspectives and ideas to be externalized, transformed, and integrated through collaborative activities (Suthers, 2005). The Knowledge Community and Inquiry model, for instance, emphasizes the development of a knowledge base accessible for revision and improvement by all members (Slotta, 2013). Facilitating the creation of and access to such a knowledge base is thus pivotal to collaborative learning.
4. Supporting intersubjective meaning making and related epistemic practices. Simply talking with each other or sharing a knowledge base is not enough for collaboration. Multiple learners bring with them diverse epistemologies, perspectives, dispositions, and roles (Järvelä & Hadwin, 2013; Scardamalia & Bereiter, 1991). Solving problems collaboratively requires intersubjective meaning making – the practice of "people in groups making sense of situations and of each other" (Suthers, 2006, p. 321). It requires more than willingness to agree, but to create shared signs, notations, and deictic references for the co-construction of

shared meanings. To achieve intersubjective meaning making, learners need to cope with possible social and epistemological contradictions they have, negotiate meanings, and create joint interpretations. The diverse perspectives and ideas in collaborative learning can cause divergence and incoherence in peer interaction (Suthers, Vatrapu, Medina, Joseph, & Dwyer, 2007). To avoid this hurdle, learners need to be able to take up each others' ideas and collectively address the central problems (Lin & Chan, 2018). These processes demand coordinated epistemic practices – practices such as asking questions, arguing from evidence, integrating different ideas, and building on one another's ideas that are essential for knowledge construction. Technological affordances are often called upon to help address these social and epistemic challenges facing collaboration, and to support knowledge processes and epistemic practices crucial for intersubjective meaning making (Suthers, 2006).

5. Coordinating, monitoring, and regulating collaborative processes. Collaborative processes could easily get complex. Collaboration can be distributed socially, spatially, and temporally, with interdependence designed between any combination of learners, processes, activities, and tools to nurture intersubjective meaning making. In order for collaborative learning processes to be productive, the planning, coordination, monitoring, and regulation of collaborative processes are necessary. For example, the Jigsaw Classroom technique assigns learners into jigsaw groups, sends each group member to one "expert group" to learn a specific topic, and invites them to bring learned information back to their jigsaw groups to develop a fuller understanding (Aronson & Patnoe, 1997). In knowledge building classrooms, learner collaboration is less "scripted" compared to the Jigsaw classroom but would still benefit from high-level coordination, reflection, and "meta-dialogues" (Resendes, Scardamalia, Bereiter, Chen, & Halewood, 2015; Zhang et al., 2018). These examples demonstrate distinct strategies for distributing coordination and monitoring responsibilities among teachers, learners, and technological agents. With technological and pedagogical support, learners are increasingly called upon to take high-level responsibilities to regulate their individual and group learning (Järvelä et al., 2015).

Supporting each of these five aspects of collaborative learning can be challenging, motivating CSCL researchers to devise technological systems to provide key affordances for collaborative learning (Jeong & Hmelo-Silver, 2016). Within these CSCL systems, artifacts such as digital texts and graphs play important roles in mediating collaborative learning processes. They help "structure the representations that groups of students use in building their intersubjective knowledge, making it visible, shared and persistent" (Stahl, Ludvigsen, Law, & Cress, 2014, p. 237). Artifacts designed for or created from collaborative learning are often multi-representational and exist in the forms of texts, graphs, tables, drawings, codes, animations, and so on. While prior research has explicated supports for collaborative learning from a technological standpoint, little work has been done to discuss representational affordances for collaborative learning. To guide future work in this area, it would be fruitful to delineate affordances provided by multiple representations for key challenges facing collaborative learning, many of which are about engaging learners with multiple perspectives.

REPRESENTATIONAL AFFORDANCES FOR COLLABORATIVE LEARNING

In CSCL environments, multiple representations are incorporated to support the expression and development of multiple perspectives of learners. While prior work has explicated functions of multiple representations for individual learning (Ainsworth, 1999, 2008; Wu & Puntambekar, 2012), little work has been done to explicitly address roles played by representations in collaborative learning. For example, while digital technologies are enabling dynamic and linked (vs. static and siloed) representations of mathematical ideas and actions, harnessing multiple representations for socially rich mathematical learning remains peripheral in the literature (Moreno-Armella et al., 2008). While individual and collaborative learning with multiple representations share general traits, we need to recognize that multiple representations also provide unique affordances for collaborative learning. An early attempt to systemize knowledge in this area lists three roles played by multiple representations for collaborative activities, including (a) initiating negotiations of meaning (when within-group agreement is deemed necessary), (b) serving as a representational proxy for purposes of contextual references, and (c) providing a foundation for implicitly shared group awareness (Suthers, 2003). More work is needed to advance our understanding about using multiple representations to support collaborative learning.

Based on a thematic analysis of CSCL systems, we discuss affordances of multiple representations for addressing the five major challenges of collaborative learning identified in the previous section. We cover exemplar CSCL systems in this section, such as Knowledge Forum (Scardamalia & Bereiter, 2003), Virtual Math Teams (Stahl, 2006), Code Breaker (White & Pea, 2011), Scratch (Resnick et al., 2009), Belvedere (Suthers, 2006), and Orchestration Graphs (Dillenbourg, 2015), but this coverage is intended to be illustrative rather than comprehensive. We also would like to note in advance that representational affordances discussed below do not operate in silos; instead, effective collaboration depends on multiple affordances working synergistically together.

Using Multiple Representations to Define and Maintain a Joint Problem Space

Multiple representations are broadly used to represent domain-specific problems. In collaborative learning, representations are used to create a joint space for problem exploration and definition. In mathematical reasoning, the Code Breaker software incorporates four dynamically linked representations – an algebraic equation, a graph, a function table, and an inverse function table – as well as three other representations to present a problem space where student groups work together to observe patterns and decipher the underlying mathematical function governing these representations (White & Pea, 2011). With Code Breaker, students are asked to act as cryptanalysts to collaboratively break or decipher codes created by the teacher or other student groups. Each problem is displayed by multiple representation tools shown on students' handheld devices; each student has direct access to a single device that displays only one or two representations designed to elicit perspectives of the problem from distinct angles. To decipher a code, a collaborative group needs to align different representations to make inferences about function parameters. These representations – dynamically linked to a same problem and socially distributed among students – help each group establish and maintain a joint problem space (White & Pea, 2011).

In argumentation, diagrams are used to represent the argumentative space to facilitate knowledge construction among students (van Amelsvoort, Andriessen, & Kanselaar, 2007). Knowledge mapping tools such as Cohere represent a knowledge space for an organization to engage in "contested discourse" detailing multiple claims, contrasting ideas, and discourse moves that advance the knowledge space (De Liddo, Sándor, & Buckingham Shum, 2012). Cohere is built with distinctive representational tools to support two key activities involving multiple perspectives. First, with Cohere installed as a browser plugin, a user can highlight a media objects in a web document and annotate it with reflective text tagged with a knowledge type (e.g., an idea, a question). Reflective ideas are represented in a browser sidebar right besides the original web document where they were produced. Second, with multiple authors making web annotations, Cohere uses knowledge mapping to help authors draw connections among annotations of different web objects and from different users. In the knowledge map, annotations and contested views are brought together to solve larger, more complex problems facing the group. Multiple representations, especially the knowledge map, represent the group's state-of-the-art understanding and help maintain a joint problem space for group inquiry (De Liddo et al., 2012).

In contrast with argumentation, CSILE/Knowledge Forum, the most widely used CSCL technology, was designed to support collaborative knowledge building. Similar to Cohere, it provides a shared two-dimensional space for learners to bring in authentic problems for discussion. In each note/post, the student can explicitly state a problem this note attempts to tackle. Replies to this note, called "build-ons" in Knowledge Forum, inherit this problem statement to keep the discourse on track (Scardamalia & Bereiter, 2003). Students can also use metacognitive scaffolds such as "I need to understand ..." to identify emerging problems of understanding. Finally, students can also design graphical backgrounds to organize the problem space and ideas (see Figure 29.1). Different graphical arrangements, such as by the time of posting, topics, or contribution types, can be applied to a same set of notes to strategically organize ideas to tackle a problem from different angles. These representations of both individual problems and larger knowledge structures helps the knowledge-building community define and continually refine a shared knowledge space (Chen & Hong, 2016; Scardamalia & Bereiter, 2003). In Figure 29.1, each square icon represents a note, and each arrow represents either a build-on or reference link. The world map is used to convey this workspace's focus on "World Issues," and multiple themes such as "Climate Change," "GDP → Inequity," and "Sexism" are identified to tag clusters of notes. Finally, statistical graphs created by students are also embedded in various areas to contextualize and substantiate their ideas.

As illustrated by these examples, representational affordances of multimedia not only enable the teacher or textbooks to present a problem to be solved by a group of learners; more profoundly, multiple representations enable the dynamic exploration, scoping, articulation, and redefinition of problems when a group of learners continually engage with the problem space.

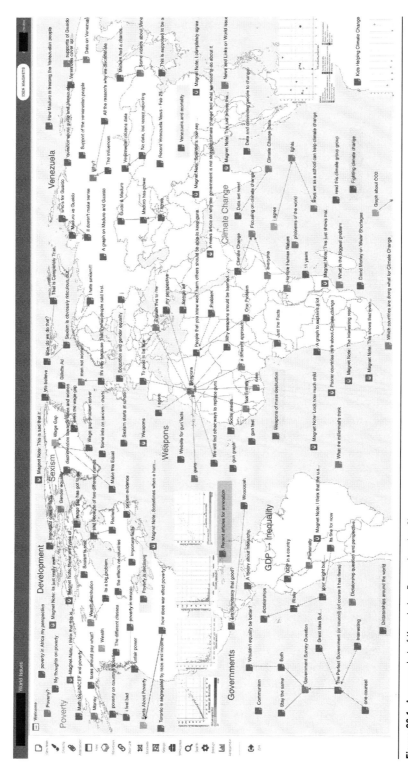

Figure 29.1 A screenshot of Knowledge Forum (version 6).

Using Multiple Representations to Support Peer Communication

In collaborative learning scenarios, communication is intertwined with the exploration of problems and the expression of ideas and is therefore also dependent on multiple representations (see also Morgan et al., Chapter 28 in this volume). While text-centric, asynchronous discussion boards (e.g., Knowledge Forum) are broadly applied to supporting group communication in collaborative learning and work, synchronous chats are also widely used. For example, Virtual Math Teams is a digital environment designed to support mathematical discourse within small groups (Stahl, 2006). Unique to this environment is a graphical referencing tool linking multiple representations of mathematical ideas in a text chat stream and a shared whiteboard drawing area (see Figure 29.2). While the chat stream supports idea exchanges within the group, the whiteboard affords rich modalities of mediated interaction. The added referencing mechanism, i.e., anchoring a chat message in a graphical object, further enriches the group's experience of intersubjectivity in group communication (Stahl, 2006).

Multimedia representations of domain perspectives are available in other CSCL environments. On Knowledge Forum, elementary school students make intensive use of drawings to communicate sophisticated science ideas (Gan, Scardamalia, Hong, & Zhang, 2010). In particular, Grade 3 and 4 students incorporated graphical representations to enhance information presented in textual notes. Analysis of student drawings found them representing sophisticated science concepts, theories, and practices; notes

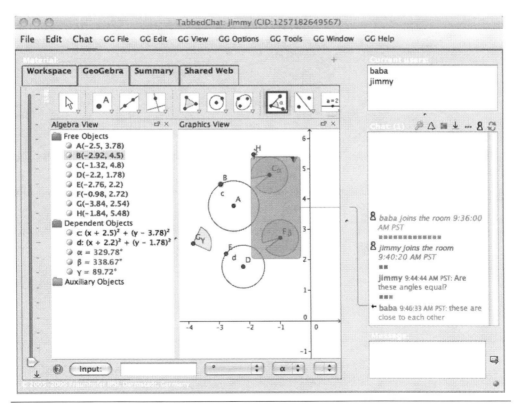

Figure 29.2 The Virtual Math Teams Software (adapted from Weusijana, Ou, Stahl, & Weimar, 2010).

with graphics also tended to be longer, include more new and unique words, and demonstrate more elaborate understanding (Gan et al., 2010). Notably, graphical representations could not only help younger learners communicate their perspectives to peers but are also conducive to richer textual communication in the online forum.

In Scratch, learners use block-based programming codes as an expressive medium for communicating their ideas (Resnick et al., 2009; Roque et al., 2016). As a programming language, Scratch uses lego-like graphical blocks to represent a wide range of programming commands; by stacking and executing these blocks, young people can create sophisticated animations, stories, and games to express their ideas (see Figure 29.3). The Scratch online community provides a space where Scratch users can share projects, browse animations rendered from shared projects, react to and comment on each other's projects, and build on peer projects through modification or remixing (Roque et al., 2016). Like in the other cases, multiple representations on Scratch afford diverse means of communicating with each other in collaborative learning.

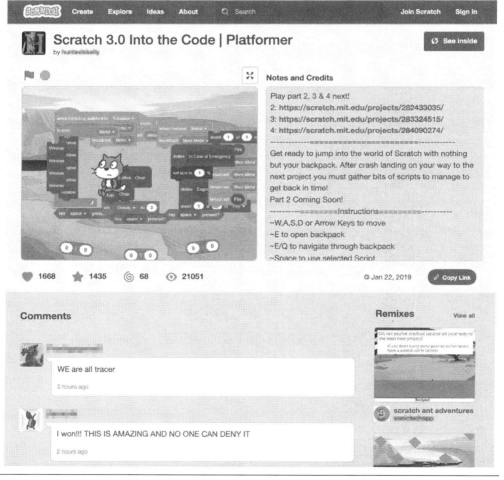

Figure 29.3 A Project Shared on the Scratch Online Community. On this screen, a user can click on the green flag to watch the rendered animation, click on "See inside" to peek into the programming code, and also comment on the shared project.

Using Multiple Representations to Maintain a Shared Knowledge Base

CSCL turns communication to substance. In individual learning, multiple representations are often used to trigger thinking that does not necessarily lead to the creation of new artifacts. In collaborative learning, because collaboration is often necessarily mediated by artifacts, communication among learners can lead to the creation of representations in artifacts, which embody learners' multiple perspectives and form a knowledge base to support future collaboration.

In the Knowledge Community and Inquiry (KCI) model, learners work collaboratively to develop a shared knowledge base by contributing multiple representations of ideas to be reviewed, negotiated, and revised by the community (Slotta, 2013). While early iterations of the KCI model used the wiki technology to sustain the knowledge base, recent work has led to the development of a specialized environment known as Common Knowledge to support collaborative inquiry following the KCI model (Fong & Slotta, 2018). Specifically, Common Knowledge is designed to support and orchestrate multiple inquiry phases including Brainstorm, Propose, and Investigate. At each phase, students are engaged to generate knowledge artifacts such as sticky notes, research proposals, topics, and tags in the communal knowledge space. Under the facilitation of teachers, these artifacts are projected on the interactive white board, reflected upon by the class, and incorporated into newer artifacts (e.g., importing sticky notes into inquiry proposals) to deepen the collective inquiry. The knowledge base is constantly at the forefront of the user interface to nurture a sense of community, facilitate the creation of rich representations of community ideas, and encourage revisions of current representations and ideas (Fong & Slotta, 2018; Slotta, 2013).

Many other CSCL environments discussed so far also mobilize multiple representations to support a shared knowledge base. In a knowledge-building community, notes in Knowledge Forum are considered as conceptual artifacts (Bereiter, 2002) that represent the state-of-the-art of current knowledge and are to be modified, built on, and risen above to achieve deeper understanding (Scardamalia & Bereiter, 2003). In the Scratch online community, shared computer codes, animations, and other rich expressive media form a diverse base of knowledge and perspectives ready to be tinkered with and remixed for the creation of new projects (Resnick et al., 2009). As such knowledge bases grow larger, meta-level representations, such as the semantic tagging system in Common Knowledge, are necessarily created to facilitate knowledge organization and discovery.

Using Multiple Representations to Support Epistemic Practices

Multiple representations are not only used in CSCL to facilitate deep conceptual understanding, but also to support engagement of epistemic practices. As mentioned earlier, we use epistemic practice to refer to the activities involved in the knowledge production process, including constructing explanations, developing models, making sense of data, using evidence to support argument, theory building, and so on (Chinn & Sandoval, 2018).

There are a variety of ways multiple representations could be used to support epistemic practices in CSCL. Multiple representations could be embedded in technology tools to structure students' thinking so that they could focus on the epistemic aspects of scientific inquiry while they work collaboratively. ExplanationConstructor is an example tool designed to structure students' efforts in co-constructing scientific explanations in their small-group inquiry (Sandoval & Reiser, 2004). ExplanationConstructor uses different representations to help students link and distinguish different epistemic entities, namely questions, explanations, and evidence. Its interface connects students' explanations to the questions they attempt to address; this particular representation supports students to link questions and explanations, a key idea of the nature of science. It also makes the representations of explanations distinct from data to support students' theory–fact understanding. These explicit epistemic representations could shape student's collaborative discourse mediated by the tool and help them focus on the epistemic aspect of their inquiry (Sandoval & Reiser, 2004). As students' questions, explanations, and evidence are explicit and open for inspection, students' discussion could not only focus on what they know, but also how they know it. They could discuss how their explanations have addressed their questions and how well their evidence has supported their claims.

Multiple representations are also used to support students' collective knowledge work through visualizing students' thinking. As another example, Belvedere is a graphical environment designed to support young students' collective construction of "evidence maps" (Suthers & Hundhausen, 2003; Suthers, Weiner, Connelly, & Paolucci, 1995). On Belvedere, students' ideas could be visualized as shapes in graphs. Different shapes are used to help students distinguish between different forms of knowledge such as theoretical claims and empirical observations (Sandoval, Bell, Enyedy, & Suthers, 2000). Students could also use links to connect different forms of knowledge to make the structure of their evidential arguments visible. These visual representations make students' group knowledge explicit, turning them into objects of co-construction, manipulation, and evaluation by the community. These representations could also facilitate intersubjective meaning making when students try to integrate their distinct perspectives and contributions to the shared knowledge space. The process of merging students' multiple perspectives involves intensive conversations and is epistemic in nature, triggering students to make sense of the epistemic categories (e.g., theory, hypothesis, claim, data) while working with the tool collaboratively (Suthers, 1998).

Using Multiple Representations to Plan, Monitor, and Regulate Group Activities

Multiple representations are used in technology-enhanced environments to mediate and coordinate micro-level group actions (see also Azevedo & Taub, Chapter 30). In the Virtual Math Teams environment, a mathematical problem is visually presented in the center of the screen to represent the problem facing a small group (see Figure 29.2). By directly manipulating the mathematical representation in the center, learners see live changes made by the group; by seeing and tweaking the representation, learners can test out different ideas and coordinate meaning-making processes (Stahl, 2006). In the Code Breaker software, multiple representations are presented on handheld devices held by each group member when they collaboratively solve mathematical problems. This software provides a unique communication feature that automatically propagates changes made on one handheld device to all the other devices in the same group. Students' face-to-face discussion is coordinated by dynamically synched multiple representations available on the devices in front of them (White & Pea, 2011). Therefore, representational tools not only support mathematical reasoning by facilitating rich links among different types of representations, but also play pivotal roles in coordinating micro-level interaction and learner discourse when they accomplish complex tasks (White & Pea, 2011). The idea of harnessing rich representational media to coordinate collaborative tasks is also represented in other contexts such as collaborative writing on Google Docs and Etherpad (Brodahl, Hadjerrouit, & Kristian Hansen, 2011) and collaborative historical reasoning with multi-touch tables (Higgins, Mercier, Burd, & Joyce-Gibbons, 2012).

Representational supports are also designed to carefully plan and execute group activities. In CSCL, collaborative "scripts" are designed to orchestrate sophisticatedly social interactions among learners, as well as data flows between activities and across levels (Dillenbourg, 2015; Fischer, Kollar, Stegmann, & Wecker, 2013). This idea leads to the development of representational technologies such as the orchestration graph that represents an idealized collaboration scenario. With an orchestration graph, sophisticated social interactions, information flows, and cross-level operations are represented. For example, Figure 29.4 illustrates a relatively simple orchestration graph designed for an online class with a tool named FROG (Fabricating and Running Orchestration Graphs). Each graph on FROG is designed to represent the temporal flow of events from left to right, as well as social configurations of activities on three social planes – individual (bottom), group (middle), and class (top). Within this graph, each rectangle represents a learning activity, whereas a circle with four arrows is called a graph operator that conducts certain orchestrative actions. For instance, the first three operations in Figure 29.4 retrieve student posts made before class, divide students into several small groups, and randomly assign posts to each group. Next, the "Text area" and "Gallery" activities involve each student group to make sense of their assigned posts shown in a gallery view and write a summary note based on their group discussion. Such orchestration graphs are used to plan and orchestrate sophisticated collaborative learning scenarios (Håklev, Faucon, Hadzilacos, & Dillenbourg, 2017).

With the rise of learning analytics (Siemens, 2013), digital traces left by collaborative activities are also harnessed to power representations of collaboration itself in order to monitor and regulate collaboration in real-time. We observe a trend of harnessing digital trace data to build adaptive support for collaborative learning (Wise et al., 2015; Wise & Schwarz, 2017). For example, multiple representations are created in teacher dashboards to enable the teacher to monitor collaboration in multiple small groups (van Leeuwen, 2015). Analytics tools are designed to track various types of discourse moves – e.g., posing a question, proposing an explanation, obtaining information – and to identify promising ideas in knowledge-building communities (Lee & Tan, 2017; Resendes et al., 2015). In social learning analytics, a combination of sociograms and word clouds are used to represent the nature of collaborative discourse (Chen, Chang, Ouyang, & Zhou, 2018). By harnessing various analytical and visualization techniques, these analytics tools attempt to make invisible things visible to aid decision making by learners, groups, and teachers. In the same vein, the Idea Thread Mapper tool enables learners to see emerging knowledge structures in their online discourse and socially regulate their collaborative work (Zhang et al., 2018). In particular, the Idea Thread Mapper enables students to first create "idea threads" representing different lines of inquiry in their knowledge-building discourse. After

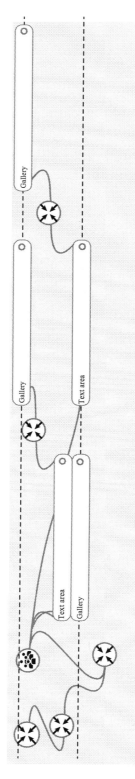

Figure 29.4 An Example Orchestration Graph Implemented in an Online Class.

its creation, each idea thread is rearranged and visualized based on the chronological order of notes; the original connections among notes are also maintained in the display. With this high-level representation, learners are asked to examine learning trajectories and emergent directions in their community. To launch the next phase of knowledge building, they compose "journey-of-thinking super notes" that rise above current ideas in an idea thread (Zhang et al., 2018). As such, rich representations of collaboration data are created to assist teachers and students to monitor and regulate learning. Well-designed representations can reveal learning patterns from different angles, assist teachers monitor multiple groups, and empower learners to take on high-level cognitive responsibility in their learning.

CONCLUSIONS AND FUTURE DIRECTIONS

Collaborative learning relies on a wide range of representational affordances to harness multiple perspectives from learners and other sources. This chapter fills a gap by systematically considering the use of multiple representations in collaborative learning environments. In particular, we discussed the use of multiple representations to address five significant challenges of collaborative learning, including (a) Defining and maintaining a joint problem space, (b) Supporting peer communication, (c) Maintaining a shared knowledge base, (d) Supporting epistemic practices, and (e) Planning, monitoring, and regulating group processes. We then discussed representational affordances provided by CSCL systems to address these five challenges. While we discussed representational affordances corresponding to each challenge, we are not suggesting representational supports for different aspects of collaborative learning can be separated. Rather, we intend to achieve two goals by taking a comprehensive look at representational affordances for collaborative learning. First, we attempt to raise awareness of a myriad of representations devised in computer systems to support collaborative learning. Second, we encourage CSCL researchers and designers to holistically consider multiple challenges of collaborative learning when devising representational tools.

Representations are fundamental to human cognition, expression, and knowledge production. With the fast evolution of digital technologies, we are facing the unprecedeced opportunity to invent new media and representational tools. There are several exciting future directions in the area of multiple representations for collaborative learning.

First, as new media such as virtual reality provide richer modalities for learners to connect and collaborate, we envision future design efforts to integrate multiple representations for more human ways of collaboration – collaboration that embraces a broader range of human sensories, bodily movements, and interaction with each other and with the physical world. For example, Dynamicland is a futuristic physical space wherein various physical objects become computational media and representational tools; instead of locking human attention to screens, Dynamicland's vision is to provide a dynamic medium for anyone to play, craft, and remix through manipulation of physical objects. With the invention of such new media, representational tools for collaborative learning could be more human, with collaborative actions and epistemic practices increasingly embodied and integrated in the physical world.

Second, we will witness significant growth of learners and citizens in their metarepresentational competence – high-level competence in critiquing, comparing, explaining, and inventing representations (diSessa, 2004). Such an increase could result from heightened efforts to promote equitable access to computing and to facilitate new media literacies among youth. For example, researchers are advancing "public computation" as a new genre of learning environments for people to directly interact with dynamic simulations and the underlying code in public spaces such as museums (Sengupta & Shanahan, 2017); the Common Open Data Analysis Platform (CODAP) put dynamically linked representations of data in the hands of young children for them to conduct computationally rich inquiry about world issues. While multiple representations are powerful tools for presenting problems to a group, collaborative learning initiatives can capitalize on the trend of engaging all learners to be creators and critical examiners of representations.

Third, as the human society is becoming increasingly connected, collaborative processes are digitally recorded in significant detail. Driven by the rise of fields such as learning analytics and educational data mining, representations of collaboration itself are constructed using trace data to provide timely feedback to learners. Using rich data from virtual and/or physical settings, we are poised to achieve "collaboration translucence" by selectively making multiple, intertwined dimensions of collaboration – physical, social, epistemic, and affective – visible (Echeverria, Martinez-Maldonado, & Buckingham Shum, 2019). We therefore anticipate representational affordances for group awareness, monitoring, and coordination continuing to grow.

To conclude, we call for research attention to various types of representational affordances for collaborative learning, design efforts to reinvent multiple representations for multiple perspectives in learning, and educational efforts to promote metarepresentational competence that is key to civic participation in modern societies.

NOTES

1. In this chapter, we use the word representation to mean external representation, which is in contrast with mental or internal representations.

REFERENCES

Ainsworth, S. (1999). The functions of multiple representations. *Computers and Education*, 33(2), 131–152. doi:10.1016/S0360-1315(99)00029-9

Ainsworth, S. (2008). The education value of multiple-representations when learning complex scientific concepts. In J. K. Gilbert, M. Reiner, & M. Nakhleh (Eds.), *Visualization: Theory and practice in science education* (pp. 191–208). Dordrecht: Springer.

Ainsworth, S. (2018). *Multiple representations and multimedia learning. In international handbook of the learning sciences* (pp.96–105). New York: Routledge. doi:10.4324/9781315617572-10

Aronson, E., & Patnoe, S. (1997). *The jigsaw classroom: Building cooperation in the classroom.* (2nd ed.). New York: Longman.

Bereiter, C. (2002). *Education and mind in the knowledge age.* Mahwah, NJ: Erlbaum.

Binkley, M., Erstad, O., Herman, J., Raizen, S., Ripley, M., Miller-Ricci, M., & Rumble, M. (2012). Defining twenty-first century skills. In P. Griffin, B. McGaw, & E. Care (Eds.), *Assessment and teaching of 21st century skills* (pp. 17–66). Dordrecht: Springer. doi:10.1007/978-94-007-2324-5_2

Brodahl, C., Hadjerrouit, S., & Kristian Hansen, N. (2011). Collaborative writing with web 2.0 technologies: Education students' perceptions. *Journal of Information Technology Education: Innovations in Practice*, 10, 73–103. doi:10.28945/1384

Chen, B., Chang, Y.-H., Ouyang, F., & Zhou, W. (2018). Fostering student engagement in online discussion through social learning analytics. *The Internet and Higher Education, 37,* 21–30. doi:10.1016/j.iheduc.2017.12.002

Chen, B., & Hong, H.-Y. (2016). Schools as knowledge-building organizations: Thirty years of design research. *Educational Psychologist, 51*(2), 266–288. doi:10.1080/00461520.2016.1175306

Chinn, C., & Sandoval, W. (2018). Epistemic cognition and epistemic development. In F. Fischer, C. E. Hmelo-Silver, S. R. Goldman, & P. Reimann (Eds.), *International handbook of the learning sciences (pp. 24–33).* New York: Routledge.

Cress, U., Moskaliuk, J., & Jeong, H. (2016). *Mass collaboration and education.* Cham: Springer. doi:10.1007/978-3-319-13536-6

De Liddo, A., Sándor, Á., & Buckingham Shum, S. (2012). Contested collective intelligence: Rationale, technologies, and a human-machine annotation study. *Computer Supported Cooperative Work: CSCW: An International Journal, 21*(4/5), 417–448. doi:10.1007/s10606-011-9155-x

Dillenbourg, P. (1999). What do you mean by collaborative learning? In P. Dillenbourg (Ed.), *Collaborative-learning: Cognitive and computational approaches* (pp. 1–19). Oxford: Elsevier.

Dillenbourg, P. (2005). Designing biases that augment socio-cognitive interactions. In R. Bromme, F. Hesse, & H. Spada (Eds.), *Barriers and biases in computer-mediated knowledge communication – and how they may be overcome.* Dordrecht: Kluwer Academic Publisher.

Dillenbourg, P. (2015). Orchestration graphs. *EPFL press.* https://infoscience.epfl.ch/record/226087

diSessa, A. A. (2004). Metarepresentation: Native competence and targets for instruction. *Cognition and Instruction, 22*(3), 293–331. doi:10.1207/s1532690xci2203_2

Echeverria, V., Martinez-Maldonado, R., & Buckingham Shum, S. (2019). Towards collaboration translucence: Giving meaning to multimodal group data. *Proceedings of the 2019 CHI Conference on Human Factors in Computing Systems, 39*(1–39), 16. doi:10.1145/3290605.3300269

Fischer, F., Kollar, I., Stegmann, K., & Wecker, C. (2013). Toward a script theory of guidance in computer-supported collaborative learning. *Educational Psychologist, 48*(1), 56–66. doi:10.1080/00461520.2012.748005

Fong, C., & Slotta, J. D. (2018). Supporting communities of learners in the elementary classroom: The common knowledge learning environment. *Instructional Science, 46*(4), 533–561.

Gan, Y., Scardamalia, M., Hong, H.-Y., & Zhang, J. (2010). Early development of graphical literacy through knowledge building. *Canadian Journal of Learning and Technology/La Revue Canadienne de l'Apprentissage et de la Technologie, 36,* 1.

Håklev, S., Faucon, L., Hadzilacos, T., & Dillenbourg, P. (2017). Orchestration graphs: Enabling rich social pedagogical scenarios in MOOCs. In *Proceedings of the fourth (2017) ACM conference on learning @ scale* (pp. 261–264). New York: ACM. doi:10.1145/3051457.3054000

Higgins, S., Mercier, E., Burd, L., & Joyce-Gibbons, A. (2012). Multi-touch tables and collaborative learning: Multi-touch tables for collaboration. *British Journal of Educational Technology: Journal of the Council for Educational Technology, 43*(6), 1041–1054. doi:10.1111/j.1467-8535.2011.01259.x

Hmelo-Silver, C. E., Jordan, R. C., Eberbach, C., & Sinha, S. (2016). Systems learning with a conceptual representation: A quasi-experimental study. *Instructional Science, 45*(1), 53–72. doi:10.1007/s11251-016-9392-y

Järvelä, S., & Hadwin, A. F. (2013). New frontiers: Regulating learning in CSCL. *Educational Psychologist, 48*(1), 25–39. doi:10.1080/00461520.2012.748006

Järvelä, S., Kirschner, P. A., Panadero, E., Malmberg, J., Phielix, C., Jaspers, J., ... Järvenoja, H. (2015). Enhancing socially shared regulation in collaborative learning groups: Designing for CSCL regulation tools. *Educational Technology Research and Development, 63*(1), 125–142. doi:10.1007/s11423-014-9358-1

Jeong, H., & Hmelo-Silver, C. E. (2016). Seven affordances of computer-supported collaborative learning: How to support collaborative learning? How can technologies help? *Educational Psychologist, 51*(2), 247–265. doi:10.1080/00461520.2016.1158654

Johnson, D. W., & Johnson, R. T. (2009). An educational psychology success story: Social interdependence theory and cooperative learning. *Educational Researcher, 38*(5), 365–379. doi:10.3102/0013189X09339057

Kay, A. C. (1991). Computers, networks and education. *Scientific American, 265*(3), 138–149. http://jstor.org/stable/24938722

Koschmann, T. (2002). Dewey's contribution to the foundations of CSCL research. In *Proceedings of the Conference on Computer Support for Collaborative learning: Foundations for a CSCL community* (pp. 17–22). Boulder, CO: International Society of the Learning Sciences. http://dl.acm.org/citation.cfm?id=1658616.1658618

Lee, A. V. Y., & Tan, S. C. (2017). Promising ideas for collective advancement of communal knowledge using temporal analytics and cluster analysis. *Journal of Learning Analytics*, *4*(3), 76–101. doi:10.18608/jla.2017.43.5

Lin, F., & Chan, C. K. K. (2018). Examining the role of computer-supported knowledge-building discourse in epistemic and conceptual understanding. *Journal of Computer Assisted Learning*, *34*(5), 567–579. doi:10.1111/jcal.12261

Moher, T. (2006). Embedded phenomena. In R. Grinter, T. Rodden, P. Aoki, E. Cutrell, R. Jeffries, & G. Olson (Eds.), *Proceedings of the SIGCHI conference on human factors in computing systems – CHI '06* (p. 691). New York: ACM Press. doi:10.1145/1124772.1124875

Moreno-Armella, L., Hegedus, S. J., & Kaput, J. J. (2008). From static to dynamic mathematics: Historical and representational perspectives. *Educational Studies in Mathematics*, *68*(2), 99–111. doi:10.1007/s10649-008-9116-6

National Research Council. (2012). *A framework for K-12 science education: Practices, crosscutting concepts, and core ideas*. Washington, DC: National Academies Press.

Resendes, M., Scardamalia, M., Bereiter, C., Chen, B., & Halewood, C. (2015). Group-level formative feedback and metadiscourse. *International Journal of Computer-Supported Collaborative Learning*, *10*(3), 309–336. doi:10.1007/s11412-015-9219-x

Resnick, M., Maloney, J., Monroy-Hernández, A., Rusk, N., Eastmond, E., Brennan, K., … Kafai, Y. (2009). Scratch: Programming for all. *Communications of the ACM*, *52*(11), 60–67. doi:10.1145/1592761.1592779

Roque, R., Rusk, N., & Resnick, M. (2016). Supporting diverse and creative collaboration in the scratch online community. In U. Cress, J. Moskaliuk, & H. Jeong (Eds.), *Mass collaboration and education* (pp. 241–256). Cham: Springer International Publishing. doi:10.1007/978-3-319-13536-6_12

Roschelle, J., & Teasley, S. D. (1995). The construction of shared knowledge in collaborative problem solving. In C. O'Malley (Ed.), *Computer supported collaborative learning* (pp. 69–97). Berlin, Heidelberg: Springer.

Sandoval, W. A., Bell, P., Enyedy, N., & Suthers, D. (2000). Designing knowledge representations for learning epistemic practices of science. Paper presented at the American Educational Research Association, New Orleans.

Sandoval, W. A., & Reiser, B. J. (2004). Explanation-driven inquiry: Integrating conceptual and epistemic scaffolds for scientific inquiry. *Science Education*, *88*(3), doi:10.1002/sce.10130, 345–372.

Scardamalia, M., & Bereiter, C. (1991). Higher levels of agency for children in knowledge building: A challenge for the design of new knowledge media. *Journal of the Learning Sciences*, *1*(1), 37–68. doi:10.1207/s15327809jls0101_3

Scardamalia, M., & Bereiter, C. (2003). Knowledge building environments: Extending the limits of the possible in education and knowledge work. In A. DiStefano, K. E. Rudestam, & R. Silverman (Eds.), *Encyclopedia of distributed learning* (pp. 269–272). Thousand Oaks, CA: Sage Publications.

Scardamalia, M., & Bereiter, C. (2014). Knowledge building and knowledge creation: Theory, pedagogy, and technology. In R. K. Sawyer (Ed.), *Cambridge handbook of the learning sciences* (2nd ed., pp. 397–417). New York: Cambridge University Press.

Sengupta, P., & Shanahan, M. C. (2017). Boundary play and pivots in public computation: New directions in STEM education. *International Journal of Engineering Education*, *33*(3), 1124–1134.

Siemens, G. (2013). Learning analytics: The emergence of a discipline. *The American Behavioral Scientist*, *57*(10), 1380–1400.

Slotta, J. D. (2013). Knowledge community and inquiry: New opportunities for scripting and orchestration. *Unpublished manuscript,*. University of Toronto. Retrieved from http://academia.edu/download/32691988/SlottaKCI120813.pdf

Stahl, G. (2006). *Group cognition*. Cambridge, MA, London: MIT Press.

Stahl, G., Koschmann, T. D., & Suthers, D. D. (2014). Computer-supported collaborative learning. In R. Keith Sawyer (Ed.), *Cambridge handbook of the learning sciences* (pp. 479–500). Cambridge: Cambridge University Press.

Stahl, G., Ludvigsen, S., Law, N., & Cress, U. (2014). CSCL artifacts. *International Journal of Computer-Supported Collaborative Learning*, *9*(3), 237–245.

Suthers, D. (1998). *Representations for scaffolding collaborative inquiry on ill-structured problems*. Paper presented at the AERA Annual Meeting, San Diego, CA.

Suthers, D. D. (2003). Representational guidance for collaborative learning. In H. U. Hoppe, F. Verdejo & Judy Kay (Eds.), *Artificial intelligence in education* (pp. 3–10). Amsterdam: IOS Press.

Suthers, D. D. (2005). Collaborative knowledge construction through shared representations. In *HICSS'05: Proceedings of the 38th annual Hawaii international conference on system sciences, 2005* (p. 5a). Waikoloa, Hawai'i: IEEE.

Suthers, D. D. (2006). Technology affordances for intersubjective meaning making: A research agenda for CSCL. *International Journal of Computer-Supported Collaborative Learning, 1*(3), 315–337.

Suthers, D. D., & Hundhausen, C. D. (2003). An experimental study of the effects of representational guidance on collaborative learning processes. *Journal of the Learning Sciences, 12*(2), 183–218. doi:10.1207/s15327809jls1202_2

Suthers, D. D., Vatrapu, R., Medina, R., Joseph, S., & Dwyer, N. (2007). Conceptual representations enhance knowledge construction in asynchronous collaboration. In C. Chinn, G. Erkens, & S. Puntambekar (Eds.), *The computer supported collaborative learning (CSCL) Conference 2007* (pp. 704–713). New Brunswick, NJ: International Society of the Learning Sciences.

Suthers, D. D., Weiner, A., Connelly, J., & Paolucci, M. (1995). Belvedere: Engaging students in critical discussion of science and public policy issues. In J. Greer (Ed.), *Proceedings of the 7th world conference on artificial intelligence in education (AI-ED 95)* (pp. 266–273). Washington, DC: AACE.

van Amelsvoort, M., Andriessen, J., & Kanselaar, G. (2007). Representational tools in computer-supported collaborative argumentation-based learning: How dyads work with constructed and inspected argumentative diagrams. *Journal of the Learning Sciences, 16*(4), 485–521. doi:10.1080/10508400701524785

van Leeuwen, A. (2015). Learning analytics to support teachers during synchronous CSCL: Balancing between overview and overload. *Journal of Learning Analytics, 2*(2), 138–162. doi:10.18608/jla.2015.22.11

Weusijana, B. K., Ou, J. X., Stahl, G., & Weimar, S. (2010). Virtual math teams: an online tool for collaborative learning in the mathematics disciplines. *Proceedings of the 9th International Conference of the Learning Sciences, 2*, 421–422. http://dl.acm.org/citation.cfm?id=1854509.1854727

White, T., & Pea, R. (2011). Distributed by design: On the promises and pitfalls of collaborative learning with multiple representations. *Journal of the Learning Sciences, 20*(3), 489–547. doi:10.1080/10508406.2010.542700

Wise, A. F., Azevedo, R., Stegmann, K., Malmberg, J., Rosé, C. P., Mudrick, N., ... Yang, D. (2015). CSCL and learning analytics: Opportunities to support social interaction, self-regulation and socially shared regulation. In O. Lindwall, P. Häkkinen, T. Koschmann, P. Tchounikine, & S. Ludvigsen (Eds.), *Exploring the material conditions of learning: The computer supported collaborative learning (CSCL) conference 2015* (vol. 2, pp. 607–614). Gothenburg: International Society of the Learning Sciences.

Wise, A. F., & Schwarz, B. B. (2017). Visions of CSCL: Eight provocations for the future of the field. *International Journal of Computer-Supported Collaborative Learning, 12*(4), 423–467. doi:10.1007/s11412-017-9267-5

Wu, H.-K., & Puntambekar, S. (2012). Pedagogical affordances of multiple external representations in scientific processes. *Journal of Science Education and Technology, 21*(6), 754–767. doi:10.1007/s10956-011-9363-7

Zhang, J., Tao, D., Chen, M.-H., Sun, Y., Judson, D., & Naqvi, S. (2018). Co-organizing the collective journey of inquiry with idea thread mapper. *Journal of the Learning Sciences, 27*(3), 390–430. doi:10.1080/10508406.2018.1444992

30

THE CHALLENGE OF MEASURING PROCESSES AND OUTCOMES WHILE LEARNING FROM MULTIPLE REPRESENTATIONS WITH ADVANCED LEARNING TECHNOLOGIES

Roger Azevedo and Michelle Taub

UNIVERSITY OF CENTRAL FLORIDA

ABSTRACT

This chapter focuses on the challenges of measuring self-regulatory processes and learning outcomes while learning from multiple representations with advanced learning technologies (ALTs). More specifically, we present challenges associated with measuring learners' processes and outcomes while using multiple representations with ALTs. ALTs are technology-based learning and training systems designed to teach learners of all ages to learn, reason, problem solve, and understand different topics and domains such as physics, math, history, biology, medicine and can include different systems such as multimedia, hypermedia, serious games, simulations, intelligent tutoring systems, immersive virtual environments and so forth. The structure of our chapter is as follows: (1) a brief overview of the major issues related to using multiple representations for learning with ALTs; (2) a description of the analytical techniques for understanding multiple representations and their goals for successful learning with ALTs; (3) a discussion of the issues associated with using multiple representations to measure and assess learning outcomes and how we can use ALTs as research tools to capture self-regulated learning; and (4) a presentation of challenges and future directions that need to be addressed by researchers.

Key words: multiple representations, advanced learning technologies, self-regulated learning, process data, learning

MULTIPLE REPRESENTATIONS DURING LEARNING WITH ADVANCED LEARNING TECHNOLOGIES

Researchers have designed advanced learning technologies (ALTs) with embedded multiple representations of information to foster different processes during learning, reasoning, and problem solving (e.g., Azevedo, Mudrick, Taub, & Bradbury, 2019; Azevedo, Taub, & Mudrick, 2018; Biswas, Baker, & Paquette, 2018; Biswas, Segedy, & Bunchongchit, 2016; D'Mello & Graesser, 2015; Graesser, 2016; Lester, Rowe, & Mott, 2013). ALTs are technology-based learning and training systems designed to teach learners of all ages to learn, reason, problem solve, and understand different topics and domains such as physics, math, biology, medicine, and can include different systems such as multimedia, hypermedia, serious games, simulations, intelligent tutoring systems, immersive virtual environments, and so forth. These environments display different types of information to learners in many ways. Thus, when we say multiple representations, we are referring to a multitude of different types of information. But what do these multiple representations display? In this chapter, we discuss three different types of information represented to learners. First, the ALT can represent domain-specific content the learner is studying, reading, or learning about (e.g., text, diagrams, video clips related to photosynthesis). Second, the ALT can represent different system elements (e.g., table of contents, dialog box, skillometer, self-regulated learning palette) the learner can engage with to facilitate learning, initiate and use diverse learning strategies, both of which allow the ALT to potentially track learning behaviors (e.g., selecting instructional materials) and processes (e.g., strategy use). And last, the ALT can display data visualizations of the learner's multimodal multichannel data (e.g., their gaze behavior collected from an eye tracker during gameplay) to allow the opportunity for learners to monitor and self-regulate their learning processes.

In this chapter, we will present challenges associated with measuring learners' processes and outcomes while using multiple representations with ALTs. Given the complexity in understanding underlying cognitive, affective, metacognitive, and motivational (CAMM) processes, we argue that using multimodal multichannel data (such as different measures within concurrent verbalizations, eye tracking, log files, facial expressions of emotions, physiological sensors, etc.) is key to capturing these complex processes while learners' internal mental representations (e.g., declarative and procedural knowledge, mental model, schema) develop, evolve, and are utilized with ALTs to impact their learning, comprehension, problem solving, and performance. The structure of our chapter is as follows: (1) a brief overview of the major issues related to using multiple representations for learning with ALTs; (2) a description of the analytical techniques for understanding multiple representations and their goals for successful learning with ALTs; (3) a discussion of the issues associated with using multiple representations to measure and assess learning outcomes and how we can use ALTs as research tools to capture self-regulated learning; and (4) a presentation of challenges and future directions that need to be addressed by researchers.

Types of Representations

ALTs afford different types of representations based on their intended learning and training objectives. These representations can range within traditional representations such as MetaTutor, a hypermedia-based intelligent tutoring system designed to enhance conceptual understanding of biological systems by providing learners with text, diagrams, and animations while fostering self-regulated learning (SRL). Besides traditional representations of domain-specific content, ALTs afford other types of representations that are designed to facilitate learning, problem solving, self-regulated learning, etc. For example, an interface element in MetaTutor allows students to set sub-goals (Harley, Taub, Azevedo, & Bouchet, 2018) to allow for monitoring of sub-goals by representing a progress bar, while MetaTutorIVH (Taub, Mudrick, & Azevedo, 2018b), another type of ALT similar to MetaTutor but with an embedded virtual human, requires learners to detect the relevancy of the text and diagrams shown by answering follow-up biology questions. Through this, the ALT fosters learners to initiate metacognitive judgments by examining the relevancy of the instructional representation (i.e., text and diagrams). Crystal Island, another type of ALT, fosters scientific reasoning by providing learners with information and clues to generate hypotheses about how to complete the game and the resources to test their hypotheses and knowledge (e.g., virtual scanner so they can test potential contaminants of an illness; Taub & Azevedo, 2018; Taub, Azevedo, Bradbury, Millar, & Lester, 2018a).

In this section, we describe different types of multiple representations across ALTs, how these representations can be used to support learners' goals and foster learning processes, and finally, assess the effectiveness of using such processes with ALTs across learners. Learners are provided with a multitude of representations during studying, learning, problem solving, reasoning, and knowledge construction with ALTs. These representations can differ based on what kinds of information they are presenting to the learner, how they present material, and who (e.g., instructional designer, researcher, embedded pedagogical agent) or what (i.e., the ALT itself) is developing the representation.

Internal vs. External Representations

ALTs allow researchers and educators to understand interactions between students' internal (e.g., declarative chunk, production rule, schema, mental model) and external representations (e.g., text, diagrams, animations) afforded by ALTs. Based on the representations, the system can provide learners with analytics to represent how they are performing with the system, such as how many content pages they have read to achieve their current sub-goal. This is presented in the form of a system element. In addition, the system can display where the student fixated on the screen for the task (Figure 30.1), which provides a heat map of where learners allocate their attention superimposed onto the instructional representation. This illustrates the text they read, diagrams they inspected, and attention allocated to the avatar who provides scaffolding prompts during the learning session. This type of external representation provided to the learner by an ALT presents a summary of where the learner focused during multimedia learning and could serve several potential functions: (1) allows the learner to visualize and reflect on their attention allocation vis-a-vis their prior knowledge of the topic, (2) enhances their metacognitive monitoring and accuracy of their evaluations including strategy use, and (3) plans for deployment of the same or different strategies to enhance their learning. Thus, learners' internal information and how they are progressing through the learning task (i.e., providing the progress bar based on

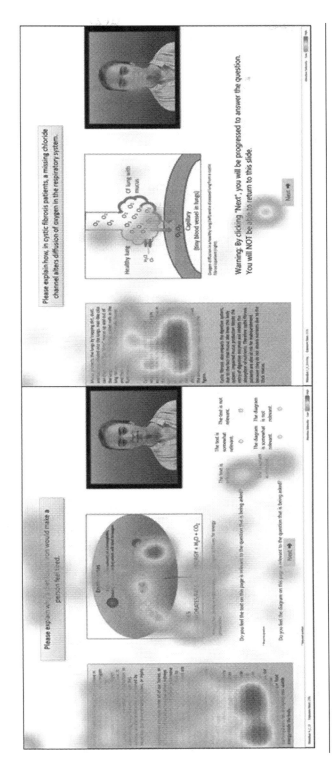

Figure 30.1 Heat Map of Learners' Attention Allocation.

the learner's individual progress or displaying the learner's emotional state) can be externally represented (the content being provided) for the learner to accomplish the learning task. We argue both types of representations are necessary for learners to monitor and regulate their learning

Static Vs. Dynamic Representations

The representations of the system content, system elements, and data visualizations can be in multiple formats. Information can be static, where everything remains stationary and cannot be manipulated. For example, static text or diagrams in an ALT allow learners to read content and inspect diagrams (i.e., a multimedia-based ALT) to accomplish a task, the table of contents remains on the interface and does not change, and a data visualization of a heat map displays the most and least fixated on areas of interest at the end of a task or trial (Figure 30.1). In contrast, information can be dynamic and change over time based on learner-system interactions. For example, an animation or embedded simulation within a hypermedia-based ALT can simulate a complex biological process (e.g., Krebs cycle). While these types of dynamic representations in ALTs are complex and can challenge learners' comprehension due to individual differences such as prior knowledge and working memory capacity (see Mayer, 2014), they can also foster self-regulation by allowing learners to metacognitively monitor and dynamically regulate their learning. For example, learners dynamically monitor and regulate their learning by manipulating a skillometer to set a new goal, take notes, or summarize as a way to regulate their metacomprehension, or test a scientific hypothesis by inserting a food item into a virtual scanner. Data visualizations can also be a real-time video of facial expressions of emotions, or display the screen recording to an expert tutor (see Figure 30.2) as in the case of MetaMentor, a system designed to study, teach, train, and foster self-regulated learning skills in students and teachers using multimodal multichannel data visualizations. All ALTs contain different amounts and types of representations that are static or can be manipulated or changed by the learner, system, or teacher, and depending on the design of the system, these amounts will vary. We argue it is important to include both static and dynamic representations to learners because there can be critical information learners must attend to in the ALT (and thus should be present), while allowing learners to manipulate or change features or actions grants them agency, which has been shown to positively impact learning (Veinott et al., 2013).

Single vs. Multiple Representations

In addition to different forms of visualizations, ALTs can range from one to many representations of the presented information. For example, the content can be displayed as text only, or the system can foster learners to engage in one self-regulatory process by, for instance, creating a causal concept map (Kinnebrew, Segedy, & Biswas, 2017) or monitoring progress on a worksheet (Taub et al., 2018b), or the data visualization can be of a single data channel (e.g., gaze behavior from eye tracking). Alternatively, the ALT can provide multiple representations; for example, to present the content, the ALT can provide text along with corresponding images of abstract concepts (Mayer, 2014). The system can also provide an SRL palette, an interface element that allows

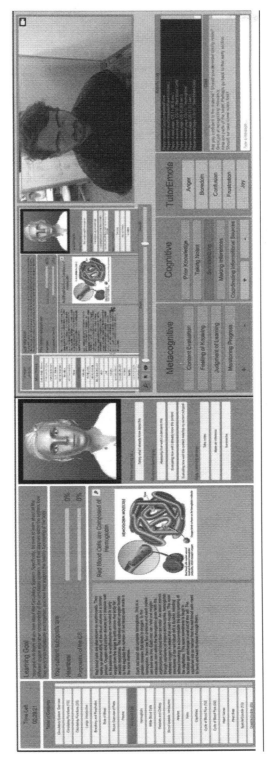

Figure 30.2 Facial Expressions of Emotions from MetaMentor.

learners to indicate to the ALT which cognitive (e.g., take notes) and metacognitive (e.g., evaluate relevance of the representation vis-a-vis current learning goal) SRL processes they plan to deploy (Azevedo et al., 2019). Additionally, the data visualization can include representations of multimodal multichannel data (e.g., gaze behaviors indicating the amount of time fixating on different areas on the screen and the frequency of making those fixations, and facial expression of emotions indicating evidence of specific learner-centered emotions, such as confusion, and emotional states, such as engagement) while students are completing a task (Figure 30.2). We argue it can be beneficial to present learners with both single and multiple representations. A single representation will reduce cognitive load (Sweller, van Merriënboer, & Paas, 2019), while multiple representations provide more detailed and contextual information about the learning session (Azevedo et al., 2018), allowing learners to process information from various representations (Mayer, 2014). However, these assumptions need to be empirically tested as we assume that providing learners with their multimodal data will allow them new unprecedented opportunities to visualize, comprehend, understand, etc. their learning processes and therefore become better self-regulators.

In this section, we discussed different types of representations of instructional content and data for individuals during learning with ALTs. It is important to focus on these distinctions in representations when designing ALTs to foster effective learning. In addition to the ways we can represent different information, ALT designers must consider the goals of the ALTs to provide the most optimal representations, depending on several factors such as prior knowledge, learning goal, type of assessment, etc. As such, we discuss the goals of multiple representations for ALTs in the next section.

Goals of Multiple Representations

Prior to incorporating specific types of representations in an ALT, a researcher must specify the aims of the ALT. These might be fostering metacognitive processes, emotion-regulation strategies, literacy skills, self-efficacy, physics learning, or many other aims, as appropriate in the ALT's design. In this section, we discuss different types of goals of ALTs. We emphasize these are not the only goals of all ALTs, nor does an ALT necessarily focus on just one goal. For example, MetaTutor fosters learning biology content while also initiating the use of SRL processes, while Crystal Island teaches concepts about microbiology and fosters SRL, literacy, and scientific-reasoning skills.

Fostering Learning

Most ALTs focus on promoting learning of a given topic where learning is predominantly operationalized by an individual's recall of factual information or conceptual understanding about said topic. For example, MetaTutor fosters learning about the human circulatory system (Azevedo et al., 2018), while MetaTutorIVH fosters learning about nine different body systems (e.g., digestive, respiratory, etc.) (Taub et al., 2018b), and Crystal Island fosters learning about microbiology (Taub et al., 2018a, 2017). SimSelf fosters learning about the hydrosphere (Taub et al., 2018b) and Betty's Brain fosters learning about ecosystems (Biswas et al., 2018). These ALTs can foster learning by providing different types of representations using static text (e.g., Crystal Island) that includes static images (e.g., MetaTutor, MetaTutorIVH, SimSelf, Betty's

Brain), or by creating simulations (Van Eck, Shute, & Rieber, 2017) and engaging in dialogue with conversational agents (Graesser, 2016), and others.

Facilitating Knowledge Acquisition

In contrast to content learning, knowledge acquisition refers to understanding the fundamental processes of a domain (declarative and procedural), how to enact these processes effectively (procedural knowledge), and when (conditional knowledge). Mostly, ALTs foster domain knowledge (i.e., content knowledge) for a range of different topics. The way in which ALTs foster procedural or conditional knowledge largely varies between ALTs, while focusing on the same or different learning processes. For example, both MetaTutor and Crystal Island foster SRL, however in MetaTutor, it is done through an SRL palette and strategic inclusion of interface elements (e.g., progress bar of the amount of material covered for a sub-goal, timer to allow for time monitoring), whereas Crystal Island fosters SRL by providing learners with tools they can use while gathering and tracking clues they need to solve the mystery (e.g., diagnosis worksheet). Additionally, the level of support can vary between and within ALTs, such that the system does not always explicitly foster procedural and conditional knowledge. For example, MetaTutor has a prompt and feedback experimental condition where pedagogical agents prompt learners to use SRL processes, but in the control condition, the pedagogical agents do not. Thus, learning how and when to engage in learning strategies is not always provided for learners, nor is it measured, making us unaware if learners are acquiring these skills and the conditional knowledge necessary to transfer these skills to the real world. Perhaps with the inclusion of data visualizations of learners' processes while using these systems, we can include their use of learning processes, such as SRL (see Figure 30.2) to foster their procedural and conditional knowledge. For example, the learner may be able to understand they did not do well on the task, based on the heat map illustrating their failure to fixate on relevant instructional content, thereby indicating their inaccurate metacognitive monitoring of relevant instructional materials.

Updating Mental Models

Some ALTs focus on learners' mental models of complex biological, chemical, physical, etc. systems that are typically examined through changes in mental representations known as mental models (Graesser, 2016). For example, Betty's Brain requires students to teach Betty about science topics by creating a causal concept map (Kinnebrew et al., 2017). Betty then takes quizzes based on the information in the map, and so students are constantly changing their map to visually represent the information they are reading. Thus, by examining the different concept maps (i.e., the additions, deletions, relationships between different concepts), researchers can investigate changes in mental models of various topics. Conceptual change can also be measured by examining changes in learners' inputted text during learning. For example, in MetaTutor, students can take notes when they are reading and inspecting diagrams. The log files capture when students are taking notes as well as the information they are writing, and so we can examine any changes or differences in students' notes from one timepoint to another during the learning session. Changes in notes or summaries can also be representative of a mental model shift based on the quality (i.e., accuracy and relevancy) of information provided (Trevors, Duffy, & Azevedo, 2014).

A similar line of work has found common misconceptions within certain topics among students. For example, McLaren, Adams, Mayer, and Forlizzi (2017) report they have identified 17 common misconceptions in math, with four specific to decimal points. Teachers constantly identify common misconceptions among their students, and so it is important for ALT researchers and developers to address these misconceptions by helping learners overcome them. ALTs can detect misconceptions by engaging learners in problem-solving tasks, where they might make a common error associated with a particular misconception, and then provide feedback on why their solution was incorrect. In McLaren et al.'s (2017) study, they developed a game and non-game version of Decimal Point, where students had to demonstrate their understanding of decimal numbers (e.g., rank order numbers from lowest to highest). When students were incorrect, they could not proceed to the next problem until they got it correct, which required students to identify their error(s) and correct them.

In this section, we have described some of the goals of ALTs, which can influence how information is represented. All ALTs foster different types, but how they approach doing so can differ. In addition, ALTs can include more than one goal. For example, ALTs can foster (1) content learning by using SRL processes (e.g., MetaTutor, MetaTutorIVH, or Crystal Island), (2) science learning while promoting conceptual changes in mental models (e.g., Betty's Brain), and (3) problem solving in math while addressing common misconceptions (e.g., Decimal Point). Thus, the goal(s) of the ALT can influence the design of the ALT as well as how these processes are measured and assessed. In the next section, we discuss different ways of measuring and assessing learning processes with ALTs that contain multiple representations.

MEASUREMENT AND ASSESSMENT WITHIN MULTIPLE REPRESENTATIONS

Given the different ways informational representations can be structured within ALTs, there are also different ways to capture various goals within an ALT. In this section, we describe various measurement and assessment techniques, and how each technique is used in current research.

Selecting a Response

In many ALTs, it is common to include activities where learners must make a selection (e.g., page quiz, self-reports). This type of representation allows learners to decide how they are going to answer a question and can be used to assess performance, emotions, metacognitive monitoring, and more. ALTs can present this type of activity (or representation) in different ways. For example, if a student is given a page or sub-goal quiz, or responding to a content pre- or post-test, the format can be multiple choice. Typically, multiple choice is structured as a four-choice option, where one answer is correct. For some grading schemes, responses are also weighted, such that there is one fully correct response, one or two partially correct responses (e.g., response includes some but not all relevant information), and one incorrect response, which does not contain any correct information. This allows for an assessment that includes a weighted score, where learners will get partial points if they knew certain aspects of the correct response.

In addition to performance, response selection can identify emotions or metacognitive judgments. For example, a self-report questionnaire can ask learners to rate how they currently feel (Harley, Bouchet, Hussain, Azevedo, & Calvo, 2015), where learners can select an option from a list or choose a number on a Likert scale for an emotion. For metacognitive monitoring, a learner can select an option to rate their understanding of content, select their response for rating the relevancy of the content to their sub-goal, or use a slider bar to indicate their confidence in selecting the correct answer. Learners can also use a drop-down menu to select their response to questions about a book they just read or select what their response is for solving the mystery. In all of these activities, learners are selecting from a list of answers based on how they want to respond to the question being asked. These selections can then be used to assess the prevalence of certain emotions, how learners judge their understanding of content and how accurate their judgment was, how their confidence relates to their performance, and whether or not they selected the correct answer from the options provided.

Writing or Inputting Information

A second type of assessment involves learners writing or inputting information into the system freely without choosing from any options. This can include writing (or typing) information such as notes or summaries, writing (or typing) everything one knows about the topic they are learning (i.e., prior knowledge activation), writing a justification for a chosen response, or answering a self-report questionnaire (e.g., overall feedback on the system) including open-ended format assessments. As described earlier, typically ALTs log all input, thus generating the learner's notes and summaries, and when these actions were initiated. Thus, we can analyze how these notes and summaries changed over time (i.e., changing mental model). We can also examine the accuracy of the notes in comparison to the content pages (e.g., by using Latent Semantic Analysis, LSA; Landauer, McNamara, Dennis, & Kintsch, 2007) to determine how similar the notes are to the page (where a value of 1 would indicate a direct copy). A justification can be coded for keywords related to either the content (e.g., phrase used to denote a change to a more sophisticated mental model such as *the pulmonary and circulatory system work in tandem to support the human body*) or learning process (e.g., phrase used to indicate metacognitive judgment related to emerging understanding of the domain such as *I do not fully understand how valves in the heart function with the electrical conduction system of the organ*), which can then be scored for accuracy in relation to the question being asked. Self-report responses can also be coded, perhaps by theme of feedback, such as level of support from the pedagogical agents (e.g., too much prompting, not enough feedback). Thus, there are many ways one can assess a learner's written response while learning with an ALT.

Drawing or Creating an Illustration

One last assessment investigates how learners are creating drawings or illustrations based on the content they are learning about. Drawings can focus on mapping out a given structure or process. For example, if a student is learning about the structure of the heart, they can map out the four chambers and their locations. This drawing can then be assessed to determine if the atria and ventricles are in the correct locations. The learner can also map out gas exchange in the blood between the heart and the lungs by either drawing it out and including the directions with arrows and add blue and red to indicate oxygenated vs. deoxygenated blood, or by creating a simulation in the ALT to show how the structures of the heart function and use it to test hypotheses about heart malfunctions (if the ALT has the functionality to allow learners to do so). Again, these drawings/simulations and other types of representations can be assessed by checking their accuracy. To check the accuracy, the researchers should seek the help of an expert (i.e., science teacher in this case) who teaches these concepts in their classrooms. Other illustrations include concept maps, which demonstrate a learner's mental model of a construct. These can be assessed by examining the links and checking for their accuracy (again, by a subject matter expert). In Betty's Brain, the maps are assessed using the quizzes Betty takes, where her ability to answer the questions depends on the accuracy of the causal concept map students generate (Kinnebrew et al., 2017). Thus, there are different opportunities that allow learners to include illustrations, which has been found to positively impact learning (Smith et al., 2019).

In addition to including an illustration tool within the ALT, a data visualization of the learner's data can include illustrations of the data that can be manipulated by the expert viewing the data visualization. For example, the expert can code the data in real-time (e.g., indicate if a student is making an accurate metacognitive judgment) (Figure 30.2), and then prompt the learner (in real-time) based on the judgment. Therefore, ALTs can strategically embed data illustrations and provide tools that afford user-centered manipulations to be effective learning tools for both learners and researchers.

These assessments can be used as proxies for researchers measuring learning, SRL, and performance with ALTs, or for the system itself to generate data visualizations to show the learner or teacher how they are progressing through the learning task. Once again, each ALT is not limited to only one type of assessment, and most ALTs do not limit learners to only one assessment. Depending on the goal of the ALT and which learning-related processes it aims to foster, some assessments might seem more beneficial than others.

In this section, we have discussed the different ways researchers can assess types of representations before, during, or after learning with ALTs. As we have seen, there are many different ways in which we can visualize information in ALTs. Selecting the most appropriate types of visualizations will largely depend on the learning processes being fostered or investigated. In the next section, we discuss using ALTs as a research tool, and how we can use multiple representations to foster learning with ALTs.

USING ALTs AS A RESEARCH TOOL TO MEASURE SELF-REGULATED LEARNING WITH MULTIPLE REPRESENTATIONS

One use of ALTs is to examine how students self-regulate their learning with different representations. By using multimodal multichannel data (e.g., eye tracking (fixations, saccades), concurrent verbalizations of emotions or metacognitive monitoring, log files (time spent per page, number of pages visited), facial expressions of emotions (evidence of confusion, proportion of engagement in a session), physiological sensors (skin conductance, heart rate)), we can collect more information about how the student is learning in real-time (Azevedo & Gasevic, 2019). To collect these data, we typically instrument our participants to capture their learning processes. In this section, we describe how we can instrument both learners and the system to measure processes and outcomes during a learning session with an ALT.

Types of Multimodal Multichannel Data

The types of data we collect can be both multimodal and multichannel in nature. Specifically, multimodal refers to the different types of data variables that can be elicited from one data channel (e.g., writing and drawing), while multichannel refers to data variables that can be elicited from more than one data channel (e.g., eye tracking and log files).

Log Files

Log-file data captures all learner–system interactions such as mouse clicks (e.g., clicking on a page, selecting different representations of information, indicating the use of a metacognitive process), keyboard entries (e.g., taking notes, activating prior knowledge by typing retrieved knowledge), or system activity (e.g., the pedagogical agent prompted the learner to make a summary, the system administered a self-report asking participants to report their current emotions). All the logged data are timestamped (e.g., typically at the s or ms-level), which informs the researcher of when the learner engaged in a particular activity, how they performed, and in what sequence. For example, the log file would inform researchers the time a learner began and completed a sub-goal quiz, the accuracy of each response on that quiz, and what occurred before and after the quiz. Thus, log files generate a time-based activity, and behavioral sequence of events during a learning session.

Eye Tracking

Eye-tracking data inform us where the learner was focusing their attention on the interface during a learning session. For example, eye tracking can reveal cognitive strategies used by learners as they select, organize, and integrate multiple representations during learning with an ALT (e.g., Taub et al., 2017). The eye tracker can generate three main types of variables: fixations, saccades, and regressions (Rayner, 2009). A fixation is defined as looking at a designated area on the screen (i.e., area of interest) for a minimum amount of time (the literature varies in what the minimum is, but a fixation ranges from 100 to 300 ms). A saccade is defined as movements between fixations (typically reading or scanning between areas of interest), and regressions are special types of saccades that are defined as reverting back to a previous area of interest (similar to rereading). The data output could be an excel spreadsheet or csv file that indicates how many times a learner fixated on a particular predefined area of interest (fixation count) and for how long (fixation duration), how many saccades were made, and between which areas of interest, etc. Eye tracking can also be represented as heat maps, which are visualizations that show the general distribution of gaze points. They are typically displayed as a color-gradient overlay on the presented image or stimulus. Red, yellow, and green colors would represent in descending order the amount of gaze points that were directed towards parts of the image (see Figure 30.1).

Videos of Facial Expressions of Affective States

Video data of learners' faces can be used to identify emotions or affective states expressed during a learning session. This is done by running the videos through facial detection software (e.g., Affdex, FaceReader, FACET, OpenFace) that identify facial-muscle movements (called action units; e.g., eyebrow lowerer, lip tightener) and the degree to which they are being activated, possibly indicating an emotion is being expressed (e.g., confusion, frustration, boredom). Variables extracted from this data channel include the evidence of a facial expression being present or the intensity of it, and the duration, frequency, and sequence of affective states during learning with an ALT. Thus, it can be beneficial to determine which facial expressions learners are expressing while learning from multiple representations during task performance. Linking affective states during learning with multiple representation is critical in understanding the role of emotions and determining their psychological basis (e.g., confusion stemming from inspecting complex diagrams).

Think-aloud Protocols

When learners are asked to think aloud, they are told to verbalize everything they are doing, thinking, and feeling during learning, including with ALTs (Greene & Azevedo, 2009; Greene, Deekens, Copeland, & Yu, 2018). This provides the researchers with information about the cognitive strategies learners are using (e.g., "I'm summarizing what is presented on this diagram") and the metacognitive processes they are engaging in (e.g., "I do not understand this paragraph and how it is related to my current learning goal"). In some cases, think-alouds can also reveal level of interest (or other motivational states and traits) in learning specific content or completing tasks successfully (e.g., "This animation of photosynthesis has some really fascinating information, I want to learn more"), and which emotions they are experiencing (e.g., "This animation of the pumping of the heart confuses me"). From this data channel, we can observe the frequency of each type of process, how long learners spent using or expressing these processes, the valence of these processes and how it changes over time (e.g., I *do not* understand this vs. I *do* understand this), and the sequence of processes during learning with multiple representations in ALTs (Azevedo et al., 2018).

Strengths and Challenges of Using Multimodal Multichannel Data

Based on the previous sections, it is evident that collecting multimodal multichannel data can provide large amounts of information toward understanding what processes learners use to comprehend, reason, and problem solve while using multiple representations embedded in ALTs, and how these processes impact their overall learning and performance. However, researchers must remember not all channels are perfect. Each channel contains its own respective strengths and weaknesses (Azevedo & Gasevic, 2019; Azevedo et al., 2019). Table 30.1 highlights the overall strengths and challenges of each data channel and we discuss them in further detail below.

Log files are advantageous data to use because they are automatically collected while a learner is interacting with a system. The generated data are timestamped, allowing the researcher to determine the sequence of events as well as their duration

Table 30.1 Strengths and Challenges of Each Data Channel Collected during Learning with Multiple Representations Embedded in Advanced Learning Technologies (ALTs)

	Strengths	Challenges
Log files	Record of all behavioral actions and events automatically collected by an ALT Timestamped Show sequence of time-based actions and events Easy to understand	Need screen recordings and other multimodal multichannel data to provide contextual information to make accurate inferences about cognitive strategies and metacognitive processes
Eye tracking	Captures what and where learners are allocating their attention and focusing on the ALT's interface Can be used to examine many underlying learning processes (e.g., cognitve strategies) Best used in a controlled setting (e.g., lab) for accurate tracking and inferences	Need screen recordings and other multimodal multichannel data to provide contextual information to make accurate inferences about cognitive, metacognitive, affective, and motivation processes Calibration errors lead to inaccuracies Lack of detection can be mind-wandering
Videos of facial expressions	Can detect and classify learners' affective states during learning Measure action units and/or emotions	Need screen recordings and other multimodal multichannel data to provide contextual information to make accurate inferences about affective, cognitive, metacognitive, and motivational processes Commercial software often does not reveal their algorithms used for detection and classification of emotions and action units Most commercial software does not detect and classify all emotions Several learner and contextual factors can influence the classification, quality, expressivity, and evidence of learners' affective states (e.g., facial occlusions, social desirability)
Concurrent think-aloud protocols	Language gives access to thoughts based on verbalizations collected in real-time during learning, reasoning, problem solving and therefore provides ground truth	Need screen recordings and other multimodal multichannel data to provide contextual information to make accurate inferences about cognitive and metacognitive processes Time consuming in transcribing, coding, re-coding verbalizations Requires trained coders to enhance accuracy Practice with concurrent think-alouds prior to learning with ALTs ensures data quality Prevents the use of other data channels such as facial recognition and EEG because of movement required for talking
Screen recordings	Critical source of data as it provides contextual information of all learner-ALT interactions	Not associated with a single data variable Better use as an additional resource to other data channels

and frequency. In addition, they are easy to understand, not requiring a large amount of training for analysis. However, the information obtained from a log file depends solely on the learner and their overt behavioral actions. For example, we do not know where they are looking on the screen since log files do not capture eyes' location. Additionally, we do not know which facial expressions learners are exerting because log files do not measure emotions learners are feeling or expressing. Finally, learners do not indicate why they are performing a certain action, and so we are not aware of their intentions during learning either.

There are many strengths of **eye-tracking data** (see Rayner, 2009). First, it can be used to capture what and where learners are focusing their attention during a task without requiring them to do any additional actions. These data can be used to infer cognitive, affective, and metacognitive processes during learning with multiple representations within ALTs. For example, eye-tracking data have been used to demonstrate if learners are engaging in monitoring or strategy use during learning (Taub & Azevedo, 2019), or if certain gaze patterns are indicative of different emotions (Jaques, Conati, Harley, & Azevedo, 2014). However, the data do not explain *why* the learner is exhibiting these eye-tracking behaviors, so making inferences about these behaviors can be challenging for researchers. Perhaps a learner is rereading because they do not understand the content (i.e., confusion) or maybe a learner is trying to waste time (e.g., off-task behavior) so they are looking around the screen (i.e., boredom). To enhance the accuracy of these inferences, a researcher is advised to collect video data of learners' facial expressions. Furthermore, although calibration is simple, there is always the chance of discrepancies in the calibration, which can lead to false positives or negatives. These discrepancies exist due to a number of factors including the size of the areas of interest (AOIs) such as when AOIs are small or dynamic like those in simulations and immersive virtual systems. When the AOIs are small, it can be difficult to ensure the learner is fixating on that area, rather than the possibility of some deviation from calibration. In addition, it cannot detect behaviors such as mind-wandering with certainty, where the learner might appear to be fixating on the screen, but is thinking about something else (Krasich et al., 2018).

Collecting **facial-expression data** has shown to be a valuable data channel, as it informs us of emotional states learners are expressing during a task such as comprehending from multiple representations. Much research has shown the impact of emotions on learning and the use of self-regulatory processes, where both positively and negatively valenced emotions have been shown to play an important role in impacting SRL process use (Loderer, Pekrun., & Lester, in press, Taub et al., in press) as well as overall learning (Sabourin & Lester, 2014). Studies have shown that different action units can be indicative of basic (e.g., joy; Ekman, 1973) or learner-centered emotions (e.g., confusion; D'Mello, 2013), however the same action unit can also contribute to many emotions (such as AU4, brow lowerer, being indicative of confusion, frustration, or mental effort; Grafsgaard, Wiggins, Boyer, Wiebe, & Lester, 2014), depending on the context. In addition, different software programs that detect facial expressions often generate different emotional states, and so at times, the software might erroneously detect an emotion. For example, commercial software that does not detect frustration might identify the learner as being angry instead. Thus, it is possible that the software does not contain the algorithms to detect some affective states, which necessitates cautious interpretations because it could result in a faulty detection. Finally, using these types of software cannot detect if learners are masking or suppressing their emotions, which research shows is a common emotion regulation strategy (Gross, 2015).

A major strength of using **concurrent think-aloud protocols** is the "ground truth" they provide, meaning the learner is overtly verbalizing what they are doing, thinking, and feeling (see Ericsson & Simon, 1993; Greene & Azevedo, 2009). This does not require researchers to infer the use of SRL processes because for the most part they are explicitly stated, but still need to be carefully coded given contextual information. However, although think-aloud protocols can explicitly provide information about what a learner is doing during a task, it requires the learner to be appropriately trained and practice how to do a think-aloud. This can occur naturally for some learners; however, it can be quite challenging for others who do not typically express themselves vocally, and the researchers might have to repeatedly prompt them to think aloud, but make sure not to influence what they are saying, which can also be challenging and requires extensive training as well (Greene et al., 2018). Additionally, coding think-aloud protocols can be quite time consuming, and relies on high inter-rater reliabilities between coders, which can be difficult as well. Thus, extensive training is required for researchers.

It is clear the abovementioned data channels and modalities have both strengths and weaknesses. But there is one overarching weakness from using all these data channels – i.e., context. Without any contextual information, we are unaware of what the learner is actually doing when exhibiting any of these behaviors, actions, or responses during learning with ALTs. Thus, it is crucial to include screen recordings in addition to any of the other data channels being measured.

It is necessary to include **screen recordings** as part of a data analytical plan as they provide contextual information of what the learner is doing during a task. Contextual information in this sense refers to information that can be used to make accurate inferences about multimodal multichannel data that typically focuses on the learner and ALT, but it can also include the learner, their peers, and teachers (in cases where classroom discourse is crucial), classroom environment, etc. For example, it informs us of which page the learner is reading, which in-game action the learner is engaging in, or which variables they are manipulating during a simulation. Without this information, we would not be able to get a full picture of what the data are telling us. If we use screen recordings alone, we would know the learner has specific content of the ALT open, but we would not know the emotions they are expressing during learning. If we wanted to determine learners' emotions, we would know the evidence or intensity of confusion, for example, but we would not know what might possibly be eliciting that confusion. The log files inform us of which actions the learner is initiating, but we would not know where system elements are located. The learner might inform us they are taking notes or making a metacognitive judgment, but we do not know which material they are taking notes on or judging their learning based on. Thus, including a screen recording adds extra contextual information that help us understand the processes learners are exhibiting while learning with ALTs.

It is important to emphasize that these are some, but not all types of data that can be collected during a learning session. We argue that using data that are both multimodal (i.e. verbal or non-verbal, physiological, video data) and multichannel (i.e., log files, concurrent verbalizations, eye tracking, facial expressions of emotions, physiological sensors) can allow us to examine learners detecting, processing, acquiring, internalizing, storing, retrieving, using, and transferring multiple representations within ALTs compared to using a single data channel. For example, the eye-tracking data inform us of where the participant is looking on screen, and with the screen recording, we know exactly what they were looking at including what they were doing (e.g., making a metacognitive judgment). Also, with the addition of videos of facial expressions, we can determine the emotions they were feeling while making that judgment. Using think-aloud protocols can inform us of which SRL processes learners are engaging in, including cognitive and metacognitive processes, as well as their motivational states (e.g., task interest, achievement goals) and expressed emotions. However, it is important to remember that selecting and weighing which data channels to use should be theoretically based and empirically driven, such that the data used should match the research questions being asked (see Azevedo & Gasevic, 2019). Typically, these data violate traditional statistical assumptions and are currently analyzed using data mining and machine learning techniques. In the next section, we discuss the theoretical assumptions for collecting multimodal multichannel data.

THEORETICAL ASSUMPTIONS FOR USING MULTIMODAL MULTICHANNEL DATA

When using multimodal multichannel data, there are also theoretical considerations that must be made when analyzing the data related to sampling rate and temporal alignment of the data. Theoretically, we use Winne and Hadwin's (Winne, 2018; Winne and Hadwin, 2008) information processing theory (IPT) of SRL that views SRL as a series of events that temporally unfold during learning. There are no limits on the length of an SRL process, but when using different data channels, they have their own sampling rates, so we need to ensure the temporal alignment includes an entire SRL event. For example, at a minimum eye trackers typically sample at 120Hz (120 data points or frames per second), facial expression detection software can sample at 30 Hz, log files and screen recordings are typically at the ms-level, think-alouds will depend on how much or how little the learner is vocalizing their actions, thoughts, or feelings. Thus, not only do we need to ensure the data are aligned with SRL events, but also with each other, such that they are temporally aligned to provide a cohesive data story.

Thus, for every second of a learning session, the data channels provide various data with different amounts of data points generated. We must then align the data channels so we can try to obtain equal amounts of data points for each second. We acknowledge that there are different sampling rates for each data channel and that several dependent variables can be extracted along various quantitative and qualitative continua ranging from frequency and duration to accuracy and efficacy (see Azevedo et al., 2019). These issues remain a challenge for interdisciplinary researchers working in this area. Companies such as iMotions (iMotions, 2018) can provide this service. For example, we can run our studies through the iMotions API platform, which includes connecting and aligning our data streams through the platform. The platform then generates a synched output file that allows us to investigate events in the dataset, calculate data variables, and run analyses to investigate processes during learning with these ALTs.

Evidence from Using Multimodal Multichannel Data

Research examining different CAMM processes during learning greatly benefits from using multimodal multichannel data because we can capture the interplay between different SRL processes as students interact with these systems. In this section, we provide some example studies that have examined SRL using multimodal multichannel data.

In a study conducted by Jaques et al. (2014), they investigated how eye-tracking sequences could be indicative of emotions during learning with MetaTutor. The researchers used machine learning to generate models where eye-gaze patterns predicted self-reported emotions (boredom and curiosity). Results revealed that they were able to predict boredom and curiosity with 69% and 73% accuracy, respectively. This analysis demonstrates how we can use multimodal multichannel (i.e., eye tracking and self-reported emotions) data to investigate learning with MetaTutor. Eye tracking has also been used with log-file data to investigate student performance during game-based learning with Crystal Island. Taub et al. (2017) used multilevel modeling to examine predictors of in-game assessment performance. Results revealed that log-file data (frequency of reading virtual books, frequency of reading each particular book) and eye-tracking data (proportions of fixations on virtual book content and virtual in-game book assessments) significantly predicted performance with a model accounting for 38.99% and 21.82% of the between- and within-subjects variance, respectively. Another study by Taub and Azevedo (2018) combined log-files and facial expression data to examine sequences of hypothesis-testing behavior during game-based learning with Crystal Island (using sequential pattern mining and differential sequence mining techniques), and whether the frequencies of the sequences differed based on how efficient students were at playing the game, and how emotionally expressive they were during gameplay. Results revealed that, in general, students who were more facially expressive and had to make many attempts to solve the mystery correctly generated the greatest amount of testing sequences, indicative of less strategic gameplay because they were testing all items instead of narrowing it down to relevant items only.

All three studies exemplify the benefits of using multimodal multichannel data to investigate SRL during learning with ALTs: if we did not include more data channels, we would not obtain this information regarding the process of how learners are interacting with these systems. It is still unclear, however, which data channel is the most effective tool for measuring learning, and we argue that depending on the specific research questions, different channels are more useful and effective. We discuss this issue in the next session.

Which Data Channel is the Most Effective for Predicting Learning?

Learning from multiple representations is complex and we argue that multimodal multichannel data is key to understanding these underlying processes. But perhaps the most difficult question posed by researchers who use multimodal multichannel data regards which data channel is the most effective for predicting learning. This is because learning is a complex task that involves many components including selecting, organizing, and integrating multiple representations (Mayer, 2014). Thus, there are many different learning-related variables a researcher might be interested in investigating. We discuss a few of these variables in this section. Different data channels will be more effective depending on what is being assessed.

Learning Processes vs. Overall Learning

We argue there is a large difference between investigating learning processes and investigating overall learning, i.e., process versus product. A learning process is typically a measure of learning as it occurs in real-time, or *during* learning. These are the type of data collected when using multimodalities and multichannels, as they investigate the actions, behaviors, thoughts, feelings, etc., exhibited by learners while they are interacting with an ALT. On the other hand, overall learning is a measure of product data. This is the overall outcome *after* learning and is typically measured by assessing post-test scores. We do not believe either measure is invaluable for assessing learning with ALTs, but measuring process data includes the use of multimodal multichannel data, while measuring product data typically does not. In addition, measuring changes in learners' internal representations while learning from external representations within ALTs is quite challenging and requires additional research effort.

Content Learning vs. SRL Learning

A second distinction we argue must be made when assessing learning relates to what type of learning is being measured. Pre- and post-tests are typically administered prior to and following a learning session. These tests typically examine domain knowledge as a learning product. However, sometimes results do not yield significant "learning" effects, with the implication that the ALT is not effective at fostering learning. The ALT may not provide direct evidence of content knowledge learning measured from pre-test to post-test due to various reasons (e.g., not enough time interacting with the ALT, level of difficulty of the tests, misalignment between test and accessibility of multiple representations in the ALT, etc.), but learners might have learned other skills that are not captured on a post-test (e.g., conditional knowledge). For example, the learners might have acquired knowledge of using SRL processes, it is just not measured in the content tests using product data. However, process data might indicate an increase in accuracy of making metacognitive judgments over a learning session, demonstrating acquisition in SRL knowledge and skill use, which can be valuable for a learner as well.

Learning vs. Performance

Another argument we believe is distinguishing between what an individual is learning when interacting with an ALT compared to how they are performing the given task. For example, when learners interact with MetaTutor, they are given an overall learning goal of learning as much as they can about the circulatory system but are then progressed through a sub-goal setting phase where they focus on two specific sub-components of the circulatory system. If they accomplish both of those sub-goals, they performed the task well; however, when administered the post-test, which contains information about all seven sub-goals in the system, they might not achieve high scores, demonstrating poor learning (Azevedo et al., 2016). This a common challenge when creating game-based learning environments as well. As a second example, the Crystal Island narrative instructs learners to solve the mystery of the outbreak on the island. However, at the end of the game, learners are given a content post-test on microbiology, which has yielded fairly low scores (Taub et al., 2018a). This poses a disconnect between learning and performance because if learners are able to solve the mystery, they demonstrate high performance, however their focus might not have been on the microbiology content, leading to poor learning outcomes. Therefore, future ALT designers should aim to eliminate this disconnect to ensure individuals are not only performing the task well but are learning the content as well. It is possible that learners who are exhibiting high performance are also learning how to self-regulate effectively, and so in addition to linking this disconnect, pre- and post-tests should also measure SRL knowledge and skills before and after a learning session.

Based on these distinctions, the question should not be, "which data channel is the most effective," but rather: which data channel is the most effective for predicting a particular process or outcome and why is using a specific data channel the most effective for predicting? Each data channel is unique and advantageous. Data channel decisions should boil down to what processes you are measuring and the research questions you are asking.

CONCLUSIONS AND FUTURE DIRECTIONS

In conclusion, while much research on multiple representations has been published by cognitive scientists, psychologists, learning scientists, STEM researchers, and others, there is still much work to be done in addressing the challenges related to measuring processes and outcomes during learning from multiple representations with ALTs. Specifically, given the complexity of the underlying cognitive, affective, metacognitive, and motivational processes, we argue that using multimodal multichannel data is key to detecting, measuring, and inferring these processes as learners acquire, develop, evolve, use, and transfer their internal representations from learning with the multiple representations that are embedded within ALTs. Future research can take advantage of new virtual, augmented, and mixed reality systems to systematically test assumptions and hypotheses regarding learners' construction of internal representations based on interactions with both physical and virtual external multiple representations within the virtual and augmented reality systems (Johnson-Glenberg, in press).

ACKNOWLEDGMENTS

This chapter was supported by funding from the National Science Foundation (DRL#1660878, DRL#1661202, DUE#1761178, CMMI#1854175, DRL#1916417) and the Social Sciences and Humanities Research Council of Canada (SSHRC 895-2011-1006). Any opinions, findings, conclusions, or recommendations expressed in this material are those of the author(s) and do not necessarily reflect the views of the National Science Foundation or Social Sciences and Humanities Research Council of Canada.

The authors would also like to thank Elizabeth Cloude, Daryn Dever, and Megan Wiedbusch for comments on an earlier version of this chapter and members of the SMART Lab at UCF for their assistance and contributions.

REFERENCES

Azevedo, R., & Gasevic, D. (2019). Analyzing multimodal multichannel data about self-regulated learning with advanced learning technologies: Issues and challenges. *Learning and Instruction, 96*, 207–210.

Azevedo, R., Martin, S. A., Taub, M., Mudrick, N., Millar, G., & Grafsgaard, J. (2016). Are pedagogical agents' external regulation effective in fostering learning with intelligent tutoring systems? In A. Micarelli, J. Stamper, & K. Panourgia (Eds.), *Proceedings of the 13th international conference on intelligent tutoring systems,* Lecture notes in computer science, 9684 (pp. 197–207). Amsterdam: Springer.

Azevedo, R., Mudrick, N. V., Taub, M., & Bradbury, A. E. (2019). Self-regulation in computer-assisted learning systems. In J. Dunlosky & K. Rawson (Eds.), *The Cambridge handbook of cognition and education* (pp. 587–618). Cambridge, MA: Cambridge University Press.

Azevedo, R., Taub, M., & Mudrick, N. V. (2018). Using multichannel trace data to infer and foster self-regulated learning between humans and advanced learning technologies. In D. H. Schunk & J. A. Greene (Eds.), *Handbook of self-regulation of learning and performance* (2nd ed., pp. 254–270). New York: Routledge.

Biswas, G., Baker, R. S., & Paquette, L. (2018). Data mining methods for assessing self-regulated learning. In D. H. Schunk & J. A. Greene (Eds.), *Handbook of self-regulation of learning and performance* (2nd ed., pp. 388–403). New York: Routledge.

Biswas, G., Segedy, J. R., & Bunchongchit, K. (2016). From design to implementation to practice: A learning by teaching system: Betty's brain. *International Journal of Artificial Intelligence in Education, 26*, 350–364.

D'Mello, S. K. (2013). A selective meta-analysis on the relative incidence of discrete affective states during learning with technology. *Journal of Educational Psychology, 105*, 1082–1099.

D'Mello, S. K., & Graesser, A. C. (2015). Feeling, thinking, and computing with affect-aware learning technologie. In R. A. Calvo, S. K. D'Mello, J. Gratch, & A. Kappas (Eds.), *Handbook of affective computing* (pp. 419–434). Oxford: Oxford University Press.

Ekman, P. (1973). *Darwin and facial expression: A century of research in review*. New York: Academic Press.

Ericsson, K., & Simon, H. (1993). *Protocol analysis: Verbal reports as data* (2nd ed.). Boston, MA: MIT Press.

Graesser, A. C. (2016). Conversations with AutoTutor help students learn. *International Journal of Artificial Intelligence in Education, 26*, 124–132.

Grafsgaard, J. F., Wiggins, J. B., Boyer, K. E., Wiebe, E. N., & Lester, J. C. (2014). Predicting learning and affect from multimodal data streams in task-oriented tutorial dialogue. In J. Stamper, Z. Pardos, M. Mavrikis, & B. M. McLaren (Eds.), *Proceedings of the 7th international conference on educational data mining* (pp. 122–129). Worcester, MA: International Educational Data Mining Society.

Greene, J. A., & Azevedo, R. (2009). A macro-level analysis of SRL processes and their relations to the acquisition of sophisticated mental models. *Contemporary Educational Psychology, 34*, 18–29.

Greene, J. A., Deekens, V. M., Copeland, D. Z., & Yu, S. (2018). Capturing and modeling self-regulated learning using think-aloud protocols. In D. H. Schunk & J. A. Greene (Eds.), *Handbook of self-regulation of learning and performance* (2nd ed., pp. 323–337). New York: Routledge.

Gross, J. J. (2015). The extended process model of emotion regulation: Elaborations, applications, and future directions. *Psychological Inquiry, 26*, 130–137.

Harley, J. M., Bouchet, F., Hussain, S., Azevedo, R., & Calvo, R. (2015). A multi-componential analysis of emotions during complex learning with an intelligent multi-agent system. *Computers in Human Behavior, 48*, 615–625.

Harley, J. M., Taub, M., Azevedo, R., & Bouchet, F. (2018). "Let's set up some subgoals": Understanding human-pedagogical agent collaborations and their implications for learning and prompt and feedback compliance. *IEEE Transactions on Learning Technologies, 11*, 54–66.

iMotions. (2018). *Attention Tool*. Version 7.1 [Computer software]. Boston, MA: Author.

Jaques, N., Conati, C., Harley, J., & Azevedo, R. (2014). Predicting affect from gaze data during interaction with an intelligent tutoring system. In S. Trausan-Matu, K. E. Boyer, M. Crosby, & K. Panourgia (Eds.), *Proceedings of the 12th international conference on intelligent tutoring systems,* Lecture notes in computer science, 8474 (pp. 29–38). Amsterdam: Springer.

Johnson-Glenberg, M. C. (in press). Embodied education in mixed and virtual realities: Results and principles for content design. In D. Liu, C. Dede, R. Huang, & J. Richards (Eds.), *Virtual, Augmented, and Mixed Realities in Education*.

Kinnebrew, J. S., Segedy, J. R., & Biswas, G. (2017). Integrating model-driven and data-driven techniques for analyzing learning behaviors in open-ended learning environments. *IEEE Transactions on Learning Technologies, 10*, 140–153.

Krasich, K., McManus, R., Hutt, S., Faber, M., D'Mello, S. K., & Brockmole, J. R. (2018). Gaze-based signatures of mind wandering during real-world scene processing. *Journal of Experimental Psychology: General, 147*, 1111–1124.

Landauer, T., McNamara, D. S., Dennis, S., & Kintsch, W. (Eds.). (2007). *Handbook of latent semantic analysis*. Mahwah, NJ: Erlbaum.

Lester, J. C., Rowe, J. P., & Mott, B. W. (2013). Narrative-centered learning environments: A story-centric approach to educational games. In C. Mouza & N. Lavigne (Eds.), *Emerging technologies for the classroom: A learning sciences perspective* (pp. 223–238). New York: Springer.

Loderer, K., Pekrun., R., & Lester, J. (in press). Beyond cold technology: A systematic review and meta-analysis on emotions in technology-based learning environments. *Learning and Instruction*.

Mayer, R. E. (2014). Cognitive theory of multimedia learning. In R. E. Mayer (Ed.), *The Cambridge handbook of multimedia learning* (2nd ed., pp. 43–71). Cambridge: Cambridge University Press.

McLaren, B. M., Adams, D., Mayer, R., & Forlizzi, J. (2017). A computer-based game that promotes mathematics learning more than a conventional approach. *International Journal of Game Learning, 7*, 36–56.

Rayner, K. (2009). The 35th Sir Frederick Bartlett Lecture: Eye movements and attention in reading, scene perception, and visual search. *Quarterly Journal of Experimental Psychology, 62*, 1457–1506.

Sabourin, J. L., & Lester, J. C. (2014). Affect and engagement in game-based learning environments. *IEEE Transactions on Affective Computing, 5*, 45–56.

Smith, A., Leeman-Munk, S., Shelton, A., Mott, B., Wiebe, E., & Lester, J. (2019). A multimodal assessment framework for integrating student writing and drawing in elementary science learning. *IEEE Transactions on Learning Technologies, 12*, 3–15.

Sweller, J., van Merriënboer, J. J. G., & Paas, F. (2019). Cognitive architecture and instructional design: 20 years later. *Educational Psychology Review, 31*(2), 1–32.

Taub, M., & Azevedo, R. (2018). Using sequence mining to assess metacognitive monitoring and scientific inquiry based on levels of efficiency and emotional expressivity during game-based learning. *Journal of Educational Data Mining, 10*, 1–26.

Taub, M., & Azevedo, R. (2019). How does prior knowledge influence eye fixations and sequences of cognitive and metacognitive SRL processes during learning with and intelligent tutoring system? *International Journal of Artificial Intelligence in Education, 29*, 1–28.

Taub, M., Azevedo, R., Bradbury, A. E., Millar, G. C., & Lester, J. (2018a). Using sequence mining to reveal the efficiency in scientific reasoning during STEM learning with a game-based learning environment. *Learning and Instruction, 54*, 93–103.

Taub, M., Azevedo, R., Rajendran, R., Cloude, E., Biswas, G., & Price, M. (in press). How are students' emotions related to the accuracy of cognitive and metacognitive processes during learning with an intelligent tutoring system? *Learning and Instruction*.

Taub, M., Mudrick, N. V., & Azevedo, R. (2018b). Strategies for designing advanced learning technologies to foster self-regulated learning. In R. Zheng (Ed.), *Strategies for deep learning with digital technology: Theories and practices in education* (pp. 137–170). Amsterdam: Springer.

Taub, M., Mudrick, N. V., Azevedo, R., Millar, G. C., Rowe, J., & Lester, J. (2017). Using multi-channel data with multi-level modeling to assess in-game performance during gameplay with CRYSTAL ISLAND. *Computers in Human Behavior, 76*, 641–655.

Taub, M., Mudrick, N. V., Rajendran, R., Dong, Y., Biswas, G., & Azevedo, R. (2018c). How are students' emotions associated with the accuracy of their note taking and summarizing during learning with ITSs? In R. Nkambou, R. Azevedo, & J. Vassileva (Eds.), *Proceedings of the 14th international conference on intelligent tutoring systems (ITS 2018)* (pp. 233–242). Amsterdam: Springer.

Trevors, G., Duffy, M., & Azevedo, R. (2014). Note-taking within metaTutor: Interactions between an intelligent tutoring system and prior knowledge on note-taking and learning. *Educational Technology Research and Development, 62*, 507–528.

Van Eck, R. N., Shute, V. J., & Rieber, L. P. (2017). Leveling up: Game design research and practice for instructional designers. In R. Reiser & J. Dempsey (Eds.), *Trends and issues in instructional design and technology* (4th ed., pp. 227–285). New York: Pearson.

Veinott, E. S., Leonard, J., Lerner, E., Perelman, B., Hale, C., Catrambone, R., … Hoffman, R. R. (2013). The effect of camera perspective and session duration on training decision making in a serious video game. In *IEEE international games innovation conference* (pp. 256–262). IEEE.

Winne, P. H., & Hadwin, A. F. (2008). The weave of motivation and self-regulated learning. In D. Schunk & B. Zimmerman (Eds.), *Motivation and self-regulated learning: Theory, research, and applications* (pp. 297–314). Mahwah, NJ: Erlbaum.

Winne, P. H. (2018). Cognition and metacognition within self-regulated learning. In D. H. Schunk & J. A. Greene (Eds.), *Handbook of self-regulation of learning and performance* (2nd ed., pp. 36–48). New York: Routledge.

Conclusion

31

THE MULTIPLE RESOURCES LEARNING FRAMEWORK
Learning from Multiple Representations and Multiple Perspectives

Peggy Van Meter
PENNSYLVANIA STATE UNIVERSITY

Alexandra List
PENNSYLVANIA STATE UNIVERSITY

Panayiota Kendeou
UNIVERSITY OF MINNESOTA

Doug Lombardi
UNIVERSITY OF MARYLAND, COLLEGE PARK

ABSTRACT

This concluding chapter reviews and integrates the points of convergence and divergence in this *Handbook* and the extant literatures on learning from multiple representations and learning from multiple perspectives. Our efforts resulted in the proposal of an integrated theoretical framework, the Multiple Resources Learning Framework (MRLF). The MRLF identifies five dimensions that are central to multiple resources learning: Context, Task and Resources, Learner Characteristics, Learner Processes, and Construction. The goal of the MRLF is to stimulate new lines of research by identifying theoretical and conceptual gaps at the intersections of these literatures.

Key words: multiple representations, multimedia, multiple perspectives, integration

INTRODUCTION

The motivation for this *Handbook* was to bring together two lines of research that have much in common yet have been pursued through separate bodies of scholarship. One of these is the study of learning from multiple representations, or multimedia. Multiple representations refers to the set of representations a person is learning from, where each representation provides some, but not all, of the to-be-learned content. These representations come in a variety of forms and modalities including spoken or written text, diagrams, graphs, and formulas. Learning from these requires understanding individual representations and integrating or synthesizing them into a connected whole. The second line of research is the study of learning from multiple perspectives. Perspectives refer to the point(s) of view reflected within a particular representation, most typically in text. For any complex topic, multiple perspectives are often involved and successful learning requires understanding, juxtaposing, and evaluating these varied ways of thinking to understand a common issue.

The commonality between these two bodies of research lies in their attention to questions of how learners acquire and construct knowledge when that knowledge is encountered across distinct, and multiple, resources. How, that is, does one construct complete and coherent mental representations when the information is given in pieces? Historically, educational research has been concerned with learning from individual resources (Britt, Rouet, & Braasch, 2012; Van Meter & Firetto, 2008), but researchers have increasingly recognized that learning from multiple resources is both ubiquitous in today's information-rich society and, in many respects, qualitatively different from learning with single resources. These qualitative differences mean that learners do not simply gain quantitatively more knowledge with each additional resource inspected. Instead, multiple resource learning requires the learner to also actively determine the relations across resources and construct a mental representation that is globally coherent and more complete than what can be achieved with a single resource alone (Ainsworth, 1999; Britt, Perfetti, Sandak, & Rouet, 1999; Wylie & Chi, 2014). And herein lies another foundational principle shared across the scholarship on learning from multiple representations and from multiple perspectives; namely, the belief that integrating across resources is desirable because it results in the construction of high-quality mental representations. Evidence across both lines of research demonstrates that integrating across resources supports performance on higher-order knowledge assessments, such as those targeting mental model revision (Butcher, 2006; Cromley, Snyder-Hogan, & Luciw-Dubas, 2010) and argumentative writing (List, Du, Wang, & Lee, 2019; Wiley & Voss, 1999). Moreover, researchers across these fields have increasingly come to recognize that integrating across resources is a necessary precondition of learning in the 21st century (Goldman & Scardamalia, 2013; List & Alexander, 2018b).

In this chapter, we identify common themes from the research on learning from multiple representations and from multiple perspectives and propose a theoretical framework that juxtaposes these two lines of work. Our primary goal is to conceptualize learning from multiple resources, regardless of the specific form these resources take; and, subsequently, draw attention to the broader theoretical, empirical, and pedagogical implications of such learning. Where do these two lines of research converge on consistent conclusions and where do they diverge? How can the research on learning from multiple representations and from multiple perspectives be aligned and what can be learned from gaps in this alignment? What new theoretical constructs emerge from comparisons across these two lines of research? The following sections present our thinking on these questions. We begin with a discussion of the major themes that emerged by juxtaposing the literatures on learning from multiple representations and from multiple perspectives. This is followed by our presentation of the Multiple Resources Learning Framework (MRLF), a framework that integrates these two areas of research and outlines future directions.

EMERGING THEMES: LINKING LITERATURES ON LEARNING FROM MULTIPLE REPRESENTATIONS AND MULTIPLE PERSPECTIVES

Our efforts to bridge the literatures on learning from multiple presentations and from multiple perspectives began by identifying major themes that arose as we read and discussed the chapters in this *Handbook*. These thematic distinctions consider (a) the resources that students have available, (b) the relations among resources that students may need to form, and (c) the tasks that students are responding to. These themes are organized according to the *differences* and *similarities* in the research on learning from multiple representations and multiple perspectives.

Learning from Multiple Representations and Perspectives: Thematic Differences

Relations among Resources and Learner Processing

The first distinction rests in how these literatures conceptualize the resources in relation to one another and what these relations mean for the learner who must translate across resources. Whether multiple representations or multiple perspectives, all resources in a set share some topic and content overlap. These two areas of research are distinct, however, in the *ways* that they view resources as varying; that is, whether learners are being asked to move between different symbolic formats or navigate different points of view. This distinction has implications for both the content of the resources and the processes a learner must execute during a multiple resource learning task.

In the research on multiple representation learning, resource representations typically vary according to symbolic format and learning requires translating and transforming these systems (Ainsworth, 1999; van der Meij & de Jong, 2011). A mathematics student, for example, has to translate between pictures and formulas when solving mathematics problems (Stylianou, Chapter 8) and expert chemists use movements between representations to support reasoning and explain concepts (Kozma, Chapter 3). Even when two representations are both visualizations (i.e., non-verbal), differences in their specific form still require fluent movement between them (Rau, Chapter 2). Although these variations present challenges for learners, an advantage is that the representations present a consistent message while each conveys some aspect of the content more effectively than some other representation (Kottmeyer, Van Meter, & Cameron, in press; Schnotz & Baadte, 2015). And, together, the representations present a more complete presentation than can be achieved with any one representation. It is the consistency across representations that underlies the prime benefit of multiple representations. A learner, that is, can leverage this consistency to map two representations onto one another so that both the overlapping content and the content unique to each representation is held in a single, globally coherent mental representation.

While the resources of multiple representations use different formats but maintain consistency in content messaging, this pattern tends to be reversed when learning from multiple perspectives. Multiple perspective resources, to this point, have been investigated as composed using the same symbolic format, typically that of written text (cf. List, 2018; Van Meter & Cameron, 2018). At the same time, multiple perspectives may be related to one another in a multitude of ways; representing overlapping, distinct yet complementary, discrepant, and directly conflicting relations introduced either across texts or within a single resource (List & Alexander, 2019; Bohn-Gettler, Chapter 15). For instance, students might encounter conflicting viewpoints when learning the history of their hometown through the perspective of different groups (Cho et al., Chapter 17) or need to balance competing economic and ecological needs when evaluating a controversial issue (List, Chapter 11).

In some cases, differences in perspectives could be mere differences in how to interpret some set of facts (Rapp, Donovan, & Salovich, Chapter 25; Lombardi, Heddy, & Matewos, Chapter 20). In other cases though, information may be deliberately misleading, one-sided, inaccurate, or false (Kendeou, Harsch, Butterfuss, Aubele, & Kim, Chapter 27). In this respect, the multiple perspectives research has often examined learning when resources are generated, not by some objective authority, but by varying sources of, at least sometimes, questionable quality (Braasch & Scharrer, Chapter 13). For the learner working with multiple perspectives then, the consistency of the verbal system can be used to connect across resources; shared words can be used to map one perspective onto another. But the learner must also determine where and how these perspectives differ and just how they can and should be related (Alexander & DRLRL, Chapter 23; Sanderson & Ecker, Chapter 26).

Of course, these differences in cross-resource relations are sensible given the goal of the respective areas of research. In the research on multiple representations, there is a recognition of the limitations of any single representational systems and questions regarding how learners can leverage a set of representations to abstract a mental model of some concept. Research on multiple perspectives recognizes that there are different ways of looking at any complex topic and questions how learners can actively corroborate, evaluate, and validate critical information. These differences in cross-resource relations found in the two bodies of research correspond to differences in some of the factors that influence what is learned. This is true despite a number of similarities in the learning processes envisioned by researchers examining learning from multiple representation and from multiple perspectives. That is, although learners in both contexts must integrate across resources to achieve global coherence, learners studying multiple representations must work to find correspondence across distinct symbolic formats and those working with multiple perspectives must recognize, evaluate, and relate potentially disparate points of view. As we worked toward our goal of connecting these two bodies of research, we recognized that these differences are non-trivial and that any synthesis of this work must leave space for these specific aspects of the learning process to be delineated and explained.

Resource Characteristics

It has long been established that learning can be affected by the surface features of a resource. Surface features refer to the *way* in which information is presented, such as its organization or appearance. However, surface features do not alter what information is presented (i.e., deep structure). Studies of text processing demonstrate that surface features such as cohesion (McNamara, Kintsch, Songer, & Kintsch, 1996), formatting (e.g., headings, Hyönä & Lorch, 2004), and text presentation, digitally or in print (Mangen, Olivier, & Velay, 2019), influence learning. Likewise, learning from visual representations can be affected by characteristics such as complexity (e.g., Butcher, 2006) and formatting (e.g., Schnotz & Baadte, 2015). The study of learning from multiple resources extends these areas of research by further considering how the surface features of a particular resource may be perceived in relation to a broader resource set. Thus, researchers studying learning from multiple resources also think about resource features that influence cross-resource global coherence. Where the research on multiple representations and multiple perspectives diverges, however, is with respect to the types of surface characteristics that ought to be manipulated in order to achieve desired learning outcomes.

As described in the previous section, multiple representations use different symbolic formats and conventions, but typically convey a consistent message. The task for one who is studying multiple representations is to determine these consistencies and use them to map the content of one representation onto another. The resource characteristics that are manipulated and tested in multiple representations research follow from the premise that effective manipulations are ones that ease the burden of locating and mapping correspondences across representations (Van Meter & Stepanik, Chapter 6). This premise has stimulated a substantial body of research on instructional design principles that can be applied to multiple representations. Learning, for example, is improved when two representations are presented in an integrated format, rather than separated (e.g., Johnson & Mayer, 2012), or when signals that explicitly mark cross-representation connections are included (e.g., Ozcelik, Arslan-Ari, & Cagiltay, 2010). Altogether, this research shows that learning improves when resource characteristics are manipulated to highlight the connections across representations that use different symbolic formats to convey a consistent, complementary message.

The resource characteristics thought to influence multiple perspectives learning are less concerned with signaling correspondence and, instead, focus on factors that influence how a learner attends to, evaluates, and uses the information presented. When two perspectives present complementary information, the learner must synthesize these. When two perspectives introduce conflicting views on some topic, the learner must evaluate the respective arguments and make some determination of how to resolve these. In cases of conflict, that is, the two resources are evaluated against one another and characteristics that influence how a particular resource fares in this comparison will ultimately influence the learner's understanding of the topic (Braasch & Scharrer, Chapter 13; Sanderson & Ecker, Chapter 26). These resource characteristics include varying the format of resource presentation in a search menu to stimulate cross-resource connection formation (Salmerón, Baccino, Cañas, Madrid, & Fajardo, 2009) and introducing indicators that identify sources as more or less credible (Kendeou et al, Chapter 27; Rapp et al., Chapter 25; Richter, Münchow, & Abendroth, Chapter 16). Emerging findings from this body of research show that resource characteristics do influence judgments of utility and credibility and that these judgments ultimately influence what is learned (Braasch & Scharrer, Chapter 13; Lombardi et al., Chapter 20).

Regardless of whether one is studying multiple representations or multiple perspectives, one thing is clear: Learning is affected by characteristics of the studied resources. When considering this point from the level of multiple resources, however, the picture becomes murkier. Our efforts to synthesize these two literatures shows that they depart at the point where specific characteristics are identified as significant. And, again, these differences are consistent with the learning objectives held within the respective areas of research. The objective when learning from multiple representations is to leverage cross-representation consistencies to construct a holistic understanding. Consequently, learning is affected by resource characteristics that influence the detection of these consistencies, with such detection often aided by explicitly linking representations to one another via referential text (e.g., inserting "See Figure 1" into a text) or color cues. While learning from multiple perspectives also requires learners to relate resources, here, the learner must be sensitive to a broader range of possible relations, including conflicts and inconsistencies. Effective resource manipulations in this context are ones that aid the learner in evaluating and validating different perspectives in order to make sense of the information provided. At the same time, resources themselves are rarely modified to create an explicit link to other resources, as authors writing from distinct perspectives rarely cross-reference one another. Instead, learners are required to construct cross-resource connections. Ultimately then, any framework that ties these two fields of study together will need to identify the importance of resource characteristics but define broadly the meaning of this category.

Learning Tasks

A third distinction that should be drawn between the research on multiple representations and multiple perspectives concerns the structure of the content that learners are asked to master and the tasks that learners are asked to complete. Here, we draw on the literature in problem solving to think about well- and ill-structured problems (Mayer & Wittrock, 1996). Whereas well-structured problems have clearly defined boundaries and expect specific solutions, ill-structured problems are more ambiguous with respect to both content and solutions. Looking across the research on multiple resource learning, we can see that multiple representations sets are typically used in service of well-structured learning goals but the introduction of multiple perspectives tends to correspond to more ill-structured, open-ended tasks.

Learning from multiple representations is typically studied in the context of STEM (i.e., science, technology, engineering, mathematics) where the objective is to learn the structures, functioning, and effects of some well-defined system. Students, for example, may learn about systems of molecules and reactions to solve chemical problems (Kozma, Chapter 3) or construct representations to learn mathematical principles (Stylianou, Chapter 8). Although open-ended probes are often used to assess higher-order abilities such as conceptual transfer (Johnson & Mayer, 2012) and mental model revision (Cromley et al., 2010), these probes are typically well-structured in nature with a clearly defined, externally determined problem space (Jonassen, 1997), and desired responses that are discrete, with clear definitions around accuracy and inaccuracy (Mayer & Wittrock, 1996).

Multiple perspective learning tasks, by contrast, are typically encountered in association with topics that are more socio-scientific in nature and with tasks that are considerably more open-ended. Consider, for example, research by Nussbaum and Edwards (2011) in which middle-school students learned about controversial issues such as causes of current climate change, raising local taxes to fight hunger, and whether torture is acceptable to obtain information from terrorists. These tasks ask students to develop some general understanding of a topic or issue and to relate this understanding to an external audience, typically through writing and with responses evaluated for quality, rather than for accuracy, *per se* (Azevedo & Taub, Chapter 30; Firetto, Chapter 14). Thus, students learning from multiple perspectives are left with the responsibility to determine which aspects of various perspectives ought to be represented for a comprehensive description of a given topic or issue.

In sum, a comparison of these respective literatures shows that the two are pursuing different types of learning tasks and objectives. In typical studies of learning from multiple representations, the goal is to organize and integrate varied representations to converge on a single solution (Cromley et al., 2013). Conversely, in learning from multiple perspectives the goal is more likely to be to organize and systematize the divergence across perspectives and a single solution may not be tenable (Daher & Kiewra, 2016; Felton & Kuhn, 2001). Responses to tasks that assess learning from multiple representations can be evaluated according to their accuracy and the completeness of the content knowledge acquired. Parallel tasks assessing learning from multiple perspectives, on the other hand, are typically scored using a much more diverse set of criteria (Firetto, Chapter 14). Attending to these variations across different multiple resource learning activities is important because they likely affect more than just the content and tasks of learning (Azevedo & Taub, Chapter 30). There are also implications for how teachers and students will understand the task and the corresponding learning goals that are set.

Learning from Multiple Representations and Perspectives: Thematic Similarities

Despite the differences described above, we remain optimistic about the potential of integrating these two literatures because there are also similarities that permit points of contact and opportunities to find convergence around questions of how learners manage and integrate multiple resources. The remainder of this section discusses these similarities around three themes that emerged from our reading of these literatures.

Theoretical Frameworks

The research on both multiple representations and multiple perspectives learning is grounded in a common set of theoretical frameworks. Specifically, both lines of research are primarily informed by cognitive and, to a lesser degree, socio-cultural theories. Cognitive theories have been used to underpin the cognitive and metacognitive operations a learner uses when studying either representations or perspectives. There are some differences in the specific processes examined across the two, such as the concern with cross-representation transitions found in the research on multiple representations (Schüler, Chapter 4) and epistemic cognition discussed in relation to multiple perspective learning (Bråten & Strømsø, Chapter 10). On the whole, however, both lines of research are grounded in common assumptions and questions about the cognitive processes underlying learning from multiple resources. A few of these include the belief that learners must attend to information in a resource to bring that information into a limited capacity working memory system where cognitive and metacognitive operations are applied to construct a mental representation. Links between new and prior knowledge are generated during this construction process as inferences to connect across resources. Ultimately, the knowledge that is constructed is stored in long-term memory where it will remain until called upon at some later time. The key point in noting the similarities between multiple representations and multiple perspectives learning is that these general assumptions hold regardless of the type of resource studied.

Socio-cultural frameworks have also been applied in both lines of research, although these have been far less prevalent than cognitive theory. In general, socio-cultural frameworks posit that learning happens in a social context, where that context holds elements such as disciplinary and conventional practices, potential collaborations, and available supports and scaffolds. Through this lens, each resource in a set is understood as an artifact of the social context that can be used to support and guide thinking. It is this theoretical framework that draws attention to such phenomena as experts' use of multiple representations during disciplinary practices (Kozma, Chapter 3) and learners' construction of representations and knowledge expressions to support thinking (Ainsworth, Tytler, & Prain, Chapter 7; Stylinaou, Chapter 8). With respect to learning from multiple perspectives, we see learners' aims for seeking out and engaging with multiple perspectives as arising from and within particular epistemic and ontic traditions, representing varied sociocultural contexts (Barzilai & Weinstock, Chapter 9; Bråten & Strømsø, Chapter 10; List, Chapter 11).

These theoretical frameworks provide a means to connect the two lines of work because they point toward shared assumptions and causal learning processes. With respect to cognitive theory, both areas of research assume that high-quality mental representations are constructed by integrating across the resources in a set. Critical questions concern just how cross-resource relations are determined and how the integration of resources can be supported. Socio-cultural theory raises questions about how multiple resources are embedded in social practices and interactions. From this theoretical perspective, all resources are inherently tools of thinking and communication, whether these be viewpoints shared on a blog or visual depictions of some system. Accordingly, application of socio-cultural theory to multiple representations and multiple perspectives learning raises similar questions of how learners understand and use resources in a socio-cultural context.

Cognitive Operations

We also find deeper connections in the specific cognitive operations identified in the two bodies of research. The research on learning from multiple representations, which has been heavily influenced by the Cognitive Theory of Multimedia Learning (Mayer, 2014; Rau, Chapter 2), has identified the selection, organization, and integration of information across auditory and visual channels and with prior knowledge as the key learning mechanisms. Although the processes involved in learning from multiple perspectives have yet to be fully articulated, chapters in this *Handbook* suggest that these may involve (a) the recognition and representation of various perspectives, (b) their comparison to one another and (c) their evaluation. The related field of learning from multiple texts introduces theoretical models that suggest that such learning involves, in part, the (a) selection, (b) processing, and (c) integration of information presented across texts (Rouet, Britt, & Durik, 2017).

Looking across, one can see commonalities in the key cognitive processes underlying learning from multiple representations and multiple perspectives. Specifically, this learning involves, at least: (1) the selection of important or relevant information from amongst a varied data stream, (2) processing that leads to the comprehension of selected information, and (3) the integration of varied data points into a cohesive whole. This latter integration process is of particular interest to us in this *Handbook*. We view this integration process as both comparative and constructive in nature, allowing disparate aspects of information to be analyzed and contrasted as well as assimilated and combined into a rich, synthetic representation. Moreover, we view this integration process expansively as carried out across representations, across new information and learners' prior knowledge, and across perspectives. We do, however, also believe that these processes are better understood as relational and comparative rather than only integrative. Our rationale for this is more fully explained in the later section of this chapter that describes the learning processes of multiple resource learning but, for now, we point out that a learner must determine just how two resources could or should be related before the two can be integrated (Alexander & the DRLRL, Chapter 23).

Task Complexity

A striking similarity between learning from multiple representations and from multiple perspectives is that the topics and tasks addressed in this research tend to be complex. In short, both of these literatures deal with students' learning about "variables and processes, that appear random, with nondeterministic outcomes" (Goldman, 2003, p. 239). In other words, multiple representations are often provided to facilitate students' problem solving and understanding of complex systems and phenomena, ones that cannot be effectively communicated through words alone (Chen & Lin, Chapter 29; Morgan, Hogan, Hampton, Lipert, & Graesser, Chapter 28). Likewise, multiple perspectives are often introduced about topics that are complex, multifaceted, or controversial in nature or topics that, by their very nature, cannot be fully encapsulated within one perspective (Britt et al., 2012). Moreover, both learning from multiple representations and from multiple perspectives often require an understanding of the domains from which these originate, with specific external representations recognized as reflecting the conventions used to communicate in different domains (Kozma, 2003), in-and-of themselves potentially constituting different perspectives on interdisciplinary topics (List, Chapter 11; Sadler, 2011; Sadler, Barab, & Scott, 2007).

We see this complexity as arising, at least in part, from the need to understand the "information diet" of today's learners, both within schools and beyond. That is, just as it would be difficult to imagine that students accessing any website on the Internet today would be presented with information via only one medium or representational format, it would likewise be unrealistic to expect learners to only encounter "objective" information, devoid of perspective. Harkening back to early definitions of texts, as authored entities, composed by someone for some purpose (Alexander & Fox,

2004), we view the information resources that students encounter today as necessarily encoded via some symbol or representational system(s) and as inherently perspective-bound. As such, integrating the literatures on learning from multiple representations and from multiple perspectives represents a much needed yet inherently complex conceptualization of the information resources available to learners today.

THE MULTIPLE RESOURCES LEARNING FRAMEWORK

While it is necessary to identify the similarities and differences across these two lines of research, a simple listing of these is insufficient to harness the potential of their synergies. Toward that goal, we propose a framework that synthesizes these two literatures by placing them within the same organizational structure. This framework, which we call the Multiple Resource Learning Framework (MRLF; see Figure 31.1), was generated by looking across the chapters in this *Handbook*, as well as our knowledge of the extant literature, and identifying common themes and points of contact. Organizing these literatures according to their commonalities permitted the major dimensions of multiple resource learning to emerge. It is clear from a reading of the chapters in this *Handbook*, for instance, that learner characteristics influence learning from both multiple representations and multiple perspectives (Bråten & Strømsø, Chapter 10; Cromley, Chapter 6; McCrudden, Chapter 12). Likewise, both literatures recognize the importance of learning within a context as well as the specific processes that the learner executes (Ainsworth, Chapter, 7; Braasch & Scharrer, Chapter 15; Chen & Lin, Chapter 29; Firetto, Chapter 14; Kozma, Chapter 3; Richter, Maier, & Münchow, Chapter 16; Schüler, Chapter 4). Ultimately, five dimensions were identified: Context, Task and Learning Resources, Learner Characteristics, Learner Processes, and Construction.

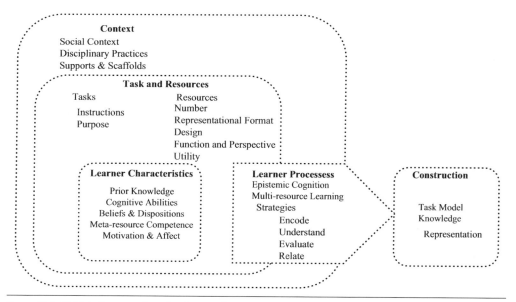

Figure 31.1 Multiple Resources Learning Framework.

We used these five dimensions to group specific constructs from the research literature (e.g., spatial ability, instructional scaffolds). Categorizing these constructs allowed us to identify factors that capture the intersections of the multiple representation and multiple perspective literatures. Constructs such as working memory, executive function, and epistemic and ontic beliefs, for example, can be grouped under a cognitive abilities factor; manipulations of the resources themselves, such as source structure (i.e., one-sided or dual position, Bohn-Gettler, Chapter 15) or changing the spatial arrangement of representations, can be grouped under the factor of resource design.

Altogether then, the MRLF organizes the literatures on multiple representations and multiple perspectives learning into a single framework comprised of five dimensions, with each dimension defined by the specific factors it contains. These factors shape the nature of multiple resource learning (see Figure 31.1). Before we describe the framework itself, we should first explain our reasoning for labeling this a framework and what we believe its utility may be. We forward a framework, rather than a model or theory, because we stop short of specifying all of the dynamic relations across factors within it. We do identify some of these in a broad and illustrative sense as we explain the framework below, but the MRLF does not specify these relations at the causal, mechanistic level necessary to generate a complete set of hypotheses as necessary for a theory or model. There are two main reasons for this. First, such a set of specifications is simply too ambitious for this single chapter. As the reader will see, the MRLF includes nearly 20 broad factors situated within five dimensions. This yields an exponential number of possible interactions and specifying each of these is well beyond both the scope of this chapter and the empirical foundation on which this framework is based. Second, models of the learning process already exist within the respective fields of study (e.g., Documents Model, Britt et al., 2012; CTML, Mayer, 2014; RESOLV, Rouet et al., 2017; ITPC, Schnotz, 2005). These models have successfully stimulated productive lines of research and we see no need to compete with them.

If the MRLF is not intended as a dynamic model, then how do we intend its use? The answer to this is two-fold. First, the MRLF can stimulate new research even though it does not specify construct-level hypotheses. This is because the MRLF does identify some compelling theoretical and empirical gaps between the two areas of research. In some cases, for example, constructs that have been vigorously pursued in one line of research have been virtually ignored in the other. Second, thinking about how points of emphasis in the two literatures can be synthesized into broader factors stimulates the conceptual thinking necessary to theorize about the nature of multiple resource learning. Such thinking, we believe, is essential to realize the potential synergies between these two independent lines of research and begin translating these into empirical and practical applications. Drawing on the 'Multiple Resource Forest through the Trees' metaphor presented in our introduction to this *Handbook* (List, Van Meter, Lombardi, & Kendeou, Chapter 1), we offer the MRLF as an opportunity to look occasionally at the multiple resource forest in which our respective representation and perspective trees are situated; to consider what might be gained by thinking of today's learner as ones who must traverse this forest, gathering resources and building log cabins within it. Just what are the landmarks and navigational aids that might support the learner and how might we design and draw learners' attention to these?

With these points in mind, the remainder of this section presents an explanation of the MRLF. The framework, which is shown in Figure 31.1, depicts the five major dimensions that influence multiple resource learning. This graphic depiction reveals three main assumptions underlying the MRLF. The first assumption is that the dimensions can be organized into different layers of influence. In particular, we see the learner, with associated Learner Characteristics, as embedded within a particular Task and Resources set. These Learner Characteristics and Task/Resources dimensions are immersed in the Context and together, these dimensions influence Learner Processes. The second assumption is revealed by the arrow-shaped box connecting Learner Processing and Construction, positioning Construction as external to the other four dimensions. We see Construction as holding the mental representations the learner builds through task engagement, with such task engagement captured in the Learner Processes. In this respect, these processes are the direct influence on what knowledge is constructed. Other dimensions, such as Context and the Task/Resources, exert their influence on Construction via these Learner Processes. Construction is externally situated because this dimension holds the constructed knowledge products that the learner is able to take away from any particular multiple resource task. The final assumption is that there are multiple, reciprocal, and dynamic relationships across dimensions. The dotted lines in Figure 31.1 depict permeable membranes to show that the flow of influence between and among dimensions is inherent in multiple resource learning. In designing the framework, our author team discussed, and rejected, the idea of depicting these relations with boxes and double-sided arrows showing multi-directional influences between separate dimensions. We rejected this depiction because it implies that each dimension is a silo, which then exerts an effect on some other silo. By contrast, the notion of permeable membranes communicates the enmeshed nature of these relationships; although each dimension can be independently defined, they all operate together.

Contained within each dimension are the factors that emerged from our review of the chapters in this *Handbook*. In the sections that follow, these dimensions are explained along with brief descriptions of how the factors, included within each dimension, have been explored in the research on learning from multiple representations and from multiple perspectives. We also discuss some of the gaps in our current knowledge of learning from multiple resources that are brought to light by the MRLF. Due to space limitations, we limit this discussion to only one or two points within each dimension, but our hope is that this partial presentation might stimulate further thought about the areas in need of additional empirical and theoretical work.

DIMENSIONS OF THE MULTIPLE RESOURCE LEARNING FRAMEWORK

Task and Resources Dimension

Table 31.1 shows the specific factors that comprise the Task and Resources dimension. This dimension captures what the learner is working on and the resources available for doing that work. The Task factors of this dimension include both the task as it is given to the learner (i.e., instructions) and the learner's own reasons, or purpose, for task completion. Tasks have been taxonomized in a variety of ways (McCrudden,

Table 31.1 Factors in the Task and Resources Dimension of the Multiple Resources Learning Framework

Factor	Category Definition and Description
Tasks	
Instructions	Externally provided task directions and definitions. May be explicit or implicit.
Purpose	Learner's reason for engaging in the task. Includes learner's understanding of instructions, the learner's goals for the task, and the standards for achieving those goals.
Resources	
Number	The number of physically separable resources. Counted by the number of physical representations or different perspectives.
Representational Format	Symbolic system of the representation, such as verbal or visual. Includes formatting of the symbol system; e.g., photograph or artist's drawing; opinion-editorial or expository essay.
Design	The instructional design and physical layout of resources. Includes instructional design manipulations to representations such as spatial layout and signals; presentation of source information (e.g., print vs. digital, single vs. multiple).
Function and Perspective	Indications in the resource set of how a resource can or should be used. Includes the intended and realized functions of multiple representations (Ainsworth, 1999) and the different areas of knowledge filled by particular viewpoints.

Magliano, & Schraw, 2011; McCrudden & Schraw, 2007), most commonly as either requiring students to locate specific information across resources or to develop a more global understanding (Cerdan & Vidal-Abarca., 2008). Tasks can further be analyzed as asking students to engage in a particular approach to processing or to produce some type of product (McCrudden & Bohn-Gettler, 2019). Across these various dimensions, task has been found to be a robust factor impacting students' multi-resource processing (see also Cromley, Chapter 6; Gil, Bråten, Vidal-Abarca, & Strømsø, 2010; Wiley & Voss, 1999).

Under the Resources factor, we consider both the (a) surface features that are used to represent information within a resource and (b) resource function and perspective, which capture the deep structure of a resource, arising from author intent in resource construction. Surface features include the three factors of number, format, and design. Each of these factors reference some surface features or physical characteristics of the resources so that these factors address the appearance and structure of the resources. At the most basic level, these characteristics reflect features of the encoding or symbol systems used within a particular resource (e.g., words, image, graphs). Each symbol system has a unique vocabulary and grammatical structure for the information that it represents. For instance, while color, shape, and size may be important in images (i.e., realistic, depictive, abstract, explanatory, Wiley, Sarmento, Griffin, & Hinze, 2017), Greek symbols and orders of operations are important in formula reading. Reviewing the various grammars that define and characterize different symbol systems has been done extensively in prior work and is beyond the scope of this chapter (e.g., Bednarz, Acheson, & Bednarz, 2006; Kress & van Leeuwen, 1996; Lemke, 1998; Serafini, 2011). Here we say only that, although these conventions serve a communicative function, they are inconsistently applied so that a surface characteristic can have different meanings in different representations (Griffard, 2013; Tversky, Zacks, Lee, & Heiser, 2000). Consequently, students must learn how these systems are used within different domains while simultaneously using these unfamiliar representations to acquire new knowledge (i.e., representation dilemma; Rau, Chapter 2).

Resources factors that align with the deep structure of a resource are the function and perspective factors. These factors address resource characteristics that support or influence the relating of resources to one another. These factors reflect the connections across resources that may be intended by authors (e.g., writing a response to an op-ed) or may be constructed by learners. In describing relations among multiple representations, Ainsworth (1999, 2006) suggests that instructional designers should be intentional about identifying one of three potential functions for the relations across resources; a complementary (e.g., providing distinct information or facilitating different processing), constraining (e.g., one representation narrows the interpretation of another), or constructing (i.e., allowing deeper understanding) function. When extended across multiple resources, the relations that can be identified are much more numerous and complex, with consistent or corroborative, complementary, conflicting, or causal information potentially presented (e.g., Anmarkrud, Bråten, & Strømsø, 2014; List et al., 2019; Wiley et al., 2009; Wolfe & Goldman, 2005). Collectively, these relations can be conceptualized according to their degree of (a) *explicitness* (e.g., semantic or representational overlap across resources, Hastings, Hughes, Magliano, Goldman, & Lawless, 2012), (b) *complexity*, in the number of resources and connections involved (List et al., 2019), and (c) *abstraction* (e.g., causal relations vis-à-vis thematic associations, Wolfe & Goldman, 2005) – with all of these features making the formation of connections across resources either easier or more challenging for the learner.

Altogether, this dimension draws attention to how manipulations to Tasks and Resources can influence multiple resource learning processing and outcomes. In the context of multiple representation learning, design is the most commonly studied of these factors. Much of this research has been influenced by Mayer's CTML (Mayer, 2014) and the instructional design principles that follow from this model (Van Meter & Stepanik, Chapter 6). These principles provide a set of recommendations on how to design representations to ease the task of processing and integrating representations. Examples of these principles include physically integrating verbal and visual information (spatial contiguity; e.g., Johnson & Mayer, 2012), cueing to indicate how two representations correspond (signaling; e.g., Scheiter & Eitel, 2015), and splitting the presentation of information across both auditory and visual channels (modality; Schüler, Scheiter, Rummer, & Gerjets, 2012). Other aspects of the Task and Resources dimensions have also been studied in relation to multiple representation learning. Under this heading, we would include, for example, research demonstrating that learning is affected by manipulations of the format of representations (Schnotz & Baadte, 2015), instructions on how to process representations (e.g., Van Meter, Cameron, & Waters, 2017), and dynamic cross-representation linking (van der Meij & de Jong, 2011).

Within the context of learning from multiple perspectives, while both task and resources have been manipulated as mechanisms for improving learning, it is the case that the former has been studied much more so than the latter. Indeed, the manipulation of task (e.g., asking students to compose an argument or pay attention to author) has been used as a way of prompting students to engage in cross-textual and cross-perspective connection formation (Gil et al., 2010; Wiley & Voss, 1999) and to more robustly evaluate author and perspective (Gerjets, Kammerer, & Werner, 2011). In contrast to task, the materials (e.g., texts) introduced to students have been manipulated to a much more limited extent. Most commonly, these manipulations have focused either on features of materials presentation to stimulate evaluation and the more balanced consideration of conflicting perspectives (e.g., presenting conflicting perspectives in a block-by-block versus interleaved fashion, Maier & Richter, 2013) or on the attribution of texts to authors holding various perspectives and degrees of expertise (Bromme & Thomm, 2016). An exception to this is more recent work, based in the Discrepancy-Induced Source Comprehension framework, which has suggested that the inclusion of conflicting information in texts prompts students' attendance to source, potentially including author perspective (Braasch, Rouet, Vibert, & Britt, 2012; Braasch & Scharrer, Chapter 13).

Future Directions

Although several task and resource characteristics have been tested in the research on both multiple representations and multiple perspectives learning, there are two particular gaps that are highlighted by the MRLF. The first of these is a conceptual gap that exists between the two literatures regarding the functions and perspectives factor. In the literature on learning from multiple representations, Ainsworth (1999, 2006) has identified three specific functions that can be realized with a set of representations. That is, representations may complement one another, one representation may constrain interpretation of another, or generating connections across representations can stimulate construction of deep understanding. Alternatively, in the research on multiple perspectives learning, different perspectives are seen as providing different information or different interpretations of the same information. Thus, the functions of multiple representations emphasize the similarities across representations or how they can be mapped onto one another while multiple perspectives draw attention to the unique and even contradictory information between and within resources. Placing these together in the MRLF, however, encourages researchers within the respective areas to consider this factor more holistically; that is to recognize that there are both similarities and differences within these resource sets and that these characteristics have implications for how learners engage with the set. Perhaps, for example, learners would be better able to integrate across perspectives if they were encouraged to identify and consider consistencies across varied points of view. Likewise, learners studying multiple representations may be more inclined to attend equally to all provided representations if they were encouraged to consider their differences. Although we will return to this point in the upcoming section on Learner Processes, for now we simply suggest that such holistic thinking is necessary to achieve effective resource design and instruction to support learners' ability to work with and use multiple resources of all types. We will not be able to tell learners how multiple resources can and should be used or how to determine which particular use is most appropriate for a given situation unless we have fully identified these points for ourselves.

The second gap that emerges from the MRLF is recognition that the learner's purpose has been largely overlooked in both areas of research. We define purpose as the learner's reason for engaging in a task and as rather distinct from any external task assignment or instructions. Participants in a study or students in a classroom may be told to "read texts to write a summary" or "study a set of representations to learn how a system works," but this does not ensure that they engage in the task with the same goal that an experimenter or classroom teacher intends. Learners, for example, may set a goal to "understand", but believe that the knowledge gained from a single resource is sufficient, provided that this information seems complete and sensible; a learner may approach the reading of different perspectives as a task requiring that the correct perspective be selected rather than attempting to understand different sides of an issue. Although these purposes for engaging in a task likely have significant influences on how that task is carried out, neither line of research has given much consideration to how learners understand multiple resource tasks and how this understanding influences learning. Efforts to improve learning, however, are unlikely to result in long-term changes in learners' independent use of multiple resource unless learners are able to adopt purposes that align with external task assignments; purposes, that is, should include learning from and integrating all resources in a set.

Context Dimension

The Context dimension contains elements of the environment in which the multiple resource task is embedded. The factors of this dimension, which are defined in Table 31.2, include the social context, disciplinary practices, and available supports and scaffolds. These factors are intended to address both the immediate context as well as longer-term participatory goals. A learner, for example, may be engaged in learning about a topic at one point in time so that, at a later point in time, he or she can participate in a discussion about that topic or apply a decision based on what was learned.

Overall, the Context dimension has received less attention in comparison to other dimensions in the MRLF as both lines of research have been historically dominated by cognitive theories. There are some efforts to apply a socio-cultural perspective, however, with this view drawing more attention to contextual variables. In the study of multiple representations, this work has highlighted the use of representations as

Table 31.2 Factors in the Context Dimension of the Multiple Resources Learning Framework

Factor	Category Definition and Description
Social Context	Captures the social, interactive dimensions of the task. Whether resources are studied independently or collaboratively and the structure of social interactions (e.g., social media, group project).
Disciplinary Practices	The ways that resources are used in the activities of a disciplinary group. This includes (1) how a learner uses the resources; e.g., constructing a representation to communicate, and (2) the author's practices underlying the development and design of a resource; e.g., refutation of a counterargument.
Supports & Scaffolds	The learning supports that are available in the context. Examples include teacher's direct actions and instruction, scaffolding prompts (i.e., tasks) embedded in materials, and design elements that facilitate resource integration (e.g., hyperlinks, dynamically linked representations).

part of disciplinary practice. One such application is the examination in Kozma, Chinn, Russell, and Marx (2000) of expert chemists' use of representations during the conduct of research. This observational study revealed that experts used and moved between representations to support their own thinking as well as to communicate their ideas to others (Kozma, Chapter 3). Such use of representations is not limited to experts. Indeed, novice students use multiple representations as both problem-solving and communication tools when working to acquire new knowledge (Ainsworth et al., Chapter 7; Stylianou, Chapter 8).

In the research on learning from multiple perspectives at least three distinct lines of work point to the contextual factors that may make a difference in students' learning from multiple perspectives. First, cultural context has been found to serve as a type of perspective, varying the information that students are able to recall when reading culturally consistent or inconsistent information (e.g., Steffensen, Joag-Dev, & Anderson, 1979) as well as changing students' Gestalt understanding, more broadly (Reynolds, Taylor, Steffensen, Shirey, & Anderson, 1982). Second, perspective has most commonly been conceptualized as a function of domain (i.e., epistemic perspective, Barzilai & Eshet-Alkalai, 2015; Kiili, Coiro, & Hämäläinen, 2016; List, Chapter 11). Finally, Rouet et al. (2017) recently undertook an effort to taxonomize the type of contextual factors that may have a bearing on students' learning from multiple texts. The RESOLV model identifies such factors as: (a) the *request* that is made, or the assigned learning task, (b) the *requester* (e.g., a parent, teacher, or peer), (c) the *audience* that is intended to benefit from the request, (d) the *supports and obstacles* for task completion included in the task context, and (e) the *self*, or learners' abilities and capabilities; with these five factors considered to jointly define the physical and social context for task completion. Although these five factors were identified to address learning from multiple texts, it is also likely that they influence students' learning from multiple perspectives. For instance, who asks students to engage with multiple perspectives, which perspectives are represented, and to whom such perspectives ought to be communicated, can all be expected to make a difference in multiple perspective learning. Nevertheless, it is important to recognize that the RESOLV model conceptualizes context much more narrowly in relation to a given task than has been defined in the broader literature on learning from multiple perspectives.

Future Directions

As we have already implied, the major need highlighted by the Context dimension of the MRLF is simply for more research that is attentive to contextual factors. Both areas of study have examined some of the instructional supports and scaffolds that might improve multiple resource learning, but few studies have considered these practices as situated within the broader context, such as a classroom of students working together. While any number of new research lines could be stimulated by this call, there are two that we find especially compelling. First, there is a need for research that examines multiple resource use in socially collaborative and interactive settings (see also Chen & Lin, Chapter 29, Morgan et al., Chapter 28). To date, the vast majority of research has examined multiple resources learning as a purely individual endeavor where both the learning itself and the expression of the knowledge gained is carried out in isolation. Yet we know that interactions with others, be they peers (Topping, 2005) or teachers

(Van de Pol, Volman, & Beishuizen, 2010), facilitate learning. Moreover, when studies are carried out in context-free, isolated settings, it is most often the case that the learners themselves (i.e., study participants) are engaging in the task in an equally context-free manner. Students recruited from their education or psychology class to participate in research where they study resources explaining an environmental issue are unlikely to engage with these resources as would students who are studying these materials as part of their ecology course. Moving more research into context-rich settings is a necessary step in moving toward the development of interventions that support multiple resource learning.

This intervention research focus is the second area of need that derives from this dimension of the MRLF. Specifically, we encourage the design and testing of interventions that teach students about the communicative and intellectual functions of resources within communities of practice. These interventions would direct students to understand resources as serving some particular function and to see how resources can be used to support thinking. While these interventions would require significant effort on the part of research teams to develop one need only look at some of the work described in the chapters of this *Handbook* to see their value (Ainsworth et al., Chapter 7; Cho et al., Chapter 17; Lombardi et al., Chapter, 20; Stylianou, Chapter 8).

Learner Characteristics Dimension

The Learner Characteristics dimension captures the individual differences that affect learning from multiple resources. As Table 31.3 shows, these factors include components of both hot and cold cognition (Pintrich, Marx, & Boyle, 1993; Sinatra, 2005). Cold cognition factors include the cognitive abilities, prior knowledge, and meta-resource competence factors while the hot cognition factors include both the motivation/affect and beliefs/dispositions factors. The factors in this dimension can also be subdivided into those that represent relatively stable trait-like factors and those that are more mutable across tasks. In particular, cognitive abilities, meta-resource competence, and beliefs and dispositions are expected to exert fairly consistent effects across corresponding tasks. Prior knowledge as well as motivation and affect, however, will shift as the topics and tasks change.

Although individual differences have received significant attention from both multiple representations and multiple perspectives researchers, there are some differences in the specific characteristics that are examined across these two lines. In the research on learning from multiple representations, the most extensively studied individual differences align with the cognitive abilities and prior knowledge factors. Specific examples of this research include demonstrations that learners with high spatial (Newcombe, 2010), working memory (Schüler, Scheiter, & van Genuchten, 2011), or diagram comprehension (Van Meter et al., 2017) abilities tend to learn more from materials than their lower ability peers. This research also shows that prior knowledge supports learning from multiple representations (Seufert, 2003), which is not surprising given the role this factor plays in learning from individual representations. In a review of this literature, Cromley (Chapter 6) concluded that reading comprehension, prior knowledge, and reasoning ability are the individual differences with the strongest demonstrated relations to multiple representations learning.

Table 31.3 Factors in the Learner Characteristics Dimension of the Multiple Resources Learning Framework

Factor	Category Definition and Description
Prior Knowledge	The learner's content knowledge of the topic. Also includes the learner's knowledge related to the task such as knowledge of disciplinary practices and task goals.
Cognitive Abilities	Stable individual differences in the information processing abilities that influence learning from multiple resources. Examples include spatial ability, reading comprehension, and working memory.
Beliefs and Dispositions	Relatively stable learner characteristics, including attitudes and tendencies. Includes individual differences such as need for cognition, epistemic beliefs, and topic interest. Also includes an individual's own perspective on a topic.
Motivation and Affect	State-like individual characteristics that fluctuate across tasks and topics. Examples include emotional responses to characteristics of resources and situational interest.
Meta-resource Competence	The individual's awareness of multiple resources and how resources can be used. Includes knowledge of the functions of different resources and how perspectives influence the content of a resource.

In the field of learning from multiple perspectives, the majority of individual difference factors considered have likewise been of a primarily cognitive nature. In parallel to research on learning from multiple representations, this has predominantly included investigating the role of prior knowledge and verbal ability in students' learning (e.g., Bråten, Ferguson, Anmarkrud, & Strømsø, 2013; Le Bigot & Rouet, 2007; Strømsø, Bråten, & Britt, 2010). Nevertheless, in an important addition to the literature on learning from multiple representations, students' epistemic beliefs, or beliefs about knowledge and knowing, have been emphasized as well (Bråten, Britt, Strømsø, & Rouet, 2011; Ferguson, Bråten, & Strømsø, 2012). Indeed, epistemic beliefs have been associated with students' decisions to corroborate information across multiple perspectives, to consider author trustworthiness in evaluating multiple perspectives, and even to elect to seek out multiple perspectives, at all (Barzilai & Eshet-Alkalai, 2015; Barzilai & Weinstock, Chapter 9; Bråten, Ferguson, Strømsø, & Anmarkrud, 2014). At the same time, stemming from work on learning from multiple texts, the literature on learning from multiple perspectives has started to examine the role of warm or affective factors as well (List & Alexander, 2017, 2018a, 2019). Most prominently, this literature has started to examine how learning is influenced not only by the perspectives put forward in a given resource but also by the learner's own perspective and how this personal perspective aligns with that of the resources available (McCrudden, Chapter 12; McCrudden & Sparks, 2014; Van Strien, Brand-Gruwel, & Boshuizen, 2014)

Future Directions

The MRLF points out one particular individual difference that has received woefully little attention in both areas of research: students' meta-resource competence. As explained by Denton, Muis, Munzar, & Etoubashi (Chapter 19): "analysis of the cognitive and metacognitive strategies individuals adopt in real time lays the groundwork to promote deeper level strategy-use and optimize the benefits of learning from multiple perspectives" (p. 325). We look to meta-resource competence as one such deeper level strategy. In particular, we define meta-resource competence by drawing on conceptual work in the multiple representations literature where representational competence refers to students' awareness of the roles and functions of different representations, including the ability to match representations to one's needs and move between different representations (Kozma, Chapter 3; Rau, Chapter 2). Despite identification of this individual difference however, little empirical work has tested either interventions to improve this competence or examined its influence on multiple representation learning. This is not to say that there is a lack of effort to understand and improve how students learn from and use representations (Schüler, Chapter 4; Van Meter & Stepanik, Chapter 6). Rather, there is a lack of research that specifically examines representational competence as an individual difference reflecting what students know about representations and how they can or should be used in service of some goal.

A "perspectives competence" construct has not been explicitly identified within multiple perspectives learning research. We do, however, see potential connections with an individual difference that has been examined in the multiple perspectives literature but largely ignored in the multiple representations' literature. This individual difference is epistemic beliefs (Hofer & Pintrich, 1997). We predict, for example, that a student who believes that knowledge is evolving and arrived at through reason and logic is also more likely to know that understanding a complex issue requires seeking and working to understand different perspectives (Bråten et al., 2011). This knowledge, we contend, is part of meta-perspective competence. As described by Barzilai and Weinstock (Chapter 9) such knowledge includes the "metacognitive epistemic understanding of the nature, legitimacy, and value of multiple perspectives" (p. 123). This competency is what Kendeou et al. (Chapter 27) deem critical to our intellectual survival in the post-truth information ecosystem.

The recommendations regarding this point are two-fold. First, we encourage further theoretical and empirical development of the meta-resource competence construct, in both areas of literature. These advances can lead to more investigations of how to improve meta-resource competence with the potential for this improvement to lead to changes in how students engage with and use multiple resources. A second, but associated, line of research is needed to explore our hypothesized relationship between meta-resource competence and epistemic beliefs. Finding such a relationship would permit the immature work on meta-resource competence to build on the more substantial work that has been done on epistemic beliefs.

Learner Processes Dimension

The fourth dimension of the MRLF highlights the role of learner processes in multiple resources learning. The factors contained in this dimension are shown in Figure 31.1 and Table 31.4 contains descriptive explanations of each. This dimension includes the internal mental operations that a learner applies toward the resources in a set. And, although these are shown in list form here, these processes are executed in a parallel and recursive manner. In this respect, a learner's effort to understand the content of some resource may prompt re-attending to another resource in order to select and encode additional information (Schüler, Chapter 4).

Table 31.4 Factors in the Learner Processes Dimension of the Multiple Resources Learning Framework

Factor	Category Definition and Description
Epistemic Cognition	Mental activities carried out in order to evaluate the quality of one's knowledge and understanding. Includes actively considering the completeness, factual accuracy, and objectivity of one's knowledge.
Cognitive Operations	
Encode	Attending to and selecting information from a resource. Necessary for further processing of that informational element.
Understand	Cognitive and metacognitive efforts to comprehend a single resource. These active processes result in construction of an organized internal representation of a resource.
Evaluate	Judging the quality of a resource for achieving task goals. Also includes evaluating the quality of one's own knowledge and understanding.
Relate	Determining and constructing the relations between resources. Includes generating connections with prior knowledge. Results in formation of an integrated internal knowledge representation.

The specific operations included under the factor of multiple resource learning operations follow from our previous discussion of the similarity in the operations identified in the two lines of research on multiple resource and multiple perspective learning. Specifically, at a minimum, multiple resource learning requires selecting relevant information, comprehending each available resource, and integrating across resources. For the MRLF we elected to label four learning operations according to processes identified by List and Alexander (2018b) as common to multi-resource and multi-modal resource learning: (a) *encoding* the salient information in each resource, including features of its symbol system(s), informational content, and its author or source, (b) *understanding* these resource features, or linking these with prior knowledge, (c) *evaluating* resources, and (d) *relating* or comparing various resources to one another. We specifically favored this processing framework for three main reasons. First, this framework explicitly conceptualized all four identified processes as carried out across resources' symbol systems, content, and sources; thereby recognizing the importance of representational format, in addition to previously examined features (e.g., source) in facilitating comprehension and evaluation. Second, this framework identifies lower-order processes involved in comprehension (i.e., encoding, understanding) alongside higher-order processes, including evaluation and relation formation. Finally, this framework is explicit in focusing on relation formation or students' active comparison and juxtaposition of resources as a processing step. That is, while integration, or the development of a coherent mental representation, has been the focus in theoretical models of both multiple representation and multiple document learning (Mayer, 2014; Rouet & Britt, 2011), the framework introduced by List and Alexander (2018b) suggests that such integration can only be achieved through the explicit connecting of multiple resources in relation to one another.

The second factor is epistemic cognition (i.e., thinking processes about knowledge and knowing; Greene, Azevedo, & Torney-Purta, 2008). Kitchner (1983) specifically referred to epistemic cognition as a meta-cognitive monitoring process (i.e., "knowing about knowing in the epistemic sense", p. 223). As such, epistemic cognition represents learners' reasoning that is reflective, explicit, and purposeful (Cartiff & Greene,

Chapter 24). Chinn, Buckland, & Samarapungavan (2011) proposed that epistemic cognition includes five broad components: (a) *epistemic aims and values* (i.e., people's goals related to inquiry and knowledge construction, as well as their perceived worth of knowledge and understanding), (b) the structure of knowledge and understanding (e.g., people's views on knowledge as either simple or complex), (c) sources and justification of epistemic achievements (e.g., a person's epistemic stance about reasons for knowledge claims, such as people's beliefs about the certainty of knowledge), (d) epistemic virtues and vices (i.e., people's character dispositions that help or hinder their epistemic aims), and (e) the processes of achieving epistemic accomplishments (i.e., the cognitive and social processes that lead to knowledge construction). For example, in considering sources and justification for knowledge, learners may find a particular messenger (e.g., an author or a speaker) lack trustworthiness and expertise, and therefore to deem the author's explanations as implausible (Barzilai & Weinstock, Chapter 9; Lombardi, Seyranian, & Sinatra, 2014). Such source evaluation may be aided by students' epistemic virtues (e.g., skepticism) and informed by their epistemic aims (e.g., acquiring accurate information). Researchers have also proposed a closer examination of the metacognitive and self-regulatory aspects of epistemic cognition as a direction for future work (Denton et al., Chapter 19).

Future Directions

The MRLF adopts the conceptualization of cognitive processes proposed by List and Alexander (2018b). This is, in part, because this conceptualization emphasizes the process of *relating* resources rather than *integrating* these. Although integration is the more common term found in long-standing models of these cognitive operations (e.g., Mayer's CTML, 2014), we argue for a shift in this terminology. As it is typically presented in the literature, integration implies that, once two or more resources have been comprehended, the learner knows how these should be connected or integrated. By contrast, the processes of relating or comparing draw attention to the fact that the learner must determine just how two resources should be connected before integration can take place. A learner studying a verbal text and a graph, for example, must determine if these two representations are informationally redundant or if the graph provides some extension of the information given in a text. A learner reading a blog post and a scientific article must determine if and how the perspectives forwarded in each align. While the similarities or consistencies across resources allow for points of contact between resources to be identified, the differences specify the unique information conveyed within each particular resource. One hypothesis generated from the adoption of relating as a key cognitive process is that multiple resource learning could be enhanced by directing learners to explicitly identify similarities and differences across resources and to use this analysis to determine how resources should be connected. In short, learners could be taught to determine the relations between resources before working toward the construction of an integrated mental representation (Alexander & the DRLR, Chapter 23).

Additional areas for future research are uncovered by the inclusion of epistemic cognition and evaluation as Learner Processes in the MRLF. With respect to the study of multiple representations learning, these processes have been largely ignored yet they are likely to have a direct impact on how learners use provided representations and, ultimately, what is learned. We base this prediction on the hypothesis that how a learner enacts his or her beliefs about the nature of knowledge and knowing and the evaluation of representations in light of those beliefs (i.e., epistemic cognition, Strømsø & Kammerer, 2016) affects how that learner directs attention to a particular representation and the efforts made toward relating and connecting that representation to other representations. Epistemic cognition has been extensively examined within the context of learning from multiple perspectives (e.g., Barzilai & Eshet-Alkalai, 2015; Kiili & Laurinen, 2018; Mason, Ariasi, & Boldrin, 2011), but this research, has, for the most part, only identified limitations in such processing and documented the relationships between learners' epistemic beliefs and processing. With respect to the study of multiple perspectives learning, there is a clear need for the development and testing of interventions that may help learners to overcome these limitations, developing more sophisticated epistemic beliefs and more readily engaging in epistemic cognition during processing (e.g., Kienhues, Bromme, & Stahl, 2008).

A third area of research suggested by attention to epistemic cognition and evaluation during multiple resource learning draws on factors from the Tasks and Resources dimension of the MRLF and points to the need to consider multiple resource learning when resources use different representational forms to convey different perspectives (i.e., when multiple perspectives are conveyed via multiple representations): When, for example, different perspectives on a historical event are conveyed via different symbolic formats (e.g., texts and political cartoons, Van Meter & Cameron, 2018) or when the formatting of different representations supports their interpretation in different ways (Schnotz & Baadte, 2015; Shah & Freedman, 2011). Resource sets, such as these, suggest that the distinction between multiple representations (i.e., different symbolic formats) and multiple perspectives (i.e., different points of view) is a false dichotomy. Instead, learners will encounter variations in both representational format and perspectives during authentic multiple resource learning. The lack of research concerning these multi-perspective, multi-representational resource sets is disconcerting because there is evidence that these resource characteristics interact. For instance, conflicting perspectives related via text may also use images or graphs to make their points of view more persuasive. Likewise, the choice of image accompanying a headline or the choice to represent quantitative information as an absolute number or a percentage may further be a matter of author perspective and intention in resource creation.

These interactions between multiple representations and multiple perspectives may be particularly tied to epistemic cognition. This hypothesis is based on evidence that learners respond differently to verbal and visual representations. Learners, for example, have generally been found to assign a great deal of "truthiness" or credibility to images, more so than to text-based content alone (Greer & Gosen, 2002; McGrew, Breakstone, Ortega, Smith, & Wineburg, 2018; Newman, Garry, Bernstein, Kantner, & Lindsay, 2012). Indeed, graphics accompanying textual content have been found to demonstrably improve students' information recall (Griffin & Stevenson, 1996), regardless of whether the information presented in such graphics has been accurate or not (Geidner & Cameron, 2017; Strange, Garry, Bernstein, & Lindsay, 2011). Moreover, students have been found to largely ignore source and perspective information when evaluating images of even controversial topics like global crises, ignoring whether a journalist or a participant (e.g., a soldier or a victim) captured a photo (Pogliano, 2015). Findings such as these point to the need to further consider the role of epistemic cognition and evaluation in students' learning from multiple resources, particularly when those resources use different representations to convey different perspectives.

Construction Dimension

The final dimension, Construction, holds the mental representation the learner generates while engaged in a multiple resource learning task. This dimension includes two primary factors, the task model and the knowledge representation that learners construct. These are described in Table 31.5. Whereas the task model holds the knowledge that drives engagement in the current task, the knowledge representation refers to the knowledge product that is constructed during learning.

The task model, which reflects the learner's reformulation and mental representation of task demands, is constructed based on information about the task and resources available for task completion and on learners' prior experiences with similar tasks (Rouet & Britt, 2011; Winne & Hadwin, 1998, 2008). The task model then, is distinct from the externally provided instructions, but holds the learner's translation of these inputs into an understanding of what the task requires and the standards for meeting those requirements. The construction that emerges as an outcome of multiple resource use results from more than just students' prior knowledge and information use. Rather, the resulting knowledge construction may be expected to reflect the task that students were asked to complete or were intending to complete, as well as the standards that students established for task completion (see the corresponding discussion under the Task and Resources dimension). In this way, the MRLF echoes the MD-TRACE as a model of learning from multiple texts (Rouet & Britt, 2011). In particular, like the MD-TRACE, the MRLF recognizes that the task model that students construct prior to multiple resource use should be viewed as translating into the ultimate mental model (i.e., construction) that students develop and its revision for task satisfaction.

Research on multiple representations learning has been largely concerned with the qualitative nature of the knowledge constructed, yet seldom measures this quality directly. On the one hand, this research is influenced by theoretical accounts of integration or global coherence formation. According to these accounts, an integrated mental representation is desirable because this holistic representation is more flexible

Table 31.5 Factors in the Construction Dimension of the Multiple Resources Learning Framework

Factor	Category Definition and Description
Task Model	Learner's internal representation of the task. Includes goals and standards for evaluating progress toward goals.
Knowledge Representation	The internal mental representation of what has been learned about the topic. These representations include knowledge derived from specific resources during study such as the internal representation of a specific document or the mental model derived from a diagram. The final knowledge representation is the internal knowledge product of the multiple resource task.

and complete than mental representations that do not inter-connect separate external representations. The most common measurement approach is to include higher-order assessments (e.g., transfer, problem solving) and draw inferences about the quality of the underlying mental representation from performance on these assessments. There are exceptions to this trend, however, with integration having been directly measured by both text-diagram multiple-choice items (Bodemer, Ploetzner, Bruchmüller, & Häcker, 2005; Van Meter et al., 2017) and sorting and transformation tasks (Kozma & Russell, 1997). Both measurement techniques have been shown to be sensitive to expected differences across participants in the studied populations. Van Meter et al. (2017), for example, found that learners who were prompted to attend to both text and diagrams scored higher on multiple-choice items assessing knowledge of content from the diagrams than participants who responded to prompts requesting verbalized self-explanations.

In the literature on learning from multiple perspectives, considerable attention has been paid to how students cognitively represent the variety of perspectives that they may encounter and the relations among them. Additionally, this literature has examined how such cognitive representations may manifest in students' performance on various objective and writing-based measures of comprehension and integration (Anmarkrud et al., 2014; Gil et al., 2010; List et al., 2019). Borrowing from the related literature on learning from multiple documents, the literature on learning from multiple perspectives has looked to the Documents Model Framework (DF; Britt et al., 1999; Perfetti, Rouet, & Britt, 1999) for a conceptualization on the ways in which various perspectives, be they presented across documents or within a single text, ought to be conceptualized. Drawing on the DF, the literature on learning from multiple perspectives may be said to evaluate the types of cognitive representations that students construct according to whether: (a) they appropriately link particular information to the perspective(s) and authors that it comes from, (b) recognize overlapping or complementary information introduced across perspectives, and prioritize it accordingly, and (c) recognize when perspectives conflict, map this conflict, and potentially understand this conflict as originating from a difference in author characteristics and perspectives (Barzilai & Weinstock, Chapter 9; Braasch & Scharrer, Chapter 13; Richter et al., Chapter 16). While the DF suggests that the constructions that students develop ought be comprehensive in nature, capturing the variety of perspectives that there may be on a given topic, more recent work by List and Alexander (2019) suggests that the constructions or cognitive representations that students develop are likely to differ in association with task. That is, we can expect that the constructions that students create when trying to *convince* someone of a given course of action will be different than those developed in response to tasks asking students to *summarize* some perspective set.

Future Directions

As apparent from both the literatures on learning from multiple representations and from multiple perspectives, greater attention is needed to the associations between the initial task models that students develop and the constructions that they ultimately form. Specifically, additional work is needed to understand how students' perceptions of task demands are tied to the cognitive representations of information that they develop as a result of multiple resource use. Additionally, while both fields recognize integration, or connection formation among disparate resources, to be a key process necessary for learning, more needs to be investigated regarding this process. This includes examining how integration may be expressed in students' task performance, rather than only assuming that successful performance is the result of integration, and further considering the various types of connections that students may need to form for effective construction.

MRLF SUMMARY

The development of the MRLF proved to be a useful tool as we analyzed and synthesized the chapters in this volume. The MRLF emerged from the many ideas presented in this *Handbook* and provided a structure for us to more easily see research gaps and opportunities to facilitate learning with multiple resources. Opportunities for meaningful research exist in all of the nested dimensions of the MRLF. For example, designing more effective instructional scaffolds requires examination of how learners can effectively integrate the functions of multiple representations with the evaluation of the various perspectives that may be conveyed through these representations. Such scaffolds could enhance learners' meta-resource and meta-perspective competencies, understudied characteristics that may have particular relevance when integrating multiple representations and multiple perspectives. Today, these meta-competencies are needed to prepare learners to face challenges associated with misinformation and fake news. For learners to be prepared, the MRLF looks toward the development of meta-cognitively guided, epistemically engaged, cognitive processes that facilitate encoding, understanding, evaluating, and relating multiple representations and multiple perspectives.

Finally, the MRLF looks at the learning environment, with specific attention to social context within and outside of traditional learning settings. For example, the effective and reliable evaluation of a controversial topic (e.g., causes of current climate change) requires understanding the society in which that controversy is situated, as well as the disciplinary practices embedded within that society. Successful integration of multiple resources (e.g., visualization of sea level rise projections and graphical interpretations of population distribution) and multiple perspectives (e.g., viewpoints from immigrants forced to move in mass migrations versus economic interests and investments in fossil fuels) are needed to construct knowledge that learners can use to address both local and global problems, and which require effective and adaptive problem solving. Many other societal challenges also require such successful integration and we view future research at the nexus of multiple representations and multiple perspectives – vis-à-vis the MRLF – to be a pathway that may help learners become more knowledgeable members of society.

CONCLUSION

In this *Handbook*, we aimed to provide the state of the art on research in two related but distinct areas, learning from multiple representations and learning from multiple perspectives. Multiple representations refer to the set of representations a person is learning from, whereas multiple perspectives refer to the point of view reflected in a particular representation. The organization of this *Handbook* reflects the state of these two lines of work. In Section 1, we invited chapters on the factors and mechanisms associated with learning from multiple representations. In Section 2, we invited parallel chapters on the factors associated with learning from multiple perspectives. In Section 3, we invited chapters focused on several characteristics and skills that learners need to be successful when learning from multiple representations and from multiple perspectives. Finally, in Section 4 we invited chapters focused on the challenges and opportunities learners encounter in the context of learning from multiple representations and perspectives, as well as emerging methodologies that allow for the investigation of these issues in complex environments.

Our review of this work has identified areas of convergence and divergence among these two independent lines of research. This review has highlighted that the core intersection lies in how learners acquire and construct knowledge across multiple resources. Several factors or dimensions influence learners' knowledge acquisition, including Task and Resources, Context, Learner Characteristics, Learner Processes, and Construction products. We articulated how these dimensions interrelate in an integrated theoretical framework, the Multiple Resources Learning Framework (MRLF). Our hope in forwarding the MRLF is that it will drive new research by identifying theoretical and conceptual gaps at the intersections of these literatures.

Among the most notable future directions, we highlighted the need to integrate work from these literatures to understand more deeply how multiple representations function when learning from multiple perspectives and vice versa. Another important direction is identifying competencies that are critical in the context of learning from multiple representations and from multiple perspectives, such as "meta-resource competence." Finally, there is also a need for more authentic, ecologically valid investigations that fully embrace the collaborative nature of learning in face-to-face and virtual environments as advances in technology (e.g., intelligent tutoring systems) and methodology (e.g., multi-trace, multi-channel data) increasingly make multi-resource learning ubiquitous and routine.

REFERENCES

Ainsworth, S. (1999). The functions of multiple representations. *Computers and Education*, 33(2), 131–152. doi:10.1016/S0360-1315(99)00029-9

Ainsworth, S. (2006). DeFT: A conceptual framework for considering learning with multiple representations. *Learning and Instruction*, 16(3), 183–198. doi:10.1016/j.learninstruc.2006.03.001

Alexander, P. A., & Fox, E. (2004). Historical perspectives on reading research and practice. In R. B. Ruddell & N. Unrau (Eds.), *Theoretical models and processes of reading* (5th ed.., pp. 33–59). Newark, DE: International Reading Association. doi:10.1598/0872075028.2

Anmarkrud, Ø., Bråten, I., & Strømsø, H. I. (2014). Multiple-documents literacy: Strategic processing, source awareness, and argumentation when reading multiple conflicting documents. *Learning and Individual Differences*, 30, 64–76. doi:10.1016/j.lindif.2013.01.007

Barzilai, S., & Eshet-Alkalai, Y. (2015). The role of epistemic perspectives in comprehension of multiple author viewpoints. *Learning and Instruction*, 36, 86–103. doi:10.1016/j.learninstruc.2014.12.003

Bednarz, S. W., Acheson, G., & Bednarz, R. S. (2006). Maps and map learning in social studies. *Social Education*, 70(7), 398–404.

Bigot, L. L., & Rouet, J. F. (2007). The impact of presentation format, task assignment, and prior knowledge on students' comprehension of multiple online documents. *Journal of Literacy Research*, 39(4), 445–470. doi:10.1080/10862960701675317

Bodemer, D., Ploetzner, R., Bruchmüller, K., & Häcker, S. (2005). Supporting learning with interactive multimedia through active integration of representations. *Instructional Science, 33*(1), 73–95. doi:10.1007/s11251-004-7685-z

Braasch, J. L., Rouet, J. F., Vibert, N., & Britt, M. A. (2012). Readers' use of source information in text comprehension. *Memory and Cognition, 40*(3), 450–465. doi:10.3758/s13421-011-0160-6

Bråten, I., Britt, M. A., Strømsø, H. I., & Rouet, J. F. (2011). The role of epistemic beliefs in the comprehension of multiple expository texts: Toward an integrated model. *Educational Psychologist, 46*(1), 48–70. doi:10.1080/00461520.2011.538647

Bråten, I., Ferguson, L. E., Anmarkrud, Ø., & Strømsø, H. I. (2013). Prediction of learning and comprehension when adolescents read multiple texts: The roles of word-level processing, strategic approach, and reading motivation. *Reading and Writing, 26*(3), 321–348. doi:10.1007/s11145-012-9371-x

Bråten, I., Ferguson, L. E., Strømsø, H. I., & Anmarkrud, Ø. (2014). Students working with multiple conflicting documents on a scientific issue: Relations between epistemic cognition while reading and sourcing and argumentation in essays. *British Journal of Educational Psychology, 84*, 58–85. doi:10.1111/bjep.12005

Britt, M. A., Perfetti, C. A., Sandak, R. L., & Rouet, J.-F. (1999). Content integration and source separation in learning from multiple texts. In S. R. Goldman (Ed.), *Essays in honor of Tom Trabasso* (pp. 209–233). Mahwah, NJ: Lawrence Erlbaum.

Britt, M. A., Rouet, J. F., & Braasch, J. L. G. (2012). Documents as entities: Extending the situation model theory of comprehension. In M. A. Britt, S. R. Goldman, & J.-F. Rouet (Eds.), *Reading: From words to multiple texts* (pp. 160–179). New York: Routledge. doi:10.4324/9780203131268

Bromme, R., & Thomm, E. (2016). Knowing who knows: Laypersons' capabilities to judge experts' pertinence for science topics. *Cognitive Science, 40*(1), 241–252. doi:10.1111/cogs.12252

Butcher, K. R. (2006). Learning from text with diagrams: Promoting mental model development and inference generation. *Journal of Educational Psychology, 98*, 182–197. doi:10.1037/0022-0663.98.1.182

Cerdan & Vidal-Abarca. (2008). The effects of tasks on integrating information from multiple documents. *Journal of Educational Psychology, 100*(1), 209–222. doi:10.1037/0022-0663.100.1.209

Chinn, C. A., Buckland, L. A., & Samarapungavan, A. L. A. (2011). Expanding the dimensions of epistemic cognition: Arguments from philosophy and psychology. *Educational Psychologist, 46*(3), 141–167. doi:10.1080/00461520.2011.587722

Cromley, J. G., Bergey, B. W., Fitzhugh, S., Newcombe, N., Wills, T. W., Shipley, T. F., & Tanaka, J. C. (2013). Effects of three diagram instruction methods on transfer of diagram comprehension skills: The critical role of inference while learning. *Learning and Instruction, 26*, 45–58. doi:10.1016/j.learninstruc.2013.01.003

Cromley, J. G., Snyder-Hogan, L. E., & Luciw-Dubas, U. A. (2010). Cognitive activities in complex science text and diagrams. *Contemporary Educational Psychology, 35*(1), 59–74. doi:10.1016/j.cedpsych.2009.10.002

Daher, T. A., & Kiewra, K. A. (2016). An investigation of SOAR study strategies for learning from multiple online resources. *Contemporary Educational Psychology, 46*, 10–21. doi:10.1016/j.cedpsych.2015.12.004

Felton, M., & Kuhn, D. (2001). The development of argumentative discourse skill. *Discourse Processes, 32*(2/3), 135–153. doi:10.1080/0163853x.2001.9651595

Ferguson, L. E., Bråten, I., & Strømsø, H. I. (2012). Epistemic cognition when students read multiple documents containing conflicting scientific evidence: A think-aloud study. *Learning and Instruction, 22*(2), 103–120. doi:10.1016/j.learninstruc.2011.08.002

Geidner, N., & Cameron, J. (2017). Readers perceive deceptive graphics as less credible. *Newspaper Research Journal, 38*(4), 473–483. doi:10.1177/0739532917739878

Gerjets, P., Kammerer, Y., & Werner, B. (2011). Measuring spontaneous and instructed evaluation processes during Web search: Integrating concurrent thinking-aloud protocols and eye-tracking data. *Learning and Instruction, 21*(2), 220–231. doi:10.1016/j.learninstruc.2010.02.005

Gil, L., Bråten, I., Vidal-Abarca, E., & Strømsø, H. I. (2010). Summary versus argument tasks when working with multiple documents: Which is better for whom?. *Contemporary Educational Psychology, 35*(3), 157–173. doi:10.1016/j.cedpsych.2009.11.002

Goldman, S. R. (2003). Learning in complex domains: When and why do multiple representations help? *Learning and Instruction, 13*(2), 239–244. doi:10.1016/S0959-4752(02)00023-3

Goldman, S. R., & Scardamalia, M. (2013). Managing, understanding, applying, and creating knowledge in the information age: Next-generation challenges and opportunities. *Cognition and Instruction, 31*, 255–269. doi:10.1080/10824669.2013.773217

Greene, J. A., Azevedo, R., & Torney-Purta, J. (2008). Modeling epistemic and ontological cognition: Philosophical perspectives and methodological directions. *Educational Psychologist*, *43*(3), 142–160. doi:10.1080/00461520802178458

Greer, J. D., & Gosen, J. D. (2002). How much is too much? Assessing levels of digital alteration of factors in public perception of news media credibility. *Visual Communication Quarterly*, *9*(3), 4–13. doi:10.1080/15551390209363485

Griffard, P. B. (2013). Deconstructing and decoding complex process diagrams in university biology. In D. F. Treagust & C. Y. Tsui (Eds.), *Multiple representations in biological education* (pp. 165–183). Amsterdam: Springer. doi:10.1007/978-94-007-4192-8_10

Griffin, J. L., & Stevenson, R. L. (1996). The influence of statistical graphics on newspaper reader recall. *Visual Communication Quarterly*, *3*(3), 9–11. doi:10.1080/15551399609363328

Hastings, P., Hughes, S., Magliano, J. P., Goldman, S. R., & Lawless, K. (2012). Assessing the use of multiple sources in student essays. *Behavior Research Methods*, *44*(3), 622–633. doi:10.3758/s13428-012-0214-0

Hofer, B. K., & Pintrich, P. R. (1997). The development of epistemological theories: Beliefs about knowledge and knowing and their relation to learning. *Review of Educational Research*, *67*(1), 88–140. doi:10.3102/00346543067001088

Hyönä, J., & Lorch, R. F., Jr. (2004). Effects of topic headings on text processing: Evidence from adult readers' eye fixation patterns. *Learning and Instruction*, *14*, 131–152. doi:10.1016/j.learninstruc.2004.01.001

Johnson, C. I., & Mayer, R. E. (2012). An eye movement analysis of the spatial contiguity effect in multimedia learning. *Journal of Experimental Psychology: Applied*, *18*(2), 178–191. doi:10.1037/a0026923

Jonassen, D. H. (1997). Instructional design models for well-structured and ill-structured problem-solving learning outcomes. *Educational Technology Research and Development*, *45*(1), 65–94. doi:10.1007/BF02299613

Kienhues, D., Bromme, R., & Stahl, E. (2008). Changing epistemological beliefs: The unexpected impact of a short-term intervention. *British Journal of Educational Psychology*, *78*(4), 545–565. doi:10.1348/000709907X268589

Kiili, C., Coiro, J., & Hämäläinen, J. (2016). An online inquiry tool to support the exploration of controversial issues on the Internet. *Journal of Literacy and Technology*, *17*(1/2), 31–52. http://literacyandtechnology.org/uploads/1/3/6/8/136889/_jlt_sp201

Kiili, C., & Laurinen, L. (2018). *Monilukutaidon mestariksi: Opettaja nettilukemisen ohjaajana [Mastering multiliteracies: Teachers supporting online reading]*. Jyväskylä, Finland: Niilo Mäki Instituutti.

Kitchner, K. S. (1983). Cognition, metacognition, and epistemic cognition. *Human Development*, *26*(4), 222–232. doi:10.1159/000272885

Kottmeyer, A., Van Meter, P., & Cameron, C. (in press). The role of representational system in relational reasoning. *Journal of Educational Psychology*, doi:10.1037/edu0000374

Kozma, R. (2003). The material features of multiple representations and their cognitive and social affordances for science understanding. *Learning and Instruction*, *13*(2), 205–226. doi:10.1016/S0959-4752(02)00021-X

Kozma, R., Chin, E., Russell, J., & Marx, N. (2000). The roles of representations and tools in the chemistry laboratory and their implications for chemistry learning. *Journal of the Learning Sciences*, *9*(2), 105–143. doi:10.1207/s15327809jls0902_1

Kozma, R. B., & Russell, J. (1997). Multimedia and understanding: Expert and novice responses to different representations of chemical phenomena. *Journal of Research in Science Teaching: the Official Journal of the National Association for Research in Science Teaching*, *34*(9), 949–968. doi:10.1002/(SICI)1098-2736(199711)34:9<949::AID-TEA7>3.0.CO;2-U

Kress, G., & van Leeuwen, T. (1996). *Reading images: The grammar of visual design*. London, England: Routledge.

Lemke, J. (1998). Metamedia literacy: Transforming meanings and media. In D. Reinking, M. McKenna, L. Labbo, & R. Kieffer (Eds.), *Handbook of literacy and technology: Transformations in a post-typographic world* (pp. 283–302). Hillsdale, NJ: Lawrence Erlbaum.

List, A. (2018). Strategies for comprehending and integrating texts and videos. *Learning and Instruction*, *57*, 34–46. doi:10.1016/j.learninstruc.2018.01.008

List, A., & Alexander, P. A. (2017). Cognitive affective engagement model of multiple source use. *Educational Psychologist*, *52*(3), 182–199. doi:10.1080/00461520.2017.1329014

List, A., & Alexander, P. A. (2018a). Cold and warm perspectives on the cognitive affective engagement model of multiple source use. In J. L. G. Braasch, I. Bråten, & M. T. McCrudden (Eds.), *Handbook of multiple source use* (pp. 34–54). New York: Routledge. doi:10.4324/9781315627496

List, A., & Alexander, P. A. (2018b). Postscript: In pursuit of integration. *Learning and Instruction, 57*, 82–85. doi:10.1016/j.learninstruc.2018.04.002

List, A., & Alexander, P. A. (2019). Toward an integrated framework of multiple text use. *Educational Psychologist, 54*(1), 20–39. doi:10.1080/00461520.2018.1505514

List, A., Du, H., Wang, Y., & Lee, H. Y. (2019). Toward a typology of integration: Examining the documents model framework. *Contemporary Educational Psychology, 58*, 228–242. doi:10.1016/j.cedpsych.2019.03.003

Lombardi, D., Seyranian, V., & Sinatra, G. M. (2014). Source effects and plausibility judgments when reading about climate change. *Discourse Processes, 51*(1/2), 75–92. doi:10.1080/0163853X.2013.855049

Maier, J., & Richter, T. (2013). Text belief consistency effects in the comprehension of multiple texts with conflicting information. *Cognition and Instruction, 31*(2), 151–175. doi:10.1080/07370008.2013.769997

Mangen, A., Olivier, G., & Velay, J. L. (2019). Comparing comprehension of a long text read in print book and on Kindle: Where in the text and when in the story? *Frontiers in Psychology, 10*, 38. doi:10.3389/fpsyg.2019.00038

Mason, L., Ariasi, N., & Boldrin, A. (2011). Epistemic beliefs in action: Spontaneous reflections about knowledge and knowing during online information searching and their influence on learning. *Learning and Instruction, 21*(1), 137–151. doi:10.1016/j.learninstruc.2010.01.001

Mayer, R. E. (2014). Cognitive theory of multimedia learning. In R. E. Mayer *The Cambridge handbook of multimedia learning* (2nd ed., pp. 43–71). New York: Cambridge University Press. doi:10.1017/cbo9781139547369.005

Mayer, R. E., & Wittrock, M. C. (1996). Problem-solving transfer. In R. C. Calfee & D. C. Berliner (Eds.), *Handbook of educational psychology* (pp. 47–62). Mahwah, NJ: Lawrence Erlbaum. doi:10.4324/9780203874790.ch13

McCrudden, M. T., & Bohn-Gettler, C. M. (2019). Contributions of processes versus product instructions in the transfer of scientific concepts. Poster presented at the annual meeting of the American Education Research Association, Toronto.

McCrudden, M. T., Magliano, J. P., & Schraw, G. (2011). The effect of diagrams on online reading processes and memory. *Discourse Processes, 48*(2), 69–92. doi:10.1080/01638531003694561

McCrudden, M. T., & Schraw, G. (2007). Relevance and goal-focusing in text processing. *Educational Psychology Review, 19*(2), 113–139. doi:10.1007/s10648-006-9010-7

McCrudden, M. T., & Sparks, P. C. (2014). Exploring the effect of task instructions on topic beliefs and topic belief justifications: A mixed methods study. *Contemporary Educational Psychology, 39*(1), 1–11. doi:10.1016/j.cedpsych.2013.10.001

McGrew, S., Breakstone, J., Ortega, T., Smith, M., & Wineburg, S. (2018). Can students evaluate online sources? Learning from assessments of civic online reasoning. *Theory and Research in Social Education, 46*(2), 165–193. doi:10.1080/00933104.2017.1416320

McNamara, D. S., Kintsch, E., Songer, N. B., & Kintsch, W. (1996). Are good texts always better? Interactions of text coherence, background knowledge, and levels of understanding in learning from text. *Cognition and Instruction, 14*(1), 1–43. doi:10.1207/s1532690xci1401_1

Newcombe, N. S. (2010). Picture this: Increasing math and science learning by improving spatial thinking. *American Educator, 34*(2), 29–43.

Newman, E. J., Garry, M., Bernstein, D. M., Kantner, J., & Lindsay, D. S. (2012). Nonprobative photographs (or words) inflate truthiness. *Psychonomic Bulletin and Review, 19*(5), 969–974. doi:10.3758/s13423-012-0292-0

Nussbaum, E. M., & Edwards, O. V. (2011). Critical questions and argument stratagems: A framework for enhancing and analyzing students' reasoning practices. *Journal of the Learning Sciences, 20*(3), 443–488. doi:10.1080/10508406.2011.564567

Ozcelik, E., Arslan-Ari, I., & Cagiltay, K. (2010). Why does signaling enhance multimedia learning? Evidence from eye movements. *Computers in Human Behavior, 26*(1), 110–117. doi:10.1016/j.chb.2009.09.001

Perfetti, C. A., Rouet, J.-F., & Britt, M. A. (1999). Towards a theory of documents representation. In H. van Oostendorp & S. R. Goldman (Eds.), *The construction of mental representations during reading* (pp. 99–122). Hillsdale, NJ: Lawrence Erlbaum. doi:10.4324/9781410603050

Pintrich, P. R., Marx, R. W., & Boyle, R. A. (1993). Beyond cold conceptual change: The role of motivational beliefs and classroom contextual factors in the process of conceptual change. *Review of Educational Research, 63*(2), 167–199. doi:10.2307/1170472

Pogliano, A. (2015). Evaluating news photographs: Trust, impact and consumer culture in the digital age. *Journalism Practice, 9*(4), 552–567. doi:10.1080/17512786.2015.1030141

Reynolds, T., Steffensen, S., & Anderson. (1982). Cultural schemata and reading comprehension. *Reading Research Quarterly, 17*(3), 353–366. doi:10.2307/747524

Rouet, J., & Britt, M. A. (2011). Relevance processes in multiple document comprehension. In M. T. McCrudden, J. P. Magliano, & G. Schraw (Eds.), *Text relevance and learning from text* (pp. 19–52). Charlotte, NC: Information Age.

Rouet, J. F., Britt, M. A., & Durik, A. M. (2017). RESOLV: Readers' representation of reading contexts and tasks. *Educational Psychologist*, 52(3), 200–215. doi:10.1080/00461520.2017.1329015

Sadler, T. D. (2011). Situating socio-scientific issues in classrooms as a means of achieving goals of science education. In T. D. Sadler (Ed.), *Socio-scientific issues in science classrooms: Teaching, learning and research* (pp. 1–9). Dordrecht: Springer. doi:10.1007/978-94-007-1159-4_1

Sadler, T. D., Barab, S. A., & Scott, B. (2007). What do students gain by engaging in socioscientific inquiry? *Research in Science Education*, 37(4), 371–391. doi:10.1007/s11165-006-9030-9

Salmerón, L., Baccino, T., Cañas, J. J., Madrid, R. I., & Fajardo, I. (2009). Do graphical overviews facilitate or hinder comprehension in hypertext? *Computers and Education*, 53(4), 1308–1319. doi:10.1016/j.compedu.2009.06.013

Scheiter, K., & Eitel, A. (2015). Signals foster multimedia learning by supporting integration of highlighted text and diagram elements. *Learning and Instruction*, 36, 11–26. doi:10.1016/j.learninstruc.2014.11.002

Schnotz, W. (2005). Integrated model of text and picture comprehension. In R. E. Mayer (Ed.), *The Cambridge handbook of multimedia learning* (2nd ed., pp. 72–103). New York: Cambridge University Press. doi:10.1017/cbo9781139547369.006

Schnotz, W., & Baadte, C. (2015). Surface and deep structures in graphics comprehension. *Memory and Cognition*, 43(4), 605–618. doi:10.3758/s13421-014-0490-2

Schüler, A., Scheiter, K., Rummer, R., & Gerjets, P. (2012). Explaining the modality effect in multimedia learning: Is it due to a lack of temporal contiguity with written text and pictures?. *Learning and Instruction*, 22(2), 92–102. doi:https://doi.org/10.1016/j.learninstruc.2011.08.001

Schüler, A., Scheiter, K., & van Genuchten, E. (2011). The role of working memory in multimedia instruction: Is working memory working during learning from text and pictures?. *Educational Psychology Review*, 23(3), 389–411. doi:10.1007/s10648-011-9168-5

Serafini, F. (2011). Expanding perspectives for comprehending visual images in multimodal texts. *Journal of Adolescent and Adult Literacy*, 54(5), 342–350. doi:10.1598/JAAL.54.5.4

Seufert, T. (2003). Supporting coherence formation in learning from multiple representations. *Learning and Instruction*, 13(2), 227–237. doi:10.1016/S0959-4752(02)00022-1

Shah, P., & Freedman, E. G. (2011). Bar and line graph comprehension: An interaction of top-down and bottom-up processes. *Topics in Cognitive Science*, 3(3), 560–578. doi:10.1111/j.1756-8765.2009.01066.x

Sinatra, G. M. (2005). The "Warming Trend" in conceptual change research: The legacy of Paul R. Pintrich. *Educational Psychologist*, 40(2), 107–115. doi:10.1207/s15326985ep4002_5

Steffensen, M. S., Joag-Dev, C., & Anderson, R. C. (1979). A cross-cultural perspective on reading comprehension. *Reading Research Quarterly*, 15, 10–29. doi:10.2307/747429

Strange, D., Garry, M., Bernstein, D. M., & Lindsay, D. S. (2011). Photographs cause false memories for the news. *Acta Psychologica*, 136(1), 90–94. doi:10.1016/j.actpsy.2010.10.006

Strømsø, H. I., Bråten, I., & Britt, M. A. (2010). Reading multiple texts about climate change: The relationship between memory for sources and text comprehension. *Learning and Instruction*, 20(3), 192–204. doi:10.1016/j.learninstruc.2009.02.001

Strømsø, H. I., & Kammerer, Y. (2016). Epistemic cognition and reading for understanding in the internet age. In J. A. Greene, W. A. Sandoval, & I. Bråten (Eds.), *Handbook of epistemic cognition* (pp. 230–246). New York: Routledge.

Topping, K. J. (2005). Trends in peer learning. *Educational Psychology*, 25(6), 631–645. doi:10.1080/01443410500345172

Tversky, B., Zacks, J., Lee, P. U., & Heiser, J. (2000). Lines, blobs, crosses, and arrows: Diagrammatic communication with schematic figures. In M. Anderson, P. Cheng, & V. Haarslev (Eds.), *Theory and application of diagrams* (pp. 221–230). Berlin: Springer. doi:10.1007/3-540-44590-0_21

Van de Pol, J., Volman, M., & Beishuizen, J. (2010). Scaffolding in teacher–Student interaction: A decade of research. *Educational Psychology Review*, 22(3), 271–296. doi:10.1007/s10648-010-9127-6

van der Meij, J., & de Jong, T. (2011). The effects of directive self-explanation prompts to support active processing of multiple representations in a simulation-based learning environment. *Journal of Computer Assisted Learning*, 27, 411–423. doi:10.1111/j.1365-2729.2011.00411.x

Van Meter, P. N., & Cameron, C. (2018). The effects of presentation format on multiple document notetaking. *Learning and Instruction*, 57, 47–56. doi:org/10.1016/j.learninstruc.2018.03.002

Van Meter, P. N., Cameron, C., & Waters, J. R. (2017). Effects of response prompts and diagram comprehension ability on text and diagram learning in a college biology course. *Learning and Instruction, 49*, 188–198. doi:10.1016/j.learninstruc.2017.01.003

Van Meter, P. N., & Firetto, C. (2008). Intertextuality and the study of new literacies: Research critique and recommendations. In J. Coiro, M. Knobel, C. Lankshear, & D. J. Leu (Eds.), *Handbook of research on new literacies* (pp. 1079–1092). New York: Routledge.

Van Strien, J. L., Brand-Gruwel, S., & Boshuizen, H. P. (2014). Dealing with conflicting information from multiple nonlinear texts: Effects of prior attitudes. *Computers in Human Behavior, 32*, 101–111. doi:10.1016/j.chb.2013.11.021

Wiley, J., Goldman, S. R., Graesser, A. C., Sanchez, C. A., Ash, I. K., & Hemmerich, J. A. (2009). Source evaluation, comprehension, and learning in Internet science inquiry tasks. *American Educational Research Journal, 46*(4), 1060–1106. doi:10.3102/0002831209333183

Wiley, J., Sarmento, D., Griffin, T. D., & Hinze, S. R. (2017). Biology textbook graphics and their impact on expectations of understanding. *Discourse Processes, 54*(5-6), 463–478. doi:10.1080/0163853X.2017.1319655

Wiley, J., & Voss, J. F. (1999). Constructing arguments from multiple sources: Tasks that promote understanding and not just memory for text. *Journal of Educational Psychology, 91*(2), 301–311. doi:10.1037/0022-0663.91.2.301

Winne, P. H., & Hadwin, A. F. (1998). Studying as self-regulated engagement in learning. in metacognition in educational theory and practice. In D. J. Hacker, J. Dunlosky, & A. C. Graesser (Eds.), *Metacognition in educational theory and practice* (pp. 277–304). New York: Routledge. doi:10.4324/9781410602350

Winne, P. H., & Hadwin, A. F. (2008). The weave of motivation and self-regulated learning. In D. H. Schunk & B. J. Zimmerman (Eds.), *Motivation and self-regulated learning: Theory, research, and applications* (pp. 297–314). Mahwah, NJ: Lawrence Erlbaum.

Wolfe, M. B., & Goldman, S. R. (2005). Relations between adolescents' text processing and reasoning. *Cognition and Instruction, 23*(4), 467–502. doi:10.1207/s1532690xci2304_2

Wylie, R., & Chi, M. T. H. (2014). The self-explanation principle in multimedia learning. In R. E. Mayer (Ed.), *The Cambridge handbook of multimedia learning* (2nd ed., pp. 413–432). New York: Cambridge University Press. doi:10.1017/cbo9781139547369.021

INDEX

Note: Page numbers in *italics* refer to figures; page numbers in **bold** refer to tables.

ability explanation 210
absolutism 129, 337
academic self-concept 355
accuracy goals 197–198
activation processes 260–261, 375, **375**, 449
active processing 40
adaptive learning systems 73
additive processes 65
advanced learning technologies (ALTs): drawing or creating an illustration 541–542; multiple representations during learning with 533–540; research using 542–548; selecting a response in 540–541; types of representations in 533–538; writing or inputting information 541
affect: changes in 388–389; defined 375; and emotions 374–375
aggregation, principle of 334
AIR model 123, 124, 127, 130–132, **131**, 134
algorithms: for bot detection 490; and fake news 487, 488; filter bubble 467; influence of on content 483–484, 485; in intelligent learning systems 385, 495, 499, 505, 546; learning 487; machine-learning 470; preference-based 467; search 124; social media 124; on websites 471
Allport, G.W. 142
ALTs *see* advanced learning technologies (ALTs)
analogies 408
analytics tools 525
animations 69, 80, 81, 95, 97, 427
anomalies 405, 408, 418
antinomy 405, 408
antithesis 405, 408
anxiety 317, 325, 374–375, 376; caused by cognitive incongruity 377, 391; class-related 365; math 373; as negative activation emotion 380, 381, 395; reducing 387; test 373, 376
Apt-AIR framework 134–137
areas of interest (AOIs) 546
argumentation fallacies 271
artificial intelligence 33, 462, 496
assessments: diagnostic 101; digital 102; drawing or creating an illustration 541–542; effective design of 455–456; formative 101; of integration 412–414; pre-intervention 456; pre-test 456; selecting a response 540–541; summative 93, 101; stealth 507; within multiple representations 540–542; writing or inputting information 541–542
attitudes: about controversial topics 335; about knowledge, knowing, and learning 334–335; defined 191, 330; learning implications for integrating 339–341; and the learning process 329–331, *331*; literature review 334–335; role of 191–193; scientific 334–335; of teachers 340–341
attributional retraining 387
authorial bias 444
authors: benevolence of 169–170; expertise of 169–170; three dimensions of 169–170
automatic processing 196, 199, 252; integrating with effortful 196–198
autonomy support 386
autonomy-control continuum 356

backfire effect 391, 435, 455, 466, 468, 482
belief-preservation 199–200
belief-revision 200
beliefs: about intelligence 348, 363; about knowledge, knowing, and learning 336–337; contextualized 157; and controversy 337–338; defined 191, 330;

dispositional 157; domain-general 151, 155; domain-specific 151–152, 155; functions of 156–157; implicit 348; influences on 157; issue-specific 412; of learners 142, 144–145, 156; learning implications for integrating 339–341; and the learning process 329–331, *331*; literature review 336–338; naïve 255; prior 154, 390, 390–393; of the reader 254; reasons for 156–157; relationship with dispositions 155–156; role of 191–193; role of (in learning) 148, 151–155; role of (in learning from multiple perspectives) 143; strength of 200; of teachers 340–341; topic-specific 151, 152–153; transformation of 337; in working memory 146; *see also* epistemic/epistemological beliefs; ontic beliefs

Belvedere 524

Betty's Brain 538–539, 540, 542

block-by-block dual position texts 248–250, 253–254, 571

bot detection 490–491

CAMM (cognitive, affective, metacognitive, and motivational) processes 533, 549

case-building 199

CBLE (computer-based learning environment) 322, 326

CIE *see* continued influence effect (CIE)

CMRs (coordinating multiple representations) 63–65, 70

co-activation 209, 213, 218, 250, 253, 449, 468

COD (Conventions of Diagrams) instruction 86, 88

CODAP (Common Open Data Analysis Platform) 528

Code Breaker 518–519, 524

cognition: cold 376, 574; constraining 34; control of 298, 300, 308; effects of emotion on 374, 393–394; enabling 34; hot 574; human 34, 157, 527; knowledge and beliefs about 319; of learners 300, 308, 499; in mathematical modeling 115; and MRC 100–101; of others 317; regulation of 318; situated 514; techno- 470–471; *see also* epistemic cognition; metacognition; need for cognition

cognitive, affective, metacognitive, and motivational (CAMM) processes 533, 549

Cognitive Affective Engagement Model 147

cognitive apprenticeship 34, 184

cognitive artifacts 35

cognitive biases 425, 432, 435, 436, 486

cognitive closure 348, 362

cognitive conflict 377; attribution of 210–211, 214; conclusions and implications 217–219; experiences of 209–214, 217, 218; origin of 208, 211; reducing 218; regulating 351; role of in learning from multiple perspectives 205–219; socio- 351

cognitive flexibility 252, 270, 306, 315, 348, 403, 500, 508; *see also* flexibility

cognitive incongruity 376, 378–379, 391, 393; anxiety caused by 377, 391

cognitive load 380; extraneous 80; germane 80; intrinsic 80

Cognitive Load Theory 66, 70, 358

cognitive neuroscience 403, 406

cognitive operations: of MERs learning 76–89; and MERs learning 88; in research 564–565

cognitive orientation 42

cognitive overload 21, 38, 40, 497–498

cognitive paradigms 50–53, 59

cognitive processes 48–59, 255, 546, 565, 582; cognitive paradigms 59; individual differences 56–57; integration of text and picture 50–53; learning from multiple inputs 302–303; in mathematical representations 109–110; and multiple representation construction 102; multiple representation construction as 93–97; for multi-representational construction 93; role of in learning from multiple inputs 302–303; studies using cognitive paradigms 50–53; studies using eye tracking 53–56, 59; studies using verbal protocols 55–56; support for 57–58; supporting understanding and learning from multiple sources 208; and text comprehension 206–215

cognitive psychology 33, 34–35, 66

cognitive resources 41, 80, 97, 145, 251–252, 266–269, 277, 339, 380, 465

cognitive skills 42, 291, 429, 499; *see also* metacognitive skills

cognitive strategies 57, 255, 280, 364, 543, 544; *see also* metacognitive strategies

cognitive theories 20–26, 40; of expertise 41; multimedia 41

Cognitive Theory of Multimedia Learning (CTML) 20–21, 49–50, 53, 59, 66, 78, 80, 564

Cohere 519

coherence 81, 199; inappropriate strategies used to re-establish coherence 211–215; standards of 196; strategies to restore 218–219

coherence effect 497

cohesion 247, 308, 309, 409, 411, 415, 417, 419, 561; context 497; source 300; text 309

collaboration 42, 73, 390, 407; defined 515; in learning 507; multiple dimensions of 528; in problem solving 508; representations of 525; using multiple representation constructions 100–102; *see also* Computer-Supported Collaborative Learning (CSCL)

collaborative problem-solving (CPS) 508

Common Core State Standards 113

Common Knowledge 523

Common Open Data Analysis Platform (CODAP) 528

communication: in collaborative learning 521–523; cultural tools of 26; disambiguation of 100; and gestures 95; improved 471; nonverbal 27–28; between peers 93, 516, 521–522; social 27; using multiple representation constructions 100–102; verbal 26–27, 28, 29
communities of learning 43
community of practice 41
compensatory processes 65
competence: epistemic 134, 138n2; lack of 210; of learners 271, 314, 355, 365, 378; meta-representational 21–22, 24–26, 28, 99, 514, 528; meta-resource 574–576, 584; perceived 378; perspectives 576; of a source 216; *see also* meta-representational competence; meta-resource competence; representational competencies
competence beliefs 355, 363
competition 388
competitive play 70
complementary perspectives 224–225, 241–242; extant research on 225–226, **227–234**, 235–237; focus and key findings 237–241
componential reading situation 263
comprehensibility 195
comprehension: component processes of 260–262; of dual-position texts 251–252; and executive function 300; models of 251; of multiple perspectives 270
computer science 33
Computer Supported Cooperative Work (CSCW) 515
computer-based learning environment (CBLE) 322, 326
Computer-Supported Collaborative Learning (CSCL) 514; challenges of 515–517; representational affordances for 518–519; research on 514–515; using multiple representations (to maintain a shared knowledge base) 523; using multiple representations (to plan, monitor, and regulate group activities) 524–525, 527; using multiple representations (to support epistemic practices) 523–524; using multiple representations (to support peer communication) 521–522; *see also* collaborative learning
conceptual change 451–454
confirmation bias 197, 199, 268, 435
conflict attribution 210–211
confusion 325, 389, 390, 391, 393
connectional fluency 23–24
conscientiousness 362, 363–364
conservation tasks 101
construction dimension 580–581, **580**
Construction-Integration model 226, 251, 263
constructionism 452
constructivism 34, 113, 340, 391, 452

Content-Source Integration (CSI) 208, 211, 215, 218
context dimension 572–573, **572**
contextual factors: classroom goal structures 366; stimulating content 366; time constraints 365–366
contiguity principle 41, 80, 82
continued influence effect (CIE) 463–464, 471; cognitive explanations for 464–465; vulnerability to 466
control, perceived 378, 385–386
control-value theory (CVT) 374, 377–382, 394; and autonomy support 386; cognitive-emotional model of emotion effects 380
controversy: beliefs in/beliefs and 154, 210, 217, 267, 270, 337–338; evaluation of 133, 382; mental representation of 268; scientific 153, 335; teaching 335
Conventions of Diagrams (COD) instruction 86, 88
coordinating multiple representations (CMRs) 63–65, 70
CPS (collaborative problem-solving) 508
credible evidence 433–434
critical thinking 321, 325, 428–429, 432; cognitive biases 435; and credible evidence 433–434; dispositions and skills **430–431**, 434–435; in domain perspective leaning 181–182; domain-general vs. domain-specific 429, 432; frameworks and multiple input integration 433–435; interventions 436; key features 433; and misinformation 469–470; philosophical frameworks 428; psychological models 428
cross-modal coordination 100
cross-representation connections 80–81, 84
Crystal Island 538, 539, 540, 549
CSCL *see* Computer-Supported Collaborative Learning (CSCL)
CSCW (Computer Supported Cooperative Work) 515
CSI *see* Content-Source Integration (CSI)
CTML *see* Cognitive Theory of Multimedia Learning (CTML)
curiosity 325, 389, 391, 393
CVT *see* control-value theory (CVT)

data visualization 35, 108, 536, 538, 539; *see also* visualization
Decimal Point 540
decoupling 126, 200
deductive reasoning 68, 73; *see also* reasoning
deep learning strategies 49, 93, 338, 352, 355, 357, 360, 381
deepfakes 462
DeFT framework (Design parameters, pedagogical Function, cognitive Tasks) 496
developmental psychology 66

diagram comprehension 86, 574
diagram-processing strategies 87
dialogic participation 281, 283
digital learning environments 48–49
digital literacy 326
digital tools 101; *see also* technology
directional goals 196–198; *see also* goals
disciplinary literacy 277, 283
disconfirmation bias 199, 435
Discrepancy-Induced Source Comprehension (D-ISC) Model 213, 218, 264, 449
disengagement 325, 409
disinformation 478; *see also* fake news; misinformation
dispositions 142, 157, 434–435; relationship with beliefs 155–156; role in learning 148–151; role in learning (from multiple perspectives) 143
DMF *see* Documents Model Framework (DMF)
documents model 226, 235, 265
Documents Model Framework (DMF) 125, 213, 215, 217–218
domain characteristics 166–167
domain literacy 185
domain perspective learning (DPL) 164–186; building deeper understanding 180–181; cautionary note on novices' 182–183; conceptualizing a single domain perspective 171; construction 171–172; critical thinking 181–182; fostering 183–186; inferential and deductive recognition and construction 172; problem solving 181; processes involved in 171–172; purpose for 180–182; recognition 171
domain perspectives 167–172; comparing conclusions across 174–175; comparison and evaluation 173; defined 166; endogenous evaluation 173–174; integration 176–179; integration (comparing approaches) 179, **180**; origin of in text 169–171; personal weighing 175–176; reasoning about 172–180; selective approach to integration 177, 179, **180**, 186; structural approach to integration 178, 179, **180**; transformative approach to integration 177–178, 179, **180**
domains, defined 166–167
DPL *see* domain perspective learning (DPL)
dual channel assumption 21
dual coding assumption 20
dual coding theory 22
dual-channel input 40
dual-position texts: addressing one or multiple perspectives 249; blocked vs. interleaved 248–256, 496–497, 571; classifying 250–251; comprehension of 251–252; neutral 248–249; situating 246–250; supporting learning from multiple perspectives 252–255; texts written to persuade the reader 248–249; utilizing refutation 249–250
Dynamicland 527

echo chambers 123, 124, 461, 466, 482–483
eco-cognitive model of abduction 97
effortful processing 154–155, 196, 308, 365, 385; integrating with automatic 196–198
elaborative processing 145, 254, 266–267, 272, 307; of conflicting information 268–271; *see also* elaboration
elaboration 42, 55, 307, 321, 325, 335, 381, 391; cross-text 149, 152, 352, 354, 364, 366; epistemic 252, 254–256; of information 268–271; relational 410; self- 238
ElectronixTutor 502–505; ASSISTments 503, 504; AutoTutor 502; BEETLE-II 503; Dragoon 503; LearnForm 503, 504; on Moodle 505; outcome possibilities **507**; Point & Query utility 504–505; screenshot *506*; static reading materials 503–504
EMMEs (Eye Movement Modeling Examples) 57–58, 71, 87
emotional contagion 379, 383, 388, 395
emotions: achievement 376; activity 376, 378; adaptive 387; appraisal-based 379; and beliefs 256; and cognition 393–394; deactivating 381; defined 374; epistemic 316–317, 324, 326, 376–377, 389, 390–392, 394; and eye tracking 549; facial expressions of *537*, 538, 542, 544, 548; of learners 548; and learning strategies 325; and mood and affect 374–375; negative 373–374; negative activating 380, 381, 382; negative deactivating 380, 382; non-cognitive induction of 379; object focus of 376, 380; origins and functions of 377–382; outcome 376; positive activating 380, 381; positive deactivating 380, 382; prospective 378; reciprocal causation 382; related to learning 376–377; retrospective 378; role of 201; role of in learning 316–317, 546–547; role of in learning (from multiple perspectives) 374, 389–393; role of in learning (from multiple representations) 374, 382–389; self-report of 394; social 377; task-extraneous positive 380; topic 377; valence and activation 375, **375**; verbalizations of 542, 544
engagement: affective 409; of learners 412, 415–417
enjoyment 325
entrainment 379, 383, 384, 393, 395
epistemic aims 130, 134, 135–137, 138n2, 316, 578
epistemic/epistemological beliefs 142–143, 158, 165, 210–211, 336–337, 348–349; complex 255–256; about deep knowledge 353; development of 337–338; domain-general 151, 155; domain-specific 151–152, 155; and epistemic emotions 391; about justification for knowing 147, 151–153, 353; of

learners 147, 153, 254–256, 269, 324, 346, 351–354, 575–576; and meta-resource competence 576; from multiple perspectives 144, 151–153, 353–354, 390–391, 575; naïve 255; role of 352–354; studies of 239, 412, 576, 579; topic-specific 145, 152–153, 211; *see also* Integrated Model of Epistemic Beliefs in Multiple-Text Comprehension
epistemic cognition 123, 180, 325, 336, 433–434, 436, 563, 577–580; AIR model of 123, 124, 127, 130–132, **131**, 134; components of 578; domain-general 436; domain-specific 180–181, 434, 436; integrated model of 353; of learners 436; of teachers 341
epistemic competence 134, 138n2
epistemic development 124, 127, 128–130
epistemic elaboration 252, 254–255
Epistemic Emotion Scales (EES) 390
epistemic engagement 281, 283
epistemic ideals 130, 131, 135
epistemic mastery 349, 351–352, 360, 362
epistemic monitoring, automatic 251–252
epistemic practices 183, 516–517
epistemic processes, 93, 130–132, 134–135, 138
epistemic reflexivity, of teachers 340–341
epistemic Stroop paradigm 261–262, 267
epistemic thinking, three components of 130–131
epistemic validation 251–252
epistemology/ies 167, 336, 444–445; apt 134–137; virtue 134
e-textiles 101
Etherpad 525
EV theory *see* expectancy-value (EV) theory of achievement motivation
evaluation, endogenous 173–174
evaluativism 129–130, 239, 337
executive functions 297–309, 403; and comprehension processes 300–302; conceptualization of 298–300; consideration of other factors 308–309; individual differences in 298, 299, 302–304; in integration of multiple inputs 303–304; in multiple representations 305–306; in multiple texts and perspectives 306–307; and reader-text interaction 301–302; roles in integration and comprehension of multiple representations **304**; roles in integration and comprehension of multiple texts and perspectives **305**; unity/diversity framework 299–300, 303
expectancies 364; and motivation 354–356
expectancy-value (EV) theory of achievement motivation 331, 332, 354–355, 356
experiences: metacognitive 319; transformative 333, 340
expert disagreement 130, 133–134
expertise reversal effect 70
expert-novice paradigm 33–35

ExplanationConstructor 523–524
Eye Movement Modeling Examples (EMMEs) 57–58, 71, 87
eye tracking 53–56, 59, 165, 264, 320–322, 326, 413, 542, 543, 546, 548, 549; *see also* gaze behavior

facial detection software 544
facial expressions: of affective states 544; data 546–547; of emotions *537*, 538, 542, 544, 548; videos of 544, 546, 549
facial-muscle movements 544
factoring assumption 20–21, 26
fair-mindedness 434
fake news: ad hominem strategy 480–481; argumentum ad populum 480; backfire effect 482; bot detection technologies 490–491; challenges presented by 478–479; creation of 479, 480–482; defined 478; detection of 485–488; diffusion patterns 487–488; and the Disease Pyramid *479*; dissemination of 483; distribution of 479, 488–491; and echo chambers 482; economic incentives for 481; educational interventions 481–482, 486; exposure to 482–485; gatekeeping 485; holding users accountable 489; human and technology challenges and solutions **480**; and the illusory-truth effect 482; key factors and phases of the news cycle 478–479; and machine learning 488; and motivated reasoning 485–486; network-based features 488; "personalized" exposure to 483–484; and political polarization 481; production of 479; sensational and emotional headlines 489; social bots 489–490; and social media 483, 487; and social pressure 482; susceptibility to 483; and trolls 487; warnings and retractions 486; *see also* misinformation; misunderstandings; understandings, inaccurate
Fake News Pyramid 479–480, *479*
fallacies 271, 416
familiarity backfire effect 468; *see also* backfire effect
feedback 74, 93; from ALTs 540; embedded 322; focused 387; from intelligent tutoring systems 499, 503; negative 363; simple 331; unexpected 392–393; using trace data 528
filter bubbles 466, 467, 471, 483–484
fixations 542, 543; *see also* eye tracking
fixed mindsets 363
flexibility 115, 299, 381, 483, 502, 504; *see also* cognitive flexibility
fluency prompts 84
focalism 435
fragmented views 446–447
freedom of speech 471

game usability 69
gatekeeping 485

gaze behavior 52, 53, 58, 533, 536, 538; *see also* eye tracking
gender differences 335
gender interaction 71, 363
gender studies 178
gestures 94, 95–96, 101
goal setting 316, 317, 325, 364, 385, 412, 550
goal structures 379, 386–387
goals: accuracy 197–198; achievement 349, 351–352, 364, 548; action/activity 351; belief-driven 197–198; classroom 366; directional 196–198; educational 270; epistemic mastery 360, 362; epistemic reading 269; knowledge-driven 197; mastery 348, 349, 351–352, 360, 365, 366; in mathematical problem solving 110; pedagogical 19; performance 355, 360, 366; performance-approach 351; personal 351; professional 18; of the reader 194–198, 207, 217, 252, 254–255, 266; of the self-regulated learner 316, 323, 326; task-based 351, 360; theory preservation 337; valuing 348; *see also* goal setting
Google Docs 525
graphical representations 97, 110, 427, 469, 521, 522
grit 363–364, 507
grounding 102, 114, 157, 428
group processes 201
growth mindsets 363

heart rate 542
heat map *535*
hedging 212
heuristics 196, 337, 435, 462, 470
hidden figures/embedded figures tests 69
historical empathy 278
historical inquiry 278
historical literacy 137, 276
hyperlinks 81
hypermedia 69, 71
hypothesis-testing behavior 549

ICAP (Interactive > Constructive > Active > Passive) framework 497
Idea Thread Mapper 525, 527
IF-MT *see* Integrated Framework of Multiple Texts (IF-MT)
illusory-truth effect 482
immersive virtual systems 546
iMotions 548
incentives 379, 386–387, 393; economic/financial 481, 482; extrinsic 386
inconsistency paradigm 52
individual differences 6, 9, 64, 66, 82–83, 146, 153, 218, 383, 385, 413, 536, 574–575; correlations of 69; dispositional 157; in executive function 298, 299, 302–304; in individual interests 364–366; in personality traits 141, 142, 157, 363–364; in processes 56–57, 239, 240, 346, 348, 351, 357;in reasoning 70; role of 361–363; and task interventions 66–67, 70–73
individual interest 147, 346, 366; and motivation 364–365
information: accuracy of 444; availability of 314, 426, 461; belief-consistent 247, 266–267; belief-inconsistent 145, 271–272; belief-related 191–201, 194, 198–200, *199*; componential 263; conflicting 264–265, 267–269; content of 3–4; credibility of 462; dissemination of 444; elaboration of 268–269; encoding 251; forms of representation 167; integration and updating 464–465; plausibility of 262; processing 78, 154; quality of 462; source 265, 270–271; static vs. dynamic 536; worldview-consistent 466
Information Disorder conceptual framework 478
information literacy 297, 469–470; and executive functions 298, 300
Information Processing Theory (IPT) 404–405, 548
informational resources 4–5; understanding 5
inhibition 298–301, 303, 305–308, 403
instruction: mathematical representations in 112–113; role of in integration 302; strategy 86–87; *see also* learning; STEM instruction
instructional design and designers 41, 43–44, 80, 385, 395, 455, 457, 534, 561, 570
instructors *see* teachers
Integrated Framework of Multiple Texts (IF-MT) 144, 147–148, 235, 403, 409; with multiple representations 411
integrated mental model 52, 67, 144, 145, 213, 306, 308
Integrated Model of Epistemic Beliefs in Multiple-Text Comprehension 144–145, 148
Integrated Model of Text and Picture Comprehension (ITPC) 20–21, 23, 49
integration: in comprehension of multiple perspective texts 262–265; defined 408–409; execution stage 410, 413–414, 416; individual differences and processes 239; of knowledge 449; measuring 237–238, 412–414; metacognitive processes during 320–326; of multiple inputs 425–426, 435–436; of multiple perspectives 582; of multiple resources 582; preparation stage 409–410, 412–413, 415; process of 409; production stage 410–411, 414, 416–419; and relational reasoning 414–419; role of instruction in 302; strategies for 327; supports for 238–239
integration processes 260–261
integrative processing: contextual factors 365–366; individual differences 361–365; levels of expectancy and motivation 354–356; motivational model of *350*; perceived costs

357–359; role of achievement goals 349, 351–352; role of epistemic beliefs 352–354; values and motivation 356–357, 359–361
intelligence: artificial 33, 462, 496; beliefs about 348, 363; and deductive reasoning 68; fluid measures of 406; individual differences in 66; verbal 466; *see also* artificial intelligence
intelligence mindsets 363
intelligent tutoring systems (ITS) 495–496, 499–500, 502; domain model 499; domains, representations, and learner interaction **501**; hybrid 502–505, 508; knowledge components 504–505; meta-analyses 500; student model 499; tutor model 499; user interface 499–500
Interactive > Constructive > Active > Passive (ICAP) framework 497
interactive processes 65
interdisciplinarity 176
interdisciplinary understanding 164–186
interleaved dual-position texts 248–256, 496–497, 571
internal attribution 210
Internet: and cognitive conflict 206; misinformation on 470, 477; multiple representations on 49; as source of information 2, 259, 326
internet trolls 487
intersubjectivity 514, 516–517
intertext model 144
intertextual commitment 280–281, 283
intertextual tasks 263
interventions: learner-driven 79; materials-driven 79–83; for MERs learning (conclusions) 88–89; prompt-driven 79
IPT (information processing theory) 404–405, 548
ITPC (Integrated Model of Text and Picture Comprehension) 20–21, 23, 49
ITS *see* intelligent tutoring systems (ITS)

Jigsaw Classroom technique 517
justification 152

KCI (Knowledge Community and Inquiry) 523
knowledge: academic 338; acquisition of 24–25, 444, 539; architecture of 445; assessment of 455; attitudes about 334–335; background 58, 208, 335; beliefs about 151; as body of interrelated concepts 144–145; certainty of 144; characterizations of 455; common 480; as complete concepts stored in memory 446–447; components of 504–505; conceptual 84; conditional 539; constellations of 447–452; construction of 133, 135–136, 322, 444, 519, 582; contemporary accounts of 445–447; content 539; context of 26; creation of 314; current 379; declarative 318, 321, 539; deep 353; desired 379; domain 218, 308, 500, 539; existing 452; expert 447; factual 451; higher-order 88; holistic accounts of 448; internal 238; justification for 144; metacognitive 317–319; modifying 447–448; multiplicity of 129; naïve 34; nature of 353, 444, 445–447; novice 447; organization of 446; perceived 206, 253; as perspective 164–186; prior 56, 67, 70, 73, 78, 84, 94, 208, 210, 213, 238, 251–252, 254, 262, 267–268, 299, 321, 412, 429, 497, 565; procedural 318, 539; of the reader 254; reconstruction of 335; revision of 250, 453; scientific reasoning 390; shared 100, 516, 523; related to source 144, 216; subject matter 499; subject-relevant 470; topic-specific 412; transfer of 404, 498; use by experts 34–35; values about 332–333; *see also* metastrategic knowledge; metatask knowledge; understandings
Knowledge Building pedagogy 516
Knowledge Community and Inquiry (KCI) 523
knowledge elaboration 321, 325
Knowledge Forum 519, *520*, 521–523
knowledge gap 316
knowledge mapping 519
Knowledge Revision Components (KReC) Framework 448–449
knowledge-in-pieces 446–447
KReC (Knowledge Revision Components) Framework 448–449

Landscape model 251, 449
language, multimodal 27, 97
Latent Semantic Analysis (LSA) 541
learner characteristics dimension 574–575, **575**
learner processes dimension 576–578, **577**
learner-driven interventions 86–87
learners: age/grade in school 70, 71; attention allocation of *535*; beliefs of 142; characteristics of 64, 574–576; dispositions of 142; engagement of 409, 412, 415–417; gender 70, 71; high knowledge 70, 73, 254; individual differences 66–67, **67**, 73; individual differences interactions 70; integration of perspectives by 238; interest of 70; judgment of truthfulness 146; low knowledge 70, 216, 254, 308; making domains and domain characteristics explicit for 184; motivation of 70, 71, 548; processes used by 576–580; support for cognitive processes of 57–58; values, attitudes, and beliefs of 339; *see also* students
learning: adaptive 73; after unexpected feedback 392–393; assessments of 549–551; authentic 426; and cognition 149; collaborative 390, 507, 516–517; by construction of multiple representations 92–103; from contradictory texts 390–392; deep 49, 93, 338, 352, 355, 357, 360, 381; digital 101, 496–498; in disciplinary classrooms 276–291; domain-specific 164–186; using dual-position texts 245–256; interventions

to support 76–89; MERs 76–89; and motivation 380; multimedia 358, 380; from multiple inputs 302–303; with multiple representations 322–323; multi-resource 583; objective 186; outcomes 381–382; personalized 495–509; role of emotions in 316–317; self-regulated 70, 71–72, 381; technology-enhanced multimedia 374; *see also* domain perspective learning; Computer-Supported Collaborative Learning (CSCL); instruction; perspective learning; self-regulated learning (SRL)

learning analytics 385, 525, 528

learning communities 17, 26, 27, 28, 43, 341

learning environments: acoustic qualities of 384; as antecedents 379; collaborative 527; computer 70, 322, 495, 499; constructionist 452; constructivist 452; digital 48, 64; game-based 551; incentives in 386; multimedia 380, 381, 383–384, 387, 496; in public spaces 528; representations in 38, 433, 498; shaping of emotions in 382; social interaction in 387–388, 582; structural features of 73, 383, 508

learning materials, satisfaction with 69

learning resources, integration of **507**

learning styles, verbalizers vs. visualizers 56–57

learning tasks 64, 395; multiple perspective 562–563; multiple representation 562–563

learning technologies, key affordances of **498–499, 504**; *see also* technology/ies

learning theories: cognitive 40; constructivist 34; multimedia theory 40; situative (socio-cultural) 40

lesson difficulty rating 69

lexical cues 127

literacy: digital 326; disciplinary 277, 273; domain 185; historical 137, 276; information and media 297, 298, 300, 469–470; scientific 151, 427; of students 97, 281, 334, 444, 470, 538

log files 542, 543, 544, 546, 548

LSA (Latent Semantic Analysis) 541

machine learning 470, 488, 548, 549

Maker Movement 101

malinformation 478; *see also* fake news; misinformation; disinformation

manipulatives 113

MASRL model 319

mastery-approach goal orientation *see* goals; motivation

materials-driven interventions 79–83; conclusions 81–83; and temporal contiguity 80–81; types of 79–80

mathematical representations 107–109; abstracted 114; background 109–110; dynamic nature of 114; in individual problem solving 110–111; in instruction 112–113; as monitoring and evaluating devices 111; as process 109–110; as product 110; as recording tools 110; as social activity 111–112; student-generated 113; symbolization and modeling in 113–115; as tools for problem solving 115; as tools to explore concepts 110–111; translation of 109; types of *108*, 109; use by experts 111, 115; use by students 111–112, 115

mathematical set theory 405

mathematics education 107–116; Principles to Actions (NCTM) 108

meaning-making 99–100; and executive function 298; intersubjective 516–517

meaning-sharing 99–100

media bias 444

media literacy 469–470

memory: and cognitive conflict 217; failure of 464–465; knowledge stored in 446; and learning strategies 381; limited capacity 40; long-term 207, 267, 348; measuring 214; *see also* working memory

memory-based processing 193–194, 196, 198–199

mental effort 70; self-reported 69

mental models 19, 21–23, 25, 260, 262, 464–465, 468, 533, 534, 542, 560; abstract 560; belief-based 254; coherent 49, 52, 195, 308, 315, 319; construction/formation of 53–54, 59, 80, 144, 195, 196, 301, 496–497, 503, 580; descriptive 21; of domain content 23; evaluation of 195; incomplete 465; integrated 52, 67, 144, 145, 196, 213, 306, 308; pictorial 21, 50; revision of 77, 88, 465, 558, 562; spatial 54; updating 195, 319, 465, 539–541; verbal 21, 50

mental representations 144

Mental Rotations Test 69

mental states 34

MERs *see* multiple external representations (MERs)

metacognition 24, 238, 317–319, 429; defined 317; epistemic 318–319, 323; role of in knowledge construction 322; and self-regulated learning 315, 317, 320–322, 326–327

metacognitive monitoring 542

metacognitive processes 327, 546; integrating multiple representations 321–322; during integration 320–326

metacognitive skills 302, 318, 319

metacognitive strategies 10, 272, 302, 307, 321, 325, 326, 364, 575

meta-competencies 582

metadata 215, 488, 490

MetaMentor 537

metamotivational framework 359

meta-representation 125–126

meta-representational competence/competencies 17, 21–22, 24–26, 28, 99, 514, 528

meta-resource competence/competencies 574–576, 583

metastrategic knowledge 318, 320, 322, 323–324
metatask knowledge 318
MetaTutor 538–539, 540, 549, 550
MetaTutorIVH 538–539, 540
microgenetic analysis 218–219
mindsets, and motivation 363–364
misconceptions 22, 34, 193–194, 302, 391–392, 404, 414, 436, 484, 540; creating 212; learner 499, 540; reader 248, 250, 252; scientific 468
misinformation 444; challenges of 466–467; classifications of 462–463; continued influence effect (CIE) 463–464; correction design 467–469; creation and distribution of 467; defined 462; detection of 470; educational approaches to 469–470; and freedom of speech 471; graphical displays 469; information and media literacy training 469–470; inoculation against 470; on the Internet 470, 477; need for social change 471; recommendations to combat 467–471; reducing the impact of 461–471; refutations 467–468; role of motivational factors 465–466; sharing of 489; susceptibility to 466, 467, 480; systemic changes 470–471; technocognition approach to 470–471; warnings 468–469; *see also* fake news; misunderstandings; understandings, inaccurate
misunderstandings 444–445, 451–452; correction of 448, 457; diverse approaches and perspectives 454–455; measuring and discussing 455–456; modifications to 456; nature of 455; *see also* fake news; misinformation; understandings, inaccurate
modality principle 41
modeling 26, 70, 98, 321; history of 116n2; in mathematical representations 113–115
modifying facts 447–452
monitoring: of behavior 403, 417; of collaborative processes 513, 517, 527, 528; comprehension 306, 307; epistemic 251; individual differences in 69; by learners 147, 302, 306, 315, 546; of MERs 78; metacognitive 316, 318, 321, 322, 534, 539, 540, 542, 577; negative 55, 239; positive 329; processes 262, 290, 464, 469; of products 323, 325; of progress 111, 322, 536; self- 319, 385; strategic 464, 469; of sub-goals 534; of time 539
mood: defined 374–375; and emotions 374–375; general and specific 376
Moodle 505
motivation: achievement 412; and achievement goals 349, 351–352; autonomous 359, 360–361; contextual factors 365–366; controlled 360–361; costs of 357–359; epistemic 351; and epistemic beliefs 352–354; and expectancies 354–356; expectancy-value (EV) theory of 332; extrinsic 361, 380; individual difference factors 361–365; interactions with tasks 70; intrinsic 359, 361; to learn 380; and misinformation 465–466; prevention 367; promotion 361; qualitatively distinct 349; quality of 359–361; of readers 252, 255; of students 277, 348, 349; and values 356–357, 359–361; variables in 67–68
motivational interactions 71
MRC *see* multiple representation construction (MRC)
MRLF *see* multiple resources learning framework (MRLF)
MSU (multiple source use) 403
multimedia 49, 81; *see also* multiple representations
multimedia learning 74, 380; autonomy support 386; cognitive theory of 59; and emotions 393; and eye tracking 53–56; incentives and goal structures 386–387; integration of text and picture 50–53; mental effort involved in 358; musical score 384; scaffolding 385–386; social interaction 387–388; task demands and clarity 385; technology-based 394; theories of 52–53; visual design 383–384
multimedia principle 41
multimedia theory 40; *see also* Cognitive Theory of Multimedia Learning
multimodal multichannel data 548–551; effectiveness of 549–551; eye tracking 543, 546; log files 543, 546, 548; physiological sensors 548; screen recordings 547; strengths and challenges of using 544, **545**, 546; theoretical assumptions for using 548–551; think-aloud protocols 544, 547; videos of facial expressions of affective states 544, 546–547, 548
Multiple Documents Task-based Relevance and Content Extraction model (MD-TRACE) 226, 235
multiple external representations (MERs) 27, 28, 35; examples of *77*; interventions to support learning from 76–89
multiple inputs: integration of 425–426, 435–436; integration using critical thinking 433–435; learning from 347–348; processing 348; *see also* multiple perspectives; multiple representations
multiple perspectives 353, 582–583; in collaborative learning 514; complementary 223–242; connections between 360; defined 315, 330, 427–428; dual-position texts 245–256, 252–255; emotions and learning from 389–393; evaluating 215–217; in expository texts *247*; and fake news 478; influence of values, attitudes, and beliefs on 330–342, *331*; integration and validation in comprehension of texts conveying 262–265; integration of 323–324, 582; of learners 516–517; learning from 141–158, 324–326, 558; learning tasks 562–563; role of validation in integrating 259–272; situating dual-position texts 246–250; *see also* multiple inputs; multiple representations

multiple representation construction (MRC) 92–103; conclusions 102–103; as constructive cognitive process 93–96; digitally supported 101; drawing 94; gesturing 94, 95–97, 101; non-linguistic 99; as representing core disciplinary practices 97–101; supporting communication and collaboration 100–102

multiple representations 582–583; application of socio-cultural theory to 564; cognitive processes involved in learning from 48–59; connections between 360; contrived vs. authentic 41–42, 43; coordinating (CMR) 63–65; in CSCL environments 518, 523–524, 527–528; cultural conventions for 28; defined 19–20, 315, 330, 426–427; DeFT framework (Design paramaters, pedagogical Function, cognitive Tasks) 496; design choices 496–497; in digital learning technologies 496–498; domain-specific 44; and educational technology 508–509; efficacy of 497; and executive functions 300–303; expert-novice studies 38–44; to facilitate knowledge acquisition 539; and fake news 478; to foster learning 538–539; goals of 18, 538–540; and guided discussion 38; ICAP (Interactive > Constructive > Active > Passive) framework 497; influence of values, attitudes, and beliefs on 330–342, *331*; and the Integrated Framework of Multiple Texts (IF-MT) 411; integration of 347; learning by construction of 92–103; learning from 62–74, 322–323, 379, 558; for learning in various ways 514–515; learning tasks 562–563; learning with advanced learning technologies (ALTs) 533–540; to maintain a shared knowledge base 523; measurement and assessment within 540–542; measuring self-regulated learning with 542–548; metacognitive processes and SRL 320–321; multiplicity and connectedness 388–389; novice use of 37–38; as overwhelming 434; to plan, monitor, and regulate group activities 524–525; problem solving in mathematics 107–116; in STEM learning 38; to support epistemic practices 523–524; to support peer communication 521–522; theoretical implications 40–43; types of 64; to update mental models 539–540; use during disciplinary practices 564; value of 18–20; verbal vs. pictorial 49; *see also* multiple external representations (MERs); multiple inputs; multiple perspectives; multiple representation construction

Multiple Resource Learning Framework *see* multiple resources learning framework (MRLF)

multiple resources, integration of 582

multiple resources learning framework (MRLF) 2, 566–568, *566*; construction dimension 580–582; context dimension 572–574; learner characteristics dimension 574–576; learner processes dimension 576–580; summary and conclusion 582–583; task and resources dimension 568–572

multiple source use (MSU) 403
multiple text integration 224, 226
multiple text proficiency 147
multiplicity 388–389
multiplism 129, 239, 337
multi-resource learning tasks, features of 5–6
musical score 384
myside bias 199

need for cognition 66, 70, 146, 148–149, 150, 155–158, 348, 361–362
negative response tendency 262
Negotiation Potentials 100
news literacy 481

object focus 376
ontic beliefs 9, 142–143, 145, 148, 153–156, 158, 567
open-mindedness 149–150, 155–156, 270
opportunity costs 358
orchestration graph *526*
overarching concepts 167
overconfidence bias 435

paraphrasing 69
passive activation 193
pattern recognition 24, 36
patterning 405
perceived ease of use 69
perceptual fluency 21–24, 25, 29; group-level 28
personality traits: big five 362; and motivation 363–364
perspective learning: acknowledging perspectives 278–279; classroom vignettes 282–289; co-constructing perspectives 279–280; comparing perspectives 279; components of 278–280; and dialogic participation 281, 283; in disciplinary classrooms 277–278; and epistemic engagement 281, 283; in a historical multisource task environment 289–291; and intertextual commitment 280–281, 283; role of multisource task environments in 280–281; *see also* multiple perspectives; perspective(s)
perspective(s) 3, 6, 9; acknowledging 278–279, 284, 286–287; alternative 124, 129, 133, 135–136; assigned 165; of the author 126, 132–133, 135–138; co-constructing 279–280; co-construction of 285–286; cognitive 97; comparing 279, 284–285, 286–287; conflicting 208, 215; contradictory 390–392; contrasting 235; defined 125, 165–166; disciplinary 132; discrepant 211; divergent 260; diverse 289; domain-specific 167–168; economic

183; external 145; importance of 124–125; knowledge as 164–186; learning about and developing 276–291; manipulating 239–240; multiple 256; non-textual 236; opposing 246, 250–251; of the reader 198; research on 236–237; role-based 166; semiotic 97, 98; socio-cultural 97; socio-semiotic 97; source 224; subjective 129; theoretical 109; *see also* complementary perspectives; dual-position texts; multiple perspectives; perspective learning; source perspectives
physiological sensors 542, 548
picture fixation 59
picture information 53–54
planned behavior, theory of 331
Plausibility Judgments of Conceptual Change (PJCC) Model 144, 146–147
post-truth 471, 477–478, 491, 576; *see also* fake news
principle of aggregation 334
problem solving 405; with advanced learning technologies (ALTs) 533; collaborative 26–27, 508; complex 407; in domain perspective leaning 181; and executive function 300; higher-order 403; interdisciplinary 183
processing: automatic 196–198, 199, 252; belief-biased 254; dual theories of 196; effortful 154–155, 196–198, 308, 365, 385; memory-based 193–194, 196, 198–199; reader-guided 194–196, 198; Type 1 and Type 2 196–197, 199; *see also* elaborative processing
prompt-driven interventions 83–86

rationalization 199–200
Raven's Progressive Matrices 406
RCA (Representation Construction Approach) 98–99
reaction time 69
reader-guided processing 194–196, 198
reading comprehension 64, 66, 67, 68, 69, 72, 73, 138, 201, 301–302, 574
reading skills 70, 150
reasoned action, theory of 331
reasoning: abductive 97; about multiple domain perspectives 172–180; analogical 408; anomalous 405, 408, 418; antinomous 405, 408, 418; antithetical 405, 408, 419; collaborative 407; deductive 68, 73; individual differences in 70; and mathematics 108; model-based 98; motivated 485–486; speculative 97; visuospatial 406; *see also* relational reasoning
reciprocal causation 382
recursive neural networks 488
redundancy effect 497
reflection prompts 322–323
reflexivity, epistemic 340–341

refutation texts 151, 152, 193–194, 245, 249–251, 253, 309, 373, 374, 390, 391, 392, 449–450, 456
regulatory focus theory 361
relational elaboration 410; *see also* elaboration
relational integration 403; *see also* integration
relational reasoning 402, 419–420; assessment of 406–407; contemporary research 402–403; discussion framework 403–404; and integration 414–419; manifestations of 405; philosophical and psychological roots 402; summations 407–408; theoretical and empirical foundations 404–405
relativism 337
representation 514
Representation Construction Approach (RCA) 98–99
representation dilemma 20, 29, 78, 88
representational competencies 20, 36, 38, 42, 43, 44, 514, 576; cognitive research on 20–22; meta- 21–22, 24–26, 28, 99, 514, 528; perceptual fluency 21–25, 28, 29; sense-making 21–23, 25
representational fluency 23–24, 498, 508
representational format(s) 3–4
representations 527; external 533; graphical 98, 110, 427, 469, 521, 522; internal vs. external (symbolic vs. visual) 19; single vs. multiple 536, 538; static vs. dynamic 536; types of in advanced learning technologies (ALTs) 533–538; *see also* multiple representations
Resonance-Integration-Validation (RI-Val) Model 261, 263, 449
reverse validity 254–255
rewards *see* incentives
RI-Val (Resonance-Integration-Validation) Model 261, 263, 449

saccades 542, 543; *see also* eye tracking
satisfaction with learning materials 69
scaffolding 26, 29, 34, 42, 321, 322, 339–341, 379, 385–386, 393, 395, 582; metastrategic 323–324; strategic 324
Science Writing Heuristic 99
scientific literacy 151, 427
Scratch Online Community 522, *522*
screen capture 326
screen recordings 547
selective exposure 268
self-efficacy 354–356, 357, 364, 366; perceived 359
self-explanation prompts 83–84
self-regulated learning (SRL) 69, 314–315, 353, 381, 550; and emotions 395; examining using multimodal multichannel data 549; information processing theory of 548; integrating multiple perspectives 323–324; learning from multiple perspectives 324–326; limitations 326–327; and

metacognition 326–327; and metacognitive processes during integration 320–326; phases of 316–317; reflection prompts 322–323; using advanced learning technologies (ALTs) to measure 542–548; *see also* executive function
self-regulation 366; metacognitive 318; *see also* self-regulated learning (SRL)
self-related explanation 210
semantic content: changing 212; creating misconceptions about 212; ignoring 212
semiotic theory 98
sense-making: connectional 25; verbally mediated 28
sense-making prompts 84
sequencing, representational 302
shifting 299, 306, 309
signaling principle 81
sign-dependent processes 98–99
SimSelf 538–539
simulations, participatory 101
situated practice 34, 42
situated theories *see* socio-cultural theories
situational interest 364
situational model *see* mental models
situative orientation 42
skill-level interactions 70–71
skin conductance 542
social bots 489–490; detection of 490–491
social interaction 387–388, 393, 395; contradictory perspectives in 390
social media: and bots 489–490; and fake news 484–485; and misinformation 466–467, 478, 483; as news sources 487
socio-cultural theories and perspectives 40, 41–42, 97, 113, 564
SOI model 226
source perspectives 3, 125–127, 224; and the AIR model 130–132; attending to 132; comprehending 131, 134–137; and epistemic development 128–130; evaluating 133; identifying 132; interpreting 133; resolving 133–134; and theory of mind (ToM) 127–128; *see also* perspective(s)
sources: credibility of 195; evaluation of 215–216, 412, 470; relation to content 126–127, *126*; strategies 206; *see also* source perspectives
spatial contiguity principle 81
spatial rotation tasks 96
spatial skills 66, 68–69, 72
SRL *see* self-regulated learning (SRL)
standards of coherence 196
STEM instruction 18, 33, 35, 38, 40, 41–43, 44, 93, 453; misunderstandings about 456
stimulating content, and motivation 366
strategies: cognitive 325; metacognitive 94, 325; to re-establish coherence 211–215; of the self-regulated learner 316; sourcing 206; text-processing 87
strategy instruction 86–87, 88
structure mapping theory 22
students: approach to relational reasoning 407; asking to read and write domain-specific texts 184–185; communication with teachers 100–101; engaging in identifying ill-structured and complex problems 185–186; high skilled 70–71; involvement in multiple representation construction 102–103; lower skilled 70; motivation of 277; written responses of 237; *see also* learners; learning
surprise 389, 391, 392
switching 299
symbolization, in mathematical representations 113–115

tangibles 101
task analysis 73
task and resources dimension 568–571, **568**
task complexity 565–566
task demands 385, 393
task environments 280–281, 291; historical multisource 282–284, 289–290
task interventions 64, 70, 72–73
teachers: communication with students 100–101; epistemic reflexivity of 340–341; expectations of 339; implications for 74; use of mathematical representations by 112–113
Teaching for Transformative Experience in Science (TTES) model 340, 341
teaching the controversy 335
technocognition 470–471
technology/ies: for bot detection 490–491; digital 514, 518; digital learning 496–498; educational 508–509; learning **498–499**; and multiple representation construction 101–102; representational 525; use to counter fake news 484–485, 487–488; use to refute misinformation 470–471; *see also* advanced learning technologies (ALTs); Computer-Supported Collaborative Learning (CSCL); intelligent tutoring systems (ITS)
temporal contiguity principle 80–81
Test of Relational Reasoning (TORR) 406, 415, 418
Test of Relational Reasoning-Junior (TORRjr) 407
text comprehension: cognitive processes in 206–215; construction-integration model 251; Landscape model 196, 251; research 52; theories of 207
texts: argumentative 248; belief-consistent/inconsistent 260, 272; block-by-block 248–250, 253–254, 571; comprehension of 260–262, 265–272, 306, 352, 354, 355, 357, 362–364; contradictory 379, 390–392; with diagrams

63–64, 66–68, 70–71, 73; expository 246–247, 256n1, 262, 302; illustrated 38, 49–53, 315, 321–322, 413; informational 334; interleaved 248–251, 253–256, 496–497, 571; with multiple perspectives 64, 262–265, 303, 306–308, 315, 347, 352, 560; neutral 248–249, 256n1; one-sided 246, 249; persuasive 248–250; processing strategies 87; referential 562; refutational/non-refutational 248, 303, 309, 392, 414, 449–450, 456; relevant 240; representations of sources 97, *170*; static 538–539; two-sided 246, 249, 250; verbal 35, 48, 49, 79; written 48, 49, 58, 79, 80, 82, 94, 236, 259, 403, 411, 558, 560; *see also* complementary perspectives; dual-position texts; text comprehension
theory of mind (ToM) 127–128
theory of personality 142
theory of planned behavior 331
theory of reasoned action 331
theory preservation goals 337
think-aloud protocols 34, 55–56, 59, 82, 132, 134, 194, 212, 240, 255, 320, 326, 392, 406, 413, 544, 547–548; concurrent 547
thinking, higher-order 402
thinking dispositions, and motivation 361–363
time constraints, and motivation 365–366
ToM (theory of mind) 127–128
TORR (Test of Relational Reasoning) 406, 415, 418
TORRjr (Test of Relational Reasoning-Junior) 407
transduction 99–100
truth value 153–154, 158, 261, 269
TTES (Teaching for Transformative Experience in Science) model 340, 341
Two-Step Model of Validation in Multiple-Text Comprehension 144, 145–146, 260, 265–269, **266**, 267–269, 270, 272; educational implications of 269–272
Type 1 and Type 2 processing 196–197, 199

UCV (Use, Change, Value) discussions 340
understandings: accurate 449; inaccurate 444–445, 448, 453, 453–455, 456; modifications to 451; sophisticated 457; *see also* misunderstandings; knowledge
unity/diversity framework 299–300, 303
updating 262, 263, 298, 298–301, 306–308, 347, 446–447, 449, 464–465, 468, 539
Use, Change, Value (UCV) discussions 340

valence 375, **375**
validation: in comprehension of multiple perspective texts 262–265; of conflicting information 267–268; epistemic 251–252; as epistemic vigilance 269; role in integrating multiple perspectives 259–272
value judgments 334
values: about conceptual topics 333–334; about knowledge, knowing, and learning 332–333; components of 356; cultural 339; defined 330; domain-specific 357; epistemic 130, 333, 339, 578; external 356, 359; individual/superindividual 331–332; intrinsic 356, 357, 359, 364; learning implications for integrating 339–341; and the learning process 329–331, *331*; and motivation 356–357, 359–361; and perceived control 378; perceived topic 357; personal 332; prevention 356, 359; promotion 356, 359; of readers 151; self-relevant 356, 357, 359; task-specific 357; of teachers 340–341; topic-specific 334; universal 175, 176
verbal ability 69
verbal protocols 55–56, 59; *see also* think-aloud protocols
verbal representations 80, 88
Verbal Test of Relational Reasoning (vTORR) 406; *see also* Test of Relational Reasoning (TORR)
verbalizations, concurrent 548; *see also* think-aloud protocols; verbal protocols
verbalizers 56–57
viewpoints: identifying 132; *see also* perspective(s)
Virtual Math Teams 521, *521*, 524
virtual reality 527
virtual systems, immersive 546
virtue epistemology 134; *see also* epistemic beliefs
visual attention 53; *see also* eye tracking
visual design 383–384
visual programming languages 101
visual representations 80, 85, 88, 97, 110
visual stimuli 413
visualization(s) 69, 95, 99, 533, 542, 582; dynamic 55; *see also* data visualization
visualizers 56–57
vTORR (Verbal Test of Relational Reasoning) 406; *see also* Test of Relational Reasoning (TORR)
Vygotskian theory 97

working memory (WM) 49, 80, 209, 213, 465; beliefs in 146; capacity of 497; dual coding assumption 20; and executive function 302; increasing capacity of 21; limited capacity of 66, 69; *see also* memory
written responses 237

zones of proximal development (ZPDs) 34

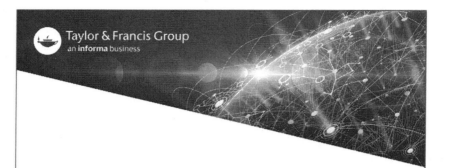